THE CULTURAL LANDSCAPE & HERITAGE PARADOX

The Cultural Landscape & Heritage Paradox

Protection and Development of the Dutch Archaeological-Historical Landscape and its European Dimension

Editors:

Tom (J.H.F.) Bloemers	Emeritus Professor of archaeological heritage and landscape, University of Amsterdam
Henk Kars	Professor of geo- and bioarchaeology, VU University Amsterdam
Arnold van der Valk	Professor in land use planning, Wageningen University
Mies Wijnen	Former secretary of the NWO PDL/BBO-programme

This publication is one of the results stemming from the NWO-programme 'Bodemarchief in Behoud en Ontwikkeling (BBO), a research programme organized by the Netherlands Organisation for Scientific Research (NWO).

AMSTERDAM UNIVERSITY PRESS

The publication of this volume has been generously supported by the following institutions and foundations (in alphabetical order):

 Consejo Superior de Investigaciones Científicas
(Spanish National Council for Scientific Research), Madrid, Spain.

 Fundación Las Médulas (Las Médulas Foundation), Ponferrada (León), Spain.

 Nederlandse Organisatie voor Wetenschappelijk Onderzoek
(Netherlands Organisation for Scientific Research), The Hague, the Netherlands.

 Rijksdienst voor het Cultureel Erfgoed (Cultural Heritage Agency),
Amersfoort, the Netherlands.

 Stimuleringsfonds voor Architectuur (the Netherlands Architecture Fund),
Rotterdam, the Netherlands.

 Van Eesteren-Fluck & Van Lohuizen Stichting,
The Hague, the Netherlands

Cover illustration: Beverwijk-Heemskerk, Broekpolder
Cover design: Magenta Ontwerpers, Bussum, the Netherlands
Lay-out and editing of illustrations: UvA-Kaartenmakers, Amsterdam
ISBN   978 90 8964 155 7
e-ISBN   978 90 4851 096 2
ISBN (CSIC)   978-84-00-09173-6
NUR   682

© Tom Bloemers, Henk Kars, Arnold van der Valk / Amsterdam University Press 2010

All rights reserved. Without limiting the rights under copyright reserved above, no part of this book may be reproduced, stored in or introduced into a retrieval system, or transmitted, in any form or by any means (electronic, mechanical, photocopying, recording or otherwise) without the written permission of both the copyright owner and the authors of the book.

Every effort has been made to obtain permission to use all copyrighted illustrations reproduced in this book. Nonetheless, whosoever believes to have rights to this material is advised to contact the publisher.

TABLE OF CONTENTS

PREFACE XI

I. INTRODUCTION 1
The Cultural Landscape and Heritage Paradox. Protection and Development of the Dutch Archaeological-Historical Landscape and its European Dimension 3
Tom (J.H.F.) Bloemers

II. INSIGHTS AND PROSPECTS OF ARCHAEOLOGICAL-HISTORICAL LANDSCAPE STUDIES 17
1. *Introduction to 'Protecting and Developing the Dutch Archaeological-Historical Landscape' (PDL/BBO)* 19
Willem J.H. Willems

2. *Planning the past. Lessons to be learned from 'Protecting and Developing the Dutch Archaeological-Historical Landscape' (PDL/BBO)* 21
Arnold van der Valk

3. *Actors and orders: the shaping of landscapes and identities* 53
Carsten Paludan-Müller

III. LINKING KNOWLEDGE AND ACTION 67
1. *Linking knowledge to action: an introduction* 69
Henk Kars

2. *The cultural biography of landscape as a tool for action research in the Drentsche Aa National Landscape (Northern Netherlands)* 83
Hans Elerie & Theo Spek

3. *From inventory to identity? Constructing the Lahemaa National Park's (Estonia) regional cultural heritage* 115
Marju Kõivupuu, Anu Printsmann & Hannes Palang

4. *A biography of the cultural landscape in the eastern Netherlands: theory and practice of acquisition and propagation of knowledge* 133
Jelle Vervloet, Roy van Beek & Luuk Keunen

5. *The protection and management of the historic landscape in Scotland in the context of the European Landscape Convention* 151
Lesley Macinnes

6. *Assessing in situ preservation of archaeological wetland sites by chemical analysis of botanical remains and micromorphology* 161
Martine van den Berg, Hans Huisman, Henk Kars, Henk van Haaster & Johan Kool

7. *The ancient quarry and mining district between the Eifel and the Rhine: aims and progress of the Vulkanpark Osteifel Project* 177
Angelika Hunold & Holger Schaaff

IV. IMAGINATION - FACTS AND CONSTRUCTIONS 187

1. *Imagination: facts and constructions. About imagination, authenticity and identity, and the value of interpretative heritage research* 189
Tom (J.H.F.) Bloemers

2. *From Oer-IJ estuary to metropolitan coastal landscape. Assessing and preserving archaeological-historical resources from 4000 years of living between land and water* 203
Tom (J.H.F.) Bloemers, Gerard Alders, Robert van Heeringen, Marjolijn Kok, Heleen van Londen, Liesbeth Theunissen & Peter Vos with an external view of Gísli Pálsson

3. *Two sorting-machines for the Oer-IJ* 239
Rob van Leeuwen

4. *Images, attitudes and measures in the field of cultural heritage in Norway* 263
Karoline Daugstad

5. *The good, the bad and the self-referential. Heritage planning and the productivity of difference* 273
Kristof Van Assche

6. *Interpretative heritage research and the politics of democratization and de-democratization. As illustrated by the plight of hard-working amateurs in the trenches of revamped policy arrangements* 291
Martijn Duineveld, Raoul Beunen & Kristof Van Assche

7. *Past pictures. Landscape visualization with digital tools* 309
Jörg Rekittke & Philip Paar

8. *Gazing at places we have never been. Landscape, heritage and identity.*
   A comment on Jörg Rekittke & Philip Paar: 'Past Pictures. Landscape visualization with digital tools'   321
   Rob van der Laarse

9. *'Green' and 'blue' developments. Prospects for research and conservation of early prehistoric hunter-gatherer landscapes*   329
   Bjørn Smit

10. *Presentation, appreciation and conservation of liminal landscapes: challenges from an Irish perspective (in response to the contribution by Bjørn Smit)*   339
    Michael O'Connell

11. *My Story – your Story: three levels for reflecting and debating the relationship between contemporary archaeological heritage management and the public. A comment from Germany*   351
    Ulf Ickerodt

V.   **SHARING KNOWLEDGE - STORIES, MAPS AND DESIGN**   363

1. *Introduction: sharing knowledge - stories, maps and design*   365
   Arnold van der Valk

2. *Revitalizing history: moving from historical landscape reconstructions to heritage practices in the southern Netherlands*   387
   Nico Roymans, Fokke Gerritsen, Cor van der Heijden, Koos Bosma & Jan Kolen

3. *The role of historical expertise in today's heritage management, landscape development and spatial planning. Comment on 'The biography of a sandy landscape' by Nico Roymans, Fokke Gerritsen, Cor van der Heijden, Koos Bosma & Jan Kolen*   407
   Jenny Atmanagara

4. *The potential of remote sensing, magnetometry and geochemical prospection in the characterization and inspection of archaeological sites and landscapes in the Netherlands*   415
   Henk Kars, Alette Kattenberg, Stijn Oonk & Chris Sueur

5. *New developments in archaeological predictive modelling*   431
   Philip Verhagen, Hans Kamermans, Martijn van Leusen & Benjamin Ducke

6. *Cultural heritage in environmental impact assessment – reflections from England and northwest Europe*   445
   Carys E. Jones

7.	On the necessity of congruent meanings in archaeological heritage management. An analysis of three case studies from a policy science perspective Anneke de Zwart	461
8.	Protection and management of Spanish archaeological-historical landscapes. Possibilities and perspectives for the application of a protective and developmental approach Maria Ruiz del Árbol & Almudena Orejas	477
9.	Knowledge and legal action: a plea for conservation. Comment on 'Protection and management of Spanish archaeological-historical landscapes. Possibilities and perspectives for the application of a protective and developmental approach' by María Ruiz del Árbol & Almudena Orejas Martin Vollmer-König	493

VI. SYNTHESIS AND CONCLUSIONS
What have we learnt?
Tom (J.H.F.) Bloemers, Henk Kars & Arnold van der Valk

501
503

VII. MANAGEMENT OF KNOWLEDGE

519

1.	The management of knowledge for integrative landscape research: an introduction Tom (J.H.F.) Bloemers	521
2.	Elephant and Delta. In search of practical guidelines for interdisciplinary and strategic research Arnold van der Valk	529
3.	LANDMARKS. A project based on transnational and interdisciplinary scientific co-operation Almudena Orejas & Guillermo-Sven Reher	545
4.	The Planarch experience John Williams	557
5.	Management of knowledge within the international and intersectoral research project 'Cultural Landscapes' Józef Hernik	565
6.	'Changing Landscapes': an interdisciplinary Danish research centre Per Grau Møller	577
7.	The PDL/BBO research programme analysed from the perspective of knowledge management Tom (J.H.F.) Bloemers	585

8. *Cultural landscapes in the mirror. What information systems reveal about information management and cultural landscape research* 605
Sophie Visser

VIII. AGENDA FOR THE FUTURE 629

1. *Agenda for the future. What do we see and what do we take?* 631
Tom (J.H.F.) Bloemers

2. *Heritage policy in spatial planning* 641
Koos Bosma

3. *Changing landscapes of archaeology and heritage* 653
Graham Fairclough & Heleen van Londen

IX. SUMMARY 671

X. APPENDIX 675
1. *List of selected abbreviations* 677
2. *Glossary of specific subject-related concepts and terms used in this book* 679
3. *Protecting and Developing the Dutch Archaeological-Historical Landscape/Bodemarchief in Behoud en Ontwikkeling (PDL/BBO): projects and programmes* 685
4. *List of authors, fields of activity and addresses* 693

SUBJECT INDEX 729
INDEX OF PLACES AND REGIONS 737

Uitgeest (NL): former Oer-IJ channel. *Photo: R. van Eerden*.

PREFACE

It is a privilege to write the preface for a book which materializes the outcome of a research programme like the PDL/BBO, which took five years to set up and lasted for ten years. It reminds us of the 'cloud of nostalgia' mentioned by one of the authors, Koos Bosma, when he is looking back to the Belvedere policy and refers to heritage perception and experience. The PDL/BBO programme and its unsuccessful pre-proposal submitted in February 1995 are a monument to the perception and experience of doing landscape and heritage research. The preface to this book also means closing an enterprise that has been made possible by the high ambitions of a few, the vision of some more and by the joint efforts of many. And by the pivotal role of Peter Schröder, former official of the Ministry of Education, Culture and Science in 1998!

This book is about the cultural-historical landscape and understanding and managing its heritage. On the European level the topicality of this theme is expressed by the European Landscape Convention and by the increasing need for integrative research. Against this general background, however, the researchers contributing to this book focus on a particular type of the cultural-historical landscape and a specific problem related to it: the (almost) invisible archaeological-historical landscapes and how to know them in order to manage them in a sustainable way. The (almost) hidden landscapes represent the majority of the cultural landscape, while what we see is only the tip of the iceberg. The hidden landscape is like the universe the astronomer is exploring, it is a resource of knowledge about past developments of people, landscape and environment with an unknown dimension and containing unimaginable information if we are prepared to look for what is hidden.

Triggered by the fascination for the unknown and by the value of landscape for present and future life, the researchers present an innovative integrative approach linking knowledge and action to deal with the particularities of the hidden landscapes. Although focused upon this specific issue, the approach is of basic value for the exploration of cultural landscapes in general and the management of its heritage in the context of the transformation of our actual environment and society. Its theoretical and methodological practice is an exemplary case for the interaction between knowledge, policy and imagination in the twenty-first century. It turns the uncertainties related to the unknown into opportunities to discover the knowable and learn through landscape.

This book is the result of a joint effort of researchers with a background in the humanities, social sciences and science and active in academic and public sectors from all over Europe. They have actively contributed by thought and action to this volume and are in this sense an example of the European inter- and transdisciplinary community of practice we envisage as a crucial condition for future landscape research, heritage management and practice. This is also reflected by the mixed group of peers, for each contribution one from the Netherlands and one from Europe outside the Netherlands, that have reviewed the manuscripts and by doing so strengthened their quality. Finally the community of practice is personified by the organizations who joined the Netherlands Organisation of Scientific Research in the funding of this publication. Interdisciplinarity is illustrated via subsidies by the Van Eesteren-Fluck & Van Lohuizen Stichting and the Netherlands Architecture Fund, the alliance between heritage research and policy by the wide ranging support of the national Cultural Heritage Agency. The generous grants from the Spanish Consejo Superior de Investigaciones Científicas and the Fundación Las Médulas not only symbolize a similar co-operation between research, heritage management and the public, but also the bond between colleagues and friends all over Europe. The editors are extremely grateful to all the colleagues and their organizations for their contributions and unlimited commitment and to Christine Jefferis and Isabelle Vella Gregory for correcting and partly translating the English texts.

Tom Bloemers, Henk Kars, Arnold van der Valk and Mies Wijnen
Amsterdam, 10 April 2010

I
INTRODUCTION

Rhineland (D): early prehistoric archaeological site excavated in opencast mining. *Photo: RAB, Bonn.*

1. The Cultural Landscape and Heritage Paradox
Protection and Development of the Dutch Archaeological-Historical Landscape and its European Dimension

Tom (J.H.F.) Bloemers[1]

ABSTRACT

This book is about the cultural-historic landscape and understanding and managing its heritage. On the European level the topicality of this theme is expressed by the European Landscape Convention and by the increasing need for integrative research. Against this background the Dutch archaeological-historical landscape is a point of reference to structure the exchange of information about it in Europe.

For the meaning of the word 'landscape' we use the definition in the European Landscape Convention: "'Landscape' means an area, as perceived by people, whose character is the result of the action and interaction of natural and/or human factors". This view fits in with the basic recognition that heritage management becomes increasingly 'the management of future change rather than simply the protection of the fabric of the past'. This presents us with a paradox, to protect or preserve our historic environment we have to collaborate with 'outsiders' and to make our expert knowledge suitable for policy and society.

In the PDL/BBO programme the Belvedere core concept 'conservation through development' has been adopted. By seeking new uses, old landscapes and buildings can be saved. The landscape-based approach is integrative research creating new insights from the integration of disciplinary knowledge. There is a need for integration between the cultural historic disciplines themselves and between these and other relevant disciplines. Two unifying concepts, 'biography of landscape' and 'action research', have been adopted to support the integration and to focus the PDL/BBO programme. The integrative approach requires a clear positioning of the involved disciplines, especially the historic ones, towards the paradigms that dominate their field. They have to accommodate the past time perspective of the archaeological-historical landscape to its meaning for the present we live in and for the future.

The insights gained from the PDL/BBO programme presented here are structured by the interaction between knowledge, policy and imagination centred around the public representing the society we are part of. The added value of considering themes in the wider European dimension is substantial. By sharing, confronting and comparing, the similarities and differences become clear and meaningful. They make us aware of the diversity of landscapes, social and institutional structures, different types of problems, approaches and ways forward. In this way landscape research and management becomes a source for the management of knowledge creation and insight in the prospects for the way forward in the near future.

KEY WORDS

Landscape and heritage, paradox, unifying concepts, European dimension

1. INTRODUCTION: "WHAT YOU SEE IS WHAT YOU TAKE"

"What you see is what you take". This quotation from the title of a paper on the perception and use of prehistoric landscape written by Roel Brandt in the mid-1980s (Brandt 1986) highlights in an extended form the basic drive leading towards the 'Protecting and Developing the Dutch Archaeological-Historical Landscape' programme (PDL/BBO; Dutch: Bodemarchief in Behoud en Ontwikkeling = BBO; Bloemers *et al.* 2001) and the volume you have in your hands. In his paper, Brandt presented the notion of perception in prehistoric societies as a factor to be considered in the research of his time to understand their exploitation and colonization of the Oer-IJ estuary. The extension of the use of 'perception' as a conceptual notion during the last 25 years is best shown by the two contributions in this volume (Ch. IV.2 and 3) on the Oer-IJ region in section IV 'Imagination: facts and constructions'. In this context it covers perception not only in the past, but also in the present and even looking forward into the future. However the connection, especially with this wetland metropolitan area northwest of Amsterdam, confronts us participants in this volume both from inside and outside the Netherlands, with a dimension of the historical environment with still much wider and fundamental implications: how and to what extent can we know past landscapes, how to avoid only considering 'what we see' as known and how to use this still hidden knowledge for actual sustainable management of landscape's cultural-historical values? The exceptional value of the Oer-IJ historical environment is that its hidden archaeological-historical landscapes extending back into a past of over 5000 years are extremely well preserved, precisely because of the rising sea level, and contain crucial information for e.g. settlement and water management problems this region is currently facing, as it did in the past. Intensive interdisciplinary research over some 50 years has opened up these invisible and unimaginable landscapes for research and policy resulting in the present challenge to link knowledge and action. However, although the Oer-IJ historical environment and the knowledge about it show exceptional qualities, they are certainly not unique. It is nothing more than a representative sample of the potential of all landscapes, wetlands and uplands in and outside Europe. In general, the crucial and very critical point is whether researchers, policy makers, practitioners and society are aware of the fact that the visible historic landscapes are literally the tip of the iceberg that is much more, diverse and older (almost) invisible landscapes (see also Bosma Ch. VIII.2 par. 3.3). Do we as a community perceive at the appropriate moments in the present time the richness and depth of the historic environment, including the invisible and unknown, as a resource in a physical and cognitive sense, as *habitat* and *habitus* for the present and the future? Do we reflect enough upon the extended meaning of the quotation "what you see is what you take", when acting in the Netherlands in the sense of the Belvedere policy and in Europe in the sense of the European Landscape Convention? What makes landscape, and archaeology, in fact so fascinating and resourceful is the combination of 'the power of place' and the challenge to the imagination to explore the invisible and unimaginable. However, grasping the right moments and opportunities very much depends on "what we see is what we take" as actors from research, policy, practice and public.

So this book is about the cultural-historic landscape, its heritage and how we as inhabitants of this landscape can understand and manage the transformations caused by our own actions and environmental influences. This issue has many dimensions like the temporal, spatial, natural and environmental, social and economic, cognitive dimensions and probably many more. It is complex because of the interactions between these dimensions through time and the many human perceptions involved. The authors of this book share for several reasons the ambition to deal with landscape and transformation from an integrated perspective. They are engaged researchers and experts who consider landscape as a fascinating source of innovative knowledge about its origins, the evolution of human society and its present-day and future management. They are also aware of the fact that they share a responsibility for landscape and heritage with society at large promoting good stewardship. Finally, they recognize that it is society that decides about the future of the landscape its members and their children will live in, as past generations did before them. In short, this book is about knowledge and action for a sustainable, meaningful and qualitatively diverse cultural-historic landscape.

But which or whose landscape? Europe is like a mosaic of many different landscapes occupied by a great variety of communities embodying numerous perceptions and memories. Each of these landscapes has its own characteristics, their inhabitants and visitors perceive them as part of their identity and behave in particular ways. Together they compose the mosaic that shapes the Europe of numerous landscapes and at the same time marks the contrast between them. From the knowledge-action perspective, this rich variety of landscapes represents as many laboratories as there are landscapes and communities. Out of this variety a number of these 'laboratories' has been presented in this book to illustrate their characteristics, the transformations these landscapes and occupants are involved in and the research themes and approaches selected. On the European level the topicality of cultural-historic landscape research and management is expressed by the European Landscape Convention as adopted by the Council of Europe in 2000 and by the increasing need for integrative research as argued for within the framework of the European Research Area.

Against this background the Dutch archaeological-historical landscape is only one of these many European 'laboratories'. In the context of this book however, it is also a point of reference to structure the exchange of information about landscape research and action in Europe. The Dutch landscape is a striking example of a wetland region showing an intensive metropolitan occupation pattern in a highly dynamic environment. The Dutch community now faces the major challenges of the twenty-first century of economic, environmental and demographic changes by innovating its centuries-old planning tradition. In 1999, by voting for the national Belvedere policy, Parliament identified the cultural historical landscape as a source of inspiration for planning and designing answers to these challenges and as a value to be 'preserved by developing' it (Belvedere 1999). At the same time a national research programme was initiated 'Protecting and Developing the Dutch Archaeological-Historical Landscape' (PDL/BBO; Dutch: Bodemarchief in Behoud en Ontwikkeling = BBO) to contribute to this policy (Bloemers *et al.* 2001; see Ch. VII.7). Both programmes were expected to explore new ways to approach these challenges and to create a body of new knowledge and experiences, which by the end of these activities in about 2008/9 should be embedded in 'normal' research, heritage and training practice.

2. THE CULTURAL LANDSCAPE AND HERITAGE PARADOX

2.1 *Cultural landscape and heritage*

For a common understanding of the meaning of the word 'landscape' we use the definition of the European Landscape Convention: "'Landscape' means an area, as perceived by people, whose character is the result of the action and interaction of natural and/or human factors." It is also useful to quote other related definitions from this Convention. "'Landscape protection' means actions to conserve and maintain the significant or characteristic features of a landscape, justified by its heritage value derived from its natural configuration and/or from human activity." Finally, "'landscape management' means action, from a perspective of sustainable development, to ensure the regular upkeep of a landscape, so as to guide and harmonize changes which are brought about by social, economic and environmental processes."

'Landscape' is not the same as 'environment'. Environment can be described as 'the complex of ecological factors that are related to the organism or person whose environment it is' (Odum 1971, 11; Udo de Haes 1984, 17-20; Ingold 2000, 193; Meier 2009). Following Fairclough, environment changes into landscape in the eyes of the beholder 'who constructs ... landscape from the material environment.' A 'cultural landscape' is "doubly cultural" since it is the product of past human cultural actions and of present-day creation by our own cultural and social attitudes (Fairclough 2008b, 409). In Schofield's view 'heritage' focuses on "the special qualities, whether natural or cultural, and the fact that we inherit it from the past." These qualities have both a tangible and intangible dimension. The interpretation of their scale and value has traditionally been on the level of a site or a building of special importance and the connotation of their protection is generally to preserve them unchanged (Schofield 2008, 18-19). Gradually, however, there is a fundamental shift in perspective going on in heritage approaches widening the scope towards landscapes and ensembles, including the 'ordinary' and recent ones and 'creating an all-inclusive concept of the 'historic environment'. Parallel with it comes the fundamental recognition that the goal of new approaches is increasingly "the management of future change rather than simply the protection of the fabric of the past" (Fairclough 2008a, 297-298).

The view represented in the Dutch PDL/BBO programme is in agreement with this wider scope and acknowledges the importance of change since the Dutch urban and rural landscape has been and is in a state of continual transformation, a process that will only be intensified in the near future. Given the wider scope as expressed by the PDL/BBO guiding concepts and respecting the important role of the historic built environment, the programme however focuses in particular on the archaeological and historic geographical landscape, here indicated as the archaeological-historical landscape. The reason for this is that the Dutch archaeological-historical resources are strongly characterized by wetland conditions and, as a consequence, are mainly subsurface. The vulnerability and invisibility of this particular Dutch landscape required, in the view of the participating funding agencies, an additional research effort to contribute in a balanced way to the national Belvedere policy and its relevance for the ratification of the European Landscape Convention by the Netherlands in 2005. At the same time, by about 2000, the programme was seen as a step towards the implementation of the principal aims of the Valletta Convention (Valletta 1992), namely the protection of the archaeological-historical resources by participation in the environmental planning policy. In this context, the PDL/BBO programme aimed at the development of scientific knowledge in order to support the sustainable development of the Dutch archaeological-historical landscape. Consequently, the strategy focused on establishing a meaningful link between scientific knowledge, archaeological-historical resource management and applied planning policy in the Netherlands.

2.2 The cultural heritage paradox and the knowledge-action nexus

The title of this book, 'The cultural landscape and heritage paradox', is a reflection of the basic dilemma professionals working in the field of cultural landscapes and the historic environment during at least the last four decades have increasingly been confronted with. It is the dilemma arising from Fairclough's statement that the new approach of heritage is increasingly 'the management of future change rather than simply the protection of the fabric of the past'. The older, that is to say my, generation has been 'educated by doing' in the world of research and legal heritage protection of the post-war decades, but has also experienced the limitations and failures connected with it. Gradually they, or we, became aware of the need for a change of strategy from 'defensive' to 'proactive' and from a sectoral towards an integrated approach of the historic environment (Bloemers/Borger 1988, 62-63; Bloemers 1990; *idem*, 1997; Groenewoudt/Bloemers 1997; Willems 1997, 9-14). The 1992 Valletta Convention on archaeological heritage is a reflection of this. During the same period archaeological fieldwork in northwest Europe was gradually scaled up from the site to the off-site and regional level evolving in what can now be called 'landscape archaeology' (Bloemers 1999; Meier 2009). These trends in archaeological research and heritage management illustrate the widening scope towards landscapes and ensembles mentioned by Fairclough before. It upgrades archaeological heritage as an asset for the European landscape and the aims of the Florence Convention (Florence 2000). This change fits very well into the overall increase of interest in environmental issues like sustainable development. Parallel with it came the new views on the relationship between government, market and public leading to a shift from government to governance and its variety of implementations in Europe (for the Valletta Convention see Kristiansen 2009). The dilemma raised by all these developments presents us with a paradox, to protect or preserve our historic environment we have to collaborate with planners, designers, developers, rural communities etc. and in order to apply our expert knowledge and new insights we have to make it accessible, and what is more, acceptable for policy and society. This is in sharp contrast with the traditional and dominant paradigms of the heritage sector and of research as an objective and independent enterprise implemented and assessed by experts. Considered together, the ways in which the dilemma and paradox are solved by the professionals and politicians in Europe will determine the degree of innovative knowledge creation and the relevance of the historic landscape disciplines for our society.

In the PDL/BBO programme the challenges stemming from this paradox have deliberately been taken up. First, it was decided from the beginning that the core concept of the national Belvedere policy, 'conservation through development', should be the guiding view for the programme. Apart from advantages of synergy between both lines there was an overall agreement between the representatives of Belvedere and PDL/BBO that this view would be a fruitful way forward. In the words of the Belvedere Memorandum: 'conservation through development' is the motto. By seeking new uses, old landscapes and buildings can be saved. However, it is just as much a question of 'development through conservation'. By using our cultural heritage in a frugal and responsible manner, we are investing in the development and strengthening of our identity, knowledge, comfort, business climate and potential for tourism." The interaction between cultural history and spatial planning and the recognition of the differences in orientation can create the condition for discovering "a new balance between retention and development", while "the process of development will create room for renewal." (Fig. 1; Belvedere 1999, 32-33).

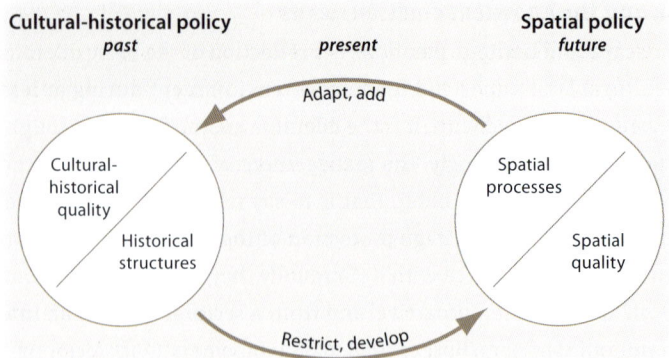

Fig. 1
Belvedere policy: the interaction between cultural-historical policy and spatial policy (*Belvedere* 1999, 32).

The other basic decision for the PDL/BBO programme was to connect research with policy. In this way new and inspiring knowledge about landscape and heritage would be created and research could have a strategic relevance for the Belvedere policy. In the background there was the view that the increasing interest of policy and society would also become 'normal' at some time in the future, as has happened with environment and nature, and that research could contribute in that phase to the level of consolidation. As a result of this decision, the relationship between research and policy had to be clarified. The view of research as an independent activity driven only by curiosity without any political or ideological motivations would not fit with this decision and create tensions. To solve this the methodology of 'action research' was adopted, which can be described as "inquiry in which participants and researchers cogenerate knowledge through collaborative communicative processes (which) … leads to social action

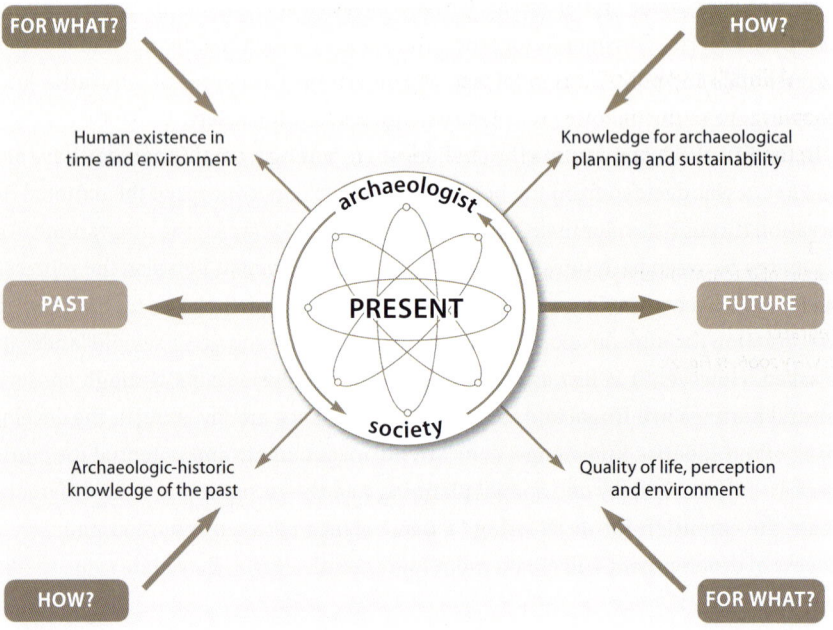

Fig. 2
Archaeology as a historic and future-oriented discipline.

... produces valid research results ... is context centred ... aims to solve real-life problems in context" (Greenwood/Levin 2003, 149). Compared with curiosity-driven research, the decision for action-driven research includes elements of a paradox regarding subjectivity of observations, reflexivity on participatory roles, evaluating results and determining research conditions. Another aspect of the relationship between research and policy is the interaction between the two groups and the rate of divergence or convergence (see Van der Valk Ch. II.2, 30-31).

The action research approach also requires a clear positioning of the involved disciplines, especially the historic ones, towards the paradigms that dominate their field. They have to accommodate the past time perspective of the archaeological-historical landscape to its meaning for the present we live in and for the future. For archaeology, and *mutatis mutandis* all disciplines dealing with the cultural landscape, these time perspectives can be accommodated by linking a historic-oriented archaeology with a future or planning-oriented environmental archaeology (Fig. 2). Its purpose should be to make the archaeological value a factor for the development of the quality of present and future human life, perception and environment (Fig. 2 right). This future-oriented archaeology does not substitute traditional archaeology but is an extension and transformation of past-oriented archaeology. The object of both archaeologies is the same archaeological value but the aims are different and consequently partly the type of questions, methods, techniques and results. Past-oriented archaeology focuses on knowledge about human existence in time and environment, future-oriented archaeology on quality and perception of the archaeological-historical landscape as part of our present-day and future environment aiming for sustainable protection. It needs the knowledge acquired through traditional archaeology to link concepts, methods and techniques from geographical and environmental disciplines. On the other hand, the future of traditional archaeology depends strongly on the effectiveness of a policy for the sustainable maintenance of the archaeological value as a primary source for past-orientated research. Therefore, these two archaeological approaches are complementary, need each other and should be integrated on the basis of mutual interest and appreciation.

2.3 *A landscape-based way of looking*

Following from the previous introductory arguments, landscape can be considered as "a way of looking" (Fairclough 2008a, 298). It directs the view on heritage as the outcome of transformations, on the

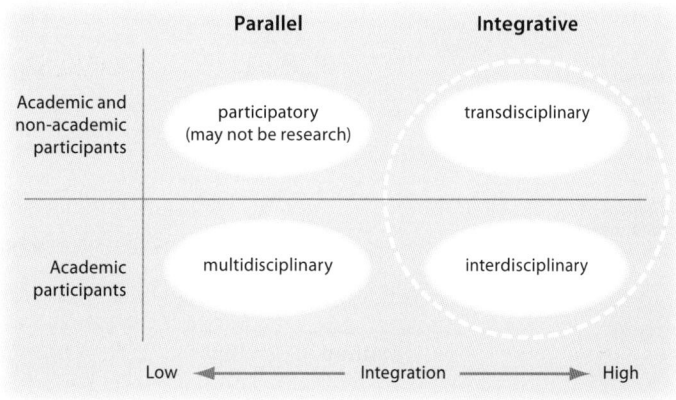

Fig. 3
Degrees of integration and stakeholder involvement in integrative and non-integrative approaches (*after Tress/Tress/Fry 2006, 17 Fig. 2*).

methodologies to cross the boundaries between research, policy and public, on the communication of knowledge, experiences and actions towards professionals and society at large. This way of looking at landscape by integrative and participatory approaches opens a wide and challenging vista, a true Belvedere, on the opportunities landscape offers for the creation of innovative knowledge and informed action.

3. HOW TO ADDRESS THE CHALLENGE OF INTEGRATIVE LANDSCAPE RESEARCH?

The way to address the challenge and exploit the opportunities of this landscape-based way of looking is integrative research, which in itself is also a challenge. Tress/Tress/Fry have presented a clear definition of integrative studies as "projects that are either interdisciplinary or transdisciplinary, in that knowledge and theory emerges from the integration of disciplinary knowledge." (Fig. 3; Tress/Tress/Fry 2006, 17; Van der Valk this volume Ch. VII.2, 534-536). It requires specific scientific competencies (knowledge, skills and attitudes) that are important for fruitful co-operation, characteristics that are underutilized in the normal practice of science.

3.1 The PDL/BBO way of integrative research
An inter- and transdisciplinary landscape approach

The aims and structure of the PDL/BBO programme are founded in a deliberate and clear vision of integrative research. Essential for the underlying knowledge organization (Fig. 4) is establishing the links between cultural or archaeological-historical heritage and planning and between research and policy with a focus on inter- and transdisciplinary interaction between both domains. The methodology follows two lines, a problem-oriented one and one on 'content' or theme. The long-term perspective is expressed by evolution indicating the origins and transformation of landscapes. The region is the entity where problems and content or themes interact and the integrative approach has to be practised. The management and transfer of knowledge is an aspect that permeates through all activities and interactions from the earliest beginning until the end of the programme. Although the focus is on the Netherlands, the world outside has to be taken into account as a wider context and source of inspiration.

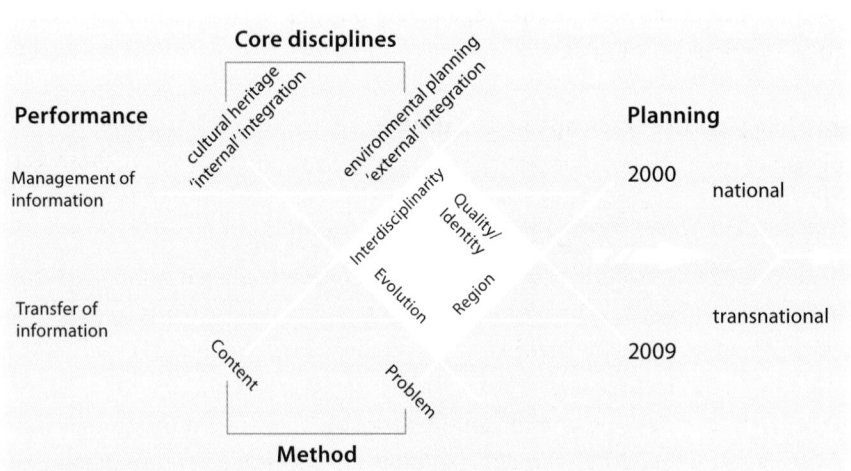

Fig. 4
The structure of the PDL/BBO programme.

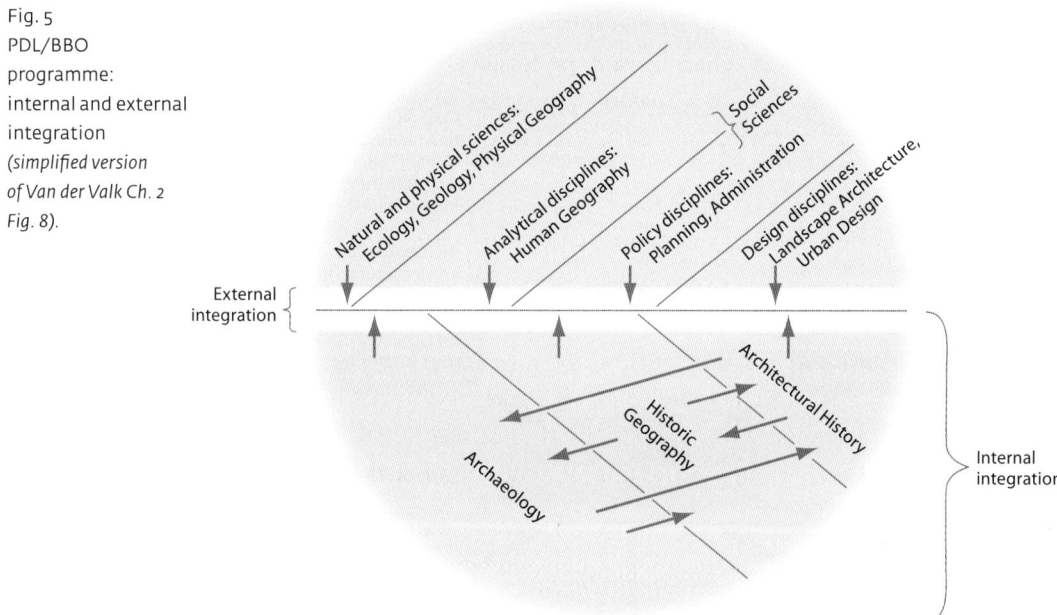

Fig. 5
PDL/BBO programme: internal and external integration
(simplified version of Van der Valk Ch. 2 Fig. 8).

The integrative ambition as applied in the PDL/BBO programme has three dimensions (Fig. 5; Van der Valk Ch. II.2, 31-34). Within the world of research there is first the need for integration between the cultural historic disciplines, the 'internal' integration, and second the integration between the cultural historic disciplines and the other relevant disciplines from the social sciences, the design and construction disciplines and the natural and physical sciences, the 'external' integration. This interdisciplinarity has confronted the participants in the PDL/BBO programme with the paradigmatic difference between the humanities and social sciences on the one side and the natural and physical sciences on the other. The third dimension has to do with integration of research with policy and public participation, a wider meaning of 'external' integration covering transdisciplinarity. This leads to the confrontation with the relationship between research, policy and society at large, between the world striving for truth and objectivity and the world of (inter)subjectivity and justness and between expert and lay knowledge (During/Elerie/Groenendijk 2001, 114; Jacobs 2006, 9-12).

Two unifying concepts: 'biography of landscape' and 'action research'
In answer to the challenge posed by the need for inter- and transdisciplinarity to fulfil the ambition of integrative research two unifying concepts have been adopted to guide and focus the PDL/BBO programme, the 'biography of landscape' and 'action research' (Bloemers et al. 2001).

'Biography of landscape' was selected because of its potential for understanding the transformations of early landscapes in the region along new lines as it was adapted during the mid-1990s by Dutch archaeologists (Van Beek et al. 2008, 179-184). Drawing on the anthropological concept of the 'cultural biography of things' they looked at landscape as a form of material culture (Appadurai 1986; Kopytoff 1986). Appadurai and Kopytoff used the biography metaphor to describe the life history of goods which circulate frequently in society and thereby go through modifications and shifts in terms of their economic functions and social meanings. Landscape archaeologists pointed out that land and landscapes in

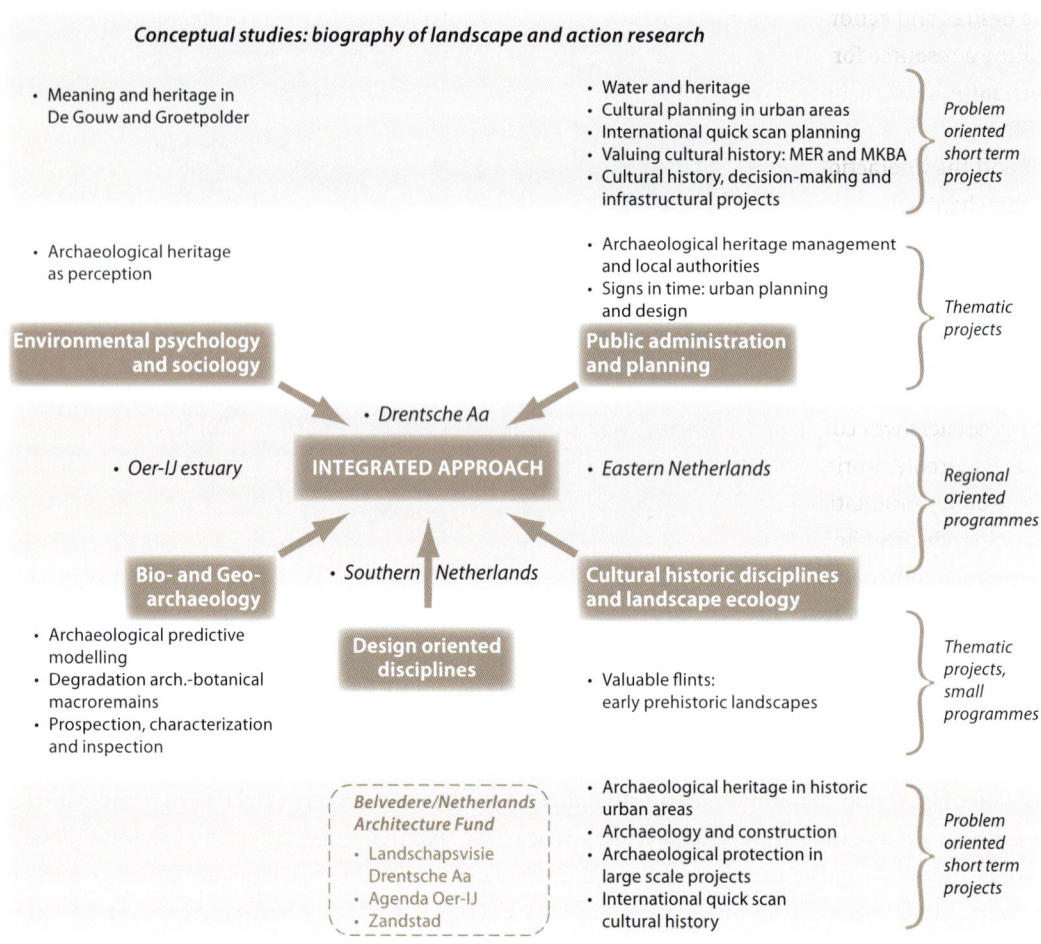

Fig. 6
PDL/BBO programme: the position of the research programmes and projects in an inter- and transdisciplinary perspective.

historic societies, although not circulating in a literal sense, were nevertheless handed down from one generation to another, frequently being transformed in the past and acquiring new functions, values and associations in the process. Given the more geographical scope as adopted in the PDL/BBO programme, the biographical approach ideally covers the long-term history of a landscape or region, 'mapping' the transformations, functional changes and shifts in meaning of the most important places and spatial structures and relating them to both social-economic developments and the history of institutions, mentalities and spatial concepts (Kolen/Witte 2007).

The landscape biographical approach has also been selected because of its potential for crossover activities between theory and practice, between science and applications such as the 'protection by development' approach, and to integrate the archaeological-historical landscape into environmental planning. Planning in itself is a discipline and activity with many roots in geography, but at the same time with a distinct character because of its connections with social sciences dealing with government and governance. Planning can be considered as a means of negotiation between the individual or market and the desires and actions of the state or community (Tewdwr-Jones 1996). To support the aim of making culture a resource for the quality of environmental development, the concept of 'cultural planning' has been introduced to unify cultural and environmental policy (Ruimte en Cultuur 2005).

The reasons for the decision to accept the methodology of 'action research' as a guiding approach to support the interaction between research, policy and public have already been explained in section 2.2 of this chapter.

The position of the PDL/BBO research in an inter- and transdisciplinary perspective
The selected and funded research proposals included four large regionally oriented programmes aiming at a fully integrative practice, four projects focusing on the development of knowledge and methods and three projects dealing with planning, public administration, sociology and cognition. The group of researchers was composed of thirteen Ph.D., seven postdoctoral and six senior researchers. In addition, ten problem-oriented short-term projects on a variety of topics were carried out as an expression of the policy orientation of PDL/BBO. They ranged from an international survey of heritage policy and planning via specific planning issues such as urbanization, infrastructure, water management, non-destructive construction techniques and assessment methods for archaeological-historical urban areas to policy-oriented studies on decision-making processes, social cost-benefit analysis and experience of regional identities. Finally one short-term project produced a mid-term assessment of the strengths and weaknesses of the application of inter- and transdisciplinarity in three regional projects of the PDL/BBO programme.

The position of the various research projects clearly reflects the inter- and transdisciplinary perspective (Fig. 6). In the centre are the four large regional programmes, since these landscapes are the platform where various disciplines come together and interact as research, policy and local people do. Smaller programmes and individual Ph.D. projects cover archaeological-historical landscape issues as seen from various disciplinary perspectives, namely cultural history, policy and socio-cognitive disciplines and geosciences. In a similar way, the ten short-term projects illustrate the inter- and transdisciplinarity, but are generally more focused on policy and practice. This overview also makes it clear that within the institutional research structure the design disciplines are completely absent, but that this has luckily been compensated by 'spin-off' projects in collaboration with the Belvedere programme.

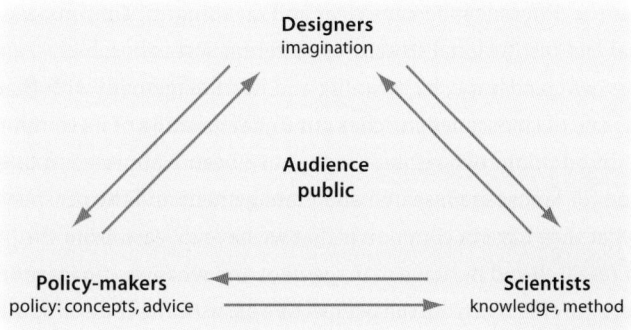

Fig. 7.
The core structure of this PDL/BBO volume: the interaction between knowledge, policy, imagination and practice (*Courtesy of Heleen van Londen*).

The interaction between knowledge, policy, imagination and practice
To do research from an integrative perspective in one programme or project has been a challenge for all participants in the PDL/BBO programme. Integrating the various strands of research in all these projects into one overarching programmatic synthesis is another challenge with a much wider dimension. This book is the result of this ambition and will hopefully illustrate many useful insights and experiences, but certainly also clear weaknesses or even failures. The structure of this synthesis focuses upon the interaction between knowledge, policy and imagination centred around the public representing the society we are part of (Fig. 7). It is the environment within which we as PDL/BBO researchers have opted to carry out our research. The types of action that characterize this relationship are threefold, the relationship between research, policy and public as expressed by 'knowledge and action' about landscape and transformation, that between research and design focusing on the role of facts and constructions in imagining the past and the future and finally the sharing of knowledge and experiences stemming from this relationship is generally mediated by stories, maps and designs to share with all actors.

4. THE EUROPEAN DIMENSION OF INTEGRATIVE LANDSCAPE RESEARCH

The European Landscape Convention and a number of other Conventions brought forward by the Council of Europe illustrate the importance European society attributes to landscape and heritage. This observation can be supported by the legal and formal regulations national, regional and local authorities apply as part of their cultural and planning policy. And finally the many publications of experts and activities by local inhabitants for museums, education, tourism and heritage management confirm the importance of landscape and its historic environment for society. It means that what has been said before about the aims and approaches of the Dutch PDL/BBO programme is of general relevance to other European countries. That is why we have invited colleagues from all over Europe to join us in presenting and discussing in-depth the issues we are confronted with, although in different contexts. Their contributions have been integrated with the Dutch ones in the structure of the three types of action to facilitate the exchange of views, problems and approaches and to provoke a critical confrontation of the Dutch approach by our colleagues from abroad.

The added value of the wider European dimension is considerable. We share the same engagement with landscape and heritage. We are confronted with similar spatial and environmental problems to those raised by demography and mobility, urban development, agriculture, nature, climate, infrastructure and exploitation of resources. We are aware of the fact that these problems cross borders of states, mountains and seas and that we need and can support each other. By comparing these various similarities the differences become clear and meaningful. They make us aware of the diversity of landscapes, social and institutional structures, different sorts of problems, approaches and ways forward. Contrasting our own landscape, its meaning and its management with that of others as part of the wider European mosaic of landscapes enriches our understanding of its component parts and as a whole.

In addition, two related issues have been elaborated, namely the management of knowledge creation for landscape research and management and the prospects for the way forward in the near future. What they have in common is that we have to learn from the past, reflecting upon our own past actions in research and heritage management and what we can learn from them for the future. It is necessary to become effective from the perspective of sustainable development in the widest sense, it is stimulating to know where we are and what we should aim for, and it responds to the basic drive for researchers: curiosity, in this case about knowledge creation by 'learning through landscape'.

NOTES

1 University of Amsterdam, the Netherlands.

REFERENCES

Appadurai, A., 1986: Introduction: commodities and the politics of value, in A. Appadurai (ed.),*The social life of things. Commodities in cultural perspective*, Cambridge, 3-63.

Beek, R. van/ Tom (J.H.F.) Bloemers/L. Keunen/H. van Londen/J. Kolen, 2008: The Netherlands, in G. Fairclough/P. Grau Møller (eds.), *Landscape as Heritage. The Management and Protection of Landscape in Europe, a summary by the Cost A 27 project 'LANDMARKS*, Bern (Geographica Bernensia 79), 177-203.

Belvedere, 1999: *The Belvedere Memorandum. A policy document examining the relationship between cultural history and spatial planning*, The Hague.

Bloemers, J.H.F., 1990: 2015 NAP+: naar een Nationaal Archeologische Beleidsplan voor een landschap met een verleden in 2015?, in J.H.F. Bloemers/C.W. van Pelt/F.A. Perk (eds.), *Cultuurhistorie en milieu in 2015. Op weg naar een landschap zonder verleden?*, Amsterdam, 68-71.

Bloemers, J.H.F., 1997: Landschaftsarchäologie und Raumordnung in den Niederlanden: aktuelle Trends und Themen, *Archäologisches Nachrichtenblatt* 2, 229-243. (Archäologische Denkmalpflege im ländlichen Raum, Kolloquium im Rahmen der Jahrestagung 1996, Bautzen, 7. Mai 1996; Verband der Landesarchäologen in der Bundesrepublik Deutschland).

Bloemers, J.H.F., 1999: Regional Research Approach since the Early 70s in the Netherlands. A Fundamental Decision with Long-term Effects, in H. Sarfatij/W.J.H. Verwers/P.J. Woltering (eds.), *In Discussion with the Past. Archaeological studies presented to W.A. van Es*, Zwolle/Amersfoort, 317-27.

Bloemers, J.H.F./G.J. Borger 1988: Cultural history and environmental planning: research and policy for the future, in L.H. van Wijngaarden-Bakker/J.J.M. van der Meer (eds.), *Spatial sciences, research in progress*, Amsterdam (Nederlandse Geografische Studies, 80), 53-67.

Bloemers, J.H.F./R. During/J.N.H. Elerie/H.A. Groenendijk/M. Hidding/J. Kolen/Th. Spek/M.-H. Wijnen (eds.), 2001: *Bodemarchief in Behoud en Ontwikkeling. De conceptuele grondslagen*, Den Haag.

Brandt, R.W., 1986: What you see is what you take. Perception and use of a prehistoric landscape, in R.W.Brandt/S.E. van der Leeuw/M.J.A.N. Kooijman (eds.), *Gedacht over Assendelft*, Amsterdam (IPP working paper 6), 51-60.

During, R./H. Elerie/H.A. Groenendijk. 2001: Denken en doen: verpachten van wijsheid of delen van kennis? Pleidooi voor de verbinding van cultuurhistorische kenniseilanden en een relatie met de sociale wetenschappen, in J.H.F. Bloemers/R. During/J.N.H. Elerie/H.A. Groenendijk/M. Hidding/J. Kolen/Th. Spek/M.-H. Wijnen, *Bodemarchief in Behoud en Ontwikkeling. De conceptuele grondslagen*, Den Haag, 111-157.

Fairclough, G., 2008a: New Heritage, an Introductory Essay – People, Landscape and Change, in G. Fairclough/R. Harrison/J.H. Jameson Jr./J. Schofield (eds.), *The Heritage Reader*, London/New York, 297-312.

Fairclough, G., 2008b: 'The Long Chain'. Archaeology, historical landscape characterization and time depth in landscape, in G. Fairclough/R. Harrison/J.H. Jameson Jr./J. Schofield (eds.), *The Heritage Reader*, London/New York, 408-424.

Florence 2000: *European Landscape Convention. Florence, 20 October 2000*, Strasbourg (Council of Europe).

Greenwood, D.J./M. Levin. 2003: Reconstructing the relationships between universities and society through action research, in N.K. Denzin/Y.S. Lincoln (eds.), *The landscape of qualitative research*, Thousands Oaks.

Groenewoudt, B.J./J.H.F. Bloemers. 1997: Dealing with significance: concepts, strategies and priorities for Archaeological Heritage Management in the Netherlands, in W.J.H. Willems/ H. Kars/D.P. Hallewas (eds.), *Archaeological Heritage Management in The Netherlands. Fifty Years State Service for Archaeological Investigations*, Amersfoort, 119-172.

Ingold, T., 2000: *The Perception of the Environment. Essays in livelihood, dwelling and skill*, London/New York.

Jacobs, M., 2006: *The production of mindscapes. A comparative theory of landscape experience*, Wageningen (Ph.D. thesis Wageningen University).

Kolen, J./M. Witte, 2007: A biographical approach to regions and its value for spatial planning, in W. van der Knaap/A. van der Valk (eds.), *Multiple Landscapes. Merging Past and Present*, Wageningen, 125-145.

Kopytoff, I. 1986: The cultural biography of things: commoditization as process, in A. Appadurai (ed.), *The social life of things. Commodities in cultural perspective,* Cambridge, 64-91.

Kristiansen, K., 2009: Contract Archaeology in Europe: an experiment in diversity, *World Archaeology* 41, 641-648.

Meier, T., 2009: Umweltarchäologie, Landschaftsarchäologie, *Historia archaeologica* 70, 697-734.

Odum, H.T., 1971: *Environment, power and society*, New York.

Ruimte en Cultuur, 2005: *Actieprogramma Ruimte en Cultuur. Architectuur- en Belvederebeleid 2005-2008*, Den Haag (Ministerie van Onderwijs, Cultuur en Wetenschappen *et al.*).

Schofield, J., 2008: Heritage Management, Theory and Practice, in G. Fairclough/R. Harrison/J.H. Jameson Jr./J. Schofield (eds.), *The Heritage Reader*, London/New York, 16-30.

Tewdwr-Jones, M. (ed.), 1996: *British planning policy in transition. Planning in the Major years*, London.

Tress, B./G. Tress/G. Fry, 2006: Defining concepts and the process of knowledge production in integrative research, in B.G. Tress/G. Tress/G. Fry/P. Opdam (eds.), *From Landscape Research to Landscape Planning. Aspects of Integration, Education and Application*, Dordrecht, 13-26.

Udo de Haes, H.A., 1984: Milieukunde, begripsbepaling en afbakening, in J.J. Boersema/J.W. Copius Peereboom/W.T. de Groot (eds.), *Basisboek milieukunde. Over de analyse en oplossing van milieuproblemen*, Amsterdam, 17-30.

Valletta 1992: *European Convention on the Protection of the Archaeological Heritage (Revised) Valetta, 16.I.1992*, Strasbourg (Council of Europe).

Willems, W.J.H., 1997: Archaeological Heritage Management in the Netherlands: Past, Present and Future, in W.J.H. Willems/H. Kars/D.P. Hallewas (eds.), *Archaeological Heritage Management in The Netherlands. Fifty Years State Service for Archaeological Investigations*, Amersfoort, 3-34.

II

INSIGHTS AND PROSPECTS OF ARCHAEOLOGICAL-HISTORICAL LANDSCAPE STUDIES

Blåvand (DK), Atlantik Wall: remote controllers. *Photo: C. Paludan-Müller.*

1. Introduction to 'Protecting and Developing the Dutch Archaeological-Historical Landscape' (PDL/BBO)

Willem J.H. Willems[1]

As chairman of the steering committee of the programme 'Protecting and Developing the Dutch Archaeological-Historical Landscape' I am honoured to introduce the publication that marks the end of the programme. Or perhaps I should say its transition to a new state, because the 2008 symposium and this volume, which is intended to position our national discussions in the context of their European background, may now be continued in a network provided by the European Science Foundation and COST.

This would be a very useful development because obviously the issues we discussed during the 2008 symposium are not national at all, or at best there are some particularly Dutch aspects to the problems and challenges that affect archaeological heritage management everywhere. The latter may well be the case because the Netherlands is one of the most densely populated countries in the world in addition to being economically strongly developed. That means that the pressure on the use of space that is evident in the entire western world, and is indeed becoming evident in the central areas of the new economic powers elsewhere, is particularly strong here. While elsewhere there are still vast open spaces or at least there is some room to negotiate, the space that is available in the Netherlands to accommodate the historical and archaeological values in competition with other needs of society is extremely limited in comparison.

Fortunately, this does not imply that the cause of preserving and enhancing the remains of our past that create our identity and that are so important in many other ways is a hopeless one. It may be somewhat more difficult than elsewhere, but on the other hand our Dutch history, thanks to the need for resilient systems of water management, has provided us with both rather tough legislation developed over several centuries and a planning system that create a strong backbone for public policies. These, of course, have first to be developed and put in place and, to cut a very long story short, our symposium here can be seen as a step in that ongoing process of becoming aware of the inadequacy of an existing policy, defining a better one, ideally through research, and putting it in place.

I was a member of the Council of Europe committee that wrote what later became the Valletta Convention (Valletta 1992) and I remember I was rather pleased that we had finally found a better response to the threats that modern development posed to archaeological heritage. I knew it would require quite a fight to get all its provisions implemented in Dutch law, though like everybody else at the time I seriously underestimated how much time would be required. But even when this fight was still going on it became clear that much more was needed. On the one hand we were busy trying to get the convention implemented, while on the other hand, archaeological resource management, or cultural resource management in general, was at the same time being redefined as 'the management of change'. How to deal with the ongoing process of change in the urban and rural and marine landscapes to ascertain the survival in some form of important historical elements? That became the question. And of course it all had to be 'sustainable' as well, the new buzzword that became fashionable in the 1990s when the message from the Brundtland Commission Report on 'Our Common Future' had sunk in.

Sometime during this period the Council of Europe started work on a new convention that would add another dimension to the Valletta Convention, i.e. the Florence Convention adopted in 2000 and which is more commonly known by its proper name, the European Landscape Convention (Florence 2000). We shall come to speak of this development in the course of this book, because obviously the concept of landscape offers an appropriate framework for archaeological heritage management. Initially its relevance was underestimated, certainly in the Netherlands where the process was handled by the Ministry of Agriculture, Fisheries and Nature Conservation, not by the Ministry of Culture. I do not mean to imply anything negative about either Ministry and I know the same thing happened in many other countries. However, this shows how relevant the sociology of decision-making and the civil service can be and, more or less parallel to all that, we were doing some exercises here locally on how archaeological remains could be integrated in the planning process in such a way that they would actually be taken into serious consideration. The problem was not that there was too much opposition but rather that, even where much good will existed, integration did not really work very well. The first exercises in this respect were not particularly encouraging, especially because of the general invisibility of archaeological and some of the historical values. The need to rethink existing relations within the cultural historical disciplines and the way they could be better tied into environmental planning and development became a central issue. And because there was indeed a lot of good will, this then led to the programme in the context of which we are here together today. It was set up by the Netherlands Organization for Scientific Research NWO and supported by the Ministry of Education, Culture and Science, as well as the Ministry of Agriculture, Nature and Food Quality, the Ministry of Housing, Spatial Planning and the Environment and the Ministry of Transport, Public Works and Water Management.

Now I would not like you to assume that all this went as smoothly as would perhaps appear from what I have just said. The establishment by NWO of a programme committee and a steering committee in 2000 was preceded by long years of hard work to get the programme established and to persuade the various ministries to participate in its financing. Even though the spirit of the time was definitely favourable, it took the perseverance of a man like Professor Tom Bloemers to actually pull this off. We have been very fortunate in that for most of the period between 2000 and 2007 the steering committee consisted of dedicated individuals from each of the ministries, who together have made a significant contribution to shaping the programme by ensuring that it would be, and would remain, relevant to the policies of those ministries. From a viewpoint of a value free research that might not perhaps seem to be such a favourable circumstance, but I disagree: we intended to connect practice and theory, knowledge and action, so it was vital for the programme not that some researchers would get their pet projects financed, but that there would be practical results that were of use to policy making so the programme would really make a difference. If it has, or will, is of course for posterity to judge.

NOTES

[1] Leiden University, the Netherlands.

REFERENCES

Florence, 2000: *European Landscape Convention. Florence, 20 October 2000*, Strasbourg (Council of Europe).
Valletta, 1992: *European Convention on the Protection of the Archaeological Heritage (Revised) Valletta,*
   16.I.1992, Strasbourg (Council of Europe).

2. Planning the past. Lessons to be learned from 'Protecting and Developing the Dutch Archaeological-Historical Landscape' (PDL/BBO)

Arnold van der Valk[1]

ABSTRACT

The results of the Dutch PDL/BBO programme are introduced and summarized for an international audience. The programme is a corollary of growing public and professional interest in cultural landscape and heritage since the 1990s. This research programme is to be perceived as the scientific counterpart of the Belvedere central government policy programme. Both programmes start from the same philosophy exemplified in the slogan 'conservation through development'. Landscape heritage in the Netherlands is under threat due to urbanization, industrialization, expansion of traffic networks and environmental degradation.

Traditional practices of government-led land-use planning no longer provide a remedy against the potentially destructive forces of the contemporary fluid and extreme mobile network society. Now attention is directed towards developments which open up opportunities for heritage conservation. These trends have been identified in field research. They encompass such diverse activities as projects for regional agricultural reconstruction, cultural heritage tourism and urban development. This change is in line with a shift from development control in planning towards collaborative developmental planning. A developmental style of planning and heritage management poses challenges to the domain of applied sciences. Positivistic evidence-based planning is complemented and gradually replaced by interpretative transdisciplinary research. Major lessons learned in the PDL/BBO programme pertain to opportunities and constraints for integrative research and border traffic between the worlds of science, government and governance.

KEY WORDS

Interdisciplinarity; landscape, heritage, preservation, development; land-use planning

1. INTRODUCTION

The Netherlands covers 41,526 km^2; 14% of the surface of the country is taken up by housing, business and infrastructure, some 70% is used as agricultural land. With a population density of 500 inhabitants per km^2, it is one of the most densely populated and urbanized countries in the world (Netherlands Environmental Assessment Agency, 2008). In an economic sense, the Netherlands has been in the top 20 of the most prosperous countries of the world for decades (Van der Horst 2007; Needham 2007). The Netherlands, though small, is the world's largest exporter of agricultural products. The combination of population density and prosperity has led to extreme pressure on the use of the environment. Comparing the appearance of cities, villages and farm lands from old postcards and topographical maps from the early 1900s with the modern appearance of the Dutch cultural landscape immediately demonstrates the enormous changes that have taken place. In the eyes of many Dutch people, this has brought advantages as well as disadvantages. Traces of the past, insofar as they have not recently disappeared, are under heavy pressure in cities and villages and outside the built-up areas. Old buildings, fields separated by hedgerows, historic patterns of land parcels, irregularities in pastures; these aspects were all too often seen as obstacles for building new housing developments, road construction or attaining more efficient organization of agricultural areas (Belvedere 1999; Eerden 2008). In the period of recovery and reconstruction after World War II, these developments were seen as necessary and inescapable, similar to the air pollution and the degradation of water quality that accompanied this process. This situation began to change in the late 1980s. A growing group of citizens and politicians began to resist this thoughtless sacrifice of the traces of the past. The interest in this historical heritage was growing. The landscape is a living, dynamic heritage (Lörzing 2001; Janssen/Pieterse/Van den Broek 2007; Pedroli/Van Doorn/De Blust 2007). The landscape which is created and used by people – the cultural landscape – is an important public good. Science is responding to this growing interest (Fairclough/Rippon 2002; Ermischer 2003; Vroom 2006; Antrop 2007). The tension between preserving and developing the landscape is being acknowledged as a social and physical problem which requires policy and science to work together to find a solution. This problem can be defined as the concern about the historical-archaeological values in the metropolitan landscape (Van den Brink/Van Dijk/Van der Valk 2006; Bloemers/Van der Valk 2007). The Netherlands is not the only country struggling with this issue; there are similar problems in much of Europe, North America and Asia (Antrop 2003).

A growing number of scientific and popular publications about cultural landscapes, regional archaeology and local history serve as illustrations of the increased interest in these topics (Duncan/Duncan 1988; Schama 1995; Antrop 2000; *idem* 2007; Fairclough/Rippon 2002; Klink/Potschin/Tress 2002; Kolen 2005; Kobylinski 2006; Kühn/Danielzyk 2006). Approximately ten years ago, a group of archaeologists, historical geographers and spatial planners determined that two aspects of this body of literature remained underexposed: invisible landscapes and the way in which historic elements can contribute to the quality of the landscape in the present. These are the central questions in 'Protecting and Developing the Dutch Archaeological-Historical Landscape' (PDL/BBO), a scientific incentives programme concerning the archaeological-historical heritage in the landscape funded by the Netherlands Organization for Scientific Research (NWO) and four ministries, the Ministry of Education, Culture and Science, as well as the Ministry of Agriculture, Nature and Food Quality, the Ministry of Housing, Spatial Planning and the Environment and the Ministry of Transport, Public Works and Water Management (Bloemers 2000; *idem* 2002; *idem* 2005; Van der Valk/Bloemers 2006). This paper discusses the aims, highlights and lessons from the programme[2].

In recent years, there has been a significant increase in the appreciation of the cultural landscape by the public and by politicians; this phenomenon is taking place in both the Netherlands and abroad (Bloemers/Borger 1988; Palang/Fry 2003; Schenk 2003; Pedroli/Van Doorn/De Blust 2007; Eerden 2008). This is shown by Dutch participation in the European Landscape Convention and the implementation of a wide-ranging policy programme (Belvedere) for the integration of cultural history in spatial planning policy at both national, provincial, and municipal levels, as well as at the level of the water management boards.

The aim of the Protecting and Developing the Dutch Archaeological-Historical Landscape programme (PDL/BBO) is to provide support for scientific reflection on practices involving policy on archaeological heritage and spatial planning in order to increase the knowledge and appreciation of the archaeological, historical-geographic and architectural-historical elements and structures of the cultural landscape

(Bloemers 2000; *idem* 2002; *idem* 2005; Bloemers/Wijnen 2002; Bloemers/Van der Valk 2007). This concerns science with a social mandate, specifically the promotion of a more cautious approach to the landscape-related heritage from a distant and more recent past. One of the assumptions underlying the PDL/BBO programme is that decision makers, designers and planners are often prepared to take account of cultural history but they do not have access to the information and knowledge they require at the time they need it.

The scientific PDL/BBO programme, like its Belvedere counterpart, has the aim of linking the conservation and development of the landscape (Bloemers/Wijnen 2002; *idem* 2007; Van Leusen/Kamermans 2005). This concerns the protection of buildings, settlements, field structures and hidden landscapes from deterioration, erosion and wear by means of reuse and by developing new economic functions. This is not a simple mandate. There is often insufficient knowledge to arrive at a value for these components (Bloemers/Borger 1988; Ruijgrok 2006). The knowledge that is available is coloured by the preferences of individual scientists and administrators, the power relations within the government apparatus and coincidental discoveries (Flyvbjerg 1998; *idem* 2001). In addition, the archaeological-cultural heritage cannot be objectively delineated (Lowenthal 1996; Van Assche 2004; Duineveld 2006). This heritage has different meanings for different groups and in different time periods. For example, several decades ago, churches and houses from the nineteenth century were considered to be less valuable products from a period when architecture was at a low point. These days, many of the same buildings, at least those that have not fallen prey to demolition, are on the protected 'built heritage' lists of the national government and municipalities. These aspects from scientific theory have been debated during the programme, not only between the researchers but also in the communication with the professional community and clients.

The ensuing discussion will first discuss the main research subject, namely the cultural landscape. This discussion takes into account the salient perspective, i.e. the search for starting points for maintaining cultural-historical values as part of desirable societal developments. The search process takes place largely in the practice of land-use planning and heritage policy. A brief characterization of the spatial policy should help the reader understand the unique aspects of the PDL/BBO programme within an institutional framework. The same applies to the subsequent characterization of two trends in the heritage policy in the Netherlands. The interaction between science and policy is explained in a section on boundary work, a concept from public administration. After this, the most important integrating concepts of the PDL/BBO programme, namely action research, internal and external integration, and the biography of the landscape will be addressed. In the final section, the main points and lessons will be summarized.

2. CULTURAL LANDSCAPE

Landscape, both visible and invisible, plays a central role in the PDL/BBO programme. Invisible landscapes are the remains of culture and nature from the past which have been covered by sediments and/or water. There are many divergent definitions of landscape. The point of departure in this programme is the definition from Article 1 of the European Landscape Convention accepted by the Council of Europe in 2000: '"Landscape" means an area, as perceived by people, whose character is the result of the action and interaction of natural and/or human factors.' In Article 2, the European Landscape Convention refers emphatically to the importance of normal, everyday landscapes from the present and past. The reference to everyday landscapes is an indication of the universal value of the landscape for people. This links up with the idea that the appreciation of cultural-historical values must not be a matter for the expert elite, but should be rooted in the experience and knowledge of the local society (Coeterier 2002; Déjeant-Pons 2002).

In the PDL/BBO programme, the focus on everyday landscapes is interpreted as a reason to search for possibilities for the sustainable conservation of elements with a high cultural-historical value as part of the process of adapting to new spatial and socio-economic developments. Sustainability can be defined as "activities, processes or structures that must continue to operate or exist indefinitely" (Allen/Tainter/Hoekstra 2002).

Sustainable cultural landscape is not an objective concept, but a subjective (or intersubjective), socially and politically determined concept (Coeterier 2002; Bastian/Steinhardt 2002; Antrop 2006). Sustainability depends on various aspects such as: 1. the time period that people choose to relate to the concept of sustainability (one, two or multiple generations); 2. the delineation of the territorial units within which the pursuit of sustainability is viewed, and 3. the selection of elements which are thought to be relevant to the study of landscape. The pursuit of sustainability provides a stimulus to search for perspective-rich combinations of modern and traditional forms of land use. This process can take place not only above ground or below ground, but also in a dry or wet environment. This pursuit is connected with a certain optimism about the plasticity ("makeability") of the environment, which is thought by some to be typically Dutch (Faludi/Van der Valk 1994; Van der Valk/Bloemers 2006; Needham 2007).

The pursuit of the conservation of historical elements and structures that have lost their original functions appears at first glance to be paradoxical. In any case, it is a recent phenomenon. Throughout history, the cultural landscape has been subjected to great changes (Lörzing 2001; Palang/Fry 2003; Kühn/Danielzyk 2006). This will continue in the future. New human activities are accompanied by new forms of land use. The history of the Dutch landscape offers outstanding examples of this process. For example, consider the deforestation, burning and grazing of the virgin forests on the sandy soil regions of the Netherlands; as a result, virtually no forests remained by the High Middle Ages (Van Beek/Keunen 2006; Van Beek/Keunen/Groenewoudt 2008). At least as drastic was the draining and harvesting of the peatlands in the western region of the Netherlands in the Middle Ages. The peatlands were first drained, excavated and then dredged below the water table. The peat was dried and used as fuel (Van de Ven 1993). A proverb goes: the Dutch have burned much of their land in their fireplaces. The tension between conservation and development has existed for a very long time. Landscape conservation is a paradoxical task because traditional cultural landscapes are the unintended product of the land being worked by owners and users (Janssen/ Pieterse/Van den Broek 2007).

Long ago, the activities that took place on the land, such as agriculture, had less drastic consequences for the structure of buildings, settlements, land parcels and the soil than they do today. Equally, there are also many examples from the distant past of new activities in agriculture, transport or obtaining raw materials that have had very drastic consequences for the landscape. The result of this process has been idealized and has led to attempts at reinforcing the results of history via conservation. If the traditional functions and forms of use have been lost or are under pressure, this is a difficult task. It is impossible to 'freeze' large-scale and complex structures in the landscape that do not have a clear function. Conservation is only effective when it focuses on concrete, well delineated artefacts. If it is impossible to preserve the landscape as heritage, why is this objective pursued so intensively in the Netherlands? The answer lies in the human need to identify with one's surroundings (Belvedere 1999; Van Assche 2004).

The experience of landscape plays a role in the well-being of people and contributes to the way in which groups and individuals to find their uniqueness. "Landscape is our basic heritage. It is all-embracing and relevant to everyone. Most of what we learn and do impinges on it," wrote the British landscape geographer David Lowenthal (Lowenthal 2003, 14). For many people, the smells and colours of the landscape are an important part of their most cherished childhood memories. These days, the landscape is an important selling point in the economic sectors of recreation and tourism. References to the landscape often characterize the region or city from which people can derive a feeling of pride or shame. Lowenthal refers to the landscape as a political glue, an academic 'open Sesame' and an avant-garde emblem in prose, music, food and folklore. These days, this beloved landscape is valued even more highly because it is threatened by skyscrapers, motorways, new housing developments, bodies of water, new 'wild' nature areas and recreational forests (Lowenthal 1996; *idem* 2003).

Since the beginning of the twentieth century, new structures have had a mono-functional, large-scale and dynamic character (Kerkstra *et al.* 2003; Janssen 2006; Janssen/Pieterse/Van den Broek 2007). Functional landscapes with an urban character offer little room for the small-scale and static traces of human activities from the past. In this context there is tension between the 'normal' dynamics in the landscape and the desire to conserve ecological and cultural-historical values. In the Netherlands, as in most other European countries, it is the responsibility of the government to safeguard and reinforce the quality of the landscape. This takes place in an interaction between the integral policy of land-use planning and the sectoral policy to conserve the archaeological-cultural heritage. It is perhaps 'typically Dutch' to assign the government a central role in the complex process of spatial development. This assumption is subject to criticism (Van Assche 2006).

3. LAND-USE PLANNING

Urbanization is the most important landscape-shaping force in the Netherlands (Faludi/Van der Valk 1994; Van der Valk 2002; Needham 2007). One glance at the topographical map shows that the central and southern regions of the country can be viewed as a patchwork of cities and open spaces. During the twentieth century the urban field has taken on the form of a horseshoe-shaped ring of densely urbanized areas surrounding a relatively open and green area; planners refer to the urbanized ring as the Randstad and the open area as the Green Heart. Amsterdam, with its airport and harbour, is located in the northern part of this urban field. In recent planning documents the region around Amsterdam portrays itself as the "Amsterdam metropolitan region". The open landscape enclosed in the mesh of this urban network is now called a metropolitan landscape (Van den Brink/Van Dijk/Van der Valk 2006). A significant part of this open landscape is still being used for traditional agriculture, especially for raising livestock. An increasing part of the open area is being assigned different types of land use, such as natural areas, woods, golf courses, water storage and cultural history. In these areas, the term 'countryside' appears to have little relevance any longer because the driving forces are related to urbanization. This occurs, for example, with respect to land prices. In the vicinity of the cities, a farmer who wants to expand his farm must pay a land price that is often two times higher, or even more, than its agricultural value (approximately € 5 per m^2). In terms of their mentality and consumption pattern, the residents of villages and farms are hardly different from the residents of the surrounding cities. This is why more and more voices are calling for the term 'countryside' to be replaced by the term 'metropolitan landscape' for areas in the urban sphere of influence, which comprises more than half of the land area of the Netherlands.

The awareness that space is in short supply has exerted a powerful effect in the Netherlands since the first half of the twentieth century (Needham 2007). For more than a century, this has provided ideal conditions for the powerful interference of government in the spatial organization of societal phenomena. Land-use planning ensures the order and regularity that have traditionally characterized the appearance of the Dutch landscape. The rational parcellation of polders and reclamation projects and the clearly delineated, compact cities and villages betray the organizing hand of government involvement. Land-use planning is an indirect form of interference with the development of the environment. This concerns facilitating the need for land, buildings and infrastructure by organizing orderly, public decision-making processes to plan the use and zoning of the land. Spatial planning is the support that is provided to this governmental activity by experts who engage in research, design and consulting (Van der Burg 2004; Needham 2007).

Government is a many-headed monster. In the Netherlands, there are three levels of government: the national government, provinces and municipalities. In the area of land-use planning and heritage policy each of these levels of government has a specific package of tasks which varies through time. The level of government that is most directly involved in land-use planning is the municipality, of which there are 441 (1 January, 2009) in total. The total number of municipalities is now declining rapidly due to voluntary and forced mergers. The municipalities can regulate the use of land by means of a zoning plan (land-use plan). This is the only plan that is binding for the individual citizen. When making a zoning plan, a municipal administration is bound to many types of strategic plans and policy documents from the national government and province in the areas of land-use planning, infrastructure, environment, economy, nature, cultural history and agriculture. Many municipalities also have their own strategic policy document, a structure (spatial) plan which broadly outlines future spatial developments. Provinces draw up regional spatial plans and strategic visions (indicative plans) which offer frameworks for the spatial development on their territory and for the actions of municipalities. National government provides legislation and establishes general terms for the desired spatial development. The Spatial Planning Act contains rules and regulations but does not stipulate substantive quality criteria; in this respect, it differs from comparable legislation in most other countries. The act was thoroughly revised between 2000 and 2008 (Needham 2007). Substantive guidelines, both binding and non-binding, for example those concerning the co-ordination of housing construction with road construction, used to be provided in national policy memoranda on land-use planning, which are updated approximately once every ten years. The most recent such memorandum, known as the National Spatial Strategy, was published in 2004 (Faludi/Van der Valk 1994; Van der Valk 2002; Van der Burg 2004; Needham 2007). After the revision of the Spatial Planning Act in the summer of 2008, substantive guidelines were legally moulded in a structural vision and a legally binding implementation decision respectively. Binding and non-binding guidelines are conceived separately. The revision of the planning act and the conception of strict guidelines on the national level marks a drastic break in Dutch planning practice. The consequences are not yet clear.

Traditionally, land-use planning in the Netherlands makes use of the zoning maps and land-use regulations that offer the government the possibility to forbid undesired forms of land use. Whether or not these powers are used is a different story. This form of planning, which uses prohibitions, is called development control planning, with an emphasis on control. Two successful examples of development control planning are the following: keeping the Green Heart open and establishing green buffer zones between urban agglomerations in the densely urbanized western region of the Netherlands (Van der Valk 2002; Needham 2007; Van der Valk/Van Dijk 2009). Development control planning, essentially the prohibition of development, is encountering growing resistance in the civil society. Co-operation between societal parties and development control planning has increased to the extent that prohibitions are accompanied by financial compensation. Previously, the care of cultural-historical values had always been linked to conservation by means of development control planning.

The more recent counterpart of development control planning is development planning. 'Development' refers to the promotion of desired developments and projects. In practical application, the term development planning is not always used consistently. The most important common characteristics are the following: taking account of the dynamics in society, centralized implementation, attention for economics, participation of the population, more attention for concrete projects than for abstract plans and co-operation between public and private actors. Often, there is extra attention for developments at a regional scale. This is referred to as integral regional development. This regional level has also been given extensive attention in the PDL/BBO programme as part of regionally oriented projects. These projects will be discussed below. Development planning is important for cultural history because the traditional pursuit of conservation, expressed in the most important government memorandum on cultural history, the 1999 Belvedere Memorandum (Belvedere 1999), has been qualified to become 'conservation through development'. This new approach is compatible with the transition of development control planning into development planning.

During the period between 1945 and 1995, the professional group of urban architects and planners showed little interest in cultural history (Nelissen/Needham 1996; Needham 2007). After World War II, attention was focused on solving the housing shortage and on the late industrialization of the Netherlands. During this period efficiency in land use regulation was a precondition for economic recovery. Cities and agricultural areas were designed strictly according to the principles of functionalism. Form followed function. As such beautification and heritage management were not a matter of great concern to planners and politicians. This indifference to the past ebbed away during the 1990s (De Haas *et al.* 1999; Reuselaars 2003; Netherlands Environmental Assessment Agency 2008). Cultural history gradually began to play a role in the pursuit of spatial quality. In the Fourth National Policy Document on Spatial Planning in the Netherlands, spatial quality is cited as a core objective of land-use planning, in addition to sustainability and economic development. Spatial quality is interpreted differently for each situation, whereby experts assign a more universal meaning to several general abstract values. The following table (Fig. 1) provides an example of a tool that is used by planners to provide an interpretation of quality in interactive decision-making processes in various regions.

The revaluation of the archaeological-cultural heritage is expressed in the use of the concept of 'cultural planning' in planning studies. Cultural planning plays an important role in the Belvedere Memorandum (Belvedere 1999; Reuselaars 2003) and in the PDL/BBO programme. First of all, this concept expresses the fact that intangible values such as beauty, diversity, historical continuity, regional use and stories play an important role in people's sense of well-being. However, not everyone agrees on the values as mediated by experts and stakeholders. The process of evaluation and valorization must take place as part of interactive policy-making processes. In this way conditions are established for creating a common image of the characteristics of the village, town or region. Design is used as a search instrument. This is an

	Economic interest	Interest to society	Ecological interest	Cultural interest
User value	Allocational efficiency	Access	External safety	Freedom of choice
	Accessibility	Equitable distribution	No negative impacts	Cultural diversity
	Incentives	Input of diverging interests	Water system in equilibrium	
	Combined use	Options for stakeholder groups	Green Networks	
Perceived value	Image	Equality	Tranquillity and space	Individuality
	Value for money	Engagement	Natural beauty	Coherence
	Attractiveness	Social safety	Healthy habitat	Cultural beauty
				Environment full of contrast
Future value	Stability and flexibility	Everyone on board	Ecological stocks	Heritage
	Agglomeration	Widespread support in society	Sustainable ecosystems	Integration
	Clustered attractions			Cultural renewal
				Identity

Fig. 1
Matrix of the interpretations of 'spatial quality' as it is used in interactive plan making; characteristics to be specified per area *(after Dauvellier 2004, 27)*.

answer to the paradox of increasing pluriformity of values combined with the increased mutual dependency in the modern network society. Identity (i.e. the specific character of an area), therefore plays an important role in the process of research, design and negotiation. Identity is a product of social construction. It acquires meaning in the midst of differences as people perceive them in their space and time. This concerns the perceived differences between 'there' and 'here', between 'before' and 'now'. In this case, identity is that which people believe has permanent value under changing conditions (Rooijakkers 1999, 301; Raagmaa 2002; Brace 2003; Lowenthal 2003).

4. HERITAGE POLICY

The Belvedere Memorandum (Belvedere 1999) provides the parameters of heritage policy in the Netherlands which continue to apply to this day. Since 2007, heritage policy has been the responsibility of the Cultural Heritage Agency of the Ministry of Education, Culture and Science. The agricultural landscape and the historical-geographical barriers fall primarily under the responsibility of the Ministry of Agriculture, Nature and Food Quality.

The relationship between heritage policy and spatial policy is not without tension (During *et al.* 2006; Eerden 2008). This can be explained in part by the 'normal' tension between integral spatial policy, which requires additional aspects to be taken into account, and sectoral policy, which focuses on a specific interest with implications for land use. This tension is also related to the divergent modes of thought on the management of archaeological and cultural heritage and corresponding opinions about the possibilities and limitations of spatial planning and design (Fig. 2). These two modes of thought are defined here as 'positivist' and 'interpretive', analogous to a frequently used dichotomy in the sociology of science.

This dichotomy runs through the Cultural Heritage Agency and the PDL/BBO research programme and explains conflicting ambitions and tendencies at the interface between science and policy. It also says something about positive and negative feelings concerning land-use planning in the cultural-historical disciplines. The positivist school of thought in heritage management generally takes a sceptical approach towards spatial policy. The underlying thought is the following: planners must weigh up the pros and cons of planning options, and experiences from the past have shown that its weak economic importance leads almost by definition to a low priority for archaeological-cultural heritage. This is partly due to the fact that planners and designers have acquired little knowledge of, and affinity with, the past during their training. This stands in contrast to an expectant attitude in a school of thought that approaches the archaeological-cultural heritage as a way to give meaning to places in the present, which is defined here as interpretive.

The first school of thought named above is the oldest. The 'positivist' label refers to scientific assumptions. Positivists have high expectations with respect to the possibility of objectively mapping out and valuing the object of concern, i.e. the stock of archaeological items, monuments and cultural landscapes, separate from preferences and time-bound beliefs. The objects of concern (the archaeological-cultural heritage) are approached as a collection of valuable relics from the past that have miraculously escaped the modern destructive urge. These relics can be valued on the basis of their rarity, representational value, condition and uniqueness. All relics together are considered to be a stock of objects with irreplaceable value. The reasoning is as follows: as the process of spatial development proceeds, with its inherent tendency towards uniformity, increasing scale, dynamics and efficiency, this stock becomes smaller. In this school of thought, the archaeological-cultural heritage must be preserved by preventing new development as much as possible. The primary characteristic of the positivist school of thought is that 'hard', preferably quantifiable values are allocated to historical objects. Analogous to the thinking about scarce environmental resources, one can also relate the pursuit of sustainability to the conservation of scarce cultural resources. This way of thinking is based on large-scale surveys and selection projects, such as the

Characteristics	Positivistic	Interpretative
Item to be conserved	Relic	Ensemble
Academic attitude and type of valuation	Quantification; reductionist	Qualitative; constructivist
Metaphor	Stock; archive	Genius loci; characteristic
Principal focus on preservation by	Protection	Development
Attitude in policy	Specialist by sector	Integrated, focused on collaboration
Bearing upon disciplines	Monodisciplinary	Multidisciplinary and interdisciplinary
Societal	Elitist	Transdisciplinary
Attitude towards spatial planning	Sceptical	Expectant
Extreme variant	Historical econometric	Historical nihilism

Fig. 2 Schools of thought within heritage management (ideal types) (Van der Valk/Bloemers 2006, 25).

built heritage survey project involving architecture between 1850 and 1960 of the former State Service for the Conservation of the Built Heritage and the initiative for an archaeological 'balance sheet' from the former State Service for Archaeological Investigations in the Netherlands (Lauwerier/Lotte 2002; Van Dockum/Lauwerier 2003).This vision of built heritage conservation results almost automatically in an argument to conserve the most valuable relics. This puts the guardians of the cultural-historical heritage in a defensive position with respect to the supporters of other interests that have demands on space.

The interpretive school of thought defines the inherited objects and their corresponding values as 'soft' mental constructions (Norberg-Schultz 1980; Ashworth/Turnbridge 1996; Kolen/Witte 2006). Values are allocated in a process of assigning meaning in the here and now, which can differ between groups and time periods. In this school of thought, traces of the past are seen as mental, subjective (or intersubjective) constructions. Coherence is important because this provides meaning. In the second, integral school of thought regarding heritage policy, the past is represented not only by exceptional physical relics, but also by all forms, memories, notions and identification sources that are inherited in and with the landscape. In this vision, the past is always and automatically a fully-fledged part of the stream of change that washes over the landscape. Residents, designers and politicians have the option of choosing various forms of sustainability or of making a break with the past. This interpretive school of thought poses new questions to the conservation of built heritage, such as:

- Is it sensible to prevent the further decline of remains from the 'milieu de mémoire' that characterize an area and to restore the characteristics of the regional landscape?
- Is it better to continue the regional tradition in a new spirit?
- Do we choose to give shape to places with new notions and associations?

In its most extreme form, this belief leads to a form of historical nihilism. In contrast, a mild variant of the second school of thought can contribute to the pursuit of cultural-historical sustainability and build a bridge to spatial planning. The remainder of this paper is primarily devoted to concepts that play a role (or could play a role) in bridging the gap between the scientific domain of cultural-historical knowledge and the domain of spatial policy. A theory from public administration is of help in acquiring a grasp on the possibilities and limitations of interaction between science and policy.

5. BOUNDARY WORK

In public administration, a theory has recently been developed about the interaction between scientists and policy makers, namely the theory of boundary work (Halffman/Hoppe 2005, 135). This theory forms the basis of the concept of 'external integration', one of the central theoretical notions (unifying concepts) in the PDL/BBO programme. According to Hoppe (Hoppe 2002; *idem* 2008) the domains of policy and science show major differences regarding the following aspects: the validity of arguments, the lines of reasoning and the way in which conclusions are drawn. Aspects such as veracity, logical consistency and clarity play a central role in the world of science, while the world of politics is based more on persuasion, vision and realism. Something that is possible in one world is not automatically relevant in the other world. Policymakers and scientists need each other. Science provides legitimacy to political decisions. In turn, scientists obtain their tasks from politics. This mutual dependency means that scientists cannot operate in a social vacuum and cannot limit themselves to the facts. Politics expects social yields,

	Primacy of science	No primacy; dialogue	Primacy of politics
Divergence	1. Science as a sweet shop; production of good ideas	2. Science as a producer of arguments for a specific aim; advocacy model	3. Science as a producer of data; bureaucracy as a neutral servant
Convergence	4. Knowledge is the power of science; technocracy	5. Community of scientists as a political role model; pragmatic learning processes	6. Power makes use of knowledge; engineer's model; social technology

Fig. 3
Types of boundary interaction between science and politics (*adapted from Hoppe 2002*).

i.e. applications. This takes place, for example, by developing new technology (conservation), contributing to scenarios for landscape development, developing systems for valuing landscape elements and contributing to the selection of valuable landscapes. Clearly, the boundary between facts and values is fluid. This makes it difficult, if not impossible, to separate political and scientific judgement.

Hoppe (Hoppe 2008) suggests that scientists should not be timorous and should keep to a prudent course midway between attraction and rejection. Scientists must deal deliberately and critically with the arguments that are exchanged and the pressure to which they are exposed in society. They must not allow politicians to walk all over them. The exchange of arguments and judgements at the boundary between science and policy is often chaotic and is accompanied by distortion. Rightly or wrongly, scientists often say that policymakers are incapable of converting the demands of society into questions that can actually be researched. In turn, politicians complain that scientists provide answers to questions that have never been asked by politics. Hoppe concludes that it is impossible and pointless to recommend a single ideal model for boundary work. He sketches a number of models, a typology based on observations in the practice of policy, where people can make a choice according to the concrete points of departure and conditions of a concrete policy situation. Figure 3 presents six models of boundary work. These models can be used to characterize the way in which the boundary interactions between cultural history and spatial policy have proceeded in the regionally oriented studies within the PDL/BBO programme.

Before the start of the PDL/BBO programme this issue had never been studied fundamentally at the interface between heritage policy and land-use planning. During brainstorming sessions, experiences and beliefs about this issue were exchanged in the PDL/BBO programme and lessons were formulated. The promotion of boundary interactions between science and policy, but also between various scientific disciplines, is the rationale behind the notion of 'integration', which is a core concept of the PDL/BBO programme.

6. INTERNAL AND EXTERNAL INTEGRATION

One of the main objectives within the PDL/BBO programme is the promotion of transfer and application of scientific knowledge about the history of the Netherlands' landscape. The transfer of expertise from the domain of science to other domains is defined here as integration. Two forms of integration are identified in this programme, internal and external integration. The difference between them may be explained by reference to the perspective of the observer. The observer is located within the cultural-

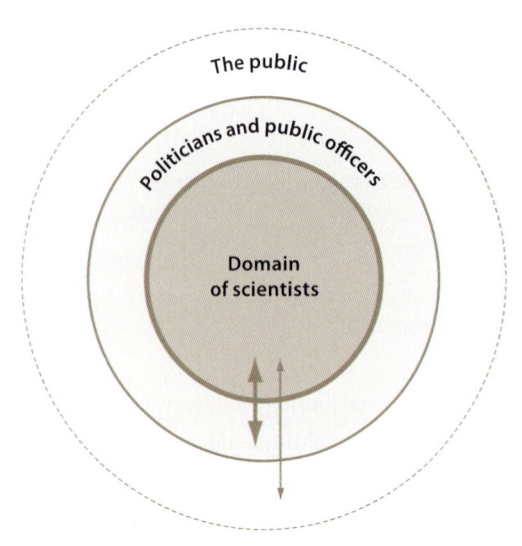

Fig. 4
Three domains of integration.

historical sciences and is looking outward, observing adjacent domains other than scientific ones. The PDL/BBO research programme focuses on three relevant domains:
1. the domain of science (core),
2. the domain of administration and policy, and
3. the domain of interested lay people.

The three separate domains of science, policy and interested lay people are pictured as three concentric circles (Fig. 4). The innermost circle exclusively comprises scientific activities. The second, larger circle borders in the domain of political decision-making, policy-making, social dialogue, negotiation with interest groups, analysis of landscape-shaping forces, the planning process and landscape design. This domain is populated predominantly by civil servants, policy advisors, politicians, representatives of interest groups and opinion leaders. The third, outermost circle comprises the domain of the popularization of scientific research, interested lay people, journalism and education.

This distinction between domains is relevant to the way information and expertise are exchanged. Each domain is separately subject to specific demands regarding the depth of expertise, the use of language, the nature of the techniques, the nature of the media and the complexity of the information. The

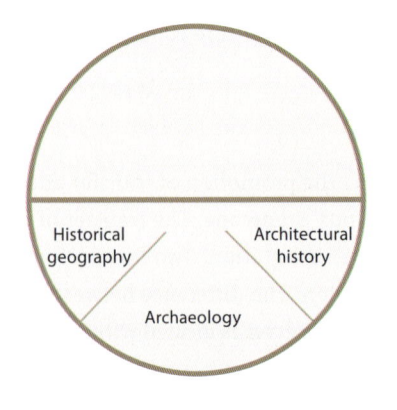

Fig. 5
Cultural history in the Netherlands.

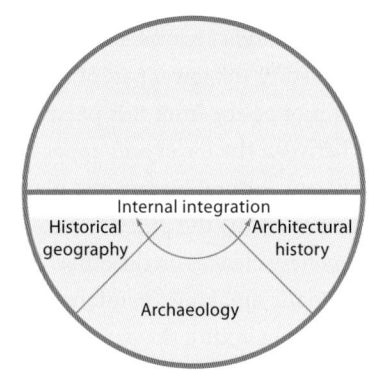

Fig. 6
Internal integration in the domain of cultural history in the Netherlands.

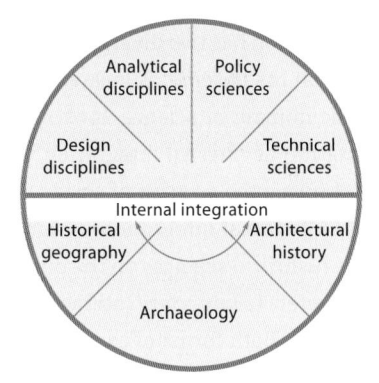

Fig. 7
Internal integration at the interface of disciplines involved in investigations in the biography of landscape.

PDL/BBO programme emphasizes the domain of science and the boundary interactions between science and policy. Communication with the general public is of secondary importance.

The PDL/BBO programme distinguishes itself from conventional incentive programmes for scientific research in the Netherlands due to its focus on issues such as the integration of knowledge and co-operation between scientists. Generating new, pioneering scientific knowledge is subordinate to disseminating and exchanging this knowledge in the form of appealing images and understandable language. The researchers make a distinction between internal and external integration. Internal integration is defined here as the co-ordination of the process of production and application of knowledge between three scientific disciplines, each of which is involved with the study of the history of the landscape, both above and below ground, i.e. archaeology, historical geography and architectural history (Figs. 5-7).

Fig. 8
Internal and external integration at the interface of humanities, social sciences, technical sciences and planning sciences.

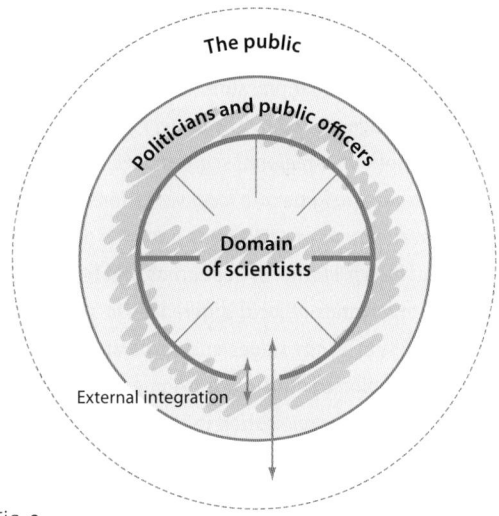

Fig. 9
External integration at the interfaces between science and policy and between the humanities and planning sciences.

II.2 INSIGHTS AND PROSPECTS • 33

External integration has two diverging connotations (Figs. 8-9). This is easier to understand if the reader remembers that the observer is located in the sphere of cultural history, the lower part of the circle representing the domain of science, looking outward to the domain of policy from this perspective. The first connotation of external integration refers to interactions between the lower and upper half of the circle representing the domain of science, i.e. the interface between cultural history and planning sciences (Fig. 8). External integration within the domain of science concerns the pursuit of co-operation between the historical sciences on the one hand and design and policy sciences on the other. The second connotation refers to boundary interactions between science and policy-making, therefore between two domains (Fig. 9). Both forms of external integration have equal weight within the programme. Within the category of the policy and design sciences an additional distinction is made between the following: design disciplines (urban design, landscape architecture), policy studies (planning studies and public administration), technical design disciplines (civil engineering, hydraulic engineering) and analytical disciplines (human geography, social-spatial analysis). Co-operation between various design and policy sciences is not self-evident (De Jonge 2009). However, inadequate integration within this group of sciences falls outside the remit of this programme, unless it has immediate repercussions for the boundary interactions between the domains of science and policy.

If representatives from the various domains are brought together with the objective of generating and applying knowledge in mutual consultation, we refer to this as transdisciplinarity. Transdisciplinarity is therefore the transboundary exchange of knowledge (Fry 2001; Tress/Tress/Fry 2003; Tress *et al* 2006).

The East Netherlands Project: a regional case study

The Eastern Netherlands Project is one out of four comprehensive regional studies exploring the intricacies of the concept of landscape biography. The biography metaphor is used as a device for boundary work. The project focuses on the cover-sand landscapes in the eastern Netherlands in the Achterhoek and Salland regions (Van Beek/Keunen 2006; Keunen in prep.). The project team is led by archaeologists and historical geographers. The areas are exposed to increasing pressures of urbanization, industrialization, water management and nature development. Because of this, cultural-historical values of this rural landscape are under pressure. A biography of this region establishes a link between the cultural historical knowledge gained by the project and daily management and planning practices. Developments are studied both on a regional scale, in order to expose broad patterns and long-term trends, and in smaller areas to gain insights into local variations. Broad patterns and general trends analysed are iron ore mining, development of settlement patterns and dispersion of isolated homesteads, road patterns and the use and interpretation of peat areas and brooks. An important conclusion attached to the broad pattern is the importance of local differences in socio-economic practices and habits due to differences in size and height of sandy ridges and dispersion of ridges and depressions in the cover-sand landscape. This gives the region a small-scale, fragmented character, which had a significant bearing on the potential for occupation and exploitation in the medieval period.

The research design implies relevance for both internal and external integration in conformity with the notions developed early in the programme (Bloemers et al. 2001).

Interdisciplinarity is incorporated in the composition and daily practices of the research team. The main framework is formed by an archaeologist and a historical geographer, both Ph.D. students, who exchange data and meet on a regular basis. Co-operation ultimately results in joint publications. Besides archaeology and historical geography, attention is paid to physical geography, palaeobotany and toponymic research. Collaborative practices between researchers, local authorities and non-governmental organizations have been established in the region from the outset. All the participants meet in a common platform where specific research questions are asked and discussed and provisional conclusions exchanged. One added value of this project is the intensive co-operation of groups of undergraduate students in landscape architecture, planning and social spatial analysis at Wageningen University. The students are capable of generating specific data for the Ph.D. students and receive training in aspects of the use of the biographical method in return.

Research methodology in this project is in line with the geographical approach in landscape biography. The core object of research is spatial phenomena and transformations within the cover-sand landscapes of the eastern Netherlands from the past to the present. The emphasis in this case study is on the physical characteristics of the region and on land use, but less on cultural interpretations and valuation. Two examples may serve to shed light on the outcomes of this study.

Interdisciplinary co-operation between archaeologists and geographers has proved most successful so far for the understanding of hitherto unexplained phenomena in medieval times. This pertains to the development of farmsteads and the adjoining field patterns. Many questions could not be answered before due to the scarcity of written records. Comparative research by archaeologists and historical-geographers has proved successful by means of the formulation and testing of a set of hypotheses using alternating disciplinary perspectives. With the help of these hypotheses and the outcomes of the micro-case study, the results of this approach can be applied to comparable situations, thus revealing a regional trend (Van Beek/Keunen 2006).

The second example pertains to the use of a detailed case study in the hamlet of Colmschate for the construction of a predictive model for the establishment of the age of common types of settlement in the research area. The model is based upon certain assumptions, for example that the largest and most fertile cover-sand ridges were the most favourable for occupation. Another assumption is that the names of farmsteads inscribed in the early medieval records of old and distinguished churches and monasteries indicate an origin in early-medieval times or slightly later. This hypothesis is being examined in archaeological field research. The provisional results from the inspection of trenches and field surveys indicate the need to revise the model regarding the prediction of the landscape elements most favourable to settlement in medieval times (Van Beek/Keunen 2006; Van Beek/Groenewoudt/Keunen 2007). The model will be used for the compilation of prospective GIS-based maps of early-medieval settlement patterns. These maps are considered to be a relevant input into the process of spatial planning and reconstruction and revitalization of rural areas. One of the sponsors of the project, 'het Overstícht', a non-governmental consulting organization active in the domain of building and planning, will use the results in its activities.

7. CO-OPERATION IN ACTION RESEARCH

Participants in the PDL/BBO programme have gained experience in co-operation by practising action research. Action research provides a template for co-operation between scientists and stakeholders. The term 'action' refers to decision making and government action. Action research is often used to allow scientists to play an active role in the process of discussion in which decisions are made. The term 'research' refers to the scientific knowledge which plays a role in that process. The concept was developed to enable researchers to participate in the complex and often chaotic process of political and bureaucratic decision-making. As part of this type of research, alternatives for the solution of societal issues are explored and the pros and cons of arguments are weighed (Senge 1990; Wenger 1997; Greenwood/Levin 1998; During/Elerie/Groenendijk 2001, 115; Argyris/Schön 1996). This method of working interactively is often used in spatial planning. Consequently there is a relatively large amount of literature on this topic. The literature on policy studies concerning the advantages and disadvantages of this form of cooperation has played a role in the reflection of the scholars active in the programme during and after the fieldwork. These reflections revolved around questions about inclusion and exclusion of disciplines and stakeholders, the articulation of problems and the role of power in decision-making.

Action research takes place within the interactive field between science and policy, between the world where objective truth is the central focus and the world where everything is concerned with making correct, i.e. responsible, decisions. In policy, values and emotions play a role that is equally important to scientific knowledge (During/Elerie/Groenendijk 2001, 114). In action research all parties concerned seek pro and con arguments about viable alternatives related to the objectives. In this way, a contribution is provided to responsible decision-making based on a realistic application of the ideal of rationality (bounded rationality) (Simon 1969; Alexander 1986, 11; Faludi 1986).

The generation of scientific knowledge about cultural history takes place by means of collecting, processing and analysing data about elements and structures in the landscape. Due to its approach, in the PDL/BBO programme the object of research is sometimes also defined as the archaeological-historical landscape. Because an expansion of perspective has occurred in the course of research, in this overview paper the subject of research will be referred to as cultural landscape. The interpretation of the collected information brings up many questions about time-linked and group-linked values. In this context impossible trade-offs must be made between disciplines, winners and losers are defined and meanings are assigned. These types of issues always play a role in the boundary interactions between science and policy. The ultimate choice of criteria for valuation systems is, or should be, a political matter. Several studies in adjoining fields that reflect on the results of action research have shown that many of these choices are made implicitly. This can easily lead to scientists complaining about manipulation, people following the pet notions of their own discipline or deliberately promoting the interests of organized professionals at the cost of amateurs (Duineveld 2006).

Action research as an operational method for interactive and transdisciplinary work has primarily been used experimentally in regionally oriented projects. These projects generate integral and region-specific knowledge and are designed in such a way as to promote internal and external integration of disciplines and societal activities. Regional studies are multidisciplinary, interdisciplinary and trans-disciplinary in nature. They are set up in order to test normative-theoretical principles in the PDL/BBO programme proposal and conceptual studies in complex situations in practice. The research design leaves ample room for learning loops and reflection in action (Schön 1983; Argyris/Schön 1996). The perspective from which the observations are made is the biography of the landscape. This concept is explained below. An integral, regionally oriented approach is intended to present multifaceted knowledge about the genesis of the landscape in such a way that it provides a stimulus for application by designers, developers and politicians. In this way, information about the landscape can play a role in the conservation of the built heritage (archaeological or otherwise), which is a task of heritage policy, and can also play a role in spatial

planning and the design of the future landscape. Four regions have been selected in the Netherlands, one from every quarter of the compass, for regionally oriented research. They serve as 'windows' on the evolution and development of the region in order to do justice to the most important archaeological and historical values in the landscape (Spek/Brinkkemper/Speleers 2006, 337). The selected regions are:
1. the region of the historical Oer-IJ in the province of North Holland;
2. the region of the Drentse Aa in the north of Drenthe;
3. the south-eastern region of the province North Brabant and
4. a region in the southwest of the province of Overijssel and the northeast of the province of Gelderland.

The process of knowledge production in the regionally oriented projects is led by both demand-driven and supply-driven factors. Demand-driven is defined here as 'driven by concrete knowledge questions from politicians and other professionals in the field'. In this context, supply-driven is defined as: 'led by knowledge questions that emerge from the practice of science, i.e. pioneering research'. Seen in retrospect, the exchange of experiences during co-operation between researchers and the discussion about varyingly successful attempts to achieve co-operation in analyses and policy proposals were among the main benefits of this programme. The results of these learning processes have only been superficially applied in the scientific publications by researchers within the programme. There are various reasons for this. First, there is a natural tendency among researchers to travel familiar paths in order to satisfy the demands for publication. Much of the fieldwork was conducted by Ph.D. students who gave priority to their dissertations. This is usually an individual project with a monodisciplinary approach. The transfer of the research outcomes into plans and other policy products requires a great deal of time and primarily takes place at the end, following the completion of the programme.

> *The example of the Southern Netherlands project: biography of landscape and action research*
>
> *Politicians attach great value to the recognizability of storylines in the biography for residents of the region. Researchers are encouraged to 'highlight' specific popular themes. Some researchers have difficulty with such a historicizing approach, while others think it is a good way to bring cultural history to the attention of the public (Kolen/Witte 2006; Van Londen 2006).*
>
> *In the Southern Netherlands project, the emphasis on recent history has been a success (Roymans/Gerritsen 2002; Kolen 2004; Bosma/Wallagh 2006; Rensink/Gerritsen/Roymans 2006). In this region, cultural-historical research takes place in the context of a large-scale reconstruction of the pig farming sector and the creation of new, environmentally benign ways for the local population to earn a living. This offers a beneficial context for making references to large-scale agriculture during the Roman era. The message is that there is nothing new under the sun. Since time immemorial, agriculture has been an important means for subsistence.*
>
> *All research teams noted that success often depended on contact with an important policymaker, a civil servant or politician. In policy jargon, such a key individual is known as a sponsor. In cases where such a sponsor is lacking, cultural history often loses out in the battle for space. In most provinces, and to a lesser extent in municipalities, cultural history plays a subsidiary role in land-use planning. Among other things, this has to do with the fact that cultural history has been assigned to the policy sector of culture within the provincial civil service apparatus. Economically powerful interests are given prior-*

ity over culture. One problem that can be reported in all regions is the disappearance of such a sponsor due to elections or reorganizations. This problem occurs more frequently at a provincial, rather than a municipal, level.

Knowledge about the institutional context and the characteristics of the region is vitally important in order to make realistic proposals. One disadvantage for cultural historians in design and policy processes is the relative unfamiliarity of archaeologists and historians with concrete legal and financial policy instruments. Knowledge of instruments determines the feasibility of concrete proposals that emerge from the biography of the landscape. A lesson learned about participation in regionally-linked projects is that expertise is required about spatial legislation, funding systems and other policy instruments. Therefore, archaeologists and historians involved in landscape biographical research are well advised to consult professional planners, economists and law experts.

8. BIOGRAPHY OF LANDSCAPE

A unifying concept in the PDL/BBO programme is the biography of landscape (Hidding/Kolen/Spek 2002, 8; Bloemers/Van der Valk 2007; Kolen 2005; Kolen/Witte 2006; Spek/Brinkkemper/Speleers 2006; Van Londen 2006). It is a concept that concerns a specification of the substantive object of research, i.e. landscape. Some researchers in the programme prefer the term 'cultural biography of the landscape', taking a leaf from the works of Kopytoff (Kopytoff 1986; Roymans 1995; Rooijakkers 1999). The addition of 'cultural' refers to one of the sources of inspiration, namely anthropological literature (Kolen/Witte 2006, 129; Appadurai 1986). The other, older source of inspiration is geographer Marwyn Samuels (Samuels 1979). There is also a third source: an approach within the psycho-social sciences that focuses on the aspect of experience. In the section below, I will address the sources of inspiration, to the extent that this throws light on the use of the concept within the PDL/BBO programme. The interpretations as they are reconstructed here are not mutually exclusive. There are differences in emphasis. In the programme, the geographical variant plays the central role.

An example of biography: the Oer-IJ region

The Oer-IJ region northwest of Amsterdam is a metropolitan wetland environment occupied by a highly dynamic society living in a typical and surprisingly rich Dutch landscape (Bloemers/Van der Valk 2007, 161; Van Londen 2006; Van de Ven 1993). The traveller arriving by land, air or water gets a striking impression of a bustling city, contrasting with a pattern of polders, canals and windmills dating back to the age of Rembrandt and before. At first glance, from the air, the main structural elements seem to be marked by colours: the grey-blue sea dotted by white-crested waves, the yellow-gold beach and dunes, and behind them the multi-coloured bulb fields and fresh green meadows perforated by lakes. Together everything seems to fit perfectly into the image created by inhabitants and visitors, that of the well organized delta landscape branded as 'Holland'. However, by looking closer and, quite literally, deeper under the surface, into the past and possible future of that environment, certain aspects of that image change. The number of dimensions has been multiplied during the continuous transformation of that landscape by the rising sea level and man's past roles. An expert in cultural history would know that many more landscape layers are invisible, hidden under the surface, and extend back in time from its origins more than 5,000 years to the landscape visible today. Planners are aware of the actual route, taken by towns, villages and rural areas, in their transformation into a metropolitan landscape of urban networks sepa-

rated by green belts (Faludi/Van der Valk 1994; Van der Valk/Van Dijk 2009). They encounter growing public concern over the management of their environment and the protection of the natural and cultural resources in the present landscape.

The idea of studying the history and transformation of landscapes with the aid of the biography metaphor originates from human geography, specifically from the phenomenological direction, better known as the humanistic school. Beginning in the mid-1970s, the members of this school opposed the one-sided quantitative approach towards human behaviour in the New Geography.[7] In this context, a pioneering article published in 1979 by the American geographer Marwyn Samuels is particularly noteworthy. It concerned the use of the biography metaphor for the study of landscape. Samuels used the concept to focus attention on humans as actors and an important landscape-shaping force. He opposed elaborate quantitative descriptions in which actions of groups and individuals remain invisible. According to Samuels, people's actions are based on specific pre-established ideas about the possibilities and limitations of their environment. He therefore made a distinction between a mental landscape (the landscape of impression) and a sensory landscape (the landscape of expression). In the life world of people there is interaction between these two spheres. The mental landscape refers to the need for ideologies and cultural representations of space and place. This includes spatial concepts of planners and designers. The sensory landscape refers to physical structures and forms:
"Landscapes of impression […] become the contexts for the making of landscape. At this point, we begin to move away from an explanation of imagery, and towards an explanation of the landscape itself. We move, in short, towards the landscape of expression" (Samuels 1979, 72).

Around the beginning of the present millennium, the geographical line of study began to acquire a following in the Netherlands via cultural geography, anthropology and landscape archaeology (Kolen/Witte 2006). A central theme here is the study of the formation and transformation of landscapes and regions during the course of time up to the present. This form of study is attractive because it promises to provide usable results for heritage policy, land-use planning and landscape design. This working method has also found a correct application in the related Belvedere programme. The integral study of the landscape with the aid of the biography concept is, first of all, a way to link up the previously dominant monodisciplinary contributions from historical geography, landscape archaeology and architectural history. The demand for such a broad approach originates from policy-makers and planners.

In the geographical approach, landscape biography works as follows. Four related characteristics can be distinguished. First, the interaction between physical structures in the surroundings and cultural values and behaviour in society is always studied. The underlying principle is that landscape and society continuously influence each other. The driving forces in the environment and society can be understood within this interaction. This form of study is closely related to a trend in planning studies and human geography in the Netherlands. A second characteristic is focusing on the reuse, reordering and reinterpretation of the traces of the past in the landscape. In this way, attention is focused on various layers in the landscape. The landscape is presented as a palimpsest, the prepared skin of a lamb, on which various texts from various times are written on top of each other and again erased. All these layers can be read with the aid of modern technology. In the same way, the landscape can be read. A third characteristic is a focus on the way in which various societies have dealt with their environment over the course of time.

How these societies act is determined by specific beliefs and behaviours, religious, socio-economic, political or otherwise. For example, the Dutch derived their identity partly from the fact that they created the landscape of the polders. Such stereotypical beliefs about the relationship between people and landscape are challenged by others in competing narratives. These days in the Netherlands, for example, there are references to the fact that nature always strikes back. The Dutch can never rest on their laurels. In this way, the Dutch are encouraged to focus serious attention on the consequences of climate change and the damage to the biological environment. A fourth characteristic of the geographical approach concerns viewing archaeological-cultural heritage as part of the environment in the experience of people. Accordingly, archaeological-cultural heritage must not be studied as a collection of objects and structures with a value that can be determined objectively, but should be studied in a historically changing cultural context. The meaning of these objects and structures changes over time, as does their influence on land-use planning and the appearance of the landscape.

A focus on the mutual influence of society and environment determines the attractiveness of the geographical approach of the biography concept for land-use planning. Critics of the biography concept point out its lack of a restricted definition and a well-described, uniform method of research. It is a 'plastic concept'. An answer to this criticism is that the breadth of the definition and the flexible application of the method are necessary in the sphere of interdisciplinary co-operation and its application in land-use planning. In this way, there is room for situation-specific modifications, debate and proposals for specialized interpretations. The use of plastic concepts characterizes the boundary interactions between the world of science and the world of policy.

In summary, the application of the geographical variant of the biography concept implies an emphasis on the following elements in the analysis. First, attention is paid to the history of the landscape or region over a long period of time. Transformations occurring in this period are mapped out and explained. This concerns not only changes in land use, but also changes in the way meaning is given to the most important places and structures. These material matters are related to socio-economic developments and the history of institutions, beliefs and spatial concepts (Bal 2002, 22). Specific attention is given to the reinterpretation of phenomena at some point in time. For example, prehistoric stone monuments have been interpreted as a giant's work in early medieval times. Finally, a great deal of attention is paid to the layered quality and the dynamic character of the concepts and experiences with which people give meaning to, and seek explanations for, the objects and structures that are part of the environment.

This biography approach is well suited for its application in the practice of spatial planning. The science of planning, with its roots in human geography and regional survey, links up well with the biographical approach. This applies especially to cultural planning where it concerns the process of increasing spatial quality by means of culturally inspired interventions, namely art, high-quality architecture or the inclusion of archaeological-cultural heritage.

As a result of the PDL/BBO programme, the biography metaphor has acquired applications in four different spheres as a framework for giving meaning (Kolen/Witte 2006; Van Londen 2006). The first sphere deals with the multiplicity of wishes and demands placed on the environment by various interest groups and visions of reality. This takes place in regional processes, where groups negotiate about future development. In such processes, spatial concepts are used to arrive at shared interpretations. These concepts usually have a fuzzy or plastic character so that there is space for different groups to search for new meanings together (Hoppe 2002; De Jonge 2009). The multivocal interpretation characteristic of such spatial concepts is an essential precondition that allows them to function as a vector of meaning for divergent groups. An example is the Sandy City concept used in the south-eastern Netherlands project (Bosma/Wallagh 2006). Another example is the Limes concept as applied in current regional development in the central parts of the Netherlands (Colenbrander 2005; Venhuizen/Van Westrenen 2006).

The second sphere is that of communication and the search for characteristics of a region, i.e. regional branding. A story about the characteristics of a region can tempt politicians and the public to focus attention on the archaeological-cultural heritage of that region. One pertinent example is the branding of Elst as the 'Stonehenge' of the Betuwe region in the paper by Anneke de Zwart (Ch. V.7). Another example pertains to the cohabitation of indigenous peoples and foreign invaders during the Roman period and the Viking age in the Oer-IJ region (Van Londen 2006).

In the third sphere, scientific research, the biography concept can provide an impulse to make visible the main aspects of the mutually linked worlds of the transformations in the landscape and the history of ideas and behaviour patterns. Of course, the history of ideas becomes more accessible for researchers as we approach the past and the written sources provide richer information. Nevertheless, archaeology can also play a role in this method, for example by explaining the secondary use of structures and objects in the landscape. The application of the biographical method can lead to divergent interpretations of the landscape that are intended for a broader public rather than just for academics. The work of the landscape biographer is to create a representation of matters that is subject to review and criticism – like every other product from the practice of science (Van Londen 2006; Kolen/Witte 2006).

The fourth sphere of application is valuation. If the landscape is described in a scientifically responsible fashion resulting in, for example, landscape characterization, a biography can help establish a valuation system that can be used when making decisions in heritage policy and spatial planning about whether or not to conserve objects and structures. A biography in the fourth sphere has a holistic character; it must aid the valuation of the landscape as a whole. The choice of the elements that are thought to be relevant for description and analysis, as well as the relationship that is assigned to these elements, must be subject to discussion. The selection criteria must therefore be made explicit (Clark/Darlington/Fairclough 2004; Van Londen 2006).

9. CONCLUSIONS AND LESSONS

The results of the programme can be divided into five categories: 1. scientific concepts and methods; 2. new forms of co-operation between scientists and lay people; 3. experience with forms of co-operation between archaeologists, historians, planners and designers; 4. in-depth disciplinary studies of specific topics, and finally, 5. the development of a national and international network of scientists and professionals. There is not enough space here for a complete summary; therefore only a few main points will be emphasized.

The first and most important results are new concepts for the description and analysis of the archaeological-cultural heritage in the landscape which play a role or will play a role in the future in heritage policy and land-use planning. The most important of these concepts is the 'biography of the landscape'. Due to the regionally oriented projects in the programme, this concept is being applied in practice, for example in the provinces of North Holland and North Brabant. This concept is also being applied in academic and higher professional education, for example at VU University and Wageningen University. In addition, the concept is also used in the international literature on planning and landscape (Antrop/

Rogge 2005; Van der Knaap/Van der Valk, 2006). This is partly due to presentations by researchers from the PDL/BBO programme at international conferences, such as the Multiple Landscape conference held in Wageningen in June 2004.

The second outcome concerns work practices and a common language which have been developed within the programme to promote internal integration in the Netherlands. This especially concerns action research that takes place with regional residents. This pursuit has borne fruit especially in the regionally oriented projects in Drenthe and south-east Brabant. Researchers and civil servants who have become acquainted with action research in one of the regionally oriented projects are now applying this method in their daily work. An important benefit stemming from this process is that by Dutch standards a large percentage of the leading archaeologists and historical geographers have become involved in some way in this programme. The most successful element of the programme is undoubtedly the experience that all participants have acquired with the internal integration of landscape archaeology and historical geography with various adjacent disciplines, such as the study of names, soil science, landscape ecology and landscape hydrology. This co-operation is not self-evident; that much has become clear. The participants in the programme, who were emphatically challenged on this point by the programme leadership, have exchanged experiences and engaged in debates several times per year.

The third outcome concerns the experiences with external integration between the archaeological-historical disciplines and the planning and design disciplines. The results in this area have been mixed. In Drenthe, south-east Brabant, eastern Netherlands and north Holland, a form of co-operation has been established via action research in the practice of land-use planning and the reconstruction of the rural area. In action research, scientific knowledge and regional knowledge from local actors are combined and processed into building blocks for spatial design and policy-making. Co-operation was structured differently in every region and has been sustainable to different degrees. In contrast to this practical success, communication between academic archaeologists and design scholars occurred only incidentally in the context of the programme. The programme committee did not succeed in getting the academic community of planners and designers involved in a structured and in-depth fashion. Among other things, this is a result of differences in academic-professional cultures.

Factors determining the success and failure of the interaction between cultural historians and policymakers are being explored in a number of dissertations. As examples, the reader can refer to the study by Van Assche (Van Assche 2004) involving historical images and symbols of a regional and national identity, and the study in this volume by De Zwart (Ch. V.7) into the factors for success and failure regarding the contribution of archaeological knowledge to policy-making at a municipal level. These studies are brought to the attention of policymakers by means of workshops and the distribution of publications.

The experiences of the researchers in the projects can be put on record as best practices. Within the programme, short-term auxiliary research projects were conducted to develop tools for action research in regional studies and devices for thematic studies. These tools encompass, among other things, explorations of international activities in the area of heritage policy, the relationship between archaeology and large infrastructure projects, decision-making about infrastructure, cultural-historical effect reports, giving meaning to the archaeological-cultural heritage and a study about interdisciplinary and transdisciplinary research.

The fourth outcome concerns thematic studies. Thematic studies are large-scale projects; in terms of duration and staffing levels, they are comparable with the regionally oriented projects. The approach is usually multidisciplinary. They are intended for filling in knowledge gaps, such as those that were ascertained at the beginning and during the course of the research programme by the programme committee. This pertains to studies in the areas of the relationship between archaeology and land-use planning, the application of cultural-historical knowledge for landscape planning, the experience of archaeological-cultural heritage, predictive modelling in the archaeological conservation of the built heritage, new methods for non-destructive prospecting for archaeological findings, the process of degradation of organic material in the soil, and the evaluation and selection of locations for excavating flint artefacts.

And last but not least, first steps were taken to develop a national and international informal network of experts. The node in this network is a community of practice which takes responsibility for the implementation, review and dissemination of ideas. In addition to and within the usual channels such as scientific journals and international conferences, the network fulfils an important role in the communication of knowledge products and experiences. The core group of this network is currently involved in the production of a policy science brief on cultural landscape research in the European Union.

In retrospect, the PDL/BBO programme is not a one-dimensional success story. It is only fair to mention at least a few flaws and pitfalls. The leadership of the programme has learned important lessons in the areas of integration between science and policy and about co-operation within scientific research teams. Friction in research methodologies can be explained via human and organizational inadequacies, such as:
- A lack of interest for other disciplines among some researchers;
- The lack of sensitivity for possibilities for practical application;
- Inadequate communication skills and a lack of curiosity about other disciplines;
- Too little feeling for the demands of scientific teamwork;
- The use of professional jargon combined with the inability to make this accessible for representatives of other disciplines and lay people;
- Lack of awareness for sensible combinations of quantitative and qualitative methods;
- Existing prejudices within every academic group;
- Inadequate respect for those who think differently in science and a lack of openness;
- Being unprepared to invest time and energy in these discussions;
- Fear of losing the connection with colleagues in one's own discipline;
- Lack of trust in one's own scientific qualities.

Some of these handicaps have been overcome due to intensive coaching and frequent in-group communication. In this respect the experiences in the PDL/BBO programme are largely in accordance with the findings of an international comparative study on the management of interdisciplinary landscape research conducted by Fry (Fry 2001; *idem* 2003).

Co-operation with residents and policymakers has provided valuable lessons in the Drenthe and the south-east Netherlands regional case studies. Coalitions between cultural historians on one side and banks, associations of recreational entrepreneurs and large landholders on the other, increase the probability of the continuation of research outcomes and spatial concepts from the ranks of cultural historians. This requires specialized expertise via social networks, facilitation, mediation and finance. Contrasts and conflicts are not harmful by definition. During action research in Drenthe and the south-east Netherlands examples of conflict situations came to light which motivated parties to develop new solutions that benefited all parties.

The success of a large integrative research programme stands or falls with the power and attractiveness of the theoretical building blocks for the researchers and the funding bodies. In this programme the following theoretical building blocks have served well: internal and external integration, thinking and doing (the knowledge-action nexus) and the biography of the landscape.

Face-to-face contact between the researchers is essential. Seminars and training sessions for young researchers on the fine points of multidisciplinary and interdisciplinary co-operation have proved indispensable. On this point, the programme has perhaps been inadequate. On the other hand, in consultation with the programme leadership a great deal of money and energy has been invested in teambuilding for the researchers, another essential precondition for successful integrative research. In this context, the appointment of a fulltime programme leader during the second phase of the programme can be seen as a crucial development. However, the most important factors are the personal involvement of the researchers with the object of research and the conviction that co-operation pays off.

NOTES

1 Wageningen University, the Netherlands.
2 An incentives programme has a scientific and practical social goal. More than half of the funding comes from various government bodies and private organizations. The national government's scientific budget provides matching funding.

    This paper makes frequent reference to publications in Dutch. The author is aware that this may be inconvenient for foreign readers. The editors have decided to accept these references keeping in mind that at least part of the readership will be interested to check secondary sources in Dutch for detailed information. After all, the *lingua franca* during the execution of the research process is Dutch.
3 Landscape architect Simon Bell (Bell 1999) provides the following definition: "(..) landscape is that part of the environment that is the human habitat, perceived and understood by us as through the medium of our perceptions." Another frequently cited definition is that for 'protected landscapes' from the International Union for Conservation of Nature and Natural Resources (IUCN) from 1994. Their definition of a protected landscape is: "a piece of land where the interaction between humans and nature over time has resulted in an area with its own character, special aesthetic, ecological or cultural values and a high level of biodiversity." The above definition is ecologically oriented and focuses on so-called nature landscapes. A definition with a more cultural-historical orientation is that of the International Council on Monuments and Sites (ICOMOS) from 1992. The ICOMOS definition reads: cultural landscapes are combined natural and human works that reflect the material evolution of civilization. In historical geography, the study of visible forms of human occupation plays the main role in the context of the physical environment. For the practitioners of this branch of science, the landscape is primarily topography, i.e. the entirety of the observable elements on and directly under the surface of the earth; settlements, roads, bodies of water, woods, fields, and pastures (Hoskins 1975, 13). In this discipline, typologies of the landscape are often linked to characteristics of soil, water and climate.

4   The European Landscape Convention (ELC) was drawn up in 2000 by the Council of Europe. The ELC went into force in 2004. The Netherlands ratified the ELC in 2005. According to Article 5 of the Convention, signatories to the ELC are obligated to take the following steps:
    - acknowledging landscape in legislation;
    - involving the general public in the development of landscape policy;
    - integrating landscape into land-use planning and other relevant policy fields;
    - implementing spatial policy for landscape planning;
    - maintaining and conserving landscapes, and;
    - engaging in international co-operation.
5   See Janssen/ Pieterse/Van den Broek 2007, 109. Conservation through development may sound paradoxical but in the cultural context of the Netherlands it is a logical idea. This has to do with the fact that the Dutch are convinced that the landscape has been made by people. This makeability is not subject to discussion. The emphasis on change and development is also indicative of a shift in the policy field of built heritage conservation and in nature conservation from conserving and protecting to transformation.
6   According to the IUCN (1994), the objective of protecting landscapes is not conservation in itself, but managing and controlling change in such a way that the acknowledged and recognizable qualities of the landscape remain preserved for future generations.
7   From the end of the 1970s humanistic geographers have opposed the dominance of quantitative research in human geography. This school of thought has arisen from a phenomenological trend in geography where explanations of human behaviour are provided by empathizing with the thoughts and motives of actors. Regarding the development of methods and techniques, humanistic geography seeks linkage primarily with cultural anthropology, literary theory and the historical sciences. Textual analysis is an important source of knowledge.
8   A complete summary of the state of affairs at the end of 2007 can be found in the publication 'Workshop: bridge between knowledge and action', compiled by the programme leadership on the occasion of the national conference in The Hague on December 7, 2007. Cf. the website of the programme: http://www.eric-project.nl/nwohome.nsf/pages/NWOA_6RZLW9. (Accessed 16 December, 2009).

REFERENCES

Alexander, E.R.,1986: *Approaches to Planning. Introducing Current Planning Theories, Concepts, and Issues*, New York.

Allen, T.F.H./J.A. Tainter/ T.W. Hoekstra, 2002: *Supplyside Sustainability*, New York.

Antrop, M., 2000: Background concepts for integrated landscape analysis, *Agriculture Ecosystems and Environment* 77, 17-28.

Antrop, M., 2003: Landscape change and the urbanization process in Europe, *Landscape and Urban Planning*, 67, 9-26.

Antrop, M., 2006: Sustainable landscapes: contradiction, fiction or utopia? in *Landscape and Urban Planning* 75, 87-197.

Antrop, M., 2007: *Perspectieven op het landschap. Achtergronden om landschappen te lezen en te begrijpen*, Gent. (Translation: Perspectives on the landscape. Materials for an understanding and reading of landscapes).

Antrop, M./E. Rogge, 2005: Valuation of the process of integration in a transdisciplinary landscape study in Pajottenland (Flanders, Belgium), *Landscape and Urban Planning* 77, 382-392.

Appadurai, A., 1986: Introduction: commodities and the politics of value, in A. Appadurai (ed.), *The social life of things. Commodities in cultural perspective*, Cambridge, 3-63.

Argyris, Ch./D. Schön, 1996²: *Organisational Learning II; Theory, Method and Practice*, Reading MA.

Ashworth, G.J./J.E. Turnbridge, 1996: *Dissonant heritage. The management of the past as a resource in conflict*, Chichester/New York.

Assche, K. Van, 2004: *Signs in Time. An Interpretative Account of Urban Planning and Design, the People and their Histories*, Wageningen (Ph. D. thesis Wageningen University).

Assche, K. Van, 2006: Crimean Tatar Heritage. On the parallel construction of heritage, history and ethnicity, in W. van der Knaap/A. van der Valk (eds.), *Multiple Landscape. Merging Past and Present. Selected Papers from the fifth International Workshop on Sustainable Land Use Planning 7-9 June 2004*, Wageningen, 101-112.

Bal, M., 2002: *Travelling Concepts in the Humanities. A Rough Guide*, London.

Bastian, O./U. Steinhardt (eds.), 2002: *Development and Perspectives of Landscape Ecology*, Dordrecht.

Beek, R. van, 2009: *Reliëf in Tijd en Ruimte. Interdisciplinair onderzoek naar bewoning en landschap van Oost-Nederland tussen vroege prehistorie en middeleeuwen*, Wageningen (Ph. D. thesis Wageningen University).

Beek, R. van/L.J. Keunen, 2006: A cultural biography of the coversand landscapes in the Salland and Achterhoek Regions. The aims and methods of the Eastern Netherlands Project, *Berichten van de Rijksdienst voor het Oudheidkundig Bodemonderzoek* 46, 355-375.

Beek, R van/B. Groenewoudt/L. Keunen, 2007: *Archeologisch veldonderzoek van boerenerven in de omgeving van Colmschate (Overijssel). De toetsing van een historisch geografisch verwachtingsmodel*, Amersfoort (Rijksdienst voor Archeologie, Cultuurlandschap en Monumenten; Beknopte Rapportage Archeologische Monumentenzorgnummer 5).

Beek, R. van/L. Keunen/B. Groenewoudt, 2008: Erven testen in Oost-Nederland, *Archeobrief. Vakblad voor de Nederlandse Archeologie* 12, 36-40.

Bell, S., 1999: *Landscape: Pattern Perception and Process*, London.

Belvedere, 1999: *The Belvedere Memorandum. A policy document examining the relationship between cultural history and spatial planning*, The Hague. Available at: http://www.belvedere.nu/download/belvedere_memorandum.pdf [Accessed 22 April, 2009].

Bloemers, J.H.F., 2000: Archäologie und Raumordnung in den Niederlanden. Ein Forschungsprogramm für den Alltag, *Archäologische Informationen* 23, 11-18.

Bloemers, J.H.F., 2001: Het NWO-Stimuleringsprogramma 'Bodemarchief in Behoud en Ontwikkeling' en de conceptuele studies. Een strategische handreiking voor onderzoek, beleid en uitvoering, in J.H.F. Bloemers/R. During/J.N.H. Elerie/H.A. Groenendijk/M. Hidding/J. Kolen/Th. Spek/M.-H. Wijnen, *Bodemarchief in Behoud en Ontwikkeling; de conceptuele grondslagen*, Den Haag, 1-6.

Bloemers, J. H. F., 2002: Past and Future Oriented Archaeology. Protecting and developing the archaeological-historical landscape of the Netherlands, in G.J. Fairclough/S.J. Rippon (eds.),

Europe's Cultural Landscape. Archaeologists and the management of change, Brussels/London (Europae Archaeologiae Consilium/ English Heritage), 89-96.

Bloemers, J.H.F., 2005: Archaeological-historical landscapes in The Netherlands: management by sustainable development in planning, in M.R. Ruiz del Árbol/A. Orejas (eds.), *Landscapes as cultural heritage in the European Research. Proceedings of the Open Workshop Madrid, 29th October 2004*, Madrid, 69-85.

Bloemers, J.H.F./G.J. Borger, 1988: Cultural history and environmental planning: research and policy for the future, in L.H. van Wijngaarden-Bakker/J.J.M. van der Meer (eds.), *Spatial sciences, research in progress*, Amsterdam (Nederlandse Geografische Studies 80), 53-67.

Bloemers, J.H.F./R. During/J.N.H. Elerie/H.A. Groenendijk/M. Hidding/J. Kolen/Th. Spek/M.-H. Wijnen, 2001: *Protecting and Developing the Dutch Archaeological-Historical Landscape*, The Hague.

Bloemers, J.H.F./A. van der Valk, 2007: The Oer IJ: A metropolitan wetland on Amsterdam's doorstep. The archaeological-historical landscape as inspiration for spatial planning, in B.Pedroli/A. van Doorn/G. De Blust (eds.), *Europe's Living Landscapes. Essays exploring our identity in the countryside*, Zeist, 161-176.

Bloemers, J.H.F./M.-H. Wijnen (eds.), 2002: *Protecting and Developing the Dutch Archaeological-Historical Landscape*, The Hague.

Bloemers, J.H.F./M.-H. Wijnen, 2007: Workshop: de brug tussen kennis en handelen. *Nationaal congres Behoud door Ontwikkeling van het Archeologisch-Historisch Landschap na 2000-2007. Vrijdag 7 december 2007*, Den Haag (NWO/BBO).

Bosma, K./G. Wallagh, 2006: *Zandstad*, Amsterdam: VU University/Bureau De Lijn. Interactive website. Available at: www.zandstad.nl. [Accessed 22 April, 2009].

Brace, Catherine, 2003: Landscape and Identity, in I. Robertson/P. Richards (eds.), *Studying Cultural Landscapes*, London, 121-140.

Bradley, R., 2002: *The past in prehistoric societies*, London.

Brink, A. van den/A. van der Valk/T. van Dijk, 2006: Planning and the Challenges of the Metropolitan Landscape. Innovation in the Netherlands, *International Planning Studies* 11, 145-163.

Burg, A.J. van den, 2004: Ruimtelijk beleid in Nederland op nationaal niveau, in R.M. van Heeringen/ E.H.P. Cordfunke/M. Ilsink/H. Sarfatij (eds.), *Geordend landschap. 3000 jaar ruimtelijke ordening in Nederland*, Hilversum, 159-189.

Clark, J./J. Darlington/G. Fairclough, 2004: *Using Historic Landscape Characterisation*, London.

Coeterier, J.F., 2002: Lay people's evaluation of historic sites, *Landscape and Urban Planning* 59, 111-123.

Colenbrander, B. (ed.), 2005: *Limes Atlas*, Rotterdam.

Dauvellier, P., 2004: Ruimtelijke kwaliteit als recept, *ROM Maandblad voor Ruimtelijke Ontwikkeling* 3, 26-29.

Déjeant-Pons, M., 2002 : The European Landscape Convention, Florence, in G.J. Fairclough/S.J. Rippon (eds.), *Europe's Cultural Landscape. Archaeologists and the management of change*. Brussels/London (Europae Archaeologiae Consilium/ English Heritage), 13-24.

Dockum, S.G. van/R.C.G.M. Lauwerier, 2004: Archaeology in the Netherlands 2002. The national archaeological review and outlook, *European Journal of Archaeology*, 7, 109-124.

Duineveld, M., 2006: *Van oude dingen, de mensen die voorbij gaan. Over de voorwaarden meer recht te kunnen doen aan de door burgers gewaardeerde cultuurhistories*, Delft (Ph.D. thesis Wageningen University).

Duncan, J./N. Duncan, 1988: (Re)reading the landscape, *Environment and Planning D. Society and Space* 6, 117-126.

During, R./M. Eerden/J. Kolen/E. Luiten/A. van der Zande, 2006: *Common Ground: Past/Planning/Future. Teaching and Research Programme and Agenda for the Belvedere Educational Network (2006-2009)*, Utrecht. Available at: http://www.belvedere.nu/download/commonground.pdf [Accessed 22 April, 2009].

During, R./H. Elerie/H.A. Groenendijk, 2001: Denken en doen: verpachten van wijsheid of delen van kennis? Pleidooi voor de verbinding van cultuurhistorische kenniseilanden en een relatie met de sociale wetenschappen, in J.H.F. Bloemers/R. During/J.N.H. Elerie/H.A. Groenendijk/M. Hidding/J. Kolen/Th. Spek/M.-H. Wijnen (eds.), *Bodemarchief in Behoud en Ontwikkeling; de conceptuele grondslagen*, Den Haag, 111-157.

Eerden, M., 2008: Observaties vanuit de Belvederepraktijk, in R. During/M. Eerden/J. Kolen/E. Luiten/A. van der Zande, *Op Historische Gronden. Erfgoed in een context van ruimtelijk ontwerp, planning en democratie*, Utrecht, 9-30.

Ermischer, G., 2003: Kulturlandschaft mehr als ein Modewort, *Berichte zur Denkmalpflege in Niedersachsen* 4, 174-179.

Fairclough, G. J./S.J. Rippon (eds.), 2002: *Europe's Cultural Landscape. Archaeologists and the management of change*. Brussels/London (Europae Archaeologiae Consilium/ English Heritage), 89-96.

Faludi, A., 1986: *Critical rationalism and planning methodology*, London.

Faludi, A./A. van der Valk, 1994: *Rule and Order. Dutch Planning Doctrine in the Twentieth Century*, Dordrecht.

Available http://books.google.nl/books?id=39xSxbWNyekC [Accessed: 22 April, 2009]

Flyvbjerg, B., 1998: *Rationality and power: democracy in practice*, London.

Flyvbjerg, B., 2001: *Making Social Science Matter. Why social inquiry fails and how it can succeed again*, Cambridge.

Fry, G.L.A., 2001: Multifunctional landscapes. Towards transdisciplinary research, *Landscape and Urban Planning* 57, 159-168.

Fry, G., 2003: Training Needs for Interdisciplinary Research, in B. Tress/G. Tress/A. van der Valk/G. Fry (eds.), *Interdisciplinary and Transdisciplinary Landscape Studies. Potential and Limitations*, Wageningen, 118-123.

Greenwood, D.J./ M. Levin, 1998: *Introduction to action research. Social research for social change*, Thousand Oaks.

Haas, W. de/R. Kranendonk/M. Pleijte, 1999: Valuable man-made landscapes (VMLs) in the Netherlands. A policy evaluation, *Landscape and Urban Planning* 46, 133-141.

Halffman, W./R. Hoppe, 2005: Science/policy Boundaries. A Changing Division of Labour in Dutch Expert Policy Advise, in S. Maasen/P. Weingart (eds.), *Democratization of Expertise? Exploring Novel Forms of Scientific Advice in Political Decision-Making*, (Sociology of the Sciences 24), 135-151.

Hidding, M./J. Kolen/Th. Spek, 2001: De biografie van het landschap. Ontwerp voor een inter- en transdisciplinaire benadering van de landschapsgeschiedenis en het cultuurhistorisch erfgoed, in J.H.F. Bloemers/R. During/J.N.H. Elerie/H.A. Groenendijk/M. Hidding/J. Kolen/Th. Spek/M.-H. Wijnen, *Bodemarchief in Behoud en Ontwikkeling; de conceptuele grondslagen*, Den Haag, 7-110.

Hoppe, R., 2002: *Van flipperkast naar grensverkeer. Veranderende visies op de relatie tussen wetenschap en beleid*, Den Haag (Adviesraad voor Wetenschaps- en Technologiebeleid. AWT-achtergrondstudie 25. Februari 2002).

Hoppe, R., 2008: Na 'doorwerking' naar 'grenzenwerk'. Een nieuwe agenda voor onderzoek naar de verhouding tussen beleid en wetenschap, *Bestuurskunde* 17, 15-26.

Horst, H. van der, 2007-6: *The Low Sky. Understanding the Dutch*, Schiedam.

Hoskins, W.G., 1975² (1955): *The Making of the English Landscape*, London.

Janssen, J., 2006: *Vooruit denken en verwijlen. De (re)constructie van het plattelandschap in Zuidoost-Brabant (1920-2000)*, Tilburg (Ph.D. thesis Tilburg University).

Janssen, J./N. Pieterse/L. van den Broek, 2007: *Nationale landschappen. Beleidsdilemma's in de praktijk*, Rotterdam.

Jonge, J. de, 2009: *Landscape Architecture between Politics and Science. An integrative perspective on landscape planning and design in the network society*, Wageningen (Ph.D. thesis Wageningen University).

Kerkstra, K./M.J. Vroom/D. Lowenthal/S.I. Andersson, 2003: *The Landscape of Symbols*, Wageningen.

Keunen, L.J., in prep.: *Het historisch cultuurlandschap van Oost-Nederland. Een landschapsbiografie van Salland en de Achterhoek*, Wageningen (Ph. D. thesis Wageningen University).

Klink, H.J./M. Potschin/ B. Tress *et al.*, 2002: Landscape and landscape ecology, in O. Bastian/U. Steinhardt (eds.): *Development and Perspectives of Landscape Ecology*, Dordrecht, 1-47.

Knaap, W. van der /A. van der Valk (eds.) 2006: *Multiple Landscape. Merging Past and Present. Selected Papers from the fifth International Workshop on Sustainable Land Use Planning 7-9 June 2004*, Wageningen.

Kobylinski, Z., 2006: Challenges, conflicts and opportunities. Cultural landscapes in Poland after the great socio-economic transformation, in W. van der Knaap/A. van der Valk (eds.), *Multiple Landscape. Merging Past and Present. Selected Papers from the fifth International Workshop on Sustainable Land Use Planning 7-9 June 2004*, Wageningen, 45-72.

Kolen, J., 2004: *De biografie van Peelland*, Amsterdam (Zuidnederlandse Archeologische Rapporten 17).

Kolen, J. 2005: *De biografie van het landschap. Drie essays over landschap, geschiedenis en erfgoed*, Amsterdam (Ph.D. thesis VU University Amsterdam).

Kolen, J./M. Witte, 2006: A biographical approach to regions and its value for spatial planning, in W. van der Knaap/A. van der Valk (eds.), *Multiple Landscape. Merging Past and Present. Selected Papers from the fifth International Workshop on Sustainable Land Use Planning 7-9 June 2004*, Wageningen, 125-145.

Kopytoff, I. 1986: The cultural biography of things. Commoditization as process, in A. Appadurai (ed.), *The social life of things. Commodities in cultural perspective*, Cambridge, 64-91.

Kühn, M./R. Danielzyk, 2006: Der Stellenwert der Kulturlandschaft in der Regional- und Raumplanung. Fazit, Ausblick und Handlungsempfehlungen, in U. Matthiesen/ R. Danielzyk/S. Heiland/S. Tzschaschel (eds.), *Kulturlandschaften als Herausforderung für die Raumplanung. Verständnisse, Erfahrungen, Perspektiven*, Hannover (Akademie für Raumforschung und Landesplanung 228), 288-296.

Lauwerier, R.C.G.M./R.M. Lotte, 2002: *Archeologiebalans 2002*, Amersfoort.

Leusen, M. van/H. Kamermans, 2005: Predictive Modelling for Archaeological Heritage Management. A Research Agenda, Amersfoort, (NAR 29).

Leusen, M. van/H. Kamermans, 2005: *Predictive Modelling for Archaeological Heritage Management. A Research Agenda,* Amersfoort (NAR 29).

Lowenthal, D., 1996: *Possessed by the past. The heritage crusade and the spoils of history,* London/New York.

Lowenthal, D., 2003: Landscape as Living Legacy, in K. Kerkstra/M.J. Vroom/D. Lowenthal/S.I. Andersson, *The Landscape of Symbols,* Wageningen, 14-37.

Londen, H. van, 2006: Cultural biography and the power of image, in: W. van der Knaap/A. van der Valk (eds.), *Multiple Landscape. Merging Past and Present. Selected Papers from the fifth International Workshop on Sustainable Land Use Planning 7-9 June 2004,* Wageningen, 171-181.

Lörzing, H., 2001: *The Nature of Landscape. A Personal Quest,* Rotterdam.

Netherlands Environmental Assessment Agency (NEAA), 2008: *Planbureau voor de Leefomgeving, Leefomgevingsmonitor.* http://www.ruimtemonitor.nl/kennisportaal/default.aspx?menucomid=26&pid=34&id=4573&themeId=329 [Accessed 22 April, 2009].

Needham, B., 2007: *Dutch land use planning. Planning and managing land use in the Netherlands, the principles and the practice,* The Hague.

Nelissen, N./B. Needham, 1996: Changes in monument care in the Netherlands, *Planning Practice and Research* 11, 391-403.

Norberg-Schulz, C., 1980: *Genius Loci. Towards a Phenomenology of Architecture,* London.

Palang, H./G. Fry (eds.) 2003: *Landscape Interfaces: Cultural Heritage in Changing Landscapes,* Dordrecht.

Pedroli, B./A. van Doorn/G. de Blust (eds.), 2007: *Europe's Living Landscapes. Essays exploring our identity in the countryside,* Zeist.

Raagmaa, G., 2002: Regional identity in regional development and planning, *European Planning Studies* 10, 55-76.

Rensink, E./F. Gerritsen/J.A.M. Roymans, 2006: Archaeological heritage management, nature development and water management in the brook valleys of the southern Netherlands, *Berichten van de Rijksdienst voor het Oudheidkundig Bodemonderzoek* 46, 383-399.

Reuselaars, I., 2003: Belvedere: Preservation of cultural heritage as part of town and country planning in the Netherlands, *Archaeologisches Nachrichtenblatt* 8, 189-202.

Rooijakkers, G., 1999: Mythisch landschap. Verhalen en rituelen als culturele biografie van een regio, in J. Kolen/T. Lemaire (eds.), *Landschap in meervoud. Perspectieven op het Nederlandse landschap,* Utrecht, 301-326.

Roymans, J.A.M., 1995: The cultural biography of urnfields and the long-term history of a mythical landscape, *Archaeological Dialogues* 2, 2-24.

Roymans, J.A.M./F. Gerritsen, 2002: Landscape, ecology and *mentalités*: a long term perspective on developments in the Meuse-Demer-Scheldt region, *Proceedings of the Prehistoric Society* 68, 257-287.

Ruijgrok, E., 2006: Cultural Heritage in Euro's; The three economic values of cultural heritage: a case study in the Netherlands, *Journal of Cultural Heritage* 7, 206-213.

Samuels, M. S., 1979: The biography of landscape. Cause and culpability, in D.W. Meinig (ed.), *The interpretation of ordinary landscapes,* Oxford, 51-88.

Schama, S.,1995: *Landscape and memory,* London.

Schenk, W., 2003: Historische Kulturlandschaften als Faktor der Regionalentwicklung, *Local Land and Soil News* 7/8, 16-18.

Schön, D., 1983: *The Reflective Practitioner*, New York.

Senge, P.M., 1990: *The Fifth Discipline. The Art and Practice of the Learning Organization*, New York.

Simon, H., 1969: *Administrative Behaviour*, New York.

Spek, Th./O. Brinkkemper/B.P. Speleers, 2006: Archaeological Heritage Management and Nature Conservation. Recent Developments and Future Prospects, Illustrated by Three Dutch Case Studies, *Berichten van de Rijksdienst voor het Oudheidkundig Bodemonderzoek* 46, 331-354.

Tress, B./G. Tress/G. Fry, 2003: Potential and limitations of interdisciplinary and transdisciplinary landscape studies, in B. Tress/G. Tress/A. van der Valk/G. Fry (eds.), *Interdisciplinary and Transdisciplinary Landscape Studies: Potential and Limitations*, Wageningen, 182-192.

Tress, B./G. Tress/G. Fry/P. Opdam, 2006: *From Landscape Research to landscape Planning. Aspects of Integration, Education and Application*, Dordrecht.

Valk, A. van der, 2002: The Dutch planning experience, *Landscape and Urban Planning* 58, 201-210.

Valk, A. van der /T. Bloemers, 2006: Multiple and sustainable landscapes. Linking heritage management and spatial planning in the Netherlands, in W. van der Knaap/A. van der Valk (eds.), *Multiple Landscape. Merging Past and Present. Selected Papers from the fifth International Workshop on Sustainable Land Use Planning 7-9 June 2004*, Wageningen, 21-33.

Valk, A. van der/T. van Dijk, 2009: *Regional planning for open space*, London.

Ven, G.P. van de, 1993²: *Leefbaar Laagland. Geschiedenis van de waterbeheersing en landaanwinning in Nederland*, Utrecht.

Venhuizen, H./F. van Westrenen (eds.), 2006: *Limes. De toekomst van de geschiedenis*, Rotterdam.

Vroom, M. J., 2006: *Lexicon of Garden and Landscape Architecture*, Basel.

Wenger, E., 1997: *Communities of practice. Learning, Meaning and Identity*, Cambridge.

WEBSITES

PDL/BBO http://www.eric-project.nl/nwohome.nsf/pages/NWOA_6RZLW9. (Accessed 12 December, 2009).

3. Actors and orders: the shaping of landscapes and identities

Carsten Paludan-Müller[1]

ABSTRACT

Our landscapes are shaped and ordered by the choices made by the actors who control the landscapes. This paper sets out to investigate three different types of actors, how they impose different types of order on the landscape, and how that order may or may not be easily discerned. The patterning of landscapes by different and discernable orders is likened to the mental process of remembering. Both can be understood as balancing acts between feeding in too much or too little information.

This paper primarily argues that power relations between actors are always reflected in the ordering of the landscapes. Since these relations are constantly changing, the landscape can never be at rest. Finally, therefore, four different scenarios are offered as a background for reflection upon how the orders in our landscapes may be affected by unfolding global developments or shifts. This is meant as a memento for those working with the issue of preserving historic qualities in the landscapes: history is still going on.

KEY WORDS

Natives, settlers, remote controllers; cultural heritage, memory; planning, scenario

1. INTRODUCTION

Landscape is a word of strong Dutch significance[2] and a phenomenon with many interpretations. It is a constantly reconfigured frame and a medium of human aspiration and action. There is always more to the landscape than meets the eye. Our perceptions of, and actions in, the landscapes are shaped by who we are, and who we are is in many ways shaped by our relationship with our physical environment, including the landscape. In other words, there is a dynamic interplay between the formation of landscape identities and that of human identities. In the following I shall first attempt a simple grouping into three of the different positions from which we can act in the shaping and interpretation of the landscape. From there I shall move on to deal with different types of order in the landscape.

2. ACTORS

2.1 Natives

The natives are those who live and work in the landscape in question. They represent, at least in their own perception, a long local continuity of use and interpretation. This is not necessarily a continuity of unchanged land use, but rather a living tradition of land use and attitudes with emphasis on whatever economic activity would make sense for the natives at a particular time. The category of 'natives' emphasizes the local community but conceals conflicts within it. These could be conflicts that manifest themselves as competing land use patterns. Such internal conflicts could also translate into fractional strategies of alliance with interests outside the local community against the interests of competing factions within the local community. In our own highly urbanized society the term 'native' holds mainly positive connotations and is commonly ascribed attributes such as immutability, ecological sustainability, and social balance or justice. Native communities are thus frequently idealized, to serve as platforms for the critique of our own civilization and its immodest dealings with landscapes, cultures, and resources.

2.2 Settlers

The category of 'settlers' covers a different approach. For them the landscape frequently represents a neglected or misused potential. It is the settlers' mission to realize the perceived potential. By implication, settling is often accompanied by a shift in land rights and land use. Often, but not always, new land use means intensification. The earlier land use as practised by the natives is sometimes characterized as wrong, neglectful, or simply unsophisticated. We often recognize such narrative patterns in the context of colonial endeavours, requiring justification for taking possession of new land. This was the case with the seventeenth to twentieth-century European settlement of the North American continent, the nineteenth-century French colonization of the Maghreb, and the twentieth- and twenty-first-century Jewish settlement in Palestine. An example to the contrary could be the change of land use from mainly agricultural to mainly pastoral in El Andalus following the late fifteenth-century Christian *Reconquista* and the subsequent expulsion of the Muslim population.

A violent contemporary example is playing itself out in Darfur in the early twenty-first century. Here, pastoral tribes that were previously semi-nomadic have become fully nomadic and have been driven from the north by climate change leading to radical loss of pasture, mainly due to drought. They are now competing with southern agricultural tribes for land. The farmers traditionally burn the grass and weed vegetation from fallow lands in a cycle to release stored nutrients from the vegetation to enable the soil to bear a new crop. To the pastoralists, this represents misuse of a grazing potential for their starving herds. This is a basic conflict over landscape resources and their use, but frequently perceived as an ethnic or religious conflict, which in fact it is, but only on the surface (Welzer 2008, 94-99).

However, there are also other forms of new settling taking place over shorter cultural and geographical distances, such as the urbanization, suburbanization, or leisurization of rural landscapes within the ever-expanding fields of gravity surrounding or separating our cities. These processes transform landscapes from fields and pastures to suburbia with new infrastructural tissues and nodes facilitating the physical flow between urban centres and between them and their fields of gravity. This brings in new people with different ways of using and perceiving the landscapes. These may or may not conflict with those of 'the natives'. Often the 'natives' are leaving, or at least abandoning, their traditional land use due to socio-economic and cultural macro-processes that have undermined their viability or attractiveness.

Settlers will sometimes acquire their new home in some sort of deal with members of the native community. This could entail buying lands from a major feudal landowner who chooses to abandon his tenants, such as much of the Jewish purchase of property in Palestine, or a deal along the lines of the famous or mythical Dutch purchase in 1626 of Manhattan Island from a native chief for the equivalent of $26. However, it could also be a more direct purchase from a small property owner selling his old village home to an urban buyer looking for a second home. Evidently, some of the purchases mentioned above are almost bound to leave themes for conflict in their aftermath as can be seen in Palestine.

A typical situation is the abandonment of traditional land use in rural or coastal settlements due to macro-economic processes. If this takes place in landscapes not too far from major population centres, it is likely to translate into a suburbanization or leisurization of the landscape. If it takes place within the urban area itself, we may see a redevelopment along the lines initiated during the 1980s in the London Docklands. It heralded a worldwide, but often uninspired, redevelopment of vast urban harbour lands that had lost their previous use in the reshuffling of global transport systems.

2.3 Remote controllers

The last category of actors in the landscape consists of those affecting it from a distance. They are a diverse group, ranging from more or less anonymous investors, developers, high-profile rulers, to planners, antiquarians, conservationists, policymakers, NGOs, activists, and artists. Increasingly, with the integration of still more local communities in the global market, decisions affecting the use of a particular landscape are taken in locations far from them. These decisions will sometimes be specifically targeted towards the particular landscape as an administrative act of planning or investment. Often, however, specific local effects will rise from general decisions about international trade, agricultural, fishery, or transport policies.

Often remote controllers act in alliances with natives, settlers, or factions of these in the pursuit of common interests against other local interests. An example could be the alliance between the central government of Sudan and the pastoral 'settlers' against the sedentary agricultural 'natives' in the current Darfur conflict. The central government is opting for the support of another type of 'remote controller', such as Chinese oil interests (Victor/Raisson/Tétart 2007, 140). In our particular context, it is worth being aware of the remote-controlling role many of us have as planners or antiquarians in the shaping of the landscapes in which other people live.

Finally it should be stressed that although remote controllers are capable of affecting landscapes and their populations from a distance, they should by no means be perceived as being in full control of the consequences of their interventions. The purpose of their intervention may or may not in each case be achieved but its collateral effects may escape their control or even be counterproductive to their interests.

3. ORDERS

Order is semantically opposed to chaos. However, in the context of landscapes it may be more rewarding to distinguish those landscapes dominated by one singular principle of order from those formed by competing, interlacing, or superimposed orders. Evidently, chaos may often be the impression conveyed to us by landscapes formed by the mixing of several orders. Nevertheless, the concept of chaos has little heuristic value to our understanding of how such landscapes took their chaotic shape.

3.1 Singular orders

When a singular ordering principle is imposed upon a landscape it implies that a single actor or a single, co-ordinated group of actors (e.g. farming villagers) defines the use of that landscape. The order imposed may extend to varying degrees in time and space. We have landscapes that in the short term may be strongly dominated or taken over by one ordering principle. This could for instance be a landscape where an army is preparing itself for battle by eradicating or manipulating as many pre-existing structures as possible and constructing new ones in order to maximize tactical advantages in the terrain. Such an order is highly unlikely to outlast the short-term perspective of the battle and is likely in its aftermath to be supplanted by a predominantly civilian (e.g. agricultural) ordering principle. However, in some cases the former battleground will (also) accommodate a new ordering principle in the form of the memorialization of the battlefield, for example as seen in certain landscapes in eastern France, where some of the bloodiest battles of the First World War were fought. In such cases the symbolic memorial dimension may become the dominant ordering principle which all other logics of land use may have to accommodate.

Other forms of symbolic landscapes may be grand designs constructed with the overriding purpose of accommodating political power in a scenography expressing the unboundedness in time and space of that power. A prominent example is Versailles, the Baroque palace, garden, and park constructed by Louis XIV outside Paris as a new residence for himself and his government, as a ceremonial stage for exercising control over the nobility, and for the radiation of French diplomatic, military, technological, and cultural power over the European continent (Fig. 1 left). With that in mind, Versailles was created as a complex networked symbolic landscape of webs and nodes of meaning arranged around a central main axis. Strong geometric order with vistas radiating far out into the landscape from focal points was an important part of the communication of unbounded power.

The Versailles plan gave inspiration to the grand design of Washington DC by Jean Pierre L'Enfant[3] at the end of the eighteenth century (Fig. 1 right). This inspiration was further emphasized in the 1901 plan. The two plans do not only share their main structures in the geometrical layout and in the use of former wetlands for the establishment of waterworks and reflective basins. They also share the principle of offering a total world interpretation reaching from the political to the cosmological through a network of interpretative nodes or 'hotspots', each addressing a particular aspect or issue. In Versailles power is expressed through a rationalistic Baroque interpretation of the world supported by state of the art landscape and hydraulic engineering and conveyed by a refined system of mythological allegories (statues) but also by media that are more readable to us such as the 'Orangerie' and the 'Menagerie' (the latter no longer exists), bringing in exotic plants and animals from distant ecospheres.

In Washington DC the enlightened, modern world interpretation is fashioned into an expression of power. Grouped along the central axis (the Mall), we find the Smithsonian Museum institutions, which each interpret a different set of phenomena (spanning from the National Museum of Natural History and the National Museum of Art to the National Air and Space Museum). And just like the 'Orangerie' in Versailles, there is a place for plants from exotic ecospheres at the US Botanic Garden. Also organized along

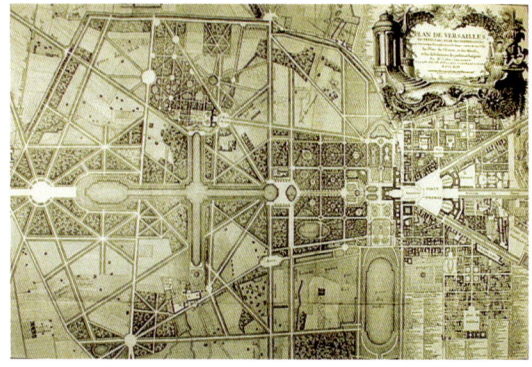

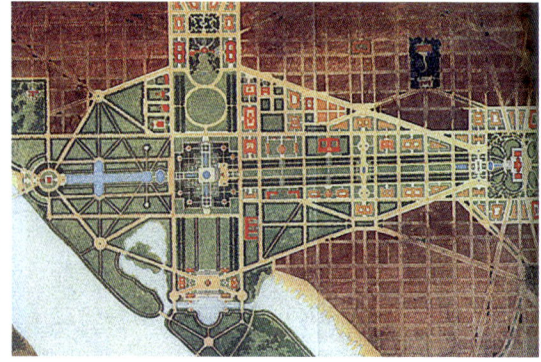

Fig. 1
The Versailles plan (left) inspired the grand design of Washington DC (right) by Jean Pierre L'Enfant at the end of the eighteenth century.

Fig. 2a
Polder landscape in the Netherlands.
Developed during hundreds of years or sometimes more, the polders are now under increasing pressure from urban growth.
Photo: W.H. Metz.

the Mall we find a system of monuments commemorating the foundation of the United States (Founding Fathers) and its expansion and rise to a dominant global position (the war memorials). In our context, the National Air and Space Museum can be seen as a particularly significant demonstration of American possession of an unrivalled technological capacity to exercise control over global space.

Versailles and Washington DC offer illuminating cases of singularly ordered landscapes. However, most of the landscapes dominated by a singular order have been designed for more mundane use than the power-symbolic representations embodied in those two.

Landscapes reclaimed for human use by controlling high energies in the natural environment

Landscapes that require a high investment of labour to accommodate a particular form of land use tend to be dominated by a singular order. Good examples would be landscapes where water management is of special importance, such as the irrigational landscapes in the arid zones or the drained and diked landscapes of the Netherlands (Fig. 2a), the Po, and Bangladesh (Fig. 2b). These landscapes may have developed over thousands of years along the same line of land use logic.

Fig. 2b
Bangladesh, Dhaka Region. Left: rice paddies during the dry season at Panam Nagar. Right: NASA image of Bangladesh during the monsoon floods. The Dhaka Region is covered in dark blue and black flood waters.

Fig. 3
Colonized land: grid-shaped field layout/property boundaries in the Midwest, USA.

The changes that have occurred may be more quantitative than qualitative in response to the need to increase agricultural output and the availability of new technologies. Sometimes however, when the environmental constraints have been pushed too far, human land reclamation may be rolled back and the landscape may revert to an earlier condition. In such cases there is no intermediate alternative between the highly organized human landscape and a landscape whose appearance is almost entirely dominated by the forces of nature.

Colonized landscapes
Landscapes settled by a new population may often have a strong regularity dominated by a singular order. Examples could be the US Midwest with its gridshaped property boundaries (Fig. 3).

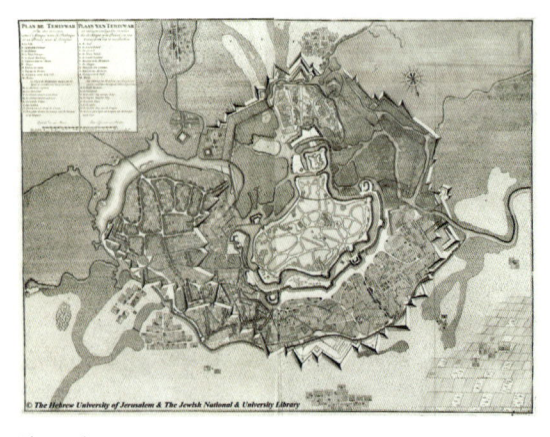

Fig. 4a-b
Left (a): A city in metamorphosis. Plan of Timisoara, a former Ottoman city at the beginning of the eighteenth century, around the time of its inclusion in the Habsburg Empire. The Dutch and French text in the legend indicates that specialists in fortification and waterworks were brought in for the purpose of developing the city and its surroundings. The layout of the new fortifications is partly represented, whereas the grid layout of the street system has yet to be designed.
Right (b): Seventeenth-century dike in the regulated riverine landscape surrounding the village of Padra near Timisoara.

58 • THE CULTURAL LANDSCAPE AND HERITAGE PARADOX

Fig. 5
Aigues Mortes: a grid street system behind strong fortifications, founded in 1240.

Another example could be the landscape around Timisoara in present-day Romania (Fig. 4b). It became the administrative centre of the Banat province, conceded to the Habsburg Empire by the declining Ottoman Empire at the Peace Treaty of Passarowitz in 1718 (Fig. 4a). Much of the province was evacuated by the Ottomans and resettled with people of various ethnicities from other parts of the Habsburg Empire. On the initiative of Maria Theresa, large-scale drainage and embankment projects were initiated in the marshy lands surrounding Timisoara. The land was dotted with regularly distributed, newly established, neatly organized road-villages. Nearly all Ottoman structures in the city of Timisoara were eradicated and an almost entirely new city was built.

The planned city

When their layout is established over a short period of time by the decision of a strong (central) authority, cities tend to be dominated by a singular order. Such planned cities are particularly characteristic of certain social and political situations and are widespread in time and space. Prominent examples are the Greek and Roman colonial cities with their characteristic grid layout. However, the grid layout was also employed in non-colonial cities like Piraeus in the fifth century BC. In Book 7 of his *Politics*, Aristotle emphasizes the advantage of new planned cities compared with the old unplanned ones such as Athens.

The grid layout recurs many times throughout history, almost as the hallmark of a strong political planning authority. Outside Europe, we find grid-shaped cities in pre-Columbian America, India, China, and Japan, whereas they are absent from the Arab concepts of urban structure.

In medieval Europe, Aigues Mortes in southern France was founded in 1240 and laid out in a grid by Louis IX (Saint Louis) to serve as the first Mediterranean port of the expanding French State and as the gathering point for the Seventh Crusade, led by King Louis (Fig. 5).

During the early modern period of centralization of the European states planned cities grew up as new foundations or re-foundations all over Europe. For instance, the Danish-Norwegian king Christian IV

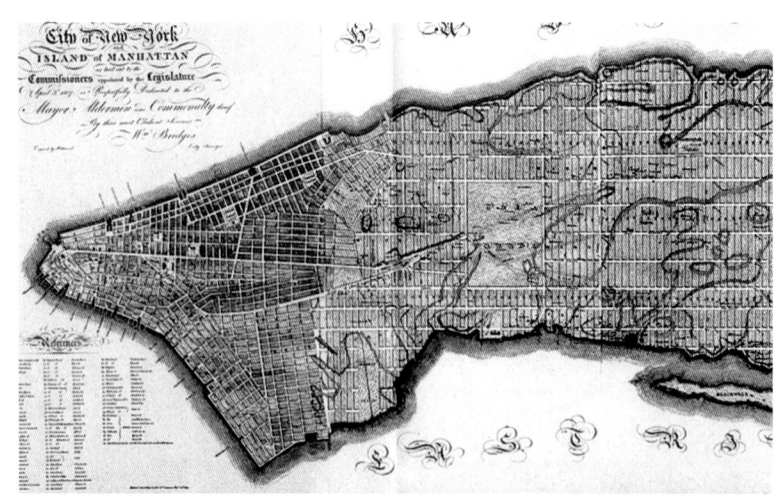

Fig. 6
The grid layout of New York City, Manhattan, developed from the southern tip of the earliest Dutch settlement (Nieuw Amsterdam), with Broadway, according to legend an old native Indian footpath, as the only major deviation (*Homberger* 2005).
New York became the city of the 20th century, an icon of urban modernity.

initiated a period of urbanization during the early seventeenth century in Norway. Prominent examples are Kristiansand, Kongsberg, and Christiania, a re-foundation and relocation of medieval Oslo (Lexau 2007).

In the United States, most of the towns founded by the colonizers were grid shaped. The best known example is New York City, Manhattan (Fig. 6).

With the regeneration of Europe after the Second World War, grandiose urban planning experienced a new flourishing. In the East, it was the new socialist planning and in the West, the welfare state which initiated urban development inspired by the ideals of Le Corbusier and driven by the rationales of mass-produced housing plus spatial segregation of work, residence, and recreation.

Since the 1970s, the concrete suburban landscapes of the welfare state have increasingly turned into social problems rather than the social solutions they were meant to be. Because of that, we now have to deal with them as heritage objects, monuments of the postwar twentieth century, as documented by English Heritage (Penrose 2007).

Redistributed landscapes: up or downscaling the number of ordering principles
Within a landscape reordering may take place as a consequence of the redistribution of land from one social group to another. In rural landscapes this may take the form of increasing or decreasing the amount of logics operating to structure the layout. For instance, the quite diverse re-regulation of rural Britain from the seventeenth to the nineteenth century referred to as 'Enclosure' generally substituted a communal pattern of land use with an individual one (Parliamentary Acts of Enclosures, passed 1750). On the one hand this left more opportunities for the individual farmer to shape his land use according to his resources and needs and greatly increased overall productivity and revenue for the landlords. On the other hand it also reduced social diversity, squeezing out the considerable fraction of poorer people in the rural population, people who had previously been able to make their modest imprint on the landscape (Newman 2001, 106-112). Similar land reforms took place over much of Europe during the same period, generally leading to increasing complexity in the ordering of the landscape and to an intensification of rural land use that went hand in hand with industrialization, urban growth, and mass migration from the rural countryside to the industrial cities and to the Americas, Australia, and New Zealand.

Today a new redistribution of rural landscapes is taking place over much of Europe and North America. This time a dramatic upscaling of the size of individual farm units has severely reduced the number of individual farm holdings. This in turn translates into a reorganization of the rural landscape that accommodates increasingly more specialized and capital-intensive farming, competing on the world market. In countries like Denmark fewer and bigger farms are responsible for the layout of the rural landscapes. This leads to an ongoing loss of diversity visually, culturally, and biologically, only modified by other regulatory mechanisms such as landscape conservation schemes.

At the other end of the scale we meet the redistribution of land through reforms that divide the properties of manorial systems and distribute them to small individual farmers. Changes like this are typically seen in revolutionary situations – they will tend to translate into a more diverse landscape with more individual orders within the same space.

3.2 Landscapes of multiple orders

With the rolling back of state power during the neoliberal last decades of the twentieth century, big planning has again retreated as the dominant choreographer of landscape. A multitude of orders has emerged, increasingly driven by global market mechanisms. This affects not only urban but also rural spaces. Global trade politics have a high impact on the viability of different types of agricultural production and therefore on the use or indeed the non-use of the rural landscapes. Urban space itself expands constantly, with more than half of the global population now living in towns. More and more agricultural zones fall within an expanding urban field of gravity and are gradually transformed and integrated into the urban zones. In many parts of Europe, it is arguable that there are no longer any rural zones as opposed to urban zones. Rather there are urban zones and then there are the transitory zones between one urban zone and the neighbouring urban zones. This is evidently the case in such densely populated areas as the Randstad[4] and other parts of the 'Blue Banana'.[5] On the other hand, outside the particularly dynamic urban areas we find vast zones where marginalization, depopulation, and functional depletion of entire landscapes and local communities are a grim reality. We meet this in the north of Scandinavia and in many of the mountain regions of central and southern Europe.

A particularly accentuated situation arises in the 'global financial cities', such as Shanghai, New York, London, and Tokyo. They have developed an economy that in many ways has decoupled the cities from the traditional hinterland. The cost of housing has ejected many ordinary citizens from the urban centres and created a high degree of social segregation in space (Graham/Marvin 2001). A classical Von Thünen hinterland-analysis would produce a map of London's economic hinterland, where spatial distance and economic distance no longer concur. The south of England has lost significant amounts of its earlier hinterland importance to places much further away. Likewise, the farmers of the Shanghai region would play a less important role in the development of Shanghai City than earlier.

If the international urban centres are decoupling from their traditional hinterlands, they are still dominating them, meaning that they take over land for urban development and on top of that, the population depends on the metropolis for jobs. In 2008 it was estimated that 19% of London's GDP was generated directly from the financial services of the City. The sector employed one third of Greater London's workforce. A significant 19% of the UK's GDP was generated by London (www.usatoday). For the Randstad, the figures for the metropolitan share of national GDP are even more dramatic, with a share of more than 50% of the GDP of the Netherlands.

Fig. 7
Two fields within which the parameters determining the shape of landscapes can be defined.

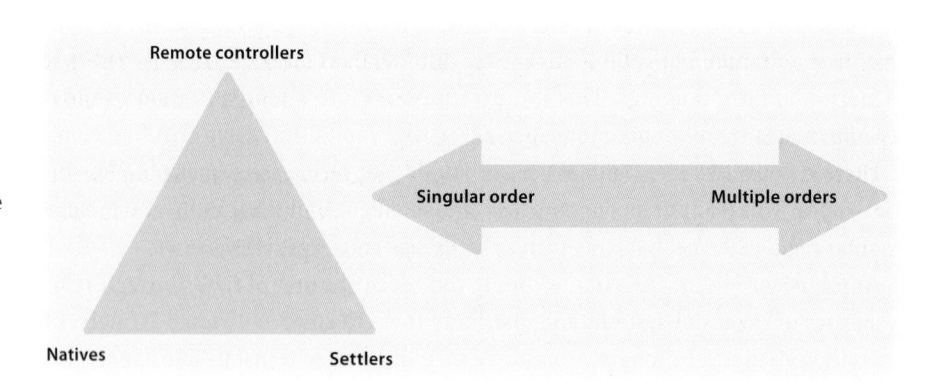

Continued growth is necessary for these urban centres, but growth potentials are determined by a volatile market and the market does not respond to long-term big planning. For this reason, urban development today is very different from urban development during the postwar heyday of the welfare state.

The Dutch architect Rem Koolhaas has dealt with the new reality of the networked global city (Koolhaas 1995). For Koolhaas, the global city is a place without a specific identity emanating from a local development. One could enhance Koolhaas' argument and claim that a localized history and cultural heritage become decreasingly relevant as a means to understand the particular development and character of a particular city in the same way as they are irrelevant to the understanding of the shape and layout of a new airport city.

To work with the long timelines of our landscapes in our present period confronts us with two fundamental challenges. First, the development of our landscapes is increasingly driven by an urban logic. Second, this urban logic is increasingly global, and freeing itself from an organic contact with a localized past. Cultural heritage may thus have to assume a different role and significance (if any), since the inhabitants of the contemporary urbanized landscapes may no longer live in memorial collectives that continue localized traditions.

4. IN LIEU OF A CONCLUSION

If the above seems defeatist to the reader, I can assure her or him that it is not meant to be so. Rather, I think it is important to sum up the observations made through this paper by pointing to the fact that the regimes that have shaped our landscapes have been constantly changing through history. I have tried to define two fields within which the parameters determining the shape of landscapes, urban or rural, can be defined (Fig. 7). One is tripolar and describes the actors and the second is bipolar and describes the nature of the order in the landscape.

The relationship between the tripolar and bipolar fields needs further investigation, beyond the limits of the present paper. It is by no means a simple and straightforward relationship. It is evident, however, that at the present time we see a regime of multiple orders affecting the landscapes in many parts of the world. It is also evident that in many parts of the world shifting configurations of remote controllers and to some extent settlers are more important in defining the premises for land use than are natives. The irony is that because all actors are operating (and competing) under the same rationale of an increasingly globalized market, the resulting palimpsest of multiple orders produces to a certain degree a monotonous repetitiveness in the arsenal of elements constituting the seemingly chaotic processes shaping our cities in ways that tend to obliterate any specific localized identity of theirs. This has been convincingly illustrated by the photographs of Peter Bialobrzeski that demonstrate the stunning similarity of urban development across the world (Bialobrzeski 2007).

There is however no reason, except for lack of imaginative power, why we should expect the present situation to be of permanence. History provides us with ample evidence for alternating periods of singular order and multiple orders dominating our landscapes. Likewise, we see periods of high mobility of people, labour, and capital alternating with periods of more contracted interaction, leaving more room for natives to form their local landscapes.

4.1   Memory and oblivion

The cognitive process of memorizing is intimately connected to a process of forgetting. If we forget nothing, we will be overloaded and unable to remember anything. The filters that relieve us from being overburdened by information also make it possible to structure and remember the information that remains in meaningful matrices that relate to or even constitute our identity. Conversely, if we forget everything, we will lose our identity. Therefore, memory is something that is formed in the interplay between remembering everything and remembering nothing (Fig. 8).

Likewise in landscapes. They are shaped in ongoing processes of deleting old structures and adding new ones. Sometimes this metabolism accelerates, and old structures are abruptly deleted over vast areas. This is what may happen when an entirely new ordering principle is introduced in a landscape, for instance with the rapid urbanization of rural landscapes. Sometimes this is done purposefully to eradicate a specific identity. An extreme example would be the Papst plan for the systematic annihilation of historic landmarks in Warsaw during the Second World War. The idea was to remould the Polish capital into a new minor regional city with a fully German identity (Tung 2001, 77-83).

An overwhelming, although slow and not complete, devouring of the past took place in Rome during the fifteen centuries following the fall of the empire. In particular, the construction of papal Rome with new monuments during the Renaissance and the Baroque took its toll on the splendour of the imperial capital. Marble from antique buildings, monuments, and statues was burned to serve as raw material for the production of high quality chalk or reshaped to ornament the magnificent new monuments of the Holy See (Tung 2001, 36-50).

Planners and antiquarians are special breeds. Emotionally we often sympathize with the natives. However, the decisions we recommend, or make, may point in many directions and do not always reflect

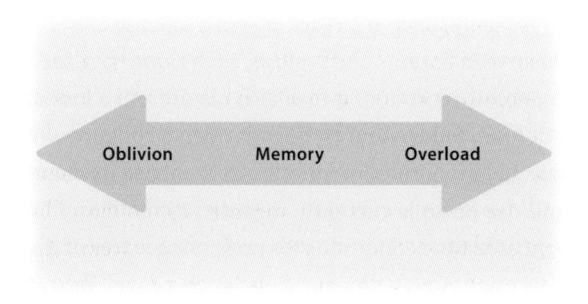

Fig. 8
Memory is something that is formed in the interplay between oblivion and overload of information.

sympathy with the natives who may often rightfully see us as belonging to the vast group of remote controllers tampering with their landscape and with their ideas of meaningful land use.

Antiquarians are generally concerned with preserving as much visible memory in a landscape as possible, sometimes even against the will and ambition of a local population more preoccupied with the future than with the past. Planners are basically concerned with planning for the future. Depending on current ideologies this may or may not include the memory of the past and its visible representation in the landscape, and it may or may not include the interests of the natives. During the heyday of modernization and big planning the ideal was certainly to shape a new and better landscape, rather than preserve traces of the shortcomings of the past. Le Corbusier's famous plan for a new Paris is one prominent example of this ambition to totally replace a historic cityscape by a completely new construct.

Under the current early twenty-first century ideological regime in Europe, both the ideal position of the antiquarians and that of the planners have been softened and frequently converge on a position where the remains of the past are seen as an asset for new development. The remains are thus seen as valuable, although not to a degree where they cannot give way to the ongoing process of rewriting the script that is our landscape. However, although the ideals may converge, the reality of the twenty-first century as it develops now and during the coming decennia may confront both planners and antiquarians with different possible dynamics and issues to address.

The following scenarios may serve as questions to reflect upon

First scenario: The current trend of urbanization continues.
We will see an increasing pressure on our landscapes, urban and interurban or rural. The pressure will be one of both volume and speed of transformation. A main challenge, also seen from an economic perspective, will be how to develop planning that allows us to develop cities that benefit from their diverse pasts as a resource for maintaining diverse identities. How do we make sure that we can still see that we are in Amsterdam and not in Hamburg? And how do we make sure that the mental ownership of the cultural heritage of a given place is open to every citizen independent of his or her ethnic affiliation?

Second scenario: The current agricultural policies continue.
We will see ever-increasing pressure for more agricultural productivity to meet the growing demands from the urban populations. The farmers will be competing on the same world market. They will be growing the same crops, breeding the same animals with the same technologies, and requiring the same productive infrastructure (buildings and field layout). How do we make sure that we will still know that we are in the farmlands of central Poland and not in those of the American Midwest?

Third scenario: The highly globalized agricultural market economy suffers a setback or even a collapse.
This may result from a growing competition for food between nations and regions, such as we have seen happen during the period prior to the onset of the economic recession. It may also result from a loss of the ability to sustain the transglobal transportation of food, fodder, and fertilizers. Such a collapse will probably translate into a lesser degree of specialization in agricultural production and impose its needs on the agricultural landscapes. Intensification of land use on soils currently regarded as too marginal may follow as a necessity. How will such a development affect the conditions for preserving traces of the past (including the current agricultural landscape)? We might find it obvious to see such a development

as favouring preservation, but is it so obvious? With the addition of climate change and the potential of gene-technology in a situation of otherwise scarce supplies we will surely not just see a reversion to pre-1950 European agriculture.

Fourth scenario: The trend of continued urban growth and concentration is broken or even reversed.
Such a scenario may result from shortages of foods and fuels on the world market. Both are needed to sustain highly urbanized populations. With the collapse of the supply lines for wheat from the provinces of Africa and Egypt during the fifth century AD, the imperial *urbs*, Rome, lost its ability to sustain its population of one million people. During the subsequent centuries Rome imploded to become a minor town with a population of no more than 30,000 inhabitants in the medieval period. Vast areas of the former imperial metropolis within the Aurelian Walls were converted into farmland and pasture. Today's megacities rely on equally vulnerable supplies of food, energy, and other goods from distant and highly specialized producers. It is a complex global logic of specialization based upon whoever has the better position to produce and ship the largest volume at the lowest cost, irrespective of geographical distance between production and consumption. Such supply chains may fail due to, for instance, rising costs of transportation or the producers' retraction of food from the world market in order to secure supplies for the home market. How do we deal with urban devolution as antiquarians and planners? It would confront us with a massive situation of functional cessation of what we would consider important urban heritage. Buildings and infrastructures would lose their economic viability and there would probably be few resources available for investment in their delicate redevelopment to accommodate new use. In such a volatile situation, authorities may focus on issues other than the preservation of cultural heritage. Documentation would probably be the better response in such a case. It may seem unfair to pose the question of how to cope with such a dystopic scenario. It is however tempting, since we are aware of the fact that history does not always stick to its overall linear course of progress and growth. Therefore let me conclude with this last scenario as a memento, while we try to prepare ourselves for the previous three scenarios, which we may like to think we should be in a better position to cope with.

Whatever the future brings, it will most probably be different from what we are capable of imagining as realistic. We do, however, know that the coming years will bring us both the direct and the indirect effects of a changing climate.

Our landscapes will accommodate new species, both domestic and wild. Our cultural heritage will be exposed to the deteriorating effects of changing sea levels, temperatures, winds, and rainfall. The landscape will need to accommodate new infrastructures that can help us adapt to the adverse effects of rising sea levels and extreme weather. Studying earlier adaptations to the dynamics of nature as witnessed by our cultural heritage may serve as an important source of insight and inspiration.

Our civil societies will have to accommodate new immigrants from distant cultures with whom we must develop the ability to share a common sense of belonging to the places we share. In this task, cultural heritage in the way it is embedded in our landscapes is an invaluable asset.

NOTES

1 The Norwegian Institute for Cultural Heritage Research, Oslo, Norway.

2   Sixteenth-century Middle Dutch *lantscap*, a term promoted widely across Europe by Dutch paintings from the period. See also Lorzing 2001, 25–26.
3   Jean Pierre L'Enfant grew up in Versailles and fought on the American side in the War of Independence. The striking thing about Washington DC is not how the architect got his inspiration for the layout, but that Versailles was accepted as a suitable model for the capital of the revolutionary American Republic. It is tempting and justifiable to read into this choice an early self-awareness on the part of the United States of its imperial potential.
4   Randstad is the name used for the circular urban conglomeration between Amsterdam, The Hague, Rotterdam and Utrecht, see Ruimte 2001, 227.
5   The "Blue Banana" is a name used among urbanists for Europe's heavily urbanized corridor stretching from Manchester in the North to Milan and Turin in the south.

REFERENCES

Bialobrzeski, P., 2007: *Lost in Transition*, Ostfildern.

Graham, S./S. Marvin, 2001: *Splintering Urbanism. Networked infrastructures, technological mobilities and the urban condition*, London.

Homberger, E., 2005: *The Historical Atlas of New York*, New York.

Koolhaas, R./B. Mau, 1995: *S,M,L,XL*, Rotterdam.

Lexau, S.S., 2007: *Kongens byer. den internasjonale bakgrunnen for Christian 4s byplanlegging I Norge*, Bergen.

Lorzing, H., 2001, *The Nature of Landscape, a Personal Quest*, Rotterdam.

Newman, R., 2001: *The Historical Archaeology of Britain c. 1450-1900*, Stroud, Gloucestershire.

Penrose, S., 2007: *Images of Change, an archaeology of England's contemporary landscape*, London.

Ruimte, 2001: *Ruimte maken, ruimte delen. Vijfde Nota over de Ruimtelijke Ordening 2000/2020*, Den Haag.

Tung, A. M., 2001: *Preserving the Worlds Great Cities, The destruction and Renewal of the Historic Metropolis*, New York.

Victor, J. C./V. Raisson/F. Tétart, 2007: *Le dessous des cartes. Atlas d'un monde qui change*, Paris.

Welzer, H., 2008: *Klimakriege. Wofür im 21. Jahrhundert getötet wird*, Frankfurt am Main.

WEBSITES

http://www.usatoday.com/marketplace/ibi/london.htm

III

LINKING KNOWLEDGE AND ACTION

Schipluiden (NL): foundations of a Roman period farmhouse. *Photo: H. van Londen.*

1. Linking knowledge to action: an introduction

Henk Kars[1]

ABSTRACT

This paper discusses a number of studies that link research-based knowledge to actions resulting in processes of decision-making, implementation and change in the protection and development of the archaeological-historical landscape. These studies on Dutch as well as on a few European regions or subjects are discussed from the perspective of sustainability, a wide-ranging term applied to economic as well as ecological systems but which also fits perfectly well to cultural resource management. It is concluded from the studies presented here that, if compared to a dozen years ago, much progress has been made in linking knowledge to sustainable action in the protection and development of the cultural landscape, while the se actions have simultaneously contributed to our knowledge about this landscape.

Research has shown that the methodology of action research is an important tool in linking knowledge to action; this paper therefore provides an overview of the characteristics of action research seen in the light of its use in cultural resource management studies where theory and practice do meet. All studies discussed here meet most, if not all, criteria of this methodology that creates situational and particular knowledge in the interaction between researchers and practitioners in cultural resource management. This interaction is most apparent in two regional studies in the Netherlands as well as in studies in Germany, Estonia and Scotland, and enables present generations to experience the archaeological-historical landscape not only as an inheritance of the past but also as a source for research and imagination for future generations.

KEYWORDS

Action research; cultural resource management; sustainability

1. INTRODUCTION

Many scientists still believe that good research is the exclusive domain of academic institutes and that the results will be taken up automatically in society where needed. Bringing the research results into the public domain by publishing in scientific journals is implicitly regarded as the end of the researcher's responsibility. This perspective has perhaps been a good characterization for the freedom and independence of basic and curiosity-driven research for a very long time, but for research that aims to influence decision-making towards generating actions with a societal impact, the reality is different. This dichotomy between curiosity-driven and use-inspired research is also seen and debated in the internationally rather small study area of cultural resource management, where research results remained mainly restricted to creating a level of public awareness instead of policy and decision-making actions.

Recently, however, it is widely recognized that in the field of sustainable development studies linking research-based knowledge to decision-making action is considered to be essential in moving forward towards solutions in reducing hunger, promoting literacy, stabilizing greenhouse-gas concentrations and many other problems. Knowledge systems in order to link knowledge to action in sustainability have therefore been presented and discussed by several authors (Cash *et al.* 2003; Van Kerkhoff/Lebel 2006), which might also be useful in sustainable development studies in cultural resource management.

The classic definition of sustainable development was provided by the World Commission on Environment and Development (United Nations 1987), which described it as a development "that meets the needs of the present without compromising the ability of future generation to meet their own needs". This has been commented on and adapted by many authors, a full discussion of which is beyond the scope of this paper. However, a widely accepted approach is that sustainable development is the process of ensuring that all people can achieve their aspirations while maintaining the critical conditions that are essential to our collective survival. Defining sustainability is therefore ultimately a social choice about what to develop, what to sustain, and for how long. It has been introduced and applied to many other fields than environment and development, and the notion of sustainability also fits remarkably well within modern views on cultural resource management. In this respect sustainability can be seen as a means to replace the longer existing rather static view on cultural *heritage* management by a more dynamic approach of cultural *resource* management.

Cultural heritage represents resources of the past that can meet the needs for present and future generations, as defined above. However, in fields where knowledge and action in sustainable development do meet, many barriers that inhibit mobilization of knowledge to effective action were encountered. This also holds for the cultural heritage field; therefore, in the research designing process of the PDL/BBO programme much attention was paid to make all participating project leaders and researchers aware of the basic concepts and methodologies of the requirement and dissemination of research-based knowledge that should lead to action in the public domain. It was realized that linking knowledge to action involves passing boundaries between multiple cultures of researchers in the inter- to multidisciplinary cultural heritage field. Moreover, it involves overcoming transdisciplinary boundaries of quite different cultures of policy and decision-makers on national, regional and local levels, of private bodies and those of the general public (Tress *et al.* 2003). The difficulty of transcending boundaries between different cultures of subdisciplines in archaeology, for instance, is illustrated by the apparently unbridgeable gap between the humanities and science (Kars 1995; Borger 2005), which might be detrimental to problem definition and research design in the early stages of the knowledge-action system discussed below. Jones (Jones 2004), referred to by several colleagues (Comments on A. Jones 2004, 2005), addresses the problem by describing the different intellectual positions of the cultural or theoretical archaeologist and the archaeological scientist towards the relationship between people and the things they used. His approach, concentrating on the cultural meaning of objects superimposed on objects as well as hidden in their material properties, might be helpful in understanding the problem from a philosophy of science viewpoint; however it does not solve it.

Moreover, the problem is seen in many other places where science and non-science-based disciplines do meet and it is perhaps an emancipatory rather than a philosophical problem. In the Dutch school system, for instance, pupils have to choose between non-scientific and science-based programmes at an early stage in their education, with the discriminating situation that pupils choosing the latter have to meet higher qualifications than those choosing a non-scientific programme.

Another important point that was recognized in linking knowledge to action is the need for, and appreciation of, unifying concepts to overcome boundaries within academic disciplines and between academia and the community of practitioners. A relevant example in studying the historical-archaeological landscape is the use of the concept 'biography of the landscape'. A common and widely accepted general perception, rather than a definition, of this concept is preferred in enhancing the imagination of all stakeholders in the knowledge-action system to avoid a Babel-like confusion of tongues of what a biography of the landscape actually is. In emphasizing the dynamics of the landscape, Vervloet, Van Beek and Keunen (Ch. III.4) note the different approaches but they concentrate in their landscape biography on measurable factors in creating academic knowledge, whereas Elerie and Spek (Ch. III.2) also stress the perception, symbolism and ideological significance in their landscape biography. It may be assumed that both approaches will be useful both for academia and non-professionals in the public domain.

In other cases, however, the parallel use of different definitions and therefore different interpretations of the same phenomenon should be accepted and mutually appreciated to avoid unworkable situations. An example is how to define landscape, which ranges from the rather positivistic definition frequently used in earth sciences (landscape by logic as it 'is', determined by measurable natural and human factors) versus the pragmatic, postmodern statement in the European Landscape Convention (landscape by argument as it is 'perceived' by people. In presenting the Vulkanpark Osteifel in this volume, Hunold and Schaaf (Ch. III.7) use the term landscape to describe the geology and geomorphology of their study area, but they also use it in a much wider sense in their paper, while Macinnes discusses the Scottish landscape seen in light of the Landscape Convention (Ch. III.5). It is clear that the strong divergence between the scientific and non-scientific definitions of landscape hinders the reconciliation of both and it seems more useful to accept several landscape definitions, a point which is also carefully discussed by Elerie and Spek (Ch. III.2).

In addition to communication and co-operation across boundaries, the actual integration of results is another challenge for creating action. Action for sustainable development of cultural heritage, including the historical-archaeological landscape, stretches across the range of scales from global UNESCO agreements to European conventions and from national legislation to provincial and municipal instructions and strategies. Integrating these scales is not always easy. The integration of cultural heritage research-based knowledge on a regional to local scale of action might, for instance, be hindered by jurisdiction since actions by the institutional bodies regarding nature or water management might have important effects on the cultural heritage strategies of other institutional bodies, often operating at different levels, a problem which is recognized in some papers in this chapter.

An important methodology used in knowledge action systems to address the above-mentioned problems is action research which was developed many years ago (Lewin 1946) and that is widely used in the social sciences. More recently it has also been successfully introduced to many other fields where theory meets practice, for instance in operations management, but the methodology has only rarely been applied in studies of the historical-archaeological landscape.

A knowledge action system is discussed below. It is the basis for describing the practical aspects of action research seen in the light of the cultural heritage studies carried out within the PDL/BBO programme. This is followed by an introduction of the papers grouped in this chapter from the perspective

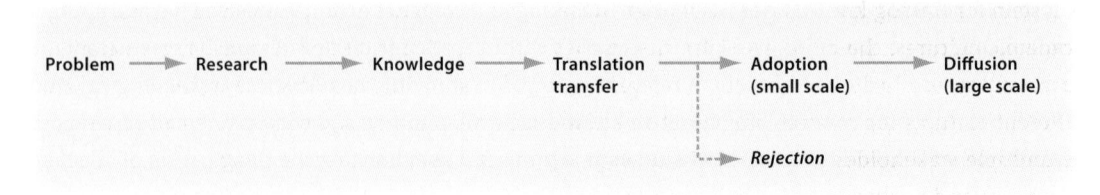

Fig. 1
The linear model of the development and transfer of knowledge. Scientists set the research agenda, do the research, and then transfer the results to the users. The results then diffuse through the community of practice. This static model had been criticized and adapted *(see Van Kerkhof/Lebel 2006 for an overview)*.

of linking knowledge to action, with action research as an important tool for the sustainable protection, maintenance, and development of the archaeological-historical landscape.

2. THE KNOWLEDGE – ACTION SYSTEM

Knowledge in general can be defined as *justifiable* belief. It encompasses knowledge generated by academic disciplines and it might also include other sources of knowledge but is justified by the adherence to a research process as defined by peers (Van Kerkhoff/Lebel 2006). In a knowledge – action system the research is oriented towards practice rather than theory. However, research programmes often continue to act as curiosity-driven projects that remain theory oriented and, for instance, in archaeology already frequently fail in the process of publication in scientific journals. For effectively designing research to serve action in the sustainable development of cultural heritage the tension has to be managed between researchers who are captured by the most exciting basic research and those who are indeed open for use-inspired research and are creating products that lead to particular solutions for practical situations.

Another problem is the fragmentation of the knowledge – action system. In the original knowledge – action chain in Fig. 1, ranging from problem definition to large-scale diffusion of the outcomes, incentives of the different stakeholders to work together are often absent because these stakeholders are in charge of different parts of the chain (Van Kerkhoff/Lebel 2006).

A third problem that has to be mentioned is the inflexibility of an academic environment which is often characterized by ignorance and surprise and this seems to be especially true of the arts and humanities. Dynamic and challenging knowledge – action programmes might be recognized, but how to initiate and implement them?

Furthermore, the link between knowledge and power is often not understood or is even denied. Francis Bacon's metaphor that knowledge is power is often underestimated by the scientific community, but when knowledge is meant to influence decisions or behaviour, knowledge is indeed power. However, the decision-makers and politicians being aware of this determine whose knowledge counts and who has influence in shaping the action. The implementation of climate change research into action, for instance, nicely demonstrates the question of how to create research-based knowledge that is both effective and equitable in global sustainable development applications, which may even lead to fraudulent treatment of data and reports by researchers and politicians!

A system for linking knowledge to action for sustainability in heritage management involves multiple academic cultures, the cultures of decision-makers and those of local and national organizations. A successful system includes individuals or organizations devoted to the task of spanning the gaps between different cultures for creating collaborative knowledge products which are jointly owned and trusted by multiple stakeholders. The central challenge for the PDL/BBO research programme therefore was to support and nurture such boundary work to produce effective and equitable science for sustainable development in the domain of the historical-archaeological landscape.

Several systems for linking research-based knowledge to action have been developed by different authors within different disciplines. A very basic one is a linear model that relates problem solving through research-based knowledge and translation towards solutions for external stakeholders who can adopt (or reject) them, but with the aim to become diffused in society (Fig. 1). This model has been criticized and adjusted in different ways, a full discussion of which is beyond the scope of this paper, but an important aspect to be noted is that this linear chain is static, having a beginning where the agenda seems to be set by the researcher, and an end, where it is hoped that the results are adopted by stakeholders leading to action and societal diffusion. Sustainable development in general, but also in heritage resource management in particular, requires a continuous process of adaptation and mitigation at all parts of the chain and the research agenda should not only be set by researchers but in close co-operation with the societal stakeholders. To present the system as a cycle instead of a chain is an important step towards creating use-inspired research leading to a societal action, while the action simultaneously contributes to our knowledge and new research questions. In achieving this cyclical process the application of the action research methodology might be extremely useful.

3. ACTION RESEARCH

Since its introduction by Lewin in 1946, many papers and books have been dedicated to the methodology and the characteristics of action research. Initially this methodology was widely accepted and used by behavioural scientists in the social sciences, but after elaborating and expanding it, action research was applied in many other areas where research and practice do meet. Defining action research is therefore not an easy task and many definitions for different areas of research and application have been proposed. A definition used in a study that aims to reconstruct the relationship between universities and society through action research might be useful here (Greenwood/Levin 2003): "Action research is inquiry in which participants and researchers cogenerate knowledge through collaborative communicative processes in which all participants' contributions are taken seriously. The meanings constructed in the inquiry process lead to social action, or these reflections on action lead to the construction of new meanings". To fully understand this definition we refer to the *Handbook of Action Research* (Reason/Bradbury 2001), which gives an excellent clarification of what action research actually is, covering the historical development of the methodology, the different philosophy of science viewpoints on the methodology, as well as a wide range of its applications.

Seen in light of the academic character of the PDL/BBO programme, the apparent paradigmatic controversy between positivistic science and action research has to be discussed. The widely accepted scientific method of positivism in science aims at creating universal knowledge, whereas action research methodologies create situational and particular knowledge in the interaction between researchers and practitioners. In action research the data are contextually embedded and interpreted, while in the positivistic philosophy of science findings are validated by reproducible measurement and logic. Action research therefore fits perfectly well within the postmodern pragmatic debate which for instance is recognized in the European Landscape Convention on how landscape is defined.

Action research is also an important tool in the modern knowledge-based economy where knowledge can be seen as a tool to produce sustainable economic benefits. Coughlan and Coghlan (Coughlan/Coghlan 2002) discuss ten major characteristics of action research applicable to operations management, which are summarized here because they are also useful in the knowledge – action system to be applied to protect, maintain and develop the archaeological-historical landscape.

1. Action researchers take action. They are not merely observing what is happening, but they are working at making things happen. Action research is more than creating awareness that is often seen in former heritage management studies, but it also has to result in action.
2. Action research involves two goals: contributing to knowledge and solving a practical problem. The challenge is to be engaged in both making the action happen and standing back from it and reflecting on it in order to contribute theory to the body of knowledge. An example in this section is the study by van den Berg *et al.* (Ch. III.6) to improve our knowledge of the preservation potential of the burial environment that leads to a method to monitor this environment by stakeholders, while the monitoring results themselves contribute to knowledge about the burial environment.
3. Action research is interactive. It requires co-operation between researchers and the societal partners in the project; both are contributing to solving a problem and to implementing solutions. This becomes clear in the study by Elerie and Spek (Ch. III.2) where they have successfully worked towards an integration of nature management, heritage management and public participation on a regional level in the northern Netherlands. This interactive approach is even more apparent in the work of Köivupuu, Printsmann and Palang (Ch. III.3) in order to create a common identity in the Lahemaa national park in Estonia, which has undergone several political and ideological changes in a short period of time.
4. Action research teams need to have a broad view of how the system works and they must be able to work with dynamic complexity and recognize multiple causes and effects over time. See, for instance, the paper by Macinnes (Ch. III.5) which deals with the historic landscape in Scotland in the context of the European Landscape Convention and also the paper by Köivupuu, Printsmann and Palang (Ch. III.3).
5. Action research is fundamentally about change and it is therefore used in understanding, planning and implementation in all kinds of scientific and non-scientific situations, which is addressed by Vervloet, Van Beek and Keunen (Ch. III.4) in their discussion regarding the use of transdisciplinarity and consensus planning in their regional study of the eastern Netherlands.
6. Action requires an understanding of the ethical framework, values and norms. This involves authentic relationships between the action researcher and all stakeholders of the system he/she works in. Values and norms that flow from ethical principles typically focus on how the action researcher works within his/her environment. It is all too clear that this is particularly applicable in the heritage field, where values and norms are a continuous subject of discussion between all stakeholders of the cultural resource management system.

7. In addition to quantitative methods, action research can include all qualitative methods of data gathering. The qualitative data collection tools such as surveys and interviews are extremely situational and subjective and this might be critical to the success or the project. This problem was, for instance, encountered in the Lahemaa National Park project presented by Köivupuu, Printsmann and Palang (Ch. III.3).
8. To be successful in action research requires a breadth of pre-understanding of the environment in which the research is performed. This is certainly true for the cultural heritage field which includes academics from different fields and a broad variety of (non-)governmental stakeholders. Research on the degradation of organic remains in soils, for instance, might be a challenge for the geochemist (Van den Berg *et al.*; Ch. III.6), but will hardly trigger other academics and certainly not stakeholders responsible for action in protecting archaeological sites and landscapes. Stagnation of this research within academia is a serious threat.
9. Action research is usually conducted in real time in order to improve existing processes and to initiate new processes, which was precisely the main rationale of the PDL/BBO programme.
10. Action research requires its own quality criteria and should not, for instance, be judged solely by the traditional criteria of the positivistic scientist. Most quality criteria will concentrate on how the research-based knowledge has reached the community of practitioners (for further discussion see section 5).

I shall now briefly introduce the papers presented in this section in light of the above-mentioned methodological criteria applied to cultural resource management.

4. LINKING KNOWLEDGE TO ACTION IN PRACTICE

Section III contains six papers which reflect different aspects of the study of the historical-archaeological landscape. Three of these were carried out within the PDL/BBO programme, two papers cover regional studies in the northern and eastern parts of the Netherlands respectively, while the third presents a methodological study on the *in situ* preservation of our archaeological resources. The three other papers in this chapter highlight situational studies on the archaeological-historical landscape in Estonia, Germany and Scotland. Though all papers can be seen from the perspective of the knowledge – action chain ranging from problem definition, the requirement and transfer of knowledge and adaptation and implementation by the relevant societal stakeholders, they are quite different. This is first of all due to the subject of study, ranging from almost curiosity-driven basic research performed by Van den Berg *et al.* (Ch. III.6), to a holistic and participative approach presented by Macinnes (Ch. III.5) with reference to landscape protection in Scotland seen in the light of the European Landscape Convention. It is also recognized that the research presented in some papers is discourse-oriented according to the methodology of action research, while others remain concentrated on the scientific empirical cycle as used within their field of study.

In addition to the papers published in this volume, four short studies carried out within the PDL/BBO programme are also briefly summarized here (Lotte 2003; Grimminck 2004; Jacobs 2005; Isarin 2007), with regard to linking knowledge to action.

Most research performed within the PDL/BBO programme addresses the relationship between the sustainable development of the archaeological-historical landscapes and spatial planning on different administrative levels. In addition, a few projects were dedicated to the occurrence and preservation of the ancient resources present in these landscapes. Comparatively little attention was paid to the legislative framework, which is a third prerequisite for the sustainable preservation and development of the resources. A positive example is a short study that evaluates the legislative basis for safeguarding the archaeological-historical values with regard to the implementation of the Valletta Treaty in the Dutch Archaeological Heritage Management Act in 2007 (Grimminck 2004; Wamz 2007). This report stresses that in the Netherlands, in addition to this Monuments Act, the Spatial Planning Act of 2008 is actually the main legal framework that provides and supports the instruments for sustainable development of the historical-archaeological landscape. It underlines that for a successful application and implementation of these instruments in archaeological-historical landscape management, all stakeholders in spatial planning must be reached in linking knowledge to action. The important role of spatial planning in sustainable development of the culture landscape also underpins the need to link this with nature development programmes in the planning process.

The region as a meeting point for nature and culture in two completely different geographical, political and mental situations is thoroughly described by Elerie and Spek for the Netherlands and by Köivupuu, Printsmann and Palang for Estonia.

In their excellent paper on the Drentsche Aa National Landscape in the northern Netherlands, Elerie and Spek (Ch. III.2) address the problem of integrating nature resource management and heritage resource management in policy and decision-making as well as in a wider societal context. During a five-year programme they successfully tried, with action research as an important methodological tool and the biography of landscape as a unifying concept, to bring together the often diverging ecological and cultural perspectives of landscape as a guide for future developments. Though not supported by examples, they claim that the inter- and transdisciplinary methods they developed for their region are now applied on a broad scale in regional environmental and planning policies and landscape management in the Netherlands. They finally mention three important building blocks for a successful integration of nature and cultural resource management: i) good collaboration between, and integration of, cultural heritage with academic disciplines; ii) good connections between expert and local knowledge, and perhaps most important of all, iii) interactive planning in which residents, stakeholders, policymakers, nature managers, researchers and designers have a balanced input.

From a Western European point of view these building blocks also hold for the intriguing and challenging paper by Köivupuu, Printsmann and Palang (Ch. III.3) which deals with the Lahemaa National Park in Estonia, some 70 km east of Tallinn. This was founded in 1971 as the first national park in the Soviet Union and was created with the idea that it should contribute to feelings of nationalism within the political framework of the time. The authors address the conceptual problem of changing identities from historical traditions through a period of representing the socialistic pride as a satellite state of the Soviet Union followed by a reappraisal of regional identities after the collapse of the USSR in the re-independent state of Estonia. Within this framework the authors propagate a new approach towards a combined management of nature conservation and cultural heritage supported by a democratic process which includes the input of the local population. They describe via knowledge gained through action, including an extensive number of interviews, how societal factors in a strongly changing political atmosphere influence the conceptual and social construction of regional identity which is determined by internal factors that are meaningful to the local inhabitants and by external factors superimposed by newcomers in the depopulated areas. An important part of their project plan was making an inventory of each village and interviewing its inhabitants using the method of dialogical anthropology. The aim is to diminish the cultural differences between the researcher and his subjects. Apart from an instrumental role in managing the achieved data, the researchers foster a relationship with the material, while being aware that the society funding the research also sets conditions for the research.

Two studies with rather different methodological approaches place the cultural landscape on the political agenda and embed it in society on both regional and national levels. The paper by Vervloet, Van Beek and Keunen (Ch. III.4) describes an ambitious research programme that has dealt with the biography of the landscape of the eastern Netherlands. In the process of acquisition and propagation of knowledge they concentrated on an interdisciplinary approach comprising of, or related to, archaeology and historical geography. This turned out to be successful in describing the "real" landscape with its different cultural elements through time. In the second part of their paper they try to frame their results in the world of decision-makers by providing a transdisciplinary overview of the historical development of awareness of the cultural landscape by different stakeholders outside academia. However, based on the paper, it seems that for this regional project the research results that were meant to be used to change the attitudes of the stakeholders have only led to an increased awareness of the cultural landscape, instead of concerted actions which guide governmental and non-governmental organizations towards a sustainable management of the cultural landscape. An important tool they mention is participatory planning involving non-professionals in all stages of the planning process rather than a traditional public consultation of a clear-cut plan that is hard to change. Baas, Groenewoudt and Raap (Baas/Groenewoudt/Raap in press), focus on a local to regional scale within the framework of the Dutch Spatial Planning Act and of the European Landscape Convention, providing a number of examples in which participation by the public, non-governmental organizations and local authorities has led to a variety of actions with sustainable protection and development of the landscape as the ultimate result. The study by Köivupuu, Printsmann and Palang (Ch. III.3) and Macinnes (Ch. III.5) described below, show that this approach has also been successful elsewhere in Europe.

In contrast to the regional approach, Macinnes describes the protection and management of the historic landscape in Scotland in the context of the European Landscape Convention by outlining a number of recent developments that contribute to a more holistic and participative approach to landscape protection, management and planning. In addition to the existing statutory and non-statutory regulations to protect the historic landscape, Macinnes mentions that historic environment measures are to some extent integrated in measures for the protection and management of the wider landscape in Scotland. She further notes that national projects on characterizing the historic landscape and historic land-use assessment, identifying historic patterns within the landscape, have been very helpful in adopting a more landscape-based approach to the conservation of the historic environment and in integrating it with other aspects of landscape management. These developments fit remarkably well within the principles of the European Landscape Convention and this consistency might lead to a structural approach in which the historic character of the landscape will be managed as an integral part of wider land-use.

Two papers and a short study (Isarin 2007) at either end of the knowledge – action chain discuss the preservation and protection of archaeological-historical resources in present and future landscapes. In addition, a short study measures the effects of large projects on the development of linear infrastructure projects (motorways, railways), surface covering projects (housing estates) or of areas for nature development on the sustainable preservation of archaeological sites (Lotte 2003). This study has, amongst other things, demonstrated that projects with a linear character in particular have a devastating effect on the *in situ* preservation of archaeological sites; only 13% of all sites threatened by the project could be fitted in for sustainable preservation. Taking into account that new motorways and railways are attractive for the establishment of trading estates and business parks, it might be expected that a large part of this 13% will be under threat again soon. A lesson to be learned is that *in situ* preservation is often an unrealistic option and that energy should be directed towards the quality of the archaeological research to be done during these projects. However, in many other cases sustainable preservation is fortunately a realistic option, which raises the urgent need for site and landscape management plans that include the actual physical protection of these sites and landscapes as addressed by Van den Berg *et al.* (Ch. III.6) and the short study by Isarin (Isarin 2007).

Whereas Van den Berg *et al.* (Ch. III.6) concentrate on knowledge acquisition regarding the physical protection of invisible archaeological sites, Hunold and Schaaff (Ch. III.7) describe the process of how to scientifically transform rather well documented archaeological-historical scars of quarrying and mining in the landscape into an educational and informative park, where people can understand the use of our natural resources in the past.

Van den Berg *et al.* (Ch. III.6) combine two studies on botanical remains in order to assess the preservation state of archaeological sites in wetlands. The first adopts a strong experimental and empirical approach to estimate the diagenetic pathway of degrading plant remains in soils using chemical analysis. The utilitarian goal of this curiosity-driven as well as use-inspired research was the development of a method for monitoring the preservation state of an archaeological site under changing soil conditions. The second is an empirical case study which describes data collection of degrading wood and its burial environment at two Neolithic sites in the Netherlands. In addition to establishing the preservation state of the wood, the conservation potential of the two different burial environments was established by examining the micromorphology of the soil. This interdisciplinary research covering different fields of earth and archaeological sciences has produced relevant knowledge; however, translation and transfer of this knowledge towards the societal stakeholders responsible for the physical protection of sites was scarce. It is beyond discussion that this kind of research is essential for a successful sustainable archaeological resource management and getting the research results adopted by heritage managers leading to action remains a challenge. Related to the paper by Van den Berg *et al.* (Ch. III.6) is a short study that reflects an inventory on the mitigation of the impact of construction on archaeological remains in the Netherlands (Isarin 2007). The effects of construction operations on different burial environments are at present poorly understood. The study presents descriptions of operations employed during the course of a development from the various works required during the pre-construction stage, through the more damaging operations during the construction stage. Maintenance activities after the construction stage, however, are rare and seldom monitored. Though successful examples of co-operation between the construction industry and heritage managers are mentioned, the most important conclusion is that more geotechnical research is needed to enhance our understanding of the subject, leading to structural action by politicians and practitioners.

In a short study dealing with preserving and protecting the cultural resources in Dutch historical towns and villages, Jacobs has evaluated the Monuments and Historic Buildings Act 1988, the Spatial Planning Act and others with respect to the feasibility of sustainable protection of archaeological remains in urbanized environments (Jacobs 2005). His main conclusion was that this legislation provides a sound basis for preserving and protecting the archaeological and historical resources. He further concluded that, due to the high economic pressure on these areas, it remains a challenge to put this legislation into practice. This is, for instance, hindered by the lack of a reliable and updated inventory of the presence and preservation state of the local archaeological-historical resources. The production of local maps showing the tangible and intangible values of these resources is essential to integrate them with the municipal scheming plan.

A beautiful example of integrating archaeological-historical values in planning on a regional level leading to preservation as well as presentation of these values is given by Hunold and Schaaff (Ch. III.7). They present the aims and progress of the Vulkanpark Osteifel Project in the ancient quarry and mining district in the Andernach-Mayen-Koblenz area in Germany. Since the Neolithic, the tephrite rocks in the Mayen area, commonly known as basalt lava, and since Roman times, volcanic tuff in the Laacher See region, were quarried and mined in huge quantities. The Mayen quarries, thoroughly described in the 1950s, were famous for their high quality millstones which are found all over northwestern Europe from the Alps to Scandinavia and Britain. For instance, large amounts of used and new unfinished querns are found in Dorestad (Kars 1980) and Haithabu (Schön 1995). Volcanic tuff was extensively used as building material and is found in almost every Roman site along the river Rhine to the North Sea coast, whereas in medieval times the tuffs were used to build churches and monasteries in Germany, the Netherlands and Denmark. Several remnants of the mines and quarries are still present and visible in many places in the landscape and are in serious danger. In realizing the international importance of this natural and cultural heritage, the Vulkanpark Osteifel project was developed in order to transform unattractive scars in the landscape into testimonies of extinct volcanic activity and of ancient exploitation of mineral resources for the general public. In a consortium of stakeholders representing academics, administration and industry, the Osteifel Vulkanpark was developed while the park is maintained with the help of many local authorities. Today this ancient industrial landscape is seen as an attractive resource for arranging the future landscape according to the European Landscape Convention with the important side-effect that it will strengthen tourism in this part of the Eifel region. Moreover, the project has led to an extensive research programme that contributes to our body of knowledge of this ancient industrial landscape.

5. DISCUSSION

This paper discusses a number of studies that link research-based knowledge to actions that should result in processes of decision making, implementation and change in the protection and development of the archaeological-historical landscape. The research presented in these studies is discussed here from two different but related perspectives. The first is sustainability, which is a wide-ranging term applied to economic as well as ecological systems on global to local scales. It is obvious that the concept of sustainability also fits the protection and development of cultural heritage perfectly well. The second is the methodology of action research which has its background in the social sciences, but since the 1990s it has also been widely applied to sustainability studies where theory and practice converge.

The discussion of the research papers concentrates on those performed within the PDL/BBO programme, most of which were dedicated to situations in the Netherlands, while the other papers provide a wider European perspective on the subject. In addition, four short studies funded by the PDL/BBO programme are evaluated.

Seen in the light of sustainability, we should first of all mention the short study by Grimminck (Grimminck 2004) which notes that, in addition to the Monuments and Historic Buildings Act 1988, the Spatial Planning Act in particular provides the instruments for sustainable protection of the archaeological-historical landscape. This is in agreement with the study by Jacobs (Jacobs 2005) on Dutch historical towns and villages, which shows that both Acts provide a sound basis for the protection of their archaeological and historical resources, although it might be hindered by the lack of knowledge with regard to the presence and preservation state of the local archaeological-historical resources. Lotte (Lotte 2003), however, arrives at the conclusion that in large linear infrastructural projects protection of sites is the exception rather than a common achievement. Additionally, Isarin's (Isarin 2007) short study shows that the effects of construction operations on different burial environments are poorly understood and that more geotechnical research is needed to enhance our understanding of the subject that leads to sustainable protection instead of excavation of sites. Based on these four studies one can conclude that there is still an enormous gap between theory and practice in the sustainable protection of cultural heritage. This appears to be supported by Van den Berg *et al.* (Ch. III.6), who concentrate on the physical preservation of our heritage. Their work shows that our knowledge with regard to the *in situ* preservation of archaeological sites in different burial environments and monitoring of the preservation state of sites under changing soil conditions is still in its infancy (Kars/Van Heeringen 2008).

However, most projects presented in this section clearly demonstrate that much progress has been made in linking knowledge to sustainable action in the protection and development of the cultural landscape, while these actions are simultaneously contributing to our knowledge about the landscape.

This is all too clear in the Drentsche Aa project presented by Elerie and Spek(Ch. III.2), who successfully merge the ecological and cultural aspects into a landscape biography which has been extremely helpful in creating a mutual understanding between researchers and the societal stakeholders for preserving the landscape in ongoing and future economic developments. Although less clear in the project presented by Vervloet, Van Beek and Keunen (Ch. III.4), similar conclusions can be drawn from their investigations in the eastern Netherlands. Based on an academic approach for the description of the landscape, they tried to create a societal basis for integrating the historical landscape in future landscape developments by participatory or consensus planning of all stakeholders in the planning process. This approach was successful in some regions in the eastern Netherlands (Baas/Groenewouldt/Raap in press).

In this paper much attention was paid to the introduction of the action research methodology as a tool of the knowledge action system that connects theory and practice in the protection and development of the archaeological-historical landscape. In evaluating the quality of action research the following questions could be asked (Reason/Bradbury 2001):
- Is the research explicit in developing praxis of relational participation between the action researcher and the community of practitioners?

- Is the research guided by a reflexive concern for practical outcomes? Is there a constant and iterative reflection as part of the process of change and improvement?
- Does action research include a plurality of knowledge which ensures conceptual-theoretical integration, extends the boundaries of knowledge and is methodologically appropriate?
- Does the research result in a new and enduring infrastructure, does sustainable change come out of the project?

It is beyond the scope of this introduction to evaluate the studies presented in this chapter separately and in detail on the above-mentioned merits with regard to meaningfully linking research-based knowledge to relevant societal actions in heritage management. It is easily seen, however, that the methodology has been successfully applied in all studies presented within this section (see Ch. VI.1, 511-513). This is particularly true for regional studies in the northern and eastern Netherlands within the PDL/BBO programme and the foreign studies by Köivupuu, Printsmann and Palang (Ch. III.3) and Hunold and Schaaf (Ch. III.7). Returning to the PDL/BBO programme, it might be concluded that the paper by Van den Berg et al. (Ch. III.6) does not meet the quality criteria for action research. This is certainly due to the basic character of the research programme that was concentrated on gathering and interpreting data with the need for additional research as a major outcome. This is in line with Isarin (Isarin 2007) on the effects of construction practices on buried sites; however, initiated by the Dutch council of municipal archaeologists, an inventory of all stakeholders is made in order to define their research needs for appropriate action in the sustainable protection of sites in highly (re-)urbanizing areas.

In conclusion, it can be stated that one of the main challenges or even prerequisites for a successful ending of the PDL/BBO programme, namely linking knowledge to societal action, has been achieved in that the archaeological-historical landscape is not only seen as a heritage of the past but also as a source for research and imagination for future generations.

NOTES

1   VU University, Amsterdam, the Netherlands.

REFERENCES

Baas, H./B. Groenewoudt/E. Raap, in press: *The Dutch approach. Public participation and the role of NGO's and local authorities in the protection, management and development of cultural landscapes in the Netherlands.*

Borger, G.J., 2005: *Afstand maakt verschil*, Amsterdam (Inaugural lecture VU University).

Cash, D./W.C. Clark/F. Alcock/N. Dickson/N. Eckley/D. Guston/J. Jäger/R. Mitchel, 2003: Knowledge systems for sustainable development, *Proceedings of the National Academy of Sciences* 100, 8068-8091.

Comments on A. Jones 2004, 2005: Archaeometry and Materiality: Materials-based analysis in theory and practice, *Archaeometry* 46, 327-338, 2004, and Reply, *Archaeometry* 47, 175-207.

Coughlan, P./D. Coghlan, 2002: Action research for operations management, *International Journal of Operations & Productions Management* 22, 220-240.

Greenwood, D.J./M. Levin, 2003: Reconstructing the relationship between universities and society through action research, in N.K. Denzin/Y.S. Lincoln (eds.), *The Landscape of qualitative research: Theories and issues,* Thousand Oaks, 131-166.

Grimminck, E.S., 2004: *Cultuurhistorie in besluitvorming en uitvoering van infrastructuurprojecten. Een juridisch onderzoek in het kader van het NWO programma Bodemarchief in Behoud en Ontwikkeling*, (internal report University of Amsterdam, Amsterdam/NWO, Den Haag).

Isarin, R., 2007: *Archeologiesparend bouwen. Waar archeologen en bouwers elkaar ontmoeten*, Woerden.

Jacobs, E., 2005: *Duurzaam beheer en behoud van archeologische waarden in het stedelijk gebied. Tussen papier en praktijk*, Amsterdam (Standaard Archeologisch Rapport 44).

Jones, A., 2004: Archaeometry and Materiality: Materials-based analysis in theory and practice, *Archaeometry* 46, 327-338.

Kars, H., 1980: Early-Medieval Dorestad, an Archaeo-Petrological Study, Part I: General Introduction. The Tephrite Querns, *Berichten van de Rijksdienst voor het Oudheidkundig Bodemonderzoek* 30, 393-422.

Kars, H., 1995: *Archeologie tussen alfa en beta*, Amsterdam (Inaugural lecture VU University).

Kars, H./R.M. van Heeringen (eds.), 2008: *Preserving archaeological remains in situ. Proceedings of the 3rd conference 7-9 December 2006, Amsterdam*, Amsterdam (Geoarchaeological and Bioarchaeological Studies 10).

Kerkhoff, L. van/L. Lebel, 2006: Linking knowledge and action for sustainable development, *Annual Review of Environment and Resources* 31, 1-33.

Lewin, K., 1946: Action research and minority problems, *Journal of Social Issues* 2, 34-46.

Lotte, R.M., 2003: *Evaluatie van grote projecten. Een studie naar het voorkomen van behoud in situ bij grote infrastructurele projecten in het kader van het NWO-Stimuleringsprogramma Bodemarchief in Behoud en Ontwikkeling (BBO)*, (internal report Cultural Heritage Agency, Amersfoort/NWO, Den Haag).

Reason, P./H. Bradbury (eds.), 2001: *The SAGE Handbook of Action Research. Participative Inquiry and Practice*, London.

Schön, V., 1995: *Die Mühlsteine von Haithabu und Schleswig. Ein Beitrag zur Entwicklungsgeschichte des mittelalterlichen Mühlenwesens in Nordwesteuropa*, Neumünster (Berichte über die Ausgrabungen in Haithabu 31).

Tress, B./G. Tress/A. van der Valk/G. Fry, 2003: *Interdisciplinary and transdisciplinary Landscape Studies: Potential and Limitations*, Wageningen (DELTA Series 2).

United Nations, 1987: *Report of the World Commission on Environment and Development*, General Assembly Resolution 42/187, 11 December 1987.

Wamz 2007: *Archaeological Heritage Management Act*, Den Haag.

2. The cultural biography of landscape as a tool for action research in the Drentsche Aa National Landscape (Northern Netherlands)

Hans Elerie[1] & Theo Spek[2]

ABSTRACT

There is a growing awareness in the Netherlands that nature management, heritage management and public participation cannot be seen in isolation and need to be tackled in a more integrated way. This not only has major practical implications, it also has a bearing on the scientific research that underpins future policy, the design and management of nature conservation sites and cultural landscapes. One of the key problems in modern landscape research and modern landscape policy lies in the fact that the ecological and cultural perspectives are far removed from one another. A second problem is that local residents are often insufficiently involved in the research and planning activities of experts. During a five-year research and action programme in the Drentsche Aa National Landscape, geologists, archaeologists, historical geographers, toponymists and ecologists put the theoretical concept of the cultural biography of landscape into practice at a regional level. The results from this exercise include an accessible and richly illustrated book and an online digital cultural atlas. The researchers also worked with residents, designers, policymakers and stakeholder organizations to develop a method of participatory planning that can be applied both regionally and locally. At regional level, an integrated landscape vision has been developed to serve as a guide for future developments. Both the cultural biography and the participatory planning method were tested at a more local level for devising development and management plans for nature conservation areas, water systems and micro-landscapes. Finally, an interactive project in three villages studied the interaction between the physical, social and mental landscape on the basis of toponyms. The interdisciplinary and transdisciplinary methods developed over the past few years in the Drentsche Aa region are now applied on a broad scale in regional environmental and planning policy and nature and landscape management in the Netherlands.

KEYWORDS

Interdisciplinarity, transdisciplinarity; landscape biography; community planning, participatory planning; landscape architecture, landscape management; field names, local knowledge

1. INTRODUCTION

The integration of heritage management and nature management poses one of the greatest challenges in Europe's rural areas over the next few years (Plieninger/Höchtl/Spek 2006). This certainly also applies to the Netherlands, whose highly urbanized society and high population density, coupled with the inevitable intensive use of space over the centuries, have meant that cultural and ecological values are closely interlinked in virtually all parts of the country. This close interweaving of values is found in almost all the National Landscapes that the Dutch government designated in 2004 (Fig. 1; Spatial Planning Memorandum 2004; Netherlands Environmental Assessment Agency 2005). More than in

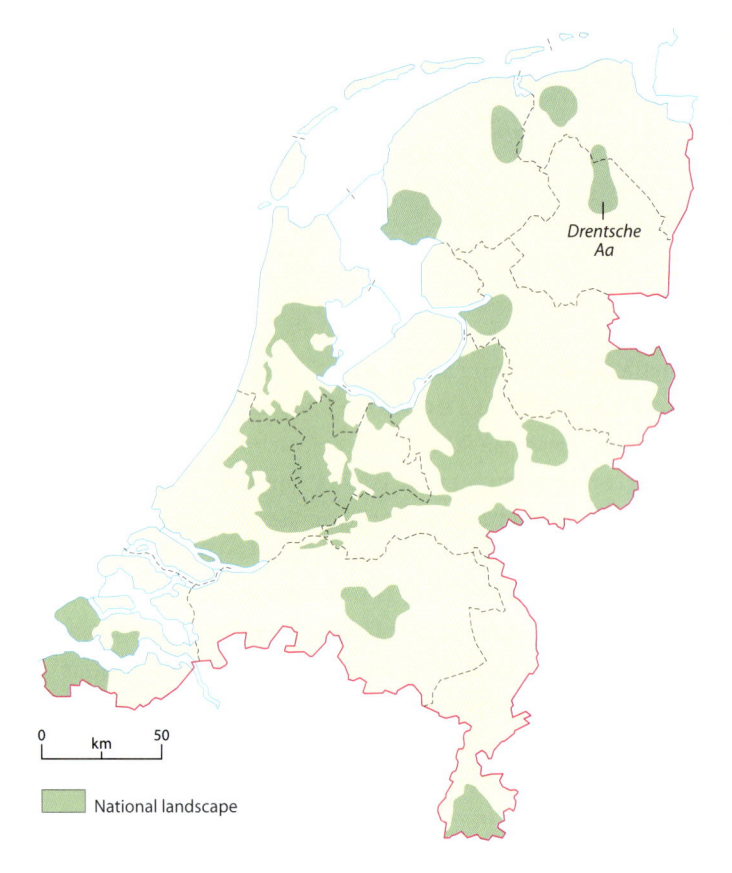

Fig. 1
National Landscapes of the Netherlands, designated by the Dutch national government in 2004.

other parts of the country, the National Landscapes have a wide range of nature conservation areas and cultural landscapes of major heritage and cultural value, usually as a result of centuries of interaction between humans and nature.

Nature conservation areas in the Netherlands almost never consist exclusively of natural ecosystems (Van Rhenen *et al.* 2005). Instead, they are made up of a broad range of semi-natural ecosystems whose diversity is determined to a large extent by the presence of or management by humans in the past. Many of these nature conservation areas were used in the distant past even more intensively than they are today, as the core of areas in which people lived and worked in prehistory and the Middle Ages. As a result, many Dutch nature conservation areas are teeming with archaeological, historical geographical and architectural sites and relics. And although they are often no longer occupied today, nature conservation areas in the Netherlands are used on a daily basis by residents and for recreational purposes by visitors. Many places and landscape features in nature conservation areas therefore have major social and emotional significance for people. In such places, nature management cannot focus exclusively on conserving and developing ecological values. It must also set out a clear vision for the preservation and development of current and past cultural values and the opportunities for residents and visitors to experience these values.

Outside conservation areas and highly urbanized areas, a large proportion of the Netherlands consists of agrarian cultural landscapes. The original historical geographical structure of many of these cultural landscapes was created in the Middle Ages and underwent several periods of radical change thereafter in response to economic and social developments. Although they are still used intensively by farmers and other land users today, natural values have been preserved in many parts of these old cultural landscapes. Examples include the many rare plant species on wooded embankments, birds in open meadows and bat populations in old military defences and on historic country estates. And to an even greater extent than in nature conservation areas, these old cultural landscapes have for many centuries been strongly associated with the identity of local residents and users. Again, nature and landscape management must take careful account of current and past cultural values (Dirkx 2004).

There is therefore a growing awareness among Dutch nature conservation organizations that nature management, heritage management and public participation cannot be seen in isolation and need to be tackled in a more integrated way. This not only has major practical implications, it also has a bearing on the scientific research that underpins future policy, the design and management of nature conservation sites and cultural landscapes. Over the next few years, nature conservation organizations will be given an increasingly important role in the management of the green spaces in the National Landscapes. Some farmers will also expand their objectives to include management of the environment and cultural landscapes. Besides agricultural nature management, they will also become engaged in cultural heritage management (Council of Europe 2000; Florence 2000). The growing importance of the housing and recreation functions in these areas is at least as important. Both residents of rural areas and urban recreationists will make greater demands in terms of the quality, accessibility and experience value of their living environment and the landscape. Nature conservation organizations, farmers' organizations and residents' groups are expected to work more with the heritage sector in the framework of regional policy. In practice, this throws up numerous dilemmas, but it also brings new opportunities to take an innovative, integrated approach. A proactive attitude is not only highly desirable, it is in fact essential in addressing the current problems in valuable nature conservation areas and cultural landscapes in many European countries and for the future management of UNESCO World Heritage Sites and European Natura 2000 areas, for example (UNESCO 1972).

This chapter examines a regional case study from the northern Netherlands, a five-year (2005-2009) research and action programme in the Drentsche Aa National Landscape (Fig. 2), exploring these issues in more depth. Under this programme, researchers, residents, designers, policymakers and managers worked closely together with the aim of achieving better integration of ecological and cultural heritage values in research, policy and management. First we shall discuss the problem addressed in the programme and the conceptual framework. We will then turn to the study area, the design of the programme and the results of four innovative projects that were carried out as part of the programme, closing with a series of conclusions and recommendations.

2. PROBLEM DEFINITION

The Drentsche Aa research and action programme, which was carried out from 2005 to 2009 as part of the NWO programme 'Preserving and Developing the Archaeological Archive' (Bodemarchief in Behoud en Ontwikkeling, PDL/BBO), focused on four major problems that had affected regional research and regional policy for many years (Bloemers *et al.* 2001).

Fig. 2
The Drentsche Aa National Landscape contains one of the best preserved brook valley systems in the Netherlands.

Alienation between cultural heritage and landscape disciplines
One of the biggest problems in regional research is the growing alienation between the various cultural heritage and landscape disciplines that has been the result of increasing specialization in academic study over the past few decades. This has not only led to a large conceptual and methodological gap between the humanities, social sciences and natural sciences (earth sciences, ecology), but also to major chronological, thematic and/or methodological specialization in the cultural heritage disciplines (archaeology, historical geography, architectural history) themselves in recent decades. This has given rise to a severe lack of unifying concepts and methods of integrated analysis.

Sectoral fragmentation of policy
In policy, too, there has been growing sectoral differentiation over the past few decades. The academic specialization mentioned above is also reflected, for example, in nature and landscape and cultural heritage management practice, a problem which was a particular focus of the Drentsche Aa programme. Preparatory inventories, area descriptions, evaluation systems, intervention impact assessments and monitoring systems are generally organized and implemented in a highly discipline-oriented way. Clients

often face the task of combining all these monodisciplinary studies into a cohesive whole. No wonder, therefore, that they have increasingly been calling for a more integrated approach.

Lack of participation by local residents in research and planning
For a long time, landscape and cultural heritage research has been almost exclusively a matter for specialists. Local residents', local amateur researchers' and land users' extensive, detailed knowledge of their area is rarely used. Since expert knowledge and local knowledge differ in many ways, and can therefore complement each other very well, this lack of interaction is a serious shortcoming. Until recently, residents had also played a very minor role in spatial planning. The traditional public inquiry procedures often led to plans that did not enjoy broad public support. This has changed in the Netherlands over the past ten years, thanks to the advent of new forms of communicative planning.

Lack of collaboration between policymakers, researchers and designers
A number of Dutch provinces undertook to produce a regional values map and guidelines to provide a source of inspiration for local authority cultural heritage policy. Products such as these have proved very useful in the many planning decisions that have to be made in rural areas, though they are less useful when it comes to producing specific future visions, spatial designs and development and management plans. Designers have a much greater need of knowledge on area-specific landscape processes and features than of values maps. Furthermore, it is not always easy to draw inspiration for plans at the local and microregional level from the broad sweep of a values map. The problem of scale differences between regional presentation and field-level implementation will become particularly apparent in the near future in the National Landscapes, where cultural heritage and landscape identity have been selected as the basis of spatial planning policy.

3. CONCEPTUAL FRAMEWORK
3.1 Landscape as a unifying concept
Both ecological and cultural heritage disciplines are concerned with the concept of 'landscape' at higher spatial levels. This is also a frequently used term in policymaking and planning circles. Since almost everyone has a certain personal association with the area where they live, work or were born, landscape plays an important role in people's perceptions. This more or less universal use of the term landscape is precisely what makes it so suitable as a unifying concept for the fields of humanities, spatial and natural sciences. It is also an obvious choice of medium for linking science and practice. Nevertheless, we must immediately acknowledge that the way in which these different parties interpret the concept of landscape can differ considerably. This divergence would at first glance seem to justify a single, widely acknowledged definition of the concept of landscape. However, given their long history in the groups with which they are associated, it is in fact more useful to assume several meanings for the term landscape in both research and spatial planning, and to place this very diversity at the centre of the dialogue between scientific disciplines and social sectors, and between academics and society.

This also ties in well with the conceptual development that the landscape-related disciplines have undergone in recent decades, particularly geography and cultural history. Almost everyone knows the traditional visual and aesthetic meaning of the term 'landscape' as scenery, 'the visible part of the Earth's surface and the sky above it, viewed from a certain vantage point'. This meaning is generally associated with the rise of landscape painting in the sixteenth and seventeenth centuries, although it has in fact recently been shown that it had its roots in Late Medieval paintings, particularly those of the Flemish Primitives (Bakker 2004). Another meaning of landscape arose in nineteenth-century geography, and was developed further in the twentieth century by geographers and landscape ecologists: the landscape as *Totalcharakter einer Gegend* ('overall character of an area'), as landscape ecologist Carl Troll (1899-1975) put it (Troll 1939). He was referring to the cohesive system of natural and anthropogenic features and genetic processes that distinguish an area from its neighbours. Until recently, this has also been both implicitly and explicitly understood as a positivistic scientific view: the landscape as an unambiguous, objective and scientifically recognizable concept. Since, in this view, landscape is the sum of individual features, structures, processes and associations, different aspects of it could be studied by a large number of disciplines and sub-disciplines.

It is precisely this reductionist and positivistic interpretation of landscape that has been called into question over the past twenty years by, among others, proponents of the New Cultural Geography. They emphasized the highly subjective nature of the term landscape (Cosgrove 1984; Olwig 1984; Lowenthal 1985; Cosgrove/Daniels 1988; Price/Lewis 1993; Wylie 2007). In the eyes of the New Cultural Geographers, the significance that individuals and social groups attribute to the term landscape depends so strongly on their personal or collective background that any single definition of the term is an illusion. In other words, every person, social group, culture and scientific discipline attributes its own specific meaning to 'landscape'. This meaning also changes over time. It depends, among other things, on the cultural period. And if each individual, social group and cultural period attributes its own specific identity to the landscape, modern researchers and policymakers cannot possibly refer to 'the identity of the landscape'. On the contrary, it forces us to exchange our uniform, positivistic concept of landscape for a more diverse and subjective interpretation. In planning processes, in particular, where the value of the various identities has to be weighed up, this leads directly to that important ethical question of which identities deserve to be given priority over others. Should priority by definition go to the identities determined by science and policy or to the local meaning attributed to the landscape by residents and users?

One interesting piece of research in this area was done by Kenneth Olwig, a Danish geographer, who explores what he holds to be the original meaning of the Germanic term 'landscape' (Olwig 1993; *idem* 2006). He believes that the Middle Dutch, and originally Germanic, term *lantscap* (with medieval variations in English, German and Danish) meant not only a piece of land in the sense of region or territory, but also the community as population associated with the region and their collective traditions and customs (Fig. 3). For centuries, these traditions and customs were passed on by word of mouth, developing continuously under the influence of the changing physical and social circumstances in the region. Customs relating to ownership and use of land, the direct link between the land and the community, played a key role. Given the highly normative character of these collective values, Olwig refers to them as "customary law", as opposed to canonical (authoritative) law, which was imposed on the region and population by a higher external power like a nation or a ruler. Interestingly, Olwig observes that customary law is a highly dynamic concept in both past and present societies. It changes in step with physical and social change in the region and is therefore an intrinsic part of the continually changing society and environment. This contrasts with the system of canonical legislation imposed by external authorities, which is more stable and therefore more conservative than local and regional customary law.

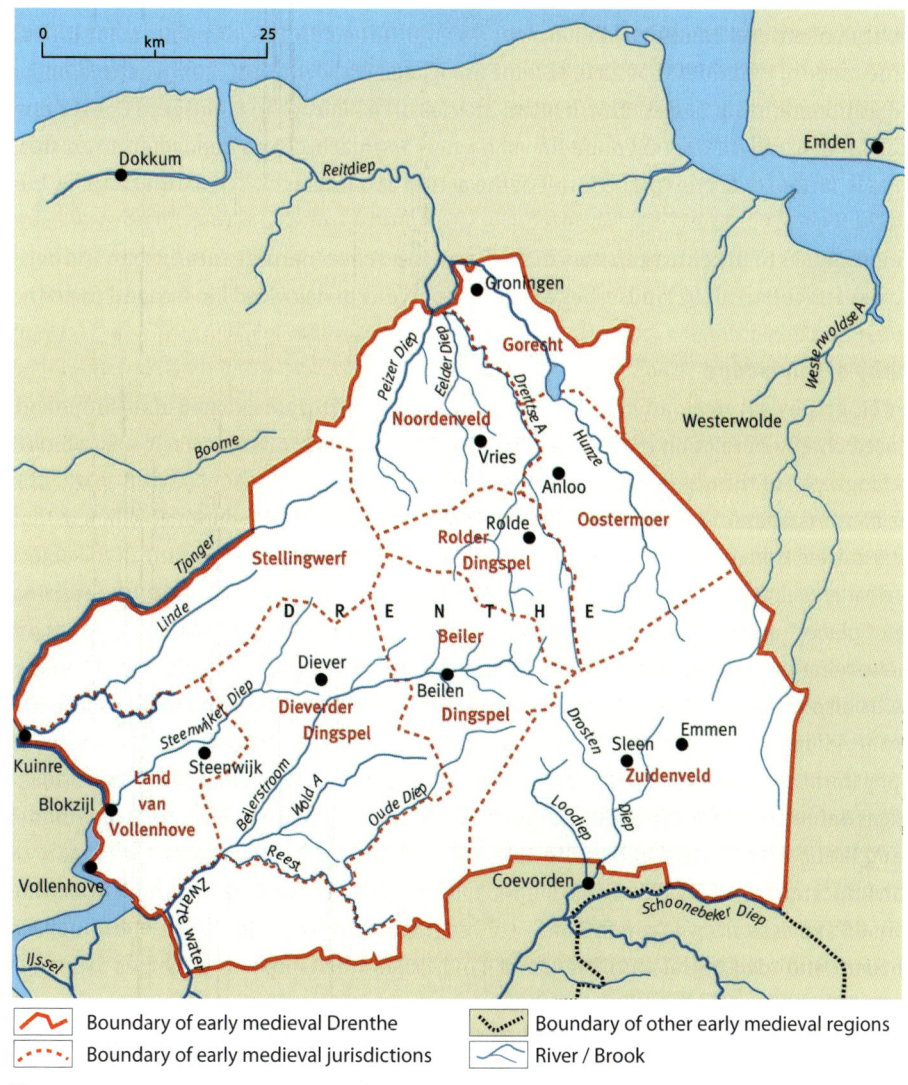

Fig. 3
The originally Germanic term *lantscap* meant a certain territory or region, but also a community associated with this region. The early medieval Landscap Drenthe was one of them. This old region was divided into nine juridical territories, called *dingspelen*.

This key difference is important not only to landscape historians but also to anyone in our current society who is involved in planning the physical environment of the future. It gives us a better insight into differences in the attribution of meaning to places, sites and micro-regions by the local population and by scientists and higher authorities. The former generally use an assessment framework that continually adjusts to new physical and social circumstances and is therefore relatively 'young', i.e. associated with the recent or sub-recent past. The latter have a more static, 'cross-period' assessment framework that is less associated with the area or local community. The roots of many past and present issues in local and regional spatial planning lie in this difference. Decisions as to which identities should be given priority in any particular planning process thus also have a major ethical dimension. More than in the past, scientists, policymakers and planners will have to be aware of the multiple, dynamic meanings of landscape and of the range of identities that have become associated with the landscape over time, shaping both its external and internal qualities. The first two articles of the European Landscape Convention (Florence 2000) can be an excellent starting point for such a new approach: "Landscape refers to an area, as perceived by people, whose character is the result of the action and interaction of natural and /or human factors" (art.1);

..."this Convention applies to the entire territory of the Parties and cover natural, rural, urban and peri-urban areas. ...It concerns outstanding landscapes as well as everyday or degraded landscapes" (art.2).

3.2 The biography of landscape

The use of the term 'biography' to refer to anything other than a human life story originated in anthropology and was initially used chiefly in relation to the often long history of prestigious objects. It was referred to as the "cultural biography of things" or the "social life of things" (Appadurai 1986; Kopytoff 1986). The key to this was the continual passing on of objects from one owner and/or user to another, which meant they also frequently shifted from one social context to another. Parallel to this, the meaning of the object was also subject to radical change. Archaeologists quickly adopted the concept of biography, referring to the "biography of places" and later also the "biography of landscapes" (Barrett 1994; Roymans 1995; Holtorf 1998). The varying perception of places and landscapes by different individuals, social groups, cultures and periods also played a key role in these terms. This 'new' way of looking at landscape did not just happen by accident. Although they did not specifically use the term 'biography', the concept of landscape biography unmistakably has its roots in the geographical work of Paul Vidal de la Blache (1845-1915), particularly his definition of the terms *pays* and *genre de vie*, and in the three-layer temporal model of historian Fernand Braudel (1902-1985) and his Annales school where, at the third level, the 'history of mentality' plays an important role (Vidal de la Blache 1903; Braudel 1966). The New Cultural Geography movement mentioned above stemmed from humanistic geography circles in the 1980s. Here, too, the perception, symbolism and ideological significance of landscapes were important themes (Samuels 1979; Cosgrove 1984; Olwig 1984; Cosgrove/Daniels 1988).

In the Netherlands the term "cultural biography of landscape" was introduced and the theory further developed by archaeologist Jan Kolen (Kolen 1993; *idem* 2005). He regards landscape biography as the progressive interplay of forces between the richly varied material landscape and the world of ideas, meanings, representations and memories. In this approach, heritage is defined in a much broader sense than merely physical relics of the past. It is also the continual process of updating and representing the past within the *Lebenswelt*, a term coined by the phenomenologist Edmund Husserl, of our modern society (Husserl 1986). In this interpretation, a landscape biography is both a description of the history of the material landscape and of the world of ideas grafted onto that landscape in various periods (Hidding/Kolen/Spek 2001).

3.3 Public participation and communicative planning

The dialogue between public authorities and experts on the one hand, and local residents and stakeholders on the other, takes place most specifically in a process referred to in the planning world as participatory planning, communicative planning, interactive planning or consensus planning (Fig. 4; Sager 1994; De Roo/Schwartz/Beukema *et al.* 2001). This method of planning has rapidly gained ground in

Fig. 4
Community planning in the Drentsche Aa National Landscape: residents, designers, nature managers and researchers discuss the first version of a development and management plan for the Balloërveld nature reserve.

the Netherlands over the past ten years in response to growing objections to the classic form of planning, with its public consultation round, whereby the authorities and property developers would launch major and highly disruptive plans without first properly consulting residents and other stakeholders. Although local residents and stakeholders can officially still influence plans at the end of the planning process in well-defined consultation procedures, in practice these procedures have rarely led to the original plans being altered. Besides the public dissatisfaction that this arouses, and the resulting damage to the originators of the plans, it is above all the extremely lengthy and costly consultation and arbitration procedures that have occasioned the need for change. Residents, landowners and stakeholder groups are now becoming involved in the planning process at a very early stage. It thus often quickly becomes clear what prerequisites they have with regard to the plans and which qualities of the existing landscape they would not want to lose or see radically altered under any circumstances. To look at it more positively, a clear analysis can then be made in the initial stages of planning of the various identities associated with the current landscape, from both a scientific and a social point of view so that they can be weighed up carefully in the actual plans.

As legal proprietors of the land they manage, nature conservation organizations enjoy a great deal of autonomy when it comes to the physical development of their sites, provided of course that they remain within the publicly established policy frameworks of local, regional and national government. Nevertheless, these organizations are also increasingly involving the public in the preparation of plans. This includes visitors and donors as well as residents and stakeholders in the region. Recent experience has shown that radical nature development plans, in particular, can prompt major local opposition, often leading to legal proceedings and damaging the image of the organization. Nature conservation organizations are therefore also increasingly inviting residents and stakeholder organizations to participate in development and management plans. Heritage organizations also play an important role if there are important cultural heritage values in the planning area.

3.4 Action research

Action research is a reflective process of progressive problem-solving led by individuals working with others in teams or as part of a 'community of practice' to improve the way they address issues and solve problems. Action research can also be undertaken by larger organizations or institutions, assisted or guided by professional researchers, with the aim of improving their strategies, practices, and knowledge of the environments within which they practice. As designers and stakeholders, researchers work with others to propose a new course of action to help their community improve its work practices (Lewin 1946; Habermas 1984/87; Sherman/Torbert 2000).

Many aspects of our landscape biography can be regarded as a form of 'action research'. They have an exploratory and experimental quality and are intended to address the tasks defined in the Drentsche Aa National Landscape's management and development plan. The field names project, which was a prime example of public participation in a cultural heritage activity, is perhaps the most appealing version of this kind of exploratory research, involving intensive exchange of local and expert knowledge. However, collaboration with landscape designers in the development of integration management and development plans for landscape reserves could also be regarded as action research. The input of historical ecological knowledge into the process not only provided passive background information, but also played a clear role in the design and future management of the sites. In this sense, action research can play an important role in renewing heritage policy and integrating it into new spatial developments.

4. GOAL AND DESIGN OF THE DRENTSCHE AA RESEARCH AND ACTION PROGRAMME

The Drentsche Aa research and action programme had four main objectives:
- To develop an integrated concept of landscape, with a corresponding conceptual framework to support the integration of the various cultural heritage specialisms and link them with ecological specialisms.
- To develop methods and techniques for linking and enriching the landscape knowledge of experts with the landscape knowledge of residents and other social and stakeholder groups, based on the integration of the material, social and conceptual dimensions of the cultural landscape.
- To develop procedures that improve collaboration between researchers, designers, residents and policymakers in terms both of substance and of process.
- To develop planning concepts that integrate all the spatial challenges of nature management, heritage management and regional environmental and planning policy.

To achieve these objectives, seven projects were developed and implemented from 2005 to 2009. They are described briefly below.

4.1 Project A: Cultural heritage inventory

In 2005 the authors of this paper produced a comprehensive inventory of the Drentsche Aa National Landscape, together with archaeologists and architectural historians. The publication and series of digital maps to which this gave rise pinpoint in detail and describe in general terms the geological, archaeological, historical geographical and historical architectural values in the area studied (Molema/Spek/Elerie 2004). This basic inventory then provided input for projects B (the landscape biography) and C (the landscape vision).

4.2 Project B: Landscape biography

The academic thread running through the entire programme was the landscape biography, an interdisciplinary project to investigate and record the long-term history of the Drentsche Aa region. The project involved a team of nine researchers (a physical geographer, a palaeobotanist, three archaeologists, two historical geographers, a toponymist and a GIS specialist, all working part-time), some 40 local volunteers (amateur archaeologists, amateur historians, nature lovers) and five undergraduate students. The resulting book, due for publication in 2010, will provide a source of inspiration for residents, stakeholder organizations, future researchers, designers and planners. More detailed information on the methodology and content of the biography can be found in section 6 (p. 97).

4.3 Project C: Landscape vision

In 2005 a bureau of landscape architects drew up a vision for the Drentsche Aa National Landscape with the aid of an agency overseeing the public participation process (Novioconsult/Strootman Landschapsarchitecten 2004). The vision describes in specific terms how a development-oriented landscape strategy can help preserve and develop the cultural heritage values in the Drentsche Aa region. The authors of this paper were closely involved in the development of this vision and had a more or less permanent contact with the landscape architect responsible. The vision was devised in close collaboration with a supervisory committee on which all stakeholder organizations were represented. The residents of the Drentsche Aa region gave their response and put forward their ideas at three well-attended public meetings. The document setting out the landscape vision now guides the policies of all involved. Several other National Landscapes organizations are now also working on a similar document, evidence of the impact that the Drentsche Aa Landscape Vision has had.

4.4 Project D: Online Cultural Atlas

The results of the research conducted in the various projects have not only been recorded in written publications. They are also to be incorporated into the Online Cultural Atlas of the Drentsche Aa National Landscape. This GIS-oriented collection of data and maps will be accessible both to professionals and to the general public. An interdisciplinary GIS system has been designed for professionals, which includes the following layers: 1. Detailed map of the physical geography; 2. Archaeological distribution map (3500 sites); 3. 1832 land register maps; 4. Georeferenced topographical maps 1812-2008; 5. seventeenth, nineteenth and twentieth century field names; and 6. Location-specific narratives. An application based on Google Earth has been developed for the general public. This will allow residents, visitors and other users accessing the Drentsche Aa National Landscape website to zoom in on the location of their choice using Google Earth and find landscape and cultural heritage information on that location.

4.5 Project E: Field names project

The field names project was the most experimental part of the programme. Together with residents, designers, artists and toponymists (place name and field name experts), the researchers investigated the role that historical field names had played in giving meaning to certain locations and sites in the Drentsche Aa region and how their meaning might play a role in the future of the region. Nine current attitudes to the cultural landscape were explored in essays, local research, design studies and art commissions. Together, they give a fascinating insight into how people perceive the current landscape.

The results of the project have been published in an attractive book for the general public (Elerie/Spek 2009). The power of imagery played a key role. In June 2009, the field names project culminated in a field names festival at the Medieval Church of St Magnus in the village of Anloo, at which poets, musicians and academics highlighted the image-rich language of the Drenthe landscape.

4.6 Project F: Biography of the water

An application-oriented project entitled 'Biography of the Water' was carried out in 2007 and 2008 in collaboration with the regional water authority and students and lecturers from a higher professional college in the region. The aim of this educational project was to allow the results of the landscape biography project to be used in qualitative and quantitative water management. Students worked together in a so-called rural atelier (Meijles 2010). Some twenty students carried out bachelor's and master's thesis research on the history of the water system, focusing on areas and themes on which the water authority will pursue an active policy over the next few years. Besides a large number of theses, this project also provided active input into a series of public design studios and five practically oriented booklets on water management in relation to landscape and heritage management.

4.7 Project G: Design by research in current planning processes

The authors of this paper actively participated in a number of planning processes in the Drentsche Aa region as researchers and programme managers. They contributed their knowledge of the landscape biography and provided ideas as to how the area might be developed and managed. This included short-term advisory roles on spatial planning, landscape management, nature management and water management, and more major contributions to development and management plans for major nature conservation areas in the region studied, a landscape remediation plan for an important stream valley and a recreational project involving the creation of *Belvederes,* viewing points (Royal Haskoning 2007). All these plans were published in beautifully illustrated books aimed at the general public, especially local residents. The studies have now gained broad recognition in Dutch and Belgian nature management circles and have prompted follow-up pilot projects on heritage management in relation to nature management.

5. THE DRENTSCHE AA NATIONAL LANDSCAPE

5.1 The landscape and its origins

The province of Drenthe is one of the three provinces that make up the northern Netherlands. Unlike the other two (Groningen and Friesland), however, it does not have a coastline. The vast majority of the province lies within the broad belt of Pleistocene sandy and moraine landscapes that extend across northwest Europe from Flanders, via the southern and eastern parts of the Netherlands, into northern Germany and western Denmark. In geological terms, the Drenthe sandy area consists largely of an extensive boulder clay plateau formed in the Saalian Ice Age and since highly fragmented by erosion, which was covered in the Weichselian Ice Age with a thin layer of coversand and, in the course of the Holocene, was 40% covered by ombrotrophic peat bogs (Spek 2004).

The Drentsche Aa National Landscape encompasses about 20% of the province, and coincides with the catchment of the Drentsche Aa brook system (*aa* = stream, small river) which drains the northern part of this old boulder clay plateau. This dense system of meandering lowland brooks transports the

Fig. 5
The Drentsche Aa National Landscape has more than 3500 archaeological sites. The oldest visible monuments are the impressive megalithic tombs from the Middle Neolithic period (3400-2800 BC).

water northwards towards the city of Groningen and then further on to the Waddenzee. The catchment, which is over 30,000 ha (300 square kilometres), has long been prized for its great diversity of geological, archaeological, historical, geographical and ecological values. The major geological values in the area are associated with the varied glacial and post-glacial geogenesis of the Drentsche Aa region and, compared with other regions, the historical and modern periods are relatively intact. Key features include the 'pingo-ruins', meltwater valleys, intact meander systems and driftsand areas. The major hydrological variation between source areas, upstream, midstream and downstream systems have also produced a great variety of flora and fauna in the brook valleys. No less remarkable is the high concentration of cultural heritage values in the region, which contains over 3500 archaeological findspots from virtually all periods in prehistory, protohistory and the Middle Ages. Characteristic archaeological features from prehistory include the *hunebedden*, megalithic tombs from the Middle Neolithic (3400-2800 BC), dozens of barrows and urnfields from the Late Neolithic, Bronze Age and Iron Age (2800-1 BC), dozens of Celtic fields (prehistoric field systems) from the period 1100 BC-AD 200, and a large number of settlement sites and ritual deposits from all these periods (Fig. 5; Spek 1996; *idem* 2007).

The foundations of the current cultural landscape in the Drentsche Aa region, known in Dutch as an *esdorp* landscape, were laid during the course of the Middle Ages. Each village district (*marke* in the Drents language) in the region traditionally has a concentric structure. At the core lay a church village

Fig. 6
Open field landscape south of the village of Gasteren in the Drentsche Aa National Landscape.

or small farming community, generally consisting of a collection of fairly dispersed farmsteads with a village green (*brink* in Dutch) at the edge of the village, where sheep would have been gathered in the past to be taken to graze on the heathland. Around the village there would have been one or more small open fields (*essen* in Drents) of 20-100 hectares, divided into small plots (Fig. 6). Each farmer would have owned several of these plots. Nearer the edge of the *marke* would have been hay meadows and pastures (*groenlanden* in Drents) in the brook valleys, and an extensive heath (*heidevelden* or *veldgronden* in Drents), interspersed with small managed areas of woodland and driftsand. Although after the advent of artificial fertilizer around 1900, this historical land use system was replaced by more modern forms of land use, and society changed with it, the village landscape still plays a major role in the social life and perceptions of residents today.

5.2 Development of landscape policy

The Drentsche Aa region has a long policy tradition. In the 1960s, the intact parts of the brook valley system were designated reserves. This initially provoked strong protests in the area, but there is no sign of dissent today. Nature managers have become just as familiar a sight there as farmers. In the late 1990s, the protests briefly reignited again when an *ad hoc* committee explored the possibility of creating a National Park there. Farmers and village residents were afraid that their interests would again be undermined by top-down planning. To break the deadlock, farmers' organization NLTO proposed a more integrated approach, with slightly less emphasis on nature. And so the Drentsche Aa National Landscape idea was born as a precursor to the government's policy of designating National Landscapes. The new approach no longer focused merely on the natural environment, but on the entire *esdorp* landscape as a source of inspiration for new policy. With its headstart in the development of policy, the Drentsche Aa National Landscape is an interesting object of study in the history of a more integrated approach to both research and policy. No fewer than 23 regional organizations are represented on the board of this National Landscape, which is chaired by the provincial authority. These organizations represent residents, farmers, nature conservation groups, leisure entrepreneurs and water authorities.

The following important quote is from the board's 2003 policy plan: "A development-oriented landscape strategy requires knowledge of the historical development of the landscape, not only institutional knowledge, but also the knowledge of residents and land users. Drawing on and linking these different areas of knowledge allows new, creative solutions to be found for development and management." The plan also describes the need for new interdisciplinary research to gather information about past ecological processes: "This will allow us to bridge the gap between ecological and cultural heritage knowledge, and to use them both in our integrated approach." (Provincie Drenthe 2003). The board also aims in its policy for a highly intersectoral and interactive approach. Current spatial planning issues are resolved as far as possible in consultation with residents and stakeholder organizations using interactive planning methods (community planning/participatory planning). This broad-ranging approach to policy also made the Drentsche Aa National Landscape a highly suitable subject for an innovative research and action programme.

6. LANDSCAPE BIOGRAPHY OF THE DRENTSCHE AA

6.1 Basic principles

The landscape biography of the Drentsche Aa combines two important approaches, a historical ecology and a historical anthropology approach. Both are concerned with the interaction between humans and the landscape but approach it from a different angle. They are also highly complementary. The historical ecology approach focuses on the long-term development of the physical landscape under the influence of changes in use and the changing perceptions of people. The historical anthropology approach focuses on the long-term development of the social and mental landscape (in other words, collective and individual perception of the landscape), under the influence of constantly changing social relations and relations with the physical landscape. Both are discussed further below.

First, the historical ecology approach. As cultural beings, humans were the main driving force behind landscape development. They design and shape their own environment based on their way of life (*genre de vie*), consciously and unconsciously manipulating the ecological process. The random self-ordering of natural processes thus becomes subordinate to human action. Historical ecology is concerned with the study of the constantly changing relationship between humans and their environment. This synthetic approach cannot accommodate the traditional culture-nature dichotomy. The focus is on studying a dynamic, anthropogenic ecosystem in the setting of a living environment (French *environnement*). Developers and managers of nature conservation areas and National Landscapes can benefit from a thorough knowledge of the history of regional and local ecosystems. Historical ecology can provide an insight into the long-term development of regional landscapes. In this process culture and nature are variables that constantly affect each other (Elerie 1998). The broad, interdisciplinary approach creates interesting opportunities for more intensive collaboration between the cultural disciplines (archaeology, historical geography, historical architecture) and the ecological disciplines (earth sciences, biology, landscape ecology), allowing a more rounded landscape biography to be produced. The historical ecology approach really comes into its own on a regional scale. In pre-modern conditions, locally organized communities still played a key role in determining the dynamics of the landscape ecology. Comparing these local processes at regional level helps us understand long-term developments in human-environment interaction. On this scale, it is also possible to study variables relating to 'site' and 'situation', interregional relationships and supralocal processes (*idem* 1998).

The historical anthropology approach must be seen as supplementary to the historical ecology approach. Besides commercial, market-oriented trade, the agricultural system of the *esdorpen* had a collective bent focused on the exploitation of common land and the maintenance of the public space. In this way, every village district or *marke* can be seen as a social space encompassing individual and collective perceptions. In this representation, field names and toponyms played an important role. The landscape of toponyms of each village is unique and can be seen as a symbolic order. The referential and narrative meanings of field names can reveal to us how past residents viewed the village landscape and the ecological setting in relation to their way of life. And because field names were also used in many written sources, such as village ordinances (*willekeuren*) and appeals, we can also find empirical evidence to underpin these historical perceptions. If enough sources are available, it is possible to produce a reconstruction of the *marke* as a mental space.

6.2 Practical implementation

These two approaches have produced a cultural landscape biography of a highly empirical nature. A wide range of primary and secondary source material from many disciplines was integrated into a cohesive account of the long-term history of the cultural landscape. Examples of the primary sources used include geological, geomorphological and soil maps (Fig. 7), additional borehole surveys, palaeobotanical and archaeobotanical data, archaeological datasets, archive data, historical maps, place names, water body and field names, aerial photographs, satellite images and laser altimetry images, historical travel writings, paintings, photographs, literature fragments and stories told by residents as part of a resident perception survey and oral history. A large body of literature from many disciplines served as a secondary source. The Drentsche Aa region has for decades been one of the most closely studied cultural landscapes in the Netherlands.

At the first level (chapters) the landscape biography is structured chronologically, while at the second level (paragraphs) its structure is thematic. In chronological terms, the landscape biography will be divided into nine chapters: 1. Geogenesis; 2. Palaeolithic and Mesolithic (< 5000 BC); 3. Neolithic to Middle Bronze Age (5000-1800 BC); 4. Late Bronze Age to Late Iron Age (1800-1 BC); 5. Roman period and Early Middle Ages (AD 1-950); 6. High and Late Middle Ages (AD 950-1600); 7. Early Modern Period (AD 1600-1800); 8. Modern Period (AD 1800-2005) and 9. Synthesis. Each period was studied by a group of two or three researchers. Given the specific knowledge of the period and sources required, membership of these groups constantly changed. Chapters 2 to 4, for example, are based on the work of an archaeologist, physical geographer and palaeobotanist, chapters 5 and 6 on the work of an archaeologist, historical geographer and palaeobotanist, and chapters 7 and 8 on the work of a historical geographer, architectural historian and archive researcher.

Although both the profile of the research groups and the emphasis vary, given the diachronic nature of the biography and in order to give it a clear structure, a fixed thematic progression will be observed

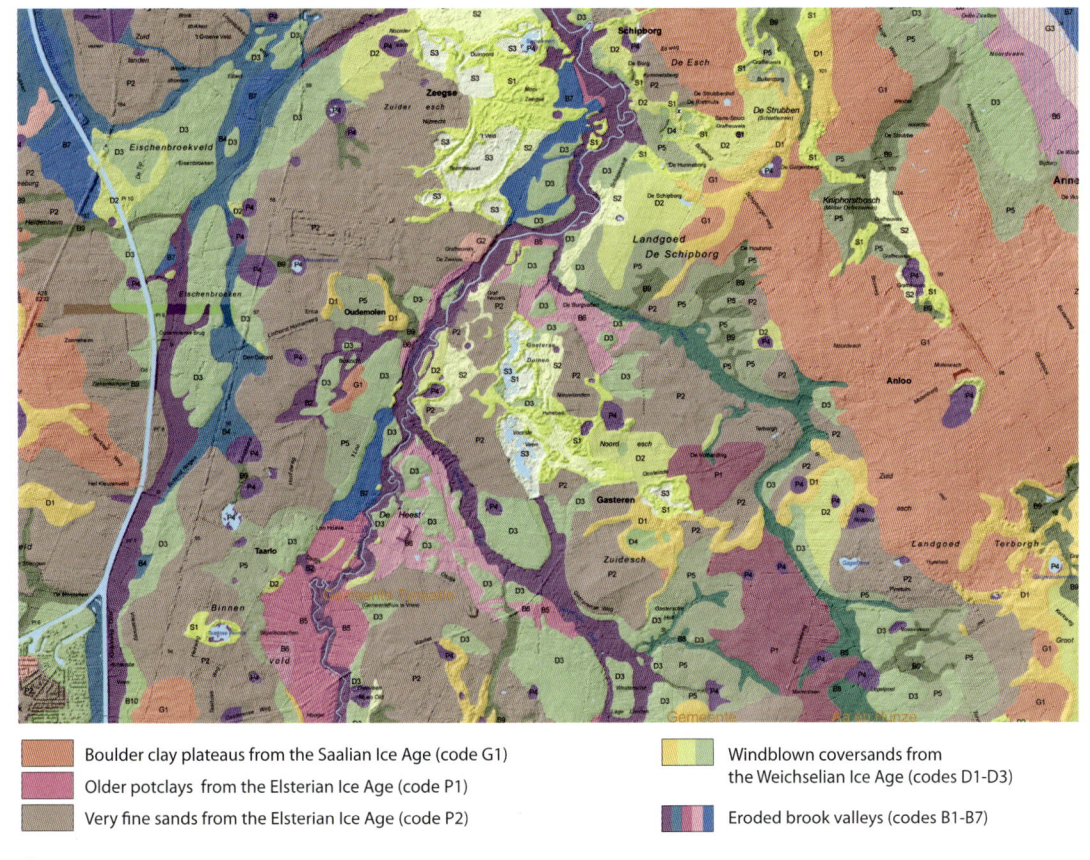

Fig. 7
One of the results of the landscape biography project was a new detailed physical-geographical map of the Drentsche Aa National Landscape by scientists from Alterra, Wageningen. The landscape patterns, shown here on a geogenetic map of the area, are dominated by glacial sediments from three different glacial periods. The large boulder clay plateaux from the Saalian Ice Age have been eroded by melting water streams, uncovering older potclays and very fine sands from the Elsterian Ice Age. These older sediments have been partly covered by windblown coversands during the last Weichselian Ice Age. Finally, the deeply eroded brook valleys dissect the older plateau landscape in many pieces.

in each chapter. Although this is still the subject of discussion and further consideration, the following structure has been proposed: Section 1. Changes in the natural and semi-natural landscape; Section 2. Occupation history and demographics; Section 3. Territory formation and boundaries; Section 4. Developments in land use; Section 5. Changes in cultural landscape patterns; Section 6. Cross-section through time (landscape reconstruction); Section 7. The social and mental landscape; Section 8. Later representations of the period and Section 9. Important places and sites.

In late 2010, a lavishly illustrated book, *A Biography of the Drentsche Aa National Landscape*, will be published, based on the many reports that have been drawn up over the past few years. It will be accompanied by an online cultural atlas. These media must be both academically sound and accessible to a larger audience, including residents, designers, policymakers and the staff and members of stakeholder organizations.

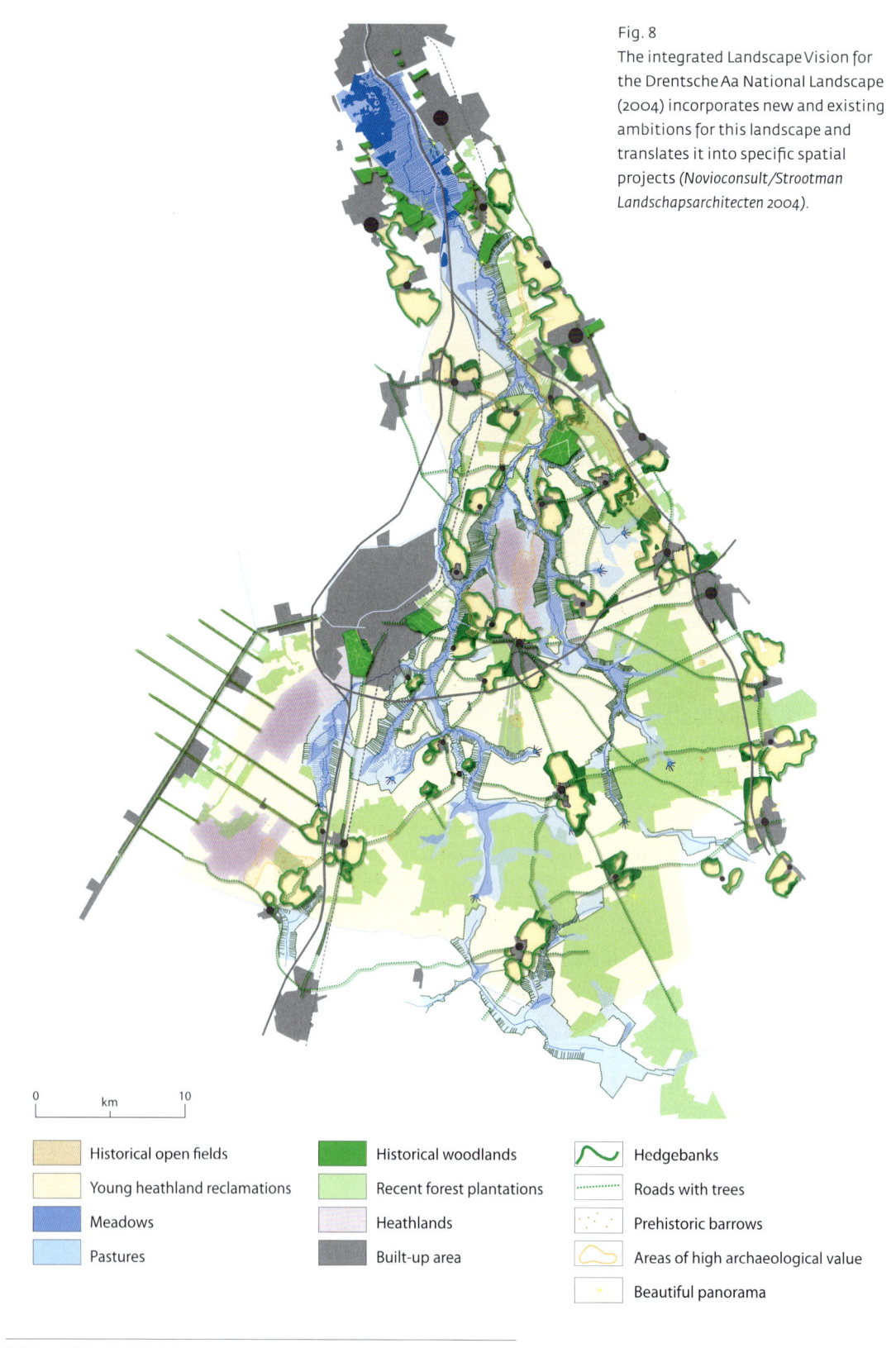

Fig. 8
The integrated Landscape Vision for the Drentsche Aa National Landscape (2004) incorporates new and existing ambitions for this landscape and translates it into specific spatial projects *(Novioconsult/Strootman Landschapsarchitecten 2004)*.

Historical open fields	Historical woodlands	Hedgebanks
Young heathland reclamations	Recent forest plantations	Roads with trees
Meadows	Heathlands	Prehistoric barrows
Pastures	Built-up area	Areas of high archaeological value
		Beautiful panorama

100 • THE CULTURAL LANDSCAPE AND HERITAGE PARADOX

7. DRENTSCHE AA LANDSCAPE VISION

At first sight, the Drentsche Aa National Landscape appears to have a rural character and a high perception value. In reality, however, it is the 'green heart' of the largest urban region in the northern Netherlands. It is a 'living landscape' where many people live and work. This means it will develop with the times, as the pace of life and society changes in the region. With this in mind, in 2003 the board of the National Landscape opted for a 'development-oriented landscape strategy'. This means that new developments must be guided and adapted so as to ensure that they help preserve and enhance the spatial quality of the region. This development-oriented approach, broadening the regular nature management policy to encompass a proactive heritage policy, signified a break with the sectoral policies pursued previously.

Over the past few decades, regional policy has become the driving force in the physical development and management of rural areas in the Netherlands. Academics who wish to tie their work in with this policy find themselves having to catch up with a development that is already well underway. In their plan of work for the landscape biography, the researchers therefore left room in their schedule to offer their services to ongoing landscape management and heritage management projects.

Shortly before it was installed, the board of the National Landscape decided to draw up an integrated *Landscape Vision* incorporating new and existing ambitions into a regional design and translating this into specific tasks (Fig. 8). Though the term 'landscape vision' appears fairly informal, it is in fact a policy document to which the members of the board have all committed. The board members are a varied mix of local and provincial administrators and representatives of farmers, nature management organizations, the Water Board, the leisure industry and residents. Alongside interactive involvement with the stakeholders in the supervisory group, the process of producing the landscape vision also included a procedure whereby residents and stakeholder groups could have input. In contrast to the regular planning procedure, the board deliberately opted for an open and broad-based interactive process. Such a broad-based approach requires careful organization and a lot of communication. A design agency (of landscape architects) and a process support agency were therefore brought in to present ideas in an appealing way, design in an integrating manner, communicate well with all parties and impart information to non-experts in a way that inspires.

For the landscape researchers, the landscape vision came at the perfect moment to prompt the best possible exchange of ideas and information with policymakers. This requires flexibility, as there is always a tendency to go off on tangents that are not consistent with the research schedule. In retrospect, direct involvement in the production of the Drentsche Aa Landscape Vision brought the research team many benefits (Novioconsult/Strootman Landschapsarchitecten 2004). Working closely with policymakers and designers gave us a front-line position in policy development. The research for the landscape biography is now used to 'deepen' policy implementation on the ground and this has attracted research funding from the regional policy budget.

The preparations for the landscape vision first involved the production of a basic inventory of the geological, archaeological and landscape values. All these features, relics and finds were then digitally recorded and broadly described in a series of thematic maps. The most important task for the landscape vision was to visualize this extensive body of data in the context of the landscape and the tasks associated with it. As in the landscape biography, this occurred on four scales:

- The highest level was the *region*, i.e. the National Landscape as a whole, with its large-scale landscape structures and processes. On this scale, the database was arranged in a series of thematic maps and explored in area plans and model studies.
- The second level was the *village landscape*, which corresponds to the historical *marke* system and the immediate vicinity of the modern village. On this level, a link was made with residents' groups' future plans for their area.
- The third level was the *terrain* or *reserve* as a historical relic of the pre-modern cultural landscape. On this scale, nature management and landscape management organizations act as proprietors and clients.
- On the fourth level, *place* was an important element of individual residents' or users', or resident/user groups' perception of the landscape. One example is the specific proposals for the development of *belvederes* (viewing points) at places with a special historical identity or group value.

The final chapter of the Drentsche Aa Landscape Vision sets out a prioritized list of projects that make clear its role in determining policy. The projects are divided on the basis of the structure of the *esdorp* landscape into brook valleys, open fields (*essen*) and fields, and by theme (archaeology, management, infrastructure, village peripheries and farming). In a separate column, the tasks are linked to the actors responsible. A substantial proportion of the projects have now been initiated or completed.

8. DEVELOPMENT AND MANAGEMENT PLANS FOR NATURE CONSERVATION AREAS

Since the Drentsche Aa Landscape Vision was published in 2004, many projects have been incorporated into the Drentsche Aa National Landscape multi-year programme and some of them have already been completed. The two authors of this chapter played an important coaching role in the next four projects as part of our action research programme:

Fig. 9
Many prehistoric burial mounds in the De Strubben-Kniphorstbosch nature reserve are overgrown with vegetation. This photomontage shows the future situation after removal of the shrubs and trees.

Fig. 10a
The Balloerveld heathland area: actual situation.

Fig. 10b
The Balloërveld heathland area: future situation after removal of trees (photomontage).

- De Strubben and Kniphorstbosch were involved in the transfer of a former military training ground to the State Forest Service (Strootman Landschapsarchitecten/Novioconsult 2008). This is a landscape reserve of major archaeological and landscape value (Fig. 9). Besides supplying a field-level database, the development and management plan also introduced the historical ecology approach in order to bridge the gap between the cultural heritage and ecology.
- The pre-modern landscape of the Drentsche Aa was known in the nineteenth century for its panoramic views. These disappeared when the heathland was reclaimed and turned into woodland. The Drentsche Aa Belvederes project is restoring the broad views and panoramas at certain high points in the landscape. We advised on the locations and physical development of the viewing points.
- The *esdorp* landscape of the Drentsche Aa has a high density of wooded embankments of all varieties. The middle and upstream sections of the stream valleys, in particular, are often enclosed by highly geometric wooded embankments. As a result of the focus on botanical nature management along the streams in recent decades, they have been poorly maintained. The Amerdiep and Anloërdiep Landscape Restoration Plan is designed to tackle this backlog in maintenance over the next 20 years (Royal Haskoning 2007).
- The Balloërveld is an extensive heath bordered on both sides by the natural stream valleys of the Rolder Diep and the Loner Diep (Fig. 10a-b and 11). The former training ground that was recently transferred to the State Forest Service has special cultural heritage and ecological values, thanks to its large size, openness and virtually undisturbed heathland vegetation. Together with the neighbouring ancient village of Balloo, visitors can experience a complete historical *esdorp* landscape in its authentic form.

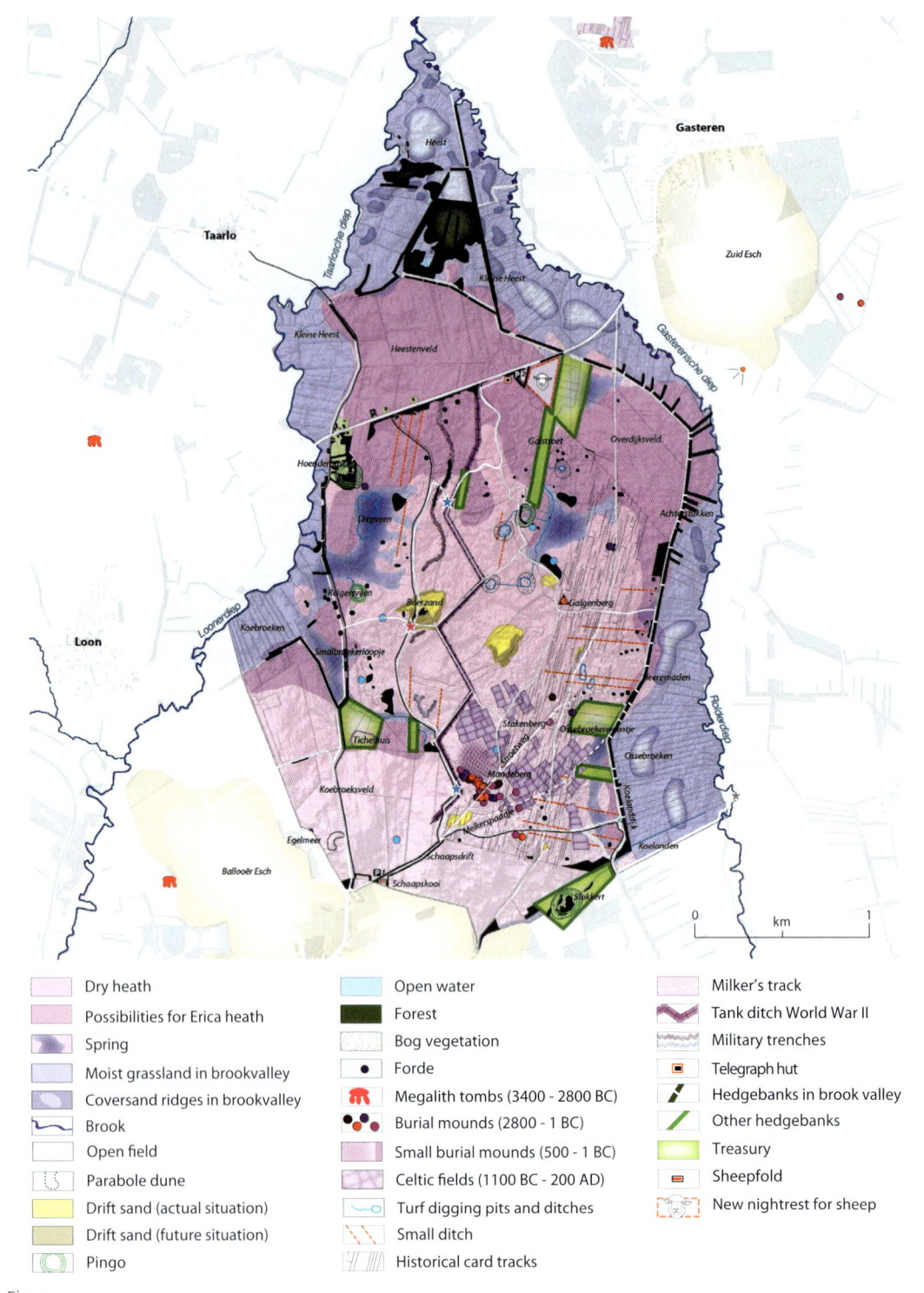

Fig. 11
The Balloërveld is an extensive heathland area that was used as a military training area between 1919 and 2005. This map shows the development and management plan of 2009 which takes into account the rich cultural heritage of this nature reserve. It is a good example of a combination of nature and heritage management (*Strootman Landschapsarchitectuur 2010*).

104 • THE CULTURAL LANDSCAPE AND HERITAGE PARADOX

Again, we incorporated our historical ecology approach into the development and management plan, in this case paying particular attention to the geological and pedological values in this intact village landscape (Strootman Landschapsarchitecten 2010).

9. FIELD NAMES AS LIVING HERITAGE

9.1 *Background*

The Drentsche Aa Landscape Biography approaches the landscape from multiple perspectives, one of which is the landscape as a living environment. How did past residents and users view their village landscape? How did their views change over time and how do current residents view that same landscape? Historical geographers often tend to focus in their analysis on the physical/spatial landscape. From their perspective, the cultural landscape is the result of human activity over time. They often regard the mental landscape, internal perceptions and symbolic ordering as a typically anthropological perspective. We believe, however, that both perspectives belong in a biographical approach to the landscape, not as separate spheres of knowledge, but complementing each other, revealing the interaction between a community and its living environment. A large proportion of the cultural heritage and ecological setting of the Drentsche Aa landscape highlights the close ties between past cultures and their living environment. It is only logical, therefore, that the biography should not only consider the history of the physical landscape, but also the village landscape as a social space.

9.2 *Method*

A field name and toponym database for an *esdorp* is a perfect way of revealing this historical phenomenological relationship. We regard this name landscape, which developed from the Middle Ages onwards as the landscape was reclaimed and is unique to each village, as the symbolic order of a working agricultural community. With their referential meaning related to the ecological setting, vegetation, land use, ownership or special places, field names form a mental map of the village district, similar to the pattern of street names in a town. And since field names are mentioned in all kinds of written sources from the seventeenth century onwards they can also tell us a lot about constantly changing perceptions of the living environment.

In our landscape biography we have used field names as a historical source and as a way of getting the public involved in the cultural heritage. Use of field names as a historical source continues a long practice in historical geographical research, where field names are used to trace the origins of settlements and landscapes. In the academic part of the landscape biography we opted for a slightly different approach, focusing on field names as a referential code for the ecological setting of the landscape. We also use the field name complex of a village district as a symbolic order through which to explore historical perceptions of the village landscape as a social and conceptual space.

In our landscape biography we especially focused on the second application of field names as internal *living* heritage. In a working agricultural community field names were a natural part of the living environment. They had a practical use in communication and spatial orientation. They formed a mental map of the village landscape with points of reference for all kinds of associations, meanings and concepts. In a modern residential village, that mental landscape has often eroded as many field names are no longer in daily use. Residents with memories of the past have often already reached an advanced age and this prompted us to conduct a detailed survey of living field names for this aspect of landscape biography.

In the survey we put the spotlight on three villages in the heart of the Drentsche Aa National Landscape. Nature management policy allowed early conservation of the old landscape along the streams and many field names have survived there. Residents gave us a glimpse of daily life in the three villages, where stories about current and past field names are still very much alive. Nevertheless, we were also forced to conclude that daily use of the remaining field names is declining in the modern residential village. The number of 'living' names fell sharply, particularly after land consolidation. However, some are fortunately enjoying a revival. Independently of the official collections in the national archives, interested villagers are compiling their own private collections. In a number of villages in the Drentsche Aa region they emerge as a curious aspect of village history or 'second-hand' identity markers in the living environment.

We may question the value of this encouraging return of field names as symbolic markers in the village landscape. Strangely enough, they barely play a role in official heritage and local policy. Nevertheless, they are evidence of a new perspective. Over the past few decades, nature management has become an important driver of developments, alongside the now declining agricultural sector. The State Forest Service, the biggest landowner in the Drentsche Aa region, has reintroduced original field names in its stream valley management policy. With the creation of the Drentsche Aa National Landscape, cultural landscape values have become associated with clear policy objectives. In this broadened perspective field names can play an important role in deepening, conceptualizing and making tangible people's perception of the landscape.

As remarked earlier, toponym experts distinguish between historical and living field names. In the present-day, pluralist village community, such a categorization is diffuse and interchangeable. An active historical society can bring dormant field names back to life by publishing them on a village website or by renaming fields. Such 'revived' field names no longer function as part of an agricultural working collective but become part of the cultural and public domain of the residential community. The village community can thus remain an important source of living field names in the future. As living heritage, field names therefore provide an excellent basis for public participation in the cultural heritage (Fig. 12). They serve a dual purpose. Local field knowledge is an indispensable part of the broad spectrum encompassed by a landscape biography, which in a methodological sense focuses not only on the 'hardware' of the physical landscape, but also on the associated 'software' of meanings, narratives and conceptualization.

9.3 Results

The living field names project has been written up in a large publication, *Van Jeruzalem tot Ezelsakker* (Elerie/Spek 2009). It is the result of two years of fieldwork, archive research, digitization, philosophizing and experimentation. Residents, local experts, students and a range of academics and artists each contributed in their own way to this lavishly illustrated picture atlas which explores the phenomenon of field names from multiple perspectives. We are grateful we were able to use the latest techniques for research both above and below ground. Together with working groups from the villages and students from Van Hall/Larenstein and the University of Groningen, we collected living and historical field names and then digitized and mapped them. Several landscape architects considered how field names might play an active role in new spatial designs. A group of eight graphic designers made creative, surprising and highly varied contributions to the development of a new imagery. Using field names as a guide, other cultural practices were explored and conceptualized. We hope this will inspire other villages to

Fig. 12
The use of historical and actual field names appears to be an excellent starting point for getting the public involved in discussion on cultural heritage and landscape. The photo shows an open air theatre performance from June 2009 inspired by the field name and local stories associated with the location.

work on their own local heritage, using new media like the Internet, Google Earth and Wikipedia. *Van Jeruzalem tot Ezelsakker* conceptualizes the various practices in ten chapters exploring different attitudes that reflect how people approach the cultural landscape. Besides essays and interviews, we also went in search of a new imagery with the aid of designers, landscape architects, photographers and poets. All these contributions, in words and images, make the book a 'work of art' in itself, an ode to field names as an example of living heritage. The book also inspired the Field Name Festival that was held in June 2009, which drew around 1200 visitors. The festival explored the cultural potential of field names and included outdoor theatre, musical impressions, exhibitions, field excursions and poetry readings.

10. CONCLUSIONS

10.1 Introduction

The five-year Drentsche Aa research and action programme not only added a great deal to the academic knowledge of this National Landscape, it also ensured that this knowledge became more accessible to residents and stakeholder organizations and more useful for policymakers, planners and managers working in the field of heritage management, nature management and regional environmental and planning policy. As such, the project took us a long way towards resolving the four academic and social problems identified in section 2. The four potential solutions are discussed briefly below.

10.2 Landscape biography as an interdisciplinary method

The operationalization of the hitherto rather theoretically defined and elaborated concept of the 'cultural biography' in an interdisciplinary and empirically-based research methodology for a landscape biography in the Drentsche Aa programme greatly improved collaboration between archaeologists, historical geographers, earth scientists and ecologists. Whereas previously these disciplines each adhered to their own research methodology, in this programme they worked closely together within a clearly defined chronological and thematic framework. The nine research themes defined in advance consultations, towards which each discipline would be expected to orient its own dataset and research methods, were the main key to success. It encouraged the researchers to move beyond the familiar confines of their own discipline and to compare their results and ideas with those working in other fields. When several disciplines reach the same conclusion it stands on much firmer foundations than could be achieved by a single discipline. If, on the other hand, they reach conflicting conclusions, this stimulates debate, often leading to interdisciplinary insights that would otherwise never have emerged. This serves as yet another illustration of the proposition that Thomas Kuhn, the philosopher of science, set out in his work *The Structure of Scientific Revolutions*, that the greatest breakthroughs occur at the interfaces between different fields of science (Kuhn 1962).

There were three key phases to our interdisciplinary landscape biography: 1. an interdisciplinary start-up phase in which the researchers held extensive consultations on the problems to be addressed and the methodology to be applied, leading to a widely supported interdisciplinary research plan; 2. a multidisciplinary research phase in which each researcher more or less went his or her own way, meeting fellow researchers from other disciplines only at prearranged times to discuss interim results; 3. an interdisciplinary final phase in which the results of the various individual studies were intensively debated, similarities and differences identified and joint final conclusions agreed.

Since the landscape biography is intended above all as a source of inspiration for residents, policymakers and organizations with a practical involvement in spatial planning, nature and landscape management and heritage management, we expressly opted to produce a piece of work which is both scientifically well-founded and accessible to a broader target audience. This meant that the language used, and the nature and quantity of images, had to meet certain requirements. We therefore opted for a three-track policy: 1. an accessibly written and well-illustrated landscape biography (in book form) for residents, policymakers, designers and stakeholder organizations; 2. an online digital cultural atlas containing all the relevant maps and datasets produced during the course of the research for the same target audiences; 3. monodisciplinary and interdisciplinary academic papers published in peer-reviewed journals and books aimed at academics.

The landscape biography strategy pursued in the Drentsche Aa programme has since been applied in many other parts of the Netherlands and Belgium. In nature management, in particular, it has become fairly common for a landscape biography to be produced prior to new development and management plans for large nature conservation areas and estates.

A landscape biography need not always come in the form of a weighty tome and a digital database. A more concise biography might be appropriate for smaller-scale planning processes, such as development and management plans for nature conservation sites. This might take the form of a summary of the data and literature in the fields of archaeology, historical geography, toponymics, ecology and earth sciences in an integrated text of no more than ten pages and one or more maps, analogue or digital. Concise publications such as this have also proved to be of great practical value to residents, designers and commissioning organizations.

10.3 New connections between nature management and heritage management

The improved collaboration between cultural heritage and ecological researchers in the Drentsche Aa region is also reflected in the integration of nature management and heritage management in the region. Current natural environments should not only be regarded as an interplay of current ecological processes, but as a result of centuries of interaction between humans and nature. This gives our modern knowledge of the landscape ecology a deeper historical dimension. In specific terms, it gives us:

1. a broader and more in-depth understanding of the cultural heritage values of nature conservation sites (archaeological sites, historical-geographical relics, historical toponyms, vegetation determined by historical ecology etc.); 2. a series of historical-ecological reference images of human-related ecosystems from earlier periods; 3. a better understanding of historical explanations for current vegetation patterns and ecological values (knowledge of the historical ecological system); 4. knowledge of the impact of historic forms of land use on soil formation and the relief of the land. Each of these four forms of new knowledge can be translated directly into development and management plans for nature conservation areas, as shown by our three specific case studies (see section 8). The historical-ecological landscape biography proved an important source of inspiration both in the management of existing nature conservation sites and the development of new ecological corridors. Sometimes the focus is on several time layers, at others it is on one particular time layer that dominates at the site in question. With careful planning, the various nature conservation sites in a single region not only display a wide variety of ecosystems and biodiversity, but also a wide variety of cultural heritage landscapes, features and narratives. Preservation and development of biodiversity can thus go hand in hand with preservation and development of cultural heritage diversity, allowing future generations to experience both the rich natural variety and the rich development history of the landscape.

10.4 Linking expert knowledge and local knowledge

While researching landscape biography, the field names project and the planning process for future development and management of nature conservation sites, we experienced time and again how important the local knowledge of residents, amateur researchers and volunteers is in supplementing the specialist knowledge of experts like scientists, policymakers and nature managers. Combining these two kinds of knowledge leads to a more complete landscape biography and to wider support for plans that determine the future of the landscape. A willingness on the part of scientists to listen to and accept the ideas of local experts is essential. This can be achieved by organizing joint design studios and field visits, involving volunteers in the compilation of databases and the production of overview maps, and taking care to provide feedback on the final results of the research process. To be in a better position to assess the reliability of the results, it is advisable to use the experience recorded in oral history and cultural geography (Ritchie 2003; Raleigh Yow 2005; Wylie 2007). Compared with scientific knowledge, local knowledge is more individually-based, more mixed with emotion, more locally than regionally determined, and more focused on a short-term genealogical perspective of one or two generations than on the diachronic development of centuries. Local knowledge also consists of a mix of historical facts, historical narratives (anecdotes, legends, folktales), images, and meanings associated with certain individuals or groups. This is also reflected in the landscape biography which reveals both the continuous biographical timeline of the scientists and the more place-oriented, unique individual narratives and meanings of residents and other local experts.

Cultural heritage and local experts have in fact increasingly been joining forces in the Netherlands over the past few years due to the growing popularity of historical societies in villages and regions. This growth in popularity can be seen both as a local and regional response to globalization and as a sign of a sharp increase in the level of education and social engagement of many village residents, partly resulting from the fact that the baby boom generation is now entering retirement. It is therefore highly likely that the connection between expert knowledge and local knowledge will prompt a thorough review of the practice of cultural heritage research and spatial planning over the next few years.

10.5 Towards more interactive landscape planning

In the various planning processes that have taken place in the Drentsche Aa region over the past few years, we have been able to gain a great deal of experience of applying the landscape biography method in practice. This has led us to the conclusion that a successful planning process that enjoys wide support requires balanced representation of the following five parties: policymakers, residents, stakeholder organizations, designers and researchers. Each of these parties has their own specific input. Policymakers define the task and the administrative and legal requirements at the outset and monitor them in a low-key way throughout the planning process. Residents and stakeholders contributed their knowledge and ideas at various points in the planning process and are important when it comes to choosing between various alternatives. Researchers not only supply information on the area in question in digestible form prior to the planning process (in the form of a landscape biography, for example), they also remain actively involved in discussion throughout the process. This differs from the common practice whereby researchers generally supply their, largely monodisciplinary, inventory reports and impact assessments prior to the planning process. The chances of success are raised, however, by a form of *design by research* whereby designers, such as landscape architects, are involved from the outset both in defining the issues and in discussing the scientific research, and researchers remain involved in planning after they have delivered their reports. The role of the designer is of course crucial in such an interactive planning process. They must not only apply their creative skills to produce an effective and appealing plan, they also have to act as a kind of mediator, balancing a variety of ideas and interests. In practice, this has proved to be such a major task that specialist process organization agencies are increasingly being brought in. Ultimately, this should lead to a plan that enjoys the support of all concerned. Public protests are much less likely than in the case of the public consultation model which was common until recently, in which residents and stakeholder organizations are asked for their opinion only after the experts have come up with a plan. Experience shows that the delays and alterations that the old method entails lead to large cost overruns and a great deal of public unrest.

10.6 Final remark

The research and action programme conducted between 2004 and 2009 in the Drentsche Aa National Landscape in the northern Netherlands has shown that there are three important building blocks for successful integration of nature management and heritage management, or in general, landscape research and landscape planning: 1. good collaboration between and integration of cultural heritage and scientific disciplines; 2. good connections between expert knowledge and local knowledge; 3. interactive planning in which residents, stakeholders, policymakers, nature managers, researchers and designers all have balanced input.

NOTES

1 Brede Overleggroep Kleine Dorpen in Drenthe, Anloo, the Netherlands.
2 Department of Landscape, Cultural Heritage Agency, Amersfoort, the Netherlands; Institute of Architectural and Art History, University of Groningen, Groningen, the Netherlands.

REFERENCES

Appadurai, A., 1986: *The social life of things. Commodities in a social perspective*, Cambridge.

Bakker, B., 2004: *Landschap en wereldbeeld. Van Van Eyck tot Rembrandt*, Amsterdam (Ph.D. thesis VU University).

Barrett, J.C., 1994: *Fragments from antiquity*, Oxford.

Bloemers, J.H.F. /R. During/J.N.H. Elerie/H.A. Groenendijk/M. Hidding/J. Kolen/Th. Spek/M.-H. Wijnen, 2001: *Bodemarchief in Behoud en Ontwikkeling, de conceptuele grondslagen*, Den Haag.

Braudel, F., 1966 : *La Méditerranée et le monde méditerranéen à l'époque de Philippe II*, 3 vols., Paris.

Cosgrove, D., 1984: *Social formation and symbolic landscape*, London.

Cosgrove, D./S. Daniels (eds.), 1988: *The iconography of landscape*, Cambridge.

Crumley, C.L., 1994: *Historical ecology. Cultural knowledge and changing landscapes*, Santa Fe.

Council of Europe, 2000: *Preamble to the European Landscape Convention. Florence, 20 October 2000*, Strasbourg (Council of Europe).

Dirckx, G.H.P., 2004: Historical ecology of Dutch cultural landscapes: references for the integration of landscape planning and nature restoration in the Netherlands, in J. Brandt/H. Vejre (eds.), *Multifunctional landscapes; Volume I Theory, values and history*, Southampton.

Elerie, J.N.H., 1998: *Weerbarstig land. Een historisch-ecologische landschapsstudie van Koekange en de Reest*, Groningen (Ph.D. thesis Wageningen University).

Elerie, H./Th. Spek (eds.), 2009: *Van Jeruzalem tot Ezelakker. Veldnamen als levend erfgoed in het Nationaal Landschap Drentsche Aa*, Utrecht.

Florence, 2000: *European Landscape Convention. Florence, 20 October 2000*, Strasbourg (Council of Europe).

Habermas, J., 1984/1987: *The Theory of Communicative Action. Volumes I & II*, Boston.

Hidding, M./J. Kolen/Th. Spek, 2001: De biografie van het landschap, in J.H.F. Bloemers/R. During/J.N.H. Elerie/H.A. Groenendijk/M. Hidding/J. Kolen/Th. Spek/M.-H. Wijnen, *Bodemarchief in Behoud en Ontwikkeling, de conceptuele grondslagen*, Den Haag.

Holtorf, C., 1998: The life-histories of megaliths in Mecklenburg-Vorpommern (Germany), *World Archaeology* 30, 23-38.

Husserl, E., 1986: *Phänomenologie der Lebenswelt*, Stuttgart (Ausgewählte Texte Band II).

Kolen, J.C.A., 1993: *The cultural biography of landscape. A re-appraisal of history*, Leiden.

Kolen, J.C.A., 2005: *De biografie van het landschap. Drie essays over landschap, geschiedenis en erfgoed*, Amsterdam (Ph.D. thesis VU University).

Kopytoff, I., 1986: The cultural biography of things: commodization as a process, in A. Appadurai (ed.), *The social life of things. Commodities in a social perspective*, Cambridge, 64-91.

Kuhn, Th., 1962: *The structure of scientific revolutions*, Chicago.

Lewin, K., 1946: Action research and minority problems, *Journal of Social Issues* 2, 34-46.

Lowenthal, D., 1985: *The past is a foreign country*, Cambridge.

Meijles, E.W., 2010 (in press): The rural atelier as an educational method in landscape studies, *Journal of Geography in Higher Education* 34 (3).

Molema, J./Th. Spek/J.N.H. Elerie, 2004: *Cultuurhistorische inventarisatie ten behoeve van de Landschapsvisie Drentse Aa*, Amsterdam (RAAP-rapport 969).

Netherlands Environmental Assessment Agency, 2005: *Natuurbalans 2005*, Bilthoven/Wageningen (Natuur- en Milieuplanbureau).

Novioconsult/Strootman Landschapsarchitecten, 2004: *Landschapsvisie Drentsche Aa*, Nijmegen/Amsterdam.

Olwig, K.R., 1984: *Nature's ideological landscape. A literary and geographic perspective on its development and preservation on Denmark's Jutland heath*, London.

Olwig, K.R., 1993: Recovering the substantive nature of landscape, *Annals of the Association of American Geographers* 86, 630-653.

Olwig, K.R., 2006: *Landscape, nature and the body politic. From Britain's Renaissance to America's New World*, Madison.

Plieninger, T./F. Höchtl/Th. Spek (eds.), 2006: European rural landscapes: land-use, biodiversity and conservation, *Environmental Science and Policy* 9, nr. 4 (special issue).

Price, M./M. Lewis, 1993: The reinvention of cultural geography, *Annals of the Association of American Geographers* 83, 1, 1-17.

Provincie Drenthe, 2003: *Beheer-, inrichting- en ontwikkelingsplan voor het Nationaal Beek- en esdorpenlandschap Drentse Aa*, Assen.

Raleigh Yow, V., 2005: *Recording Oral History: A Guide for the Humanities and Social Sciences*, Lanham/Oxford.

Rhenen, T. van/M. van Bavel/C. Graveland/T. Selnes, 2005: *Putting nature on the EU political agenda: a review of four policy dossiers*, Den Haag (Rapport Landbouw Economisch Instituut, Domein 6, Beleid 6.05.05).

Ritchie, D., 2003: *Doing oral history. A practical guide*, New York.

Roo, G. de/M. Schwartz/G. Beukema, 2001: *Omgevingsplanning, een innovatief proces. Over integratie, participatie, omgevingsplannen en de gebiedsgerichte aanpak*, Den Haag.

Royal Haskoning, 2007: *Landschapsherstelplan Amer- en Anloërdiep*, Groningen.

Roymans, N., 1995: The cultural biography of urnfields and the long-term history of a mythical landscape, *Archaeological Dialogues* 2, 2-24.

Sager, T., 1994: *Communicative planning theory*, Aldershot.

Samuels, M.S., 1979: The biography of landscape. Cause and culpability, in D.W. Meinig (ed.), *The interpretation of ordinary landscapes*, New York/Oxford, 51-88.

Sherman, F.T./W.R. Torbert, 2000: *Transforming Social Inquiry, Transforming Social Action. New paradigms for crossing the theory/practice divide in universities and communities*, Boston.

Spatial Planning Memorandum, 2005: *Wet op de Ruimtelijke Ordening 2005*, Den Haag (Ministerie van VROM).

Spek, Th., 1996: Die bodenkundliche und landschaftliche Lage von Siedlungen, Äckern und Gräberfeldern in Drenthe (nördliche Niederlande). Eine Studie zur Standortwahl in vorgeschichtlicher, frühgeschichtlicher und mittelalterlicher Zeit (3400 v. Chr. - 1500 n. Chr.), *Siedlungsforschung* 14, 95-193.

Spek, Th., 2004: *Het Drentse esdorpenlandschap. Een historisch-geografische studie,* Utrecht (Ph.D. thesis, Wageningen University).

Spek, Th., 2007: Kulturlandschaftsentwicklung in den Eschdörferlandschaften der nordöstlichen Niederlanden (Provinz Drenthe), in W. Schenk/R. Bergmann (eds.), *Historische Kulturlandschaftsforschung im Spannungsfeld von älteren Ansätzen und aktuellen Fragestellungen und Methoden. Institutioneller Hintergrund, methodische Ausgangsüberlegungen und inhaltlichen Zielsetzungen,* Bonn (Siedlungsforschung 24), 219-250.

Strootman Landschapsarchitecten/Novioconsult, 2008: *Strubben-Kniphorstbosch. Inrichtings- en beheerplan,* Amsterdam/Nijmegen.

Strootman Landschapsarchitecten, 2010: *Balloërveld. Inrichtings- en beheerplan,* Amsterdam.

Troll, C., 1939: Luftbildplan und ökologische Bodenforschung, *Zeitschrift der Gesellschaft für Erdkunde zu Berlin* 1939, 241-298.

UNESCO, 1972: *UNESCO World Heritage Convention,* Florence.

Vidal de la Blache, P., 1903 : *Tableau de la géographie de France,* Paris.

Wylie, J., 2007: *Landscape,* Abingdon/New York.

3. From inventory to identity? Constructing the Lahemaa National Park's (Estonia) regional cultural heritage

Marju Kõivupuu[1], Anu Printsmann[1] & Hannes Palang[1]

ABSTRACT

The Lahemaa National Park in Estonia is a somewhat special case among national parks due to its controversial history. Its creation was seen as outwitting the Soviet system, serving simultaneously as an object of national as well as socialist pride, being the first of its kind in the Union of Soviet Socialist Republics (USSR). The national park's contested nature collapsed along with the USSR and its identity as resistance needs to be reviewed. With Estonian independence the property restitution reform was carried out in conjunction with many others leaving many gaps in the legislative system. Today Lahemaa faces a building demand and set out to make an inventory of the present situation as the most urgent problem is to draft guidelines for newly built houses in order to maintain the 'traditional' look. Traditionality is a very difficult concept to express in words and measures. Our suggestion after extensive fieldwork is that in maintaining or searching for a new regional identity, the bottom-up approach need not focus on rural built heritage but on creating a new vision of combined nature conservation and cultural heritage by democratic process. This is not to say that material heritage (buildings and settlement structure) does not influence the conceptual heritage and social construction of regional identity but the management of this should be done in accordance with the local population.

KEY WORDS

Lahemaa National Park; planning; heritage, nature conservation, local identity

1. INTRODUCTION

This paper departs from the interlocked trinity of landscape, culture and heritage and addresses a set of paradoxes including protection/development, past/future and science/policy (Palang/Fry 2003). The regional example here, namely Lahemaa National Park (LNP) in Estonia, conjoining nature and culture, exemplifies how knowledge gained through action can contribute to regional identity shaped both by orders from 'above' and local actors.

The aim of the paper is to sketch the specific situation of the LNP to explain how societal factors alongside natural and especially material cultural heritage like rural buildings and settlement systems influence the conceptual and social construction of regional identity.

We rely on data gathered by the project entitled Basic Research for Management Plan of the Lahemaa National Park and Inventory of Coastal Villages (2007-2009) that was set up to consider how much free space there is to construct new buildings in order not to ruin the traditional landscape and if so, identify the local architectural traits to adhere to when erecting these. These data should have surfaced if more than 6000 houses and their surroundings in 31 coastal villages were thoroughly scrutinized in addition to land use and settlement development analysis. The LNP now covers over 725 km^2, of which 251 km^2 is the sea (www.estonica.org). The complex task demanded an interdisciplinary team consisting of ethnographers, anthropologists, folklorists, geographers, landscape planners and specialists in built heritage. The high-handed inventory was unavoidably accompanied by public participation in the form of focus group and individual in-depth interviews.

Doing this unprecedented extensive fieldwork gave us plenty of material to consider, leading us to far-reaching conclusions that the seemingly innocent task of inventory and laying out building and planning suggestions actually re-contributes to the make-up of Lahemaa's regional identity. We found that the importance of every particular building, household or even a village may be deemed incompatible with the public representation of Lahemaa, that being entangled in detail, common sense and a bigger picture is missing. Identifying what is 'proper' and what is not to Lahemaa would have meant coining the essence of Lahemaa, which had not been done in four previous decades and seemed imposturous. Thus, controversially, we see that the administration of the LNP should come up with a clear vision of what Lahemaa is about, not forgetting the natural aspects and communicating this with local inhabitants, underpinning the mentality of the LNP instead of materiality. This is not to say that inventorial data concerning built environment do not matter but the added value coming from conversing with local inhabitants is more meaningful.

In order to further explain our far-reaching conclusions we need to delve into the specificity of the LNP and elucidate why rural built heritage plays a crucial role there.

2. THE BACKGROUND OF THE LAHEMAA NATIONAL PARK

2.1 *The peculiarities of the foundation of the Lahemaa National Park*

Traditionally, landscape has been a concern of natural sciences in Estonia (Palang *et al.* 2000; Peil *et al.* 2004), but nature conservation in the 1960s and 1970s tried to unite both natural and cultural heritage, having nationalistic undercurrents as a resistance movement during a totalitarian regime which peaked in 1971 when the LNP was established (Smurr 2008; Caddell 2009). It was the first national [sic] park in the Union of Soviet Socialist Republics (USSR) soon to be followed by many others (e.g. Bunkše 1992; *idem* 1999; Schwartz 2006; see the special issue "From Phosphate Springs to 'Nordstream': Contemporary Environmentalism in the Baltic States" in the *Journal of Baltic Studies*, 2009).

The attempts to create a national park originate from nineteenth century tsarist Russia when, following the ideas of Herder, the (Baltic) Germans saw "their landscape, and especially their nation were perceived as entirely organic, that is, natural" (Smurr 2008, 402). 'Heimatkunde' resonated with the Estonian nationalistic awakening movement. The developments resemble those existing in the Unites States, the United Kingdom or Scandinavia. During the inter-war independent republic period the discussions continued with more focus on natural diversity. "Arguably, those who promoted the park during the uncertain Soviet era might have deemed its founding more critical than would have their more confident pre-war predecessors" (*ibidem* 2008, 402) and the hub of negotiations shifted back to nationalistic emotions.

The original name Lahemaa for the region was proposed by the Finnish geographer J.G. Granö, founder of Estonian geography, in 1922 (Granö 1922). Lahemaa can be translated from Estonian as 'land of bays', but also 'cool land' referring both to natural and cultural features. Lahemaa comprises four peninsulas stretching into the sea between four bays (Fig. 1) scattered with erratic boulders and has been a favourite holiday place for the intelligentsia and artists since the end of the nineteenth century, facilitated by the St Petersburg–Tallinn railway.

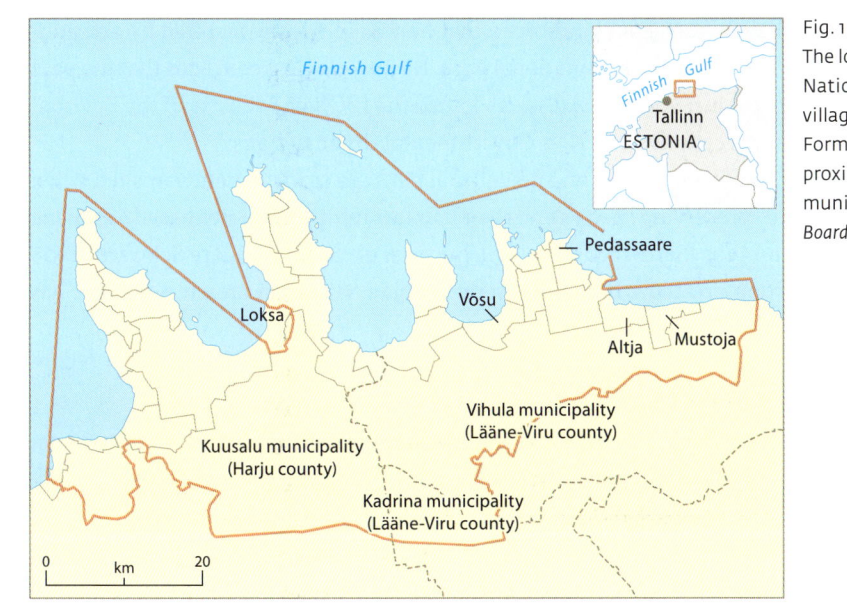

Fig. 1
The location of Lahemaa National Park and its coastal villages.
Former church parishes are proxies for contemporary municipalities *(data: Estonian Land Board, 01.01.2009)*.

Historically, the LNP area has belonged to different administrative units dependent on political organization. Nowadays, the LNP belongs to two counties, three municipalities and 77 villages. As to traditional settlement pattern, the borders of villages have been constantly redrawn depending on the existence of private property (see Palang *et al.* 2006), yet the nuclei of villages have persisted in the same spot, in some occasions even for millennia.

Thus, the interplay of identities happens on two levels: Lahemaa's regional identity as a late construct is fuzzy, while the LNP contributed greatly to Estonian (ethnic) national identity during the Soviet period. "Estonian founders strove to have the park project a national culture that was nearly devoid of socialist content. Whereas Moscow appeared willing to tolerate a park that was natural in form provided it was socialist in content, Estonians ultimately succeeded in creating a park that was both natural in form and national in content. It is in this context that the USSR's first national park presents us with an intriguing paradox: Lahemaa appealed to the anti-modern nationalist sentiments of its intended, primarily Estonian, audience, but it did so in an era, and under the observant eye, of a more 'modern' and 'international' promethean-minded overlord (Smurr 2008, 400).

The designation of the LNP has been recognized in local literature (Smurr 2008) as an endeavour of a few 'founding fathers', making it an elitist project like elsewhere. One of these men, Jaan Eilart (1933-2006), held the chair of the Eastern-European Committee of the International Union for Conservation of Nature (IUCN) from 1982 to 1990 and was nominated for the honorary presidency of Eastern-European Committee on Education of IUCN (www.elks.ee). He had to be familiar with contemporary developments of the definition of national parks but he promoted the nineteenth century connotation: "The park had everything to do with Estonians and their culture and nothing to do with nature". But the Estonian culture Eilart sought to protect was a traditional peasant culture tied intimately to the land in accordance with the Ratzelian idea of unity of land and people, people taking root in soil by sweat and blood. Thus, despite his contention to the contrary, the park was also about nature. "It was a place where the natural and built environments served as congenial complements to one another" (*ibidem*, 411; compare Bunkše

1992; *idem* 1999 for Latvia). "Eilart insists [1998], however, that he was in no way inspired by any anti-Soviet sentiment when he conceived the idea for a national park. He nevertheless concedes that the park eventually did assume that role" (Smurr 2008, 418). Estonia joined the IUCN on Ministry of the Environment level as late as 2007; it was preceded by two Non-Governmental Organizations.

The approach of combining nature conservation and cultural heritage management vanished when nature protection turned towards preserving species and their habitats into biodiversity-based European Union directives and policies in 1990s (Sepp *et al.* 1999; Wilshusen *et al.* 2002; compare Schwartz 2006 for Latvia) and heritage protection created a heritage reserve outside the urban area in 1987 that has remained until now a singular case.

2.2   *Defining the Lahemaa National Park*

When comparing the aims of the LNP back in 1971 and the contemporary IUCN definition of national parks, perhaps stressing natural values and biodiversity as stated in the primary objective, they are not poles apart.

First out of six of the LNP's primary goals and tasks is: "to protect and preserve nature in the national park, especially the larger natural associations (forests, bog systems, and others), particularly noteworthy natural objects (alvars, stone fields, rare plants and animals, etc.), cultural landscapes together with historical and cultural monuments, as well as ethnographically and architecturally worthy buildings and structures" (Lahemaa Rahvuspargi põhimäärus 1971 cit. Smurr 2008, 404). The other goals underpin the need for research, education among visitors, local inhabitants and especially the youth, preserving pristine nature and enabling recreation in anticipated places.

In the IUCN definition national parks "are large natural or near natural areas set aside to protect large-scale ecological processes, along with the complement of species and ecosystems characteristic of the area, which also provide a foundation for environmentally and culturally compatible, spiritual, scientific, educational, recreational, and visitor opportunities" (www.iucn.org). The strength and weakness of IUCN definition lies in its imprecision, e.g. immeasurable criteria like "near natural areas", "in as natural a state as possible" (objective one), "viable", "functional", "sufficient", "integrity", "resilience" (objective two), the question of scale of "large-scale ecological processes" and "ecosystems characteristic of the area" etc. and flexibility in time, such as fast-changing concepts of what constitutes natural.

Mels (Mels 2002) has shown how in Sweden the drive for pristine nature in national parks is a rhetorical mediation that secures the naturalization and nationalization of park spaces. The illusion of empty wilderness is even more remarkable in colonized areas (Adams/McShane 1992; Neumann 1995; Schama 1995; Neumann 1998; Spence 1999). As Olwig (Olwig 1996, 380) has observed, "[n]ational parks would seem to be as much about the nature of national identity as about physical nature" (Nash 1973; Runte 1979; Schwartz 2006, 45; Smurr 2008, 411).

"After all, many of the park's 'noteworthy objects', such as its glacial erratic boulders, flora and fauna, already enjoyed protected status under the republic's 1957 nature protection law, but the surrounding built environment, that is the larger cultural context, did not" (Smurr 2008, 405). Yet "… the territory of the park still remained one of Estonia's most pristine natural environments. /…/ In 1980, for example, Lahemaa's average population density [13.7 inhabitants/km^2] was but one-third of that for Estonia as a whole [31.6]" (*ibidem*, 406 and 417). As of 1 January 2009, Estonian population density is 30.9 and declining; c. 400,000 of 1.34 million are living in the capital Tallinn (www.stat.ee). "Lahemaa did quickly become a shaped, rendered and beloved place not merely for the park's founders but also for the entire Estonian nation. By the mid-1980s, for example, an estimated 200,000 tourists visited the park annually, a figure that approximates one-fifth of all Estonians" (*ibidem*, 412). There were supposedly no objections for the establishment of the national park from the local population since the Soviet regime had nationalized all private property.

The importance of the LNP was based on the biological and landscape diversity in the LNP as expressed by important habitats for spawning salmon and trout, by its comparatively rich bird life as a result of its thick forests and the presence of brown bear and lynx. This diversity needed protection from large-scale desk-top-designed forest drainage, land reclamation projects and planned growth of recreational facilities (Smurr 2008). The IUCN requirement for ecosystems characteristic of the area is met by four landscape regions (www.estonica.org) out of 25 (Arold 2005) so that "Estonians from any region of the country could discern something familiar, something local, in the park" (*ibidem*, 406). In this way Lahemaa was presented as a small model of Estonia.

Lahemaa became the subject of research and training. "Specialists conducted extensive archaeological surveys in the early years of the park and thereby helped to reveal many of Lahemaa's abundant scientific and cultural treasures. Due to the region's long history of settlement and land tenure, specialists suggested that it was 'particularly in Lahemaa' where one could find 'the most diverse picture of the development of agriculture and folk culture' characteristic of Estonia" (Smurr 2008, 405). While many students have received their natural sciences or ethnographic field training there, for example by compiling reports on building details, the few attempts to generalize all available material have failed. Although the focus on ethnic issues was rather innovative at that time in the USSR, the studies continued the local pre-World War II practice, the methods copied the ones spread elsewhere in the USSR and were mainly descriptive, lacking systematic analysis and publication due to ideological reasons. At that time maps were not available, photographing and other recording devices were rare and their quality is often unsatisfactory.

Lahemaa was partly transformed into something that resembled folk art on a grand scale, into a "ceremonial landscape", an "open-air museum" (compare Crang 1999) for public enjoyment. Visitor centres, guest houses, closely regulated campsites and newly built trails all ensured that even this enormous museum could direct visitors' attention to the art that the park's administrators chose to emphasize (Smurr 2008).

2.3 The importance of rural built heritage

Landscape has been considered as a natural entity in Estonia (Palang *et al.* 2000; Peil *et al.* 2004) whereas heritage tends to belong to the cultural sphere dealing with landmarks. A monument, as defined by the Heritage Conservation Act (2002), is movable or immovable, a part thereof, a group of things or an integral group of structures; it will be under state protection because it is of historical, archaeological, ethnographic, urban developmental, architectural, artistic or scientific value or of value in terms of religious history or of other cultural value. Monuments may be classified as archaeological, architectural, artistic, industrial or historical monuments, meaning 'cultural', not 'natural' (Printsmann /Palang 2008).

Focussing on monuments has its origins in the Soviet era which completely erased previous landmarks or changed their meanings, e.g. gyms in churches, while other socio-economic formations have done so to lesser degrees. An object could be protected so that it had no link with the people. The outcome is alienation.

In Estonia, as elsewhere in the world, activities concentrating around heritage protection and management have become more active when the society is going through some sort of major change (Cosgrove 1984; Lowenthal 1985; Pickard 1997; Palang et al. 2006). It was at the turn of the nineteenth and twentieth centuries, characterized by urbanization replacing agrarian life-styles, Russification, wider spread of education and Estonia gaining independence in 1918, when oral and material heritage was gathered enthusiastically. This rather thin layer of higher culture in the Estonian language has turned the agrarian life-style and the desire for it into an icon of Estonianness and materials gathered into archives are taken far too seriously. This is the era which has been publicly accepted as an etalon, a yardstick against which traditionality is measured. A second phase in the 1970s and 1980s is connected with the stagnation of Soviet power, when people again turned to their roots by the combination of nature and heritage conservation, and an authentic folklore movement comprised all things that had an officially forbidden political hue. The third phase since the regaining of independence in 1991 and the years after has turned us back to the past once again.

Landscape and heritage can only be understood in their historic-cultural context (Jones 1991; Palang et al. 2006) and in the Estonian case they are very much ideology-laden, politicized and administratively separated (Printsmann/Kõivupuu/Palang 2010). Heritage can be natural and cultural, material and mental; natural material heritage is often described or explained in cultural mental heritage, done so universally. This oral heritage or folklore has remained largely alien to and ignored by the republic's more recent Slavo-Soviet arrivals (Smurr 2008), whereby the peculiarity and difference of Estonianness represented in the LNP could not be actuated. The material cultural heritage in the form of rural built heritage could not be ignored and the difference in cultural context was perceived as self-explanatorily distinguishable from Slavic traditions (Fig. 2). The importance of rural built heritage in the LNP has served Estonian ethnic and national identity, underpinning the cultural context's inseparability from natural settings while regional level variations have been quite forgotten.

Time is one of the most important dimensions of identity. From this point of view, identity reaches the past through narratives that emerge from our experiences (Cohen 1993). In a similar way it also reaches the future through our personal and cultural expectations (Gover 1998). Promoters of identity "often seek ways to present the old within the new" (Smurr 2008, 400) as heritage has always served contemporary ends. Tradition could be understood not only as the heritage from the past, but as a consistency created in the present that leans on the past. Therefore traditionality should not be understood as something that never changes but rather as something that still persists. However something can only persist when it changes flexibly and constantly (Smith 1995). So when life changes, folk culture should also change, part of it loses its functionality and disappears. In this way tradition is a process that balances change and sustains ways of thinking, expressing and acting. The selection of what perishes and what persists becomes socially determined in time (Hobsbawm/Ranger 1983).

Fig. 2
Käspri farm in the village of Mustoja was built in the nineteenth century and has been renovated three times (1956, 1970 and 2000). This type of house is called a sea-captain's house and formerly they were all painted white. The peaceful districts of sea-captains' houses are assigned as valuable milieu area nominations and are one of the trademarks of Lahemaa. The heir to the captain's house fled to Sweden from the Soviets. The present landlady has been working in the house as a maid since the end of 1930s and her hobby is local history. *Photo: Marju Kõivupuu, 31.07.2008.*

3. LAHEMAA IN WINDS OF CHANGE

3.1 *Administrating change*

When looked at closely enough, every region becomes contested and the LNP is no exception here. The general belief is that since the formation of the national park the landscape did not undergo many changes till the 1990s and Estonia's re-independence. Following the collapse of the USSR, new modernizing 'Western winds', rapid societal and spatial developments along with legislative and planning vacuum resulting from land restitution, and economic considerations took over the place of national idealism, blurring both the ethnic and regional identity of the LNP.

Lahemaa as an elitist recreational area only an hour's drive away from Tallinn serves nowadays as its daily suburbanized hinterland, whereas summer house building activities have never stopped. With the re-emergence of private property, the previous land use structure is in peril as former subsistence gardens are replaced by front lawns and the former large plots become divided among friends. Discontent with possible fragmentation and building density may appear later with realization that the landscape that attracted them in the first place has changed. Furthermore, new or thought-to-be-traditional construction styles and materials are being introduced. The building boom is perceived by the LNP administration as 'threatening' characteristic national and regional culture and heritage, meaning traditionality or authenticity which the park should maintain according to Protection Rules. The main pressure is on coastal areas.

Since there are certain gaps in the national legislation that do not define clear priorities between conservation and planning laws, the conflicts between protection, management and development are inevitable. Classically, all this often happens at the expense of the local people.

Since 1998, the national park has been in a situation where the Protection Rules have to be updated and the Management Plan needs compiling. Despite the improvement of technology, the overview of the state-of-the-art of landscape, settlements and architecture was lacking, even though the employees of the national park possess everyday practical knowledge about it. In order to evaluate the national park's assets concerning cultural material heritage (buildings and settlement structure) in coastal areas, an inventory as a basic research for recommendations for the Management Plan was ordered by the park administration. Relying on a 'solid scientific database', the Project should ultimately specify regional conditions for natural and cultural development including local guiding principles proposing where to build and how to sustain or create regional (and national?) 'characteristic' traits in remodelled or new houses.

The ambitious Project foresaw a range of activities but was hugely downsized mainly due to time, financial, personnel constraints and rational claims. The following tasks were carried out:

1. The exploration of the existing archive, database, literature, scientific, legislative materials (general and theme plans of counties and municipalities, the national park's management zones, detail plans and building blueprints, orthophotos, Estonian Base and Basic Map, cadastral map, available historical maps to identify traditional settlement structure and village type) for analysing the development, change and current situation of landscape, road network and village settlement structure and milieu characteristic of the area. This information had to be used to pinpoint villages' landscape values and characteristic settlement structure coming from different historic periods.
2. A synthesis combining contemporary map data, the digital map layer of road networks and Lahemaa buildings, comparing them with building registry and creating the database for village settlement structure and architecture, including data about the historic change in settlement structure and land use.
3. The formation of the database based on fieldwork inventorial measurements and photographs.
4. The definition of characteristic traditional architecture (area, height, cubage, material, proportions and basic architectural solutions) and village settlement structure (density, plot size, number of buildings on the plot, distance between buildings and yards, configuration of houses on the plot) and supported by architectural restoration and construction recommendations alongside schemes for further development (condense or expand, direction and range) where applicable; however, creating new residential developments is not an option according to current Protection Rules (ruining traditional settlement pattern).
5. To list and describe architecturally, historically, culturally and ethnographically valuable buildings and ruins and give restoration recommendations.
6. To list and describe small cultural heritage features and give recommendations for their maintenance.

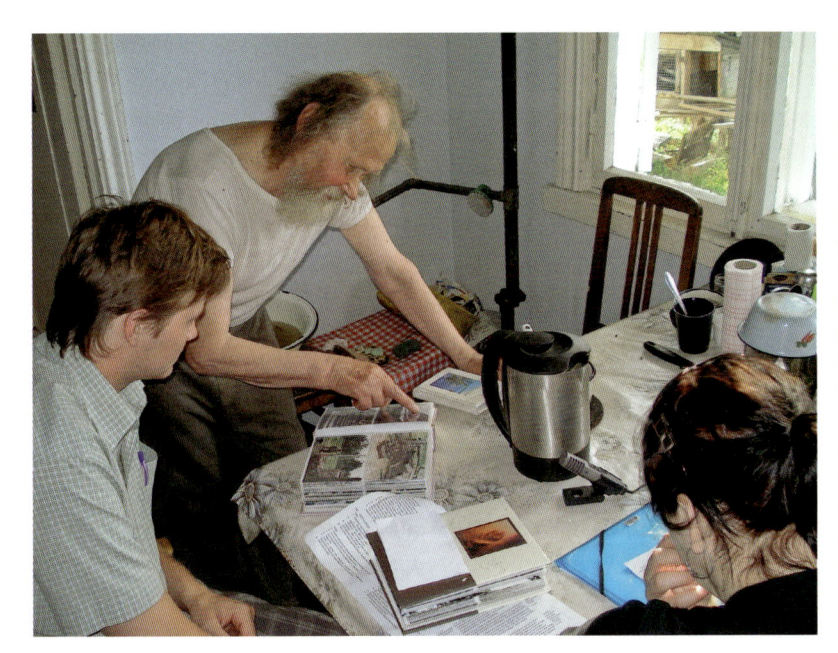

Fig. 3
Dialogical anthropology in the village of Pedassaare. Dialogical anthropology focuses on the diminishing of the cultural differences between the researchers and the researched in a situation where the researcher has many roles: he/she has a personal relationship with the material, an instrumental role in forming the data within the rules of a research and has obligations to the society which pays for and sets conditions for the research *(Honko 1990)*.
Photo: Marju Kõivupuu, 12 August 2008.

This kind of project needs a village-wise approach as similar village settlement structures can result from different processes, but similar processes can create different patterns (Widgren 2004). We carried out a frontal expedition which resulted in inventorying households and interviewing some inhabitants. The data collection was accompanied by interviews (Fig. 3) not demanded by the LNP administration in order to gain understanding of how the locals define, understand and value heritage as part of their daily lives in the LNP. As a rule, each household was represented by 1-2 persons, usually from the eldest generation who had lived there for a long time and had survived all power changes. Since the narratives were not of interest to the park management, the interviews proved to be the side-product. Visual observations also reveal that the built heritage (houses, fences etc.) do not follow any regularities, the households do not form settlements of uniform architecture.

A participatory approach coming from planned economy is not obvious to the society (Printsmann/Palang 2008). In our case the problems mostly arise because the social system is left apart and the interest focuses only on material objects. The Management Plan has to be publicly available before ratification, but the sooner the locals get involved, the better. Many of their concerns are not new but it is intriguing to see how some of the etic topics intersect into everyday life.

3.2 Emic problems in contemporary Lahemaa

IUCN is also concerned with issues of settled populations, their livelihood and compensation mechanisms and commercialization of land and water (www.iucn.org), which are also problematic in the LNP.

The settled LNP population has been decreasing because of the lack of available jobs due to urbanization and changed mentality. Most of the inhabitants are seasonal, some of them originating from the region. In the village of Mustoja of c. 40 households only around five were inhabited throughout the year. The first concern of the populace is that the village life should continue.

With regard to livelihood in coastal areas, the main occupation has been fishing. As Lahemaa was situated on the Soviet Union's western border, it was under double protection as a border zone and a national park. A border zone in general meant that none other than residents would have a permit to enter the zone, but as Lahemaa had previously gained fame as a recreational area it was developed as a health resort for progressive Soviet workers. After the establishment of the national park, the barbed wire was removed from the beaches but access to certain areas was still restricted. Fishing, ship-building, trade and seafaring were cancelled in the fear of people fleeing to Finland, gaining extra individual income and for other ideological reasons.

"How many of the world's national parks, after all, can one find in a highly contested border region that is demarcated, in part, by searchlights, barbed wire, guard towers, and a training facility for tracking infiltrators and refugees?" (Smurr 2008, 400). Curiously, the Soviet military heritage does not concern local inhabitants as their interests have been elsewhere for a very long time. What is remembered and most talked about are outwitting the officers and haggling with them.

The traditional way of life survived in the oral memories of the people, on postcards and photographs, in literature and in coastal villages that had been turned into open-air museums that illustrate the lifestyle at the beginning of the twentieth century.

Today access to the sea is again obstructed, this time due to re-emergent private property as most minor roads were privatized together with surrounding lands in the early 1990s. Getting along with neighbours is important as they will grant the permission to trespass their properties. Friendly relations are not easy to come by, as very often there is a feeling that expensive plots by the seaside are acquired not quite legally. Another twist in fishermen's lives has been new legislative regulations to be fulfilled, e.g. a fishing exam and buying fishing permits. These are viewed unfavourably because they are seen to undermine self-esteem and the wallet.

A different 'traditional' livelihood since the mid-nineteenth century has been renting out summer rooms. This quasi-legal extra income became especially handy during the Soviet era when the traditional fishermen's livelihood could not be continued. In market economy circumstances the centralized summer holiday homes (e.g. in Võsu) for different enterprises and pioneer camps collapsed and the desire for private property is not satisfied with a room any more, people want a house and a segment of beach.

The contemporary narratives tell stories about conflicts with nature and heritage conservation authorities as their activities are seen as an intrusion into the right of management on private property. Their precepts constrain land use and building decisions thus hindering everyday life and development. One extra activity the locals do not understand and ridicule is that the national park restores natural plant communities on former agricultural land. They argue that there has never been nature, it has always been cultivated land.

3.3 Etic problems with contemporary Lahemaa

As the region is well-researched regarding folklore (see for example Ahven 1957; Nõmmsalu 1977; Tarvel 1983), the strong traditions and identity are clearly distinguishable among three former church parishes. Next to centralized institutions and a museum dealing with history and memory, local initiatives have now taken up the task of collecting and preserving oral history (Piikmann 2008; Sandström 1996), a task that was not possible during the totalitarian regime. Including the seasonal population, the link with the older layer of landscape (Cosgrove 1984; Palang *et al.* 2006) and its everyday intangible cultural heritage like micro-toponyms is in some cases being replaced by elitist traditions retrieved from easily accessible archives. For a newcomer heritage is obtained via buildings, the lifestyle he/she has learnt from different sources and information of 'how things were in the good old times'. This knowledge is eclectic and not necessarily based on specific local knowledge. Dependent on the empathy of a newcomer, he/she either gets assimilated by the community and learns the survival strategies or, vice versa, does not. In the latter case, he/she will always be a stranger in the village. The locals assume these people should somehow be directed and controlled. Sometimes the toughest fighters for local customs or lore have settled in that area only recently or even live somewhere else.

The ineluctable change in a way of life, lack of job positions in fishery and agriculture contribute to emptying villages and urbanization alters rural built heritage and land use affecting traditional landscapes. The vast majority of houses are now used as second homes. Our study suggests that about one-third of the buildings have been erected (or seriously renovated) during the last 40 years, while the remaining two-thirds originate from earlier times. This change also means that there is no need for granaries, barns, sheds etc. and these are being turned into cottages where people can sleep during the warm season. The need for seasonal lodging in turn means changes in the details of the buildings, windows get enlarged and installed into buildings that previously had no windows, additional storeys are being attached, traditional roof and wall materials are replaced by modern or thought-to-be-traditional ones. The preconception of what a coastal village should look like directs reality (Olwig 2004) and local or regional building traits are often not acknowledged, resulting in log-houses and reed-roofs not historically typical of Lahemaa. Buildings that are not needed are left alone to deteriorate or more often torn down, the average number of buildings per household is decreasing despite the fact that plots are being fragmented among friends. Newly-formed gated communities do not seem to disturb other local inhabitants as there is not much communication with newcomers, save for accessing the seaside.

Decline of agriculture means lands formerly cultivated become overgrown and this tendency, in our view, clearly hinders the national and regional identity of the LNP, not to mention the threat on biodiversity in semi-natural coastal meadows. Many authors (Callegari/Vallega 2002; Pinder/Vallega 2003; Vallega 2003; Granö 2007) have indicated that more attention should be paid to sensitive coastal areas which ask for a balanced approach to biodiversity, ecological and economic sustainability together with tourism and heritage management. On the one hand, support schemes are available for maintaining these lands, on the other, domestic animals are much better stewards of rural landscape than any lawn mower and there is a clear lack of animals these days to keep the views open and the countryside tidy, pleasing tourists.

It is difficult to conceptualize Lahemaa's regional identity as an addition to an administratively diverse background which embodies several natural and cultural aspects, such as peninsulas and bays scattered with erratic boulders, secluded coastal idylls with shabby net-sheds amplified by artists and writers, simple beaches and romantic forests, sea views, restored manor houses, rustic village life, peaceful sea-captains' houses and vernacular serial granaries with fences, renowned as a summer holiday place (Printsmann/Kõivupuu/Palang 2010).

From the outsider's point of view (Relph 1976), everything that is located within the boundaries of the national park could, and should, be considered natural and cultural, national and regional heritage. From the locals' point of view, the landscape is foremost the arena of their everyday practices, a stage where progress is to be made and a memory device that stores all the changes resulting from their activities.

Controversially, what does not comprise Lahemaa is very clear. Loksa, an industrial town, does not fit into that perceived cultural image of Lahemaa and indeed Loksa is excluded from the national park. Within the borders of the LNP there are Soviet military remains that are currently circumvented by locals (like gated communities) and park administration. However, this Soviet heritage could serve as an attraction for foreign tourists. Another puzzle for administration includes the so-called neo-ethnographical type-models envisaged by renowned architects during the 1980s, inspired by remaining buildings of paupers unaffected due to poverty and Soviet period border zone restrictions since the 1940s. The dilemma is whether to cherish them as a nationalist outburst during oppression or treat them as extreme kitsch (Printsmann/Kõivupuu/Palang 2010).

While the LNP's regional identity is not yet fixed, we suggest incorporating the Soviet military heritage and neo-ethnographic summer homes as witnesses of the recent past, showing what Estonians have 'endured', without 'freezing' the landscape as an open-air museum of the fishermen village period. On the other hand, it is important to identify when to stop building in order to preserve the Lahemaa's natural characteristics.

4. DISCUSSION

The eternal interplay of emic and etic concerns where the positions are never totally fixed, e.g. the emic viewpoint of locals may be torn by opposing views, brings forward many other issues and some surprising results. The most unexpected finding was that local inhabitants do not have any problems with seasonal residents or tourists despite them forming the majority (Kizos 2007; Tress 2007) except in terms of social injustice to gain better plots, closing access to the sea and challenging architectural precepts since the resulting fines are minimal. The main concern is that village life would not end altogether.

The emic trepidation in livelihood changes and etic aspects of how this affects landscape and rural built heritage both have impact on regional identity. Heritage is not the first thing that comes into one's mind in everyday situations. If legislation regarding fishing would ease up within the realm of nature protection supporting the traditional lifestyle, the romantic shabby net-sheds need not to be mere decorations any more, resulting in a continuity of the idea instead of form (Gustavsson/Peterson 2003; Jones 2004).

Both the locals and park administration tend to ignore twentieth century alterations like Soviet military heritage and neo-ethnographic summer homes which distinguish Lahemaa from the rest of the world. Luckily, the resort culture survives as a result of the rise of living standards despite global recession. As typical in a post-socialist society where the past has not been thoroughly discussed, the previous layer in the landscape, i.e. the Soviet era, is ignored and earlier features are praised (Alumäe/Printsmann/Palang 2003).

Tourists view Lahemaa as a small model of Estonia and this perception has its drawbacks on regional identity, for example logs as building material may be traditional for Estonia but are not characteristic of Lahemaa. Observers might attach importance to very different issues than insiders (Cohen 1993). As the national park itself has historically belonged to different administrative units, its material as well as mental culture is not uniform (Anderson 1983). Furthermore, the general understanding of folk culture is based on idealized stereotypes. Thus we speak about peasant culture as an independent, harmonious and well functioning system and do not try to analyse the hierarchies, conflicts and competition in it. The biggest problem however is that the model is used to define the lifestyle of the country folk, ignoring landless people, craftsmen, tradesmen and intellectuals that comprised considerable part of society. This way of thinking is shaped by the nineteenth century bourgeoisie, which was a rather dynamic societal group that needed forefathers and prehistory to counter the aristocracy. To counterbalance the inherited status, people started propagating the social status gained from one's achievements. The term 'free peasant' obtained a mythical dimension and started to cover both largely unexplored prehistoric times as well as the contemporary situation, which needed no balanced depiction. The question of what is tradition also raises the question of whose tradition (Honko 1990).

Outsiders might have clear and specific visions, but they can also imitate local influential people thereby seeking authoritative support for their actions. This is a psychological problem, describing culture in a certain way means claiming the culture under the describer's protection. When a cultural community is unable to defend itself against these issues, the result is usually asymmetry where the community remains on the loser's side. This puts a remarkable responsibility on the outsiders, they should realize this asymmetry and try to relieve it (Honko 1990).

The outsiders' vision constitutes the national importance of the LNP. Locals have to take care not to lose their regional peculiarities. Local inhabitants cannot constantly think that they live in the realm of natural and cultural heritage, they should carry on their daily activities safeguarding the heritage as taken-for-granted so that everybody could win from that situation. On the other hand we were quite reluctant to give very specific renovation and building recommendations in order not to stagnate development and possibly enable the emergence of new local traditions. In this case, heritage comprises both a natural and cultural context which gives value to the forms, i.e. processes and functions beneficial to the landscape of Lahemaa should be maintained (Widgren 2004), rather than remain solely focused on the decorative forms of rural built heritage (Fig. 4).

Fig. 4
The tavern of Altja, authentic illusion at work: preservation of the idea is preferred to the conservation of form (see Gustavsson/Peterson 2003). The Altja village is the most 'traditional' one resembling an open-air museum and thus becoming one of the tourist hotspots in Lahemaa. The tavern is a popular place for lunch. The original tavern burned down, the current one was 'imported' from outside of the national park.
Photo: Anu Printsmann, 29 January 2008.

5. CONCLUSIONS

The LNP poses an intriguing problem where ethnic and national identity has overshadowed a regional identity which started as an elite project. Despite nearly 40 years, local understanding what constitutes the park or region is vague. The identity of the LNP is being degraded as the expected traditionalist image does not coincide with rather contemporary reality. The local people are not a uniform group but they should not be made tourists in their homes. The socio-economic formation, during which the LNP was created, has ceased. The aura of resistance must be substituted with something new. It is much more difficult to stand *for* something than against. The LNP administration is still struggling to find its way out of the chaos caused by the collapse of the USSR, when old rules ceased to be enforced and new ones were not yet created. The pendulum has shifted to the other end and local inhabitants fear strict reconstruction, restoration and building precepts. Heritage protection has started to outweigh nature conservation, but tradition has the same quality as naturalness, both meanings change over time.

It is in this context of an interplay between protection/development, past/future and science/policy, that the inventory of rural built heritage in coastal areas was carried out in order to formulate recommendations for a Management Plan. The knowledge gained from interviews with locals gave a more material dimension than a quantitative inventory to the real problem, i.e. a lack of vision of regional cultural heritage and therefore regional identity. Villages are different and there is no correct answer when it is the right time to freeze development in order not to lose traditional settlement patterns or natural values. The quantitative approach should be supplemented by in-depth analysis that only local inhabitants themselves could carry out and it seems that this policy is currently considered favourable. Locals are the ones who have to dwell in their landscapes (Luz 2000).

Lahemaa should be more than a vernacular housing district. To establish Lahemaa's identity, one must consider the rural built heritage and also other aspects of natural and cultural heritage, especially social and conceptual constructions gained by communicating with local inhabitants.

ACKNOWLEDGEMENTS

Our special thanks for their help in preparing the paper to Rasmus Kask, Kaarel Kõivupuu, Liilia Laanemann, Elo Lutsepp, Joosep Metslang, Heiki Pärdi, Grete Tammetalu, Estonian Land Board and all the Lahemaa people we met during the fieldwork and two very thorough anonymous reviewers.

Financial support came from the European Union through the European Regional Development Fund (Centre of Excellence in Cultural Theory) and Estonian Ministry of Education target-financed project SF0130033s07 *Landscape Practice and Heritage*.

NOTES

1 Tallinn University, Tallinn, Estonia.

REFERENCES

Adams, J.S./T.O. McShane, 1992: *The Myth of Wild Africa: Conservation without Illusion*, Berkeley.
Ahven, H. (ed.), 1957: *Pajatusi põhjarannikult. Valimik korrespondentide murdetekste 2*. Tallinn.
Alumäe, H./A. Printsmann/H. Palang, 2003: Cultural and historical values in landscape planning: locals' perceptions, in H. Palang/G. Fry (eds.), *Landscape Interfaces: Cultural Heritage in Changing Landscapes*, Dordrecht (Landscape Series I), 125-145.

Anderson, B., 1983: *Imagined Communities. Reflections on the Origin and Spread of Nationalism*, London.

Arold, I., 2005: *Eesti maastikud*, Tartu.

Bunkše, E.V., 1992: God, thine earth is burning: nature attitudes and the Latvian drive for independence, *GeoJournal* 26, 203-209.

Bunkše, E.V., 1999: Reality of rural landscape symbolism in the formation of a post-soviet, postmodern Latvian identity, *Norsk Geografisk Tidsskrift – Norwegian Journal of Geography* 53, 121-138.

Caddell, R., 2009: Nature conservation in Estonia: from Soviet Union to European Union, *Journal of Baltic Studies* 40, 307-332.

Callegari, F./A. Vallega, 2002: Coastal cultural heritage: a management tool, *Journal of Cultural Heritage* 3, 227-236.

Cohen, A.P., 1993: Culture as identity: an anthropologist view, *New Literary History* 24, 195-209.

Cosgrove, D.E., 1984: *Social Formation and Symbolic Landscape,* Madison.

Crang, M., 1999: Nation, region and homeland: history and tradition in Dalarna, Sweden, *Ecumene* 6, 447-470.

Gover, M., 1998: The narrative emergence of identity, in J. Knuf (ed.), *Proceedings of the Fifth International Conference on Narrative. Lexington, Kentucky, October 18-20, 1996*, Lexington.

Granö, J.G., 1922: Eesti maastikulised üksused, *Loodus* 5, 277-278.

Granö, O., 2007: Coastal studies in Finland. Reciprocal relations between the coastal environment and institutional structures, in T. Koff/A. Raukas (eds.), *Eesti Geograafia Seltsi aastaraamat* 36, 156-177.

Gustavsson, R./A. Peterson, 2003: Authenticity in landscape conservation and management – the importance of the local context, in H. Palang/G. Fry (eds.), *Landscape Interfaces: Cultural Heritage in Changing Landscapes,* Dordrecht (Landscape Series I), 319-357.

Hobsbawm, E./T. Ranger (eds.), 1983: *The Invention of Tradition,* Cambridge.

Honko, L., 1990: Folkloreprosessi, *Sananjalka* 32, 93-121.

Jones, M., 1991: The elusive reality of landscape: concepts and approaches in landscape research, *Norsk Geografisk Tidsskrift – Norwegian Journal of Geography* 45, 229-244.

Jones, M., 2004: Tycho Brahe, cartography and landscape in 16th century Scandinavia, in H. Palang/H. Sooväli/M. Antrop/G. Setten (eds.), *European Rural Landscapes: Persistence and Change in a Globalising Environment*, Dordrecht, 209-226.

Journal of Baltic Studies 2009, 40 (3): Special issue on "From Phosphate Springs to 'Nordstream': Contemporary Environmentalism in the Baltic States".

Kizos, T., 2007: Island lifestyles in the Aegean Islands, Greece: heaven in summer, hell in winter? in H. Palang/H. Sooväli/A. Printsmann (eds.), *Seasonal Landscapes*, Berlin, 127-150.

Lahemaa Rahvuspargi põhimäärus, *ENSV Teataja* 1971, 26, 285.

Lowenthal, D., 1985: *The Past is a Foreign Country,* Cambridge.

Luz, F., 2000: Participatory landscape ecology – a basis for acceptance and implementation, *Landscape and Urban Planning* 50, 157-166.

Mels, T., 2002: Nature, home, and scenery: the official spatialities of Swedish national parks, *Environment and Planning D: Society and Space* 20, 135-154.

Nash, R., 1973: *Wilderness and the American Mind,* New Haven.

Neumann, R.P., 1995: Ways of seeing Africa: colonial recasting of African society and landscape in Serengeti National Park, *Ecumene* 2, 149-169.

Neumann, R.P., 1998: *Imposing Wilderness: Struggles over Livelihood and Nature Preservation in Africa,* Berkeley.

Nõmmsalu, F., 1977: *Lahemaale sündis rahvuspark.* Tallinn.

Olwig, K.R., 1996: Reinventing common nature: Yosemite and Mount Rushmore – a meandering tale of a double nature, in W. Cronon (ed.), *Uncommon Ground: Rethinking the Human Place in Nature,* New York.

Olwig, K.R., 2004: "This is not a landscape": circulating reference and land shaping, in H. Palang/H. Sooväli/M. Antrop/G. Setten (eds.), *European Rural Landscapes: Persistence and Change in a Globalising Environment,* Dordrecht, 41-67.

Palang, H. /G. Fry, 2003: Landscape interfaces, in H. Palang/G. Fry (eds.), *Landscape Interfaces: Cultural Heritage in Changing Landscapes,* Dordrecht (Landscape Series I), 1-14.

Palang, H./Ü. Mander/O. Kurs/K. Sepp, 2000: The concept of landscape in Estonian geography, in J.-M. Punning (ed.), *Living with Diversity. On the Occasion of the 29th International Geographical Congress,* Tallinn (Estonia. Geographical Studies 8), 154-169.

Palang, H./A. Printsmann/É. Konkoly Gyuró/M. Urbanc/E. Skowronek/W. Woloszyn, 2006: The forgotten rural landscapes of Central and Eastern Europe, *Landscape Ecology* 21, 347-357.

Peil, T./H. Sooväli/H. Palang/T. Oja/Ü. Mander, 2004: Estonian landscape study: contextual history, *BelGeo* 2-3, 231-244.

Pickard, R.D., 1997: Post-independence in Eastern Europe: managing the built heritage; the Belarus example, *International Journal of Heritage Studies* 3, 81-94.

Piikmann, V.J., 2008: *Lahemaa rannakülade lugusid,* MTÜ Eru Lahe Rannarahva Selts.

Pinder, D./A. Vallega, 2003: Coastal cultural heritage and sustainable development: introduction, *Journal of Cultural Heritage* 4, 3-4.

Printsmann, A./M. Kõivupuu/H. Palang, 2010: The dual character of landscape in the Lahemaa National Park, Estonia, in Z. Roca/P. Claval/J. Agnew (eds.), *Landscapes, Identities and Development,* Farnham, *in press*.

Printsmann, A./H. Palang, 2008: Estonia, in: G. Fairclough/P. Grau Møller (eds.), *Landscape as Heritage. The Management and Protection of Landscape in Europe, a Summary by the COST A27 Project "Landmarks",* Bern (Geographica Bernensia G79), 61-76.

Relph, E., 1976: *Place and Placelessness,* London (Research in Planning and Design).

Runte, A., 1979: *National Parks: The American Experience,* Lincoln.

Sandström, H.,1996: *Lahemaa randlased,* Tallinn.

Schama, S., 1995: *Landscape and Memory,* New York.

Schwartz, K.Z.S., 2006: "Masters in our native place": the politics of Latvian national parks on the road from communism to "Europe", *Political Geography* 25, 42-71.

Sepp, K./H. Palang/Ü. Mander/A. Kaasik, 1999: Prospects for nature and landscape protection in Estonia, *Landscape and Urban Planning* 46, 161-167.

Smith, A.D., 1995: The formation of national identity, in H. Harris (ed.), *Identity – Essays Based on Herbert Spencer Lectures Given at the University of Oxford,* Oxford, 129-154.

Smurr, R.W., 2008: Lahemaa: the paradox of the USSR's first national park, *Nationalities Papers* 36, 399-423.

Spence, M.D., 1999: *Dispossessing the Wilderness: Indian Removal and the Making of National Parks,* Oxford.

Tarvel, E., 1983: *Lahemaa ajalugu,* Tallinn.

Tress, G., 2007: Seasonality of second-home use in Denmark, in H. Palang/ H. Sooväli/A. Printsmann (eds.), *Seasonal Landscapes,* Berlin, 151-179.

Vallega, A., 2003: The coastal cultural heritage facing coastal management, *Journal of Cultural Heritage* 4, 5-24.

Widgren, M., 2004: Can landscapes be read? in H. Palang/H. Sooväli/M. Antrop/G. Setten (eds.), *European Rural Landscapes: Persistence and Change in a Globalising Environment,* Dordrecht, 455-465.

Wilshusen, P./S. Brechin/C. Fortwangler/P. West, 2002: Reinventing a square wheel: critique of a resurgent "Protection Paradigm" in International Biodiversity Conservation, *Society and Natural Resources* 15, 17-40.

WEBSITES

www.elks.ee = Eesti Looduskaitse Selts (Estonian Nature Conservation Society), Accessed 14 December, 2009.

www.estonica.org = Encyclopedia about Estonia (Accessed 3 August, 2009).

www.iucn.org = International Union for Conservation of Nature (Accessed 14 December, 2009).

www.stat.ee = Eesti Statistikaamet (Statistics Estonia) (Accessed 15 December, 2009).

4. A biography of the cultural landscape in the eastern Netherlands: theory and practice of acquisition and propagation of knowledge

Jelle Vervloet[1], Roy van Beek[2] & Luuk Keunen[3]

ABSTRACT

For many years, archaeologists and historical geographers have been aware of a significant 'lacuna in research on the eastern Netherlands. Currently, urbanization, industrialization, water management measures and nature development projects have a growing impact on the landscape of this region. The Eastern Netherlands Project has two main objectives.

The first is to construct a comprehensive image of the biography of the cultural landscape. Second, it is essential that knowledge be exchanged with policymakers, planners, landscape architects and the local population in order to ensure that the information gathered has an impact on the way cultural heritage values are dealt with in spatial planning. We focus principally on the experiences that have been gained with the implementation of the central concepts of the programme, namely biography of the landscape, interdisciplinarity and transdisciplinarity. Biography of the landscape is a concept that is open to many interpretations. This project emphasizes the dynamics of a landscape that has been affected by human interaction. Essentially this leads to a diachronic scientific description of the morphological aspects, namely objects, patterns and structures in the manmade environment. Interdisciplinarity is essential for research into the origins of the cultural landscape. Various kinds of expertise are needed to discover what developments caused the complex landscapes of the eastern Netherlands. Transdisciplinarity primarily concerns problems of a philosophical and communicative nature. What is the relationship between the knowledge of the 'experts' and the 'common people' and how does this affect future developments?

Finally, this paper presents the final results from the three leading concepts, showing the new understanding gained from this research.

KEYWORDS

Eastern Netherlands; archaeology, historical geography; landscape biography; cultural heritage, spatial planning

1. INTRODUCTION

For many years, archaeologists and historical geographers have been aware of a significant lacuna in research on the eastern Netherlands. The region is among the least well known areas of the Netherlands and often appears as a 'white space' on the research maps used in both disciplines. Currently, urbanization, industrialization, water management measures and nature development projects have a growing impact on the landscape. This trend is very likely to continue over the coming decades, implying that a scientific catch-up operation is needed in order to create a reliable basis for the proper management of cultural heritage values in the future. This is the main reason why an interdisciplinary project entitled 'A cultural biography of the coversand landscapes in the Salland and Achterhoek regions' was launched in 2004 by Wageningen University and the State Service for Archaeological Investigations in the Netherlands

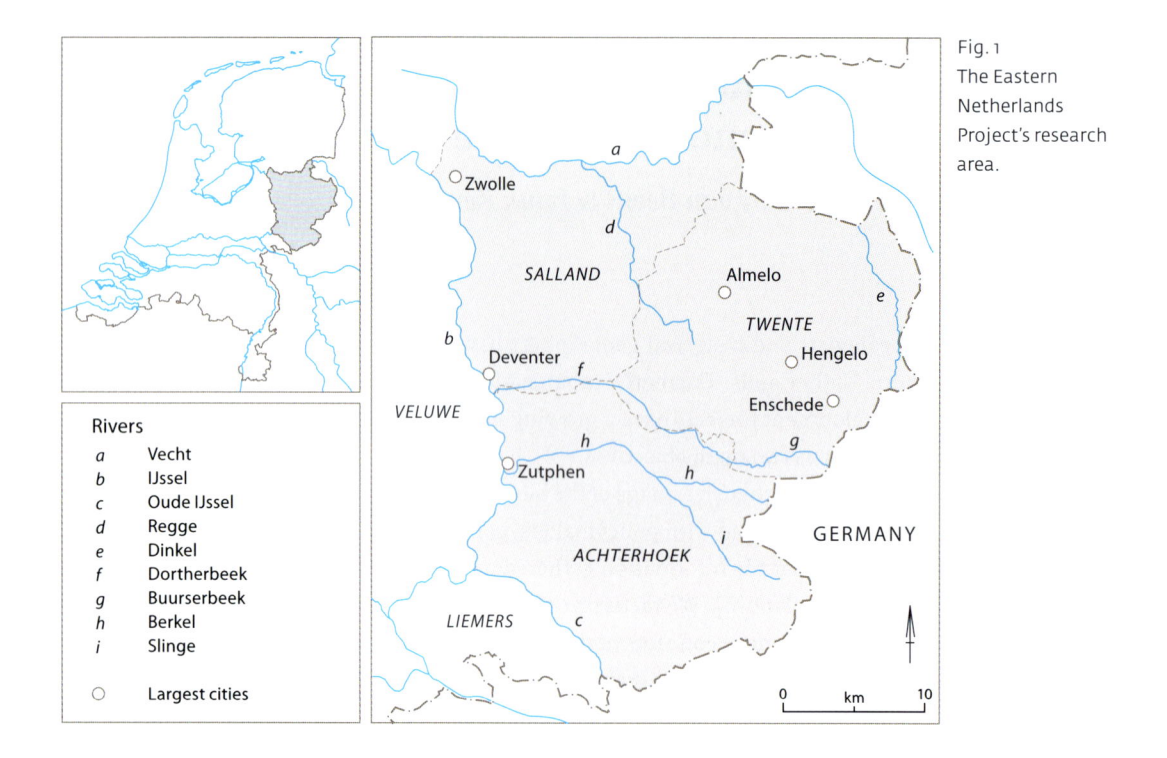

Fig. 1 The Eastern Netherlands Project's research area.

Rivers
a Vecht
b IJssel
c Oude IJssel
d Regge
e Dinkel
f Dortherbeek
g Buurserbeek
h Berkel
i Slinge

○ Largest cities

(nowadays the Cultural Heritage Agency) in Amersfoort (Van Beek/Keunen 2006a). This research is known for short as the Eastern Netherlands Project and forms one of the regional projects which are part of the 'Protecting and Developing the Dutch Archaeological-Historical Landscape' incentive programme by the Netherlands Organization of Scientific Research.

The research area in the present project is situated in the eastern part of the Netherlands (Fig. 1). It consists of a large part of the province of Overijssel and the eastern part of the province of Gelderland. The latter area is known as the Achterhoek region, while the investigated part of Overijssel is divided into the Salland (west) and Twente (east) regions. The research area is defined by the rivers Vecht (north), IJssel (west) and Oude IJssel (south) and by the border with Germany in the east. The landscape of the research area is characterized by a very high degree of diversity and variation. Large parts of the Salland and Achterhoek regions can be described as coversand landscapes. The same applies to smaller parts of the Twente region. The landscape in large parts of Twente is dominated by ice-pushed ridges, with a considerable variation in size, height, structure and orientation. In particular the origins and character of the eastern part of the Achterhoek are markedly different. This so-called 'Eastern Netherlands Plateau' has its origin in tectonic processes during the Mesozoic Period and was further shaped by glacial processes during the Saalian Period.

The Eastern Netherlands Project has two main objectives. The first is to construct a comprehensive biography of the cultural landscape by means of interdisciplinary research. Second it is essential that knowledge be exchanged with policymakers, planners, landscape architects and the local population to ensure that the information gathered has an impact on the way cultural heritage values are dealt with in spatial planning (external integration). This applied part of the project is also known as transdisciplinary or 'action' research.

In our contribution we focus principally on the experiences that have been gained from the implementation of the central concepts of the programme, namely biography of the landscape, interdisciplinarity and transdisciplinarity (Bloemers *et al.* 2001).

Biography of the landscape turns out to be a concept that is open to many interpretations. Which is the most viable alternative in our position and in what way do we apply this concept in heritage management?

Interdisciplinarity is essential for research into the origins of the cultural landscape. We are dealing with a complex history and reality. Various kinds of expertise are needed to discover what developments caused this complexity. Is it possible to work together and what are the results of this approach? Transdisciplinarity primarily concerns problems of a philosophical and communicative nature. What is the relationship between the knowledge of the 'experts' and the 'common people' and how does this affect future developments of the landscape?

2. THE USE OF THE BIOGRAPHICAL CONCEPT IN THE STUDY OF THE CULTURAL LANDSCAPE OF THE EASTERN NETHERLANDS

What is a landscape biography? Various interpretations are possible. Discussions between different participants in the 'Protecting and Developing the Dutch Archaeological-Historical Landscape' incentive programme led to different viewpoints:
- Landscape biography considered from the perspective of the present inhabitants and users or consumers of the landscape.
- Landscape biography considered from the perspective of the inhabitants and users of the landscape from a recent or distant past.
- Landscape biography considered as the narrative of the landscape, whereby all developments based on scientific research are depicted as completely as possible.

In the first approach the perception of the history of landscapes by 'ordinary' citizens, inhabitants and visitors is the central point of departure. Stories about individuals, families and events connected to certain objects and regions play an important role. This way of looking at the (pre)historical background of landscapes is not the result of scientific study of primary sources such as written records or archaeological finds. 'Truth' is mingled with a lot of sound and unsound fantasy. This interpretation of landscapes can be defined as *het waarachtige landschap* or the 'authentic landscape' (Jacobs 2002).

The second approach is the study of the perception of the environment by past generations. This can be a major method to understand spatial patterns and activities of humankind in prehistory and history. It is probable that decisions about place and structure of settlements, the arrangement of farmland and of infrastructural facilities were not only based on pure socio-economic considerations. Also important is the memory of the location of burial grounds of ancestors or even earlier people and of other mysterious and holy places. Old myths, folk tales and faiths, transferred from generation to generation, certainly played a role (Gerritsen 2003; *idem* 2004).

In the third approach the dynamics of the landscape, since people put it into use, are emphasized. Essentially this leads to a diachronic scientific description of morphological aspects, namely objects, patterns and structures of the human environment of a region. This interpretation of landscapes can be defined as *het ware landschap* or the 'real landscape' (Jacobs 2002).

In order to explain the different developments it is inevitable that the effects of a lot of determining physical and social factors in the course of time must also be analysed. In this way this approach is very comprehensive and demanding. In real terms it is not possible to study the whole range of disciplines or all available resources of information. Selection is necessary. Often this process is rather pragmatic and subjective. To some extent this approach looks like working on a traditional biography: 'an account of a person's life written by another' (Webster 1993). Factually this comparison of course falls short because the biography of a person inevitably ends because the subject of investigation is mortal. A landscape however is virtually immortal and as such, a landscape biography is a never-ending story.

We chose the third approach, 'the real landscape' as defined by Jacobs, chiefly because scientifically underpinned basic information about the diachronical development of the cultural landscape in the eastern Netherlands was not yet available. With this approach an important step towards academic knowledge development could be taken. Nevertheless, some attention was directed towards the second approach also as a result of the discovery of two archaeological sites related to pre-Christian worship.

3. THE USE OF INTERDISCIPLINARITY IN THE STUDY OF THE CULTURAL LANDSCAPE OF THE EASTERN NETHERLANDS

3.1 *Interdisciplinarity*

Our research revolves around archaeology and historical-geography. However, numerous other supporting disciplines are also included because the expansion of knowledge is also dependent on geomorphology, soil science, hydrology, palaeo-ecology, place-name etymology, genealogy and medieval historical research. The first four are important for obtaining insight in the alternating natural circumstances in which human habitation occurred, the last three aim to clarify the various social processes through time. The main aim of our project is to develop and apply research methods, especially with regard to the reconstruction of long-term processes in settlement patterns and landscape dynamics. Knowledge of these developments and insight into the origin of the modern-day cultural landscapes will prove to be of great value for the proper management of cultural heritage in the near future.

Landscape history requires interdisciplinary collaboration in order to gain balanced scientific results. Landscape is a complex entity which is established by many actors, powers and conditions. We stress the importance of collaboration, of hearing each other out and of paying attention to solving each other's problems because it is the only way interdisciplinarity can bear fruit. Interdisciplinarity strives to be more than the sum of its parts. Less desirable is multidisciplinarity, whereby various disciplines are applied, but there is a lack of communication (Vervloet/Renes/Spek 1996).

The project is positively characterized by interdisciplinarity. Two Ph.D. candidates, an archaeologist and a historical geographer, responsible for the biographical research, have co-operated where possible. As a result they have published numerous articles about several aspects of their work in progress. Both Ph.D. theses (Van Beek 2009; Keunen in prep.) refer to each other's study results as often as possible in order to create a continuous storyline in the spirit of our interpretation of the term 'biography' as a diachronic description of a cultural landscape.

3.2 Occupation

The Ph.D. candidates spent a lot of their time together studying the level of continuity of settlements from the early Middle Ages, a period in which the fields of knowledge of archaeology and historical geography overlap each other. This research is known as the 'farmstead-test'. Situated on the flanks and edges of coversand ridges and river dunes, old single farmsteads with a group-like distribution form a defining element in the present landscape of the eastern Netherlands (Uhlig/Linau 1972). Until recently there was only very little scientific knowledge about the origins of this typical habitation pattern. Some studies showed that construction parts from the oldest farm buildings that still exist today date from the fifteenth or sixteenth century at the earliest (Van der Waard 1997; Enderman 2002). Archaeological research of medieval settlements in the countryside shows, however, that the majority of excavated house plans and other buildings date from the twelfth or thirteenth century at the latest. This raises the question whether the late medieval 'gap' between the two can be bridged so that a continuous habitation history is formed. It will be argued that this matter can only be solved by interdisciplinary research, especially by incorporating detailed historical geographical research into the picture.

Until the present day, with virtually no exceptions, excavated sites were central to the medieval archaeology of the eastern Netherlands. During or after archaeological research occasional attempts were made to 'identify' excavated medieval structures with the help of historical sources such as archives or manuscript maps (Van Beek/Keunen 2006b). In some cases such a link is established quite easily when archaeologically excavated features are situated close to still existing farmsteads. These obvious links are quite rare and in many cases it proves to be quite difficult to connect archaeological sites with still existing farmsteads or farmsteads that are known to have existed from historical sources. Therefore, within the Eastern Netherlands Project the possibilities of a different, reverse way of research were explored (Van Beek/ Groenewoudt/Keunen 2007). In this pilot study historical geographical data were given a central place and they defined both the problem and research method. The research was based on the results of Keunen's historical geographical study of an area directly east of the city of Deventer which offered detailed information on the development of the cultural landscape since the Middle Ages (Keunen in prep.). One of the most important conclusions is that several 'time layers' can be discerned in the foundation dates of farmsteads, which makes it possible to reconstruct a phased landscape development.

Making use of various criteria (including the ownership situation, earliest appearance in historical sources and geophysical setting), it proved possible to make educated guesses as to the age of specific farmsteads in Keunen's research area. It was decided to test these hypotheses by small-scale archaeological research on thirteen farmstead locations in the vicinity of Deventer. At each location one or two small test pits with a surface of six square metres were dug in strategic places, in the direct vicinity of the present-day farm buildings and on adjacent lower parts of the coversand ridges. Assuming that farmsteads have not shifted over very large distances since the Late Medieval Period and the earliest reclamations will have taken place on adjacent parts of the higher sandy soils, these locations are the most likely ones to yield archaeological material of value to date the oldest occupation phases (Fig. 2). When possible, field surveys were also carried out on arable fields in the direct vicinity of the research locations. Taking into account the fact that very small amounts of pottery and other finds might have been brought to the site with manure and sods from other locations, the density, character and stratigraphical position of the finds were used as the most important criteria in determining whether it concerned settlement refuse from a local farmstead.

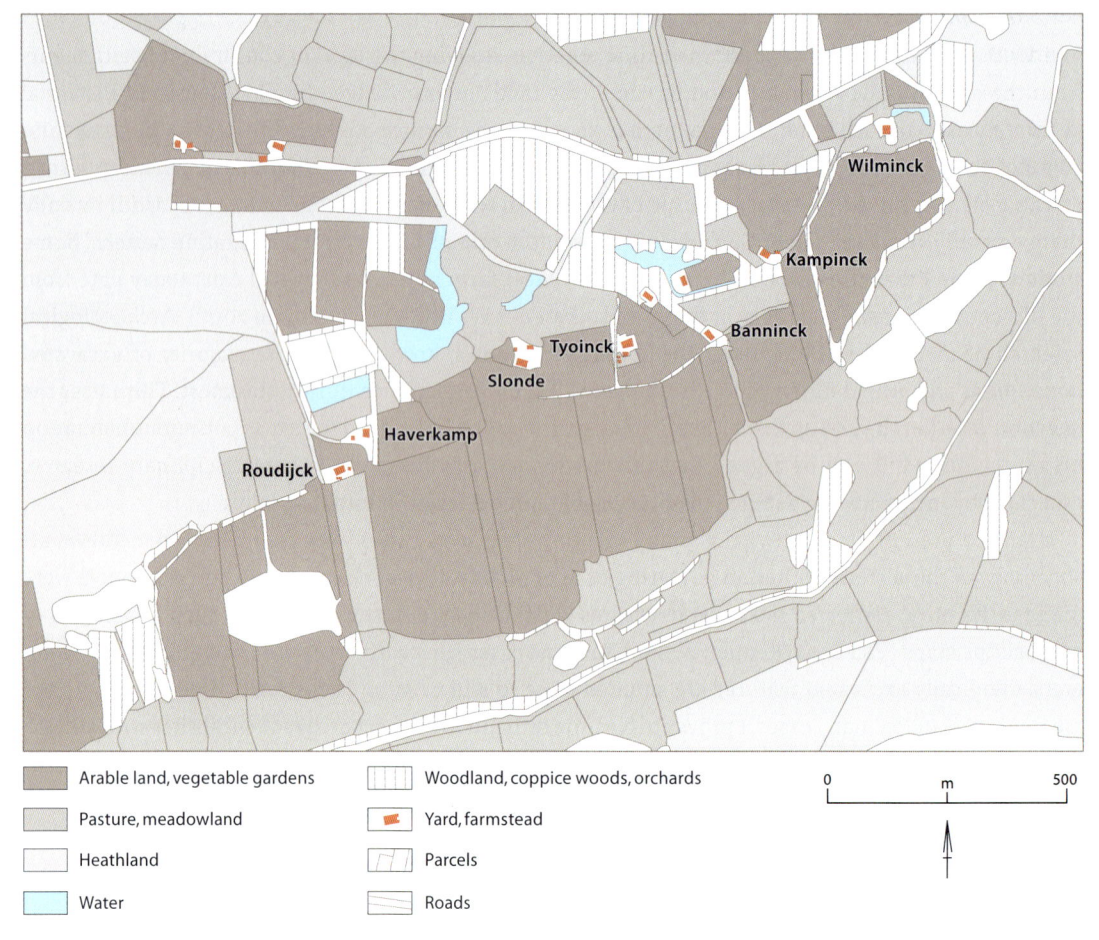

Fig. 2
Series of farmsteads situated along the edges of an elongated coversand ridge southeast of the city of Deventer (Essener Enk). The shape of the coversand ridge can be clearly recognized in the location of arable fields. Medieval settlement remains are most likely to be present in the direct vicinity of the farmsteads and adjacent parts of the arable fields.

In the next stage of research, the established archaeological dating of the earliest recognizable occupation phases were compared with the historical geographical expectation model. At most locations, sufficient material could be collected for a first archaeological indication of the foundation date of the farmstead. Dates show that occupation was mainly between the ninth or tenth and thirteenth centuries. A point of interest concerning the recognition of 'time layers' within farmsteads is that none of them precede the ninth century. This observation correlates with the results of earlier archaeological research in the eastern Netherlands, which has shown that from the eighth and ninth centuries onwards settlements 'shifted' to the lower parts of the landscape. They also became increasingly fixed to one place. Most of the farmsteads that were investigated seem to have been founded in a slightly later phase, however, between the tenth and thirteenth centuries. Obviously, it has to be noted that different farmsteads might have different occupation histories or 'biographies'. This applies for instance to the moment of foundation and (often related to that) the specific location that was chosen. Some farmsteads were abandoned at a certain point, while others remain inhabited until the present day. The new interdisciplinary research method has proved useful in reconstructing these 'farmstead biographies' in greater detail than before. The same applies to the reconstruction of the origins of habitation patterns and the medieval cultural landscapes of the eastern Netherlands in general.

Because of this, a better insight was gained into the location of the farmsteads at various moments in time. As it turned out, the farmsteads showed continuity by a gradually shifting position in the landscape. From this, patterns can be distinguished that offer pointers for predicting models (Van Beek/Groenewoudt/Keunen 2007).

3.3 Vegetation, hydrology and physical geography

Another interdisciplinary research theme was to put together the biography of the development of the vegetation in the landscape in order to understand the changing ecological environments in which people lived in this part of the Netherlands. To tackle this question, a new palynological research was set up making use of samples taken from wells and pools from excavated settlements in the western part of the eastern Netherlands (Groenewoudt/Van Haaster/Van Beek/Brinkkemper 2008). The main goal was to reconstruct developments on the higher sandy soils, as well as the adjacent lower parts of the landscape in the direct vicinity of settlements. There is one disadvantage involved with these samples. They do not offer a diachronological image of the vegetation development, but for a snapshot of vegetation structure at a certain point in time in each settlement. This problem has been solved by selecting tens of samples from different sites that altogether cover the time span between the Late Bronze Age and Late Medieval Period (1100 BC-1500 AD). Based on the analysis, large-scale deforestation of the higher parts of the landscape could be demonstrated, showing how it accelerated during the Iron Age and Roman Period. This deforestation can be easily read from the sharp decrease of oak pollen and the increase of heather and grasses. It is almost certain that this trend has its origins in the later phases of the Neolithic Period, even though appropriate sample locations are not yet available. The present data indicate that during the Neolithic settlements lay like small islands in the closed deciduous forest. Between the Iron Age and Roman Period the situation was completely reversed (Fig. 3). The landscape in the immediate vicinity of settlements changed into a semi-open park landscape, with only some small remnants of forest spread out here and there. There are no indications for a substantial forest regeneration during the Early Medieval Period, and from the Late Medieval Period onwards human influence on vegetation and landscape in general only increased.

Various studies have undertaken to reconstruct hydrological developments, in particular tracing disappeared raised bogs since the Medieval Period (De Rooi 2006). Expansion of the areas covered with

Fig. 3
Schematic image of the reversal of landscape structure between the Middle Neolithic Period (left) and the Roman Period. In the former, settlements (light) lay like islands in closed deciduous forests (dark). In the latter, woodland remnants formed small islands in open and semi-open landscapes.

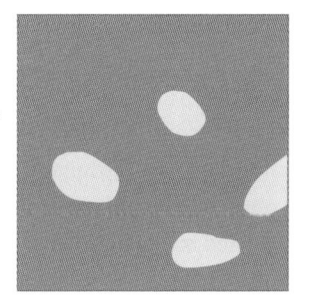

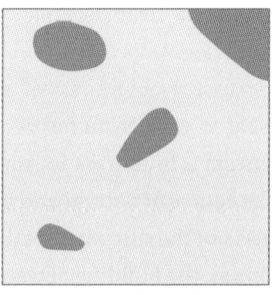

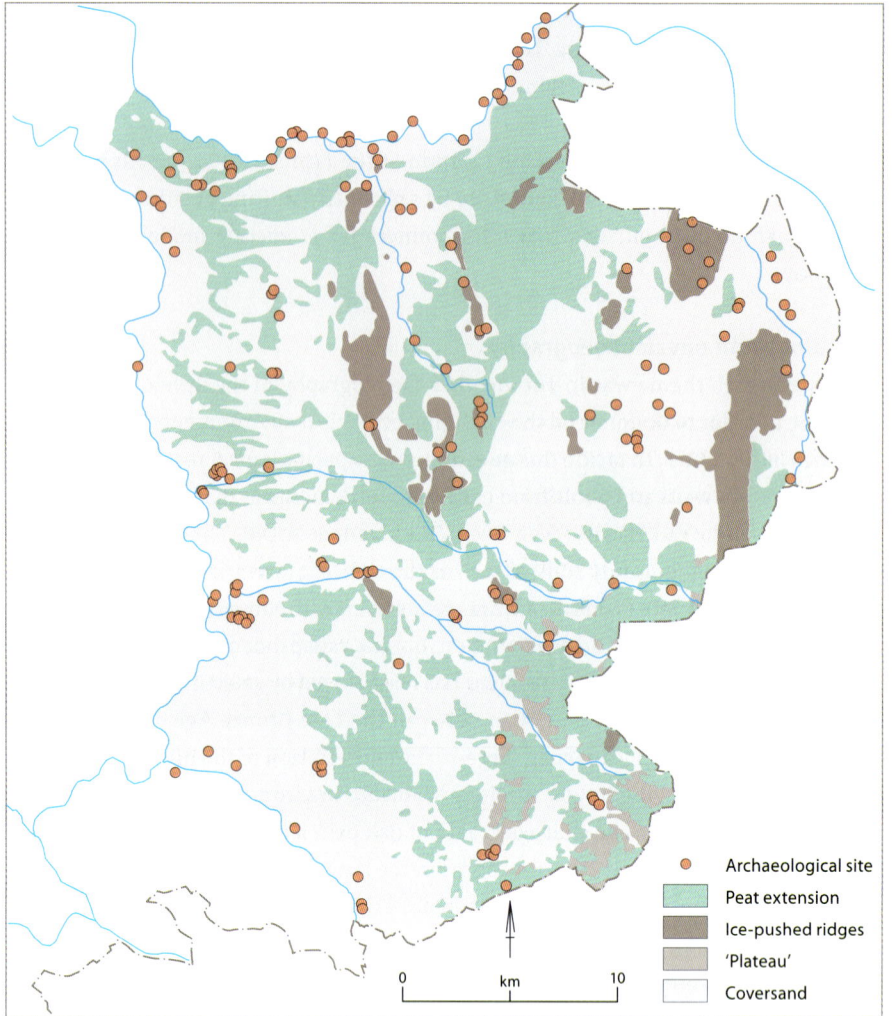

Fig. 4 Reconstructed maximal peat extension in the eastern Netherlands and archaeological sites dating from the Roman and Early Medieval Periods *(peat extension partly based on De Rooi 2006; Vos in prep.)*.

peat was one of the most important landscape processes during the Holocene, especially from the Atlantic Period onwards. It has been demonstrated by interdisciplinary research based on a combined study of soil information, ancient topographical maps and old historical documents, that nearly 30% of the Achterhoek region was at one point covered with peat, implying that the importance of peat extension as a factor within landscape and habitation history has been severely underestimated in past research. The maximal peat extension in the eastern Netherlands, which was reached during the Medieval Period, displays a clear negative correlation with settlement patterns between late prehistory and the Middle Ages (Fig. 4).

Next to vegetation history and the reconstruction of peat extension, the development of the drainage system is important for understanding past settlement, land use and infrastructure. A detailed study of the course of natural and dug-out streams supported our need for this knowledge (De Rooi 2005). Large parts of the discharge pattern turned out to have been radically influenced by people via, among other things, the building of water mills and enhancing the discharge.

To get a better understanding of the physical factors determining the establishment of human settlement, a physical-geographical map of the eastern Netherlands was produced by the research institute Alterra. It is a combined map in the fields of soil science and geomorphology (Maas/Makaske 2007). This map offers a means for the analysis of habitation and land use from prehistory until more recent times, connecting important physical factors such as soil fertility, water balance, land degradation and geographic relief. It also offers promising possibilities for the implementation in predicting modelling for archaeological heritage management, which is important in the context of transdisciplinary application.

3.4 Place and fieldnames

No less important for our research is the study of place and fieldnames. The meaning of names offer indications when determining the age of the reclamation, the way society was structured, the natural condition of the terrain and land use (Ter Laak 2005). In particular, Late Prehistoric, Early Medieval and Late Medieval patterns of habitation, discovered by archaeological detection, are supported by place name evidence.

4. THE USE OF TRANSDISCIPLINARITY IN THE STUDY OF THE CULTURAL LANDSCAPE OF THE EASTERN NETHERLANDS

4.1 Transdisciplinarity

Transdisciplinarity concerns the position of cultural history and heritage management in a modern, rapidly changing society (Vervloet 2008). Various parties are involved, including experts, governments, non-governmental organizations (NGOs) and the inhabitants living in the cities and the surrounding countryside. All these different actors have a vision about what is valuable and what should be preserved for the future. Their aspiration is to preserve, as expressed by Jacobs, *het juiste landschap* ('the correct landscape') (Jacobs 2002).

The main issue is which of these actors eventually decide on the correctness of the choice of our heritage. Until the recent past, this used to be absolutely clear. Decision was in the hands of the government, advised by expert archaeologists, structural engineers and historical geographers. With the help of their scientific expertise, policy documents were written deciding which areas, terrains, buildings and elements were designated for preservation. In this way, science almost automatically obtained primacy over policy-making. The scientists laid down the cultural-historical significance from above. This fitted the idea of a socially engineerable society that was popular at that time.

The values that the scientists attached to areas and objects, however, were not always recognized or acknowledged as such by the population itself (Van den Berg/Casimir 2002). Many inhabitants, especially farmers, felt that their existence was threatened by these claims. In their opinion, to 'freeze' the structure and the content of landscapes would result in stagnation and stagnation automatically leads to decline. They not only feared for their income, but were also suspicious about the state subsidies offered to overcome the deadlock they were in since subsidies imply financial dependency and a restriction of free enterprise. People would rather not be stigmatized as park keepers (Denig 1975).

Dissent over these policies was voiced as early as in the 1970s. Wooded banks that had been appointed for preservation were cut down almost directly by the involved farmers, causing considerable consternation among civil servants and scientists. The 'ignorant people' revolted. In reality, government and science were largely out of touch with the desires of the local inhabitants (Vervloet 2008).

Independent of our judgement of the motives and principles of those who developed the policies and carried out the inventories, it makes sense to ascertain how the population itself experiences the cultural history of the landscape and how this can be implemented in future policy concerning the landscape (Vervloet 2007). When discussing questions concerning what ignites the population's interest, we must consider the standards upon which people base their choices and their motives. Furthermore, we need to ask which objects they prefer and whether their preferences correspond with the ideas and plans of scientists, the governments and NGOs (Coeterier 2000; Van Assche 2004; Koedoot 2004; Duineveld 2006).

This process of change is not new. It started with the introduction of the term *inspraak* (participation). This was followed by the establishment of *draagvlak* (public support), and now people are busily engaged in *participatieve planvorming* (participative planning), whereby the population is directly involved in reflecting upon future town and country planning (De Poel *et al.* 2000; Ministerie van LNV 2000). A gradual shift from top-down to bottom-up can be discerned in planning, as shown by the way the policy on town and country planning is structured in the Netherlands. These plans used to be drawn up by the central government, but nowadays this administrative rank is responsible only for setting general planning guidelines. The lower administrative ranks, like municipalities, are closer to the public and therefore formulate concrete planning proposals (Woltjer 1992; Hendrikx 1999).

We notice a similar shift at successive conferences of historical geographers. The number of contributions on the assessment systems based on a positivistic scientific perspective is on the decrease in favour of contributions with a more postmodern slant and which first consider the manner in which the inhabitants experience the historical aspects of the landscape. In this framework, other disciplines and approaches, such as cultural anthropology, steadily play a more important role (Schavemaker 2008).

Correct assessment is no longer only a matter of a technically intrinsic evaluation based on flawlessness, rarity or distinctive characteristics by experts. Instead, it is also a matter of, for instance, which parts of the landscape are considered by the inhabitants or land-users as having historical significance and thus warrant being preserved in some form or another (Jacobs 2002; Duineveld 2006). In addition, these days many people want to preserve an object or an area because there is a nice anecdote attached to it. For them, an object or an area only counts if it is supplied with a historical narrative that appeals to their imagination (Kolen 2005). The conclusion is that our vision about what is a 'correct landscape' has shifted considerably. The emancipation of the 'public' has resulted in a plurality of 'correct landscapes'.

In order to fathom the consequences of this paradigm-change for our cultural history and for the preservation of monuments and landscapes, we addressed three related themes that might help us to gain a clearer understanding of the way in which people experience their history and heritage:
- the historical backgrounds of mutual knowledge development between scientists and local experts on history and archaeology,
- the role of regional and local historical associations in striving for landscape preservation in the east of the Netherlands.
- the way various actor-groups perceive the cultural history of the landscape.

4.2 Scientists and local experts

The relationship between scientists and local experts has varied in the course of time. It is a time-honoured tradition to suggest that there is a large gap between science and 'public' interests, more precisely the historically interested public. The well-known 'ivory tower' is often used to symbolize this. This problem is elaborated on the basis of an historiography of landscape research in the eastern part of the Netherlands. Our main question is, in what way has the position of scientific researchers changed throughout time? To tackle this problem we distinguish connections on the input side, namely the determination of research objectives and the gathering of data and connections on the output side, namely the adoption of results and theoretical frameworks of scientific research by the public.

Until the early 1930s, no detailed research was carried out at Dutch universities on the historical development of the rural landscape of the eastern part of the Netherlands. Only the historian Bouwmeester (Bouwmeester 1911) paid some attention to this issue during the first decade of the twentieth century.

The next step was taken in the thirties by Miss Heeringa, a Ph.D. student of Professor Van Vuuren, a human geographer at the University of Utrecht. Heeringa's research focused on the landscape of the Achterhoek, one of the regions in the eastern Netherlands (Heeringa 1934). The result of her study was a typology of landscapes, with a strong emphasis on the 'ancient' mid-nineteenth century and earlier landscapes in contrast with the 'modern' landscapes that had originated in connection with recent developments in agriculture.

Another part of her research is much more important for our issue. It was one of the first studies on the relationship between the *scholtenboeren* (extensive feudal farmers) living in the neighbourhood of Winterswijk and the development of the landscape they dwelled and worked in. Thanks to Van Vuuren's support, Heeringa was assisted by a student from the Agricultural University of Wageningen (now Wageningen University), a descendant of a dynasty of *scholtenboeren*, who introduced her to numerous *scholten* families. In this way she explicitly tried to get in contact with the local inhabitants and she intensively used the local oral and written tradition of the farmers. Her dissertation is still one of the pillars of research about *scholtenboeren* and the scenic landscapes they produced. It largely determines the socio-historical and touristic identity of the area as well as the local-historical discourse. In this way we are able to point out a link between Heeringa's study and the public on both the input and the output side (Keunen 2007).

Another of Van Vuuren's students at this time was Keuning. In 1936 he published an elaborate article on landscape and village types on the Pleistocene sandy soils east of the IJssel river (Keuning 1936). Significant to this model formation was the theoretical framework that had been developed earlier by the German geographer Martiny (Martiny 1926). The systematic study of the terminology of settlement types he developed is still regularly used in local historical publications and policy reports. However, they are no longer common in science, although similar terms are still used in German literature. In contrast with Heeringa, the relationship between Keuning, the public and the government lies mostly on the output side of research.

A similar relationship between scientific output and the public can be found in the work of Slicher van Bath, a descendant of a family living in the eastern Netherlands. His dissertation *'Mensch en Land in de middeleeuwen'* ('Man and Land in the Middle Ages 'examines settlements in the eastern Netherlands (Slicher van Bath 1944). Just like Keuning, he based his theoretical framework largely on the work of

Martiny, who could therefore be considered to be the founder of the oldest scientific vision of the landscape history in the eastern Netherlands. Slicher van Bath adopted interdisciplinary methods, combining place names and archaeological finds with historical data to construct a regional colonization model of the eastern Netherlands before 1500 AD.

After 1950, scientific research on the eastern Netherlands landscape experienced a decline. For decades, regional and local historians were the only ones to decide which subjects were studied. Scientists from abroad ignored the area. Scientists and people interested in local history and landscape became alienated from each other. At the same time, the debate within historical geography increasingly inclined towards a static approach to the landscape. The landscape of the early nineteenth century was considered to reflect the ancient situation from the Middle Ages and before.

At the end of the 1960s we see a cautious turn in the scientific world because of the increase in archaeological research into settlements in the east of the Netherlands by the well-known archaeologists Van Es and Verlinde, among others. As a result of this work, new regional habitation models were constructed (Van Es/Verlinde 1977). These models, however, hardly ever reached the local literature. Nonetheless, the establishment of local departments of the *Archeologische Werkgemeenschap Nederland* (the Dutch association for Amateur Archaeologists), for instance in the region of Deventer in 1968, heralded a turn for the better in the relationship between scientific archaeology and the local experts (Van Beek 2009).

In this period the only scientific input in the local historical geographical debate came through the contributions of a few scientists, such as Palmboom (Palmboom 1983), Vervloet (Vervloet 1983), Van de Westeringh (Van de Westeringh 1972; *idem* 1979) and Van den Brandt (Van den Brandt *et al.* 1981), to local monographs. Apart from that, scientific historical geography hardly ever focused on the eastern part of the Netherlands.

Unconsciously, however, archaeologists fulfilled a second role in the last decades of the twentieth century. Their settlement research opened the eyes of historical geographers to the dynamics in settlement development. This revolution led to the notion that the landscape was almost always on the move. The findings of agricultural historians on the dynamics of agriculture only enhanced this notion. Historical geographers became convinced that research on a local scale was absolutely vital as this type of research could reveal the differences underlying the diversity.

4.3 Regional and local historical associations

This scientific emancipation at a local research level was parallel to a similar trend in the amateur world. Besides the regional associations which had been established in the late nineteenth and early twentieth century as a result of the emancipation of regional awareness, local associations were now also being formed. In the eastern part of the Netherlands their numbers increased rapidly from the late 1970s onwards, influenced by the increasing interest of the common people in the history of their region.

The role of regional and local historical associations in the transfer of knowledge and emancipation of awareness has recently been recognized as an undisputed fact. For quite some time it was claimed that the natural backing for the preservation of cultural historical phenomena in the landscape should also be sought in the circles of the local and regional historical associations (Rooijakkers 2000). In order to substantiate this claim, research was carried out in the eastern part of the Netherlands to systematically take a closer look at associations that have been active on a local and regional level for a considerable time (Groot 2008).

The results were remarkable. In only a very limited number of cases did the associations actually react to plans proposed by the government. Local and regional history clubs hardly functioned (if at all) as platforms for protests against interventions in the landscapes. In general, they adopted a neutral attitude. Within this type of association, the unity of the village community or the region they claim to represent is the first matter of importance. Interventions in the landscape, for example through house-building or the construction of roads, could all too easily grow into a subject that causes discord between the members. Local politicians from several parties are frequently also members of the historical associations. Therefore, they rather look into the past than into the future. The associations will only contact the town council if it is expected that virtually all members will see eye to eye on a certain matter. This explains a protest against the felling of a *kroezeboom* (an age-old tree with a highly symbolic value), where village meetings are still held on special occasions.

What the local clubs are interested in is the history of the individual farms. This is tied up with the history of generations of farmers, whose descendants often still live in the village. Genealogical research is central at a local level. As people search for their roots, they come across farmsteads that carry their family name. These farmsteads are the point of departure for research. For local historians they are the stepping stones to their family trees.

The rural landscape outside the farmsteads receives a lot less attention. For historical geographers it is also interesting to investigate how much land was owned, where this land was situated and which fieldnames were given to the various parcels, as this helps them form an image of historical rural land use. However, the selected local researchers are hardly interested in that particular knowledge. Most of them have no understanding of the cohesion between farmsteads and the surrounding landscape.

4.4 *Actor groups*

The experience of cultural history is connected to education, income and background. In order to shed more light on the way people perceive the cultural history in the landscape, we also studied how different actor groups experience the cultural history in the landscape.

We view actors as representatives of groups that are involved with the cultural historical aspects of the landscape. In a monograph, two students looked at the relationship between the experience of the landscape in the east of the Netherlands and the cultural-historical phenomena in it (De Keijzer/Van der Wal 2006). Experience is understood as information processing leading to the attribution of meaning. This process is all about the attribution of the correct meaning to the incoming information so that a proper behavioural reaction can be selected. This study dealt with the perception and valuation of the landscape by various groups in society. The experience of cultural history and landscapes stems from deeper motives and incentives. Next to knowledge, income and similar factors, experience also stems from emotional involvement, the susceptibility to aesthetics, the functional fulfilment of needs and the degree of economic dependence. By making a distinction based on these motives and incentives, a typology of various social groups is presented. Founded on interviews, the monograph presents a view of the landscape by seven different groups, divided into thirteen subgroups. For practical reasons, in this contribution we consider a select sample of salient results.

An interesting group of actors are the policymakers and the people who implement the policies. Each of these actors has a different focus on their subject. The policymakers ask themselves which phenomena are of cultural-historical value and which can be fitted into the policy. For the people who implement the policies, cultural historical information of landscapes is only valuable when it is in line with the intended policy.

Experts on the other hand are only focused on the content. This actor group experiences the landscape primarily out of the desire to find out more about the origins of the landscape through research. Moreover, inside this group we can distinguish two subgroups, the academic scientists and the applied researchers. The objective of the academic is to amass knowledge for the sake of knowledge. This actor is not exactly interested in *de facto* preservation of cultural historical elements; instead, publishing is his or her main objective. The objective of the applied researcher is to conduct brief studies and pass the results on to, for instance, policymakers. From this perspective, the Ph.D. students involved in our research project played an active role. In order to reach their goal they acted both as academics and as applied researchers, which was not always easy.

Another way of handling the history of landscape is by consuming. People involved in this activity are mainly interested in 'beautiful stories', whether or not these are offered by travel guides. Their main goal, however, is peacefulness and quietness. No matter how rich the landscape is in cultural history, if it lacks tourist infrastructure like hotels and campsites, the tourists will not turn up. In our research two subgroups in this category are distinguished, namely the persons interested in the past, visiting an area in order to learn something about its history. The second subgroup seeks entertainment in the landscape without really caring about the environment. This latter group is in it for the activity, not for the area where the activity takes place.

Other people have a vision of cultural history based on a purely economic perspective. Two subgroups can be distinguished here. The first group consists of people who profit from the richness of cultural history without offering anything in return. Examples of these people are hotelkeepers, property developers and estate agents, who extol the virtues of their goods based on the presence of cultural-historical remnants, but leave the preservation thereof to the public domain. A specific group are people who use their metal detectors to search for valuable finds in the soil in order to sell these to antique dealers or directly to collectors of antiquities.

5. CONCLUSIONS

Until now, knowledge of the long-term development of settlement patterns in the eastern Netherlands was very limited. Even though quite a large quantity of archaeological and historical data was available, general overviews were almost completely lacking. The Eastern Netherlands Project has offered a scientific framework as well as a first diachronological and interdisciplinary view of the most important patterns and developments. Furthermore, insight was gained in the local and regional variety of the countryside of this part of the Netherlands. Obviously, these data are crucial in several respects. Without a wider framework it is almost impossible to assess the importance of a specific archaeological or historical site, let alone a cultural landscape in general. The location of archaeological sites can be predicted in more detail than before as well.

The insight that the countryside has a clear historical stratification that can be reconstructed in detail by interdisciplinary research could play a vital role in the radical changes in function taking place in the eastern Netherlands. The new scientific insights can be used in the selection of historically important objects and structures and be a source of inspiration for the landscape planning of the future countryside.

Considering the viewpoint of the ever-continuing change our surroundings go through, we can ask ourselves if we are actually doing the right thing in continuing to put preservation (or preservation through development, which is essentially the same thing) first. What heritage remains has hardly ever been preserved intentionally in the last millennia, but is mostly based on coincidence. Indeed, heritage management also has to contend ever-changing policy and uncertain processes.

It seems to be important to be aware of such matters beforehand. This will support the credibility of our 'thinking' and 'acting' to the outside world and also gives us an idea of where we stand as scientists.

The themes 'protecting and developing' as highlighted in the title of the incentive programme at least force us to reflect on this matter. This realization has to have great consequences for the transdisciplinary sides of our project.

The transdisciplinary approach shows that groups and individuals vary greatly as regards their commitment, experiences and preferences. The shift from expert knowledge to public support and participative planning is a clear development. Archaeologists and historical geographers active in assessment procedures and the production of applied landscape studies should be aware of this fact.

A relationship between science and the historically interested public has in fact existed throughout the entire twentieth century, even if it was not particularly widespread in the mid-twentieth century. In some cases the link was more on the input side, such as the involvement of the public with the collection of data, while in other cases the output of the research was received so well that it remained common knowledge for those interested as well as policy-makers for decades and it even turned out to be difficult to replace with new theories.

If one were to go into the country and ask people what they would like to happen to their cultural heritage, the answers would be far from clear-cut. In the framework of our programme this was lucidly clarified again by Duineveld's dissertation (Duineveld 2006) on the connection between the existence of several 'cultural histories' in a specific area, which is in turn dependent on the social group one consults.

Participative planning could be a solution, where planning is determined from the bottom. The cultural-historical diversity is bound to increase because of bottom-up planning because every group or individual is able to design the cultural-historical environment that makes him or her feel at home. Consequently, in principle an unlimited amount of responsible answers is possible.

Cultural history comes up with each intervention. A nicely comprehensive origins story, a biography of the development of the landscape, will be able to offer help and inspiration.

NOTES

1. Wageningen University, Wageningen, the Netherlands.
2. Cultural Heritage Agency, Amersfoort, the Netherlands.
3. RAAP Archaeological Consultancy, Zutphen, the Netherlands.

REFERENCES

Assche, K.A.M. Van, 2004: *Signs in time. An interpretive account of urban planning and design, the people and their histories*, Wageningen (Ph.D. thesis Wageningen University).

Beek, R. van, 2009: *Reliëf in Tijd en Ruimte. Interdisciplinair onderzoek naar mens en landschap in Oost-Nederland tussen vroege prehistorie en middeleeuwen*, Wageningen (Ph.D. thesis Wageningen University).

Beek, R. van/ B. Groenewoudt/L.J. Keunen, 2007: *Archeologisch veldonderzoek van boerenerven in de omgeving van Colmschate (Overijssel). De toetsing van een historisch-geografisch verwachtingsmodel*, Amersfoort (Beknopte Rapportage Archeologische Monumentenzorg 5).

Beek, R. van/L.J. Keunen, 2006a: A cultural biography of the coversand landscapes in the Salland and Achterhoek Regions. The aims and methods of the Eastern Netherlands Project, Berichten van de Rijksdienst voor het Oudheidkundig Bodemonderzoek 46, 355-375.

Beek, R. van/L.J. Keunen, 2006b: Van huisplattegronden en historische erven, *Overijssels Erfgoed. Archeologische en Bouwhistorische Kroniek 2005*, 83-111.

Berg, A. E. van den/T. Casimir, 2002: *Landschapsbeleving en Cultuurhistorie; een theoretische en empirische verkenning van de invloed van cultuurhistorie op de beleving van het landschap*, Wageningen.

Bloemers, J.H.F. /R. During/J.N.H. Elerie/H.A. Groenendijk/M. Hidding/J. Kolen/Th. Spek/M.-H. Wijnen, 2001: *Bodemarchief in Behoud en Ontwikkeling. De conceptuele grondslagen*, Den Haag.

Bouwmeester, W.L., 1911: *De ontwikkeling van Nederlands landschappen. Bijdrage tot de geschiedenis van Nederlandsche beschavingstoestanden, zooals die onder wisselwerking van bodem en mensch zijn ontstaan*, 's-Gravenhage.

Brandt, S.T.H. van den/M. van den Bosch/D. Hamhuis/W. van de Westeringh, 1981: *Winterswijk, Landschap en vegetatie. Deel 1. Ontstaan en opbouw van het landschap*, Hoogwoud (Wetenschappelijke mededelingen K.N.N.V. 147 – juni 1981).

Coeterier, J.F., 2000: *Hoe beleven wij onze omgeving? Resultaten van 25 jaar omgevingspsychologisch onderzoek in stad en landschap*, Wageningen.

Denig, E., 1975: *Boer of parkwachter. Enige gedachten over nationale landschapsparken*, Den Haag (Agrarische Reeks, Ministerie van Landbouw en Visserij).

Duineveld, M., 2006: *Van oude dingen, de mensen die voorbij gaan. Over de voorwaarden meer recht te kunnen doen aan de door de burgers gewaardeerde cultuurhistories*, Delft (Ph.D. thesis Wageningen University).

Enderman, M., 2002: De ontwikkeling van de boerderij in de Achterhoek, in P.J. van Cruyningen/A. Punt/J.A. van Zuilen (eds.), *Historisch boerderijonderzoek 2002*, Stichting Historisch Boerderij-Onderzoek Jaarverslag 2001, Arnhem, 39-45.

Es, W.A. van/A.D. Verlinde, 1977: Overijssel in Roman and Early-Medieval Times, *Berichten van de Rijksdienst voor het Oudheidkundig Bodemonderzoek* 27, 7-89.

Gerritsen, F., 2003: *Local Identities. Landscape and community in the late prehistoric Meuse-Demer-Scheldt region*, Amsterdam (Amsterdam Archaeological Studies 6).

Gerritsen, F., 2004: Leven te midden van het verleden. Veranderende ruimtelijke ordeningen in het prehistorische landschap, in R.M. van Heeringen/E.H.P. Cordfunke/M. Ilsink/H. Sarfatij (eds.), *Geordend Landschap. 3000 jaar ruimtelijke ordening in Nederland*, Hilversum, 13-30.

Groenewoudt, B.J/H. van Haaster/R. van Beek/O. Brinkkemper, 2008: Towards a reverse image. Botanical research into the landscape history of the eastern Netherlands (BC 1100 – AD 1500), *Landscape History* 29, 17-33.

Groot, M., 2008: *Het verleden telt in het heden. Verkenning naar heemkundekringen en hun rol in de ruimtelijke ordening in de Achterhoek*, Wageningen (Thesis Wageningen University).

Heeringa, T., 1934: *De Graafschap; een bijdrage tot de kennis van het cultuurlandschap en van het scholtenprobleem*, Zutphen (Ph.D. thesis Rijksuniversiteit Utrecht).

Hendrikx, J.A., 1999: *Cultuurhistorie van stad en land. Waardering en behoud,* Utrecht.

Jacobs, M.H., 2002: *Landschap 3. Het ware, juiste en waarachtige landschap. Expertisecentrum Landschapsbeleving,* Wageningen.

Keijzer, M. de/D. van der Wal, 2006: *Ik zie, ik zie, wat jij niet ziet! Onderzoek naar de beleving van cultuurhistorie in Salland en de Achterhoek door verschillende actorgroepen*, Wageningen (Thesis Wageningen University).

Keunen, L.J., in prep.: *Eeuwig grensland. Een historisch-geografische studie van Salland en de Achterhoek*, Wageningen (Ph.D. thesis Wageningen University).

Keunen, L.J., 2007: Tetje Stark-Heeringa (1905 -1995). Leven en werk van een vergeten sociaal-geografe, *Historisch-geografisch tijdschrift* 25,120-127.

Keuning, H.J., 1936: Nederzettingsvormen in diluviaal Nederland ten noorden en ten oosten van de IJssel, *Tijdschrift voor Economische Geographie* 193, 49-55; 73-88; 97-115.

Koedoot, M., 2004: *Het Neolithicum van nu. Over de alledaagse betekenis van archeologisch erfgoed in de polder De Gouw en de Groetpolder,* Wageningen.

Kolen, J., 2005: *De biografie van het landschap. Drie essays over landschap, geschiedenis en erfgoed,* Amsterdam (Ph.D. thesis VU University).

Laak, J.C. ter, 2005: *De taal van het landschap. Pilotproject toponiemen in de Berkelstreek. Een verkennend onderzoek naar de bruikbaarheid van geografische namen voor het reconstrueren van de geschiedenis van het Oost-Nederlandse landschap. ROB-themaprogramma 'kennis voor beleid' 2: Archeologie en landschap. Themaproject 2.1 Biografie van het Oost-Nederlandse dekzandlandschap*, Amersfoort (Rapportage Archeologische Monumentenzorg 123).

Maas, G./B. Makaske, 2007: *Het natuurlijke landschap van Oost-Nederland. Geomorfologische detailkarteringen van de gebieden Deventer-Colmschate, Neede-Eibergen, Markelo-Rijssen, Zutphen-Warnsveld en Ruurlo*, Wageningen (Intern Rapport Alterra).

Martiny, R., 1926: Hof und Dorf in Alt-Westfalen. Das westfälische Streusiedlungsproblem, *Forschungen zur deutschen Landes- und Volkskunde* 24, 287-301.

Ministerie van Landbouw, Natuurbeheer en Visserij (LNV), 2000: *Natuur voor mensen, mensen voor natuur. Nota natuur, bos en landschap in de 21e eeuw*, Alkmaar.

Palmboom, E., 1983: De nederzetting in de middeleeuwen, in C.O.A. Schimmelpenninck van der Oije (ed.), *Over stad en scholtambt Lochem. Een beschrijving na 750 jaar (1233 – 1983)*, Lochem, 55-77.

Poel, K.R. de/N.P. van der Windt/J. Kruit/J.N.H. Elerie/T. Spek, 2000: *Essen in perspectief. Een interactieve planningsbenadering in Spier, Wijster en Drijber,* Wageningen.

Rooi, C-J. de, 2005: *Water stroomt waar het niet gaan kan. De ontwikkeling van het bekenstelsel in de Achterhoek*, Wageningen (Thesis Wageningen University).

Rooi, C-J. de, 2006: *Waar de venen groeiden. De situering en transformatie van veengebieden in de Achterhoek*, Wageningen (Thesis Wageningen University).

Rooijakkers, G., 2000: Mensen en dingen. Materiële cultuur, in T. Dekker/H. Roodenberg/G. Rooijakkers (eds.), *Volkscultuur. Een inleiding in de Nederlandse etnologie*, Nijmegen, 110-172.

Schavemaker, H., 2008: *Een analyse van 'The permanent conference' for the study of the rural landscape*, Wageningen (Ph.D. thesis Wageningen University).

Slicher van Bath, B.H., 1944: *Mensch en land in de middeleeuwen. Bijdrage tot een geschiedenis der nederzettingen in Oostelijk Nederland*, 2 vols., Assen.

Uhlig, H./C. Linau (eds.), 1972: *Basic material for the terminology of the agricultural landscape. Volume II Rural settlements. International Working Group for the Geographical Terminology of the Agricultural Landscape*, Giessen.

Vervloet, J.A.J., 1983: Het landschap van Lochem tot omstreeks 1830, in C.O.A. Schimmelpenninck van der Oije (ed.), *Over stad en scholtambt Lochem (1233 – 1983). Een beschrijving na 750 jaar*, Lochem, 79-110.

Vervloet, J.A.J., 2007: Some remarks about the changing position of landscape assessment, in Z. Roca/T. Spek/T. Terkenli/T. Plieninger/ F. Höchtl (eds.), *European Landscapes and Lifestyles. The Mediterranean and Beyond*, Lisbon, 433-438.

Vervloet, J.A.J., 2008: The Position of Cultural History and Heritage Management in a Complex Society, in H. de Haan/R. van der Duim (eds.), *Landscape, Leisure and Tourism*, Delft, 63-70.

Vervloet, J.A.J./J. Renes/T. Spek, 1996: Historical Geography And Integrated Landscape Research, in F.H.A. Aalen (ed.), *Landscapestudy and management. The Office of Public Works Dublin,* Trinity College Dublin, Department of Geography, 112-122.

Vos, P., (in prep.): *Palaeogeografische kaart van Nederland 800 na Christus,* Deltares, RACM TNO Bouw en Ondergrond 2009 (concept).

Waard, F. van der, 1997: Oplecht wark. De oudste boerderijconstructies in Oost-Nederland , Monumenten en Bouwhistorie, *Jaarboek Monumentenzorg 1996*, 8-18.

Webster, 1993: *Webster's Universal Dictionary and Thesaurus,* New Lanark, Scotland, 67.

Westeringh, W. van de, 1972: Landschap en landbouw in het Winterswijkse, *Natuur en landschap* 26, 23-46.

Westeringh, W. van de, 1979: De ontwikkeling van het agrarisch cultuurlandschap in een zandgebied (Winterswijk), *Cultuurtechnisch Tijdschrift* 18, 199-210.

Woltjer, J.J., 1992: *Recent verleden: de geschiedenis van Nederland in de twintigste eeuw,* Amsterdam.

5. The protection and management of the historic landscape in Scotland in the context of the European Landscape Convention

Lesley Macinnes[1]

ABSTRACT

This paper explains Scotland's holistic view of the historic environment, the main policy measures for its protection and management and the valuable new spatial approaches of historic landscape characterisation and historic land-use assessment. It considers the place of the historic environment and the characterisation processes in the context of policy measures for landscape, noting that these are moving towards a greater level of integration that is in keeping with the spirit of the European Landscape Convention. The paper assesses the impact of the ELC in Scotland and takes the view that the trend towards integration is developing as a consequence of the new national planning policy and the Scottish Government's Strategic Objectives, rather than in direct response to the ELC itself. Nevertheless, these current developments are broadly in line with the principles of the ELC and should lead Scotland to a more holistic, informed and participative approach to landscape protection, management and planning.

KEY WORDS

Scotland; historic environment, landscape characterisation, historic land-use assessment; integration

1. THE NATURE OF THE HISTORIC LANDSCAPE IN SCOTLAND

Many physical traces of past human impact can be seen in the landscape across Scotland. As elsewhere, a wide range of buildings, sites and monuments survive spanning the period since the last Ice Age. Scotland also has a rich legacy of relict landscapes, particularly deserted landscapes of the post-

Fig. 1
A historic landscape: Scott's View, Scottish Borders.
The landscape visible from Scott's View is famed for its association with Sir Walter Scott. It is designated as a National Scenic Area for its scenic qualities, but it is also a rich archaeological landscape that includes the prehistoric hill-fort of Eildon Hill North, the Roman military complex at Newstead, and the medieval abbey and town of Melrose (© *Lesley Macinnes and Historic Scotland*).

Fig. 2
A relict landscape: St Kilda, Western Isles. This abandoned 19th century settlement on St Kilda, now a World Heritage Site, clearly shows the close relationship of the natural and cultural landscape. The visible remains show houses strung along a central street, surrounded by field systems and associated structures, including some of earlier date, all nestling within the natural arena of the bay framed by the sharp rise of hills and the ocean beyond (© *Lesley Macinnes*).

medieval period that were abandoned as a result of wholesale restructuring and land improvements in the eighteenth and nineteenth centuries. These can cover extensive areas on the ground, especially in the less improved uplands (Fig. 1).

Other landscape elements are also the product of, or have been heavily influenced by, human actions in the past, but may be less well recognized. These include designed landscapes, which were explicitly planned for human appreciation of the natural landscape; semi-natural woodland, which has survived largely as a result of human management; and field boundaries, many of which date back to the eighteenth century and sometimes even earlier. Much more, of course, lies hidden beneath the ground surface, for example beneath agricultural land or within wetlands, obscured by natural processes and subsequent human activity (Fig. 2).

This past use contributes significantly to the present character of the landscape of Scotland. It is encapsulated by the umbrella term 'historic environment', which is defined in the Scottish Historic Environment Policy 2009 (Historic Scotland 2009) as:

"Our whole environment, whether rural or urban, on land or under water, has a historic dimension that contributes to its quality and character. It has been shaped by human and natural processes over thousands of years. This is most obvious in our built heritage: ancient monuments; archaeological sites and landscapes; historic buildings; townscapes; parks; gardens and designed landscapes; and our marine heritage, for example in the form of historic shipwrecks or underwater landscapes once dry land. We can see it in the patterns in our landscape, the layout of fields and roads, and the remains of a wide range of past human activities. ...

The context or setting in which specific historic features sit and the patterns of past use are part of our historic environment. The historical, artistic, literary, linguistic, and scenic associations of places and landscapes are some of the less tangible elements of the historic environment. These elements make a fundamental contribution to our sense of place and cultural identity."

This definition guides policy and practice for the protection and management of the historic aspects of the Scottish landscape. It fits well with the definition of the broader landscape contained within the European Landscape Convention (ELC; Florence 2000): "Landscape means an area, as perceived by people, whose character is the result of the action and interaction of natural and/or human factors."

2. PROTECTION AND MANAGEMENT OF THE HISTORIC LANDSCAPE

The historic environment and historic aspects of landscape are principally protected through the statutory designations of scheduled monuments, listed buildings and conservation areas, through the non-statutory Inventory of gardens and designed landscapes, and as world heritage sites. In addition, a non-statutory Inventory of historic battlefields of national importance is currently in preparation. These protected sites can cover large areas of land and take account of the landscape setting of individual sites, but only some are directed towards heritage landscapes *per se* (Macinnes 2006a).

Listing identifies the architectural and historic importance of historic buildings and structures so that this can be taken into account when change is planned. Listed buildings are designated by Historic Scotland on behalf of Scottish Ministers for the guidance of the local planning authorities that are in the main responsible for their regulation through the planning system. The policy aim is to ensure that no listed building is unnecessarily damaged or destroyed.

Scheduling seeks to protect nationally important monuments, ruinous structures and archaeological sites of all periods, some covering extensive areas of land, particularly in rural contexts. Scheduled monuments are designated by Historic Scotland on behalf of Scottish Ministers and Historic Scotland is also responsible for subsequent controls of works affecting them. Local authorities have no formal role except in relation to planning-related impacts on the setting of scheduled monuments. The policy aim is to conserve scheduled monuments as found and manage change with minimum intervention.

Areas of historic or architectural interest can be designated as Conservation Areas. These are designated by local planning authorities and regulated through the planning system. Their purpose is to define areas of particular historic character and to seek to preserve and enhance that character: character appraisals help to define character and guide change. Conservation areas can be extensive, though most are in urban rather than rural contexts. An important exception to this is the important battlefield at Culloden, which is designated as a rural conservation area.

The Inventory of Gardens and Designed Landscapes is compiled by Historic Scotland. It is non-statutory, meaning that there is no legal requirement to protect Inventory sites. However, they are a material consideration in the development planning and management process, regulated by the local planning authorities in consultation with Historic Scotland.

Scotland's inscribed World Heritage Sites are Edinburgh Old and New Towns, New Lanark, The Heart of Neolithic Orkney and St Kilda, which is also inscribed as a natural site. In addition, the Antonine Wall has recently been inscribed as part of the transnational World Heritage Site, Frontiers of the Roman Empire. There are currently no sites inscribed in Scotland under the cultural landscape category. While sites are inscribed for inclusion on the World Heritage List by the UK Government, their accompanying management plans are linked to existing mechanisms for spatial planning and land-use management and involve local planning authorities and other relevant land management organizations.

An Inventory of Historic Battlefields is currently being developed by Historic Scotland. As with the Inventory of Gardens and Designed Landscapes, this will be non-statutory but will make battlefields a material consideration in the development planning and management process, regulated by the local planning authorities in consultation with Historic Scotland.

In addition to the process of designation, the historic environment is also protected through the spatial planning process. The management of the historic environment in the context of spatial planning is set out in Scottish Planning Policy. This policy explains how the protective measures outlined above operate in relation to the planning process. Local authorities can use their land-use development plans to define a suite of protective policies for the historic environment, including historic landscapes, which inform, and are implemented through, the development management process. This is supported by the tools of Strategic Environmental Assessment and Environmental Impact Assessment, which help ensure that strategic and major development plans take adequate account of the historic environment, including its landscape aspects.

3. INTEGRATION INTO WIDER LANDSCAPE MEASURES

Historic environment measures are also integrated to some extent within measures for the protection and management of the wider landscape in Scotland. The principal national landscape designations are National Parks and National Scenic Areas (NSAs). The conservation and enhancement of the cultural heritage forms one of the principal aims of Scotland's two National Parks and is addressed by the National Park Authorities in their park plans and associated management strategies. The prime purpose of NSAs is the protection of areas of scenic or natural beauty, but recent legislative amendments recognize cultural heritage among their special qualities and so allow for historic aspects of the landscape to be included within any future management strategies. While NSAs are national designations, implementation is primarily regulated through the planning system by local planning authorities.

National landscape designations are complemented by a range of local landscape designations which are areas identified by local planning authorities for their importance for landscape, natural or cultural heritage qualities. Recent guidance on these from Historic Scotland and Scottish Natural Heritage, the national agency responsible for the natural heritage, encourages a more holistic approach to their designation and management in accordance with the principles of the ELC (Historic Scotland and Scottish Natural Heritage 2005).

National planning policy for landscape is included within the Scottish Planning Policy, alongside that for natural heritage, while the National Planning Framework for Scotland recognizes the importance of landscapes in a way that is in line with the ELC:

> "In their rich diversity, Scotland's landscapes are a national treasure. They provide the context for our daily lives and are a major attraction for our tourist visitors. As settings for outdoor recreation they are a source of refreshment and inspiration for many. They bear witness to the activities of our forebears and are a critical element in defining Scotland's identity. ... The aim should be to build environmental capital and pass well-managed, high quality landscapes on to future generations."

In addition to provisions within the spatial planning process, key land-use strategies and plans also relate to landscape management, principally the Scottish Rural Development Programme and the Scottish Forestry Strategy. These are increasingly becoming more holistic in approach, giving better recognition to both landscape and historic environment.

4. CHARACTERIZING THE HISTORIC LANDSCAPE

Conservation measures for the historic environment are underpinned by recording and investigation. Area-based and thematic survey is undertaken by Royal Commission on the Ancient and Historical Monuments of Scotland (RCAHMS), while Historic Scotland conducts surveys in relation to its protection programmes. Our understanding of the historic landscape at a broad scale is regularly enhanced through individual projects, often supported by grants from Historic Scotland. The resultant information is held within the national historic environment record, curated by RCAHMS, and local historic environment records maintained by local planning authorities or heritage trusts.

This work is complemented by the characterisation approach to landscape conservation and planning that has become established in recent years. Historic landscape characterisation (HLC) is the process of depicting land-use from the point of view of its historic origin, to show how land-use has changed over time and the extent to which evidence of past use can still be traced in the modern landscape. Precise approaches vary in different countries (for a range of examples see Fairclough/Rippon 2002; Macinnes 2004; Rippon 2004), but all underline both the dynamic nature of landscape and the considerable 'time-depth' within it.

Most approaches result in digital data-sets which are capable of interrogation to show different aspects of the landscape, for example type of use or period of use. This allows curators to show what is characteristic or distinctive about a given area, and enables comparison between areas, highlighting their similarities and their differences both now and over time. This in turn allows management of the historic environment to be broader in scale, moving beyond its traditional focus on specific sites, and at the same time more targeted to the particular issues in a given area. It also enables landscape planning and management strategies to be informed by a better understanding of the historic development of the landscape and to consider the importance of its historic character and time-depth when change is proposed (for practical examples see Clark/Darlington/Fairclough 2004).

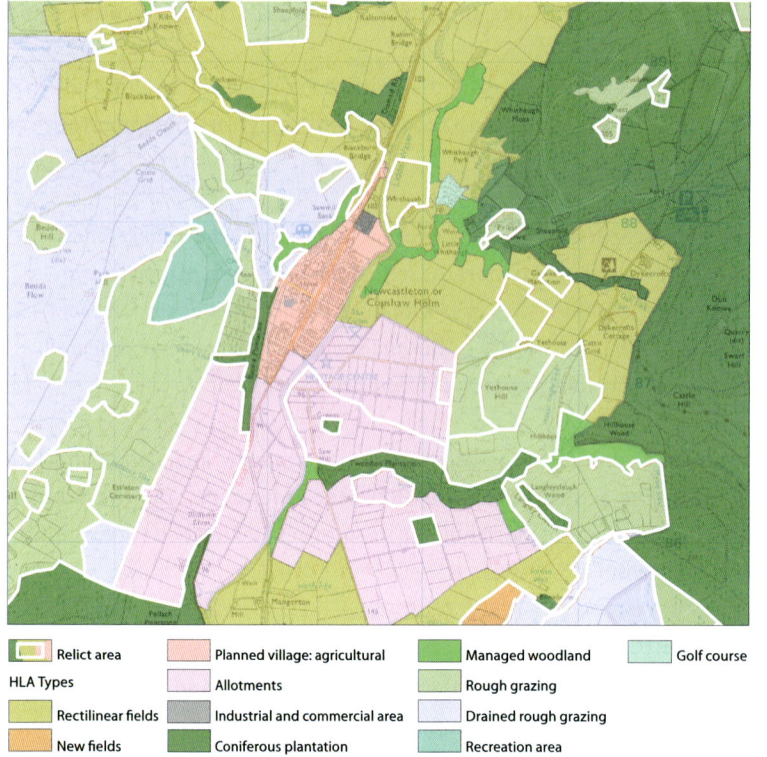

Fig. 3
Newcastleton HLA.
This shows the historic land-use types around the village of Newcastleton in the Scottish Borders. The HLA characterises units of lands by their form, function and period of origin and indicates areas of relict land-use, including historic landscapes over 1 ha in extent (© *Crown Copyright: RCAHMS and Historic Scotland*).

5. HISTORIC LAND-USE ASSESSMENT (HLA)

In Scotland, the characterisation approach is being carried out through historic land-use assessment, a joint project between Historic Scotland and RCAHMS. This is identifying historic patterns within the landscape and is enabling us to adopt a more landscape-based approach to the conservation of the historic environment than was previously possible, as well as improving integration with other aspects of landscape management.

The HLA is a digital dataset that provides an overview of the historic nature of the landscape by mapping the extent of past and present land-uses at 1:25,000 scale and indicating their date of origin or currency (Fig. 3). It is based on the analysis of key data sources, such as early maps, aerial photography and survey results. Some 55 individual historic land-use types have been identified, grouped under 14 thematic headings or categories. HLA also depicts relict land-use and archaeological landscapes greater than 1 hectare in extent. The data can be readily viewed on the website, HLAmap, and can be interactively interrogated on suitable GIS applications.

Over 70% of the country has now been covered by HLA, and it is expected that national coverage will be completed over the next few years. Areas covered to date include the two National Parks, most National Scenic Areas and the most recent World Heritage Site. In urban areas the HLA is complemented by the separate assessment processes of Conservation Area Character Appraisals and the Scottish Burgh Surveys.

Within designated landscapes, HLA has been used to help define the special qualities of the landscape of the Loch Lomond and the Trossachs National Park and to inform the recent landscape character assessment for the Cairngorms National Park. This work will underpin the landscape strategy for each Park. HLA has helped in the development of pilot management strategies for National Scenic Areas in Wester Ross and the Solway Coast. Within World Heritage Sites, it was integrated into a landscape capacity study in the Heart of Neolithic Orkney, and was used in defining the buffer zone for the Antonine Wall, part of the Frontiers of the Roman Empire. It is regularly used by some local authorities to inform their development management, seeking in particular to retain the footprint of significant patterns of earlier phases of settlement and land-use within a changing landscape.

The use of the HLA in the two National Parks illustrates its contribution to landscape and land-use management. In the Loch Lomond and the Trossachs National Park, the HLA demonstrated a clear contrast between the southern, lowland fringe of the Park and the upland territory to the north: the south is dominated by evidence for the impact of human design, whereas to the north human settlement has always been more constrained by the topography and land quality. In the HLA this contrast appeared as a high concentration of designed landscapes and a strong pattern of later rectilinear fields relating to the period of land improvement in the eighteenth/nineteenth century to the south; while to the north the human influence was less marked and showed greater survival of the less regular patterns of pre-improvement settlements and field systems that had been lost further south.

The mountainous region of the Cairngorms National Park is generally considered to be a fairly natural area with limited human intervention. However, the HLA clearly demonstrated that some areas have been significant nodal points of settlement through time and continue to be so today. In one particular area the settlement and land-use pattern that seems to have originated in the late medieval period is still dominant now, with little modern expansion. HLA data also demonstrated that the hill-passes have been important route-ways across the Park area for long periods, even though they appear unexploited today.

The HLA data have enabled both Park Authorities to develop landscape strategies that incorporate the historic environment spatially and much more fully than would have been possible without it. Working alongside geological, ecological and settlement and landscape data, the HLA helps facilitate an integrated approach to landscape that is better informed about historical development and significance.

In general, it is the landscape scale and land-use base of HLA that enables its historic environment data to be linked more effectively with other aspects of landscape planning and management. This enables the historic environment to be taken into account more easily in integrated approaches to landscape conservation and management, and helps to inform future policies for the Scottish landscape. Alongside landscape character assessment, it is seen as an essential tool for applying the principles of the ELC in Scotland. HLA is also establishing a baseline for assessing impacts on the historic aspects of the Scottish landscape, which will be invaluable for monitoring future change.

When national coverage is complete, analysis of the HLA data will help bring out the diversity of historic land-uses across Scotland, identifying what is typical and what is rare at national and regional levels, and drawing out local character and distinctiveness. Some consideration is now being given to clarifying the management implications of key historic land-use types with a view to building these into future land management schemes.

To support the application of HLA data in a variety of planning and land management contexts, a suite of guidance material is being developed and will be made available through the website, HLAmap. This website includes a bibliography of HLA and related publications, though summaries and lists of HLA publications can also be found in Fairclough/Macinnes 2003; Macinnes 2004; *idem* 2006b.

6. THE IMPACT OF THE EUROPEAN LANDSCAPE CONVENTION

The ELC (Florence 2000) was ratified by the UK Government on the basis that the UK was already meeting the essential requirements of the Convention through existing measures for landscape planning, protection and management. A UK-wide monitoring group liaises on progress and co-ordinates reports for the Council of Europe, but the devolved administrations have responsibility for developing their own implementation action plans. In Scotland an ELC co-ordination group has recently been established to help ensure a more co-ordinated approach to landscape among key agencies in accordance with the principles of the ELC. This builds on a report for the Scottish Government by the erstwhile Scottish Landscape Forum and by commissioned research on how the ELC has been implemented elsewhere in Europe (Scottish Government report 2007).

Any work to implement the ELC in Scotland must sit within the Scottish Government's 5 Strategic Objectives which aim to focus "Government and public services on creating a more successful country, with opportunities for all of Scotland to flourish, through increasing sustainable economic growth." These objectives aim to make Scotland "Safer and Stronger, Healthier, Wealthier and Fairer, Smarter and Greener" (Scottish Government Strategic Objectives). The strategic objectives are underpinned by 15 national outcomes, some of which are relevant to landscapes and the principles of the ELC, particularly

> "We live in well-designed, sustainable places where we are able to access the amenities and services we need. We value and enjoy our built and natural environment and protect it and enhance it for future generations."

Also relevant to the principles of the ELC is the recognition by the Scottish Government that landscape and heritage play an important role in national identity, that people and place are closely linked and that more decision-making should be carried out at local level.

7. CONCLUSION

While the long-term formal impact of the ELC in Scotland remains to be seen, the various recent developments outlined in this paper should help promote a more holistic, informed and participative approach to landscape protection, management and planning consistent with the principles of the Convention. The place of the historic environment in this will be greatly enhanced by the national completion and wider application of the HLA, as this enables historic character to take its place as an integral part of wider landscape character and to be managed as an integral part of wider land-use.

This paper has concentrated on Scotland, but the initiatives outlined here in relation to historic characterization and integrated spatial planning are mirrored across Europe. These will surely help achieve the holistic approach to landscape advocated by the ELC and enable landscape planning and management strategies to embrace Europe's rich and varied historic character in future change.

NOTES

1. Historic Scotland, Edinburgh, Scotland.

REFERENCES

Clark, J./J. Darlington/G. Fairclough, 2004: *Using Historic Landscape Characterisation*, English Heritage and Lancashire County Council.

Fairclough, G./S. Rippon (eds.), 2002: *Europe's Cultural Landscape: archaeologists and the management of change*, Brussels (Europae Archaeologiae Consilium Occasional Paper 2).

Fairclough G./L. Macinnes, 2003: *Understanding Historic Landscape Character*, Topic Paper 5 published by the Countryside Agency and Scottish Natural Heritage, September 2003. This can be downloaded at http://www.landscapecharacter.org.uk/node/82

Florence, 2000: *European Landscape Convention. Florence, 20 October 2000*, Strassbourg (Council of Europe).

Historic Scotland: *Scottish Historic Environment Policy*. This can be downloaded at http://www.historic-scotland.gov.uk/shep-july-2009.pdf.

Historic Scotland and Scottish Natural Heritage, 2005: *Guidance on Local Landscape Designations* can be downloaded at http://www.snh.org.uk/pubs/results.asp?q=local+landscape+designations&rpp=10

HLAmap: can be viewed at http://jura.rcahms.gov.uk/HLA/start.jsp

Macinnes, L., 2004: Historic Landscape Characterization, in K. Bishop/A. Phillips (eds.), *Countryside Planning: New Approaches to Management and Conservation,* London, 155-69

Macinnes, L., 2006²a: Archaeology and land use, in J. Hunter/I. Ralston (eds.), *Archaeological Resource Management in the UK, an Introduction,* Stroud, 339-357

Macinnes, L. 2006b: From past to present: understanding and managing the historic environment, in R.A. Davidson/C.A. Galbraith (eds.), *Farming, Forestry and the Natural Heritage: towards a more integrated future,* Edinburgh.

National Planning Framework for Scotland 2: Discussion Draft can be downloaded at http://www.scotland.gov.uk/Publications/2008/01/07093039/0

Rippon, S., 2004: *Historic Landscape Analysis: Deciphering the Countryside,* CBA Practical Handbook in Archaeology 15: http://www.britarch.ac.uk/pubs/handbooks.html

Scottish Forestry Strategy: can be viewed at http://www.forestry.gov.uk/sfs

Scottish Government report, 2007: Identifying Good Practice from Countries Implementing the European Landscape Convention (Project Reference ICP/001/07) can be downloaded at http://www.scotland.gov.uk/Publications/2009/06/11091754/0

Scottish Government's Strategic Objectives: can be viewed at http://www.scotland.gov.uk/About/purposestratobjs

Scottish Landscape Forum, 2007: Scotland's Living Landscapes. Places for People, Report to Scottish Ministers (March 2007) can be downloaded at http://www.snh.org.uk/pdfs/strategy/landscapes/Report%20to%20Ministers%20-%20March%202007-2.pdf

Scottish Planning Policy: can be downloaded at http://www.scotland.gov.uk/Publications/2008/10/28115149/0

Scottish Rural Development Programme: can be viewed at http://www.scotland.gov.uk/Topics/farmingrural/SRDP

6. Assessing *in situ* preservation of archaeological wetland sites by chemical analysis of botanical remains and micromorphology

Martine van den Berg[1], Hans Huisman[2], Henk Kars[1], Henk van Haaster[3] & Johan Kool[4]

ABSTRACT

Archaeological botanical remains are prone to deterioration in many burial environments and play an important role in assessing the preservation state of scheduled sites. Two projects that deal with these remains are presented here. The first is an experimental study on the degradation patterns of macroremains using instrumental analytical techniques. After the visual inspection of samples of more than 60 species the chemical profiles were determined using pyrolysis-gas chromatography/mass spectrometry and thermochemolysis. Only a few species have characteristic chromatograms, therefore recognizing plant species based only on their chromatograms is not a viable method. Degradation estimated by visual inspection so far has not shown a correlation with chemical degradation.

The second project encompasses two case studies applying micromorphology to study the preservation potential of archaeological soils. The first deals with a Neolithic wooden trackway in a peat extraction area. Since the 1980s, the water table was often far below large parts of the trackway and test pits from 2004 showed that the wood was heavily degraded by erosion bacteria but not by fungi. Micromorphological research showed that peat layers above the trackway are occasionally heavily degraded by microbes and soil fauna but that most of the peat is well preserved. It was concluded that the trackway was not in direct danger, thanks to the strong water retaining capacity of peat. The second case study concentrated on a series of Early Neolithic sites found on clayey fluvial levees with thick layers of organic-rich material. The sites have a complex post-depositional history, they were flooded in a freshwater environment and peat was formed. This was followed by flooding by the sea, turning the area into a brackish and then to a saline inland sea. After reclaiming in the 1960s, the sites are at shallow depths in a heavily drained agricultural area. In 2004, a site assessment was carried out. Wood samples showed strong decay by erosion bacteria but no traces of fungi. Redox probes, soil chemical analyses and micromorphological research showed that (sub)oxic conditions reached the top of the archaeological layer, while the deeper parts were still reduced. Organic matter appeared to be unaffected and had well-preserved cell structures. Micromorphological research also showed the presence of diagenetic minerals, reflecting good past and present preservation conditions for wood. However the sites from both projects are under threat from oxidation-related processes and monitoring is advised in order to keep track of their state of preservation.

KEYWORDS

Archaeological resource management; archaeobotany, micromorphology; wetlands, in situ preservation; the Netherlands

1. **INTRODUCTION AND BACKGROUND**

Archaeological botanical remains, such as (cultivated) food plants, weeds (mainly occuring as seeds), pollen and wood are commonly found and are therefore well suited for systematic research of the past. These materials and their anthropogenic and natural context in archaeological soils provide relevant archaeological data and important contextual information on the occupation history by reflecting, among other things, the ecological setting at that time, food economics, dietary habits and (ship) building practices. These organic materials, however, are also very prone to deterioration in common soil conditions and therefore play an important role in estimating the preservation state of archaeological sites and in monitoring scheduled sites.

In the near and further future paradigms and research concepts in archaeology may change and methods and techniques will improve, which means that the information value of the archaeological resources will change and increase with time (Fig. 1). Good examples are the development of the radiocarbon method in the 1950s and the application of ancient DNA studies today. The modern concept of archaeological resource management in Europe is therefore aimed at preserving the archaeological record where it is, in the burial environment. However, this policy of *in situ* preservation is rather hazardous because it can be safely assumed that a loss of information will happen due to the deterioration of one or probably more components of a site. This is certainly true for highly dynamic urbanizing landscapes in the Netherlands, but it also holds for more remote and rural areas in, for instance, Sweden, where field archaeologists note that the physical quality of artefacts encountered during recent excavations is much worse than expected when compared with material recovered from the same area many years ago (Mattsson *et al.* 1996). This confronts decision-makers in archaeological resource management with a basic dilemma. If it cannot be guaranteed that a critical amount of information in a site is preserved, the policy of *in situ* preservation has failed (Fig. 1). This means that degradation mechanisms of all kinds of archaeological materials must be understood in order: i) to be able to make a risk assessment of a site under changing soil conditions; ii) if excavation is not an option, to develop mitigation measures responding to these changing conditions and; iii) to develop cost-effective monitoring methods to measure unforeseen changes in the soil conditons at scheduled sites.

Since the 1990s, this risk of deterioration has been recognized by several archaeological heritage institutions in northwestern Europe. In addition to national research projects this has led to a number of EC-funded research programmes which focused on the degradation process of archaeological materials

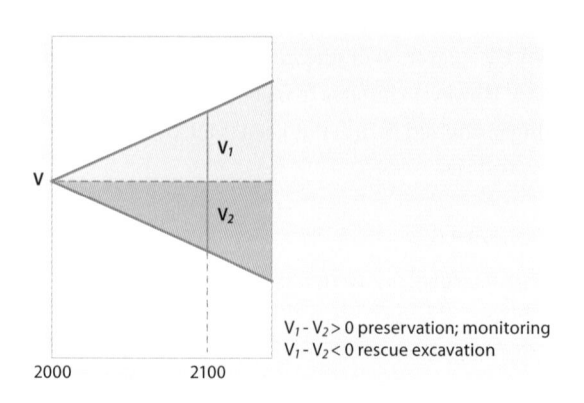

Fig. 1
Schematic representation of the change in value of an archaeological site over time. In practice both the increase and the decrease will be intermittent rather than showing a linear relationship. A good example for a sudden increase was the development of the radiocarbon method in the 1950s, while a change in the groundwater level might lead to a sudden decrease in the physical quality of the site.

$V_1 - V_2 > 0$ preservation; monitoring
$V_1 - V_2 < 0$ rescue excavation

in soils and the diagenetic pathways manifested in these materials, i.e. metal artefacts (Wagner *et al.* 1997), bone (Kars/Kars 2002) and wood (Klaassen 2005). It has also led to the international Preservation of Archaeological Remains In Situ (PARIS) conferences (Corfield *et al.* 1998; Nixon 2004; Kars/Van Heeringen 2008) bringing together specialists in this field from all over the world. At this moment the mechanisms behind deterioration in most archaeological materials are empirically identified and roughly broadly understood (Huisman 2009). An important conclusion is that various materials react in different ways under changing conditions in the burial environment. The soil parameters of this environment which are instrumental in providing conditions to either preserve or to deteriorate the archaeological remains are mostly governed by the behaviour of soil moisture and groundwater. Therefore, when also seen in the light of the expected effects of climate change, an important next step is to investigate national and international water management policies (Van den Berg/Hatzmann 2005). In addition to this more insight has to be gained into the applicability of geohydrological models on the artefact-soil system in different soil types.

During the last few decades a number of measuring techniques for assessing and monitoring the conditions of the burial environment have been developed and applied in the Netherlands (e.g. Van Heeringen/Mauro/Smit 2004; Smit/Mol/Van Heeringen 2005) and the results gained so far are summarized and transformed into guidelines in the 'Archaeological Monitoring standard' (Smit/Van Heeringen/Theunissen 2006). The number of monitoring schemes applied to scheduled sites is seen to increase and it is expected that this development will evolve into a structural branch within commercial archaeology (e.g. Hill/Mc Kenna/Vorenhout 2008; Vorenhout 2008).

Since oxygen availability and water (moisture) regime are among the most important factors that determine the preservation potential of the burial environment, especially of organic remains, the most commonly used techniques are using dipwells and probes for measuring redox potential, oxygen content and moisture levels. In addition, at some sites soil chemical analyses are done in order to determine the processes that are active in the soil. The consequence of this approach, however, is that the degradation of the archaeological remains is only indirectly determined; measurements of the environmental conditions function as a proxy and provide circumstantial evidence for the state of preservation of a site. There is an additional need for a direct manner of assessing the degradation that could have been taking place on a site which can be performed systematically without damaging the site.

Botanical macro-remains, wood and undefined organic matter present in features are extremely sensitive to degradation in an oxidizing environment and are therefore a good indicator for any change in the state of preservation of a site. In this paper two examples of projects that deal with the preservation state of a site are given. The first one concentrates on botanical macro-remains by gaining insight into their degradation patterns using instrumental analytical techniques. The second project comprises two case studies stressing the importance of the application of micromorphology on archaeological soils; a technique which is unfortunately declining in traditional soil science.

2. THE PRESERVATION OF BOTANICAL MACRO-REMAINS

Well-preserved organic remains are generally found in a reducing soil environment but deteriorate dramatically in the presence of oxygen. Apart from wood, little is known about the pathway of degradation of organic matter on a more detailed level. The natural sciences offer various research techniques and approaches to support a direct assessment and evaluation of the deterioration of organic remains based on their morphological features and chemical characteristics.

2.1 Methodology

A large number of samples of different kinds of macro-remains from sixteen wetland sites, representing both domesticated species and wild plants, were selected in order to investigate their morphological state of preservation and their chemical profiles (Fig. 2.a-b). Special care was taken to select plant species that are encountered more commonly than others at archaeological sites to ensure that the findings and recommendations are valid for a wide variety of sites. All analysed remains comprise seeds, which are in general the most resistant part of the plant and are most commonly found in archaeological soil samples. In addition, seeds display the most reliable morphological diagnostic features by which the species can be determined. In a strict botanical sense a seed is composed of an embryo, a supply of nutrients for the embryo (storage tissue), and a seed coating (testa) that in most cases is the only part preserved in archaeological samples. Many species show structures attached to their seeds. Often parts of the fruit (in which the seeds are formed) or even parts of the flower remain attached to the seed (i.e. endocarp, mesocarp, exocarp, pseudocarp, perianth). These seeds are actually fruits in which the seeds are included. The morphology and the preservation state of all seed remains were macroscopically investigated by the archaeobotanist, based on the classification system of Jones, Tinsley and Brunning (Jones/Tinsley/Brunning 2007). This system has the advantage of being easy to use during the classification; it further provides information which can be roughly attributed to physical and chemical/biological deterioration of the seed remains. It is also possible to compare this classification with the system developed by Vernimmen (Vernimmen 2002) which is used in Dutch archaeology.

All samples were inspected in order to establish if any non-charred remains are present and, if present, to count the number of species present in the samples. This was followed by a morphological inspection on species level according to Vernimmen (Vernimmen 2002) on a scale from 1 (no uncharred material present) to 5 (with very good preserved uncharred material, i.e. intact surface, clearly visible cell patterns, etc.). Alternative to this approach was to estimate the amount of weathering of the surface of the grains (from A < 25% weathered, to C > 50% weathered), combined with the amount of fragmentation (from a < 25% fragmented grains to c > 50% fragmented grains) (Jones/Tinsley/Brunning 2007).

After the visual inspections the chemical profiles, the so-called biomarkers, were analysed and determined. Chemical analyses on the sample material were performed using pyrolysis-gas chromatography/mass spectrometry (Py-GC/MS). This method is very suitable to detect changes in high molecular compound such as lipids, proteins, sugars and lignin molecules that are the main compounds in the macro-remains. Approximately 60 plant species from sixteen sites were analysed. They are shown in Fig. 2a while the sites and their archaeological characteristics and type of soil are given in Fig. 2b. The seeds were treated as a whole and chemical signals are derived from the elementary seeds and in a number of cases also from the attached fruit or flower parts. A substantial number of the plant species was also subjected to thermochemolysis, which has the advantage, among other things, of avoiding secondary reactions and of a greater sensitivity compared to conventional pyrolysis.

With this as a background the possibilities of distinguishing species from one another were investigated and the pathway of chemical deterioration of macro-remains in relation to various soil conditions was explored. Finally the project explored the possibility of using Py-GC/MS to measure the state of degradation of botanical macro-remains and to use this as a proxy of degradation of other materials on an archaeological site.

As noted in the introduction the material cannot be studied alone, but must be seen in a system composed of the material and its surroundings, the burial environment. Therefore the relevant soil parameters of each site were assessed. Important soil parameters are the phreatic groundwater level, pH and redox potential (e.g. Kars/Smit 2003). A huge part of the data used was gathered during previous research campaigns (Van Heeringen/Theunissen 2002; Van Heeringen/Mauro/Smit 2004; Smit/Mol/Van Heeringen 2005; Doesburg/Mauro 2007; Vorenhout/Smit in prep.). Some additional fieldwork and laboratory measurements are carried out to gain data on the grain size, lime content, siderite content, organic carbon content and C/N ratio. Additional data on groundwater levels was available in the TNO database (DINO) and the databases of the water boards 'Zuiderzeeland' and 'Zeeuwse eilanden'.

2.2 Results

Apart from wood (Klaassen 2005), little was known until now about the chemical characteristics of botanical archaeological remains, in particular seeds. The analysis of approximately 60 plant species using Py-GC/MS to establish the reference database showed that typically aliphatic and lignin cellulose compounds are found together (see as an example Fig. 3), though for certain plant species only one of either group of compounds was found in high abundance. The analysed remains comprise various parts of a plant; besides the testa, the pericarp was often present. Perianth, pseudocarp, endocarp and mesocarp were less frequently part of the samples. The trend is that testa correlate with aliphatic compounds and that the pericarp is more associated with lignin cellulose compounds. A few species have very characteristic chromatograms, but this is rare. Although the chromatograms mainly comprise the same compounds, there is a diversity in their abundances which cannot be explained by species type. This proved that recognizing individual plant species based on their chemical signal in pyrograms is not a promising technique and that losing the ability of macroscopical identification of the remains is catastrophic with the current state of technology.

There are pronounced differences between samples of the same plant species from the various sites. However, these differences are not necessarily attributable to differences in the preservation state between sites and might also be the result of other factors such as the growing conditions of the plant, that have to be studied in more detail. Moreover, pathways of degradation may also be influenced by differences in the composition of the micro-organism community present in the soil.

Though it was hoped that degradation estimated by macro- and microscopical means would show a comparative and distinct pattern in chemical degradation, such a correlation could not, unfortunately, be demonstrated within the time scheme of the project and the research activities moved from the chemical analysis of the remains towards the study of the burial environment, in particular the water management at sites.

An important part of the original project was to establish the site-specific hydrological regime and hydrological processes to understand the environmental conditions of the site, which could be of help in predicting the conditions of the burial environment under changing circumstances. This has been done for a few sites within the project and when it was realized that the aims of the original project in describing detailed pathways of degradation for botanical remains using chemical analysis could not be reached, an in-depth study of the relationship between water management and the preservation of

Scientific Name	Common Name	Sample Origin, see Fig. 2b
Crops		
Atriplex patula / prostrata	common orache / spear-leaved orache	AHR0, BGM1, LRN0, SNK0, WMH0 (2x)
Avena¶	oat	AMD0
Brassica rapa	turnip	BGM1, LRN0, VLG0
Fagopyrum esculentum	buckwheat	GRM1, KUI0
Hordeum vulgare	six-row barley	SNK0
Linum usitatissimum	cultivated flax	BGM0, VKK0
Secale cereale¶	rye	ODZ1
Triticum aestivum¶	bread wheat	-
Nuts and fruits		
Corylus avellana	hazel	VKK0, VLG0
Fragaria vesca	wild strawberry	VLG0
Juglans regia	walnut	VLG0
Prunus avium	gean / wild cherry	KUI0
Prunus domestica subsp. insititia	vullace	KUI0
Prunus persica	peach	VLG*
Rubus idaeus	raspberry	-
Vitis vinifera	grape-vine	KUI0
Wild plants		
Bidens tripartita	trifid bur-marigold	LRN1
Bolboschoenus maritimus¶	sea club-rush	AHR0, SNK0
Calluna vulgaris	heather / ling	ODZ0
Cannabis sativa	hemp	GRM1
Centaurea cyanus	cornflower	KUI0
Ceratophyllum demersum	rigid hornwort	LRN0
Chenopodium album	fat-hen	AKA0, LRN0, ODZ0
Cirsium arvense / palustre	creeping thistle / marsh thistle	LRN0
Cladium mariscus¶	great sedge / saw-sedge	BGW0
Fallopia convolvulus	black bindweed	VKK0
Galeopsis speciosa / tetrahit	large-flowered - / common hemp-nettle	LRN1, ODZ0
Lamium album / maculatum	white dead-nettle / spotted dead-nettle	ODZ1
Leontodon autumnalis	autumnal hawkbit	SNK0
Mentha aquatica / arvensis	water mint / corn mint	LRN1
Myrica gale	bog-myrtle / sweet gale	BGW0
Nuphar lutea	yellow water-lily	LRN0, MRD0
Oenanthe aquatica	fine-leaved water-dropwort	LRN0, VLG0
Persicaria hydropiper	water-pepper	LRN0, VLG0
Persicaria lapathifolia	pale persicaria	BGM0, LRN1, ODZ0, VKK0, VLG0
Persicaria maculosa	persicaria / red shank	AKA0, LRN1
Phragmites australis¶	common reed	AHR0
Polygonum aviculare	knotgrass	AHR0, BGM0, LRN0, WMH0 (2x)
Potentilla anserina	silverweed	SNK0
Ranunculus acris / repens	meadow buttercup / creeping buttercup	LRN0
Ranunculus repens	creeping buttercup	AMD0

Fig. 2a
Overview of the plant species found during various archaeological excavations for which Py-GC/MS traces were obtained from their seeds.

Ranunculus sardous	hairy buttercup	AHR0, BGM1, SNK0
Raphanus raphanistrum	wild radish	AKA0 (2x), BGM0
Rosa	rose	VLG0
Rumex acetosella	sheep's sorrel	ODZ1, VKK0
Rumex crispus	curled dock	AKA0, LRN0
Rumex maritimus / palustris	golden dock / marsh dock	LRN0
Sambucus nigra	elder	-
Scleranthus annuus	annual knawel	KUI0, ODZ1, VKK0
Solanum nigrum	black nightshade	ODZ0, VLG0
Sonchus arvensis	corn sow-thistle / per. sow-thistle	SNK0
Stellaria media	chickweed	AKA0, BGM1, LRN0, ODZ0
Suaeda maritima¶	annual-seablite	BGM1
Thlaspi arvense	field pennycress	AKA0
Triglochin maritima	sea arrowgrass	AMD0, BGM0, WMH0
Urtica dioica	stinging nettle	AKA0
Urtica urens	annual nettle	ODZ0, VKK0

Fig. 2a continuation

Code	Site	Age (AD)	Site type	Feature type	Soil type
AHR0	Harnaschpolder	250	Settlement	Well	Silty clay
AKA0	Alphen Kerkakkers	500 -1600	Settlement	Well	Pleistocene cover sands
AMD0	Amsterdam	1700 -1800	Town	Stable	Clay, peat
BGM0	Beetgumermolen	1150-1200	Artificial dwelling hill	Well	Tidal mud-flat deposits, sea clay
BGM1	Beetgumermolen (m272)	1150 - 1200	Artificial dwelling hill	Well	Tidal mud-flat deposits, sea clay
BGW0	Bodegraafseweg (m3)	100	Settlement	Pit	River deposits, natural levee
GRM1	Gorinchem (m34)	1675 - 1775	Town	Well	Natural levee
KUI0	Kuinre	1650	Town	Cesspool	Pleistocene sand
LRN0	Leidse Rijn (35, m88)	100	Settlement	Channel	River deposits, channel
LRN1	Leidse Rijn (35, m300)	1100 - 1200	Settlement	Ditch	River deposits, natural levee
ODZ0	Oldenzaal (m136)	1042	Town	Well	Pleistocene sand, push moraine border
ODZ1	Oldenzaal (m141)	1065	Town	Well	Pleistocene sand
SNK0	Sneek (m76)	1100 - 1200	Artificial dwelling hill	Well	Sea clay
VKK0	Vinkenkamp (m890)	800 - 900	Settlement	Well	Pleistocene sand
VLG0	Vleugel	1500 - 1700	Farmstead	Ditch	Natural levee
WMH0	Warmenhuizen	800 - 900	Artificial dwelling hill	Ditch	Tidal mud-flat deposits, sea clay

Fig. 2b
Site and context of the analysed sample, cf. Fig. 2a.

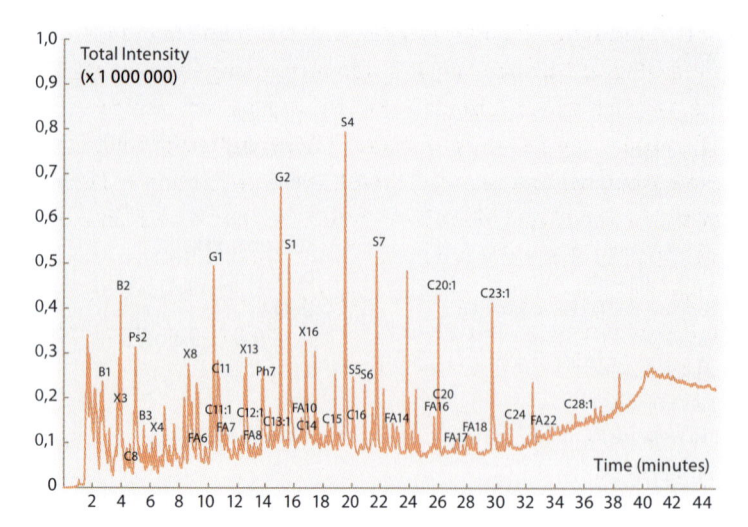

Fig. 3
Total ion chromatogram of *Persicaria lapathifolia (Pale Persicaria)* found at a site located between Vleuten and Houten (the Netherlands) dated 1500-1700 AD. Guaiacol (G) and syringol (S) compounds are derived from lignin. Alkanes (Cx:0), alkenes (Cx:1) and fatty acids (FAx) are aliphatic compounds, usually derived from plant waxes.

archaeological resources was designed and is under way (Van den Berg in prep.). An overview of most of the hydrological features of Dutch burial environments is provided by Van den Berg, Aalbersberg and Van Heeringen (Van den Berg/Aalbersberg/Van Heeringen 2006), while an inventory of the various instruments and actions within Dutch water management and the implications for archaeological heritage management are given by Van den Berg and Hatzmann (Van den Berg/Hatzmann 2005).

For the forthcoming years it will remain a challenge to heritage and water managers to harmonize the archaeological needs with planned water-actions and to include this knowledge in the archaeological heritage management cycle and in monitoring programmes.

3. SOIL-MICROMORPHOLOGY AND *IN SITU* PRESERVATION

3.1 Methodology and site information

Soil micromorphology is a method that originates from the field of soil science and was developed to study soil formation processes. Since the 1980s it occasionally also became a tool in geoarchaeological research, but its application for assessing and monitoring the preservation state of a site remains scarce and has not yet been fully appreciated. Examples of micromorphological studies applied to archaeology and archaeological resource management in the Netherlands are published by Exaltus and Soonius (Exaltus/Soonius 1994; *idem* 1997a; *idem* 1997b); Exaltus (Exaltus 2000); Exaltus *et al.* (Exaltus *et al.* 2003), Van Heeringen and Theunissen (Van Heeringen/Theunissen 2001; *idem* 2002), and Smit, Van Heeringen and Theunissen (Smit/Van Heeringen/Theunissen 2006). This paper presents two case studies which assess the transformation and degradation processes in anthropogenic soils from two Neolithic sites. It demonstrates that micromorphological techniques are a powerful means in understanding anthroposols and the effects of changing soil conditions on these sites.

Micromorphological study of soils and sediments requires non-disturbed soil samples which are impregnated with a polyester resin and sawn to c. 30 μm thickness. By studying these thin sections under the (polarizing) microscope, the mineralogical contents, the (micro-) structure, the organic matter contents and its characteristics and the changes in the soil induced by man can be investigated (e.g. Courty/Goldberg/Pacphail 1989).

The first case study presented here deals with the Neolithic wooden trackway found in the 1950s in the Nieuw-Dordrecht peat extraction area (Fig. 4). The trackway is c. 400 metres long and consists of a large number of wooden logs placed next to each other horizontally. Since the 1980s, increasing worries about the condition of the trackway have arisen, especially since the water table was often far below large sections of it. It was feared that these low groundwater levels would result in the desiccation and oxidation of the peat overlying the trackway and in wood degradation by bacteria and fungi. An elaborate and costly rescue plan was designed, involving subsurface water supply to save the wood. In 2004, a series of small test-pits were made to study the type and intensity of the decay on site (Fig. 5). The study combined groundwater and redox-measurements with pore water extraction, wood sampling and micromorphological samples from the soil profile. For a more detailed description we refer to Theunissen *et al.* (Theunissen *et al.* 2006).

The second case study is situated in the region around Swifterbant (Fig. 4), where a series of Early Neolithic sites are found on clayey fluvial levees. The sites consist of thick layers (up to 1 m) of organic-rich material, containing large amounts of bone fragments, burnt plant material, pottery and flint. The sites have a complex post-sedimentary history. After abandonment, they were flooded in a freshwater environment and peat was formed. The area turned into a freshwater lake until c. 1200 AD. Then, an open connection with the sea was formed, turning the lake into a brackish and then to a saline inland sea, the Zuiderzee. In 1932 a dam was constructed, again making it a freshwater lake, IJsselmeer. In 1959 the Swifterbant area was drained and reclaimed and became part of the Flevoland polders. The Neolithic

Fig. 4
The locations of the sites.

Fig. 5
Test pit at the Nieuw-Dordrecht site. The exposed wooden logs of the trackway are clearly visible.

sites nowadays lie at relatively shallow depths, within 1 m below the surface in an extensively drained agricultural area. A series of excavations between 1959 and 1979 revealed large amounts of well-preserved organic and inorganic archaeological finds, including several human burials. There are concerns on the state of preservation of the unexcavated scheduled sites since the drainage of the area was likely to have led to desiccation and subsequent degradation of the organic components. In 2004 a site assessment was carried out on one of the sites (S2) in order to establish to what extent the site was under threat. Wood samples were studied to assess the present state of preservation. Redox probes, soil chemical analyses and micromorphological research were used to assess the present burial conditions. The thin sections were also studied to establish the influence of the past burial environment on the site. Moreover, micromorphological research was also done on a neighbouring site (S4).

3.2 Results

At Nieuw-Dordrecht groundwater levels often drop to depths below the trackway's level. The redox potential was oxic to suboxic at levels at or below the trackway (Fig. 6), whereas nitrate was found to penetrate into the level of the trackway. The wood was heavily degraded by erosion bacteria but did not contain traces of fungal degradation. This is surprising since the overall feeling until the start of this project was that the trackway was in a bad condition due to the actions of wood-degrading fungi (Theunissen *et al.* 2006). Micromorphological research showed that the peat layer above the wood contained layers that were heavily degraded by microbes and soil fauna. However, such layers occurred between and below layers that showed very well preserved organic remains (Fig. 7). The lack of degradation and the overall structure of the peat demonstrated that desiccation and degradation had not taken place since these

Fig. 6
Redox profiles at the Nieuw-Dordrecht site. The location of the trackway is indicated.

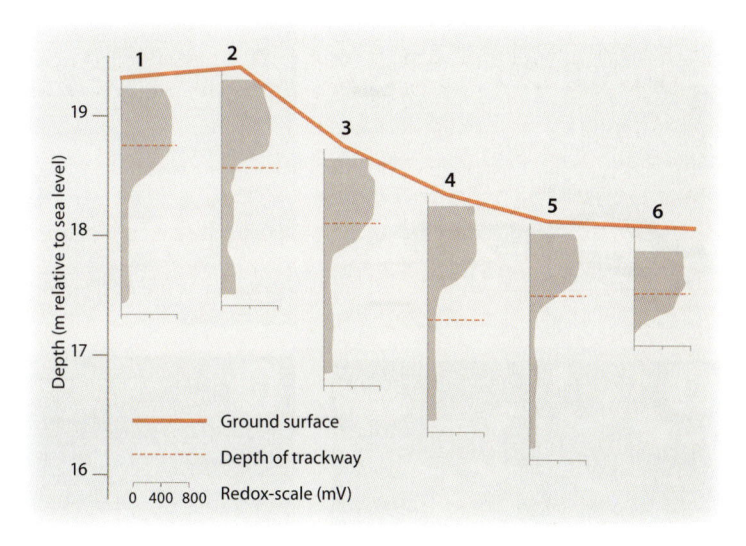

layers were formed. The degradation as observed in other layers probably originated from drier phases during the growth of the peat. It was concluded that the trackway was not in direct danger. This was thanks to the strong retention capacity of the peat which prevented desiccation and fungal activity.

At Swifterbant wood showed strong decay by erosion bacteria but no traces of fungi were found. Oxic or suboxic conditions reached into the top of the archaeological layer but did not penetrate far into it. The deeper parts of the profile were still reduced and still showed some traces of salt from the pre-1932 Zuiderzee saline water. In the thin sections (Fig. 8), the organic matter appeared to be unaffected by degradation and in general it looks pristine, with well-preserved cell structures and clear birefringence.

Furthermore, large amounts of secondary iron Fe-minerals appeared to be present in both the upper and deeper layers of the site, with different minerals related to different phases in the post-sedimentary history of the site. Vivianite (iron phosphate) and, less frequently, siderite (iron carbonate) occur in the deeper layers. At some depths these minerals are restricted to the soil mass and at others they are concentrated in pores and cracks. Vivianite and siderite can only form in slightly basic, reducing, sulphate-poor environments with high contents of iron and bicarbonate or phosphate, e.g. lake bottoms and organic-rich deposits where iron and phosphate are supplied by upwelling reduced (deep) groundwater. Their presence is therefore diagnostic for preservation conditions containing wooden remains and the environmental mechanisms behind preservation. In the Swifterbant case, they probably formed shortly after burial of the site. The soil mass surrounding root channels, cracks and other pores that penetrate the archaeological layer show accumulation haloes ('hypocoatings') of iron oxyhydroxides. They probably formed synchronous with or shortly after the formation of the vivianite as a result of the transport of oxygen through pores into the reduced groundmass. Pyrite (iron sulfide) occurs throughout the layers studied but is restricted to pores, cracks and root channels. The highest concentrations are often found in connection with organic matter. Often vivianite and iron oxyhydroxides can be seen to be (partly) transformed into pyrite. In the upper layers of the site, in the range where oxygen penetration can occur, pyrite is oxidized. Since the sediments that make up the site contain calcium carbonate, mostly in the form of shells, the sulphuric acid formed by the oxidation of pyrite is readily transformed into gypsum. At the same time, the presence of calcium carbonate prevents decreasing pH levels, while pyrite will not

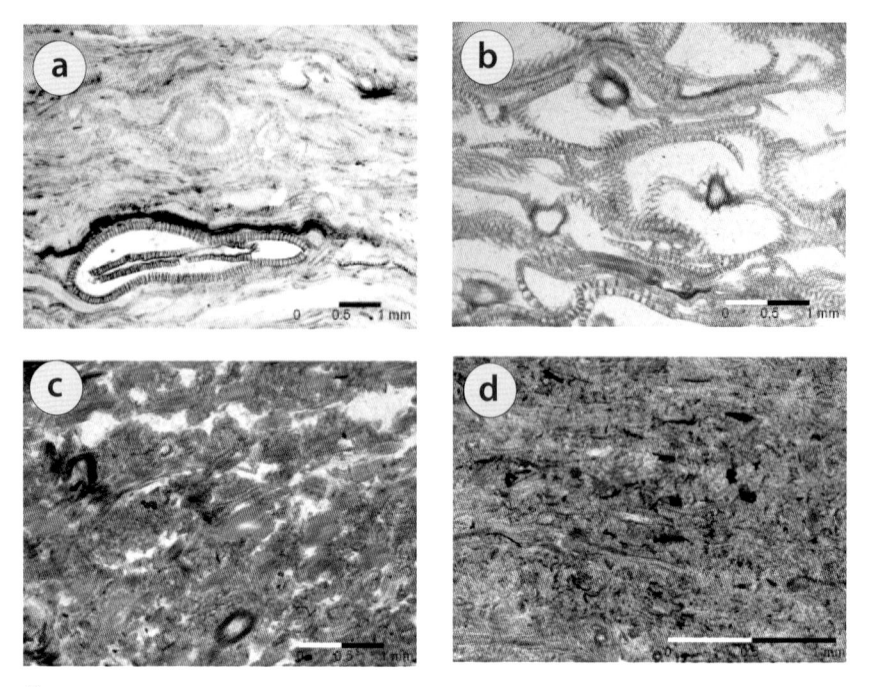

Fig. 7
Photomicrographs showing the variations in the degree of degradation of peat in thin sections from Nieuw-Dordrecht.
a: Well-preserved material. Cell walls and plant fragments can be clearly recognized. Most of the plant remains are birefringent (not shown), which indicates that the cellulose is still preserved in (semi) crystalline form.
b: Very loosely packed moss peat, with an estimated 80% (water filled) pore space and no traces of biological degradation.
c: Peat, strongly degraded by soil fauna. Plant remains are fragmented and degraded. Some layering or structure seem to still be present.
d: Strongly fragmented and degraded peat due to soil fauna activity.

oxidize completely. The iron produced is not well soluble at high pH values and forms a protective skin of iron oxyhydroxides surrounding a kernel of pyrite that is not affected any further. Furthermore, the occurrence of various labile mineral species in the groundmass indicates that the clay in which the site is embedded is remarkably impermeable and has successfully sealed most of it from outside detrimental factors such as oxygen. Although the archaeological site is sealed and the pyrite oxidation does not result in overall pH decrease that could damage archaeological remains, the site remains under threat from oxidation-related processes. In addition, the formation of gypsum can seriously deform and fragment wood. A monitoring plan is therefore advised in order to keep track of the oxidation processes in the Swifterbant area.

4. GENERAL DISCUSSION AND CONCLUSIONS

So far, the results of the molecular research on the botanical macro-remains did not greatly contribute to the understanding of the degradation pathway. Variability in chromatograms was found but it appeared that determination of chemical changes does not necessarily represent the morphological degradation.

Fig. 8
Well-preserved organic matter at Swifterbant. Plane polarized light (a) and crossed polarized light (b). The good conservation of the structure is clearly visible, as is the strong birefringence in b, indicating well-preserved cellulose.

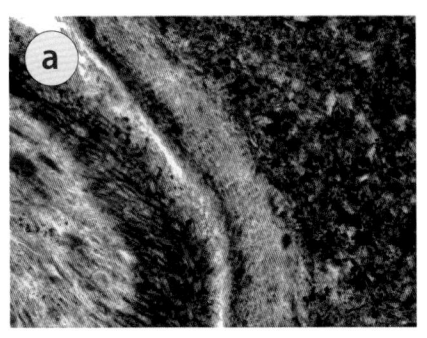

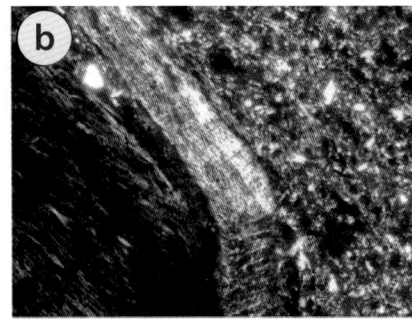

It also remained unclear whether chemical degradation is related to differences in the rate of chemical degradation, to differences in the pathway of degradation, to environmental differences during life or to a combination of these three factors. It is expected that the exact mechanisms behind degradation are too complex to comprehend. It is therefore recommended that the molecular differences between the individual molecular assessments must be systematically compared to environmental conditions in order to gain empirical evidence on detrimental environmental conditions. We also conclude that, at least at this stage of research, as long as the chemical signals as shown in the chromatograms are not understood with regard to reconstructing diagenetic pathways, systematic molecular determination of macroremains is not a promising tool for monitoring and we have to rely on visual inspection of the remains. Some species were, however, shown to be more suitable for monitoring degradation than others because they contain more of the compounds known to be reflective of chemical degradation.

Micromorphological research, on the other hand, has proved to be a more powerful tool for the assessment of the deterioration and preservation of wood, peat and botanical macroremains. The Nieuw-Dordrecht and Swifterbant cases demonstrate how micromorphological research can be used in assessing the threat of degradation to archaeological wetland sites. It must be stressed, however, that micromorphological research cannot replace methods that are now in use (groundwater level monitoring, redox probes, soil and water chemistry). It should rather be seen as one of a series of valuable tools. The examples presented here demonstrate two important aspects related to site conditions and burial environment that can be studied. Firstly, micromorphological analyses provide a direct impression of the quality of organic remains that are present within the archaeological site. These are not necessarily of archaeological origin. However, when it can be shown that the latter have experienced the same burial environment as the archaeological remains, they might be a fair proxy for the condition of the organic component of the site. Secondly, the presence of diagenetic minerals, especially various iron-bearing minerals, reflect past and present soil conditions like reduction-oxidation ratios and salinity. The great advantage of micromorphology next to bulk analyses is that it is possible to determine the distribution of these minerals in relation to the soil structure and each other. By including this information it is possible to reconstruct past changes in the burial environment from the diagenetic minerals present and determine which (potentially detrimental) processes are active now. An additional advantage of the use of micromorphology in wetland site monitoring is that the thin sections can be stored, enabling comparisons with future sampling at the site.

ACKNOWLEDGEMENTS

This paper actually combines two projects which were presented during the final Symposium of the PDL/BBO programme (Lunteren 20-23 May 2008). Written versions of both presentations were reviewed in detail by Jim Williams (English Heritage, Northampton, UK) for which he is greatly acknowledged. This final paper was reviewed by two anonymous peers.

NOTES

1 VU University Amsterdam, the Netherlands.
2 Cultural Heritage Agency, Amersfoort, the Netherlands.
3 BIAX Consult, Zaandam, the Netherlands.
4 Koolistov, Hendrik-Ido-Ambacht, the Netherlands.

REFERENCES

Berg, M.M. van den (in prep.): *The Dutch water-system and the implications for in-situ preservation of the archaeological record,* Amsterdam (Ph.D. thesis VU University).

Berg, M.M. van den/G. Aalbersberg/R.M. van Heeringen, 2006: *Archeologische kwaliteit op peil. Bestaande grondwatermeetnetten en het erfgoedbeheer,* Amsterdam (Geoarchaeological and Bioarchaeological Studies 5).

Berg, M.M. van den/E.A. Hatzmann, 2005: *Water en archeologisch erfgoed,* Amersfoort (Nederlandse Archeologische Rapporten 30).

Corfield, M./P. Hinton/T. Nixon/M. Pollard, 1998: *Preserving archaeological remains in situ. Proceedings of the conference. London 1994,* London/Bradford.

Courty, M.A./P. Goldberg/R. Macphail, 1989: *Soils and micromorphology in archaeology,* Cambridge.

Doesburg, J. van/G.V. Mauro, 2007: *Onderzoek en archeologische begeleiding op en rondom Schokland; een kleinschalig onderzoek aan het Enserkerkje en archeologische begeleiding van de herstelwerkzaamheden aan de kerkresten, de waterput op de Zuidert en de aanleg van de hydrologische zone,* Amersfoort (Rapportage Archeologische Monumentenzorg 142).

Exaltus, R.P., 2000: *Bescherming bodemarchief Limmen-Heiloo; monitoringonderzoek januari 1997 tot en met juni 1999,* Amsterdam (RAAP-rapport 557).

Exaltus, R.P./C.M. Soonius, 1994: *Bescherming antropogeen waardevolle terreinen t.b.v. de uitvoering Bijdragenregeling Bodembeschermingsgebieden. Opstartnotitie t.b.v het deelproject Waterland onderzoeksfase eerste jaar,* Amsterdam (RAAP-rapport 91).

Exaltus, R.P./C.M. Soonius, 1997a: *Bescherming antropogeen waardevolle terreinen t.b.v. de uitvoering Bijdragenregeling Bodembeschermingsgebieden. Eindverslag deelproject Limmen-Heiloo, monitoring 1994-1996,* Amsterdam (RAAP-rapport 188).

Exaltus, R.P./C.M. Soonius, 1997b: *Bescherming antropogeen waardevolle terreinen t.b.v. de uitvoering Bijdragenregeling Bodembeschermingsgebieden. Eindverslag deelproject Waterland, monitoring 1994-1996,* Amsterdam (RAAP-rapport 189).

Exaltus, R.P./C.M. Soonius/S. Moolenaar/M.C.A. van Waijen, 2003: *Bescherming bodemarchief Waterland-Oost en Waterland-Midden; eindrapport monitoringsonderzoek 1994-2001,* Amsterdam (RAAP-rapport 928).

Heeringen, R.M. van/G.V. Mauro/A. Smit, 2004: *A Pilot Study on the Monitoring of the Physical Quality of Three Archaeological Sites at the UNESCO World Heritage Site at Schokland, Province of Flevoland, the Netherlands*, Amersfoort (Nederlandse Archeologische Rapporten 26).

Heeringen, R.M. van/E.M. Theunissen, 2001: *Kwaliteitsbepalend onderzoek ten behoeve van duurzaam behoud van neolithische terreinen in West-Friesland en de kop van Noord-Holland*, Amersfoort (Nederlandse Archeologische Rapporten 21).

Heeringen, R.M. van/E.M. Theunissen, 2002: *Dessication of the Archaeological Landscape at Voorne-Putten*, Amersfoort (Nederlandse Archeologische Rapporten 25).

Hill, T./R. Mc Kenna/M. Vorenhout, 2008: *Beckingham Marshes, Nottinghamshire: A palaeoenvironmental evaluation of fluvial deposits associated with the River Trent*, University of Birmingham.

Huisman, D.J., 2009: *Degradation of archaeological remains*, Den Haag.

Jones, J./H. Tinsley/R. Brunning, 2007: Methodologies for assessment of the state of preservation of pollen and plant macrofossil remains in waterlogged deposits, *Environmental Archaeology* 12, 71-86.

Kars, H./R.M. van Heeringen, 2008: *Preserving Archaeological Remains In Situ Proceedings of the 3rd conference December 2006, Amsterdam*, Amsterdam (Geoarchaeological and Bioarchaeological Studies 10).

Kars, E.A.K./H. Kars, 2002: *The Degradation of Bone as an Indicator in the Deterioration of the European Archaeological Property*, Brussels/Amersfoort (Final Report, with Appendices A-H; Project ENV4-CT98-0712).

Kars, H./A. Smit, 2003: *Handleiding Fysiek Behoud Archeologisch Erfgoed, Degradatiemechanismen in sporen en materialen. Monitoring van de conditie van het bodemarchief*, Amsterdam (Geoarchaeological and Bioarchaeological Studies 1).

Klaassen, R. (ed.), 2005: *Preserving cultural heritage by preventing bacterial decay of wood in foundation poles and archaeological sites*, Brussels (Final Report, with Appendices, Project EVK4-CT-2001-00043, internal report, European Commission).

Mattsson, E./A.G. Nord/K. Tronner/M. Fjaestad/A. Lagerlöf/I. Ullén/G.Ch. Borg, 1996: *Deterioration of archaeological material in soil. Results on bronze artefacts*, Stockholm (Konserveringstekniska Studier 10),.

Nixon, T., 2004: *Preserving Archaeological Remains In Situ? Proceedings of the 2nd conference, September 2001 London*, London.

Smit, A./G. Mol/R.M. van Heeringen, 2005: *Natte voeten voor Schokland. Inrichting hydrologische zone, Archeologische Monitoring 2003-2004, Een evaluatie van de waterhuishoudkundige maatregelen*, Amersfoort (Rapportage Archeologische Monumentenzorg 124).

Smit, A./R.M. van Heeringen/E.M. Theunissen, 2006: *Archaeological Monitoring Standard. Guidelines for the non-destructive recording and monitoring of the physical quality of archaeological sites and monuments*, Amersfoort (Nederlandse Archeologische Rapporten 33).

Theunissen, E.M./D.J. Huisman/A. Smit/F. van der Heijden, 2006: *Kijkoperatie in het veen. Kwaliteitsbepalend onderzoek naar de neolithische veenweg van Nieuw-Dordrecht (gemeente Emmen)*, Amersfoort (Rapportage Archeologische Monumentenzorg 130).

Vernimmen, T., 2002: The preservation of botanical remains in archaeological sites on Voorne-Putten, in R.M. van Heeringen/E.M. Theunissen (eds.), *Dessication of the Archaeological Landscape at Voorne-Putten*, Amersfoort (Nederlandse Archeologische Rapporten 25), 137-162.

Vorenhout, M., 2008: *Grondwaterstand en -kwaliteit rond twee verschillend ingekuilde wrakken (25H-20 en -21, Almere)*, Amsterdam (IGBA rapport 2008-02).

Vorenhout, M./A. Smit (in prep.): *Monitoring Aardenburg*, Amsterdam (IGBA rapport).

Wagner, D.M./M. Kropp/K.A.N. Abelskamp-Boos/F. Dakoronia/N. Earl/C. Ferguson/ W.R. Fischer/ C. Hills/H. Kars/R. Leenheer/R. Meijers, 1997: *Soil archive classification in terms of impacts of conservability of archaeological heritage*, Brussels/Amersfoort (Final report EV5V-CT94-0516).

7. The ancient quarry and mining district between the Eifel and the Rhine: aims and progress of the Vulkanpark Osteifel Project.[1]

Angelika Hunold[2] & Holger Schaaff[2]

ABSTRACT

The landscape of the Osteifel between the towns of Andernach and Mayen in the north of Rheinland-Pfalz, Germany, is characterized by quaternary volcanism. In the course of the eruptions valuable raw materials were produced, including basalt lava, tuffstone and pumice. People first used the volcanic resources in prehistoric times. One of the most extensive mining districts north of the Alps in the ancient world developed here during the Roman period. Millstones of basalt lava and building material of tuff were extensively traded over many centuries into large parts of Europe.

Quarrying, which has been carried out up to the present day, is a great burden on the landscape of the Osteifel but at the same time it provides opportunities. Thus, thanks to enormous mining profiles, deep geological windows have developed which allow a detailed view into the history of the earth. At the same time, previously unknown ancient quarries and mines have been located in the last 150 years by means of modern mining techniques. Brought to light by the mining, the sites could, at least for a short time, be examined without danger.

The importance of the unique geological and archaeological heritage of the region led to the idea of Vulkanpark Osteifel. Founded in 1996, the project follows a dual aim, scientific research on the one hand and economic strengthening through tourism on the other. To realize this goal, a GmbH (Limited Company) was founded whose shareholders are the district council of Mayen-Koblenz and the Römisch-Germanisches Zentralmuseum in Mainz, an international research institute for archaeology. Today, more than 20 monuments and three information centres have been established.

With the implementation of the Vulkanpark, the legacy of the stone industry has for the first time been considered as a cultural heritage worthy of protection.

KEY WORDS

Volcanology; archaeology; stone industry; ancient quarrying; cultural landscape; Vulkanpark; mining

1. INTRODUCTION

One of the largest mining areas for mineral resources in the ancient world was to be found in the north of Rheinland-Pfalz, Germany, between Andernach on the Rhine and Mayen on the border of the Eifel, in use in Roman times and the Middle Ages (Fig. 1). Millstones of basalt lava, blocks made from tuff and clay crockery were absolute top export goods for hundreds of years. These were then transported on the Rhine to customers in Switzerland, Britain and Scandinavia. Even now in the twenty-first century, the regional economic and social structure is characterized by the mining and processing of the valuable raw materials. Mining has increased over the years, resulting in a lasting change in the landscape. This ongoing development is briefly described below.

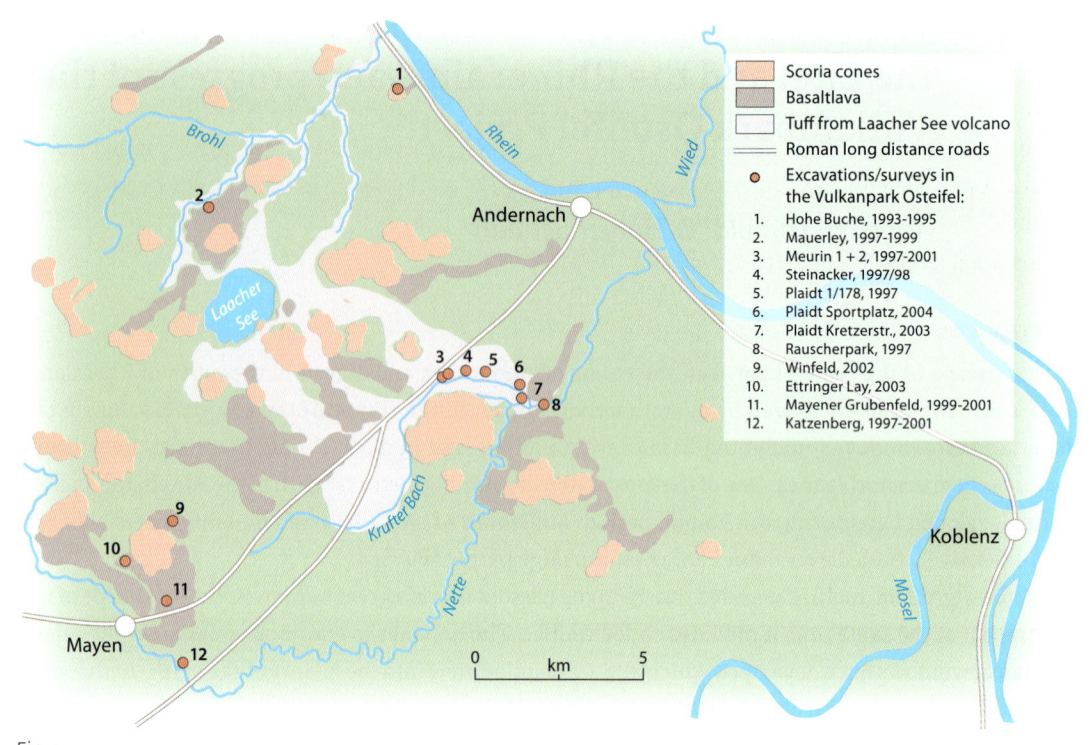

Fig. 1
The mining area for mineral resources between Andernach and Mayen (Germany). In the course of the Vulkanpark Osteifel project many ancient quarries were investigated. *Graphic: Forschungsbereich VAT.*

2. LANDSCAPE CONDITIONS

The region consists of a large part of the so-called Osteifel Volcanic Field which comprises approximately 100 volcanoes. The eruption from the Laacher See volcano, the largest in the new age of the geological history of Central Europe, took place approximately 13,000 years ago (Jöris/Weninger 2000; Schmincke 2000, 170-178). Enormous quantities of ash and pumice were thrown more than 30 kilometres high into the stratosphere and were carried towards Sweden in the north and Italy in the south. Metre-high pumice deposits covered the landscape surrounding the volcano. The bordering river valleys were filled with deposits from pyroclastic flows. Over time the resulting tuff deposits in the Brohl valley and the Krufter Bach valley reached depths of up to 35 metres and more. Pumice and tuff later proved to be valuable raw materials for humankind. Almost 2,000 years later the Ulmener Maar in the west Eifel erupted (Zolitschka/Negendank/Lottermoser 1995), marking the provisional end of volcanic activities in the Eifel highlands.

Osteifel volcanism dates back more than half a million years. Rieden volcano, Wehr volcano and finally the Laacher See volcano mark the three main volcanic phases in the geological era of the quaternary (Van den Bogaard/Schmincke 1990a; Baales 2002, 49). The resulting craters formed by highly explosive pumice and ash eruptions can still be seen today as extensive calderas in the landscape. Due to the rising of glutinous magma around the Riedener Vulkan, so-called domes have been created (Van den Bogaard/Schmincke 1990b; Meyer 1994, 369-378).

Mostly however, it is the distinctive volcanic form of the numerous scoria cones that dot the landscape (Schmincke 1988, 36-47; *idem* 2000, 124-126). They were formed during the main volcanic phases approximately 400,000 years and 200,000 years ago. Magma, rich in gas, was expelled from the chimney in the form of pieces of lava and fountains. After hardening to scoria, the characteristic ramparts were formed. During such magma eruptions hot liquid lava streams broke out and when they cooled down produced the valuable basalt lava deposits. Bellerberg volcano near Mayen, with its three lava streams, is a striking example of this phenomenon (Harms/Mangartz 2002).

Discovered by modern mining, maars and tuff rings can now be seen beneath many scoria cones in the Osteifel. They show the beginning of volcanic eruptions, when contact between magma and water caused violent steam explosions and phreatomagmatic eruptions. In Nastberg near Andernach-Eich we can most clearly see beneath the dark scoria layers the red tuff layers of an earlier eruption phase (Ippach/Mangartz/Schaaff 2002, 29-51). Maars and scoria cones can simultaneously erupt next to each other, as the example from the Booser Vulkan in the far west of the region illustrates (Lorenz 1973).

Today, the Eifel volcanism is by no means considered to be extinct. Rather, according to recent geological research, there will be future activity so that a periodical monitoring of the volcanoes makes sense (Schmincke 2000, 210-212). At present, noticeable signs of active volcanism are CO^2 exhalations on the Laacher See shores and the fact that the region is an earthquake zone.

3. THE USES OF VOLCANIC ROCK

Many thousands of years passed before humans first began to use the volcanic raw materials. Approximately 7,000 years ago, the first simple grain grinding stones were produced in the lava streams of the Bellerberg volcano near Mayen, thereby laying the foundation for stone quarrying in this region (Hörter/Michels/Röder 1950/51; *idem* 1954/55).

The quality of the basalt lava and the proximity to the river Rhine resulted in early extra-regional trade in stone products. In the Roman era, the Mayen millstone developed into an absolute export best seller. The trade reached Britain as well as the Alps. The lava streams in Mayen developed into the largest production works for grinding stones north of the Alps (Mangartz 2006; *idem* 2008). Quarrying was carried out in opencast mining in well-organized stone quarries (Fig. 2). In the Middle Ages, a change in underground mining took place. Over hundreds of years huge underground mining halls, so-called rock cellars, were formed in Mayen and in the Mendig lava stream (Mangartz 2003; Wehinger 2004; Kling 2006). The quarrying of basalt lava has continued to the present day. In the last 200 years, the production of building stones has come to the fore, although today millstones are still occasionally produced.

Although the basalt industry can look back on very old local traditions, the beginning of tuff stone production was triggered by technology from the Mediterranean. Roman soldiers were responsible for the start of the organized quarrying of the rich tuff layer areas around the Laacher See 2,000 years ago (Röder 1957; Schaaff 2000). They were knowledgeable about building with stone and, from their country of origin, they also knew the value of the tuff stones which were light and easy to work with. In cities such as Pompeii and Herculaneum these stones were used for building (Ciro Nappo 2004, 24-25). The foundation for the native building stone industry was laid. From the start, mining took place in widespread underground mining works. From the harbour in Andernach, tuff stone went on to reach the province of

Fig. 2
A Roman millstone quarry within a lava flow from the Bellerberg volcano near Mayen. *Graphic: Fanny Hartmann, Bern.*

Germania Inferior, which was very poor in stone, and further up to the North Sea coast. One is unlikely to find a Roman town, castle or settlement along the Rhine without tuff stone buildings (Schäfer 2000). Tuff mining reached its second heyday in the eleventh to the thirteenth centuries with the building of churches and monasteries (Haiduck 1992). Large quantities of the material were shipped to Denmark. Mining in underground tunnel systems continued until 1858, when it was replaced by the less dangerous opencast mining (Schaaff 2002).

4. THE EFFECTS OF THE MODERN STONE INDUSTRY

Today, the landscape between the towns of Andernach and Mayen is marked by industrial mining. Over the last 150 years, the modernization of mining techniques has led to a permanent change in the shape of the landscape. Extensive opencast mines are now found in the area of basalt and tuff deposits. In the course of modern mining, the old mining works were in danger of becoming extinct.

Even more serious are the consequences of pumice mining. From about 1845, volcanic glass, a product of the eruption of the Laacher See volcano, has been used as a basic material for the production of breeze blocks (Röder 1956). The mining of this material constitutes a considerable intrusion in the landscape. It is a fact that the archaeological preservation of historical monuments is affected (Von Berg 1995). Many archaeological sites from the past 13,000 years have been lost forever.

Another raw material, the basalt scoria from numerous volcanoes, has been intensively used since the 1930s (Fig. 3). This is sorted into different sizes and then used in road-building, the light cement industry, sewage plants and road grit. Whole volcano cones have disappeared as a result of mining.

The mining which is still taking place is a great burden on the landscape of the Osteifel. However, it provides opportunities for the region by causing conditions which set this region apart from many others. It provides the possibility for scientific exploration and documentation of historical monuments which would not otherwise have been discovered. Thus, thanks to enormous mining profiles, deep geological windows have developed which allow a detailed view into the history of the earth. A good example of this is the Eppelsberg, which is a half-mined scoria cone (Fig. 3). Here, one can see the eruption process of a typical Osteifel volcano (Ippach/Mangartz/Schaaff 2002, 3-27). The most famous geological exposure in our region is the Wingertsbergwand near Mendig. The deciphering of the more than 40-metre-high tephra deposits of the Laacher See volcano contributed greatly to the detailed reconstruction of the complicated set of past events which occurred during the eruption (Schmincke 2000, 170-178).

At the same time, in the last 150 years ancient quarries and mines have been discovered by means of the modern mining techniques. The millstone quarries from Mayen and Mendig as well as the extensive underground tuff stone mines in the Krufter Bach valley are well known in the world of archaeological research. Brought to light by mining, there was, at least for a short time, the possibility to examine the sites without danger. However many of the so-called 'Old Men' were later destroyed by the continuing mining (Von Berg/Wegner 1995).

5. VULKANPARK OSTEIFEL

The concept behind the Vulkanpark Project was born in the district of Mayen-Koblenz, an area which comprises a large part of the East Eifel mining region (Fig. 1). Scientific advice was sought to certify the international importance of the local heritage, which was the most important condition for the project. Indeed the region offers unique testimonies both in the fields of volcanology and archaeology. On the one hand we have one of the rare cases of intra-plate volcanism in the world, on the other the development of an industrial landscape which started in the Neolithic period and has changed continually up to the present day. By means of the Vulkanpark, this unique heritage was firstly to be researched and secondly

Fig. 3
Eppelsberg volcano near Nickenich in the year 2000. *Photo: Forschungsbereich VAT.*

Fig. 4
Interior view of Römerbergwerk Meurin near Kretz. *Photo: Forschungsbereich VAT.*

made accessible and understandable to the public. The key themes of the project are the origins of the landscape, humans living in the landscape and humans changing the landscape.

In this context one should mention the continuous decline in the economic development of the stone industry which has resulted in ever decreasing jobs for the people living in the region. New economic stimuli are needed. The Vulkanpark project follows two aims, namely scientific research and economic strengthening through tourism. Although neighbouring regions are traditional tourist destinations, the East Eifel was long considered to be unattractive because of its extraction activities. Here, the task was to transform this assumed disadvantage into an advantage by awakening an understanding of the history and development of this landscape.

To realize this goal, a GmbH (Limited Company) was founded in Koblenz in 1996. Fifty per cent of the shareholders consist of the association of local authorities Vulkanpark from the district of Mayen-Koblenz. These represent the interests of the various villages and towns in Vulkanpark. The Römisch-Germanisches Zentralmuseum, Forschungsinstitut für Vor- und Frühgeschichte, which is based in Mainz is the other shareholder. This innovative constellation, an international research institute and a district council, makes it possible to unite scientific interests and tourism and promote and represent these interests equally.

In practice, the work on the project proceeds as follows. A site, such as a volcano or an ancient quarry, is selected to be a Vulkanpark site. Following selection by scientists from the Römisch-Germanisches Zentralmuseum in collaboration with local agents, the approval of the corresponding town or municipal council must be sought. Criteria for the decision on a site are its scientific importance as well as its suitability for opening to the public. Moreover, practical aspects such as the permission and support of the landowner have to be taken into account. In our experience, agreements with landowners or stone industry companies are often more effective than insisting on legal protection.

In any case, research has to be carried out on a site before the practical work can start. The measures depend on the nature of a site, a volcano will first be prospected while in a quarry an archaeological excavation is often necessary. After the exploration, the knowledge acquired is presented to the public. Scientists draw up a concept for each site and work out a series of information charts (Fig. 2). These are placed along trails leading through the site.

Within Vulkanpark, individual visitors can find their way with the help of information trails. Nevertheless, guided tours for groups of visitors are very much in demand. Therefore, Vulkanpark guides are trained from time to time by the scientific staff so that a pool of guides is always available. Moreover, a pool of teachers takes care of special pupil programmes. These teachers also run a school website so that schools, as one of the most important groups of users, are integrated in an optimal way.

The limited company's other partner, the association of local authorities Vulkanpark, is in charge of marketing, management and maintenance. Employees of the local authorities are in charge of tasks on the local level. In this way, a lot of work can be done by a small Vulkanpark staff. Moreover, local agents are always involved in the process of planning and implementing a site.

Most of the sites are freely accessible. Entrance fees only apply for the information centres and the 'Römerbergwerk Meurin' site (see below). The Vulkanpark Osteifel is integrated with wider networks, for example, the Nationaler Geopark Vulkanland Eifel, which unites three neighbouring Vulkanpark projects.

Finally, it has to be mentioned that the most important condition to make the project work is the cooperation of science, administration and industry. Only the permanent interplay of these actors, not just during an initial phase, provides the durable quality of the Vulkanpark monuments.

6. THE DEVELOPMENT OF VULKANPARK OSTEIFEL

At the moment, more than 20 monuments and three information centres have been established. Each information centre gives general information about the sites and facilities in Vulkanpark, but one section in each of them is dedicated to a special subject, for example volcanism or stone production. The sites in the landscape are accessible by several routes. They include volcanoes and quarries, a Late Roman fortification, Roman tomb monuments and several local museums. Some are also part of nature reserves and thus Vulkanpark Osteifel offers a great variety of subjects to the visitors, including geology, archaeology, history and biology.

The site of Römerbergwerk Meurin, situated in the middle of modern tuff stone works in the Trasswerke Meurin, (Fig. 4) is a good example of this (Schaaff 2005). It is the only place in the Krufter Bach valley where tuff stone is still being mined today. Here you can find the last remnants of widely branched tunnel systems which stretch across the valley for kilometres. The main parts of these underground quarries, the oldest of which date back to the beginning of the Christian era, were destroyed with the arrival of the extensive open mining systems in 1860.

As a result of very close team work with the landowner, it was possible to research, protect and make available to the public a small but representative part from the early phases of this industry. The development of the European stone mining methods since the Roman age provides a good example of this. It comprises the beginning of stone quarrying by the Roman army and long distance trade and the building boom in the Middle Ages up to the modern stone industry. Because of this the site received the European Union Prize for Cultural Heritage/Europa Nostra Award 2003.

Further research has also developed since the start of the project. The investigation of the Vulkanpark sites has not only led to their presentation to the public but has also formed the basis for an extensive research programme named 'The origin and formation of an industrial landscape, the ancient quarry and mining district between the Eifel and the Rhine'. Up to fifteen archaeologists and mineralogists work on individual projects within the programme. Besides volcanism and stone mining, mineral resources, especially clay for ceramic production, are now the focus of attention.

With the implementation of the Vulkanpark, the legacy of the stone industry has for the first time been considered as a cultural heritage worthy of protection. Consequently, the local population's appreciation of the heritage of their own landscape has increased. As a result the cultural resources are increasingly regarded not only in a historical dimension, but also as a source for arranging the modern and future landscape, for example in making landscape-planning decisions. In this sense, the Vulkanpark project meets the aims of the European Landscape Convention.

7. FUTURE ACTIVITIES

Another aspect of land use stemming from a case study in a limited area next to the Mayen quarries has provided another piece of heritage to protect. We would like to understand how the supply of the great number of workers necessary in quarries and mines was managed and what influences on the environment can be detected.

An aspect relevant to both the area of Vulkanpark Osteifel and a wider region beyond its borders is the impact of the Laacher See pumice on the landscape in the Middle Rhine basin and the extensive industrial use of this raw material in modern times. Therefore, a pumice museum is planned as a common project of the districts of Mayen-Koblenz and Neuwied and the pumice federation, an association of entrepreneurs.

NOTES

1 This contribution is an extended and modified version of a lecture first given at the International Conference *Cultural Heritage and Landscapes in Europe* in Bochum 2007; see Schaaff 2008.
2 Römisch-Germanisches Zentralmuseum, Mainz, Germany.

REFERENCES

Baales, M., 2002: Vulkanismus und Archäologie des Eiszeitalters am Mittelrhein. Die Forschungsergebnisse der letzten dreißig Jahre, *Jahrbuch RGZM* 49, 43-80.

Berg, A. von, 1995: Archäologische Denkmalpflege und wirtschaftliche Flächennutzung im Neuwieder Becken. Die besondere Problematik archäologischer Denkmalpflege im nördlichen Mittelrheingebiet, *Berichte zur Archäologie an Mittelrhein und Mosel* 4, 313-326.

Berg, A. von/H.-H. Wegner, 1995: *Antike Steinbrüche in der Vordereifel*, Koblenz (Archäologie an Mittelrhein und Mosel 10).

Bogaard, P. van den/H.-U. Schmincke, 1990a: Die Entwicklungsgeschichte des Mittelrheinraumes und die Eruptionsgeschichte des Osteifelvulkanfeldes, in W. Schirmer (ed.), *Rheingeschichte zwischen Mosel und Maas. Deuqua-Führer 1*, Hannover, 166-190.

Bogaard, P. van den/H.-U. Schmincke, 1990b: *Vulkanologische Karte der Osteifel 1:50 000*, Koblenz.

Ciro Nappo, S., 2004: *Pompeji. Die versunkene Stadt*, Köln.

Haiduck, H., 1992: *Beginn und Entwicklung des Kirchenbaues im Küstengebiet zwischen Ems- und Wesermündung bis zum Anfang des 13. Jahrhunderts*, Aurich (Quellen zur Geschichte Ostfrieslands 15).

Harms, E./F. Mangartz, 2002: *Vom Magma zum Mühlstein. Eine Zeitreise durch die Lavaströme des Bellerberg-Vulkans*, Mainz (Vulkanpark-Forschungen 5).

Hörter, F./F.X. Michels/J. Röder, 1950/51: Die Geschichte der Basaltlavaindustrie von Mayen und Niedermendig, *Jahrbuch für Geschichte und Kultur des Mittelrheins und seiner Nachbargebiete* 2/3, 1-32.

Hörter, F./F.X. Michels/J. Röder, 1954/55: Die Geschichte der Basaltlavaindustrie von Mayen und Niedermendig, Teil II, *Jahrbuch für Geschichte und Kultur des Mittelrheins und seiner Nachbargebiete* 6/7, 7-32.

Ippach, P./F. Mangartz/H. Schaaff, 2002: *Krater und Schlackenkegel*, Mainz (Vulkanpark-Forschungen 6).

Jöris, O./B. Weninger, 2000: ^{14}C-Alterskalibration und die absolute Chronologie des Spätglazials, *Archäologisches Korrespondenzblatt* 30, 461-471.

Kling, J., 2006: Die unterirdischen Mühlsteinbrüche von Niedermendig/Deutschland. Historische Kartographie und Detailinventarisierung, in A. Belmont/F. Mangartz (eds.), *Mühlsteinbrüche. Erforschung, Schutz und Inwertsetzung eines Kulturerbes europäischer Industrie (Antike-21. Jahrhundert), Internationales Kolloquium Grenoble 22.-25. September 2005*, Mainz (RGZM-Tagungen 2), 133-144.

Lorenz, V., 1973: On the formation of maars, *Bulletin volcanologique* 37, 183-204.

Mangartz, F. 2003: Abbau und Produktion rheinischer Basaltlava-Mühlsteine vom Mittelalter bis 1900, in *Meules à grains. Actes du colloque international de La Ferté-sous-Jouarre, 16-19 mai 2002*, Paris, 160-168.

Mangartz, F., 2006: Vorgeschichtliche bis mittelalterliche Mühlsteinproduktion in der Osteifel, in A. Belmont/F.Mangartz (eds.), *Mühlsteinbrüche. Erforschung, Schutz und Inwertsetzung eines Kulturerbes europäischer Industrie (Antike-21. Jahrhundert), Internationales Kolloquium Grenoble 22.-25. September 2005*, Mainz (RGZM-Tagungen 2), 25-34.

Mangartz, F., 2008: *Römischer Basaltlava-Abbau zwischen Eifel und Rhein*, Mainz (Monographien des Römisch-Germanischen Zentralmuseums 75; Vulkanpark-Forschungen 7).

Meyer, W., 1994³: *Geologie der Eifel*, Stuttgart.

Röder, J., 1956: Die Frühzeit der Bimsindustrie (Die Schwemmsteinindustrie), in *Rheinische Bimsbaustoffe. Entstehung und Entwicklung der Rheinischen Bimsbaustoffindustrie*, Wiesbaden/Berlin, 39-53.

Röder, J., 1957: Die antiken Tuffsteinbrüche der Pellenz, *Bonner Jahrbuch* 157, 213-271.

Schaaff, H., 2000: Antike Tuffbergwerke in der Pellenz, in *Steinbruch und Bergwerk. Denkmäler römischer Technikgeschichte zwischen Eifel und Rhein*, Mainz (Vulkanpark-Forschungen 2), 17-30.

Schaaff, H., 2002: Rätselhafte Stollen bei Plaidt (Kr. Mayen-Koblenz). Zeugnisse der frühen Trassindustrie in der Pellenz, *Acta Praehistorica et Archaeologica* 34, 281-291.

Schaaff, H., 2005: Unterirdische Arbeitswelten – Das Römerbergwerk Meurin, *Archäologie in Deutschland* 2005, 64-65.

Schaaff, H., 2008: The Origin and Formation of an Industrial Landscape – The Ancient Quarry and Mining District between the Eifel and the Rhine, in Ch. Bartels/C. Küpper-Eichas (eds.), *Cultural Heritage and Landscapes in Europe – Landschaften: Kulturelles Erbe in Europa. Proceedings of the International Conference, Bochum June 8-10, 2007*, Bochum (Veröffentlichungen aus dem Deutschen Bergbau-Museum Bochum 161), 499-508.

Schäfer, K., 2000: Andernach – Drehscheibe des antiken Steinhandels, in *Steinbruch und Bergwerk. Denkmäler römischer Technikgeschichte zwischen Eifel und Rhein,* Mainz (Vulkanpark-Forschungen 2), 99-109.

Schmincke, H.-U., 1988: *Vulkane im Laacher See-Gebiet. Ihre Entstehung und heutige Bedeutung,* Haltern.

Schmincke, H.-U., 2000²: *Vulkanismus,* Darmstadt.

Wehinger, A., 2004: Der Obere Niedermendiger Basaltstrom. Lagerstätte und Bergbau, *Mainzer geowissenschaftliche Mitteilungen* 32, 113-132.

Zolitschka, B./J.F.W. Negendank/B.G. Lottermoser, 1995: Sedimentological proof and dating of the Early Holocene volcanic eruption of Ulmener Maar (Vulkaneifel, Germany), *Geologische Rundschau* 84, 213-219.

IV

IMAGINATION - FACTS AND CONSTRUCTIONS

Cooney Lough (IE): lake coring in the Neolithic landscape. *Photo: M. O'Connell*.

1. Imagination: facts and constructions

About imagination, authenticity and identity, and the value of interpretative heritage research

Tom (J.H.F.) Bloemers[1]

ABSTRACT

This introduction reflects on three themes selected from the contributions in this section: imagination, authenticity and identity, and interpretative heritage research.

Imagination covers facts and constructions and their relationship. The tension between these can be understood by adopting the concepts of 'superstructure' and 'infrastructure'. In our case, superstructure is the 'narration' of the archaeological-historical landscape story by applying the metaphor of 'biography of landscape', infrastructure is the methodical way towards this narration, exploring the sources. Action research creates a platform to apply these concepts for linking (the production) of facts and constructions.

Authenticity and identity represent aims, effects or outcomes of imagination and are expressed by images of the archaeological-historical landscape. They are constructs with a dynamic and fluid character related to the time and the context they belong to. In the specific context of linking cultural-historical heritage, planning and design various concepts are available to assess this heritage, namely the biography of landscape, protection by development, the canon and historic landscape characterization. Identity is a key notion in the interaction between practice and imagination.

Interpretative heritage research is the reflection on the way people relate to past elements and structures. Issues like effectiveness of implementations, transparency of procedures, attracting public interest or the closure and openness of the system can 'further the democratization of heritage policy'. The introduction of the Valletta Convention in the Netherlands and its effects on the role of amateur archaeologists, self- and hetero-reference and the value of a philosophy of science for the heritage disciplines show that more basic reflective issues can also be the subject of interpretative research.

Finally the issue of the ethics of pragmatism is introduced as an urgently needed condition to frame heritage studies and management within modern society.

KEY WORDS

Imagination; authenticity, identity; interpretative heritage research; self- and hetero-reference, reactivity, ethics

1. INTRODUCTION

The core theme of this section is 'imagination'. Imagination as used in this section primarily covers the 'images' of the archaeological-historical landscape, the images themselves and the process of creating and perceiving these images, i.e. imagination in and about the past, the present and the future. However, it can also indicate the meaning of images for those dealing with and living in the landscape in the past and the present, the actors' involvement in ordering, analysing and interpreting landscapes and for the relationship between actors as part of the communication about different views on and the relationship between various interests in that landscape.

This introduction reflects on three themes selected from the contributions in this section, namely imagination, authenticity and identity, and interpretative heritage research. Imagination covers facts and constructions and their relationship. Authenticity and identity represent aims or effects or outcomes of imagination and are expressed, among other things, by images of the archaeological-historical landscape. Interpretative heritage research is the reflection on the way people relate to past elements and structures, for example by implementing and legitimizing heritage policy.

2. IMAGINATION

2.1 Facts and constructions: sources of images and carriers of imagination such as the biography of landscape

Imagination covers facts and constructions, they are a source of images and carriers of the process of imagination and interpretation respectively. What is generally indicated by the word 'fact' is the result of any form of observation, while construction can be considered as an interpretation or perception of such an observation giving meaning to it. In research the relationship or interaction between them is supported by the application of some sort of hypothesis or assumption that can be 'tested' and adapted in an iterative procedure that is commonly referred to as the 'empirical cycle' (Bloemers/Van Dorp 1991, 139-156).

Referring to Van der Valk's contribution (see Ch. II.2, 28-30), the constructivistic aspect of this procedure is of great relevance for our theme, especially the role or the position of the biography of landscape concept (see Ch. I) and its relationship with the 'facts' or 'data' about the archaeological-historical landscape. Accepting the importance of the constructivistic view, Van Londen (Van Londen 2004, 8-9) has adopted Goldstein's *Historical knowing* (Goldstein 1976) of 'superstructure' and 'infrastructure' as outcomes of the research procedure. In our case, superstructure is the 'narration' of the archaeological-historical landscape story by applying the metaphor of 'biography of landscape'; infrastructure is the methodical way towards this narration, exploring the sources. The biography as superstructure embodies its unifying potential by its role in the cultural planning activity in the Oer-IJ programme where archaeology, landscape architecture and planning have merged in a metaphoric view on the region's future development (see Ch. IV.2. Bloemers *et al.* and Ch. IV.3 Van Leeuwen). The narrative unifies various relevant strands of knowledge and perception, it supports communication and regional characterisation and it presents a framework for research and landscape assessment (Van Beek *et al.* 2008, 184). It can do justice to the specific qualities of the archaeological-historical heritage in general and the regional characteristics, in particular its long-term time depth, invisibility, materiality, cultural and natural transformation. The infrastructure as a methodical way facilitating the composition of the landscape biography covers a wide range of 'normal' practices in archaeological research and heritage policy within their specific context, such as those listed for the Oer-IJ programme in Fig. 1 (conventional) (Ch. IV.2. Bloemers *et al.*, 208). They range from developing new techniques for monitoring degradation processes or exploring geomorphology to preparing inventories of sites and areas for assessment. In this way the ambitions and possibilities of the various actors and institutions involved can be exploited.

2.2 The relationship between statements in science and policy: truth and justness in the conceptual studies presented at the start of the PDL/BBO programme in 2001

During has characterized science and (planning) policy as acting in the domain of truth and justness respectively (During/Elerie/Groenendijk 2001, 114; for an application on landscape in general, see Jacobs 2006, 9-12). Science aims for objectivity in the process of institutionalized knowledge production, policy for intersubjective exchange of opinions in the process of legitimated social decision-making.

In the context of research, policy and management of the archaeological-historical landscape there is no relevant discussion about this topic. Consequently we have turned to history. In historical terms the criteria for truth are 'correspondence' and 'coherence'. Correspondence means that a statement is true when that statement is in agreement with the state of art in (historic) reality; coherence indicates that a statement is true when it is connected with one or more other statements already accepted as true (Ankersmit 1984, 99-103). 'Justness' might be compared with the basic issue discussed in history about social engagement and the role of historians as social agents (Ankersmit 1984, 299-307). Rigney points to the two key issues of partiality and subjectivity that 'have become foregrounded in recent theoretical debates as part of what is loosely called post-modernism.' In her view the tension between scholarship and social commitment is 'endemic to historiographical practice' but needs to be discussed once more since a number of trends in cultural practice compel historians to do so, namely the desire to make history socially relevant, the growing public interest in collective memory and lived experience and the outside competition of alternative forms of history by multi-media museums, heritage sites and films (Rigney 2000, 7-9).

Although the topic of truth and justness of archaeological statements and decisions is not a widely discussed issue in archaeology, it is of relevance for various daily practices in archaeology all over Europe, namely when assessing and selecting the elements and structures in the archaeological-historical landscape for heritage management and planning, the presentations of the past in museums, popular books and the 'living history' enactments. Ankersmit's criteria can fill this hiatus for archaeology as well as for history.

In the PDL/BBO programme we have regularly encountered the tension between facts and constructions and between research and policy. In the Oer-IJ programme researchers criticized the way in which responsible authorities presented the 'popular story' of the region using 'ethnic identities' or were only partially prepared to participate in the assessment and selection process, having no formal responsibility. At the same time it had to be recognized that the researchers had no monopoly on knowledge or 'facts' but that colleagues in the policy field and amateur archaeologists also possessed expert or lay knowledge.

2.3 Action research: a platform for linking facts and constructions

The concept of 'action research' is discussed in chapter III.1 by Kars. We will summarize only what we consider as relevant for its use as a method for relating research and decision-making in policy and practice in the way it has been presented in contributions in this section. The interaction between research and policy is based on the notions of inter- and transdisciplinarity as defined in chapter I (p. 9 Fig. 3).

The critical factors influencing success or failure in the co-operation between various actors and institutions have to do with harmonizing differences in paradigms, operational context and synchronization of actions.

First, we will discuss the problem of the divide between paradigms.

The differences between researchers of the archaeological-historical landscape or its heritage (Ch. II.2: Van der Valk's 'internal integration') and the social, technical and planning sciences (Ch. II.2: Van der Valk's 'external integration') are recognizable both in the structure of research and policy institutions. The disciplinary divide between university research and teaching is paralleled in policy organization by the divide in sectors and political strategic documents.

A first major step towards inter- and transdisciplinary co-operation is recognizing and accepting the differences in the operational context of the involved actors, both institutions and individuals. The aims, means, tempi, results and their valorization are fundamentally different in research and policy, even when the same or similar methods and language are used. A next very critical step is to find out in what sort of actions research and policy can co-operate and what degree of integration is needed. This influences the form, methods and relationship between participants in specific actions. Are research and policy on equal footing or is one leading and the other supplying, one on 'top' and another on 'tap'? (Hoppe 2002).

Another recognition of major relevance is the fact that research and policy processes generally each have their specific phasings which do not normally run parallel. This can cause many problems, such as funding and approval, the time availability of participants and information, changes in human resources or political constellation effecting continuity in co-operation etc. Often researchers are seen by the policy sector as delivering their contribution too late and not well suited for the policy context.

Unifying concepts like cultural planning (more or less the same as Van Assche Ch. IV.5: heritage planning) and biography of landscape can help to overcome these critical factors. Not only do they help to cross the boundaries between the paradigms, they can also help to maintain the continuity in transfer of knowledge and experiences over successive research and policy cycles. This is crucial since the Belvedere and PDL/BBO programmes have made it clear that the transformation from a sectoral to an integrative heritage approach and its embedding in research and policy takes several research and policy cycles covering one or two decades from its start. Apart from that, the ambition to integrate the archaeological-historical landscape as a factor of quality, inspiration and sustainability in spatial planning is a long-term process to be implemented at the local and regional level.

Given the critical factors in the co-operation between research and policy, the time span of a planning process and implementation while maintaining continuity over one or two decades are a critical factor. This requires intermediary strategies aiming at the mediation between knowledge creation and policy-making that cover several policy cycles. The actors involved must have access to new knowledge and current policy developments. Such strategies can take various, not mutually exclusive, forms operating at the local or regional level but supported by formal policies at the provincial or national level. There are various examples of such intermediary roles, for example the public-private or semi-governmental institution (like the Erfgoedhuis, Steunpunt etc. in the Netherlands), the contract company, the local expert (see chapter II.2 Drentsche Aa) or the local society or action group. It is surprising that many participants in the PDL/BBO programme gradually arrived at the opinion that some form of local or regional organization is needed to function as long-term intermediary between science, policy and implementation to ensure the Belvedere and PDL/BBO aims.

2.4 Conclusions

Tensions in the relationship between research and policy will always be present. However, they can be handled when the various contexts in which the actors operate are recognized and the actions and degree of integration are clearly defined. The managing of changes in insights, policy and actors over several research and policy cycles is crucial to maintain the integration process's long-term continuity.

3. AUTHENTICITY AND IDENTITY

Authenticity and identity or identification are issues always explicitly or implicitly present in historic landscape research and policy and the interaction between facts and constructions. In what follows, we will discuss questions like who owns the past and the knowledge about the past, the expression of authenticity and identity/identification, the conceptualization and instrumentation of images and imagination and their consequences for assessment and selection.

3.1 Who owns the past and knowledge about the past?

Archaeologists are generally well aware of the question of who owns the past and that knowledge about the past can be appropriated and manipulated. Indeed, Colin Renfrew and Paul Bahn dedicate a whole chapter to the issue (Renfrew/Bahn 2000³ Ch. 14: Whose past? Archaeology and the public) and identity is one of the issues discussed.

Although anyone will readily agree that both professionals and the public claim ownership (of the knowledge) of the past, reality is somewhat more complex. Professionals are educated experts who have access to specific information and techniques and are well organized in institutions and disciplinary networks. Their main job is generally to use these abilities and potential for research, policy and management. Of course, the transfer of knowledge is part of the professionals' job by teaching and communicating, but there will always be a gap between expert and lay knowledge. On the other hand, research, policy and management need public and political support for a wide range of reasons varying from finances to engagement and from social well-being to disciplinarian self-respect. On its part, the public is not only interested in this knowledge but, as a consumer and visitor, is increasingly becoming a major influence in the presentation of the past. Most of all, the public is a factor that is a value in its own right as a political factor demanding a policy that facilitates the quality conditions for its daily life. The shift from government towards governance and the buzz word 'democratization' are expressions of this trend. The tendencies for professionalization and democratization seem to represent opposing trends. The action research approach is a way to reconcile these oppositions, but it also creates tensions within research itself, between basic and applied research. As Duineveld has shown (Duineveld 2006, 47-49 and Ch. IV.6), these opposing trends can be analysed in terms of power and the aims and objectives of the actors involved leading to, for example, the unintended exclusion of amateur archaeologists from the new archaeological system recently introduced in the Netherlands.

3.2 Authenticity and identity/identification: a time and context related dynamic construct

Authenticity and identity are in our view constructs of which form and content are related to the time and the context they belong to, consequently they have, even if continuity may be observed, a dynamic and fluid character. This is well illustrated by Daugstad's contribution (Ch. IV.4) on her views on Norwegian heritage in the nineteenth century and the effects on present-day landscape policy.

Authenticity refers in general to the truthfulness of the origins and attributions of objects and images and their perception (Kianicka/Buchecker 2006, 115-119). Elements and structures of the archaeological-historical landscape are the result of (long-term) transformations and of what has been preserved in the past. These transformations are determined by natural and cultural factors. One of the cultural factors is how past societies experienced, assessed and 'managed' the relics of the past in their own time and environment, often indicated as 'the past in the past', and eventually anticipated on their future. As Ickerodt has argued elsewhere (Ickerodt 2005), the perception and the social effect of the past is not dependent on this aspect and causes a certain variability and instability. However, the use of land and landscape has always been related to an already existing landscape and consequently landscape can be perceived as a layered system with stories, institutions, networks of occupation and infrastructure embedded in an ecological system (Hidding/Kolen/Spek 2001, 9-14). This layeredness of the archaeological-historical landscape complicates the definition of its authenticity and how to measure it. Is it the visible past of elements like church towers, field systems, rivers or dikes? Or is the invisible past hidden by later extensions and restorations of buildings or by later sedimentations or erosions? Apart from that, there is the tension between preference for the original as the supposed expression of authenticity and the actual experience of it creating its own artificiality, the 'staged authenticity' referred to by Van der Laarse in his comment on Rekittke and Paar's contribution (Ch. IV.8).

The conclusion must be that archaeological-historical landscape formation has and always will be founded on what was there before and that it logically leads towards a continuation of this 'tradition', recognizing "the powerful fact that life must be lived amidst that which was made before" (Meinig as quoted by Hidding/Kolen/Spek 2001, 21). The Belvedere concept of 'conservation through development' is one form of expressing this awareness. However, one also has to recognize that this assumption is not always justified or effective and that there are situations where this awareness is weak or absent. It can come under pressure when a social system loses touch with rural space because of its metropolitan background. Globalization might influence the transformation of landscapes, either indirectly by decisions made in other parts of the world, or directly, by national or local decisions based on global economic thinking. Awareness may also be absent because of a long time gap between present inhabitants and prehistoric land use. This is the case with Neolithic landscapes in the north of Holland that almost 'disappear' behind the identification of present-day 'West Frisians' with their medieval roots (Koedoot 2004, 20-29 and 59).

Identity and identification are a social construction and process with the outcome of the interaction between a person, a group and a place equating personality, culture or polity and space (Van Assche 2004, 168-169). Images of the past play an important role in identity constructions in general, they reflect time-bound perceptions of the past and archaeology is one of the sources frequently used (Hobsbawm/Ranger 1983; Ickerodt 2005). In the heritage sector, identity constructions are superior to authenticity since the focus is often not on the preservation of the object or structure but on the symbolic function (Van der Laarse 2005, 14). In this context, the interface between real and virtual landscapes as facilitated by powerful computer programmes like the 3D landscape visualization in Rekittke and Paar's contribution (Ch. IV.7) is becoming increasingly complex. They can strongly support the intermediary role of design in the process of integrating cultural-historical landscape qualities in planning as is promoted by the Belvedere policy. The images created in this way can also function as prosthetic memories to raise public interest in past landscapes, how they were used and what happened there (Kolen 2005, 6-8). Kolen raises the question whether the historical experience is changed by these images rather than diminished. Arguing that the challenge lies in differentiating between 'mythological' and 'scientific' perceptions of the past, Ickerodt demonstrates how genealogical and evolutionary approaches are still applied to the conceptualization of burial mounds and these have remained largely unchanged since the nineteenth century and their condensed form during the Third Reich (Ickerodt 2005).

Especially interesting for archaeological heritage is that it is now possible to make the invisible virtually visible. A combination of Smit's 2D hunter-gatherer landscape (Ch. IV.9) with Rekittke and Paar's 3D model showing the vegetation of the gradient zones with camp sites would be very appealing. It can help establish a link between an ecological and archaeological heritage policy for sustainable landscape management, as Smit indicates. Moreover, it could also bridge the gap between present inhabitants and prehistoric land use by raising awareness of a forgotten or neglected past. The complexity of the relationship between real and virtual landscapes lies not only in the blurring of transition between both worlds, but also in the powerful potential of manipulating past landscapes and implicit or hidden ideological intentions as we know them from our recent history. In archaeology the issue of 'ethnicity' as a particular aspect of identity has great topicality (Renfrew/Bahn 2000[3], 189 and chapter 14) as has been shown by the discussions among the researchers in the Oer-IJ programme about the focus on the Frisians in the public activities organized by the provincial authorities.

To our conclusion about authenticity we can now add those about identity and identification. Identity is a dynamic construct related to a time-bound context and identification is a process of reshaping knowledge, interpretation and experience. Experience related to the social and economic use of space evolved as a product of multiple feedback relations. The archaeological heritage existing in the unknown, the invisible or the unassessed is not generally involved and this can limit the input of archaeological heritage on planning and landscape design. This differentiation appears to be crucial because the invisible may represent an important aspect of the use of landscapes, for example as forbidden areas etc. Finally, there is a tension between assessing the authenticity of archaeological-historical landscapes as the outcome of past transformations and the process of identification on the basis of selected elements and structures and the perception of their meaning for identity.

Conceptualization and instrumentation to assess the archaeological-historical landscape
The function of concepts in planning can be cognitive, intentional, institutional, communicative or active and these functions are not mutually exclusive in their application (Zonneveld 1991). The same applies to their use in the specific context of linking cultural-historical heritage, planning and design. There are various concepts available, including the biography of landscape, protection by development, the canonical and historic landscape characterisation.

The biography of landscape has already been discussed in this chapter and in the introduction to this volume (Ch. I, 11-13). Kolen has pointed out that the application of this concept following a geographical line is most appropriate for the study of spatial (trans)formations within landscapes and regions. Van Londen listed the variety in uses of the biography concept depending on the context, namely managing heterogeneity, supporting communication and regional branding as a context for research and as framework for valorization (Van Beek et al. 2008, 179-184). As Kolen states, the biography concept recognizes that 'spatial (trans)formations always involve interactions between physical structures and changes in cultural values and mentalities; in this sense landscape is never simply a *habitat* or static built environment, but a *habitus* reflecting, transmitting and renewing the spatial habits and values of culture.' An example of this is the way 'water' can be applied in the biography concept since, in the context of the Dutch landscape, 'water' is a feature that always comes to the forefront. Water as a metaphor is frequently used in a planning context and it is a determining factor in the origin of the Dutch archaeological-historical landscape, which makes it a strong unifying concept to link both worlds (cf. Flood 2005; Kolen 2005, 9). However, to make it a characteristic and meaningful feature of a regional landscape, the diversity of water and its meaning in a regional context have to be taken into account. The sea, lakes, moors, wells, rivers and canals have particular qualities and are perceived differently in time and space.

The Belvedere Memorandum (Belvedere 1999, 32-33) has developed the concept of 'conservation through development' as a strategic vision: 'By seeking new uses, old landscapes and buildings can be saved. However, it is just as much a question of "development through conservation". By using our cultural heritage in a frugal and responsible manner, we are investing in the development and strengthening of our identity, knowledge, comfort, business climate and potential for tourism.' In the interaction between cultural history and planning, the first has both a restricting and a developing influence, the second has an adaptive and additive function.

The Dutch 'cultural canon' with fifty 'windows' from prehistory to the present (Van Oostrom 2007) is another concept of integration. The canon is accompanied by a list of statements about what it is intended for and how it should be used. History has to be seen as a source of inspiration, 'a story of the country we live in', it can 'contribute to citizenship', it is 'based on identity and/or citizenship', but the canon and national identity are 'not one and the same' (Van Oostrom 2007, 16 and 27-31; Bazelmans 2009). The canon concept has been taken up by many regions and even other disciplines like earth sciences and physics have presented their own canon. A series of canons has already been produced (Adams/Hendriks 2007), including for landscape (Van den Ancker 2008; Van Blerk/Harsema 2008) and Roman monuments (Bus/De Vries 2008, 9).

The Historic Landscape Characterisation is an 'all inclusive' approach for the management of present change affecting the historic landscape developed by English Heritage and its partners (Clark/Darlington/Fairclough 2004, 6-7; Fairclough 2008, 413). Its methodology is integrative because it includes all aspects of the present-day landscape, takes into account the human perspective of nature and culture, considers the people's views and aims at integration with spatial and environmental planning. It serves various goals like extending the scope from site to landscape, giving research data a new context and encouraging public awareness. Applying 'normal' archaeological heritage methods, the additional value of this approach lies in the concept of 'characterization'. Characterization expresses the aim to arrive at an understanding of the development of a specific landscape from the past into the present. In this way it is a prerequisite for taking sensible conservation and development decisions leading to a strengthening of the qualities of a landscape. Historic Landscape Characterisation clearly belongs with the 'infrastructure' as described by Van Londen, but it also prepares the ground for the application of the biography concept. Together they could be an interesting combination of approaches giving legitimacy to the final process of assessment and selection.

All the approaches previously described lead to the inevitable step of assessment and selection of archaeological-historical elements and structures in the present-day landscape resulting in their preservation, development or destruction. Generally, assessment and selection are applied on the site level, using criteria related to perception, physical condition and intrinsic value or comparable aspects (Deeben *et al.* 1999). Historic Landscape Characterisation and biography of landscape focus on landscape scale, long-term developments and related characteristic elements and structures. By this integrative 'holistic' approach, the invisible, mostly archaeological, elements and structures, can 'profit' from visible ones since their attraction can raise the interest in the historic landscape and, once this has succeeded, the scope can subsequently be widened towards the invisible layers.

3.3 Conclusions

The tendencies for professionalization and democratization appear to represent opposing trends. Here, the action research approach is a way to reconcile these oppositions. However, this approach might sometimes also be confronted with tensions within research itself, between basic and applied research.

The archaeological-historical landscape as *habitat* and *habitus* is the result of (long-term) adaptation processes causing transformations and of what has been preserved in the past. This justifies the collaboration of the heritage sector with planning and design in a joint effort for 'conservation through development'. 'The powerful fact that life must be lived amidst that which was made before' obliges planners and designers not only to use the past as a source of inspiration, but also to take care of it, even in the case of the unknown, the invisible or the unassessed. A meaningful synergy between methodological infrastructure and interpretative superstructure can produce an effective balance between practice and imagination. In the interaction between practice and imagination, identity as a key notion and as a social construct is generally dominant over criteria of authenticity.

4. INTERPRETATIVE HERITAGE (RESEARCH)

4.1 Introduction

In his contribution, Duineveld (Ch. IV.6) introduced the notion of interpretative heritage research. He describes this as "to study ... the way people relate to them [the past or relics]... construct and interpret [them]... One branch... is policy implementation studies." In his words this type of research "can provide insights in the societal impact of heritage management strategies, the multiple perspectives on heritage politics and on the subjects of these policies, and provide recommendations for the implementation of archaeological heritage protection." Issues like effectiveness of implementations, transparency of procedures, attracting public interest or the closure and openness of the system can "further the democratization of heritage policy". Duineveld has illustrated his approach with a study of the introduction of the Valletta Convention in the Netherlands and its effects on the role of amateur archaeologists, a well organized group with a long tradition of active and supportive participation in Dutch archaeology. These organizations have been formally excluded from a range of professional activities such as excavations. Not only has this raised a lot of discussion and lack of understanding in this group, but it could also lead to a loss of public support for archaeology in general.

The relevance of interpretative heritage research is great and it is a new field, certainly for archaeology and historic geography. Its relevance has to do with the increasing policy and public interest as expressed by the Valletta Convention (Valletta 1992), the European Landscape Convention (Florence 2000) and, in the Netherlands, the Belvedere policy. During the past years, several studies have been published in the Netherlands that can be classified as 'interpretative'. Some of them focus on the Belvedere policy and the conditions that have to be fulfilled to make it a success (Wallagh 2005; Bosma 2008), others analyse the state of the art and the effectiveness of (archaeological) heritage management by quantifying data and monitoring various processes (Lauwerier/Lotte 2002; Zoetbrood/Van Rooijen 2006; Beukers 2009). A fine example of such a study in England with a great strategic impact is the Monuments at Risk Survey (Darvill *et al.* 1998).

The contributions to this section by Van Assche on self- and hetero-reference and by Ickerodt on the value of a philosophy of science for the heritage disciplines show that more basic reflective issues can also be the subject of interpretative research. Finally, the issue of ethics is introduced as a condition urgently needed to frame heritage studies and management.

4.2 Self- and hetero-reference as conditions for crossing disciplinary boundaries

The concept of self- and hetero-reference discussed by Van Assche touches on the major issue of the shift from the historic oriented to the heritage approach of the archaeological-historical landscape and the paradigmatic obstacles encountered (see Van der Valk Ch. II.2). Crucial is the understanding of the value and difficulties of trespassing boundaries in heritage planning as an inter- and transdisciplinary endeavour and 'in understanding the value of conflict and cultivated differences in the planning process' as Van Assche states.

Self-reference indicates that every social system such as, for example, a discipline reconstructs the world in its own terms in a process of 'autopoiesis' using solely its own structures, elements and programmes. The effect is an 'operational closure', i.e. the drawing of system or disciplinary boundaries and mechanisms to maintain these boundaries. The success of inter- and transdisciplinary approaches like the PDL/BBO programme aiming at integrative problem-solving depends on the ability to cross these boundaries and develop a meaningful synergy without losing sight of the intrinsic and relevant qualities of the specific discipline. This requires an openness towards other disciplines and the capacity to respond and adapt to them. This capacity and the observations made by it are founded in the ability for self-reference and consequently self- and hetero-reference go hand in hand. It may be clear that there always will be a tension between self-reference, with its operational closure as a condition for 'autopoiesis', and hetero-reference based on the capacity for openness. It will also be manifest that it needs at least 'two to tango' in inter- and transdisciplinarity and that what has been stated applies to both parties.

As Van Assche (Ch. IV.5) states "in heritage planning, this can be translated as an argument for the inclusion of actually different perspectives in a planning process, as opposed to the imposition of one disciplinary or bureaucratic perspective ...". In heritage planning, experts play a significant role and the boundary interactions between science and policy and between heritage and planning are critical. Applying action research, the recognition of possible productive differences between sectors and disciplines can be considered more as an asset than as a liability. We have however learned from the PDL/BBO programme that heritage experts and managers have to be aware of the fact that hetero-reference of the heritage sector will not 'automatically' produce hetero-reference by planners to include cultural history in planning deliberations. Projected on the heritage aims of preservation and development, the balance between operational closure and openness must be the outcome of the interaction in an arena with all stakeholders.

4.3 Reactivity: the interference of society and heritage research and management

The issue of openness is also very relevant for the position of the archaeological discipline regarding research and heritage management and its attitude towards modern society. The interference between science in general and society is referred to in sociology as 'reactivity'. Using this concept, Ickerodt (Ch. IV.11) has explored the way archaeology is at present dealing with this interference. He states that archaeology is facing the questions for whom and for what aims is 'heritage conservation management' is undertaken. One of them is socio-political: "to ensure individual identity in Europe, the population of which is growing closer together." And, as we may add, the chances the Valletta Convention and the European Landscape Convention offer compel us to answer many more specific questions. They influence not only the type of archaeological research as identity-creating factor and formal partner in spatial planning, but also the mentality of the discipline and its members. How does archaeology handle this political task?

Archaeologists have to be aware that the discipline needs a view on archaeological heritage management that 'is based both on scientific discoveries as well as on social categories', which are rapidly changing as a result of aging, migration, mobility and shifts in (types of) economic activities. Sociology of science can support the evaluation of various visions of archaeological heritage management and help clarify the role archaeology plays in society. Topics which can be thus evaluated include the meaning of archaeological sites and landscapes for society, the way decisions about heritage are taken and the communication of policies, actions and their aims and effects.

4.4 Ethics

Ethics as a theme of research or policy is not frequently or directly referred to in the various contributions in this section but is often implicitly present in the background. An exception is Ickerodt's contribution (Ch. IV.11), in which he remarks that "… the scientific-cum-social issue should serve quality management of… how to communicate archaeological information to the public in a way that will be understood. This requires the evaluation of the social background so that the possible ways of understanding the communicated historical facts are not left to intercultural or intersubcultural arbitrariness and are understood within certain limits. Since this step has a social effect, it should only be taken if based on previously defined scientific and ethical standards." Taking these implicit and explicit notions into consideration it can be concluded that ethics of heritage is a neglected theme that is needed to frame and justify actions.

The PDL/BBO programme offers a number of observations illustrating this need and its urgency. Various cases show tensions in the relationship between research, policy and the public regarding for example the relationship between (the roles of) the actors, the justification of decisions affecting assessment and selection of heritage relics and the selection and use of historic images for communication towards policy and public (e.g. Van Londen 2006, 174-176). These tensions sometimes lead to normative statements, disruption of co-operation etc. founded in individual views and emotions, but not embedded in intersubjective deliberations framed by professional ethical thinking. These cases illustrate the need for prescriptive ethics for norms, values and behaviour in the specific context of heritage research, policy and management. The development of such ethics should be founded in a dialogue encompassing theory, concept, strategy and practice of experiences in heritage research and management. Apart from ethical codes for professional behaviour as have been formulated in several countries and various organizations during the past decades, there is a limited number of publications on this theme. These mainly focus on the specific North American context but the European continent probably needs its own or at least adapted form of ethics.

The Dutch research programme on Ethics and Policy (NWO *Stimuleringsprogramma Ethiek & Beleid*) can act as a source of inspiration and an example of how to make a start towards the formulation of specific heritage ethics. A promising approach might be found in 'pragmatism', an approach which recognizes practice as a source of moral knowledge and appreciates the role of intuition and experience. To conceptualize the relationship between practice and ethics, two models are discussed in this programme, i.e. the reflective equilibrium model and pragmatic hermeneutics (Van Delden *et al.* 2005). The first offers a structure for solving moral problems or the quest for justifying of a moral theory (*ibidem*, 36). In this approach a person tries to arrive at a balanced coherent view of all relevant considerations via reflection and argumentation. The second approach recognizes the situatedness of human existence and understanding and consequently values practice and experience as a source for ethics developed out of a learning process (*ibidem*, 88-89). The two approaches link moral consciousness and a contingent historical practice. During an ESF/COST workshop about interdisciplinary landscape research in Brussels (November 2008), Keulartz presented four methods of pragmatism, namely gradualization by breaking up unproductive dualism, reframing by recasting and reconnecting things and relations in the perceptual and social field, common ground dialogue looking for deeper shared values, and boundary objects belonging to several intersecting parts of the social world and consequently suited to satisfy the informational requirements of each part.

4.5 Conclusions

Reflection and pragmatism are ways forward to understand tensions and support an integrative approach. Interpretative heritage research is a crucial field of research for the social relevance of archaeological-historical landscape research and management. The archaeological-historical disciplines have to find a balance between operational closure and openness in their inter- and transdisciplinary activities, for example by reflecting on these relationships from the perspective of reactivity. Pragmatism might indicate the way forward towards ethics framing inter- and transdisciplinary approaches to archaeological-historical landscape research and management.

NOTES

1   University of Amsterdam, Amsterdam, the Netherlands.

REFERENCES

Adams, T./M. Hendriks, 2007: *Culturele canonvorming. Een eerste inventarisatie*, Amsterdam.

Ancker, J.A.M. van den, 2008: *Het ontstaan van het Nederlandse landschap. Een canon in 12 thema's in 50 vensters*, s.l.

Ankersmit, F.R., 1984: *Denken over geschiedenis. Een overzicht van moderne geschiedfilosofische opvattingen*, Groningen.

Assche, K, Van, 2004: *Signs in time. An interpretive account of urban planning and design, the people and their histories*, Wageningen (Ph.D. thesis Wageningen University).

Bazelmans. J., 2009: 50+3. De historische canon en de voor- en vroegste geschiedenis van Nederland, *Vitruvius* 2, 20-25.

Beek, R. van/J.H.F. Bloemers/L. Keunen/H. van Londen/J. Kolen, 2008: The Netherlands, in G. Fairclough/P. Grau Møller (eds.), *Landscape as Heritage. The Management and Protection of Landscape in Europe, a summary by the Cost A 27 project 'LANDMARKS*, Bern (Geographica Bernensia 79), 177-203.

Belvedere, 1999: *The Belvedere Memorandum. A policy document examining the relationship between cultural history and spatial planning*, The Hague.

Beukers, E., et al. (eds.), 2009: *Erfgoedbalans 2009. Archeologie, monumenten en cultuurlandschap in Nederland*, Amersfoort.

Blerck, H. van/H. Harsema (eds.), 2008: *Canons van het Nederlandse landschap*, Wageningen.

Bloemers, J.H.F./T. van Dorp (eds.), 1991: *Pre- & Protohistorie van de Lage Landen*, Houten.

Bosma, K., 2008: *Het post-Belvederetijdperk: Cultuurhistorisch beleid verankerd in de ruimtelijke ordening en in de ontwerpopgave*, Den Haag.

Bus, M./B. de Vries, 2008: *Monumenten van Romeins Nederland. Beschermingsagenda Archeologie 2008*, Zwolle.

Clark, J./J. Darlington/G. Fairclough, 2004: *Using Historic Landscape Characterisation, s.l.*, English Heritage and Lancashire County Council.

Darvill, T./A.K. Fulton/M. Bell/K. Anderson, 1998: *The Monuments at Risk Survey of England, 1995. Main Report*, Bournemouth/London.

Deeben, J./B.J. Groenewoudt/D.P. Hallewas/W.J.H. Willems, 1999: Proposals for a practical system of significance evaluation in archaeological heritage management, *European Journal of Archaeology* 2, 177-199.

Delden, H. van/L. van der Scheer/G. van Thiel/G. Widdershoven, 2005: *Ethiek en Empirie. Theorie en methodologie van empirisch ethisch onderzoek*, Maastricht.

Duineveld, M., 2006: *Van oude dingen, de mensen, die voorbij gaan. Over de voorwaarden meer recht te kunnen doen aan de door burgers gewaardeerde cultuurhistories*, Wageningen (Ph.D. thesis Wageningen University).

During, R./H. Elerie/ H.A. Groenendijk, 2001: Denken en doen: verpachten van wijsheid of delen van kennis? Pleidooi voor de verbinding van cultuurhistorische kenniseilanden en een relatie met de sociale wetenschappen, in J.H.F. Bloemers/R. During/J.N.H. Elerie/H.A. Groenendijk/M. Hidding/J. Kolen/Th. Spek/M.-H. Wijnen, *Bodemarchief in Behoud en Ontwikkeling. De conceptuele grondslagen*, Den Haag, 111-157.

Fairclough, G., 2008: 'The Long Chain'. Archaeology, historical landscape characterization and time depth in landscape, in G. Fairclough/R. Harrison/J.H. Jameson Jr./J. Schofield (eds.), *The Heritage Reader*, London/New York, 408-424.

Flood, 2005: *The Flood*, Rotterdam (Catalogue 2nd International Architectural Biennale).

Goldstein, L.J., 1976: *Historical knowing*, Austin.

Hidding, M./J. Kolen/Th. Spek, 2001: De biografie van het landschap. Ontwerp voor een inter- en multidisciplinaire benadering van de landschapsgeschiedenis en het cultuurhistorisch erfgoed, in J.H.F. Bloemers/R. During/J.N.H. Elerie/H.A. Groenendijk/M. Hidding/J. Kolen/Th. Spek/M.-H. Wijnen, *Bodemarchief in Behoud en Ontwikkeling. De conceptuele grondslagen*, Den Haag, 7-109.

Hobsbawm, E./T. Ranger, 1983: *The invention of tradition*, Cambridge.

Hoppe, R., 2002: *Van flipperkast naar grensverkeer. Veranderende visies op de relatie tussen wetenschap en beleid*, Den Haag (Adviesraad voor het Wetenschaps- en Technologiebeleid).

Ickerodt, U., 2005: Hobsbawms erfundene Traditionen – Archäologie als soziales Phänomen, *Archäologisches Nachrichtenblatt* 10, 167-174.

Jacobs, M., 2006: *The production of mindscapes. A comparative theory of landscape experience*, Wageningen (Ph.D. thesis Wageningen University).

Jameson J.H. Jr./J. Schofield, (eds.), *The Heritage Reader*, London/New York, 408-424.

Kianicka, S./M. Buchecker, 2006: The experience of authenticity in the Swiss Alpine landscape – 'outside' and 'inside' gazes, in W. van der Knaap/A. van der Valk (eds.), *Multiple Landscape. Merging Past and Present. Selected Papers from the fifth International Workshop on Sustainable Land Use Planning 7-9 June 2004*, Wageningen, 113-124.

Koedoot, M., 2004: *Het Neolithicum van nu. Over de alledaagse betekenis van archeologisch errfgoed in de polder De Gouw en de Groetpolder*, Wageningen.

Kolen, J., 2005: De 'geheugenprothese' en andere verhalen. Over de historische ervaring in het tijdperk van massaconsumptie, in R. Brons/J. Rodermond/G. Wallagh (eds.), *Een cultuur van ruimte maken. Ontwerpen aan geschiedenis*, Rotterdam, 6-13.

Laarse, R. van der, 2005: Erfgoed en de constructie van vroeger, in R. van der Laarse (eds.), *Bezeten van vroeger. Erfgoed, identiteit en musealisering*, Amsterdam, 1-28.

Lauwerier, R.C.G.M./R.M. Lotte, 2002: *Archeologiebalans 2002*, Amersfoort.

Londen, H. van, 2004: *Culturele biografie van het landschap. Tussen kennisoverdracht en belangenbehartiging. Essay over de definitie en het toepassingsbereik van het concept*, Amsterdam (manuscript presented at the NWO/BBO meeting 21-22.4.2004 in Amsterdam, University of Amsterdam).

Londen, H. van, 2006: Cultural biography and the power of image, in W. van der Knaap/A. van der Valk (eds.), *Multiple Landscape. Merging Past and Present. Selected Papers from the fifth International Workshop on Sustainable Land Use Planning 7-9 June 2004*, Wageningen, 171-181.

Oostrom, F. van, 2007: *A Key to Dutch History. Report by the Committee for the Development of the Dutch Canon*, Amsterdam.

Renfrew, C./P. Bahn, 2000[3]: *Archaeology. Theory, Methods and Practice*, London.

Rigney, A., 2000: Introduction: Values, Responsibilities, History, in J. Leerssen/A. Rigney (eds.), *Historians and Social Values*, Amsterdam, 7-15.

Wallagh, G., 2005: Urgentie gezocht. Belvederebeleid te ver verwijderd van alledaagse realiteit, in R. Brons/J. Rodermond/G. Wallagh (eds.), *Een cultuur van ruimte maken. Ontwerpen aan geschiedenis*, Rotterdam, 19-22.

Zoetbrood, P./C.A.M. van Rooijen, 2006: Monuments in Balance. An Overview of the Stock of Archaeological Complexes at Archaeological Monument Sites, *Berichten van de Rijksdienst voor het Oudheidkundig Bodemonderzoek* 46, 171-179.

Zonneveld, W., 1991: *Conceptvorming in de ruimtelijke planning*, Amsterdam.

2. From Oer-IJ estuary to metropolitan coastal landscape

Assessing and preserving archaeological-historical resources from 4000 years of living between land and water

[1]Tom (J.H.F.) Bloemers[a], Gerard Alders[b], Robert van Heeringen[c], Marjolijn Kok[d], Heleen van Londen[e], Liesbeth Theunissen[f] & Peter Vos[g] with an external view by Gísli Pálsson[h]

ABSTRACT

The subject of this paper is the study of the wetland Oer-IJ area northwest of Amsterdam. The application of 'action research' and the cultural biography are outlined and followed by two specific aspects of water, the religious meaning and the relevance for degradation.

The analysis of the context of the action illustrates that the 'conventional' activities fit into Hoppe's 'engineers' model with policy 'on top' and researchers 'on tap' creating tensions between policy and research. The 'unconventional' activities complied more with the policy-oriented learning models based on equal partnership.

The cultural biography of the Oer-IJ has been named 'the forgotten delta' and presents a case to explore this concept in the context of planning. Before implementing the narrative definition, methods and context of use are explained. By its geological transformation, present-day landscape structure and the long-term development of landscape patterns, the buried delta itself offers the strongest regional identity possible. People's relationship with water while living on the 'wet' land has been dominant and determined by the principles behind the long-term development of the estuary.

A specific research topic was to make predictive maps of ritual activities in the pre- and protohistoric period. It was assumed that in the Oer-IJ ritual activities took place within the wet low-lying parts of the landscape. All 499 known archaeological sites from the pre- and protohistoric period were re-evaluated. A total of 22 sites in wet low-lying parts of the landscape were interpreted as offering sites. From these findings a model was made in which the time, place and find complex of offering sites were combined for the predictive modelling of the offering sites.

Another specific project focused on the degradation of archaeological sites in the Oer-IJ wetland. On selected sites the position and condition of the cultural layer was noted and sampled. The groundwater level was studied by divers, dataloggers and in dipwells. Furthermore, the redox potential was fixed as a measure of the presence of oxidizing substances. In addition the soil pH was sampled at several depths at each monitoring location. An important conclusion is that a rise in the groundwater level is not always favourable for the archaeological remains. Depending on the local hydrology, this can lead to the reversal of a seepage situation to an infiltration environment.

Pálsson compares the Oer-IJ approach with research in the Arctic and Iceland. His perspective is to find a middle ground between highly modern management schemes and avoid engagement with the environmental problems. The Dutch cases represent interesting attempts by engaging a variety of 'stakeholders' and at the same time engaging with comparison, theory, and critical and self-conscious reflection.

KEY WORDS
Oer-IJ; (un)conventional actions; forgotten delta, predicting ritual places, monitoring degradation

1. THE PDL/BBO/OER-IJ PROGRAMME
   (Tom Bloemers and Robert van Heeringen)

1.1 Introduction

The subject of this paper is one of the four regionally oriented studies of the PDL/BBO research programme dealing with the Oer-IJ area northwest of Amsterdam. First the programme as a whole will be outlined, followed by various subthemes, namely the two conceptual approaches of the PDL/BBO programme 'action research' and the cultural biography followed by two specific aspects of water, the religious meaning and the relevance for degradation, and an external view on the Oer-IJ programme.

Incorporated are the results of the research by Gerard Alders (formerly Province of North-Holland, now Cultureel Erfgoed Noord-Holland) dealing with the historical landscape, and Peter Vos (Deltares) who is responsible for the fine sequence of palaeographical/geomorphological maps of the past Oer-IJ landscapes.

1.2 Subject, context, aims and organization[2]
Subject, context and aims

The PDL/BBO/Oer-IJ research programme aims at developing an integrated approach for the sustainable development of archaeological-historical values as part of the environmental planning process. The programme started in April 2002 and will gradually come to an end in 2009/10.

The Oer-IJ area lies northwest of Amsterdam and on the west is bordered by the North Sea. It is a good example of the environmental problems currently faced by the western part of the Netherlands such as expanding urbanization and intensive economic activities resulting from the functional transformation of rural areas. This occurs in the wider background of global warming, rising sea level and the need for up-to-date water management. It is also a good example of the unexpected richness of the archaeological-historical complexes in the wetlands and the difficulties of assessing and protecting them.

The Oer-IJ area derives its name from a former estuary. It has been the object of intensive, systematic geological and archaeological research over the past 50 years. Its complex origins and the relationship between people and the environment over time are among the best studied cases in northwest Europe. The evolution of the landscape has been determined by a rise in sea level of more than 5 m over the past 5000 years. Coastal barriers protect the land from the sea and behind them lies the estuary that, until early historic times, linked the northern branch of the Rhine with the sea. East of the estuary stretches an extensive peat zone.

The Oer-IJ area is the focus of this programmatic case study supporting and studying the role of the province of North Holland as an intermediary between the national and regional levels for the implementation of the national Belvedere policy. The cultural policy of the province, as formulated in the Cultuurnota 2005-2008 (Cultuur Verbindt 2004), is facilitated by a specific form of planning called 'cultural planning'. Among other things, it exploits the potential of the archaeological-historical landscape for spatial quality and identity, resulting in a series of pilot projects (Beleving 2005).

To assess the potential of the archaeological-historical resources and their quality, three research activities were planned:
- the formulation of habitation/land use models supported by palaeogeology/palaeoecology for the origins and cultural transformation of the landscape from 2000 BC to post-medieval times;
- the assessment of the present-day condition of archaeological-historical sites and ensembles of sites;
- the development of predictive maps based on the habitation/land use models and quality assessment results.

The concept of 'cultural biography of landscape' has been applied to the Oer-IJ estuary and a process oriented organization model will be developed. This model will be based on the analysis of the application of the concept of 'heritage management by research and action' in order to facilitate internal (within cultural history) and external (with environmental planning) integration.

1.3 Organization of the PDL/BBO/Oer-IJ research and actions

The programme is a co-operation between the former National Service for Archaeological Heritage (now Cultural Heritage Agency), the Amsterdam Archaeological Centre of the University of Amsterdam (UvA) and the Province of North Holland. The funding is based on matching contributions from these three partners with PDL/BBO financing to a total amount of almost € 600,000. The research group comprises two Ph.D. researchers appointed by the University and the Province for a period of four years, two part-time senior researchers appointed by the University of Amsterdam and the Cultural Heritage Agency for three years, and two applicants from the University and the Cultural Heritage Agency. The research focuses on the following themes:

Habitation/land use models and palaeogeology/palaeoecology (Ph.D. researchers G. Alders, UvA/ Province North Holland and M. Kok/UvA)

Various studies have been made of the origins and trajectory of the Oer-IJ estuary, from c. 2000 BC onwards (*inter alios* Hallewas 1981; *idem* 1987; Van Es/Sarfatij/Woltering 1988, 69-101). This has led to an implicit deterministic designation of what 'marginal' land was in the past, whereby survey and excavation have tended to concentrate on higher lying areas, rather than low-lying 'marginal' places. Cultural land use, of whatever area of the estuary, has not been modelled for continuing use from later prehistory through to the post-medieval period. However, there are also strong indications that prehistoric settlement and ritualized landscape affected later patterns of village and urban patterning.

The research aims at a greater integration and testing of new results concerning prehistoric and historical land use in relation to the specific (past and present) wetland environment and the present land use. The two main aims that will be achieved through integration are:
- creating a refined, and possibly redesigned, model of the use and habitation of the region from the later prehistoric period to post-medieval periods and their relationship to our modern patterns of use through evaluating and testing concepts by exploiting different data sets;
- the model will be predictive in nature and thus of value for provincial and state policy with regard to archaeological-historical site evaluation and cultural resource management.

The Oer-IJ estuary can be divided into three types of landscape; the coastal barriers and dunes, the estuarine zone and the peat area (Fig. 2-3). Each zone has its own characteristic geological and archaeological-historical structure and development through the last four millennia. Nevertheless the relationship between these zones is essential for their proper understanding (Vos 1983; Westerhoff/De Mulder/De Gans 1987). Within the overall framework of the Oer-IJ estuary, each type of landscape has micro-regions containing sites where large-scale archaeological fieldwork has been carried out in the last decades. These data will be used to test the generalized statements on the archaeological-historical habitation/land use models from 2000 BC onwards.

Two Ph.D. researchers are involved in selected aspects of defining and modelling transformations and continuity. Marjolijn Kok studies the importance of peat and watery places in the pre- and protohistoric landscape as a specific regional variation within the broader northwestern European context (see section 4). Gerard Alders concentrates on characterization of habitation/land use for the historic phases. He analyses the peat area reclamation, the arrangement of the polder landscape, the relationship between the rural landscape and the villages and towns, and the role of defence.

Quality, assessment and prediction (Senior researcher L. Theunissen, Cultural Heritage Agency)

The specific heritage problem of the Oer-IJ programme is the gradual degradation of archaeological sites and ensembles of sites by intensive land use, lowering of the groundwater level and the fragmentation of the cohesion of ensembles, substrate and surroundings. This affects the quality of archaeological resources in a direct and irreversible manner and is extremely serious, for the wetland environment contains a high proportion of organic material and is very vulnerable. An appropriate and early assessment of high-quality sites and landscapes, including the conservation conditions for organic material, is crucial for sustainable heritage management. The use of predictive modelling is another means of timely identification of archaeological resources and assessment of their quality. Since predictive modelling is partly based on the structure and development of the physical landscape as an environment for human behaviour, it is crucial to have proper insight into the geo-genesis of the Oer-IJ estuary and its relationship to the archaeological-historical sites and ensembles of sites. Bound to present preservation policy, such facets as 'where' exactly flooding occurred, how long settlements were divided by a natural boundary of the Oer-IJ, and how continuity in settlement pattern and land use could be achieved through to the early Middle Ages must be further specified.

The purpose of this theme is to develop an 'instrument' for identification, assessment, selection, protection and conservation in the form of a cultural resource map, preferably at a scale of 1:10,000, which contains information about the physical conditions and the character of archaeological sites and ensembles. In this way conditions are created for the adjustment of a national heritage policy on a provincial level.

The research method covers the following steps:
- actualization and production of the Archaeological Monuments Map 1:25,000 (or 1:10,000) with more specific data about the physical and intrinsic archaeological quality of sites and ensembles, which requires an adaptation of the mapping procedures on a scale of 1:25,000;
- developing and testing of predictive maps for the archaeological-historical habitation/land use models covering the (pre-)historic time span and the relationship with the palaeo-geographical structures and

processes. To avoid a bias towards high-lying areas on which research has traditionally been focused, special attention will be given to the aspect of low-lying 'peaty and watery' marginal areas;
- identifying present patterns of land use and those recommended for the future which combine sustainable preservation of the archaeological-historical resources with agricultural exploitation, nature conservation, recreation and education.

An integrated policy for the sustainable development of archaeological-historical resources (Senior researcher H. van Londen, UvA)

The problem of this project is the realization of an integrated approach for the sustainable development of archaeological-historical values on a regional or provincial scale. The provincial, regional and local levels are crucial for the success and variability of ways to implement the national policy. When the involved actors with their very different competences are taken into account, this process with its various forms and dimensions of integration is complex and unusual in archaeological resource management at the time of its initiation.

The aim is to carry out a pilot study for an effective integrated approach
- by applying the concept of the cultural biography of landscape in the case of the Oer-IJ estuary to arrive at a powerful and region-specific archaeological-historical project which supports internal and external integration on a regional scale;
- by developing an organizational model utilizing the co-operative experience of the institutions involved via action research.

2. THE ACTION RESEARCH APPROACH
(Tom Bloemers & Heleen van Londen)

The implementation of 'action research' in the PDL/BBO/Oer-IJ programme is based on the close co-operation between Tom Bloemers and Heleen van Londen and the result of interaction and discussions during the past years. First we will present the context and the various actions of the provincial policy which are relevant to the PDL/BBO/Oer-IJ programme as described above. This will be followed by the analysis of our experiences.

2.1 The context of the action and the actors involved

The context of the action is the province of North Holland's policy to implement the national Belvedere policy on a regional level from 2001 onwards. In anticipation of this policy, the PDL/BBO/Oer-IJ programme has presented itself as a partner to develop an integrated approach for the sustainable development of archaeological-historical values as part of the environmental planning process. This context has two dimensions; first the interface between archaeological-historical heritage management and environmental planning, and second the interface between archaeological-historical policy-makers and archaeological-historical researchers.

Three groups of actors are directly involved in this context, namely the provincial policy-makers responsible for heritage management and environmental planning, the PDL/BBO researchers from the university and the national heritage institute Cultural Heritage Agency, and the landscape architects as private entrepreneurs mediating and visualizing the Belvedere policy in their designs. There are also archaeological companies as private entrepreneurs contracted for *ad hoc* activities.

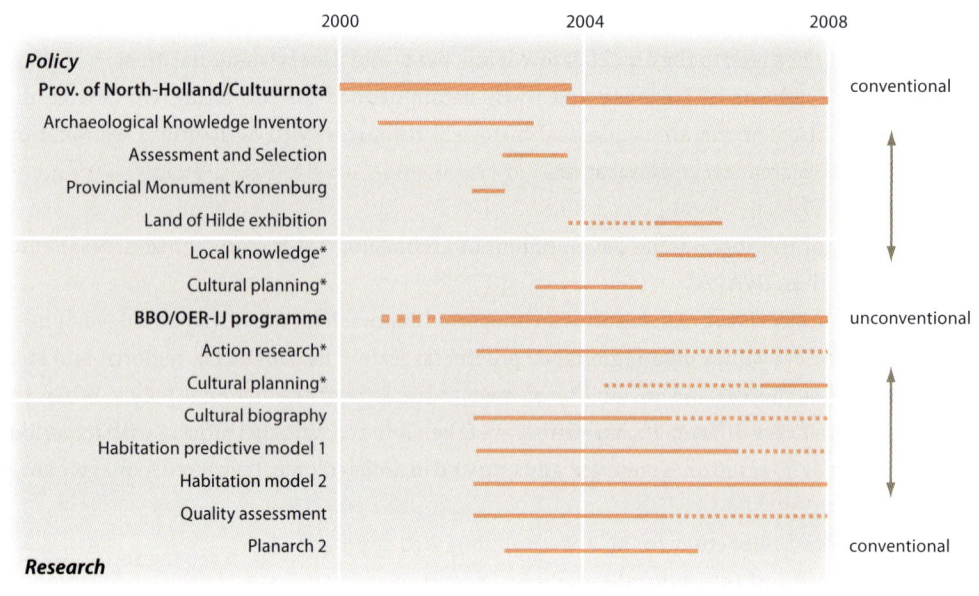

	2000	2004	2008	
Policy				
Prov. of North-Holland/Cultuurnota	———————————	———————————————	conventional
Archaeological Knowledge Inventory	————			
Assessment and Selection		—		
Provincial Monument Kronenburg	—			
Land of Hilde exhibition		············———		
Local knowledge*		———		
Cultural planning*		———		
BBO/OER-IJ programme	■ ■ ■ —————————————————	unconventional
Action research*		————————————·
Cultural planning*		····················
Cultural biography		——————————··········
Habitation predictive model 1		————————————········
Habitation model 2		———————————————
Quality assessment		——————————········
Planarch 2		—————————	conventional
Research				

*) Transdisciplinarian activities

Fig. 1
Overview of actions by the Province of North Holland and the PDL/BBO programme.

The action's time span covers nine to ten years from 2000 until 2009. The time frame of the provincial policy and actions and of the PDL/BBO programme are not synchronized and the tempi vary considerably. During this long period the institutional scene has seen several fundamental changes such as the restructuring of the legal and organizational framework, roles and budgets or the exchange of individuals on a political and official level. These changes are part of real practice that can be characterized by slogans like 'more market, less administration', 'nearer to the citizen' and 'quality of life and environment'.

2.2 The actions of the Province of North Holland and the PDL/BBO/Oer-IJ research programme (Fig. 1)

The actions of the Province of North Holland described below are expressions of the cultural policy as formulated in the central provincial document, the Cultuurnota. During the PDL/BBO/Oer-IJ research two such documents were issued, the first focusing upon a more 'conventional' heritage approach by listing and assessing archaeological values to preserve them by various measures and the second is characterized by the more unconventional Belvedere approach aiming at 'conservation through development' by creating a new form of planning labelled as 'cultural planning'.

The more 'conventional' heritage approach has been implemented by producing an 'Archaeological Knowledge Inventory' (AKI; Lange/Besselsen/Van Londen 2004) between 2001 and 2003, followed in mid-2004 by an assessment and selection of 163 sites resulting in 70 preliminarily selected sites (BBAV; Van Eerden 2004). The assessment was preliminary in the sense that a classification of priorities was limited to the depth of sites and thus to their risk of physical destruction. A broader assessment using 'technical, scientific and policy' criteria has been postponed. Two general recommendations have been made for the physical preservation of the sites, i.e. integrating them in environmental planning and developing specific site management instruments linked with financial compensation for the (agrarian) user. The provincial pilot for this policy and 'show case' is the 28-hectare settlement site of the former castle Kronenburg at Castricum, where in 2003, for the first time, the instrument of legal protection was combined with financial compensation.

The policy of preservation should be supported by activities aiming at the mobilization of public interest and support. For this reason an exhibition and a lavishly illustrated book entitled *Land of Hilde* were prepared and presented to the public in mid-2006 (Dekkers/Dorren/Van Eerden 2006). The exhibition was located in an information centre for nature and environment and attracted over 100,000 visitors from mid-2006 to mid-2007.

Researchers from the PDL/BBO/Oer-IJ programme were involved in these activities in various ways, such as producing the AKI inventory, advising on assessment and commenting during the preparation of the exhibition and the book. In addition, they produced a research report on the archaeological monitoring of one of the major archaeological sites, the Broekpolder/Heemskerk-Beverwijk (Van Heeringen/Theunissen 2004).

Related to the more 'unconventional' Belvedere policy, the new concept of cultural planning was presented in the national cultural policy document 2001-2004, but without a clear definition and methodology (Cultuur als confrontatie 2000). In the cultural planning approach, cultural heritage has not only to be preserved, but also to be used as a source of inspiration for environmental development and quality. Provinces were stimulated by this national policy and the related funding to determine implementation according to specific needs. The Province of North Holland initially implemented policy between 2001 and 2004, followed by a special cultural planning project during 2004 and 2005 (Beleving 2005). This project was led by the external project leader Maarten van Wesemael, who presents himself as urban curator. He created the conditions for transdisciplinary co-operation between Heleen van Londen as PDL/BBO/Oer-IJ researcher and an external designer, Jeroen van Westen, adopting the biography of landscape as 'unifying concept'. This led to the interpretation and transformation of the data from the archaeological inventory and assessment into a meaningful characterization of the Oer-IJ landscape presented in simple, but appealing, verbal and visual language. When the project was finished in 2005, van Wesemael left the project since his contract had expired. Early in 2008, participants of the cultural planning project, including Van Wesemael, PDL/BBO researchers and landscape architects, followed it up by assessing the first project and preparing an approach for an integrated landscape view which will hopefully be used in the regional planning policy from 2009 onwards, the so-called 'Oer-IJ Agenda' (Bloemers/Husken/Van Leeuwen 2009). This follow-up is a PDL/BBO/Oer-IJ initiative funded by Belvedere/the Netherlands Architecture Fund, the Province of North Holland and PDL/BBO/Oer-IJ and aims at embedding the new cultural planning approach in regional planning. The pivotal role however is played by a semi-public institution, Cultural Heritage North-Holland. This organization functions as intermediary between the province and the local authorities, for example by advising local authorities how to implement the integrated landscape view in their local planning policy. This intermediary role is facilitated by the fact that one of the PDL/BBO/Oer-IJ researchers, Gerard Alders, is senior staff member at Cultureel Erfgoed Noord-Holland (Cultural Heritage North Holland). The integration of the cultural planning with regional planning is supported by a narrative landscape biography and recommendations for regional landscape planning based on the analysis of eight regional and local plans and designs (see Van Leeuwen Ch. IV.3).

2.3 Action research: the analysis of the interaction between the province of North Holland and the PDL/BBO/Oer-IJ programme

'Action research' is, as the term implies, the combination of 'research' and 'action' (see also Kars Ch. III.1). It is an approach to generate knowledge about complex social problems and processes by becoming actively involved in them and contributing to their solution, i.e. creating change by action. It requires an iterative process of interaction between theory and practice. The ambition of the PDL/BBO/Oer-IJ programme is to participate in the complex process of integrating cultural historical knowledge in environmental planning policy at the regional level.

For the analysis we use three supporting notions from the social sciences. The first is the awareness that 'correct' scientific research aims for objectivity and 'truth' by exploiting formal and institutionalized knowledge. In social practices, the subjective perception of values and their intersubjective assessment are recognized as essential elements of correctness in the process of coming to social and political judgments (During/Elerie/Groenendijk 2001).

The second relates to the discourse between science and policy. This is influenced by the mutual views about each other's roles and relationships; the technocratic view views science as dominant actor, the engineers' model considers policy 'on top' and researchers 'on tap' and the policy-oriented learning models are based on equal partnership (Hoppe 2002; also Van der Valk Ch. II.2, 30-31).

The third involves the notion of transdisciplinary research, where academics from various fields collaborate closely with non-academics in order to achieve certain research objectives and to develop new knowledge, usually negotiated knowledge such as the common definition of problems, the identification of facts and the development of strategies (Tress *et al.* 2003).

In this analysis we again distinguish between the 'conventional' heritage approach and the 'unconventional' Belvedere policy expressed by the concept of 'cultural planning'.

The PDL/BBO/Oer-IJ activities of the two Ph.D. researchers presenting their archaeological-historical habitation/land use models and the assessment of the physical quality of wetland sites fit into the 'conventional' heritage approach. These studies present information belonging to the domain of objective scientific 'truth', which is welcomed without discussion by the archaeological policy-makers as valuable new information. The meaning given to it is at least congruent for both partners, but knowledge is dominant over policy (Hoppe 2002).

The same applies to the inventory commissioned by the Province as the first step of its policy. However, with the next step of assessing and selecting the sites, the balance gradually shifted from the scientific to the social and political domain, from 'objectivity' to 'subjectivity', from 'positivistic' to 'interpretative' (Van der Valk Ch. II.2, 28-30). Symptoms of divergence between the archaeological researchers and their colleague policy-makers do now appear. The assessment project has been carried out by an archaeological company contracted by the Province. The selection was limited to the 'objective' physical condition, 'subjective' scientific and policy selection was postponed. The reasons for the role as advisors of the PDL/BBO/Oer-IJ researchers could be various and not mutually exclusive; were they expected not to be able to finish this job in time, did they decline the responsibility or the mix of science and policy or were they invited for the sake of legitimacy? The Province as principal is the dominant actor and a more or less clear cut division between science and policy has been established. The specific new form of site management for Kronenburg is a remarkable act of provincial policy and clearly lies in the domain of intersubjective assessment which has been the outcome of a legitimized political and democratic process.

The exhibition and book were mainly focused on 'conventional' historically oriented archaeology with a very limited reference to the cultural planning approach. The implementation of the archaeological-historical story temporarily created a divergence between research and policy.

The 'cultural planning' line shows a surprisingly different picture. Co-operation between the archaeological researcher, the project leader and the designer is on the basis of equality. Although they represent completely different disciplines and adopt an unexplored unifying concept (biography of landscape), they enter a spontaneous learning process. This process is the interaction between the scientific domain of objectivity and the social domain of subjectivity leading to a synthesis in the use of design. Crucial in this process is the convergence of meanings given to the biography concept by story telling and imagination using the metaphor 'Oer-IJ treasury', a notion introduced in the assessment and selection project of the 'conventional' heritage approach. This results in the presentation of the characteristics of the Oer-IJ landscape through time and an invitation to exploit it for environmental planning. In this way the 'empty' concept of cultural planning has also been given a content that can be presented as the typical North Holland brand of the Belvedere policy.

2.4 Conclusion

One conclusion in this case is the shifting interaction between knowledge and policy, depending on the type and timing of an action, through various relationships, as equal partners in a dialogue or not, as noted by Hoppe (Hoppe 2002). Hoppe's technocratic model views science as the dominant actor, the engineers' model as policy 'on top' and researchers 'on tap' and the policy oriented learning models are seen as based on equal partnership. It is remarkable that the interaction between the actors in the 'conventional' and 'unconventional' lines must have been limited.

This conclusion can be combined with a SWOT analysis to identify the strengths, weaknesses, opportunities and threats of the present situation (Jain/Triandis 1997, 253-254). A strong factor is the ambition and the factual intensive co-operation between knowledge and policy and the explicit use of 'unifying concepts' like biography of landscape and cultural planning to construct bridges.

One weakness is that at the start of the process the content and the use of these concepts were unclear to the actors and their development has been part of the process. Related to this is that the various actors had no clear prior view of their roles and the changes in their positions during the successive actions. The shift in the role of the 'action researcher' from analytical observer to participating actor is sometimes confusing. Communication and discourse are a very weak spot because of the relationship between supply and demand, expectations and aims, progressive insights and changing contexts. This applies to both the relationship between the individuals from both groups and to that between institutions and inside institutions. The exhibition and book were very successful from the perspective of the 'conventional' heritage approach but they did not exploit and present the results from the 'cultural planning' approach to the public. The focus on the 'Frisians' gave rise to discussion among the researchers about the complex issue of ethnicity.

The opportunity arose to integrate the two lines in the next phase of provincial cultural policy and planning from 2009 onwards. The relationship between the Province as 'policy-maker' and the semi-public Cultural Heritage North-Holland as intermediary for implementation towards local authorities will be crucial for success. The metaphor 'Oer-IJ treasury' should be further exploited as a concept unifying the different levels and interests of various actors.

The new political hype recently initiated by the national government to formulate a national and provincial 'canon' could become a threat if it leads to a simplified and polarizing view of history instead of an understanding of how the past is related to the present. A major threat however is if no meaningful relationship between the supply of knowledge and demand for policy on the regional and local level can be established. And the greatest threat is undoubtedly when researchers and policy-makers think that the aims for the 'protection by development' of the archaeological-historical landscape have already been achieved, because we shall need at least another decade to institutionalize a new approach and attitude towards our environment!

3. THE FORGOTTEN DELTA: THE CULTURAL BIOGRAPHY OF THE OER-IJ ESTUARY
(Heleen van Londen)

3.1 Introduction

The Oer-IJ estuary was chosen as a case-study to explore the concept of cultural biography in the context of planning to attain sustainable landscape development. The former estuary, located north of Amsterdam, is now covered and invisible to the untrained eye. The region is subject to high development pressure for industry, housing and the expansion of Schiphol airport. Various planning projects are to be realized in the area. Development leads to problems of unattractiveness and lack of local support. The present-day landscape becomes increasingly unstructured.

At the provincial level, much priority has been given to the notion of cultural planning, including in relation to the former estuary. Today, hardly anyone is familiar with the ancient estuary. The purpose of this Oer-IJ story is to make people remember what was forgotten. Dissemination of knowledge regarding the rich long-term history is vital for protection through development. The estuary forms a magnificent landscape structure, still visible if you are willing to look (see Ch. IV.3, Fig. 1). The landscape structures such as that of the old delta itself can be used in planning, but there are also other development principles to be learned. The concept of cultural biography has been chosen to communicate knowledge about cultural landscape transformation.

3.2 Setting the context for the use of the cultural biography of landscape in the Oer-IJ estuary

History of research

At the start of this research in 2002 and 2003, a clear-cut definition of the concept of 'cultural biography of landscape', theory and methods was lacking, although conceptual studies were available (Bloemers *et al.* 2001). As a consequence, attention has been given to the development of a theoretical and methodological framework (Van Londen 2004; *idem* 2006; Van Beek *et al.* 2008).

In the same period, a regional inventory was made of the present state of archaeological knowledge (Lange *et al.* 2004). Here, a first attempt was made to define an overview of the major developments in the region's history over a time period of c. 5000 years.

The research programme contained activities in the field of action research. The user context was studied through active participation in several provincial policy projects. A firm realization was that archaeologists should be changing paradigms from the more or less objective stance of preservation to the subjective construction of heritage (Van Londen 2006; Flamman/Van Londen 2008). Subjectivity and the role of constructions not only by experts, but also by policy-makers, politicians and the public are part of the strategic game (Bartels *et al.* 2008). It follows that research activities in transdisciplinary contexts must be regarded as strategic research, that is research with preset goals of influencing others. When the goal is clear and the target group is defined there is a thin line between politicizing, lobbying and valorizing research results. It is clear that in the interaction between groups all parties use whatever seems available for their purpose.

Definitions and method

The 'cultural biography of landscape' is a metaphor referring to the history of landscape, using various disciplines, that can be used to express the value even if it is hidden underneath the surface (Kolen 2006; Van Beek *et al.* 2008). The biography is about story telling and can in my view be ranked within the school of narrativism. Like any literary biography, the author shapes an image of the subject and therefore chooses story elements to make a point. The selection of story elements is the direct result of the image that is chosen and has to be made explicit (Van Londen 2004; *idem* 2006). Any other point of view will lead to a different story about the region's landscape. This is certainly the case in regions with a very rich history that is multi-layered and detailed, such as the Oer-IJ region. Stories can be seen as the superstructure of the construction, while the infrastructure may be seen as the entire set of data, methodology and argumentation that lies behind it (Goldstein 1976, 140; Ankersmit 1996, 96-136; Van Londen 2004). Stories without the infrastructure are more or less unaccounted for. So for the Oer-IJ estuary biography, the purpose of the story and the image that needs to be carried across should be made explicit. This means that the present-day context in which the story is going to be parachuted must be analysed. In the case of the 'Oer-IJ Agenda' that context is the strategic aim of embedding cultural planning in next generation regional planning policy (Bloemers/Husken/Van Leeuwen 2009; Van Leeuwen Ch. IV.3). The biography of landscape represents the superstructure, its narration has been adapted to the policy context of use and corresponds to the infrastructure as explained below.

The approach towards applying the concept of the biography of landscape for the Oer-IJ estuary is based on the empirical methodology that is normal in research procedures and will be structured the following way:
- analysis of the context of use;
- the forgotten delta: geological transformation, present-day landscape structure (topography), landscape ensembles and transformation;
- framing the story: regional identity;
- development principles.

Analysis of the context of use

The biography of landscape can be viewed as a way to disseminate historical knowledge. In the case of the Oer-IJ estuary, two contexts of use can be identified, both in the field of policy; these are planning and archaeological heritage management. Both contexts need a firm topographical basis because they deal

Tidal landscapes

Sub-tidal landscape

▭ North Sea, estuary and large tidal channels

Intertidal landscape

▭ Mud flats

Inter- and supratidal landscape

▭ Beach sands and wash-overs

Supra-tidal landscape

▭ Salt marshes

Terrestrial landscapes

Coastal dune landscape

▭ Coastal barriers and low dunes

▭ Coastal plain generally filled with peat

Peat landscape

▭ Reed peat landscape (eutrophic)

▭ Sphagnum and heath peat (meso- and oligotrophic)

▭ Medieval reclamation dating to the tenth century A.D.

Supra-tidal landscape

▭ Former mud flats

▭ Former wash-overs and salt marsh heights

▭ Former creek ridges

▭ Former salt marsh plains

Stagnating water

▭ Fresh water lakes

▭ Brackish water lagoons

Line symbols

⋯⋯ Uncertain border

⋯⋯ Mediocre certain border

——— Certain border

Point symbols

• Archaeological site

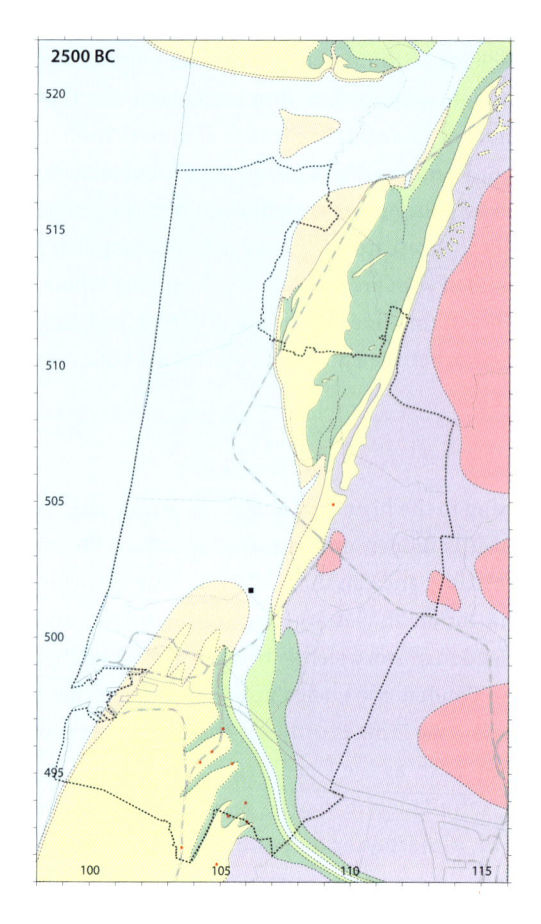

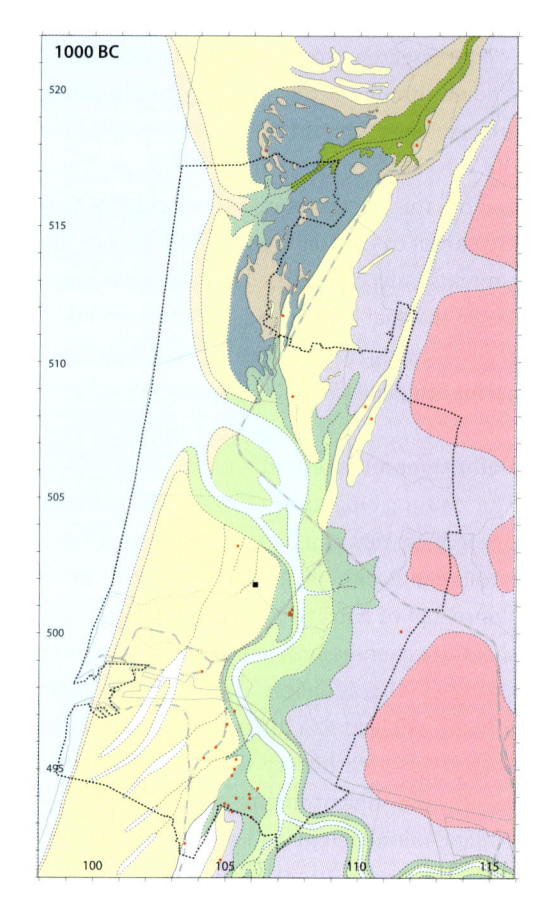

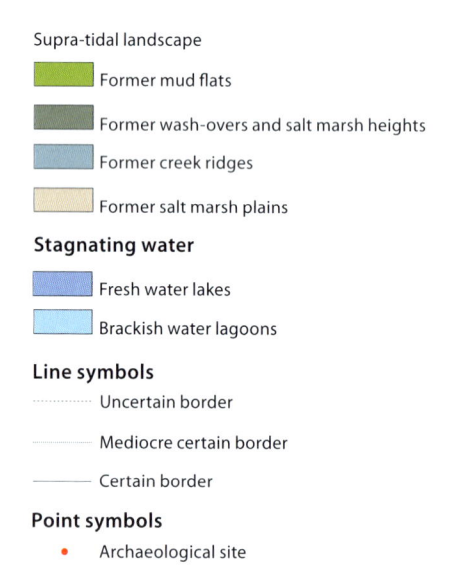

■ Location of planning area

214 • THE CULTURAL LANDSCAPE AND HERITAGE PARADOX

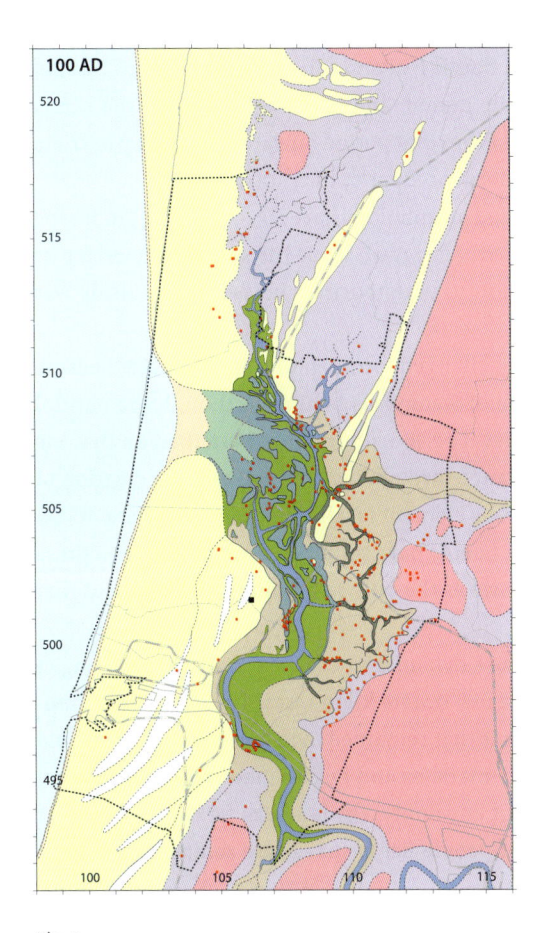

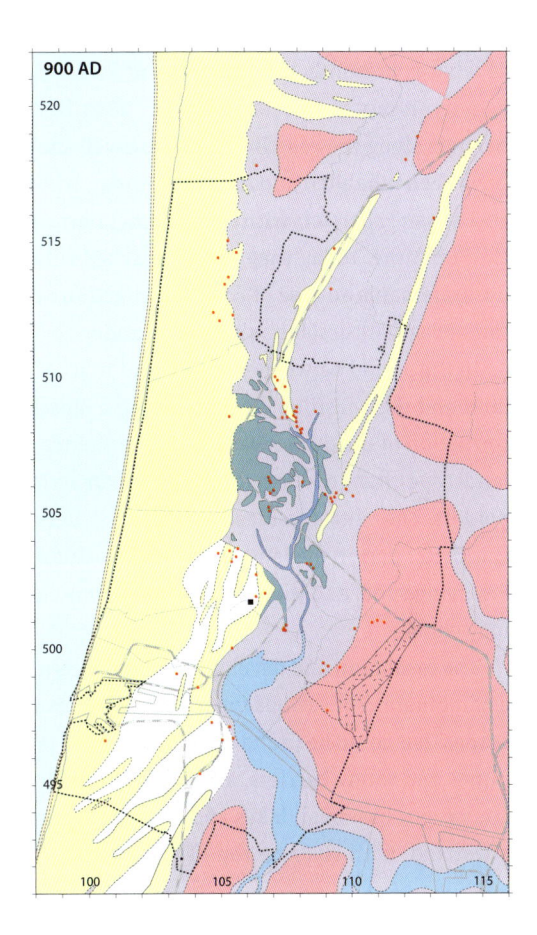

Fig. 2
Landscape formation of the Oer-IJ estuary in four phases (*Lange et al. 2004, 31-35*).

primarily with space. It follows that maps need to be carriers of landscape history. The incorporation of old landscape elements in new landscape design means that the analysis of the landscape history should result in development principles underlying the shaping of the landscape and in this way will continue to safeguard its integrity.

In the field of archaeological heritage management it is paramount to legitimize the reasons for protection in the light of the pressure on land. This characteristic is probably dependent on local spatial development and might be a specifically Dutch problem of the metropolitan region. Because of this need, strong meaning needs to be developed and communicated, culminating in a regional landscape identity.

3.3 *The forgotten delta*
Geological transformation

The story of the Oer-IJ estuary must start with the natural formation of the estuary. The delta is a direct remnant of the coastal formation in the Netherlands during the last 10,000 years, a geological period also known as the Holocene. Between 5000 and 3000 BC, large parts of the coast were literally below the water table as a result of the sea level rise. The sea caused sedimentation that led to an island structure of what is presently the provinces of Zeeland, North and South Holland. The first evidence of human activity in our region dates from c. 2850 BC, the Neolithic period, and is mainly found on the sandy barriers along the coastline that were well above sea level. From that period onwards, the sandy barriers have been inhabited and used until today, which is a long-term occupancy of c. 5000 years.

The sandy barriers with their slender north-south oriented morphology have structured the landscape through time. Today, they are jam-packed with towns and urban sprawl, while the seaside known for its dunes remains an area of coastal protection and natural reserve with tourist value and the landside was mainly agricultural but is presently under development.

In the period between 3000 BC and 1050 AD the estuary changed form rapidly (Fig. 2). Water became land and the coastline closed, leaving a close-knit system of waterways behind. Although the natural formation of the dunes was of great influence in the medieval period, it is mainly from then on that the landscape changed form through human activity, for instance through reclamation and the creation of polders. The delta, fossilized as it is, is a structuring landscape element just like the sandy barriers. Today the lowest part in the land is that of the estuary. Until now, people have refrained from building on these low-lying spots and therefore the estuary is easy to recognize as the only remaining open area. But that may change.

The formation and development of the estuary reads like a dynamic landscape formation resulting in a combination of various types of landscapes within just a few square kilometres. Typical natural landscapes that could be found through time are terrestrial lands that remained high and dry such as the old dunes and sandy barriers, areas under tidal influence like marshes and gullies, and stagnating watery landscapes like small lakes and swampy fenlands. Without any doubt, the land can be characterized as a wetland, with layer on top of layer containing traces of people before us. These remains have been

Fig. 3
Main structure of the Oer-IJ landscape in the present landscape.

1. Dunes, now mostly nature and water reserve
2. Sandy barriers, now mostly urban area
3. Oer-IJ river, now mostly grazing land
4. Peat, now mostly grazing land
5. A9 motorway

The Oer-IJ area under study is marked by a black contour.
Source: Google Earth.

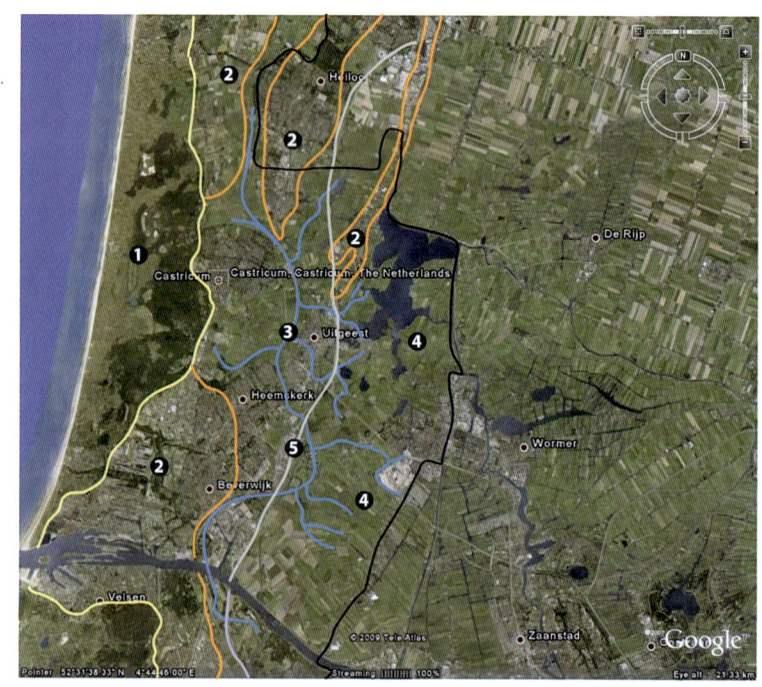

Fig. 4
Earliest evidence of a landscape structure dating from the Bronze Age to later periods in the Velserbroek area (after Therkorn 2008, 152).

1-2. Burial mound
3. Group of burial mounds
4-6. Settlements

- Occupied areas (Archaeologically determined)
- Track way (Archaeologically determined)
- Track way (Archaeologically supposed)
- Oer IJ
- Polders
- VELSEN Name of present settlement

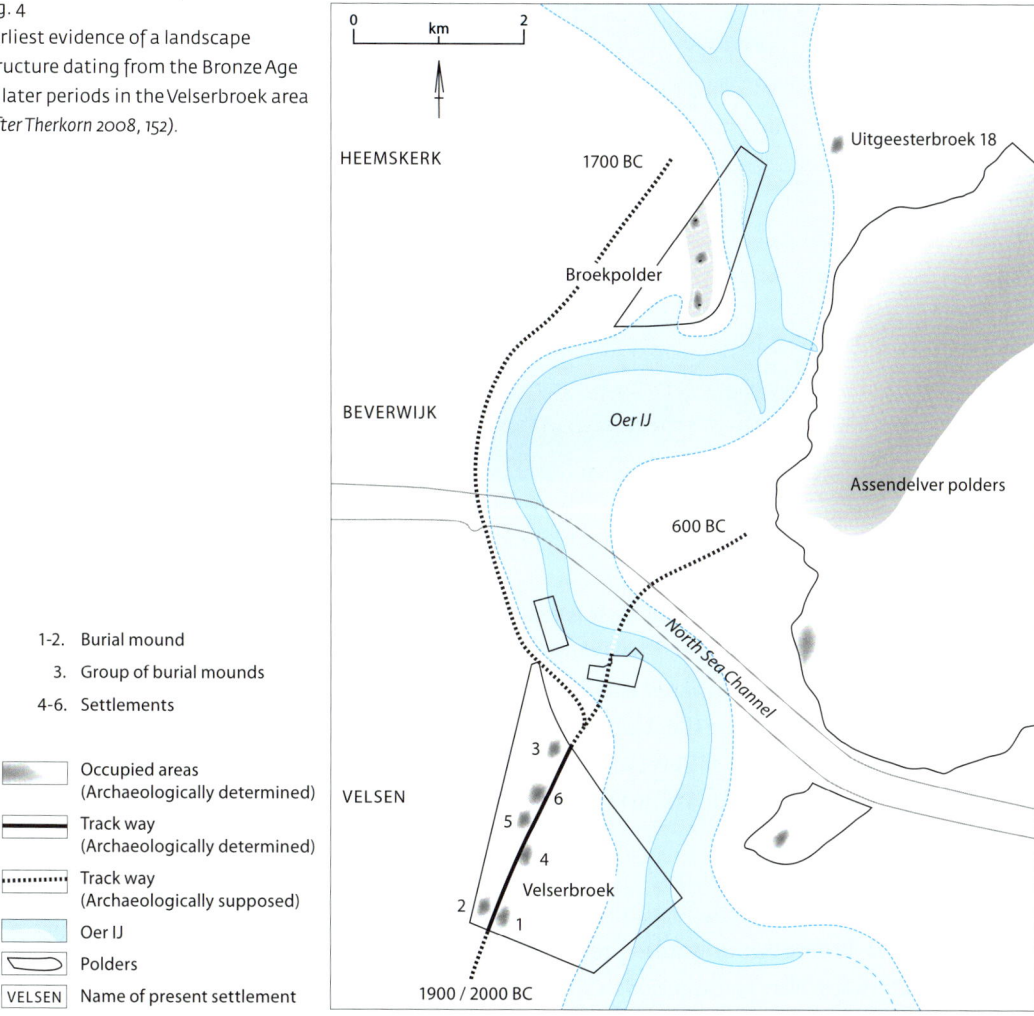

preserved in an excellent condition because of the high water table. In that sense, the area is a cultural historic gold mine.

Present-day landscape structure

The topography today can be well understood in relation to the geology. The coastal strip (Fig. 3.1) consists of dunes formed from the Middle Ages onwards (c. 900 -1000 AD). The area is presently used for coastal defence, nature, recreation and water reserve. Building is prohibited. Before the formation of the dunes, the sandy barriers (Fig. 3.2) were the natural sea walls. On both sides of the barriers older dunes were formed and on the sea side various farming and fishing hamlets emerged dating to the Early Middle Ages (Merovingian and Carolingian periods). The coastal strip covers these hamlets, which are literally buried in sand. It is these sand storms dating to c. 1000 AD that made people leave the coast for the eastern hinterland, the peat marshes, which they started to drain from then on to make them suitable for

Fig. 5
Assendelft site 56: a cut for turf and deeper clay extraction (to the left are two excavated medieval pits f157, f158, fig. 15)
(Therkorn et al. 2007, 20).

settlement. This means that the peat reclamation can only be understood in relation to the occurrences on the coastline.

Looking at the present-day topography, it is clear that the contours of the sandy barriers (Fig. 3.2) define much of the built environment. The sandy barriers and old dunes (Fig. 3.1-2) have been used continuously from the Neolithic onwards and have the most complex layered archaeology in the region. They have been used to structure the road systems, field systems, settlements, burial mounds, churches, castles and villages. Especially at Beverwijk and Heemskerk, due to the increased demand for building new houses, housing has extended from the good quality sandy soils towards the low-lying clay deposits of the former estuary (Fig. 3.3).

By mapping levels, the contours of the estuary are easily recognized (see Ch. IV.3, Fig. 1). After its formation, the estuary gradually fossilized, offering more and more opportunities for habitation and land use from the Bronze Age onwards. It remained a wetland through time, harbouring various watery places and waterways. New research shows that some of these watery places were used as offering sites and can provide insight into the religious beliefs of ancient cultures. The creek levees were intensively used for habitation in the late Iron Age and Roman period. In fact, in the Roman period the area was rather densely populated, leaving a great number of traces behind.

The creeks and small peat rivers are still recognizable in the field patterns in the peat area (Fig. 3.4), as they formed the structuring lines during reclamation. For many hundreds of years these polders were used for cattle grazing. The layout of the polders is historic, but nonetheless still apt for its purpose.

The last landscape structure that needs to be addressed is the A9 motorway (Fig. 3.5). It is our present-day variety in a line of many historic roads that have been oriented this way from the Neolithic onwards. Today this motorway can be seen as the eastern limit of development, as most of the development is concentrated between the dunes and this motorway. These two limits leave a linear area which is a combination of sandy barriers and estuary deposits.

Long-term development of landscape patterns

Traces of human activities have been found mainly on the terrestrial lands from the Neolithic until the Bronze Age (2850-1800 BC). On the sandy barriers there is evidence of trackways and burial mounds.

The combination of roads and burial mounds forms the first human structuring of the landscape and is oriented along the coastline (Fig. 4). On the old dunes we find arable land and cattle enclosures. Marshes (Fig. 2 brown) bear traces of arable lands, fences, ditches and pits. Remarkable is the lack of evidence for any kind of settlement. Until today, the dwelling places from this period have not yet been found. Not much is known about the principles structuring the Neolithic landscape.

The use of coastal barriers remains mostly the same in the following period from the Bronze Age to the Iron Age (1800-250 BC). The archaeological evidence corresponds with that found in the north and east of the Netherlands. The first settlements were located in the old dunes and there are activities pointing to the exploitation of salt. From the seventh century BC onwards, the fenlands (Fig. 2 purple) become inhabited. Rows of farmsteads form aligned ribbons of habitation. Houses on peat are tremendously well preserved. People cut peat for fuel, influencing the natural balance (Fig. 5). As before, the marshes were exploited for agriculture, but a new insight is the use of stagnant pools as places of offering. From the content of these watery deposits we can learn about the world of ideas (Fig. 6). In the Oer-IJ river deposit a canoe was found dating to the Iron Age. It is the first evidence of traffic on water, but of course this method of transport must be much older.

Fig. 6
A model for expected sites in watery places (Kok 2008, app.1).

1. Green: small wet low-lying areas not exactly located, offerings from all periods can be expected
2. Dark blue: wet areas between old dunes and coastal barriers, offerings from all periods can be expected
3. Light blue: wet areas with a greater circumference, between dry land, offerings from all periods can be expected
4. Light purple: areas bordering the Oer-IJ, offerings are expected from the end of the Late Iron Age onward
5. Purple: the Oer-IJ, offerings are expected from the end of the Late Iron Age onward
6. Bright pink: creeks and creek systems, offerings are expected from the end of the Middle Iron Age onward
7. Red: creeks in peaty areas, offerings are expected from the end of the Middle Iron Age onward

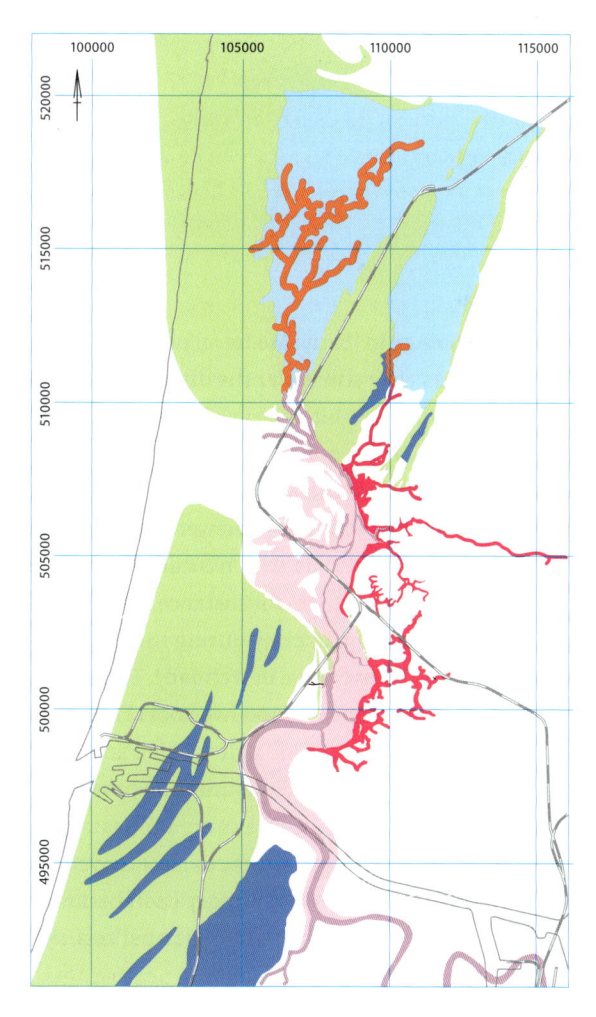

Fig. 7
Strategic location of the Roman fort Velsen (*Castellum Flevum*) and projected shipping routes (*Broesi 2005, 84*).
The connection to the sea north of *Flevum* is in a geological sense already blocked in the Roman period (*Vos/Van Eerden/De Koning 2009*).

In the Iron Age to (Early) Medieval period (250 BC-1050 AD), much of the estuary became marshland, but large areas were still under the direct influence of the tides. The gullies fossilized and all landscape types were either inhabited or used in some way. There seems to have been an enormous increase in population, as was the case in most parts of the Netherlands in this period. Besides settlements, we find agricultural activities with storage places, cattle enclosures, field systems, pathways and pits. The places of offering from the former period were continuously used and point to long-term traditions. However, we have no traces of burials, which is odd and leads to ongoing speculation as to what people were doing with their dead at the time, for instance sending them to sea. In the early first century AD, the region was visited by the Roman army during the Elbe strategy, which aimed to extend the frontier of the Roman Empire to the river Elbe in Germany. Two military harbours were founded near the town of Velsen, securing transport of people and livestock. The location of the harbours meant that the waterways could be navigated (Fig. 7). The Elbe policy failed and the frontier was placed to the south of the region along the river Rhine. Most of the Romanization processes found in the south are absent north of the frontier, which means that the Iron Age communities continued well into the Roman period. In the late third and fourth century, people appear to have moved to the dry lands of the old dunes and sandy barriers. We have reason to believe the estuary itself became increasingly wet, leading to peat growth. However, during the Merovingian and Carolingian periods, the terrestrial areas were covered with farmsteads and fishing hamlets. The region became part of Franconia with the emergence of Christianity and the forming of a local nobility.

From the Late Medieval period until the present (1050-1850 AD) only a few lakes remain from what was once an estuary. The small hamlets in the dunes were affected by drift-sand which resulted in what is known in geological terms as the young dunes. People moved to the fenlands in the east and began to reclaim the peat area (Fig. 8). More water management was introduced in the form of dike construction to keep the water at bay. The first dike dates from c. 1000 AD. The sandy barriers were chosen for main roads (again), hamlets, villages, churches and castles. Twelve castles built from the thirteenth century onwards were aligned, forming a strategic structure. More and more information becomes available about the social and economic situation, such as the conflicts between the church and the nobility and about the miraculous endeavours of saints saving the local community from Vikings and other threats.

Special attention must be given to the Golden Age, the seventeenth century. Making use of the most sophisticated knowledge at the time, ring dikes were built along a selection of lakes with windmills on top of them, pumping them dry, much to everybody's admiration. The city of Amsterdam flourished because of the successful trade in the East Indies. Rich tradesmen invested in these polders. The Beemster polder, now a World Heritage Site, was designed after the ideal city and contained quite a few estates with stylish gardens that were used as country houses (Alders *et al.* 2006, 215-218). The area can only be understood in relation to Amsterdam, world trade and the incredible wealth stemming from it.

Modern times, dating from c. 1850 until the present, saw the construction of a second World Heritage Site in the environs of Amsterdam, the Stelling van Amsterdam. It is a ring structure of military bunkers and inundation fields around Amsterdam, a strategic military construction from the late nineteenth cen-

Fig. 8
Polder landscape dating from medieval reclamation onwards.
Source: Google Earth.

tury that was never used. The central idea was to flood the land around Amsterdam to build a physical barrier. In this phase, the area was dominated by industrialization, starting along the river Zaan. The opening of the North Sea Channel in 1876 and development of the sea port of IJmuiden stimulated the importance of the region. The economic growth has led to intensive land use and a fragmentation of the older landscape structures. Major roads, rail roads, industry and housing have cut into and filled up the area.

3.4 *Framing the story*
Regional identity
Framing the region today, one has to admit that the buried delta itself offers the strongest regional identity possible. Throughout its history, people's relationship with water while living on the 'wet' land has been dominant. Of course, the delta can be seen as a natural wetland, but its watery places have been used over the long term in a religious context as places of offering. Water has been a threat as well as an opportunity, leading to the drainage of the fenlands through reclamation and the building of dikes. People also tamed it by pumping water away, creating in fact a reverse cascade. Several authors, such as Aldous Huxley and the famous Dutch poet, Joost van den Vondel (1587-1679), have sung the praises of the miracle of the Beemster polder. A good example is Van den Vondel's poem *De Beemster*, written for Karel Looten, an important inhabitant of the polder. The poem describes how the dangerous mass of water was pumped away by windmills and the lake was transformed into a flowery and fertile land, where people lived a prosperous life (Alders *et al.* 2006, 216). As a metaphor, the Beemster is represented by a young woman who, just like Venus, was born out of the foam of the sea with the help of the wind and was then dressed with the fruits of the earth. Manipulating the land gave a sense of power and control.

The estuary has been a source of life on 'wet' land with fishing and seafaring. A network of waterways gave access throughout the area, and allowed for industry later. The wealthy gained status by building canals around their castles and ponds in their gardens. Water was chosen by the military as an ally, being able to flood the area at will. Today, the North Sea Channel functions as the entrance to the world around us. The estuary has brought together land and sea. It is still there for those who wish to see.

Development principles
The principles behind the long-term development of the Oer-IJ region can be found on different scales depending on the amount of detail that historical research will offer. Scales can be viewed as layers, some have a clear materialization, others offer a more theoretical structure. Geology for instance gives a firm zoning of the area, offering a strong structure for further development. The estuary can be made visible again, perhaps by bringing water back into the estuary basin. Historical topography of the surface landscape offers structures of land reclamation and water management, such as the repetitive patterns of ditches in the polders, the dikes and windmills. These structures are also clear and dominant. It is more difficult to understand the spatial structures formed by ideology, such as the distribution of places of offering and later churches, or the structure of fancy villas and castles. If these historically developed patterns in the landscape are used for future landscape design, detailed studies of these structures can be used.

The defence structure of the Stelling van Amsterdam is a large scale and dominant landscape object that needs to be respected since it has become a World Heritage site. It represents various scales. It unifies town and country through time. It reflects ideologies and their transformation culminating in a World Heritage landscape structure.

4. WATER AND THE RELIGIOUS LANDSCAPE: A QUALITATIVE PREDICTION OF OFFERING SITES IN THE OER-IJ AREA

(Marjolijn Kok)

4.1 Introduction

One of the tasks of this Ph.D. research within the PDL/BBO/Oer-IJ programme was to make predictive maps of ritual activities in the pre- and protohistoric period. In Dutch archaeology in general, ritual activities are not part of predictive models as they are considered less easy to detect, especially through core-boring (Tol *et al.* 2004, 21), the first field phase in most prospection research in the Netherlands. Predictive models usually focus on settlements (for example, IKAW map with archaeological predictive values for the entire Netherlands, Soonius/Verhagen/Bekius 2005). I am not aware of any predictive models in the Netherlands that focus specifically on ritual practices, like offering sites. Fortunately within the PDL/BBO-programme there is also the project 'Stategic research into, and development of best practice for, predictive modelling on behalf of Dutch Cultural Resource Management' (see Ch. V.5) that, although not specifically dealing with offering sites, has produced many useful insights for the development of a predictive model of offering sites in the Oer-IJ area. The baseline report produced by this research group (Van Leusen *et al.* 2005) has been used as a starting point. In this contribution I want to show that a combination of environmental and socio-cultural factors with an emphasis on landscape perception can create a qualitative predictive model for offering sites.

4.2 Research background

Large-scale archaeological research in the Oer-IJ area has led to the assumption that ritual activities took place within the wet low-lying parts of the landscape. In order to understand this phenomenon, research focused on analysing these rituals in the local landscape and the wider northwestern European tradition of offerings in water in the pre-and protohistoric period. A theoretical framework combining a social and cognitive perspective was proposed (Kok 2008, chapter 1). The cognitive perspective enabled the formulation of clear definitions concerning religion and ritual. In short, religion is a world view which incorporates Culturally Postulated Superhuman agents (CPS agents; Lawson/McCauley 1996, 5) and religious rituals are actions that involve these CPS agents. Offerings are a specific type of ritual in which a person offers a gift to a CPS agent. An offering site is a locality where at least one offering has taken place. The social perspective places religion in the wider social context and enables the analyses of ritual practices as social practices. As this theoretical framework does not inform us about the actual shape specific rituals take and the study of offerings in the Netherlands is still in its infancy, a wider background was needed. From the long research tradition into offering sites in northern Germany, Denmark and southern Sweden, 100 published sites were analysed. It became clear that there is no checklist against which we can determine whether specific archaeological remains are the result of offering practices, but general trends could be observed. All 499 known archaeological sites in the Oer-IJ area from the pre- and protohistoric period were re-evaluated. Locality, placement, time frame and similarity and difference with other find complexes were taken as determining factors in establishing whether a site could be interpreted as an offering site. A total of 22 sites within the Oer-IJ area were interpreted as offering sites in wet low-lying parts of the landscape. From these findings a model was made in which the time, place and find complex of offering sites were combined (Kok 2008, Fig. 4.48). This model was used in the predictive modelling of the offering sites.

4.3 Predictive modelling
Basics

The minimum definition of predictive modelling as defined by Kohler and Parker still stands: "a technique used to predict, at a minimum, the location of archaeological sites or materials in a region, based either on the observed pattern in a sample or on assumptions about human behaviour" (Kohler/Parker 1986 cited in Van Leusen et al. 2005, 26). The aim of the predictive model for the Oer-IJ area is "to predict the locations with offerings in the wet low-lying parts of the landscape. The predictive model can be used as a tool in archaeological heritage management and at the same time test the scientific model of the Oer-IJ itself. A better scientific model will lead to better predictions and thereby strengthen its usability in cultural heritage management." (Kok 2008, chapter 5).

Van Leusen et al. (2005) address six themes that are important for the development of predictive models: quality and quantity of the data; environmental input factors; inclusion of socio-cultural factors, higher spatial temporal resolution, spatial statistics; and testing. Due to the number of offering sites the use of spatial statistics was not justifiable. While testing was planned, it unexpectedly proved impossible due to problems accessing selected sites. This has meant that the predictive model is of a qualitative nature. In other words, zones in the landscape where offerings are likely to be found are not given a probability value, but a possibility value. The other four themes are elaborated on within this research project.

Vos updated four palaeogeographical maps and made a new palaeogeographical map to strengthen the environmental input and increase the temporal and spatial resolution. Furthermore he created a geogenetic map of the area with an emphasis on wet areas. The quantity and quality of the data for the area were evaluated as all 499 recorded sites within the Oer-IJ area were reviewed in the light of the purpose of the predictive model.

The socio-cultural factors were emphasized as it was considered necessary to determine whether there were any cultural rules that could indicate how the landscape was used. From the specific uses it might be possible to deduce which elements were of importance in the perception of the landscape.

Assumptions

By analysing the known offering sites and other sites in relation to the landscape, a model was made from which five assumptions were formulated that were used for the predictive model. The assumptions made in the predictive model are the following:

a. Human activities are patterned in various ways and scales (Van Leusen et al. 2005, 32).

This assumption is applicable to all predictive models. The theoretical background that it is based upon influences the nature of the various ways and scales. Here a dynamic theoretical framework of structuration theory is used in which "History is the structuration of events in time and space through the continual interplay of agency and structure: the interconnection of the mundane nature of day-to-day life with institutional forms stretching over immense spans of time and space." (Giddens 1995,

362). Because there is a constant movement between agency and structure this is not a deterministic model as it involves the decisions of actors, but at the same time allows for patterns to exist as the actors manoeuvre within the rules of social life. These rules of social life can be regarded as 'techniques or generalizable procedures applied in the enactment/reproduction of social practices.' (*ibidem*, 21). It is these social rules that need to be studied so that predictions can be made that can be used in the understanding of past communities and their spatial expression. It is these spatial expressions that point towards the localization of actions in the landscape. Here the term regionalization can be of use as it refers "to the zoning of time-space in relation to routinized social practices." (*ibidem*, 119). In other words, social practice is not just based on what is proper to do but also on where it is proper to act in a certain way.

b. Offerings were not made in salt water.
On the basis of the known offering sites it is assumed that offerings were not made in salt water (Kok 2008 chapter 4 § 4.3.1). Other excluded areas include waters under tidal influence. This assumption on the avoidance of salt water seems to be strengthened by the broadening of the use of the landscape through time as the amount of salt water in the estuary diminishes. Offering sites appear in new wet low-lying parts of the landscape as soon as the water turns from salt or brackish to fresh. As the location of salt or fresh water changes through time, the predictions also change through time. New parts of the landscape are continually added, while the old areas remain in use.

c. The wet low-lying offering sites were at close proximity to settlements and fields.
The assumption that offering sites were close to settlements and fields is based on the known sites from larger excavations. The fields appear to be situated between the settlement and the offering sites. This is probably due to the relief of the landscape with the settlements at the highest and driest parts, the fields at the flanks, and the offering sites in the wet lower parts (Kok 2008 chapter 4 § 4.8). The offering sites, however, remain within sight and easy walking distance of the settlements. Offering sites can be situated directly next to settlements depending on the local landscape. In fields, when the constellation Pegasus is expressed in pits and/or gullies, an offering site can be expected southwest of it (*ibidem* chapter 4 § 4.3.2).

d. The wet low-lying offering sites seem to be associated with barrows and embankments.
There appears to be an association between wet low-lying offering sites and earthworks such as barrows and especially embankments. This association is not just nearness in space, but the earthworks and offering sites seem to refer to each other (Kok 2008 chapter 4 § 4.4.1). This can be done either through stake rows or the direction of the embankment. Wet low-lying areas near the earthworks should therefore be expected to contain offerings.

e. Although anything could be considered an offering, there are certain preferences.
The diverse character of the different offering sites makes it clear that a broad range of items were considered suitable for offerings. Patterns in the artefact distribution do suggest certain preferences when offerings are made (Kok 2008 chapter 4 § 4.7). When these preferred items are encountered it becomes more likely that an offering site is present. These preferred items are: human bone (specifically from head, leg and arm), metal artefacts, complete vessels, a selection of wood (from different parts of the landscape), and stones. The likelihood of there being an offering site becomes stronger when these items are recovered from a natural layer (*ibidem* chapter 5).

Mapping

These assumptions were mapped on the palaeogeographical maps of the different periods (Kok 2008, Fig. 5.4-5.8) and combined into a single predictive map (Fig. 6) that can be used as a starting point for research.

The colours on the map indicate a specific type of prediction. The colours do not represent a scale of less to more probability of encountering an offering site as on most predictive maps, but the colours stand for specific expectations. Green areas are expected to contain small wet low-lying areas due to the morphology with small shifting dunes and valleys that are not yet precisely located. In these small wet areas offerings from all periods can be expected. Dark blue areas are known wet areas near or between the old dunes and former coastal barriers. In these areas offering sites from all periods can be expected. Light blue areas are wet areas with a greater circumference, but still between dry land. Offering sites can be expected from all periods but the size of the area somewhat reduces the chance of finding an offering site. The borders are the most likely areas but they shift through time. Light purple areas border the Oer-IJ and offerings are expected to be present from the end of the Late Iron Age onwards. Purple areas represent the Oer-IJ. Offering sites can be expected from the end of the Late Iron Age onwards. Bright pink areas represent creeks and creek systems. From the Middle Iron Age onwards, offering sites can be expected here, especially when other uses of specific places are known. Red areas are creeks in peaty areas. Here offering sites can be expected from the Middle Iron Age onwards.

This map should be used as an initial indication of where offering sites can be expected. For specific areas the separate maps should be used to give a more detailed prediction. The large peat area in the east of the Oer-IJ is not included in the predictions because of its relatively scant information on offering sites (Kok 2008 chapter 5).

4.4 Past perception of the landscape

Although the combined predictive map may not give much information about the perception of the landscape, it has been essential for the shaping of the map. I will elaborate on assumptions b.-e. to make my point clear. Although assumptions b. and c. do not seem directly or necessarily related, their combination shows us something about where offerings should take place, namely in those parts of the landscape where people are busy on a daily basis, literally the cultivated landscape. As soon as water turns fresh the surrounding areas are used. It is, however, striking that this use is often preceded by the offering of objects into the water, especially in the early periods. Furthermore, all offering sites that are part of large-scale excavations are near fields and settlements. This location indicates that offerings were made in places that were not distant or remote. The CPS agents were part of the inhabited world. A rigid spatial separation of the CPS agents and human agents is difficult to envisage within this framework. Although northern European mythology indicates that the salt water sea accommodated CPS agents of all kinds, they did not seem to receive any offerings in the landlocked salt water of the estuary.

Assumptions d. and partly e. are based on the idea that people in the Oer-IJ area were not only aware of the local differences in the landscape but saw the landscape as a whole as expressed through their earthworks and deposition of materials, especially wood and bone. There was a constant effort to bring together material from different places representing the wet and dry elements within the landscape. They also seem to have placed special value on the malleability of their landscape as some of the offerings consist of especially hard foreign material.

I have tried to show that cultural rules can be used as a tool for making predictive maps. Although the assumptions are based on known sites, the predictive map is not site-based. The map is a combination of geological information and cultural rules.

5. WATER AND THE HERITAGE LANDSCAPE: PRESERVING THE RESOURCES OF PAST CULTURAL AND NATURAL LANDSCAPES
(Liesbeth Theunissen)

The Oer-IJ is a structure subtly surviving in the landscape and rich in cultural history. Interpreting the oldest traces of settlement in a dynamic landscape is impossible, even to the trained eye. The oldest cultural layers lie deep below the surface. This position means that the archaeological evidence is often cut off from oxygen and consequently well preserved. When the landscape-creating dynamics of this area decrease in the Roman period, human influence increases. The inhabitants' intervention in their environment produces ever more traces, some of which, filtered by time, are still recognizable today. These traces of habitation are often found just below the surface, at the division between waterlogged or saturated zone (well preserved) and permeable or unsaturated zone (degradation). This critical layer of the archaeological resource in a wetland environment is very vulnerable to degradation. As degradation leads to the loss of information, the call for proper management of this hidden heritage is growing stronger.

Within this degradation project the research focus was directed towards the different landscapes of the Oer-IJ wetland; from the coastal barriers and dunes in the west to the creek systems and peat area in the east. This broad variation in landscapes combined with a rich soil archive makes the Oer-IJ an ideal study area. Some of the main questions were: what is the present quality of this varied resource and what is the sustainability of these hidden landscapes?

5.1 *In situ preservation and monitoring of archaeological sites*

During the last decade a growing number of initiatives has been undertaken to develop research strategies for the sustainable preservation of Dutch wetland sites (Smit *et al.* 2006). Good management of wetland sites is only possible if we have a quantitative insight into the effects of the burial environment on the materials and features that make up findspots. Determination of the sensitivity of various archaeological remains, their rate of degradation and their current physical quality are crucial in this evaluation, together with the properties of the burial environment.

In the analysis of archaeological remains for monitoring purposes several issues are important. First, the archaeological remains at the site, obtained from an *in situ* context. This tells us what materials are present (or can be expected), what conversion and degradation processes are active and how advanced they are. It is important to bear in mind that the distribution of archaeological material is often very heterogeneous. The question of representativeness should therefore be assessed during sampling. Besides that, it is also important to realize that it is difficult to determine whether degradation processes are still active or merely a reflection of past burial conditions or re-burial decay.

5.2 *Characterization of the landscapes studied*

In the BBO substudy the preservation capacity of the soil was investigated on the basis of the quality determination at findspots in three subareas. These were the Broekpolder, the Uitgeester-/Heemsker-

Fig.9
In the landscape of Weijenbus and Vroonmeer the house terps can be recognized as slight elevations in the pasture land.

kerbroekpolder and the Castricummerpolder, three polder landscapes each with its own history and present-day dynamics.

The Broekpolder is an area that has undergone a rapid change. Over the past years it has been transformed from an agrarian to an urban landscape. Prior to its development into a Vinex location, extensive preliminary archaeological research was carried out. When it became apparent that the Broekpolder contained a considerable amount of archaeological evidence, part of it was designated as a legally protected monument and investigated in three excavation campaigns from 1998 to 2000 (Therkorn *et al.* 2009). The archaeological investigation revealed that a high, broad marsh bar centrally situated in the old salt marsh landscape was sporadically inhabited around 1700 BC and from 400 BC onwards the site was continuously inhabited by farming communities. A part of this sandy ridge measuring 5.7 hectares has been left open in the residential area as a listed monument (see Ch. IV.3, Fig. 3). It is one of the few examples where physical measures have been taken to protect archaeology. The scheduled monument is surrounded by a high-water ditch and the area will be transformed into a park.

The Uitgeester-/Heemskerkerbroekpolder is a clay-on-peat area which still has an open character. Parcels in the north, in the vicinity of the Weijenbus and the Vroonmeer, belong to Stichting Landschap Noordholland and Staatsbosbeheer (Dutch Forestry Commission). The water balance in this meadow bird pasture land is regulated together with Hoogheemraadschap Noorderkwartier to ensure a more natural water level management. In this extensive pasture land the old creek landscape with house terps from the Roman period is still easily recognizable (Fig. 9).

The Castricummerpolder is situated in the middle of the Oer-IJ estuary, which after silting up was transformed into a strand plain. This region is characterized by gradual urbanization and related infrastructural intensification. In this area, just as in the Uitgeesterbroekpolder, parcels which had for decades been used as pasture land are now being transformed into arable land for maize cultivation. The archaeological wealth of this former estuary of the Oer-IJ is remarkable. The former sandy tidal deposits on or just below the surface were attractive sites for settlement, particularly in the Roman period and Early Middle Ages.

Together they offered a fine, wide range of old landscape elements within the Oer-IJ estuary; from broad creek ridges and creek systems to a strand plain they formed suitable settlement sites for former farming communities over the centuries.

5.3 Method: selection of sites and baseline measurement sampling

Taking the Oer-IJ section of the Archaeological Monuments Map (AMK) of North Holland as a starting point, fourteen sites of (very) high value were selected for qualitative research. They represented a total of over 100 hectares of archaeologically valuable landscape. An important criterion in this selection was the condition that research had already been done there to enable a comparison in time. Another requirement was the presence of a cultural layer, which is the matrix in the soil for measurements.

From March 2002 to November 2004, monitoring locations were set up and measurements carried out in a baseline survey. At each site investigated, the starting point was the known archaeological findspot in relation to the geological subsoil. The planned bore hole survey per site was oriented so that it would run right through the findspot at right angles to the deposits in the soil such as the sandy deposits of the creeks or other geological units chosen as settlement sites by the former inhabitants. During this bore hole survey the position and condition of the cultural layer was noted (Fig. 10). Samples were taken of the cultural layer drilled up so that the quality of the botanical macroremains could be established.

The ground water level was followed by divers (dataloggers) in dipwells. The dipwells used, plastic tubes with a length of 2 metres, had a filter of 80 cm. Dataloggers were hung in the tubes. Once a month the water table was manually checked to verify the measurements of the diver. The datalogger measurements give a detailed picture of the fluctuations in the water table. The redox potential of the soil, that is a measure of the presence of oxidizing substances, was also fixed. Oxygen is the best known and most damaging, but nitrate, sulphate, iron, and manganese oxides are also important oxidizers in the soil. The redox potential has an important bearing on the preservation potential of the soil for materials that can be lost due to oxidation. The last parameter in the assessment of the burial environment was the soil pH (degree of acidity). Like the redox measurements, samples were taken at several depths at each monitoring location.

Fig. 10
A gauge filled with the cultural layer from a site near Castricum.
This slightly darker layer is created when occupation remains are mixed with the soil substrate.

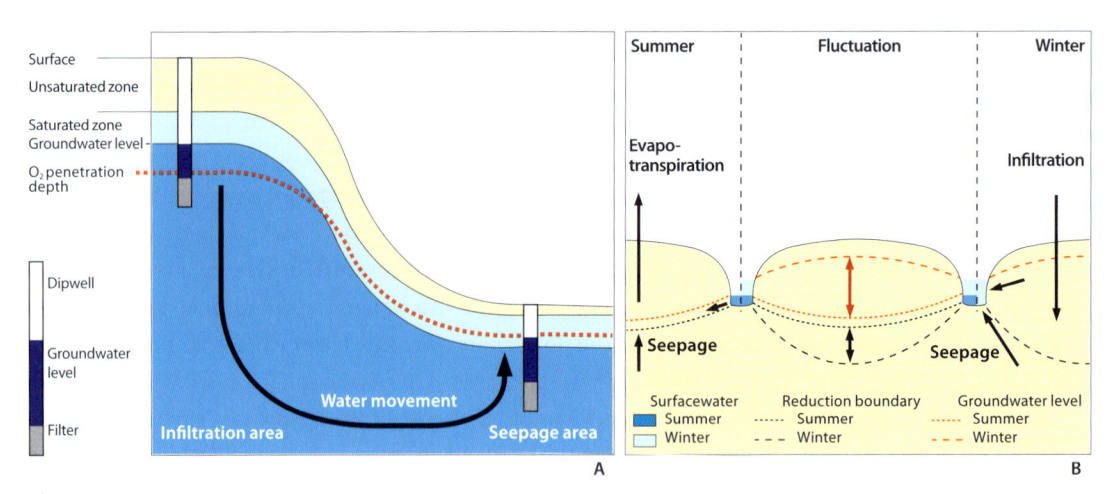

Fig. 11
Schematic representations of the relationship between water tables, unsaturated and saturated zones (*after Huisman 2009*).
A. Differences in infiltration and seepage areas.
B. Seasonal fluctuations in lowlands with ditches, based on higher levels of precipitation and less transpiration in winter and less precipitation and greater transpiration in summer.

5.4 Results, conclusions and recommendations

The soil environments investigated in the Oer-IJ give an interesting picture of the preservation capacity of the various landscapes. Differences in hydrological situations and the soil environment become clear when one works from a landscape-oriented approach. The results from the locations measured can be fairly easily translated to landscape elements. However, it is clear that a definition of the preservation capacity with resulting unequivocal recommendations is tricky because many aspects are inextricably linked. Thus the groundwater regime is a combination of factors such as precipitation and evaporation, the supply of seepage water and the polder level in combination with the porosity of the soil (Fig. 11). All these environmental aspects influence each other. The influence of seepage pressure and seepage water is substantial in the former Oer-IJ landscape. In a number of places clear effects of seepage have been observed which have a favourable effect on the quality of the organic remains in the archaeological soil archive. The oxygen-poor seepage water provides good preservation conditions. At other locations it was observed that the poor porosity of the soil in some places leads to dehydration in the summer months. Generally speaking, the groundwater level does not drop to more than 30 cm below polder level.

The soil environment containing the archaeological remains is alkaline for the first metre below the surface, which is often a favourable environment for most categories of material. The top of it is acid. In an acid soil environment the preservation chance of unburnt bone and metals is small. Acidification is not only caused by precipitation or animal faeces, for dehydration also leads to (temporary) changes in the pH value, certainly in soils with a low organic matter content. Whether this acidification penetrates further into the soil environment depends on a number of factors. The supply of alkaline seepage and agrarian liming appear to slow down this acidification process.

The measurements also showed that dehydration, especially in the summer months, leads to a highly oxidizing soil environment. The redox potential for a number of sites was reducing in the winter but, generally speaking, the soil environment of the three polders can be said to be oxidizing. Another conclusion of the research was that a favourable, slightly alkaline degree of acidity in the cultural layer is sometimes the result of agrarian liming. Continuous agrarian use of parcels, with regular liming, can produce a favourable soil environment. When a parcel is taken out of cultivation, allowance must be made for the fact that the degree of acidity may drop in the course of time causing the quality of certain categories of material in the soil, especially metals, to decline.

An important conclusion is that raising the groundwater level is not always favourable for the archaeological remains. Depending on local hydrology, a rise can lead to the reversal of a seepage situation to an infiltration environment. Such an inversion is usually linked with a rise in the redox potential, which in turn eventually leads to oxidation of the organic material. This rise in redox potential is the result of infiltration water transporting dissolved oxygen from the surface downwards.

To complete the project, a pilot study was carried out in conjunction with other parties to determine the possibilities of mapping the preservation capacity. Methods were sought to convert the data obtained into comprehensive knowledge about the preservation capacity. The development of the geological/pedological model was opted for, the 3D layer model, in which there is a link between the subsoil and the archaeological cultural layers in relation to the groundwater and other soil parameters, such as the redox potential and the degree of acidity. Changes in the groundwater dynamics can thus be simulated, revealing the effects on the soil environment and the archaeological remains. Generated maps showing the preservation capacity can be used as policy maps in spatial planning.

Because detailed data on the Dutch (Holocene) soil are limited and the geological and pedological map images are extrapolations, the scale on which this type of potential map can be used is subject to restrictions. The preservation capacity map has the greatest power of expression over the expected physical quality of the potential archaeological values in a certain type of landscape. This model reflecting the preservation potential has not yet been validated, which therefore must be considered as proof of a concept.

6. AN EXTERNAL VIEW OF THE PDL/BBO/OER-IJ PROGRAMME
(Gísli Pálsson)

My brief commentary is focused on four themes, namely the Dutch heritage management scheme, transdisciplinary projects and collaboration more generally, the notion of cultural biography and my own wetlands project.

6.1 *The Dutch cases*

In his book *Seeing Like a State*, Scott (Scott 1998) explores state-sponsored management schemes. He suggests that 'high modernism' is represented by "supreme self-confidence about continued linear progress, the development of scientific and technical knowledge, ... the rational design of social order, the growing satisfaction of human needs, and, not least, an increased control over nature (including human nature) commensurate with scientific understanding of natural laws" (*ibidem*, 89-90). Nature, then, is presented as an inherently logical and linear domain and, accordingly, the project of the resource manager is likened to that of the engineer or the technician. Some of the management schemes of high modernism have been successful while others have collapsed. While the rhetoric of high-modernism promises too much, somehow we have to act with respect to environmental problems. The alternative, avoiding engagement and simply indulging in analyses of social constructions, is equally unrealistic and irresponsible.

To me, the Dutch cases represent interesting attempts in finding a middle ground, seriously engaging with the environment and a whole series of 'stakeholders' while at the same attending to comparison, theory, and critical and self-conscious reflection. Developing this middle ground is not easy but somehow we have to muddle through.

6.2. Transdisciplinarity and collaboration

The Dutch cases raise useful questions about the nature of collaboration across disciplines and between 'lay' persons and experts and the problems and challenges and the tensions and opportunities involved. The projects and their aims necessarily suggest collaborations of this kind, but these are also times of interdisciplinarity, if not postdisciplinarity. The collapsing of nature and culture in post-modernity, by definition, reshuffles the academic landscape and the separation and hierarchy of 'lay' and expertise.

Collaborative approaches are not new to my field, anthropology; for decades there has been much talk and experimenting on rapport, dialogue and consultancy, partly drawing upon earlier developments in feminist scholarship and critical ethnography (Pálsson 2008). Thus, Heath, for instance, suggested the notion of "modest interventions" to refer to "translocal engagements that reveal, perturb, and perhaps transform the constructed boundaries between local, situated knowledge" (Heath 1997,68). However, "collaboration" is now being formulated with more force and precision than before. Lassiter argues (Lassiter 2005) the tide is turning as ethnographers increasingly apply the term to the entire research process, from research design to the dissemination of results. For him, this has much to do with the shifting context of fieldwork and the growth of multi-sited ethnography.

An interesting parallel to the Dutch collaborations is that of heritage management and presentation in the Inuit and Yup'ik Arctic. Clifford (Clifford 2004) has explored the collaborations of academics and Alaskan Natives on heritage projects, pointing out that while sometimes they lean towards a multivocal model juxtaposing Native and non-Native views, some collaborations are more community-based, primarily reflecting Native perspectives. Taking the collaborative model seriously may necessitate innovative thinking and radical restructuring of academic institutions and research practices. In his discussion of the work of anthropologist Ann Fienup-Riordan, which experiments with close collaborations with Yup'ik people, Clifford comments: "It is arguable that her choice to remain unaffiliated with any university or governmental institution has given her the flexibility to pioneer collaborative styles of work, engaging in relations and projects which might have seemed 'unprofessional' *before they became, under pressure, the norm*" (*ibidem* 2004, 12; added emphasis).

Questions that need to be addressed in collaborative research include how to define a community and how to deal with differences in perspectives and interests. How should projects deal with different opinions on research design and the interpretation of results, the potential clash between the perspectives of researchers and the ethnopolitics of the 'lay' people involved? Forms of collaboration, no doubt, will depend on context, researchers and the kind of research in question.

6.3 The notion of cultural biography

It seems to me the notion of cultural biography opens several avenues. One of these avenues is that outlined by Van Londen, avoiding linear chronology and emphasizing "a narrative of transformation

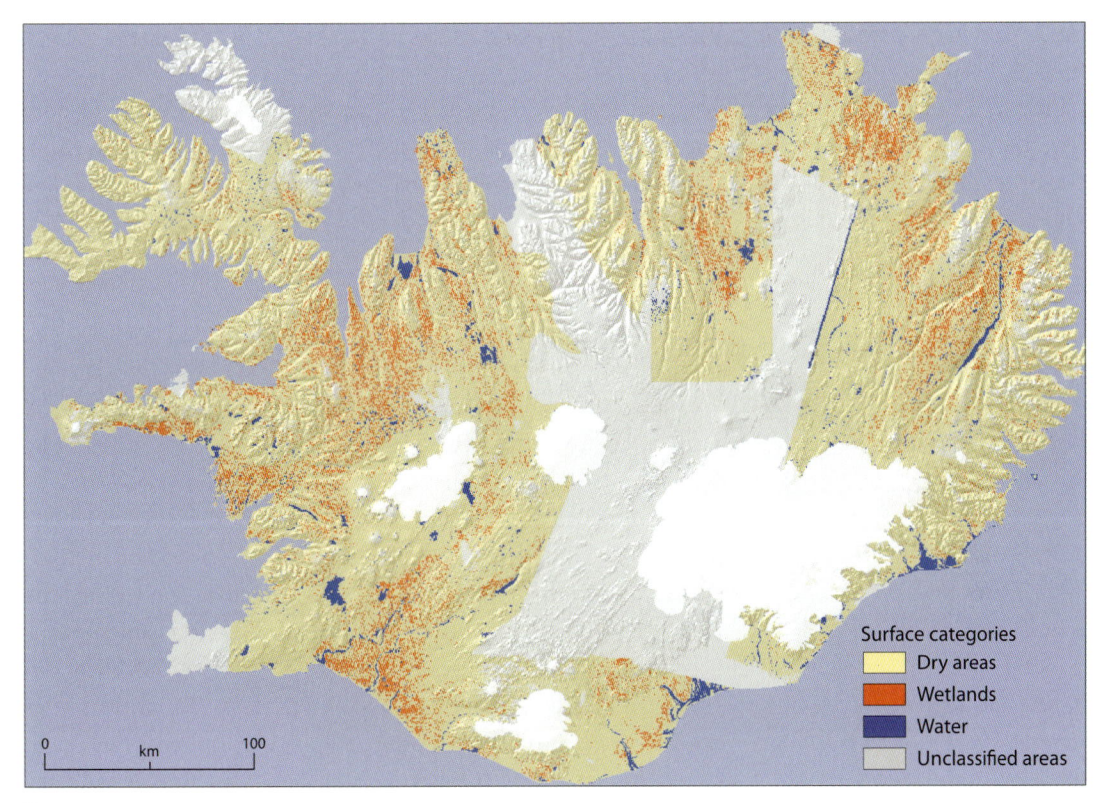

Fig. 12
Icelandic wetlands.
Source: The Agricultural College of Iceland, The Icelandic Farmland Database 2006.

of meaning through time" (Van Londen 2004; *idem* 2006). The construction of narrative, as pointed out by Van Londen, is necessarily an interpretive exercise. Another related avenue is that by Appadurai, Kopytoff and some others focusing on the biography of things and landscapes (Appadurai 1986). Such a perspective grants the environment an element of agency, a point emphasized by environmental historians such as Cronon (Cronon 1996).

Interestingly, the social sciences and the humanities, including anthropology, have seen a general 'turn' to biographical methods (see for instance Chamberlayne/Bornat/Wengraf 2003), focusing on private lives and the ways in which they constitute and are constituted by context. Much of this literature resonates with the narrative approach to cultural biography in that it tries to reveal what is hidden beneath the surface. A growing body of literature, for instance, emphasizes the importance of showing how the management of intimacy in European colonies, usually a highly secretive thing, was part of imperial politics; one example is Stoler's book *Carnal Knowledge and Imperial Power: Race and the Intimate in Colonial Rule* (Stoler 2002). If sentiments, as Stoler argues, are the "real stuff" of official archives, biographies deserve careful attention, illuminating contexts and regimes through private lives, at the intersection of self and history. Stoler's work seeks to outline the "microphysics of colonial rule" (Stoler 2002, 7) through a colonial reading of Foucault.

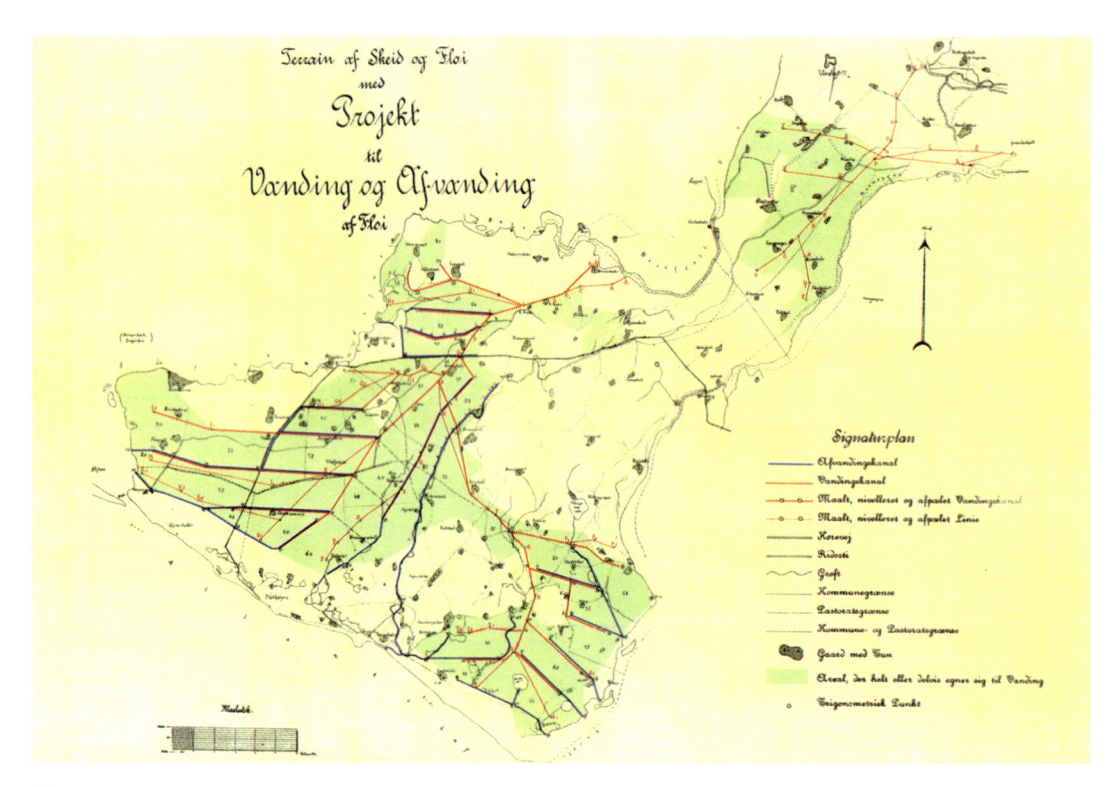

Fig. 13
The irrigations plan for Flói in southwest Iceland.

6.4. An environmental anthropology of Icelandic wetlands

Currently, I am engaged in a research project on wetlands. Drawing upon archival material, twentieth century literature and interviews with farmers, policy-makers, scientists, and environmentalists, the project emphasizes the phenomenology of landscape, the symbolism of water and the politics of drainage, protection and reclamation. The major goal is to explore environmental and social histories of wetland areas in Iceland, human perceptions of landscape change and the politics of rural societies within the background of present-day concerns regarding sustainable development and the 'preservation' of nature. Specifically, emphasis will be placed on charting changes in landscapes and ecosystems as a result of human activities. The project outlines the logic of modernism, the views and politics that shaped the course of events and their impact and re-evaluation during recent years in light of environmentalism.

While the project considers the Icelandic context in general (Fig. 12), emphasizing official policy and general concepts, a further focus on specific sites will provide the opportunity for a detailed analysis of local processes in diverse environments.

Nowadays, there is a strong movement for the protection and reclamation of wetlands on both aesthetic and environmental grounds. Not only, it is argued, will reclaiming make the landscape more 'natural', it will also reduce the emission of CO_2 and other gases contributing to global warming. Indeed, wetlands, one of the most vulnerable natural features on earth, play an important ecological role. Quite appropriately, wetlands have sometimes been described as 'organic machines', the 'kidneys of the environment' and 'biological supermarkets'.

The theoretical take on wetlands emphasizes the phenomenology of landscape, the role of perception and the senses, the biography of things and the politics of modernism and the patriarchal state.

In Iceland, much change occurred during the last century with the application of modernist perspectives in agriculture with its emphasis on order, design, and efficiency. Around 1870, a grand hydraulic scheme in the Flói region in southern Iceland was extensively discussed locally and at state level (Fig. 13). Enthusiastic plans were drawn up suggesting the channelling of water through a complex artificial maze for the purpose of advancing efficiency in agriculture. The hydraulic system involved was accepted by the state and detailed planning began in 1914. The agricultural results, however, were meagre and disappointing, leaving behind much bitterness among farmers and permanent changes in the land. In 1933, when the Icelandic Parliament closed the accounts by paying the debt of the local community, one political commentator observed: "Parliament, it is now clear, walked into a … trap by accepting the Flói project in 1917. All the lofty promises associated with it have completely collapsed" (see Kjartansson 1988, 354).

ACKNOWLEDGEMENTS

We thank LindaTherkorn (University of Amsterdam), Rob van Eerden (Provincie Noord-Holland), Maarten van Wesemael (urban curator) and Sacha Husken (Cultureel Erfgoed Noord-Holland) for their supportive engagement with the PDL/BBO Oer-IJ programme.

NOTES

1. [b] Cultureel Erfgoed Noord-Holland, Haarlem, the Netherlands;
   [a, d, e] Amsterdam Archaeological Centre, University of Amsterdam (UvA), Amsterdam, the Netherlands;
   [c] previously Cultural Heritage Agency, Amersfoort; presently Vestigia Archeologie en Cultuurhistorie, Amersfoort, the Netherlands;
   [f] Cultural Heritage Agency, Amersfoort, the Netherlands;
   [g] Deltares, B&O, Utrecht;
   [h] Department of Anthropology, Faculty of Social Science, University of Iceland.
2. This section is a shortened version of the original research proposal written for the 2001 grant application.

REFERENCES

Alders G./H. Renes/H. van Londen/J.H.F. Bloemers, 2006: Beemster: A Reclaimed lake with a Classical Landscape, in L. Lévêque/M. Ruiz del Árbol/L. Pop/C. Bartels (eds.), *Journeys through European Landscapes/Voyages dans les paysages européens*, Ponferrada, 215-218.

Ankersmit, F.R., 1996: *De spiegel van het verleden. Exploraties I: Geschiedtheorie*, Groningen.

Appadurai, A. (ed.), 1986: *The Social Life of Things: Commodities in Cultural Perspective*, Cambridge.

Bartels, C./M. Ruiz del Árbol /H. van Londen/A. Orejas (eds.), 2008: *Landmarks. Profiling Europe's Historic Landscapes*, Bochum.

Beek, R. van/J.H.F. Bloemers/L. Keunen/J. Kolen /H. van Londen/H. Renes, 2008: Managing and protecting by developing the landscape in the Netherlands: an overview of current policy and research, in G. Fairclough/P. Grau Møller (eds.), *Landscape as Heritage. The Management and Protection of*

Landscape in Europe, a summary by the Cost A 27 project 'LANDMARKS, Bern (Geographica Bernensia 79), 177-203.

Beleving 2005: *Beleving en verbeelding door culturele planologie. Twee jaar integratie van kunst en ruimtelijke inrichting in de provincie Noord-Holland. Provinciaal Bestuur van Noord-Holland,* Haarlem (Oer-IJ: 34-43).

Bloemers, J.H.F./R. During/J.N.H. Elerie/H.A. Groenendijk/M. Hidding/J. Kolen/Th. Spek/M.-H. Wijnen, 2001: *Bodemarchief in Behoud en Ontwikkeling. De conceptuele grondslagen*, Den Haag.

Bloemers, T./S. Husken/R. van Leeuwen 2009: *Een agenda voor het Oer-IJ. Het Oer-IJ op het snijvlak van cultuurhistorisch kennen en handelen*, Haarlem.

Broesi, R., 2005: De limes als netwerk, in B. Colenbrander (ed.), *Limes Atlas*, Rotterdam.

Chamberlayne, P./J. Bornat/T. Wengraf (eds.), 2003: *The Turn to Biographical Methods in Social Science: Comparative Issues and Examples,* London.

Clifford, J., 2004: Looking several ways: Anthropology and native heritage in Alaska, *Current Anthropology* 45, 5-30.

Cronon, W. (ed.), 1996: *Uncommon Ground: Rethinking the Human Place in Nature,* New York.

Cultuur als confrontatie, 2000: *Cultuur als confrontatie. Uitgangspunten voor het cultuurbeleid 2001-2004,* Den Haag.

Cultuur Verbindt, 2004: *Cultuur Verbindt. Cultuurnota 2005-2008 Provincie Noord-Holland*, Haarlem.

Dekkers, C./G. Dorren/R. van Eerden, 2006: *Het land van Hilde. Archeologie in het Noord-Hollands kustgebied*, Haarlem/Utrecht.

During, R./H. Elerie/H.A. Groenendijk, 2001: 'Denken en doen: verpachten van wijsheid of delen van kennis? Pleidooi voor de verbinding van cultuurhistorische kenniseilanden en een relatie met de sociale wetenschappen', in J.H.F Bloemers/R. During/J.N.H. Elerie/H.A. Groenendijk/M. Hidding/J. Kolen/Th. Spek/ M.-H. Wijnen , *Bodemarchief in Behoud en Ontwikkeling. De conceptuele grondslagen*, Den Haag, 111-157.

Eerden, R.A. van, 2004: *Behoud en beheer van archeologische vindplaatsen in het Oer-IJ-gebied,* Haarlem.

Es, W.A. van/H. Sarfatij/P.J. Woltering (eds.), 1988: *Archeologie in Nederland. De rijkdom van het bodemarchief*, Amsterdam/Amersfoort.

Flamman, J. P./H. van Londen, 2008: Archeologische monumentenzorg en duurzame ontwikkeling, in J.P. Flamman/E. Besselsen (eds.), *Het verleden boven water. Archeologische Monumentenzorg in het AHR-project,* Delft, 345-364.

Giddens, A., 1995² (1984): *The Constitution of Society: Outline of the theory of structuration*, Cambridge.

Hallewas, D.P., 1981: Archaeological Cartography between Marsdiep and IJ, *Berichten van de Rijksdienst voor het Oudheidkundig Bodemonderzoek* 31, 219-272.

Hallewas, D.P., 1987: The geology in relation to the record of occupation and settlement, in R.W. Brandt/W. Groenman-van Waateringe/S.E. van der Leeuw (eds.), *Assendelver Polder Papers* 1, Amsterdam (Cingula 10), 23-38.

Heath, D., 1997: Bodies, antibodies, and modest interventions: Works of art in the age of cyborgian reproduction, in G. Downey/J. Dumit (eds.), *Cyborgs and citadels: Anthropological interventions in the borderland of technoscience,* Santa Fe, 67-82.

Heeringen, R.M. van/E.M. Theunissen, 2006: The threat of dessication - recent work on the *in situ* monitoring of archaeological wetland sites in The Netherlands, in L. Dyson/E. Heppell/C.

Johnson/M. Pieters (eds.), *Archaeological Evaluation of Wetlands in the Planarch Area of North West Europe*, Maidstone, 64-71.

Hoppe, R., 2002: *Van flipperkast naar grensverkeer. Veranderende visies op de relatie tussen wetenschap en beleid*, Den Haag (Adviesraad voor het Wetenschaps- en Technologiebeleid).

Huisman, D.J., 2009: *Degradation of archaeological remains*, Den Haag.

Jain, R.K./H.C. Triandis, 1997: *Management of research and development organization. Managing the Unmanageable*, New York etc.

Kohler, T.A./S.C. Parker, 1986: Predictive models for archaeological resource location, in M.B. Schiffer (ed.), *Advances in Archaeological Method and Theory 9*, New York, 397-452.

Kjartansson, H.S., 1988: Áveiturnar miklu á Skeið og Flóa, *Skírnir* 162, 330-360.

Kok, M.S.M., 2008: *The homecoming of religious practice. An analysis of offering sites in the wet low-lying parts of the landscape in the Oer-IJ area (2500 BC-AD 450)*, Amsterdam (Ph.D. thesis University of Amsterdam).

Kolen, J.C.A., 2005: *De biografie van het landschap: drie essays over landschap, geschiedenis en erfgoed*, Amsterdam (Ph.D. thesis VU University).

Lange, S./E. Besselsen/H. van Londen, 2004: *Het Oer-IJ estuarium. Archeologische Kennisinventarisatie (AKI)*, Amsterdam (AAC-publicaties 12).

Lassiter, L.E., 2005: *The Chicago guide to collaborative ethnography*, Chicago.

Lawson, T.E./R.N. McCauley, 1996 (1990): *Rethinking religion: connecting cognition and culture*, Cambridge.

Leusen, M. van/J. Deeben/D. Halewas/H. Kamermans/P. Verhagen/P. Zoetbrood, 2005: A baseline for Predictive Modelling in the Netherlands, in M. van Leusen/H. Kamermans (eds.), *Predictive Modelling for Archaeological Heritage Management: A research agenda*, Amersfoort (Nederlandse Archaeologische Rapporten, 29), 25-92.

Londen, H. van, 2004: *Culturele biografie van het landschap. Tussen kennisoverdracht en belangenbehartiging. Essay over de definitie en het toepassingsbereik van het concept*, Amsterdam (manuscript presented at the NWO/BBO meeting 21-22.4.2004 in Amsterdam, University of Amsterdam).

Londen, H. van, 2006: Cultural biography and the power of image, in W. van der Knaap/A. van der Valk (eds.), *Multiple Landscape. Merging Past and Present*, Wageningen, 171-181.

Pálsson, G., 2008: Genomic Anthropology: Coming in from the Cold?, *Current Anthropology* 49(4), 545-568.

Provincie Noord-Holland, 2006: *Beleidskader Landschap en cultuurhistorie Noord-Holland*, Haarlem.

Scott, J., 1998: *Seeing Like a State: How Certain Schemes to Improve the Human Condition Have Failed*, New Haven.

Smit, A./R.M. van Heeringen/E.M. Theunissen, 2006: *Archaeological Monitoring Standard. Guidelines for the non-destructive recording and monitoring of the physical quality of archaeological sites and monuments*, Amersfoort (Nederlandse Archaeologische Rapporten 33).

Soonius, C.M./J.W.H.P. Verhagen/D. Bekius, 2005: *Buitengebied gemeente Castricum. Een archeologische verwachtings- en advieskaart*, Amsterdam (RAAP-rapport 1211).

Stoler, A. L., 2002: *Carnal Knowledge and Imperial Power: Race and the Intimate in Colonial Rule*, Berkeley.

Therkorn, L.L., 2008, Marking while taking land into use: some indications for long-term traditions within the Oer-IJ estuarine region, in A. Arnoldussen/H. Fokkens (eds.), *Bronze Age settlements in the Low Countries*, Oxford.

Therkorn, L.L./E.A. Besselsen/J.F.S. Oversteegen/J. Slopsma, 2006: *Assendelver Polders revisited. Excavations 1997*, Amsterdam (AACpublicaties 36).

Therkorn, L.L./E. Besselsen/M. Diepeveen-Jansen/S. Gerritsen/J. Kaarsemaker/M. Kok/L. Kubiak-Martens/J. Slopsma/P. Vos, 2009: *Landscapes in the Broekpolder: excavations around a monument with aspects of the Bronze Age to the Modern (Beverwijk & Heemskerk, Noord-Holland)*, Amsterdam.

Tol, A./P. Verhagen/A. Borsboom/M. Verbruggen, 2004: *Prospectief boren. Een studie naar de betrouwbaarheid en toepasbaarheid van booronderzoek in de prospectiearcheologie*, Amsterdam (RAAP-rapport 1000).

Tress, B./G. Tress/A. van der Valk/G. Fry (eds.), 2003: *Interdisciplinary and Transdisciplinary Landscape Studies: Potential and Limitations*, Wageningen.

Vos, P.C., 1983: De relatie tussen de geologische ontwikkeling en de bewoningsgeschiedenis in de Assendelver polders vanaf 1000 voor Chr., *Westerheem* 32, 54-80.

Vos, P.C./R.A. van Eerden/J. de Koning, 2009: *Paleolandschap en archeologie van het PWN duingebied bij Castricum. Rapportage van een multidisciplinair onderzoeksprogramma, uitgevoerd naar aanleiding van geologische en archeologische veldopnamen in acht bouwputten gelegen binnen het waterwingebied van PWN bij Castricum*, Utrecht (Deltares rapport, kenmerk 0912-0242).

Westerhoff, W.E./E.F.J. de Mulder/W. de Gans, 1987: *Toelichting bij de geologische kaart van Nederland 1:50.000, Blad Alkmaar West (19W) en Blad Alkmaar Oost (19O)*, Haarlem (Rijks Geologische Dienst).

3. Two sorting-machines for the Oer-IJ

Rob van Leeuwen[1]

This tug of war between memory that pulls and oblivion that pushes, a useless contest, for oblivion and forgetting always win in the end.
The world is so forgetful, that it even fails to notice the absence of what has been forgotten.

José Saramago, The year of the death of Ricardo Reis

ABSTRACT

The article is a transcription of two chapters of a study report on the archaeology of the Oer-IJ area. The report was aimed at enlightening the *behoud door ontwikkeling* (conservation through development) strategy and concluded by constituting an implementable policy agenda for the area based on this strategy.

This article focuses on two models. One is designed to distinguish between the abstract domain of policy-making, the world of language, and the (designed) results of these policies in the material world. Six levels were distinguished to research the relation between policy and outcome: policy concepts, policy aims, policy measures, design concepts, design repertoires and (executed or executable) designs. One finding is that there is so little exchange between the distinguished levels that there is no way to assess whether what is designed has anything to do with what was aimed at; a second finding is that the concepts tend to take the form of dogmatic, denial-proof statements.

The second model is a section of the first and distributes the designed results in relation to their claim to historical authenticity and their existence in the material world. This model is designed to be able to define the possible results of the *behoud door ontwikkeling* strategy as authentic historical representations distinguished from stories, art, falsifications and kitsch.

KEY WORDS

Conservation by development; Oer-IJ, cultural history; policy concept, aims, measures; design concept, design repertoire, design; policy and space; cupboard, matrix, forgetting

1. INTRODUCTION

The Belvedere Memorandum was published in 1999 (Belvedere 1999). In this document, the national government of the Netherlands assigned a guiding role to cultural history on the policy agenda for spatial development. Everyone supported this initiative, no one was against it. The national government, provinces, municipalities and water boards were unanimous in their conviction that it is better when the past is recognizable in spatial development than when it is not. This also applied to the Oer-IJ, the region in the province of North Holland where, on the surface and underground, traces can be found of the former estuary of the IJ (Fig. 1), of its ever-changing creeks and channels, of the fixation thereof, and incorporation in an occupation pattern and of the decor and attributes of the life that took place there.

The study *Een agenda voor het Oer-IJ* (Bloemers/Husken/Van Leeuwen 2009; 'An agenda for the Oer-IJ') was the result of an initiative of the PDL/BBO research programme dealing with the Oer-IJ area to pro-

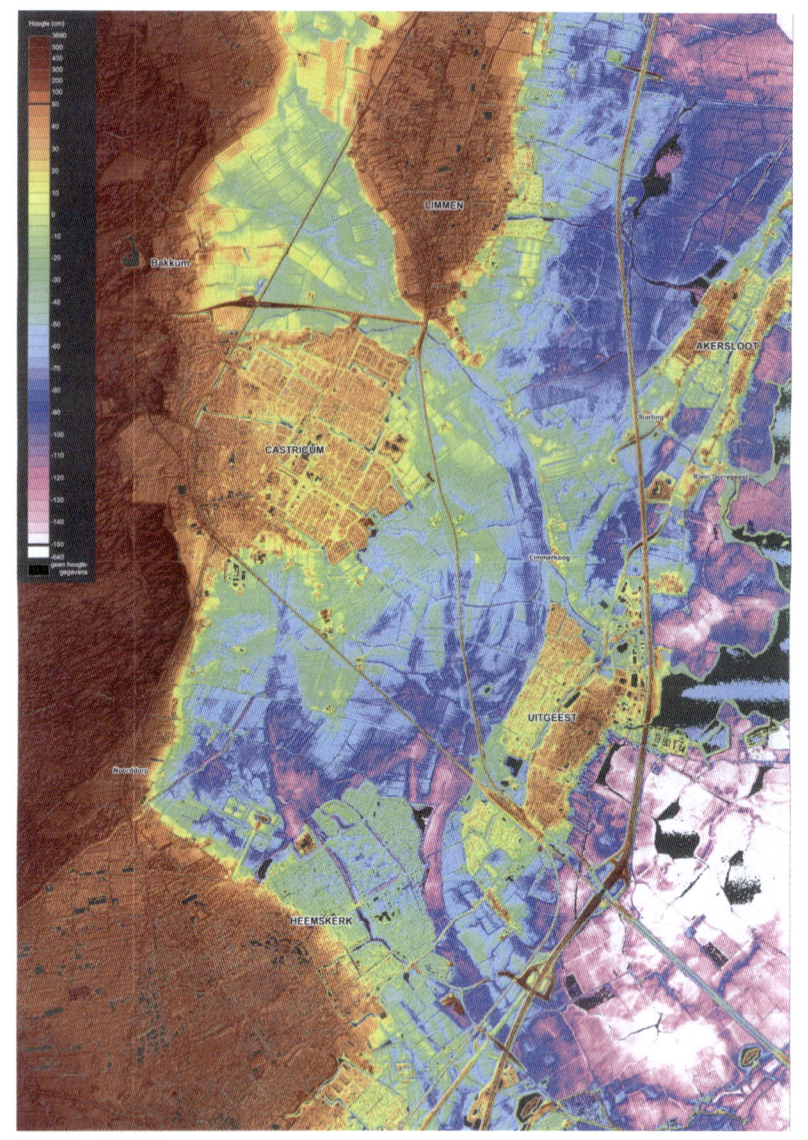

Fig. 1
The Oer-IJ between Heemskerk and Limmen. Elevation map (dark red: high; purple: low) showing the dunes (west), the river (middle) and the peat plain (east) *(De Ruijter et al. 2005)*.
Graphic: Ben Bom, Provincie Noord-Holland.

vide advice to the province of North Holland on the way cultural-historical identity could be created in the Oer-IJ region, and more specifically, how this process could be used to give content and shape to the attractive but largely unspecified motto 'conservation through development'.

Conservation of historical monuments is stipulated by law, no advice is required for this. But how should the conservation of aspects other than objects be created? Which development creates which content? Which part of cultural history is relevant, which creation leads to identity?

As with every study, the authors first looked at what was already there, which 'wheels had already been invented' in this domain. After the Belvedere Memorandum, a lot of policy had been formulated on the topic of the cultural ambition in land-use planning and a number of projects had also been implemented under this policy. A conspicuous result of this initial scan was the essentially uniform but abstractly formulated policy that led to a great diversity of form in its implementation without making clear where this diversity of form sprang from. This led to the central question of this article, is that which has been implemented also that which was intended when the policy was formulated?

This article, a summary of part of the study *Een agenda voor het Oer-IJ*, addresses the connection between policy and implementation. Did the policy actually intend the implementation that it received? Did the implementation meet the ambitions of the policy? Do policy makers have an idea or even a vision of the result of their policy?

Two 'sorting-machines' have been designed as methods to answer these questions. The first, the 'cupboard with shelves' (section 2), was created to shed light on the transition from policy to implementation; the second, the 'matrix' (section 5), to classify the results of policy implementation. These 'sorting-machines' were developed during the study from attempts to organize the material. The two sorting-machines are the subject of this article.

2. THE CUPBOARD
2.1 *The material world and the world of policy*

The Oer-IJ exists in two worlds, matter and language. One world is the landscape and what lies under it, the soil archive. This world lies in the domain of matter. The other world is the policy world of the Oer-IJ, the collection of wishes, aspirations, resolutions and agreements about dealing with the Oer-IJ. This world lies in the domain of language. Both worlds exist equally but separately.

Many events in the material world have no predecessor in the world of policy and many aspirations in the world of policy have nothing to do with the material world. However, our attention is focused on the connection between the two worlds, policy that affects space. Based on policy, something must be created in space, a road, a residential area, a harbour, a nature reserve. This takes place in a series of steps; a policy resolution becomes a draft, the draft becomes a plan, the plan becomes a set of specifications and specifications are implemented. Stated more formally, the language of policy is transformed into the matter and form of the space. Language becomes matter, this is the essence of the transformation of abstract policy into material space.

How do these steps work? What lies between policy and material space? What are the transformation stages of a policy idea into material form? To answer these questions, a series of projects in the Oer-IJ region recorded in publications are studied to determine the relationship between intent and result. These publications are selected using the following keywords: cultural planning, archaeology, Oer-IJ and projects. The research method is simple: collect and distinguish. We harvested information from two worlds, the world of policy where the intention originates and the material world, i.e. the physical space where the result manifests itself. In between we distinguished six stages, three of which exist in the language world of policy and three in the material world. They are:
- policy concepts;
- policy wishes;
- policy measures;
- design concepts;
- design repertoire;
- implementation designs.

The underlying idea is simple, we assume that policy concepts are expressed in policy wishes and on this basis measures are taken that lead to spatial plans. Every plan is based on a design concept which calls for a design repertoire that is appropriate for realizing the design concept. Based on the design concept, the final design is made and implemented. If the process worked well, this design reflects what, at the very beginning, was intended in the policy concept. But is it?

2.2 The cupboard

The first sorting-machine has the form of a cupboard, a standing cabinet with horizontal shelves. Each shelf represents one of the six stages. The publications collected are searched for the presence of each of these six stages and for the content of the stages. Why this grouping? We looked for extremes and transitional forms between extremes. The extremes are the components that entirely and exclusively occur in one of the two worlds, language and matter; the language shelf is therefore the uppermost shelf and the matter shelf is the lowermost shelf. The transitional forms are the components that either point from one world to the other or appear in both worlds and are located in the four interim shelves. Moreover, there is a hierarchy because what happens on the shelf above determines what happens on the shelf below. The transformation of policy into space has the form of a descent through the cupboard.

The six compartments in the cupboard were used to sort the collection as follows. The policy concepts were sorted into the uppermost compartment. Policy concepts are words about what is good. An example is a statement such as "cultural-historical identity contributes to spatial quality". At this level, little can be said about the truth of this statement; policy concepts primarily have meaning in the domain of language where they chiefly say something about the words from which they are constructed. They are formulated as a creed, in a manner that is simultaneously compelling and coercive. The structure is usually elliptical, it is good to do good. In the example above, truth is achieved when the quality of space is defined by the presence of cultural-historical identity; the proposition proves itself. Policy concepts are therefore apodictic, axiomatic statements and are not subject to refutation and discussion. If someone were to state that cultural-historical identity does *not* contribute to spatial quality, that statement would be considered unacceptable and rigorous proof would be demanded, far more rigorous than if someone were to state that cultural-historical identity indeed contributes to spatial identity. It is important to distinguish this apodictic characteristic because on this cupboard shelf a definition of what is good is established, a definition that can no longer be ignored or disputed at a lower level.

What do policy concepts do? They stipulate the topic for conversation, in this case cultural history. Once the topic has been introduced into the conversation everyone wants to have their say. The policy concepts set the agenda, although it is not clear where the process following that agenda leads to. On the one hand the policy concept in the example above expresses a certain respect for the material past; on the other hand it leads the way to a colourful procession of actions and projects which, as long as they claim to be applicable to the initial policy concepts, are thereby legitimized as a result. The procession becomes visible in the lower compartments of the cupboard. For that matter, there are not *many* policy concepts in the collection of documents about the Oer-IJ: the above example summarizes them rather well.

The second compartment proceeding downward contains the policy wishes. Policy wishes formulate the aims which are pursued. They describe the outcome of the axiomatic good which is formulated in the policy concepts. For example, "we want to give cultural and cultural-historical values a full-fledged role in land-use planning tasks and put them on the stand to serve as a starting-point or inspiration for the spatial developments that our province faces in the future, conservation through development" (Streekplan 2003).

The policy wishes also exist almost entirely in the domain of language. They describe the desired future. They expand the policy concepts with verbs, something must be created. The word 'must' is universally present. The desired future must be. As a result, they break through the elliptical, self-referential structure of the policy concepts. It is replaced with semantic vagueness, the policy wish does not make it clear what is there, if there is what must be.

What do policy wishes do? They specify the agenda that is proposed by the policy concepts. They provide words with which, on the lower levels of the cupboard, the actions and projects can be explained. This offers no guarantee however, if a project explains itself in accordance with the policy wishes there is no criterion in this domain to confirm or deny the validity of that assertion.

The third compartment proceeding downward contains the policy measures. Policy measures are the actions that are taken to achieve the aims formulated in the policy concepts and policy wishes, for example "pursuing an integral spatial quality programme, linked to the instrument of the aesthetic quality plan"[2] (Cultuur op de kaart 2008). The distinction between policy measures and policy wishes is not always entirely clear but it is clear enough to be assigned its 'own' shelf in the cupboard; not only is there something that must be in the future, but we are also going to do something to achieve it. This compartment contains the actions.

The policy measures establish a bridge between the world of language and that of space and matter. Policy measures state that we are going to create something that can be described with the words of the policy concepts and policy wishes and that will make a difference in the material world. The semantic vagueness that characterizes the policy wishes still shines through in the policy measures in the words that describe the aims, but a more tangible 'interim target' is also formulated; in the above example, this is the programme and the aesthetic quality plan.

What do policy measures actually do? They mark the border of the domain of language and they create the transition to the material domain.

The fourth compartment proceeding downward contains the design concepts. Design concepts are ideas formulated in language, and sometimes in images, about the aspects in the design that can be in accordance with what is intended in the three compartments above. Examples include "the parcellation plan must be inspired by historical patterns" (Offenberg 2003) and "make the asymmetry of the line of the Stelling van Amsterdam [Defence Line of Amsterdam] (dry inside – wet outside) recognizable. Protect the slow dynamics, the emptiness and the silence" (Fig. 2; H+N+S landschapsarchitecten 2001).

Design concepts are generic, they provide a generally applicable approach but do not specify what the results must look like. Design concepts are images of words, they are located on the bridge between the domain of language and the material world. They are somewhat related to the policy concepts in the sense that they are apodictic, there is no basis for refuting their validity, neither is there a basis for accepting it.

Fig. 2
The Stelling van Amsterdam, five different approaches *(H+N+S Landschapsarchitecten 2001)*.

What do design concepts actually do? They indicate the components of space to which the policy wishes refer, i.e. what the policymakers actually want. The design concepts are interpretations of the policy wishes and policy concepts.

The fifth compartment going downward contains the design repertoire. The design repertoire is created as a generic specification of the design concepts and consists both of applicable images and instructions regarding their application. An example is, "leave the contours of the plain of the Oer-IJ area intact and empty as an archaeological buffer zone, and treat the other archaeological sites as islands (archaeological 'stepping stones', with a different function)" (Beleving 2005; De Ruijter *et al.* 2005).

Especially notable are specifications where the visual concepts do not aim to create a material situation but a mental one, i.e. the presence of knowledge, a story, interest or feeling. They are also, as stowaways, sorted into this compartment and the distinction will be worked out below, in the matrix.

The design repertoire is a specification and concretization of the design concepts which is applied in a general sense to an actual space, e.g. a region, programme or object. As a concretization of the design concepts the content of the design repertoire is a potential topic for discussion, is this really the best way to fulfil the policy ambitions? In fact, however, this discussion seldom takes place, partly as a result of the inability of the potential discussion participants to understand one another. Top-down, from the policy domain, people are already very pleased that something tangible is appearing. In any case, no specific image existed of what was wanted down the line in that domain. Bottom-up, from where the designers are, there is no criterion to test the cultural-historical validity of the design repertoire. As long as it is well designed, it is good.

The cultural historians also have little to say. They only feel competent regarding the actual historical objects and their judgement about the design repertoire is close to being a matter of personal taste. What does the design repertoire do? It indicates how and with which means the policy-based initiatives, the four compartments above this compartment, can be accommodated.

The bottom compartment, the sixth from above, contains the implementation designs. These are not only the implemented plans but also the designs that exist purely on paper and have not (yet) been im-

Fig. 3
Beverwijk-Heemskerk.
Vlaskamp park on the site of the protected archaeological monument in the Broekpolder (*Buro Adrichem* 2004).
Elevated areas have been made on the site ('tidal marsh'), on which trees are planted along lines that correspond with the orientation and size of the old fields. A sacrificial location is symbolized with meandering square-cut hedges in front of a water constellation (see Fig. 5).

plemented. To connect the contents of this compartment with those of the other compartments it is very important to distinguish between facts and opinions. This compartment shows only the facts. For example, the Vlaskamp park in the new residential area Broekpolder, "Elevated areas have been made on the site ('tidal marsh'), on which trees are planted along lines that correspond with the orientation and size of the old fields (Fig. 3). A sacrificial location is symbolized with meandering square-cut hedges" (Offenberg 2003). What we see are varying elevations, tree lines and square-cut hedges, in a specific pattern.

Implemented designs are things, forms, linked to matter and the topography. This compartment also contains the tangible projects that focus on creating a mental situation. Implementation designs are located entirely in the material world. A story is usually involved which is initially provided as an explanation. However, the daily user generally never gets the story, he or she just encounters tree lines and square-cut hedges. This compartment is the apotheosis of everything that came before, the concretization of the design repertoire and the design concepts and, in that sense, the materialization of the policy. At this point the cultural-historical identity that contributes to the quality of the space can be perceived. The contents of this lowermost compartment are subject to additional consideration in the matrix (section 5).

3. THE ANTHOLOGY

As part of the study *Een agenda voor het Oer-IJ*, 30 documents of projects in the Oer-IJ region were studied and sorted with the first sorting-machine. These were policy documents as well as design reports and reports of experiments with cultural planning were also included. The Province of North Holland placed cultural-historical inspiration on the policy agenda; municipalities made development plans, for example for new residential areas, with which they attempted to satisfy these aspirations. Not all the documents will be presented in this article but the ones chosen for discussion are mentioned in both text and images in this article.

This section presents a limited, but we hope representative, selection of the anthology which was collected as part of the study *Een agenda voor het Oer-IJ*. Below, the first sorting-machine can be witnessed in operation. The compartments exclusively present quotations from the 30 documents, which have occasionally been modified to benefit the readability of the formulations. As to the content, they have been left intact.

3.1 Policy concepts

'Spatial quality' is the central policy concept in this document. One component of spatial quality is cultural history: because identity and recognizability are key concepts for the development of the northern region in the North Holland Province. Cultural-historical values play an important role in determining identity (Ontwikkelingsbeeld 2004). Preservation and development of cultural-historical values is thus one of the main spatial policy tasks for the region (Streekplan 2003). By using cultural planning as an instrument, present-day culture and cultural history are included in land-use planning processes. As a result, the quality and the liveability of the urban and rural landscape environment are improved (Cultuur verbindt 2004).

3.2 Policy wishes

The quality and liveability of the environment can be increased by using culture and cultural history (Cultuur verbindt 2004). We believe it is important to conserve the cultural and cultural-historical values of North Holland not only by protecting them, but also by providing space for development (Streekplan 2003). The cultural-historical values must be surveyed at an early stage of planned development, used in the design and taken into consideration before being established (Ontwikkelingsbeeld 2004). This development-oriented approach means conserving existing quality and developing new quality. The developments must be worked out in such a way that the history of the landscape remains readable (Beleidskader 2006). This involves strengthening the cultural-historical basic structure of the Oer-IJ and giving a place to the recognizability of cultural-historical structures (OD 205 stedenbouw onderzoek en landschap 2006).

For this purpose the coherence and interweaving of architecture and urban design, visual arts, built heritage conservation, landscape management and archaeology are required as part of a design practice that focuses on aestheticizing the living environment by integrating cultural history, architecture, nature and visual arts (Actieplan 2000).

The history of the landscape will be expressed in the green structure (Offenberg 2003). The district park must establish a relationship with the past (Bureau Adrichem 2004).

3.3 Policy measures

To achieve all of the above, the following measures have been approved.

Sustainable conservation of cultural-historical qualities is assured through policy-based anchoring in national spatial policy in the provincial Spatial Structure Vision and in zoning plans (Belvedere 1999). The creation of a protection contour (comparable with the Green Contour of the Fifth National Policy Document on Spatial Planning, but with the inclusion of 'red (urban)' elements) (H+N+S landschaps-architecten 2001) is part of this process.

Where provincial cultural-historical importance is established in the provincial Spatial Structure Vision, projects are initiated as inspiration for other parties, including substantive review and dissemination of knowledge and expertise (Cultuur op de kaart 2008). In that context, the map of cultural-historical values is specified in the Policy Framework for Landscape and Cultural History (Streekplan 2003).

For regions where development and intervention in land-use planning are allowed, an aesthetic quality plan is mandatory. This includes the basic assumptions for the quality dimensions that planners must comply with. As part of new developments, the aesthetic quality plan aims to preserve and strengthen the cultural-historical and landscape values and offer a guarantee for spatial quality based on the idea of identity in a community or coherent region. Elements that must be included in the aesthetic quality plan are:
- characteristics of the built-up area;
- inclusion in the landscape;
- differentiation in the residential segment;
- cultural history;
- spatial diversity (Ontwikkelingsbeeld 2004).

For the Stelling van Amsterdam[3] a Project Bureau will be established with the following tasks:
- preparing a development plan;
- preparing a *Polder atlas* as the basis for a restoration plan;
- purchasing land (H+N+S landschapsarchitecten 2001).

Cultural-historical characteristics of the planned area are being integrated in the design. In any case, this means strengthening the cultural-historical basic structure of the Oer-IJ and preservation of:
- old and often vulnerable dikes;
- wooded estates;
- the archaeological value of the landscape (OD205 stedenbouw onderzoek en landschap 2006).

3.4 Design concepts

The cultural-historical elements (in the region to be transformed into a residential area between Heiloo and Limmen, RvL) contain linear landscape elements (orientation), wooded banks and hedges (rooms), ditches and channels (direction, pattern) and civil engineering elements. Regarding these material shapes, the plan uses cultural-historical references to forms, materials, choice of types, colours and atmosphere of these elements (OD205 stedenbouw onderzoek en landschap 2006).

The cultural-historical characteristics of the planned area between Heiloo en Limmen will be integrated in the design. In any case, this means the following:
- emphasizing the difference between the open polder and the closed coastal barrier;
- maintaining the north-south oriented structure and the remaining transitions from East to West (OD205 stedenbouw onderzoek en landschap 2006).
- making the asymmetry of the dike line (dry inside – wet outside) recognizable.
- making the coherence between the components visible (H+N+S landschapsarchitecten 2001).

Some of the new bearers of identity for the green area have been selected from the different time layers. In chronological order these are:
- the levee from the Oer-IJ period is the oldest layer. Traces of the farming culture of the proto-Frisians from the early and late Iron Age can be found in the soil;
- de Kil (a former channel, RvL) from the period of the Hollandveen (ancient peat layer);
- the strip land parcelling and the dikes from the medieval moorland reclamation landscape;
- the medieval moorland reclamation.

These aspects are 'revalorized' and included in the design (Vista 2006).
In addition, new elements are introduced:
- Recognition symbols, such as a new dike post that marks the new parts of the dike.
- 'Scars' at the site of short interruptions and long re-routings of the dikes. The interruption scar is strongly accentuated and visualized (Van Westen 2005).

3.5 Design repertoire

The following design tools are relevant in the plan for the park in the new Broekpolder residential area (in the municipalities of Beverwijk and Heemskerk, RvL). The original elevation difference from dune to

Fig. 4
Beverwijk-Heemskerk.
The centre of the new Broekpolder district in the form of a medieval fortress town. *Source: unknown*.

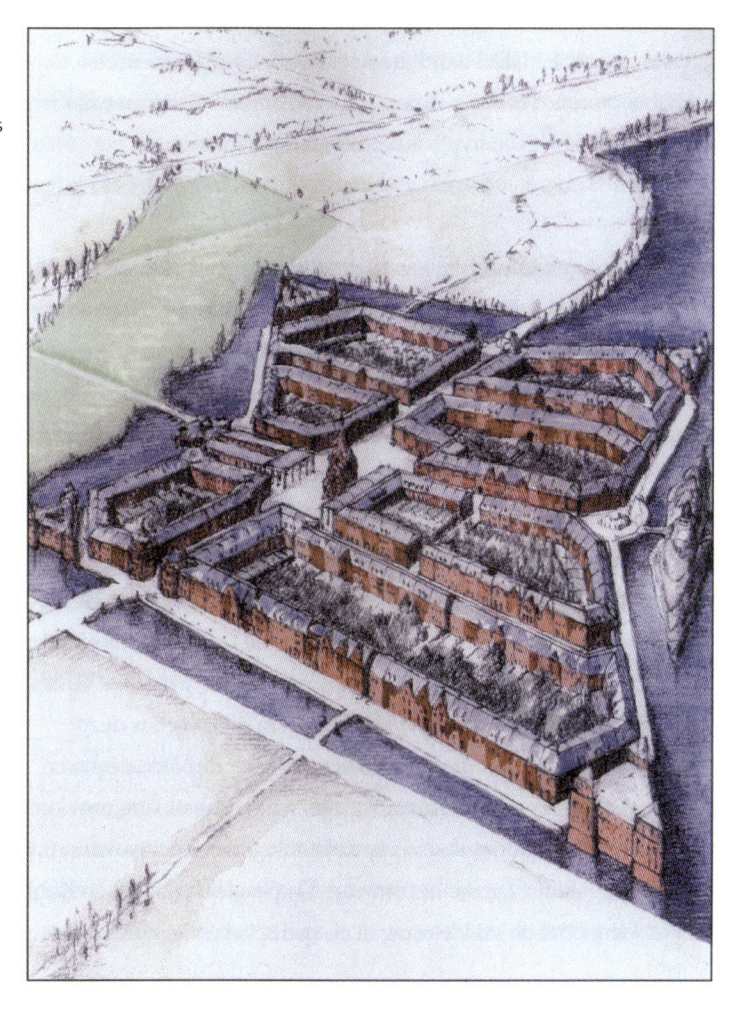

moorland is expressed in the terrain. The orientation of the tidal marsh is used. The archaeological house locations are expressed with follies[4] (Bureau Adrichem 2004). The development of the new residential area links up with the more diffuse and all-round parcel orientations of the clay and peat-soil area. The remains of the Oer-IJ and the remaining micro-relief are used for water retention.

In the development of the district park, that is situated on top of an archaeological monument that rests in the ground (no excavation was executed, it's all still there), the parcel orientations of the initial land reclamation were expressed in the surface design; the evocation of an archaeological sacrificial location is part of the programme. The previous course of the Oer-IJ is shown with 'IJ landmarks' and 'IJ follies' (Beleving 2005; De Ruijter *et al.* 2005). 'Field units', a new addition that refers to the Stelling van Amsterdam, are installed at 1000 m from the forts in the Stelling, 1000 m being the artillery range from the forts (H+N+S landschapsarchitecten 2001), The design of the field units refers to the spatial aspects of the forts. The dimensions are 160 x 300 m and ⅓ of this area is water. Each unit has a rotated base and an asymmetrical design. One side borders with vegetation and on the open side there is a long and narrow construction (20 x 200m, 10 m high) built of wood (Gebiedsaanpak 2006). Each archaeological site has

Fig. 5
Beverwijk-Heemskerk.
Water constellation representing the Great Dog *Canis major*, adjacent to the Vlaskamp park in the new Broekpolder district (*Eekhout/De Kort 2004*).

an information board (like a bus-stop sign); at the more important sites, the information is housed in a kind of 'bus shelter'.

Special media created for the purpose are used to place the IJdijk, the still operational flood defence, on the mental map. The electronic information boards, used for dynamic traveller information in buses, refer to the presence of the IJdijk with brief facts or lines of poetry when the bus passes the dike. When mobile phone users dial the information number 06-IJDIJKEN they can choose to make contact. In another cell phone use the traveller is given unexpected image-based information about the IJdijken as a sort of spam (Bureau Alle Hosper et al. 2006).

3.6 Implementation of designs

The centre of the district (Broekpolder, RvL) is given the form of a medieval fortress town surrounded by quay walls with water, a reference to the rich history of the region (Fig. 4). In one area, elements of traditional farms are used in the design of the houses. Green profiled wooden boarding refers to the Zaanse Schans.[5] In another part, the houses are built somewhat above street level as a reference to living on the levee in this former salt marsh (Bureau Adrichem 2004). The levee in the new residential area of Saendelft, near Assendelft, will be developed as a park as part of the transition from residential area to countryside (Vista 2006). The border of the residential area contains 'bastions', clusters of sport facilities, which delineate the residential area from the city and accentuate the openness of the landscape. In between are the 'donjons'[6], clustered residences where openness is assured by their mutual distance (Streekplanuitwerking 2004).

In the park on an archaeological monument in the new Broekpolder residential area, the subterranean tidal marsh ridge is represented by a long elevated area, the prehistoric farmhouses are represented by three 'flax fields', the prehistoric parcel shapes are represented by tree lines perpendicular to the 'bank' and the creek is represented by a skating rink also located perpendicular to the bank. A probable prehistoric sacrificial location is symbolized by meandering square-cut hedges on the water which separate the park

Fig. 6
Masterplan for the
Stelling van Amsterdam
(H+N+S
Landschapsarchitecten
2001).

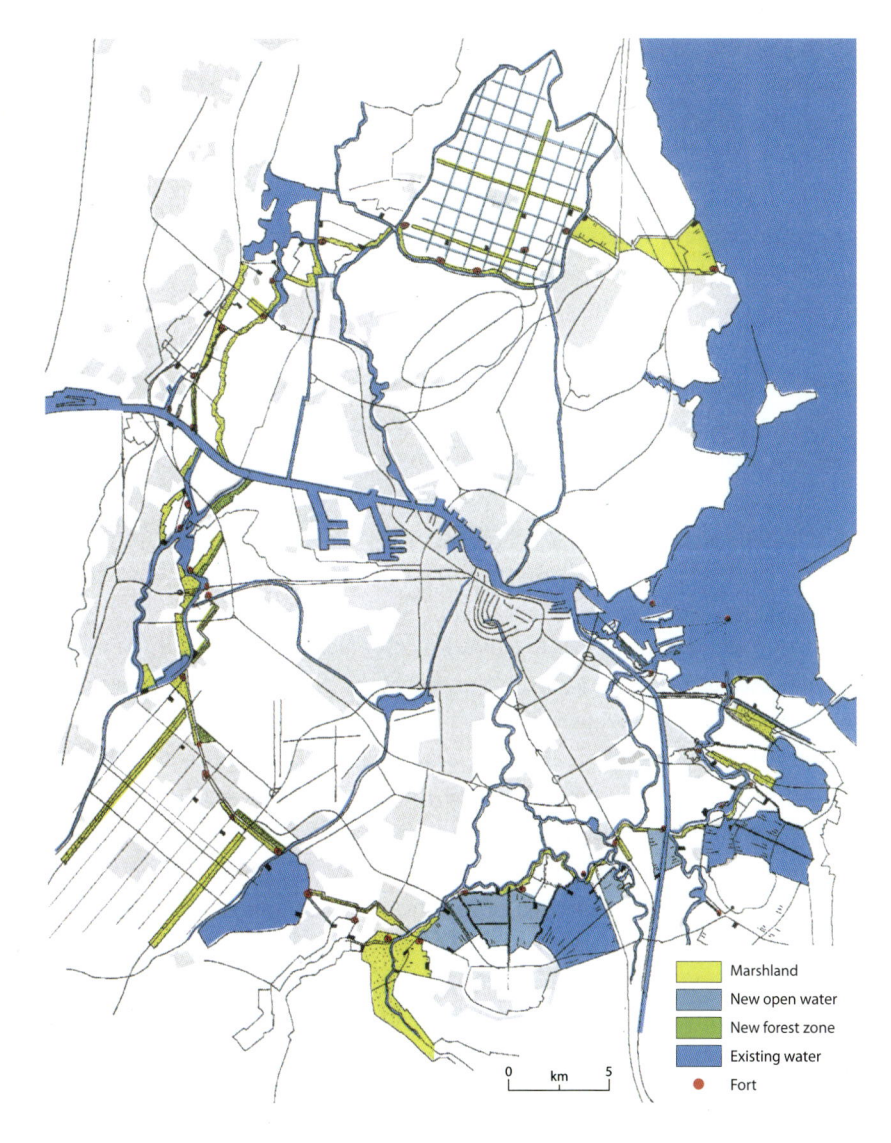

Marshland
New open water
New forest zone
Existing water
Fort

from the residential area (Offenberg 2003). A uniquely designed historical Monument Bicycle Route circles through the park and is accompanied by information panels (Fig. 3; Bureau Adrichem 2004).

In the Broekpolder residential area, a commission to create art with cultural-historical information led to 'water sacrifice stones', a spring and a drain, salt marsh islands as constellations and prehistoric vegetation. The water sacrifice stones are small flat pebbles with a spiral carved on top. Residents of every new household receive a water sacrifice stone upon arrival. The water sacrifice stone is accompanied by the story of the 'water offerings' which were thought to have occurred in prehistoric times on the banks of the Oer-IJ. The water sacrifice stones are intended to establish a ritual, if residents move to a different location they offer the stone at a special location in the park. As a result the stones are collected in this location, creating material for archaeologists in the future (Eekhout/De Kort 2004).

The spring and the drains are actually drawings with clay and shells in the grass at the centre of two roundabouts; one that turns outward, the spring, and one that turns inward to the central point, the drain, as symbols of the origin and destination of the water in the district.

Four islands in the watercourse that flows through the Broekpolder area, 'salt marsh islands' in the 'Offer Canal', are shaped according to three 'water constellations,' Hydra, Pisces and Cygnus. The fourth constellation (Auriga, the Charioteer) represents a ford in the Oer-IJ (Fig. 5). The banks of this watercourse are planted with Water Horsetail (*Equisetum fluviatile*), a relatively common species that "elicits associations with the ancient estuary". It can be found in fossils and has not changed much over millennia.

In the Oer-IJ region, the Stelling van Amsterdam is developed into a park-like green zone (Fig. 6; H+N+S landschapsarchitecten 2001). Trees have been planted behind the line of defences. A bicycle path running along the line of defences looks like a cart track, an asphalt strip with two strips of paving stones (Gebiedsaanpak 2006).

A through bicycle route also runs along the crown of the former sea dike (IJdijk) along the Oer-IJ. Interruptions of this dike are explicitly shown by means of 'symbols' in basalt (Bureau Alle Hosper *et al.* 2006). A series of projects to restore the old sea dike, which is now almost invisible, into the mental map has been implemented:

- Dijkschouw. All the residents in houses on or along the IJdijk have been sent a postcard. The picture side of the postcard has panorama photos of the IJdijk and the address side has a brief message which states that they are living on the IJdijk and are invited to join in a storytelling tour of the IJdijk.
- Dijkstalen. Despite all the changes, it is possible to indicate a series of characteristics usable to trace the line of the ancient dikes. In image and text the characteristics of the dikes are shown on a 'fan' of cards. With these cards in hand it becomes possible to read the landscape and cyclists or walkers can discover a route themselves.
- There is a website containing all historic stories and future plans of residents, project developers, associations, the port water boards and municipal administrations. By visiting the website you can find out everything about the present and past of the IJdijk.
- Game. A simulation where the decisions of the player determine the development of the landscape and culture of the Oer-IJ until far into the twenty-first century (Van Westen 2005).

The anthology ends here. What can we make of it?

4. THE FIRST HARVEST

What does the cupboard provide? We harvested two fields, the policy field where the intention originates and the field of physical space where the result manifests itself. The first harvest was made from the policy field. Before being classified, the harvest in physical space will pass through the matrix (section 5).

The defining concept in the world of policy, and the adage of cultural planning, is the requirement that culture and cultural history must provide direction and inspiration for the treatment of space. This can mean almost anything because culture and cultural history are malleable concepts. In the world of policy we find in our anthology five modes within which culture, and especially cultural history, are given their guiding position.

Valuation, status and conservation
Certain parts of space are attributed a value, on the basis of which they are assigned a status by the government and are conserved as a result. Examples are archaeological sites which are conserved *in situ*. This is the familiar procedural routine of laws and treaties from which the concept of conservation through development attempts to escape. Valuation is often conducted by professionals. As a result, confusion between professional interest ('science') and general interest can occur, a phenomenon that also occurs in nature protection.

Organization and money
The Stelling van Amsterdam is one example. There is a project bureau with a budget and there is a Stelling Committee. The Stelling is being developed to become its own museum. The development task falls largely within this organization. The Stelling Committee influences the design and development of the other plans for the Stelling region.

The Oer-IJ Experiment (Beleving 2005; De Ruijter *et al.* 2005) is a second example. There was a project leader with a budget who established projects or supported them. Preconditions for setting up such an organization are the presence of a clearly recognizable valued object, in the case of the Stelling the forts, enthusiastic propaganda for the contribution of this object to the environment and the public and a commissioning body that takes this field of action as its core task.

Procedures
The policy establishes fixed and obligatory procedures to ensure that the guiding role is effective. An example is the requirement, set down by the province in a regulation, for an aesthetic quality plan for all new developments in the rural area.

Agendas
In these procedures the government establishes a substantive 'list' of the topics that must be dealt with, without specifying what this dealing should lead to. An example is the table of contents of the aesthetic quality plan prescribed by the province:
- characteristics of the built-up area,
- adaptation to the landscape,
- differentiation in the residential segment,
- cultural history,
- spatial diversity.

The assumption is that this list ensures that identity will be created in relation to cultural history and that without this list this would probably not be the case.

Programme combinations
Culture and cultural history are being made part of programmes that have other objectives. An example is cultural history attached to programmes for landscape, nature and water. The idea is that alliances will be created where multiple objectives support each other.

This harvest comes directly from the anthology. In addition, a conclusion emerges that we make with less certainty, but still do not leave out. This is the conclusion of blind policy.

Analysis means dissection, cutting something apart. Our cupboard has been made by cutting a more or less continuous process into slices. The cutting creates the cupboard. There is a pitfall, it is tempting to think that these slices also exist in reality, that the compartments of the cupboard provide insights into characteristics that are also present in the integral process. Perhaps we do, perhaps we don't, but not by definition. Due to the process of dissection itself properties can be created that perhaps would not be there without the dissection, especially at the cutting edges.

Nevertheless, it appears that there are conceptual gaps between the six compartments in our cupboard. Particularly striking is the absence in the policy field of any image of what a cultural-historical identity could be in the material world and, in relation to that, the ease with which proposals from the designers' world are accepted as suitable answers to meet the demands from the policy field. Policy is blind, anything can be served.

Consequently, it comes down to the fact that the policy field, at all three layers (concepts, wishes and measures), asks for commitment. If there is sufficient commitment and the policy measures indicate when it is sufficient, the policy field is quickly satisfied. Commitment to cultural history, in any form, is in itself a desirable result of cultural planning.

5. THE MATRIX

To organize the harvest in the lowermost compartment of the cupboard, the second sorting-machine was developed. The first sorting-machine created the distinctions between the world of policy and the results in the material world. The results are wishes that have come true, the result is what you get if the policy wish is the guiding principle.

What do we find in the lowermost compartment of the cupboard? Surveying the harvest, one is struck not only by the diversity of forms but also by the diversity of strategies. Conservation, transformation, reference, inspiration, imitation, stories, rituals, games, everything imaginable, and which would not have been there if cultural actors and factors had not played a guiding role. No criterion can be derived from policy concepts and policy targets that we can use to evaluate the harvest or judge it in some other way. There is no distinction between good or bad, valid or invalid, useful or useless. Putting cultural history on the agenda and coercing commitment to cultural history appears to be the primary task of cultural planning, not the evaluation of the result.

We have therefore designed the second sorting-machine, which sorts the harvest in the cupboard's sixth compartment into four categories (Fig. 7). Each of these categories has two of four properties. They are either spatial (material) or non-spatial and they are either related to the actual past or to an imaginary past (the 'idea' of history). The sorting-machine was just like the cupboard developed during the research process, the anthology preceded the sorting-machine. The process of designing the second sorting-machine had an effect on the author of this article which the first sorting-machine did not have. He could not repress the urge, when he thought of something not collected in the anthology that could

	Actual past	Imaginary past
Spatial	Conservation through development	Fine arts
Non-spatial	Information	Stories

Fig. 7
Second sorting machine for the harvest of the sixth compartment.

be placed in this matrix, to go ahead and do it, even if it had nothing to do with the Oer-IJ. This is perhaps irresponsible but it was done nevertheless. How are the implemented designs distributed in the matrix?

5.1 Conservation through development

Results that have a special dimension and have something to do with the actual past are placed in the compartment labelled 'conservation through development'.

What does 'conservation through development' mean? It is a simple observation, something has been made (development, the implementation of a plan) and something has been conserved (a trace from the past). In language this is correct, but is it also in the material world? 'Conservation through development' is a paradox as development destroys what should be conserved. However, one can escape from the paradox when conservation does not concern the object itself, but an image of the object. 'Conservation through development' does not conserve the actual past because then 'through development' would not be included in the creed and there would also be no causal 'through' link, but it conserves an image of the past. To be placed in this compartment, however, that image must refer to the actual past (otherwise nothing is conserved), but the image is not the actual past.

The ambition in this compartment is that the image is a reliable representation of the decor of history. It is not the real decor, but it does evoke the real decor. The background is the idea that a design gains recognizable identity if specific, location-linked historical elements are made visible.

Here the authenticity issue, which emerges directly from the concept of 'conservation through development', does play a role. How do we know that the image provides a reliable representation of the actual past? Between the actual old object and the image of the old object lies a human interpretation which is always questionable. Interpretation can also be wrong, then the cultural-historical contribution creates a history that did not actually occur. This lies close to the dilemma that always accompanies history; it is over, we cannot look at it again.

This category (spatial, historical) includes all results that concern the 'memory of the landscape'; not the facts, but a (hopefully responsible) image of something that happened in the past. What does this compartment contain? The anthology harvest of 'conservation through development' can be divided into six categories.

Preserving the spatial structure

The Oer-IJ conditioned a cultural-historical landscape that is characterized by a primary structure composed of the Oer-IJ flood plain, its edges, the meander of the old channel and the remaining parts of the course of the Oer-IJ itself. That is the essence. If developments are designed in such a way as to conserve this structure, cultural history is honoured. For example small-scale expansions of villages on the course of the Oer-IJ are given the shape of 'islands' on the plain. The edges of the plain are left intact and empty (Beleving 2005; De Ruijter et al. 2005).

Conservation of representative ensembles

This is what people sometimes call the Asterix strategy, everything changes but a small reserve of originality is conserved. The development is allowed to erase the surrounding cultural-historical decor because 'style rooms' are exempt. These are locations where the decor of cultural history still exists and which are not protected by other regulations. An example outside the Oer-IJ concerns the environs of

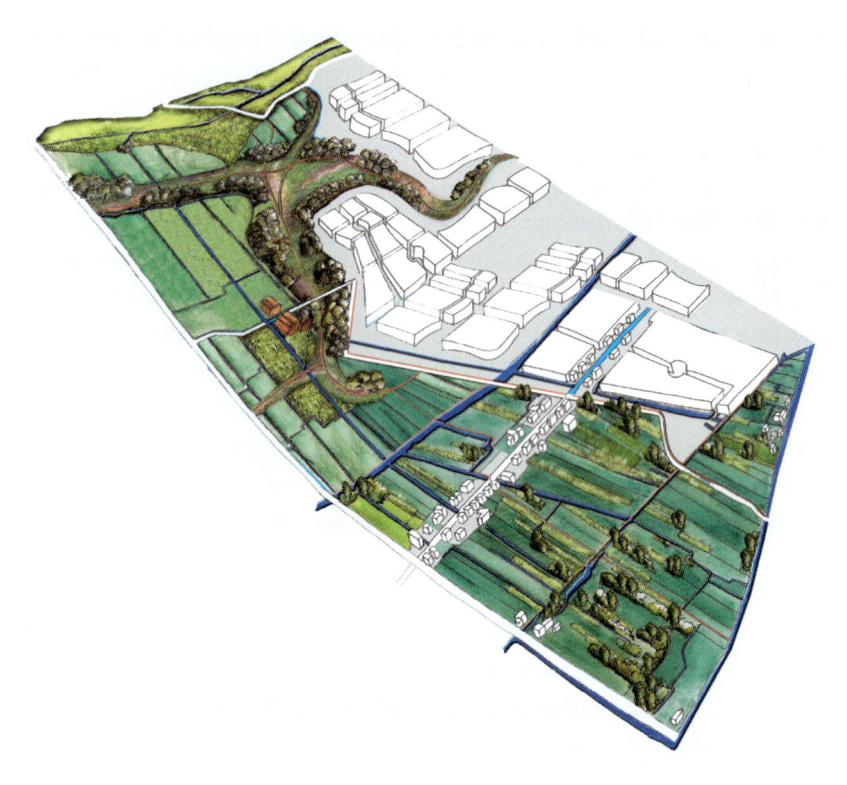

Fig. 8
Assendelft. Design of the De Omzoom urban garden in Saendelft (Vista 2006).

the Nieuwendam sluice near Amsterdam, where the dike, sluice, outport, dike buildings and hinterland comprise an image that is a powerful evocation of the former landscape.

Reusing parts of the decor

Parts of the previous decor are reused to structure the present-day assignment, essentially remodelling the previous decor. The underlying idea is that the development in the past, events in cultural history, have brought forth spatial elements that can be filled in with new, different programmes and can still evoke the past. The evocation of history takes place through the combination of old and new elements. An example is using an old vanished channel of the Oer-IJ as a watercourse in Saendelft or zoning the modernized agricultural landscape to become an urban garden (Fig. 8; Streekplanuitwerking 2004). For this purpose, the agricultural landscape within the current pattern is made to look 'old'. It is transformed into an image of the former agricultural landscape and is equipped with a recreational programme.

In architecture there are many examples of remodelling old buildings by expanding them with new components which often have a strongly contrasting design. Examples include the Koldinghus in Denmark, where a ruin was included in a museum about the ruin, and the Dominikanerkerk in Maastricht, a former church in which a modern bookstore has been built.

A special type of such reuse concerns theatrical activities of local people whereby the old decor is used, thus pulling it into the present-day world of experience and restoring it to life. An example is the project LangsteLenteLicht (LongestSpringLight) by Bruno Doedens's SLEM foundation, where people living along the Overijsselsch Canal lit a series of torches and lanterns along the entire 20 km canal on the first night of spring in 2008 (Doedens/Vogels 2009). The old space is given meaning not with a new programme but with a new ceremony.

Imitating form

The idea is that a design acquires *'genius loci'* if the cultural history or the archaeological soil archive is represented in the design in something other than its original, conserved old form. In this category the cultural-historical origin is symbolized by images that correspond with one, but not all, characteristics of something that has disappeared but about which knowledge, or alleged knowledge, exists about how it was in the old days. This can be considered a type of image rhyming over time. For that matter, it is an unintelligible rhyme because the original rhyming word is lost in time, one of the rhyming words does not exist.

An example of such imitation is using the forms of a creek system for other functions, such as parks, roads or parcel shapes. It is not the creek itself that is used, nor its location, but its form, a meander. Another example concerns linking up with the land parcel orientations of the clay and peat soil region, not the land parcels themselves, but their orientation.

Replicas

An object that has disappeared is built again and in this way provides an image of the past. In principle, the creek in Saendelft park is a replica, it is an imitation without the original context but with a form that would not have been designed if the old creek had not existed (Streekplanuitwerking 2004). The replica can be an accurate copy in the same way that bombed inner cities have been restored as accurate copies, or a stylized copy, such as the Delftse Poort in Rotterdam, a steel frame in the shape of the old gateway.

The distinction between this category and the previous one is not always clear-cut, but it comes down to this; replicas are 'complete' reconstructions while the previous category contains only forms that show a single aspect of form.

Transformations

New elements in the landscape are not shaped following the model of the existing (or old) elements, but 'in the way of the old'. For example, the 'field units' added to the Stelling van Amsterdam to make the initially invisible Stelling visible were sited according to dimensions that emerged from the use of the Stelling, like the artillery range, and constructed of forms that appeared in the Stelling but in a different, modern and functional composition.

Here as well, the dilemma of interpretation looms in the same way that Peter Schat, a twentieth century composer observed that the music of Rosemary Brown[7], which is made of musical citations, had less to do with Mozart's music than his own, modern sounding compositions.

5.2 *Information*

Results that have no spatial dimension, but do have something to do with the actual past, are placed in the compartment labelled 'Information'. 'No spatial dimension' does not mean that no matter is used but that this matter itself does not represent anything and only serves to transmit nonmaterial aspects.

'There can be no museum without signs'. A series of possibilities for information provision is proposed for the Oer-IJ region. The most physical proposal concerns the *Haltepalen*, posts like bus-stop signs with information placed next to every archaeological site; at more important sites, a 'bus shelter' with information is proposed (Beleving 2005; De Ruijter et al. 2005). The digital and telephone information also falls into this category (Bureau Alle Hosper et al. 2006). The information is educational, a form of history teaching. Some of the information is in the form of stories, narratives of events of which sometimes only parts of the decor still exist, sometimes not even that. "It happened here". The underlying idea is that when people know facts about the location where they are they acquire a feeling of being anchored in time and that this feeling is desirable. All proposals focus directly on regular people, not on professionals in land-use planning.

5.3 Fine art

Results that have a spatial dimension and elicit a past that did not actually exist are placed in the compartment labelled 'Fine Art'. In the Oer-IJ region, fine art refers to an imaginary history that did not take place. There is development, but no conservation. Instead of conservation, there is creation, the imaginary history is invented. Sometimes this imaginary history can consist of images that refer to a past that actually existed, but somewhere else. But if that was not in the past of the Oer-IJ, we call this fabricated history, forged is another, angrier word for this.

The image of the imaginary past refers to a history that did not take place. This is the core of the distinction between 'conservation through development' and 'imaginary past'. For that matter, the imaginary past is neither better nor worse than the actual past. We simply place the visual references to an imaginary past in the domain that is involved with creation of imaginary images, the fine arts. Mythology, a different form of an imaginary past, is also located in that domain. And yes, religion resides there as well.

The nomenclature of this compartment does not imply that all fine arts are being considered as a reference to an imaginary history. There is more than this in the arts. Moreover, the reverse proposition, that all references to an imaginary history belong to the fine arts, is not true either. Religion is not art. The crux is the spatial dimension. What is the harvest in this part of the matrix?

Art

The central aspect is an idea of history (old, traditional) or an image of the primal landscape which exists in the mind and consists primarily of assigned meaning, the representation of a primal feeling. Examples include the IJ-landmark, the IJ-folly and the water sacrifice stones – this is fine art where inspiration is expressed in the form of a reference. In general the meaning, cultural-historical or otherwise, is linked to the object with a story. If the story is not included then the intended meaning is not evoked, but of course any other meaning can be assigned.

Replicas of a non-existent past

A special form in this category, where art should perhaps be called craft, is the representation of a non-existent past or at any rate non-existent in the past of the relevant location, such as the Citadel and the Zaandam building style in the Broekpolder area (Offenberg 2003). The form refers to an imaginary cultural history and romanticizes it, coming close to the definition of kitsch.

5.4 *Stories*

Results that have no spatial dimension and do not refer to the actual past are placed in the compartment labelled 'Stories'. As with most history, the stories belong to the domain of literature and not to the domain of the physical environment.

Names

A special form of story is where names are used to create historical meaning. In this way, 'regular' parts of the residential area are given special names so that they will be designed in a special way and consequently acquire a place in cultural history. One example is the Vinex residential project *Stad van de Zon* (City of the Sun) in Heerhugowaard.

Game

In the 'IJ game', the Oer-IJ, the stories and history are all imaginary; nevertheless, an image of the cultural history is created.

6. TO CONCLUDE

Both sorting-machines arose from the need to acquire some clarity about the enigmatic phenomenon of the ease with which personal interpretations are accepted as authentic representations of cultural history. This enigma has not been fully explained. However, it has become apparent that there is a significant gap between the world of policy and the world of the design. This gap leads to mutual incomprehensibility which partly explains the enigma. If we return to the initial question, i.e. is that which was implemented indeed that which was intended when the policy was formulated, the answer is no but in a special way. When the policy was formulated nothing spatial whatsoever was intended. Perhaps we have been chasing a phantom, maybe it is sufficient just to show commitment to cultural history and lip service is sufficient.

At the level where the policy statements are generated it seems that there is scarcely any imagination of what the physical results of that policy will be. It is good to honour cultural history but there is no perception of how this should be done. This explains why both conservation, and conservation through development, and fantasy are equally acceptable. In the domain of language there is no actual standard for quality in space.

In this context it is also interesting to illuminate the apodictic character of policy and design concepts. In both categories statements are formulated in such a way that they avoid refutation. This is not because they are truer than their negation but because they are cloaked in a moralistic, socially correct or irresistibly expert-sounding veil which makes them invisible to the critical eye. There is no negation. It cannot do any harm to investigate this phenomenon further.

Neither the cupboard nor the matrix have truly been tested. They were designed and adapted as we proceeded and have not yet shown that they can withstand the test of criticism. The question remains whether these divisions are the most suitable ones or whether the correct distinctions have been made between the collected groups. In the meantime it appears that these divisions, or similar ones, are a good way to create distinctions in the multiplicity of results that emerge from a relatively simple policy adage.

We are not yet finished. For example, a question has arisen from the matrix which would not perhaps have been asked without the matrix. If we put aside the categories of fine arts and stories, a set of design instruments becomes visible that concerns actual history. If we want to remain in these two columns because we believe a reference to actual history is important, then how will we deal with conservation in relation to conservation through development? If it turns out that a replica of the past is a better representation than the half-perished original, should we discard the original?

'Conservation through development' is a form of conservation. It results that this form also has many variations, such as 'simply' keeping something, conserving something by including it in something else, conserving something other than the original and conserving something by means of a replica. We must become accustomed to this. In the meantime, the fine arts and stories that have been set aside cannot be declared irrelevant as they also represent cultural history. We consider them as by-products, the result of the cultural process that was previously unknowable. If it contributes to the identity of the Oer-IJ, then the by-product is also legitimized.

Ultimately, the issue of the scientifically ascertained truth content of the harvest is a moral question. All things considered, there is no reason to declare one finding more important than another. And one day, all will be forgotten.

NOTES

1. RBOI, Rotterdam, the Netherlands.
2. An aesthetic quality plan is a policy document that explicitly formulates certain aspects of spatial quality as a review framework. The aesthetic quality plan compels the author of the plan to concretely refer to spatial quality and compels the government to promote its realization. See also Bloemers 2009.
3. The Stelling van Amsterdam is a ring of fortifications and potential inundations surrounding Amsterdam that was built at the end of the nineteenth and beginning of the twentieth centuries. It is a World Heritage site. Part of the Stelling is located in the Oer-IJ region.
4. The word folly (literally: foolishness) is used in landscape architecture to denote an ostentatious, over-ambitious and useless structure, preferably with a wildly improbable local legend attached to it (Headly/Meulenkamp 1986, xxi).
5. The Zaanse Schans is an open-air museum near Zaandam where demolished buildings from the Zaanstreek are rebuilt.
6. A donjon is a medieval tower-like structure within a castle, fortress or citadel used as a refuge for the final defence.
7. A twentieth century English lady who created compositions which she believed were 'channelled' to her by Wolfgang Amadeus Mozart (1756–1791).

REFERENCES

Actieplan, 2000: *Actieplan Cultuurbereik 2001-2004*, Den Haag (Ministerie van OCenW).

Beleving, 2005: *Beleving en verbeelding door culturele planologie. Twee jaar integratie van kunst en ruimtelijke inrichting in de provincie Noord-Holland. Provinciaal Bestuur van Noord-Holland*, Haarlem (Oer-IJ: 34-43).

Beleidskader, 2006: *Beleidskader Landschap en Cultuurhistorie,* Provinciaal Bestuur van Noord-Holland, Haarlem.

Belvedere, 1999: *The Belvedere Memorandum. A policy document examining the relationship between cultural history and spatial planning*, The Hague.

Bloemers, J.H.F., 2009: Archaeological heritage management and the instrument of the Image Quality Plan (Beeldkwaliteitplan). The case of the Broekpolder development scheme in: L.L. Therkorn et al., *Landscapes in the Broekpolder. Excavations around a monument with aspects of the Bronze Age to the Modern (Beverwijk & Heemskerk, Noord-Holland)*, Amsterdam (AAC/Projectenbureau Themata 2), 205-209.

Bloemers, T./S. Husken/R. van Leeuwen, 2009: *Een agenda voor het Oer-IJ*, Haarlem.

Bureau Adrichem, 2004: *Wijkpark De Vlaskamp op het beschermd archeologisch rijksmonument in de Broekpolder,* IJmuiden.

Bureau Alle Hosper/Jeroen van Westen/H+N+S Landschapsarchitecten/RBOI Rotterdam, 2006: *IJdijken, een dijk van een dijk,* Haarlem.

Cultuur op de kaart, 2008: *Cultuur op de kaart. Cultuurnota 2009-2012,* Provinciaal Bestuur van Noord-Holland, Haarlem.

Cultuur Verbindt, 2004: *Cultuur Verbindt, Cultuurnota 2005-2008,* Provinciaal Bestuur van Noord-Holland, Haarlem.

Doedens B./F. Vogels, 2009: *Temporary landscapes/tijdelijke landschappen*, Deventer.

Eekhout, M./P. de Kort, 2004: Wateroffers in waterrijke wijk. Broekpolder Beverwijk-Heemskerk, in Beleving 2005: *Beleving en verbeelding door culturele planologie. Twee jaar integratie van kunst en ruimtelijke inrichting in de provincie Noord-Holland. Provinciaal Bestuur van Noord-Holland*, Haarlem, 73-75.

Gebiedsaanpak, 2006: *Gebiedsaanpak Stelling van Amsterdam, Inspiratieboek,* Provinciaal Bestuur van Noord-Holland, Haarlem.

Headly, G./W. Meulenkamp, 1986: *Follies,* London

H+N+S landschapsarchitecten, 2001: *Een langzame buitenring (in de snelle metropool); ruimtelijke strategie voor de Stelling van Amsterdam,* Utrecht.

OD205 stedenbouw onderzoek en landschap 2006: *Wonen in het groen Heiloo/Limmen, Beeldkwaliteitsplan*, Delft.

Offenberg, G.A.M., 2003: *Broekpolder, een archeologisch monument op een VINEX-locatie,* Amsterdam.

Ontwikkelingsbeeld, 2004: *Ontwikkelingsbeeld Noord-Holland Noord (streekplan vastgesteld oktober 2005,* Provinciaal Bestuur van Noord-Holland, Haarlem.

Ruijter, G. de/P. de Ruyter/T. van Vliet/M. van Wesemael/J. van Westen, 2005: *Oer-IJ, voorbij het verleden. Culturele planologie van het Oer-IJ. Werkboek*, Provincie Noord-Holland, Haarlem.

Saramago, J., 1991 (1984): *The year of the death of Ricardo Reis,* San Diego/New York/London.

Streekplan, 2003: *Streekplan Noord-Holland Zuid,* Provinciaal Bestuur van Noord-Holland, Haarlem.

Streekplanuitwerking, 2004: *Streekplanuitwerking Randzone Saendelft,* Provinciaal Bestuur van Noord-Holland, Haarlem.

Vista, 2006: *Groengebied de Omzoom. Voorlopig ontwerp,* Amsterdam.

Westen, J. van, 2005: *Aanscherpen van het geheugen,* Werkboek.

4. Images, attitudes and measures in the field of cultural heritage in Norway

Karoline Daugstad[1]

ABSTRACT

Policies and measures towards the upkeep of cultural heritage are influenced by historical processes and priorities as well as pressing contemporary issues. This article explores measures and attitudes towards the cultural heritage of agriculture in Norway. Relying on recent studies and concrete examples, it shows how 'ideal landscapes' as depicted by painters in the national Romantic era are part of the frame of reference for public managers and probably also influence the way in which people in general view agrarian landscapes. However, the pattern of 'favoured landscapes' in the context of agri-environmental measures and in local practical landscape management projects is also strongly influenced by the development of farming as such, the development of the agrarian landscape and people's aesthetic or practical preferences on a general level. Heritage cannot be defined and taken for granted once and for all. Heritage is dynamic. At the same time, cultural heritage management as a public responsibility needs to prioritize different forms of heritage. What is of great importance is to critically reflect around decisions taken and acknowledge the variety of views and definitions.

KEY WORDS

Cultural heritage; measures, landscape management; landscape values; farming

1. INTRODUCTION

Cultural heritage as a concept, a field of research, public management responsibility and as a part of human practice and lifeworld is multi-faceted. Views, definitions, assessments and measures are numerous. Several actors or interests influence how cultural heritage is defined and valued and how it is physically manifested in our surroundings. This paper will address examples of 'appointed heritage' in a past and present context based on recent research and heritage policy trends within a Norwegian setting.

2. THE EMBLEMATIC STATUS OF AGRICULTURE'S CULTURAL HERITAGE

National cultural heritage in a Norwegian context is strongly linked to rurality and to agricultural practices, objects and landscapes. This can be explained by several interrelated factors. Firstly, due to the natural conditions at the northern fringe of Europe, the economy has traditionally relied on primary businesses, especially pastoral systems adapted to the abundance of outlying lands in forests and mountains and the scarcity of lowland areas suitable for arable production. Agro-pastoral systems have developed in many forms and also in combination with fisheries and forestry. Secondly, Norway was late to industrialize and urbanize and an agrarian based and partly subsistence economy had a stronghold for a long time. Thirdly, the agricultural cultural history and the Norwegian farmer became a symbol of national pride and identity defining 'true Norwegianness' in the nineteenth century. When Norway gained its independence from Denmark in 1814 after centuries of Danish rule, a 'national project' developed in the following decades where an elite of politicians, major landowners, merchants, artists and prominent scientists set out to define what was truly Norwegian (Berggreen 1989; Østerud 1990; Eriksen 1997). This coincided with the national Romantic movement in the mid-nineteenth century. The appointed 'personified upholder' of national identity came to be the independent farmer struggling with nature and surviving in a harsh climate due to virtues like pride, independence, purity and hard work (Daugstad 1999). This image was to a large extent a deliberately designed image relatively removed from the situation of many farmers whose debt, heavy taxation and a crofting system resulted in the opposite of independence, as pointed out by Keller (Keller 1990).

In accordance with the heroic status of the Norwegian farmer, the national emblematic landscape became the farmer's landscape especially in the interior of the country and the upper valleys close to the mountains where remnants of a 'true Norwegian culture' were seen as relatively untouched by Danish culture. Strongly influenced by the Romantic focus on pastoral idylls and scenic views, the national emblems of a proud agrarian nation were physically depicted by painters (Daugstad 1999).

The mismatch between the symbol and the reality had to do with more than the issue of the independent farmer, it also applied to the focus on the inland agrarian communities despite the fact that a large part of the population was living in coastal areas where fisheries and trade, often in combination with agriculture, were an important part of economic life. In short, the deliberate design of national emblems ended up being far from 'the real life situation' for the majority of the population (Berggreen 1989; Daugstad 1999). The phenomenon of the romantic glorification of a rural population and the pastoral idyll is not exclusive to Norway and it has also been described and documented in other northern and western European countries (Short 1991; Frykman/Löfgren 1992; Osborne 1992).

3. PRESENT STATUS AND CONCERNS

More than 150 years after the 'national project' was set in motion and after the restructuring and modernization of Norwegian agriculture, especially during the last 50 years, the personified upholders of the cultural heritage of agriculture (i.e. the farmers) have decreased considerably in number and the emblematic landscape they were once seen as caretakers of has changed. A total of 2.6% of the national workforce is now employed in agriculture (Statistics Norway 2008), a total of about 51,000 farms have an agrarian production (compared to 210,000 in 1949 and 125,000 in 1979). Over the last seven years, 28% of the farms have been closed down (Daugstad 2007). The land under cultivation has more or less stayed the same due to new cultivation in the most intensively used areas and covers only 3.2% of the land area (Statistics Norway 2008). In general, Norwegian agriculture is small-scale and the average farm size is about 14 hectares (Statistics Norway 2002). As an illustration of the natural conditions, 36% of the land area is higher than 600 metres above sea level and ⅓ of the land area is covered by forest (Statistics Norway 2006).

In the contemporary discourse on cultural heritage in Norway, much concern is related to the state of the cultural landscape formed by agrarian practices. More specifically, how the agrarian influenced landscape changes character with increasing speed, representing loss of landscape values like scenery and recreational value, historic value or cultural heritage value and loss of biodiversity upheld by culture. This development has been acknowledged as jeopardizing national and even internationally significant landscape values by the environmental, cultural heritage and agricultural authorities for decades (Daugstad/Rønningen 2004). The landscape change is induced by changes in farming practices in the direction of more intensive methods and by an opposite process of downscaling farming in other areas where agrarian landscapes and buildings are left to decay and to overgrowth. This situation has initiated public agri-environmental measures aimed at slowing down the process and 'repairing' the negative effects.

At the same time the rural economy as such is under pressure and new 'productions' in relation to 'multifunctional agriculture' or a 'multifunctional countryside' emerge. The latter mainly means tourism-related activities and concerns where the authorities increasingly stress that rural Norway has heritage qualities attractive to tourists and that rural inhabitants, especially farmers, should act entrepreneurially and develop rural tourism (Daugstad 2008).

4. MANAGING THE LANDSCAPE PAINTING

Given the historic position of the agrarian heritage and the actual development in agriculture as a business over the last half century, what type of heritage targeted by the public managers in charge of the agrarian landscape is given priority through the different agri-environmental schemes?

As documented by Daugstad (Daugstad 1999), the landscape painting of the bucolic pastoral idyll framed by snow-covered mountains is still present as a more or less conscious ideal for public managers when dealing with plans for protection, special measures or other incentives directed towards agrarian influenced cultural landscape and heritage (Fig. 1). From the environmental, cultural heritage and agrarian public sectors there is a clear focus on landscape as heritage as something visually and aesthetically pleasing. However, other landscape qualities are also underlined. Typically these include biodiversity conditioned by culture from the Directorate for nature management and the cultural landscape as a physical manifestation of history and an element in people's identity as underlined by the Directorate for cultural heritage.

When public managers implement agri-environmental schemes, does the nineteenth-century version of agriculture's cultural heritage get priority? Agri-environmental schemes focussing on environmental and heritage values in the cultural landscape of agriculture have been in operation in Norway for the last 20 years. These measures can be divided into general environmental measures and specific measures requiring a more targeted activity by the farmer to uphold and manage specific landscape features or heritage objects. On a national scale, the specific measures coming from the agricultural authorities are the main support system for agriculture's cultural heritage. Cultural heritage in this context means agrarian buildings or other built structures (on farm land as well as mountains and other outlying land), archaeological objects and sites, and pastures and fields with biodiversity conditioned by culture (Daugstad/Rønningen/Skar 2006).

A recent study analysed the distribution of specific measures towards agriculture's cultural heritage from the years 2000-2002 (Skar/Rønningen 2006; Daugstad 2007). A striking pattern emerging from the analysis regarding the uptake of these measures was a belt across southern Norway where the uptake was very high. These areas correspond to the core areas of emblematic status from the national Romantic period. The inland agrarian communities and valleys where the Romantic painters depicted what was 'true Norwegian' come out as the winners when it comes to agri-environmental measures. An equally striking finding is that the northern parts of the country as well as the coastal areas have a considerable lower uptake of the same measures. Can this be explained by actual variation in agrarian practices and development or is it also a question of mentality? Regarding the actual conditions for farming, the high

Fig.1
A 2008 mountain farm landscape confirming the emblematic agrarian landscape heritage.
Photo: the author.

uptake belt coincides more or less with an agricultural system based on dairy production with use of cultivated and uncultivated pastures. This is, roughly speaking, 'a cultural heritage friendly' practice where cultural heritage objects are not a major hindrance to run the system effectively (as opposed to grave mounds or dry stone walls giving agricultural lands a fragmented character which represents an obstacle to effective harvesting) and where extensive grazing to a certain extent keeps 'the landscape painting' relatively intact. However, the pastoral economy has also been dominant in large parts of northern Norway without the same uptake pattern being present. The latter might be explained by the fact that some of the northern counties have traditionally had an economy based on fishery and reindeer herding, often in combination with agriculture, and agriculture has to a larger extent than in many other parts of the country been abandoned during the last half century either due to depopulation or business specialization.

Given these explanatory factors more or less in terms of agronomy there are, however, qualitative studies supporting the fact that the national distribution of agri-environmental measures also has to do with attitudes or perceptions of what is 'proper' agrarian cultural heritage. In coastal as well as northern Norwegian communities, farmers do not see themselves as bearers of agriculture's cultural heritage because the connotation with the national Romantic painting style of cultural heritage as something belonging to inland agrarian communities is so strong (Rønningen/Flø/Fjeldavli 2005). This influences motivation for the uptake of schemes and contributes to upholding a geographical pattern with a certain national Romantic bias.

5. LANDSCAPE AND HERITAGE FROM THE VIEWPOINT OF TOURISTS AND LOCALS

The above-mentioned increased focus on cultural heritage as part of the multifunctional countryside and as an asset for rural tourism makes it relevant to investigate how tourists view the emblematic landscapes of Norway and how the same landscapes are viewed by local inhabitants.

A recent study (Daugstad 2008) parallels the views of (mostly Norwegian) tourists, rural tourism providers, farmers and agricultural authorities on the agriculturally influenced cultural landscape in the mountain areas of Norway, in other words in the core areas of emblematic status. The following actors have been studied, the Norwegian Tourist Association (NTA, a hikers' organization), the Norwegian Rural Tourism and Traditional Food Organization (NRTTF, members' organization for rural tourism and niche farm-food production), the Norwegian Farmers' Union (NFU) and the Ministry of Agriculture and Food (MAF). The aim of the study was to investigate landscape as a field where different views and perceptions are negotiated between landscape 'producers', being the farmers, and the landscape 'consumers', represented by the tourists. The empirical basis is a content analysis of the NTA members' magazine and website, the NRTTF catalogues and website, the NFU members' newspaper and the MAF website, campaigns and recent reports addressing cultural landscape related to tourism. A point of departure for the study was to see whether the stereotype insider – outsider dichotomy could be found in the material. According to this dichotomy the farmer can be seen as an insider in the landscape, living off and in it, with local knowledge and a business approach to landscape. The stereotype outsider on the other hand would be the tourist with a visual approach to landscape, viewing it from a distance with limited knowledge of local processes. In a world where farmers are pushed towards tourism as an additional source of income and where an emerging tourist segment is seeking 'real rural experiences' and 'the authentic countryside', it is of special interest to see whether or not it is possible to detect the outsider – insider dimension. A striking result from the study is that even if the tourists uphold a form of outside view of the cultural landscape confirming the stereotype of visual consumption from a distance, the tourists, tourist operators and the agricultural sector unite over a major concern, namely the overgrowth of vegetation in the landscape due to discontinuation of agriculture and lack of mowing and grazing in the mountain areas. "The changing agricultural land use, which has the potential to turn the scenic and highly regarded landscape mosaic into forest, is a major concern for all actors in this study. The mechanism behind this landscape change is also acknowledged: active farming is needed to prevent the loss of the culturally defined landscape and all it symbolizes. Here, the perspective of insiders and outsiders is the same" (Daugstad 2008, 419). In other words, losing the landscape painting is a common concern for tourists, tourism providers and farmers.

A number of examples exist where local authorities, communities or interest groups give weight to the same emblematic landscapes that the elite defined 150 years ago. An illustrative example of this is the small village of Geiranger in the fjord district of western Norway where several research projects have documented landscape status, landscape change and landscape views and interpretations (Fig. 2; Daugstad/Svarstad/Vistad 2005; Vistad/Daugstad/Svarstad 2006; Holm/Daugstad/Frisvoll 2007; Vik 2008). Geiranger is a traditional agrarian community where dairy production (cows and goats) has produced a spectacular landscape with farms located at the confined flat areas close to the fjord and in small 'shelves' in the steep slopes along the fjord. Since the late nineteenth century this heterogeneous mosaic-style landscape framed by majestic mountain peaks has been the focus of attention for foreign tourists, many of them British, Dutch and German. One regular visitor was the German emperor Wilhelm

Fig. 2
The iconic Geiranger landscape.
Photo: the author.

II who visited Geiranger eight times in the period 1890-1908 (Aasheim/Bruaset 2001). Until the last decades agriculture and a growing tourism sector have developed in a symbiosis that is taken for granted. Farmers have kept the heritage landscape in optimum condition and hotels have made money out of the scenery and have provided an additional income for the farm household (the female members have traditionally been seasonally employed at the hotels). However, due to the difficult circumstances for upholding a sound agrarian production, the symbiosis has been disturbed. The farmer earns very little by continuing to farm the steep slopes and additional employment needs to be found outside the village. Most of the farmers feel sad about giving up agriculture and not upholding the character of the cultural landscape but see no other option. Farming is discontinued and the landscape changes its character when the spectacular farms on the shelves are abandoned and the fields quickly become overgrown with forest. As a consequence, the view from the cruise ship or the car becomes more or less free from the cultural imprints on nature diminishing the heterogeneous character of the landscape. This worries the hotel owners and cruise companies who are afraid of losing customers (Daugstad/Svarstad/Vistad 2005; Holm/Daugstad/Frisvoll 2007).

Over the last years the local branch of the Norwegian Farmers' Association has initiated a cultural landscape project called 'An open Geiranger'. Along the main road to the village the view has been re-opened by cutting trees overgrowing former pastures. There have also been attempts to revive the longstanding tradition of keeping goats due to the effect that their grazing has on keeping bushes and small trees from invading pastures. However, in order to secure a landscape effect in the long term, the farmers' association stresses the need for public support. The argument raised is that one cannot expect farmers or other inhabitants to use their spare time keeping the view open for tourists. Given the fact that in 2005 this landscape received Unesco World Heritage Status due to the dramatic gradient fjord-mountains, the cry for state support has become louder. The argument now stated not only by farmers but by local inhabitants in general and leading local politicians is that being put on the world heritage list must guarantee public support to the population living in and upholding the world heritage area.

A number of projects from other parts of rural Norway, regionally and locally initiated, further indicate that ordinary people are concerned about the visual qualities of their surroundings. For example, as documented by Daugstad/Forbord/Rønningen (2006), an open well-kept cultural landscape is an important quality for the rural population's sense of well-being and important in defining identity and a sense of belonging. This finding can be seen in relation to recent national opinion polls where the population in general is concerned for the re-growth of small-scale open farmlands and loss of landscape quality. Opinion polls from 2003 report that 16% of the respondents express a 'major concern for re-growth of cultural landscapes' and in 2006 the figure increased to 19% (Landbruks- og matdepartmentet 2006). The Open Geiranger project has been accompanied by several similar projects around the country, all characterized by an initiative from public authorities at county or municipal level but strongly supported by the population in general, and where the aesthetic and visual aspects of cultural landscape are highlighted as a frame of reference for identity and well-being. One example is the Open landscapes project in Sogn og Fjordane county where the County Governor's Office has been in charge. Over a three-year period, 96 field projects have been initiated all over the county and of these, 63 have focussed on clearing cultural landscapes from re-growth close to main roads in order to 'give back the view' to both inhabitants and tourists (Kusslid 2008).

6. DISCUSSION

There is, not surprisingly, a link between the national project defining the landscape and heritage symbols and the upholders of 'Norwegianness' in the mid-nineteenth century to what has actually been receiving attention from environmental and cultural heritage authorities in the epoch of agri-environmental schemes. To what extent this has biased the view on valued cultural heritage in the average Norwegian is hard to say, but obviously deeply embedded ideals in a culture influence people whether one is aware of it or not. The examples in this paper have shown that when locals get to prioritize landscape and heritage management there is a striking resemblance to 'old ideals'. To explain this as people being slaves to 150-year-old ideals is hard to support scientifically, as well as being somewhat patronizing. Most likely there is a dialectic process of exchange and mutual influence between actual landscape development, underlying structures of ideology and people's preferences.

On the other hand there has been a detectable change in the heritage policy during the last decades towards a diversification of 'the favoured heritage' of the national project in the nineteenth century. This policy shift has been reflected in the Cultural Heritage Act, in strategies and projects run by the Directorate for Cultural Heritage and from the cultural heritage authorities at county level (Lidén 1991; Daugstad 1999; Myklebost 1999). The national cultural heritage attention should reflect ethnic variation (for example the Sami cultural heritage was not given legal protection through national law until 1978), all sectors should take responsibility for cultural heritage and cultural heritage should be acknowledged in the everyday and ordinary landscapes as well as in more iconic landscapes. Whether a democratic and multicultural shift to cultural heritage management and legislation actually leads to a shift in mentality towards the same is another question. However, there are indications from studies in Denmark that preferred landscapes and, hence, potential future heritage, might shift due to generations. A study by Højring (Højring 2000) documents that young Danes prefer open and almost industrial agricultural

Fig. 3
The future agrarian heritage of Norway? A combined meat and milk production farm in southwest Norway.
Photo: the author.

landscapes to small-scale diverse landscapes with hedges and patches of wood. Perhaps this is an indication that Norway's emblematic landscapes may change if the rhetoric of a more democratic heritage policy from the Directorate for cultural heritage comes into action (Fig. 3).

Cultural heritage understood as 'culture' in the widest sense of the word and 'heritage' as being everything from 'before' meaning even recent years heritage, can be seen as something always up for negotiation. However, if cultural heritage is to continue as a public responsibility regulated by national law, policies and more specific instruments, cultural heritage managers will always be in a position to give some forms of cultural heritage different status from other cultural heritage. What seems to be of inevitable importance is to critically reflect around decisions taken and acknowledge that there is no such thing as a unanimous heritage of a people or a nation that is taken for granted once and for all. Heritage is dynamic.

ACKNOWLEDGEMENTS

The author thanks Jozef Keulartz for his thorough and constructive comments during the Lunteren symposium and the final preparation of this paper.

NOTES

1   Norwegian University of Science and Technology, Trondheim, Norway.

REFERENCES

Aasheim, A./O. Bruaset, 2001: *Geiranger – Juvel i fjordlandet*, Drammen.
Berggreen, B., 1989: *Da Kulturen kom til Norge*, Oslo.

Daugstad, K., 1999: *Mellom romantikk og realisme. Om seterlandskapet som ideal og realitet*, Trondheim (Centre for Rural Research Report 16/99).

Daugstad, K., 2007: Jordbrukets rolle som kulturbærer; hvem, hva og hvor?, *Jord og Gjerning*, Årbok, Norsk Landbruksmuseum, 9-21.

Daugstad, K., 2008: Negotiating landscape in rural tourism, *Annals of Tourism Research* 35, 402-426.

Daugstad, K./M. Forbord/K. Rønningen, 2006: *Bioenergi og kulturlandskap: resultater fra en intervjuundersøkelse i Møre og Romsdal*, Trondheim (Center for Rural Research 7/06).

Daugstad, K./K. Rønningen, 2004: Landskapet som felles gode og privat ressurs, in G. Setten (ed.), *Det levende landskapet*, Trondheim, 111-129.

Daugstad, K./K. Rønningen/B. Skar, 2006: Agriculture as an upholder of cultural heritage? Conceptualizations and value judgements – A Norwegian perspective in international context, *Journal of Rural Studies* 22, 67-81.

Daugstad, K./H. Svarstad/O.I. Vistad, 2005: Geiranger-Herdalen: Lang dags ferd mot vern, *PLAN* 3-4, 58-64.

Eriksen, A., 1997: Norge – en naturlig historie, *Historisk Tidsskrift* 1, 76-86.

Frykman, J./O. Löfgren, 1992: *Den kultiverade människan*, Stockholm (Skrifter Etnologiska sällskapet i Lund), 21-132.

Højring, K., 2000: Hvordan ser gymnasieelever landskabet? Park og landskab vidensblade, Planlægning, *Skov og landskab* 3, 12-5 April 2008.

Holm, F.E./K. Daugstad/S. Frisvoll, 2007: Verdensarven etter festen, *PLAN* 3-4, 56-61.

Keller, C., 1990: Fornminnevernets ideologiske grunnlag - en anakronisme? in *Norges allmennvitenskapelige forskningsråd: Kulturminnevernets teori og metode. Status 1989 og veien videre. Utstein kloster 8.-11. mai 1989*, Oslo (Seminarrapport. NAVFs program for forskning om kulturminnevern), 47-61.

Kusslid, L. A. N., 2008: *Prosjekt Opne landskap. Sluttrapport for hovudprosjekt mars 2005-april 2008*, Fylkesmannen i Sogn og Fjordane (Rapport 4).

Landbruks- og matdepartementet, 2006: *Kulturlandskap: Flere bekymret for gjengroing*, Newsletter from the Ministry of Agriculture and Food. (www.odin.dep.no/lmd/norsk/tema/jordbruk/nyheter/049051-211945/dok-bu.html. Accessed 4 April, 2006).

Lidén, H-E., 1991: *Fra antikvitet til kulturminne. Trekk av kulturminnevernets historie i Norge*, Oslo.

Myklebost, D., 1999: Utviklingen av kulturminnevernet gjennom 1900-tallet. Noen hovedtrekk og noen framtidsvyer, *Fortidsminneforeningens Årbok* 153, 9-34.

Osborne, B. S., 1992: Interpreting a nations's identity: artists as creators of national consciousness, in R.H. Baker/G. Biger (eds.), *Ideology and landscape in historical perspective. Essays on the meanings of some places in the past*, Cambridge, 230-254.

Rønningen, K./B.E. Flø/E. Fjeldavli, 2005: *Multifunksjonelt landbruk – hva slags legitimitet har fellesgodeproduksjon innad i landbrukssektoren*, Trondheim (Centre for Rural Research Report 6/05).

Short, J. R., 1991: *Imagined country. Environment, culture and society*, London/New York.

Skar, B./K. Rønningen, 2006: 'Kulturarvkartet': En analyse av forholdet mellom kulturlandskapsmidler og status for den fysiske kulturarven, in K. Daugstad (ed.), *Jordbrukets rolle som kulturbærer*, Trondheim (Centre for Rural Research Report 8/06), 59-80.

Statistics Norway, 2002: Store strukturendringer i jordbruket. (http://www.ssb.no/emner/10/04/10/jtl999/. Accessed 5 December, 2003).

Statistics Norway, 2006: Statistikkområde jordbruk. (http://www.ssb.no/aarbok/. Accessed 1 December, 2006).

Statistics Norway, 2008: Tema Areal og Tema Jordbruk. (http://www.ssb.no/areal/main.shtml; http://www.ssb.no/jordbruk/main-shtml. Accessed 29 February, 2008).

Vik, M. L., 2008: *'There is always a reverse of a medal': A narrative approach to area designations, farming and tourism in Geiranger, Western Norway*, Trondheim (Centre for Rural Research, Report 9/08).

Vistad, O. I./K. Daugstad/H. Svarstad, 2006: Store verneområde med lokal forvaltning: Funn og refleksjonar, UTMARK 1/2006. (http://www.utmark.org/utgivelser/pub/2006-1/).

Østerud, Ø., 1990: Norge i våre hjerter? Internasjonaliseringen og det nasjonale, *Tidsskrift for samfunnsforskning* 31, 211-225.

5. The good, the bad and the self-referential
Heritage planning and the productivity of difference

Kristof Van Assche[1]

ABSTRACT

Heritage planning as an integrated approach to dealing with traces of the past in the ongoing organization of the landscape cannot be but a transdisciplinary endeavour. As such, the insights gained in work on interdisciplinary and transdisciplinary knowledge production and application should inform any methodology of heritage planning. Bridging differences between scientific disciplines and between sciences and law, administration, politics and economy is a continuous challenge. We argue that Niklas Luhmann's social systems theory, with its sophisticated understanding of society as an evolving and multiplying population of social systems and his insights into the identity and difference of those systems, prove very useful indeed in understanding the value and difficulty of trespassing boundaries in heritage planning and in understanding the value of conflict and cultivated difference in the planning process.

In an attempt to apply Niklas Luhmann's social systems theory to heritage planning, we will reflect on mechanisms of self-reference and self-reproduction that are active within the scientific (heritage-related) disciplines, (planning) administrations, politics and law. These mechanisms are not in essence negative, they are necessary for the production of the kind of knowledge that is specific for the system or organization.

However, in planning, where some form of co-ordination of interests and types of knowledge is strived for, an acute awareness of these forms of self-reference in all the actors in the planning system is crucial. Without resorting to easy-escape consensus models, we would like to argue for an approach to heritage planning that avoids self-reference in the planning system as a whole while accepting and cherishing the self-reference of the elements, the actors. This, we argue, is necessary to create decision spaces where plans can be made that are truly site-specific, where various forms of heritage can acquire various roles, making different types of knowledge important in different situations.

KEY WORDS

Heritage planning; knowledge; disciplines; self-reference; systems theory, Luhmann

1. ACTORS IN HERITAGE PLANNING

Heritage planning is an integrated approach to dealing with traces of the past in the ongoing organization of the landscape (compare the contributions in Ashworth/Howarth 1999). In current practice, the traces of the past dealt with usually represent a small part of those traces, a subset that is labelled 'heritage' in the administrative/scientific establishment of the country or region at stake. Sometimes there is a strong connection with the heritage as defined in broader cultural circles, sometimes not, depending on the closeness of the scientific observations present in the planning system to the observations and valuations made in society at large. In that current practice, when there is a category of planning that could be seen as heritage planning, it is usually spatial planning for well-defined sites with heritage values. The heritage planning we would argue for looks beyond the recognized heritage sites, includes a much larger subset of traces of the past in its deliberations and is sensitive to heritage as defined by different communities (Van Assche 2004; Duineveld 2006; Van der Valk Ch. II.2). Heritage in turn is seen as those products of a group that are connected with the identity of that group, as well as sites where the group experienced or produced something deemed significant (Van Assche/Weijschede 2009). Sites are naturally relevant for spatial planning, defined as any organized decision-making on future spatial organization, but some of the heritage-as-product can also be relevant as well, such as buildings, ruins, festivals, regional products and other traditions with more spatial implications than direct spatial form.

Nowadays, after many waves of reform in planning practice and theory, most planners would agree that planning necessarily involves the co-ordination of interests of various stakeholders (Allmendinger 2002; Hillier 2002). In Europe academia is generally more acknowledged as a stakeholder in planning than in the United States and heritage planning generally bears the mark of a strong scientific input (Van Assche/Leinfelder 2008). Disciplines like archaeology, art history, geography, anthropology, history and sociology are often seen as valuable both in the study and assessment of heritage and in the decision-making regarding the future spatial organization of heritage sites. As Van der Valk argues (Van der Valk Ch. II.2), this produces added value but at the price of interdisciplinary confusion.

Part of the mentioned wave of planning reforms consisted of the (re-)introduction of local knowledge and perspectives in the decision-making. Evidently, people do not agree simply because they are local and such a re-articulation of the local as opposed to the state, science and big business, comes with its own risks. A local community with a pre-existing consensus, or a consensus that can easily be brokered by planners, cannot be assumed (Soja 1997). Identities of people and groups are complex and variable, as are the networks people are embedded in. However it is constructed and however it plays out, local inhabitants are nowadays mostly assigned a more important role in planning processes because they are seen as actors who cannot be ignored (Healy 1997; Innes/Booher 1999).

Actors also include members of administration, politics, economy and law. Planning administrations are not the only factor and other departments can influence the way sites are handled, such as economic development agencies and nature conservation departments. Several scales can be distinguished in politics and administration, with some places having an even distribution of powers and responsibilities while others lean very much towards one of the levels articulated. Politics, administration, law and economy influence planning in every country, but the relative influence of each, and the form of the relations between them, will vary greatly (King/Thornhill 2003). Generally, planning law in the United States will be weaker than in Europe and, conversely, property rights will be stronger in the United States. US planning-related administrations will be weaker, political decisions regarding planning mostly centre on issues of property rights protection and economic development.

2. NIKLAS LUHMANN, SOCIAL SYSTEMS THEORY AND THE *AUTOPOIESIS* CONCEPT

The way different actors in heritage planning were briefly introduced above comprises elements from a social systems perspective. Social systems theory was pioneered in the 1980s by Niklas Luhmann and economy, law and administration are prime examples of what he calls function systems, i.e. specialized social systems typical of modern society. In the following paragraphs, we will elaborate on a few concepts from Luhmann's theory that can be relevant for our present analysis of heritage planning (derived from Luhmann 1990; *idem* 1995; *idem* 2000), after which we will focus on the concept of self-reference in planning.

Luhmann sees society as consisting of a multitude of social systems with function- systems, organizations and interactions (conversations) as main categories. Important to note right from the start is that neither people nor actions (as in the functionalism of Parsons 1964) but communications are the elements of social systems. People are not less important than the social systems, his theory is not anti-humanistic, rather they form a different category of systems, psychic systems, that is not theorized by him and exists in the environment of social systems. Again, this existence in the environment does not imply inferiority in any sense. System environment is a basic distinction in social systems theory and systems are seen as environments to each other. Every system has a set of environments that supplies external complexity from which to draw in establishing internal complexity. Any system evolves in a continuous adaptation to various environments and structure and function are elements of a system which can only be explained by its specific history of adaptations to a set of specific environments, in turn adjusting to each other (Luhmann 1995).

Such an evolutionary perspective is typical for Luhmann and needs to be understood in conjunction with another concept fundamental to his theory, *autopoiesis*. A social system is autopoietic when its structures, elements and programmes are produced solely using the structures, elements and programmes of the system itself. This seems trivial, but it is not. In an evolutionary perspective it introduces strong path dependencies because every evolution of and adaptation to environments will be shaped by the previous history of adaptations, reflected in all the features of the system. A certain path of adaptation will be visible in the structure and content of the system and will allow for certain future adaptations but not others. Determinism is not a word which aptly describes this situation since nothing is predictable.

Autopoiesis entails the self-reproduction of every system using materials in and of the system. Social systems require constant dynamism since without reproduction and adaptation, systems simply disintegrate. Constant communication is necessary in the sense that communications need to link to previous communications in the system as well as produce possible connections for future communication. Every past or future situation however is interpreted in terms of the present and interpretations of past and future are therefore bound to change continuously. The environment, any other social system and the 'natural environment', always interpreted through the lens of other social systems, can lead to rephrasing and revision of past and future, but those reinterpretations always derive from the present state of the system (Van Assche 2006).

3. SELF-REFERENCE AND HETERO-REFERENCE

Changes in environments are reconstructed within a system according to the codes, semantics and structures of the system. Every system reconstructs the whole world in its own terms so the environment cannot have a direct influence on the observing and adapting system. This is what Luhmann calls operational closure, i.e. the differentiation and origins of a system entails the establishment of a specific *autopoiesis* and requires the drawing of systems boundaries and mechanisms to maintain those boundaries. The legal system could only differentiate from politics and religion by an operational closure, by articulating itself on the basis of the distinction, *Leitdifferenz*, legal/illegal. Every action of the other systems is interpreted in terms of that distinction. Programmes in the legal system are there to reduce other observations to combinations of legal/ illegal assignments. In that sense the legal system, as any other social system, is self-referential.

Luhmann is often criticized for proposing a systems concept that is entirely closed and therefore blind and static. Nothing, however, could be farther from the truth. As briefly explained above, systems require constant change in order to reproduce themselves. Systems emerge and dissolve, are embedded in each other, constantly observe each other and form new connections with each other. Psychic and social systems are the product of structural coupling and co-evolution. Closure in this sense is a productive closure because it means that a boundary is needed for the *autopoiesis* to start and for the system to acquire an identity. It means that everything in the system is the product of its own operations. Direct introduction of elements of the environments into the system, or a response to an environment dictated by that environment (as distinct from interpreted first) would interrupt the *autopoiesis* of the system. It would not be able to make sense of that alien element, to attribute informational value to those disturbances and to adequately respond to them. Therefore, operational closure is a requirement for openness to environments and for the capacity to respond to them. Systems observe each other and those observations are framed in terms of the system. No observation would be possible without these terms and without operational closure the system would dissolve into the environment, instead of adapting to it.

After this explanation, it is clear that the self-referential character of a social system does not exclude the possibility of a hetero-reference, a reference to external environments. On the contrary, self-reference and hetero-reference always go hand in hand. Adaptation to environments asks for observation, observation requires hetero-reference, hetero-reference is necessarily grounded in self-reference. Self-reference has to be the solid foundation of the theory since systems are defined as self-organizing entities. Nature and reality are not denied existence anywhere by Luhmann, it is just that all realities accessible to us are produced in and by social systems. Here, Luhmann falls in line with Foucault and the other post-structuralists, see for example Foucault 1968. Social systems produce what we accept as knowledge while simultaneously structuring society. Self-reference in a highly differentiated modern society, with people participating in a host of social systems simultaneously, organizations being embedded in various function systems and increasingly differentiated functions allows for a series of very specialized observations to arise in society. Thus modern society became typified by a wide variety of types of knowledge and action that allow for flexibility and adaptation. Self-reference allows for the development of this variety of perspectives because it is essentially productive.

The social system of science could not have developed without a specific *autopoiesis* based on the distinction true/untrue, based on self-formulated procedures to determine what truth is and how to find and test it. Scientific findings can only be communicated if presented as emerging from accepted procedures and referring to accepted theories and facts. Scientific communications will only be recognized as such, and link to further communications, when adhering to the semantics developed in science to describe external reality and itself. The imposition of religious, political and aesthetic criteria on science interrupts its self-reproduction. It does not lead to an enriched science but to a dissolution of science. A radical constructivist epistemology goes well with a strict delineation of science (Seidl 2005).

Within science, the continuing differentiation of society can be observed in the multiplication of disciplines. A discipline is a social system, a subsystem of science, that covers more than a piece of a predefined and agreed-upon external reality. It reconstructs the whole of reality in a way that at least slightly differs from the perspectives developed in other disciplines. Once neighbouring disciplines are observed, competition and identity politics lead to further differentiation, to the underlining of differences and a growing distance between disciplines. Art history and archaeology both deal with old objects, yet feel very different. They often stress their differences, use different assumptions and procedures to establish facts, define objects or value them and come up with different strategies to deal with them. Both disciplines can however add insights of their own because of the specificity of their perspective and the specific nature of their elements, programmes, structures and codes. In other words, this happens because of their specific *autopoiesis* grounded in self-reference. The multiplication of disciplines mentioned is a multiplication of self-references, simultaneously a multiplication of hetero-references and a specialization that enriches the observational capacity of society as a whole.

4. PLANNING AND PRODUCTIVE SELF-REFERENCE

Based on the perspective discussed above, planning as co-ordination of stakeholders in working towards a vision for spatial futures starts to look a little different. Planning involves numerous interactions (conversations), organizations and function systems. Planners as persons need to be able to switch swiftly from one discipline to another and need at least to be able to communicate key aspects of the findings of several disciplines. They need to be able to include various function systems in the ongoing decision-making. What is an 'actor' in this perspective? Any social system that wants to be included in the decision-making counts. Around the table one typically finds people, not social systems, but the planning process should try to be inclusive of social systems. Of course, which systems, organizations, function systems and disciplines are allowed is in itself the result of previous decisions hopefully based on an inclusive and agreed-upon democratic procedure (Van Assche/Verschraegen 2008). In general, Luhmann does show us that a more inclusive deliberation includes more perspectives and social systems, reducing blind spots of every individual system while allowing the specific findings and valuations of systems to confront and enrich each other in mutual adaptation (Dunsire 1996; Evans 1995).

In social systems terms, actors are neither the drivers of communication in a social system, nor the elements of a social system. Communication is the elements of any social system and both actions and actors are semantic ascriptions made by social systems. What counts as an action and as an actor is the result of a process of categorization within a social system. If planning aims to co-ordinate actors or stakeholders, it also aims to co-ordinate actors and their stories as produced in a variety of social systems. This makes planning as total co-ordination of spatial strategies an impossible task since no system can have a comprehensive overview of society and no semantics can integrate unambiguously the semantics of all the social systems included in a planning process.

Still, a Luhmannian analysis of participatory planning does elucidate the potential of such a form of planning. A more inclusive deliberation in an upgraded participatory planning effort could result in a spatial strategy based on a richer model of external realities and possible futures to adapt to. Such a strategy would stand a better chance to address the desires of various groups in society and a better chance to deal with changes (Van Assche/Verschraegen 2008). Luhmann overall is critical of centralized planning and the steering capacity of any system, for example a planning administration or public-private planning organization, but planning is still possible in his theory. It would have to happen through programming, organizations and the manipulation of relevant contexts.

The argument for inclusiveness and decentralization is not unlike many arguments made by proponents of a move from government to governance in policy studies and the proponents of participatory planning (see for example Healy 1997; Soja 1997; Hillier 2002). However, social systems theory does warn us not to make the same mistakes with participatory planning as earlier on with centralized planning. Organizations as social systems and disciplines and function systems produce their own images of the future. None of them can predict the behaviour of the other social systems and the future state of their environment. In addition, there is the difference between the images of futures consciously present in the social system versus the history of previous adaptations as integrated in the current structure of the system driving its *autopoiesis* towards a possibly different future.

This makes perfect planning procedures perfectly adaptable procedures. Participation by itself is no solution to planning's earlier issues with democratic legitimacy and efficacy. An extensive and powerful participatory planning system can even undermine the legitimacy and *autopoiesis* of the political system. For Luhmann, politics imply a delegation of power, allowing politics to use power in brokering collectively binding decisions on the boundaries between different function systems (Luhmann 1990). Accumulation of power in a network of organizations co-ordinating spatial futures outside the arena of politics can undercut the reproduction of the political system using the medium of power.

Therefore, social systems theory sees self-reference as productive, as the motor of differentiation that can later be included in discussions again (King/Thornhill 2003), an observation with direct relevance to participatory planning. It sees steering as indirect steering and planning as an exercise in reflexivity and flexibility.

In heritage planning this can be translated as an argument for the inclusion of actually different perspectives in a planning process as opposed to the imposition of one disciplinary or bureaucratic perspective. It should also be distinguished from a process where the various disciplinary perspectives are selected and reinterpreted by one discipline, for example policy studies summarizing the findings of archaeology or archaeology dismissing the findings of art history. The value of the different perspectives lies exactly in their difference and the essence of their difference is a different type of self-reference which produces different constructions of reality. People sitting around a table in a planning process can switch from one social system to another and are, for example, never entirely embedded in a discipline. This allows for flexibility in the process and for an openness in communication that would not be there if social systems were to sit around an imaginary table. The role of planners in such a process can vary but we argue that the planner should develop a strong sense of the difference between disciplines and actors as well as common ground. In traditional consensus-building models which often underly communicative and participatory planning theories, the focus is on the shared meanings, interests and values (e.g. Forester 1999; Innes/Booher 1999). Here we argue that even where consensus is possible, the depth and variety of insights behind the consensus can be greatly deepened when there is also an understanding of the structural differences in the various actors' perspective and an insight into the specific self-reference that is grounding their respective *autopoiesis*. This might also avoid dissatisfaction with a specific planning process and later with planning in general when people find out that the consensus arrived at is shallow, or means something very different to different actors and will lead to different actions (Allmendinger 2002; Van Assche 2004).

5. NON-PRODUCTIVE SELF-REFERENCE: PLANNING AND DE-DIFFERENTIATION

The planner can therefore increase an awareness of the differences between actors, social systems and perspectives. This simultaneously entails an increased awareness of self and others since an awareness of the difference will highlight both self and other (Van Assche/Leinfelder 2008). We argue that such an increased awareness can also avoid the non-productive self-reference mentioned earlier. At various points in his work, Niklas Luhmann deplores (he is normative there) what he calls de-differentiation, an undoing of the painfully acquired complexity by erasing differences, more specifically by trespassing the boundaries of one system by another, therefore disrupting the *autopoiesis* of the invaded system (Van Assche 2006). If politics take over the economy and legal system, for example in the old USSR, then the function of economy and law are lost and they cannot reproduce themselves anymore according to their own logic. With that effacing of boundaries, society's capacity to handle external and internal complexity is decreased and economy's role in dealing with scarcity and the law's role in stabilizing expectations are not carried out adequately. Environmental changes cannot be responded to in ways that are specific to the legal and economic system, and economic and legal environments are much harder to predict for the political system than for the systems in question. Therefore, according to Luhmann de-differentiation destabilizes society and cannot but throw it back into an older, more primitive type of organization.

One way to produce an unfortunate de-differentiation is by means of an increased self-reference. Spatial planning can also be seen as a set of organizations working towards spatial organization, which in this case we will term the planning system. We know now that both organizations and function systems are social systems in Luhmann's theory. Every organization is steeped in several function systems and no function system is restricted to one organization. When Luhmann analysed de-differentiation he mostly talked about the colonization of one function system by others (for example in his critique of the welfare state, Luhmann 1990), yet his definitions apply to other systems such as for instance organizations.

When planning in society can be interpreted as the co-ordination efforts of various function systems, regarding spatial organization, then this should take place mostly at the level of organizations and programming (rules, laws, visions; Van Assche/Leinfelder 2008) Organizations have their own logic and *autopoiesis* driven by decisions as a special type of communication, yet they also embody the function systems (Seidl 2005). No organization is restricted to one function system, but no function system can be observed without its embodiment in organizations. If and when the organizations in a planning system, whether they are economic, legal, political, bureaucratic, artistic or scientific, are all tied together for a long period of time by means of a colonizing bureaucracy (or conversely by an unregulated economy), then one risks a de-differentiation. This risk is located not just at the level of organizations ('forgetting' their original identity and goal and gradually losing their added value to the whole) but also in the participating function systems. The boundaries of market, legal, political and artistic domains are blurred in an enforced consensus.

Such a situation represents a form of self-reference since the planning system as a whole acquires the tendency to refer to itself, not to external environments (Van Assche 2006). All the participating organizations are supposed to correct and enrich each other and simultaneously allow for a continuous adaptation to changes in external environments. Changes in citizens' preferences should find their way into the political system and administration should become part of the conversation between organizations in a planning system, for example when those organizations forget about their specific goals and become part of a symbiosis where ideas thrive because they fit a shared ideology, the mutually corrective mechanisms wither away and the adaptive capacity decreases. When planners, architects and historians know how it's supposed to be done, then in fact all those people stopped thinking as planners, architects and historians and became mere representatives of the ideology of the planning system. That ideology might work, even work well, for a while but, as a matter of logic, the chances that it will be well-adapted to environments will systematically decrease. It will tend to become more rigid and less adapted. Whether the shared ideology came from an originally interactive process between organizations or represents the power of one organization over the others does not really matter for the diagnosis of de-differentiation as unproductive self-reference (Luhmann 1995).

6. HERITAGE PLANNING

In heritage planning, more than in many other forms of planning, the role of experts is significant. Most actors agree that this is crucial. The interest in depth and content is strong. People in the process, as well as outsiders, want to be convinced that one is 'really' dealing with heritage, something old and relevant to us now, and that the people sitting around the table really know what they are doing, know what is what, how valuable it is and how it should be used in plans. One can agree on an investment in heritage or on a restriction on other uses if the experts unequivocally tell us what, how and why (Fischer 1997; Van Assche 2004). Luhmann would point at the overestimation by other systems of the certainty produced by science, a misunderstanding of the axiomatic discursive structure of all scientific knowledge and its self-referential nature (Dunsire 1997). Different scientific disciplines come up with different definitions, valuations and strategic views of heritage grounded in the discipline-specific self-reference. Historians will refer back to historical research, producing values based on historical arguments etc. (Ashworth/Howarth 1999; Van Assche 2004; Duineveld 2006)

Revisiting our distinction between productive and non-productive self-reference, we could say that productive self-reference can become non-productive and turn into de-differentiation in several scenarios:
1. When one scientific discipline dominates the planning process (broader: system) and marginalizes the other disciplines.
2. When science marginalizes other perspectives (systems).
3. When science is marginalized by other perspectives (systems).
4. When a symbiosis between organizations has evolved in the planning system.

In all four cases, the boundaries of the various function systems are overstepped in a planning process. Social systems theory shows that every system constructs a reality in its own narrowly focussed and self-referential way. This is not a problem but the result of a positive evolution towards a more differentiated society where the number and variety of social systems allows for a much greater production of knowledge and a much more refined mutual balancing and adaptation than ever before. A narrowing focus in a growing number of systems is balanced by the flexibility of the whole. No system has an overview of all the others and no system can steer all the others. Science, economy, law or art cannot tell us how exactly to organize space, incorporate the old into the new and to refer to the old in the new (Luhmann 2000; Van Assche/Verschraegen 2008).

Planning as an activity needs to be the site of co-ordination of all these perspectives and one can only envision the possibilities of those perspectives if their differences are acknowledged (Soja 1997; Hillier 2002). Ignoring and overstepping the boundaries of the perspectives and systems leads to de-differentiation and non-productive self-reference in the sense that the planning system will create its own world, untouched by changing external realities and unable to be touched by them. The variety of perspectives that would allow for a variety of observations of external environments, and a variety of ways to import those observations into the planning system, that variety has gradually disappeared. Rigidity will be introduced. The four scenarios mentioned above are paths in planning towards de-differentiation. Flexibility is lost in these scenarios and planning without flexibility is bound to fail.

A company can go bankrupt, an organization can fail or disappear, but a planning system cannot afford to fail since the co-ordination of spatial organization affects the whole society. Flexibility needs to be high on the agenda since non-adaptation and dissolution are not an option. Recent post-socialist history has shown that centralized planning systems do collapse and can be replaced by amalgams of socialism, capitalism and opportunism (Wilson 2005). In systems theoretical terms this can be described as a transition from one mode of de-differentiation to another (Hough 1972; Taubman 1973). The evolutionary process towards differentiation never took place and even the rigorous legal-political disciplining of EU membership cannot replace such evolution, as a gradual stabilization of expectations, a gradual crystallization of power relations, a gradual clarification of interdependencies and roles. A smooth transition from one form of co-ordination to another is possible and is conceivably democratically legitimate. Such a situation, even marked by a high transaction cost, might still be termed adaptation, not disintegration. By disintegration we refer to the collapse of any mechanism of co-ordination of spatial organization, for example a co-ordination of a free market and legal system by means of zoning laws and local zoning boards. Such a disintegration, we argue, necessarily comes at a high cost for society, including dysfunctional markets, a distrusted legal system and opaque politics (Verdery 2004; Wilson 2005).

Rigidity therefore leads to de-differentiation and de-differentiation can ultimately lead to a loss of co-ordination. In the case of heritage planning, the value attributed to the scientific perspectives cannot be allowed to lead to such rigidity and de-differentiation. On the other hand, a mere dismissal of the scientific perspectives would seriously narrow down the options for heritage planning and undermine the democratic legitimacy of the planning effort (since many people agree on its importance). In a broader sense it would also undermine the concept of heritage and the self-identification of a community which views heritage, contributing to a sense of self (Ashworth/Howarth 1999; Hidding/Kolen/Spek 2001; Van Assche 2004).

7. HERITAGE PLANNING, DEPTH AND FLEXIBILITY

How to balance depth and flexibility? How to avoid non-productive self-reference while cherishing productive self-reference? We argue that the balance should be different in every planning process and a process can be dominated by the artistic, scientific, economic, heritage, archaeological or historical geographical principle.

A truly inclusive planning system that optimally utilizes the capacity of a differentiated society does not include all systems in every planning process, which would overburden the planning process and would probably lead to a de-differentiated standard approach.

Inclusive therefore means including different perspectives in different cases and acknowledging the difference between those perspectives. As generalists in spatial organization capable of communicating with representatives from different scientific disciplines and function systems, planners can be essential go-betweens in these situations (Forester 1999; Van der Valk Ch. II.2). One of their key functions would be to increase the self-awareness of the actors in a process (Van Assche 2003) and the awareness of the specificity of their autopoietic self-reference. Such an approach might stand in the way of a quick consensus but it is also productive because the actors can rely on their own devices to contribute to the discussion. It also reduces the chance of de-differentiation.

Another role of the planner would be to facilitate the design of the decision spaces and the selection of actors around the table (Van Assche 2008). Flexible selections of actors are needed to produce site- and issue-specific plans but there is always the question as to who is making the selection. An infinite classic regression lurks here and in a practical sense there is also an overburdening of planning administrations and the other actors by complicating the procedures. There is no final answer to the question as to who is making decisions. Luhmann would probably place the definition of the role of planners in shaping the processes and selecting the actors in the hands of politicians, capable of making collectively binding decisions at the intersection of the other systems (Luhmann 1990; King/Thornhill 2003). If a planner's role is defined in politics and becomes part of administration while allowing the planner to make flexible selections of actors according to certain procedures, then that role is legitimate as long as citizens accept it and do not contest it in such a way that the political system feels the need to adjust that role. Of course, the way politics respond to signals also depends on the chosen model for a democracy, a lobby-driven civil society model would not allow for a powerful planner (Van Assche/Leinfelder 2008). Such a reference to politics takes away the infinite regression and re-introduces flexibility to the second degree.

8. REFLECTIONS ON AND CONNECTIONS WITH THE PDL/BBO RESEARCH PROGRAMME

The argument for flexibility and depth in heritage planning, made from a systems theoretical perspective and conveying the productive potential of different genres of self-reference, is in line with some of the key findings of the Netherlands Organization for Scientific Research programme 'Protecting and Developing the Dutch Archaeological-Historical Landscape' (PDL/BBO), the results of which are presented in this volume. In the following discussion, we will analyse a few of the guiding concepts for the PDL/BBO programme through the lens of Luhmannian self-reference (Bloemers 2001; Hidding/Kolen/Spek 2001; Van der Valk Ch. II.2, 30-31).

8.1 Transdisciplinary work

Van der Valk, referring to Hoppe and others, speaks about the necessity of 'boundary work' in the necessarily transdisciplinary endeavour of heritage planning (Van der Valk Ch. II.2, 30-31) and on the varied character of that boundary work. Science and politics can converge or diverge and can be in superior, inferior or equal positions of power vis-à-vis each other. The inclusion of scientific knowledge in planning practice will depend on the type of boundary interaction that occurs. In a social systems perspective the number of boundary interactions is multiplied by bringing law, economy and education into the picture, therefore the number of potential relations. Luhmann can also clarify some of the similarities between boundary work appearing when leaving or entering science and the efforts to cross disciplinary boundaries within science. Both scientific disciplines and function systems (law etc.) are social systems, autopoietically self-reproducing and maintaining their boundaries (Luhmann 1995).

The various research projects within PDL/BBO clearly showed that working towards a politically, legally, scientifically and economically reasonable heritage planning entails the identification of various stakeholders with various interpretations of and interests in historical remains or old places and including them in a planning process where those interests and interpretations can be presented, confronted and deliberated. It became clear that heritage planning has to be a transdisciplinary effort and that it cannot be driven by the interpretations and valuations of science or one scientific discipline (see already Bloemers 2001; Hidding/Kolen/Spek 2001). Simultaneously, in several projects the realization occurred that science itself cannot guide the interactions with the other function systems. Disciplines and science as a whole can lobby for a larger role of science in the planning system, but lobbying is not a scientific activity as such (Forester 1999; Hillier 2002; Van Assche 2004). One can take a scientific look at the game of lobbying and the planning game as a whole; however, such a reflection needs to be amoral, in the sense that no values can be allowed to enter the observation. In other words, the self-reference of one of the heritage disciplines leading to greater and distinct insights in heritage matters is very unlikely to produce the hetero-reference that is most helpful in persuading other actors to include more historical matters in the planning deliberations.

8.2 Reflection and action/action research

In anthropology and sociology, action research is usually a type of participant observation that places a strong emphasis on the participatory side. Typically, researchers work in an organization they try to improve by means of their research outcomes. Some of the projects in PDL/BBO could be placed in this category (e.g. De Zwart Ch. V.7) and other projects (like mine, leading to Van Assche 2004) reflected on the potential and limitations of action research in heritage planning through theoretical and case-study research. The remarks on boundary work and disciplines already point at some of the limitations. Organizational learning, for example in a planning agency or conservation agency, will be delimited by the *autopoiesis* of the organization and the *autopoiesis* of the dominant disciplines and function/systems in and embodied by the organization (see also Seidl 2005; Van Assche/Verschraegen 2008). This means that first one needs to understand the organization, then come up with viable ways to 'improve' its functioning (in case the improvement is not biased from the start), followed by grasping the specific organizational culture and the culture and the conceptual framework of the dominant discipline and the relationship with the conceptual framework of the discipline one is immersed in.

A lack of understanding of the specific self-reference of the observed organization and discipline will produce a flawed image to base improvements upon and, if implemented, these improvements could prove highly disruptive for the organization. Duineveld (Duineveld 2006) studied how a restructuring of heritage protection agencies at the national level, with an associated clash of organizational cultures, produced an exclusion of amateur archaeologists, their knowledge and valuations and a loss of their goodwill. That perspective could only be obtained by taking a critical distance from the agencies while observing. At the same time, the insights gained could be applied and lead to an improvement of the organization in terms of economic efficiency and political legitimacy. The term 'action research' as used over the years in the PDL/BBO programme refers rather to this kind of reflexive applied research, a method that partly developed within the framework of the programme.

This broader concept of action research in a radically interdisciplinary programme with transdisciplinary aspirations taps into the productive potential of action research by highlighting the prevalent cross-disciplinary observations and participations with planners and sociologists observing and participating in heritage organizations and archaeologists, historians and geographers taking part in planning processes. As such, the PDL/BBO project created a field of observational experiments and a number of shifting perspectives aimed at improving the inclusion of heritage in Dutch planning practice which experience the potential and limitations of the boundary work they were doing. As a whole however, the consistent collective reflection on the practices of action research brings the variety of the boundary work to the surface and reintroduces a new image of the whole (i.e. the heritage planning world) into the scientific project organization. In Luhmannian terms, derived from logician Spencer-Brown, this is a re-entry whereby an image of the whole environment is introduced in the system, in this case project organization, allowing for a redirection and a new series of adaptations to that environment.

The regular project meetings, with discussion and reflection on the variety of applied research experiences crossing the same set of disciplines in different directions, did produce a new concept of action research which took into account the diversity of perspectives in a society of many autopoietic social systems. In the case of the discipline of planning it must be said that the added value of this new concept of action research is substantial since planning still grapples with a legacy of high modernism, a lack of interest in local knowledge and in the specificity of scientific disciplines and function systems. Just a few years ago, one of the leading Dutch planning academics proclaimed that the world needed something like 'political anthropology' to deal with these issues, thereby completely overlooking the existence of that field for about a century. In the case of archaeology, the bureaucratic web of the Dutch planning system proved a new field of observation and there too the observational methods provided by the discipline proved insufficient.

The presence of geography, sociology, anthropology and philosophy in the programme utilized a variety of methods and concepts that smoothened the inevitable confrontation of perspectives in programme meetings. These disciplines considerably added to the tools for constructing an action-research methodology specific for heritage planning, the specific mix of disciplines and non-scientific practices and for accepting and interpreting action research observations. The singular and valuable experience of PDL/BBO, an experience that does not occur often elsewhere, should be capitalized on and one way to do so would be a reflection on the bumpy but successful process of developing, confronting and synthesizing action research methods for heritage planning. One of the conclusions I drew from the experience is the value of regular cross-disciplinary work, collective reflection on that work and, in the process, a recognition of productive difference. Ignoring the system-specific self-reference in the project and reducing one perspective to another would lead to methodologies and conclusions that would be ignored by various actors in the field. However, cultivating the difference in the project and looking for avenues to transfer insights over boundaries can maintain the image of the larger world and the system boundaries there in the project organizations. Group-speak at the end of a project is often a false consensus that would not hold in the larger world so the lack of a complete consensus and a completely accepted common project language has to be considered more of an asset than a liability. It is a sign that productive self-reference was indeed maintained while avoiding the de-differentiated type of self-reference described above. Conflated perspectives do not produce synergies.

8.3 *Conservation and development*

Probably the main overall goal of the PDL/BBO programme, as testified by its name, is the identification and promotion of strategies to combine conservation of archaeological and historical remains, traces, places and structures in the landscape with economically, politically and legally realistic development. This is in the context of understanding that change always occurs and that time never stands still. From the start, the programme opted to substitute a pure conservation approach with one that allowed for mutual enrichment of history and place. Planning and design strategies that are respectful of the heritage were envisaged, as well as uses of the heritage to increase the spatial quality of the planned/ designed area (Bloemers 2001; Hidding/Kolen/Spek 2001; Van Assche 2004; Van der Valk Ch. II.2, 28-35).

One thing that became glaringly obvious in the course of the project is that this can only happen with plans specific to a site, history, legal, economic, political and cultural context. The balance between conservation and development will differ significantly in different places. The value and the fragility of the traces of the past will be different in every case and will be contested differently in various places. This can be due to competition with other interests (valuable ecology, high building pressure) or because the interest in a particular form of the past, or in the past in general, is weak in a certain community (Van Assche 2007; see also Hamm 1976 and Ziegler 2006 for striking examples in the East).

In other words, the balance between conservation and development that is most appropriate cannot be the result of the scientific calculations of one discipline or interdisciplinary research, but will have to be decided in an arena where other stakeholders are represented. In this process of finding a balance context is both limiting, and it is guiding. The landscape context and the cultural/political context are and should be considered as substantial constraints to development. They can be guiding in the design of planning procedure and the design of the actual space. A good plan in heritage planning will use history and landscape as values to be respected, sometimes as sites to be avoided, but it can also use history and landscape (history) as sources of inspiration and as assets for the design (Van Assche 2004; Ashworth/ Howarth 1999; Van der Valk Ch. II.2, 27-28). Landscape architecture, planning and architecture all bring their skills to the table in the interpretation of old places and buildings, and their potential for a new plan. Archaeology, art history and, historical geography can bring in their interpretations and assessments, that can in turn be of value for the more spatial disciplines. This being 'of value', it was argued, should take place in the frame of a planning process where a confrontation and cross-fertilization can potentially emerge, not in a place where one discipline is already in a leading position because of embeddings in administration, and not or in a place where simplified interpretations of buyer's preferences marginalize all other considerations, as in the United States (Throgmorton 1996).

Not every planning project will be able to include the wide array of disciplines present in the PDL/BBO programme and thus the desired productive confrontation of difference cannot be repeated as a whole. In planning practice some procedures will be simplified and some of the guiding principles will be legal, economic or political. The realities of the function systems will assert themselves quickly, as will the realities of an administrative practice that developed simplification procedures to control the complexities of planning. All this will delimit the number of options on the table in a planning process, the number of actors around the table and the amount of knowledge that is actually confronted. In principle, we do not see this as a problem because as long as the rule of thumb of flexibility and depth is applied, it is possible to design a confrontation of types of knowledge and to allow the resulting process and plan to lean towards a specific combination of perspectives. This requires active and interested citizens and a network of organizations in civil society (Putnam 1993; Kornai/Rose-Ackerman 2004).

9. CONCLUSION

The template design of the planning process should be such that any type of knowledge can be *potentially* introduced in the process and can be allowed to enter the conversation without being assigned a predetermined role. Only then can the final result be weaned off a predictable mix of land-use functions, design elements and some aspects of the preservation of ecologica, historical, cultural or polluted factors.

Indeed, it is impossible to be both comprehensive and context-sensitive at the same time and to include all actors and a selection of actors, but it is possible to espouse planning procedures that allow for the inclusion of *potentially* all fields of knowledge. It is also possible to envision openings in the procedures for a broad field of actors to enter, including some previously unrecognized or non-existent actors. Planners should therefore not press for comprehensiveness in every procedure but mediate the selection process of actors and disciplines that is locally legitimate and capable of plans acceptable to citizens and experts alike. Heritage planning in this perspective is a process of ongoing experimentation in a field of shifting power relations. According to Luhmann, differentiation of society entails an ever-increasing number of checks and balances and a continuous readjustment of the power of various geographical scales. A key issue in Dutch heritage planning will be the planning power of local politics and municipal councils versus the power of regional and national administrations richly populated with expert knowledge. Giving one of the scales dominance in heritage planning reduces the flexibility of the system and is disingenuous to the functioning of checks and balances. Conflicts between municipal politics and regional or national expert administrations are a sign of the proper functioning of democracy.

Former Dutch national landscape advisor Dirk Sijmons and prominent landscape architect Adriaan Geuze (West 8) regularly asserted that the uniformly, boring character and ruthless disregard of context in much of twentieth century Dutch urban development is not a product of a lack of space, inferior design skills or the result of an inherently boring landscape. Rather, they argued, it is the product of the Dutch planning machine, marked by a bureaucratic culture that was powerful enough to override politics, economy and the sciences that were not integrated in the administration.

A greater leeway for local politics as a check on national bureaucratic power and a source of local knowledge to localize plans are now traditional remedies for the ills of such centralized planning. The American planning experience, radically localized and privatized from the early days, shows that the cure can be worse than the ailment. Many features of spatial organization desired by citizens and recommended by experts (like bike lanes) are almost impossible to materialize in a situation where local politics and free market parties dominate. Many actors and forms of knowledge are almost impossible to include in the process. In other words, to address the concerns of Sijmons and Geuze and produce context-sensitive local plans, local politics cannot routinely trump scientific expertise and national bureaucracy. The flexible planning procedures argued for, allowing for case-based combinations of actors and disciplines, will hinge on a flexible distribution of planning powers over the scales of politics and administration. It will also depend on an easy availability of scientific expertise and design skills at the lower levels of politics and administration. More local power can produce more diversity in design but it can also produce uniformity because of larger market powers, the power of tradition and limited access to science and design.

Coming back to Dutch planning traditions, we have to add that in the course of the twentieth century more scientific disciplines, aided by political momentum and international recognition, entered the planning process. Ecology came back, especially since the Seventies and historical disciplines gained momentum in the last decade of the century. At the same time a slow reorientation towards participatory planning, a slow reappraisal of local knowledge and citizen preferences are taking place within planning, starting with planning academia (Healy 1997; Hillier 2002; Van Assche 2004; Duineveld 2006). This amounts to a repositioning of administration versus politics and law and it will and should influence the way the more recent scientific arrivals in the planning world, the historical disciplines, will be treated.

From the perspective of the heritage disciplines, it is understandable that their recent success and greater weight in Dutch planning procedures make them resistant to greater inclusion of local knowledge and citizen perspectives in those planning procedures. From a planning perspective, however, there is a danger of increasing de-differentiation and increasing the power of the standardizing planning machine by turning the contribution of the 'new' disciplines into new bullets on the checklist of the planning process into pre-defined new limitations for developers, architects and landscape architects. The Dutch interpretation of the Valletta Convention should avoid such a new and greater disregard for historical context. Citizens should be able to choose different mixes of knowledge and values in different plan/design scenarios, including scenarios that sacrifice some nature for archaeology and some old buildings for new ones, scenarios where the ambition levels of landscape architecture are higher or lower and so forth. In the end, citizens do decide how much they want to sacrifice for history and heritage but equally they also decide how they want to see plans and designs use history and heritage as an asset in the creation of new living environments and new spatial quality.

Making site-specific plans means capitalizing on the differentiation of society to do so, to analyse the specificity of site and issues and to come up with planning and design strategies for that site and issue. Planning always involves a co-ordination of interests and a multiplicity of knowledge. What exactly the planner can do, depends on the political and administrative context, e.g. the presence or absence of social democracy. Yet we have also argued for a planner with considerable skills freedom, a freedom however that can be redefined politically all the time (Miller 2002; Van Assche 2004). In the continuous redistribution of planning power over the scales of administration and, consequently, between politics, administration, law and science (Luhmann 1990; *idem* 1995; Shore/Wright 2002), the planner will be assigned very different tasks, such as making way for a landscape architect or bringing developers and archaeologists or local politicians and regional experts. In all this diversity, however, the requirements of planning in a differentiated society do produce uniformity in the desirable role of the planner.

A planner should be able to encourage self-awareness in the actors while observing the dangers of de-differentiation. He/she can contribute to the selection of actors that, in their acknowledged self-reference, can contribute to the drafting of heritage plans that are truly site specific. This implies that in different situations, different definitions of heritage are allowed and that various forms of heritage can acquire various roles in the plans, making various types of knowledge important in different situations.

NOTES
1   St Cloud State University, Minnesota, USA.

REFERENCES
Allmendinger, P., 2002: *Planning theory,* Basingstoke.
Ashworth, G./P. Howarth (eds.), 1999: *European heritage planning and management,* Bristol.

Assche, K. Van, 2003: Understanding the nature of disciplinary boundaries as a reason for success in interdisciplinary research, in B. Tress/G. Tress/A. van der Valk/G. Fry (eds.), *Interdisciplinary and trans- disciplinary landscape studies. Potential and limitations*, Wageningen, 100-106.

Assche, K. Van, 2004: *Signs in time. An interpretive account of urban planning and design, the people and their histories*, Wageningen (Ph.D. thesis Wageningen University).

Assche, K. Van, 2006: *Over goede bedoelingen en hun schadelijke bijwerkingen. Flexibiliteit, ruimtelijke ordening en systeemtheorie*, Utrecht.

Assche, K. Van, 2007: Planning as/and/in context. Towards a new analysis of context in interactive planning, *Middle Eastern Technical University JFA* 24, 105-117.

Assche, K. Van, 2008: 'Amenez-nous les citoyens et incluez-les!' Les chemins tortueux de la participation citoyenne dans les théories et les pratiques de l'urbanisme contemporain, in M. Hubert/F. Delmotte (eds.), *La cité administrative de l'état à la croisée des chemins. Des enjeux pour la ville et l'action publique à Bruxelles*, Brussels, 279-298.

Assche, K. Van/H. Leinfelder, 2008: Nut en noodzaak van een kritische planologie. Suggesties van Nederland en Amerika op basis van Luhmann's systeemtheorie, *Ruimte & Planning* 28, 28-38.

Assche, K. Van/G. Verschraegen, 2008: The limits of planning. Niklas Luhmann's social systems theory and the analysis of planning and planning ambitions, *Planning Theory* 7, 263-283.

Assche, K. Van/T. Weijschede, 2009: Over de productiviteit van versplinterde kennis: discursieve constructies van het verleden in de ruimtelijke ordening, in A. van der Zande/R. During (eds.), *Erfgoed en ruimtelijke planning*, Den Haag, 91-107.

Bloemers, J.H.F, 2001: Het NWO-Stimuleringsprogramma 'Bodemarchief in Behoud en Ontwikkeling' en de conceptuele studies. Een strategische handleiding voor onderzoek, beleid en uitvoering, in J.H.F. Bloemers/R. During/J.N.H. Elerie/H.A. Groenendijk/M. Hidding/J. Kolen/Th. Spek/M.-H. Wijnen, *Bodemarchief in Behoud en Ontwikkeling. De conceptuele grondslagen*, Den Haag, 1-7.

Duineveld, M., 2006: *Van oude dingen, de mensen, die voorbij gaan*, Delft (Ph.D. thesis Wageningen University).

Dunsire, A., 1996: Tipping the balance: autopoiesis and governance, *Administration and society*, 28, 299-334.

Evans, B., 1995: *Experts and environmental planning*, Avebury.

Fischer, F., 1990: *Technocracy and the politics of expertise*, Avebury.

Forester, J., 1999: *The deliberative practitioner. Encouraging participatory planning processes*, Cambridge.

Foucault, M., 1968: *Les mots et les choses*, Paris.

Hamm, F. (ed.), 1976: *The city in Russian history*, Lexington.

Healy, P., 1997: *Collaborative planning. Shaping places in fragmented societies*, London.

Hidding, J./J. Kolen/Th. Spek, 2001: De biografie van het landschap. Ontwerp voor een inter- en multidisciplinaire benadering van de landschapsgeschiedenis en het cultuurhistorisch erfgoed, in J.H.F. Bloemers/R. During/J.N.H. Elerie/H.A. Groenendijk/M. Hidding/J. Kolen/Th. Spek/M.-H. Wijnen, *Bodemarchief in Behoud en Ontwikkeling. De conceptuele grondslagen*, Den Haag, 7-109.

Hillier, J., 2002: *Shadows of power. An allegory of planning in land- use planning*, London.

Hough, J., 1972: Soviet urban politics and comparative urban theory, *Journal of comparative administration*, 311-334.

Innes, J./D. Booher, 1999: Consensus building as role playing and bricolage. Toward a theory of collaborative planning, *Journal of the American Planning Association* 65, 9-26.

King, M./C. Thornhill, 2003: *Niklas Luhmann's theory of politics and law*, New York.

Kornai, J./ S. Rose-Ackerman (eds.) 2004: *Building a trustworthy state in post-socialist transition*, New York.

Luhmann, N., 1990: *Political theory in the welfare state*, Berlin.

Luhmann, N., 1995: *Social systems*, Stanford.

Luhmann, N., 2000: *Art as a social system*, Stanford.

Miller, H., 2002: *Postmodern public policy*, New York.

Parsons, T., 1964: *The social system*, New York.

Pressman, J./A. Wildavsky, 1984: *Implementation*, Berkeley.

Putnam, R., 1993: *Making democracy work. Civic traditions in modern Italy*, Princeton.

Seidl, D., 2005: *Organisational identity and self-transformation*, Aldershot.

Shore, C./S. Wright, 2002: *Anthropology of policy. Critical perspectives on governance and power*, London.

Soja, E., 1997: Planning in/for post-modernity, in G. Benko/U. Strohmayer (eds.), *Space and social theory in interpreting modernity and postmodernity*, Oxford.

Taubman, W., 1973: *Governing Soviet cities. Bureaucratic politics and urban development in the USSR*, New York.

Throgmorton, J., 1996: *Planning as persuasive story-telling. The rhetorical construction of Chicago's electrical future*, Chicago.

Verdery, K., 2004: *The vanishing hectare. Property and value in post-socialist Transylvania*, Ithaca.

Wilson, A., 2005: *Virtual politics. Faking democracy in the Post-Soviet World*, New Haven.

Ziegler, K., 2006: *Städtebau in Georgien - vom Sozialismus zur Marktwirtschaft*, Kaiserslautern.

6. Interpretative heritage research and the politics of democratization and de-democratization
As illustrated by the plight of hard-working amateurs in the trenches of revamped policy arrangements

Martijn Duineveld[1], Raoul Beunen[2] & Kristof Van Assche[3]

ABSTRACT

Interpretative heritage research (IHR) can be used to increase the effectiveness and improve the democratic character of archaeological protection policies. Taking an interpretive heritage research approach, we argue that the apparently successful implementation of the Valletta Convention in the Netherlands has effectively excluded amateur archaeologists, a group of semi-experts often deemed essential to the protection and development of archaeological heritage. This in turn has caused unnecessary discussion and frustration, undermining public support for the initial policy goal of heritage conservation. Our analysis links up with recent academic debates on the policy-practice nexus in processes of Europeanization where implementation of European policies is viewed as a form of uncontrolled evolution. As such, implementation processes are unpredictable and frequently produce unanticipated consequences. Reducing negative side effects and re-targeting policies for greater efficacy and democracy requires insight into the pathways of implementation which can be acquired by means of interpretive heritage research.

KEY WORDS

Malta Treaty (Valletta Convention), archaeology; policy implementation, amateur archaeologists; power, exclusion, subjugation

1. INTRODUCTION: THE POLITICAL IMPERATIVE OF INTERPRETATIVE HERITAGE RESEARCH

The scientific practices of historians, archaeologists, historic geographers and art historians can be described as interpreting the remains from the past (such as artefacts, documents and relics) and using these interpretations to construct new knowledge about the past (Lorenz 1998; Ashworth/Graham/Tunbridge 2007). There are also academics who do not study the past or relics but rather the way in which people relate to them. Society, science, policy and science-policy interfaces are objects of study for the social scientist. One can scientifically interpret and analyse the ways people construct and interpret the past and its material remains (Bloemers *et al.* 2001). Academics in this field perform what we call interpretive heritage research (IHR). This form of research is practised in disciplines such as anthropology, sociology, planning and cultural and tourism studies, but also in disciplines that interpret the past (history, art history etc.). Topics include the meanings of Greek monuments for local inhabitants (Caftanzoglou 2001), the visitors of heritage sites (Gable/Handler 2003), the spiritual significance of cathedrals (Shackley 2002), the struggle for the appropriation of Stonehenge (Bender 1998), the relationship between heritage and identity of the Crimean Tatars (Van Assche 2004), as well as lesser-known studies such as the touristification of Auschwitz (Lennon/Foley 2000).

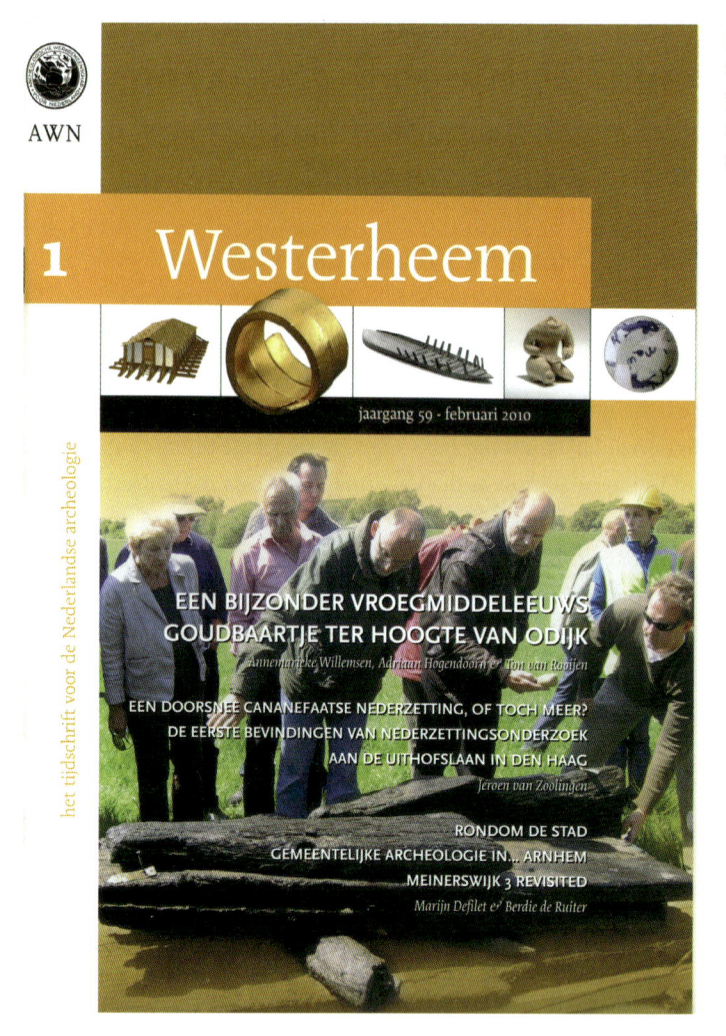

Fig. 1
Cover of a 2010 issue of the magazine for the Dutch Archaeological Working Community (Archeologische Werkgemeenschap voor Nederland AWN).

The increasing scope, magnitude and variety of IHR can be explained by the scientific value of these studies and their political and social or 'extra-academic' incentives (see also Low 2002; Duineveld 2008). IHR can provide insights into the societal impact of heritage management strategies, the multiple perspectives on heritage policies and the subjects of these policies and provide recommendations for the implementation of archaeological heritage protection. One branch of IHR that can be particularly valuable to policy-makers and citizens alike is policy implementation studies. We will demonstrate the scientific and political potential of IHR by analysing the implementation of the essential EU treaty on archaeological heritage, the Valletta Convention (also known as the Malta Treaty; Valletta 1992), in one of its most compliant member states, the Netherlands.

Though the socio-political legitimacy of IHR has hardly been tested, various studies into the extra-academic use of scientific knowledge in public administration (Turnhout 2003; Hoppe 2005), philosophy, sociology and anthropology of science have made similar arguments (Bourdieu 1981; Bourdieu/Wacquant 1992; Gibbons 1994; Biagioli/Galison 1999; Pestre 2004). These studies have shown that scientific research is used in practice "for various objectives" or, depending on the chosen vocabulary, "can play several roles", "be effective", "can be valorized" or "can be applied". Depending on the chosen categorization, various "uses" can be distinguished. For instance, a distinction can be made between the instrumental, strategic and conceptual use of knowledge. Turnhout, Hisschemöller and Eijsackers (Turnhout/Hisschemöller/Eijsackers 2007, 224) distinguished "four different roles that knowledge can have in policy (problem solver, problem signalling, accommodation and advocate (...)." Elsewhere it is argued that six types of use of IHR can be distinguished, namely democratization, legitimizing, problem solving, deconstruction, problem identification and the dissemination of knowledge (Duineveld 2008).

In this chapter we will focus on using IHR to further the democratization of heritage policy, specifically Dutch archaeological heritage policy. This makes a good case for IHR since the call for transparent representation and better citizen participation (in short for democratization) has been heard for decades in various policy domains in various welfare states (Fischer 1990; Flyvbjerg 1998; Pierre 2000; Hajer/Wagenaar 2003; Latour 2004). This trend can also be seen in Dutch heritage policy. A number of studies and policy initiatives aimed at increased citizen involvement and inclusion of lay interpretation and valuation of heritage have appeared (Poel *et al.* 2000; Duineveld 2006; Van der Zande 2006). IHR is already contributing to this trend and could conceivably contribute more by mapping out peoples' knowledge and values and their use and interpretation of space and history. The results of these studies can subsequently be integrated into policy and consequently contribute to the democratization of the heritage policy system (Low 2002).

IHR can also contribute to this democratization through critical reflection on the closure and openness of the policy domain. IHR is superbly positioned to study mechanisms of inclusion and exclusion in heritage policy. It can unveil whose heritage is being protected, under whose rules and based on whose knowledge. In our case study on the implementation of the Valletta Convention in the Netherlands we analysed the relationships between amateur archaeologists and the state. In-depth interviews for a discourse analysis (Howarth/Torfing 2005, for a methodological framework see Hajer 2005) were conducted in 2005, 2006 and 2007 with 15 amateur archaeologists (all were members of the Dutch Archaeological Working Community/ Archeologische Werkgemeenschap Nederland (AWN) and 20 civil servants at local, regional and national tiers of government. Most of the latter worked for the National Service for Archaeological Heritage, which merged with the State Service for the Conservation of the Built Heritage (RDMZ) in 2007 to form the present-day Cultural Heritage Agency. We also analysed the 1995-2005 volumes of *Westerheem* (Fig. 1; Archeologische Werkgemeenschap voor Nederland 2004), the monthly magazine for and by amateur archaeologists, and other formal and informal documents.

We found that the amateur's relationship with the government has changed since the signing of the Valletta Convention. They feel sidelined. We studied this changing relationship between amateur archaeologists and government to gain insight into the inclusion and exclusion of non-governmental initiatives by governmental agencies in heritage policy. Our study reinforced the argument that there is a political imperative for IHR.

2. A THEORY OF POLICY IMPLEMENTATION: ON EVOLUTION AND UNINTENDED CONSEQUENCES

Policy-making in EU member states is increasingly shaped and restricted by EU legislation and policy such as directives and conventions. The European Union has become an important institution for co-ordinating, integrating and stimulating joint efforts by member states to deal with issues of common concern, such as environmental quality, biodiversity conservation and the protection of archaeological heritage. The objectives of directives and conventions can be procedural, substantial or both. These objectives are often achieved through complex and lengthy processes. Besides positive outcomes, there are concerns about implementation and enforcement of EU policies (Barnes/Barnes 1999). In order to critically discuss and constructively judge European policies, careful and critical monitoring of the impact of EU policy on the daily practices of policy making, interpretation, adaptation and combination is required in conjunction with enforcement by the other tiers of government (Wallace/Wallace 1996; Olson 2000; Beunen/Knaap/Biesbroek 2009).

Majone and Wildavsky (Majone/Wildavsky 1979) have presented and analysed policy implementation as an evolutionary process. They argued that the results of an implementation process are not predictable. An element of surprise is always present and the outcomes are likely to be different from those sought by any single participant. To argue that policies can develop in several ways during implementation, they used the metaphorical comparison between a policy and an organism that evolves through interaction with its environment and that is partly constrained by the original policy. They proposed that a policy can be seen as an idea or a set of ideas about a specific policy item. Policy implementation then becomes the struggle for the realization of these ideas. Ideas about how a policy should be interpreted and how it should be applied evolve during the implementation process. From this perspective, the meaning of a policy is not an intrinsic element of a policy, rather people who interpret and apply the policy give it meaning. This implies that the struggle for the ideas that characterize policy formulation does not stop once a policy is drawn up but continues during its implementation. Implementation can thus be seen as a process in which the different actors who are involved in the implementation process constantly interpret and reinterpret the 'original' policies, laws or directives. Nevertheless, the outcomes of an implementation process often retain some relationship to the policy's original ideas, which suggests that the interpretation and application is somehow guided by the policy. "Policy content shapes implementation by defining the arena in which the process takes place, the identity and role of the principal actors, the range of permissible tools for actions, and of course by supplying resources" (*ibidem*, 174). Initial policy choices may restrict subsequent evolution so that a kind of path dependency influences the course of policy (Pierson 1996). Simply stated, policy shapes implementation but it does not determine it.

In the evolutionary process of implementation actors, ideas, decisions, actions and outcomes are all considered to be potentially interrelated. It is only when we can gain more insight into these multiple relations that it becomes possible to see why a certain policy works in a specific way and gives specific results. According to Jensen and Richardson (Jensen/Richardson 2004), this insight is necessary before the quality of a policy and its desirability and transformational power can be discussed, "Understanding more about the interweaving of policy discourse with our continuous making and remaking of everyday lived space seems an attractive and necessary challenge" (*ibidem* 2004, preface x). This amounts to recognizing the importance of context in the interpretation, and therefore implementation, of any policy. We began our analysis of the effect of the Valletta Convention on the Netherlands at the point when this convention started to affect the routines of amateur archaeologists.

3. THE IMPLEMENTATION OF THE VALLETTA CONVENTION

The Cultural Heritage Agency estimates that 30% of the Dutch archaeological soil archive has vanished since World War II (www.noaa.nl). This is mostly due to anthropogenic activities, such as the development of villages, cities, roads and canals, and the disturbance of fertile soils for agricultural activities. The growing awareness that Dutch archaeology needed to be protected and that archaeological research needed to be more properly regulated gave rise to the Dutch Monuments and Historic Building Act in 1961. Archaeological research was only to be conducted by those in possession of a licence. This included the National Service for Archaeological Heritage, the Dutch National Museum of Antiquities, a few universities and a number of municipalities (Willems/Brandt 2004; Bazelmans/Hilberdink/Lange 2005).

Because much of the archaeological heritage was lost during post-war urban renewal, several local authorities established municipal archaeologists and archaeological services in the 1970s. The conservation of archaeology was not integrated in spatial planning in those days and the archaeologists primarily occupied themselves with emergency excavations. This was partly because the previous Monuments Act did not require local authorities to have an archaeological policy.

The Valletta Convention was signed in 1992 as a reaction to the disappearance of the soil archive. According to De Jonge (De Jonge 2005), who compared the implementation of the Convention in the Netherlands, France and Norway, the treaty has been implemented in different countries in various ways.

"Although the three States speak unanimously 'through' the Preamble of the Convention, in their own legislation we could clearly see influence of the national circumstances and priorities. Especially in the Netherlands, restrictions upon the rights of an owner are not lightly imposed. In France and Norway protection mechanisms are more sophisticated or at least more enforceable. In the division of financial responsibility and promotion of public access by the State one can clearly see the starting point that archaeology is a public responsibility in France and Norway, whereas the Netherlands chose for liberalization and privatization."

In the Netherlands, the Convention was incorporated into national legislation in the form of the new Archaeological Heritage Management Act (Wamz 2007). The results of that process can be summarized as six basic principles:
1. Conserving and protecting archaeological heritage in the soil as much as possible (*in situ*). This was the overall goal.
2. Improving the integration of archaeological interests with spatial planning. Statutory changes were made in this regard.
3. Decentralizing responsibilities to a municipal level.
4. Passing on the costs of archaeological activities to the person or institute causing the disturbance of the soil.
5. Liberalizing archaeological excavations, which implied that commercial companies with a permit would be allowed to do archaeological research and conduct excavations.
6. Imposing an obligation on authorities and executive institutes to provide information (Bosch 2008).

Even though the Monuments and Historic Buildings Act did not come into force until 1 September 2007, the archaeological policy system had been transforming itself in accordance with the demands of the new act ever since the Convention was signed in 1992 (Valletta 1992; Willems/Brandt 2004).

Before the Convention, the Dutch archaeological community was made up of 150 professional archaeologists working at four national services, six universities, nineteen provincial institutes and museums, fifteen local councils and museums and a few other museums and institutions. More than ten years later, the archaeological policy system has completely changed. Dozens of commercial archaeological agencies and hundreds of people are now working in archaeology due to the liberalization of archaeological research. Many responsibilities of the former National Service for Archaeological Heritage have been transferred to the local councils. Together with the Cultural Heritage Agency and the provinces, they are largely responsible for archaeological policy (Hessing 2002). Whenever there is a change in the zoning plan, local councils are required to investigate whether these locations contain valuable archaeological heritage. If it does not employ qualified people itself, the local council can hire a commercial agency.

Information about archaeological heritage at specific locations can be found, among other ways, by checking Archis, a computer-based Archaeological Information System (www.racm.nl/...asp). Maps indicating locations and structures with archaeological value can also be consulted here. If the outcome of the assessment and selection procedures indicates the presence of valuable archaeological heritage, the potentially responsible party is expected to preserve the site or to have it archaeologically excavated. Either the municipality or a commercial agency can conduct the excavation. Based on the archaeological study, a municipality can decide to classify valuable sites that require protection. The excavations have to meet certain quality standards as described in the Quality Norm Dutch Archaeology (KNA). The State Inspectorate for Archaeology checks whether a civil council, commercial agency or university meets the standards (www.erfgoedinspectie.nl). These standards are described in the Dutch Archaeology Quality Standard (Willems/Brandt 2004).

In summary, within only a decade after the Valletta Convention was signed, a system of heritage protection and an archaeological system were established in the Netherlands which have strongly influenced how archaeology is dealt with at the national and local policy levels. This was viewed as a very successful way of integrating archaeology into the Dutch planning system. However, this success also had a negative outcome in that it partially excluded an important group of citizens in Dutch society who had always been very active and useful within the archaeological system.

4. THE EXCLUSION OF AMATEUR ARCHAEOLOGISTS

In the mid-1980s, according to Ribbens (Ribbens 2002, 112-113, translated by the authors), the Netherlands had

> "(...) over 540 organizations that occupy themselves with the practice and promotion of local and regional historical research. Most organizations pay attention to a broad spectrum of historical aspects. Some are predominantly aimed at the conservation and management of historically valuable landscapes, monuments and other immovable objects, others at genealogy and heraldry, archaeology, vernacular languages and dialects. The majority of these associations have between 50 and 300 members. The number of members of most associations has only increased over the past ten years. (...) In 1997, (...) researcher Jos de Haan demonstrated that 3% of the Dutch population over 16, so more than 300,000 people, was a member of an association for regional and local history or of an archaeological society."

Amateur archaeologists, united in associations such as the Dutch Archaeological Working Community (AWN), form a specialized group of historically committed citizens. Approximately 4,000 volunteers are active in the world of Dutch archaeology today. The AWN has around 2,400 members (www.awn-archeologie.nl). The number of archaeology clubs is estimated at between 150 and 300 (De Haan 1997, 86). These amateur archaeologists were and are beneficial for Dutch archaeological heritage. They think so themselves and the policymakers and professional archaeologists agree (www.minocw.nl/toespraken).

Amateur archaeologists make various contributions to archaeological knowledge (Duineveld 2006). They search the surface of the land for relics, for instance in fields where archaeological remnants have resurfaced after ploughing. As a result, new sites are discovered and archaeological relics are saved from erosion and ploughing damage. Some of these relics are considered to be of great value within the archaeological system in terms of indication of archaeological remains. Amateurs also conduct excavations, both in collaboration with professional archaeologists and by themselves.

Some of the excavations are done out of sheer necessity. This is to say that they save archaeological heritage in danger of being lost due to disturbance of the soil. In the past, the National Service for Archaeological Heritage has made grateful use of these search and excavation activities. The amateurs helped the National Service free of charge and large areas of the Dutch soil archive were mapped with their help. The amateurs also contributed to knowledge development by acting as 'the eyes and ears of archaeology' (Band/Cordfunke 2001). Amateurs have been the first to spot many finds or indications for possible finds.

Some amateurs are even seen as authorities by professional archaeologists. They acknowledge that some amateurs are more knowledgeable about certain histories and archaeology than they are themselves. Some amateurs generate knowledge following the same procedures scientists do but outside of the academic disciplines and organizations. They read and refer to academic publications and their studies lead to scientifically sound knowledge (Archeologische Werkgemeenschap voor Nederland 2004).

Professional archaeologists regularly make use of the amateurs' expertise (Cultuur als confrontatie 2000, 36). A great deal of archaeological knowledge is exchanged and archaeological heritage is salvaged because amateurs and employees of municipalities, provinces and the Service for Archaeology, Cultural Landscape and Built Heritage maintain good communication with one another. Amateurs also add to the public awareness of archaeology. They bring it to the attention of Dutch citizens by giving hundreds of lectures every year and by publishing articles in local newspapers.

At the same time, amateur archaeologists actively try to influence various tiers of government, particularly the local tier. Many municipalities never had a specific policy on archaeology. Partly thanks to the amateurs, a number of municipalities started to pursue a structural archaeological policy (Verhagen 2003; Krauwer 2004). These direct and indirect contributions by amateurs are largely due to informal contacts between amateurs, professional archaeologists and local governments (Duineveld 2006).

The implementation of the Valletta Convention has strongly influenced the practices of amateur archaeologists. This becomes apparent from the letters and articles that appeared in the *Westerheem*, the magazine for members of the Dutch Archaeological Working Community (2003-2005). These letters and articles clearly show that amateur archaeologists do not favour some of the changes in the archaeological policy system (see for instance: De Grood 2003; Houkes 2003a; *idem* 2003b; *idem* 2003c; Verhagen 2003; Vissers 2003; Houkes 2004). One amateur even conducted a survey to sound out his colleagues' dissatisfaction about these changes, "The amateurs' emotions on this subject are alarming" (De Grood 2003, translated by the authors). The interviews held with amateur archaeologists stress their concerns expressed in the *Westerheem*. The implementation of the Convention has thus affected the roles of amateur archaeologists.

According to the amateurs, the transformation of archaeology policy has serious consequences for them. The problem is not that there is not any work left for them. So much of the soil archive has already been disturbed that in theory there would be enough material for every amateur. The main problems, they believe, are the regulations and their rigid enforcement (Hoekstein 2001; De Grood 2003). Amateur archaeologist Jan Verhagen also provided a number of examples from actual practice that illustrate how the field of archaeology treats amateur archaeologists (Verhagen 2003). These authors, as well as our own analysis of the implications of the Valletta Convention, show that amateurs view the procedural requirements of the statutory system as being unfavourable to them and the conservation of the soil archive.

Despite the successful implementation of the Valletta Convention, there are some unintended negative consequences. The new statutory system has broken the close mutually supportive relationships that existed between the policy system and the amateurs. This has caused frustration amongst the amateurs and has led to a negative impact on the protection of archaeological heritage and on the public support for conservation policies. The National Service confirms this notion in the draft proposal 'Vision National Service for Archaeological Heritage on the involvement of amateur archaeologists with the AMZ' (Visie ROB 1999, translated by the authors).

> "Amateurs would like (…) the re-establishment of the structural contact with the professional world through, among other things, the National Service for Archaeological Heritage (…) amateurs don't feel they're being taken seriously (…) miss clear expert contact points and personal contacts (…) miss clarity on the division of tasks in the new establishment (…) feel threatened by the professionalization and the rise of companies (…) aren't getting sufficient feedback when they report finds (…) are too often passed over by the National Service for Archaeological Heritage and the provinces at emergency situations or for advice (…) don't wish to be considered as cheap labour (…) would like more opportunities to take part in excavations (…) are not being involved or too little involved in the execution path (…)."

5. EXCLUSIONARY MECHANISMS

It is obvious that the implementation of the Convention has caused amateur archaeologists and the archaeological policy system to drift apart to a certain extent. How did this process of closure and exclusion come about?

5.1 *Organizational transformations and the increasing bureaucracy*

First and foremost we have to mention the reform of the National Service for Archaeological Heritage. Since the beginning of the 1990s, this national service has changed from an archaeological institute focusing on excavations to a knowledge institution aiming at the conservation of archaeology. Because of this, many of its former tasks have been passed on to provinces, local councils and commercial excavation companies. Before the implementation of the Valletta Convention, the National Service often depended on amateurs for emergency excavations. At that time it was easy for many professional archaeologists in the National Service for Archaeological Heritage to gather a large group of amateurs in a short amount of time. The National Service for Archaeological Heritage almost completely stopped excavating in 1997. Its position was no longer reactive, trying to salvage whatever could be salvaged. Instead it became proactive, wishing to conserve *in situ* what could be conserved. This change has rendered the amateurs virtually useless for the purposes of the National Service for Archaeological Heritage and it therefore no longer offers them direct support.

Connected to this mechanism is the increase in rules and formal procedures, i.e. the growing bureaucracy of the archaeological policy system. Nearly all those interviewed, both amateur archaeologists and employees of the National Service, acknowledged this. According to an employee of the National Service, the archaeological system has become too rigid, noting that "as an amateur, you sometimes have to go through a great deal of trouble to salvage the heritage, while in the meantime a contractor is moving a few cubic metres of earth. So a growing bureaucracy here only weakens the connection with the amateurs."

5.2 Severed and closed networks

The fabric of relationships between people, organizations and between people and organizations can be described as a network in terms of relational ties that allow people a certain access to material sources, knowledge and power (Hillier 2002, 85). Whoever belongs to a network can gain access to the knowledge, information, capital and goods that are exchanged within the network. Networks can therefore be open or closed to a certain degree and thus either include or exclude people, knowledge, capital, values etc. (Castells 1996; Kickert/Klijn/Koppenjan 1997). The archaeological policy system is also made up of networks, partly internal and partly external, such as the networks involving the amateurs.

An important, formalized external network between the archaeological system and the amateurs was the correspondents' system. This officially linked the amateurs to the National Service for Archaeological Heritage. Correspondents of the National Service received a card acknowledging their special status as a correspondent. Many amateurs were very appreciative of this acknowledgement by the government. The correspondents' system no longer exists today. It was discontinued in 1997. Besides the disappearance of this formal network, the implementation of the Valletta Convention also caused the discontinuation of many informal networks between amateur archaeologists and local, regional and national civil servants, especially within the National Service for Archaeology, Cultural Landscape and Built Heritage. In this way, many contacts between amateurs and the National Service were severed due to the disappearance of the 'traditional' provincial archaeologists. These archaeologists used to work for the National Service and were funded in part by the provinces. These traditional provincial archaeologists had a great deal of contact with the amateurs and served as liaisons (Duineveld 2006).

5.3 The selective accessibility of the policy instruments

The selective accessibility of some of the policy instruments contributes to the exclusion of amateurs. An example of such an instrument is Archis. This system is exclusively accessible to people and organizations connected with the archaeological field. Those who are not connected will now have to report their finds indirectly. They cannot consult Archis to find out whether a site has archaeological heritage and thus "Archis2 is not accessible to amateur archaeologists" (www.racm.nl/...toc=). The selective accessibility of the instruments is partly due to the fact that their use implies certain skills, e.g. "for Archis2 is so complex that the programme cannot be used without having taken a course" (www.racm.nl/...n4-6).

Those who do not have these skills either have no access at all to the instrument or can only access it with difficulty. The same applies to the digital files of archaeological maps, such as the Indicative Map of Archaeological Values (IKAW). In short, the production and selective use of some instruments causes some knowledge and values to be excluded.

5.4 Commercialization

Likewise, the selective accessibility mentioned above is connected to the commercialization of a large part of archaeological research. Officially, amateurs still have the possibility to assist commercial agencies. However, it is up to the agencies to determine whether or not an amateur is allowed to participate (www.erfgoedinspectie.nl/…faq). According to a managing director of a large excavation company, the contribution of amateurs is usually not seen as a way to expedite or reduce the price of the work. One of the things complicating collaboration is the fact that commercial businesses work during office hours and amateurs are usually available outside office hours. In practice, many commercial agencies are not very enthusiastic about help from amateurs.

5.5 Selective reproduction of knowledge and values in instruments

Archaeological value maps are one of the instruments that can be used to determine whether there might be valuable archaeology at a certain site. An important value map within the archaeological policy system is the Archaeological Monuments Map. It shows the most important archaeological sites in the Netherlands (www.racm.nl/…n4-8). These maps are predominantly produced by incorporating the knowledge and values of professional archaeologists (Foucault 1994). When these instruments are used, for example to include valuable sites in a zoning plan, the knowledge and values of archaeologists are automatically reproduced. The use of this instrument thus leads to the selective reproduction of certain knowledge and values while simultaneously excluding all knowledge and values not incorporated in it, such as those of amateurs.

5.6 Marginalizing the knowledge of amateurs

An important set of rules within archaeology is described in the Dutch Archaeology Quality Standard. This regulates who is allowed to do excavations, produce knowledge and assign value to old things. The Standard places professional archaeologists in a clear hierarchy with one another (Kwaliteitsnorm 2005). Only professionally trained archaeologists are officially authorized to excavate, perform research and determine the value of archaeological finds. Amateur archaeologists and other non-experts have no place in this qualification system. This is the case despite the fact that some amateurs use the same methods and procedures as professionals, despite the fact that their studies often lead to scientifically sound knowledge and despite the fact that amateur and professional archaeologists both acknowledge that amateurs often have more and better knowledge of the local cultural history than professional archaeologists. It is possible that a professional archaeologist could be authorized to make statements about the significance and value of the archaeological heritage somewhere, while a more knowledgeable amateur would have no formal authority to interfere.

6. THE SELF-REFERENCE OF A PARTIALLY CLOSED SYSTEM

An important co-ordinating mechanism behind the ones mentioned above is self-reference. Groups and individuals (but also cultures, organizations and systems) observe their surroundings, attach meaning and value to them and act within the notions, practices and discourses they take for granted. Ecologists, for example, often think they know exactly which ecology is valuable and which is not without realizing that their assessments are based on assumptions internalized in their ecological knowledge; knowledge and assessments refer to each other in the self-referential system of the ecological discipline. Planners think that their ideas about landscape quality and proper spatial planning are well-founded in rationality (Van Assche/Verschraegen 2008). All disciplinary interpretations and valuations are grounded in tautology since the basic premises are not directly affected by new observations and the valuations by a discipline are 'true' because they emerge from disciplinary inquiry. Ecological values are there because of ecological investigations, legal decisions are based on other legal decisions, a Greek vase is valuable because a value is attached to it by Greek vase experts.

The same applies to the archaeological policy system. This system is set up in such a way that it is dominated by the professional archaeologists' ideas on what relics from the past are valuable and how they need to be handled. Self-reference leads to naturalization. Within this system constructed values are presented as natural, normal and objective and as intrinsic quality, i.e. as non-constructed (Barthes 1957; Luhmann 1987; Barnes/Duncan 1992). People tend to forget that values are produced by and within self-referential frameworks and are not revealed or discovered in some external reality. Naturalizing one construction means veiling other constructions and other views, knowledge, ideas and values go unnoticed or are regarded as inferior. Veiling, forgetting or marginalizing can be the consequences (Foucault 2003).

The post-Valletta Convention archaeological system in the Netherlands can be characterized as partially closed. Knowledge and values produced within this system dominate, while other knowledge and values hardly play a role. Officially, the government archaeologists do not have the power to make political decisions. Theoretically, this power lies with politicians in the national, provincial and local tiers of government. Reality is different. Even though politicians are officially independent of the archaeological field, archaeological policy is primarily based on the advice of the archaeological policy system and the decisions are made in consultation with it. In addition, politicians mostly leave it up to the archaeological field itself to steer its functioning. : "What is good archaeology? The archaeological field itself is best equipped to decide ('self-regulation')" (www.minocw.nl/malta).

People and organizations that are part of the archaeological field are also the predominant influence in the decision process at the local level (Hessing 2002). The role of local politics is usually limited to approving or disapproving the bylaws drawn up by the professional archaeologists, stating which places they define as valuable. A partially closed policy field has emerged that can operate largely independently of political decision-making and groups of citizens such as the amateur archaeologists and this is a form of depoliticization.

Depoliticization is a broader phenomenon and moreover one that is not new. Depoliticization fits the increasing professionalization and scientification of Dutch administration, a development that allows a selection of expert knowledge to dominate government policy (Fischer 1990; Frissen 1996; Fischer 2000). As early as 1994, Lengkeek wrote about incapability of recreation policy to do justice to the desires and passions of citizens. According to him, this is due to the fact that the policy is produced within a system world following rationalities that can hardly do justice to the thinking and acting of people in their everyday environment. Many non-governmental organizations and representatives have been sidelined because of the changes in government policy (Lengkeek 1994). The know-how that was built up by private organizations was rendered useless because their contact points with the authorities were abolished (Lengkeek 1994, 176). More recently Wissink (Wissink 2000), Turnhout (Turnhout 2003), Van Ark (Van Ark 2005), Van Assche (Van Assche 2004) and Buizer (Buizer 2008) have argued in their dissertations that politics, authorities, universities, research institutes and businesses in the system of spatial planning are closely interwoven. In the planning practices they studied, the knowledge, values and problem definitions of politicians, government experts, public servants and interest groups dominated. The problems and solutions signalled in spatial planning are therefore sometimes largely detached from the desires of the wide range of users in the Dutch landscape. The initiatives of citizens, public organizations and businesses to influence the content of the policy are often obstructed by the closed character of the policy systems. Cultural sociologist Corijn aptly remarked that the closure characterizing policy fields and the considerable power of experts within them is partly responsible for a crisis in representative democracy (Magits/Steene 2003). To avert this crisis, authorities need to create more openness. In the case of the amateur archaeologists this implies, for example, that with the production of the value maps, more justice will be done to their and other peoples' opinions of which heritage is valuable. The same goes for the other instruments within this field. More openness can also be created by adjusting rules and procedures and by recreating networks between amateurs and professionals and governmental professionals.

7. CONCLUSION: DEMOCRACY AND THE SOCIO-POLITICAL IMPERATIVE OF IHR

The dedication of many citizens to the conservation and development of the heritage they value is something that cannot be overlooked by the state (Bargeman 1996; Rhodes 1996; Lengkeek 2000; Weber/Chistophersen 2002; Wollebaek/Selle 2002; Sela-Sheffy 2006; Dam/Eshuis/Aarts 2008). The argument here is both practical and democratic. The Valletta Convention increased the closed character of the archaeological heritage policy system, though there seems to be hope on the horizon. In recent years the amateur archaeologists kept fighting for their approach to heritage. Their struggle created new forms of openness. In this vein, and thanks to an AWN initiative, a consultation platform was formed in 2004 to discuss the problems of amateur archaeologists. Both people from the National Service for Archaeology, Cultural Landscape and Built Heritage and the AWN board participate in this platform.

Developments such as these seem to offer hope for the future. They show that the archaeological policy system is constantly changing. The level of openness and closure is therefore dynamic. The dynamic is limited, however, because the mechanisms governing opening and closing are codified and embodied in organizations, laws, rules, instruments and procedures. Certain knowledge and values are incorporated in these organizations and as such they will in turn determine the positions and behaviour of the actors in the system. As a result, the self-reference of the archaeological policy system is 'materialized' and preserved. Given the already very institutionalized character of the way archaeology is dealt with, it will not be easy to create more openness in the foreseeable future and to take socially important associations into account. An unfortunate path dependency can obstruct this process (Luhmann 1987). Laws and practical objections stand in the way of openness. This system-theoretical wisdom does not mean that interpretive heritage researchers working on the negative side-effects of policy implementation should give up their jobs. Their findings can be used to indicate and reformulate problems and place them on the political agenda. Publishing the results of interpretative heritage research might lead to the placement of problems on societal and political agendas.

Of course, we still need to determine whether the responsible governments incorporated these questions and problems. That is something a researcher can only influence to a certain extent. For that reason we have spoken about the ways in which IHR could be used since it is usually impossible to predict whether or not the extra-academic objectives will lead to the envisaged extra-academic effects. One can discern certain degrees of predictability because the production, reproduction and use of the knowledge depend on the context of its use (Duineveld et al, 2009). This is because studies can be ignored, selectively used or may have only a very indirect influence on extra-academic practices.

This conclusion might feed the scepticism of people who think socio-scientific research, including IHR, is a useless activity by sociologists and similar academics who mostly occupy themselves with using difficult words to describe things everybody already knows. The opposite is true. Scientific research and socio-scientific research have played many political, administrative and social roles and will continue to do so in the future. It is difficult to predict what extra-academic role the IHR will play in the Netherlands. However, we believe it is now evident that IHR holds the promise of being able to critically analyse the relationship between the state and its citizens in the field of heritage politics.

NOTES

1 Wageningen University, Wageningen, the Netherlands.
2 Wageningen University, Wageningen, the Netherlands.
3 St Cloud State University, Minnesota, USA.

REFERENCES

Archeologische Werkgemeenschap voor Nederland, 2004: Westerheems op CD-ROM. All volumes 1952-2004, Amsterdam
Ark, R.G.H. van, 2005: *Planning, contract en commitment: naar een relationeel perspectief op gebiedscontracten in de ruimtelijke planning*, Delft.
Ashworth, G./B. Graham/J. Tunbridge, 2007: *Pluralizing Pasts: Heritage, Identity and Place in Multicultural Societies*, London.
Assche, K. Van, 2004: *Signs in time. An interpretive account of urban planning and design, the people and their histories*, Wageningen (Ph.D. thesis Wageningen University).
Assche, K. Van/G. Verschraegen, 2008: The Limits of Planning: Niklas Luhmann's Systems Theory and the Analysis of Planning and Planning Ambitions, *Planning Theory* 7, 263-283.
Band, A.P. van den/E.H.P. Cordfunke (eds.), 2001: *Archeologie in veelvoud, vijftig jaar Archeologische Werkgemeenschap voor Nederland. Jubileumboek AWN*, Utrecht.
Bargeman, B., 1996: Associaties in de vrijetijd, *Vrijetijdstudies* 14 (2), 34-49.
Barnes, P.M./I. Barnes, 1999: *Environmental Policy in the European Union*, Cheltenham.
Barnes, T.J./J.S. Duncan, 1992: *Writing worlds: discourse, text and metaphor in the representation of landscape*, London.
Barthes, R., 1957: *Mythologies*, Paris.

Bazelmans, J./K. Hilberdink/G. Lange, 2005: *Sectoranalyse Universitaire Archeologie (3e concept)*, Amersfoort (Rijksdienst voor het Oudheidkundig Bodemonderzoek).

Bender, B., 1998: *Stonehenge: making space*, Oxford.

Beunen, R./W.G.M. Knaap/G.R Biesbroek, 2009: Implementation and Integration of EU Environmental Directives. Experiences from the Netherlands, *Environmental Policy and Governance* 19, 57-69.

Biagioli, M./P. Galison, 1999: *The science studies reader*, New York.

Bloemers, J.H.F. /R. During/J.N.H. Elerie/H.A. Groenendijk/M. Hidding/J. Kolen/Th. Spek/M.-H. Wijnen, 2001: *Bodemarchief in Behoud en Ontwikkeling. De conceptuele grondslagen*, Den Haag.

Bosch, J., 2008: *Waar met beleid gegraven wordt... Een onderzoek naar de mate van doorwerking van de nieuwe Wet op de archeologische monumentenzorg op het ruimtelijk beleid van de Nederlandse gemeenten*, Nijmegen (Afstudeeronderzoek Radboud Universiteit).

Bourdieu, P., 1981: The specificity of the scientific field, in Ch.C. Lemert (ed.), *French Sociology: rupture and renewal since 1968*, New York.

Bourdieu, P./L.J.D. Wacquant, 1992: *An invitation to reflexive sociology*, Chicago.

Buizer, I. M., 2008: *Worlds apart. Interactions between Local Initiatives and Established Policy*, Wageningen.

Caftanzoglou, R., 2001: The shadow of the sacred rock: Contrasting discourses of place under the Acropolis, in B. Bender/M. Winer (eds.), *Contested landscapes: movement, exile and place*, Oxford, 21-35

Castells, M., 1996: *The rise of the network society*, Oxford.

Cultuur als confrontatie 2000: *Cultuur als confrontatie*, Den Haag (Ministerie van Onderwijs, Cultuur en Wetenschap).

Dam, R. van/J. Eshuis/N. Aarts, 2008: *Transition starts with people*, s.l. (Unpublished paper).

Duineveld, M., 2006: *Van oude dingen, de mensen, die voorbij gaan. Over de voorwaarden meer recht te kunnen doen aan de door burgers gewaardeerde cultuurhistories*, Delft (Ph.D. thesis Wageningen University).

Duineveld, M., 2008: The Socio-political Use of Environmental Perception, Interpretation and Evaluation Research, in H. Haan/R. van der Duim (eds.), *Landscape, Leisure and Tourism. Socio-spatial Studies in Experiences, Practices and Policies*, Delft.

Duineveld, M./R. Beunen/R. During/K.Van Assche/R. van Ark, 2009: It holds a promise... The relation between description and prescription in transition-research, in K. Poppen/K. Termeer/M. Slingerland (eds.), *Transitions Towards Sustainable Agriculture, Food Chains, in Peri-urban Areas*, Wageningen, 133-147.

Fischer, F., 1990: *Technocracy and the politics of expertise*, Newbury Park.

Fischer, F., 2000: *Citizens, experts and the environment: The politics of local knowledge*, London.

Flyvbjerg, B., 1998: *Rationality and Power: Democracy in Practice*, Chicago.

Foucault, M., 1994: Truth and juridical forms, in J.D. Faubion (ed.), *Power. Essential works of Foucault 1954-1984. Volume 3*, New York, 1-89.

Foucault, M., 2003: *"Society must be defended"*, Picador USA (Lectures at the College de France, 1975-76).

Frissen, P.H.A., 1996: *De virtuele staat. Politiek, bestuur, technologie: een postmodern verhaal*, Schoonhoven.

Gable, E.R. Handler, 2003: After authenticity at an American heritage site, in S. M. Low/D. Lawrence-Zunga (eds.), *The anthropology of space and place: locating culture*, Oxford, 370-386.

Gibbons, M., 1994: *The new production of knowledge: the dynamics of science and research in contemporary societies*, London.

Grood, J., de, 2003: *De amateur in het veranderende archeologisch bestel*, Archeobrief 2003, 25-26.

Haan, J. de, 1997: *Het gedeelde erfgoed: een onderzoek naar veranderingen in de cultuurhistorische belangstelling sinds het einde van de jaren zeventig*, Rijswijk.

Hajer, M., 2005: Coalitions, Practices, and Meaning in Environmental Politics: From Acid Rain to BSE., in D.R. Howarth/J. Torfing (eds.), *Discourse Theory in European politics: Identity, Policy and Governance*, Basingstoke, 297-315.

Hajer, M./H. Wagenaar (eds.), 2003: *Deliberative Policy Analysis: Understanding Governance in the Network Society*, Cambridge.

Hessing, W., 2002: *Voorbeeldbeleidsplan gemeentelijke archeologische monumentenzorg*, Amsterdam (Convent van Gemeentelijke Archeologen).

Hillier, J., 2002: *Shadows of power: an allegory of prudence in land-use planning*, New York.

Hoekstein, J., 2001: *Amateurs zijn onmisbaar*, Groningen.

Hoppe, R., 2005: Rethinking the science-policy nexus: from knowledge utilization and science technology studies to types of boundary arrangements, *Poiesis & Praxis: International Journal of Technology Assessment and Ethics of Science* 3, 199-215.

Houkes, R., 2003a: De grenzen van de wet, *Westerheem* 52, 170-172.

Houkes, R., 2003b: De grenzen van de wet (2), *Westerheem* 52, 211-213.

Houkes, R., 2003c: De grenzen van de wet (3), *Westerheem* 52, 245

Houkes, R., 2004: De grenzen van de wet (4), *Westerheem* 53, 21-23.

Howarth, D.R./J. Torfing (eds.), 2005: *Discourse Theory in European politics: Identity, Policy and Governance*, Basingstoke.

Jensen, O.B./T. Richardson, 2004: *Making European Space: Mobility, Power and Territorial Identity*, London.

Jonge, B. de, 2005: *Protection of Archaeology after 'Malta': One Treaty, Different Interpretations*, Amsterdam.

Kickert, W.J.M./E.H. Klijn/J.F.M. Koppenjan, 1997: *Managing complex networks: strategies for the public sector*, London.

Krauwer, M., 2004: Amateurarcheologie blijft toekomst hebben!, *Westerheem* 53, 25-27.

Kwaliteitsnorm, 2005: *Kwaliteitsnorm Nederlandse Archeologie versie 2.2*, Den Haag (College voor de Archeologische Kwaliteit).

Latour, B., 2004: *Politics of nature: how to bring the sciences into democracy*, Cambridge (Mass.)/London.

Lengkeek, J., 1994: *Een meervoudige werkelijkheid: een sociologisch-filosofisch essay over het collectieve belang van recreatie en toerisme*, Wageningen.

Lengkeek, J., 2000: Commercial and club marinas: Pay money or do the chores, *Loisir et société* 23, 371-388.

Lennon, J./M. Foley, 2000: *Dark tourism*, London.

Lorenz, C.F.G., 1998: *De constructie van het verleden: een inleiding in de theorie van geschiedenis*, Meppel.

Low, S. M., 2002: *Assessing the Values of Cultural Heritage*, Los Angeles (The Getty Conservation Institute Research Report).

Luhmann, N., 1987: *Soziale Systeme: Grundriss einer allgemeinen Theorie*, Frankfurt am Main.

Magits, V./S. van de Steene, 2003: *Interview met Prof. Dr. Eric Corijn. Filosoof en cultuursocioloog aan de VUB en de UA*, Sint-Lambrechts-Woluwe.

Majone, G./A. Wildavsky, 1979: Implementation as Evolution in J. Pressman/A. Wildavsky (eds.), *Implementation*, Berkeley, 163-180.

Olson, J.P., 2000: Organising European Institutions of Governance. A Prelude to an Institutional Account of Political Integration, in H. Wallace (ed.), *Whose Europe? Interlocking dimensions of integration*, London, 2-37.

Pestre, D., 2004: Thirty years of science studies: knowledge, society and the political, *History and Technology* 20, 351 - 369.

Pierre, J., 2000: *Debating governance, authority, steering, and democracy*, Oxford.

Pierson, P., 1996: The Path to European Integration: A Historical Institutionalist Analysis, *Comparative Political Studies* 29, 123-163.

Poel, K.R. de/J. van der Windt/N. Kruit/H. Elerie/T. Spek, 2000: *Essen in perspectief: een interactieve planningsbenadering in Spier, Wijster en Drijber (Midden-Drenthe)*, Groningen.

Rhodes, R.A.W., 1996: The New Governance: Governing without Government[1], *Political Studies* 44, 652-667.

Ribbens, K., 2002: *Een eigentijds verleden: alledaagse historische cultuur in Nederland, 1945-2000*, Hilversum.

Sela-Sheffy, R., 2006: Detachment and Engagement: Israelis' Everyday Verbal Representations of the Israeli Person' and the Contest for the Right to Condemn a Collective Identity, *Social Identities* 12, 325-344.

Shackley, M.L., 2002: Space, sanctity and service: the English Cathedral as heterotopia, *International Journal of Tourism Research* 4, 345-352.

Turnhout, E., 2003: *Ecological indicators in Dutch nature conservation. Science and policy intertwined in the classification and evaluation of nature*, Amsterdam.

Turnhout, E./M. Hisschemöller/H. Eijsackers, 2007: Ecological indicators: Between the two fires of science and policy, *Ecological Indicators* 7, 215-228.

Valletta, 1992: *European Convention on the Protection of the Archaeological Heritage (revised),Valletta 16.I.1992*, Strasbourg (Council of Europe).

Verhagen, J.G.M., 2003: Amateur-archeologie: van negatief gevoel naar positieve actie?, *Westerheem* 52, 229-268

Visie ROB, 1999: *Visie ROB op de betrokkenheid van amateur-archeologen bij de AMZ (concept)*. Amersfoort (Rijksdienst voor het Oudheidkundig Bodemonderzoek).

Vissers, P., 2003: Opgravingen door amateur-archeologen waren al passé!, *Westerheem* 52, 169-170

Wallace, H./ W. Wallace (eds.), 1996: *Policy-Making in the European Union*, Oxford.

Wamz, 2007: *Wet op de archeologische monumentenzorg*, Den Haag.

Weber, N./T. Chistophersen, 2002: The influence of non-governmental organizations on the creation of Natura 2000 during the European Policy process, *Forest Policy and Economics* 4, 1-12.

Willems, W./R.W. Brandt, 2004: *Dutch Archaeology Quality Standard*, Den Haag (State Inspectorate for Archaeology).

Wissink, B., 2000: *Ontworpen en ontstaan: een praktijktheoretische analyse van het debat over het provinciale omgevingsbeleid*, Den Haag.

Wollebaek, D./P. Selle, 2002: Does Participation in Voluntary Associations Contribute to Social Capital? The Impact of Intensity, Scope, and Type, *Nonprofit and Voluntary Sector Quarterly* 31, 32-61.

Zande, A.N. van der, 2006: *Het landschap verandert! Naar een mooi 21e eeuws landschap,* Wageningen (Inaugural lecture Wageningen University).

WEBSITES

www.awn-archeologie.nl/awn/watdoenwe.htm.
www.erfgoedinspectie.nl.
www.erfgoedinspectie.nl/page/archeologie/faq.
www.minocw.nl/malta/factsheets/fact1.html.
www.minocw.nl/toespraken/2001/034.html.
www.noaa.nl/content/nieuwe-content/hst2/h2.1.xml.asp.
www.racm.nl/content/xml_racm%5Cpd_archis-ii.xml.asp?toc=n4-6.
www.racm.nl/content/rubriek-n4-6.asp.
www.racm.nl/content/xml_racm%5Cpd_bk_amk-00.xml.asp?toc=n4-8.
www.racm.nl/content/xml_racm%5Cpd_archis-ii-03.xml.asp?toc=.

Note: All websites accessed 8 March, 2008. Most of these websites are still accessible via www.web.archive.org

7. Past pictures. Landscape visualization with digital tools

Jörg Rekittke[1] & Philip Paar[2]

ABSTRACT

'A picture is worth a thousand words.' Computer software and digital tools are increasingly used for the production of scientific and correct, data-based landscape visualizations. Some of the applied techniques are following old and time-tested rules of visual communication while others explore new fields of visual imagination. Many results of digital visualization depict future developments or scenarios but comparatively few generated pictures are related to the past. What can be used for projections of the future can also be utilized to look into the past. Past pictures can contribute to a better understanding of a wide range of scientific works. Archaeologists and historians by now definitely profit from the canon of available technology. The paper discusses the potential of state-of-the-art visualization techniques and presents selected scientific projects of past-related sophisticated landscape visualization.

KEY WORDS

Landscape visualization, before-after-representations, 3D vegetation, interactive promenade, 3D landscape models

1. INTRODUCTION

The lion's share of visualizations in the vast field of digital representation depict the future. Designers, investors and financiers are focusing on planned or projected results. Sciences however, most notably archeology and history, are also interested in visual representations and visual models of things from the past that became lost, buried or are uncertain. Landscape visualization with advanced digital tools can contribute to the understanding and exemplification of past landscapes and natural as well as man-made settings of all scales.

Landscape planning and design are not exactly known for being cutting-edge disciplines, utilizing newest technologies or to be first to apply available state-of-the-art tools. In these disciplines the theme 'visualization' is often still equated with 2D cartography and perspectives. Well-established Geographic Information Systems (GIS) even promoted this common perception because the 3D potential of this technology is only marginally utilized. In most ecological landscape projects the world is still considered as a flat disc which evokes quite a negative effect on the spatial sense and imagination and consequently on the acceptance of people and decision-makers. Furthermore, there is the difficulty that a multiplicity of space-oriented problems can only be represented in a rudimentary way by graphical illustration if they are not even invisible and thus undepictable (Paar/Rekittke 2003). "Even though the circles of planners in particular harp on about information and participation, there is still a lack of intelligible images. With a view to a more comprehensible and less abstract visualization by the planning disciplines, planners have to increase their effort to work with the third dimension." (Lange 1999, 9; translated for the present paper by the authors).

The generation of comprehensible three-dimensional depictions and models of landscapes, related to scientifically obtained data, is a field that goes well with the research scope of protecting and developing the archaeological-historical landscape (PDL/BBO). Hitherto the potential connection of digital 3D landscape visualization and archaeological landscape research is not being executed at a satisfactory rate. The examples described in the present paper might provide an impulse for some ideas of closer co-operation.

2. BEFORE AND AFTER-REPRESENTATION OR RATHER A THEN AND NOW-VIEW

Perspective drawings and illustrations as well as before and after representations in open space planning can look back on a long tradition. It was the landscape designer Humphry Repton (1752-1818), an innovative man not only in the range of project visualization but also in marketing and handling of technology for surveying and alignment (Carter *et al.* 1982; Petschek 2005), who first presented his designs and ideas to the clients by dint of beautiful watercolour picture books which became renowned as Red Books. Repton painted the as-is state of his projects on a moveable cover. By turning that cover back and forth, like the partial page of a book, the client could compare the subjacent planned scenario in an innovative way. With the aid of this special technique, Repton (Repton 1803), denoting his pictures as "slides", combined conventional media like books and sketches with a basic form of user interactivity, the viewer had to flip the partial pages again and again to see all details of the before and after effect. This met with great professional and economic success. This historical form of analogue landscape visualization (Fig. 1) set a methodological standard which is still relevant today.

Fig. 1
Red Books, vignette of a suggested landscape garden *(VercellonI 1994)*.
Above: as-is state of landscape; below: designed state of landscape.

Fig. 2
Mannahatta Project, New York City. Left: Split screen image of Manhattan 1609/today. Right: Manhattan 1609 and present day Times Square. *Source: Mannahatta Project.*

The powerful tool of before and after representation is the precursor of no less impressive then and now views. Imagining past landscapes is as difficult and challenging as figuring future scenarios. This is where the well-known proverb 'a picture is worth a thousand words' applies. One of the most recent and spectacular examples of a then and now view of a vanished landscape is represented by the ongoing 'Mannahatta Project' (Sanderson/Brown 2007) which compares the landscape of Manhattan in 1609 and today. Sanderson, a member of the Wildlife Conservation Society in New York City, and Brown, from the Department of Geography, Hunter College, City University of New York, show in their research (Fig. 2) that Manhattan formerly hosted a rugged topography watered by over 108 km of streams and at least 21 ponds flowing in and out of wetlands that covered nearly 10% of the island in the late eighteenth century. These features are largely representative of the landscape prior to European settlement. The scientists used ecological features interpreted from the British Headquarters Map and additional historical, ecological and archaeological information to hypothesize about the ecosystem composition of the pre-European island. "We suggest that 54 different ecological communities may once have been found on the island or in nearby waters, including chestnut-tulip tree forests, Hempstead Plains grasslands, freshwater and tidal marshes, hardwood swamps, peatlands, rocky headwater streams, coastal-plain ponds, eelgrass meadows, and culturally derived ecosystems, such as Native American village sites and fields. This former ecosystem mosaic, consisting of over 99% natural areas, stands in sharp contrast to the 21st-century state of the island in which only 3% of its area is dedicated to ecological management" (*ibidem* 2007, 545).

3. COMPUTER GRAPHICAL INTERACTIVE LANDSCAPE VISUALIZATION

Ever since the rediscovery of perspective drawings and illustrations in the Renaissance and the second spring of before and after representations in the computer era, methods of landscape visualization have only been moderately influenced by common technological progress (Danahy 2001). Pioneering work in the field of digital perspective landscape visualization is represented by first applications of 2D photomontages, also referred to as photosimulation, in the context of environmental impact studies, environmental assessment and planning as well as impact regulation under nature protection law. Two main aspects argue against the use of photosimulation in complex planning processes: 1. the empty promise of reality in so-called 'photo-realistic' images that are categorically dependent on the author's artistic and technical skills and subject to artistic freedom and 2. the inflexibility of custom-made images because of their non-conjunction to changing data resulting from updated analyses and ongoing planning process. The sole use of freeze images and pre-produced animations is scientifically questionable because these products mostly show just the best side of planning qua postcard beauty.

Whereas photomontages merely represent a small extract of reality seen from a fixed position of the beholder, interactive 3D models like in the Mannahatta project, can enable the beholder to enter space and to define an own critical viewpoint. "It is solely the possibility of the viewer to look around and move about which allows an intellectual examination within the spatial context (...) precisely because a discerning reflection and debate on spatial resolution models demands the possibility of experiencing correlations between landscape elements as well as spatial-temporal dependencies" (Danahy/Hoinkes 1999; translated for the present paper by the authors). Interactivity means freedom of choice and liberty of action. Interactivity prevents tendentious precooked visuals and idealistic embellished imagery.

The combination of digital geometric modelling and picture processing, so-called 'texture mapping', helped to get computer-graphical 3D landscape visualization broadly accepted (Danahy 2001). Detailed and realistic data, for example the leaf-texture of a 3D plant model, are extracted from the real world by scan or photography. Over the years, image quality could be significantly improved and doors were opened towards interactive real-time representations of virtual landscape models. The plant, principal performer at visual landscape simulations, is the element that proved to be one of the biggest challenges in virtual landscape representation. Recent examples (Deussen/Lintermann 2005; Rekittke/Paar 2006) indicate the viable level of detailed representations of plants and vegetation (Fig. 3).

When the application of digital representation techniques in landscape visualization processes is discussed, a differentiation regarding purpose of application and data availability should be made. Is it about support of analysis and assessment, planning visualization in participatory processes or landscape representation in marketing and public relations, for example tourism or fundraising? In other words, "who is the visualization for? What has to be shown, and how? What is really important? What is less relevant?" (Paar/Rekittke 2006, 516; translated for the present paper by the authors).

Sheppard (Sheppard 1999) states intelligibility, reliability and impartiality as three fundamental items for landscape visualizations. In many cases correct accurate landscape data are lacking, a fact that is disguised by extremely realistic looking visualizations. The more an alleged photo-realism is achieved, the deeper the insight that photo-realistic images are not categorically an appropriate solution for the communication of visual information (Ervin 2001; Rekittke/Paar/Coconu 2004; Paar/Rekittke 2006).

Fig. 3
3D visualization of a moor meadow, UNESCO Biosphere Reserve Entlebuch, Switzerland. *Source: Lenné3D and ETHZ 2005.*

4. THE DIGITAL EARTH AS MEDIUM AND PLATFORM

In his speech on a Digital Earth Al Gore (Gore 1998) said, "I believe we need (...) a multi-resolution, three-dimensional representation of the planet, into which we can embed vast quantities of geo-referenced data." In the meantime such visions have become digital reality. More and more local authorities, scientific groups, administrative institutions and all sorts of businesses think about possibilities to jump on the bandwagon of Google Earth, the most popular public digital globe on the Internet. They position themselves in an adequate and geographically correct way and offer reliable information to citizens, tourists, clients and others. For that purpose, the open Google Earth interchange KML format is well suited. It is supported by the Google-owned 3D CAD SketchUp and meanwhile by other companies in the GIS- and CAD-branch of trade. By dint of KML, pictures, maps, links to web pages and 3D-models can be placed on the earth's surface of Google Earth. If the user clicks a link on a web page or in an email, a KML-data file is loaded from an Internet server and Google Earth is launched if necessary. The user will be automatically guided to his/her destination. Just as easily, users can import the KML-data file back to a CAD-programme for editing. Up to now there is no digital rights management or other safety mechanism that would protect KML data providers against data thieves. At present a wild hotchpotch of 3D models is generated in Google's 3D Warehouse by public upload and use, exempt from charges. In Google Earth or similar interactive software systems, gardens and landscapes can so far only be represented in a quite rudimentary way. Some computer games, such as the successful German production *Far Cry* or the academic software Lenné3D-Player (Fig. 4), which was specially created for sophisticated interactive visualizations of vegetation and landscape, represent available state-of-the-art technology.

Fig. 4
Castle and virtual reconstruction of Gütergotz garden (Güterfelde). *Source: Christoph Hendrich/Lenné3D 2006.*

5. LENNÉ3D-PLAYER AND BIOSPHERE3D

The open-source project Biosphere3D (www.biosphere3d.org) supports multiple scales on a digital globe and focuses on real-time rendering of landscape scenery and convincing visualization of vegetation cover. The main target scale of the academic predecessor Lenné3D-Player was visualizing landscape from an eye-level perspective, enabling the user to wander through the planned or predicted landscape (Seiler/ Rekittke/Paar 2005). In 2005, numerous constraints like limited size of terrain and deficient scalability motivated the developers to restart from scratch. In the most recent version of Biosphere3D unlimited terrain can be visualized due to the use of a spherical terrain model and optimized data management. Satellite images and raster digital elevation models (DEM) can be combined with complex 3D models of vegetation to create photorealistic views and schematic visualizations of planned or past landscape scenarios (Fig. 5), virtually reconstructed historic gardens etc.

From October 2009 to 2012 (3 years runtime), Biosphere3D will be adopted and further developed for archeological and museum applications within the German research project *Berliner Skulpturennetzwerk* to create and contextualize an integrating virtual model of Pergamon, including the ancient city, surrounding landscape and marmoreal statues. Since Biosphere3D is free and open it can be extended to meet specific requirements and interfaces.

6. BACK TO THE FUTURE 01. THE VISUALIZATION OF WREST PARK GARDEN

Wrest Park Garden (Bedfordshire, England) is a rare relict of a formal garden, many of which have been redesigned into the style of the English landscape garden popular at the end of the eighteenth century. Today the visitor enters a 50-hectare garden that had once been part of an estate of 250 hectares. With its compositions of water and groves, Wrest Park Garden is regarded as one of the most beautiful gardens in Great Britain. After the end of the Second World War an agro-scientific institute made use of Wrest Park and for a short time it was administered by English Heritage (EH), the English national institution for cultural heritage and monument conservation. Even though the formal design elements like axes, paths, summer houses and channels have been largely conserved to this day, the park lost its original coulisse, the outer park. Today, visual axes direct into space, avenues end short and monotone fields have replaced the erstwhile wooded pasture land. In 2006, a pilot project for digital modelling and 3D visualization of Wrest Park was launched. It was accomplished by co-operation between English Heritage and Lenné3D GmbH, a research oriented company specializing in digital landscape visualization. The reason for the choice of Wrest Park as a case study was set up by the availability of archive material and a recent vegetation mapping that could identify most of the shrubs and trees in the park. The modelling of different time slices of the 300-year-old park history as well as the 3D computer visualization permitted the illustration of the lost and modified garden structures in an interactive, freely explorable mode (Fig. 6). Both the central part of the garden and the designed proximity, in its role of being an essential element of the ensemble, were modelled and visualized. Though the original structure of the main garden at Wrest Park is to a large extent conserved, the visualization aimed at allowing a better and scientific comparison of today's landscape and its former occurrence.

Therefore the viewer was confronted with the opportunity of a 'familiar' way of orientation in the garden space and an 'interactive promenade' (Fig. 7). With the aid of that special method of visualization the main aspects of maintenance could be clearly communicated to the viewer. These aspects comprise the conversion of the designed landscape coulisse (outer park), constructional elements and vegetation elements in the Old Park, the over-aged and too compact groves, visual axes and avenues that are blocked by growth of vegetation or have lost their particular reference point. Furthermore, the great many statues and other nineteenth century addenda which adulterated the style of the original garden (Way 2005), could be highlighted or blanked out in the digital visualization.

Fig. 5
Biosphere3D: Kimberley Climate Change Adaptation project, virtual scenario view from Taylors Mill.
Source: Olaf Schroth, University of Vancouver, 2009.

Fig. 6
Wrest Park Garden (1882) in a scientific 3D landscape model.
Left: Rowan Blaik/Lenné3D 2006 and Ordnance Survey Bedfordshire 1st edn. and (right) seen today via Google Earth.

7. BACK TO THE FUTURE 02. THE VISUALIZATION OF HEROD'S PALACE AND SURROUNDING LANDSCAPE

This case study[3], led by Agnes Kirchhoff (Lenné3D GmbH), is an example of a virtual reconstruction and visualization of an archaeological excavation using GIS, CAD and the open-source landscape scenery globe Biosphere3D. The aim was to virtually reconstruct Herod's winter palace and gardens near Jericho and to get a fact-based idea of its embeddedness in the ancient cultural landscape setting. The 3D models were visualized in an interactive real-time computer environment. The third Palace, a vast complex of buildings and gardens, was built from 15 to 10 BC. Historic sources including the Bible describe the area as fertile land supplied with water via irrigation systems (Garbrecht/Netzer 1991). The palm plantations surrounding the palace buildings were of great economic importance while the gardens inside the palace complex conveyed wealth and prestige. From 1973 to 1987, Prof. Dr Ehud Netzer lead the excavations of the palaces. For the visualization, resources like his archaeological data and attendant garden-archaeological excavations were used, as well as information deduced from historic references (Gleason 1987-1988; Netzer 2001-2004).

Fig. 7
Principle of an interactive promenade in Lenné3D *(sketch by Mele Brink in collaboration with Jörg Rekittke).*

Fig. 8
Virtual reconstruction of Herod's Third Winter Palace and Oasis in Jericho (*modelling by Jochen Mülder, Philip Paar, Agnes Kirchhoff*).

Firstly, a digital elevation model was constructed based on archaeologists' drawings and current, coarse-grain terrain data. ArcGlobe ESRI GIS data and archaeological maps were spatially combined with global ground data from NASA, satellite images and land use data. Next, the palace buildings were outlined in Google SketchUp. Each digital building model is based on the most detailed maps and archaeological drawings available. Measurements and proportions of isometric sketches were taken into consideration (Netzer 2001-2004). In a third step, the Palace gardens, the surrounding plantations and the natural vegetation in historic times were digitally reconstructed. A fieldwork-based species list was compiled and a plant distribution map was generated. Details of the gardens are just adumbrated since the visualization could not rely on consolidated findings. In such a situation omission is better than wild guesses. Finally, the elevation model, buildings and vegetation were loaded into Biosphere3D to simulate the ancient cultural landscape structure and scenery. The landscape reconstructions compose a vivid model and the 3D plant models in the scenery exemplify the interaction of buildings and land use, demonstrating the important role of the vegetation in its historical context (Fig. 8).

8. CONCLUSION

Two important points need to be discussed. First, the original landscape reality and beauty can never be digitally simulated in a truly convincing way. Nature, especially the beauty of nature, is utterly not reproducible. Second, media and techniques of representation have one axiomatic thing in common, their invention and development never result in the complete replacement of their forerunners but merely in the suppression or rather supplementation of them (Paar/Rekittke 2006). Progressive digitalization will not bring forth the extinction of conventional model making or hand-drawn sketches. On the contrary, it will perhaps result in a renaissance and increased appreciation of handcraft and drawing skills.

Nevertheless well-produced 3D landscape visualizations make sense. They are appropriate to translate data from past or present landscapes or gardens into intelligible pictures for experts and the public. Administrators, archaeologists and historians may profit from visualization tools that can be used to build up an interactive virtual working model. The biggest advantage of digital working models is their possibility of being constantly updated without loss of data or working time. Long-term activities, being a daily occurrence in past-oriented projects of archaeology and history, can be effectively supported by application of digital databases and visualization techniques. Organizations such as English Heritage are interested in the systematic application of digital visualization techniques and tools for future planning in the context of the preservation of historical garden monuments. It would definitely have been advantageous if a visualization project like Wrest Park could have been based on GIS-friendly data right from the start. A significant amount of work was invested in the conversion of fragmented CAD-data that had been on hand without referenced attributes like species/cultivar or elevation. If not already standard, it is commendable to use and archive data in GIS formats that should be combined with meta data. Google SketchUp has proved its worth as a fast and effective tool for the 3D modelling of constructional elements based on floor plans, historic illustrations or photographs.

Interactive landscape visualizations on Digital Earth have the potential to be developed into a perceptually efficacious, somehow 'natural' user interface for both experts and the general public. Planners, landscape architects and archeologists can publish their projects 'on earth', georeferenced and with time specification. Currently, mainstream tools and media like Google Earth already offer an easy and wide access to Internet users. Still, the digital tool box lacks professional features such as multiple terrains, digital rights management for user data and support for state-of-the-art representation of vegetation. However Google Earth is particularly powerful in that geo-data can be presented in a visually attractive mode intelligible to all and sundry. If interconnected, all media like historic maps, aerial photographs, photographs, paintings, movies etc. form important sources for grassroots examinations of local, regional and global landscape development. In the future, these media will be increasingly used as implemented 'layers' in interactive 3D landscape models.

Landscape visualization is more than picture production. Large scale past or future landscapes, such as the past landscape in place of today's urban Manhattan, are difficult to 'imagine'. Digital landscape visualizations and past pictures are helpful in initiating such imagination. Even if they can never show the truth, they can expand the limits of human imagination and this is something that modern archaeology and modern science is often dependent on. Past pictures can form a benchmark or starting basis for scientific discussion, formulation of working theses and public communication of research results. Correct visualizations can enlarge the scientific point of view. In the virtual reconstruction of Herod's Third Winter Palace and Oasis in Jericho, the visual inclusion of the past landscape and vegetation could deliver some new answers to architecture-related questions. Knowledge of landscape features and ecological circumstances sometimes leads to insights that would not be possible without having the bigger picture.

A society constantly exposed to visual media literally begins to expect the supply of visual products in any situation, independent of rationality or unreasonableness. Even the hardest science can no longer hide behind the lack of reliable data because scientists have to deliver some 'interesting' pictures, publish or perish. The systematic application and the careful and reasonable use of digital visual tools might allow a constant learning process concerning the critical handling of these seductive and dangerous eye-catchers. Dispelling them seems to be a hopeless undertaking. A picture is worth a thousand words, a trivial statement, but thoroughly true.

NOTES

1 National University of Singapore, Singapore.
2 Berlin, Germany.
3 A research project by the Leibniz Centre for Agricultural Landscape Research (ZALF) and Lenné3D GmbH, Berlin, supported by the German Israeli Foundation in collaboration with the University of Bayreuth.

REFERENCES

Carter, G./P. Goode/K. Laurie, K., 1982: *Humphry Repton Landscape Gardener 1752-1818*, Norwich.
Danahy, J.W., 2001: Technology for dynamic viewing and peripherical vision in landscape visualization, *Landscape and Urban Planning* 54, 125-137.
Danahy, J./R. Hoinkes, 1999: Schauen, Bewegen und Verknüpfen, *Garten+Landschaft* 11, 22-27.
Deussen, O./B. Lintermann, 2005: *Digital Design of Nature – Computer Generated Plants and Organics*, New York.
Ervin, S.M., 2001: Digital landscape modeling and visualization: a research agenda, *Landscape and Urban Planning* 54, 49-62.
Garbrecht, G./E. Netzer, 1991: *Die Wasserversorgung des geschichtlichen Jericho und seiner königlichen Anlagen*, Braunschweig (Leichtweiss-Institut für Wasserbau der Technischen Universität Braunschweig, Mitteilungen 115).
Gleason, K. L., 1987-1988: Garden Excavations at the Herodian Winter Palace in Jericho 1985–87, *Bulletin of the Anglo-Israel Archaeological Society* 7, 21-39.
Gore, A., 1998: The Digital Earth: Understanding Our Planet in the 21st Century. The Digital Earth Vision. Speech of the former US Vice President, California Science Center, Los Angeles. (URL http://portal.opengeospatial.org/files/?artifact_id=6210. Accessed 19 April, 2009).
Lange, E., 1999: Thema Visual Landscape, *Garten und Landschaft* 11, 9.
Netzer, E., 2001-2004: Hasmonean and Herodian Palaces at Jericho, *Final Reports of the 1973–1987 Excavations*, Jerusalem.
Paar, P./J. Rekittke, 2003: Geplante Landschaft – wie sie der Spaziergänger kennt. Lenné3D – Entwicklung eines Programms zur Landschaftsvisualisierung, *Stadt+Grün* 11, 26-30.
Paar, P./J. Rekittke, 2006: Nachhaltige Aufklärungsmethoden für die Informationsgesellschaft. Diplomatische Trittsteine zwischen landschaftlicher Realität und Vision, *Tagungsband CORP*, Wien, 511-518.
Petschek, P., 2005: Terrain Modeling with GPS and Real-Time in Landscape Architecture, in E. Buhmann/P. Paar/I.D. Bishop/E. Lange (eds.), *Trends in Real-time Visualization and Participation*, Heidelberg (Proc. at Anhalt University of Applied Sciences), 168-174.
Rekittke, J./P. Paar, 2006: Digital Botany. Thinking Eye, *Journal of Landscape Architecture* 2, 28-35 & cover.
Rekittke, J./P. Paar/L. Coconu, 2004: Dogma 3D. Grundsätze der non-photorealistischen Landschaftsvisualisierung, *Stadt+Grün* 7, 15-21.

Repton, H., 1803: *Observations on the theory and practice of landscape gardening: including some remarks on Grecian and Gothic architecture,* London/Oxford (facs.).

Sanderson, E.W./M. Brown, 2007: Mannahatta: An Ecological First Look at the Manhattan Landscape Prior to Henry Hudson, *Northeastern Naturalist* 14, 545-570.

Seiler, M./J. Rekittke/P. Paar, 2005: Spaziergang in einem verschwundenen Garten. Einsatz des Visualisierungssystems Lenné3D zur Reanimation des "Italienischen Kulturstücks" im Park von Sanssouci, *Die Gartenkunst* 1, 161-167.

Sheppard, S. R.-J., 1999: Regeln für die Nutzung der digitalen Kristallkugel, *Garten+Landschaft* 11, 28-32.

Vercelloni, V., 1994: *Historischer Gartenatlas. Eine europäische Ideengeschichte,* Stuttgart.

Way, T., 2005: *Wrest Park, Bedfordshire: Review of 1993 Masterplan,* Massachusetts (Ph.D. thesis).

WEBSITES

www.biosphere3d.org

8. Gazing at places we have never been. Landscape, heritage and identity

A comment on Jörg Rekittke and Philip Paar: 'Past Pictures. Landscape visualization with digital tools'.

Rob van der Laarse[1]

ABSTRACT

Acknowledging the paradigmatic impact of new digital techniques, this contribution questions the depoliticized conceptualization of landscape in modern landscape visualizations from a theoretical and historical perspective. Long after the earlier periods of formal gardening and landscaping, the present-day heritage focus on landscapes is looked upon as the real shift in the perception of landscapes, representing an appropriation by tourists and other groups of people without any historical connection to their history and nature.

KEY WORDS

Landscape, heritage; memory, sites, visual culture; national identity, authenticity, taste, cultural biography

1. INTRODUCTION

Landscapes are markers of personal as well as national taste, memory and identity. Reflecting on the topic of landscape visualisation, such as presented in this volume by Rekittke and Paar (Rekittke/Paar 2008; Ch. IV.7), I find it fascinating to see how the visual and spatial turns in cultural sciences are radiating into the field of landscape studies. Of course, this should not surprise us since visualisation has always been pivotal to landscape planning and design. That landscapes are not simply there, but shaped and reshaped by human activities, has been well known since Marc Bloch (Bloch 1931) and Hoskins (Hoskins1955) introduced their constructivist views on the making of French and English landscapes. This was still the basic paradigm of the following interpretative methods of landscape-*reading* used by historical geographers such as Meinig (Meinig 1979) and Cosgrove (Cosgrove 1984). Yet, what we see today is a shift from visual analysis to virtual reality or, to put it differently, from semiotics to *experience*. Swapping 2D cartography for 3D computer simulations, new methods of landscape visualization are closely related to modern heritage practices and produce experiences by commodifying the past as *sites*. This might be demonstrated by catchwords like 'staged authenticity' (MacCannell 1976), 'tourist gazing' (Urry 1991; *idem* 2002), 'consumption of places' (Urry 1995; Ashworth 2005), '*lieux de mémoire*' (Nora 2002[2]), 'destinisation' (Kirshenblatt-Gimblett 1998), '*Erinnerungsräume*' (Assmann 1999) and 'prosthetic memory' (Landsberg 2004). What we consume as heritage are brand new fabrications (Lowenthal 1998) which help us to experience 'our' culture rooted in nature and history, or more precisely in landscapes (Fig. 1).

2. LIVING AND VISUAL LANDSCAPES

Such a dynamic approach of both the production, consumption, making and experiencing of historical landscapes confronts us with at least two paradoxes. First, landscapes are cultural artefacts with many

Fig. 1
Amsterdam heritage students gazing at the Netherland's only (reconstructed) Baroque garden from the roof of the Het Loo Royal Palace near Apeldoorn.
Photo: author, 2006.

pasts forgotten and remembered (Holtorf/Williams 2006). Second, there is probably nothing more local than a living landscape and nothing more global than European landscape identities (Agnew 1998). Provided that it is not used in a Hegelian way as a layering of stages, the metaphor of cultural biography (Samuels 1979; Kopytoff 1986; Kolen 2005) seems to me an ideal tool to deal with such contradictions. Landscapes are after all presentist constructions which use local stories and place memories for the fabrication of regional identities while applying universal meanings to stereotyped heritage-scapes such as 'the Alps', Tuscany or 'Holland'.

This is of fundamental importance for a better understanding of what we name a landscape because the idea of landscape (Johnson 2007) refers at the same time to the material (or godly) creation of a living landscape, as expressed in the Dutch and German notion of 'land-shaped', and to the mental perception of a visual landscape, as expressed in the English notion of 'land-scape'. While all land is man-made and owned, only the second meaning offers the possibility of external aesthetic representations and touristic appropriations. In other words, what we visualise as a landscape is not identical to the landscape as perceived by its makers and inhabitants. Although developed in a long-term process of generational path dependence, a landscape becomes decontextualised when commodified as a tourist experience. Reading an 'authentic' historical landscape is therefore quite the opposite of gazing at a heritage site.

3. REPRESENTATIONS

Landscape is thus a hybrid concept which historically refers to both human environments and specific religious and aesthetic representations. Whether idealised as an Arcadian paradise, propagated as a cradle of picturesque patriotism or feared as a sublime, inhospitable place, landscapes have for centuries been attributed with meanings. However, there is also an element of hyper reality in the perception of environments *as* landscapes.

The idea of landscape goes back to Renaissance art and scholarly tradition in which nature has been conceptualised as *ordo et varietas,* a twofold representation of God's harmonic order and the infinite multiplicity of His Creation (Whyte 2002; Bakker 2004). In the early modern period, in particular in Italy,

France and the Netherlands, the idea of cultivating nature by order and symmetry played an important role in the creation of courtly gardens (Fig. 2; De Jong 2001; Bezemer Sellers 2003) in which political power was represented by impressive sculptures, vistas and waterworks visualised in bird's eye views (Mukerji 1997; Cosgrove 2008). With the Enlightenment's focus on sensitivity, however, these Italianising French or Dutch Baroque gardens gave way to English landscape gardens designed according to the laws of nature. As these natural gardens were made for walking, the gaze from above gave way to an experience from below.

Because the modern idea of landscape goes back to this revolution of taste at about 1800, it is tempting to see William Gilpin's *Cult of the picturesque* or Humphrey Repton's *Red Books* as forerunners to the modern packaging of the past. No doubt their landscape visualisations by way of 3D scenic compositions, perceived as living landscape paintings, lay the foundation for contemporary landscape design and experiential heritage tourism (Prentice 2001). Surely one could even find parallels with present-day experience economy in which work is regarded as theatre and business as stage (Gilmore/Pine 1999). Yet, such parallels overlook that landscapes are always representations of specific mindscapes (Löfgren 1999). Just as landscaping in the past was more than merely a technique of visualisation, present-day digital landscape visualisations should not be simply regarded as the repackaging of old ideas. The Rousseauan mindset expressed a longing for a purity (Van der Laarse/Labrie/Melching 1998) that is completely absent in both the seventeenth century formal gaze of Cartesianism as well as that of present-day tourists.

To be sure, wild landscapes during the picturesque decade were no less designed at the drawing table than pre-modern Baroque gardens or postmodern heritage-scapes, as might be illustrated by the well-known engraving of Repton with his theodolite or *Kippregel*. We seldom see landscape gardens, however, represented by 'imperialist' bird's eye views or other imprints of power. Instead of copper engravings and oil paintings or film and photography in our period, watercolours were the usual medium for the representation of landscape gardens. This fast technique belonged to a world of picturesque tours in

Fig. 2
Reconstructed vista of the Dutch Oranienbaum garden in Kulturstiftung Dessau-Wörlitz, Germany.
Photo: author, 2006.

which visitors moved from scenery to scenery appealing to different emotions or sentiments (Fig. 3; Van der Laarse 2005a; *idem* 2007). And this *movement* across the landscape was precisely what Repton's *Red books* showed in their sequential designs of estate properties (Rogger 2007).

4. HERITAGE AND IDENTITY

Unfortunately, heritage designers are not trained in historical contextualisation and hardly pay attention to conflicting visual narratives (Gross 1985). Transformed into sites, the cultural biography of places is often reduced to an iconic period, such as the Dutch Golden Age and the Second World War. Though offering fascinating possibilities for interactive museum experiences, this also holds true for most 3D computer models of historical buildings and landscapes. Every spatial staging of the past needs framing. By singling out one period, existing traces of other periods may even be wiped out by heritage visualisations of *invisible* pasts, e.g. simulacrums of Celtic fields, the Roman *limes* (Fig. 4), Baroque gardens or battlefields.

As such at every heritage site we have to deal with conflicting notions of authenticity and identity. On the one hand a nostalgic longing for authenticity ask for timeless, place-bound experiences in a post-modern consumer society (Gilmore/Pine 2007), while on the other hand sites are permanently 'under construction'. In spite of the common Dutch metaphor of history frozen under the cheese cover, heritage landscapes are continuously transformed in form and meaning by repeating appropriations of competing inheritors. Instead of offering such a dynamic interpretation of landscapes as permanently gazed, framed, mapped and staged by acts of signification, however, most heritage reconstructions end up in a cultural vacuum with the exclusion of politics. In fact, this apparent depolitisation marks the difference between earlier garden and landscape architecture and postmodern heritage design.

Propagating the power or taste of their creators, gardens in the past were above all political landscapes (Warnke 1994). While this was obvious in the Baroque era, it also applies to the picturesque. Although our idea of landscape owes much to the sentimental taste of the landlords of this later period who

Fig. 3
Landscaping of the coastal estate of Bergen (province North Holland) with the Zeeweg designed by Leonard Springer who was commissioned by the Van Reenen family *(from Van der Laarse, 2001)*.

Fig. 4.
Roman watchtower at Vechten, the Netherlands.

literally owned the land, modern heritage experts and landscape designers, however, lack a natural bond or attachment with their sites. While landscaping was primarily an active ideological project aimed at the material and aesthetic appropriation of 'picturesque' environments by self-proclaimed national elites (Bermingham 1994; Van der Laarse/Kuiper 2005c), heritage experts may be regarded no more than protectors of the former creations of these connoisseurs by pedigree.

However, in practice heritage-scapes are also political. Instead of protection and conservation most heritage interventions opt for new reconstructions and developments. The politics of heritage could therefore be very useful in periods of war and nation building. By far the most radical appropriation of this sort was the German *Ostplanung* of 1939-1945, which transformed Polish landscapes and Jewish *sjtetls* into 'age-old' Teutonic 'Heimat'-landscapes (Wolschke-Bulmahn 2003; Van der Laarse 2009). In the Israeli occupied territories nowadays it is striking to notice a similar coalition of ideologists, colonists and planners legitimating a Zionist mapping of Palestinian land by historical claims on the Holy Land supported by archaeological excavations of ancient Jewish palaces in the Jordan valley in the West Bank. Less contested, however, comparable politics of identity might be found in many countries. Thus in the Netherlands, recently shook to its foundations by a wave of populism, the government has singled out nine highway panoramas, chosen by 'the people' in Internet polls, for protection as national landscapes (Van der Laarse 2008). Just as landscape has been regarded as a pivotal marker of national identity in Europe since early nineteenth century Romanticism, the nationalisation of the masses (Mosse 1975) has been reinforced almost everywhere by a nationalisation of history and nature.

5. CONCLUSION

The tensions exposed between living and visible landscapes, contrasting representations of order and experience and the longing for authenticity and identity make clear that landscapes cannot be reduced to fixed forms and meanings. Extrinsic similarities may conceal intrinsic differences. This also applies to landscape visualisations. Therefore, the present-day idea of a heritage experience is completely unfamiliar with the cult of the picturesque. What landscaping was opting for was an elitist invention of an upper class hunting paradise by radically *breaking* with the past, while heritage management in the present is opting for the *reinvention* of a purified and canonised past, packaged for touristic consumption and identity politics. If landscapes are mindscapes then postmodernity is not represented in traditional ordinary landscapes but in sites referring to them in the form of heritage-scapes. Instead of mourning about what is lost in present-day landscapes, we might therefore better question the fetish of the original and ask who owns and *dis*owns the place. As heritage is always about loss and appropriation and biased by ethics and politics, it is by definition using the past for the present (Van der Laarse 2005b; Smith

2006). In other words, what is on the map is just as important as what is left out. The growing popularity of Google Earth, computer games and 3D models of historical environments seems to me a perfect demonstration of this virtual identification with the appropriated heritage of others, allowing more and more people to experience 'their' past by gazing at places they have never been.

NOTES

1 University of Amsterdam, the Netherlands.

REFERENCES

Agnew, J., 1998: European Landscape and Identity, in B. Graham (ed.), *Modern Europe. Place, Culture & Identity*, London, 213-33.

Ashworth, G., 2005: Heritage and the Consumption of Places, in R. van der Laarse (ed.), *Bezeten van vroeger. Erfgoed, identiteit en musealisering*, Amsterdam, 193-206.

Assmann, A., 1999: *Erinnerungsräume. Formen und Wandlungen des kulturellen Gedächtnisses*, München.

Bakker, B., 2004: *Landschap en wereldbeeld van Van Eyck tot Rembrandt*, Bussum.

Bermingham, A., 1994: System, Order, and Abstraction: the Politics of English Landscape Drawing around 1795, in W.J.T. Mitchell (ed.), *Landscape and Power*, Chicago/London, 77-102.

Bezemer Sellers, V., 2001: *Courtly gardens in Holland 1600-1650. The House of Orange and the Hortus Batavus*, Amsterdam/Woodbridge.

Bloch, M., 1956³ (1931): *Les caractères originaux de l'histoire rurale française*, Paris.

Cosgrove, D.E., 1984: *Social Formation and Symbolic Landscape*, Wisconsin.

Cosgrove, D.E., 2008: *Geography and Vision. Seeing, Imagining and Representing the World*, London/New York.

Gilmore, J. E./B. Joseph Pine II, 1999: *The Experience Economy. Work is Theatre & Every Business a Stage*, Boston.

Gilmore, J.E./B. Joseph Pine II, 2007: *Authenticity. What consumers really want*, Boston.

Gross, L.,1985: Life vs. Art: The Interpretation of Visual Narratives, *Studies in Visual Communication* 11, 2-11.

Holtorf, C./H. Williams, 2006: Landscapes and memories, in D. Hicks/M.C. Beadry (eds.), *The Cambridge Companion to Historical Archaeology* , Cambridge, 235-254.

Hoskins, W.G., 1955: *The Making of the English Landscape*, London.

Johnson, M., 2007: *Ideas of Landscape*, Oxford.

Jong, E. de, 2001: *Nature and Art. Dutch garden- and landscape-architecture, 1650-1740*, Philadelphia.

Kirshenblatt-Gimblett, B., 1998: *Destination Culture. Tourism, Museums, and Heritage*, Berkeley.

Kolen, J., 2005: *De biografie van het landschap. Drie essays over landschap, geschiedenis en erfgoed*, Amsterdam (Ph.D. thesis VU University).

Kopytoff, I., 1986: The cultural biography of things: commodization as process, in A. Appadurai (ed.), *The Social Life of Things*, Cambridge, 64-91.

Laarse, R. van der, 2001: Ten geleide. Notabele levensvormen, in R. van der Laarse (ed.), *Van goeden huize. Elite in en rondom Alkmaar in de negentiende eeuw*, Alkmaar, 7-32.

Laarse, R. van der, 2005a: De beleving van de buitenplaats. Smaak, toerisme en erfgoed, in R. van der Laarse (ed.), *Bezeten van vroeger. Erfgoed, identiteit en musealisering*, Amsterdam, 59-87.

Laarse, R. van der, 2005b: Erfgoed en de constructie van vroeger, in R. van der Laarse (ed.), *Bezeten van vroeger. Erfgoed, identiteit en musealisering*, Amsterdam, 1-28.

Laarse, R. van der, 2007: Burgers als buitenlui. Het landschap der notabelen, in J.H. Furnée (ed.), *Stijlen van Burgers*, Groningen, 7-38.

Laarse, R. van der, 2008: Panorama's op vroeger. De culturele dynamiek van het landschap, *Levend erfgoed. Vakblad voor public folklore & public history* 5, 10-20.

Laarse, R. van der, 2009: Kunsten, kampen en landschappen. De blinde vlek van het dadererfgoed, in F. van Vree/R. van der Laarse (eds.), *De dynamiek van de herinnering. Nederland en de Tweede Wereldoorlog in een internationale context*, Amsterdam, 169-195.

Laarse, R. van der/Y.B. Kuiper (eds.), 2005: *Beelden van de buitenplaats. Elite en elitevorming in Nederland in de negentiende eeuw*, Hilversum.

Laarse, R. van der/A. Labrie/W. Melching (eds.), 1998: *Het verlangen naar zuiverheid. De cultuur van Europa*, Amsterdam.

Landsberg, A., 2004: *Prosthetic Memory. The Transformation of American Remembrance in the Age of Mass Culture*, New York.

Lowenthal, D., 1998: Fabricating Heritage, *History & Memory* 10, 1-16.

Löfgren, O., 1999: *On Holiday, A History of Vacationing*, Berkeley.

MacCannell, D., 1999² (1976): *The Tourist. A New Theory of the Leisure Class*, London.

Meinig, D.W., 1979: Reading the landscape. An appreciation of W.G. Hoskins and J.B. Jackson, in D.W. Meinig (ed.), *The Interpretation of Ordinary Landscapes. Geographical Essays*, New York/Oxford, 195-244.

Mosse, G., 1975: *The Nationalization of the Masses. Political Symbolism and Mass Movements in Germany from the Napoleonic Wars trough the Third Reich*, New York.

Mukerji, C., 1997: *Territorial ambitions and the gardens of Versailles*, Cambridge.

Nora, P. (ed.), 2002² (1984): *Les lieux des mémoires*, Paris.

Prentice, R., 2001: Experiential Cultural Tourism: Museums & the Marketing of the New Romanticism of Evoked Authenticity, *Museum Management and Curatorship* 19, 5-26.

Rekittke, J./P. Paar, 2008: Descriptive landscape visualization – old wine in new skins. Methods of landscape visualization (Paper *Interactive NWO-BBO Symposium The Protection and development of Dutch archaeological-historical landscape: the European dimension*, Lunteren 20-23 May 2008).

Rogger, A., 2007: *Landscapes of Taste. Humphrey Repton's Red Books*, London.

Samuels, M.S., 1979: The Biography of Landscape. Cause and Culpability, in D.W. Meinig (ed.), *The Interpretation of Ordinary Landscapes. Geographical Essays*, New York/Oxford, 51-88.

Smith, L., 2006: *Uses of Heritage*, London/New York.

Urry, J., 1995: *Consuming Places*, London.

Urry, J., 2002² (1991): *The Tourist Gaze*, London.

Warnke, M., 1994: *Political Landscape. The Art History of Nature*, London.

Whyte, I.D., 2002: *Landscape and History since 1500*, London.

Wolschke-Bulmahn, J., 2003: 'Teutonic' Landscape Heritage: The Search for National Identity in Early-twentieth-century German Landscape Design, in R. Shannan Peckham (ed.), *Rethinking Heritage. Cultures and Politics in Europe*, London/New York, 139-154.

9. 'Green' and 'blue' developments. Prospects for research and conservation of early prehistoric hunter-gatherer landscapes

Bjørn Smit[1]

ABSTRACT

This article discusses the possibilities of future research of early prehistoric remains within large-scale nature management and water management developments. It is especially in these projects within the Archaeological Heritage Management that a landscape approach can be used. The landscape approach is seen as a crucial way of researching remains of communities from early prehistory. These large-scale development projects take place in landscape zones where archaeological remains might be found which hint at the social and ritual use of the landscape in early prehistory. This new information has to be integrated in existing (mainly economic) models of early prehistoric land use. This information can eventually be used to communicate the way of life of these early prehistoric communities and their large-scale land use to a wider public.

KEY WORDS

Early prehistory; nature development, water management; multidisciplinary research; northern Netherlands

1. INTRODUCTION

About 50% of the time span of our cultural history consists of activities and land use by early prehistoric hunter-gatherers. Unfortunately, the archaeological remains of these activities hardly seem spectacular at first sight. In this article the focus will be on surface scatters roughly dating to the Late Palaeolithic and Mesolithic (c. 12,300-4,900 cal BC). In particular, on dry Pleistocene coversands in the Netherlands these remains consist of nothing more than several flint scatters or pits filled with charcoal which presumably functioned in terms of food preparation. Based on these remains a picture may emerge of early prehistoric people spending their time digging pits, burning fire and knapping flints. It is believed that this is a meagre and uniform picture which does not resemble reality.

2. THE NATURE OF EARLY PREHISTORIC SOCIETIES

Analysis of the enormous quantitative number of, at first sight, uniform Stone Age sites presents a picture of societies with a huge spatial, diachronic and synchronic variation in for example migration patterns, resource procurement strategies and probably site types. One of the most important characteristics of early prehistoric hunter-gatherer societies is their large-scale land use and certain degree of mobility (Kelly 1995). From ethnography we know that sizes of home ranges can vary to an enormous degree, for example the Nunamiut Inuit have a home range area of 5400 km² (Binford 1983; Jochim 2003). There were probably different degrees of mobility so this did not mean that there was no special attachment to particular places like burial grounds or central places. The existence of these locations is known from

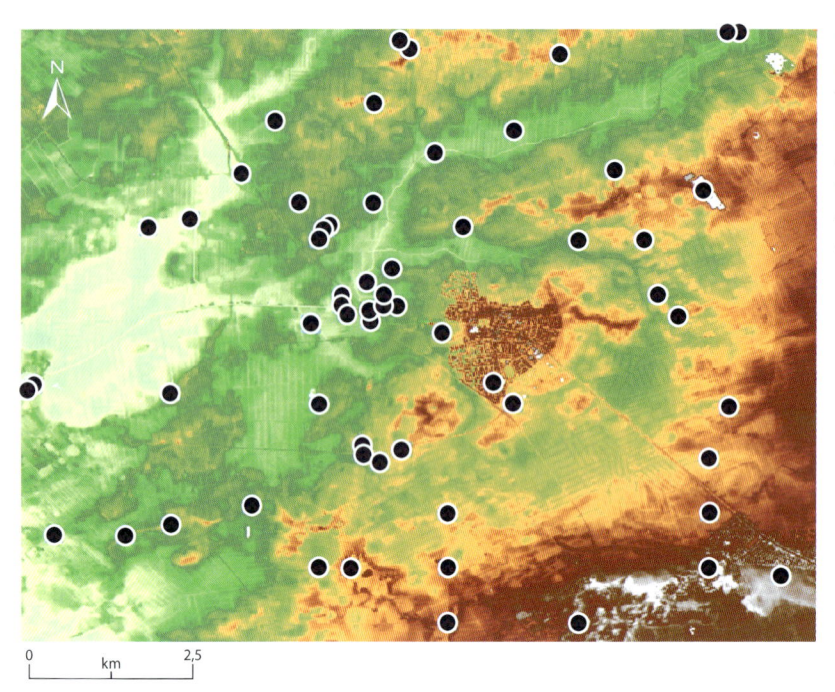

Fig. 1
Friesland, Tjonger Valley. The red zones are the high areas and the green zones the lower areas, the black dots depict the archaeological sites in the area. *Figure: B.I. Smit.*

ethnography but the archaeological record of the northern Netherlands is meagre in this aspect, so-called palimpsests (multi-component sites) being the exception.

The reason for mobility is largely due to the fact that these hunter-gatherer societies used resources which were available at different places at different times in their surrounding environment. Besides this purely economic factor which produces mobility, the formation and maintenance of social relations with other social groups in their environment also results in mobility. Mobility entails the movement of different social units within society, like the movement of families to yearly aggregation camps or the more specific mobility of task groups which go on hunting trips of several days for which they leave the residential settlement. Mobility therefore acts on differential spatial and temporal scales.

The definition of one particular spatial scale which fits our archaeological dataset is very difficult because of the enormous time depth of different sites with archaeological material. It is almost impossible to establish synchronic relations between different sites. However the number of sites known suggests a widely spaced use of the landscape in early prehistory, both economically as well as socially (this latter aspect is predominantly derived from ethnography on hunter-gatherer communities). Therefore we might imagine that in early prehistory activities took place in enculturated landscapes the size of which can only be guessed. In terms of archaeological research and the combination of relevant information one should think of research areas of one or even several square kilometres.

The archaeological material which is the result of these activities throughout the landscape is formed by different small to large flint clusters, dump zones of organic material like animal remains and indications for active transformations of the environment such as the intentional burning of reeds of trees to create open spaces, attract wild animals or improve growth conditions for favourable plants (for a general review of Dutch Stone Age archaeology see Deeben *et al.* 2005; Louwe Kooijmans *et al.* 2005).

The archaeological and palaeobiological remains which provide information on these activities may be encountered on different landforms, like cover-sand ridges, cover-sand dunes, brook valleys and perhaps near or in pingo ruins. This substantiates the view that early prehistoric people used several different landscape zones or environments. By use, I mean the use of the landscape in its widest form, so not only from a economic viewpoint but also from other viewpoints such as social and probably ritual (Verhart/Arts 2005). Unfortunately, the archaeological record of the dry Pleistocene soils (surface scatters) is dominated by inorganic remains from which only the economic sphere of communities can be reconstructed. For example, only a few locations are known which might be interpreted as burial sites, the same goes for locations where ritual depositions were made in the Late Palaeolithic and Mesolithic. Therefore only sparse remains are discovered that hint at other than the economic use of the landscape, which is definitely the result of research bias amongst other things.

Research on early prehistoric societies therefore benefits the most when a landscape approach is adopted during research. "The landscape paradigm is a strategy/approach which archaeologists can use as a pattern which connects human behaviour with particular places and times." (Anschuetz/Wilshusen/Scheick 2001, 157). In such an approach all aspects of daily life, whether economical, social or ritual, can be integrated.

In particular, transitions between landscape zones have been favourable activity zones and these are described as gradient zones. Research in the former peat colonies in the province of Groningen and the brook valleys in the northern Netherlands has provided clear indications for occupation in the available gradient zones (Groenendijk 1997; De Boer/Roymans 2002; Peeters/Niekus 2005; Stapert 1985; *idem* 2005). These gradient zones are formed by relief steps between different landscape units, such as transitions between cover-sand ridges and cover-sand plateaus or between cover-sand dunes and brook valleys. Everyone familiar with the Dutch landscape will realize that these changes in relief are very limited. However, in these gradient zones marked differences in vegetation are present and were presumably present in the past. This is not to suggest that this vegetation has remained the same throughout history. These gradient zones contained a rich variety of flora and fauna which probably changed from season to season. The connection between these gradient zones was formed by several different 'paths' which criss-crossed the entire landscape, in particular streams, brook valleys and track ways were relevant communication arteries (Mc Glade 1999, 476). It is believed that future research on brook valleys may result in (preferably organic) finds which can be interpreted beyond the economic aspects of early prehistoric communities and perhaps hint at ritual and social dimensions.

The relationship between flint sites and gradient zones is illustrated in Fig. 1. In this picture, several Stone Age sites are plotted on a digital elevation model of a part of the Tjonger brook valley in the southeast part of the province of Friesland.

In 1981 a hunting/kill site dating to the Late Mesolithic (c. 7000-4900 cal BC) was discovered in the Tjonger brook valley. Research conducted in 1981, 2002 and 2003 shows that at least four aurochs were slaughtered at this site. This slaughtering was probably initially aimed at subsistence needs but indications for sacral or ritual use of the landscape were also found (Prummel *et al.* 1999; Prummel/Niekus 2005). These finds are just one example as the ethnographic record shows that on some occasions hunter-gatherers perceive their environment as sacred or enculturated (Zvelebil 2003).

The early prehistoric landscape can be visualized as a rich varied landscape in terms of dynamics, relief, flora, fauna and use by prehistoric people compared to the subsequent predominately agricultural landscape which has evolved into the current monotonous modern agricultural landscape. An early prehistoric landscape can be summarized as a large-scale landscape in which small-scale activities occurred.

3. TOWN AND COUNTRY PLANNING IN THE NETHERLANDS: OPPORTUNITIES FOR RESEARCH AND DEVELOPMENT OF EARLY PREHISTORIC REMAINS?

The Netherlands is one of the most densely populated countries in the world (Van der Heiden 2005; Rensink/Deeben/Peeters 2006). It needs no elaborate discussion that town and country planning practices play a significant role in government policy. Although densely populated, farmland and meadows still contribute to 60% of the total land surface. A specific characteristic of the Netherlands is the long agricultural and cultural history of this man-made landscape (Haartsen 1995). By stating this characteristic implicitly, the legacy of past hunter-gatherer societies is ignored. The Dutch landscape is seen as a predominantly agricultural landscape. The general belief is that history started with the advance of agriculture (Waterbolk 1999). From this moment onwards, prehistoric people are envisaged as households with houses, some fields and cattle instead of groups of wandering people who performed activities in their surrounding environment. In modern western societies hunter-gatherers are generally not accepted as the cultural ancestors of our modern society (Raemaekers 2006; Zvelebil/Moore 2006; Peeters 2007). The first farming communities did not arrive in an empty landscape and aspects of early prehistoric hunter-gatherer societies and their land use should be integrated in the story of prehistory which is spread to the general public. It could even be stated that information on this early part of our prehistory can contribute to a more realistic picture of the development of the present appearance of the Netherlands in the past and present.

In my opinion, several opportunities are present within current and future town and country planning projects from which the research and heritage management of early prehistoric landscapes may benefit. Currently two major aspects within town and country planning are relevant, these are the so-called 'blue' and 'green' developments (see also Rensink/Gerritsen/Roymans 2006; Spek/Brinkkemper/Speleers 2006). In the course of history and in the present, water management has always been an important feature of the Netherlands. Besides water management, nature development is also a relevant theme in country planning projects both in terms of creating recreational facilities as well as providing safe havens for different floral and faunal species. The formation of a National Ecological Network (*Ecologische Hoofdstructuur*) is a nationwide initiative to create a network of interlinked nature reserves. The spatial scale of these developments provides an excellent podium for the integration of initiatives which try to unravel and preserve the normally hidden early prehistoric landscapes. These landscapes can literally be covered because of sedimentation of younger deposits but in several instances these landscapes are metaphorically covered because their appearance is not known or broadcast to a wider public.

The scale of many land development practices provides possibilities of creating connections between the past and the present. Most developments are aimed at large areas such as landscapes, landscape units or geomorphologic entities like cover-sand ridges, brook valleys etc.

On the one hand 'green' organizations like the State Forestry Service (*Staatsbosbeheer*) or the Dutch Society for the Protection of Nature Monuments (*Natuurmonumenten*) initiate the development of large environmental landscapes of nature reserves which are connected through several nature corridors. On the other hand 'blue' organizations such as the Department of Waterways and Public Works

(*Rijkswaterstaat*) and water-board districts (*waterschappen*) initiate numerous projects to facilitate and improve water management. These projects are primarily aimed at aspects of storage and drainage. However, in these plans nature development is often integrated as a secondary objective particularly when retention facilities are transformed into large nature areas.

A final common factor in these processes is an ambition to create or facilitate recreational facilities or opportunities in these restructured areas. In these recreational zones the Dutch public can retreat and relax when they want to escape their urban environment. With reference to the National Ecological Network, the Ministry of Agriculture, Nature and Food Quality (Ministerie van Landbouw, Natuur en Voedselkwaliteit) website states that "large nature reserves provide many opportunities for recreation. (…) Large nature reserves have a growing importance in terms of water management." (www.minlnv.nl, November 2007; my translation).

4. EXPANDING RESEARCH POSSIBILITIES

These developments in water management and creation of nature reserves in combination with recreational ambitions offer opportunities to integrate the elements of early prehistoric societies in these projects. They provide a means of enlarging the awareness and valuation of the early prehistoric period. In these projects archaeological research may be integrated on a landscape scale instead of a site focussed approach which in most cases only brings attention to hardly attractive archaeological remains.

As stated previously, the daily life of early prehistoric hunter-gatherers was focussed on their surrounding environments and their activities were performed in different landscape zones. Their life was not solely dominated by flint knapping as current archaeological research may sometimes suggest. These lives took place in different environments and the same environments or comparable gradient zones are at present the areas in which water and nature development plans are initiated. Projects by 'blue' and 'green' organizations usually intersect several gradient zones. During the execution of these projects it is likely that archaeological remains dating to early prehistory may be detected in zones which in the past have largely been ignored (Gerritsen/Rensink 2004; Roymans 2005; KNA 2007). It is also believed that material other than flint remains will be present in the project areas because of the fact that the majority of these projects are planned in the 'wetter' zones of the present landscape (like brook valleys or fens). In these wet zones it is likely that potentially well preserved organic remains dating to the early prehistory may be present (Groenewoudt *et al.* 2001; Gerritsen/Rensink 2004; Rensink/Gerritsen/Roymans 2006; KNA 2008 on the potential and research methods of brook valleys; Prummel *et al.* 2002; Prummel/Niekus 2005 for specific finds from the Tjonger brook valley). Analyses of these remains could enrich our knowledge about the environment and other aspects of early prehistoric societies. Peeters' study of early prehistoric remains in the Flevoland province provides ideas on which types of data can be gathered, both archaeological, ecological and environmental, and which types of remains other than lithics may be expected in these 'wetter' zones (Peeters 2007).

5. THE BIOGRAPHY OF LANDSCAPES

One could argue that the current interest in gradient zones is comparable to the interest in these zones in early prehistory, although of course the activities employed are different. This long-term land use can effectively be described in a so-called biography of landscapes (Roymans 1995; Rooijakkers 1999; Hidding/Kolen/Spek 2001). In these biographies the different functions and use of these gradient zones and the principles determining them in the past and present are presented and substantiated and are hopefully an inspiration for development initiatives.

A positive aspect is the fact that the terms or concepts used in nature development plans can easily be adopted or adapted and used by archaeologists when formulating a biography of an early prehistoric landscape, thereby avoiding conflicts and miscommunication between different parties. The goal within nature development plans is to enlarge the number and variation of species within landscape zones and the connection between different ecological zones to counter landscape fragmentation is promoted. Additionally in these projects the focus on restoration and conservation of specific characteristics of landscapes, the general vision of conservation and protection will probably be approved by many archaeologists. In the National Ecological Network, which is often integrated in nature development plans, a connection between different ecological zones is propagated which should lead to the establishment of a system of nature reserves which provide a sound base for the flourish of flora and fauna in the Netherlands. Besides the National Ecological Network, also National Parks and National Landscapes, specifically designated nature/landscape reserves with specific ecological and landscape characteristics larger than 1000 hectares may be used to communicate a cultural biography of landscapes to the general public which recognizes in an appropriate way the early prehistoric hunter-gatherers.

The National Ecological Network consists of a network of landscapes or landscape units which are described by the concepts core areas, corridors and stepping stones. These concepts or terminology can be compared with concepts used in studies on early prehistoric archaeological remains. In my view core areas could be synonymous with (residential) settlements, corridors are the paths or communication

Fig. 2
Flevoland. Shipwreck sign.
Photo: B.I. Smit, 2007.

Fig. 3
View of a small lake.
Photo: M. Beumer, 2007.

arteries used by prehistoric societies and stepping stones could be used for smaller areas where specific activities, both economic and perhaps ritual/sacral, occurred as presented in the following scheme:

National Ecological Network	Biography of early prehistoric landscapes
core areas	(residential) settlement areas
corridors	paths/communication arteries
stepping stones	small activity areas

6. APPRECIATION OF EARLY PREHISTORIC LANDSCAPES AND SOCIETIES

In the section above two positive aspects of the integration of nature development plans with research of early prehistoric remains have been suggested. The creation of recreational facilities in many of the areas which are being developed by 'blue' or 'green' organizations provide a third excellent opportunity to present the scale and contents of prehistoric societies and landscapes to a wider public instead of current initiatives which only focus on archaeological sites.

The appreciation of the scale of prehistoric landscapes may, among other options, easily be established through the creation of paths or trails throughout the present landscape or in present or future planned nature reserves and water management areas (Zvelebil/Moore 2006). By doing this a connection may be created between the past and the present. Through these paths the ecological, geographical and social diversity of different areas might be unlocked, thus strengthening the cultural identity of these areas. The intersection of different landscape units by these corridors provides a means of presenting the scale of early prehistoric landscapes.

The unravelling of early prehistoric landscapes does not necessarily translate to site reconstruction or information panels, since sites could for instance be marked by artwork or markers. For example, fields in the province of Flevoland where shipwrecks are found are marked by a simple sign (Fig. 2). Furthermore, the reconstruction of early prehistoric landscapes and re-enactment of early prehistoric lives aimed at a general public are a difficult endeavour (as several PDL/BBO related studies have shown, e.g. Duineveld 2006; Zvelebil/Moore 2006; Peeters 2007) and is beyond the scope of this article.

Fig. 4
Prehistoric encounter?
Photo: M. Beumer, 2007.

Similar signs could be envisaged for Stone Age sites using a relevant iconography. Recently, a model of a canoe was erected in the Tjonger brook valley to draw the passing public's attention to the presence of early prehistoric remains in the brook valley. Besides simple markers, small clearings in the vegetation can be created, functioning as peep-holes or loop-holes to see or to spy on other landscape features or fauna. For example, clearings in shrubbery may be created through which waterfowl may be seen (Fig. 3). Finally in some areas a sense of a prehistoric encounter might be established (Fig. 4).

7. CONCLUSIONS

In this paper I have tried to provide some thoughts on the possibility of an active integration of archaeological research and heritage management, especially of early prehistoric hunter-gatherer landscapes within the projects of 'green' and 'blue' organizations. It is believed that both the archaeological research, our archaeological knowledge and the possibilities of communicating the results to a general public will benefit from this integration. Furthermore, it is believed that research in zones where these developments are planned are likely to reveal new and other archaeological remains which could give insight into the social and ritual dimensions of early prehistoric communities and their connection or communication with the landscape. In the end this should lead to a better understanding of a substantial part of our cultural heritage, the early prehistory, and the long-term developments in landscape development and human land use.

NOTES

1 Cultural Heritage Agency, Amersfoort, the Netherlands.

REFERENCES

Anschuetz, K.F./R.H. Wilshusen/C.L. Scheick, 2001: An Archaeology of Landscapes: Perspectives and Directions, *Journal of Archaeological Research* 9, 157-211.
Binford, L.R., 1983: *In pursuit of the past. Decoding the archaeological record*, New York.

Boer, de G.H./J.A.M. Roymans, 2002: *Ruilverkavelingsgebied Land van Thorn: een archeologische verwachtings- en advieskaart*, Amsterdam (RAAP-rapport 802).

Deeben, J./E. Drenth/M.-F. van Oorsouw/L. Verhart (eds.), 2005: *De steentijd van Nederland*, Meppel (Archeologie 11/12).

Duineveld, M., 2006: *Van oude dingen, de mensen, die voorbij gaan. Over de voorwaarden meer recht te kunnen doen aan de door burgers gewaardeerde cultuurhistories*, Wageningen (Ph.D. thesis Wageningen University).

Gerritsen, F./E. Rensink (eds.), 2004: *Beekdallandschappen in archeologisch perspectief: een kwestie van onderzoek en monumentenzorg*, Amersfoort (Nederlandse Archeologische Rapportages 28).

Groenendijk, H.A., 1997: *Op zoek naar de Horizon. Het landschap van Oost-Groningen en zijn bewoners tussen 8000 voor Chr. en 1000 na Chr.*, Groningen (Regio- en landschapsstudies 4).

Groenewoudt, B.J./J. Deeben/B. van Geel/R.C.G.M. Lauwerier, 2001: An early Mesolithic assemblage with faunal remains in a stream valley near Zutphen, The Netherlands, *Archäologisches Korrespondenzblatt* 31, 329-348.

Haartsen, A., 1995: Natuur versus Cultuur? Natuurontwikkeling, landschapsbehoud en de identiteit van het cultuurlandschap, *Landschap* 12, 31-34.

Heiden, H.A. van der, 2005: Ecological restoration, environmentalism and the Dutch politics of 'New Nature', *Environmental Values* 14, 427-46.

Hidding, J./J. Kolen/Th. Spek, 2001: De biografie van het landschap. Ontwerp voor een inter- en multi-disciplinaire benadering van de landschapsgeschiedenis en het cultuurhistorisch erfgoed, in J.H.F. Bloemers/R. During/J.N.H. Elerie/H.A. Groenendijk/M. Hidding/J. Kolen/Th. Spek/M.-H. Wijnen, 2001: *Bodemarchief in Behoud en Ontwikkeling. De conceptuele grondslagen*, Den Haag, 7-109.

Jochim, M., 2003: Regionalism in the Mesolithic of Southern Germany, in L. Larsson/K. Knutsson/H. Kindgren (eds.), *Mesolithic on the move*, Oxbow, 323-330.

Kelly, R.L., 1995: *The Foraging Spectrum. Diversity in Hunter-Gatherer Lifeways*, Washington.

KNA, 2007: *Leidraad Archeologisch onderzoek van Beekdalen (ontwerpversie 0.1)*. www.sikb.nl. (Accessed January, 2008).

KNA, 2008: *Kwaliteitsnorm Nederlandse Archeologie (versie 3.1)*. www.sikb.nl.

Louwe Kooijmans, L.P./P.W. van den Broeke/H. Fokkens/A.L. Van Gijn, 2005: *The prehistory of the Netherlands*, Amsterdam.

Mc.Glade, J., 1999: Archaeology and the evolution of cultural landscapes: towards an interdisciplinary research agenda, in P.J. Ucko/R. Layton (eds.), *The archaeology and anthropology of landscape: shaping your landscape*, London, 458-482.

Peeters, J.H.M., 2007: *Hoge Vaart-A27 in context: Towards a model of Mesolithic-Neolithic land use dynamics as a framework for archaeological heritage management*, Amersfoort (Ph.D. thesis University of Amsterdam).

Peeters, H./M.J.L.Th. Niekus, 2005: Het mesolithicum in Noord-Nederland, in J. Deeben/E. Drenth/M.-F. van Oorsouw/L. Verhart (eds.), *De steentijd van Nederland*, Meppel (Archeologie 11/12), 201-234.

Prummel, W./M. Niekus 2005: De laatmesolithische vindplaats Jardinga (Fr.): de opgravingen in 2002 en 2003, *Paleoaktueel* 14/15, 40-45.

Prummel, W./M.J.L.TH. Niekus/A.L. van Gijn/R.T.J. Cappers, 2002: A Late Mesolithic Kill Site of Aurochs at Jardinga, the Netherlands, *Antiquity* 76, 413-424.

Raemaekers, D.C.M., 2006: *De spiegel van Swifterbant,* Groningen (Inaugural lecture).

Rensink, E./J. Deeben/H. Peeters, 2006: Early prehistoric sites and landscapes in the Netherlands. Building frameworks for archaeological heritage management, in E. Rensink/H. Peeters (eds.), *Preserving the Early Past. Investigation, selection and preservation of Palaeolithic and Mesolithic sites and landscapes,* Amersfoort (Nederlandse Archeologische Rapporten 31), 201-226.

Rensink, E./F.A. Gerritsen/J.A.M. Roymans, 2006: Archeological Heritage Management, Nature Development and Water Management in the Brook Valleys of the Southern Netherlands, *Berichten van de Rijksdienst voor het Oudheidkundig Bodemonderzoek* 46, 383-399.

Rooijakkers, G., 1999: Mythisch landschap: verhalen en rituelen als culturele biografie van een regio, in J. Kolen/T. Lemaire (eds.), *Landschap in meervoud. Perspectieven op het Nederlandse landschap in de 20ste/21ste eeuw,* Utrecht, 301-340.

Roymans, J.A.M. 2005: *Een cultuurhistorisch verwachtingsmodel voor Brabantse beekdallandschappen: Een mogelijke toekomst voor het verleden van de beekdalen,* Amsterdam (MA thesis VU University).

Roymans, N., 1995: The cultural biography of urnfields and the long term history of a mythical landscape, *Archaeological Dialogues* 2, 2-38.

Spek, Th./O. Brinkkemper/B.P. Speleers, 2006: Archaeological Heritage Management and Nature Conservation. Recent developments and future prospects, illustrated by three Dutch case studies, *Berichten van de Rijksdienst voor het Oudheidkundig Bodemonderzoek* 46, 331-354.

Stapert, D., 1985: A small Creswellian site at Emmerhout (province of Drenthe, the Netherlands), *Palaeohistoria* 27, 1-65.

Stapert, D., 2005: Het Laat-Paleolithicum in Noord-Nederland, in J. Deeben/J., E. Drenth/M.-F. van Oorsouw/L. Verhart (eds.), *De steentijd van Nederland,* Meppel (Archeologie 11/12), 143-169.

Verhart, L./N. Arts, 2005. Het mesolithicum in Zuid-Nederland, in J. Deeben/E. Drenth/M.-F. van Oorsouw/L. Verhart (eds.), *De steentijd van Nederland,* Meppel (Archeologie 11/12), 235-260.

Waterbolk, T. 1999: De landschappen in mijn omgeving: cultuur en natuur in Noord-Nederland, in J. Kolen/T. Lemaire (eds.): *Landschap in meervoud. Perspectieven op het Nederlandse landschap in de 20ste/21ste eeuw,* Utrecht, 95-116.

Zvelebil, M., 2003: Enculturation of Mesolithic Landscapes, in L. Larsson/H. Kindgren/K. Knutsson/D. Loeffler/A. Akerlund (eds.), *Mesolithic on the Move. Papers presented at the Sixth International Conference on the Mesolithic in Europe, Stockholm 2000,* Oxford, 65-73.

Zvelebil, M./J. Moore, 2006: Assessment and representation: the informative value of Mesolithic Landscapes, in E. Rensink/H. Peeters (eds.), *Preserving the Early Past. Investigation, selection and preservation of Palaeolithic and Mesolithic sites and landscapes,* Amersfoort (Nederlandse Archeologische Rapporten 31),151-165.

WEBSITE

http: www.minlnv.nl: Ministry of Agriculture, Nature and Food Quality. (Accessed November, 2007).

10. Presentation, appreciation and conservation of liminal landscapes: challenges from an Irish perspective
(in response to the contribution by Bjørn Smit)

Michael O'Connell[1]

ABSTRACT

This paper considers the challenges for archaeologists and environmentalists in elucidating past landscapes and presenting them effectively and in an attractive manner to the public within an Irish context. Ireland is rather exceptional in western Europe in that it was only in the last decade that it experienced strong economic development that involved large-scale infrastructural works. While such works inevitably result in destruction of parts of the natural and built heritage, they have also led to many new findings regarding Irish environment and heritage. Many of the new findings have been brought to public attention through well illustrated, attractive and readily available publications. In turn, this has led to increased public awareness of heritage and engagement with conservation and related issues. While these developments are briefly reviewed, the main focus is on liminal landscapes associated with peatlands and the challenges in highlighting the importance of these extensive landscapes and presenting them attractively to the public. Three such landscapes are considered in some detail, namely (i) Lough Boora Parklands, Co. Offaly, where the early Mesolithic environment has been recreated *in situ*; (ii) Céide Fields, north Mayo, where a Visitor Centre serves to explain the significance of an early Neolithic extensive field system hidden by blanket bog; and (iii) Barrees, Beara Peninsula, west Cork, where recent detailed archaeological survey and excavation and palaeoecological investigations have elucidated many aspects of a liminal landscape with rich but largely hidden evidence of past human activity and settlement.

KEYWORDS

Liminal landscapes, blanket bog; Mesolithic, Neolithic, Iron Age; human impact; Ireland

1. INTRODUCTION

Establishing a 'cultural biography of landscapes' is a major challenge for practitioners involved in the interpretation, presentation and conservation of cultural landscapes. The challenge arises from the multi-faceted character of landscapes that makes it difficult to view landscapes in a holistic way whether the practitioners are archaeologists, environmentalists, educators or planners.

In this paper, some of the difficulties and possibilities are discussed from an Irish context and in the light of the considerations put forward by Bjørn Smit in his paper on the challenges facing Dutch authorities in improving awareness by the general public and planners of pre-farming cultures and specifically Mesolithic hunter/gatherer societies. Envisaging how these societies functioned and related to their environment is not easy and conveying this to the general public is particularly difficult given the overall urban character of society, especially in Europe where urban dwellers far outnumber those involved in farming. As a result, there is a loss of a sense of connection between human survival, nature and overall landscape characteristics. Indeed for the majority of people today, nature and landscape are merely backdrops to living, which contrasts with the situation in earlier societies where local environments were pivotal to survival in that they were the immediate source of all food and shelter and also formed the spiritual coulisse to human life (cf. McCartan *et al.* 2009 for examples from the Mesolithic).

2. THE NETHERLANDS AND IRELAND: GENERAL REMARKS

The Netherlands, comprising some 41 500 km^2, has an area similar to that of Munster, the southernmost of the four provinces of Ireland, but it has a population of over 16.5 million which contrasts with about 6 million for the island of Ireland. Though its population density is more than five times that of Ireland, strict planning has ensured that some 60% of its land surface is available for agriculture but this does not preclude high importance being attached to nature conservation. Wetlands, for instance, cover some 82,000 ha; within the EU only Germany has assigned a more extensive area to this important conservation category (Statistics Netherlands 2009).

The dense population of the Netherlands is sustained by a highly developed economy that capitalizes on a pivotal location beside the strongest economies in Europe. Ireland, on the other hand, with its peripheral European location, has only recently, in the context of the so-called 'Celtic Tiger' (1995–2007), experienced a period of strong economic development (Ní Mháille Battel 2003). The high level of economic activity gave rise to both opportunities and challenges. On the one hand, it necessitated large-scale developments particularly as regards transport infrastructure of all types. While planning policy dictated that archaeological features and environmentally important habitats be avoided where at all possible, inevitably large-scale transport and other developments also involved alteration and/or destruction of familiar landscapes but, in so doing, were instrumental in revealing previously hidden archaeological, geological and environmental features. Legal obligations to make comprehensive records of all archaeological sites ensure that survey, excavation and conservation of artefacts and other material remains are carried out to a high standard while environmental impact assessments provide new information on habitats and especially rare species distributions. The requirement for archaeological and environmental assessments relating to developments has spawned a consultancy industry that is now delivering in terms of publications of both primary data and also syntheses (for examples see http://www.nra.ie/Publications). The initiation of public-interested, tailored publications, such as *Seanda* which, now in its third issue (http://www.nra.ie/Archaeology/Seanda-NRAArchaeologyMagazine), is an important development in that it serves to bring to wide public attention the most important findings from excavation and survey arising from construction of new National Routes. *Archaeology Ireland*, the popular quarterly archaeological magazine that began publication in 1987, i.e. several years before the phenomenon of the 'Celtic Tiger', fulfils a similar but wider brief in that it includes short, well illustrated articles and reviews on a wide range of subjects but again accessible to the general reader and invariably topical. In the environmental field, publications such as *Biodiversity Ireland*, again in its third issue (http://www.biodiversityireland.ie), highlight biodiversity issues and the need for conservation of the natural as distinct from the built environment. As a result of these and other initiatives, infrastructural and related developments have given rise not only to many new discoveries but also a general heightening of awareness of the archaeological richness and environmental diversity of the country, notwithstanding some heated controversies relating to particular infrastructural projects such as the M50/Carrickmines debacle in south Co. Dublin and the M3 Motorway/Skryne Valley/Hill of Tara controversy in Co. Meath (Newman/Strohmayer 2007; Leonard 2008).

3. PEATLANDS AND THE HIDDEN ANCIENT LANDSCAPES OF IRELAND

While the eye-catching activities referred to above tend to be very much in the public domain, often as a result of controversial decisions regarding precise routing of new roads, the hidden side of past Irish landscapes tends to be either ignored or largely forgotten. Rather than being occluded by cover-sands and marine deposits as is often the case in the Netherlands, Ireland's ancient landscapes are often hidden as a result of peat growth. The bogs of Ireland, which originally covered 17% of the land-surface, have long been recognized as a rich archive not only of archaeological structures and artefacts but also as a source of environmental information about the bogs themselves, their hinterland and past climates (Feehan/O'Donovan 1996).

Close monitoring of the once extensive raised bogs of the Irish midlands has revealed much archaeological evidence for past settlement and an intricate communication system in the form of extensive trackways that span most of the prehistoric farming period, i.e. from the Neolithic to the end of the Iron Age (Raftery 1990; *idem* 1996; Gowan 2005). Still more sensational has been the discovery, beneath blanket bog, of intact landscapes that include stone-walls (presumed usually to constitute field boundaries). That at Céide Fields, near Ballycastle, is the most noteworthy in that here the area involved is particularly extensive (up to 1,000 ha) and includes a highly regular co-axial system of stone-wall field boundaries

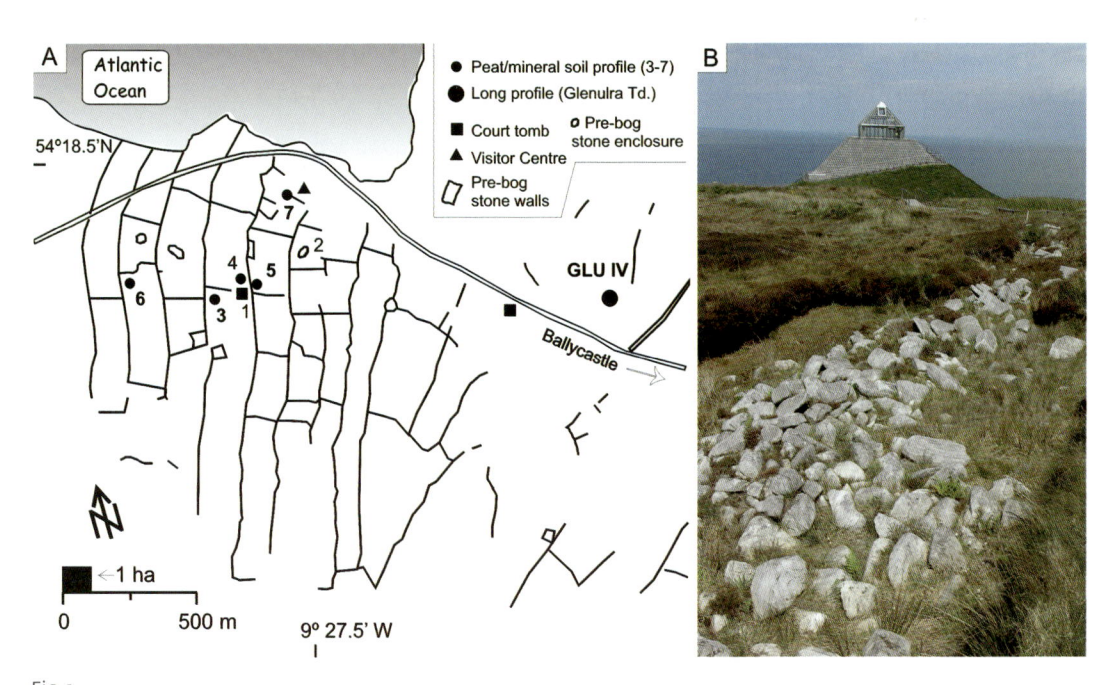

Fig. 1.
Céide Fields, north Mayo.
A. Map showing the stone-wall pattern in the main part of the pre-bog field system at Céide Fields and other features including pollen sampling locations (field system based on maps by S. Caulfield).
B. Part of an excavated pre-bog stone-wall (partly overgrown) in the foreground and Visitor Centre in the background (view to the north. *Photo: 27/05/2008*.

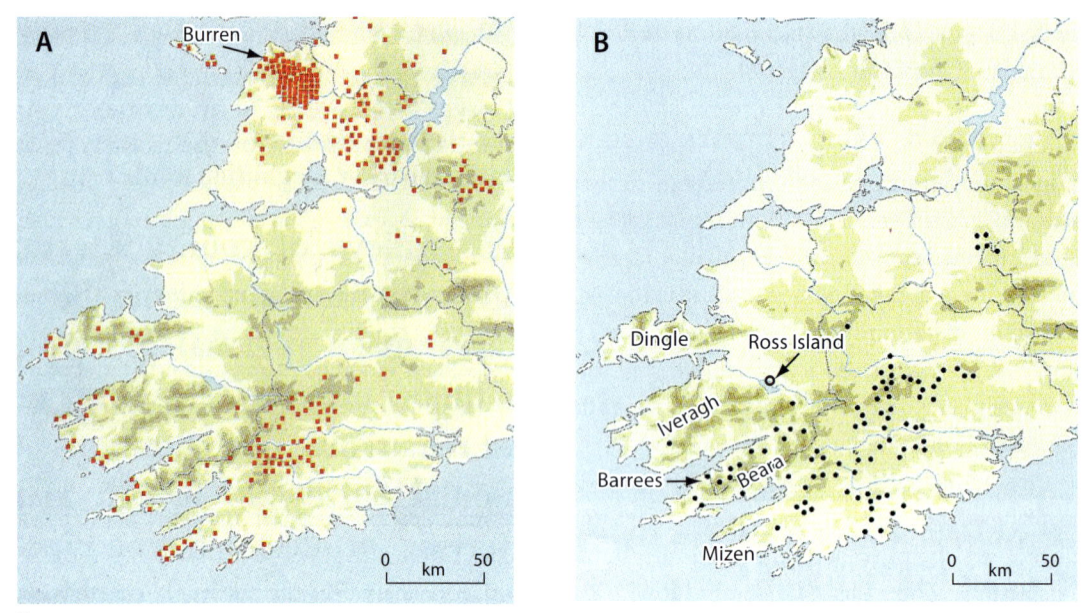

Fig. 2.
Map of south-west Ireland showing wedge tomb (A) and stone-circle (B) distributions (filled-in circles) and Ross Island (open circle) *(after Aalen et al. 1997)*.

that has been shown to date to the earlier Neolithic (*sensu* British/Irish contexts), i.e. to the period 3700-3200 BC (all dates calibrated) which is exceptionally early as regards enclosed, farmed landscape in Atlantic Europe (Caulfield 1978; Molloy/O'Connell 1995; Fig. 1A).

3.1 Contrasting approaches to presentation of landscapes: Céide Fields, North Mayo and Lough Boora Parklands, Co. Offaly

Whilst the importance of many of the discoveries associated with peatlands is widely recognized, the evidence, though spectacular, does not provide iconographic images on a par with megalithic tombs such as the passage tomb at Newgrange, promontory forts with spectacular siting such as Dún Aonghasa on Inis Mór or even the much more modest wedge tombs that dot the Burren, the karstic region of north Clare (Fig. 2A). Indeed it can be argued that without suitable on-site interpretation, the significance of many peatland sites would be lost to the general public. Céide Fields is a case in point. Here a visitor centre, with an award-winning pyramidal design and close to spectacular cliff scenery, plays a vital role in communicating to the public the significance of this peat-covered landscape as evidence for early farming in Ireland (Fig. 1B). Similarly a visitor centre at Corlea, Co. Longford, where a stretch of mid-Iron-Age timber trackway (148 BC) is displayed, brings home the impressive nature of these trackways and their role in communication and transport across open expanses of bog in periods when much of the countryside was still heavily wooded. A very different but perhaps even more exciting development is the large-scale environmental engineering project by Bord na Móna (Irish Peat Board) at Boora, Co. Offaly (Fig. 3; http://www.loughbooraparklands.com; planning and management issues are discussed by Collier/Scott 2009). Here, on a lake shore, the site of an early Mesolithic encampment was discovered in 1977 in the course of industrial large-scale peat removal by Bord na Móna (Ryan 1980; pollen analytical data in O'Connell 1980; for an overview of the Mesolithic in Ireland see Woodman 2009). In the meantime, the bog has been largely cut away and the extensive area it once occupied has been allowed to revert to quasi-natural ecosystems that include aquatic, fen, reedswamp and carr (woodlands on peat) habitats (for an overview see Higgins 2006), i.e. systems analogous to those experienced by Mesolithic peoples in this part of Ireland ca. 9,600 years ago (Fig. 3). The visitor to the Park thus gains a first-hand experience of the palaeoenvironment without recourse to physical structures other than signposts and display boards. The available information, however, might have a much stronger environmental slant, especially in view of the interesting palaeoenvironmental component that has been highlighted by the excavation results (e.g. the importance of hazelnuts and eel fishing for the Mesolithic communities; Little 2009; McComb 2009). An opportunity has thus been missed of forging strong links for the visitor between environments of today and those experienced by a fisher/hunter/gatherer-based culture in the past.

While the efforts described above to present the archaeology of peatlands are most worthwhile and proving popular, such an approach will inevitably be limited given the cost of design and construction of

Fig. 3.
Lough Boora Parklands and surrounds. Clockwise from top left-hand side: large-scale industrial harvesting of milled peat (north of Boora); traditional domestic use of turf continues in the area; Bog Track (2005) by Johan Sietzema, created from fossil oak trunks as part of Sculpture in the Parklands permanent exhibition; wildlife in a wetland amenity area created after industrial removal of peat; a simple stone monument marks the site of the Mesolithic hearths (peat harvested and natural succession taking place) with a large fossil oak trunk nearby. *Photo: 16/09/2009.*

Fig. 4.
Overview of Barrees landscape, Beara Peninsula, showing part of Loch Beag in the immediate foreground, and pasture and oak woodland fragments in lower mid view, followed by hummocky ground with rough pasture, heath and bog where most of the archaeological sites lie (October 2004).

interpretative centres and the recurrent costs connected with maintenance and staffing. It cannot therefore serve as a model for interpretation and presentation on a large scale, especially given the widespread occurrence of bogs worthy of conservation in Ireland. Blanket bog, the most extensive peatland type, covers some 8000 km² (11% of the Republic of Ireland) and constitutes a major landform in western Ireland and especially west Cork/Kerry, Clare, Galway, Mayo and Donegal. It thus remains a challenge to increase awareness of the archaeological and environmental importance attaching to such bogs among the general public. In this regard, the conservation work of the Irish Peatland Conservation Council (IPCC), founded in 1982, deserves high commendation. Many of the features associated with these blanket bogs are low-key (cf. Céide Fields above), seldom in the public domain and the landscapes in question are usually marginal in terms of present-day farming. Indeed, these blanket bog and heath-covered landscapes may best be described as liminal, i.e. occupying a space at the edge or periphery (cf. L. *limen* threshold), at least in modern-day contexts though not necessarily in the past. Yet, such landscapes are rich as regards archaeology and environment. By way of illustration, one such system in southwestern Ireland that has been recently studied in some detail is briefly described and the contribution that such studies can make to the biography of a landscape is briefly discussed.

3.3 Barrees, a liminal landscape in the Beara peninsula, SW Ireland

The Beara peninsula, lying between Kenmare Bay and Bantry Bay, is the southernmost of the three large peninsulas that define the outline of southwest Ireland (Fig. 2B). It is some 40 km in length, 17 km at its widest and consists mainly of bog and heath-covered uplands (80% is at or above 200 m altitude; geology: Devonian Sandstone), with the more fertile land confined to the mainly narrow coastal fringes. The west Cork/Kerry region, of which Beara is part, is known for its high concentration of field monuments and other evidence for Bronze Age activity. Indeed, this region is one of the great megalith centres in Europe with some 500 chamber tombs, stone circles, stone rows and related monument types (wedge type chambered tombs and stone circle distributions are shown in Fig. 2), as well as 600 single standing stones (Power 1992; Aalen *et al.* 1997; O'Brien 1999). It has also provided the earliest evidence for Bronze Age copper mining in Britain and Ireland at Ross Island, Killarney (as well as evidence for a Mesolithic presence at this site, recently reported by Gibbons *et al.* 2007), while the Mizen peninsula, to the east of Beara, constituted a major centre for Bronze Age copper mining (O'Brien 1996; *idem* 2004; Fig. 2B). The region is also noted for the high frequency of burnt mounds (*fulachta fiadh*) that typically date to c.

A. Pair of Standing Stones (late Bronze Age) within a large stone-walled enclosure (Late Iron Age).

B. Stone-wall (BAR3) partially covered by peat. Wall construction was followed by substanial soil erosion (colluvium on LHS) and peat growth (mid and later first millennium AD, respectively).

C. Cultivation ridges (lower elevation than A and B; probably late 19th/earlier 20th century) presumably used for potato cultivation. Oak woodland fragments in the middle distance.

Fig. 5.
Selected features, Barrees, Beara Peninsula, south-west Ireland.

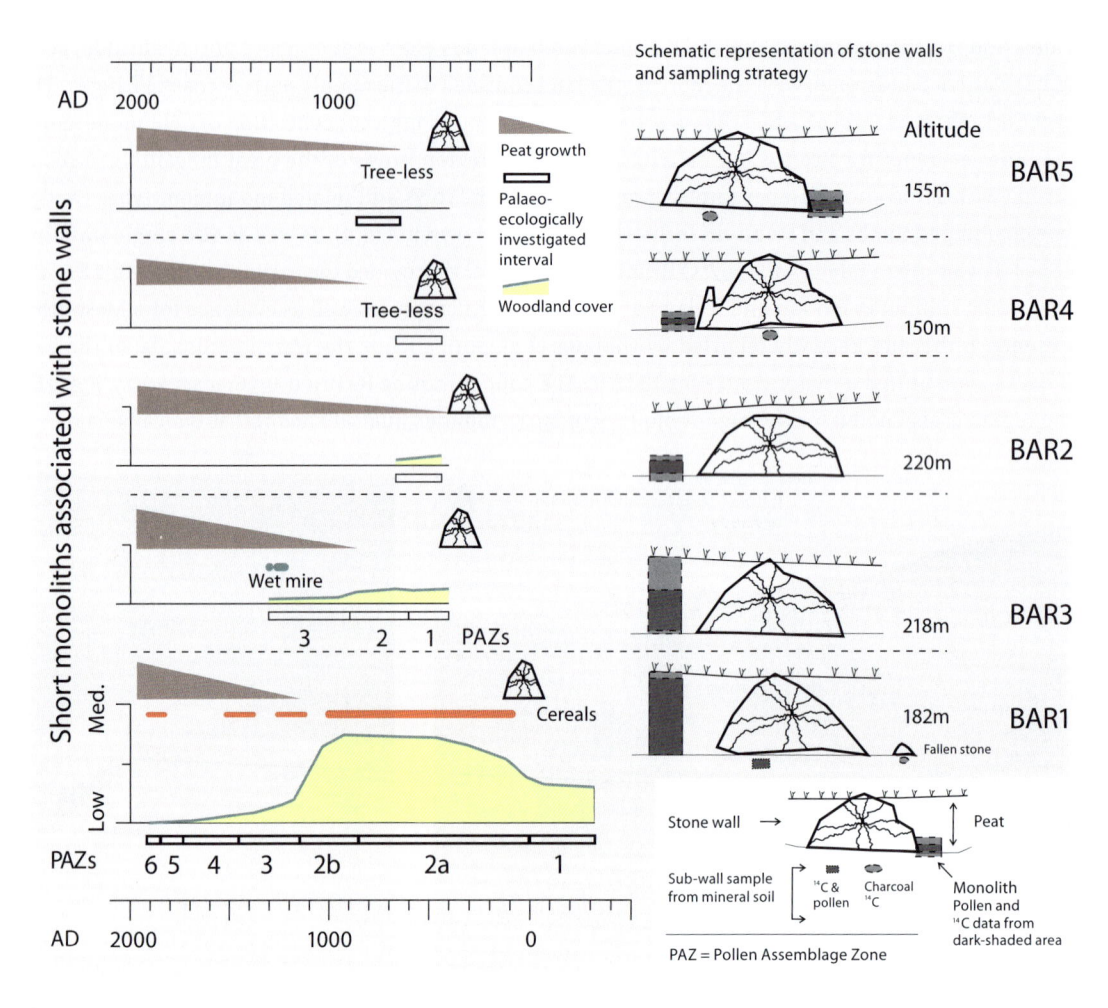

Fig. 6a.
Schematic representation of the results of archaeological and palaeoecological investigations at Barrees, Beara Peninsula, south-west Cork.
Information derived from investigations of short soil/peat monoliths (BAR1–5) from excavation trenches through partially peat-covered stone walls is presented.

1600-1000 BC (almost half of the known Irish sites are in Co. Cork; Waddell 2000) and as a centre for ogham stones (datable to the early centuries AD, i.e. end of the Iron Age/beginning of the Christian period; Monk/Sheehan 1998). With respect to natural history, the region, with its mild and humid climate, is famous for its Atlantic oak woodlands especially the woodlands of Killarney and Glengarriff that have been likened to tropical rainforest on account of their rich bryophyte and fern flora (see below). Its blanket bog and heathlands harbour many of the more distinctive elements of the flora such as the greater butterwort (*Pinguicula grandiflora*) and Irish spurge (*Euphorbia hyberna*) (Preston et al. 2002).

We here focus attention on the townland Barrees where most of the elements mentioned above are present and located in a quite spectacular landscape (Fig. 4). Widespread bog and heath, however, tend to obscure many of the archaeological features and especially the stone walls that are frequent in the uplands (Figs. 4 and 5). Despite the long-term interest in stone-wall systems associated with peatlands in

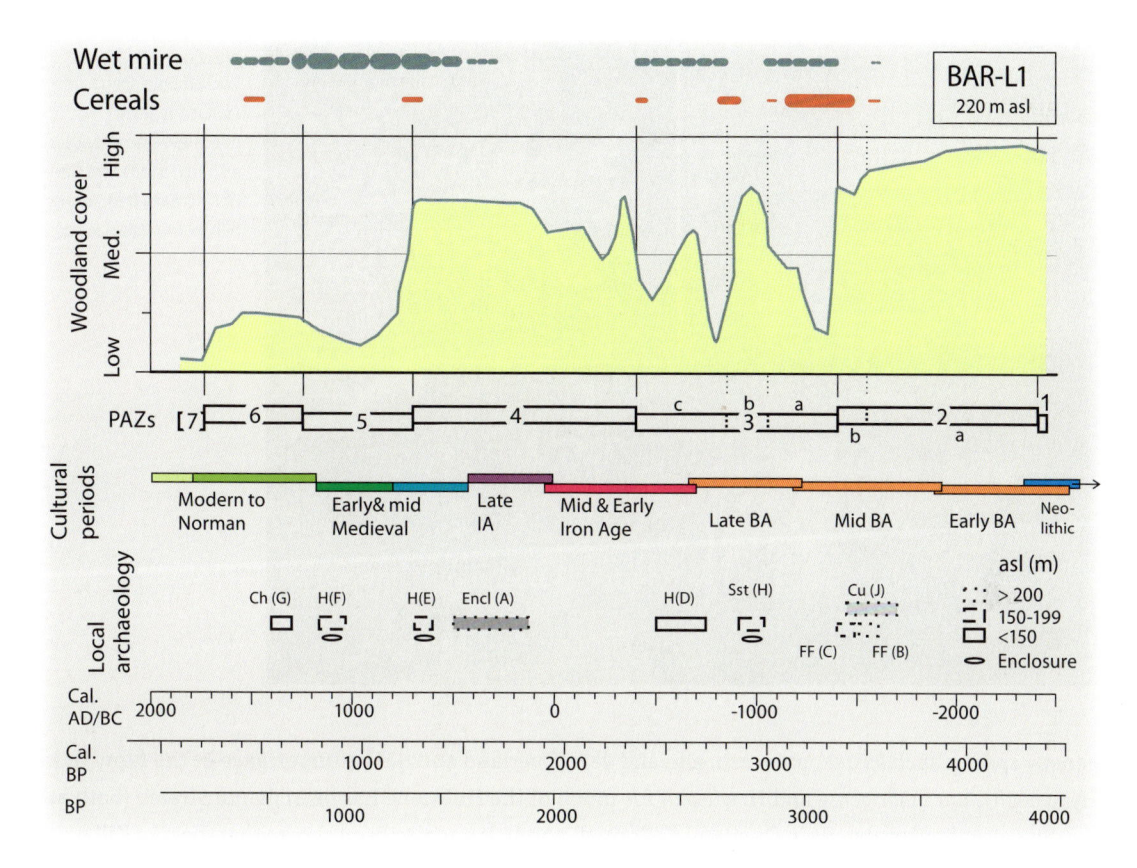

Fig. 6b.
Schematic representation of the results of archaeological and palaeoecological investigations at Barrees, Beara Peninsula, south-west Cork.
Reconstructions derived from the long peat core BAR-L1, cultural periods, archaeological features in the study area and time scales are presented *(for details see Overland/O'Connell 2008)*.

Ireland, it is only recently that low-profile systems, such as those at Barrees, have received attention (but cf. Lynch 1981; Mitchell 1989).

Investigations at Barrees have involved detailed, fine-spatial palaeoecological investigations carried out in the context of an archaeological programme of survey and excavation (Overland/O'Connell 2008; O'Brien 2009). A pollen profile from a small lake (Fig. 4), situated at low elevation and towards the periphery of the study area, has provided a more or less complete Holocene record for the low-lying area near the lake. A small peat basin, 700 m distant and at somewhat higher elevation (140 m asl), has given a pollen profile (BAR-L1) that spans the critical period from the late Neolithic to recent times. A series of short profiles (BAR1–5), taken where stone walls and the underlying mineral soils were sectioned in the course of archaeological excavations, completes the picture and enabled details such as the chronology and circumstances of wall construction and peat growth to be pencilled in (Figs. 5 and 6).

The palaeoecological investigations also shed light on woodland dynamics and the history of some of the more noteworthy floristic elements. At lower elevations, i.e. in the vicinity of Loch Beag, woodland with a high species diversity persisted well into the first millennium AD while at more elevated locations woodland, if it survived at all, was dominated mainly by alder and birch and was largely devoid of tall

Fig. 7.
Trichomanes speciosum (Killarney fern; overview and detail) in a shady, moss and fern-rich stream bed, Beara peninsula (May 2004).

canopy species such as oak, pine, ash, elm and yew (Overland 2007). The importance of the filmy ferns *Hymenophyllum tunbrigense* and *H. wilsonii* for much of the Holocene has been demonstrated (both are locally present today; details in Overland/O'Connell 2008). It has also been shown that the rare Killarney fern (*Trichomanes speciosum*; Fig. 7) was most likely also present locally (today it still persists at a few locations on Beara). As might be expected, increased representation of spores of filmy ferns in the pollen diagrams are positively correlated with periods of woodland regeneration, i.e. reduced human impact. These and other investigations at Barrees have enabled a detailed biography of this liminal landscape to be reconstructed with particular reference to the last two millennia (Overland/O'Connell 2008; O'Brien 2009).

4. CONCLUSION

Establishing the biography of any landscape, and more especially liminal landscapes, requires intensive multidisciplinary investigations with a high level of co-ordination (cf. the classical study in this genre by Berglund 1998). The advantage of such investigations, however, are manifold not only on account of the comprehensive information that accrues but, more especially, the possibility that is afforded for testing various hypotheses and reconstructing past environments at a level of sophistication that otherwise would be impossible. While the detailed publications from such investigations may be beyond the reach of a general readership, illustrated booklets, web-based presentations and information packs, as well as overview well-illustrated accounts, such as the recent volume on cultural landscape development in northern Germany by Behre (Behre 2008), can effectively convey the overall significance of landscape at various spatial and temporal scales to the interested public and especially local communities who, ultimately, are the best conservators and also the custodians of the memories that form an integral part of such landscapes.

NOTES

1 National University of Ireland Galway, Galway, Ireland.

REFERENCES

Aalen, A./Whelan, K./Stout, M. (eds), 1997: *Atlas of the Irish rural landscape*, Cork.

Behre, K.-E., 2008: *Landschaftsgeschichte Norddeutschlands. Umwelt und Siedlung von der Steinzeit bis zur Gegenwart*, Neumünster.

Berglund, B.E. (ed.), 1998: *The cultural landscape during 6000 years in southern Sweden – the Ystad project*, Copenhagen (Ecological Bulletins 41).

Caulfield, S., 1978: Neolithic fields: the Irish evidence, in H.C. Bowen/P.J. Fowler (eds.), *Early land allotment in the British Isles. A survey of recent work*, Oxford (BAR British Series 48), 137-143.

Collier, M.J./M. Scott, 2009: Conflicting rationalities, knowledge and values in scarred landscapes, *Journal of Rural Studies* 25, 267-277.

Feehan, J./G. O'Donovan, 1996: *The bogs of Ireland. An introduction to the natural, cultural and industrial heritage of Irish peatlands*, Dublin.

Gibbons, M./J. Higgins/M. Gibbons, 2007: A consideration of late Mesolithic settlement on Ross Island, Killarney National Park, *Journal of the Kerry Archaeological and Historical Society*, Ser. 2, 7, 5-14.

Gowan, M. (ed.), 2005: *The Lisheen Mine archaeological project 1996–8*, Bray.

Higgins, T., 2006: Returning to the wild: creating lakes on industrial cutaway peatlands in Ireland, *Sil News*, 48, 1-4.

Leonard, L., 2008: *The environmental movement in Ireland*, Berlin.

Little, A., 2009: Fishy settlement patterns and their social significance: a case study from the northern Midlands of Ireland, in S. McCartan/R.Schulting/G. Warren/P. Woodman (eds.), *Mesolithic Horizons*, Oxford, 698-705.

Lynch, A., 1981, *Man and environment in south-west Ireland, 4000 B.C.–A.D. 800*, Oxford (BAR British Series 85), 1-175.

McCartan, S./R. Schulting/G. Warren/P. Woodman (eds.), 2009: *Mesolithic Horizons*, Oxford.

McComb, A.M.G., 2009: The ecology of hazel (*Corylus avellana*) nuts in Mesolithic Ireland, in S. McCartan/R. Schulting/G. Warren/P.Woodman (eds.), *Mesolithic Horizons*, Oxford, 225-231.

Mitchell, F., 1989: *Man and environment in Valencia Island*, Dublin.

Molloy, K./M. O'Connell, 1995: Palaeoecological investigations towards the reconstruction of environment and land-use changes during prehistory at Céide Fields, western Ireland, *Probleme der Küstenforschung im südlichen Nordseegebiet*, 23, 187-225.

Monk, M.A./J. Sheehan, (eds.), 1998: *Early Medieval Munster. Archaeology, history and society*, Cork.

Newman, C./U.Strohmayer, 2007: *Uninhabited Ireland. Tara, the M3 and public spaces in Galway*, Galway.

Ní Mháille Battel, R., 2003: Ireland's "Celtic Tiger" economy, *Science, Technology and Human Values* 28, 93-111.

O'Brien, W., 1996: *Bronze Age copper mining in Britain and Ireland*, Princes Risborough.

O'Brien, W.F., 1999: *Sacred ground. Megalithic tombs in coastal south-west Ireland*, Galway (Bronze Age Studies 4).

O'Brien, W., 2004: *Ross Island. Mining, metal and society in early Ireland*, Galway (Bronze Age Studies 6).

O'Brien, W., 2009: *Local worlds. Early settlement landscapes and upland farming in south-west Ireland*, Cork.

O'Connell, M., 1980: Pollen analysis of fen peat from a Mesolithic site at Lough Boora, Co. Offaly, Ireland, *Journal of Life Science (R. Dublin Soc.)*, 2, 45-49.

Overland, A., 2007: *Palaeoecological investigations of lake sediments and peats towards reconstruction of long-term environmental changes at Barrees, Beara Peninsula, south-west Cork*, (Ph.D. thesis National University of Ireland Galway).

Overland, A./M. O'Connell, 2008: Fine-spatial paleoecological investigations towards reconstructing late Holocene environmental change, landscape evolution and farming activity in Barrees, Beara Peninsula, southwestern Ireland, *Journal of the North Atlantic* 1, 37-73.

Power, D., 1992: *Archaeological inventory of County Cork. Volume 1: West Cork*, Dublin.

Preston, C.D./D.A. Pearman/T.D. Dines (eds.), 2002: *New atlas of the British and Irish flora*, Oxford.

Raftery, B., 1990: *Trackways through time: archaeological investigations on Irish bog roads, 1985–1989*, Rush (Co. Dublin).

Raftery, B., 1996: Trackway excavations in the Mountdillon Bogs, Co. Longford, 1985–1991, *Irish Archaeological Wetland Unit (Crannóg Publication), Transactions*, 3, 1-461.

Ryan, M., 1980: An early Mesolithic site in the Irish Midlands, *Antiquity*, 54, 46-47.

Statistics Netherlands, 2009: Web Magazine, 03 February 2009 15:00. (http://www.cbs.nl/en-GB/menu/themas/natuur-milieu/publicaties/artikelen/archief/2009/2009-2685-wm.htm. Accessed 15 September, 2009).

Waddell, J., 2000^2: *The prehistoric archaeology of Ireland*, Bray.

Woodman, P.C., 2009: Ireland's place in the European Mesolithic: why it's ok to be different, in S. McCartan/R. Schulting/G. Warren/P. Woodman (eds.), *Mesolithic Horizons*, Oxford, xxxvi–xlvi.

11. My story – your story: three levels for reflecting and debating the relationship between contemporary archaeological heritage management and the public
A comment from Germany

Ulf Ickerodt[1]

ABSTRACT

The existing German[2] and to some extent European archaeological heritage protection agencies are, as far as their routine work is concerned, torn between the demands of academic research and their mandate as administrative bodies. The preference tends towards academic research. In this article I wish to examine two main questions. Firstly, who benefits from archaeological heritage management, i.e. who is it done for? Secondly, what is the social purpose of archaeological heritage management? When tackling these questions we must keep three important factors in mind, namely the current demographic changes, the increasing mobility of modern societies and the accelerating changes that are taking place both in world economics and land-use structures.

KEY WORDS

Archaeological heritage management, public involvement, cultural heritage, regional planning, potential aims

1. INTRODUCTION

It is now almost three decades since archaeological research in Germany and its administrative arm, archaeological heritage management, began to become aware of the social effects of their work. Towards the end of the 1980s there was increasing interest in the political misuse of archaeology in the Third Reich. This issue made both academic and administrative archaeological circles conscious of the problem of reactivity.

In sociology this term is used to describe the interference of society and science which, in fact, opened up a new field of research for archaeology. This step in the direction of a discipline dealing with the sociology of science not only opens up completely new perspectives for archaeological interpretation, it also permits a distinction to be made between social and scientific interpretation patterns or modes. It also represents the first step in a new form of enquiry about the content of our own discipline, which of course also bears on the influence of archaeological research work on the contemporary social environment. In this sense, the contemplation of the social dimension of archaeology permits a completely new view of the evolution of archaeology itself. This now involves both aspects of research history and also its effect on mentality development and co-related problems of the ethics of science (Ickerodt 2004).

These must be taken into consideration when one is faced with the questions 'For whom is archaeological heritage management undertaken?' and 'What are the social aims of archaeological heritage management?'

We therefore have two related problems that must be addressed much more extensively and carefully in the future by archaeological research and, seen from a research historical German viewpoint, its sub-discipline archaeological heritage management. The reason for this lies in the two issues themselves. Apart from their official administrative mandate to protect cultural heritage, the various cultural heritage institutions have a socio-political mandate. On a broader scale this is to ensure individual identity in Europe, whose population is growing closer together. We now have touched on two important task fields which it will be vital to address in the future.

These two issues with their associated problems influence archaeological research and the practice of archaeological heritage protection, not only in Germany, on three levels (e.g. Hermann 1978; ARL 2001; Bertelsmann Stiftung 2004; Brunnengräber/Klein/Walk 2005; Kaufmann 2005; NIW 2005; ROOK 2005; Stiftung Niedersachsen 2006; Bauerochse/Haßmann/Ickerodt 2007; Ickerodt 2007; *idem* 2008b; Ickerodt/Maluck 2008).

1. The level of archaeological heritage management.

    Here one must deal with the consequences of the increasingly dynamic nature of world economics; for example in some growth areas the infrastructure can no longer cope and is collapsing, whereas other regions face a strong decline in inhabitants, economy, infrastructure, etc. Another aspect is the changing legal framework. Cultural heritage laws are not only becoming increasingly international, but also administrative cultural heritage work and the way it is carried out is being politically reinterpreted (liberalization, public involvement etc.).

2. The regional planning level of archaeological heritage management.

    At this level, archaeological heritage management should co-operate much more extensively in long-term planning procedures than it has done previously by following its own overall aims and it should weld new alliances with other interested parties. In addition, it is necessary that governments stress the aspect of public involvement, particularly in connection with local development concepts. As far as archaeological heritage management is concerned this means making its own long-term decisions which, apart from other things, have a selective effect on the archaeological landscape. These decisions commit one to a special historical narration which exists in the form of the archaeological remains and will thus be preserved for future generations.

3. The philosophy of science level.

    The facet of the identity- and mentality-forming effect of archaeology is commonly used in the political field and it is precisely this facet which involves new scientific challenges. They should be viewed against a background of an increasingly mobile society and fundamental demographic changes (Kaufmann 2005; Stiftung Niedersachsen 2006).

2. THE LEVEL OF PRACTICAL ARCHAEOLOGICAL HERITAGE MANAGEMENT

Current archaeological heritage management as the administrative arm of academic archaeological research, in both the methodological and the scientific-ethical sense, clearly has its origins in the nineteenth century. At that time the foundations were laid and these are, more or less, still valid today. Heritage protection is often seen by outsiders as being of a restorative and/or defensive nature and mostly as unchallengeable, i.e. not open to discussion. They aim at an uncompromising preservation of the actual substance of cultural heritage.

On the opposite side we have routine archaeological heritage management itself. In contrast to the outsider's view mentioned above, it is characterized by a multitude of compromises between academic and management wishes and the reality of political feasibility. Archaeological heritage management must succeed in straddling the gap between the bare facts of reality and its own romantic ideas.

Against a background of the expansion of world-wide economics at the beginning of the 1990s, there was a certain feeling of confidence or euphoria with respect to the introduction of the principle of the perpetrator in German archaeology. It was possible after German reunification to carry out an enormous number of rescue digs, in particular in the eastern part of Germany. This meant that a huge number of operations was carried out while permanent staff and financial shortages inside the archaeological heritage management institutions could be observed.

Seen as a whole, German archaeological heritage management is on the brink of a comprehensive socio-political change in structure which is a challenge to its own innovative capabilities. One can identify various factors, interrelated through feedback, that need a common strategy by the different German organizations dealing with cultural and/or archaeological heritage management.

a. With respect to recent developments in world economics, commonly referred to as globalization, we see that there is growing pressure on the landscape as well in terms of land use and land abandonment affecting settlement activities and agricultural production structures. A central issue here is the economization of environment exploitation that is related to individual economic interests steered by worldwide investment possibilities that may cause regionally varying, increasingly rapid changes in economic aims, trade routes and/or production goals influencing:

   a.1 agricultural production (melioration, changes in the agricultural industry, sowing fallow land or abandoning it completely, introducing different crops, deserted farmsteads, scale enlargement of agricultural land, introduction of industrial methods in agricultural production, etc.);

   a.2. increasing use of agricultural land for other purposes (urban development, commercial centres, industrial areas, extraction of construction raw materials, etc.);

   a.3. extension of the infrastructure (harbours, roads, railways, canals, etc.);

   a.4. energy industry (opencast mines, production of energy crops, etc.);

   a.5. mass tourism (large blocks of holiday flats, etc.).

b. In addition we see the social effects of changes within economic structures on social behaviour depending on one's own economic basis and aims. With the growth of the service society, the economy is beginning to be divorced from the surrounding social, geographic and historical environment. This kind of development is visibly expressed by office blocks and factories which are primarily oriented on economics and profit and less on a relationship with the local surroundings. This whole development leads to increasingly strong and rapid changes in the environment and increases the pressure on society to adapt and therefore change. A direct consequence of this development, which is invariably counterproductive for resource conservation, is the short-term nature of the land-use concepts. Thus, new financial investment causes structures that are hundreds or thousands of years old to be abandoned, only to realize in a few decades or years that this was wasted effort since business had left the district on account of the changing economic framework.

c. Economic developments also generate changes in society which have a knock-on effect on space perception and land-use characterized by an increasing individualization, an increase in the monetary aspect of space perception and a changing understanding of national identity and the duty of the state.

In this last case the government right and/or mandate to steer is given up in favour of deregulation. The argument used is that the market will regulate itself. This process has an especially bad effect on institutions that do little or no lobby work, as is the case in German archaeological heritage management. Therefore a government controlling body needs to be set up which, from a German archaeological heritage management point of view, has the well-being of the whole population in view and moreover will act as a buffer to the world economy, which is unrelated to the various regions and/or, at a concrete level, to investors that have no relationship to locality. A tool may be the development of archaeological management goals and principles of decision-making that render the process of decision-making transparent and have to be adhered to by individual decision-makers.

d. Another influencing factor is demographic change, which today is often described in Germany as 'our population is becoming multi-ethnic and old'. It is accompanied by growing social mobility and the related loss of local ties. In the future, therefore, archaeological heritage management should not only confine itself to its original target group, i.e. the parties to an approval procedure, as in fact is commonly done. Rather, it should make contact with other groups, evaluate them and if possible involve them in decision processes. A difficulty here is that suitable structures do not exist at a German national level in which possible solutions can be developed and carried out in order to present cultural and archaeological heritage protection interests to policy-makers and the public. This applies at both state and federal levels as well as with respect to attaining some recognition in European institutions. It also comprises the job of introducing cultural heritage interests more effectively into laws and opinion-making processes, i.e. lobbying.

3. PRACTICAL ARCHAEOLOGICAL HERITAGE MANAGEMENT AT A REGIONAL PLANNING LEVEL

Archaeological heritage management in Germany is active at parish, state and federal levels and constitutes a part of regional planning. According to its official mandate it must make its interests heard, although in this sense it is only one of many actors. Its work is characterized by many internal, external, legal, administrative and political premises and influencing factors.

Partly in contrast to this, its own interpretation of its mandate, i.e. the highest aim of archaeological heritage management, is the protection and conservation of the common cultural heritage in the ground. Naturally, archaeological heritage protection places particular emphasis on soil protection since the soil is an archive of natural and cultural history (on a federal level BbodSchG § 2 Abs. 2 Nr. 2). It is essential to reduce the continuous erosion of this irreplaceable archive and, by extension, reduce the rate of land consumption by developers. The success of such a reduction is of vital importance for the conservation of the cultural landscape and its archaeological content. An important prerequisite for this work is an adequate archaeological and methodological basis as well as the development of feasible and sustainable protection goals. Thus management is inclined to give precedence to its own research aims and results at the expense of administrative work.

This attitude is borne out by the fact that, from the research history point of view, the aspect of archaeology as a component of spatial planning[3] has so far rarely been a topic of theoretical reflections and of project reports. The administrative aspect is of peripheral importance in academic archaeological teaching. It is a similar situation on the administrative side of archaeological heritage management. This is normally taught during voluntary work or via on-the-job learning. This leads to a kind of internal split in archaeological heritage management since one tends to think that it is possible to distinguish between research and administration. This widely held view is based on the mistaken idea that protection is passive and thus makes cultural heritage protection appear as a defensive activity to outsiders.

As a counter measure and influenced by European policies, a more active form of archaeological heritage management began to be adopted several years ago. At the forefront is the participation of government cultural heritage protection in long-term regional planning procedures (federal regional planning, state regional planning, visions for cross-border planning projects and landscape framework plans).

An important step at the planning level is the active participation of archaeological heritage management in regional projects at an early stage in environmental impact assessments (EIA) or strategic environmental assessments (SEA). At the European level, the first steps in this direction have already been taken with the Planarch (Waugh 2006) and LancewadPlan (www.lancewadplan.org) projects. As far as Germany itself is concerned, aims and visions have to be formulated and implemented in the different regional planning levels. These concern tasks such as finding a compromise between different interests, the drawing up of protection zones, etc.

A prerequisite for effective co-operation by the cultural heritage protection in regional planning is a clear and unambiguous evaluation criteria and philosophy which must be understandable to outsiders. This includes statements of aims and delegated aims which should not only be relevant to the various levels but also have an inspirational or guiding function for archaeological heritage management work. Without such a general framework it is quite likely that aims are developed by individual archaeologists and are then mistakenly considered to be given aims. In addition, archaeological heritage management should not only concentrate on participation in planning procedures but should go on the offensive and integrate the aims of the target groups involved in the planning procedure into their own plans. In this process it is important to be creative and innovative when drawing up protection strategies.

The interpretation suggested in this paper requires a shift from exclusive cultural heritage protection to planning-oriented strategies covering several or all sectors, such as those currently practised in a few other countries. In this respect, a start was made in the last few years by Lower Saxony in co-operation with the Netherlands, Schleswig-Holstein and Denmark within the framework of the European Union LancewadPlan programme to compile an inventory of the structures existing at present and to develop concepts and strategies for solving problems. Such an active form of archaeological heritage management, which characteristically takes the initiative, does not involve the above-mentioned problem that the issues tend to be addressed from one's own very individual viewpoint. It relies much more on dialogue and co-operation with other organizations and stakeholders and allows the claims on the land by other sectors to be evaluated and then incorporated into one's own work. The model used in this case is the Integrated Coastal Zone Management.

This form of archaeological heritage management is no longer confined to the original target groups, i.e. the parties to the approval procedure, but wishes to, and must, identify other affected groups. The routine day-to-day business of archaeological heritage management, therefore, must be seen in its socio-economic environment and the requirements of the various affected groups must be understood, compared and made compatible with one's own archaeological heritage management aims. This work can be expanded so much that public involvement, which is promoted by the European Community, as discussed earlier in this connection, must be addressed. Active public involvement on the European and national level constitutes the central quality factor of political steering (Bertelsmann Stiftung 2004). It is for this reason that the involvement of representatives of the various stakeholders as well as the local population is incorporated in the European Landscape Convention. Particularly in the case of archaeological as well as cultural heritage management, public involvement promotes a large degree of sustainability in the way we look after our environment.[4] This step is necessary from the point of view of European individualization as well as to counter the trend whereby industry becomes severed from its social environment with the consequent loss of local ties.

The LancewadPlan project (www.lancewadplan.org) can be mentioned here once again as an example. The project aims at establishing a uniform and locally anchored, cross-border consciousness for the protection of the common natural and cultural heritage, taking account of the special local characteristics. The project is intended to involve regional planners and cultural heritage managers on the one hand, and on the other hand non-governmental organizations (NGOs) which are concerned with cultural heritage and natural protection (Brunnengräber/Klein/Walk 2005). Thus, existing networks should be improved and new synergies created and co-operation between these bodies should preferably be modelled on clear concepts.

This development, however, brings with it a fundamental potential danger for archaeological heritage management. The function of governmental archaeological heritage management is, like that of building laws, rather similar to a referee or a judge. It is therefore the ultimate factor that puts a brake on free, unrestricted land-use. We should contemplate what would happen if, owing to pressure from the public or from NGOs, authentic cultural heritage or archaeological landscapes were abandoned in favour of fictitious historical landscapes.

This leads us to a core problem confronting archaeological or cultural heritage management. As noted earlier, archaeology is seen by archaeologists as a pure and strict science and, subsequently, is seen from an archaeological point of view mediated in this pure so-called 'scientific sense' despite all its social bonds and metaphysical uncertainties (Ickerodt 2004; *idem* 2008a; *idem* 2008b). Archaeologists and cultural heritage landscape researchers feel an obligation to facts, not fiction.

However, as the German philosopher and sociologist J. Habermas (Habermas 1976) pointed out more than three decades ago, it is crucial to understand that archaeological research and the mediation of historical knowledge in terms of metanarratives are related to different systems of understanding and therefore have to obey totally different social constraints. While archaeologists and cultural heritage are dealing with historical sources, the non-archaeological world experiences archaeological sites as a place of remembrance where past social experiences are memorized. This aspect is closely related to a thesis that the American historian W. McNeill (McNeill 1986,164) developed in relation to the social impact of the historical sciences. He formulated that "if historical interpretation is a form of myth-making, the myths help to guide public action and are a human substitute for instinct."

While examining the social determination of this thesis with respect to (1) the level of archaeological heritage management and (2) the regional planning level of archaeological heritage management, one has to take into account the different levels of historical mediation. One has to differentiate between archaeological/ historical research and the social function of the creation of historical narratives via spatial planning. The latter seems to be the response to the process of myth creation within a secular, respectively science based society that helps create social identity and harmonize social behaviour (e.g. Ickerodt 2004; *idem* 2005; *idem* 2006; *idem* 2008a; *idem* 2008b). The reason for this is that both myths and historical narratives can be identified by content as a form of reflection of origins with the aim to pass on experience of the past to forthcoming generations. Both mythologically and historically legitimated forms of social behaviour have, in different ways, a self-constituting and legitimating function. They explain how our world has become the place that it is today. In this way, both may legitimate social institutions and social behaviour. They help to stabilize people's existence and provide legal social security. Swiss philosopher Angehrn (Angehrn 1996, 307) stated, *"Die Verwurzelung in der Herkunft ist eine Strategie der Identitätssicherung. Wer weiß, woher er kommt, weiß, wer er ist."* ("Recognizing one's own origins is a strategy to secure identity. Who knows where he comes from or who he is?" (translation by the author), as stated by the Swiss philosopher Angehrn (Angehrn 1996, 307).

In more general terms this approach is closely related to a phenomenon that was named "invented traditions" by the British historian E. Hobsbawm (Hobsbawm/Ranger 1992; cf. Ickerodt 2005). The historically young social organizations that comprise European nation states needed to legitimate their almost recent forms of social organization by shaping them as almost ancient.

This changing social framework explains the sudden and genuine development of archaeology in the nineteenth century that S. Piggott (Piggott 1937, 31) saw as a "natural outcome of the social and industrial background of the period" to a key science.[5] What are the consequences for archaeological research and archaeological heritage management? In order to answer this question one must consider the philosophy of science level.

4. THE PHILOSOPHY OF SCIENCE LEVEL

The discussions in the two previous sections are necessary to understand the practical input of these ideas for archaeological research and archaeological heritage management. In politics, consciously or unconsciously as well as positively or negatively, archaeology and the cultural heritage landscape are often used as identity-creating factors *sensu* McNeill or Hobsbawm. In this context, archaeological research is underestimated as a mentality-forming influence and in some cases this is not recognized at all (Ickerodt 2008a; *idem* 2008b).

How can the archaeological sector, whether archaeological heritage management or the academic side, tackle such a political task and adopt its social responsibilities? What aims should be attained by archaeological heritage management? What sort of identity should be created and whose history told? And how detailed should such a picture be? What happens if, in a mobile society, there is a radical change in the population?

It is extraordinarily difficult for archaeological heritage management, when incorporated in administrative or political structures, as well as for academic research, to evaluate the consequences of these questions for its own work and these problems are often considered to constitute a separate research field. One reason for this difficulty may be that archaeological heritage management tends to focus its work on Level (1) (see above). However, this practice should be discontinued so that Level (2) can be addressed at the same time. It is essential to persuade archaeological heritage management at an early stage that evaluation of its own visions is based on both scientific discoveries as well as on social categories with its different levels (from local/regional up to state level). In this respect, the central or decentralized steering of the communication process in which visions are developed and compared is particularly important. This is even more relevant since the aspect of public involvement together with all its special requirements is becoming increasingly important (Fig. 1).

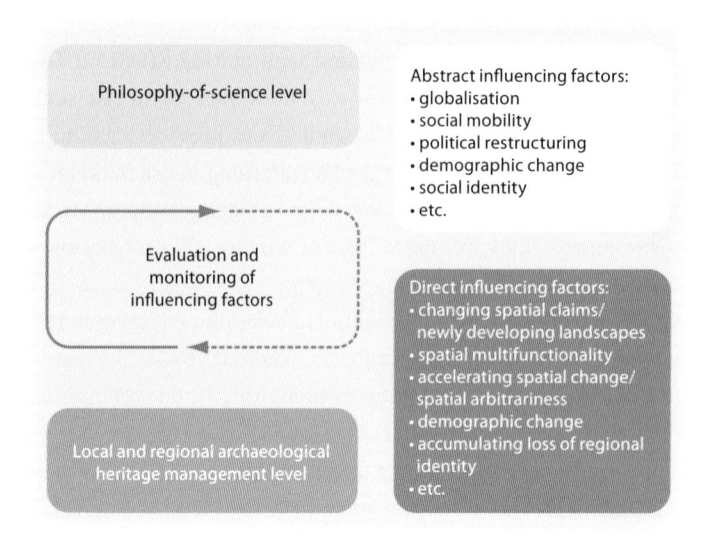

Fig. 1
The philosophy of science level as a tool to evaluate and steer the interaction between archaeology and society.

How can social cohesion be created and promoted via archaeological and cultural heritage management? What influence does archaeological research have on the generation and establishment of social norms and values? And last but not least, how can the process of communication of values be carried out in a responsible manner above personal interests?

These problems require the two fields of archaeological heritage management and academic research to open up completely new fields of research (Fig. 2). Indeed research on the social influence of archaeology is, even with respect to methodology, in the initial stages. For this reason it has already been suggested that this complex theme be dealt with under sociology of science. Sociology of science assists archaeological heritage management research in understanding what role archaeology plays in society and this understanding helps archaeological heritage management in steering its own communication work.

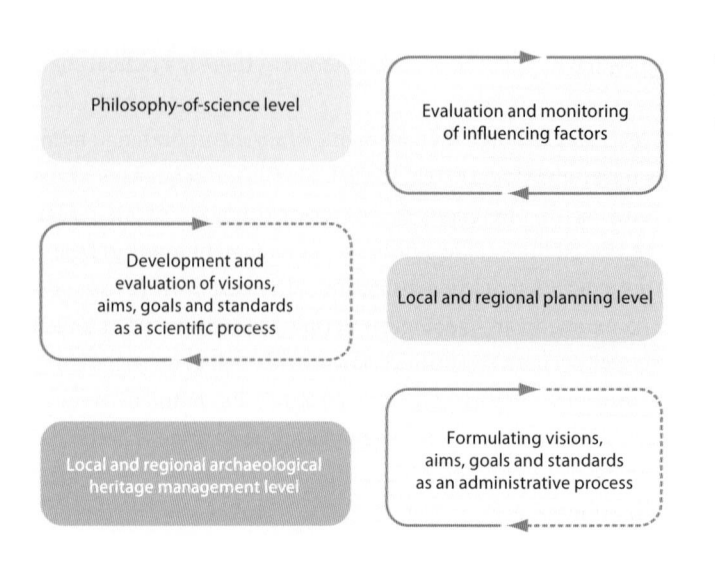

Fig. 2
The interaction levels of the different research fields of archaeological heritage management.

358 • THE CULTURAL LANDSCAPE AND HERITAGE PARADOX

In this context there is a multitude of aspects to be contemplated by the archaeological heritage management side. An archaeological site is primarily an archaeological archive and thus a historical source and, on a more abstract level, a site of memories. From the scientific view it possesses a historical value which should be evaluated for the time levels present. In contrast, the social value of an archaeological site depends on entirely different factors which are subjective and may change through time. It is closely connected with the field of identity creation. It answers the question 'where do we come from?' in the context of the typical Western fixation on the future origination in the nineteenth century 'where are we going?' (e.g. Ickerodt 2008a; *idem* 2008b).

Decisions in archaeological heritage management that favour a cultural heritage site or permit it to be destroyed, as the case may be, define historical narrations in public space and these in turn influence our space-time understanding. Archaeological sites and objects communicate history and therefore do not only provide a historical picture of national relevance. They can just as well readily become a marketable product and in an extreme case stem from historical make-believe, fantasy or imagination.

From the archaeological heritage management viewpoint this leads to a fundamental problem. Which time period should one portray? Which aspect should be stressed at the expense of others?

Even though the dimensions of the problem mentioned above in section 2 can only be touched on, it seems clear to me that a satisfactory solution requires a considerably more complex evaluation. A historical narrative should not be based on chance finds but on the evaluation of its significance for the global history of humankind in the sense of Herder or for local or regional history. There is always a danger for cultural heritage protection that it will be picked up by public interest and become its willing servant. The reason for this is that archaeological discoveries (find, sites, knowledge) are communicated to and understood by the public via social criteria. On a practical level, the scientific-cum-social issue should serve the quality management of communication work (didactics of archaeology). This requires an initial basic step to define a suitable publicly anchored type of reading (semiotics), i.e. how to communicate archaeological information to the public in a way that will be understood. This requires the evaluation of the social background so that the possible ways of understanding the communicated historical facts are not left to intercultural or intersubcultural arbitrariness and are understood within certain limits. Since this step has a social effect it should only be taken if based on previously defined scientific and ethical standards. Thus, this question is not altogether new.

5. CONCLUSIONS

Many might think that the answers to the questions tackled in this paper are self-evident. However, this paper concerns the protection of cultural heritage. This protection work is based on academic knowledge whose roots go back to the nineteenth century. For this reason, as far as its work is concerned, archaeological heritage management today is caught between the claims of academic research and its mandate as an administrative organization. Currently one can see a trend towards the wish to undertake academic research.

Independently of this, our society is changing via an accelerating process of restructuring and reorientation. At the beginning of the nineteenth century about 75% of the working population was employed in agriculture and today the figure is lower than 5%. The rapidly expanding service and information sectors, with their specific needs, have long ago superseded industry as the source of livelihood in urban and globalized post-war postmodern society.

This development has two components which can only be separated by analysis, but both have a massive influence on cultural heritage protection. On one level (1) 'practical cultural heritage protection', we see a growing demand for land and a reduction in the period of use, i.e. residence time. There is a simultaneous improvement and expansion of the infrastructure in the sense of spatial multifunctionality. The direction of these changes is dictated by world trade routes, the international money market and individual interests.

The second component is the social framework. Altogether one can detect an increasing decoupling of business from the social and local or regional environment. This process is not only accompanied by demographic change ('older and more ethnically diverse') but also by a changing perception of space. As argued in section 1, 'practical archaeological heritage management' is characterized by concepts of 'individualization' and 'economization' of spatial perception and is accompanied by a changing national identity. In this way the government's right to influence everyday life should be reduced. The political side naturally wishes to counter this influence (Eurek, European Landscape Convention, etc.) and stresses the aspect of local and regional identity protection.

Against this background the answers to 'for whom is archaeological heritage management carried out?' and 'what social task does archaeological heritage management have?' are considerably more difficult since the answers themselves are not unambiguous. In the case of Germany it is possible to say that archaeological heritage management, with respect to the available personnel and within the current financial framework, is most successful where it contributes directly to the preservation of regional identity. This is particularly true of the eastern part of Germany after reunification.

On the theory of science side, this development is turning out to be highly problematic since the relevant content and formal questions have not been sufficiently studied or understood. This is even truer since archaeological heritage management needs a clear concept and clearly specified aims according to identifiable criteria if it is going to co-operate in long- and medium-term planning procedures. Moreover these aims must be achieved in co-operation with the public in a sustainable way. In this context it is not only essential to develop quality standards but also scientific and ethical standards. This step in the direction of sociology of science opens up completely new perspectives for archaeological interpretation since it permits a distinction to be drawn between social and scientific interpretation patterns and understanding systems. In addition, this proves to be an important tool for ensuring the quality of work by archaeological heritage management and archaeological research.

NOTES

1 Archäologisches Landesamt Schleswig-Holstein, Schleswig, Germany.
2 As a federal state consisting of sixteen states without a centralized institution concerned with archaeological heritage management, Germany can be indicative of very different problems and approaches. They may vary in the different regions and states and in some ways can therefore serve as a model.
3 The 17th General Meeting of UNESCO in Paris in November 1972 was a turning point at which the concerns of cultural heritage protection were incorporated into regional planning. At the end of the Meeting the "Convention concerning the protection of cultural and natural heritage" was signed. Only three years later the "Union International des Sciences Préhistorique et Protohistorique" (Weimar 3-6.11.1975) also discussed this issue. The conference proceedings were published under

the title "Archaeological monuments and environmental management" (Hermann 1978). These two conferences are seen as a reaction to the development described in paragraph 2.

4   With respect to the incorporation of cultural heritage protection interests as part of regional planning, the work of English Heritage appears to have played the role of a forerunner in Europe. The main reason for this step forward was that in England the traditional cultural heritage protection issues and concepts, with respect to the designation of conservation areas, came to the limits of their possibilities in the 1990s and thus cultural heritage protection orders had to be co-ordinated with the political concepts of sustainable development and participation (Ickerodt 2007; Went 2007).

5   An example of this development is the so-called *ethnische Deutung* (ethnical interpretation) developed by G. Kossinna. It was created as a scientific method to explore the self and can be defined as a bourgeois tool of self-legitimation while the contemporaneous North American direct historical approach was developed to explore the past of the native north Americans. Nevertheless, the logic of this approach of ethnic self-exploration functions as legitimation through history, things are the way they are because they succeeded in competition or in the struggle for life (Ickerodt 2008b).

REFERENCES

Angehrn, E., 1996: Ursprungsmythos und Geschichtsdenken, in H. Nagl-Docekal (ed.), *Der Sinn des Historischen. Geschichtsphilosophische Debatten* (P. Nanz [ed.], Philosophie der Gegenwart), Frankfurt am Main, 305-332.

ARL (Akademie für Raumordnung und Landesplanung) (eds.), 2001: *Die Zukunft der Kulturlandschaft zwischen Verlust, Bewahrung und Gestaltung,* Hannover (Forschungs- und Sitzungsberichte Akademie für Raumordnung und Landesplanung 215).

Bauerochse, A./H. Haßmann/U. Ickerodt (eds.), 2007: *Kulturlandschaft. administrativ – digital – touristisch.* Osnabrück.

Bertelsmann Stiftung, 2004: *Politische Partizipation in Deutschland. Ergebnisse einer repräsentativen Umfrage,* Bonn (Bundeszentrale für politische Bildung Schriftenreihe 471).

Brunnengräber, A./A. Klein/H. Walk, 2005: *NGOs im Prozess der Globalisierung. Mächtige Zwerge – umstrittene Zwerge,* Bonn (Bundeszentrale für politische Bildung Schriftenreihe 400).

Bundesbodenschutzgesetz (Gesetz zum Schutz vor schädlichen Bodenveränderungen und zur Sanierung von Altlasten; BbodSchG; German Soil Protection Act. (http.://bundesrecht.juris.de/bbodschg/_2.html)

Habermas, J., 1976 (1990[5]): Geschichte und Evolution, in J. Habermas, *Zur Rekonstruktion des Historischen Materialismus,* Frankfurt am Main, 200-259.

Hermann, J., (ed.), 1978: *Archäologische Denkmale und Umweltgestaltung,* Berlin (Veröffentlichungen des Zentralinstituts für Alte Geschichte und Archäologie der Akademie der Wissenschaften der DDR 9).

Hobsbawm, E./Ranger, T., 1992: *The Invention of Tradition,* Cambridge.

Ickerodt, U., 2004: *Bilder von Archäologen, Bilder von Urmenschen. Ein kultur- und mentalitätsgeschichtlicher Beitrag zur Genese der prähistorischen Archäologie am Beispiel zeitgenössischer Quellen,* Bonn (Ph.D. thesis Martin-Luther-Universität Halle-Wittenberg). (http://sundoc.bibliothek.uni-halle.de/diss-online/05/06H070/ index.htm).

Ickerodt, U., 2005: Hobsbawms erfundene Traditionen – Archäologie als Soziales Phänomen, *Archäologisches Nachrichtenblatt* 10, 167-174.

Ickerodt, U., 2006: The term "cultural landscape", in T. Meier (ed.), *Landscape ideologies,* Budapest (Archaeolingua Series Minor), 53-79.

Ickerodt, U., 2007: Bodendenkmalschutz als Teil des Kulturlandschaftsschutzes, *Nachrichten aus Niedersachsens Urgeschichte* 76, 305-318.

Ickerodt, U. 2008a: "Oh schaurig ist's, übers Moor zu gehen" – Zur gesellschaftlichen Wahrnehmung des Moorleichenfundes Moora, dem Mädchen aus dem Uchter Moor, in A. Bauerochse/H. Haßmann/K. Püschel (eds.), *Moora – eine Moorleiche aus der Eisenzeit aus Niedersachsen 1,* Raden in Westf. (Materialhefte zur Ur- und Frühgeschichte Niedersachsens 37), 111-130.

Ickerodt, U., 2008b: The spatial dimension of history: propagation of historical knowledge via open-air museums, leisure parks and motion pictures, *The Public Journal of Semiotics* 2, 73-102. (http://www.semiotics.ca/issues/pjos-2-2.pdf. Accessed 24 April, 2009).

Ickerodt, U./M. Maluck, 2008: LANCEWADPLAN – The Consideration of specific Processes in Landscape Development on the Wadden Sea Coast in an integrated Management of Cultural Heritage, in C. Bartels/C. Küppers-Eichas (eds.), *Cultural Heritage and Landscapes in Europe. Landschaften: Kulturelles Erbe in Europa. Proceedings of the International Conference, Bochum June 8-10, 2007,* Bochum, 401-423.

Kaufmann, F.-X., 2005: *Schrumpfende Gesellschaft. Vom Bevölkerungsrückgang und seinen Folgen,* Bonn (Bundeszentrale für politische Bildung Schriftenreihe 508).

NIW (Niedersächsisches Institut für Wirtschaftsforschung((eds.), 2005: *Regionalbericht Norddeutschland 2005. Aktuelle wirtschaftliche Entwicklungen in den Regionen von Schleswig-Holstein, Niedersachsen und den angrenzenden Hansestädten sowie in den 16 Bundesländern,* Hannover.

McNeill, W. H., 1986: *Mythistory and other Essays,* Chicago.

Piggott, S., 1937: Prehistory and the Romantic Movement, *Antiquity* 11, 31-38.

ROOK 2005: *Raumordungskonzept für das niedersächsische Küstenmeer. Herausgegeben vom Niedersächsisches Ministerium für den ländlichen Raum, Ernährung, Landwirtschaft und Verbraucherschutz - Regierungsvertretung Oldenburg - Landesentwicklung, Raumordnung. Stand 2005.*

Stiftung Niedersachsen (eds.), 2006: *älter, bunter, weniger. Die demografische Herausforderung an die Kultur,* Bielefeld.

Waugh, K., 2006: *Archaeological Management Strategies in the Planarch Area of North West Europe,* Maidstone.

Went, D., 2007: Painting a bigger picture – an overview of Historic Landscape Characterisation in England, in A. Bauerochse/H. Haßmann/U. Ickerodt (eds.), 2007: *Kulturlandschaft. administrativ – digital – touristisch,* Osnabrück, 145-161.

WEBSITES

www.lancewadplan.org

V

SHARING KNOWLEDGE - STORIES, MAPS AND DESIGN

Mayen (D), Vulkanpark: quarry landscape with electric crane. *Photo: A. Hunold.*

1. Introduction: sharing knowledge - stories, maps and design

Arnold van der Valk[1]

ABSTRACT

This section focuses on questions related to the role of maps, images and metaphors in the process of knowledge creation for cultural landscapes and heritage. Images and metaphors play a pivotal role in the creation of planning support systems and the dissemination of information and interpretation of geographically tagged data. The author emphasises the value-laden character of images and the need to specify underlying frames of reference. Raw data do not speak for themselves no matter how seductively they may be packed. Processing of data and information into knowledge is dependent upon anticipated uses in the domains of science and policymaking. In science, truthfulness is the leading principle. In policy, other values such as legitimacy, applicability and transparency are equally relevant. Framing of knowledge is an emerging theme in scientific research in the aftermath of the European Landscape Convention and its recognition of the importance of the human dimension in landscape valorisation and evaluation.

KEY WORDS

Landscape, preservation, development; images, metaphors, spatial concepts; knowledge-action nexus; European Landscape Convention

1. RATIONALE OF SHARING KNOWLEDGE

1.1 Data and knowledge

Raw data do not speak for themselves. Data have to be interpreted in order to make sense or transformed into meaningful information or knowledge (Popper 1966, 260). Interpretation starts from a theoretical frame of preconceived notions. That is where disciplines, discourses and power conflicts enter scientific narratives which help us make sense of the world we live in (Gibbons *et al.* 1994; Gieryn 1999). After the science wars in the 1990s a growing number of scientists aired their doubts about the rigidity of the old positivistic divide in facts and values (Funtowicz/Ravetz 1990; Flyvbjerg 2001; Ravetz 2007). The papers in this section are all linked in some way by questions pertaining to the processing of knowledge and the transfer of knowledge to the domain of heritage management and spatial planning. The translation of scientific knowledge into policy considerations by way of evaluation, policy design and monitoring opens an amalgam of epistemological and ontological questions (Friedmann 1987; Argyris/Schön 1996[2]; Hisschemöller/Hoppe 1995). Policy is defined here as taking preparatory actions to create a framework for operational decisions. Operational decisions preclude interventions by governmental bodies which may be taken in co-operation with non-governmental organizations. Policy-making encompasses goal setting, data collection, interpretation, valuation, design, choice of means, implementation and monitoring. Knowledge creation is intricately interwoven with the process of policy-making. Knowledge production is supposed to be about facts. Policy making starts from values and norms. This may explain dilemmas with respect to the straightforward application of knowledge in archaeological heritage conservation and landscape planning in the papers in section V.

Data feed our understanding of the empirical world if packed in theoretically informed devices such as thematic maps, models, drawings and narratives (Schön 1987; Nonaka/Takeuchi 1995; Lawson 2006[4]). This section emphasizes the relative importance of images for presentation, analysis and application of knowledge. Images are a powerful tool in communication between scientists and policy-makers and other user groups (Lynch 1998[26]; De Jonge 2009). However, images do not speak for themselves. It takes knowledgeable people to make sense of the patterns, white spots, limits, the parts and the whole. Knowledge is encapsulated in media. It takes experts to make sense of the message and help non-experts such as policy makers and stakeholders to interpret the consequences of their options. The medium is not supposed to be the message. The contributions to this section explore facets of narration and imagination of the landscapes of the past, present and future with a focus on the means for sharing knowledge. First of all we need shared definitions in order to exchange information in a meaningful way. That is why the authors of this volume have agreed to adopt the definition of landscape as perceived in the European Landscape Convention. The PDL/BBO programme researchers present some more unifying concepts such as archaeological-historical landscape, landscape biography, landscape heritage, protection by way of development, prospection, extended peer communities and heritage impact assessment.

1.2 Core questions

Core questions in the introductory text to this section dealing with knowledge and communication extend toward ways of understanding information. First we will dwell upon the potential and limitations of the use of maps. Second, the processing of data and information into knowledge is dependent upon anticipated use in the domains of science and policy-making. In science, truthfulness is the leading principle. In policy, other values such as legitimacy, applicability and transparency are equally relevant (Hoppe 1999; Hillier 2002). Finally the introductory text will explore the scope for learning in international comparative research. These issues will be considered in relation to the topics of the contributions in this section.

Communication between scientists and policy-makers is fraught with complaints from both sides about misunderstandings (Schön 1983; Friedmann 1987; Ravetz 2007). These are aptly illustrated in the contributions by De Zwart and Verhagen *et al.* in this volume. This is not a vice of archaeologists, landscape historians, historical-geographers and practising heritage managers, planners and landscape architects. Creating pathways crossing the boundary between science and policy is a lucrative niche for scholars in contemporary policy science and knowledge sociology. Researchers in the PDL/BBO programme have taken a leaf from the book of boundary work in order to outline the potential for integrative studies (Gieryn 1999; Hoppe/Huijs 2003; Van Londen 2006). The methodological intricacies of this type of work as perceived by the researchers in this programme are outlined by Van der Valk in Ch. II.2 of this volume. Policy-makers, planners and architects may interpret information which is presented to them by way of planning support systems slightly differently from archaeologists, art historians or historical-geographers. Diversions in interpretation may be attributed to a lack of expert knowledge, diverging frames of understanding, different value systems or conflicting legal frames. Confusion and conflict are not a natural state of things in the protection and development of archaeological-historical landscape but the result of mistaken expectations. Conflict can be avoided by deliberation and joint learning in action research as shown in the contributions by Roymans *et al.*, Atmanagara and De Zwart in this volume (cf. Argyris/Schön 1996[2]; Weggeman 2001).

Planning support systems play an important role in the process of boundary work between science and policy-making (Stillwell/Geertman/Openshaw 1999; Couclelis 2005; De Wit 2005; Carsjens 2009). The contribution by Verhagen *et al.* (Ch. V.5) reveals some of the technical, institutional and epistemological shortcomings attached to the transfer of knowledge from one domain to the other. Prospection may be an objective and impartial device in the eyes of scholars but it takes a community of scientific practice or even an extended peer community in order to establish new policy practices and acceptance of the newly devised planning support system for the prospection of archaeological sites.

The paper by Roymans *et al.* in this section (Ch. V.2) touches upon another related obstacle in the communication between science and policy. Policy may take the shape of landscape planning and heritage management. Policy is defined here in line with the European landscape convention as an expression of the competent public authorities of general principles, strategies and guidelines that permit the taking of specific measures. Planning in the public domain is supported by expert knowledge outlining the pros and cons of alternative anticipated courses of actions (Friedmann 1987). Scholars in archaeology and historical geography have high expectations about the application of archaeological and historical knowledge in planning and design, provided that the planning support systems to be applied meet with scientific and legal standards for information management. Furthermore, they assume that planners and landscape architects are able and willing to process the data they have produced. This is not self-evident as is shown in De Zwart's paper in this volume (Ch. V.7). Planners and landscape architects are caught in a comprehensive balancing act directed by politicians and interest groups. Diverging disciplinary perspectives and professional discourses may pose an obstacle towards common understanding. De Zwart offers striking proof of misunderstanding between archaeologists, planners and politicians which is due to diverging frames or discourses (Howarth 2005). Archaeologists and historians may prefer simple sectoral rules over complex integral legal frameworks for environmental and spatial planning. Planners tend to prefer the statutory planning system and sticking to more rigid sectoral rules as a last resort. Designers tend to prefer knowledge which opens up new creative options and does not close off space for action. Therefore sharing knowledge among participants in the planning process, even among experts in the domain of archaeology alone, is not simple. Archaeological and historical maps and models are filtered on the road to action. One way to prevent confusion and conflict is the use of comprehensible yet broadly applicable definitions by way of constructing a common language. The European Landscape Convention may serve as a case in point.

2. IMPACT OF THE EUROPEAN LANDSCAPE CONVENTION

2.1 *The European Landscape Convention*

The European Landscape Convention adopted in Florence in 2000 is a Council of Europe project (Florence 2000; Landscape Character Network 2008; Council of Europe 2008). The Landscape Convention is a comprehensive complement to the 1992 Valletta Convention on archaeology. Although the Landscape Convention has not yet been signed by all European countries and leaves ample room for derogations and exceptions for national legislative bodies, it is considered to be a major step on the road to sustainable landscape management. The definition of landscape as used in the convention does not exclude the hidden or covered traces of the past which tend to be easily overlooked by experts and decision-makers trained outside the domain of archaeology. Landscape is delimited as "an area, as perceived by people, whose character is the result of the action and interaction of natural and/or human factors". This definition reflects a growing recognition of landscape being an important condition for quality of life, an ingredient of sustainable development of the human environment and a building block for local, regional, national and European identity.

Countries which have signed the convention commit themselves to engage in landscape protection, management and planning. For most countries this is not a brand new task (Howard *et al.* 2007); however, the general idea is to integrate the landscape dimension in a wide range of territorial policies and apply a long list of general principles. The issues covered are manifold. First, the convention takes a comprehensive perspective on territory. Second, it emphasizes the fundamental role of knowledge. Third, it promotes public awareness. Fourth, it encompasses a specific conception of landscape quality objectives and strategies. Fifth, it advocates integration of landscape in spatial planning and integration of landscape in sectoral policies while making use of public participation. The broad definition of landscape does not distinguish between rural, urban and peri-urban environments. It takes into consideration physical, cultural, social and economic dimensions. Most importantly it encompasses the sensory and emotional relations people develop with their environment. Thus they become aware of particular historical and cultural features which serve as constituting parts of the identity of a territory's population.

The convention urges for protection in order to conserve and maintain significant or characteristic features of the landscape. It does so by way of recognition of the need to manage landscape change. Change is caused by driving physical, social and economic forces which impact upon the use of land. Management is a tool for continuous action in order to bring about planned modifications keeping intact basic values. These are made explicit in landscape policies and plans combining ecological, archaeological, historical, cultural, perceptive and economic perspectives. The spirit of the convention is strongly in favour of smart development avoiding the dangers of rigid protection schemes. The convention lays emphasis on the drawing up of specific landscape policies and landscape planning. Landscape planning is defined as "(..) strong forward-looking action to enhance, restore and create landscapes." (Landscape Character Network 2008, 4). These phrases create ample opportunity to link landscape planning to people's ordinary life worlds, taking into account ongoing developments, degraded environments and shared ambitions. Bringing landscape closer to people's knowledge of their environment as a source of inspiration for planning is an explicit goal of the Landscape Convention. In this context, the PDL/BBO's objectives fit in nicely with the Convention's goals. Therefore definitions of the objects of research in the programme are squared with definitions in the Landscape Convention. The spirit of the Convention is a powerful presence in most of the papers in this volume.

A core argument about the importance of the Landscape Convention pertains to the potential of landscape as a unifying concept for people's commitments to their environment, to the dedication of a wide range of scientific disciplines and to sectors of government (Howard *et al.* 2007). It refers to the need to synthesize a wide range of perspectives in order to promote good causes, i.e. quality of life, sustainability and creation of identity. Landscape raises associations to widely diverging worlds of understanding and/or action labelled respectively 'matterscape', 'powerscape' and 'mindscape' by social scientist and philosopher Maarten Jacobs (Jacobs 2006). Reference to landscape as matterscape focuses attention on the description and analysis of physical characteristics such as soils, traces of human activities, hydrology, actual and historical vegetation, biotopes for living creatures, parcellation and property. Matterscape is the object of research in empirical science. In the domain of matterscapes, scientists prevail. It is explained best in covering laws and quantitative models. Landscape framed as powerscape directs attention to institutional regimes and organizational structures giving direction to the uses of land and the management of changes. The language of powerscape is the jargon of politicians, architects, planners and policy scientists. It is full of narratives, metaphors and imagery. The electorate has a final say in the creation of powerscape. Landscape perceived as mindscape sheds light on the emotional and sensory relations between people and their territory. Mindscapes mirror value judgements and perceptions of individuals and groups. As such, mindscapes are explored and interpreted by artists, tourists, philosophers and psychologists. The European Landscape Convention encompasses all three domains and attempts to link them up.

The Convention further emphasizes the importance of knowledge as the basis for action. This echoes the contemporary spirit of evidence-based policy-making (Nowotny/Scott/Gibbons 2001; Davoudi 2006; Faludi/Waterhout 2006). Planning and government intervention is in need of neutral and objective argumentation thus applying the rationality principle and separation of values and facts. In spite of growing opposition to the modernistic or positivistic paradigm in science and government, these principles are still valued by practitioners and deeply rooted in popular images of good government. Both modernist and postmodernist tendencies in science adhere to the principle of evidence-based planning as the predominant form of legitimizing political choices. The philosophy of evidence-based planning encompasses the continuation of efforts to discern facts, values, means and objectives respectively pertaining to the worlds of science and politics.

2.2 Framing of knowledge

The underlying concept of knowledge production in this text is a cumulative process in three steps. The first step pertains to the collection of data and primary classification. This may be a process of trial and error. The second step is ranking and bringing tentative order, thus upgrading data into information. The third and final step focuses on the creation of meaning for the users. In the empirical sciences this may refer to the testing of preconceived theories pertaining to covering laws and cause-effect chains. In the humanities the process of knowledge management may also focus on the construction of interpretations and narratives. During the science wars between positivists and social-constructivists in the 1990s the positions of both tendencies in science were opposite. In archaeology, the science war raged between adherents of processual versus post-processual archaeology (Bloemers 1991a; *idem* 1991b; Preucel 1994; Jones 2004). The PDL/BBO participants have extensively reflected upon the methodological consequences of the divide between explanatory and interpretative sciences and tendencies. The 2008 Lunteren conference reflected a shared feeling of distance from this unproductive controversy. Non-archaeologists present at the Lunteren conference noted it was revealing that archaeologists are only marginally aware of the links with similar paradigmatic debates in adjacent disciplines such as urban and regional planning, policy sciences, geography and landscape ecology (Balducci/Bertolini 2007a; *idem* 2007b). This is evident in the contribution by Verhagen *et al.* (Ch. V.5). Jones (Jones 2004) is perceived by the editors of this volume as the leader of an emerging tendency in archaeology which combines the best of the two worlds.

It is clear that tailor-made knowledge is a key resource in the identification, analysis and assessment of landscape quality. Decision-making presupposes an adequate knowledge base but the creation of knowledge is not the privilege of trained scientists. The Landscape Convention promotes the (post) modern notion of joint learning. Guidelines for implementation, adopted by the Committee of Ministers from the European Council's member states, explicitly address means of collaboration between experts and stakeholders. The section about knowledge makes reference to many innovative and conventional practices in the process of landscape knowledge creation. The conventional approach of planning is the expert model, encompassing episodes of survey, analysis and plan-making in precisely that sequence. Survey, e.g. producing landscape atlases, precedes the valuation of landscape structures and decision making. However the valuation of landscape is not the sole responsibility of a specific category of experts, be they ecologists or archaeologists. These documents are supposed to be a means to an end, and no more than that, in the process of communication with stakeholders. What is innovative is the special emphasis which rests on the promotion of integration of different types of territorially bound knowledge production. Ease of access, clarity and transparency of data and methods of knowledge production are explicitly demanded. This is for the sake of securing public involvement in landscape policy choices. In this way, the convention mirrors modern societal preferences for governance and bottom-up decision-making as opposed to traditional top-down government where scientists are supposed to speak truth to power, paraphrasing policy scientist Aaron Wildawsky (Wildawsky 1987). The PDL/BBO Programme brings these principles into practice, adopting a dialogical approach.

3. CONDITIONS FOR SUCCESS IN LANDSCAPE DIALOGUE

3.1 Introduction

Dialogue about the analysis, planning and design of cultural landscape legacy is not a minor detail. Various groups of experts, stakeholders and people in power are involved in surveying, interpretation, diagnosing problems and providing solutions and all adopt their own specific perspective, using their own jargon and telling their stories about past, present and future. According to Roymans *et al.* and Atmanagara (Ch. V.2 and 3) landscape legacy is not so much about the past as about the present and the future of cultural landscape. We will dwell upon this subject a little longer, but first we turn our attention to the role of information and knowledge in landscape dialogue. Knowledge is defined here as processed information, ready for use by anticipated consumers. A recurrent question in this volume pertains to discrepancies between the knowledge producer's expectations and the consumer's actual needs. We will address this question by identifying conditions for success in communication between producers and consumers.

Databases, maps, character assessments and other knowledge resources constitute a common reference framework and a common language for collaboration between various fields of expertise, various groups of stakeholders and decision takers (Council of Europe 2008). This demand is explicitly addressed throughout the Planning and Developing Programme and has been discussed intensively in the concluding international Lunteren conference.

3.2 Conditions

Creating a body of shared knowledge among a wide variety of disciplines is a major effort (Fry *et al.* 2003; De Boer *et al.* 2006). Sharing knowledge is a complex process of communication touching on questions of framing, interpretation, signification, disciplinary conventions and bringing together diverging scientific paradigms. The papers in this volume bring forward a wide range of best practices and guidelines showing necessary conditions for successful interdisciplinary and transdisciplinary work. These are the conditions for success or failure.

First it takes unifying concepts which are accessible for all the participating scholars and the consumers of knowledge. The unifying powers may be attributed to openness and flexibility combined with clarity. This boils down to somewhat paradoxical demands. Elements securing immunity to misinterpretation are coupled with provisions for the integration of various discourses. Biography of landscape is an example of a unifying concept in the Protecting and Developing Programme, being a vehicle for common understanding. Biography is a powerful metaphor which leaves ample scope for slightly diverging interpretations as shown in the regional studies in the PDL/BBO programme presented in this volume by Bloemers *et al.* (Ch.IV.2), Elerie/Spek (Ch. III.2), Roymans *et al.* (Ch. V.2) and Vervloet *et al* (Ch. III.4). The use of similar concepts and jargon by all of the participants of a research programme does not provide guarantees about convergence in meanings attached to the words. Although it is not sufficient, the use of mutually familiar words, images and concepts helps in creating common understanding among the participants. This specifically applies to key concepts which are explored and defined in a process of open discussion. The contribution by Roymans *et al.* in this section focuses attention on a promising vehicle for the origins of unifying concepts in collaborative policy development, i.e. the creation of extended peer communities.

A second necessary condition for the creation of shared knowledge is an open mind, frequent group meetings and the capacity to show empathy. Experts show a tendency to consider their norms and values as superior to competing disciplines. Heritage experts are no exception to this rule. Well developed branches of science which demand a high degree of specialization and education are less inclined to an exchange of knowledge and joint learning than less well developed disciplines. Sociologists make mention of certain characteristics of established scientific professions. These include a well defined body of knowledge, a professional platform, professional journals, professional ethics and quality assessment (Gold 1976). The divide between fully-fledged professions and semi-institutionalized disciplines shows some coherence with the divide in science between empirical and technically oriented scientists and conceptual scholars.

In this section of the volume, the papers by Kars *et al.*, Verhagen *et al.* on the one hand, and the papers by Roymans *et al.* and De Zwart on the other hand, feed a (biased) suspicion of a divide between competing discourses in modern landscape science. Notice the differences in the use of methods, the appreciation of precision in the treatment of data, the application of technology and the use of words and numbers. During the implementation of the programme the basis for communication between the extremes in the programme has been broadened due to a growing understanding of the necessity of open minds, frequent meetings and empathy. The presence of a broad range of mixed empirical-conceptual disciplines such as environmental sciences, landscape archaeology and landscape ecology, as exemplified in the contributions of Atmanagara, Jones and Ruiz del Árbol and Orejas, shows various ways to bridge the gaps between scientific disciplines and their associated professions.

The third necessary condition which may be deduced from best practices revealed in the PDL/BBO programme is the relevance of shared ideals. Most participants feel the need to enhance the role of archaeology and historical geography in landscape planning and design. They also advocate promotion of public awareness. Other participants profess their explicit support for sustainable development, improvement of quality of life for inhabitants or strengthening local and regional identity. Scientific ambitions and social goals are intricately mixed in this volume, which seems appropriate for the final report of a strategic and applied research programme. Taking social values into consideration raises challenging epistemological, methodological and ethical questions. The contributions by Atmanagara, Ruiz del Árbol, Vollmer-König and De Zwart show facets of the emerging questions and dilemmas.

A fourth condition is the acceptance of applied research methods among scholars. Verhagen *et al.* and Kars *et al.* make reference to the institutional barriers against a proliferation of state of the art research techniques and models for prediction and prospection. Discussions in the aftermath of the synthesis of the constitutive projects of the PDL/BBO programme have resulted in disagreement among archaeologists and policy-makers about the validity, the possibilities for generalization and the practical value of regional case studies. On the positive side we notice a growing consensus with respect to the sophistication of impact assessment methods, see for example the contribution by Carys Jones in this section about the design of assessment devices for archaeological heritage management in the UK. Maria Ruiz del Árbol raises interesting questions about the opportunities and obstacles for the application of Dutch research and assessment methods to the Spanish multi-tiered system of landscape assessment, heritage management and landscape planning. Vollmer-König attaches less weight to the acceptance of well established survey methods. He prefers a practical goal-oriented strategy for all-inclusive landscape protection taking an administrative point of view. Bothering about state of the art research technology, calibration of models and sophistication of data management is not his major concern as an administrator. Awkward though this may sound to scholars, Vollmer-König's position is supported in the ranks of practising planners, designers and lawyers.

A fifth condition implicitly seen in a range of contributions in this section and the volume as a whole is the need for a thorough understanding of the relationship between diverging branches of research, planning, design and policy. This pertains to boundary work in between the worlds of science and action. A common source of confusion is the idea that high quality survey and research automatically produce excellent policy guidelines. The adjective 'excellent' refers to logically deduced and thus scientifically sound. In contemporary policy sciences this axiom is considered to be a product of old school positivism. Judging by the views expressed during the Lunteren conference, the group of adherents to this axiom is decreasing.

One more source of confusion is the equation of heritage with history. Planners, architects and non-experts in the domain of history and archaeology are inclined to take the equation for granted, much to the detriment of common understanding. Roymans *et al.* and the Lunteren conference participants make a rather more strict divide. Landscape history is defined as an intellectual interest in the past *per se*. It is the domain of experts par excellence. Heritage is defined as a practice designed to situate the past in, or adapt it to, the present. History and heritage trigger diverging types of research questions. History focuses primarily on revealing true stories about the past. Heritage revolves around group identity, inclusion and exclusion. Questions about landscape legacy always imply questions about whose legacy. A seemingly innocent definitional component in the European Landscape Convention making reference to "landscape as perceived by people" is bound to evoke mind-boggling questions about appropriation, changing preferences and dominant discourses and a range of other socio-political and ethical issues.

3.3 Past Particulars and Grounded Theory

According to Roymans *et al.* and Atmanagara, historians will have to give up some more popular convictions in order to improve their performance in the process of interaction with planners, stakeholder groups and the polity. They specifically refer to the idea of repetition in the unfolding of landscape history and the probability that history will repeat itself in the future. As a consequence, historical knowledge is deemed highly relevant for the interpretation of actual landscape dynamics and the formulation of inherent planning proposals. This is a faulty perspective on history according to Roymans *et al.* because it omits human agency and free choice. Roymans and Atmanagara are in agreement about the fallacy of the underlying premises. History can make an important contribution to the analysis of things past but not necessarily by deducing predetermined scenarios.

Roymans and Atmanagara are aware of the complexities of the process of communication between heritage scholars and planners-designers. They emphasize the importance of maps, images and metaphors as powerful devices in the process of communication. However, the pictures do not speak for themselves. They are interpreted by the receivers of information. Contrary to a premise held by naïve positivists, Roymans acknowledges obstacles to communication due to diverging frameworks and unspecified roles and ambitions. The process of communication is fraught with complexities which so far have been under-researched. Roymans' paper underlines the role of landscape designers as mediators between historians and design professionals, as well as the importance of stakeholder participation in the plan-making process. The professed goal of applying storylines uncovered by historical disciplines in heritage management and landscape planning is a complex task. Atmanagara makes it clear that part of the problem pertains to differences in the outlook of historians and planners. The needs and goals are basically different. Historical disciplines are interested in the production of knowledge about the substance of landscape and human and natural forces shaping it. Planners and landscape designers show an interest in narratives and images which may help in developing attractive concepts and alternative scenarios and strategies.

Roymans and other authors on landscape biography in this volume produce many pages of insightful information based on case studies. The problem is we have no clue as to the general relevance of best practices depicted in laboratory situations such as 'Biography of De Zandstad' and 'Biography of Peelland'. Atmanagara surmises that the Brabant experience offers promising hypotheses for international comparative research. Here she makes reference to lessons from the 'Landscape Typology for Switzerland' implemented at the Institute of Geography in Bern in the context of the Cost A27 LANDMARKS programme. The construction of a body of empirically founded knowledge about necessary and sufficient conditions for sharing knowledge remains a core question. We are in need of grounded theory of a knowledge-action nexus in heritage management and landscape planning (Strauss/Corbin 1997; Flyvbjerg 2001; Charmaz 2006; Seaman 2008).

This volume identifies building blocks but the bulk of the scientific and practical work seems to lie ahead of us. We may add to this that national and regional cultural factors tend to obscure generic conclusions. This is to be perceived as encouragement towards international comparative research.

4. LANDSCAPE RESEARCH AND PLANNING: STORYTELLING AND MAPPING

The authors of this volume, be they archaeologists, historians, geographers, planners or architects, all share the ambition of making a contribution to contemporary planning. But do they all share the same concept of landscape research and landscape planning? The reader may feel tempted to make his/her own judgement.

One particular perspective on archaeological and historical landscape research deserves special attention, i.e. storytelling. This fits in with the needs expressed by many a planner and architect during the Lunteren conference. Historians feel inclined to focus on the properties of landscape *per se*, thus deepening the understanding of shaping forces of landscapes. In a dialogue with planners and stakeholders this is not necessarily a recipe for success, since the others may perceive the historians´ truth as irrelevant to their needs and interests. This of course does not mean that historians are advised to refrain from collaborative working processes, but they had better reflect upon their role and refrain from imposing their view of heritage on stakeholders. Roymans encourages archaeologists and historians to perform as academically trained storytellers. Landscape biography may be perceived as the medium for this enterprise. Writing a landscape biography is an integral part of the process of enforcing or weakening group identities. Historians are supposed to provide resources for the creation of constructions of identity in societal dialogue. They are well equipped to identify which layers of meaning are attached to the landscape. This leaves the decisions to the people in power. Archaeologists and historians are in a position to exert influence by mediating meaningful stories to consumers of knowledge. Looking at the transfer of archaeological and historical knowledge from this angle, truthfulness is not the only and probably not the first criterion for success. The historians' vocation may be to broaden the understanding of past landscapes, thus presenting a wider scope of options for choice for the future landscape to planners, architects and stakeholders.

Spatial planners take pride in scanning past, present and future social needs and patterns of land use in order to devise strategies to solve discrepancies between aspired and actual patterns (Elmore 1979; Forester 1999; Hillier 2002; Needham 2007). Thus perceived planning focuses on backward mapping and forward mapping of land use, needs and interventions. Associated types of research bring with them special demands which appear rather awkward to academically trained archaeologists and historians. Backward mapping means establishing the need for, and character of, actions in the present which will lead to specific goals encapsulated in concepts of preconceived futures. The future is the point of departure. Forward mapping implies the mapping of trends and actual needs and extrapolation of scenarios into the distant future. According to Atmanagara, knowledge about the distant past is not terribly relevant in planning survey because demography, technology and the economy have changed profoundly in the twentieth and twenty-first century. Planners are particularly interested in the establishment of consequences of anticipated actions. Thus they map out opportunities and obstacles taking into account power structures. This goes to show that archaeological-historical research does not automatically qualify as planning research. The ultimate goal of landscape inquiries is the creation of landscape awareness among planners including notions of dynamics, strata, structure and transformations in time. In this context action research is identified as a promising road forward. Action research is a reflective process of interactive research and problem solving aimed at the promotion of learning processes on the job (Argyris/Schön 1996[2]; Yanow 2003).

5. PROGRESS IN SCIENTIFIC RESEARCH IN ARCHAEOLOGY AND THE UNFOLDING OF DECISION SUPPORT SYSTEMS

5.1 Decision support systems

The 1992 Valletta Convention has strengthened the foundations for a shared body of scientific knowledge and applied technology for archaeological-historical heritage. Papers in this section written by Jones, Kars *et al.* and Verhagen *et al.* deal with aspects of the origins of a body of advanced archaeological-historical technology based on state of the art science. They also demonstrate the existence of strong cultural-institutional barriers in the world of conventional scholars, practitioners and policy-makers. Here we surmise the relevance of concepts taken from the domain of planning sciences, such as boundary work, uncertainty management and the role of planning support systems (Funtowitcz/Ravetz 1990; Hoppe 1999; Friend/Hickling 2005[3]; Carsjens 2009).

One core issue is the image of scientifically underpinned decision-making in public policy (Friedmann 1987; Faludi/Van der Valk 1994). The dominant view of decision-making underlying the Valletta Convention is the rational central-rule approach to decision-making (Van Gunsteren 1976). This view starts from the notion of a planning subject which is geared to weigh all options and the impacts attached to it, taking into consideration a fixed set of policy goals. The planning subject is supposed to choose the best option under consideration as far as discernable within the limits of its intellectual, cultural and political frames. Herbert Simon, Amitai Etzioni and Andreas Faludi have developed this decision rule into full-blown planning decision methods under the aegis of the bounded-rationality principle (Camhis 1979; Faludi 1986; Simon 1997; Friend/Hickling 2005[3]). In practice this comes down to the successive elimination of low-score options. The subject's frame of reference changes over time and varies according to place. What stands out in this scientific approach to planning is the high esteem for evidence-based planning, i.e. scientific evidence. The evidence is presented by way of the classic devices of normal science, i.e. quantitative models of geographically tagged data (Couclelis 2005; Davoudi 2006; Faludi/Waterhout 2006). These are the main sources of inspiration for the booming business of impact analysis. With the help of the Valletta Convention, archaeologists and historians are on the road to emulate the successes of environmentalists and ecologists.

5.2 Environmental Impact Assessment

The paper by Carys Jones (Ch. V.6) reports on progress in the field of assessing cultural heritage impacts in the wider context of environmental impact assessment. Her findings are based on the Planarch study funded by the European Union and on selected best practices in northwestern Europe. The basic question is, is the growing interest in heritage management translated into European, national and regional legislation directives and finally put into practice? The proof of the pudding is in the eating. Jones explores the field, focusing on regional and local cases of environmental impact studies. The English case studies are a rich source of in-depth study of key actors and flaws in the decision-making process.

The fieldwork results from the UK are presented in the context of six episodes of the process of impact assessment. The stages reflect popular models of evidence-based planning in the tradition of the rational planning paradigm as recounted earlier. Comparison of the outcomes with classic analyses of complex decision-making processes in the domain of spatial and environmental planning holds a promise for future research. The aim of this type of research can be the articulation of a grounded theory of heritage impact analysis comprising of building blocks from contemporary generic theories of impact analysis in planning theory and policy science (Allmendinger 2002; Charmaz 2006; Van Dijk 2008).

Jones distils the dos and don'ts of a grounded theory-in-the-making from a wide range of carefully selected case studies. Grounded theory in policy sciences and the humanities holds a mix of empirically validated analytical concepts as well as normative precepts (Flyvbjerg 2001; Bal 2002; Creswell 2003; Seaman 2008). The professed goal of cultural heritage assessment is raising the profile of cultural heritage by enhancing the knowledge of participants in the policy process. This pertains to different tiers of government and levels of decision-making. The underlying premise is the sharing of knowledge among key actors in spatial planning as a necessary condition for success in the protection and development of cultural heritage.

Decision-making under the rule of the bounded-rationality principle in planning favours quantitative methods of the articulation of consequences of anticipated actions over qualitative methods (Allmendinger 2002). So far, the methods used in historical impact assessment compare unfavourably to the results of most other branches of applied research in planning. Unlike demographic research, economic analysis or environmental research, the results of historical landscape analysis cannot easily be translated into generic and comparable criteria. The lack of uniform quantitative criteria puts landscape history in a relatively weak position in the emerging broad field of policy impact assessment (RebelGroup 2007). Archaeology is in a relatively privileged position due to progress in the establishment of legally sanctioned quality norms. In the Netherlands, policy impact analysis has been standard practice in the domain of spatial planning, environmental planning and economic planning for decades. Recently, EU legislation and national regulation have substantially broadened and deepened the playfield of impact analysis (Van Dijk 2008).

5.3 Social Cost Benefit Analysis

The relatively backward situation in historical impact assessment has triggered the management committee of the PDL/BBO programme to commission an exploratory research project by economists Ruijgrok and Nillesen (Nillesen 2004). They were asked to scan the state of historical impact assessment and develop methods for measuring impacts in various domains of historic amenities with the help of a uniform monetary standard. They have produced a pilot study which resulted in a series of further studies on the quantification and standardization of social-cultural values (Ruijgrok/Brouwer/Verbruggen 2004; Ruijgrok 2006; Ruijgrok/Bel 2008). This series encompasses recent in-depth studies on landscape valuation for the Dutch Ministry of Agriculture, Nature and Food Quality and reports on the valuation of aspects of built heritage for the Ministry of Education, Culture and Science. The 2004 exploratory inquiry combines the worlds of heritage research and socio-economic cost-benefit analysis. The report introduces methods and standards (such as hedonic pricing and contingent valuation methods) which are so far unknown to the vast majority of scholars in archaeology and heritage research. The common denominator in these methods is an attempt to attach a price to products and services which are not traded in a free market. They are commonly considered to be public goods and services. As a consequence, policy-makers are not able to attach a clear weight to the goods. In the community of heritage managers and spatial planners today the idea is gaining ground that ultimately soft values will never be on par with hard quantifiable values. Thus, the development of uniform monetary standards for landscape heritage management puts archaeology and landscape history on an equal footing with ecology.

The establishment of fixed and uniform criteria raises intriguing questions about underlying scientific and social premises. For example, criteria are based upon expert judgement and best practices. Expert judgement reflects dominant power structures in science and government. What is considered best practice may change overnight due to alleged failures or success stories. We are well advised to take into consideration that the trend towards quantification fits in with a trend in government and policy sciences known as new public management. The body of knowledge bringing up well founded criticisms against the economization of government has been growing recently. For the time being, social cost-benefit analysis is perceived as a promising field of research for economists with an interest in heritage and land use planning (European Commission 2002).

5.4 *Prospection and predictive modelling*

One issue in the PDL/BBO programme's complex knowledge-action nexus in archaeological heritage management and spatial planning requiring further in-depth research is the evaluation and application of state-of-the-art scientific prospection of archaeological sites and predictive modelling (Kamermans/Van Leusen/Verhagen 2009). This section presents the results of recent explorations in predictive modelling and new technology for prospection by research groups led by Hans Kamermans and Henk Kars respectively.

New and improved technology holds promise for the development of more effective and more efficient planning support systems. Leading archaeologists underpin the need for scientifically valid devices for exploration with arguments such as a rough estimate shows that known archaeological resources stand at 5% of the total amount (known and as yet unknown). High quality prospective and predictive data are an indispensable source for archaeological heritage management and the determination of excavation strategies.

Kars *et al.* (Ch. V.4) have developed multi-disciplinary methods for prospection focusing on the application of non-destructive techniques which are deemed suitable for various soil types. This pertains to geophysical, geochemical and magnetic prospection combined with remote sensing techniques. Thus researchers produce images on maps. Maps tell a story of the character of sites and the conditions of material heritage in its actual physical context. This type of data provides clues as to a desirable conservation strategy and/or excavation in line with policy guidelines in the Valletta Convention.

The promise of sophisticated predictive modelling as researched by Verhagen *et al.* (this volume Ch. V.5; Kamermans/Van Leusen/Verhagen 2009) within the context of the PDL/BBO programme is a story which has not yet resulted in broad recognition in practice. Predictive modelling is a technique that tries to predict the location of archaeological sites in a region based on analysis of samples or on fundamental notions concerning human behaviour. Predictive models use the best knowledge available within financial, human and technical constraints in archaeological heritage management in the era of implementation of the Valletta Convention. In their contribution in this section, Kamermans *et al.* make a forceful plea in favour of state-of-the-art predictive modelling technology for the sake of more effective and efficient handling of scarce human and financial resources in archaeological heritage management.

So far, research has produced encouraging results from a methodological and technical point of view. In his contribution Ducke endorses the scientific merits of the inquiries by Verhagen *et al.* For over twenty years the results have been perceived as most promising by the peer community in science. However, old prejudices in the Dutch community of archaeological heritage management practitioners and scholars are still in place. Practitioners have upheld their scepticism of the application of alleged state-of-the art technology such as Bayesian statistical analysis. As yet, the methodological and theoretical complexities of predictive modelling are perceived as unmanageable by the community of practice. The criticisms focus on three issues, namely defective statistics, unsatisfactory theories of human behaviour and lack of data. Verhagen *et al.* confirm the criticisms but they argue that their state-of-the art science provides a means to overcome the shortcomings. The problem is that so far they have not been able to convince the Dutch peers. As a consequence, improved technology has not yet been implemented in practice.

The objective of the research effort has been the development of predictive modelling into a full-blown risk assessment tool for archaeological heritage management and spatial planning. A major breakthrough is the application of Bayesian statistical techniques for the provision of numerical accurate estimates and intervals based on expert judgement and data as opposed to the traditional maps based only on expert judgement, designating zones of low, medium and high probability of presence of sites and artefacts. Although not all scientific and technical intricacies have been solved so far, the results have been very promising in the eyes of the authors and their international peers. They have produced predictive models showing high accuracy and designation of fields and levels of uncertainty (Deeben *et al.* 1997; Kamermans/Van Leusen/Verhagen 2009).

The Achilles heel of methods currently in use is non-reliable data. With the present low level of reliability, advanced statistical technology cannot come to fruition. Here Kamermans and his research group meet with a paradox. Predictive models are developed with the aim of reducing the amount of expensive survey in low probability zones, but for reasons of statistical rigour intensive research in these zones is a necessary condition. Zones of low probability are in fact zones where little archaeological research has been conducted. Now the further development of predictive models into full-blown risk assessment tools is at stake. Reliable datasets for model testing have so far proved to be a major obstacle. Expert judgement cannot replace accurate quantifiable data based on representative samples. Focusing research on high probability zones is the equivalent of bringing more water to the sea in predictive modelling. Improving predictive modelling with the help of accurate techniques and data holds promise for the eagerly awaited production of archaeological impact assessment maps with a facility for prediction of archaeological costs and benefits specified in euros. So far, institutional obstacles have stood in the way of technological innovation. From an interdisciplinary perspective, the story of the reception of predictive modelling in archaeological heritage management attracts attention to possible lessons to be learned from generic innovation and technology studies. Planning scholars will easily find analogies between the defective application of predictive modelling in archaeological heritage management and the problematic implementation of state-of-the art planning support technology in spatial planning.

Both archaeology and planning science are confronted with the divide between normal and postnormal science as well as an evolution from mode 1 science to mode 2 science. Normal science revolves around conventional disciplinary puzzle solving. Post-normal science practises methods of inquiry which are appropriate for cases where facts are uncertain, stakes high and decisions urgent. This implies extended peer review by a mixed group of scholars, practitioners and stakeholders (Funtowitcz/Ravetz 1990; Ravetz 2007). The concept of an evolution of science coming from traditional mode 1 science was put forward by sociologist of science Michael Gibbons and his team in 1994 (Gibbons *et al.* 1994; Nowotny/Scott/Gibbons 2001). Mode 1 science is conventional academic, researcher-initiated, peer-reviewed, discipline-based knowledge production. Mode 2 science has evolved since the middle of the twentieth century in centres for applied research and has gradually conquered strongholds in academia. Research is practice oriented, problem focused and interdisciplinary.

6. LANDSCAPE HERITAGE AND PLANNING CONTEMPORARY LANDSCAPES: POWERSCAPES

6.1 *Communication breakdown and congruency*

New perspectives on the evolution of science such as those mentioned above open up windows on the world of power. Traditional scientists stick to facts and objectivity, they feel their role is speaking truth to power (Wildawsky 1987; Hoppe 1999). Postmodernists and scholars versed in mode 2 science are more sensitive to the role of values and interests in research and decision-making. De Zwart's contribution to this section (Ch.V.7) shows the outcomes of in-depth case studies of the mechanisms of decision-making in the realm of archaeological heritage management and spatial planning in the Netherlands. She outlines a grounded theory of knowledge sharing. Her case studies provide rich and detailed information about the appropriation and implementation of archaeological heritage management in the aftermath of the Valletta Convention. Her inquiries exemplify the aim of interdisciplinary research. Being an archaeologist by training, she explores promising theories about framing and learning as developed in policy sciences. These theories were applied to the explanation of dilemmas, anomalies and conflicts in local and regional planning practice during the 1990s.

She builds her analysis of the unfortunate sequence of miscommunications between archaeologists, planners and local authorities on the concept of diverging frames, thus taking a leaf from the works of Chris Argyris and Donald Schön (e.g. Schön 1983; *idem* 1987; Argyris/Schön 1996[2]) on organizational learning. Archaeologists, planners and politicians have different world views and problem definitions. Starting from diverging frames they develop diverging interpretations of heritage, statutory rules and opportunities for development and conservation. Archaeologists, planners and politicians are inclined to act from different rationales, they use different jargon and they belong to different discursive communities. De Zwart has reconstructed three discursive communities which are manifestly present in her case studies. The clash between discourse communities explains conflicts and missed opportunities in the domain of archaeological heritage management. She develops a conceptual framework of congruency as a means to overcome miscommunication. The creation of congruent meanings between actors is considered to be a sufficient condition for joint action. The definition of congruence is that the meaning of a concept is not so much fully shared between actors but perceived as making sense on a basic level of understanding. A theory of the creation of congruent meanings provides clues for prudent strategies in heritage management and spatial planning. The theory of congruency between conflicting discourses in spatial planning and archaeological heritage management offers a promising perspective for comparative interdisciplinary research.

6.2 *Heritage management and landscape planning in southern Europe*

The existence of an elaborate statutory system of planning and heritage management offers no guarantees for effective and efficient landscape development and preservation. This message is clear in the paper by Ruiz del Árbol and Orejas in this section (Ch. V.8). They set their analysis of heritage management and landscape planning in southern Europe against the backdrop of the Dutch preservation-by-way-of-development doctrine and the concept archaeological-historical landscape. They express the feeling that the core concepts of the PDL/BBO programme offer an analytical framework and guidelines for the improvement of landscape planning in the Mediterranean.

They spot a dilemma which touches upon our key issue of sharing knowledge. In their view, embedding knowledge about archaeological-historical monuments in the broader context of landscape studies is a necessary condition for success in comprehensive spatial and environmental planning. In southern Europe protective strategies for listed monuments prevail. Protection by way of development is virtually unknown. The developmental dimension can be an eye-opener because of the potential to put an end to established practices of inherently unproductive practices of listing and protecting isolated amenities. This practice all too often ends in a rigid protective regime causing landowners and other stakeholders to oppose preservation. In the worst case it leaves the region vulnerable to economic stagnation. A developmental perspective opens up windows towards new sources of income, innovation and societal dialogue.

The northern European tradition of landscape research thus contrasts sharply with that in southern Europe. The Spanish example is analysed by way of identifying idiosyncrasies of the southern approach and the underlying landscape concept. The Spanish understanding of cultural landscape stems from a composite, multidisciplinary interpretation. The problem with the multifaceted world of landscape studies in Spain is the detachment of scholarly work and landscape policies. Landscape policies do not reflect the vibrant diversity of cultural landscape studies. Landscape heritage management is conceived in various ways in Spanish semi-autonomous regions. Most regions show an inclination to keep heritage management and environmental protection separate. Natural heritage and cultural heritage are subject to different regimes. Integrative landscape policy in the spirit of the European Landscape Convention is a distant goal. National Spanish laws keep intact a traditional sectoral approach. However, current practices in other regions offer proof of changes for the better in terms of the unfolding of an inter- and transdisciplinary approach of cultural landscapes. Some regions have issued specific legislation for the protection and management of the archaeological-historical landscape. Other regions in Spain opt for integrative landscape policy guidelines and the production of landscape visions.

According to Ruiz del Árbol and Orejas, the multi-vocality of the landscape choir is not an impediment to the creation of unifying concepts. Contemporary landscape studies in Spain represent various discourses labelled aesthetic, morphological, environmentalist and socio-synthetic. In the Lunteren discussion, after the presentation of the draft paper discussants raised questions about the alleged unique character of the complex and inclusive character of the Spanish landscape concept. Ruiz del Árbol and Orejas appreciate the multifaceted research effort in Spain as a source of inspiration. In their view it does not cause confusion. The colourful community of landscape archaeologists and historians is supposed to show new roads of understanding for the benefit of a new trend towards integrated cultural resource management and the inclusion of heritage management in comprehensive environmental planning.

6.3 Heritage and power play

In his contribution Vollmer-König (Ch.V.9) defends a diametrically opposed position with respect to protection of archaeological heritage in the context of the cultural landscape. In his view a developmental perspective linked to educational initiatives cannot bring about a change of minds in society. These ideas of Ruiz del Árbol and Orejas are labelled an academic chimera by Vollmer-König. By the time this strategy produces results, the legacy of the past will be wiped out by the forces of modern agriculture, urban development and traffic engineering. Writing in the language of the legal expert, Vollmer-König launches an ardent plea for legal action. He is not afraid of accusations of legalistic action, on the contrary, he is inclined to exhaust all statutory possibilities in the domain of environmental protection, heritage preservation and nature conservation.

He brings up an issue which is particularly pressing in Germany, namely a widening gap between the academic sphere in archaeology and the sphere of public administration. The inhabitants of both worlds direct their endeavours towards different goals and speak different languages. The divide reflects a widespread misconception of archaeologists as primarily excavating researchers. This enforces the popular bias in planning of archaeologists as professionals who are eagerly awaiting an opportunity for uncovering archaeological artefacts. Vollmer-König presents arguments in favour of a conservationist discourse. Academic archaeologists are encouraged to leave their ivory tower and actively support heritage management strategies. Archaeologists cannot avoid active involvement in comprehensive environmental planning and landscape planning for the sake of salvation of their resources. They must provide as much informational ammunition as possible to their counterparts in administration and not get lost in scientific squabbles. The proper approach to better archaeological heritage management is professional conduct in planning and approval procedures.

Some critical remarks cross the reader's mind with reference to Vollmer-König's black-and-white plea for a strategy of preservation by all possible means. Does it convince landowners and developers who are inclined to fight protective measures in courts of justice? Can it be conform with popular objections against legalistic aberrations? Does it not put archaeologists in an extremely defensive position? Environmentalists have paid their dues for their invariably defensive tactics and rhetoric in the 1980s and 1990s. A knightly battle against the omnipresent foe of development can easily evolve into a battle against windmills. The author may reply that these critical remarks are born from airy academic considerations with respect to ideal procedures and the calibration of behavioural models for heritage management and spatial planning.

7. CONCLUSIONS

Sharing knowledge implies sharing meanings. Meaning is transferred in language, be it words or images. The participants of the PDL/BBO programme have accumulated valuable insights and skills in the transfer of knowledge from the domain of landscape heritage research to that of planning and design. This volume brings forth a selection of the lessons learned and puts them in an international perspective.

This section holds the current state of knowledge transfer over the border between science and policy (archaeological heritage management and spatial planning) as perceived through the eyes of the community of scientific practice. Special attention goes to the means of transportation in cross-border traffic, i.e. narratives and imagery. Narratives provide verbal interpretations of the world around us and the elements we value as heritage. Here we face a serious communication problem between sender (archaeologists, historians) and receiver (planner, designer, politician, stakeholder). The words used for description, analysis and explanation of the phenomena studied transfer different meanings for various professions.

One important aspect of the flaws in communication is the use of signs and signification (Van Assche 2004). Planners and designers do read the verbal signs of archaeologists and historians but they interpret them from a different mindset. They perceive different patterns of opportunities and threats in the landscape. Archaeologists and historians focus on heritage which is linked up with their particular field of expertise and special interest. Planners and designers will not discuss the relevance but their frame is set on the identification of spatial patterns which fit with the actual needs of politicians and stakeholder groups. Heritage tends to be a minor detail in the everlasting process of adaptation of the environment to human needs. Words, i.e. narratives can be extremely helpful in the transfer of meaning but imagery is even more important. Imagery takes different shapes such as metaphors, spatial concepts, schemes, symbols, zones, border-patterns and networks and passes the message along with the help of state-of-the-art technology in geographical information systems and 3D-software or with traditional maps and drawings. One of the lessons learned in the programme is that we face a lack of knowledge about frameworks and consequently a lack of skills among archaeologists and historians to make use of power-play and creative design.

NOTES

1 Wageningen Universiteit, Wageningen, the Netherlands.

REFERENCES

Allmendinger, P., 2002: *Planning Theory*, Basingstoke.
Argyris, Ch./D. Schön, 1996[2]: *Organisational Learning II; Theory, Method and Practice*, Reading.
Assche, K. Van, 2004: *Signs in Time, an Interpretative Account of Urban Planning and Design, the People and their Histories*, Wageningen (Ph.D. thesis Wageningen University).
Bal, M., 2002: *Travelling Concepts in the Humanities. A Rough Guide*, London.
Balducci, A./L. Bertolini, 2007a: Interface: Reflecting on Practice or Reflecting with Practice? *Planning Theory & Practice, 8*, 532-533.
Balducci, A./L. Bertolini, 2007b: Comparing Views: What Sort of Knowledge Does Planning Need and How Can it Best Be Developed? *Planning Theory & Practice, 8*, 2007, 553-555.
Bloemers, J.H.F., 1991a: Drie archeologische paradigma's, in J.H.F. Bloemers /T. van Dorp (eds.), *Pre- & Protohistorie van de Lage Landen*, Houten, 63-72.
Bloemers, J.H.F., 1991b: Systemen en processen, in J.H.F. Bloemers/T. van Dorp (eds.), *Pre- & Protohistorie van de Lage Landen*, Houten, 73-82.
Boer, Y. de/A. de Gier/M. Verschuur/B. de Wit (eds.), 2006: *Building Bridges. Researchers on their experiences with interdisciplinary research in the Netherlands*, Utrecht.
Camhis, M., 1979: *Planning Theory and Philosophy*, London.
Carsjens, G.J., 2009: *Supporting Strategic Spatial Planning. Planning support systems for the spatial planning of metropolitan landscapes*, Wageningen (Ph.D. thesis Wageningen University).
Charmaz, K., 2006: *Constructing Grounded Theory. A practical guide through qualitative analysis*, London.
Couclelis, H., 2005: Where has the future gone? Rethinking the role of integrated land-use models in spatial planning, *Environment and Planning A 37*, 1353-1371.
Council of Europe, 2008: *Recommendation CM/Rec(2008)3 of the Committee of Ministers to member states on the guidelines for the implementation of the European Landscape Convention. Adopted by the Committee of Ministers on 6 February 2008 at the 1017th meeting of the Ministers' Deputies.* (Retrieved on 12-12-2009 from http://www.landscapecharacter.org.uk/files/pdfs/ELC-Guidelines-For-Implementation.pdf).
Creswell, John W., 2003-2: *Research Design. Qualitative, quantitative and mixed methods approaches*, London.

Davoudi, S., 2006: Evidence-based Planning, in *disP 165*, 14-24.

Deeben, J./D.P. Hallewas/J. Kolen /R. Wiemer, 1997: Beyond the Crystal Ball. Predictive Modelling as a Tool in Archaeological Heritage Management and Occupation History, in: W.J.H. Willems/H. Kars/D.P. Hallewas (eds.), *Archaeological Heritage Management in the Netherlands. Fifty Years State Service for Archaeological Investigations*, Assen, 76-118.

Dijk, J. M. van, 2008: *Water and Environment in Decision-making. Water Assessment, Environmental Impact Assessment, and Strategic Environmental Assessment in Dutch Planning. A Comparison*, Wageningen (Ph.D. thesis Wageningen University).

Elmore, R.F., 1979: Backward mapping: implementation research and policy decisions, *Political Science Quarterly 94*, 601-616.

European Commission, 2002: *Unlocking the Value of Cultural Heritage. The DigiCULT Report. Technological Landscapes for Tomorrow's Cultural Economy. Executive summary.* Luxembourg. (Retrieved on 23 12 2009 from: http://digicult.salzburgresearch.at/).

Faludi, A., 1986: *Critical rationalism and planning methodology*, London.

Faludi, A./A.J. van der Valk, 1994: *Rule and Order; Dutch Planning Doctrine in the Twentieth Century*, Dordrecht.

Faludi, A./B. Waterhout, 2006: Insights into Evidence-Based Planning. Guest Editorial, *disP 165*, 4-13.

Flyvbjerg, B., 2001: *Making Social Science Matter. Why social inquiry fails and how it can succeed again*, Cambridge.

Florence, 2000: *European Landscape Convention. Florence, 20 October 2000*, Strasbourg (Council of Europe).

Forester, J., 1999: *The Deliberative Practitioner; Encouraging Participatory Planning Processes*, London.

Friedmann, J., 1987: *Planning in the Public Domain. From Knowledge to Action*, Princeton.

Friend, J./A. Hickling, 2005^3: *Planning under Pressure. The Strategic Choice Approach*, Oxford.

Fry, G./B. Tress/G. Tress/A.J. van der Valk (eds.), 2003: *Interdisciplinary and Transdisciplinary Landscape Studies: Potential and Limitations*, Wageningen.

Funtowicz, S.O./J.R. Ravetz, 1990: *Uncertainty and Quality in Science for Policy*, Dordrecht.

Gibbons, M./C. Limoges/H. Nowotny/S. Schwartzman/P. Scott/M. Trow, 1994: *The New Production of Knowledge: The Dynamics of Science and Research in Contemporary Societies*, London.

Gieryn, T. F., 1999: *Cultural Boundaries of Science: Credibility on the Line*, Chicago.

Gold, H., 1976: The dynamics of professionalization, the case of urban planning, in G.K. Zollschau/W. Hirsch (eds.), *Social Change. Explorations, Diagnoses and Conjectures*, New York, 835-863.

Gunsteren, H. R. van, 1976: *The Quest for Control. A Critique of the Central-Rule Approach in Public Affairs*, London.

Hillier, J., 2002: *Shadows of Power; An Allegory of Prudence in Land-Use Planning*, London.

Hisschemöller, M./R. Hoppe, 1995: Coping with intractable controversies: the case for problem structuring in policy design and analysis, *Knowledge Technology and Policy 4*, 40-60.

Hoppe, R., 1999: Policy analysis, science, and politics: from 'speaking truth to power' to 'making sense together', *Science and Public Policy 26*, 201-210.

Hoppe, R./S. Huijs, 2003: *Werk op de grens tussen wetenschap en beleid: paradoxen en dilemma's*, Den Haag.

Howard, P. /M. Jones/K.R. Olwig/J. Primdahl/I. Sarloev Herlin, 2007: Multiple interfaces of the European Landscape Convention, *Norwegian Journal of Geography 61*, 1-10.

Howarth, D., 2005: Applying Discourse Theory: the Method of Articulation, in D. Howarth/J. Torfing, Discourse Theory in European Politics. Identity, Policy and Governance, Basingstoke, 316-349.

Jacobs, M., 2006: *The production of mindscapes. A comprehensive theory of landscape experience*, Wageningen (Ph.D. thesis Wageningen University).

Jones, A., 2004: Archaeometry and materiality: Materials-based analysis in theory and practice, *Archaeometry 46*, 327-338.

Jonge, J. de, 2009: *Landscape Architecture between Politics and Science. An integrative perspective on landscape planning and the design in the network society*, Wageningen (Ph.D. thesis Wageningen University).

Kamermans, H./M. van Leusen/Ph. Verhagen (eds.), 2009: *Archaeological Prediction and Risk Management. Alternatives to current practice*, Leiden.

Landscape Character Network, 2008: *The European Landscape Convention and its Explanatory Report side by side*, London: Landscape Character Network. Retrieved on 12-12-2009 from: http://www.landscapecharacter.org.uk/files/pdfs/ELC-LCN.pdf

Lawson, B., 2006[4]: *How designers think. The design process demystified*, Amsterdam.

Londen, H. van, 2006: Cultural biography and the power of image, in W. van der Knaap/A. van der Valk (eds.), *Multiple Landscape. Merging Past and Present. Selected Papers from the fifth International Workshop on Sustainable Land Use Planning 7-9 June 2004*, Wageningen, 171-182.

Lynch, K., 1998[26]: *The Image of the City*, London.

Needham, B., 2007: *Dutch land use planning; planning and managing land use in the Netherlands, the principles and the practice*, Den Haag.

Nonaka, I./H. Takeuchi, 1995: *The Knowledge-Creating Company. How Japanese Companies Create the Dynamics of Innovation*, Oxford.

Nowotny, H./P. Scott/M. Gibbons, 2001: *Rethinking Science. Knowledge and the Public in an Age of Uncertainty*, Cambridge.

Popper, K.R., 1984[5] (1966): *The Open Society And Its Enemies. Volume 2: the high tide of prophecy: Hegel, Marx, and the aftermath*, London.

Preucel, R.W., 1995, The post-processual condition, *Journal of Archaeological Research 3*, 147-175.

Ravetz, J., 2007: Towards a non-violent discourse in science, in G.E. Frerks/B. Klein Goldewijk (eds.), *Human security and international insecurity*, Wageningen, 249-263.

RebelGroup, 2007: *Digitale handleiding Belvedere en financiering*, Utrecht: Belvedere. Website retrieved 08 12 2009: http://belvedere.nu/page.php?section=05&pID=6&mID=9

Roymans, N./F.Gerritsen/C. van der Heijden/K. Bosma/J. Kolen, 2009: Landscape Biography as Research Strategy: The Case of the South Netherlands Project, *Landscape Research 34*, 337-359.

Ruijgrok, E.C.M., 2006: *Kentallen waardering natuur, water, bodem en landschap; hulpmiddel bij MKBA's*, Rotterdam.

Ruijgrok, E./D. Bel, 2008: *Handreiking Cultuurhistorie in m.e.r. en MKBA*, Deventer (Uitgebracht in opdracht van RACM & Projectbureau Belvedere. Eindversie).

Ruijgrok, E.C.M./R. Brouwer/H. Verbruggen, 2004: *Waardering van natuur, water en bodem in maatschappelijke kosten baten analyses: een handreiking ter aanvulling op de OEI-leidraad*, Den Haag.

Schön, D.A., 1983: *The Reflective Practitioner. How Professionals Think in Action*, New York.

Schön, D.A. 1987:, *Educating the Reflective Practitioner. Toward a New Design for Teaching and Learning in the Professions,* San Francisco.

Seaman, J., 2008: Adopting Grounded Theory Approach to Cultural-Historical Research: Conflicting Methodologies or Complementary Methods? *International Journal of Qualitative Methods* 7, 1-17.

Simon, H., 1997[4] (1947): *Administrative Behaviour. A Study of Decision-Making Processes in Administrative Organizations,* New York.

Stillwell, J.S./S. Geertman/S. Openshaw, 1999: Developments in geographical information and planning, in: J. Stillwell/S. Geertman/S. Openshaw (eds.), *Geographical Information and Planning,* Heidelberg, 3-22.

Strauss, A.C./J. Corbin, 1997: *Grounded Theory in Practice,* London.

Vroom, M. J., 2006: *Lexicon of Garden and Landscape Architecture,* Basel.

Weggeman, M., 2001[4]: *Kennismanagement. Inrichting en besturing van kennisintensieve organisaties,* Schiedam.

Wildawsky, A., 1987[2] (1979): *Speaking Truth to Power: The Art and Craft of Policy Analysis,* New Jersey.

Wit, B. de, 2005: *De methodologie van grenswerk. Programmeren van onderzoek, kennismanagement, analyse van kennis infrastructuur en kennisnetwerken: wat, hoe en waarom?* Den Haag.

Yanow, D., 2003: Accessing local knowledge, in M. Hajer/H. Wagenaar (eds.), *Deliberative Policy Analysis. Understanding Governance in the Network Society,* Cambridge, 28-246.

WEBSITES

Text of European Landscape Convention: http://www.landscapecharacter.org.uk/files/pdfs/ELC-LCN.pdf. Accessed on 12 December, 2009.

Text of European Landscape Convention and Explanatory Text by Landscape Character Network http://www.landscapecharacter.org.uk/files/pdfs/ELC-and-expl-rep-LCN.pdf. Accessed on 12 December, 2009.

Recommendation of the Committee of Ministers to member states of the Council of Europe on the guidelines for the implementation of the European Landscape Convention http://www.landscapecharacter.org.uk/files/pdfs/ELC-Guidelines-For-Implementation.pdf. Accessed on 12 December, 2009.

2. Revitalizing history: moving from historical landscape reconstructions to heritage practices in the southern Netherlands

Nico Roymans[1], Fokke Gerritsen[1], Cor van der Heijden[2], Koos Bosma[1] & Jan Kolen[1]

ABSTRACT

This paper presents the outline of a biographical approach to landscape as developed in the Netherlands during the last 15 years by archaeologists that focuses on the study of the *longue durée* interrelationships between spatial transformations, social and economic changes and the construction of regional and local identities in the region. This approach offers interesting possibilities for application in the sphere of heritage management, landscape design and spatial planning. The implementation of this biographical approach to landscape is illustrated by presenting a case study for the southern Netherlands, a semi-urban region which ranks among the most intensively studied cultural landscapes of western Europe.

KEY WORDS

Landscape biography; cultural history, archaeology, heritage transmission; southern Netherlands

1. INTRODUCTION

There is a long tradition of regional landscape research in Dutch archaeology. By combining large-scale excavations with synthesizing academic research, the South Netherlands Project has established a special place within this tradition. This is the name often given to a loose collaboration of three archaeological institutes that have made this region a focal point of almost uninterrupted activity over the past thirty years (Fokkens 1996; Roymans 1996) Within various NWO-funded research programmes, we have constantly produced syntheses striving for theoretical and methodological innovation. As a result, the sandy landscape of the southern Netherlands now ranks among the best studied cultural landscapes in western Europe (Fig. 1).

The rapid development of landscape archaeological research in the southern Netherlands over the past three decades must be seen in conjunction with a major physical characteristic of Pleistocene sandy soils, that is the almost complete absence of a vertical stratigraphy in settlement traces. All traces from the Bronze Age to the modern era are generally found in a single excavation layer beneath the (pre-)modern arable top soil. This condition means that large surface areas on sandy soils can be excavated relatively cheaply, making the landscape ideal for research from a landscape archaeological perspective. The surge in archaeological excavations in past decades should also be understood in the light of recent dynamic economic growth which has seen the region rapidly transformed from a rural to a semi-urban landscape, a process that is still in full swing.

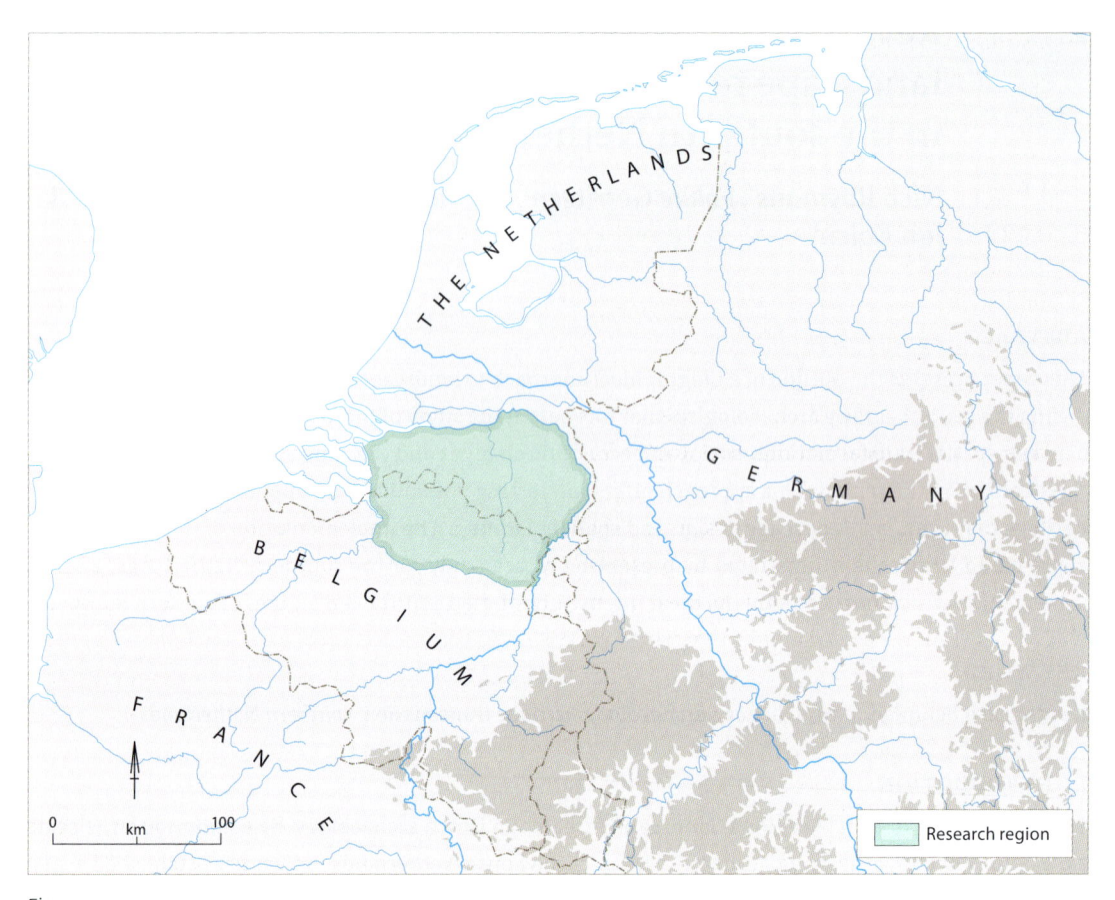

Fig. 1
The northwest European plain showing the south Netherlands research region.

The programme 'The biography of a sandy landscape: cultural history, heritage management and spatial planning in the southern Netherlands', run by VU University Amsterdam, is the most recent phase of the South Netherlands Project. It has two objectives:
a) the elaboration of a long-term cultural history of the region from the Bronze Age to the present based on a biographical perspective of the landscape;
b) the study of possible applications of this landscape biography to heritage management and spatial planning.

The programme combines archaeological research with historical and historical geographical research in order to extend the biography into modern times. The outline and results of this approach are presented below in greater detail.

2. THE BIOGRAPHY AS A PERSPECTIVE ON THE LANDSCAPE

What then are the core elements of the landscape biography approach as aspired to within this project? We would like to enumerate five points. Our notion of biography:
a. is a historicizing one. We seek to gain an understanding of changing patterns in the way that a landscape's inhabitants used, organized and gave meaning to that landscape. This approach therefore dif-

fers from constructivist approaches often adopted in heritage practices based on the belief that the biography should refer primarily to the sense of identity and the self-image of present day communities, or in post-processual studies of past landscapes from a phenomenological perspective.

b. does not focus on chronological periods as closed cultural time frames. It looks at continuities, breaks and rapid changes from the past to the present.

c. does not employ a sectoral approach but aims to combine archaeological, historical geographical and historical sources and methods.

d. aims to build an understanding of the historical layeredness within the landscape in the past and present. This layeredness is the result of continuous processes of addition and erasure of traces of human activity.

e. focuses on the study of local communities. It continually seeks to explore links between the lived environment of local communities and *structures de longue durée* in a community's dealings with the landscape.

Prominent focuses within our approach are the identity constructions of local communities and the role of the landscape in identity formation. Processes of remembering and forgetting have always been formative principles in the organization of the lived environment both today and in the past. It is true of all periods that life must be lived amidst that which was there before, which brings us to the theme of the past in the past. Inasmuch as archaeologists and historians have been able to make reconstructions, societies have always been fascinated by things in their environment which they knew, or intuitively sensed, had survived many generations (Bradley 2002; Frijhoff 2007). This fascination could lead to the emergence of specific landscapes of memory and *lieux de mémoire*, such as the barrow landscapes from the Bronze and Iron Ages. Although these landscapes and places were not exclusively intended for commemorations and historical experiences, their spatial order, social meanings and economic functions were to a large extent laden with historical values, shared memories and notions of origin and ancestry.

The ways in which prehistoric and historic communities built up an existence amidst all the things left behind in their living environment by preceding generations and how they dealt with that past in concrete terms offer new insights into the historical layeredness of present and past landscapes, as well as the culture-specific arrangement and interpretation of that space and the transformations that occur within it. With regard to interpreting the landscape, we must bear in mind the different, possibly even conflicting, perspectives of groups of inhabitants (and outsiders). This can be specified in more detail for the historical periods.

Since landscape biography does not make a sharp break between past and present, present-day heritage practices are also studied from this perspective. In the modern period dealing with the past within the landscape is an integral part of the spatial condition of societies and hence of spatial transformations (Kolen 1995; *idem* 2005, 225-295). This implies that heritage is always a dynamic process involving people, with processes of cultural transmission and the construction of values and identities being inextricably bound with one another.

3. THE LONG-TERM HISTORY OF LAND APPROPRIATION

A characteristic feature of the landscape biography approach is its ability to shed light on a broad range of themes. Just as a biographical study of a person will emphasize certain lines of development, revealing how certain characteristics or early experiences continue to reverberate in that person's later life, in the same way a landscape biography also makes choices, imposing a structure on the many possible narratives.

In the Biography of a Sandy Landscape Project, we look at the ever-changing relationships between 1) the use and layout of the landscape; 2) the representation and interpretation of the landscape and 3) the identities of the individuals and communities inhabiting the landscape. Our underlying assumption is that the relationships between these three dimensions together constitute a key impetus in the long-term history of the landscape. This article looks more closely at one phenomenon that plays a part in many of the relationships between these three landscape dimensions, namely land appropriation. Our concern here is with three separate periods and we make no attempt to describe a complete, unbroken line from the Bronze Age to the present. The theme of land appropriation does lend itself to this, however, and as such it forms a *leitmotif* in the monographs currently being written as part of the project. The periods discussed represent critical transformation stages. They are the later Urnfield period (c. 700-400 BC), the period of the Christianization of the landscape in the High Middle Ages (c. 1000-1300 AD), and the period of large-scale heathland reclamation (c. 1850-1950 AD).

4. SHIFTING FARMSTEADS AND STABLE URNFIELDS IN LATE PREHISTORY

For people today, the notion of continuity of the inhabited space is almost axiomatic. Although this space may be constantly changing, this almost always involves an expansion of the inhabited area and almost

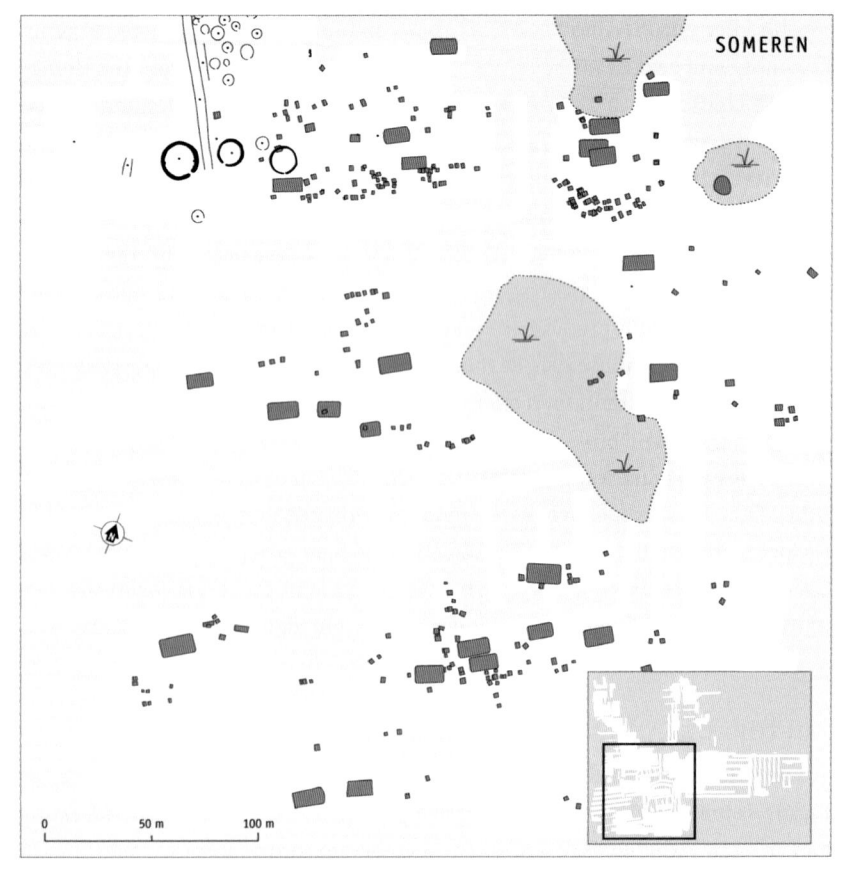

Fig. 2
Multiple generations of shifting farmhouses (dark grey rectangles) from the Early/Middle Iron Age at Someren, south Netherlands.

never the return of settlement units to nature. It is therefore difficult for us to imagine a tradition of habitation that is not founded on the idea of stability of location but rather on that of periodic relocation of house and yard. Nevertheless, archaeological data from the first millennium BC oblige us to conclude that this was the norm at the time (Gerritsen 2003, chapter 3). Farmsteads rarely remained in the same location in the landscape for more than a single building phase. Successive generations constantly selected new sites on which to establish a new farmstead without 'roaming' over large distances (Fig. 2). The archaeological pattern is so clear that we are able to conclude that the regular abandonment of an inhabited site was a key feature of the habitation traditions of local communities and that the meanings and values associated with this were of immense importance. Whereas the periodic relocation of houses might come across to us as something altogether unfamiliar, the type of house that people inhabited in the Iron Age, the byre house with people and cattle under one roof, continued to be a familiar type of farmhouse in the southern Netherlands until just a few generations ago.

If we try to imagine the role of appropriation and identity in a system of shifting farmsteads, then the most likely scenario is that a personal, intimate bond will have formed between the inhabitants (probably with a single nuclear family at the core) and the farmstead, and possibly the surrounding fields (Gerritsen 2007). The labour expended on the building of house and yard and the daily work on and around the farmstead for the purpose of food supply will have led people to view that location as their own (in other words, appropriation) and will have contributed to feelings of solidarity and shared identity within the group of inhabitants. It is important to point out, however, that this does not assign a key role to memories of earlier generations or to traces from the past. After all, people did not live on a farmstead established by their grandparents or earlier ancestors and neither were they custodians who had to maintain the family property and pass it on to later generations. The appropriation of land by individuals and families was based on the understanding that this was for a limited time only. Entering into a bond was inextricably linked to breaking it off again and to abandoning associated identities.

However, we must also bear in mind that there were places in the territory of each local community that could be identified as former farmsteads, thanks to the presence of ruined buildings, fencing or midden remains or perhaps just different vegetation. Tracing back generations of forebears through memory was akin to making an imaginary journey through the territory.

We can say with a high degree of certainty that individual families did not move about the landscape as isolated units. On the contrary, the local community constituted an important unifying social element. At this point in late prehistory we should think in terms of small groups of 20 to 50 people and the relationships between landscape, appropriation and common identity were shaped in a very different way. It would appear that descent and continuity were core values, expressed in the fixed location of the shared cemetery. After cremation, the community's dead were interred in the cemetery, usually called an urnfield because of the ceramic urns that were used. The majority of the dead had their own funerary monument in the form of a round mound enclosed by a ditch or sometimes a long barrow.

Many of the urnfields were in continual use in the Late Bronze Age (1100-800 BC) and Early Iron Age (800-500 BC; Roymans/Kortlang 1999; Gerritsen 2003, 118 ff.). Over the centuries, despite the small size of the associated living communities, this created vast cemeteries which must have dominated the landscape as important landmarks (Fig. 3 and 4). Monumental older barrows were regularly chosen as the location for a new urnfield. While not every individual grave was monumental, urnfields as a whole were elements in the landscape that could not be overlooked. Long, open strips through cemeteries or a location near a natural crossing in a stream valley show that paths ran alongside and through cemeteries (Gerritsen/Rensink 2004). Travellers and local inhabitants were thus constantly being confronted with the past. The urnfield landscape connected the living, their immediate ancestors and the mythical founders of the local community to one another in a physical, tangible way. Moreover, the urnfield emphasized the community's inalienable rights to the land through the long-term stability of location. Other meanings, either opposing or complementary, appear to have been attributed to the peripheral zones of settlement territories, as attested to by finds of depositions, especially in stream valleys and peat bogs (Fontijn 2003). Although the ritual deposition of metal objects and other goods was less customary in the Iron Age than in the Bronze Age, rare examples suggest that, as in the previous period, wet zones occupied a special place in the scheme of perception that local communities had of their landscape.

Fig. 3
Ground plan of the Iron Age urnfield of Someren showing dense clusters of small barrows enclosed by ditches.

392 • THE CULTURAL LANDSCAPE AND HERITAGE PARADOX

Fig. 4
Nineteenth century heath landscape with urnfield barrows. *Painted by J. du Fief, c. 1870.*

We can say that the combination of dynamics and discontinuity of the shifting farmsteads and the ideology of stability as a core value behind the local community and the local settlement territory had a significant impact on the arrangement and interpretation of the landscape in this period. Naturally, it could not have been foreseen that the effects of this combination would still be evident more than two thousand years later, but the habitation traditions in the Urnfield period have given rise to a physical landscape structure which we can identify to this day and which over the centuries has repeatedly played a part in different ways in the relationships between the above-mentioned dimensions of use, interpretation and identity.

A striking phenomenon marked the end of the Early Iron Age and the beginning of the Middle Iron Age, virtually all urnfields fell into disuse. After about 400 BC, the dead were interred in the old urnfields on only an incidental basis. Moreover, in a substantial portion of these cases there is nothing to indicate continuity of habitation in the area around the cemetery. In other known cases, although the urnfield may have fallen into disuse, habitation continued and even appears to have intensified. Earlier research has established that Iron Age habitation ceased in zones of (former) pre-modern heathland and that habitation continued in zones of (former) medieval field complexes (Roymans/Gerritsen 2002). In the former instance, this involves relatively inferior, loam-poor sandy soils in the form of secondarily formed heath podzols, and in the latter more loamy soils that had not been degraded by secondary podzolization. It seems clear that those settlement territories abandoned in around 500-400 BC had initially been able to thrive on the loam-poor soils but gradually had to contend with increasingly unproductive fields and a decline in the fertility regeneration levels of the soil, even with lengthy fallow periods. Although we cannot say with any certainty what vegetation then grew on the abandoned cultivated land, and how much of this was heathland, we know for a fact that these zones continued as uninhabited outlying areas from the Middle Iron Age until the period of large-scale heathland reclamation in the nineteenth century. As a consequence of the over-use of loam-poor soils by local communities during the Urnfield period, from the Middle Iron Age onwards there was always a bipartite division in the structure of the landscape, with inhabited cultivated zones versus wastelands (Roymans/Gerritsen 2002). In large tracts of the southern Netherlands these wastelands covered much bigger areas than the intervening cultivated zones (Fig. 5).

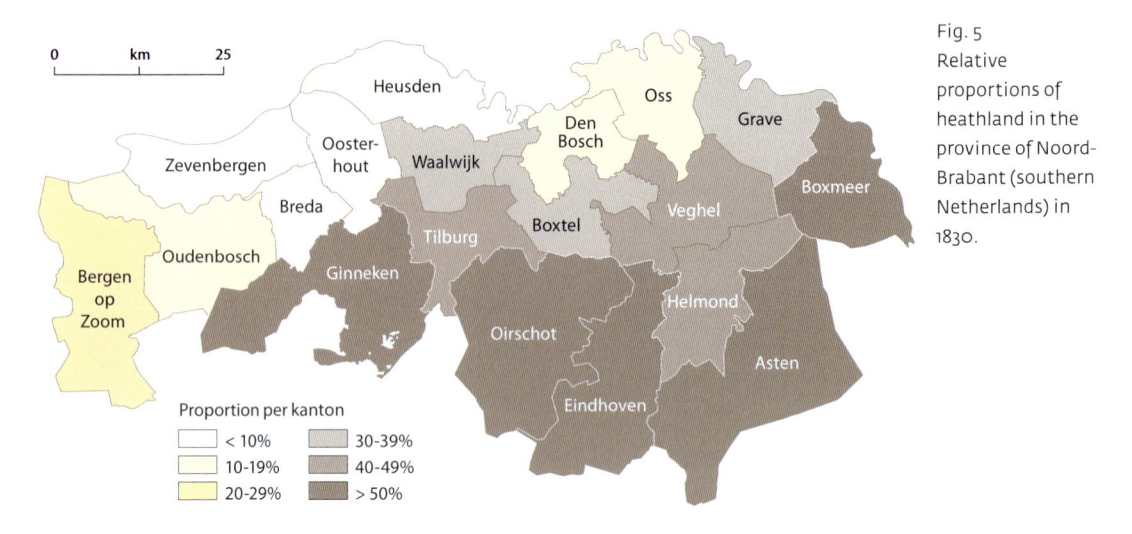

Fig. 5 Relative proportions of heathland in the province of Noord-Brabant (southern Netherlands) in 1830.

5. THE CHRISTIANIZATION OF THE LANDSCAPE

It is a known fact that Christianity was introduced into the Low Countries in a slow process taking place over many centuries (Mostert 1993). We also know that in the initial phase changes in religious beliefs and in the associated lifestyle were largely confined to the elite and that it took a long time for the rural population to make the new religion an integral part of their everyday lives. It is only recently that we have begun to study Christianization as a process that did not only happen in people's heads but ultimately also gave shape and substance to their religious and everyday activities. This approach shows that through these activities Christianization also influenced the organization and interpretation of the landscape. Landscape archaeological research thus enables us to study aspects of the Christianization of the countryside, whose inhabitants have largely remained outside the written sources.

During the phase in which Christianity was probably still of limited importance to local communities on the sandy soils of the southern Netherlands, these communities were nevertheless already part of a system of large-scale land ownership and land exploitation in which ecclesiastical bodies played a key role (Roymans/Theuws 1999, 19). Much of the land was owned by monasteries and the Christianized nobility whose power base was situated outside the area. An important strategy by which the nobility secured their own salvation and that of their descendants was to donate landed property to the church (Bijsterveld 1999), although it is difficult to establish the extent to which this had an impact on the daily practices of local communities. Here we see an example of different perspectives of the elite and the local communities on the landscape that can co-exist and lead to different forms of appropriation.

In the Early Middle Ages, churches were thinly scattered across the sandy soils of the southern Netherlands. The High Middle Ages (11th-13th centuries) saw the emergence of a dense network of parish churches, with a cemetery attached to each church. One outcome was that the annual and weekly church calendar began to structure the lives of the rural population and the church became the central location for key life-cycle rituals of individuals, in particular baptism, marriage and death. The church, particularly if it was built of tuff stone, or from the fourteenth century onwards of brick, and sported a church tower, became a focal point in the landscape, the symbol of the local community which thus defined itself as a Christian community. This visual message became more powerful in the Late Middle Ages when the wastelands were exploited with increasing intensity and the expanding heath vegetation created a more open landscape. In addition, church bells were an auditory means by which a temporal structure was imposed on the Christianized landscape (Corbin 1994).

However, the formation of a Christianized landscape was not just a question of adding Christian elements. It also entailed the removal of pagan elements from the landscape (Roymans 1995). In archaeological terms, a reasonable case can be made for the levelling of prehistoric barrows and urnfields, particularly in the High Middle Ages. This mainly occurred in the immediate vicinity of villages in landscape zones that were inhabited and cultivated. Although pagan relics situated further away from the church in the wasteland zones were left physically untouched, they became demonized, probably also from this time. This is the origin, according to this model, of later associations of prehistoric funerary monuments with heathen powers (devils, witches, cats, dwarfs), which continued into the twentieth century. It is interesting to point out here that in the Middle Ages locations where criminals were executed, and sometimes also buried, were always situated in the wasteland zone, often on old prehistoric barrows ('gallow mounds'). Although of great economic importance for farming and later also for sheep farming and wool production, the wastelands became the un-Christianized periphery.

In summary, we can say that Christianization led to a radical reinterpretation of the landscape (Fig. 6). This was based on a contrastive harmony between a Christianized civilized inner world with the parish church at its centre, and a savage outer world of swamps, heathland and old barrows in which anti-Christian forces had their earthly domicile.

6. RECLAIMING THE HEATH (1850 – 1950)

In the nineteenth century the heath was frequently described as a desert to be traversed as quickly as possible in order to reach the oasis of cultivated land. Travellers found the endless brown expanses in the southern Netherlands silent and threatening, places of deathly desolation. While this may have been the perception of urban dwellers, the heath had an important economic significance for farmers on the sandy soils (Van der Heijden/Rooijakkers 1993). It was the area where they grazed cattle, cut heath sods for use as fertilizer, excavated sand, located their beehives and gathered fuel in the form of turfs.

The first two were the most universal and important activities but they gradually declined in significance when farmers switched to buying cattle fodder and artificial fertilizer, especially after 1880

Fig. 6
Perception model of a Christianized landscape in the southern Netherlands based on nineteenth century folkloric evidence.
After Roymans 1995, Fig. 13.

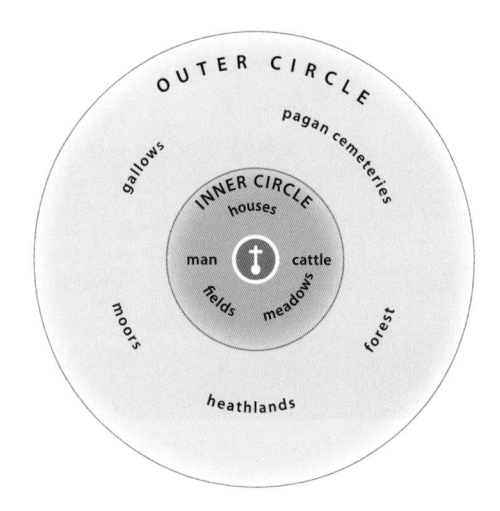

(Crijns/Kriellaars 1987; *idem* 1992). Artificial fertilizer was not yet widely used, however. Thanks to the growing quantity of fertilizer produced on the farmers' own land and the option of buying fertilizer, there were greater opportunities for heathland reclamation. At this early stage, however, reclamation was seldom carried out on a grand scale and generally involved the fringes of the heath, leaving the centres untouched. This was because the heathland continued to play a role in the agricultural system, albeit one of much reduced importance.

Because much of the heathland in the southern Netherlands belonged to municipalities, it was they who switched to reclamation, on a small scale, in the second half of the nineteenth century. Instead of converting the wasteland into cultivated land, they forested it, usually in the context of unemployment relief projects (Trienekens 1993). This changed after 1890, when it became possible to develop large areas of heath in their entirety (Fig. 7). This was due in part to the involvement of entirely new supralocal agencies which carried out the work using different methods (Thissen 1993). Particular mention should be made here of De Nederlandsche Heidemaatschappij (Dutch Moor Company).

The technologies introduced or improved by the Heidemaatschappij included soil research, deep ploughing using bullocks (Fig. 8) and steam-powered vehicles and the generous application of artificial fertilizer. Initially, this type of work was mainly carried out on country estates but after the turn of the twentieth century farmers who no longer needed their heathlands began for the first time to establish completely new farms on the heath.

Stimulated by improved transport opportunities, the spread of technological expertise with regard to reclamation, high prices for agricultural products, the greater availability and falling prices of artificial fertilizer and the work of the Heidemaatschappij in this area, many people enthusiastically switched to

Fig. 7
Labourers reclaiming heathland in the southern Netherlands, c. 1915. *Photo: private collection*.

Fig. 8
Large-scale heathland reclamation by the Dutch Moor Company using two teams of six bullocks for deep ploughing. C. 1900.
Photo: Gelders Archief.

reclamation. In fact, these years witnessed a veritable boom involving enthusiastic speculation with land that was newly reclaimed or about to be developed.

Greater accessibility through roads, drainage, the conversion of heathland to agricultural land and forest and the establishment of new villages were all seen in relationship to one another. In the 1930s a new professional group employed by provincial authorities, town and country planners, drew up the first regional plans to take account of this. This did not yet amount to very much but it was just one of the signs of the national government's growing involvement in reclamation.

After 1920 a great deal of land was reclaimed in the southern Netherlands. Although economic reasons for doing so were weak, this was compensated for by the high population pressure in the countryside. Countless sons of farmers wanted to start their own farm and many were forced to move onto the heath. After 1920 it was almost exclusively local farmers and farmers' sons who reclaimed land with the support of the authorities.

It was not purely rational economic considerations, however, that drove the colonization of new tracts of land (see Olwig 1984). People in the province of North Brabant resisted things that were regarded as 'un-Brabant', such as large-scale landownership, tenant farming and religions other than Catholicism. Because they owned the land, local authorities were able to play an active role in putting this 'policy' into practice. For instance, in 1904 local councils in the De Kempen area still owned a large share (more than 80%) of the wasteland. The provincial government also had its finger in the pie thanks to its power to give consent to council land sales. As an example, in an attempt to prevent a sizeable area of reclamation land from falling into Protestant hands, the provincial authorities wrote the following to the Wanroy council in the 1930s, 'the religious aspect implies that no farmers with a different way of thinking may be settled there' (Thissen 1993).

It was in the 1920s and 1930s that the government seized the legal opportunities at its disposal to play a leading role in urban and regional planning. In 1931 the intercouncil regional plan gave the province an instrument for directing and co-ordinating developments. They believed that if they did not intervene quickly to regulate matters, the unplanned growth of both town and countryside would eventually result in a region that was chaotic and unworkable. It quickly became apparent that the scientifically-based plans of the professionals (like de Casseres; Bosma 2003) were at odds with what politicians and administrators had in mind. For urban planners, the city had priority over the countryside. However, this vision did

Fig. 9
Reconstruction of ancient river meanders in the Beerze valley, southern Netherlands. *Photo: K. Tomei, Flying Camera, Eindhoven.*

not mesh with the subsidiarity principle adhered to within Brabant Roman Catholic circles which saw municipal autonomy as paramount and, for cultural and religious reasons, the city at best as the crown on the countryside.

North Brabant saw the emergence of a strict form of what is termed 'Catholic planning' (Janssen 2002; *idem* 2006) and more specifically 'Catholic reclamation' (Thissen 1993). United within Brabantia Nostra, intellectuals and writers of the 1930s, all with excellent Catholic credentials, constantly aimed their barbs at 'the city' as a wild and corrupt place and as a 'cesspool of vice'. Those who left their mark on the layout of the outlying areas included urban planners like Granpré Molière, Buskens and Margry, provincial governors like Van Rijckevorsel and De Quay, men of letters like Coolen and Van Duinkerken and clerical leaders like Father van den Elsen and rector (later bishop) Bekkers. What they had in common was a view of Brabant as a rustic, Arcadian and Catholic rural society. It was a one-sided story full of contradictions. Catholicism was contrasted with Protestantism, the village was elevated above the town and harmony was preached above social polarization. The chapel or church was often the first thing to be built in the new villages, it was then surrounded by other amenities and the homes of the farmers and the town and country people. Sometimes even the name of the new settlement (e.g. St Jozefparochie, Elsendorp; Janssen 2006,

92) expressed the need to safeguard Brabant's Catholic rural identity and to protect it from the menace of urban mentality and culture.

After World War Two, when it became clear that North Brabant's rapidly increasing population, which had increased from 559,000 in 1900 to 1,267,000 in 1950, could no longer be accommodated in the villages, the 'village mentality' continued to be a dominant force. It was decided to expand the existing towns in parish fashion, which meant that plans for new residential areas had to be based on a parish size of about 6,000 inhabitants. Each area had to have a clearly defined territory and the amenities there, with the church as the central element, had to be grouped in such a way that the inhabitants would need to go outside their own familiar environment as little as possible. Single-family dwellings were given priority in the plans because this was where family life could best flourish.

The early twenty-first century has seen the return, in a modified form, of these ideological concepts in the recently launched large-scale restructuring of rural areas. The notion of regional identity constantly recurs in memoranda and plans, expressions of a heightened urban longing for an Arcadian idyll that are inextricably linked to the transition of the Brabant countryside towards a consumer landscape. Specific projects within the Reconstruction of the Sandy Soils Project have sought to literally reconstruct 'the original identity' of the Brabantian countryside (Fig. 9) and in so doing to keep alive the memory of old Brabant (Janssen 2006).

7. CONCLUSION

The above analysis illustrates the potential of the biographical approach to generate powerful innovative narratives about the ways in which local communities have used, organized and interpreted the landscape over time. We are confronted with surprisingly potent long-term structures but also with important moments of transformation in land appropriation. The Middle Iron Age saw the emergence of a landscape arrangement, the dichotomy between uninhabited wastelands on degraded soils and inhabited cultivated zones on more loamy soils, that continued to operate as a referential framework for human activities right up to the nineteenth century. The intensified Christianization of local communities in the High Middle Ages led not only to the introduction of Christian cult places like churches, but also to an ideological reinterpretation of the landscape as a whole. The landscape underwent a substantial metamorphosis in the period 1850-1950 through large-scale reclamation of the wastelands. It can be demonstrated that this enthusiasm for reclamation cannot be understood in purely economic terms. Ideas about the identity and central values of local communities played a decisive behind-the-scenes role. The same theme of identity and regional character also crops up in the current debate and policy on landscape organization and spatial planning.

The narratives generated by landscape biography illustrate in a unique way the principle of the historical layeredness of landscapes and the notion of the past in the past. In all periods of prehistory up to the present, the landscape has been shown to play an active role in the identity constructions of individuals and communities. This offers clues for the application of landscape biography to present-day heritage management. It is intriguing to observe that, far from being a modern theme, the relationship between heritage and awareness of identity and the associated spatial 'policy' was also one that intensely preoccupied societies in the past.

8. FROM LANDSCAPE BIOGRAPHY TO PRESENT-DAY HERITAGE PRACTICES

It is generally a big step for archaeologists and historians to go from the historical study of landscapes to making an active contribution to contemporary heritage practices. This feeling is further reinforced by the sharp distinction frequently made between history and heritage (Lowenthal 1996). After all, history is often defined as an intellectual interest in the past *per se*, whereas heritage is viewed as a practice designed to situate the past *in* or adapt it *to* the present. By this definition, heritage often says more about present-day society than the historical one and is perhaps less a research field for landscape historians than it is for anthropologists, social geographers or planners (Ashworth 2005). Nevertheless, in landscape biography the step from historical interpretation to heritage practice is smaller than this distinction would suggest (Kolen/Witte 2006).

This is largely because heritage transmission is part of the spatial condition of all communities and as such is always a form of human activity. We refer here once again to Donald Meinig's (Meinig 1979, 40) well-known premise that societies, at all times and in all places, have to organize their existence amidst the traces left behind in their living environment by previous generations. In the case of heritage, culture-specific meaningful processes of transfer and transmission come into play, with successive heirs each time employing different interests and attaching new values and meanings to heritage (Bender 1993; Kolen 2005, 225-295). For this reason a changing society always makes different choices when it comes to remembering and forgetting, as is already apparent in the long-term perspective outlined for the southern Netherlands' landscape. Changes in late prehistoric society, the Christianization of the southern Netherlands communities in the Middle Ages and landscape modernization from the end of the nineteenth century were accompanied each time by a new appreciation of the past, a different 'past in the past' (Bradley 2002, 14-16). There are no compelling reasons for assuming that this is any different in the southern Netherlands region today. Therefore, from a biographical perspective on landscape, heritage is never an objective historical given but is closely tied to the social construction of values and identities in contemporary society.

This does not make things any easier for archaeologists and historians. Among other things it implies that they are just one of many groups participating in present-day heritage practices and that their contribution does not by definition offer a greater degree of objectivity. At the same time, however, it is clear that historians do have a special role to play in this process, one that can enrich, broaden or deepen dialogue on cultural heritage. Indeed, that role can be found in the special position of archaeologists and historians as socially valued story tellers who are also academically trained, which lends them a certain authority no matter what. The anthropologist Tim Ingold once expressed this role very nicely when he said, "it is part of an archaeological training to learn to attend to those clues which the rest of us might pass over, literally, when they are below the surface – and which make it possible to tell a richer or fuller story[...]". But despite this, he added, "insofar both seek the past in the landscape, the dweller and the archaeologist are engaged in projects of fundamentally the same kind" (Ingold 2000, 189-190).

9. A CLOSER LOOK AT TWO REGIONAL HERITAGE PROJECTS

This somewhat theoretical consideration also outlines the contribution that landscape biography can make to current heritage practices. Strictly speaking of course, writing a landscape biography is already an example of present-day heritage practice. After all it is about producing a story about the landscape. As an explicit act of remembrance, this story produces a chronicle of life and dwelling in the region for

Fig. 10
Matrix of topics and transformations of the Biography of De Zandstad website (www.zandstad.nl).

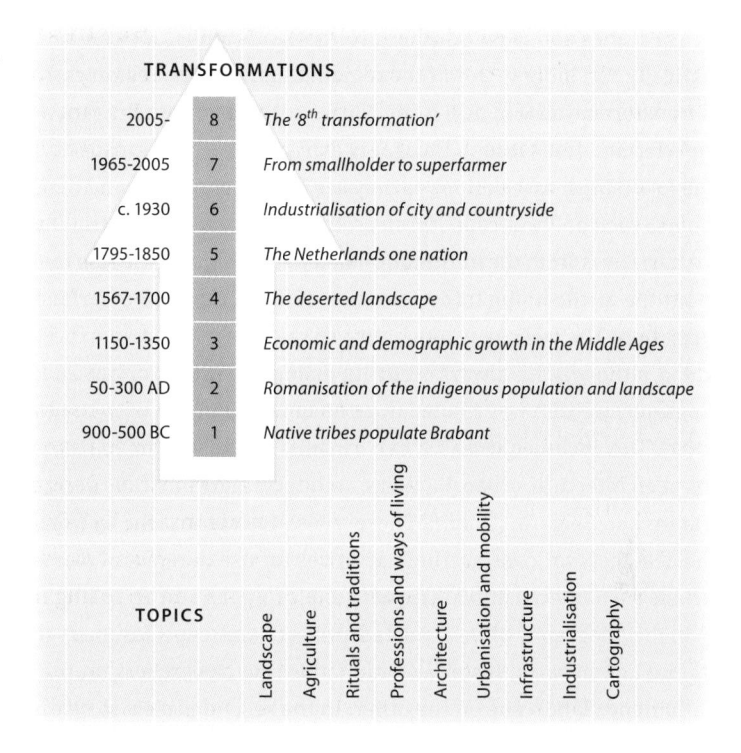

TRANSFORMATIONS		
2005-	8	The '8th transformation'
1965-2005	7	From smallholder to superfarmer
c. 1930	6	Industrialisation of city and countryside
1795-1850	5	The Netherlands one nation
1567-1700	4	The deserted landscape
1150-1350	3	Economic and demographic growth in the Middle Ages
50-300 AD	2	Romanisation of the indigenous population and landscape
900-500 BC	1	Native tribes populate Brabant

TOPICS: Landscape, Agriculture, Rituals and traditions, Professions and ways of living, Architecture, Urbanisation and mobility, Infrastructure, Industrialisation, Cartography

present-day society. In the South Netherlands Project, however, we have gone several steps further especially in terms of giving a new form to the material past in the southern Netherlands landscape. We have of course attempted to create some distance here. In all cases, researchers in the project entered into dialogue with different interest groups who ultimately acted as cultural mediators in present-day landscape developments. We will briefly outline two projects that follow this procedure, The Biography of De Zandstad and The Biography of Peelland.

The aim of the first project, the Biography of De Zandstad, was to draw its findings to the attention of the specific target group of architects and landscape designers (Brons 2007). Experience with design projects in recent years has taught us that these groups are critically important for the transmission of landscapes and traces contained within landscapes, as it is they who to a significant degree create the spatial conditions for the contemporary transmission or construction of memories. However, landscape designers cannot fully utilize traditional descriptions of monuments, archaeological research reports and historical geographical analyses as these are too descriptive, textual and specialist in character to serve as sources of inspiration for spatial design. Moreover, such reports are drafted from a one-sided perspective on preservation. This means that too little attention is paid to possibilities for reorganization and development, although in many cases this is precisely what is needed to preserve the social and economic vitality of the southern Netherlands landscape for its inhabitants, visitors and other users of the space. For this reason, a decision was taken in the Biography of De Zandstad project to develop a regional historical website (www.zandstad.nl) whose experimental, associative and interactive nature would make it particularly useful for designers (cf. Belvedere 1999).

The website's experimental features include its graphic design and frequent use of text-based as well as image-based stories. The website is associative because of the way that information is structured. Historical stories about the southern Netherlands landscape can be arranged spatially, temporally or thematically and biographies of the region or parts of the region can be constructed using seven moments of transformation (Fig. 10), from 'Native tribes populate Brabant' (900-500 BC) to 'From smallholder to superfarmer' (1985-2005). Designers can adopt both a retrospective and a prospective approach and are free to establish associations as they see fit. Places, stories and developments can be linked by searching themes such as 'landscape', 'profession', 'rituals' and 'industrialization,' thereby generating very different narratives from the information on offer. Designers are also invited to think further along these lines about the forthcoming transformation of the southern Netherlands region, known as the eighth transformation. The website is interactive in that the users' own expertise, experiences or memories can be added, although this always occurs in dialogue with historians and landscape researchers. The Zandstad Biography website was trialled in 2006 in co-operation with the Netherlands Architecture Fund (Brons 2007). This included research experiments by more than 70 historians, historical geographers, historians of architecture, urban planners, architects and landscape designers from six universities in the Netherlands and Belgium (Ghent). These trials indicate that the website offers good possibilities for planners and designers for constructing narratives for use in regional plans and landscape designs, whereas historians encountered difficulties with exploring the site and using the various databases.

In the 'Biography of De Zandstad' project, landscape designers therefore act in a mediating role. They are the link between historians and landscape researchers on the one hand and users of the southern Netherlands landscape on the other. In the second project to be discussed here, The 'Biography of Peelland' (Kolen 2004), this role is mainly played by inhabitants with a special interest in the landscape and the history of the region.

This second project covering the De Peel reconstruction area has been conducted within the context of a programme for rural regeneration, referred to as the Reconstruction of the Brabant Countryside (Provincie Noord-Brabant 2001; Janssen 2006). In addition, the project is designed as a platform for all kinds of smaller-scale local initiatives in the field of cultural heritage and landscape development. The principal aim of reconstruction is to increase the sustainability and quality of life of the agricultural areas, especially by offering new possibilities for farming, by creating zones without intensive cattle breeding and by improving the quality of the lived environment. This will provide new opportunities for landscape, nature and cultural heritage. The De Peel reconstruction area is situated in the southeastern corner of North Brabant and covers over 56,000 hectares. It has traditionally been characterized by the presence of high moorland and other wet biotopes, such as fens and wet heathland landscapes, moving into a drier cultural landscape.

The Biography of Peelland is highly participative in character. The concrete potential for applying landscape biography to regional developments is tested in collaboration with many inhabitants who have knowledge of local history and landscape. Using their expertise and that of the archaeologists and historical geographers involved in the project, a plan is then drawn up for the sustainable transmission of the region's spatial characteristics. Special emphasis is given to fourteen landscapes that together give a good picture of the developmental history of Peelland. Moreover, the participants are of the view that these landscapes are representative of the spatial diversity and historical layeredness of present day Peelland. Descriptions of the landscapes, also a joint product, explain historical development and spatial features and outline the development trajectories that can help preserve the social and economic vitality of the landscapes.

The Biography of Peelland is included in regional government projections outlining how the region should look in the near future. Perhaps it is even more important for the project outcomes to be shared with a network of participants, some of whom are active in local politics. The project has led to the development of a wide range of local landscape plans, a number of which have since been started or even completed. In these instances the Biography of Peelland also offers tools for evaluating small-scale transformations, such as changes at the level of individual properties or the village, from a long-term perspective on regional developments.

Thus both projects have created a platform encouraging different groups into a dialogue about the past and future of the southern Netherlands' landscape. Moreover, people other than historians are acting as mediators to translate the results of that dialogue into the actual practice of reshaping and managing areas. In this model the historian is one of the co-authors of the memories and historical narratives that are relevant to everyday practice. This does not mean, however, that the special role of the historian is thereby lost. The biographies of both De Zandstad and Peelland also present 'expert' stories and themes exposing unexpected 'layers' that have been only superficially reclaimed in the social representation and collective memory of inhabitants or planners. Two examples can help elucidate this. Most people in the region still regard the heath as an ancient natural landscape that has remained largely outside the sphere of human influence. However, ecologists, archaeologists and historical geographers have long known that heathland is an unstable phase in the succession of vegetation, one which has in fact been created through human land-use activity. Before the heathland reclamation, in other words in the nineteenth century, the heath belonged to the communally managed land of the southern Netherlands villages and had a wide range of agricultural uses. Moreover, as we have already seen, the heath occupied a specific place in the Christian structuring of the living environment and was therefore part of the cultural landscape.

Archaeologists, historical anthropologists and historical geographers are also able to lend depth, nuances or alternative stories to other widely-held views of the landscape. A case in point is the one-sided association of Peelland with the history of peat bog reclamation or with Catholic rural life. Archaeological and historical research shows that the landscape has also been formed and passed down (Lowenthal 1998) by societies with fundamentally different economies, social structures, religions and rituals and experiences of the living environment, including the role of the past.

Thus the projects are not concerned with tame consensus but with producing alternative histories and perhaps even unwanted or unpopular accounts of the past. Although not all of these readings eventually find their way into formal policy, they are nevertheless evident in the diversity of landscape designs for a single locality or area and of course in the dialogue conducted within the projects.

10. PUTTING THE PIECES TOGETHER: THE LANDSCAPE AS A MULTILAYERED LIVING ENVIRONMENT

One theme of landscape biography is always paramount in the heritage projects discussed here, namely the elaboration of the historical layeredness of the lived environment. The notion of layeredness stands firstly for the fact that the temporality of landscape has not just a diachronological but a synchronic dimension. At any moment in time earlier transformations of the landscape can be read in their continuing effect on the contemporary environment and by means of the palimpsest of objects and structures produced in that process. It is tempting to think principally of material traces here, but of course the memories, stories and meanings attached to the lived environment also undergo change. Secondly, layeredness in landscape biography stands for the multivocal character of the past. The past of the southern Netherlands' landscape contains beautiful grey and black tones. Different groups and individuals raise very diverse questions about regional history (Bender/Winer 2001). Furthermore, memories and heritage are experienced and valued in constantly changing ways because the perspective and self-image of individuals and groups are subject to change (Bender 1998). Until now, heritage and design projects have not adequately acknowledged the dynamic way in which the regional past is perceived and dealt with. Instead, traditional heritage management is a closed system, with a small group of insiders deciding which aspects of the past are valuable and which are not. In landscape biography this system has been prised open to create room for the memories and historical associations of other interested groups (Kolen 1995).

Thus the historical layeredness of the region functions as a barometer of the sustainability of spatial transformations while at the same time saying something about the region's capacity for creating a climate for differentiated appreciation of heritage. In both cases, landscape biography is an appropriate concept for interpreting the lived environment historically, for deepening existing historical experiences and for considering the social values inherent in this, as well as for studying further possibilities for landscape development. This gives rise to opportunities to profile the region in terms of more varied images of the past than the historical icons and canons that are currently often featured by influential minorities at the local and regional level.

NOTES

1 Research Institute CLUE, VU University, Amsterdam, The Netherlands.
2 Hulsel, The Netherlands.

REFERENCES

Ashworth, G., 2005: Heritage and the Consumption of Places, in R. van der Laarse (ed.), *Bezeten van Vroeger. Erfgoed, Identiteit en Musealisering*, Amsterdam, 193-206.

Belvedere, 1999: *The Belvedere Memorandum. A policy document examining the relationship between cultural history and spatial planning*, Utrecht.

Bender, B., 1993: Stonehenge – contested landscapes (medieval to present-day), in B. Bender (ed.), *Landscape – Politics and Perspectives*, Oxford, 245-280.

Bender, B., 1998: *Stonehenge: Making Space*, Oxford.

Bender, B./M. Winer 2001: *Contested landscapes: movement, exile and place*, Oxford.

Bosma, K., 2003: *J.M. de Casseres. De eerste planoloog*, Rotterdam.

Bradley, R., 2002: *The past in prehistoric societies*, London/New York.

Brons, R. (ed.), 2007: *Podcasting cultuurgeschiedenis. Case: de toekomst van de Zandstad*, Rotterdam (Stimuleringsfonds voor Architectuur).

Bijsterveld, A.A., 1999: Gift exchange, landed property, and eternity. The foundation and endowment of the Premonstratensian priory of Postel, in F. Theuws/N. Roymans (eds.), *Land and Ancestors*.

Cultural dynamics in the Urnfield period and the Middle Ages in the southern Netherlands, Amsterdam (Amsterdam Archaeological Studies 4), 309-348.

Corbin, A., 1994: *Les cloches de la terre: paysage sonore et culture sensible dans les campagnes au XIXe siècle*, Paris.

Crijns A.H./F.W.J. Kriellaars, 1987: *Het gemengde landbouwbedrijf op de zandgronden in Noord-Brabant, 1800-1885*, Tilburg.

Crijns A.H./F.W.J. Kriellaars, 1992: *Het gemengde landbouwbedrijf op de zandgronden in Noord-Brabant, 1886-1930*, Tilburg.

Fokkens, H., 1996: The Maaskant project. Continuity and change of a regional research project, *Archaeological Dialogues* 1996, 196-215.

Fontijn, D., 2003: *Sacrificial landscapes. Cultural biographies of persons, objects and 'natural' places in the Bronze Age of the southern Netherlands, c. 2300-600 BC*, Leiden (Analecta Praehistorica Leidensia 33/34).

Frijhoff, W., 2007: *Dynamisch erfgoed*, Amsterdam.

Gerritsen, F., 2003: *Local identities. Landscape and community in the late prehistoric Meuse-Demer-Scheldt region*, Amsterdam (Amsterdam Archaeological Studies 9).

Gerritsen, F.A., 2007: Relocating the house. Social transformations in late prehistoric Northern Europe, in R.A. Beck (ed.), *The Durable House. House Society Models in Archaeology*, Carbondale (Center for Archaeological Investigations Occasional Publication 34), 154-174.

Gerritsen, F.A./E. Rensink (eds.), 2004: *Beekdallandschappen in archeologisch perspectief. Een kwestie van onderzoek en monumentenzorg*, Amersfoort (Nederlandse Archeologische Rapporten 28).

Heijden, C. van der/G. Rooijakkers, 1993: *Kempische boeren en Vlaamse vissers. Kunstenaars en volkscultuur omstreeks 1885: Victor de Buck en Joseph Gindra*, Eindhoven.

Ingold, T., 2000 (1993): The temporality of landscape, in T. Ingold, *The perception of the environment. Essays in livehood, dwelling and skill*, London/New York, 189-208.

Janssen, J., 2002: Nostalgic landscape. Planning between conservation and modernisation, *OASE/Architectural Journal* 60, 77-110.

Janssen, J., 2006: *Vooruit denken en verwijlen. De (re)constructie van het plattelandschap in Zuidoost-Brabant, 1920-2000*, Tilburg.

Kolen J., 1995: Recreating (in) Nature, Visiting History. Second thoughts on landscape reserves and their role in the preservation and experience of the historic environment, *Archaeological Dialogues* 2, 127-159.

Kolen, J., 2005: *De biografie van het landschap. Drie essays over landschap, geschiedenis en erfgoed*, Amsterdam (Ph.D. thesis VU University).

Kolen, J. (et al.), 2004: *De Biografie van Peelland*, Amsterdam (Zuidnederlandse Archeologische Rapporten 13).

Kolen, J./M. Witte, 2006: A biographical approach to regions, and its value for spatial planning, in W. van der Knaap/A. van der Valk (eds.), *Multiple landscape. Merging past and present. Selected Papers from the fifth International Workshop on Sustainable Land Use Planning 7-9 June 2004*, Wageningen, 125-147.

Lowenthal, D., 1996: *Possessed by the past. The heritage crusade and the spoils of history*, New York/London.

Lowenthal, D., 1998: The past is a foreign country: for the motion (1), in T. Ingold (ed.), *Key debates in anthropology*, London, 206-212.

Meinig, D.W., 1979: The beholding eye. Ten versions of the same scene, in D.W. Meinig (ed.), *The interpretation of ordinary landscapes: geographical essays*, New York/Oxford, 33-47.

Mostert, M., 1993: De kerstening van Holland (zevende tot twaalfde eeuw). Een bijdrage aan de middeleeuwse religieuze geschiedenis, *Holland* 25, 125-155.

Olwig, K.R., 1984: *Nature's ideological landscape. A literary and geographic perspective on its development and preservation on Denmark's Jutland Heath*, London.

Provincie Noord-Brabant, 2001: *Reconstructie aan zet. Koepelplan reconstructie concentratiegebieden*, 's-Hertogenbosch.

Roymans, N., 1995: The cultural biography of urnfields and the long-term history of a mythical landscape, *Archaeological Dialogues* 2, 2-38.

Roymans, N., 1996: The South Netherlands project. Changing perspectives on landscape and culture, *Archaeological Dialogues* 3, 231-245.

Roymans, N./F. Gerritsen 2002: Landscape, ecology and mentalités: a long-term perspective on developments in the Meuse-Demer-Scheldt region, *Proceedings of the Prehistoric Society* 68, 257-287.

Roymans, N./F. Kortlang, 1999: Urnfield symbolism, ancestors and the land in the Lower Rhine Region, in F. Theuws/N. Roymans (eds.), *Land and ancestors. Cultural dynamics in the Urnfield period and the Middle Ages in the Southern Netherlands*, Amsterdam (Amsterdam Archaeological Studies 4), 33-62.

Roymans, N./F. Theuws, 1999: Long-term perspectives on man and landscape in the Meuse-Demer-Scheldt region. An introduction, in F. Theuws/N. Roymans (eds.), *Land and ancestors. Cultural dynamics in the Urnfield period and the Middle Ages in the Southern Netherlands*, Amsterdam (Amsterdam Archaeological Studies 4), 1-32.

Thissen, P.H.M., 1993: *Heideontginning en modernisering in het bijzonder in drie Brabantse Peelgemeenten, 1850-1940*, Utrecht.

Trienekens, G., 1993: Integrale geschiedenis in wording. Aarle-Rixtel en Wanroij in de negentiende en het begin van de twintigste eeuw, in J.A. van Oudheusden/G. Trienekens (eds.), *Een pront wijf, een mager paard en een zoon op het seminarie. Aanzetten tot een integrale geschiedenis van oostelijk Noord-Brabant 1770-1914*, 's-Hertogenbosch, 211-313.

3. The role of historical expertise in today's heritage management, landscape development and spatial planning
Comment on 'The biography of a sandy landscape' by Nico Roymans, Fokke Gerritsen, Cor van der Heijden, Koos Bosma & Jan Kolen

Jenny Atmanagara[1]

ABSTRACT

Cultural landscapes undergo constant transformations over time. The determinants influencing this development and the stakeholders involved in the process have been analysed by Roymans *et al.* (Ch. V.2). Their approach to biographical studies of landscapes was applied in the South Netherlands project and considered both research and practice of heritage management.

The biography approach delivers an interesting landscape genesis based on historical narrative. This knowledge provides additional information by combining different methods and can complement quantitative approaches to landscape research. It points out continuities and breaks in landscape development and the underlying reasons. Therefore, the biography approach elaborates the historical layeredness of a landscape with a focus on the community level.

This comment analyses and interprets the core themes addressed by the authors and evaluates their applicability with regard to the necessities in today's heritage management, landscape development and spatial planning. The focus of this comment is on the opportunities and constraints of inter- and transdisciplinary research on landscapes.

In addition it presents some results from the 'Landscape Typology for Switzerland', a project conducted within the action COST A27 LANDMARKS. Though Switzerland has less than half of the population of the Netherlands, i.e. 7,667,715 persons on a surface area of about 41,000 km^2 (http://epp.eurostat.ec.europa.eu. Accessed on 11 May, 2009), the country faces similar challenges, particularly with increasing urbanization as well as climate change and their impacts on landscape development and spatial planning.

KEY WORDS

Cultural landscape, heritage management; spatial planning, socio-cultural determinants; landscape typology; knowledge transfer; sustainable development

1. STORY LINES: LINKING PAST AND PRESENT

Roymans *et al.* (Ch. V.2) illustrate the biographical approach of landscape studies in the South Netherlands project alongside three narratives from the Urnfield period (700-400 BC), the Christianization period (1000-1300 AD) and the period of large-scale heathland reclamation (1850-1950 AD). These narra-

tives highlight several core themes which are also relevant for today's heritage management, landscape development and spatial planning:
- land appropriation and land use;
- identity constructions of the local communities;
- socio-cultural determinants of landscape change including aspects of institutional regime and participation; and
- polarization between intensification and extensification of land use.

Though focussing on very diverse periods in the past, the results by Roymans *et al.* underline the compliance of major historical issues with many of today's requirements. With regard to land appropriation the European societies have been used to sedentary occupation and fixed homesteads during the last centuries; however, this is currently changing with the ongoing trends of globalization and increased mobility. For landscape designers and planners this issue generates new challenges, such as the need for flexible homes or recreation facilities, and underlines their professional approach to constantly developing landscapes.

The example of shifting farmsteads and shared urnfields in late prehistory emphasizes the importance of religious symbols and landmarks for the identity construction of the local communities and as a unifying element in an unstable environment. The loss of identities, meanings and values associated with a particular landscape were compensated by imprinting the society's values in the built environment. Nowadays the challenge for designers and planners consists in making these symbols and landmarks accessible and valuable to today's society by re-interpreting them in a modern way, adapting them to the needs of today's society and embedding them in the everyday life of (groups of) individuals.

Furthermore, socio-cultural determinants affect the transformation of landscapes as shown by the example of Christianization and the situation of the Protestants in the North Brabant province. Land property rights, the inclusion and exclusion of social groups and the institutional regime influence the way how landscapes are interpreted and organized and how conflicts between different land users are managed. The long-lasting persistence of attitudes and values in a society becomes apparent today with the immigration of new social groups who bring along their own culture, attitudes and values which influence their perception and handling of their living place. The political and economic participation of immigrants is an important precondition for integration and acculturation.

Finally, the example of heathland reclamation illustrates the bipartite division of the landscape's structure into cultivated zones and wastelands. In this period (1850-1950), demographic trends such as the migration of young farmers due to population pressure in other areas and innovations in technology and transport fostered the rapid change of these landscapes. In today's societies the polarization between intensification and extensification of land use is a widespread phenomenon. It presents one of the major challenges for landscape planners and managers and puts heritage managers in intensively used areas under pressure since their valuable sites often have to give way to more profitable forms of land use. In spite of the dynamics and discontinuity of landscape transformations, there is a need for stability and identity within many societies and these factors are regarded as an integral part of quality of life.

2. APPLICABILITY OF THE CORE THEMES: MERGING RESEARCH AND PRACTICE

Which role can the expertise from archaeological and historical studies play in today's spatial planning, landscape development and heritage management?

Roymans *et al.* exemplify the applicability of the biographical approach and the role of landscape design and planning by two heritage management projects. The first one, Biography of De Zandstad, underlined the role of landscape architects and designers as mediators between historians, landscape researchers and the landscape users. They require narratives which are comprehensible to non-experts and can be easily transferred into design and planning in order to create the contemporary and future spatial conditions for landscape development. The second project, Biography of Peelland, focussed on the participation of local communities in the region. Here the local stakeholders served as cultural mediators who gave their knowledge and expertise to the project and brought up alternative stories about the past. The project provided new instruments, e.g. an interactive website as a platform for local initiatives and tools for evaluating landscape transmissions. Both projects can be regarded as laboratories to study best practices in heritage management, landscape development and spatial planning.

The applicability of the core themes (see section 1) in today's heritage management, landscape development and spatial planning is ambivalent. Past narratives framed the preconditions under which landscape transformations take place, thus they can serve as a reference for similar developments today. However, they cannot provide solutions for today's and future challenges (as it is intended in landscape management and spatial planning), since the determinants have changed both in their quantity and quality. For example, with regard to demographic trends the number of inhabitants is much higher and the local societies are much more diverse than ever before.

Land appropriation and land use today take place in a sphere of multiplied influences, conflicts between different land users, high dynamics and an accelerated tempo. This makes planning in the classical sense almost impossible and calls for a flexible and process-oriented steering. A conservative approach, as it is often claimed by nature conservationists and heritage managers, inevitably leads to an attitude of defensiveness, particularly in dynamic urban and peri-urban areas. It drives these professions and their objectives into less dynamic peripheral or remote areas. However development, including heritage planning, in both urban and rural areas seems increasingly to take place by coincidence rather than deliberate planning.

In this context the valuable contribution of historical narratives lies in their potential to bring closer the everyday life of former societies and the experiences of their individuals. This helps us to understand the determinants that formed landscapes in the past. However, it is hardly possible to transfer these stories to the present. As mentioned above, today's societies and groups of individuals living in particular landscapes have changed to a great extent. This concerns not only their formation but also their values and attitudes which constitute their 'mental landscapes'. Formerly important landscape symbols and landmarks have sometimes lost their importance or have been given a different meaning by new social groups. While this phenomenon is wellknown with regard to the internal migration from urban areas to rural areas and the differences in landscape perception of suburbanites and villagers, knowledge of the perception and experience of European landscapes by external migrants is still poor. Lessons might be learnt from non-European countries which have more experience with large-scale migration. For example Stephenson (Stephenson 2008) studied how the Maoris and the European settlers in New Zealand perceive their environment and everyday landscape. She found out that the settlers mainly realigned to the 'surface values' (perception of physical landscape elements, forms, relations and practices), whereas the natives oriented themselves more on 'embedded values' (awareness of inclusive values, narratives, symbols, memories and emotions).

The integration and acculturation of new social groups provide new chances and challenges. Despite the trend towards more diverse societies the political participation of migrants is still minor. With regard to heritage management this means that even if the local stakeholders are included in the process, this does not necessarily mean that new inhabitants are reached. Cultural differences, language barriers and the digital divide might be reasons for this issue. Economic participation is even less common since many newcomers work in less attractive jobs, face insecure residence status and social security and mostly have neither the networks nor the property for social advancement. Hence, the interpretation of landscape elements, the organization and planning of land use and the valorization of landscapes remain largely with those who have inhabited these areas for many generations.

In these dynamic surroundings landscapes face a difficult role. Since cultural landscapes usually develop slowly over a long period of time, the adaptation to new determinants and the accelerated tempo and dynamics is often impossible. The landscape with its typical elements is changed rapidly or falls behind. As a consequence the total area is polarized into intensively used and extensively used areas. However, such a development is not necessarily negative because it can also open up new chances and possibilities while blocking or hindering others. The emerging mosaic of landscapes with diverse qualities and speeds of development poses an exceptional challenge to heritage management, landscape development and spatial planning. These disciplines will need to develop new objectives for landscape management in a more flexible and process-oriented approach.

Merging the worlds of landscape research and practice has been an important concern for many years. However, to apply the narratives discovered by the historical disciplines in today's heritage management, landscape development and spatial planning seems to be more difficult than it appears at first glance. Whereas historians, archaeologists and historical geographers are primarily interested in the landscape *per se*, i.e. in producing new knowledge and gaining insight in the transformations of the past, landscape designers and planners usually assess the status quo and develop alternative designs and future concepts for landscapes and places. Hence, the aims and needs of landscape designers and planners differ from those of researchers. Designing or planning landscapes includes normative objectives, visions and guidelines for future developments. Certainly, the objectives that have driven landscape development in the past are not the same as nowadays. It is impossible to infer from the past if development in the future will be similar. Despite these restrictions, historical narratives can still serve as a source of inspiration for landscape designers and planners. For this purpose the stories produced by local stakeholders and interpreted by historians and archaeologists need to be practicable and useful for landscape designers and planners in order to be considered in current plans.

3. LANDSCAPE TYPOLOGY: COMBINING QUANTITATIVE AND QUALITATIVE APPROACHES

The need to develop new quality objectives for landscape management (see above section 2) requires the demarcation and detailed analysis of representative landscapes, as applied by Roymans *et al.* (Ch. V.2) in the Peelland project. On the one hand this kind of research can deliver an impression of both the spatial diversity and the historical layeredness of a region. On the other hand it provides information on the potential of a region and its landscape for future development. This basic idea was the stimulus for the

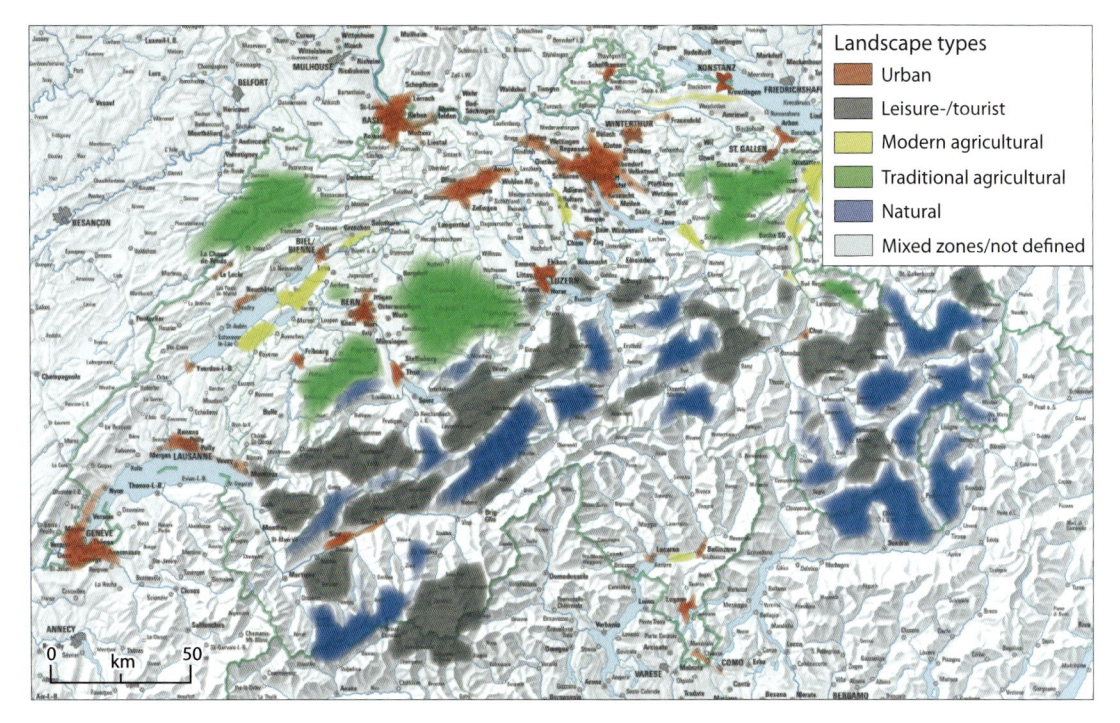

Fig. 1
Spatial distribution of the core areas of different landscapes in Switzerland.

Landscape Typology for Switzerland project briefly described below. The project was implemented by the Institute of Geography in Bern from 2006 to 2008 as a sub-project within the action COST A27 LANDMARKS (see Orejas/Reher Ch. VII.3).

The project's objective was to develop a typology of cultural landscapes that occur in Switzerland and to study the type of the traditional agrarian landscape in detail. For this purpose integral landscape types were defined and their core areas demarcated. These areas needed to fulfil diverse criteria including having a specific minimum size. The GIS analysis of the traditional agrarian landscape was done for different points in time in two case study areas, the Franches Montagnes (Jura) and the Napfgebiet (Upper Midland). It was based on the indicators forest areas, road network, topography and settlement development (Essig *et al.* 2008).

Five main landscape types were identified in Switzerland:
- urban landscapes;
- recreation and tourism landscapes;
- modern agrarian landscapes;
- traditional agrarian landscapes;
- semi-natural landscapes.

Furthermore, there are mixed zones in which different landscape types appear but which do not achieve the minimum size required to be demarcated as a separate core area. Some areas could not be assigned to a specific landscape type due to the indicators used (Fig. 1).

The quantitative results were complemented by a questionnaire survey, including landscape photographs, among the inhabitants of the case study regions. The inhabitants widely confirmed the different landscape types (Essig *et al.* 2008).The results of the diachronic analysis in the case study areas for the years 1870, 1950 and 2000 showed that forest areas increased in steep terrain. Furthermore, the population numbers increased in the larger municipalities and decreased in the smaller ones, i.e. there is a trend towards the concentration of settlements. These are primarily located in areas with a gradient of less than 5% (Essig *et al.* 2008).

The results of this project serve as basic information for landscape management and its integration into spatial planning in Switzerland. It delivers the concept, a number of methods and relevant findings to deduce objectives for the future development of the different landscape types. Hence, this landscape typology is in line with several political approaches of the Swiss government and administration, such as the Swiss Landscape Concept (BUWAL/BRP 1998; BUWAL 2002), the Report on the Swiss Planning Policy Guidelines (ARE 1996) and the draft of the Spatial Concept Switzerland (ARE 2008). These public policies aim at a sustainable spatial development and the integration of cultural landscapes into spatial planning.

4. CONCLUSIONS

The biographical study of landscapes is a concept which elaborates narratives that have influenced landscape development during different periods from the past. These narratives can contribute to the understanding of cultural landscape transformations and should be integrated into today's heritage management, landscape development and spatial planning.

The narratives provide knowledge and insight about former societies and their everyday life and how their interests, strategies and actions impacted the landscapes inhabited by them. Furthermore, these narratives help us understand how these societies construct their common identities and which role the landscape played in identity construction. Therefore, this approach delivers valuable information to complement and interpret other results from landscape research, particularly from quantitative approaches such as GIS analyses.

The core themes identified (land appropriation and land use; community identity; socio-cultural determinants of landscape change; polarization between intensification and extensification of land use) made it clear that the perception, use and adaptation of landscapes and land use forms cannot be examined without considering the socio-cultural background of the inhabitants. The societies and their values are constantly changing, as are the landscapes. Symbols and landmarks play an important role in landscapes, an aspect which has been widely neglected in landscape research so far. With increasing globalization and mobility, societies are nowadays more diverse and of a temporary nature. Individuals living in these societies often face not only one identity but several. This makes both identity construction and planning in the classical sense almost obsolete. Instead strategies are needed which are flexible and suitable to create living landscapes for varying social groups. Such an approach contributes to the well-being of the inhabitants and the quality of life within a region.

In today's societies landscape development often leads to conflicts between utilization and protection. Here the narratives from the past can raise awareness for landscape changes both among decision-makers and the population, thereby, helping maintain or even increase the identity of the inhabitants with respect to their living environment. However, accessibility to the landscapes is a precondition for identity construction, both in the sense of opening up an area as well as the inclusion of diverse social groups.

The knowledge transfer from research to practice is reasonable on the regional level where the local population can participate. It requires research results that are presented in a comprehensible and interesting manner for non-experts, new methods and instruments for participation and the openness of the researchers for different opinions and alternative stories. In this context the co-operation between different disciplines as well as with policies and the general public poses a specific challenge. Since these groups usually follow diverse objectives and come from different starting points, the applicability of historical knowledge in today's heritage management, landscape development and spatial planning is a difficult task. Finding a common language, developing suitable theories and methods and combining quantitative and qualitative results seem to be important tasks in order to achieve an effective and efficient handling of this inter- and transdisciplinary field.

In the broader sense, it can be concluded that the concepts of cultural landscape and biography are suitable ways to study the issues involved as their analysis helps us understand and explain the development of a region. According to the definition provided by the Swiss landscape concept[2], cultural landscapes cover the whole area of a region, are not limited to open landscapes but include the settlements and traffic infrastructure. This holistic approach makes the cultural landscape concept an appropriate approach to evaluate landscape transformations in space and time and to operationalize the concept of sustainable development, e.g. by considering short-term and long-term perspectives or the dynamic process. In this context, the integration of historical expertise into the relevant public policies allows a broad perspective with some distance from the everyday problems in planning and design.

NOTES

1 Institute of Geography, University of Bern, Switzerland.
2 "Landscape comprises the entire space within and outside settlements. It is the sum of the past and of the future emerged through the natural factors like underground, soil, water, air, light, climate, fauna and flora in interaction with cultural, social and economic factors (BUWAL/BRP 1998)".

REFERENCES

ARE - Bundesamt für Raumentwicklung (ed.), 1996: *Grundzüge der Raumordnung Schweiz*, Ittigen.

ARE - Bundesamt für Raumentwicklung (ed.), 2008: *Raumkonzept Schweiz. Eine dynamische und soziale Schweiz. Entwurf*, Ittigen.

BUWAL – Bundesamt für Umwelt, Wald und Landschaft (ed.), 2002: *Landschaftskonzept Schweiz LKS. Reporting 2002*, Bern.

BUWAL/BRP - Bundesamt für Umwelt, Wald und Landschaft; Bundesamt für Raumplanung (eds.),1998: *Landschaftskonzept Schweiz. Teil 1 Konzept, Teil 2 Bericht*, Bern.

Essig, M./J.Atmanagara/P. Flury/H.-R. Egli, 2008: *Landschaftstypologie Schweiz: Vorindustrielle Landschaften – Definition, räumliche Abgrenzung, Wahrnehmung und Bewertung. - Ein Projekt im Rahmen der europäischen Aktion COST A27 LANDMARKS*, Bern (manuscript, not published yet).

Roymans,N./F. Gerritsen/C. van der Heijden/K. Bosma/J. Kolen: Revitalizing history: moving from historical landscape reconstructions to heritage practices in the southern Netherlands, this volume Ch. V.2.

Stephenson, J., 2008: The Cultural Values Model. An integrated approach to values in landscapes, *Landscape and Urban Planning* 84,127-139.

WEBSITES

Total population of European countries on 1 January 2009:

http://epp.eurostat.ec.europa.eu/tgm/table.do?tab=table&language=en&pcode=tps00001&tableSelection=1&footnotes=yes&labeling=labels&plugin=1. (Accessed on 11 May, 2009).

4. The potential of remote sensing, magnetometry and geochemical prospection in the characterization and inspection of archaeological sites and landscapes in the Netherlands

Henk Kars[1], Alette Kattenberg[2], Stijn Oonk[3] & Chris Sueur[4]

ABSTRACT

This paper summarizes the findings of three studies dealing with the application of remote sensing techniques, magnetometry and geochemical prospection in Dutch archaeology. The section on remote sensing presents a short study based on a literature review and on interviews with specialists and stakeholders in the field of heritage management. It is concluded that remote sensing techniques are widely applicable in different landscapes in the Netherlands and offer great opportunities; however, so far their application in modern prospective archaeology is mainly restricted to the use of digital elevation models.

The study on magnetometry is, in addition to the measurement of the magnetic susceptibility of many soil samples, based on a magnetometer survey of 31 sites in order to perform an assessment of the use of magnetic methods for locating and mapping archaeological sites. Areas in different geogenetic environments in the Netherlands were identified where use of the method will be successful and the method should therefore be added to the toolkit of the archaeological prospector.

The section on geochemical prospection presents, in addition to literature reviews, the application of state of the art techniques for the recognition of inorganic and organic chemical fingerprints in archaeological soils. The investigations showed that even in densely occupied areas with soils containing subrecent to modern anthropogenic signals, archaeological soils and features could be determined. The analysis of soils using mass spectrometer proteomics showed that proteinaceous matter reflects the presence of keratin which probably derives from ancient hair and skin. It is argued that the use of biomarkers in archeological prospection is a challenging subject for future research.

It is concluded that, in sharp contrast to field surveys, coring and test trenching, the described non-destructive techniques are only rarely used in archaeological prospection in the Netherlands. One reason might be the lack of a master's degree programme in prospective archaeology at Dutch universities. Another reason often mentioned is that these methods are not cost-efficient, which might be true for advanced geochemical prospection techniques but does not hold for magnetometry and remote sensing methods. A third reason might be the argued reliability of these methods; however, despite their restrictions they have proved to be very useful in other countries.

KEYWORDS

Archaeological science; magnetometry, remote sensing, geochemical prospection; the Netherlands

1. INTRODUCTION

Recent developments in archaeological resource management in the Netherlands, induced by the regulations of the Valletta Convention (Valletta 1992) and recently implemented in the Dutch Archaeological Heritage Management Act (Wamz 2007), have had a tremendous impact on views regarding the sustainable protection and development of our archaeological resources. However, both scientists and policymakers in the archaeological heritage field realize that there are several gaps in our knowledge needed for the implementation of these new views. One of the gaps deals with the inventorization and valuation of archaeological sites and landscapes (Fig. 1).

It might be safely assumed for northwestern Europe that more than 95% of the archaeological record is hidden in the soil and invisible to the untrained eye, which means that in terms of its perception by the general public the cultural value of this hidden and invisible part of the record is close to zero. The value, therefore, is restricted to its intrinsic qualities. How can the information present in features and artefacts in the soil tell us something about the past? These intrinsic qualities are mainly determined by two parameters: i) the age and character of an archaeological site; and ii) the physical quality of the site, how much of the original site is preserved and the state of preservation. A solid and reliable knowledge of both these parameters is essential in the decision-making process regarding excavation or *in situ* preservation. Property developers and others dealing with the interests of the archaeological resources in the planning process are, therefore, in nearly all cases obliged to perform prospective investigations of threatened sites on paper and in the field (see also Verhagen *et al.*, Ch. V.5). The first aim of these investigations is to establish if any archaeological site is present and, if present, to determine the character and preservation state of these sites. In addition, they might be of great help in determining excavation strategies as well as strategies for *in situ* preservation, while prospection methods can also be used in monitoring scheduled sites. This requires: i) the availability of a number of mostly non-destructive techniques which; ii) provide

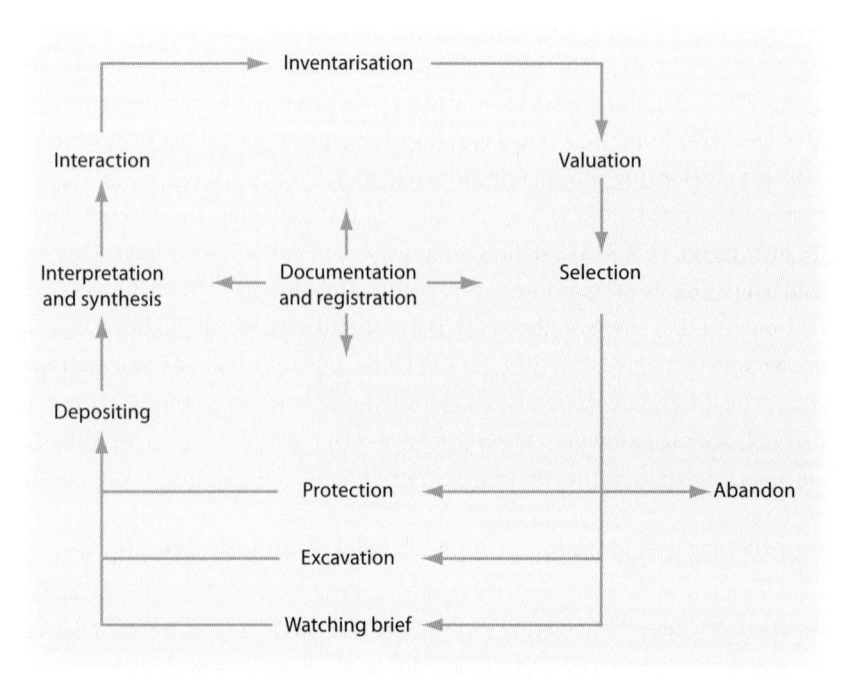

Fig. 1 The cyclical process of archaeological resource management. Archaeological prospection plays a key role in the assessment and valuation of archaeological resources (Willems 1997; idem 2008).

sound and reproducible information, representative of the archaeological phenomena present and iii) that can be used in a time- and cost-effective way.

The first decades of archaeological prospection in the Netherlands were dominated by the investigation of manifestations of the buried archaeological record on the surface, i.e. incidentally by aerial photography and more structurally by surface collection during field surveys. In general, however, archaeological remains that are buried under thick natural or anthropogenic deposits and remains representing earlier phases of multi-phase sites cannot be seen in aerial photographs. Surface collection has similar limitations since this prospection technique only provides information about superficial sites and sites that are buried at shallow depth and are damaged by post-depositional processes. Moreover, the relationship between the manifestations of an archaeological site on the surface and the buried archaeological site is unclear.

During the 1980s and 1990s the methodological focus in Dutch archaeological prospection gradually shifted to hand augering because of its success rate. With some exceptions, limited attention was paid to established techniques like aerial photography or novel geophysical and geochemical methods. Methodological research was concentrated on investigating the instrumental variables that influence the discovery of an archaeological site by augering, namely grid spacing, type of grid, type and size of auger (Groenewoudt 1994), the effectiveness of mechanical drills (Tol *et al.* 2004) and a qualitative comparison of mechanical and manual augering (Hissel/Van Londen 2004).

Though the great potential of augering is not denied, there is no one specific method that meets all demands at the same time and our knowledge with respect to the functionality of a certain method is far from complete and needs to be improved to satisfy the demands of archaeological prospection within modern archaeological resource management. The overall objective of the research project, which is summarized in this paper, was the improvement of prospective archaeology in the Netherlands by the development of non-destructive methods for different soil types, which in other countries were shown to have a great potential for the detection of a wide range of archaeological phenomena in similar or slightly different pedological settings.

The objectives of the project were defined in three subprojects and are as follows:
i. To describe the state of the art and the potential of remote sensing applications in Dutch archaeology.
ii. To investigate and to test the application of magnetic methods for detecting, mapping and evaluating archaeological sites and landscapes.
iii. To develop a cost-effective geochemical prospection method with emphasis on the refinement of phosphate prospection by testing different extraction methods and using multi-element analysing techniques.

The first and rather small subproject is based on a literature review and on interviews with different stakeholders in the heritage field to define future needs and opportunities in remote sensing applications in the Netherlands (Sueur 2006).

The subproject on geophysical prospection, designed as a Ph.D. project, was dedicated entirely to the use of magnetometry (Kattenberg 2008). This decision was made because in the 1990s a study was carried out on the application of electric resistivity methods in the Netherlands which, unfortunately, was not published. Due to the development of new GPR antennas with exciting new results in gaining high resolution data, an interesting next step could be to investigate the applicability of ground penetrating radar techniques in Dutch archaeological resource management.

The geochemical study, also designed as a Ph.D. project, drifted away from the originally chosen methodology using inorganic methods towards applying organic geochemical methods for tracing anthropogenic signals in soils. This has led to cutting-edge research that raised numerous intriguing questions which also deal with the preservation of organic archaeological remains in soils.

This paper aims to summarize the results of the whole project. The research questions, conclusions and recommendations of the three subprojects are described with regard to their implementation in modern archaeological resource management.

2. REMOTE SENSING APPLICATIONS IN DUTCH ARCHAEOLOGY

Airborne and spatial remote sensing techniques generally provide information about archaeological remains that are buried at shallow depth in the form of crop marks or shadow marks, for example the so-called Celtic fields (Brongers 1976) or, in the case of soil marks, are directly visible on the surface. However, the aerial photography section of the Universiteit Gent has demonstrated that crop marks can originate from archaeological features that are covered with a one-metre-thick layer of soil, but these situations are rare (J. Bourgeois, pers. comm.).

Airborne remote sensing is the science of acquiring information about the earth's surface and the zone immediately beneath it from the air without physical contact with it. Black-and-white and colour photographs have been successfully tested to detect, monitor and protect archaeological sites in Dutch archaeology (De Vries-Metz 1993). However, until now, monochrome and colour images have been applied sporadically in the Netherlands. Near-infrared and thermal images have not been tested systematically and are therefore not yet accepted as prospecting or monitoring tools. The positive thing to mention, however, is that digital elevation models by airborne laser scanning is already fully implemented in Dutch archaeological resource management (Waldus/Van der Velde 2006; KNA 2007).

Spatial remote sensing images are collected by satellites orbiting at high levels in the ionosphere or troposphere. To date, experiments with archaeological spatial remote sensing have not been executed in the Netherlands. Since the resolution of the scanners has increased dramatically, up to 1 metre, this method has become potentially useful for archaeological purposes.

Based on the literature inventory and interviews, remote sensing images should be used as an overlay in a geographical information system (GIS) and linked to topographical maps, cultural heritage maps, indicative maps of archaeological values, soil maps and so on. In doing so, remote sensing techniques might be highly relevant as is summarized (Sueur 2006) for:
- The inventorization and valuation of historical-archaeological sites and landscapes.
- Exploring the research area via office-based pilot studies.
- Determining the most effective strategy for the selection and use of prospection methods in the field and the positioning of test pits and trenches.
- Interpreting spatial data from an excavation in context of the landscape on a regional level.
- Monitoring the slow but ongoing degradation processes of scheduled monuments and historical-archaeological landscapes.
- Predictive modelling and risk assessment as an instrument for selection (Kamermans/Van Leusen/Verhagen 2009; Verhagen *et al.* Ch. V.5).

It is also stressed that airborne and spatial remote sensing could successfully be matched with geophysical techniques, as is already done in the United Kingdom and Germany. It is noted that per square kilometer both airborne and spatial remote sensing are very cost effective compared to other techniques.

Though people are aware of these opportunities, the situation remains that, apart from the application of digital elevation models, remote sensing techniques are only rarely used in Dutch archaeological resource management and there are no real signs that this situation will change soon.

However, an exciting new initiative to stimulate the application of remote sensing techniques in Dutch archaeology is the establishment of the Dutch Expertise Centre for Archaeological Remote Sensing (DECARS). So far, this initiative is mainly based on the enthusiasm of co-workers with different backgrounds and from different institutes. Creating a more structural network that is professionally related to an academic institute is the next important step to take.

3. THE APPLICATION OF MAGNETIC METHODS IN DUTCH ARCHAEOLOGICAL RESOURCE MANAGEMENT

This subproject aimed to assess the possibilities of the application of magnetic methods for mapping and evaluating archaeological remains in the Netherlands. Within this aim the following objectives were defined (Kattenberg 2008):
- To assess the use of magnetic methods for mapping archaeological features and sites.
- To assess the use of magnetic methods for archaeological landscape prospection.
- To define areas within which magnetic methods can and cannot be used within the framework of archaeological resource management.
- To develop a quick soil sample based method to predict whether a magnetometer survey can provide information about archaeological remains.

3.1 *Methodology*

The principle of magnetic prospection lies in the contrast between archaeological features and objects and the matrix they are embedded in. This contrast can be *remanent*, being caused for instance by subjecting soil material to high temperatures, or *induced*, depending on differences in magnetic susceptibility. Buried archaeological features like pits and ditches with a magnetic contrast can acquire a magnetic field around them which, depending on volume, depth of burial and contrast of the features, can be measured on the surface with a magnetometer.

Used alongside hand augering, magnetometry can obtain a much better resolution in the same time. Moreover, archaeological features are mapped in the horizontal plane. For example, the features of those archaeological sites that are found during a hand augering prospection can be made visible in a magnetometer survey. At present, traditional prospection methods like augering and test trenching are often used in cases where a magnetometer survey would produce better data when compared to augering and would be less intrusive when compared to test trenching.

On extensive sites magnetometer surveys can be used next to excavations in order to gain information from the unexcavated part of the site or to plan future excavations. Archaeological or geological features like ditches and creeks that have sufficient magnetic contrast can be quickly mapped over great lengths.

Within the framework of this study, 31 archaeological sites spread over different geogenetic environments in the Netherlands and covering different archaeological periods from the Bronze Age onwards,

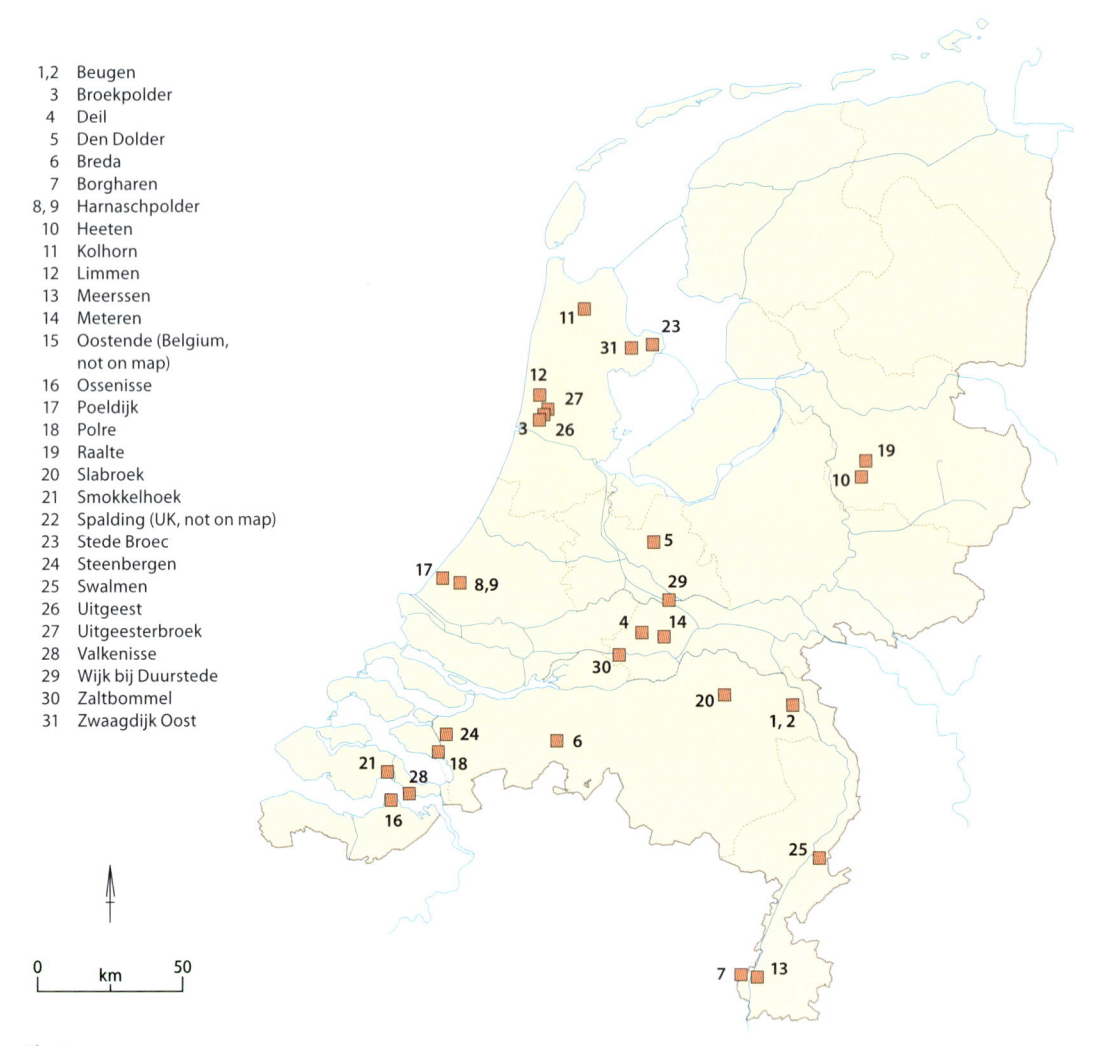

1,2	Beugen
3	Broekpolder
4	Deil
5	Den Dolder
6	Breda
7	Borgharen
8, 9	Harnaschpolder
10	Heeten
11	Kolhorn
12	Limmen
13	Meerssen
14	Meteren
15	Oostende (Belgium, not on map)
16	Ossenisse
17	Poeldijk
18	Polre
19	Raalte
20	Slabroek
21	Smokkelhoek
22	Spalding (UK, not on map)
23	Stede Broec
24	Steenbergen
25	Swalmen
26	Uitgeest
27	Uitgeesterbroek
28	Valkenisse
29	Wijk bij Duurstede
30	Zaltbommel
31	Zwaagdijk Oost

Fig. 2
The location of the sites investigated in this study
(Kattenberg 2008).

were investigated (Fig. 2). Field studies consisted of a magnetometer survey in combination with hand augering and magnetic susceptibility sampling. All the magnetometer surveys that are performed within this study have been carried out with fluxgate gradiometer instruments (Geoscan FM36 fluxgate gradiometer and Bartington GRAD601 fluxgate gradiometer, both with resolutions of 0,1 nT). Magnetic susceptibility measurements and more advanced magnetic measurements were conducted in the laboratory (Kattenberg 2008).

3.2 Results

Conclusions about the possible use of magnetic methods to measure induced anomalies caused by magnetic susceptibility contrasts in the fill of archaeological features depend on the lithological composition of the soil matrix in which these features are found. The analytical results of the 31 investigated sites have therefore been grouped with regard to the different geogenetic areas of the Netherlands in which they were located.

Magnetometer surveys on estuarine deposits did not prove successful in mapping archaeological pits and ditches. It is thought that the lack of contrast between the archaeological and the non-archaeological deposits is the result of post-depositional processes like gleying and sea waterlogging. Because of these findings, magnetometer surveys on estuarine soils are not recommended. One exception is archaeological sites that are buried under saline or brackish groundwater, as the preferential formation of iron sulphides in organic deposits could make these sites very good targets (Kattenberg/Aalbersberg 2004; Kattenberg 2008).

Magnetic susceptibilities and contrasts were very low on the archaeological sites investigated on the Weichselian coversands of the eastern and the southern part of the country. The reason for the lack of differentiation in these sandy soils is likely to be found in the fact that magnetic susceptibility enhancement is difficult to achieve and is easily lost in coarse grained sediments.

Both of the sites that were studied on loess and on coastal dune deposits, however, had very good magnetic susceptibility contrasts. The data that have been collected here are too limited to judge the suitability of these environments for the use of magnetic methods as an archaeological prospection tool but the results are promising and these areas should certainly be selected for a follow-up study.

The fluvial environment produced mixed results. In the river Rhine area and its tributaries, sites with and without clear magnetic contrasts were observed and further investigations are needed to assess which factors have enabled the formation, preservation and deletion of magnetic contrasts on these sites. Consistently good magnetic contrasts were detected in the Meuse valley, making this valley the most suitable starting point for the integration of magnetic methods into the current suite of prospection methods.

Features and objects with a remanent magnetization will always cause a magnetic anomaly in the earth's magnetic field. In archaeological terms these features include brick walls, kilns, hearths and feature fills that consist mainly of brick. The only constraints for the magnetic detection of these features are their contrast, size and depth of burial. The certainty of the presence of a magnetic anomaly that is caused by the above-mentioned features and materials alone could be an incentive to use magnetic methods more frequently in archaeological prospection in the Netherlands.

For this reason and in addition to the geogenetic approach, in her thesis Kattenberg (Kattenberg 2008) presents a wide range of archaeological features which have been successfully visualized by magnetic mapping within different archaeological contexts. This includes settlements (pits, ditches, walls and wells), off-site structures (plough marks, ditches and watering pits), funerary structures (graves, tumuli), industrial activities (peat ties and extraction pits, iron production and iron working furnaces) and infrastructure (roads).

The knowledge that was gained during this study is aimed to constitute the basis for the integration of magnetometry into the archaeological prospection toolkit. A proposed phased introduction of magnetometer surveys into the framework of Dutch archaeological resource management is presented in Fig. 3. With this study it has become much clearer under which circumstances a magnetometer survey can be successfully applied, which will give a focus to the integration of this novel technique into the existing archaeological prospection toolkit.

Phase I	• Include magnetometry in the KNA* as the method of choice for the prospection of metal working sites and sites at which kilns or furnaces are expected to be present. • Propose geophysical guide (leidraad geofysica) for the KNA. • Magnetometer surveys to be conducted alongside other archaeological prospection methods in all Meuse valley surveys in which archaeological remains are expected to be possibly present in the top metre of the soil.	In this first phase magnetometry is embedded in the framework of the KNA* in which ARM work is usually conducted. Consistent magnetometer surveys in an environment that is expected to show good results can create a (local) base for the integration of magnetometry as a prospection tool.
Phase II	• Magnetometer surveys to be conducted alongside other archaeological prospection methods in all surveys on loess in which archaeological remains are expected to be possibly present in the top metre of the soil.	In phase II and III the application radius of the magnetometer is increased, again using areas in which good results are expected.
Phase III	• Magnetometer surveys to be conducted alongside other archaeological prospection methods in all surveys on dune sands in which archaeological remains are expected to be possibly present in the top metre of the soil.	

Fig. 3
A proposed introduction of magnetometry surveys in Dutch archaeological resource management.

* KNA Kwaliteitsnorm Nederlandse Archeologie (Dutch Archaeology Quality Standard).

4. THE APPLICATION OF GEOCHEMICAL PROSPECTION METHODS FOR DUTCH ARCHAEOLOGICAL RESOURCE MANAGEMENT

In view of one of the aims of this subproject's research programme, i.e. to develop a cost-effective geochemical prospection technique, it was already concluded in the early stage of the project that an evaluation of cost-effectiveness could only be done for the longer existing, semi-quantitative method of estimating phosphate concentrations in soils. For the application of more advanced geochemical prospection in archaeological resource management, however, basic research concerning analytical strategies and methods was needed and the investigations were focused on the following issues (Oonk 2009):

i. to assess general chemical characteristics of archaeological soils in different lithological environments;
ii. to determine the information yield of various analytical methods, including chemical and mineralogical methods;
iii. to acquire knowledge on geochemical processes with respect to the formation of archaeological soil features, and
iv. to assess the value of organic biomarkers, especially proteins to study archaeological soils.

4.1 Methodology

In archaeological environments soils often reflect an alternative chemistry if compared to non-archaeological soils, mainly because of the waste that is released in the soil during habitation (Holliday/Gartner 2007; Wells/Terry 2007). The realization that soils are a sink for anthropogenic matter, together with the possibility that associated (in)organic components are retained by soils, has given rise to various approaches to chemically analyse soils in order to detect and/or interpret archaeological sites or features (Fig. 4). It is also demonstrated by several studies that specific human activities leave chemical fingerprints in the soil which can also be used to study former space use on archaeological sites (e.g. Entwistle/ Abrahams 1997; Entwistle/Abrahams/Dodgshon 1998; *idem* 2000; Barba 2007; Oonk/Slomp/Huisman 2009).

Phosphorus is most widely used as an anthropogenic indicator in archaeological soils. This is because phosphorus is normally prevalent in plant and animal tissue, bones, urine and faeces and thus a key element in occupation waste. In addition, phosphorus is relatively stable in most soils. Although anomalous levels of phosphorus have been found in archaeological soils all over the world, sub-recent to modern phosphorus coming from the application of (artificial) manure or sewage effluents often intermixes with archaeological phosphorus. There is ongoing debate on how to differentiate between archaeological and modern phosphorus and which phosphorus forms should be used as anthropogenic indicators. In addition to the current lack of knowledge on the range of geochemical reactions that have occurred after phosphorus inputs, little is known about the modern history of land-use and the effects that recent anthropogenic soil inputs have on the chemistry of buried archaeological soils. The co-occurrence of phosphorus and other presumed anthropogenic elements in archaeological soils may, however, give an indication of the nature of phosphorus.

Fig. 4
Overview of anthropogenic inputs and basal geochemical processes in archaeological soils
(Oonk 2009).

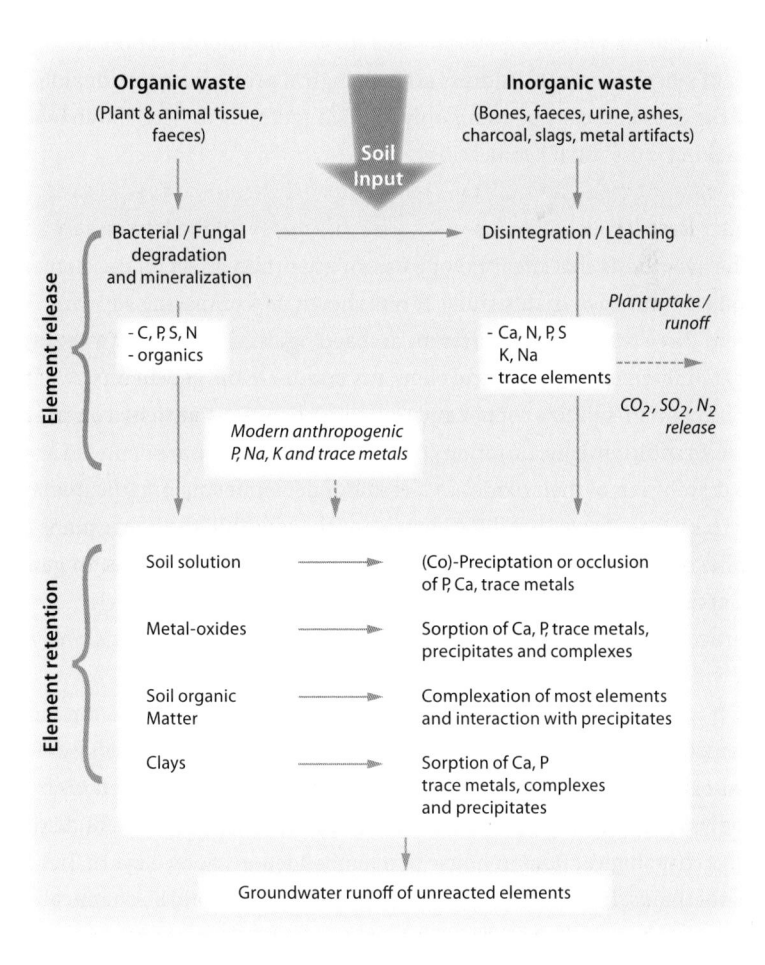

During the last decade archaeological soils have increasingly been studied using other elements besides phosphorus. Such methods can unveil the complexity of archaeological soils through specific soil extraction techniques and multi-element analysis. Despite the increasing interest in multi-element approaches, phosphorus analysis remains an important tool. This is not only due to the relative simplicity of phosphorus analysis but also because the archaeological value of most other elements has not yet been established (Oonk 2009).

In recent years research has also focused on new approaches using organic soil components as archaeological biomarkers, i.e. lipids, nucleic acids and proteinaceous compounds. In this context, archaeological biomarkers are recalcitrant molecules or molecular complexes that originate from organic matter added to the soil by human action and thus can be used to locate habitation sites and assess the source of organic matter in archaeological soils. The latter aspect of archaeological biomarkers is of special importance because detailed knowledge on the origin of organic matter on site may provide unprecedented information on, for instance, the social use of space and land use management in the past.

Various methods to extract and analyse anthropogenic elements and biomarkers in archaeological soils have been developed and used under laboratory and field conditions. The results obtained by using these methods are by no means definitive and show great variation in anthropogenic composition. It remains unclear whether this variation is a method effect or a sample effect, i.e. soil type, environmental conditions or sampled material. This makes the interpretation of data challenging and the applicability of soil chemistry to address archaeological problems questionable. Consequently, an understanding of the pros and cons of commonly applied methods to detect archaeological soils and chemical source tracking is essential (Oonk 2009).

4.2 Results

The hypothesis that site lithology has an important effect on the element composition of archaeological soils is confirmed in this study. It was shown, by comparing soil multi-element analyses of house plans from three lithologically different archaeological sites with off-site samples and regional backgrounds, that different sets of chemical elements dominate the geochemistry of these sites, whereas only concentrations of metals like copper and tin seem universally enriched on site and refer to an anthropogenic input. In addition, concentrations of iron and manganese are depleted at all three sites which might be due to dissolution of their oxides as a result of decomposing organic matter (Oonk *et al.* 2009a). In addition to this it was shown that different uses of space within the house plans embedded in sands and medium-to-heavy clays was evidenced by specific element distributions. In general, geochemical interpretation of archaeological house plans is feasible but as anthropogenic element signatures differ from site to site care must be taken not to jump to conclusions too easily. Oonk (Oonk 2009) therefore advocates the use of widely available regional background data.

It was recognized that in separating anthropogenic signals from natural background soils, the selection of the right extraction method for preparing different soil phases for analysis is essential. A sequential extraction method was therefore developed and combined with chemical and mineralogical soil analysis in order to assess the origin and diagenetic pathways of distinct greenish soil features within an archaeological Roman house plan embedded in sandy clays at Tiel-Passewaay, central river area, the Netherlands. In doing so all archaeological features could be chemically distinguished from background soils (Oonk *et al.* 2009b). The results also suggest that anthropogenic element inputs were more or less identical for all examined soil features with calcium, copper, phosphorus and zinc as the key elements. Phosphorus with amorphous iron and calcium phases were seen as coatings on mineral grains in the archaeological soils. The formation of such mineral coatings is suggested to result from the presence of an in-house barn. This approach demonstrates that this finer scale of detail gained from geochemical data provides insight into the function of buildings, use of space within farmhouses or specific on-site activities.

To investigate the geochemical fingerprints of ancient habitation in a high probability archaeological area but affected by sub-recent pollution at Borgharen, southern Netherlands, spatial soil profiling was applied by means of factor analysis and cluster analysis of geochemical data from three soil horizons at respectively 20 cm, 40 cm and 60 cm below the surface. The results show that the horizons differ significantly with respect to concentrations of presumed anthropogenic elements. Factor and cluster models indicate that at least two anthropogenic processes have altered the soil chemistry and they appear to be related to inputs of i) copper, lead and zinc and; ii) copper and phosphorus, especially at a soil depth of 40 cm. The first process probably reflects modern pollution whilst the latter is indicative of an ancient habitation horizon at 40-60 cm soil depth, as was confirmed by archaeological research (Oonk et al. 2009b). Apparently, archaeological soils can be seriously influenced by pollution and geochemical fingerprints of both ancient and modern human activities may be reflected throughout soil profiles.

The organic geochemical part of the study was mostly concentrated on the potential role of mass spectrometry-based soil proteomics in archaeological prospection and site interpretation. Given the novel character of soil proteomics and the range of analytical problems to be encountered while studying archaeological soils, efforts were made to examine the effects of some protein isolation agents and basic soil constituents on peptide mass fingerprinting by matrix assisted laser desorption/ionization mass spectrometry (MALDI-MS). In these experiments various artificial soils spiked with bovine serum albumin were used (Oonk/Cappellini/Collins in press). The preliminary results showed that proteins can only be partly isolated from soils and at present the prospect is low for successful archaeological soil proteomics. However, application of newly developed (sequential) protein isolation methods seems promising, whereas enhanced protein purification and separation techniques are suspected to improve protein identification in (archaeological) soils (Oonk/Cappellini/Collins in press).

Based on these results, the proteinaceous composition of soils from some Dutch archaeological house plans was assessed using amino acid (racemization) analysis and MALDI-MS of sequentially isolated soil proteinaceous matter. Detectable concentrations of hydrolyzable amino acids were present in all soils, independent of soil type or archaeological context. As amino acids probably stem from proteinaceous matter, these results suggest the presence of proteins in archaeological soils. Relative protein age was assessed using their state of degradation as reflected by amino acid racemization. Matrix assisted laser desorption/ionization mass spectrometry confirmed the presence of proteinaceous matter in the examined archaeological soils, whereas peptide mass fingerprinting could significantly link the protein signals to keratins. Keratins are widely and abundantly distributed in habitation environments and may survive degradation in soils and it is plausible to suggest that keratinaceous matter has been incorporated into the studied house plan soils during occupation. Keratin proteins could therefore play a significant role in prospection and site interpretation studies (Oonk/Cappellini/Collins in press).

5. CONCLUSIONS

Both the institutional world of archaeological resource management and the commercial companies in field archaeology stress that there is a need for sound, reliable and cost-effective non-destructive prospection techniques. Compared to other countries, like Germany and the UK, but also in the Mediterranean where a wide range of techniques is used, archaeological prospection in the Netherlands is mainly restricted to hand augering.

This paper, based on three monographs, presents the great potential for the application of remote sensing techniques in Dutch archaeological resource management and argues it should not only be restricted to the use of digital elevation models. It also presents the merits of the use of the magnetometer in Dutch archaeology, particularly in assessing the value of known sites. Used alongside hand augering, magnetometry can obtain a much better resolution in the same time, approximately one hectare per day on a resolution of 0.25 x 1 metre. Another advantage is that it maps archaeological features on a horizontal plane as opposed to a vertical stratigraphy. For example, the features of those sites that are found during hand augering prospection can be made visible in a magnetometer survey. On extensive sites magnetometer surveys can be used next to excavations in order to gain information from the unexcavated part of the site or to plan future excavations. Archaeological or geological features like ditches and creeks that have sufficient magnetic contrast can be quickly mapped over great lengths. Although the study was concentrated on magnetometry, other geophysical methods like electric resistivity methods and ground penetrating radar might also be useful for archaeological prospection in the Netherlands. Several internal reports by commercial companies mention encouraging results.

The geochemical study contributed to a better understanding of various archaeological soils in the Netherlands. It outlined possibilities and limitations of a range of organic and inorganic (geo)chemical and mineralogical methodologies for the prospection and interpretation archaeological sites. A universally applicable geochemical method, however, could not be formulated and this study advocates treating archaeological sites within their lithological context individually and defining tailor-made analytical approaches towards solving the problem. This seems to be in sharp contrast with a primary objective of Dutch archaeological resource management, namely the development of an out of the box, fast and cheap prospection/interpretation method. As is the case with the more traditional prospection tools (e.g. hand augering and test trenching), geochemical methods by themselves rarely provide enough information to answer archaeological questions.

It can be concluded that both geochemical and geophysical methods are best suited to assess size, shape and character of known archaeological sites rather than locate previously unknown sites, whereas remote sensing techniques might be of great help in recognizing unknown sites. Geochemical and geophysical methods can thus best be used alongside augering to increase the resolution of (geo)archaeological data in general.

More than with geophysical methods, detailed knowledge on soil formation and ancient anthropogenic inputs can be obtained by chemical investigation of archaeological soils and this increase in detailed knowledge can be regarded as an important merit of chemical methodologies. In particular, biomarker research proves essential in providing detailed information for site interpretation. Although acquiring geochemical data is a rather time-consuming and expensive effort, relatively cheap and fast geochemical methods, such as hand-held XRF, may be employed as a first phase geochemical reconnaissance of archaeological sites or features, whereas further chemical or mineralogical investigations can be planned and conducted in view of these data.

The establishment of the *Kwaliteitsnorm Nederlandse Archeologie* (KNA; Dutch Archaeology Quality Standard) has unfortunately reinforced the dominance of hand augering and test trenching over alternative prospection methods. This study shows that other methods, ranging from already rather long existing airborne remote sensing techniques, but also geophysical techniques, as well as newly achieved advancements in geochemical prospection may contribute to an integrated approach of archaeological prospection in the Netherlands. One wonders why non-destructive techniques are only rarely used in archaeological prospection, in sharp contrast to field surveys, coring and test trenching. One reason might be the lack of a master's degree programme in prospective archaeology at Dutch universities which hinders the emancipation of archaeological prospection within field archaeology in the Netherlands. Another often mentioned reason is that these methods are not cost-efficient, which might be true for advanced geochemical prospection techniques but does not hold for magnetometry and remote sensing methods. A third reason might be the assumed lack of reliability of these methods; however, although they have their restrictions as mentioned above, they have proved to be very useful not only in other countries but also in the Netherlands.

ACKNOWLEDGMENTS

This project was mainly financed by the NWO PDL/BBO programme (Project no. BBO.01.10) with substantial support from the Amsterdam Archaeological Centre and the Faculty of Humanities of the University of Amsterdam and the Cultural Heritage Agency of the Netherlands (Amersfoort).

Dr B. Ducke (Oxford Archaeology, Oxford, UK) is greatly acknowledged for reviewing an earlier draft of this paper.

NOTES

1 VU University, Amsterdam, the Netherlands.
2 Orkney College, Kirkwall, Orkney.
3 TNO Defence, Security and Safety, Delft, the Netherlands.
4 Buro de Brug, Amersfoort, the Netherlands.

REFERENCES

Barba, L., 2007: Chemical residues in lime-plastered archaeological floors, *Geoarchaeology* 22, 439-452.

Brongers, J.A., 1976: *Air photography and Celtic field research in The Netherlands,* Amersfoort (Nederlandse Oudheden 6).

Entwistle, J.A./P.W. Abrahams, 1997: Multi-Element Analysis of Soils and Sediments from Scottish Historical Sites. The Potential of Inductively Coupled Plasma-Mass Spectrometry for Rapid Site Investigation, *Journal of Archaeological Science* 24, 407-416.

Entwistle, J.A./P.W. Abrahams/R.A. Dodgshon, 1998: Multi-Element Analysis of Soils from Scottish Historical Sites. Interpreting Land-Use History Through the Physical and Geochemical Analysis of Soil, *Journal of Archaeological Science* 25, 53-68.

Entwistle, J.A./P.W. Abrahams/R.A. Dodgshon, 2000: The Geoarchaeological Significance and Spatial Variability of a Range of Physical and Chemical Soil Properties from a Former Habitation Site, Isle of Skye, *Journal of Archaeological Science* 27, 287-303.

Groenewoudt, B.J., 1994: *Prospectie, waardering en selectie van archeologische vindplaatsen: een beleidsgerichte verkenning van middelen en mogelijkheden*, Amersfoort (Nederlandse Archeologische Rapporten 17).

Hissel, M./H. van Londen, 2004: *De kwaliteit van de waarneming; een vergelijking van boormethoden voor archeologisch inventariserend veldonderzoek*, Amsterdam (Rapport AAC/Projectenbureau).

Holliday, V.T./W.G. Gartner, 2007: Methods of soil P analysis in archaeology, *Journal of Archaeological Science* 34, 30-333.

Kamermans, H./M. van Leusen/Ph. Verhagen (eds.), 2009: *Archaeological prediction and risk management. Alternatives to current practice*, Leiden (Archaeological Studies Leiden University 17).

Kattenberg, A.E., 2008: *The application of magnetic methods for Dutch Archaeological Resource Management*, Amsterdam (Geoarchaeological and Bioarchaeological Studies 9) (Ph.D. thesis University of Amsterdam).

Kattenberg, A.E./G. Aalbersberg, 2004: Archaeological prospection of the Dutch perimarine landscape by means of magnetic methods, *Archaeological Prospection* 11, 227-235.

KNA 2007: Protocol Bureauonderzoek, Kwaliteitsnorm Nederlandse Archeologie versie 3.1. d.d.01-01-2007, SIKB, Gouda.

Oonk, S., 2009: *The application of geochemical methods for Dutch Archaeological Resource Management*, Amsterdam (Geoarchaeological and Bioarchaeological Studies 11) (Ph.D. thesis VU University).

Oonk, S./E.C. Cappellini/M.C. Collins, in press: Insights from protein-spiked artificial soils into the value of mass spectrometry based soil proteomics as to study archaeological soils, *Journal of Organic Geochemistry*.

Oonk, S./C.P. Slomp/D.J. Huisman, 2009: Geochemistry as an aid in archaeological prospection and site interpretation: current issues and research directions, *Archaeological Prospection* 16, 35-51.

Oonk, S./C.P. Slomp/D.J. Huisman/S.P. Vriend, 2009a: Effects of site lithology on geochemical signatures of human occupation in archaeological house plans in The Netherlands, *Journal of Archaeological Science* 36, 1215-1228.

Oonk, S./C.P. Slomp/D.J. Huisman/S.P. Vriend, 2009b: Geochemical and mineralogical domestication of domestic archaeological soil features at the Tiel-Passewaay site, The Netherlands, *Journal of Geochemical Exploration* 101, 155-165.

Sueur, C., 2006: *Remote sensing voor archeologische prospectie en monitoring*, Amsterdam (RAAP-rapport 1261).

Tol, A./P. Verhagen/A. Borsboom/M. Verbruggen, 2004: *Prospectief boren, een studie naar de betrouwbaarheid en toepasbaarheid van booronderzoek in de prospectiearcheologie*, Amsterdam (RAAP-rapport 1000).

Valletta, 1992: European Convention on the Protection of the Archaeological Heritage (Revised) Valetta, 16.I.1992, Strasbourg (Council of Europe).

Vries-Metz, W.H. de, 1993: *Luchtfoto-archeologie in oostelijk West-Friesland*, Amsterdam (Ph.D. thesis University of Amsterdam).

Waldus, W.B./H.M. van der Velde, 2006: *Archeologie in vogelvlucht. Toepassingsmogelijheden van het AHN in de archeologie,* Amsterdam (Geoarchaeological and Bioarchaeological Studies 6).

Wamz, 2007: Archaeological Heritage Management Act, Den Haag.

Wells, E.C./R.E. Terry, 2007: Introduction to the special issue: Advances in geoarchaeological approaches to anthrosol chemistry, Part I: Agriculture. *Geoarchaeology* 22, 285-290.

Willems, W.J.H., 1997: Archaeological heritage management in the Netherlands: Past, present and future, in: W.J.H. Willems/H. Kars/D.P. Hallewas (eds.), *Archaeological Heritage Management in the Netherlands: fifty years state service for archaeological investigations*, Assen, 3-17.

Willems, W.J.H., 2008: Archaeological resource management and preservation, in H. Kars/R.M. van Heeringen (eds.) *Preserving archaeological remains in situ. Proceedings of the 3rd conference 2006, Amsterdam,* Amsterdam (Geoarchaeological and Bioarchaeological Studies 10), 253-60.

5. New developments in archaeological predictive modelling

Philip Verhagen,[1] Hans Kamermans,[2] Martijn van Leusen[3] & Benjamin Ducke[4]

ABSTRACT

In this paper the authors present an overview of their research on improving predictive modelling into true risk assessment tools. Predictive modelling as it is used in archaeological heritage management today is often considered to be a rather crude way of predicting the distribution of archaeological remains. This is partly because of its lack of consideration of archaeological theory but also because of a neglect of the effect of the quality of archaeological data sets on the models. Furthermore, it seems that more appropriate statistical methods are available for predictive modelling than are currently used. There is also the issue of quality control, a large number of predictive maps have been made but how do we know how good they are? The authors have experimented with two novel techniques that can include measures of uncertainty in the models and thus specify model quality in a more sophisticated way, namely Bayesian statistics and Dempster-Shafer modelling. The results of the experiments show that there is room for considerable improvement of current modelling practice but that this will come at a price because more investment is needed for model building and data analysis than is currently allowed for. It is however doubtful whether archaeological heritage management in the Netherlands will have a true need for this.

KEY WORDS

Predictive modelling; archaeological heritage management, expert judgement; uncertainty, statistics

1. INTRODUCTION

Predictive modelling is a technique that at a minimum tries to predict 'the location of archaeological sites or materials in a region, based either on a sample of that region or on fundamental notions concerning human behaviour' (Kohler/Parker 1986, 400). Predictive modelling departs from the assumption that the location of archaeological remains in the landscape is not random but is related to certain characteristics of the (natural) environment. The precise nature of these relations depends very much on the landscape characteristics involved and the use that prehistoric people may have had for these characteristics. In short, it is assumed that certain portions of the landscape were more attractive for human activity than others. If, for example, a society primarily relies on agricultural production it is reasonable to assume that the actual choice of settlement location is, among other things, determined by the availability of land suitable for agriculture.

Archaeological location models have been made with two types of aims in mind. In most academic projects the goal is to model the locational behaviour of different functional, chronological and cultural types of occupations. By contrast, the goal of most archaeological heritage management projects (AHM) has been to conserve archaeological remains and limit costs by identifying areas with and without these remains, regardless of their nature.

Whilst in theory the academic and heritage management aims might be achieved in different ways, in practice there is little difference between the approaches adopted. Predictive modelling was initially developed in the United States of America in the late 1970s and early 1980s, evolving from governmental land management projects in which archaeological remains became regarded as 'finite, non-renewable resources', and gave rise to considerable academic debate (Carr 1985; Savage 1990). Until the start of the 1990s the emphasis of this debate was on the statistical methods used to evaluate the correlation between archaeological parameters and the physical landscape (e.g. Kvamme 1985; *idem* 1988; *idem* 1990; Parker 1985). European academic interest in predictive models using GIS grew out of its long-standing concern with locational models in general and has been partly directed at an understanding of the modelling process itself. The primary result of this has been a series of papers critical of the inductive AHM-oriented approach common in Dutch predictive modelling (Van Leusen 1995; *idem* 1996; Kamermans/Rensink 1999; Kamermans/Wansleeben 1999). At the same time alternative methods and techniques were also explored (Wansleeben/Verhart 1992; *idem* 1997; *idem* 1998; Kamermans 2000; Verhagen/Berger 2001; Verhagen 2006). More recently, researchers have begun to concentrate on the incorporation of social variables into their predictive models (Wheatley 1996; Stančič/Kvamme 1999; Whitley 2005; Lock/Harris 2006).

In general, academic archaeologists have always been sceptical of, and sometimes even averse to, predictive modelling practised in AHM. The models produced and used in AHM are not considered sophisticated enough and many of the methodological and theoretical problems associated with predictive modelling have not been taken onboard in AHM (see e.g. Ebert 2000; Woodman/Woodward 2002; Wheatley 2004; Van Leusen *et al.* 2005). At the same time the production and use of predictive models has become a standard procedure in Dutch AHM and it has clearly attracted interest in other countries as well (see e.g. Kunow/Müller 2003).

In post-Valletta Convention archaeology, the financial, human and technical resources allocated to archaeology have increased enormously. At the same time these resources have to be spent both effectively and efficiently. Archaeological predictive models will tell us where we have the best chances of encountering archaeology. Searching for archaeology in the high probability areas will pay off as more archaeology will be found there than in low probability zones. It is a matter of priorities, we cannot survey everything and we do not want to spend money and energy on finding nothing. There is also the political dimension, the general public wants something back for the taxpayers' money invested in archaeology. It is not much use telling politicians to spend money on research that will not deliver an 'archaeological return'.

How can we be so sure that the low probability zones are really not interesting? Where do we draw the line between interesting and not interesting? These are difficult choices indeed for those involved in AHM. Archaeologists who do not have to make these choices can criticize the current approach to predictive modelling from the sidelines but do not have to come up with an alternative.

Within the PDL/BBO programme we have been trying to provide such an alternative to the archaeological community (see Van Leusen/Kamermans 2005; Kamermans/Van Leusen/Verhagen 2009). However, after five years of research we have to conclude that we have only been partly successful. In this paper we will briefly explain the research that we have undertaken and venture to offer some explanations for the lack of success of new approaches to predictive modelling in AHM up to now.

2. THE DEBATE ON PREDICTIVE MODELLING

Over the past twenty-five years, archaeological predictive modelling has been debated within the larger context of GIS applications in archaeology (see e.g. many of the papers in Lock/Stančič 1995; Lock 2000) and the processual/post-processual controversy that has dominated the archaeological theoretical debate. This debate has centred on the perceived theoretical poverty of what has sometimes been termed ecological determinism, usually contrasted with the theory-laden humanistic approaches advocated by various exponents of post-modernist archaeology. The arguments for and against ecological determinism in the context of GIS modelling were first set out by Gaffney/Van Leusen (Gaffney/Van Leusen 1995) and the significance of the dichotomy was debated by Kvamme (Kvamme 1997) and Wheatley (Wheatley 1998) in the pages of the *Archaeological Computing Newsletter*. As a dispassionate evaluation of the practical differences in approach between the two sides in this debate shows, the only significant difference is in the use of 'cognitive' variables (see also the brief discussion by Kvamme (Kvamme 1999, 182). As such, predictive modelling remains clearly rooted in the processual tradition, with its emphasis on generalization and quantitative 'objective' methods and its lack of interest in the subjective and individual dimensions of archaeology. In itself, this is not a matter of 'bad' versus 'good' archaeology and within the context of AHM, generalized maps are necessary tools to bring back the enormous complexity of archaeology to manageable proportions.

However, the lack of real interest in using spatial technology and statistical methods in post-processual academic archaeology has certainly slowed down the development of predictive modelling as a scientific method. The feeling that processual approaches no longer offered a real contribution to the advancement of archaeological science has left predictive modelling somewhat lost in space. This is a pity because even if we do not want to use predictive modelling in an AHM context, there still is a lot of potential in spatial technologies (GIS) to develop and test theories of spatial patterning of settlements and human activities. Two decades of extensive studies and practical experience in the field of predictive modelling have resulted in some of the most stringent, verifiable and thorough research work known to our discipline (Judge/Sebastian 1988; Zeidler 2001; Van Leusen/Kamermans 2005; to name just a few), speaking strongly in favour of predictive models as an essential tool in efficient heritage management.

It appears then that the continuing controversy over whether predictive models actually do anything useful is at least as much about wrong expectations, misunderstandings and maintaining the old processualist vs. post-processualist struggle as it is about real-life performance of the models. One only needs to consult the long-term statistics for projects such as the Mn Model to verify that they do indeed achieve their objectives (http://www.mnmodel.dot.state.mn.us). While academics have the liberty to limit the space-time scale of the archaeological record to their personal window of interest, AHM's foremost obligation is to assess and preserve the overall archaeological value of the landscape, indiscriminately, under heavy time and money restrictions. Clearly we have here a clash of two very different space-time scales of interest and this includes the choice of methods and practice.

The criticism of predictive modelling in scientific literature has focused on three main issues, statistics, theory and data. In all three areas predictive modelling as it stands today is considered by various authors to insufficiently address the complexity of the matter (see e.g. Van Leusen 1996; Ebert 2000; Woodman/Woodward 2002; Wheatley 2004; Whitley 2005). Statistical methods are used uncritically, often using a limited number of techniques that are not the best available. Archaeological theory, especially where it concerns the human and temporal factors in site placement, only plays a marginal role in selecting the variables used for predictive modelling. Archaeological data, which we all know have various degrees of reliability, are used without much source criticism.

While this is all very much true and many archaeological predictive maps are rather coarse representations of a complex archaeological reality, these criticisms mask a more fundamental question, what is the required quality of a predictive model? This is precisely why models are made that are not very sophisticated from a scientific point of view, they are considered good enough for the purposes they are made for. We do have to wonder however about the demand for more complex models. A commonly held view in science is that the simpler model should be preferred whenever possible as it offers the best interpretability and the least undefined behaviour. It also eases communication of requirements and results. Increased complexity usually serves to compensate for lack of structural knowledge.

3. DEVELOPING PREDICTIVE MODELS INTO RISK ASSESSMENT TOOLS

Our one fundamental problem with predictive modelling is therefore the issue of quality. No one seems to know what constitutes a 'good' model and no tools are available and used to make the quality of the models explicit. This takes us to the mathematical aspects of our framework, necessary to connect critical components like predictive models and survey data into a full risk assessment tool set. A requisite is the incorporation of a formal quantitative notion of uncertainty, such as probability, confidence intervals, residuals or belief values. Within our research project we have tried to focus on these issues by looking at the potential of new statistical techniques for incorporating uncertainty in the predictions (Van Leusen/Millard/Ducke 2009) and by studying the best ways of testing the models (Verhagen 2007). Our first foray into the uncharted waters of model quality concerned the role of expert judgement in a quantitative framework. When the first criticisms of predictive modelling appeared in the late 1980s, it quickly became clear that a fully inductive approach was in many cases unsatisfactory (see e.g. Brandt/Groenewoudt/Kvamme 1992; Dalla Bona 1994). The lack of reliable survey data in many areas of the world basically ruled out a rigorous statistical approach unless vast amounts of money were invested in survey. The pragmatic solution therefore was to stop using statistical methods for developing predictive models and instead rely on expert judgement and see if the experts' views were corroborated by the available archaeological data (see e.g. Deeben/Hallewas/Maarleveld 2002). However, in doing so a major advantage of statistical methods was neglected, namely the ability to come up with estimates in real numbers and the calculation of confidence intervals around the estimates. Expert judgement models only classify the landscape into zones of low, medium and high probability without specifying the numbers involved. How many archaeological sites can we expect in a high probability zone? How certain can we be of this estimate with the available data? Statistical methods will provide these numbers, expert judgement will not.

4. BAYESIAN STATISTICS

Bayesian statistical techniques are very well suited to provide numerical estimates and confidence intervals on the basis of both expert judgement and data. Bayesian inference differs from classical statistics in allowing the explicit incorporation of subjective prior beliefs into statistical analysis (see e.g. Buck/Cavanagh/Litton 1996). This makes it an effective method for predictive modelling using expert (prior) opinions. A Bayesian statistical analysis produces an assessment of the uncertainty of the calculated

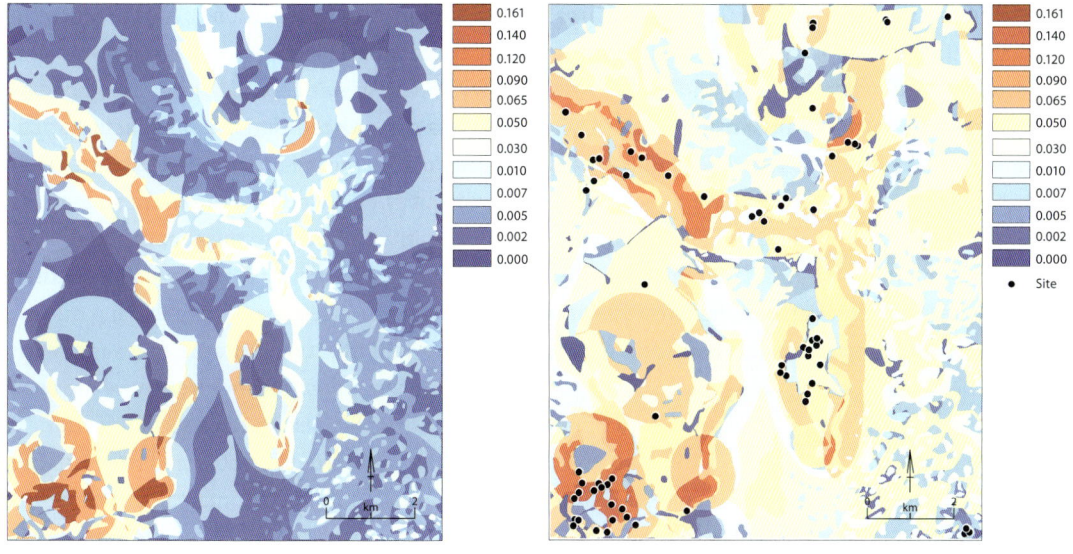

Fig. 1
An example of Bayesian predictive modelling. Relative site density according to expert judgement (prior proportions, a cell with a value of 0.12 is twice as likely to contain a site as a cell with a value of 0.06).

Fig. 2
Relative site densities following inclusion of 80 observed sites using the same legend as Fig. 1 (posterior proportions with sites overlaid).

probabilities in the form of standard deviations and credibility intervals. It also provides a simple framework for incorporating new data into the model.

Bayesian inference, while conceptually straightforward, has only enjoyed widespread application after the advent of powerful computing methods. In archaeology Bayesian inference is predominantly used in 14C dating for calibration purposes. However, up to now it has not been extensively used in predictive modelling. The number of published applications is limited to two case studies (Van Dalen 1999; Verhagen 2006). In addition, two other papers (Orton 2000; Nicholson/Barry/Orton 2000) consider survey sampling strategies and the probability that archaeological sites are missed in a survey project given prior knowledge of site density, such as might be gained from a Bayesian predictive model. This lack of application is probably due to the relative complexity of the calculations involved. There are very few archaeologists who can perform these calculations even though computing power is now no longer an obstacle. We have however proved that it can be done (see Van Leusen/Millard/Ducke 2009) and we see Bayesian statistics as a very powerful and useful tool for predictive model building. Figs. 1 and 2 show the resulting maps from the pilot study that was done in the area of Rijssen-Wierden, using the opinions of three different experts as input to the model and updating it afterwards with archaeological site data from the area.

5. DEMPSTER-SHAFER MODELLING

We also tested the potential of Dempster-Shafer modelling, which has been suggested as an alternative to standard statistical methods. While the results of earlier predictive modelling studies indicated that it performed better than most statistical tools (Ejstrud 2003; *idem* 2005), it has no inherent mechanism to accommodate expert judgement. Furthermore, its conceptual basis is rather complex. We will not go into detail in this paper (see Van Leusen/Millard/Ducke 2009 for more background), but it suffices to say that Dempster-Shafer modelling is more controversial in statistical science than Bayesian statistics and it is more difficult to understand. The Dempster-Shafer Theory of evidence (DST) was developed by Dempster (Dempster 1967) and Shafer (Shafer 1976) and takes a somewhat different approach to statistical modelling. It uses the concept of belief, which is comparable to but not the same as probability. Belief refers to the fact that we do not have to believe all the available evidence and we can make statements of uncertainty regarding our data. The specification of uncertainty is crucial to the application of DST. Unlike Bayesian inference, DST does not work with an explicit formulation of prior knowledge. Rather, it takes the existing data set and evaluates it for its weight of evidence. The reasons for believing the evidence or not may be of a statistical nature (a lack of significance of the observed patterns, for example), or they may be based on expert judgement (like knowing from experience that forested areas have not been surveyed in the past). DST modelling offers a framework to incorporate these statements of uncertainty. It calculates a measure called plausibility, which is the probability that would be obtained if we trust all our evidence. The difference between plausibility and belief is called the belief interval and shows us the uncertainties in the model. Finally, the weight of conflict map identifies places where evidence is contradictory. Different beliefs for different parameters can easily be combined using Dempster's rule of combination.

DST modelling is incorporated in Idrisi and GRASS GIS and is used for a number of GIS applications outside archaeology. In archaeological predictive modelling it has been applied in case studies by Ejstrud (Ejstrud 2003; *idem* 2005). It is better incorporated in GIS and predictive modelling than Bayesian inference. There are clear similarities between DST and (Bayesian) probability theory as both provide an abstract framework for reasoning using uncertain information. The practical difference is that in a DST model belief values do not have to be proper mathematical probabilities and much simpler quantifications, such as ratings, may also work (Lalmas 1997).

6. IMPLICATIONS

The results of our modelling exercises show that Bayesian inference and DST modelling are both capable of including and visualizing uncertainty in predictive modelling. Because the DST modelling applied in our case study used different environmental factors from the Bayesian modelling, we could not perform a direct comparison between the two. We can however assume that even with a comparable input the results of the methods will be different, which begs the question of what will be the best approach. The answer should consider practical issues of versatility, robustness, computational performance and interpretability of model results more than mathematical accuracy as the latter is adequate in both cases.

Given the preference of DST modelling for using existing data sets instead of formulating prior knowledge, we can assume that Bayesian modelling will be the most appropriate when few data are available. It will then show us where the experts are uncertain and this could imply targeting those areas for future survey. Bayesian modelling however does not supply a clear mechanism for dealing with (supposedly) unreliable data, while the DST approach implements this by simply stating that these data can only partially be trusted and hence will only have a limited effect on the modelling outcome. The Dempster-Shafer concept of belief supersedes that of mathematical probability and the latter in turn underlies statistical confidence intervals and residuals so that a Dempster-Shafer-based framework could accommodate a Bayesian predictive model, sources of uncertainty and survey information. The

U P	High	Medium	Low
High			
Medium			
Low			

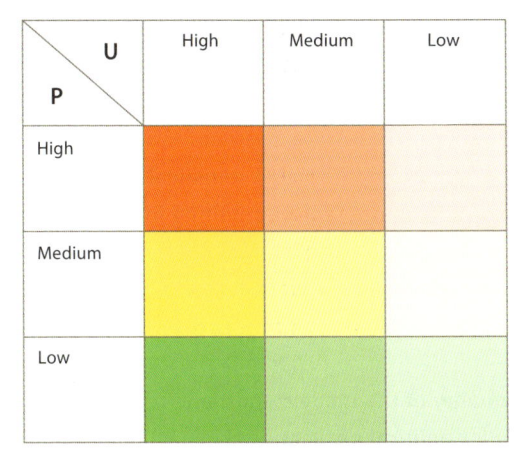

Fig. 3.
Simplified scheme for representing predicted site density (p) and uncertainty (u) in predictive mapping.

hardest challenge lies in compressing the diverse sources of evidence and uncertainty into one decision criterion. Ideally, there should be a single simple decision map. Anything else would mean a regression in practical applicability.

For practical purposes the results of the models will have to be translated into clear-cut zones. In a simple matrix (Fig. 3) the possible 'states' of the model can be shown, with 9 different combinations of predicted site density and uncertainty. For end users of the models, who have to decide on the associated policies, this means that the number of available choices increases from 3 to 9. A reduction to 4 categories might therefore be preferable, only distinguishing between high and low site density and uncertainty. After all, why do we still need the medium class? Usually, this is the zone where we 'park' our uncertainties so a binary model plus an uncertainty model should achieve the same results. The end users then only need to specify how (un)certain they want the prediction to be.

However, even if tools like Bayesian statistics can build a bridge between expert judgement and quantification, we still need reliable data to have it deliver its potential. The testing issue is therefore of primary importance to predictive modelling. What is probably most problematic in this respect is the lack of attention by archaeologists to the simple statistical principle of data representativity. No matter what statistical method is used, this issue needs to be addressed first before attempting to produce a numerical estimate of any kind. While it is possible to reduce the bias encountered in existing archaeological survey data to an acceptable level, in order to have reliable archaeological predictive models we also need to survey the low probability zones. So here we are facing a real paradox, predictive models are developed to reduce the amount of survey (or even skip it) in low probability zones, yet statistical rigour tells us to do a survey there as well.

Our approach has been to re-assess the value of using statistical methods in predictive modelling. We are convinced that this is necessary and think that it can offer a valuable contribution to AHM. If we can base the models on sophisticated statistical methods and reliable data, then we can really start using predictive models as archaeological and/or economic risk management tools. However, we have not been able to get this message across to the AHM community in the Netherlands. While we have not done an exhaustive survey among our colleagues, we think that the following reasons may be responsible for it:
- The innovations suggested are too complex. While it is sometimes said that statistics are not very difficult, but only very subtle, in practice most archaeologists do not work with them on a daily basis.

Some even have difficulty grasping the most fundamental principles of quantitative methods. This makes it hard to get the message across as it does not really help when we have to bridge a large gap in knowledge between the statistical experts and the people who have to use the end results of statistical models.
- Shifting from the current expert judgement approach to a more sophisticated statistical approach is too expensive. Improving the models in the way we suggest does not replace anything in the current way of dealing with predictive modelling, it only adds to it. So on top of the things we already do, like gathering and digitizing all the available information and interviewing the experts, we now also need to have a statistical expert doing the modelling, a data analysis programme to detect and reduce survey bias and perhaps even a test survey.
- It is irrelevant. While we may be bothered about the quality of the models, most end users are not. They trust the experts. In particular, those responsible for political decision-making will not care as they only need clear lines drawn on a map telling them where to survey and where not. If the archaeologists are happy with it, then they are as well.
- This ties in with our last explanation, archaeologists may have reason to be afraid of more transparent methods that will give non-archaeologists insight into the uncertainties of predictive models. When anyone can judge model quality, they will lose their position of power in dealing with politicians and developers.

We may not have been assertive enough in the presentation of our research to our colleagues and we certainly did not have enough time to fully develop these new approaches into practical working solutions. As long as the relevance of these new methods is not acknowledged, it will only remain an interesting approach from a scientific point of view.

7. DISCUSSION

Predictive modelling as it stands today is a tool with strengths and weaknesses. Its strong points can be summarized as follows:
- Predictive models are cost-effective tools for archaeological heritage management as they allow us to make transparent and well-founded choices when confronted with the question where to invest money for archaeological research. The approach that is taken in e.g. the United Kingdom, where these decisions are taken on the basis of (expert) knowledge of the *known* archaeological site sample, is in our view an irresponsible approach to AHM. It increases the archaeological risks involved by not taking into account the zones where no previous archaeological research has been done.
- As the models explicitly detail where to expect archaeological remains, they are open to scrutiny and criticism from archaeologists and non-archaeologists. In this way they can also stimulate a debate on how to deal with the areas where uncertainties exist.
- Predictive models, though not often considered as such, are also inherently heuristic tools with a clear scientific value. In the process of constructing a predictive model we are forced to clearly specify and reconsider hypotheses and theories concerning the distribution of archaeological remains and, ultimately, past human behaviour in the landscape.

However, we can also identify some clear weaknesses:
- The models and resulting predictions are only as good as the data and theories that are put into them. The garbage-in, garbage-out principle is relevant to any type of model but becomes even more important for predictive models when they are used for real-world decision-making. Using bad models has potentially undesired consequences for both archaeological research and society. In particular, the lack of attention to testing of the models is, in our view, a serious flaw and the absence of norms with regard to predictive model quality is a worrying aspect of current AHM in the Netherlands.
- Related to this, the emphasis on predicting settlement sites at the expense of other archaeological phenomena means that the use of archaeological predictive models will lead to the protection and investigation of ever more settlement sites, thereby reinforcing the predictions made and leading to a vicious circle of self-fulfilling prophecies. While we want to emphasize that there is no reason why predictive models could not also predict other types of archaeological remains, it is true that current models do not usually take this into account.
- The actual AHM decisions taken on the basis of predictive models may not always be to the archaeologists' liking. We find it hard to judge whether this is a true weakness of the models or of the process by which these decisions are arrived at. In the end, archaeology is only one of the issues that have to be dealt with in spatial planning and in a democratic society it will always be weighed against other interests. We have the impression that some archaeologists feel that predictive models should be used as weapons against the pressures from politics and if this fails they are dissatisfied with the weapons at their disposal rather than with the way in which the decision-making process operates and the role that archaeology plays in it.

There are some interesting developments in the debate on whether to continue developing predictive models and in which direction. The archaeological site as it is traditionally perceived in our discipline is changing its very status from being an object of almost esoteric, clandestine curiosity to a measurable, quantifiable, predictable and assessable resource (see e.g. Verhagen/Borsboom 2009). It will take some effort to establish this notion in general archaeological research. At the same time the definition of the archaeological site itself is under direct attack from modern landscape archaeology that increasingly sees archaeology as the study not only of the places that humans occupied in the past, but also of the landscape that they lived in. In this holistic concept of landscape archaeology, the site itself becomes an almost meaningless entity. Therefore, we can expect a considerable tension between the development towards a better understanding of the physical characteristics of archaeological remains in terms of feature and finds density and size and the fact that a broader vision of landscape archaeology implies that virtually everything in the landscape is worth investigating. In this view, predictive modelling might still be of some use for deciding on the strategy to follow for a survey campaign but it should no longer be used to exempt areas from survey. It is clear that this point of view will create tensions between archaeologists and developers and politicians who would like archaeological research to be manageable in terms of both finance and planning and who currently depend on predictive models to do much of this job for them.

Furthermore, much of the discussion on predictive model quality will probably become less relevant in the future, at least from a practical point of view. Many of the dichotomies debated in archaeological predictive modelling are leftovers from a time when calculations were time-consuming and heading down the less efficient road could waste precious resources. In the digital age the effects of mistakes and inefficiencies in research design and during the research process have become less severe as models can be re-run, data restructured and results easily updated. Software knows no hard boundaries between data and information, quantity and quality, deduction and induction, belief and knowledge. This has never been more clearly visible than with today's powerful and visually persuasive applications. Anyone who needs proof should try some data mining software. Indeed, archaeology is still in the middle of a digital (read: quantitative) transition where nothing seems uncontested, everything is in flux and many developments will turn out to be dead ends. Considerable stamina is still needed, especially given the small number of archaeologists active in the statistical and computational fields. Nevertheless, with powerful computing technology and mathematical tools at our disposal we are now closer than ever to providing truly efficient, user-friendly (Gibson 2005), reliable archaeological resource management tools and should thus forge ahead.

In our view another important development is the vigorous debate on the merits of regulation of all aspects of archaeological heritage management. In recent years Dutch archaeology has witnessed the birth of national quality norms regarding the execution of excavation, followed by norms for survey, digital data storage and curation and the level of education and experience that archaeologists need to be allowed to do archaeological research. National and local research agendas that try to specify the desired scientific outcome of archaeological fieldwork are recent additions to this expanding web of guidelines, norms and regulations. No doubt there will be more to come and predictive modelling may be one of the issues included. As a matter of fact, we do not see much future in imposing standardized predictive modelling procedures for the whole country. The history of the national Indicative Map of Archaeological Values (IKAW) shows that this is undesirable since a standardized product can never meet local needs (Van Leusen *et al.* 2005, 48-51). Nevertheless, we do think that clear norms are necessary where it concerns the correct use of input data, the methods applied and the required output of the models. However, experience shows that more regulation does not necessary imply a better quality of work and we will therefore have to see how Dutch public archaeology will cope with the tension between taming its bureaucracy and maintaining professional integrity in a fiercely competitive market.

NOTES

1 CLUE, VU University, the Netherlands.
2 Faculty of Archaeology, Leiden University, the Netherlands.
3 Institute of Archaeology, Groningen University, the Netherlands.
4 Oxford Archaeological Unit Ltd, Oxford, England.

REFERENCES

Brandt, R.W./B.J. Groenewoudt/K.L. Kvamme, 1992: An experiment in archaeological site location: modelling in the Netherlands using GIS techniques, *World Archaeology*, 268-282.

Buck, C.E./W.G. Cavanagh/C.D. Litton, 1996: *Bayesian Approach to Interpreting Archaeological Data*, Chichester.

Carr, C., 1985: Introductory remarks on Regional Analysis, in C. Carr (ed.), *For Concordance in Archaeological Analysis. Bridging Data Structure, Quantitative Technique, and Theory*, Kansas City, 114-127.

Dalen, J. van, 1999: Probability modeling: a Bayesian and a geometric example, in M. Gillings/D. Mattingley/J. van Dalen (eds.), *Geographical Information Systems and Landscape Archaeology*, Oxford (The Archaeology of Mediterranean Landscapes 3), 117-124.

Dalla Bona, L., 1994: *Ontario Ministry of Natural Resources Archaeological Predictive Modelling Project*, Thunder Bay.

Deeben, J./D.P. Hallewas/T.J. Maarleveld, 2002, Predictive Modelling in Archaeological Heritage Management of the Netherlands: the Indicative Map of Archaeological Values (2nd Generation), *Berichten van de Rijksdienst voor het Oudheidkundig Bodemonderzoek* 45, 9-56.

Dempster, A. P., 1967: Upper and lower probabilities induced by a multivalued mapping, *The Annals of Mathematical Statistics* 38, 325-339.

Ebert, J.I., 2000: The State of the Art in "Inductive" Predictive Modeling: Seven Big Mistakes (and Lots of Smaller Ones), in K.L. Wescott/R.J. Brandon (eds.), *Practical Applications of GIS For Archaeologists. A Predictive Modeling Kit*, London, 129-134.

Ejstrud, B., 2003: Indicative Models in Landscape Management: Testing the Methods, in J. Kunow/J. Müller (eds.), *Symposium The Archaeology of Landscapes and Geographic Information Systems. Predictive Maps, Settlement Dynamics and Space and Territory in Prehistory*, Wünsdorf (Forschungen zur Archäologie im Land Brandenburg 8), 119-134.

Ejstrud, B., 2005: Taphonomic Models: Using Dempster-Shafer theory to assess the quality of archaeological data and indicative models, in M. van Leusen/H. Kamermans (eds.), *Predictive Modelling for Archaeological Heritage Management: A research agenda*, Amersfoort (Nederlandse Archeologische Rapporten 29), 83-194.

Gaffney, V.L./P.M. van Leusen, 1995: GIS and environmental determinism, in G. Lock/Z. Stančič (eds.), *GIS and Archaeology: a European Perspective*, London, 367-82.

Gibson, T.H., 2005: Modeling and management of historical resources, in M. van Leusen/H. Kamermans (eds.), *Predictive Modelling for Archaeological Heritage Management: A research agenda*, Amersfoort (Nederlandse Archeologische Rapporten 29), 205-223.

Judge, J.W./L. Sebastian (eds.), 1988: *Quantifying the Present and Predicting the Past: Theory, Method, and Application of Archaeological Predictive Modeling*, Denver.

Kamermans, H., 2000: Land evaluation as predictive modelling: a deductive approach, in G. Lock (ed.), *Beyond the Map. Archaeology and Spatial Technologies*, Amsterdam (NATO Science Series), 124-146.

Kamermans, H./M. van Leusen/P. Verhagen (eds.), 2009: *Archaeological Prediction and Risk Management. Alternatives to Current Approaches*, Leiden (ASLU 17).

Kamermans, H./E. Rensink, 1999: GIS in Palaeolithic Archaeology. A case study from the southern Netherlands, in L. Dingwall/S. Exon/V. Gaffney/S. Lafflin/M. van Leusen (eds.), *Archaeology in the Age of the Internet. Computer Applications and Quantitative Methods in Archaeology*, Oxford (BAR International Series 750), 81 and CD-ROM.

Kamermans, H./M. Wansleeben, 1999: Predictive modelling in Dutch archaeology, joining forces, in: J.A. Barceló/I. Briz/A. Vila (eds.), *New Techniques for Old Times - CAA98. Computer Applications and Quantitative Methods in Archaeology*, Oxford (BAR International Series 757), 225-230.

Kohler, T.A./S.C. Parker, 1986: Predictive models for archaeological resource location, in M.B. Schiffer (ed.), *Advances in Archaeological Method and Theory, Vol. 9*, New York, 397-452.

Kunow, J./J. Müller (eds.), 2003: *Symposium The Archaeology of Landscapes and Geographic Information Systems. Predictive Maps, Settlement Dynamics and Space and Territory in Prehistory*, Wünsdorf (Forschungen zur Archäologie im Land Brandenburg 8).

Kvamme, K.L., 1985: Determining empirical relationships between the natural environment and prehistoric site location: a hunter-gatherer example, in C. Carr (ed.), *For Concordance in Archaeological Analysis. Bridging Data Structure, Quantitative Technique, and Theory,* Kansas City, 208-238.

Kvamme, K.L., 1988: Development and Testing of Quantitative Models, in J.W. Judge/L. Sebastian (eds.), *Quantifying the Present and Predicting the Past: Theory, Method, and Application of Archaeological Predictive Modeling,* Denver, 325-428.

Kvamme, K.L., 1990: The fundamental principles and practice of predictive archaeological modelling, in A. Voorrips (ed.), *Mathematics and Information Science in Archaeology, Volume 3,* Bonn, 257-295.

Kvamme, K.L., 1997: Ranters Corner: bringing the camps togethers: GIS and ED, *Archaeological Computing Newsletter* 47, 1-5.

Kvamme, K.L., 1999, Recent Directions and Developments in Geographical Information Systems, *Journal of Archaeological Research* 7, 153-201.

Lalmas, M., 1997: Dempster-Shafer's Theory of Evidence Applied to Structured Documents: Modelling Uncertainty, in *SIGIR '97: Proceedings of the 20th Annual International ACM SIGIR Conference on Research and Development in Information Retrieval, July 27-31, 1997,* Philadelphia, 110-118.

Leusen, P.M. van, 1995: GIS and Archaeological Resource Management: A European Agenda, in G. Lock/Z. Stančič (eds), *Archaeology and Geographical Information Systems,* London, 27-41.

Leusen, P.M. van, 1996: Locational Modelling in Dutch Archaeology, in H.D.G. Maschner (ed.), *New Methods, Old Problems: Geographic Information Systems in Modern Archaeological Research,* Carbondale (Occasional Paper 23), 177-197.

Leusen, M. van/J. Deeben/D. Hallewas/H. Kamermans/P. Verhagen/P. Zoetbrood, 2005: A Baseline for Predictive Modelling in the Netherlands, in M. van Leusen/H. Kamermans (eds.), *Predictive Modelling for Archaeological Heritage Management: A research agenda,* Amersfoort (Nederlandse Archeologische Rapporten 29), 25-92.

Leusen, M. van/H. Kamermans (eds.), 2005: *Predictive Modelling for Archaeological Heritage Management: A research agenda,* Amersfoort (Nederlandse Archeologische Rapporten 29).

Leusen, M. van/A.R. Millard/B. Ducke, 2009: Dealing with uncertainty in archaeological prediction, in H. Kamermans/M. van Leusen/P. Verhagen (eds.), *Archaeological Prediction and Risk Management. Alternatives to current approaches,* Leiden (ASLU 17), 123-160.

Lock, G. (ed.), 2000, *Beyond the Map,* Amsterdam (NATO Science Series).

Lock, G./T. Harris, 2006: Enhancing Predictive Archaeological Modeling: Integrating Location, Landscape and Culture, in M.W. Mehrer/K.L. Wescott (eds.), *GIS and Archaeological Site Location Modelling,* Boca Raton, 41-62.

Lock, G./Z. Stančič (eds.), 1995: *Archaeology and Geographical Information Systems,* London.

Nicholson, M./J. Barry/C. Orton, 2000: *Did the Burglar Steal my Car Keys? Controlling the Risk of Remains Being Missed in Archaeological Surveys,* Paper presented at the Institute of Field Archaeologists Conference, Brighton, April 2000. (http://eprints.ucl.ac.uk/archive/00002738/01/2738.pdf. Accessed 10 May, 2010).

Orton, C., 2000: A Bayesian approach to a problem of archaeological site evaluation, in K. Lockyear/ T. Sly/V. Mihailescu-Bîrliba (eds.), *CAA 96. Computer Applications and Quantitative Methods in Archaeology*, Oxford (BAR International Series 845), 1-7.

Parker, S., 1985: Predictive modelling of site settlement systems using multivariate logistics, in C. Carr (ed.), *For Concordance in Archaeological Analysis. Bridging Data Structure, Quantitative Technique, and Theory*, Kansas City, 173-207.

Savage, S.H., 1990: GIS in archaeological research, in K.M.S. Allen/S.W. Green/E.B.W. Zubrow (eds.), *Interpreting Space: GIS and archaeology*, London, 22-32.

Shafer, G., 1976: *A Mathematical Theory of Evidence*, Princeton.

Stančič, Z./K.L. Kvamme, 1999: Settlement Pattern Modelling through Boolean Overlays of Social and Environmental Variables, in J.A. Barceló/I. Briz/A. Vila (eds.), *New Techniques for Old Times - CAA98. Computer Applications and Quantitative Methods in Archaeology*, Oxford (BAR International Series 757), 231-237.

Verhagen, P., 2006: Quantifying the Qualified: the Use of Multicriteria Methods and Bayesian Statistics for the Development of Archaeological Predictive Models, in M. Mehrer/K. Wescott (eds.), *GIS and Archaeological Site Location Modeling*, Boca Raton, 191-216.

Verhagen, P., 2007: Predictive Models Put to the Test, in P. Verhagen (ed.), *Case Studies in Archaeological Predictive Modelling*, Leiden (ASLU 14), 115-168.

Verhagen, P./J.-F. Berger, 2001: The Hidden Reserve: Predictive Modelling of Buried Archaeological Sites in the Tricastin-Valdaine Region (Middle Rhône Valley, France), in Z. Stancic/T. Veljanovski (eds.), *Computing Archaeology for Understanding the Past. CAA2000. Computer Applications and Quantitative Methods in Archaeology*, Oxford (BAR International Series 931), 219-231.

Verhagen, P./A. Borsboom, 2009: The design of effective and efficient trial trenching strategies for discovering archaeological sites, *Journal of Archaeological Science* 36, 1807-1816.

Wansleeben, M./L.B.M. Verhart, 1992: The Meuse Valley Project: GIS and site location statistics, *Analecta Praehistorica Leidensia* 25, 99-108.

Wansleeben, M./L.B.M. Verhart, 1997: Geographical Information Systems. Methodical progress and theoretical decline? *Archaeological Dialogues* 4, 53-70.

Wansleeben, M./L.B.M. Verhart, 1998: Graphical analysis of regional archaeological data. The use of site typology to explore the Dutch Neolithization process, *Internet Archaeology* 4. (http://intarch.ac.uk/journal/issue4/wansleeben_index.html. Accessed on 10 May, 2010).

Wheatley, D., 1996: Between the lines: the role of GIS-based predictive modelling in the interpretation of extensive survey data, in H. Kamermans/K. Fennema (eds.), *Interfacing the Past. Computer applications and quantitative methods in Archaeology CAA95* (Analecta Praehistorica Leidensia 28), 275-292.

Wheatley, D., 1998: Ranters Corner: Keeping the camp fires burning: the case for pluralism, *Archaeological Computing Newsletter* 50, 2-7.

Wheatley, D., 2004: Making Space for an Archaeology of Place, *Internet Archaeology* 15. (http://intarch.ac.uk/journal/issue15/wheatley_index.html. Accessed 10 May, 2010).

Whitley, T., 2005: A Brief Outline of Causality-Based Cognitive Archaeological Probabilistic Modelling, in M. van Leusen/H. Kamermans (eds.), *Predictive Modelling for Archaeological Heritage Management: A research agenda*, Amersfoort (Nederlandse Archeologische Rapporten 29), 123-137.

Woodman, P.E./M. Woodward, 2002: The use and abuse of statistical methods in archaeological site location modelling, in D. Wheatley/G. Earl/S. Poppy (eds.), *Contemporary Themes in Archaeological Computing,* Oxford, 22-27.

Zeidler, J.A. (ed.), 2001: *Dynamic Modeling of Landscape Evolution and Archaeological Site Distributions: A Three-Dimensional Approach,* Fort Collins. (http://www.cemml.colostate.edu/assets/pdf/SEEDfin rep.pdf. Accessed 10 May, 2010).

WEBSITES

http://www.mnmodel.dot.state.mn.us

6. Cultural heritage in environmental impact assessment – reflections from England and northwest Europe

Carys E. Jones[1]

ABSTRACT

This paper considers experiences of assessing cultural heritage impacts within the EIA process in England and northwest Europe based on findings from the Planarch study funded by the European Regional Development Fund Interreg IIIB programme. Overall whilst there are examples of good practice, cultural heritage has a relatively low profile in EIA in the countries studied. Nevertheless, cultural heritage is important and makes wider contributions to society beyond its intrinsic value. Therefore, the profile of cultural heritage needs to be raised both within the planning process and EIA and also in the minds of decision-makers, other specialists and the wider public. Ten guiding principles provide a first step in promoting the assessment of cultural heritage in EIA and also to include the consideration of cultural heritage into more strategic planning decisions through SEA.

KEYWORDS

Environmental impact assessment (EIA), strategic environmental assessment (SEA); cultural heritage, archaeology; England, Europe

1. INTRODUCTION

In recent years the threat to cultural heritage within Europe has increased due to the increasing pressures of development, changes in farming techniques and the impact of natural processes. It is also important to remember that whilst sustainable development explicitly focuses on the broad themes of social, economic and environmental factors, cultural heritage is also an essential component that cuts across these three themes. Therefore there is a need to identify what is important about the historic environment and manage it appropriately for the benefit of present and future generations.

Previous studies on cultural heritage in environmental impact assessment (EIA) focussed on Europe and the USA and indicated shortcomings related to lack of guidance (Lambrick 1993; King 2000; Braithwaite/Hopkins/Grover 2001), narrowly focused and limited definitions of what constitutes cultural heritage (King 2000; Bond et al. 2004), and a failure to identify potential cultural heritage impacts during the early stages of EIA in either screening or scoping (Lambrick 1993; King 2000; Braithwaite/Hopkins/Grover 2001; Teller/Bond 2002). In Europe deficiencies were apparent in methods and approaches used to assess effects on cultural heritage, with inconsistencies in the role played by cultural heritage in decision-making and little involvement of the public in the consideration of cultural heritage (Bond et al. 2004).

This paper presents some of the findings, relating primarily to England, from a study carried out by the Planarch partnership, funded by the European Regional Development Fund Interreg IIIB programme (Jones et al. 2006; http://www.planarch.org for further details of the Planarch study; Jones/Slinn 2008 for the findings from all the participating countries). The Planarch initiative supported the better integration of cultural heritage in spatial planning and the development of methodologies and systems to lead to more cost effective management of cultural heritage both in the individual regions and across the partnership area as a whole. This paper mainly utilizes the findings from England (Kent, Essex, Somerset and Derbyshire) on the treatment of cultural heritage in EIAs with a primary focus on archaeology but with reference to the historic built environment, palaeo-environmental deposits and historic or cultural landscapes. The other countries involved were France (Nord Pas-de-Calais), Belgium (Wallonia and Flanders), the Netherlands and Germany (the Rhineland).

The following sections discuss the framework adopted in gathering data and information and the approaches to protecting and managing cultural heritage in England followed by implementation of EIA. Key findings on practice in integrating cultural heritage into EIA studies are described in terms of the coverage of cultural heritage in the EIA process, assessment of cultural heritage impacts and the role of specialist expertise and public participation in consultation. Finally, conclusions are drawn followed by reflections on future developments to improve practice, including the ten 'Guiding Principles for Cultural Heritage in EIA' developed as part of the Planarch study.

2. THE APPROACH

An overview of the EIA process in England (Lambrick et al. 2005) was undertaken as part of the Planarch study to evaluate the quality of assessment of cultural heritage through exploration of EIA activity and the review of selected environmental impact statements (EISs). Similar studies were undertaken for the other countries in varying degrees of detail. This provided detailed coverage of EIA activity and practice in the assessment of effects on archaeology and wider cultural heritage. The findings were drawn together to evaluate the EIA process for:
- its coverage of cultural heritage,
- the assessment of impacts on cultural heritage, and
- the roles played by experts and the public.

The overall analysis was based on a total sample of 428 EISs submitted during the period 1997-2004 (135 EISs from England covering 1999-2003), comprising a wide range of project types as shown in Fig. 1. The majority of the EISs were in the infrastructure (30%), extractive industry (15%) and road and rail (12%) project categories, together with land use plans[2] (10%).

Other relevant documentation was used to support the information and data in the EISs, such as government and practice guidelines, inception/scoping reports, archaeological studies, correspondence, findings from consultation and participation and decision letters. A more detailed analysis of 43 case studies was undertaken in England, plus 25 case studies in the Netherlands, to explore in greater depth the approach to assessment of cultural heritage. This involved interviews with key practitioners, exploration of decision-making and monitoring outcomes and examination of key issues and trends in practice.

3. PROTECTION AND MANAGEMENT OF CULTURAL HERITAGE

A number of international agreements directly or indirectly cover cultural heritage components, indicating the importance of this area (for further details see Teller/Bond 2002; Jones et al. 2006). These include those of the Council of Europe, particularly the Valletta Convention on the Protection of the Archaeologi-

Fig. 1
Project types analysed from England, the Netherlands, Rhineland and Wallonia.

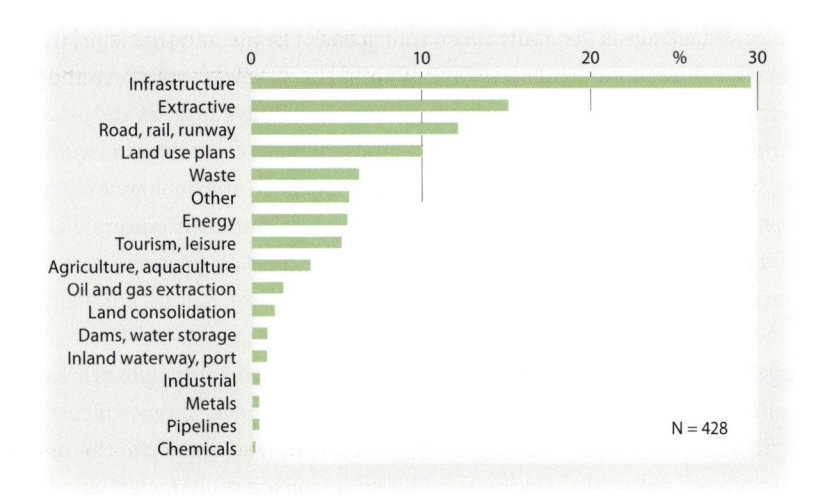

cal Heritage (Valletta 1992) and of the United Nations Educational, Scientific and Cultural Organization (UNESCO), which are binding in those countries that have ratified them; together with the International Council on Monuments and Sites presiding over good practice to be adopted whenever possible.

More recently the European Landscape Convention has indicated a more holistic view of the wider environment where "landscape means an area, as perceived by people, whose character is the result of the action and interaction of natural and/or human factors" (Florence 2000). Cultural heritage, in both its physical and less tangible forms (for example, memories, values), is clearly a key contributor to this character of an area and is important in defining such a sense of place.

These agreements all emphasize the need to integrate cultural heritage protection into land use planning procedures and for international collaboration on technical and procedural issues. A further characteristic of all these agreements is the definition of cultural heritage in broad terms, sometimes going beyond the coverage of heritage protection legislation of signatory states.

There are no European Union (EU) directives dealing solely with cultural heritage and in particular the historic environment. However, the EIA Directive provides a framework to address any standards and objectives set on a national basis. Two key principles affirmed in the preamble of the EIA Directives (85/337/EEC and as amended by 97/11/EC) are also fundamental to internationally accepted principles for management of the cultural heritage, namely that best environmental policy consists of:
- preventing (...) nuisances at the source rather than subsequently trying to counteract their effects;
- recognizing the need to take effects on the environment into account at the earliest possible stage in all the technical planning and decision-making processes.

Both these statements underline the three key factors in addressing the uncertainties that are inherently part of addressing the potential impacts of development on archaeology. These are the primacy of the principle of preservation *in situ* for cultural heritage studies, the need for careful technically competent specialist consideration of the issues and the importance of gathering adequate baseline information demonstrating the cultural heritage features of the area that might be affected by a proposed development project (where necessary) through stages of field investigation.

Cultural heritage is generally taken into account in the national legislation and spatial planning guidance for all European countries. In England, this is through statutory and non-statutory designations of archaeological sites and monuments, historic buildings and areas and places. In addition, the policy planning process for development plans and development control for individual projects also covers cultural heritage. National planning policy guidance exists on archaeology, built heritage and the wider historic environment. Early consultation with relevant local authority cultural heritage experts is recommended as standard good practice in order to agree frameworks for evaluation. Well established professional standards exist for gathering information through desk studies and fieldwork guided by specifications provided or approved by local authority cultural heritage experts. There are various standards for assessing the importance of cultural heritage resources and the principle of *in situ* preservation is enshrined in policy. English Heritage acts as a statutory advisor to government for cultural heritage.

Historic landscape is an important issue in England and since the mid-1990s English Heritage has instituted a national programme of historic landscape characterization for England which has been developed and carried out by local authorities for sustainable heritage management. The objective is to ensure that change is managed in ways that respect the historic character of places that people value. The European Landscape Convention also focuses on this approach.

In other European countries cultural heritage and archaeology are dealt with through the planning system (e.g. Flanders and Walloon regions of Belgium) or through specific legislation at the national (e.g. France) or federal levels (e.g. Germany). In France the EIA process is a fundamental requirement funded by a tax on the developer in obtaining information to deal with archaeological remains. In the Netherlands, the Belvedere philosophy adopts a 'preservation through development' stance which requires cultural heritage always to be taken into account in cases of spatial development.

4. IMPLEMENTATION OF EIA

The EIA process is a widespread legislative requirement to assess the impact of new developments upon the environment prior to their implementation (European Commission 1997). As such it is a key means of assessing the value of cultural heritage assets and also of the impact of land use changes on cultural heritage resources.

The EIA process is widely implemented through a series of stages, either mandatory or less formal, generally involving:
- screening – deciding if an assessment is required;
- scoping – deciding on the coverage of the assessment;
- preparation of an Environmental Impact Statement (EIS) – the document that records much of the process of assessment together with its findings and includes descriptions of the project and environment, predictions of impacts and evaluations of significance, mitigation measures;
- reviewing – of the EIS and other supporting documentation by competent authorities with consultation and public participation;
- decision-making – by competent authorities using EIS and other information;
- monitoring – follow-up of project if implemented.

This process covers a range of potential impacts and the European EIA Directive 97/11/EC, indicates that assessments should: ...identify, describe and assess the direct and indirect effects (...) on the following factors:
- human beings, fauna and flora;
- soil, water, air, climate and the landscape;
- material assets and the cultural heritage;
- interaction between these factors (European Commission 1997, Article 3).

EIA therefore covers a wide range of impact types, including cultural heritage and primarily biophysical components but also physical and social aspects. The treatment of these different impact types in the assessment process and their relative importance in making a decision on the project can vary according to the type of project and its particular context. This, together with the complexities of dealing with interactions between the impacts, can lead to inconsistencies in approach.

Even within the framework of the EIA Directive, there is considerable variation in EIA activity between European Union member states (European Commission 2003). The range in numbers of EIAs, taking into account different levels of population and GDP, highlights the different national and regional contexts in which the framework EIA Directive was implemented. Different approaches to the implementation of a framework directive are inevitable given the variations in legal systems, governance and culture. Thus, concerns have been raised about inconsistencies in the application of the Directive across the member states (European Commission 2003).

Legal implementation of EIA varies from specific EIA legislation (Belgium), EIA regulations under a broader environmental management remit (France and the Netherlands), to the UK's use of the planning system. Similarly, responsibility ranges from the regional level in Belgium, to the federal states in Germany and to a range of levels in the UK (national to local).

Typically around 400 EIAs are currently undertaken each year in the UK and in England, as elsewhere in the UK and in most member states, developers are responsible for undertaking and financing these EIAs, often commissioning consultancies to assist them. In the Flanders region developers choose relevant specialists, e.g. in archaeology, from a register of competent organizations that can prepare EISs. Their qualifications are reviewed by a commission. In the Netherlands an EIA Commission assists in scoping, reviews the adequacy of EISs and receives monitoring information, the Flanders Commission performs similar functions.

The decision as to whether a project should proceed is the responsibility of the competent authority in Flanders, Rhineland and England (usually the local planning authority in the latter). Statutory bodies (dealing with nature conservation and landscape, environmental quality and protection) provide information to developers on request and also have a role in providing advice to decision-makers. In England, English Heritage will occasionally provide advice on the EIA process but is only a statutory consultee for EIAs covering highways, water resources and uncultivated land projects. However, it is a statutory consultee for strategic environmental assessments.

5. CULTURAL HERITAGE IN EIA IN ENGLAND

5.1 Stages of EIA and cultural heritage

All potential impacts on the environment, including cultural heritage, should be considered throughout the EIA process and the EIA Directive makes specific provisions for this during screening and the prediction and evaluation of impacts (Teller/Bond 2002). However, in England it seems that cultural heritage issues play a relatively minor role in most stages of the EIA process.

Cultural heritage did not feature prominently in screening decisions, the Directive focuses more on the characteristics of the proposed development (as set out in Annexes I and II, European Commission 1997) rather than of the receiving environment at this early stage, so this is not surprising. It was very rare that cultural heritage considerations were used as a principal reason for requiring an EIA in the Planarch study, with England providing the only three examples of such cases.

The EIA Directive does not formally require scoping but does allow for voluntary provision and inevitably this has led to great variation in its treatment across the Europe Union. Therefore, in Flanders, the Netherlands and Wallonia it is a compulsory stage, in Norway (Jerpåsen/Omland/Lindblom 2008) it is undertaken by the environmental authority, whilst it remains a voluntary activity for developers in the UK. The case studies indicated that scoping discussions focused on information requirements for establishing the baseline, but much less on exploring methods for impact assessment. However, cultural heritage was rarely 'scoped out' of, or excluded from, EIAs. This perhaps reflects the uncertainty involved in assessing archaeological potential at this early stage. In seven of 15 cases where cultural heritage issues were scoped out in England, the decision appeared unjustified and, in two of these cases, archaeological deposits were subsequently discovered.[3] Overall, the effectiveness of scoping appeared variable and even where scoping happened routinely, difficulties included resource provision by statutory bodies, short timescales and lack of wider consultation (see also EIA Centre and Land Use Consultants 2006; Wood/Glasson/Becker 2006).

Although decision-making did seem to give greater weight to important sites, reflecting specific statutory protection of such sites, the overall profile of cultural heritage impacts in deciding if a project should proceed seemed to be low. This perhaps reflects the restricted role of cultural heritage in screening and scoping and therefore its lower profile in the remit of various stakeholders. The fact that further information on cultural heritage issues was required at this late stage in the EIA process for approximately 40% of the case studies in England again highlights the consequences of lack of attention to cultural heritage earlier in the process. This extra information was mainly to address flaws in the baseline data and impact prediction analysis. Interestingly, six cases were identified where cultural heritage issues were important reasons for refusal of consent.

Monitoring and follow-up are not required under the EIA Directive and, unsurprisingly, there was a low general level of activity (see also Bond/Langstaff/Ruelle 2002). However, there was widespread use of monitoring at the project site as the development commenced to check for archaeological finds. This can be regarded as a form of impact mitigation that acknowledges the inherent uncertainty in dealing, in particular, with buried remains and for appropriate action if discoveries are made.

5.2 Assessing impacts on cultural heritage

In Europe, the responsibility for the EIA process and the production of the EIS generally lies with project proponents, usually assisted by one or more consultancies. Although specialist expertise was usually employed for cultural heritage studies in England, non-specialists were often found to have conducted desk studies of available published information. Where external specialists were sub-contracted, in 37% of cases in England, this seemed to lead to better quality EISs than where work was undertaken in-house by non-specialists. In Flanders the registers of approved experts in cultural heritage indicate the importance of using specialist knowledge.

EIA is a baseline-led process and the baseline studies should be guided by the outcome of the scoping stage. The treatment of cultural heritage in establishing the baseline tends to be based around its constituent elements:
- archaeology – buried physical remains, earthworks and ruined standing structures;
- built heritage – buildings and built-up areas of historic interest that remain in use;
- historic landscapes – areas of designed landscape and the historic character and features of the wider countryside, and
- cultural landscapes – landscapes indicative of human activity over time.

This sub-division, together with overlaps with other study areas, particularly landscape and visual studies, nature conservation and noise, tends to complicate the establishment of a baseline.

The most popular means of gathering information was the simplest, using desk studies (see above) but was often supplemented by walkover surveys. More intrusive surveys and investigations were less common in England, although these are gaining in popularity in other countries such as France and Germany.

Most studies of cultural heritage in England focused on archaeological issues, followed by studies of the historic landscape and the built environment (Fig. 2). In Norway, where the cultural heritage baseline is viewed as a much broader entity due to the wide ranging definition of cultural heritage, there is still a tendency to consider it a specific issue rather than its role in the wider landscape (Lund-Iversen 2009).

Fig. 2
Coverage of cultural heritage types in baseline studies in England and other European countries.

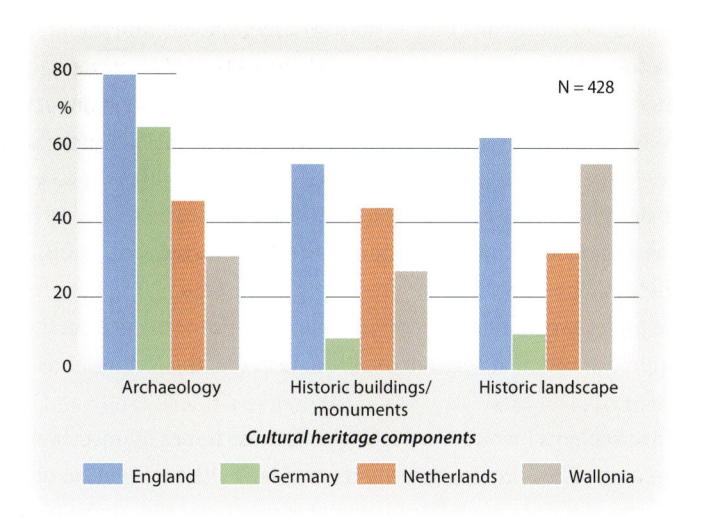

A unique and difficult aspect of dealing with cultural heritage impacts relates to the treatment of any unknown cultural heritage, especially buried archaeological sites, and how this might be affected by a development. In England, where there are good grounds for suspecting that archaeological remains may exist, surveys can be required even where little or nothing is definitely known. In other countries the potential of the unknown can play a much stronger role as a driver for assessment, as in the Belgian regions and the Rhineland.

The lack of a standard framework for the assessment of potential effects on cultural heritage can be regarded as positive in that it allows flexibility to deal with the wide range of circumstances that may occur (Braithwaite/Hopkins/Grover 2001) including both:
- direct effects, e.g. the destruction or loss of cultural heritage, and
- indirect effects, e.g. changes in drainage consequently affecting a standing structure or the condition of buried remains.

Most studies in all the countries covered direct adverse effects and were restricted to a relatively small range of impacts (see also Tweed/Sutherland 2007). There was little evidence for a wider appreciation of impacts and their evaluation through, for example, the concept of people as receptors of cultural heritage effects. Visual intrusion, an obvious impact, was often explicitly evaluated, but the wider concepts of setting were rarely addressed. Similarly, despite its broader view of the environment and its components, Norway struggles to deal with impacts at the landscape level (Jerpåsen/Omland/Lindblom 2008). As well as this restricted approach to assessing impacts, the coverage of indirect, cumulative and beneficial effects was also poor, reflecting EIA studies more generally (Barker/Wood 1999; Gray/Edwards-Jones 2003). This restricted approach to assessing cultural heritage impacts is disappointing as EIA provides the opportunity to move beyond the consideration of development impacts on just protected cultural heritage sites and to consider the wider implications for a whole range of cultural heritage effects in the landscape (King 2006; Erikstad *et al.* 2008).

Of more concern was the treatment of the impacts that were addressed, with impact magnitude and significance of effects on cultural heritage being variable and often weak. This may well counter the potential flexibility of a lack of standard approaches and perhaps highlights the need for more objective methods and explicit recognition and treatment of the uncertainty surrounding the buried and undocumented remains. In the English EISs judgements on the importance of cultural heritage assets affected were, in 30% of cases, based on designation aspects related to other legislation on protection of such assets. In this context it is not surprising that EIA takes on board the priorities inherent in the approach to designation (King 2006). These criteria tend to be relatively limited in scope and take little account of the wider local context (Turnpenny 2004; Erikstad *et al.* 2008). In addition, the various procedures and methodologies utilized for predicting and assessing impacts, in common with some other environmental topics, were seldom reported systematically or in detail in the EISs (Bond *et al.* 2004). This descriptive approach was also noted in the Rhineland and the Netherlands.

The problems involved in dealing with these issues of uncertainty and unknown cultural heritage assets become of key importance when considering the mitigation of impacts. Inevitably, excavating archaeological remains generally means the partial or total destruction of the cultural heritage asset concerned.

The relative importance of any resources under consideration, including cultural heritage, together with the pressures for development are likely to influence any judgements and practice in preserving these resources. Although English national planning guidance notes for cultural heritage provide clear advice on the importance of preservation *in situ*, particularly for nationally important assets, this did not appear to be common practice and there was a general acceptance that mitigation through investigation and recording is justifiable. Thus, mitigation in the UK context focuses on evaluating and recording both prior to, and during, construction, known as a 'watching brief'. Information is thus preserved, even if the asset concerned is not. This potential trend of moving away from rigorous baseline studies prior to the decision on the project may be problematical and has led to at least one legal challenge. The premise of EIA providing information for decision-making is rather compromised if the information is only available after the decision has been taken. An example relates to gathering baseline information for a protected bat species colony after development consent was given (Communities and Local Government 2004). The proposed mitigation measures were less of a feature in the Netherlands and Rhineland, although the Belgian regions adopted a more structured approach.

5.3 Consultation: specialist expertise and public participation

The role of cultural heritage expert bodies in providing specialist advice at all stages of the EIA process seems to be widely recognized, but to varying degrees even within the same jurisdiction. Encouragingly, it seemed to occur mainly in the early stages of EIA during scoping, a voluntary stage in England, but where it is common to consult the appropriate bodies responsible for cultural heritage, predominantly archaeologists, and also during the mandatory consultation phase during decision-making (Fig. 3). Decision-makers are usually able to draw on the advice of at least one expert body with cultural heritage responsibilities, but as with all statutory consultees in the EIA process difficulties are experienced with resource constraints. Other functions and responsibilities often take precedence and therefore any involvement tends to be prioritized based on the point in the process where the most impact can be made.

Fig. 3
Consultation of statutory cultural heritage bodies in EIA process in England, Germany and the Netherlands.

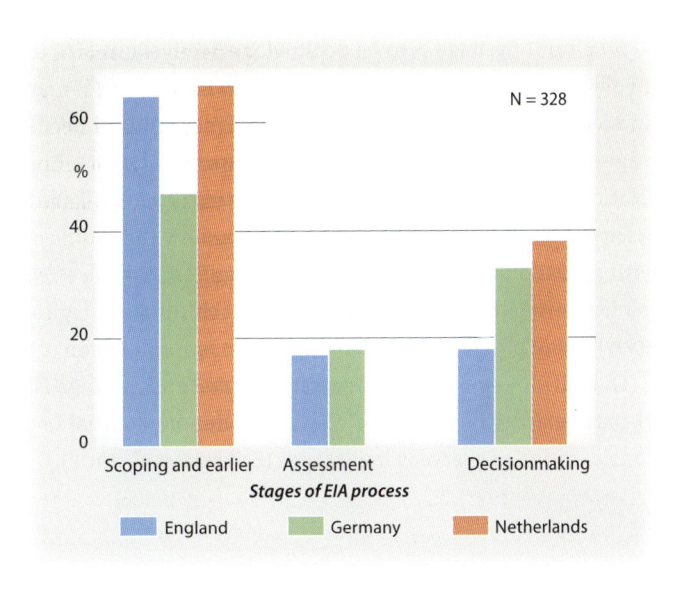

In addition, involvement can be restricted if developers or decision-making bodies themselves have a limited perception of who should be consulted at particular stages. In England screening decisions would not routinely involve the bodies responsible for custodianship of the cultural heritage.

Public participation in the EIA process is only required by the EIA Directive at the decision-making stage. The public should be able to access the EIS and have the opportunity to submit comments to the competent authority to feed into the decision-making process. In England the public rarely mentioned cultural heritage as a concern. This may relate to the relative profile of the many aspects of cultural heritage when compared with biodiversity issues or the more direct impact of developments on people, such as air quality.

6. CONCLUSIONS AND FUTURE DEVELOPMENTS

In England overall levels of satisfaction with the treatment of cultural heritage in EIA were regarded as broadly positive. Just over half (58%) of the EISs studied were considered to meet or exceed the minimum requirements of the EIA regulations (in the Rhineland a level of 71% was expressed). The main good practice elements were the involvement of cultural heritage statutory bodies in the process and providing a specific cultural heritage baseline.

However, the same weaknesses reported in earlier studies on Europe (King 1996; Teller/Bond 2002) and the USA (King 2000) still seem to exist. In particular, the narrow and often superficial assessment of impacts relating to loss or damage of cultural heritage resources was a recurring theme. Moreover, the more detailed analysis of case studies indicated that even where identification and evaluation of effects occurred it was not always effective in accurately assessing effects on cultural heritage resources. A stronger focus on key cultural heritage issues at the early stages of the EIA process, together with drawing on the expertise of specialists and using properly trained staff for undertaking assessments, would help ameliorate some of these recurring weaknesses. Such problems are not restricted to cultural heritage and other impact areas also face these difficulties. Therefore, whilst the protection of the most important sites is clearly a priority in assessments in England, overall the assessment of impacts on cultural heritage has a relatively low status within EIA in England.

If cultural heritage is to be dealt with effectively in EIA, those with the appropriate skills need to be involved in assessment and also in review of information and findings and in consultation. A clearer understanding of the potential vulnerability of cultural heritage resources at the screening and scoping stages, by planners and specialists alike, would allow a more informed consideration of alternatives in relation to development projects (Kværner/Swensen/Erikstad 2006). More broadly, the cultural heritage discipline as a whole may need to reflect on how the profile of the subject can be raised and maintained with spatial planning professionals. In addition, a more effective engagement of the wider community in recognizing the importance and value of cultural heritage assets (Turnpenny 2004; Tweed/Sutherland 2007) would provide additional impetus for consideration of cultural heritage.

Overall, there needs to be *integration* of cultural heritage issues into the stages of the EIA process (Fig. 4), particularly where designated sites or sites of potential importance are concerned, but also including consideration of everyday landscapes (Erikstad et al. 2008).

Fig. 4
Integration of cultural heritage in the EIA process.

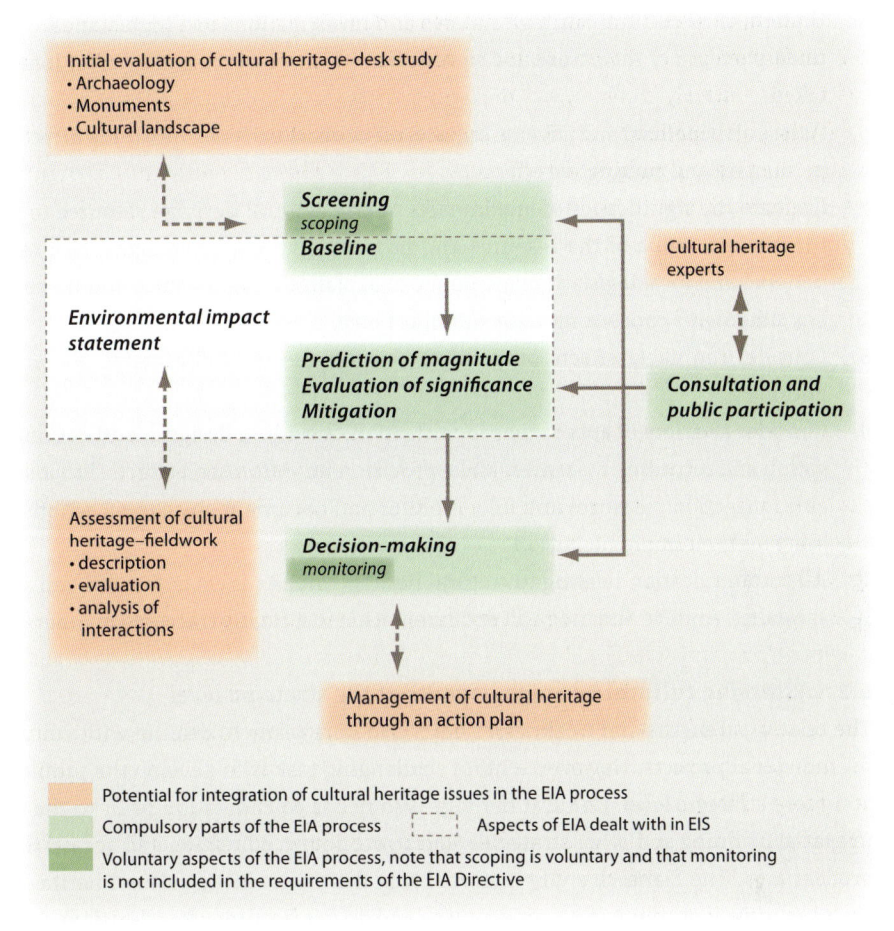

Initial evaluation of cultural heritage–desk study
- Archaeology
- Monuments
- Cultural landscape

Screening
scoping
Baseline

Environmental impact statement

Prediction of magnitude
Evaluation of significance
Mitigation

Cultural heritage experts

Consultation and public participation

Assessment of cultural heritage–fieldwork
- description
- evaluation
- analysis of interactions

Decision-making
monitoring

Management of cultural heritage through an action plan

- Potential for integration of cultural heritage issues in the EIA process
- Compulsory parts of the EIA process
- Aspects of EIA dealt with in EIS
- Voluntary aspects of the EIA process, note that scoping is voluntary and that monitoring is not included in the requirements of the EIA Directive

6.1 Guiding principles for cultural heritage in EIA

A key outcome of the Planarch initiative was the ten guiding principles which aimed to provide a framework to sensitize all stakeholders to the need for the appropriate treatment of cultural heritage in the EIA process. These principles provide a platform to improve understanding of cultural heritage (by planners, developers, consultancies and the public) and the contribution it can make to the broader sustainability agenda. A key step that needs to be addressed is moving cultural heritage as a concern beyond the professional specialist cultural heritage community and into the wider public sphere.

Guiding Principles for Cultural Heritage in EIA

1. Cover all aspects of cultural heritage.
2. Integrate cultural heritage expertise into all stages of EIA, from screening through to implementation.
3. Describe the project requiring assessment clearly and in sufficient detail to allow identification of all impacts that could affect the cultural heritage.
4. Define a suitably large study area to allow a clear understanding of the cultural heritage and the extent of potential impacts upon it.

5. Undertake all cultural heritage surveys and investigations to a high standard so as to ensure a full understanding of the nature and significance of the resource and to allow informed decisions to be taken.
6. Assess all beneficial and adverse impacts on cultural heritage, including direct, indirect, temporary, permanent and cumulative effects.
7. Evaluate the significance of any impacts on the cultural heritage resource to take account of both the intrinsic value of the resource and how much it will be changed. Use relevant international, national and local legislation and policy to explain the significance and make explicit the basis for any statements concerning value or importance.
8. Consider the likely effects on cultural heritage assets of alternative scenarios, including doing nothing.
9. Consider a variety of approaches to mitigation, including design modification, appropriate investigation and recording measures. Make provision for unforeseen effects. Propose realistically achievable mitigation measures and fully monitor and document any agreed actions, including responsibility for their implementation.
10. All communication relating to cultural heritage in EIAs is clear, focused and accessible to the non-specialist. Archive and index all documentation in a clearly traceable manner.

6.2 Assessing cultural heritage impacts at the strategic level

The relative strengths and weaknesses described here relate to dealing with cultural heritage impacts for individual projects. However, a more challenging task is to develop the profile of cultural heritage at a more strategic level. Cultural heritage also needs consideration prior to the initiation of projects in spatial planning and other strategies (social, economic, education and access) likely to affect a much broader area. The Planarch study indicated that the treatment of cultural heritage impacts, with their seemingly lower profile, can become routine and do not feature in key decisions during the EIA process. Whilst cultural heritage assets do not appear to have suffered unduly due to this situation, the potential to explore interactions with other impact areas (required by the EIA Directive but seldom investigated in detail), properly assess indirect and cumulative effects and to develop innovative design of projects have been neglected.

There is a requirement for cultural heritage to be addressed in implementation of the SEA Directive (European Commission 2001) in judging which plans and programmes are to be evaluated and in ensuring that information on cultural heritage is included in the subsequent environmental report (Teller/Bond 2002). An incorporation of cultural heritage in strategic planning would also assist in fulfilling the requirements of the Valletta Convention that cultural heritage should be integrated at all levels of planning.

The rapidly developing implementation of the SEA Directive in the European member states provides an opportunity to embed cultural heritage in thinking at this level of planning and avoid the relative marginalisation it has experienced at the EIA level. In particular, the importance of early engagement and consultation seem particularly relevant, particularly in exploring the notion of vulnerability of cultural heritage assets at a more strategic level (Kværner/Swensen/Erikstad 2006) and including the public (Tweed/Sutherland 2007).

6.3 The future

Cultural heritage contributes strongly to people's sense of place and identity and should be recognized as both a non-renewable and valuable resource. It is therefore an essential part of considerations relating to sustainability, contributing to economic and social aspects and broader quality of life. Thus it has the potential to play an important role in community development, regeneration and in other strategic actions dealing with access, leisure and tourism.

Currently, more attention is being paid to integrated approaches to assessments, such as sustainability appraisal or sustainability impact assessment (Gibson et al. 2005; Jay et al. 2007) and these approaches may offer a route for less mainstream areas to be given more explicit and relevant attention. In addition, a stronger focus on interactions between impacts in such an integrated approach would also permit the profile of cultural heritage to be enhanced. For example, the Planarch study indicated that potential linkages between cultural heritage and biodiversity were under-explored and such an approach might help promote more holistic thinking about the landscape (King 2006), particularly where land use has been less intensive. Similarly, conducting an assessment from the standpoint of a resource or the wider landscape (Erikstad et al. 2008) or tracing the network of consequences from a specific project action, for example the potential consequences of land drainage for both biodiversity and archaeology, would allow consideration of development impacts beyond particular environmental compartments. The European Landscape Convention may also provide another vehicle for a more integrated and holistic consideration of impacts.

Therefore, in the immediate term the quality of assessment of cultural heritage in EIA needs to be improved and its role in SEA has great potential for development. In the longer term, the pursuit of win-win scenarios in the context of sustainability appraisal might yield improved approaches and outcomes for cultural heritage itself and related social and economic matters.

ACKNOWLEDGEMENTS

The author would like to thank Dr John Williams, Casper Johnson and Paul Slinn. The support of the European Commission in funding the Planarch study through the European Regional Development Fund Interreg IIIB programme is also acknowledged. However, the views expressed in this paper are those of the author and as such should not be attributed to any other individual or organization.

NOTES

1. University of Manchester, Manchester, England.
2. Legislation implementing the EIA Directive in the Netherlands and Wallonia covers land use plans as well as projects.
3. Other research on EIA in England has revealed that such 'scoping out' of impacts judged to be less important to the decision on a project is rare (EIA Centre and Land Use Consultants 2006).

REFERENCES

Barker, A./C. Wood 1999: An evaluation of EIA system performance in eight EU countries, Environmental Impact Assessment Review 19, 387-404.

Bond, A.J./L. Langstaff/R. Baxter/H.W.J. Kofoed/K. Lisitzin/S. Lundström, 2004: Dealing with the cultural heritage aspect of environmental impact assessment in Europe, *Impact Assessment and Project Appraisal* 22, 37-45.

Bond, A./L. Langstaff/C. Ruelle, 2002: *Monitoring and post-evaluation of the cultural heritage component of environmental assessments*, (SUIT Position Paper 4, October). (http://www.lema.ulg.ac.be/research/suit/Reports/Public/SUIT5.2d_Paper.pdf. Accessed 26 March, 2010).

Braithwaite, R./J. Hopkins/P. Grover, 2001: Archaeological and other material cultural assets, in P. Morris/R. Therivel (eds.), *Methods of Environmental Impact Assessment*, London, 122-144.

Communities and Local Government, 2004: 'Scoping', *Note on environmental impact assessment directive for local planning authorities*, 19 April 2004. (http://www.communities.gov.uk/planningandbuilding/planning/sustainabilityenvironmental/environmentalimpactassessment/noteenvironmental/. Accessed 26 March, 2010).

EIA Centre and Land Use Consultants, 2006: *Evidence Review of Scoping in Environmental Impact Assessment*, Department for Communities and Local Government, London. (http://www.communities.gov.uk/publications/planningandbuilding/evidencereview. Accessed 26 March, 2010).

Erikstad, L./I. Lindblom/G. Jerpåsen/M.A. Hanssen/T. Bekkby/O. Stabbetorp/V. Bakkestuen, 2008: Environmental value assessment in a multidisciplinary setting, *Environmental Impact Assessment Review* 28, 131-143.

European Commission, 1997: *Council Directive 97/11/EC of 3 March 1997 amending Directive 85/337/EEC on the assessment of the effects of certain public and private projects on the environment Official Journal No. L073, 14/03/1997, p. 0005.* (http://eur-lex.europa.eu/LexUriServ/LexUriServ.do?uri=CELEX:31997L0011:EN:HTML. Accessed 26 March, 2010).

European Commission, 2001: *Directive 2001/42/EC of the European Parliament and of the Council of 27 June 2001 on the Assessment of the Effects of Certain Plans and Programmes on the Environment Official Journal No. L197, 21/07/2001, p. 0030.* (http://eur-lex.europa.eu/LexUriServ/LexUriServ.do?uri=CELEX:32001L0042:EN:HTML. Accessed 26 March, 2010).

European Commission, 2003: *Report from the Commission to the European Parliament and the Council on the Application and Effectiveness of the EIA Directive (Directive 85/337/EEC as amended by Directive 97/11/EC) - How successful are the Member States in implementing the EIA Directive* (Impacts Assessment Unit, Oxford Brookes University) DG Environment. (http://ec.europa.eu/environment/eia/pdf/report_en.pdf. Accessed 26 March, 2010).

Florence, 2000: *European Landscape Convention. Florence, 20 October 2000*, Strasbourg. (http://www.coe.int/t/dg4/cultureheritage/heritage/Landscape/default_en.asp. Accessed 26 March, 2010).

Gibson, R.B./S. Hassan/S. Holtz/J. Tansey/G. Whitelaw, 2005: *Sustainability Assessment – criteria, processes and application*, London.

Gray, I./G. Edwards-Jones, 2003: A review of environmental statements in the British forest sector, *Impact Assessment and Project Appraisal* 21, 303-312.

Jay, S./C. Jones/P. Slinn/C. Wood, 2007: Environmental impact assessment: retrospect and prospect, *Environmental Impact Assessment Review* 27, 287-300.

Jerpåsen, G./A. Omland/I. Lindblom, 2008: Norway, in G. Fairclough/P.Grau Møller (eds.), *Landscape as Heritage - The Management and Protection of Landscape in Europe, a summary by the Cost A27 project "Landmarks"*, Bern (Geographica Bernensia G79, 205-227.

Jones, C.E./P. Slinn, 2008: Cultural Heritage in EIA - Reflections on Practice in North West Europe, *Journal of Environmental Assessment Management and Planning* 10, 215-238.

Jones, C.E./P. Slinn/P. Burggraaff/K.-D. Kleefeld/G. Lambrick, 2006: *Cultural Heritage and Environmental Impact Assessment in the Planarch Area of North West Europe*, Maidstone. (http://www.planarch.org/downloads/library/action_3a_final_report_english.pdf. Accessed 26 March, 2010).

King, A., 1996: Environmental impact assessment; reviewing process and product, *European Water Pollution Control* 6, 29-37.

King, T.F., 2000: What should be the 'cultural resources' element of an EIA? *Environmental Impact Assessment Review*, 20, 5-30.

King, T.F., 2006: Cultural heritage preservation and the legal system with specific reference to landscapes, in L.R. Lozny (ed.), *Landscapes Under Pressure: Theory and Practice of Cultural Heritage Research and Preservation*, New York, 243-254,.

Kværner, J./G. Swensen/L. Erikstad, 2006: Assessing environmental vulnerability in EIA – The content and context of the vulnerability concept in an alternative approach to standard EIA practice, *Environmental Impact Assessment Review* 26, 511-517.

Lambrick, G.H., 1993: Environmental assessment and the cultural heritage: Principles and practice, in I. Ralston/R. Thomas (eds.), *Environmental Assessment and Archaeology*, Birmingham, 9-19.

Lambrick, G./J. Hind/G. Hey/K. Spandl, 2005: *A Review of Cultural Heritage Coverage in Environmental Impact Assessments in England*, Oxford Archaeology, Oxford. (http://www.planarch.org/downloads/library/england_eia-report.pdf. Accessed on 26 March, 2010).

Lund-Iversen, M., 2009: *Handout 24. February*, Oslo (Norwegian Institute for Urban and Regional Research NIBR).

Teller, J./A. Bond, 2002: Review of present European environmental policies and legislation involving cultural heritage, *Environmental Impact Assessment Review* 22, 611-632.

Turnpenny, M., 2004: Cultural heritage, an ill-defined concept? A call for joined-up policy, *International Journal of Heritage Studies* 10, 295-307.

Tweed, C./M. Sutherland, 2007: Built cultural heritage and sustainable urban development, *Landscape and Urban Planning* 83, 62-69.

Valletta, 1992: *European Convention on the Protection of the Archaeological Heritage (Revised)*, 16.I.1992, European Treaty Series 143, Council of Europe, Strasbourg. (http://conventions.coe.int/Treaty/en/Treaties/Html/143.htm. Accessed 26 March, 2010).

Wood, G./J. Glasson/J. Becker, 2006: EIA scoping in England and Wales: practitioner's approaches, perspectives and constraints, *Environmental Impact Assessment Review* 26, 221-241.

7. On the necessity of congruent meanings in archaeological heritage management
An analysis of three case studies from a policy science perspective

Anneke de Zwart[1]

ABSTRACT

In this paper I discuss the debate between local authorities, planners and developers on the one hand and archaeologists on the other. The focus is on three cases in the Dutch river landscape, the Betuwe, where the municipalities are planning new housing and archaeologists want to preserve selected sites deemed important.

I try to explain the conflicts that arise and their consequences by taking an interpretive stance using concepts such as frame of meaning, levels of judgement, shared meanings and congruent meanings.

The argument I will develop is that if archaeologists seriously want to integrate archaeological sites in the public space in a successful and significant way, they should acknowledge the necessity of congruent meanings of the archaeological record. The examples used show how the archaeologist can employ the theoretical concept of congruent meanings to engage in the practice of planning processes in a more fruitful way.

I conclude that although congruent meanings of the archaeological record appeared to arise on several occasions, this did not result in a shared solution because different actors did not attempt to understand the motivations of the others.

KEYWORDS

Planning, archaeological record, heritage management, congruent meanings, frame of meaning, Valletta Convention

1. INTRODUCTION

It will be no surprise that in a densely populated country like the Netherlands conflicts over land use arise on many occasions. In this paper I will deal with a specific type of conflict, cases where new housing is planned on top of a site that is also (highly) valuable from an archaeological point of view. Theoretically speaking, an integration of both interests is quite possible, and moreover the 1992 Valletta Convention (Valletta 1992) expressly asks for such an integration. In practice, however, the parties involved find it very difficult and consequently very often do not succeed in attaining such a meaningful integration.

I will try to explain why this is so difficult and will do so in such a way that my explanation points at a pattern of thinking to handle these types of conflicts. My explanation will rely on literature from the policy sciences, especially the work of Donald Schön (Schön 1983), Frank Fischer (Fischer 1995) and John Grin and Henk van de Graaf (Grin/Van de Graaf 1996; Van de Graaf/Grin 2001). The empirical data in this paper are mainly taken from a case study in the municipality of Elst in the Dutch river landscape, the Betuwe. Some additional data are taken from case studies the neighbouring cities of Arnhem and Nijmegen.[2]

In order to provide the context of the conflicts discussed later on, I will start with a short overview of policy in the fields of spatial planning and archaeological heritage management in the Netherlands.

2. SPATIAL PLANNING AND ARCHAEOLOGICAL HERITAGE MANAGEMENT

In 1990 the Dutch government issued a comprehensive White Paper on Spatial Planning, the so-called VINEX document (Vinex 1990), a major development scheme covering all the main issues of the time and strongly influenced by the concept of sustainable development. Spatial planning is seen as a vehicle for economic development while at the same time covering questions of the environment, infrastructure and transport. Moreover, the White Paper is a large-scale housing project aiming to diminish the continuing housing shortage in the Netherlands by building 650,000 houses.

The spatial concept used to determine how and where to build is in the tradition of Dutch spatial ordering. One of the basic principles of the planning discourse, the concept of orderly and compact urbanization, is the guideline for choosing large-scale locations on the outskirts of existing towns in order to keep open spaces (Faludi/Van der Valk 1994; Wissink 2000). The presence or timely availability of high-grade public transport is another criterion. However, the effect is rather to be seen as a suburban development taking up a large amount of space, including farmland and orchards.

In the VINEX document much emphasis is put on the living quality of the planned new extensions. In this respect the document devotes some passages to cultural and historical places of interest as well as archaeological values. They are considered to contribute to the spatial quality of the new built-up areas and so, according to the VINEX document, to enhance the living quality. They also help to prevent landscapes and villages from becoming dull and monotonous.

In line with the Dutch law on spatial ordering, the overall structure of spatial development is a task of the national government. With regard to new housing, the implementation of this overall structure is left to the municipalities involved. Thus, the municipalities of Elst, Arnhem and Nijmegen have the obligation to create the new extensions. Although the VINEX document stipulates the importance of archaeological values for the environmental quality, no policy directions are given. This amounts to delegating the question to the local municipalities.

The 1992 Valletta Convention expresses the increasing public interest in archaeology and the preservation of archaeological monuments in the Netherlands as well as in Europe. The Convention recognizes the increasing number of major planning schemes seriously threatening the archaeological record. Thus, solutions for the protection of the archaeological heritage should be found in land-use planning via conservation *in situ*, when feasible, by reconciling the requirements of archaeology and spatial planning. The means to this end is a participatory approach, archaeologists should participate in the various stages of planning policies to ensure well-balanced strategies for the protection and conservation of archeological sites. The implementation of the Convention's objectives is left to the political judgement of national governments. Yet the Convention indicates that changes in the handling of the archaeological record in spatial policy are in most cases unavoidable.

Until then, archaeology or the Archaeological Preservation of Monuments (Archaeological Heritage Management or AMZ in Dutch) was a policy area more or less unknown within spatial planning. Tradi-

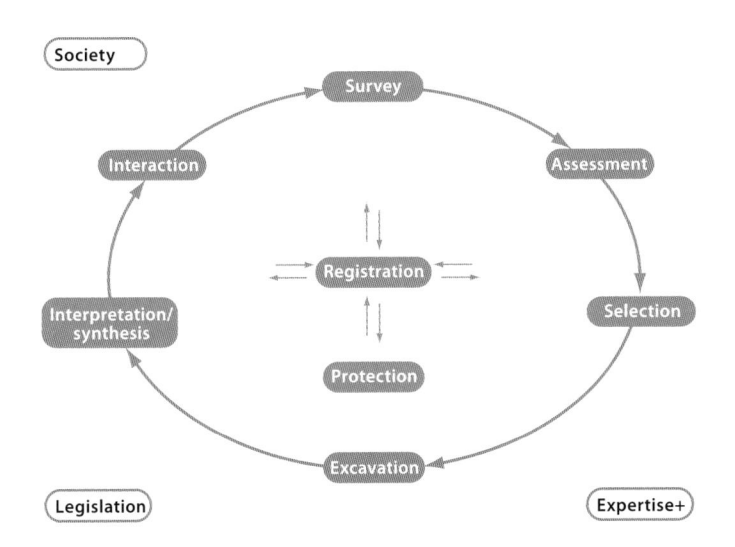

Fig. 1
The AMZ (Archaeological Heritage Management) cycle (ROB/OCW 1995; also Willems/Kars/Hallewas 1997, 4).

tionally, AMZ aimed at saving the archaeological record by excavating and, occasionally, by applying for legal protection. Consequently, concepts such as archaeological sites, archaeological record or heritage have literally no meaning or value for (local) policy-makers and planners.

Since the Valletta Convention, AMZ has focussed on spatial planning with the goal of achieving good management of the archaeological record and a preference for *in situ* preservation. The implementation of the new policy in the Vinex locations is one of the main focuses of the Service for Archaeological Heritage (ROB). This is done by setting the AMZ cycle, as depicted in Fig. 1, in motion (ROB/OCW 1995).

The AMZ cycle as conceived of by ROB is an example of a closed system's theoretical action model whose primary aim is to obtain more knowledge about the past by means of the stated actions. Protection is understood as both legal and planners' protection (in Dutch: *planologische bescherming*). The latter kind of protection assumes that planners will fit in archaeological sites in the land use plan if prior knowledge of highly valued sites is available. *In situ* preservation is the general term for both forms of protection. *In situ* preservation is the most problematic element in the cycle because new choices between excavating now and protecting a potential source of knowledge for the future have to be made again and again.

It can be concluded that increasing knowledge of the past is the main focus of the AMZ cycle. As a consequence, the strategy that ROB has chosen to influence local administrations in favour of *in situ* preservation is to convince them of the value of the archaeological record. This value lies in the fact that it contains remnants of the past that must be preserved for future generations. Future generations of archaeologists, that is, who must be given the opportunity to search the archaeological record with better techniques and their own questions.

For local administrations the arguments put forward by ROB are only one of the considerations to be taken into account. They also have other obligations, such as building the quota of houses prescribed by the government and comply with other provisions of the VINEX document. Furthermore, their ambition is not just to build houses, their ultimate objective is to create a 'good' living and residential environment.

3. FRAMING

3.1 *Practitioners*

Donald Schön (Schön 1983) conducted extensive empirical research about how practitioners act in real life. A reflective practitioner faced with a problem does not take it for granted, but appreciates the situation at first glance, 'seeing' its possibilities in a flash. The problem is intuitively defined, suggesting certain solutions. However, the situation 'talks back', the unintended and side effects of the first framing of the situation come into view generating other appraisals and solutions. This goes on in a reiterative process of reflection-in-action till a satisfactory outcome is attained. The practitioner, or professional as Schön alternatively calls them, is guided in this process by his/her expert knowledge, experience and what Schön calls "overarching theories" and "appreciative systems including tacit knowledge". That is what I call the practitioner's frame of thinking.

In the case descriptions below we will meet three types of practitioners: the archaeologists trying to protect the archaeological heritage, the project developers or planners who have the task of planning the new extension in accordance with all the quantitative and qualitative requirements set for them by the local authorities and the local policy-makers responsible for the quality of the new extension and the quality of living in their municipality as a whole.

Using Schön's observations about the framing of a problem in the context of the situation and Fischer's (Fischer 1995) model of four discursive levels on which deliberation, argumentation and judgement can take place, we can build frames based on the research of Grin and Van de Graaf (Grin/Van de Graaf 1996; Van de Graaf/Grin 2001).

A frame of a policy actor, according to Fischer, can be visualized in two orders. The first order relates to a specific situation where a certain policy in question is divided into two levels. At the first level the judgement of a policy actor about the effects, efficiency and costs is at stake, at the second level the actor's definition of the problem is under scrutiny. The second order regards the more generic notions applying to a broader policy field and again consists of two levels. The first level concerns the value systems and ideologies by which actors look at the situation to make sense of it, guided by their preferences about the social order at the second level.

The logic of this four-levelled frame of policy actors can also be used to describe a frame of non-policy actors such as, in this case, archaeologists and planners, the policy actors of course being the local authorities. The system and the structure of the frame of professionals are the same except for the content (Fig. 2).

The analytic use of the reconstruction of frames is twofold; the levels on which it is structured function as levels on which the debate is pursued but also as elements of the debate that can crystallize into views and notions. They become commitments serving actors as guidelines in knowing how to act. Since the debate is ongoing, these commitments can be broken open and changed till new outlooks and other commitments arise. This ongoing dialectic takes care of the dynamics of the process, in other words notions and conceptions are not static or fixed. The first use of portraying the frames of the actors involved is a better understanding of the debate by constructing the different backgrounds that lie behind it and secondly, it is a heuristic approach to trace changes and to get a better insight if and where room for changes can be found. As an example, I briefly describe the frames of the local authorities, archaeologists and planners along the lines of Fig. 2 to substantiate my method.

Element of the frame	Policy-maker	Archaeologist	Planner
Judgements on solutions	Judgements on effects, side effects and costs of policy-options	Judgements concerning the handling of the archaeological record	Judgements on effects and consequences of various designs and models of the planning area
Problem definitions	What is the policy problem in this case? Meaning of the grounds claimed by archaeologists as archaeological record	What is the 'archaeological' problem?	What is the planning problem in this area? Meaning of the grounds claimed by archaeologists as archaeological record
Empirical and normative background theories	Value systems and worldviews (ideologies) experience in policy making	Views about archaeological science, heritage and their relation; appreciation systems	Planning theories; spatial organization principles; notions from the social sciences
Normative ontological preferences	Preferences about the social order (relation government/market/citizens; ways of decision making, etc.)	Meaning of the grounds as archaeological record for archaeologists	Preferences about the spatial order

Fig. 2 Frames of meaning of policymakers, archaeologists and planners. *After Grin/Van de Graaf 1996, 2001.*

3.2 Practitioners in AMZ

Local authorities

On the first level the local authorities' reasoning is as follows. A planning process organized in phases and a gradual production of houses shall in the course of 10-15 years deliver the preferred residential area consisting of a differential housing supply creating a favourable market position. In the case of Elst, the problem for the local authorities is to develop a new housing estate in such a way that an attractive living environment comes into being, doing justice to the historical value and identity of the village in the Dutch river landscape. The grounds claimed by archaeologists as valuable parts of the archaeological record are viewed on a scale from negative to positive contributions in the realization of housing estates. The background theories on the third level hold respect for cultural landscape, nature and environmental values next to attention to sustainable energy and building. The preferences of the local authorities on the fourth level concern the well-being of the local citizens and the creation of a good living and residential environment in a physical and social way.

Archaeologists

The judgement by archaeologists on the first level about the best way to handle the archaeological record is to proceed according to the AMZ cycle (Fig. 1) and to learn more about the local record in order to make final decisions as to which sites should be excavated or preserved *in situ*. This reasoning is consistent with the preferred meaning on the fourth level, a meaning reflecting the scientific function of the archaeological record as a source of knowledge about the past. Increasing this knowledge is the ultimate objective. Not surprisingly, the problem is to prevent the local archaeological record from disappearing unobserved and to save the information. The related problem is how to deal with local authorities seen by the archaeologists as 'disturbers'. Trying to convince the local authorities of the scientific value of the sites and threatening to seek legal protection for selected sites are the means to this end on the first level. The background theories on level three are in line with the solution for the problem, AMZ is subservient to archaeological science.

Planners

The solutions of the planners concern the gradual designing of a housing development plan by the production of successive plan documents which meet the requirements of the local administration. Starting with a basic structure for the future housing area, the plan will be elaborated and in due course satisfy the demands of a good residential environment (first level). By doing so the urban developers are imposing order on space, disciplining it according to their preferences about the spatial order. In the case of Elst, after positioning the village as a core with open spaces between the big cities of Nijmegen and Arnhem, the next step is to structure the housing estate within the region and the landscape. The housing estate itself is structured along the same principles, from compact building near the village to a more extended green area, encompassing the concept 'from culture to nature' (level four). The existing historical structures do have a part in their first plans but archaeological monuments or sites are excluded. On the contrary, the urban developers perceive the meaning of the grounds claimed by archaeologists as valuable parts of the archaeological record as an obstacle and a complicating factor for the realization of the plan (level two). The urban developers' obvious predilection for planning as a process is a planning theoretical notion known as the incremental approach (level three).

3.3 How does this overview of frames of the different types of actors help us to understand what is going on in their debates?

At first it is crucial to notice that the archaeological record has a different meaning for archaeologists, planners and local authorities. The meaning of the *only* common policy object, the grounds claimed as archaeological record by archaeologists, as assigned by the actors involved is situated on different levels of the frames described. For both planners and local authorities it is instrumental. Its function may be an end or a means in their assessment of the situation or it may be perceived as contrary to their goals. Depending on their background theories it can play different roles, from an impediment to an enhancement in the realization of the housing estate.

The meaning of the archaeological record is for archaeologists the source of inspiration and motivates their actions towards the local authorities. It follows that the only common policy object, the grounds claimed by archaeologists as archaeological record, is in general not capable of creating shared meanings between these actors. However, in cases like this where actors are involved operating from different rationalities, these actors can still develop a common action perspective focused on a result that is both desirable and feasible. To achieve such a result the actors do not need to struggle to achieve consensus on the values in question or reach a compromise. From this point of view congruent meanings will suffice to bring about jointly supported solutions. The concept of congruent meanings introduced by Grin and Van de Graaf (Grin/Van de Graaf 1996) refers to a form of agreement that is reached when each of the actors involved allocates a positive meaning to the local archaeological record that is both sensible and practical according to all the parties involved but for each in its own way. For policy actors and planners such a part of the record has a sensible meaning if it somehow contributes to the solution of their problems. On the other hand the archaeological record must also preserve a significant meaning for the archaeologists.

I will therefore focus the analysis of the case materials on the occurrence of such congruent meanings and the conditions under which they (seem to) appear and eventually disappear. In doing so I will elaborate the concept itself and try to find out what different actors can do to stimulate the emergence of congruent meanings.

4. FOUR CASES

4.1. *Elst Westeraam*

We let the story begin in 1994 the moment of the first confrontation between ROB and the local authorities. The local authorities devised the first design of the master plan in connection with upgrading the area of the railway station at the southwestern edge of the area. Their interest lay in a quick decision because of a timely request for a grant from the EU. The problem was a planned access road going right across an archaeological monument (40C-36N, see Fig. 3), protected by the Monuments Act in 1985. The site was given the status of monument based on three drillings revealing traces of settlements from the Roman period and the Middle Ages, but nothing is visible except for an elevated part of an ancient riverbank. It took more than a year for the problem to be temporarily solved. At first, neither party was willing to compromise. ROB stated that the local authorities knew beforehand the monument was there to stay, while the local authorities maintained that the design would lose its quality with every adaptation. In order to determine the boundaries of the monument the parties agreed to investigate the monument in a more detailed way by the use of test trenches. As customary in AMZ in those days, the whole parcel in which the remains were found was protected. More detailed investigations might therefore result in a more limited size of the monument. The mayor however saw no reason to alter the plan and not to apply for a building license with regard to the monument, although ROB strongly advised against doing so.

The lack of an EU grant helped reduce tensions. A newly appointed urban planner presented a new design which anticipated the new Master Plan. In his plans the monument was saved as an open space. In the meantime RAAP Archaeological Consultancy prospected the development area for archaeological traces detecting seven more sites (see the numbers in Fig. 3; Stichting RAAP 1996). The question of what to do with these new finds is anticipated by RAAP in the report giving advice on every site. However they missed the remains of a Roman temple which was only discovered in 2002 (see section 4.2). The so-called site 2, near the spot where the temple was later to be found, was subject to a resistance investigation and showed up possible stone wall remains which were not recognized as Roman. Further prospecting was thus deemed unnecessary, although parties did not agree to investigate two of the other sites (nos. 4 and 6).

The local authorities started the development of the necessary plan documents. The main concepts used were quality, sustainability and identity. They perceived Elst as a village in the Dutch river landscape whose rural character must be preserved, but at the same time the village should acquire an urban style. The historical characteristics such as the old neighbourhoods, farms and archaeological monuments underpinned the basic assumption in the Master plan. They became large open spaces.

The new draft zoning scheme (*bestemmingsplan*, July 1997) heralded a new period. While everything looked perfect on paper, the groundwork proved to be more complex as it required different data concerning the physical preservation of the monuments and the other archaeological sites, such as the actual depths of the artefacts. A lot of confusion resulted between the actors, particularly at ROB. It was hard to provide the required data on time. Meanwhile, in 1999 planners made a second version of the zoning scheme which included a school and parking lot on top of the monument and the laying of underground

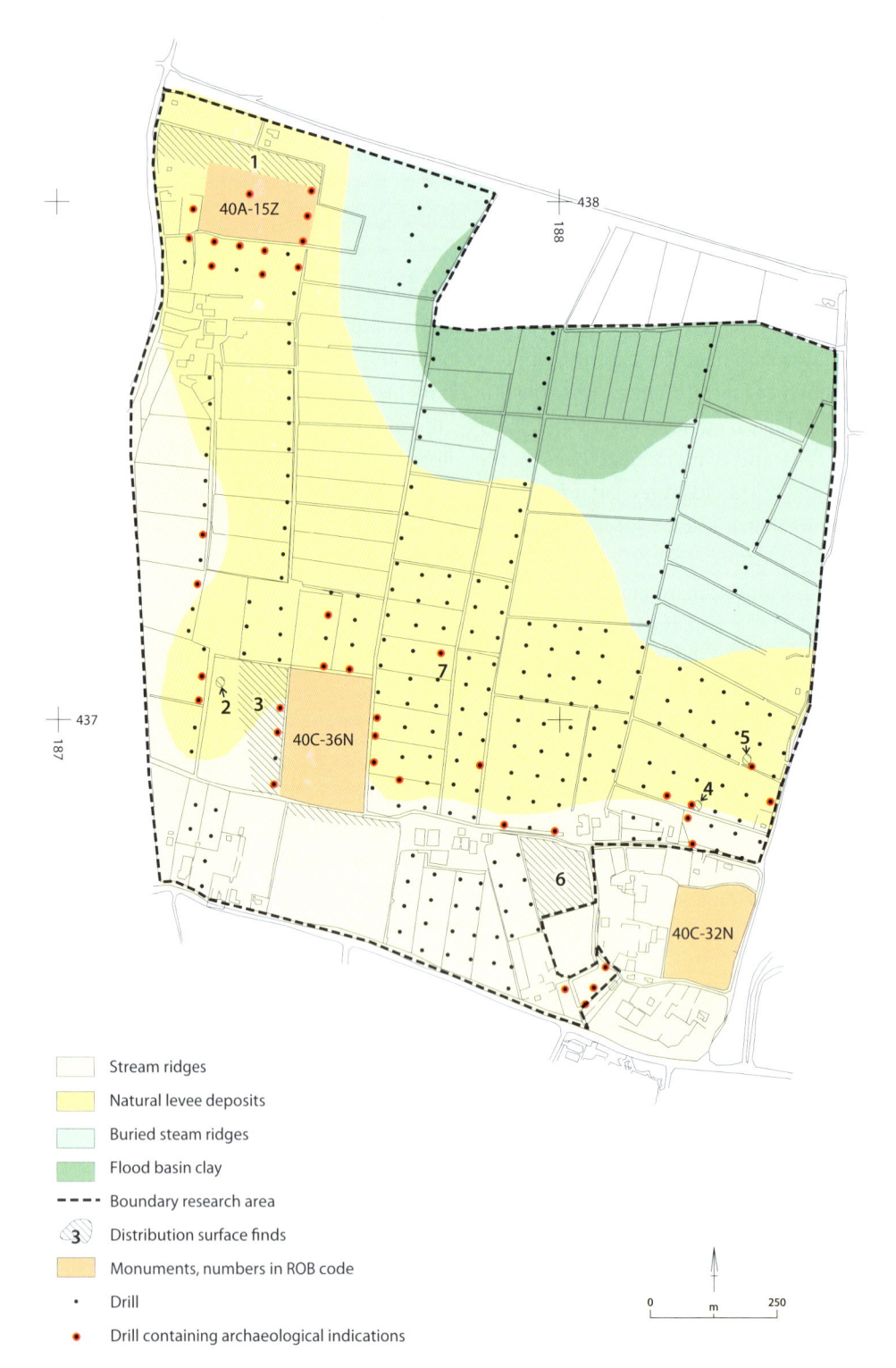

Stream ridges
Natural levee deposits
Buried steam ridges
Flood basin clay
– – – Boundary research area
Distribution surface finds
Monuments, numbers in ROB code
· Drill
• Drill containing archaeological indications

Fig. 3
Elst-Westeraam.
Survey of the planning area at Westeraam. *Source: Stichting RAAP 1996.*

cabling. Two years later the problem remained unsolved. Research was required into building appropriate foundations and an imaginative plan involving the monument which would make history tangible.

Analysis

There were already three legally protected monuments in Westeraam before the planning process for the new area began. After some initial squabbling between the municipal authorities and ROB, the three monuments were integrated as open spaces into the new plan's zoning scheme. The open spaces allocated to the monuments only exist because they serve the function of making the past visible (see Fig. 4). However, in the eyes of politicians and planners the presence of an invisible monument is in itself not enough to improve the quality and allure of the new area. Any further elaboration of how to make the past visible in the open spaces failed to materialize. It is therefore not surprising that in a second version of the zoning scheme one of the open spaces was allocated to other functions.

At first congruent meanings appeared to emerge. The monuments in Elst were given a positive meaning, for local authorities they had a function in the plan as public space, while their meaning as an important part of the archaeological record was retained for archaeologists. However, in the end congruent meanings did not really materialize and thus the chance to provide congruent meanings for the monuments disappeared. The main reason is that ROB failed to see that visibility of the archaeological value was a necessary condition for the open spaces to contribute to the local authorities' ultimate motive, i.e. to create a good residential environment.

A complicating factor is that the municipal authorities and the planners have a different view of archaeology from the view held by archaeologists. They mainly think in terms of material remains (see the pots and bones in Fig. 4). If they are to obtain a more realistic view, municipal authorities will need ROB's knowledge and support to help them adjust their ideas. In order to maintain congruent meanings, ROB in particular must make an effort to make history accessible in a way that enables it to fulfil a function in shaping the quality of the living environment.

4.2. Elst Westeraam: The Temple dilemma

On June 4, 2002, contractors were busy with their draglines while amateur archaeologists were examining the resulting holes, in which they discovered the remains of stone foundations belonging to a Roman building dating from the first century A.D. The find was immediately reported to the provincial authorities and by the next day archaeologists from the archaeological department of the city of Nijmegen started an emergency investigation. The remains were first interpreted as a villa complex although it soon became clear that they were dealing with a temple, probably of the Gallo-Roman gallery type. The ROB declared the temple of national interest, resulting in a complex situation. The municipal council had already passed the final zoning scheme and the first houses were scheduled to be built in three months' time.

During a meeting, ROB argued that since the discovery of the temple was unexpected, the local authorities could not be blamed and should not be forced to adapt their plans. While agreeing, the provincial archaeologist wanted to know what lessons could be learnt from this incident and asked the local council to reconsider conservation *in situ*. ROB argued that unless time and funds were made available for further investigation, it would have to enforce the law. The development company, speaking in the interest of public housing, wanted to excavate the site and was willing to facilitate the archaeological research under certain conditions. They wanted to know exactly when, where, what kind of research

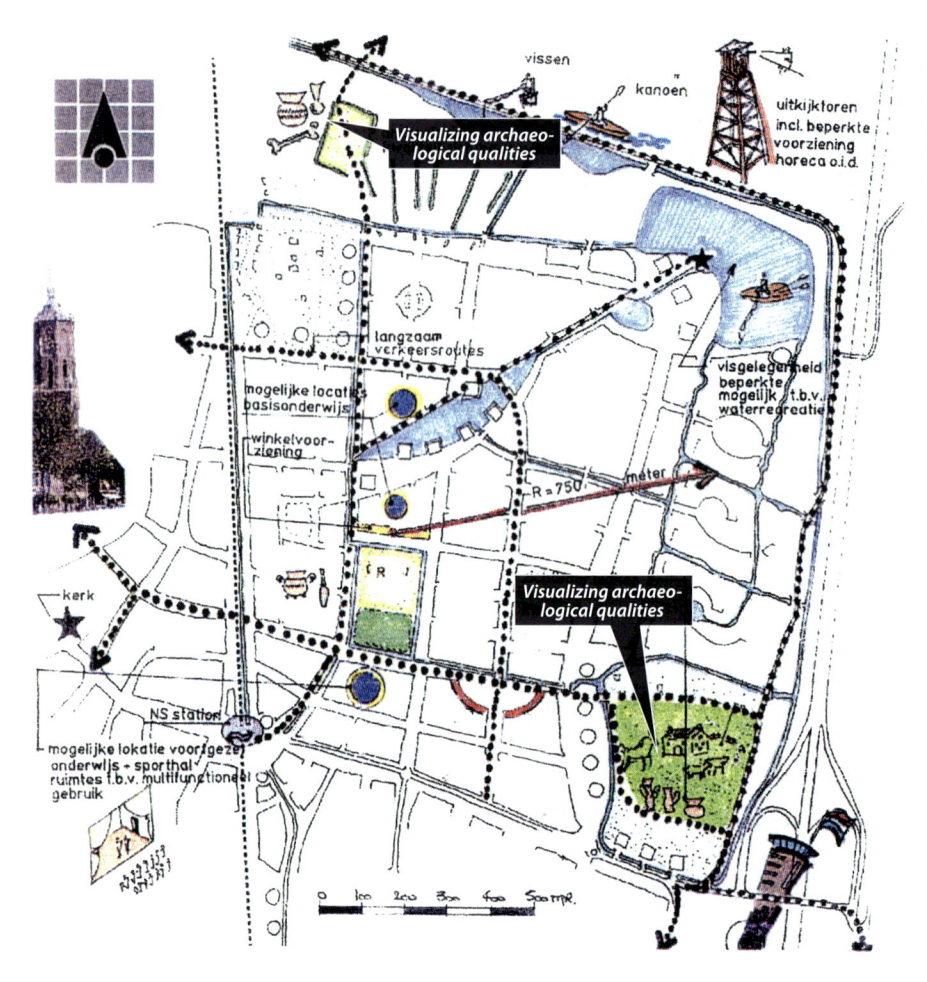

Fig. 4 Elst-Westeraam, zoning plan version 2, December 1999. Source: Buro 5 Maastricht.

and what impediments were to be expected. In the meantime the building process could be stopped. The archaeological operations were also brought to a halt in anticipation of the Programme of Requirements. At this point it was unclear as to who would pay necessary expenses.

Anticipating the decision of the local authorities in favour of excavating appeared to be right. The authorities, stating that they were proud of the discovery, were worried about the progress of house building and decided against *in situ* conservation. Meanwhile the estimated budget for excavation was available so investigations officially went ahead even if the repartition of the costs was still not completely clear. The local authorities requested subsidy from the national government. The development company paid some expenses but expressly refused to pay for further scientific investigation.

The situation was drastically altered by two events in early August 2002. First there was another unique find, a small wooden building, probably an earlier temple, within the walls of the already visible temple. Secondly, the local authorities wanted to reinvestigate the possibilities of *in situ* conservation. In particular, the alderman was enthusiastic about preserving the temple. He had a vision of Elst as a 'Stonehenge in the Betuwe', an important religious centre in the region, with implications for the local population and tourists. He argued that although the costs might be high, the archaeologists themselves had declared the temple of national and even international importance and thus relevant powers should contribute to the costs. He proposed the removal of four planned building plots. The alderman, perhaps somewhat late, discovered the Valletta Convention and ordered his civil servants to study it carefully, claiming that "we know the Convention's spirit but not yet the details". The alderman further claimed that preservation was enthusiastically supported by local inhabitants, who started a movement and quickly founded a *Preserve the Roman temples at Westeraam* committee, collecting 750 signatures.

The decision by the mayor and aldermen had many consequences. The excavation was stopped. The development company wanted an expert commission to investigate whether the archaeological world at large set great store on keeping the temple *in situ*. According to the development company the costs would increase significantly by many millions of euros. Unsubtly, perhaps, the development company argued that the party wishing to change the existing plans should be the one to foot the bill. Archaeologists wanted to continue the excavation, the argument being the technical impossibility of preserving the remains of the temple. Contact with the open air would destroy the relics within a year. This argument convinced the mayor and aldermen, who decided to conform.

The committee was very disappointed and a speaker stated that "archaeological investigations are destructive. You do have to demolish to see what is there". The committee asked for a proper investigation into the possibilities of preserving the temple. This request was impossible in one week, the time between the proposition and the final decision. Questions were asked at the council meeting at the end of August, with some arguing that the decision-making process is obscure and that opportunities for future research must be left open. Others argued that the history of the place must be made visible for the citizens, prompting a second petition. The alderman declared that the case was not closed and that he was considering proposing a 'heritage plan'. In this plan something would be made visible by means of a reconstruction incorporating authentic materials. In the end everybody had to be satisfied with the promise of a plan.

Analysis

The amazing thing in this case is that congruent meanings were not achieved although, as the alderman pointed out, the possibilities were there for the taking. He saw the temple remains as an instrument for strengthening Elst's historical identity as a village in the wake of its incorporation into the new municipality of Overbetuwe. The new meaning that the alderman hereby constructed of the find, in which the temple remains would serve to contribute to the quality of the living environment, touches the essence of the Valletta Convention to which the alderman referred in order to support his proposal. For ROB as policy actor, preservation would have meant potential knowledge for future generations of archaeologists.

The explanation for not achieving congruent meanings in this case is to be found in the AMZ cycle, the inherent ambivalence of a policy in which two opposing acts - excavation or protection - have the same intended goal to prevent parts of the archaeological record from disappearing without first having been seen by archaeologists. For archaeologists, this 'rescue discourse' (Van der Laarse 2005, 12) serves to legitimate their actions but they seem insensitive to the consequences of whichever approach they choose for the other actors involved, even though this choice clearly makes a great difference to these other actors.

In this case ROB preferred the role of 'archaeologist' to that of policy actor. From that point of view, the academic value was the most important. Here there was a unique opportunity to increase knowledge of the religious landscape at the time of the Romans and Batavians. Even though the temple was an accidental find, this case still poses questions with regard to the *in situ* preservation policy. If something is really interesting for archaeologists, then excavation is the preferred option.

4.3 Arnhem Schuytgraaf

The design for Schuytgraaf is based on the existing landscape. The architect sought to find a connection with the old parcelling patterns in order to recreate the expansion location as a landscape park. The assignment was to create 25 varied residential areas with varying densities. The centre of the new residential area was to be next to the railway station that had not yet been built and where a much higher living density had been planned. This design had a certain degree of flexibility which allowed archaeological sites to be taken into account.

The so-called site 10 was not yet known when the first design was made. It was discovered in the third survey by RAAP Archaeological Consultancy. This Stone Age site is exactly in the heart of the new centre, in front of the railway station and on the only collector road in the neighbourhood. The site therefore formed a huge obstacle. Despite this, the Urban Development Department (*Dienst Stadsontwikkeling*) in consultation with the newly appointed municipal archaeologist saw an opportunity to save the site as much as possible and make it an open space, a large square in front of the railway station. It was clear from the beginning that this would be an enormous task because the area covered by the site was in fact too large to function solely as a station square. It was also where the most expensive ground was located and building had less severe financial consequences. The situation became really problematic, however, when a new survey by RAAP revealed that the site was even larger than had originally been thought. This was a step too far for the planners, especially when ROB announced its intention to seek legal protection for the site. The talks came to a standstill.

Analysis

This case shows one of the effects of the AMZ cycle in practice, namely the exclusive focus on increasing knowledge leads to more research and larger claims on the space. The result is conflict and that protection of the archaeological record by means of fitting in the site in the spatial plan is ultimately not provided. *In situ* preservation is not forthcoming unless the Monuments and Historic Buildings Act is applied. With this law at their disposal, ROB has no urgent need to explore possibilities for giving the archaeological record a function that could be recognized by the local authorities.

Naturally, conflicts about space are not unique. Comparable tensions arise in diverse areas of policy. Policy scientists have thought about similar situations wherein actors operating from different rationalities can still develop a common action perspective focused on a "result that is both desirable and feasible" (Grin 2006, 122). However, it takes two parties, not just one, to achieve such a result.

4.4. Nijmegen Waalsprong

In Nijmegen the local authorities took the initiative to promote the search for congruent meanings. The municipal authorities decided to adjust their plans in reaction to criticism of the Structure Plan for Waalsprong. To meet the objections from a cultural heritage perspective, the authorities made a well-considered decision to take a different participatory approach to the problem. This political choice for a participatory approach demonstrated the municipality's preference for interactive policy-making when dealing with cultural heritage values. The guidelines on how to handle these values look as if they would be more at home in the Belvedere ideas of preservation by development than in a sectoral approach. This participation was given concrete form by setting up workshops that met regularly over the course of one year. The participants from the cultural heritage camp were ROB, the State Service for the Conservation of the Built Heritage (RDMZ), the provincial authorities and the Gelders Genootschap, in addition to the designers of several of the sub-plans. Another workshop was set up for the members of various local historical societies.

Analysis

By setting up workshops the municipal authorities created the conditions for a learning process, the act of consciously searching for congruent meanings. The workshops provided the time and space to give cultural heritage elements and site locations a positive function in the plan. It was then possible to develop ideas and proposals together with the designers that contributed to improving the everyday home and work environment. ROB and RDMZ participated in the process but did not see the space and opportunity, either physically or discursively, to contribute to the quality of the plan by applying knowledge about the past. They remained fixated on the meanings that represented scientific interests and were oblivious to the social heritage significance. Ignoring the local authorities' wish to find a solution other than legal protection, ROB turned to the law.

5. CONCLUSIONS

In each of the four cases discussed above, attaining congruent meanings was not impossible. In Arnhem congruent meanings were still far away but the city took a first step by planning an open space in front of the railway station which could have saved at least part of site 10. In the case of the Roman temple in Elst, congruent meanings were just for the taking but ROB preferred a scientific point of view rather than a contribution to the quality of the new extension of Westeraam. In the case of monument 40C-36N, also in Elst, ROB failed to see that achievement of congruent meanings was in need of an active contribution on their part to make the past visible. The city of Nijmegen deliberately set up a learning process to achieve congruent meanings, but here ROB let this opportunity pass.

All this happened after the 1992 Valletta Convention. The cases show that the implementation of the Convention is not self-evident. Before the Convention, ROB was already assigned the task of preserving and protecting monuments but even so perceived itself as a primarily scientific institution. A lot of excavating was done, strongly motivated by the threats faced by the archaeological record due to the ever increasing intervening operations in the soil. However the need to legitimize the great amount of excavating is felt. Excavations are considered rescue operations. Here the image of the guardian of the archaeological record comes to the fore (archaeologists as guardians) because society at large "does not give a damn" (Roebroeks 1993, 40 ; see also Van Es/Sarfatij/Woltering 1988). When constantly produced and reproduced this way of seeing becomes a sort of truth and gets a life of its own. This outlook also gives an indication how local authorities are approached.

The Valletta Convention was greeted with mixed feelings by the archaeological community. On the one hand archaeologists expressed amazement at no longer being allowed to excavate, on the other hand they were happy that at last funds were made available for excavations. The views of academic archaeologists range from worrying about the possibilities to continue their pure scientific research to developing new research paths (Knoop 1993; Bloemers 1994; *idem* 1997; Willems/Kars/Hallewas 1997). These first spontaneous reactions show that the Convention is capable of various constructions regarding its meaning. All the different outlooks affect how problems are constructed and how to act.

Which perspective did the Ministry and ROB choose? Their commitment relates to the sustainable conservation of visible or invisible archaeological values in the landscape. First priority is conservation *in situ* and excavations are only an option when this is not feasible. The reason beyond this aim is the possibility for future generations of archaeologists to investigate the archaeological record with research questions of their own. A policy directed at the prevention of destroying the archaeological record is the means to achieve the mentioned objectives (OCW/ROB 1995). Thus, the official policy is focused on preserving sites *in situ*, but in the ensuing debates the prospect of funding for research and excavations to be paid by governments and the private sector plays an important role. Reflecting on article 6 of the Valletta Convention, this prospect is captured in the phrase 'the disturber pays' (Knoop 1996; Van Marrewijk/Brandt 1997; Aten 2003).

For the time being the implementation of the Convention means the continuation of the existing practices. During the dispute about monument 40C-36N the archaeologists tried to prevent every act that would damage the archaeological record. However, they failed to contribute to the policy process by offering something in return. Negotiation is therefore difficult. If one views the policy process as a game, the archaeologists appear to win. However the outcome of the process is nothing more than a compromise. A compromise is metaphorically speaking something like a truce, the battle can begin again at any moment, as the story illustrates. The local authorities are not convinced of the importance of the monument. So not surprisingly there is no question of a breakthrough of new insights in what can be done with the monument other than keeping the physical space open.

The introduction of the Valletta Convention implies two ways of re-orientation for the archaeologists working at ROB, first from excavating to preservation *in situ* and second from conservation to 'development'. The second move reflects the ideas of the Belvedere policy on preservation by development, but already mentioned as the enhancement of archaeological sites in article 5 of the Valletta Convention. Complicated though it is, it further illustrates all the more the necessity of looking for congruent meanings doing justice to the Convention's principles. The search for new meanings of the archaeological record is certainly a task for archaeologists themselves, especially for the responsible government department and the State Service. It amounts to the question how new meanings sensible for both can be constructed in the debate with local authorities with regard to the archaeological record. In the case of Elst, reflection-in-action is needed, archaeologists should have reflected on the possibilities of the new meaning as envisioned by the alderman. But as the meaning of the archaeological record is a second order notion this will not be easy, certainly not in a context of urbanization. On the other hand an example of another Vinex extension location, Leidsche Rijn, shows us how, in a laborious debate, the city archaeologist and landscape architect constructed congruence of meaning. Here the archaeologists wanted to excavate a medieval tower, a *donjon,* with the explicit goal not to destroy it but to make it visible as a reminiscence of the past. The landscape architect whose professional design notions and aesthetical values did not allow for straight reference to the past, could see a sensible meaning in contrasting the authentic 'old' with a new design. However, ROB intervened and the plan was not executed (Van Assche/Duineveld 2003).

The analysis illustrates that congruence of meaning can be attained even when conflicting interests are at stake. It also shows the necessity of learning among the actors involved. In the case of the temple in Elst, the circumstance of the chance find played a role in bringing the different actors together in favour of an excavation. The example of Leidsche Rijn on the other hand gives us a clue as to how a synthesis between actors with different views can be realized. Congruent meanings are to be discovered through a specific debate about the archaeological record in which all parties are involved. Only in a deliberate quest for new meanings of the archaeological record, which is a learning process, can justice be done to the Valletta Convention's principles. This implies a change "from speaking truth to power to making sense together" (Hoppe 1999, 201).

NOTES

1 University of Amsterdam, the Netherlands.
2 A full account of the case studies will be given in my Ph.D. thesis, forthcoming.

REFERENCES

Assche, K. Van/M. Duineveld, 2003: *Groot Archeologiepark Leidsche Rijn: Over de rol van cultuurhistorie in planning en ontwerp*, Wageningen.

Aten, N,. 2003: Malta in Duitsland, *Archeobrief* 26, 15-19.

Belvedere, 1999: *The Belvedere Memorandum. A policy document examining the relationship between cultural history and spatial planning*, The Hague.

Bloemers, J.H.F., 1994: De gemeentelijke archeoloog tussen maatschappijgerichte en wetenschappelijke archeologiebeoefening, *Archeologisch Informatie Cahier* 7, 25-31.

Bloemers, J.H.F., 1997: Landschaftsarchäologie und Raumordnung in den Niederlanden: Aktuelle Trends und Themen, *Archäologisches Nachrichtenblatt* 2, 229-243.

Es, W.A. van/H. Sarfatij/ P.J. Woltering (eds.), 1988: *Archeologie in Nederland: De rijkdom van het bodemarchief*, Amsterdam/Amersfoort.

Faludi, A./A. van der Valk, 1994: *Rule and Order: Dutch Planning Doctrine in the Twentieth Century*, Dordrecht.

Fischer, F., 1995: *Evaluating Public Policy*, Chicago.

Graaf, H. van de/J. Grin, 2001: Variëteit in rationaliteit en de legitimiteit van beleid, in T. Abma/R.J. in 't Veld (eds.), *Handboek Beleidswetenschap*, Amsterdam.

Grin, J., 2006: Elk speelt zijn rol en krijgt zijn deel. Van compromis of consensus naar creatieve congruentie, in J. Grin/M. Hajer/W. Versteeg (eds.), *Meervoudige democratie, Ervaringen met vernieuwend bestuur*, Amsterdam.

Grin, J./H. van de Graaf, 1996: Implementation as communicative action: An interpretive understanding of interactions between policy actors and target groups, *Policy Sciences* 29, 291-319.

Hoppe, R., 1999: Policy analysis, science, and politics: from "speaking truth to power" to "making sense together", *Science and Public Policy* 26, 201-210.

Knoop, R. (ed.), 1993: *Archeologie, Maatschappij en Ethiek*, Leiden (Archeologisch Informatie Cahier 5).

Knoop, R., 1996: Malta: de stand van zaken, *Archeobrief* 1, 5-7.

Laarse, R. van der (ed.), 2005: *Bezeten Van Vroeger. Erfgoed, identiteit en musealisering*, Amsterdam.

Marrewijk, D. van/R. Brandt, 1997: Dreaming of Malta, in W.J.H. Willems/H., Kars/D.P. Hallewas (eds.), *Archaeological Heritage Management in the Netherlands. Fifty Years State Service for Archaeological Investigations*, Assen/Amersfoort, 58-75.

ROB/OCenW, 1995: *Het Verleden Zeker: Naar een meer effectieve archeologische monumentenzorg in Nederland*, Amersfoort.

Roebroeks, W., 1993: Naar een politieke discussie in de Nederlandse archeologie, in R. Knoop (ed.), *Archeologie, Maatschappij en Ethiek*, Leiden (Archeologisch Informatie Cahier 5), 39-42.

Schön, D.A., 1983: *The reflective practitioner: How professionals think in action*, New York.

Stichting RAAP, 1996: *Westeraam, een archeologische kartering, inventarisatie en waardering*, Amsterdam (RAAP-rapport 115).

Valletta, 1992: European Convention on the Protection of the Archaeological Heritage (Revised) Valetta, 16.I.1992, Strasbourg (Council of Europe).

Vinex 1990: *Vierde nota over de ruimtelijke ordening Extra deel 1: ontwerp planologische kernbeslissing*, Den Haag.

Willems, W.H.J./H. Kars/D.P. Hallewas (eds.), 1997: *Archaeological Heritage Management in the Netherlands: Fifty Years State Service for Archaeological Investigations*, Assen/Amersfoort.

Wissink, B., 2000: *Ontworpen en Ontstaan: Een praktijktheoretische analyse van het debat over het provinciale omgevingsbeleid*, Den Haag.

8. Protection and management of Spanish archaeological-historical landscapes
Possibilities and perspectives for the application of a protective and developmental approach

María Ruiz del Árbol & Almudena Orejas[1]

ABSTRACT

The present practice in Spanish cultural heritage protection and management is marked by the high presence of historical and archaeological landscapes in research and theoretical formulations and by the fragmentary presence of these conceptions in territorial strategies of protection and development. This situation that, in general terms, can be presented as paradigmatic of Mediterranean countries, contrasts with the situation in the Netherlands and in northern Europe in general, where the transformation of the present-day landscape has opened the opportunity of establishing closer links with sustainable management of the archaeological-historical elements and structures of the cultural landscape.

In this paper we propose to explore the possibilities and perspectives of applying PDL/BBO and Belvedere concepts such as "conservation through development" to the Spanish context and we analyse to what extent Spanish practices can take advantage of the PDL/BBO experience. After presenting an overview of the treatment of archaeological-historical resources in current Spanish cultural heritage management policies, we take into consideration the PDL/BBO research programme's aims and structure with the aim of developing new ways of thinking about the sustainable development of archaeological-historical landscapes in Spain following the successes of the PDL/BBO programme.

KEYWORDS

Mediterranean countries, cultural landscapes, landscape research traditions, legal dispositions, cultural parks

1. INTRODUCTION: GOAL AND PROBLEM

Landscape has, for several decades, been fully incorporated into Spanish archaeological research (see synthesis in Orejas 1995). However, the development in the last 10 years of archaeological landscape studies and the implementation of transdisciplinary research projects have allowed the recent revision of theoretical concepts and the development of methods and techniques of landscape analysis. Landscape is nowadays the core object of several historical and archaeological projects that consider it a spatial synthesis of social relations (see for example Criado/Parcero 1997; Burillo 1998; and more recently, Sánchez-Palencia/Orejas/Ruiz del Árbol 2005).

This situation in research contrasts with the present practice in the protection and management of Spanish cultural heritage in which archaeological and historical landscapes have little weight or a fragmentary presence in a background in which the protection and development of the territory is the domain of environmentalists or urban planners. At first glance the state of the art of Spanish landscape protection and management and the integration of archaeological-historical landscapes contrasts with the situation in the Netherlands, where the transformation of the present-day landscape is linked with sustainable management of the archaeological-historical elements and structures of the cultural landscape. What are the possibilities and perspectives of applying PDL/BBO concepts such as "protection by development" to the Spanish case? Can current Spanish practices take advantage of the PDL/BBO experience? What are the prospects of applying such a perspective to the Spanish context?

In this paper we aim to access the possible contribution of the Dutch experience and successes to our landscape management policies and practices in Spain. First, we will present an overview of the treatment of archaeological-historical resources in current Spanish cultural heritage management policies with the intention of synthesizing approaches and main lines of action. Second, and taking into consideration the PDL/BBO Research Programme's aims and structure, we will analyse the possibilities of applying the concepts of a past- and future-oriented archaeology in Spanish regions for the sustainable development of archaeological resources by giving them a function and meaning in environmental policies (as expressed in Bloemers 2002, 90). This is done in a context in which the recent entry into force of the European Landscape Convention in Spain (1 March, 2008) opens up new perspectives and grounds for discussion. Our final objective is to try to develop new ways of thinking about the sustainability and sustainable development of archaeological-historical landscapes in Spain through the results and experiences of the PDL/BBO programme.

The structure of the paper is inspired by the PDL/BBO programme structure. The scope of problems will be presented using a regional approach with attention to the diversity of the Spanish landscape, its political organization and associated policies and current initiatives that deal with landscape management. A comparative approach will be employed. We consider that, in general terms, current attitudes in Spanish cultural heritage administration can be presented as paradigmatic of Mediterranean countries. This is, of course, a general statement. Contrary to Spanish laws, Italian laws, for example, included the notion of historic environment and cultural landscape in the protection of cultural heritage at an early date (Breda/Bernardi 2001, 37-41; see also Settis 2002). However, like Spain, and despite its tradition and growing interest in landscape, current Italian policies do not integrate landscape into cultural heritage policies to any great extent (Cecchi 2001). Similarly, countries such as Greece, France and Portugal, where a theory of the archaeological-historical character of landscape has been successfully developed, find it difficult to integrate the archaeological-historical character of landscapes into the daily practice of cultural heritage policies and measures generally remain restricted to environmental policies (see Breda 2001; Doukellis/Mendoni 2008). This is why, for the purpose of this paper and its final considerations, we consider that Spain can be labelled paradigmatic of southern European thinking about archaeological heritage and traditions of protection and management.

From the beginning of our collaboration with colleagues from the Netherlands, mainly developed within the COST A27 LANDMARKS project (www.soc.staffs.ac.uk), a knowledge of the approach adopted in the PDL/BBO Research Programme "Protecting and Developing the Dutch Archaeological-Historical Landscape" has been very stimulating for us and our work on historical landscapes. Also, through COST A27, we have had the opportunity to study other European approaches to the protection and management of landscapes (for example Norway, the United Kingdom and Germany), experiences structured and designed from different traditions and closer to the Dutch case. In this sense The Netherlands can, in our view, be considered paradigmatic of northern traditions and policies on landscape.

Expected bonuses of this approach are, first of all, the critical consideration of our Spanish practices, limitations and advantages compared with, in our opinion, a successful approach to the protection and development of archaeological landscapes such as the Dutch one. Second, is a reflection on the possibilities of establishing a European community of practice and its utility for the application and sharing of concepts and ideas. Can the reflection and discussion between diverging traditions (or experiences) and the construction of different communities of practice (such as the European Science Foundation/COST Synergy on Landscape Studies) find realistic common points of interest and mutual help between southern and northwestern Europe? In the background several constraints will be found, such as dominant traditions, concepts and methods determining approaches in archaeological practices and landscape studies.

2. CONCEPTUALIZING LANDSCAPE. DIVERGING TRADITIONS AND COMMON THEMES IN SPANISH ACADEMIC PRACTICE IN LANDSCAPE STUDIES

The Spanish academic tradition concerning understanding and explaining landscapes is marked by the convergence of different disciplines. Among these geography has traditionally had considerable weight (for a good and a recent example see Martínez de Pisón 2009) although archaeology and history have also played an important role in the development of concepts related to the historical depth of landscapes. As a result, nowadays the concept of landscape embraces a wide variety of values. However it can be said that, among these, landscape's cultural relevance is an essential factor for its comprehension and valorization. In accordance with this, the concept of cultural landscape (*paisaje cultural*, used more and more frequently in landscape archaeology approaches) synthesizes the variety of manifestations produced by the interaction of people and environment throughout history. This concept of landscape, including its historical depth and cultural character, is not however very widespread in other fields of research or disciplines more closely related with the environmental aspects of the landscape. The result is that the Spanish case is marked by different visions of landscape.

However, the complex and inclusive character of landscape encourages the convergence of different practices and disciplines in present Spanish landscape practice. There is today a diversity of approaches to landscape and its cultural study. Focusing more specifically on Spanish archaeological-historical landscape research, four main trends can be easily discerned in the current situation (Orejas 1998; synthesized in Ruiz del Árbol/Orejas 2008, 229-230). First is the presence of what can be called aesthetic views, mainly based on the consideration of past elements as monuments in their surroundings. Landscape is considered a static frame, a scenario in which archaeological-historical elements are located. Second are morphological views, which are centred on the study of the elements that structure the landscape. These views risk restricting archaeological study to the identification of these elements without getting very far with their interpretation as a product of social relations. Third are the environmentalist or economic views that often incorporate palaeoenvironmental and geoarchaeological studies. Characteristic of these approaches is the idea that landscape equates with human-made and natural-environmental reconstruction. Fourth are the synthetic views which consider landscape as part and product of society. Different sub-traditions can be distinguished here, the sociological line explains landscape as a means and product of social processes and the socio-cultural line considers landscape as the manifestation of social practices, both material and imaginary.

Current Spanish landscape archaeology and history is characterized by a combination of these approaches. The diversity that results is a strong asset for the archaeological study of landscape (Orejas 1998) and demonstrates the dynamism and potential of archaeologists' contribution to understanding landscape.

In spite of this, archaeological and historical aspects of landscape are still very unequally reflected in protecting and planning policies in Spain although the relevance of landscape for cultural heritage policies is not disputed within the research community. Many scientific disciplines (geography, biology, ecology, geology etc.) are involved in understanding and protecting the landscape and, among these, many archaeologists have fully engaged with the topic (see examples collected in Ruiz del Árbol/Orejas 2005; and in Lévêque *et al.* 2006, 81-108). In fact, archaeology has contributed enormously to emphasizing the crucial place occupied by cultural landscape in relation to history, identity and sustainable development.

3. PROBLEMS ASSOCIATED WITH LANDSCAPE TRANSFORMATION, HERITAGE MANAGEMENT AND SPATIAL PLANNING IN SPAIN

As can be said for almost any region of Europe, Mediterranean landscapes are in a state of continual transformation, a process that is becoming more intense as time goes by. The degree of transformation of agricultural space has intensified considerably in the last 50 years with the following tendencies affecting the traditional rural landscape, abandonment of fields and settlements, flattening of rural paths and tracks, simplification and trivialization of the landscape by homogenization of crops and productive practices and the removal of singular elements like hedges, walls, terraces etc. (for the specific case of terraces and landscape disorganization processes in Spain see Asins-Velis 2006; *idem* 2008).

The current Spanish situation is a good example of the extent of these processes in southern European countries. In the last 40 years the population of small municipalities in Spain with under 10,000 inhabitants has dropped from 57% of the Spanish population to only 23% (Fig. 1). Rural areas account for more than 80.2% of the nation's total area. By contrast, artificial environments are growing in coastal provinces, uncontrolled urban expansion being the most characteristic feature. Furthermore, the emulation of urban models in rural areas related to second homes is very much altering the configuration of these communities. The Mediterranean coast of Spain and the Autonomous Community of Madrid are the areas most affected as a result of this uncontrolled urbanization (Sostenibilidad 2007). Other serious problems are linked to desertification processes and the appearance of peripheral spaces. More than a third of Spanish land has a very high, high, or medium risk of desertification, particularly in the Canary Islands and the southern part of the Iberian Peninsula.

In this context and following Zoido (Zoido 2006a, 8-9), we can identify the main general negative processes in Spain that together result in the deterioration of Mediterranean landscapes:
- Environmental, such as climate changes and other generalized processes like increasing consumption of non-renewable natural resources, air, water and soil pollution related to the use of energy. These have a particular impact on landscapes as fragile and rare as those of the Mediterranean.
- Technological changes and structural economic changes by intensification in some places and abandonment in others that radically modify the forms of land use and management of rural landscapes.
- Transformations related to the increasing movement of goods and peoples (infrastructures, urbanization processes).

Fig. 1.
La Balouta, an example of a small abandoned rural village in the province of León (Autonomous Community of Castilla y León). *Photo: Miguel Lage.*

- Changes in outlook and behaviour, such as changes in the way of life, spatial forms and specific symbolism.

These processes are also present in other parts of Europe but they need to be considered in relation to relatively small, fragmented and developed territories such as those of Mediterranean Europe (Zoido 2006a, 9). The current Mediterranean situation is thus characterized by the fast deterioration of its landscapes accompanied by an insufficient institutional response. In Spain a substantial part of territorial planning is promoted by private companies and, at the same time, environmental and planning offences have grown enormously (Sostenibilidad 2007).

In this scenario several problems associated with heritage management arise. First, as already stated, the current state of Spanish research on historical and archaeological landscapes contrasts with their scarce presence in protection and management policies. Spanish policies for the protection and management of archaeological-historical resources do not generally consider landscapes as products of the interaction between people and the environment and therefore as cultural-historic resources relevant to cultural heritage protection and development. Second, measures and actions concerning cultural heritage are usually disconnected from other policies such as environmental or territorial planning.

This deterioration requires urgent action in terms of protection, development and management policies. In our view the best solution is to work on their re-orientation, at a time when action in other countries, as the Dutch situation shows, and the European context and especially the European Landscape

Convention have prepared the ground for this to be done. In this context, which is pressing even for Mediterranean countries such as Spain, a double opportunity for archaeology emerges. On one hand is the chance to widen the notion of archaeological historical resources from the single monument to the whole landscape and thus initiate action on the spatial and conceptual scale of cultural landscapes. On the other is the opportunity for archaeology to acquire a new role in the processes of decision-making with regard to planning and development policies. In this context the need for profound reflection on the concept of landscape and its archaeological-historical dimension is quite clear. At the same time, as Martin Vollmer-König correctly stated in his comment on our paper and during the discussions during the PDL/BBO symposium held in Lunteren, there is a need both to study suitable strategies for adequate protection that take Spanish academic and planning traditions into account and to find a legal basis for protecting the cultural landscape other than cultural heritage legislation. With this purpose in mind, we shall now consider how Spanish cultural heritage provisions and regulations work and how these are integrated with other landscape protection and planning strategies.

4. INSTITUTIONAL FRAMEWORK

The Spanish scenario is characterized by the particular situations in each of Spain's seventeen Autonomous Communities, the administrative territories into which Spain is divided. These regions having considerable self-government and autonomy in several areas such as Cultural Heritage, Environment, Transport, Agriculture, Planning and Tourism. It is also characterized by the consequent fragmentation and dispersion of initiatives and legal provisions.

Landscape is taken into account in Spanish law by references to it in nature conservation laws, urban regulations and other provisions such as legislation on roads (for a general view, in Italian and English, of landscape policies in Spain, see Ottone 2001). Consequently, policies aimed at the protection, management and valorization of landscapes are fragmentary and scarce. Within this context, however, there are some clauses in existing legislation that enable archaeological-historical landscapes to be recognized and incorporated as an essential component of landscape planning and management (for a fuller review of these see Ruiz del Árbol/Orejas 2008, 233-242). To better understand this point it is advisable to summarize the treatment given to both cultural and natural heritage in the Spanish legislative system (Querol 2003):

- Cultural or historical heritage is conceived as a set of tangible and intangible assets created by society in the course of history and which are considered worth protecting. Their defining characteristic, therefore, is the human hand, they are assets made or manipulated by people.
- Natural heritage is defined as a set of environmental assets which have not been altered or manipulated by human hand and are thus the product of nature.

These are, as Querol correctly states, two different concepts of heritage with two different sets of legislation, two different administrations governing them, two specific forms of education and information and, above all, two completely different degrees of impact, very strong for natural heritage but very weak for cultural heritage.

The Spanish Historic Heritage Law (*Ley de Patrimonio Histórico Español*) enhances the legal and administrative consideration of cultural, historic or historic-cultural heritage. This law (published in 1985) expanded the concept of cultural heritage, traditionally centred on artistic monuments, and also improved its social background by enabling any element used and known by the public, not just what was declared officially, to be considered historical heritage.

From 1990, following these advances, and always in addition to the Spanish Historic Heritage Law, the Autonomous Communities, using some of their newly given powers, started creating their own laws for cultural or historical heritage. In 2009 there were fourteen specific laws. Although each is different, especially with regard to the nature and terminology of the types of heritage and the specific treatment of each type, they have many points in common, particularly with regard to the concept of cultural assets. One of these is the establishment of three levels of protection, the maximum, generally called BIC (*Bien de Interés Cultural* = Asset of Cultural Interest), the intermediate (Inventoried or Catalogued) and the minimum, mainly consisting of integrating assets of cultural heritage. Cultural assets are classified as *inmuebles* (fixed, non-movable), *muebles* (movable) and *inmateriales* (intangible). There is also an added category of special heritage (archaeological, ethnographic, documentary, bibliographic and even industrial).

The BICs are classified in several categories. The purpose of this classification is to determine their nature and characteristics in order to define their protection and management. For the purposes of this paper we consider it useful to focus on the non-movable BICs. These include monuments,[2] historic gardens,[3] historic ensembles,[4] historic sites[5] and archaeological areas.[6] Practically all Autonomous Communities have elaborated on these five and have introduced many more, such as monumental complex, place or area of ethnographic or ethnological interest, palaeontological area, natural place, cultural place, archaeological protection area, etc.

The tradition of protecting environmental assets is as old as the protection of archaeological and historical heritage in Spanish law. Currently, the environmental equivalent to the Spanish Historic Heritage Law is the 1989 Law on the protection of natural areas and flora and fauna. According to the Spanish Constitution, the promulgation of laws protecting the environment is the exclusive prerogative of the State, although the Autonomous Communities can draw up additional legislation on protection. As a result in Spain the rules and legal parameters are completely different for cultural heritage and natural heritage. However, it must be said that the categories established by environmental laws such as national parks, natural parks and nature reserves, which are widely accepted, have in recent years been reproduced and emulated by cultural laws as cultural parks, cultural areas, archaeological parks, etc. and by the creation of promotion and management instruments such as cultural parks or cultural spaces structured in the form of networks of these parks and spaces.

One fundamental difference between the Spanish Historic Heritage Law of 1985 and the Environmental law of 1989 is that the latter is much more detailed in terms of administrative organization and development of protected areas. In fact, this law enforces the need to draw up plans for protecting natural resources before they are specifically declared to be protected areas. The bodies in charge of managing these must draw up use and management plans and these overrule previous urban planning. In case of incompatibility, the latter must adapt. Apart from that, a National Commission for the Protection of Nature was created to enable the co-operation of central government and Autonomous Communities, similar to the Cultural Heritage Council created by the Spanish Historic Heritage Law.

Given the current situation, co-ordination of these mechanisms seems the first reasonable step towards successfully protecting archaeological-historical landscapes. However, at first glance, natural and

Fig. 2.
The Las Médulas Roman gold mine is an excellent example of a cultural landscape in which archaeological-historical elements are curated on the basis of their protection and development. The dual system of protection (directed by cultural and environmental administrations) causes several problems, mainly due to the lack of co-ordination mechanisms between administrations and political levels (from the local to the national). *Photo: Miguel Lage.*

cultural heritage do not share a common approach. Some co-ordination in the management of several regions does exist in practice, depending on the personal commitment and good relations between the staff of the administrations concerned.

Environmental law declares that its objectives are to protect, preserve and use nature in an ordered manner (when it has not been manipulated, altered or created by the human hand). Both formally and in its intentions, this law clearly separates what is 'cultural' from what is 'natural', although in actually applying the law, cultural heritage is also taken into consideration by environmental administrators. Furthermore, cultural heritage rulings are generally not very promising when we try to find connections with natural heritage. However, and following Querol (Querol 2003), certain promising signs can be seen. First, several laws mention the need to protect the surroundings of cultural heritage sites in relation to the BIC protection process of a historic ensemble or a non-movable element of cultural heritage. The law itself allows for the inclusion within "surroundings" of topographic and natural elements around the site, although there are no criteria for defining their extent and landscape is treated as subsidiary to what is singular or monumental. The cultural heritage laws of some Autonomous Communities can be somewhat different and in some there is a meticulous concern for the environment. Some have introduced the concept of cultural spaces or cultural parks with the aim of establishing the territorial management of cultural assets (good examples are the initiatives developed by some Autonomous Communities, such as Andalusia and Aragon, see Verdugo 2008; Hernández/Pereta 2008).

The second promising sign is the concept of BIC, established by the Spanish Law on historic heritage in order to provide the highest level of protection for the most prominent cultural assets. In general, the concept of BIC has been maintained by the Autonomous Communities in the laws they have subsequently introduced and we can say that it is the only form of protection with true social consequences. The inclusion of a cultural asset in the BIC category implies that its protection must be set out in a special protection plan. In the case of non-movable assets it entails the cancellation of all building permits until new planning approval has been granted. Even though this is a general law, some Autonomous Communities have used this degree of protection for other things, for instance the Autonomous Community of Madrid uses the BIC to define large areas (archaeological areas) in order to force all developers to produce an archaeological report before starting any building or public works.

By analysing the definitions given for the different types of BIC (see notes 2-6), it can be seen how some are very close to natural heritage jurisdiction, making them useful for their potential for providing protection and management of cultural landscapes. This is the case of sites such as the Roman gold mine of Las Médulas, a World Heritage Site, an area that has been declared and protected both as a natural monument by environmental legislation and as a BIC under the definition of archaeological area by the cultural law. Here the convergence of concepts offers the potential to co-ordinate environmental and cultural management, although actually in daily practice these concepts contrast and contradict each other (see Ruiz del Árbol/Orejas 2008, 238-240) (Fig. 2). Another useful example is the case of the Autonomous Community of Cantabria, where the BIC approach tries to combine the natural and the cultural under the heading of cultural landscape. It is defined as "specific parts of a territory formed by the combination of the work of people and nature, illustrating the evolution of human society and its settlements in space and time and which have acquired socially-recognized values on different territorial levels thanks to tradition, technology or their description in literature and works of art". There will be special consideration for the so-called *paisajes de cercas*, enclosed microproperty landscapes, and mosaic structures in rural areas of Cantabria.

5. CURRENT PRACTICES, GOOD MOVES AND DEFICIENCIES

The existence of all these specific provisions does not really solve the problem of either co-ordination or integration of the archaeological-historical landscape in environmental policies. Each Autonomous Community ministry has exclusive competence in the areas with which it is concerned (nature, culture) and establishes the limits defined by the law. In some cases responsibilities are shared by regional commissions and territorial services. In these cases the very fact that experts in cultural management must sit down with those in environmental management is a promising step towards co-ordination. However, the fragmentation of Spanish laws and the different initiatives of the various Autonomous administrations make it harder to implement and integrate the protection of historical landscapes and make it difficult to enhance the public role of archaeological-historical landscape and to promote support for its protection, management and development. As shown in the previous pages, holistic protection and management of landscape and its archaeological-historical dimension is not present in the basic Spanish legislation.

Despite these deficiencies three main tendencies can be defined within Spanish territorial actions and policies (some make a real difference and are a step forward in the protection and management of landscapes).

First, some Autonomous Communities have incorporated specific legislation for the landscape. In these cases, however, archaeological-historical values are less integrated into landscape policies. More specifically two regions, the Autonomous Community of Valencia (in 2004) and the Autonomous Community of Catalonia (in 2005) have developed special laws concerning the landscape, in some points clearly influenced by the European Landscape Convention. Valencia's action on landscape is based on

Fig. 3.
Las Médulas: an information panel at the area of Lake Somido, a Roman waste evacuation canal.
Photo: Jimena Martinez.

the law for Territorial Planning and Landscape Protection; in Catalonia on the law for the Protection, Management and Planning of Landscape. In fact, both laws tend towards convergence with the European Landscape Convention and seek integration of all planning instruments relating to all types of territories and the active participation of their inhabitants. Landscape studies are proposed in all aspects of territorial planning (covering units, resources, identities, the participation of local population and visitors, visibility and landscape quality) as well as studies for landscape integration, landscape inventories and management programmes.

Other regions have not introduced laws on landscape but have partially incorporated European Landscape Convention recommendations and are working on an integrated view of landscape. This is the case at the Andalusian Institute for Historical Heritage (the body responsible for cultural heritage action in the Autonomous Community of Andalusia) which has developed some interesting initiatives and studies (for example Salmerón 2005). Recently, a Centre for Landscape and Territory Studies has been created with the participation of all the Andalusian Universities (www.paisajeyterritorio.es) and the administration has set up a cultural landscape laboratory. In the Andalusian region the connection between research and action is worthy of mention and is producing interesting results (Zoido 2006b; a specific example in Ruiz del Árbol *et al.* 2005).

The third group of tendencies is represented by most Spanish regions which have not yet incorporated a landscape-integrated approach into their planning and spatial policies. Thus, some initiatives show that when archaeological-historical and environmental assets are integrated they result in interesting projects. Most initiatives are linked to protection strategies based on selecting a collection of the more representative or relevant archaeological-historical elements and legal entities such as archaeological parks (as in Castilla La Mancha Autonomous Community, see Ortiz/Caballero 2007), networks of sites (as is the case of Galician Autonomous Community, see Tallón et al. 2005) or the promotion of cultural spaces (for example the Castilla y León Autonomous Community, for recent work on Las Médulas see Sánchez-Palencia et al. 2008) (Fig. 3).

The recent ratification of the European Landscape Convention (Spain ratified it on 26 November, 2007 and it entered into effect on 1 March, 2008) makes it an accepted legal instrument needed in Spain and clarifies main areas of action and jurisdiction. Irrespective of regional differences and trajectories and the convergence of different factors and processes as described in previous pages, it recommends the adoption of landscape policies that are defined and articulated for the whole of Spain (Zoido 2006c). The promising interest by the Ministry of Culture in a project for a national plan on cultural landscapes is worth mentioning (see www.mcu.es/patrimonio).

6. LESSONS AND RECOMMENDATIONS TAKEN FROM THE PROTECTION AND DEVELOPMENT PROGRAMME

Spain still has a great deal of work to do to recognize the importance of the historical value of landscape and its public interest role in the cultural and social fields. In this process archaeologists and historians are responsible for communicating first, that archaeological-historical values are present everywhere in our environment and as a consequence are everyone's responsibility and second, that their protection and management are worth all the effort needed because they enhance our present and future environment. Moreover, their work would open the way towards the development of new understanding and insights in the field of integrated cultural resource management and interaction with environmental planning and public discussion (as stressed by Bloemers 2002, 93). At this point an initial matter for reflection arises (and allows us to make a relevant link with our commenter's suggestions and the discussions held during the sessions at Lunteren), to make archaeology a past- and future-orientated activity is not only a matter of creating or adapting laws and procedures but also of changing attitudes.

The protection and sustainable development of archaeological-historical landscapes within the framework of environmental planning policy is a very complex problem and, as the Dutch experience has shown, it must be achieved through several lines of action.

First this should be done through the promotion of research in this field aimed at the construction of theories and concepts capable of connecting fundamental research to applied projects that put into practice specific proposals for sustainable protection and management. Nowadays we face historical and management problems shared by many European research teams and institutions. In our opinion there is an urgent need in Mediterranean landscape action to strengthen the connection between landscape research and protection and development of the landscape. The national research programme PDL/BBO is, in our opinion, a good example of how to create a scientific basis for the applied approach. Important issues for research in PDL/BBO (Bloemers 2005, 83), such as the fundamental appreciation of cultural historical resources as meaningful elements in the quality of human environment or the development of well-founded and effective methods for survey, evaluation, selection and protection are already well developed in Spain and applied to specific projects. Other issues developed within PDL/BBO such as the operational definition of sustainability in relation to archaeological-historical resources and the development of concepts and instruments to integrate them with historical landscapes and buildings in environmental and spatial planning offer a good lesson that the PDL/BBO programme suggests could be incorporated into our current practices.

Second, we should integrate cultural assets into landscape development. From our point of view and experience one of the important lessons that could be taken from the PDL/BBO programme is that cultural elements not only need protection, but also need to function as elements in the development and exploitation of the modern urban and rural landscape. We need to make archaeological values a factor in the development of the quality of present and future human life, perception and environment. The traditional Spanish approach to protection and development is based on the delimitation of closed areas. The ideas of landscape or the enhancement of the surroundings of cultural monuments in recent years have promoted the creation of protected areas or the revision of existing ones in which elements of archaeological and historical heritage are protected within their environment. This has been done, in many cases, using concepts such as cultural landscape, cultural areas or archaeological parks, despite the fact that very often there has been no real change in attitude towards the protection of archaeological landscapes apart from these initiatives. In our view, the cultural landscape concept should not be used to legitimate the creation of new protected areas or to colour the management of those that already exist. On the contrary, it seriously obliges us to work for the protection and management of archaeological-historical resources on a different level on the basis of criteria that take into consideration the complexity, problems and possibilities of landscapes as something more than the mere spatial context of heritage sites (an idea with strong roots in Mediterranean academic and management traditions). In this context, the concept of protection by development that links the distant past with the present and future use of the environment (Bloemers 2002, 92) is of very great interest to us. In fact, the fundamental notion of cultural and historical values as a resource for experiencing and expressing identity through conservation, innovation and design (*ibidem*, 92) is quite different from the principal actions undertaken under Spanish cultural and environmental policies.

Third we should develop and legally formalize a deliberately preventive archaeological heritage policy that integrates archaeological values into normal spatial planning concepts and procedures (Bloemers 2002, 89), a task that is urgent in Spain. A good recommendation taken from the PDL/BBO programme is the urgent need to develop a Spanish national plan on cultural landscapes. This has already been proposed by our Ministry of Culture but is still only a draft which needs the contribution of other Ministries (Environment, Housing, Transport). In fact, the experience of the PDL/BBO programme encourages us to assert that the consistent collaboration by Spanish institutions and administrations interested in landscape policies would enable research work to be efficiently organized and common initiatives developed. However, we believe that the best level of action is closer to the implementation of urban and rural planning. In the case of Spain the role of the national government must be limited to frameworks, general policies, financing and general rules or models. Spain, due to its history and administrative structure, has a long and excellent history of regional and local action that will serve as a good basis for this approach.

Within this context we consider the European Landscape Convention to be the right framework for developing new visions of landscape understanding and management in Spain. Both the rich Mediterranean cultural heritage and the aspirations for creating an authentic knowledge-based society form an integral part of the development of the ideas and concepts relating to the sustainability of landscapes, very well developed in the Netherlands, in the general context of European integration.

ACKNOWLEDGEMENTS

This article has very much benefited from the suggestions and comments by Arnold van der Valk and Tom Bloemers. We are very grateful for their remarks and advice as editors. We would also like to thank Tom Bloemers for his invitation to participate in the Lunteren symposium. We are also indebted to Miguel Lage, photographer of Figs. 1 and 2, who travelled to La Balouta to take recent pictures of the village for this article.

NOTES

1 Research Group "Social Structure and Territory-Landscape Archaeology", Centre for Human and Social Sciences (CCHS), CSIC. This paper has been written in the framework of the research projects "Formation and transformation of the *civitas* in the Iberian Northwest" (*Formación y disolución de la civitas en el Noroeste peninsular*, CIVITAS) (AR2008-06018-C03-01/HIST) and CONSOLIDER "Research Programme on Technologies for the conservation and valorization of Cultural Heritage" (*Programa de Investigación para la conservación y revalorización del Patrimonio Cultural*, TCP) (CSD2007-0058).
2 The law defines monuments as those non-movable assets that constitute architectural or engineering structures or very large works of sculpture that are of historical, artistic, scientific or social interest.
3 Historical garden is, according to the Law, a defined space produced by human management of natural elements, sometimes complemented with masonry structures, and considered of interest in terms of its origin or past history and its aesthetic, sensory or botanical values.
4 Historic ensemble is the grouping of non-movable assets that form a unit of settlement, continuous or dispersed, whose physical structure is representative of the evolution of a human community because it is a testament to its culture or is valued for its use and enjoyment by the community. A historic ensemble may also be any individual collection of non-movable assets included in a larger unit of population that displays the same characteristics and can be clearly defined.
5 Historic site is a natural place or site associated with events or memories of the past, popular traditions, cultural or natural creations and works by people, which possess a historical, ethnological, palaeontological or anthropological value.
6 Archaeological Area is a natural place or site where there are movable or non-movable assets that can be studied using archaeological methods, whether or not they have been excavated and whether they are found on the surface, in the subsoil, or in Spanish territorial waters.

REFERENCES

Asins-Velis, S., 2006: Linking historical Mediterranean terraces with water catchment, harvesting and distribution structures, in J. P. Morel/J. Tresserras/J. C. Matamala (eds.), *The archaeology of crop fields and gardens*, Bari, 21-40.

Asins-Velis, S., 2008: Abandono de terrazas agrícolas: procesos de erosión y desorganización del paisaje, in Recuperación, *Recuperación de paisajes de terrazas y prevención de riesgos naturales. Jornades sobre terrasses i prevenció de riscos naturales, Mallorca, 14-16 setembre 2006*, Mallorca, 285-296.

Bloemers, J.H.F., 2002: Past- and future-oriented archaeology: protecting and developing the archaeological-historical landscape in the Netherlands, in G. Fairclough/S. Rippon (eds.), *Europe's*

Cultural Landscape: archaeologists and the management of change, Brussels/London (Europae Archaeologiae Consilium and English Heritage; EAC Occasional Paper 2), 89-96.

Bloemers, J.H.F., 2005: Archaeological-historical landscapes in the Netherlands: management by sustainable development in planning, in M. Ruiz del Árbol/A. Orejas (eds.), *Landscapes as Cultural Heritage in the European Research. Proceedings of the Open Workshop (Madrid, 29th October 2004)*, Madrid (Biblioteca de Ciencias 22), 69-85.

Breda, M. A., 2001: Francia. Nuovi strumenti per la pianificazione e il governo del paesaggio, in L. Scazzosi (ed.), *Politiche e Culture del Paessaggio. Landscape policies and cultures. Nuovi confronti. New Comparisons*, Roma, 99-104.

Breda, M. A./C. De Bernardi, 2001: La tutela del paesaggio in Italia: normativa e strumenti, in L. Scazzosi (ed.), *Politiche e Culture del Paessaggio. Landscape policies and cultures. Nuovi confronti. New Comparisons*, Roma, 37-66.

Burillo, F. (ed.), 1998: *Arqueología del paisaje. Comunicaciones presentadas al 5º Coloquio Internacional de Arqueología Espacial (Teruel, 14-16 de septiembre de 1998)*, Teruel.

Cecchi, R., 2001: Presentation, in L. Scazzosi (ed.), *Politiche e Culture del Paessaggio. Landscape policies and cultures. Nuovi confronti. New Comparisons*, Roma, 7.

Criado, F./C. Parcero (eds.), 1997: *Landscape, Archaeology, Heritage*, Santiago de Compostela (Trabajos en Arqueología del Paisaje, TAPA 2).

Doukellis, P.N./L.G. Mendoni, 2008: Greece, in G. J. Fairclough/P. Grau Moller (eds.), *Landscape as Heritage. The management and Protection of Landscape in Europe, a summary by the COST A27 project "LANDMARKS"*, Bern, 129-144.

Hernández, M.A./A. Pereta, 2008: Los Parques Culturales de Aragón, in VV.AA., Hacia la gestión territorial del patrimonio cultural. Bienes, paisajes, itinerarios, *PH, Boletín del Instituto Andaluz del Patrimonio Histórico*, 65, 64-71.

Léveque, L./M. Ruiz del Árbol/L. Pop/C. Bartels (eds.), 2006: *Journeys through European Landscapes*, Ponferrada.

Martínez de Pisón, E., 2009: *Miradas sobre el paisaje*, Madrid (Colección Paisaje y Teoría).

Orejas, A., 1995: *Del "marco geográfico" a la Arqueología del paisaje. La aportación de la fotografía aérea*, Madrid.

Orejas, A., 1998: El estudio del Paisaje: visiones desde la Arqueología, in F. Burillo (ed.), *Arqueología del paisaje. Comunicaciones presentadas al 5º Coloquio Internacional de Arqueología Espacial (Teruel, 14-16 de septiembre de 1998)*, Teruel, 9-19.

Ortiz, J.R./Caballero, A., 2007: Los parques arqueológicos de Castilla-La Mancha. Nuevo modelo de gestión del patrimonio arqueológico, *IV Congreso de Rehabilitación Sostenible del Patrimonio Cultural. Arqueología y Mecenazgo*, Salas, 61-76.

Ottone, C., 2001: Politiche e cultura del paesaggio in Spagna, in L. Scazzosi (ed.), *Politiche e Culture del Paessaggio. Landscape policies and cultures. Nuovi confronti. New Comparisons*, Roma, 79-96.

Querol, M.A., 2003: Patrimonio Cultural y Patrimonio Natural. Una relación con futuro, in: A. Moure (ed.), *Patrimonio Cultural y Patrimonio Natural. Una reserva de futuro*, Cantabria, 31-45.

Ruiz, A./M. Molinos/A. Sánchez/M.L. Gutiérrez, 2005: Between History and Landscape: a Journey to the Time of Iberians, in M. Ruiz del Árbol/A. Orejas (eds.), *Landscapes as Cultural Heritage in the*

Ruiz del Árbol, M./A. Orejas (eds.), 2005: *Landscapes as Cultural Heritage in the European Research. Proceedings of the Open Workshop (Madrid, 29*[th] *October 2004)*, Madrid (Biblioteca de Ciencias, 22), 145-159.

Ruiz del Árbol, M./A. Orejas (eds.), 2005: *Landscapes as Cultural Heritage in the European Research. Proceedings of the Open Workshop (Madrid, 29*[th] *October 2004)*, Madrid (Biblioteca de Ciencias, 22).

Ruiz del Árbol, M./A. Orejas, 2008: Spain, in G.J. Fairclough/P. Grau Møller (eds.), *Landscape as Heritage. The management and Protection of Landscape in Europe, a summary by the COST A27 project "LANDMARKS"*, Bern (Geographica Bernensia 79), 229-248.

Salmerón, P. (ed.), 2005: *Guía del Paisaje Cultural de la Ensenada de Bolonia. Cádiz. Avance*, Seville.

Sánchez-Palencia, F.J./A. Orejas/M. Ruiz del Árbol, 2005: Social Structure and Territory. Landscape Archaeology: from Regional Projects to European Co-operation, in M. Ruiz del Árbol/A.Orejas (eds.), *Landscapes as Cultural Heritage in the European Research. Proceedings of the Open Workshop (Madrid, 29*[th] *October 2004)*, Madrid (Biblioteca de Ciencias, 22), 23-35.

Sánchez-Palencia, F.J./A. Orejas/ Mª.D. Fernández-Posse/M. Ruiz del Árbol/I. Sastre, 2008: Las Médulas (León, Spain). A Rural and Mining Landscape, in C. Bartels/M. Ruiz del Árbol/H. van Londen/A. Orejas (eds.), *Landmarks. Profiling Europe's Historic Landscapes*, Bochum, 113-124.

Settis, S., 2002: *L'assalto al patrimonio culturale*, Torino.

Sostenibilidad, 2007: *Presentación del informe sobre Sostenibilidad en España, 2007*. (www.sostenibilidad-es.org/Observatorio+Sostenibilidad. Accessed 25 March, 2008).

Tallón, M.J., Infante, F./Rey, J.M./Rodriguez, F., 2005: The Galician Archaeological Heritage Network, in M. Ruiz del Árbol/A. Orejas (eds.), *Landscapes as Cultural Heritage in the European Research. Proceedings of the Open Workshop (Madrid, 29*[th] *October 2004)*, Madrid (Biblioteca de Ciencias, 22), 133-143.

Verdugo, J., 2008: Red de Espacios Culturales de Andalucía, in VV.AA, Hacia la gestión territorial del patrimonio cultural. Bienes, paisajes, itinerarios, *PH, Boletín del Instituto Andaluz del Patrimonio Histórico* 65, 46-51.

Zoido, F., 2006a: Paisaje y ordenación territorial en ámbitos mediterráneos, *Jornadas sobre el paisaje mediterráneo: opciones de multifuncionalidad*, 1-14. (www.paisajeyterritorio.es. Accessed 19 March, 2008).

Zoido, F. (ed.), 2006b: *Estudio sobre la relevancia paisajística de Madinat al–Zahra*, Sevilla.

Zoido, F., 2006c: Bases para la aplicación del Convenio Europeo del Paisaje en España, in: www.coe.int (we have consulted the version published at: www.paisajeyterritorio.es. Accessed 19 March, 2008).

WEBSITES

http://www.mcu.es/patrimonio/MC/IPHE/PlanesNac/PlanPaisajesCulturales/PaisajesCult.html

http://www.paisajeyterritorio.es

http://www.soc.staffs.ac.uk/jdw1/costa27home.html

9. Knowledge and legal action: a plea for conservation

Comment on 'Protection and management of Spanish archaeological-historical landscapes. Possibilities and perspectives for the application of a protective and developmental approach', by María Ruiz del Árbol & Almudena Orejas

Martin Vollmer-König[1]

ABSTRACT

Facing the worldwide melting of archaeological heritage everybody knows that we have to slow down this process as well as possible. But concerning the way to reach this aim the accordance already ends. Do we first need a better common awareness of archaeological heritage to achieve more preservation or would better archaeological heritage protection cause a change of awareness? What significance should legal protection have? Why are aspects of protection, conservation and management nearly absent in the common view on archaeology? What are the reasons for the common view on archaeologists as primarily excavating researchers? Do we have to choose between research and heritage protection? Are archaeologists able to act successfully in planning and approval procedures claiming to respect the archaeological heritage?

Such questions and a short discussion of different aspects and incisive positions point to structural deficiencies in archaeology. A few examples of planning procedures shall illustrate that forceful and competent use of all judicial possibilities in the procedures is indispensable to reach the successful inclusion of the archaeological heritage.

KEYWORDS

Legalistic archaeological action and protection, planning and approval procedure, conservation, Rhineland cases

1. TWO OPPOSING POSITIONS ON ARCHAEOLOGICAL HERITAGE STRATEGIES

The PDL/BBO symposium showed that there are two opposing positions in archaeology towards the way in which archaeological heritage should be protected. One refuses legal protection and legalistic action. The protection and management of archaeological-historical resources has to happen on a different level (Ruiz del Árbol/Orejas Ch. V.8, 487). This position is based on the idea that protection can only be accomplished if accompanied by a change of mind in society. A new understanding of the value of archaeological heritage should make everyone feel responsible. However, for the other position, definitely mine, it is indispensable to exhaust all legal possibilities of planning and approval procedures in order to attain the maximum care of archaeological heritage. In this context the method of procedure should definitely include legal protection as much as possible because it improves the preconditions for appropriately considering archaeological heritage in the procedures.

1.1 Interactive approach

Why do advocates of the interactive approach look so sceptically at legalistic action? On the one hand they fear that legal protection would cause resistance instead of appreciation. On the other hand they assume that comprehensive protection areas would result in an insufficient reduction of the landscape to meet archaeological needs. To meet the complexity of cultural landscape we should be in need of a social dialogue and of co-operation with the other actors who determine the use and creation of landscape. At the same time they look with reservation at narrow legal protection because it would not meet the importance of the archaeological-historical values which were present everywhere in our environment (Ruiz del Árbol/Orejas Ch. V.8, 482-485).

From my point of view, this approach is an expression of an academic sphere in archaeology which has very little contact with the everyday heritage action of the administration sphere. Sometimes when this approach is brought forward one could receive the impression that everything could be ruled in perfect harmony. In this context the use of the term legal action as something more formal and correct than reasonable content, as well as the claim for a balanced relationship between legal protection and the ideals of the Valletta Convention, imply that it would be a matter of alternatives. This appears to be a choice between the heedless enforcement of particular interests of archaeological heritage versus the co-operation with partners in an integrated cultural resource management that would lead to a change of mind.

This does not hold true. I do agree with the idea that awareness of the value of archaeological heritage has to grow but I believe that this is the wrong method of implementation. We do not have to change the awareness to reach better protection of archaeological sources but we do have to ensure better archaeological heritage protection to change the awareness. At first this means putting the conservation of archaeological sites at the centre of our work. There is a common perception of archaeologists as primarily excavating researchers. We are to blame for it because archaeology communicates this image while aspects of protection, conservation and management are nearly absent. We support this perception with every popular book and publicity about new excavation results. Similarly, in planning procedures we first encounter the idea that the natural destiny of archaeological sites is their excavation. It is regrettable how common this imprudent concept is among archaeologists.

1.2 Legal protection

In trying to change this image, the legal protection (besides its judicial impact) plays a significant role. It very clearly documents the claim that archaeological sites have to be conserved in the long term and must not be damaged. Thus, the legal status already underlines the value of the archaeological heritage because something that is under protection has to be valuable. Furthermore, if many people think that archaeology only happens in Greece, legal protection makes it clear that it also exists here. Thus every protected archaeological site or monument, especially if attractively presented, reveals the archaeological background of a modern rural and urban landscape and helps to change the way of thinking.

The proper approach to better heritage management is naturally a professional handling of planning and approval procedures. Thereby I agree that we are in need of concerted action in cultural and natural heritage that will lead to comprehensive landscape protection. However, today agreement is mostly lacking and occasionally a contradiction between both is even constructed in procedures. This is especially regrettable because the German nature conservation law includes the opportunity for a comprehensive approach. It claims the preservation of historic cultural landscapes and the function of soil as an archive of cultural history.

We archaeologists certainly will not reach an adequate positioning of archaeological heritage in environmental planning on a different level, but only by forceful and competent representation of our interests on every level of governmental planning and approval procedures. This already starts when planning executives are unaware of the fact that archaeological heritage institutions have to be involved obligatorily. Let's tell them! Furthermore, the examination of archaeological heritage in environmental impact assessments is often forgotten or just formally completed without checking it in fact: 'known archaeological sites do not exist'. Let's claim a serious handling! To get access to procedures and to put in claims you certainly have to give judicial reasons and here we spot a fundamental deficiency in archaeology, too many archaeologists do not have sufficient knowledge of relevant laws and how they must be applied in planning and approval procedures. In this regard the apprenticeship at the universities fails the demand.

An important instrument for successful heritage is legal protection which gives much more weight to archaeological sites. Especially in the Rhineland, owing to legal regulation, sites are comprehensively considered only when legally protected. Without protection their destruction is almost unavoidable if competing use appears. Only legal protection allows us to implement archaeological procedures if a new use makes them necessary. Therefore it is not only a question of spatial planning or big intentions regarding the countryside but also of limited projects in urban space, like the building of a house, the installation of a pipe or the reconstruction of a road. For the administration sphere there is no doubt that every legal protection of an archaeological site or monument helps to preserve archaeological heritage. It does not matter if it concerns wide protected areas or the protection of isolated objects. Nature, landscape and water protection areas show how it works. So why should we hesitate to put archaeological sites under protection? Besides, it is incomprehensible that we have to look for the right balance between legal protection and the ideals of the Valletta Convention. This agreement explicitly binds the subscribers to create archaeological reserves. Furthermore, the risk of a constricted view of the landscape from the archaeological perspective does not exist. Quite the contrary, comprehensive solutions in terms of protection by development can be best created on the basis of a strong position. Finally, experiences with professional archaeological heritage protection by planning agencies, investors and administrative representatives lead to more acceptance and a better awareness of the existence and value of the archaeological heritage.

2. EXPLAIN, CLAIM AND ASSERT: THREE EXAMPLES FROM THE RHINELAND

It is evident what archaeological heritage protection has to do: explain, claim and assert rights. Three examples from the Rhineland show how successful, but at the same time constructive and integrating, forceful action in planning and approval procedures can be.

Fig. 1 Kranenburg: the ditches of the Alde Borg and the genesis of the planning.

2.1 First example: a building development in Kranenburg

When we received the plans for a new building area in the town of Kranenburg the name of an adjoining street, Alde Borg ('old castle'), indicated that we had a problem. The houses would be constructed on the site of the old castle that had formed the origin of Kranenburg 800 years ago (Fig. 1 bottom left). The ditches of the main castle and the bailey were clearly visible in an aerial photograph (Fig. 1 top). It was absolutely clear that this archaeological site had to be put under legal protection and should not be damaged by the intended use (Vollmer-König 2008).

The town's reaction was defensive because half of the planning area was affected. They did not believe that any archaeological substance was preserved. An archaeological survey was carried out to resolve their doubts. Ditches and post-holes of the ancient buildings in the trial trenches verified our prediction. It is very honourable that the township then realized the significance of the *Alde Borg* and looked seriously for a solution to the problem. The result is particularly encouraging. The archaeological site was put under legal protection and defined as a green space in the development plan. The building area now respected the protection zone (Fig. 1 bottom middle). In a further step the structure of the prospective development was adapted to the ancient ditch system. Now it surrounds the medieval site like a growth ring

(Fig. 1 bottom right). Finally, the historical ditches, hitherto not visible on the surface, will be carefully modulated. They will absorb the surface water of the surrounding development. Attractive information media will explain their structure and the history and relevance of the castle. A schematic partial reconstruction is planned so the *Alde Borg* can be better experienced.

What we got in the end is not only the preservation of a valuable archaeological site. Building in accordance with the natural situation and preserving the historical identity of the place created a special quality of living. The historical origins of Kranenburg have become a point of reference for modern development.

2.2   Second example: a dike reconstruction in Rees

The modern reconstruction of dikes almost always means totally rebuilding the old dike. Thus, when we had to appraise the planned reconstruction of the Rhine dike in the town of Rees, we knew the extent of the digging. In contrast it was unknown how far there would be relics of the historical fortification. Because a map from 1825 still showed most of its structure we had to anticipate finds and features. Therefore, archaeological procedures were indispensable. When the planning executive refused this claim we enforced the legal protection of the fortification against the opposition of the investor and the town. Because of the new judicial situation now the planning executive had to change its permission and the investor now had to ensure the archaeological support of the reconstruction. Unfortunately, this did not prevent the beginning of digging without accompanying archaeologists. This was immediately reported. The mechanical excavator had uncovered massive brickwork in the old dike. About 18 metres had already been destroyed before the building site was shut down (Fig. 2). The rest of the vault, about 33 metres long and 7.50 metres wide, was then professionally explored and documented. Historical maps made it clear that it had been a so-called *Bär* (bear), a building to control the water inflow from the Rhine into the moats (Wroblewski/Zeune 2002).

Fig. 2
Rees: the Bär after exposure (left) and conservation (right).

With its exposure we had a new problem. The dike reconstruction presupposed the destruction of the *Bär* which, as an important archaeological site, had necessarily to be preserved. Building stopped again, time was short, the contention about preservation or destruction was short but intensive. It was resolved by a change in the reconstruction planning. The trace of the new dike was displaced and the preservation of the *Bär* was secured. Now the wind had changed. The excavation of the fortification had caught the interest of the citizens of Rees. People realized the potential to make their town more attractive for tourism. The proposition to conserve the ruin and to present it within a concept was accepted (Fig. 2). Today the *Bär*, together with other parts of the fortification, forms part of a popular historical tour of the town. Following this episode, archaeological aspects in dike reconstruction procedures are now being continuously included.

2.3 Third example: a flood retention basin in Mönchengladbach

When we heard about the intended construction of a flood retention basin in the city of Mönchengladbach, the planning of the project had already been going on for more than 20 years without taking archaeology into account. Thus, the concept planning and the rough planning were ready, alternative locations had been checked, the environmental impact assessment concluded and the approval concept including the accompanying landscape conservation plan was finished. Even the planning approval procedure had been concluded without the obligatory participation of the archaeological heritage protection. The waterboard 'Niersverband' was waiting for the licence to begin the construction. After we had complained about the incorrect procedure, we received the plans for appraisal (Vollmer-König 2004).

We found out that there was an important Stone Age site in the central part of the basin in the water meadow of the River Niers. More than 12,000 artefacts had already come to light from here and another adjoining site. They spanned a period of c. 40,000 years from the Palaeolithic to the Neolithic. This time span covers the change from the Pleistocene to the Holocene, the change of landscape from the glacial tundra to complete afforestation, the replacement of Neanderthals by Homo Sapiens and the development from hunters and gatherers to farmers and stockbreeders. From a trial trench and pollen analyses we knew that in the subsoil there were the sediments and layers of the landscape development, almost completely preserved since the end of the Ice Age. Embedded in them were flint artefacts in several layers. The soil conditions were ideal for the conservation of organic archaeological finds and features, for pollen and other floral relics and also bones (Gerlach *et al.* 1999). We expected that this archaeological site would be much larger than the known finds from the surface suggested.

The basin with an extension of 1,600 by 300 metres was to be constructed by digging up almost the whole area and building a wall with deep foundations around it. We categorically refused the plans because their realization would have destroyed the archaeological site. To underline our position we invoked the legal protection of the area in which the surface finds had been made. To verify the assumed continuance of the site in the area of the basin, a geo-archaeological survey was commissioned by the investor. It attested, with 225 drill-holes and pollen analyses, that potential relevant layers existed in the subsoil of the whole basin (Meurers-Balke 1999).

What to do? Alternative locations did not exist. An approximate calculation of an archaeological excavation generated a demand of 5 years of fieldwork and 2.5 years of evaluation. The costs added up to 5.2 million euros. Influenced by these figures, the plan was readapted. The new construction did not need any digging and provided a bulkhead instead. The surrounding wall was now only intended to cover the above-ground part of the bulkhead and was to be placed on the actual surface. With this solution, the preservation of the archaeological site was ensured. Moreover, the new use of the area would even allow for better conservation of the archaeological site. While hitherto the site had been damaged by ploughing, now it was to be used as extensive grassland. Because the area was also subject to nature and water conservation, the construction was also a better solution for the local ecology.

Finally, we can say that the serious search for alternatives led to a solution that not only preserved the archaeological site and landscape, but resulted in no higher costs than the original construction would have caused. The expenses for planning and the procedure before the participation of archaeological heritage could have been avoided completely. So just one question remains, why not do it straight away?

3. CONCLUSION

What do these examples show? Surely the success only results from the forceful and competent use of all judicial possibilities in the procedures. Indispensable in all cases was legal protection that made it impossible to ignore the archaeological interests in planning, procedures and construction. Certainly, they also show that we do not have the time to wait for the creation of landscape management concepts or a change in thinking because the daily damage to archaeological sources would be much greater than it already is. Finally they attest that forceful, but at the same time concrete and calculable action, results in a better awareness of the archaeological values both by the public as well as in planning and approval procedures.

All in all, this subject makes clear that there are two spheres in archaeology with very little contact. On the one hand is the academic sphere, acting in basic research and creating models of managing monument conservation, and on the other is the administration sphere which has to manage sections of the cultural landscape dependent on the particular planning. It works in a narrow framework, limited by a lot of procedures and a lack of time. Intensive research as a basis for comprehensive heritage protection is normally not possible. At the same time the administration sphere often does not have any (immediate) access to new research results by other institutions. We therefore need better communication between academia and administration to utilize concepts and research results in a practical manner in everyday monument protection management.

NOTES

1   Rheinisches Amt für Bodendenkmalpflege, Bonn, Germany.

REFERENCES

Gerlach, R./M. Heinen/B. Kopecky/M. Vollmer-König, 1999: Eine Herausforderung: Der mesolithische Fundplatz Geneicken, *Archäologie im Rheinland 1998*, Köln, 35-38.

Meurers-Balke, J., 1999: Die Pollenanalyse als Instrument zur Datierung von Auenablagerungen, *Archäologie im Rheinland 1998*, Köln, 145-149.

Vollmer-König, M., 2004: *Das archäologische Kulturgut in zwei wasserrechtlichen Verfahren am Beispiel Mönchengladbach-Geneicken*, Hamm (UVP-Report 18 (2 + 3)), 116-119.

Vollmer-König, M., 2008: Schützen, pflegen, sinnvoll nutzen - Bodendenkmalpflege und Planung, *Archäologie im Rheinland 2007*, Stuttgart, 29-31.

Wroblewski, J.-H./J. Zeune, 2003: 'Dem Feind die "Bärenkrallen" gezeigt' - die Festungsruine in Rees, *Archäologie im Rheinland 2002*, Stuttgart, 165-166.

VI

SYNTHESIS AND CONCLUSIONS

Bathmen (NL): locals and experts on plaggen soils. *Photo: L.J. Keunen.*

VI. Synthesis and conclusions
What have we learnt?

Tom (J.H.F.) Bloemers[1], Henk Kars[2] & Arnold van der Valk[3]

ABSTRACT

The synthesis and conclusions follow the thematic structure of the previous sections based on the interaction between knowledge, policy, imagination and practice (see Ch. I, 13 and Fig. 7 and sections III-V). In the synthesis the conditions, focus and characteristics of the interaction and the components of knowledge creation will be considered, mainly based on the PDL/BBO results and experiences. The conclusions deal with the value for the various groups of users of the relevant knowledge acquired by the PDL/BBO programme and combine this with the contributions from Europe to identify the factors influencing success and failures and to present the 'lessons'.

In the synthesis (section 2) we take into consideration the actors and users that embody the knowledge supply-demand relationship within research and between research, policy and practice. Woven into the texture of the synthesis is the understanding of the knowledge creation process as defined by Weggeman. For its various components the key notions resulting from the PDL/BBO programme are presented in catchwords in Fig. 1-4. The most relevant acquired knowledge covers the interpretative heritage approach, the best practice for the application of the biography concept and action research, the potential abilities that are already available but have to be adapted and new ones that have to be developed, and the need for a community of practice.

In the concluding section 3 we will assess the value of the PDL/BBO programme for the various user groups. Together with the contributions from Europe the factors are identified that influence success and failures of integrative landscape heritage research and management and create opportunities and threats. Finally the 'lessons learned' are presented to cope with the cultural landscape and heritage paradox and the knowledge-action nexus. In the present phase of transition from site- towards landscape-oriented approach, the region is the proper scale and entity to link knowledge and action and to develop, test and apply the integrative action research methodology. Imagination can be fully exploited when it is framed in the duality of super- and infrastructure and democratic legitimation. This can create the conditions for co-operation resulting in a community of practice for cultural planning, but it should be supported by various forms of interpretative reflection. The well-balanced combination of thematic c.q. problem-oriented and regionally oriented studies has proven to be a fruitful balance of depth and breadth of approaches.

KEY WORDS

Synthesis, specific knowledge creation; 'lessons learned', region, legitimation, community of practice

1. INTRODUCTION

Research activities in the field of cultural landscape heritage and management as presented in the sections before have often been stimulated and legitimated by the Valletta Convention (Valletta 1992) and the European Landscape Convention (Florence 2000). In turn the initiation and acceptance of these conventions reflect the growing awareness in the late 1980s and 90s among researchers and policy-makers of the need for anticipatory and integrative approaches of landscape transformation. The core issue now is what progress we have made in achieving the goals and ideas represented by these conventions and other formal statements on landscape planning and integrative research policy.

This year the Council of Europe will celebrate the tenth anniversary of the European Landscape Convention. In 2012 it will be twenty years since the Valletta Convention was signed by the European member states. For both policies the time is coming to reflect upon past progress and present results. This should be done on the European level, but first of all on the national because the member states are the ones who committed themselves to implementing these conventions. In the Netherlands, as one of the European 'laboratories' mentioned in the introduction to this book (Ch. I, 5), during the last decade the Belvedere policy has given the main and formal impetus towards the implementation of the Landscape Convention. In 2007, after ten years of consultation and debate, a new heritage law was passed which legitimated the implementation of the Valletta Convention (Wamz 2007). In 2009 a detailed heritage review of the state of the archaeological-historical heritage in the Netherlands was published (Beukers 2009).

On the threshold of the next decade we see the immense changes in the roles of institutions and the struggle to implement the new ways forward. In light of these developments, our synthesis and conclusions should make a useful contribution towards their consolidation. The synthesis and conclusions follow the thematic structure of the previous sections based on the interaction between knowledge, policy, imagination and practice (see Ch. I, 13 and Fig. 7 and sections III-V). In the synthesis the conditions, focus and characteristics of the interaction and the components of knowledge creation will be considered, mainly based on the PDL/BBO results and experiences. In the conclusions we deal with the value of the two PDL/BBO concepts and the value for the various groups of users of the relevant knowledge acquired by the PDL/BBO programme. Together with the contributions from Europe we finally identify the factors influencing success and failures of integrative landscape heritage research and management and present the 'lessons learned' to cope with the cultural landscape heritage paradox and the knowledge-action nexus.

2. SYNTHESIS: $K=f(I.EVA)$

In the synthesis mainly based on the PDL/BBO results and experiences we take into consideration the actors and users that embody the knowledge supply-demand relationship as indicated by the internal and external levels of integration (Van der Valk in chapter II.2) representing this relationship within research and between research, policy and practice. Woven into the texture of the synthesis is the understanding of knowledge (K) as "the partially unconscious capacity that is represented by the metaphoric function of Information (I), Experience (E), Ability (V in Dutch: *vaardigheden*) and Attitude (A) of someone" (Weggeman 2001[2], 28-41 and expressed in the 'formula' $K=f(I.EVA)$. Weggeman defines the various components of the knowledge creation process as follows:

- information is meaning given to observed data, i.e. symbolic representations of quantities, facts and opinions;
- experience is the set of events a person has seen during his/her life;
- abilities have two forms: "exogenous" abilities of external communication and expression and "endogenous" or 'cerebral' abilities being analysis, intuition, imagination and reflection;

- attitude is the set of basic beliefs framing values and norms.

This results in the sorting out of crucial insights for the knowledge-action nexus stemming form the PDL/BBO programme and European research presented in this book. The insights formulated in catchwords are grouped in Fig. 1-4. They are selected by the editors of the sections III-V covering the themes linking knowledge-action, imagination: facts and constructions and sharing knowledge: stories, maps and designs. The authors of the various contributions to these sections might select different aspects.

2.1 The interaction between knowledge, policy, imagination and practice: conditions, focus and characteristics

The thematic structure of the previous sections has been derived from the types of action that characterize the interaction between knowledge, policy, imagination and practice (Fig. 1; see also Ch. I, 13 and Fig. 7):
- the relationship between research, policy and public as expressed by 'knowledge and action' about landscape and transformation (section III);
- the interaction between research and design focusing on the role of facts and constructions in imagination of the past and the future (section IV);
- the sharing of knowledge and experiences stemming from this interaction which is generally mediated by stories, maps and designs to share them with all actors (section V).

Reflecting upon the papers contributing to these themes of action and the introductory commentaries, we have identified and schematically presented the following conditions that determined the approach and its outcomes and some specific characteristics or issues of the actions involved that we are confronted with. The arrangement of the key notions reflects their importance for the specific theme of action but by definition their relevance is not limited to one of them. Because of the interaction between knowledge, policy, imagination and practice as conceptualized here and the integrative research approach many key notions are also relevant to the other types of actions depending on the type of study involved.

For the clarity of the analysis there is no need to comment on most of the key notions since this has already been done in the introductions to the three types of action (section III-V). Only one important issue still has to be clarified, the so-called gap between the sciences and social sciences and humanities discussed in the introduction to section III on the knowledge-action nexus. In discussing this topic, Kars

Type of action	III knowledge-action	IV imagination	V sharing knowledge
Conditions	• action research methodology - quality - situational	• constructivistic approach • truth-justness = science-policy	• unifying concepts • open mind • shared ideals and methods • understanding relation research-planning
Focus	• sustainable development • various landscape views/definitions: an asset	• authenticity, identity • reflection	• joint learning and exploring
Characteristic	• knowledge-action chain linking research-society • sciences v. social sciences /humanities: compatible in common relevant social problem	• recognizing perception and meaning, exploiting creativity • respecting facts and constructions	• knowledge: production, communication, sharing

Fig. 1 Conditions, focus and characteristics of the three types of action (section III-V).

Type of action	III *knowledge-action*	IV *imagination*	V *sharing knowledge*
Information (I)	• culture and nature: (re)in-interpretation available data • degradation: new physical data	• critical views on available data/existing practices	• predictive modelling: critical methodology • prospection: integration of techniques and data
charged by the 'central concepts'			
• cultural biography	• region as cultural-historic meaningful entity/scale	• geographic context • super-/infrastructure	
• action research	• situational • real time	• conservation through development • historic landscape characterisation	• joint learning • boundary work • uncertainty management

Fig. 2
Types of action: concepts giving meaning to the data resulting in information (I) related to specific issues.

states that Jones' contribution "via the use of the concept 'materiality' 'might be helpful in understanding the problem from a philosophy of science viewpoint but is not solving it." (Kars Ch. III.1, 70). If so, the relationship between the sciences and social sciences and humanities still has to be described in the context of interdisciplinary research: is it existent in one way or another or non-existent? We will try to present a way forward in section 3.2 (p. 511-512).

2.2 The interaction between knowledge, policy, imagination and practice: components of knowledge creation

Components of knowledge creation

Applying the interpretation of knowledge creation described above, we analyse the way in which researchers have approached the different components of this process (Fig. 2).

To create information researchers from the PDL/BBO programme used both already available data and completely new data collected for the purpose of the research. Existing data were either reinterpreted by applying different theories or concepts from those applied before or the methodology of the research procedure and the use of the results were critically reviewed and upgraded. On the one hand the result has been new information about a variety of aspects concerning the cultural-historic landscape and the management of its heritage. On the other hand, we have now learned from practice the ways in which the concept of biography of landscape can be applied and how action research focused on the cultural-historical landscape issue can be implemented and which aspects are crucial for success. The combination of thematic and problem-oriented studies with regionally oriented programmes has produced diverse and detailed results on a variety of important issues.

Assessing the Experiences (E) and Abilities (V) of the knowledge creation process, it becomes clear that landscape research and management cover a very wide spectrum of these two components that can support and strengthen each other, such as narratives and 3D landscape visualization (Ch. IV.7). However, it is not always necessary for them to be relevant to each other, they can also operate independently as in science-based degradation research (Ch. III.6). Sometimes they also raise contradictions or might even be incompatible. Not everyone trusts the approach of interactive or communicative heritage planning and prefers to follow the way of legal action (Ch. V.9). The variety of experiences and abilities can be deduced from the introductory chapters of the three sections and they are too numerous to be considered here.

Fig. 3
Types of action: critical attitude (A) related to specific issues.

Type of action	III knowledge-action	IV imagination	V sharing knowledge
Attitude (A)	• participatory • inter-/transdisciplinarity • heritage management oriented	• self-/heteroreference • reactivity	• congruency

It is stated here that the last knowledge component, Attitude (Fig. 3), is probably the most important factor influencing successful integrative knowledge creation because it is about people and first of all about researchers, although it also concerns the wider group of professionals in policy and practice. The basic engagement with the historic environment and the management of its transformation in a committed and accountable way result in a fruitful interaction between research, policy, practice and public. The interests of many members of these actor groups can for various reasons be triggered by the combination of landscape and history, even when they do not often allow themselves to admit this. This is why the historic landscape is a platform that opens the way towards the solution of potential conflicts of interest in the sense of the Belvedere motto 'conservation through development'. The participatory approach towards the local or regional society is a well proven way to create public engagement and exploit valuable lay knowledge. Interactive or communicative heritage planning can create the conditions for the implementation of the 'conservation through development' concept but it needs a congruency of meanings as has been concluded from the case studies of the development schemes in Arnhem, Elst and Nijmegen (De Zwart Ch. V.7). However, to obtain the required attitude the members of the research and professional groups, especially those belonging to the cultural-historic one, have to reflect about their own domain, the existing paradigms and the interaction between policy and society. This is where issues like self- and hetero-reference and reactivity come in, as has been discussed by Van Assche (Ch IV.5) and Ickerodt (Ch. IV.11) and this is a very delicate and complex topic because of the effects on existing institutional structures and balances of power.

Synthesis

Now we can synthesize the knowledge and insights acquired from the three types of action (section III-IV) that characterize the interaction between knowledge, policy, imagination and practice based on the previous steps of analysis. This acquired knowledge (Fig. 4) comprises knowledge specifically related to the three themes of action as schematically represented below. In addition the acquired knowledge and insights relevant for all three actions has been presented.

The insight that the duality of region and place is of great importance for the knowledge-action chain of integrative research (section III) might at first glance seem to be self-evident. To some degree this is true, since the awareness of the crucial role of the region for integrative research was present before the start of the PDL/BBO programme leading to the decision to give the regional approach a central place in the programme. However, the assumption of its relevance has now been 'tested' and approved not only by Dutch research, but also by the international contributions showing its application in the wider European context. The region, however exactly defined, is the scale and entity of effective interaction between research, policy, imagination and practice for three reasons. First the region is the scale where people can experience the 'power of place' in all its dimensions of daily life, of political action, of the cultural and natural environment, of perception and emotion confronting them with the past origins

Type of Action	III *knowledge-action*	IV *imagination*	V *sharing knowledge*

Acquired Knowledge (K)	• region: 'power of place' (*Handlungsraum*)
	  - cultural-historic meaningful entity/scale
	  - local knowledge
		• 'embedded' imagination
		  - truth-justness-truthfulness
		  - infrastructure
		  - historic landscape characterisation
			• boundary work
			  - framing signs and signification
			  - story telling
			  - legal framing

	General • interpretative heritage approach • best practice for the application of the biography concept and action research • abilities: already available, to be adapted and new to develop • community of practice		

Fig. 4
Types of action: acquired knowledge (K).

and roots and with perspectives on the presence and the future. The cultural landscape creates a space for action (*Handlungsraum*) in the present that links the future with the past in a meaningful way and that links up with the concept of regional governance (Fürst *et al.* 2008, 11-17). It is here that plans about actual and future land use are made and discussions are held leading towards decisions about changes. Historic landscape research has convincingly shown that in the past the region has also been a meaningful scale for understanding the way communities function, although in a long-term perspective the size and use have varied from the past to the present. It is here that local lay and expert knowledge can meet and interact in a fruitful way as has been shown in the Drentsche Aa programme.

The insight that imagination (section IV) is another crucial asset for integrative research and action is also not very surprising when one considers the strong focus since its inception in 1999 by the Dutch Belvedere policy on urban and landscape design. The decision to give the biography of landscape concept a central role in the PDL/BBO programme is another illustration of the early awareness of the 'power of imagination'. The added value from our research is, however, the clear recognition that the use of this powerful capacity has to be embedded in a conceptual framework for its interaction with research, practice and actors. The products of imagination, be it a scientific interpretation stemming from a hypothesis, a political statement, a feature or story of the biography of landscape or a landscape design, have to be validated in the epistemological sense. The frame of reference for it is the tripartite series of true, just or truthful statements as has been adapted for a theory of landscape experience by Jacobs (Jacobs 2006, 9-12). The biography of landscape concept as a product of imagination can be considered as superstructure with a malleable character that must be founded on an methodological infrastructure as a source for the chosen narrative. The Historic Landscape Characterisation approach can be considered as such an infrastructure that frames the biography.

The third insight is about the value and constraints of boundary work linking knowledge and policy (section V) as consequence of the decision and need for integrative research approaches (see Van der Valk Ch. II.2 section 5). A fruitful approach to integrative action research is founded on interaction based on dialogue and convergence. The interpretation and valuation of the meaning of words and notions by partners on both sides of the boundary is crucial. These meanings are modelled, 'framed', by the world of ideas and norms held by the various partners and when they are unaware of it this might easily lead to serious misunderstandings (Van Assche 2004, 18-21; De Zwart Ch. V.7). Storytelling, the biography of landscape as narrative, might help create a sphere of understanding, trust and engagement, but needs to be founded on a clear and accountable infrastructure as exemplified in this volume. Maps and designs can easily be misinterpreted without the intention of manipulating them. It must be stressed that the interactive and communicative approach with its democratic engagement as expressed by the change from government towards governance must be legitimated by public laws and regulations to formalize the role of the representatives, professionals and lay people involved with the historic environment and strengthen their position amid conflicting interests. The instruments of heritage or planning law have to be used carefully and not frivolously since they can sharpen tensions considerably with unexpected outcomes and loss of credibility. Legal regulations and rules of professional best practices can contribute to the conditions for effective boundary work.

Finally for all three types of action the following acquired insights derived from the PDL/BBO experience are relevant.
- The naming and description of an interpretative heritage approach which by the potential coverage of its fields of attention reflects the capacity for self- and hetero-reference and reactivity about the position of the heritage domain within research and society. Eventually this will lead to formulation of an ethics on landscape research and heritage management.
- The experience with landscape action research and the use of the biography of landscape concept has resulted in the facilitation of the internal and external integration and a specification of integrative methodology for the context of archaeological-historical landscape.
- Abilities to practice integrative research and heritage management can be strengthened and developed in two ways. Many methods and techniques are already available and have only to be adapted, integrated or focused on the specific problem (for example historic anthropology and ecology, predictive modelling, EIA and 3D visualization). It means that considerable progress can be made with small investments and in a short time. For specific important fields of research and heritage management new methods and techniques have to be developed or structurally adapted for the specific problem as in geo- or bioarchaeological sciences and economic valuation using for example Social Cost/Benefit Analysis. This, however, requires substantial investments and time before they are ready for daily practice.
- A community of practice covering research, policy, practice and public on different scales ranging from the local to the European level is easily created in the digital age by linking networks. Such multi networks facilitate the exchange of information and joint learning in order to capitalize on the knowledge-action bond.

3. CONCLUSIONS

In this concluding section we will assess the value of the two concepts adopted for guiding the PDL/BBO programme and what value the acquired knowledge and insights have had for the various user groups. Of general relevance for the Dutch and European level are the factors that influence the success or failure of integrative landscape heritage research and management and create opportunities and threats.

3.1 *The value of the two PDL/BBO concepts: biography of landscape and action research*
Fundamental for the implementation of the PDL/BBO programme has been the role of the two main concepts formulated before the start of the programme to facilitate the integrative ambitions and as guiding

points of reference: the biography of landscape as a metaphor and action research as a methodology. By opting for these concepts it has been assumed that they would substantially contribute to the implementation of the integrative ambition but it was also clear from the beginning that it would be necessary to develop ways of applying them in the practice of the specific setting of landscape heritage research and management. They were concepts that had to be shaped as instruments for landscape research and management while this research was underway.

As stated in the introductory chapter (Ch. I section 2.3), landscape can be considered as a way-of-looking. From the rich series of studies presented in this volume it is clear that there are many ways-of-looking at landscape. Accepting the definition of landscape formulated by the European Landscape Convention, "'Landscape' means an area, as perceived by people, whose character is the result of the action and interaction of natural and/or human factors", various meanings can be given to its use and various weights can be attributed to its components and the role of people depending on disciplinary or professional approaches towards a type of research or policy problem (see e.g. Elerie/Spek Ch. III.2 section 3.1). Common to all views is that the human observer is an integral part of the landscape that he/she observes, landscape is people's life world (Ingold 2000, 209; Meier 2009, 703-706).

The two central concepts of the PDL/BBO programme represent such a way of looking, deliberately chosen and consistently applied to develop them for practice and to learn about their effectiveness for integrative landscape research and management. It has been shown by practice that there is a variety of ways in which the biography of landscape as a geographical line (Van Beek *et al.* 2008, 180) has been used in the four regional case studies. From the four potential context-given ways of use described by Van Londen (Van Beek *et al.* 2008, 184) namely, planning, communication, research and valorization, a changing mix reflects the factual implementation in the regional programmes. The context for communication and research is frequent which seems to be logical since the decision for this form is in the hands of the group of researchers involved and their partners and the effects of its use are more in the sphere of engagement and raising interest than in direct decision-making. The use in planning and valorization has a more formal character, the effects can have policy consequences and as a result one might be more reluctant to apply the concept. In this context the biography concept has also shown its value for policy practice, as exemplified in the eastern Netherlands by its integration in the Landscape Development Plan exploiting the old name Berlewalde as a metaphor for regional landscape identity (Baas/Groenewoudt/Raap in press).

The action research approach has been fully applied in at least six of the eleven programmes and projects of the PDL/BBO programme following the criteria as summed up by Kars in his introduction to section III (Ch. III.1, 74-75; Reason/Bradbury 2001). Apart from the research on predictive modelling and hunter-gatherer landscapes, all the four regional programmes followed the action research model almost by definition because of their integrative aims. The power of action research lies in the situatedness of research and the embeddedness of the data in a specific context. This creates a direct feedback between research and application in a specific landscape planning or management context and opens the way for community-based engagement. The Drentsch Aa programme might be the finest example of this methodology and demonstrates that the union between qualified expert and engaged local inhabitant as personified by Hans Elerie is an extremely favourable condition. In general, however, the present state is that initiatives for integrative regional landscape heritage planning programmes come from regional or provincial authorities and, at least in the Netherlands, their realization is often contracted out to private consultancy companies. To supplement this top-down way of working with a bottom-up basis it is recommended that an additional aim of these programmes should be to establish a local expert group or centre to secure continuity and follow up the programme on a voluntary basis after its formal end.

3.2 The value of relevant acquired knowledge for the various groups of users

Relevant acquired knowledge is divided into general and specific knowledge. The user groups are those engaged in the internal cultural historical integration, in the external interdisciplinary integration and in the wider external integration with policy and public (Ch. II.2 Fig. 4). This primarily affects those in the Netherlands because of the specific focus of the PDL/BBO programme but also similar groups in Europe since the knowledge acquired in projects comparable to the Dutch context is relevant to all of them.

General knowledge relevant to all user groups includes the scientific and professional notions, methods and techniques for applied integrative research and the policy concepts for research, development and management of visible and invisible archaeological-historical landscape presented in the previous chapters. It encompasses, among other things, the forms of conducting integrative research, the development of a common language and the reflection about roles, framing and meanings as part of communication processes. For policy and practice, the empirical basis of collected cultural landscape data is very valuable for all cases where concrete information is necessary. However, it has been shown that the use of this knowledge very much depends on the compatibility of views between research and policy (Ch. II.2, 30-31 and Fig. 3). For research, this basis can be important for the development of grounded theories that can be tested and validated (Glaser/Strauss 1967). The best practice approach has created another type of empirical knowledge which, however, has often not been documented but stored in the minds and memories of the researchers and their partners. It would be wise to make this tacit knowledge explicit and to integrate it in heritage handbooks.

Three issues appear to be relevant in the context of acquired specific knowledge and insights about integrative research namely, collaboration between the sciences and the social sciences and humanities, interaction between cultural history and the design disciplines and the diversity of the regional programmes.

The first and most basic one has to do with collaboration in integrative research between the natural and physical sciences on the one hand and the social sciences and humanities on the other. For a long time during the PDL/BBO programme a feeling prevailed that there was a serious divide between them because of the value of the positivistic and objective research methodology for science and the constructive and subjective methodology for the social sciences and humanities. Gradually it became clear that this was an important issue that could not be neglected, although it was not taken for granted that it could be solved in an acceptable way. Kars has stated in his introductory chapter III.1 that the strength of the argument about materiality as a form of rapprochement between sciences and social sciences and humanities is not convincing. As a consequence another line of argumentation to bridge the gap is presented here based on the experiences and best practice of the PDL/BBO programme.

It is recognized that every domain of disciplines has its own paradigms, theories and methodologies and that they have to be respected simply because these domains function that way, satisfying the ambitions and producing 'justifiable' knowledge and beliefs. However, in the context of integrative action research the three scientific domains meet each other in the context of a research problem that reflects the demands from society and the curiosity of the researcher. The decision to select this type of problem and approach is the result of the negotiation between the demand and supply side, satisfying more or less the paradigms of the partners. The context of action research determines the formulation of the research problem influencing the selection of appropriate methods and techniques and resulting in data and analyses that are valuable for the 'action' partner. The action context neither influences the validity of the scientific theory and methodology nor the justification of the acquired knowledge. In the situation that science researchers collaborate with the social sciences or humanities researchers in an integrative action research programme, all participating disciplinary domains have to maintain their own standards, but the common negotiated research problem forces them to integrate data and analysis. They have to aim for integrated knowledge, which is justifiable within the context of an integrative paradigm and will consequently be of a different kind from mono- or multidisciplinary research.

The interaction between cultural history and the design disciplines is another problem of interdisciplinarity. During the PDL/BBO programme it gradually became clear that the approach towards the design disciplines would fail since after two calls for proposals no qualifying research projects were proposed. It was assumed that this had to do with the absence of a research tradition in that domain that could be linked with the domains and their procedures represented in the Netherlands Organization for Scientific Research. This explanation might still be valid but the problem seems to be more fundamental. Recently, landscape ecology science has recognized that it has to strengthen its effectiveness in transferring knowledge to society. By extending the pattern-process paradigm with a third party design, an analytic framework based on the concept of knowledge innovation is developed. In applying this framework in two case studies, design functioned as a boundary concept between science and practice (Nassauer/Opdam 2008). This resembles the use of design in the Belvedere policy and leads towards a reinterpretation of the background for the failure for participation of the design disciplines within the PDL/BBO programme. At that time, about 2000, there was no paradigmatic condition favouring the collaborative research between the archaeological-historical domain and the design disciplines. This situation has changed now, as can be illustrated by the Belvedere chair for design at Delft University (Cerutti 2008, 8), the impressive results of the Drentsche Aa Landscape Vision (Novioconsult/Strootman Landschapsarchitecten 2004) and similar projects related to the PDL/BBO regional programmes (Ch. I. Fig. 6).

In particular the series of four regional integrative programmes illustrates as a whole the diversity of archaeological-historical landscapes, regional environmental challenges, planning policies and the approaches influencing the form the programmes have taken. The Drentsch Aa, Oer-IJ and southern Netherlands could all start from a thorough knowledge about the long-term history and character of their heritage, while the eastern Netherlands programme started in a reputedly limitedly known region. The planning in the Drentsche Aa was focused on the nature-culture development in a low dynamic area, while the Oer-IJ is situated in a high dynamic metropolitan wetland area. The eastern and southern Netherlands show great overall similarities as archaeological-historical landscapes, but in various stages of spatial development. The former still mainly shows an agricultural character on the edge of urban expansion while the latter experienced this expansion and industrialization during the past three or four decades. Consequently, the four regional programmes show considerable differences in integrative character as do the outcomes, a diverse result that was originally aimed for when formulating the PDL/BBO programme.

The combination of regional integrative programmes has also yielded unexpected insights in a methodological sense related to the ways of interaction. For example, in the Drentsche Aa the integrative research followed a pragmatic phasing from an interdisciplinary start-up via a multidisciplinary research phase ending in an interdisciplinary final phase. In the Oer-IJ it has been concluded that the interaction between knowledge and policy shifts, depending on the type and timing of an action, through various relationships, as equal partners in a dialogue or not. It also appeared that the shift in the role of the action researcher from analytical observer to participating actor sometimes caused confusion. A striking and valuable observation has been that real integrative interaction was especially successful in what have been called 'unconventional' activities like special programmes on cultural planning on the fringe of 'conventional' sectors. All programmes were confronted in one way or another with the problem of the 'real' time of the research cycle and the policy cycle, which were not and could not be synchronized. Synchronization was impossible since the two cycles started at different points in time that were dependent on the actions of two completely unrelated authorities, the Netherlands Organization for Scientific Research and the relevant Provincial authority. The solution was found in more flexibility and a longer factual duration of the research programmes covering almost eight years instead of the planned four to five, that is two policy cycles. In this way, the chance increased that windows of opportunity for integrative actions were opened during the 'real' time processes in the research and policy cycles, in this way transforming 'real' time into what is called 'kairos' time (Dunne 1993, 355; De Jonge 2009, 34-37).

3.3 *Factors influencing successes and failures of integrative landscape heritage research and management*

We will now look back at the PDL/BBO programme, taking into consideration its Dutch context characterized by the national Belvedere policy and also the European contributions to this volume taking into account their European context characterized by the European Landscape Convention. To structure this we use a SWOT model to sort out the relevant observations and value them from a strategic perspective. A SWOT model encompasses the strengths, weaknesses, opportunities and threats of an organization, where the first pair of concepts focuses on the internal aspects and the second on the external ones. In our case the issue is the research of the historic environment and its management given its socio-political context and the ambition of the domain of researchers to contribute to the sustainable development of the historic environment by linking knowledge and action (Jain/Triandis 1997, 253). The perspective is strategic because, as stated in section 1, after a decade or more of activity by the actors in the national and European heritage domain it is crucial to demonstrate what progress has been made to the actors, especially those affected by the external integration of research, policy and public. What can be learned from all these activities and could or should be the way forward? The decade 2010-2020 lying ahead of us will certainly be characterized by some form of consolidation if things go well, or failure if not.

In the following discussion the observations are presented for each type of action but only discussed in detail when necessary. In many cases the argument has already been presented in this chapter, in the introductory chapters to the three sections (III-V) or the individual contributions. The underlined observation covers the issue of the historic environment and its management in general.

Type of action	III *knowledge-action*	IV *imagination*	V *sharing knowledge*
Strength	• linking science and heritage • action research=participatory • region as *Handlungsraum*	• narrative and visualisation	• joint learning • open mind
	General • landscape as a way-of-looking creates a platform and focus for integrative research and action resulting in a 'community of practice'.		

Fig. 5
Types of action: strengths.

Strengths (Fig. 5)

The field has a range of strong assets that it is exploiting in different ways and which have to be strengthened to make the most of it. A basic condition to realize this is the idea of landscape as a way of looking which creates a platform and focus for integrative research and action. The outcome aimed for should be the community of practice on various levels from local to European.

Weaknesses (Fig. 6)

Some of the weaknesses of an action type are of general value. The integration between science, social sciences and humanities is problematic. The problem of synchronization of the sequences of research and planning is present overall, but especially so when basic research is involved in the case of a serious lack of data. This has been the case not only in the eastern Netherlands programme but it also applies to the basic research on the degradation of archaeological sites. The other weakness is the lack of effectiveness of planning and design activities. Much of it must for various reasons remain desk top products with no or limited effects in practice. Apart from that, the manifold commissioners and contractors involved in spatial construction represent as many risks for misinterpretation or reducing the core idea behind the original plan or design.

In general it can be stated that knowledge among landscape researchers and heritage professionals about the interaction between research, policy and public is very limited. In combination with a limited capacity for a balanced self- and heteroreference this seriously weakens the position of the field regarding its own organization, priorities and socio-political acceptance.

Opportunities (Fig. 7)

The specific type of action related to imagination is of general value in terms of the external opportunities. There is an overall need in planning for strengthening spatial quality expressed by issues like

Type of action	III *knowledge-action*	IV *imagination*	V *sharing knowledge*

Weakness	• real time: incompatible time
	sequences of research and
	planning
		• Real vs. virtual complexity:
		  manipulation
		• cultural history and design:
		  'living apart together'
		• lack of effectiveness of
		  planning and design
			• limited experience in
			  inter-/transdisciplinarity
			• lack of knowledge of
			  framing and power
			• communication

	General • integration between sciences and social sciences and humanities • synchronisation of planned vs. real time • effectiveness of plans and actions • balance between self-/heteroreference • balance between thruth vs. justness founded in truthfulness (*Jacobs 2006*)		

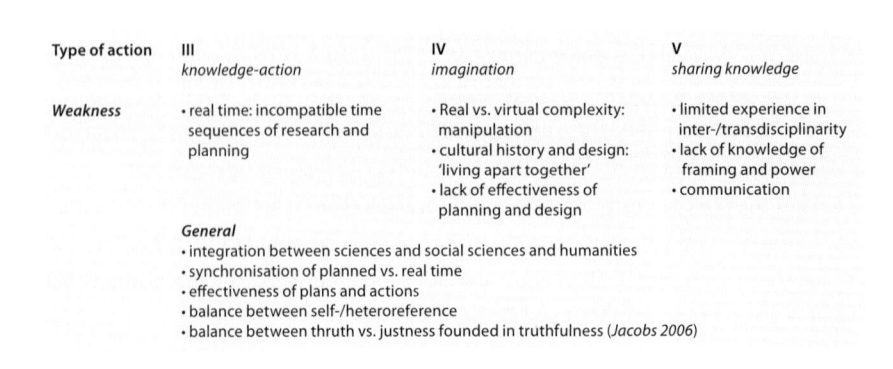

Fig. 6
Types of action: weaknesses.

Fig. 7
Types of action: opportunities.

Type of action	III knowledge-action	IV imagination	V sharing knowledge
Opportunity	• going along with planning	• design as way towards effective practice	
	General • opening towards design disciplines in policy and paradigm • research policy aiming for integrative research • from government to (regional) governance supported by informed action		

sustainability, cohesion, diversity and identity. Cultural history can contribute to this demand in a very meaningful and appealing way. Landscape and urban design have a high potential to play an intermediary role between cultural history and planning because of the ability to translate knowledge into imagination and plans into practice. The Belvedere policy has prepared the window of opportunity and, paradigmatically, an opening has been made.

Two general trends offer excellent opportunities for all types of action. In research policy interdisciplinary and socially relevant approaches are strongly favoured. The expectation is that in this way innovation is fostered and major social issues like social cohesion and mobility, economic development, natural diversity and environmental challenges can be handled in a sustainable way. A more or less parallel development is the gradual move from top-down government towards a more regionally and locally based form of governance. This fits perfectly with many of the strengths described above.

Threats (Fig. 8)

All sorts of threats ranged under the various types of action have a more general value. The trend towards further professionalization of the heritage sector exemplified by the commercialization of the archaeological profession in some European countries might, temporarily, be in contrast with the tendency towards decentralization and governance stimulating democratic interaction. The focus on perception and meaning of cultural values fitting into a post-modern view on subjectivity should be embedded in scientific and institutional structures to prevent *laissez faire* behaviour. While respecting the importance of new forms of interactive and communicative planning supporting the conservation by development concept, it should never be forgotten that heritage legislation and regulation are crucial for the heritage domain to be considered as a serious and formal partner in the power play of interests.

There is probably only one general really serious threat that the landscape heritage domain has to face, namely that it does not recognize the opportunities policy and society offers in a timely manner or does not come up with the proper answers to their demands and needs at the right moment. This can

Fig. 8
Types of action: threats.

Type of action	III knowledge-action	IV imagination	V sharing knowledge
Threat		• professionalization vs. democratization	• post-modernity: 'anything goes' • neglect/weakening of legal and formal regulations
		General • Research and education do not recognize timely the opportunities arising from demands and interests of policy and public	

be the case if dominant paradigms do not allow the development of new ideas or frustrate the careers of talented and unconventional professionals.

A final aspect of the strategic value of this analysis is the focus on the management of knowledge as presented and discussed in the next section (VIII). By this is meant the focus on the basic research aim, creating new integrative knowledge and insights within the proposed topic and its ambitions, in our case of integrative research. Some of the recommendations resulting from this section are already mentioned here, namely special attention on leadership and co-ordination, external communication and adequate training. The effect should be to get more value for the invested creativity and money.

3.4. Lessons learned from PDL/BBO and its European context
From the analysis of the previous synthesis and concluding discussion we are now able to abstract some final observations that can be considered as lessons learned with an overall value for integrative research in the field of landscape heritage and management. They cover general trends, relevant theories, methods and concepts, the implementation in the specific context of the knowledge-action nexus and the opportunities available.

A clear overall trend can be observed in European landscape research and policy where attention shifts from a site or object-focused and mono- or multidisciplinary cultural historical approach towards landscape and ensemble-focused integrative, inter- and transdisciplinary approaches. The contributions in this volume not only exemplify this trend, but above all show how the comprehensive landscape focus can be deepened and implemented in theory and practice and what new perspectives for future research and policy become visible (see Fig. 1). A decade or more after the conceptualization of the Belvedere policy in the Netherlands and the European Landscape Convention in Europe we have moved from ambitions towards practice and learning by 'doing landscape'. We now have hands on experience of how to cope with the knowledge-action nexus while at the same time exploring and exploiting the action research methodology and the power of place for action. In this way the insights and experiences presented here will hopefully appear to be a milestone in the transformation of the conceptualization and practice of landscape heritage research and management from the twentieth into the twenty-first century.

It is crucial for assessing its full meaning and importance to recognize that European landscape research and policy by its comprehensive character has two dimensions in which researchers and practitioners can operate and that determine its potential. First is the generic dimension covering aspects and issues that it shares with other themes like climate change or health, such as the knowledge-action nexus, the management of knowledge and the divide between disciplines and sectors. The second dimension is related to the specific characteristics of landscape as people's life world as a theme in its own right. These include the cultural-historical environment, the complex interaction between place and time and people's perception and behaviour and the ways of acquiring and assessing knowledge, all of which have their specific forms of manifestation and conceptualization. These two dimensions condition the process of knowledge creation about landscape research and policy. In the PDL/BBO programme the input of concepts, experiences (E) and abilities (V) derived from theory has been combined with the programmatically postulated outward-oriented attitude (A). The application in practice aiming at the integrative approach has produced a variety of experiences and results about the factors and limitations that influence results, successes and failures (Fig. 2-3).

Basic knowledge has been acquired how to operate in the field of interaction between knowledge, policy and imagination centred around the public (see Ch. I Fig. 7), which in the long run might result in the formation of a community of practice. As results in the form of acquired knowledge (K) (Fig. 4) we have gained insights of general value for the European scale and of specific relevance to the PDL/BBO programme.
Of general value are:
- The confirmation that in the present phase of transition from site or object-centred towards landscape-oriented approach, the region is indeed the proper scale and entity to link knowledge and action and to develop, test and apply the integrative action research methodology. This transition differs in form and process over Europe showing that there are many possible and appropriate ways to make diversity a valuable asset.
- The awareness that imagination can be exploited when it is framed in the duality of super- and infrastructure in appropriate processes and rules for democratic legitimation and top-down bottom-up interaction.
- The experience that appropriate interaction and communication based on the sharing of knowledge can create the conditions for co-operation resulting in a community of practice for cultural planning but should be supported by various forms of interpretative reflection.
- The well-balanced combination of thematic c.q. problem-oriented and regionally oriented studies has proven to be a fruitful balance of depth and breadth of approaches.

There are three fundamental observations relating to the PDL/BBO programme in the Dutch context:
- The usability of the two PDL/BBO concepts of cultural biography and action research. The type of use of the biography concept in relation to the regional setting depends on the context of planning, communication, research and/or valorization and consequently can be applied in various ways. Action research is an effective approach to facilitate the interaction on the regional and local level and to embed the use of the biography concept. However it is crucial for the follow-up to establish a local expert group or centre or any other form of community-based knowledge-action unit to secure continuity.
- The validity has been confirmed of the assumption made at the start of the PDL/BBO programme that the diversity of the regionally oriented programmes is a valuable asset, not a disadvantage. This diversity is expressed by the archaeological-historical landscapes, regional environmental challenges and planning policies and by the approaches and creativity of the involved actors.
- Finally it has become clear that real integrative interaction was especially successful in special programmes related to cultural planning apart from the conventional planning process. All programmes were confronted in one way or another with the problem of the differences in 'real' time of the research cycle and the policy cycle. The (lack of) synchronization was crucial to discover the window of opportunity or to change 'real' time in 'kairos' time. Of course the compatibility of views of actors in the knowledge-action chain also plays a crucial role in reflecting the variety of interactions in boundary work.

NOTES
1 University of Amsterdam, Amsterdam, the Netherlands.

2   VU University, Amsterdam, the Netherlands.
3   Wageningen University, Wageningen, the Netherlands.

REFERENCES

Assche, K. Van, 2004: *Signs in time. An interpretive account of urban planning and design, the people and their histories*, Wageningen (Ph.D. thesis Wageningen University).

Baas, H./B. Groenewoudt/E. Raap (in press): The Dutch approach. Public participation and the role of NGO's and local authorities in the protection, management and development of cultural landscapes in the Netherlands, Springer Verlag.

Beek, R. van/Tom (J.H.F.) Bloemers/L. Keunen/H. van Londen/J. Kolen, 2008: The Netherlands, in G. Fairclough/P. Grau Møller (eds.), *Landscape as Heritage. The Management and Protection of Landscape in Europe, a summary by the Cost A 27 project 'LANDMARKS*, Bern (Geographica Bernensia 79), 177-203.

Beukers, E. et al. (eds.), 2009: *Erfgoedbalans 2009. Archeologie, monumenten en cultuurlandschap in Nederland*, Amersfoort.

Cerutti, V., 2008: *Leerstoelen in de etalage. Review Onderwijsnetwerk Belvedere*, z.p.

Dunne, J., 1993. *Back to the rough ground. 'Phronesis' and 'Techne' in Modern Philosophy and Aristotle*, London.

Florence, 2000: *European Landscape Convention. Florence, 20 October 2000*, Strasbourg (Council of Europe).

Fürst, D./L. Gailing/K. Pollermann/A. Röhring (eds.), 2008: *Kulturlandschaft als Handlungsraum. Institutionen und Governance im Umgang mit dem regionalen Gemeinschaftsgut Kulturlandschaft*, Dortmund.

Glaser, B.G./A.L. Strauss, 1967: *The discovery of grounded theory: strategies for qualitative research*, Dordrecht.

Ingold, T., 2000: *The Perception of the Environment. Essays in livelihood, dwelling and skill*, London/New York.

Jacobs, M., 2006: *The production of mindscapes. A comparative theory of landscape experience*, Wageningen (Ph.D. thesis Wageningen University).

Jain, R.K./H.C. Triandis, 1997: *Management of research and development organization. Managing the Unmanageable*, New York etc.

Jonge, J. de, 2009: *Landscape Architecture between Politics and Science. An integrative perspective on landscape planning and design in the network society*, Wageningen (Ph.D. thesis Wageningen University).

Meier, T., 2009: Umweltarchäologie, Landschaftsarchäologie, *Historia archaeologica* 70, 697-734.

Nassauer, J.I./P. Opdam 2008: Design in science: extending the landscape ecology paradigm, *Landscape ecology* 23, 633-644.

Novioconsult/Strootman Landschapsarchitecten, 2004. *Landschapsvisie Drentsche Aa*, Nijmegen/Amsterdam.

Reason, P./H. Bradbury (eds.), 2001: *The SAGE Handbook of Action Research. Participative Inquiry and Practice*, London.

Valletta, 1992: *European Convention on the Protection of the Archaeological Heritage (Revised) Valetta, 16.I.1992*, Strasbourg (Council of Europe).

Wamz, 2007: *Archaeological Heritage Management Act*, Den Haag.

Weggeman, M., 2001[4]: *Kennismanagement. Inrichting en besturing van kennisintensieve organisaties*, Schiedam.

VII

MANAGEMENT OF KNOWLEDGE

Wiśniowa (PL): rural village. *Photo: J. Hernik.*

1. The management of knowledge for integrative landscape research: an introduction

Tom (J.H.F.) Bloemers[1]

ABSTRACT

Knowledge is defined as "the partially unconscious capacity that is represented by the function of Information, Experience, Ability and Attitude of someone" (Weggeman 2001[4], 28-41). Since the subject of the cultural landscape covers many different disciplines and research, practice and policy, the need for specific management of knowledge is evident. The contributions to this section are analyzed from this perspective. They represent a balanced mixture of types of research programmes, national ones, transnational Interreg programmes, a European COST A27 programme and one on information systems for cultural-historical landscapes.

For successful integrative research five aspects should be given attention: project design, integration, communication (leadership, clear role of participants and personal chemistry), output/results and SWOT analysis.

Some specific recommendations are made to support management of knowledge of integrative research programmes:
- timely attention for theory, conceptualization and methodology supporting integrative research practice;
- specific funding of leadership and co-ordination focused on the creation of integrative knowledge;
- specific funding for external communication to avoid a one-sided focus on the own group;
- adequate training for acting as a researcher in integrative programmes.

KEY WORDS

Management of knowledge; (trans)national research programmes; leadership, communication, training

1. WHY A SECTION ON THE MANAGEMENT OF KNOWLEDGE FOR INTEGRATIVE LANDSCAPE RESEARCH?

It is useful to explain why a special section of this book on integrative landscape research and heritage practice is devoted to the theme of knowledge management and what is understood by this term.

Knowledge management as it is used in the context of this section is not only the usual development of research themes within a particular research policy and the organization of the appropriate assessment of research proposals, the allocation and control of the money flow and of reporting about progress and output. This is of course a basic condition for implementing research focused on specific new themes or lines and selected in a competitive environment, a task generally fulfilled by the funding research authority.

Knowledge management must also take into account the other basic research aim, creating new knowledge and insights within the proposed topic and its ambitions. In this context knowledge is defined as "the partially unconscious capacity that is represented by the function of Information, Experience,

Ability and Attitude of someone" (Weggeman 2001[4], 28-41). Knowledge creation within a programmatic setting is primarily the responsibility of the leader(s) of the research programme or project, generally participating researchers themselves. To my big surprise this does not seem to be a specific field of interest in the academic world, or at least in the humanities (but see also Cultplan 2007). However, since the subject of the cultural landscape by its nature covers many paradigmatically different disciplines and involves research, practice and policy, the need for some form of specific knowledge management is evident. This feeling of urgency is strengthened by the overall trend in research policy on national and international levels to stimulate integrative research and practice, which forces disciplines to consider their traditional *raison d´être* and the opportunities and threats the integrative policy trend presents to them. The humanities cannot escape the confrontation with these developments as is shown by many policy documents on all institutional levels.

The answer to this need is, as a first step, to make explicit the experiences and tacit knowledge of researchers involved in relevant landscape research programmes that can be exploited for further analysis and generalizations. The contributions to this section are not selected with the intention to cover what is going on in Europe and might be relevant, they are probably not even representative from this perspective. They reflect the network within which some of the PDL/BBO researchers have participated and consequently there is a bias towards archaeology. On the other hand they are a balanced mixture of types of research programmes now possible within Europe, such as national ones, transnational Interreg programmes and a European COST A27 programme. At first glance, Sophie Visser's paper is somewhat deviant since it focuses not on one specific research programme but on selected information systems for cultural-historical landscapes, foremost the Netherlands. However, these systems are often instrumental to the research programmes discussed here and they reflect aspects of knowledge management as discussed in this section.

2. FROM LANDSCAPE RESEARCH TO CULTURAL-HISTORICAL LANDSCAPE PLANNING AND MANAGEMENT

The management of knowledge for integrative landscape research has to do with crossing boundaries between disciplines and paradigms. This can be illustrated by the description of what landscape is in the European Landscape Convention and in landscape ecology. The European Landscape Convention defines landscape as "an area, as perceived by people, whose character is the result of the action and interaction of natural and/or human factors" and in identifying landscapes, assessment should proceed by "taking into account the particular *values* assigned to them by the interested parties and the population concerned". In landscape ecology a landscape is seen as "a distinct, measurable unit defined as a cluster of interacting ecosystems that corresponds to a distinct level of biological organization or hierarchy." (Florence 2000). The first description focuses on the human perspective, the last one on a systems approach. The two views or paradigms might not be incompatible, but at present they are at best either not united by an integrative approach or in the worst case work separately from each other. Other complicated boundaries to be crossed in integrative research are those between research, policy, practice and public (see Van der Valk Ch. II.2 section 5 and Ch. VII.2 section 5) and in the case of international programmes those between nations, languages, law systems etc. and the physical distance between them.

All considered together, knowledge creation in integrative research is confronted with so many barriers that, to be successful, special attention has to be given to it.

To structure the content of the contributions to this section on knowledge management we have followed the studies by Tress/Tress/Fry (Tress/Tress/Fry 2006a; *idem* 2006b) by using their definitions for various disciplinary forms of research and the challenges for integrative research. Integrative research is either inter- or transdisciplinary. Interdisciplinary research involves collaboration between various unrelated academic fields for the express purpose of crossing boundaries so that researchers can create new knowledge and achieve a common research goal. Here the adjective 'unrelated' indicates that the disciplines in question differ with regard to their research paradigms, for example differences regarding quantitative, qualitative, analytical or interpretative approaches. In transdisciplinary research, academics from different unrelated disciplines collaborate closely with non-academics in order to achieve certain research objectives and to develop new knowledge. This approach is participative and usually leads to negotiated knowledge such as a common definition of problems, the identification of facts and the development of strategies (Tress/Tress/Fry 2006a, 15-17). Integration is described as "that knowledge cultures are bridged and their knowledge fused together when answering a research question… integration needs to lead to the development of new common methods and theory and finally to new knowledge."(*idem* 18).

Ten steps to deal with challenges are recommended for successful integrative research (Tress/Tress/Fry 2006b). Here they have been paraphrased to structure the content of the contributions to this section.

a. *Project design*
- research design
- institutional structure
- process of selecting participants

b. *Integration*
- conflicting epistemologies
- development of common theory and methods
- finding a common research question
- agreement on concepts and terminology

c. *Communication*
- communication and contact
- additional time demand
- leadership, clear role of participants and personal chemistry
- (lack of) training and education

d. *Output/results*
- application and consultancy
- achieving integrated products
- publishing

e. *SWOT analysis*

A final self-reflective balance based on a SWOT analysis has been added, namely the strengths and weaknesses of the programme itself and opportunities and threats of the environment in which the programme is operating.

3. THE EXAMPLES OF INTEGRATIVE LANDSCAPE RESEARCH

As noted earlier, the contributions to this section are not selected with the intention to cover what is going on in Europe and might be relevant, they are probably not even representative from this perspective. Only the Interreg funding scheme of the European Union, which because of its regional focus is of great value for landscape research, shows a great variety of programmes on culture (Cultplan 2007, 23-25). Common to all is the focus on the cultural-historical landscape and on basic or applied research from the supply side, and on policy, user and public from the demand side. The mix of these aspects of course varies considerably. All authors were asked to focus on the items paraphrased from the challenges listed above (Tress/Tress/Fry 2006b). In general this structure has been followed in a liberal way and reflecting the particularities of the relevant programme and the personal experiences of the authors as responsible leaders.

Without intending to summarize the contributions some observations about them are made to characterize their value for this section.

Van der Valk's paper presents the particularities of integrative research, especially what is indicated as strategic research which aims to contribute to policy, society, industry or commercial issues. The PDL/BBO programme belongs in this category. Consequently, the interaction between science, policy and society is clarified and the type of research is indicated as hybrid since it operates in the area between fundamental and applied research. His argument is in line with that of Tress *et al.* and their ten recommended steps for successful integrative research to face the challenges (Tress/Tress/Fry 2006b) that structure the contributions.

Orejas and Reher's paper deals with the COST A27 LANDMARKS programme focused on mining and rural landscapes in Europe. An important goal has been to exploit the added value of co-operation on a European scale. At the start of the programme in 2002, 11 countries and 44 researchers were participating, at its end in 2008 their number had grown to 21 countries and over 150 participants. Managing this dynamic growth and the diversity of cultures between the various groups has been a crucial task for the programme's success. Although the collaborative production of publications has yielded integrative results the authors confess that "true interdisciplinarity requires much more co-operation and the identification of common research goals" (Orejas/Reher Ch. VII.3, 551). They also state that interdisciplinarity needs specific disciplinary achievements and that finding a fruitful interaction within common methodological frameworks is important. Outward communication and visibility both in the scientific and policy community have been weak, although both specific publications and a website were produced for this purpose. Given the geographical spread, the number of participants and the complexity of the research activities it is clear, although not explicitly stated, that the management of this programme has consumed much more time than was funded and made visible by the COST budget. In particular the lead partner, the Spanish Consejo Superior de Investigaciones Científicas, must have made considerable additional personal investments which created the conditions for success.

The two transnational Interreg III programmes are examples of collaborative applied research. The combination of these two programmes facilitates the comparison between the western European 'Planarch' and the eastern European 'Cultural Landscape' approaches.

Planarch started as an Interreg II initiative evolving in a follow up with a clear research concept focussing on archaeological heritage management and planning. The partners, all from 'old' member states of the European Union, had a background in northwest European archaeological heritage agencies. They had a more or less clear vision about the importance of integrating meaningful archaeological values in the decision-making of the planning processes in a highly dynamic metropolitan region on both sides of the southern North Sea. This resulted among other things in a set of Guiding Principles "intended to provide a rigorous, robust and reasonable framework for ensuring that cultural heritage is appropriately treated in the EIA process" (Planarch 2006). A set of overviews of the use of Environmental Impact Assessment instruments in the partner countries and a synthesis of the results created a solid background information for the Guiding Principles. Reflecting upon Planarch, Williams (Ch. VII.4, 563) confesses that communication with stakeholders was a weak spot by "not engaging planners, developers and other non-historic environment specialists more in its deliberations."

The Cultural Landscape programme is a first generation Interreg programme initiated by partners from four 'new' or non-EU member states and one 'old'. The institutional background is an interesting combination of three universities among which the University of Agriculture in Kraków is the lead partner, three heritage associations, two municipalities, a museum and an educational training unit. The programme aimed at "the identification of the iconic features that composed those landscapes, incorporating a number of pilot projects." An important result with an integrative effect is the *Catalogue of Cultural Landscape Elements with a Glossary of Terms*, a catalogue of elements together with photographs and descriptions and the so-called mapping key which can be used as a methodological instrument (Ch. VII.5, 570). Interesting examples of the outcomes of applied pilot projects are those with the Municipality of Wiśniowa in southern Poland on a small historical retention basin as significant historical heritage and local landscape asset, the contribution to the Regional Development Concept 'Middle Saale Valley' in German Thuringia and the training scheme for opinion leaders and decision-makers involved in projects to protect cultural landscape and a programme for managers and technical personnel in tourism.

Two research programmes represent the national scale, 'Changing Landscapes' from Denmark and PDL/BBO from the Netherlands.

Changing Landscapes is a large-scale Danish research programme carried out between 1997 and 2002 with the "aim ... to create a scientific basis for understanding the historical background to the appearance of the present landscape. Equally important is to comprehend the processes of change occurring in the landscape." (Ch. VII.6) The programme has been organized in the form of a centre as a group of researchers called Changing Landscapes with the subtitle 'Centre for strategic studies in cultural environments, nature and landscape history'. The research centre was strategic, involving governmental research institutions and museums and furthermore background groups were established with researchers, administrators, landowners and organizations. Grau Møller, the programme leader, states in his paper that multidisciplinarity is the most appropriate word to characterize the centre's research. He says that interdisciplinarity gradually unfolded within the six research projects and was stimulated by the preparation of a book on five interdisciplinary questions. His conclusion is that interdisciplinary research needs time to develop relevant research questions involving all disciplines. Good co-operation existed between the widespread researchers which continued after the end of the centre and programme. Unfortunately, the political situation in Denmark changed shortly after the end of the programme and the synergetic effects of good co-operation could not be used because funding for environmental research was radically diminished.

The 'Protecting and Developing the Dutch Archaeological-Historical Landscape' (PDL/BBO) programme started in 2000 and was primarily aimed at the development of scientific knowledge in order to support the sustainable development of the Dutch archaeological-historical landscape. Consequently, the strategy focused on establishing a meaningful link between scientific knowledge, archaeological-historical resource management and applied planning policy in the Netherlands. It has a strategic focus as is illustrated by the composition of the funding bodies and its complementary role regarding the national Belvedere policy. Two unifying concepts were used to establish a meaningful link between scientific knowledge, archaeological-historical resource management and applied planning policy, the (cultural) biography of landscape and the action research approach. Much attention has been given to the communication within the group of researchers as to the co-ordination of joint research efforts. Outside communication however has been a very weak spot and consequently the visibility is limited. The creation of new knowledge in this research programme has been analysed with the help of the definition of knowledge as "the partially unconscious capacity that is represented by the function of Information, Experience, Ability (Dutch: *vaardigheden*) and Attitude of someone" (Weggeman 2001[4], 8-41) and expressed in the formula K=f(I.EVA). The organization of the PDL/BBO research programme can be described as inherently dynamic, a 'fuzzy structure' in Weggeman's terminology.

A position in its own right within this section on knowledge management is the contribution by Sophie Visser on the content and usability of information systems for cultural historical landscapes as they are currently used in the Netherlands and compared with the situation in Germany and England. In particular she focuses on historical geographic values and also considers archaeological values in information systems. Information in this context is defined as 'communicated knowledge or content'; knowledge has to be differentiated in basic descriptive and derived knowledge like values. In particular, cultural landscape information systems show an "emphasis on external communication, with other organizations (or their information systems) or with 'outside' people." (Ch. VII.8, 607). A well-designed information system is composed of three integrated levels, the computer-based technical level and the intermediate logical level connecting the technical with the third conceptual semantic level. In her analysis Visser considers the wider context within which an information system functions, issues of management of information and the quality of expertise and awareness of informational principles and management. Her conclusions are very important, but surprising and worrying at the same time. There is generally a clear lack of the right expertise about helpful insights from the information system's discipline. Conceptual thinking is also generally a weak point resulting in, for example, the mix-up of knowledge and values. The usability of information systems for cultural historical landscapes is limited because of one-way communicative thinking instead of two-way. Finally the organizational situation is very complex since various institutions have their own external and internal needs and views. As for the state of the art we have arrived at in the Netherlands these observations are somewhat disappointing after almost 20 years of investment! It is an illustration of the need for giving attention to the management of knowledge in order to make the management of heritage resources effective.

4. CONCLUSIONS

To conclude this introduction to the section on knowledge management I follow the paraphrased structure of ten recommended steps towards successful integrative research discussed above (Tress/Tress/Fry 2006b): project design, integration, communication, output/results and SWOT analysis.

The research design is generally clear, which is a *conditio sine qua non* for a programme proposal granted in a competitive context. Frequently, research institutions and heritage agencies are joint partners. The crucial issue of the selection of partners shows an essential difference between COST and Interreg programmes and the national research programmes. In the last group the access to the programme is based on some form of more or less free competition within the limits of the funding scheme, resulting for PDL/BBO in about 30-40% acceptance of presented research proposals. The access to the first group is based more on a coalition of willing participants and as in the COST A27 LANDMARKS programme resulting in a considerable growth of the number of participants during the programme and about one-third of no show members.

Integration as an expression of the inter- and transdisciplinary approach is a core issue, but considering the various programmes there is still a long way to go. All programmes show useful experiences depending on their aims and activities ranging from fundamental issues to action research oriented activities, but none seems to have tackled integration in all its aspects. There is a clear lack of explicit knowledge and experience about integrative theories and methods. Sometimes unifying concepts or the construction of a common terminology have been a formal part of the research to facilitate integration on different levels. Probably all programmes show what Weggeman calls an 'emergent strategy'. The research starts with the intended explicit and formal strategy, during the process an emergent strategy appears in an informal and opportunistic way while at the end it gradually becomes clear which actions had a strategic value and have been realized (Weggeman 2001[4], 134).

Communication is mainly inwardly focussed towards the own group of involved researchers and disciplines. Even when explicitly aimed for, contacts with outside disciplines like planners or landscape architects are at the best limited and at the worst neglected. The same applies for policies and the public. Aside from all sorts of practical reasons, two conditions might reflect the structural barriers integrative research is facing. Within research the paradigmatic dominance of traditional mono- and multidisciplinary research and training is so strong that it limits the visibility of integrative research considerably, not so much on the level of research policy but in a disciplinary context. The other reason relates to the interaction between research and policy. Policy tends to long for quick solutions to actual problems where even applied research needs more time or deeper information than asked for. Or research asks questions or raises issues that are not welcomed by policy. Policy and research have different frameworks and tempi and their synchronization or articulation are critical for integrative ambitions.

Co-ordination and leadership are, in all programmes, more or less clearly structured as a result of the formal procedures for a successful application of research proposals. However, it remains unclear to what extent staff, time and money for co-ordinating a programme have formally been part of the funding and planning. Probably the lead partners have contributed a substantial amount of the co-ordination work load from their own resources, either as formal matching or just because of their strategic decision for the initiative. The same applies for specific training or education for integrative research co-operation which seems to have been generally absent. It can be concluded that the engagement of the leadership and the partners must have contributed to a great extent to the conditions for a successful accomplishment!

Considering the output, the preparation of collaborative publications has been a great stimulus for integrative research results. Effects on policy and practice seem to be much more limited or take more time before they become visible. Planarch's Guiding Principles for the Environmental Impact Assessment or the training course of the Cultural Landscape programme are good examples, as may be the application of research in planning processes on a regional scale in the PDL/BBO programme or the management of archaeological parks as exemplified in COST A27 LANDMARKS.

To conclude, some specific recommendations derived from the previous observations can be made. Regarding integrative research aims the following aspects should be structural parts of its programming to support the management of knowledge:
- timely attention for theory, conceptualization and methodology supporting integrative research practice;
- specific funding of leadership and co-ordination focused on the creation of integrative knowledge;
- specific funding for external communication to avoid a one-sided focus on the own group;
- adequate training for acting as researcher in integrative programmes.

The effect should be that better results are achieved. At the same time however, one should be aware that innovative research needs its freedom to flourish in an environment that has been labelled by Weggeman as a 'fuzzy structure'. So, in the end it comes down to finding a fruitful balance between freedom and integration.

NOTES

1 University of Amsterdam, Amsterdam, the Netherlands,

REFERENCES

Cultplan, 2007: *Cultural Differences in European Cooperation. Learning from Interreg Practice*, Wageningen.

Florence, 2000: *European Landscape Convention. Florence, 20 October 2000*, Strasbourg (Council of Europe).

Planarch, 2006: *Guiding Principles for Cultural heritage in Environmental Impact Assessment (EIA)*, s.l.

Tress, B./G. Tress/G. Fry, 2006a: Defining concepts and the process of knowledge production in integrative research, in B.G. Tress/G. Tress/G. Fry/P. Opdam (eds.), *From Landscape Research to landscape Planning. Aspects of Integration, Education and Application*, Dordrecht, 13-26.

Tress, B./G. Tress/G. Fry, 2006b: Ten steps to success in integrative research, in B.G. Tress/G. Tress/G. Fry/P. Opdam (eds.), *From Landscape Research to landscape Planning. Aspects of Integration, Education and Application*, Dordrecht, 241-75.

Weggeman, M., 2001[4]: *Kennismanagement. Inrichting en besturing van kennisintensieve organisaties*, Schiedam.

2. Elephant and Delta. In search of practical guidelines for interdisciplinary and strategic research

Arnold van der Valk[1]

It was six men of Indostan
To learning much inclined,
Who went to see the Elephant
(Though all of them were blind),
That each by observation
Might satisfy his mind.

John Godfrey Saxe (1816-1887)

ABSTRACT

This paper is about co-operation between practitioners of various disciplines in the humanities, natural sciences and social sciences. The author explores the intricacies of integrative research, building upon his personal experience. First he analyses three cases selected more or less arbitrarily from Dutch planning practice because they were well documented and seemed promising since by 2003 they showed analogies with the emerging Protecting and Developing Programme. The cases provide building blocks for a provisional middle range action theory for the direction of interdisciplinary research. The building blocks are compared to lessons learned and recommendations produced by researchers of practices in contemporary interdisciplinary research associated with the Wageningen Delta Programme for Integrative Landscape Research (1999-2004). The author was its research leader. The lessons from the Delta Programme are both positive and negative. Lessons are compared with experiences by Fry and others in the field of landscape research. The author deduces tentative guidelines which have been a source of inspiration for the leadership of the PDL/BBO programme between 2003 and 2010.

KEY WORDS

Multi-disciplinarity, interdisciplinarity, transdisciplinarity; integrative landscape research, best practices, strategic research

1. INTRODUCTION

A popular Dutch saying has it that two heads are better than one. Unfortunately, this does not always apply to science. The situation in scientific research all too often shows more similarity with an old Indian fable in which six blind men investigate the phenomenon which people who can see refer to as an 'elephant'.

The blind men jointly investigate something which for them is an abstraction. They are keen to explore an elephant by getting in touch with it, literally, thus collecting empirical evidence for its existence. They hear that the thing is standing in front of them and take turns exploring the contours. The first blind man walks forward, stumbles and falls against the flank of the animal. He observes that the elephant is solid and hard like a wall. The second blind man investigates the front of the animal and grasps the tip of the tusk. He is convinced that the elephant is to be associated with a spear. The third blind man touches the coiling trunk. He is convinced that the elephant is something like a snake. The fourth blind man touches the animal's leg below the knee, and immediately compares it to a tree. Number five touches an ear and thinks of a gigantic fan. The final blind man grasps the tail and discovers a striking resemblance to a thick rope. They become involved in a heated discussion about the composition of an elephant. The phenomenon of an elephant, as observed by sighted people, remains a mystery to the stubborn blind men.

Like the blind in the story, scientists must often work together to overcome limitations of a specialized view of one aspect of an infinitely complex reality. Such reduction of reality and continuing specialization within disciplines is necessary to achieve depth. At the same time, specialization leads to a fragmentation of knowledge. As a result of this, scientists are often unable to answer complex social and technical questions. Consumers of scientific knowledge repeatedly complain that scientists answer questions that have not been asked. Even worse, all too often they are unable to provide any answer at all to complex questions. A cynical view of the lack of coherence in the inventory of scientific knowledge is that society has questions while science has disciplines and research departments (Winder 2003).

This article addresses the issue of co-operation in science. It is initially based on the author's personal experiences as a leader and participant in an integrative landscape research programme initiated by Wageningen University and Research Centre in 1999 (Tress/Tress/Van der Valk 2003). One of the goals of this programme was reflecting on interdisciplinary researchers-in-action. Before going into more detail on this programme, three cases will be analysed to outline some of the intricacies of co-operation in landscape science. Landscape science is particularly interesting because it encompasses efforts in co-operation between highly contrasting domains of science such as humanities, natural sciences and social sciences. Mention is made of participation by lay persons and policy-makers. The examples provide an inventory of issues which have been systematically researched in the Wageningen programme mentioned above. Lessons learned from the Wageningen programme have applied to the PDL/BBO programme. Thus the author of this paper has accumulated over ten years of experience in interdisciplinary landscape research. The accumulated knowledge is presented in the recommendations at the end of the paper and in an appendix which reproduces in detail the lessons from the Wageningen programme. These may be used and tested in future projects since the underlying reasoning and basic assumptions require further review and refinement (De Jonge 2009; Nassauer/Opdam 2008).

2. EXAMPLES

People learn by doing. Research into possibilities of scientific co-operation to solve societal issues begins with the critical review of examples from practice. Three examples are presented below.

The first example concerns a programme on the consequences of flooding of the major rivers in the Netherlands, initiated by the Ministry of Transport, Public Works and Water Management.[2] The aim of this programme was to develop a comprehensive methodology to evaluate damage from river flooding from different perspectives such as economy, safety, heritage management, spatial planning, hydrology, agriculture and traffic. The central questions, freely summarized, were the following: what are the consequences for societal activities if something goes wrong with the water management of the major rivers? What perspectives on the risks are conceivable, taking into account the divergent values and interests in society (Immink 2007; Van Dijk 2008)?

During the first phase, the researchers aimed to establish an integrated model for cost-benefit analysis. The purpose of the model was to make the economic, hydrological, toxological, ecological, pedological, agricultural, regional planning, geo-morphological and culture-historical effects of flooding measurable and comparable. By using such a model, the Directorate General for Public Works and Water Management expected to be able to map out the risks of flooding in greater detail in both qualitative and quantitative terms. The model is intended to play a role in evaluating choices regarding various ways to keep the rivers under control or to let them run their own course. The first part of the research was assigned to a consortium of technical research institutes in Delft (civil engineering), Twente (legal aspects and policy) and Wageningen (ecological, agricultural and landscape aspects).

In this project the commissioning body and researchers struggled with the different languages spoken by natural scientists and engineers and social scientists and landscape architects. A frequently heard complaint from the hydrological engineers was that cost-benefit assessment research produces comparisons between apples and oranges. There was a great deal of scepticism about the possibilities of converting a wide range of effects into one single measurable unit: money. An attempt to reduce all consequences to monetary value conflicts with standard practice of engineers at the Directorate General for Public Works and Water Management. They are accustomed to working with hydrological models in which flow velocities and quantities are the standard units. Disciplines such as historical geography and geomorphology, which do not have access to easily quantifiable models, are viewed with suspicion. In the programme, technical disciplines held a dominant position. Among technicians, proposals by public administrators and planners to map out problems and solutions in collaboration with the involved parties from society could count on little sympathy. According to the traditional hydrological engineers, the safety of citizens can never be decided by political consensus. A frequently heard statement from the engineers in the programme was that first we deal with the rational scientific side and only afterwards with emotional arguments.

According to critics, the research programme into the risks of flooding lacked a vision of the coherence between the questions and methods of various disciplines. At the beginning of the programme coherence was assumed to be self-evident. The process of accounting for scientific quality was left to prominent scientists who had earned their reputation in a specific discipline. At the same time, the exact sciences enjoyed more prestige than the humanities and social sciences. The question about added scientific value of the whole with respect to the individual components within the programme remained unanswered. The research reports contained a comprehensive summary of non-comparable physical and social activities. A series of questions were answered which had never been asked.

The second example concerns co-operation between hydrologists, ecologists, geographers, economists, planners and landscape architects in a research project exploring possibilities for water storage in new urban expansion areas, the Aquatic Contours project.[3] In this project research was conducted into possibilities for multifunctional use of space, a hot issue in land-use planning then and now. Various experts studied actual building locations near the towns of Zaandam and Amstelveen in the vicinity of Amsterdam looking for innovative options to combine water storage with residential functions, natural habitats and recreation. Calculations by hydrologists on the minimum and maximum needs for water storage during wet and dry periods were used as the point of departure for the study. At Zaandam hydrologists calculated that 80 hectares of new water basins were required to eliminate the hazard of flooding. Social geographers calculated spatial needs for housing, commercial use and parks. An innovative aspect of this project was that landscape architects questioned experts about the tenability of all kinds of commonplace assumptions about the compatibility, or lack thereof, of terrestrial and aquatic aspects of land use. These assumptions had been included in rules of thumb for land use and in indicators in the standard vocabulary of geographers and hydrologists.

The Aquatic Contours project used intellectual and financial stimuli to create dialogue between various specialists. The project leadership encouraged researchers to formulate joint research questions. In this way the project promoted an understanding of the possibilities and limitations of expertise from other disciplines. Participants referred to a growth process and there were creative moments when breakthroughs were achieved. At these times, all the specialists in the team were asked to take themselves outside the terrain of their trusted models. They were asked to stand in the shoes of other experts, policymakers and citizens. An important part of the process of developing transdisciplinary thinking was working together on a new spatial concept: the aquatic/hydrological contour.[4] A spatial concept is a schematic representation of a desirable and possible development of an area. The concept also contains an indication of how the proposal can be implemented (Faludi/Van der Valk 1994, 18). A spatial concept or design concept has an analytical side and an intentional side. In an analytical sense, a spatial concept shows similarities with a scientific theory. Geographers emphasize the analytical testable side. Planners and designers, in contrast, pay particular attention to the creative mind-expanding effects of a spatial concept.

The third example concerns research into the past, present and future of old open fields (in Dutch: *essen*) in the villages of Wijster, Drijber and Spier in the Dutch province of Drenthe (De Poel *et al.* 2000; Hidding/Kolen/Spek 2001, 102). In this project which took place in 1999 and 2000, historical geographers, archaeologists, architectural historians, ecologists, planners and landscape architects worked together with residents to map out qualities of the landscape surrounding these villages. This information was used to address the issue of desired spatial development of the area while retaining cultural-historical values. A unique aspect of this project was the involvement of residents in the scientific exploration of the cultural-historical values. By doing this on their own initiative, scientists showed that they do not pretend to have exclusive rights to the truth. From the beginning to the end of the project, the role of the residents was decisive. During the initial phase emphasis was on collecting information, at the end there were primarily discussions about developing policy and taking concrete measures. The result of this process was a broadly supported vision of the desired future of the characteristic open fields in the region. In this vision a balance was achieved between future liveability for the village residents and conserving and strengthening the cultural-historical values that were present. All parties involved were convinced that the implementation of the proposed projects and measures would encounter little resistance from the population.[5] The implementation of several subprojects by private parties confirmed this assumption.

Now by way of reflection I will draw attention to a number of striking issues in these examples.
- First, the success of the programmes initially depended on the extent to which the researchers could develop a coherent vision of the full range of the issue. This range was determined by the commissioning

body, i.e. the client and by societal actors. Combining observations from various relevant disciplinary approaches requires more than simple addition.
- Second, scoring tables are used when determining and evaluating the consequences of activities. In such a table, various and divergent variables are placed in a column. The aim of this approach is to visualize conceivable effects of various measures or forms of development.
- Third, filling in the cells of such a table as a whole is based on a combination of scientific considerations and social choices. The choices include the question of which disciplines will participate and which societal parties will be consulted.
- Fourth, the above-mentioned choices can be traced to vested interests, rules and regulations and other institutions. Customs, standards and rules can often be justifiably questioned. A debate on the institutional preconditions can open up new perspectives for solutions to complex problems. Pluriformity of opinions can be used under certain circumstances to enrich the spectrum of plausible options in a decision-making process.
- Fifth, searching for acceptable solutions to complex societal issues requires interweaving knowledge management and process management. Thinking from a single discipline or a single societal interest seldom provides a solid basis for solutions in a pluriform society.
- Finally, in the above examples virtually no role is given to fundamental curiosity-driven research. At the same time, it must be noted that the applications of science elicit questions about the scientific quality of the knowledge that was used.

In the following section answers to two questions will be considered. The first question is how can the gap between fundamental science and application be bridged? The second question is what is the best way to co-ordinate the production and consumption of knowledge? The answer to the first question is addressed here under the heading strategic research. The second question is addressed in the section on multidisciplinary, interdisciplinary and transdisciplinary research.

3. STRATEGIC RESEARCH

The PDL/BBO incentive programme may be categorized as strategic research. Scientific research is interpreted here as the collection of data and information which is categorized, analysed, interpreted, tested and fed back into the academic community. According to the 2001 UK Research Assessment Exercise, research is original investigation undertaken specifically to gain knowledge and understanding. It may encompass work of relevance to the needs of industry, commerce, government and the public. Knowledge is perceived as explicit knowledge, as opposed to tacit, i.e. individual knowledge. Explicit knowledge is expressed in language fit for interpersonal communication, accessible and put in a collectively shared frame of reference (Tress/Tress/Fry 2006, 22).

In the PDL/BBO programme research is supposed to contribute to the policy issue of including archaeological-historical monuments in spatial development. In this way science, policy and society can be linked together in a viable fashion. In the jargon of policy reports, the term 'strategic research' is generally used to indicate a hybrid form of research. This concerns research that operates in the area between fundamental, curiosity-driven research and applied research (Tress/Tress/Fry 2006, 21) Strategic research, like applied research, is expected to contribute to supporting well-considered societal actions. At the same time, scholars involved in strategic research cherish the idea that they comply with high scientific standards. Often, but not always, strategic research involves combining and integrating knowledge from various scientific disciplines. The necessity of integration emerges from the necessity to study social problems as much as possible in their full complexity and in relation to each other (De Jonge 2009, 28; Gibbons *et al.* 1994).

The demand for strategic research arises from society or politics not from the community of scientific practitioners (Fig. 1), as in the case of fundamental scientific research (Nowotny/Scott/Gibbons 2001). There are scientific disciplines that justify their existence from the contribution they provide to strategic research, such as public administration, planning studies and landscape architecture. During the past century, many classical academic disciplines produced offshoots that focus on applied and strategic research, such as cultural history, landscape ecology, applied geography and environmental science. In these disciplines the field of view shifts from the practice of science to social action. In strategic research, creativity and intuition play an important role. When answering specific questions, this is combined with the precision of the exact sciences (Kars 1995; Tress *et al.* 2001; Antrop 2006).

Strategic research tries to combine the best aspects of a technical scientific approach with the best aspects of interpretative social sciences and humanities. However, this endeavour all too often produces confusion about jargon. Practitioners of strategic research must be crystal clear in using definitions and terminology. Also they must be willing to show extra-ordinary empathy. This places high demands on the management of strategic research.

- The knowledge of laypersons sometimes plays a role in strategic research. This concerns knowledge about local matters held by residents, users, owners and visitors in a specific area or region.
- Another frequently occurring characteristic is the process of 'editing' knowledge. This is the process of combining concepts, models and data from various disciplines by so-called knowledge brokers. This practice has grown rapidly in research on landscape planning and land-use planning.
- A final characteristic of strategic research is its explicit attention for directing focused questions emerging from applied science to fundamental science.

The practitioners of strategic research believe it is their special task to ask conscientious questions about the quality of knowledge. They continually ask themselves and their application-oriented colleagues questions such as:

- is your scientific knowledge up-to-date?
- do you distance yourself sufficiently from the opinions and beliefs of your client?
- do other combinations of knowledge have a greater chance of providing promising solutions?
- is there sufficient room for creativity or is there a risk that the same scientific trick will simply be repeated?

The figure (Fig. 1) illustrates the relationship between science, politics and society as embedded in the concept of strategic research used in this article. Co-operation between scientists, policy makers and societal actors has a central place in strategic research. Unfortunately, there is often a lack of clarity about the possible and desirable forms of co-operation. In the following section a proposal is made to arrive at a clearer delineation and unequivocal definitions.

4. DELINEATING INTEGRATIVE RESEARCH

There is permanent tension between society and the practice of science (Halffman/Hoppe 2005). Society has problems and science explores these problems via disciplines and research organizations. However,

Fig. 1
Simplified relationship between society, policy and science.
Diagram based on Rotmans 1998, 5.

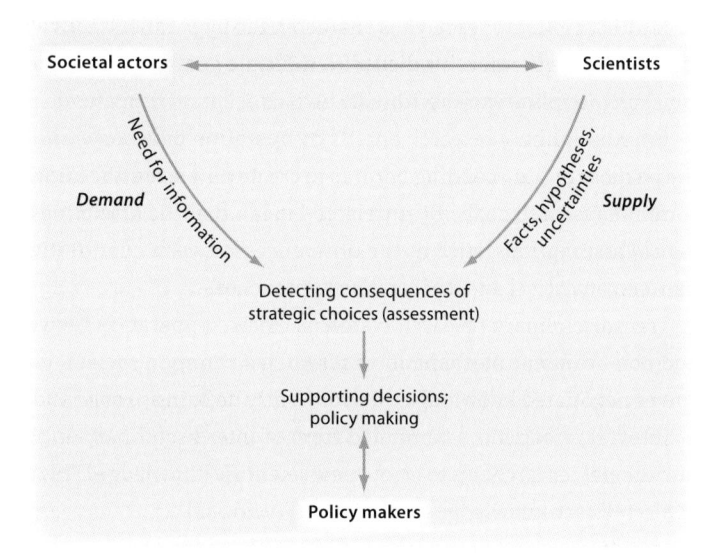

society and science connect poorly with each other. All too often scientists are accused of answering questions that are not relevant to society. From their perspective, scientists are frequently confronted with clients commissioning research where the answer is already given in the research brief. Furthermore, during negotiations about projects, interest groups often show no interest whatsoever in the warnings of scientists (Nowotny/Scott/Gibbons 2001; Rotmans/Van Asselt/Vellinga 2000; Tress/Tress/Fry 2005a; *idem* 2005b).

Division of labour in science is a necessary evil (Tress/Tress 2002). Due to forms of organizational parcellation, scientists are capable of transforming data, information and observations into scientific knowledge. Specialization inevitably occurs at the expense of a broad view of the correlation between the research object and socially relevant details.

Society assigns great value to co-ordination and co-operation between disciplines. In fact, policymakers and research managers all too frequently believe that co-operation is the ultimate answer to all knowledge questions (Tress/Tress/Van der Valk 2003). One could even say that society inserts a standard mistrust clause in its dealings with science in terms of the saying 'he who pays the piper calls the tune'. Generally speaking, three arguments play a role in the call for co-operation and co-ordination (Schanz/Spies/Oesten 1999). The first argument is that co-operation provides a means to repair the limitations resulting from science being organized into disciplines. The second argument is that co-operation prevents scientists from conceiving of partial solutions to complicated societal and technological problems. The third argument is that innovative insights occur exactly at the interface between disciplines.

A wide variety of definitions and the abstract character of the material make it impossible to arrive at a description of divergent forms of co-operation based on the largest common denominator of the standpoints. To escape from the confusion of terminology, Tress and Tress and Fry (Tress/Tress/Fry 2006) have proposed the following definitions, building on extensive international research of the pros and cons of interdisciplinary landscape research.

Disciplinary research takes place within the bounds of a single currently recognized academic discipline although disciplinary boundaries are subject to change over time.

Multidisciplinary research is characterized by parallel tracks within academic disciplines. Interaction is limited. One theme is studied with multiple goals in mind. Knowledge is exchanged but not integrated. Each discipline works within its own conceptual framework, using its own methods.

Interdisciplinary research entails co-operation between various unrelated academic disciplines with the purpose of transcending borders to create new scientific knowledge, unifying concepts and realizing common research goals. By unrelated I mean that the disciplines differ in their methods and epistemological assumptions, such as the differences between quantitative and qualitative research methods or between analytical and interpretive approaches.

Transdisciplinary research concerns close co-operation between scientists from various disciplines and non-academic participants to research a common societal goal and create new knowledge. This involves negotiated knowledge, such as jointly defining problems and developing strategy and actions.

Integral research is a combined form of interdisciplinary and transdisciplinary research. The aim of the integral researcher is to create new scientific knowledge. This knowledge results from the integration of disciplinary knowledge (Tress/Tress/Fry 2005a).

This classification is based on a simple distinction between more ambitious and less ambitious forms of co-operation. The more ambitious forms of co-operation are characterized by the creation of new scientific knowledge, unifying concepts and a shared aim. This can be explained by the metaphor of playing music. In multidisciplinary research, musicians study their parts for specific instruments in separate rooms. There is no co-operation and co-ordination based on a unifying concept, such as performing a composition for multiple instruments. But this is the case with interdisciplinarity and transdisciplinarity. In musical terms, interdisciplinarity means that several musicians come together in a room to perform a piece of music as a trio or quartet. They interpret the piece of music under the leadership of one of the musicians. Transdisciplinarity is comparable to an orchestra in which musicians perform a piece of music. They are led by a conductor.

In the following section the author will specifically draw upon his personal experience as research leader of the Delta programme for interdisciplinary landscape research, commissioned by Wageningen University and Research Institute in the Netherlands within the frame of the corporate research and development. This incentive programme was initiated in 1999 and completed in 2004. Various Ph.D. papers and papers in scientific journals originating partially or fully from the Delta research programme have already been published, the last ones in 2009 (Van der Valk 2000; *idem* 2003; Tress/Tress/Fry 2005b; Van der Valk/Van Dijk 2009).

5. LESSONS LEARNED FROM THE WAGENINGEN DELTA PROGRAMME

The Wageningen Delta programme for interdisciplinary and transdisciplinary studies in landscape-related fields is a representative example of a large-scale and complex programme for strategic research. The goals of the programme show striking similarities with the PDL/BBO programme, namely exploring new roads in interdisciplinary and transdisciplinary landscape research, developing innovative concepts and theories and conceiving and testing new research methods and technologies. Participants in both programmes aim to make a contribution to the solution of complex societal problems by informing land use planners, landscape architects and policy advisers. The projects in both programmes are linked to the preservation and development of open spaces in metropolitan areas. The researchers take an integrated approach to physical and societal processes in open spaces in western countries with the aim of contributing to landscape planning and design in the future. Preserving cultural-historical values in the landscape is part of the pursuit of sustainability and spatial quality, two central aims of landscape planning.

The Delta programme's research brief had three main aims.
- First, the codification of successful interdisciplinary co-operation between proponents of the humanities, the natural sciences and the social sciences. This concerns both analytical and intentional action (research in practice, design and policy-making) as well as the investigative work on which this is based.
- Second, critical reflection on those practices based on theoretical notions from fields such as systems engineering, planning methodology and theory of science.
- Third, developing methodology and guidelines for interdisciplinary work.[6]

The Delta Programme may not qualify as an exemplary programme but nevertheless is an interesting case for reflection on interdisciplinary work in action. From the perspective of commercial research management the results were considered to be poor. The estimated turnover of the project between 1999 and 2004 is the equivalent of 3 million euros. Money invested by third parties was about 60%. The remaining 40% was research and development money funded by Wageningen University and Research Centre. As so many programmes which start out with high ambitions and precise targets, the exact outcomes of the programme are as yet largely unknown because the project's managers did not commission an independent assessment of the commercial outcomes. From a scholarly perspective the programme has been extremely successful because it gave the incentive to Ph.D. projects which have produced some 50 scientific papers and ten Ph.D. theses. The scientific publications have triggered many innovations in Dutch planning practice and Wageningen's research programme on landscape research and planning. Before the Delta programme, the number of papers and Ph.D. theses in this domain was only a fraction of the production during the programme and afterwards.

The programme was initiated in 1998 by a project group with managers and researchers from various Wageningen research institutes (from both the University and the departmental Agricultural Research Service, DLO). Expectations were high. It was expected to establish firm foundations for an interdisciplinary and transdisciplinary approach to scientific research at Wageningen. The label 'delta' does not refer to soil conditions or the hydrology of the Netherlands but to the fourth letter of the Greek alphabet. The alpha, beta and gamma refer to the humanities, the natural sciences and the social sciences respectively in Dutch academic jargon. Interdisciplinarity was perceived by the board of directors as a trademark of the Wageningen knowledge complex. The delta approach is based on the desire to bring the humanities, natural sciences and social sciences closer together. The delta approach is founded on the idea that cooperation which transcends the limits of disciplines leads to a better knowledge product, subject to the condition that the concrete needs of the client and the possibilities of the knowledge-creating organization are taken into account. Co-operation is no longer an aim in itself, but a means to an end.

The knowledge of laypersons is considered to be an essential ingredient in the development of system innovations. Good communication between scientists and societal actors is a must in the Delta philosophy. The pre-scientific experiential knowledge of the interested parties is a source of inspiration in designing solutions. It enables scientific advisers to devise customized solutions and to operate outside the well-worn technological pathways. Examples include the Aquatic Contours project in the province of North Holland and the open fields project in the province of Drenthe.

Much attention is paid to theory development. Theory development focuses on merging high-quality (disciplinary) building blocks to form an integral theory of the landscape (Antrop 2006). This theory has empirical and normative dimensions. It is not inconceivable that a new scientific discipline, landscape science, will emerge from this theory. The theory in formation partly serves as material for future professionals who are being trained at the University.

The delta approach has no fixed narrowly defined substantive themes within the broad research object of landscape. According to the varying needs of society, new themes will be taken up and treated in a spirit of collaboration.

The delta approach emphasizes scientific competencies (knowledge, skills and attitudes) that are important to fruitful co-operation. Participants in the delta approach research are selected for characteristics that are underutilized, admittedly with good reason, in the normal practice of science. Consider the following:
- Authentic interest in other disciplines;
- Sensitivity to practical application possibilities and societal needs;
- Communication-orientation with the aim of learning to understand the representatives of other disciplines;
- Sensitivity to the demands of scientific teamwork;
- Desire for simplicity and clarity in professional jargon;
- Ability to see sensible combinations of quantitative and qualitative methods;
- Ability to distance oneself from the prejudices that exist in every academic group;
- A respectful and open approach to those who think differently in science;
- Preparedness to invest time and energy in context;
- No fear of losing the connection with colleagues in one's own discipline;
- Trust in one's own scientific qualities.

The Delta programme both acquires the approval of external parties and participants and also elicits their criticism. A distinction can be made between criticism based on scientific theory and scientific practice.

Scientific theoreticians aim their criticism at the holistic ideal. They argue that the pursuit of a unified science is doomed to failure. Interdisciplinarity should not be confused with practising science with the aid of a scientific variant of the mixer. The core of science is the pursuit of truth. Mixing scientific points of view distracts the practitioner from pure science. Scientific practices that have the single goal of transcending the limits of our knowledge must be distinguished from practices in which knowledge, in one form or another, is used in the service of policymaking, technology and other forms of societal action. According to the counter-argument, it is not the process of generating knowledge that requires co-operation, but defining the problems and choices and applying scientific knowledge.

A second objection is that the desire to involve societal parties and policymakers in the process of knowledge formation detracts from the pursuit of objectivity in science. This objection is often heard from the technocratic corner. The counter-argument is that science is never value-free. A pragmatic approach, in which scientists and policymakers jointly explore the limits of action, is preferable to the belief that science can place objective limits on human action.

Practical counter-arguments are linked to doubts about assuring the scientific quality of the products. Natural scientists, academics from the humanities and social scientists often have divergent beliefs about science.[7] The body of knowledge of practical disciplines, such as archaeology, human geography, public administration and planning studies, contains little 'hard' knowledge. This takes nothing away from the societal relevance of these disciplines. However, this observation can be interpreted as encouragement to pursue an increased level of scientific content. This concerns requirements such as careful formulation, keeping causes and results separate, being consistent, identifying testable statements and distinguishing between facts and values.

6. LESSONS

Based on international experience, Fry (Fry 2001; *idem* 2003) has drawn a number of conclusions and formulated lessons about the possibilities and limitations of interdisciplinary research programmes which have landscape as a subject. My own experiences in the Delta programme are along the same line.

Interdisciplinary research into the landscape must be supported by theory development. Landscape ecology, archaeology and historical geography offer good building blocks for a comprehensive theory of the landscape. New disciplines, such as landscape architecture, planning studies and public administration, have fallen behind in this area. Interdisciplinarity is not a trendy phenomenon but a bitter necessity for supporting important decisions about dealing with natural resources or developing the environment for purposes such as nature management, recreation, agriculture and water management. Interdisciplinary research cannot cure all ailments. Interdisciplinarity cannot eliminate conflicts about land use. Science can provide advice about what we can do and what we should not do, but it never provides a definitive answer about what we must do. Interdisciplinarity can weaken a sector-based interest (such as cultural history) because it promotes understanding of other viewpoints and interests. Finally, it is important to understand that not all situations can be transformed so they benefit all parties involved. Choices still have to be made.

International research has provided indications for factors that are decisive to the success of interdisciplinary research programmes into the landscape.
1. The development of theoretical building blocks is paramount. Landscape ecology offers a good point of departure for a broad theory about landscape in which both people and nature are addressed.
2. Research training for young researchers is an essential precondition.
3. Training for research leaders and teambuilding are essential.
4. Without extraordinary motivation for co-operation and personal involvement with the subject of the landscape, interdisciplinarity is doomed to failure.

From the above a number of practical indications can be derived for the approach to interdisciplinary landscape research (Fry 2001; Van der Valk 2003):
- Determine if there is an actual need for interdisciplinarity with respect to the subject of study.
- If there is a demonstrable need, then interdisciplinarity must become an explicit aim of the programme.
- Begin the process of integration at the start of the programme, not at the end.
- The commissioning body (client) and financiers should find out how the desire for interdisciplinarity will be given substantive shape.
- Do not take on a subject that is too big or too broad. More disciplines and more participants lead to a greater risk of friction.

- Pay attention to interpersonal chemistry.
- All researchers must have the courage to question the way in which they define their object of research.
- All researchers must be prepared to go beyond the framework of their own field of research.
- Use joint targets and products in order to strengthen the links between disciplines.
- Emphasise mutual respect between disciplines and divergent approaches.
- Look at the possibilities for jointly developing theoretical notions within the specifications of the interdisciplinary programme.
- Be aware of practical objections (money, personal differences, distance between colleagues).
- Be aware of academic obstacles (merit system, external review committees).
- Share literature, study facilities and problems.
- Maintain periodic contact with professional colleagues via conferences and seminars.
- Accept the fact that interdisciplinarity takes more time but does ensure the periodic generation of research outputs.
- Support studies of the interdisciplinary work process (possibilities and limitations).
- Develop quality criteria and use peer review for interdisciplinarity.
- Reward quality in interdisciplinarity.

NOTES

1 Wageningen University, Wageningen, the Netherlands.
2 This example is based on an interview conducted in 2002 with Dr. Irene Immink, a participant in the programme on behalf of the Alterra research institute.
3 The example is reconstructed from multiple interviews conducted in 2002 with project leader, physical geographer Dr. Kees Kwakernaak from the Alterra Institute. These interviews were conducted during the compilation of a booklet on experiences with multidisciplinary and interdisciplinary research at Alterra.
4 In Dutch the contour is known as blue contour. This makes sense because it was loosely associated with popular concepts in Dutch national planning shown via red and green contours. Red contours were used in regional and national plans to designate urban growth boundaries. Green contours were advocated by nature preservation organizations for the designation of preservation areas.
5 The information is taken from literature quoted in the text and interviews in 2002 with Dr. Theo Spek, who at the time was a doctorate candidate at the University of Wageningen.
6 In a report of the outcomes of the programme (Van der Valk 2003), the following were reported:
   – research and reflection based on best practices;
   – initiating Ph.D. research based on tender financing;
   – initiating and co-financing scientific reflection in the applied research at DLO institutes;
   – organizing courses, seminars and lectures for participants and interested parties from the Netherlands and abroad;
   – publishing scientific and professional publications;
   – building an international expertise network for interdisciplinary and transdisciplinary landscape research;
   – developing models and software;

contributing to other research projects to promote thinking about interdisciplinarity and transdisciplinarity.
7 Scientific knowledge is frequently offered in the form of models or a system. This involves a simplification of complex reality. A model offers the possibility of providing access to the best available knowledge in a useful form to benefit professional practice. Unfortunately, the fact that models can never cover all of reality is often disregarded. Excessively complex models (too many variables) become unrealistic. Excessively simple models provide insufficient answers to the questions with which policymakers are struggling. It is a technocratic misunderstanding to believe that we can eliminate uncertainty with the aid of the latest scientific findings. This is endorsed by every scientist with integrity. But what should we do about uncertainty? We must clearly see the possibilities and limitations of the best knowledge that is currently available. Uncertainty should actually be a central focus in policymaking so that we can deal with it very deliberately. Many forms of uncertainty with which we struggle in societal action cannot be completely reduced by science.

REFERENCES

Antrop, M., 2006: From holistic landscape synthesis to transdiciplinary landscape management, in B. Tress/G. Tress/G. Fry/P. Opdam (eds.), *From Landscape Research to Landscape Planning; Aspects of Integration, Education and Application*, Dordrecht, 27-50.

Dijk, J. M. van, 2008: *Water and Environment in Decision-making. Water Assessment, Environmental Impact Assessment, and Strategic Environmental Assessment in Dutch Planning. A Comparison*, Wageningen (Ph.D. thesis Wageningen University).

Faludi, A./A.J. van der Valk, 1994: *Rule and Order; Dutch Planning Doctrine in the Twentieth Century*, Dordrecht.

Fry, G.L.A., 2001: Multifunctional landscapes: towards transdisciplinary research, *Landscape and Urban Planning* 57, 159-168.

Fry, G.L.A., 2003: Training Needs for Interdisciplinary Research, in G. Fry/B. Tress/G. Tress/A.J. van der Valk (eds.), *Interdisciplinary and Transdisciplinary Landscape Studies: Potential and Limitations*, Wageningen, 118-123.

Gibbons, M./C. Limoges/H. Nowotny/S. Schwartzmann/P. Scott/M. Trow, 1994: *The new production of knowledge: the dynamics of science and research in contemporary societies*, London.

Halffman, W./R. Hoppe, 2005: Science/policy Boundaries. A Changing Division of Labour in Dutch Expert Policy Advise, in S. Maasen/P. Weingart (eds.), Democratization of Expertise? Exploring Novel Forms of Scientific Advice in Political Decision-Making. *Sociology of the Sciences* 24, 135-151.

Hidding, M./J. Kolen/T. Spek, 2001: De biografie van het landschap. Ontwerp voor een inter- en transdisciplinaire benadering van de landschapsgeschiedenis en het cultuurhistorisch erfgoed, in J.H.F. Bloemers/R. During/J.N.H. Elerie/H.A. Groenendijk/M. Hidding/J. Kolen/Th. Spek/M.-H. Wijnen, 2001: *Bodemarchief in Behoud en Ontwikkeling. De conceptuele grondslagen*, Den Haag, 7-110.

Immink, I., 2007: *Voorbij de risiconorm. Nieuwe relaties tussen water, ruimte en risico*, Delft.

Jacobs, M., 2006: *The production of mindscapes. A comprehensive theory of landscape experience*, Wageningen (Ph.D. thesis Wageningen University).

Jonge, J. de, 2009: *Landscape Architecture between Politics and Science. An integrative perspective on landscape planning and design in the network society.* Wageningen (Ph.D. thesis Wageningen University).

Kars, H., 1995: *Archeologie tussen alfa en bèta; inaugurele rede,* Amsterdam (VU University).

Nassauer, J.I./P. Opdam, 2008: Design in science: extending the landscape ecology paradigm, *Landscape Ecology* 23, 633-644.

Nowotny, H./P. Scott/M. Gibbons, 2001: *Rethinking Science. Knowledge and the Public in an Age of Uncertainty,* Cambridge.

Poel, K.R. de/N.P. van der Windt/J. Kruit/J.H.N. Elerie/Th. Spek, 2000: *Essen in perspectief; een interactieve planningsbenadering in Spier, Wijster en Drijber (Midden-Drenthe),* Wageningen.

Rotmans, J., 1998: *Geintegreerd denken en handelen; een noodzakelijk goed,* Maastricht (Inaugural lecture Maastricht University).

Rotmans, J./M.B.A. van Asselt/P. Vellinga, 2000: An Integrated Framework for Sustainable Cities, *Environmental Impact Assessment Review* 20, 265-276,

Schanz, H./G.V. Spies/G. Oesten, 1999: Forstwissenschaft oder Forstwissenschaften: Interdisziplinarität zwischen Zwangsläufigkeit, Vision und Utopie, *Forstwissenschaftliche Centralblatt* 118, 368-380.

Tress, B./G.Tress, 2002: Disciplinary and meta-disciplinary approaches in landscape ecology, in O. Bastian/U. Steinhardt (eds.), *Development and Perspectives of Landscape Ecology,* Dordrecht, 25-37.

Tress, B./G.Tress/H. Décamps/A. d'Hauteserre, 2001: Bridging human and natural sciences in landscape research, *Landscape and Urban Planning* 57, 137-141.

Tress, B./G. Tress/G. Fry, 2005a: Researchers' experiences, positive and negative, in integrative landscape projects, *Environmental Management* 36, 792-807.

Tress, B./G. Tress/G. Fry, 2005b: Integrative studies on rural landscapes: policy expectations and research practice, *Landscape and Urban Planning* 70, 177-191.

Tress, B./G. Tress/G. Fry, 2006: Defining concepts and the process of knowledge production in integrative research, in B. Tress/G. Tress/G. Fry/P. Opdam (eds.), *From Landscape Research to Landscape Planning; Aspects of Integration, Education and Application,* Dordrecht, 13-26.

Tress, B./G. Tress/A.J. van der Valk, 2003: Interdisciplinarity and transdisciplinarity in landscape studies – the Wageningen Delta approach, in G.Fry/B. Tress/G. Tress/A.J. Van der Valk (eds.), *Interdisciplinary and Transdisciplinary Landscape Studies: Potential and Limitations,* Wageningen, 8-17.

Valk, A.J. van der, 2000: *Deltaprogramma Groene Ruimte. Koepelthema: gebiedsgericht, ontwerpgericht en op integratie gericht onderzoek,* Wageningen.

Valk, A.J. van der, 10 april 2003: *Aandachtspunten deltabenadering vanuit het perspectief van de programmaleider,* Wageningen (Notitie voor de directie van het Centrum Landschap van Wageningen UR).

Valk, A. van der/T. van Dijk, 2009: Rethinking Open Space Planning in Metropolitan Areas, in A. van der Valk/T. van Dijk, *Regional planning for open space,* London, 1-20.

Winder, N., 2003: Successes and problems when conducting interdisciplinary or transdisciplinary (= integrative) research, in G. Fry/B. Tress/G. Tress/A.J. van der Valk (eds.), *Interdisciplinary and Transdisciplinary Landscape Studies: Potential and Limitations,* Wageningen, 74-90.

Appendix 1: Lessons learned from the Wageningen Delta programme for interdisciplinary and transdisciplinary studies in landscape-related fields (1999-2003)

Organization of the programme
- Realize that the foundation for real co-operation is established during the initial phase of the programme.
- Reflection on the desired form of co-operation between the practitioners of various disciplines in the programme as a whole is essential within the project. This process should be continuous.
- Choose projects based not only on substantive thematic considerations, but also pay attention to the methodological aspects of integration.
- When designing the programme, pay attention to the comprehensibility of the programme as a whole and the coherence between the projects.
- Avoid conflicting aims.
- Ensure a realistic budget for the programme
- Establish priorities and work with a contingency plan.
- Try to prevent co-operation from becoming ritualistic. Pay attention to theory development that transcends the borders of disciplines.
- Creating innovations involves a time span of years, not of months (as desired by research programmers).
- Develop a practical form of knowledge management for exchanging data, analyses, models and theoretical concepts between projects and between the research projects and the parallel policy activities in archaeological policy, integral conservation of cultural history and land-use planning.
- Encourage serious scientific publication from the outset. Provide good scientific quality assurance for the work.
- Offer a meeting place for researchers inside and outside the university while taking into account the cultural differences between academics, application-oriented researchers and policy officials.
- Ensure a compensation system with positive stimuli for co-operation. Offer compensation for the missed opportunities in a disciplinary career to young researchers who waive the possibility of specialization and choose co-operation instead.

Forming networks
- Work on acquiring key positions in international networks for excellent interdisciplinary oriented research.
- Develop a quality test for integrative studies. Before designing such a test, it is advisable to establish a network of international experts (a community of practice).
- Promptly develop a showcase to display the most important knowledge products to the commissioning bodies (clients) and other users.

Competencies of research leaders
- The leadership must use clear definitions of core concepts such as multidisciplinarity, transdisciplinarity, interdisciplinarity and interactivity.
- Do not underestimate the organizational conditions for integrality.

- Promptly establish the research management with an eye to the special demands of integration in strategic research. This is essentially different from fundamental disciplinary research and applied research to benefit policy.
- Pay attention to the human factor. Excellent scientists are often difficult people to deal with. Each discipline has its own language and culture.
- Innovation requires courage, vision and willingness to invest from all levels of management in a scientific organization.
- The desire to reduce overhead costs by cutting back on programme management can entail major disadvantages. Overhead is difficult to control because it is primarily determined by the commissioning bodies (clients). A complex programme automatically has high overhead costs.

Competencies of researchers
- In co-operation between natural scientists and social scientists, be aware that major differences in culture must be overcome. The greater the diversity in a group of researchers, the lower the probability of a successful result.
- Give researchers the opportunity to acquire experience with integration before holding them to account in this regard.
- Integration requires new competencies. Much learning takes place by trial and error.
- Attention should be paid to developing practical forms of integration. The thinking about integration is the interdisciplinary cement between the disciplinary building blocks.

3. LANDMARKS. A project based on transnational and interdisciplinary scientific co-operation

Almudena Orejas & Guillermo-Sven Reher[1]

ABSTRACT

Action COST A27 LANDMARKS has been a successful attempt at establishing an effective transnational interdisciplinary project around the theme of landscapes. Running from 2004 to 2007, and coordinated from Madrid, A27 has proven extremely fruitful: 17 conferences and workshops, 13 edited publications. The best result, however, has been the establishment of working networks across fields and national borders.

In this chapter we revise the scientific environment in which this project was conceived and generated, as well as the internal organisation it adopted. Our intention, though, is not to congratulate ourselves for our good work. We want to go over the important challenges faced, how they were met, and what lessons can be learned for future collaborative European projects.

In order to achieve transnational and interdisciplinary integration, the internal structure of the project was organised around objectives and work packages which required side-by-side collaboration. Some problems, though, were encountered, particularly relating to the different degree of involvement of different partners, which tended to be self-defeating. Another problem is the lack of visibility of that research given the nature of COST publishing.

In conclusion, landscapes as a theme are a good way to push interdisciplinarity and transnationality forward in a field which is still being created and which requires these two to be in full swing.

KEY WORDS

LANDMARKS, landscapes, heritage; European collaborative projects; interdisciplinarity, transnationality

1. INTRODUCTION

LANDMARKS was conceived as a scientific co-operation project with two converging lines of interest, sharing research experiences and expertise on the historical dimension of cultural landscapes and generating tools based on that knowledge that would assist their management and foster the dissemination of scientifically-based programmes. That is why the participation of academic institutions was combined with administrative bodies and local/regional development organizations. In this way the project intended to extend the knowledge of the past into today's management strategies with a keen interest in preserving landscapes threatened by the abandonment of traditional lifestyles. Both approaches were part of one unified project and they were not hierarchically articulated but designed as complementary and interdependent facets of the collective research activity.

2. THE ACTION COST A27 LANDMARKS: UNDERSTANDING PRE-INDUSTRIAL STRUCTURES IN RURAL AND MINING LANDSCAPES

2.1 *Motives and origins of LANDMARKS*

The combination of research on landscape and cultural heritage had been clearly identified during the 5th and 6th Framework Programmes as one of the key areas where scientific development and co-operation was necessary (Review 2004). A series of projects started their development within these frames: SENSOR (Sustainability Impact Assessment: Tools for Environmental, Social and Economic Effects of Multifunctional Land Use in European Regions), SUIT (Sustainable Development of Urban Historical Areas though an Active Integration within Towns), PICTURE (Pro-active management of the Impact of Cultural Tourism upon Urban Resources and Economies), APPEAR (Accessibility Projects. Sustainable Preservation and Enhancement of Urban Subsoil Archaeological Remains) and DEMOTEC (Development of a Monitoring System for Cultural Heritage through European co-operation). As a next step, the protection of archaeological sites and cultural landscapes is explicitly taken into account in the 7th Framework Programme (in the Environment theme of the Co-operation work programme).

During the same period the Congress of Regional and Local Authorities of the Council of Europe had worked on an agreement on common mores involving local and regional stakeholders in relation to landscape. That effort culminated in 2000, when the European Landscape Convention was approved by the Council of Europe (CoE), a document gradually ratified by thirty of the forty-seven countries who form the Council. In any case, the implementation of the ELC is a far-reaching reform which would ensure the protection of Europe's landscapes by involving different public and private bodies, as well as academic and non-academic spheres. The CoE established that "the aims of this Convention are to promote landscape protection, management and planning, and to organize European co-operation on landscape issues" (Florence 2000 art. 3). As a consequence of this, it is considered a way of creating new opportunities for sustainable development in any kind of region as well as a key to understanding and protecting cultural heritage. Landscape is a recognizable form of common heritage for Europe and public policy was pointing the way forward for the scientific community. Previously, the UNESCO had recognized cultural landscapes as a form of heritage in 1992, an important precedent. The World Heritage Convention became the first international legal instrument to recognize and protect cultural landscapes as combined works of nature and of people. Cultural landscapes could be included in the World Heritage List under three main categories: clearly defined landscape designed and created intentionally by people, organically evolved landscape (including two sub-categories: relict (or fossil) landscape and continuing landscape) and associative cultural landscapes (Operational Guidelines 2008).

These two processes synthesize the research and socio-political contexts where LANDMARKS was conceived.[2] The impulse behind Action COST A27 was based on two main stimuli. First, many of the partners enjoyed previous experience in relevant national research programmes and international projects funded by COST and ESF. Second, the urgent need to implement the ELC required the development of scientifically-based activities that would result in a crystallization of collaboration as well as outcomes within that frame. As a consequence, many of the Action's activities are directly related with developing ELC policy.

Action COST A27's project proposal was centred on a principal objective, the identification and evaluation of pre-industrial elements in the European landscape threatened by the abandonment of traditional agricultural and mining activities. There are two main tasks related to this, the intellectual examination of regional and local practices in the framework of broader historic processes and the understanding of the evolution of the present-day landscape through a diachronic reading of the landscape (MoU 2004; Orejas/Mattingly/Clavel-Lévêque 2009a, 28-29).

In order to achieve its objectives, LANDMARKS had to focus on the heritage potential of landscapes from the way they change in time, how their endangerment is a risk for social identity and non-renewable heritage and in what way they can be incorporated into twenty-first century society as improved spaces.

2.2 The scientific structure of LANDMARKS: specific objectives and Working Groups

However, A27 revolved around a series of more specific objectives which were achievable within the frame of the Action (MoU 2004). These were:
- Analysis of the morphological elements and models of integration in the landscape of today.
- Analysis of the technologies related to the historical use of landscapes.
- Diachronic study of specific legal and administrative practices.
- Analysis of landscape perception throughout history by the communities that inhabited and made use of them.
- Provision of mechanisms for the public presentation of landscapes and the optimization of their cultural heritage-related resources.

Achieving these objectives was facilitated through the creation of four Working Groups (WGs) with specific tasks, coordinators and goals. This key structure ensured interdisciplinary collaboration aimed at meeting specific WG goals, harnessing co-operation while making full use of varied expertise. The first two working groups revolved around the types of landscapes dealt with directly in A27, rural and mining areas. After activity ceases at any point in time, mining tends to be very destructive of both the environment and the dependent social structures which it had generated. By producing documentation from sampled mining areas of Europe, WG1 expected to offer valuable advice about how these areas can be turned into cultural landscapes.

The loss of traditional land use in rural areas has opened the door to new risks such as fires and erosion. WG2 elaborated a sample inventory of traditional landscape markers which could draw attention to this abandonment. In this way the countryside's fate could be turned around by making that traditional land use a new opportunity for sustainable development. Both WG1 and WG2 developed joint initiatives based on these principles.

The other two WGs were created as transversal harnessers. WG3 would work on the production of efficient tools for the management and presentation of information, focusing on the application of innovative geo-information systems to the study and presentation of cultural landscapes based on good practice case studies. WG4 was created to ensure that the activities and results of all WGs were made visible beyond A27 and by designing joint activities. The existence of joint meetings or workshops and trans-WG publications guaranteed the integration of all four Working Groups.

3. ACHIEVING INTEGRATION

3.1 Countries and disciplines

Part of the logic behind the European added value concept is that scientific initiatives must cross borders of every type (Muldur *et al.* 2006, 183-222). The diversity of European cultures, academic structures and research priorities implies that a negotiation towards a common ground is a necessary first step. This dialogue must take place between different countries as well as disciplines. Thus, *transnationality* and *interdisciplinarity* are synonymous with European collaborative projects. In addition, the participation of partners outside the traditional central-western European academic circles is always stimulated. These requirements posed serious challenges which were tackled during the inception and design of Action COST A27 in the following way.

COST stipulates that Actions must have a Management Committee (MC) and allows a Working Group (WG) internal structure. In the case of LANDMARKS the MC included representatives of all countries and disciplines involved in the project. The four WGs had 3 coordinators each, appointed at the start of the project. Apart from COST standard structure, A27 decided to incorporate two elements to ensure adequate co-ordination, a core group and evaluation panels.

The core group was composed of the Chair and two Vice-chairs and the WG coordinators. This committee was at the heart of all dialogue between MC and WGs, allowing for common strategy and ensuring fluid dialogue both bottom-up and top-down. This group, which had no meetings of its own, worked as an intermediate structure, allowing for the organization and common design of both MC meetings and WG strategies and making the adoption of some decisions more efficient. Evaluation panels were created to assess both Short Time Scientific Mission beneficiaries and Training School candidacies.

The MC held regular plenary A27 meetings which the WGs could use to have particular meetings of their own. This communication rhythm ensured a strict control of timetables, working programmes and intra-WG dialogue. All in all, participation in MC and WG co-ordination involved 47 researchers from all signatory countries.

The initial project was submitted in 2002 with 44 partners from 11 countries expressing interest (MoU 2004, 18-25). In 2004, when A27 began its work, 14 countries had signed. The final number of participating nations reached 21 by the end of the Action in 2008. These national delegations included more than 80 institutions and the permanent involvement of over 150 researchers.

3.2 Working plan: scientific joint activities

COST avails its Actions of certain instruments which help consolidate coordinated actions. Among these are the meetings, workshops and conferences. A27 held 17 MC/WG meetings between June 2004 and September 2008 in nine locations (9 MC/WG joint meetings and 8 specific WG meetings). In addition, and open to non-members, six workshops and six conferences were held. Their topics ranged from highly specialized meetings such as that on geoarchaeology of river sedimentation processes (Ghent-BE, 09/2006=Vermeulen/De Dapper 2009), to broader themes such as landscape heritage research (Madrid-ES, 10/2004=Ruiz del Árbol/Orejas 2005) and socio-economic implications (Funen-DK, 05/2005 and Samos-GR, 05/2006). Variety can also be seen in the topics discussed ranging from ancient or contemporary perception (Le Mans-FR, 12/2006=Compatangelo-Soussignan *et al.* 2008), legal traditions (Naples-IT, 11/2005=Reduzzi 2007) to historic mining (Aberystwyth-UK, 09/2007). A thorough list of these events can be found in the Final Report (Final Report 2008, 7-10).

While management meetings enabled the daily organization of work within the Action, the WG meeting became the forum for specific discussions and programming of particular activities. Open workshops and conferences exposed the Action to other academic and non-academic spheres and stimulated the involvement of participating institutions.

The participation of junior researchers through Short Term Scientific Missions (STSMs) was encouraged, resulting in 20 transnational visits. Training schools offered high-profile scientific preparation concerning two specific issues covered by A27, analytical techniques regarding mining landscapes (Aberystwyth-UK, 09/2007) and the application of science and technology for cultural heritage (Genova-IT, 09/2007). In fact the Genova Training School involved all COST Actions focusing on diverse aspects of cultural heritage through the COST Group of Interest on Cultural Heritage. In addition, another two training activities were participated in directly by the Action, the Complutense University summer school on landscape archaeology and heritage (San Lorenzo de El Escorial-ES, 08/2005) and ARCHAIA training seminar on archaeological planning, conservation and management (Bologna-IT, 05/2008).

Finally, thirteen publications intended as a vehicle for integrating project members, were edited by Action members to ensure the visibility of A27's objectives and nature. These were therefore always required to comply with the following conditions: collaborative, international, integrating junior and senior researchers, involving other academic institutions, involving local institutions and directed at different audiences. Like the themes of the meetings that they were sometimes the proceedings of (see above), the themes of the publications were quite varied. One was an edited translation and study of a Roman land survey technical treaty (Behrends *et al.* 2005), another dealt exclusively with geo-information technologies applied to cultural landscapes (Bender *et al.* 2008) or their modern perception (Lévêque/Ruiz del Árbol 2010), while others sought to demonstrate different casestudies of good practice in cultural landscape management (Lévêque *et al.* 2006; Bartels *et al.* 2008; Fairclough/Møller 2008). As a culmination of the Action the last collective publication sought to synthesize this integrative spirit with a transnational co-authorship policy which reflected joint research activity, ongoing debates, or emerging themes or approaches (Orejas/Mattingly/Clavel-Lévêque 2009b).

All these activities were oriented towards the close collaboration of partners across borders and disciplines. People from different backgrounds had to come together and work side by side in order to establish a fluid communication. That is why the work oriented to the preparation of these collective publications has often been as fruitful as the production of the books themselves, namely to reach an agreement on the structure, criteria, the thematic, geographical or chronological limits or the selection of exemplary case studies has been the core of intense discussions in order to identify a common ground while allowing room for differences.

4. HIGHLIGHTS, LETDOWNS AND SOME LESSONS FOR THE FUTURE

Was A27 successful in responding to the challenge behind the European added value, transnationality, interdisciplinarity, integration of all types of partners? After initial drawbacks in finding a common basis, progress was made from 2006 onwards. All WGs adapted common ideas that enabled common case study presentations and recommendations for future advancement. Certainly one of the highlights in the scientific debate was to stress that landscape reflects the non-sectorialization of pre-industrial society, which entails the need for landscape studies to adopt an integrative and diachronic approach that includes society and territory as structural frames. It could be seen as obvious, but it is not so easy to articulate the strongly sectoral reading of contemporary landscapes and the integrative perspective required in the study of pre-industrial phases. A purely stratigraphic approach is not enough. LANDMARKS is full of suggestive proposals for the future integration within landscape studies of the scientific community, stakeholders, policy-makers and local and regional actors.

Another important challenge has been to connect Action A27 with ongoing or potential national and local/regional programmes. The consensus found within the Action is in stark contrast with the diversity of approaches and administrative frameworks in those programmes. Though LANDMARKS has stimulated a dialogue between them, the European framework that would make this co-operation possible is still to be developed. The Action has been instrumental in the creation of a European network of cultural landscapes, some of them already formalized as cultural or archaeological parks, as a way of linking scientific results and strategic issues on the European scale.

LANDMARKS finished nearly a year ago, in 2008. We feel that some honesty is in order to assess the successes and failures of the project so that valuable lessons can be learned for the future. First, we will evaluate the behaviour of the project in certain axes already discussed such as transnationality, interdisciplinarity, participation and scientific results, followed by some suggestions based on our experience.

4.1 Challenges faced

Transnationality

Considering the importance of cross-border networking as a way for the EU to build a solid scientific structure that can compete with Japan, the USA, China, etc., it is undoubtedly a vital requirement for the European added value concept. The risks come when numbers become a more important requisite than quality when building collaborative networks. Co-operation has often been unable to overcome both horizontal and vertical segmentation, stifling adequate science and technology policy development, a problem already identified by Grande/Peschke 1999.

In Action A27 there was a nucleus of partners which had already worked together before and had contributed to the project's design. In general terms these would remain very active participants throughout the duration. In addition, some new partners who joined the project in the early stages, attracted by the objectives and design, proved to be very active and collaborated by updating the working plan and enlarging the scope of scientific perspectives. The result was a community of practice among many of the partners which sustained the project's structure. This community of practice has demonstrated not only its efficiency for cooperative production in the frame of the Action (publications, meetings, strategic documents, specific working groups), its permanent effects will be visible in the following years both in new common projects and in the common language shared by different national initiatives. The low level of participation of other partners was due to various reasons including a peripheral involvement in the project, later integration in the Action, personal scientific profile or interests, institutional scientific policy, etc. (a common problem, see Bachtler 2008). In general terms one-third of the members was strongly involved, one-third was clearly collaborative and one-third was scarcely interested in the Action. Whatever the reasons for this imbalance, non-involvement has a tendency to become a very negative self-fulfilling prophecy.

Interdisciplinarity

Dialogue tends to be much more difficult across disciplines than between different countries. In this sense LANDMARKS can be considered a success involving historians, archaeologists, environmental experts, scientists, geologists, biologists, mathematicians, geo-information specialists, literature experts, geographers, spatial planners and heritage managers. Many conferences and publications comprising contributions from all partners required close collaboration in their organization and edition. As is common with this challenge, we feel many opportunities were missed. True interdisciplinarity requires much more co-operation and the identification of common research goals as well as problems to be broached, which in turn makes European participation fundamental. Sometimes cutting across both types of boundaries, national and disciplinary, requires a double effort which partners often consider unrewarding.

Participation

The integration of different academic disciplines within Europe is closely related to the issue of transnationality. The fundamentals of the European Research Area were conceived from the central and western academic traditions and institutional frames. However, the ERA is in fact built on a plurality of trajectories, with the differences increasing throughout the twentieth century parallel to the development of administrative frames for research and teaching. Scientific communication between some subsets of European countries, in part sustained by common trajectories, has not necessarily entailed the creation of co-operation programmes, though it has generated a sort of scientific regionalization which cannot be ignored. The requirements or recommendations to include as many countries as possible in the projects directly address the ERA objective of building a common research community. That is the reason for considering the geographical balance a key element in the articulation of collaborative projects. However, the number and nationality of the participants should not weigh more than the involvement they can provide within the project. Often, the problems related with international collaboration are further complicated by the subsidiary role that some partners tend to adopt. The reason for this adoption has to do both with the smaller role they are willing and able to carry out and with their self-defeating absence from management positions within the project which only hampers any possibility of having a greater role in the future.

Many institutions or research groups used their, sometimes insignificant, participation in international projects as a platform with which to improve their competitive standing within national funding programmes. Particularly in these cases the rewards were far beyond the demands.

Scientific results

A total of 30 joint activities have been developed in the frame of LANDMARKS, including workshops, conferences, publications and training schools. A27 is particularly proud of the integration of early-stage researchers and the active co-ordination efforts carried out within national and regional research programmes. At the same time, a special effort was made to edit many publications and a brochure that was distributed throughout Europe in different languages. Their editorial boards have ensured the quality of publications and the MC has sought the equilibrium on topics and audiences targeted. Nevertheless the platforms chosen made this output hardly visible to the scientific community as a whole. This is related to the nature of these publications and the poor distribution they get. In a similar way, the usually poor internet profile combined with tardiness or lack of interest, virtually amounts to academic invisibility.

4.2 Lessons learned

Some of the lessons for the future which we extract from our experience are implicit in the previous discussion but we will proceed to explicitly point out some aspects. Sometimes we are dealing with a paradoxical situation. On the one hand, researchers and scientific bodies feel the need for internationalization and it has become a strong tool for the evaluation of academic activity. On the other hand, we are often conscious of the scarce profitability of projects requiring an enormous investment in co-ordination and management not proportional to the real production of innovative knowledge. Reconsidering transnational solidarity or geographical balance, i.e. involving a reasonable number of truly active partners and adapting the project's scale to the scientific focus and aims, would also reduce the perception that European projects require double the work and are half as effective in achieving scientific impact. They are often considered as an afterthought, a perception which turns this into a structural problem.

This is not the right forum for reviewing some general problems detected in the European research programmes related to the selection of topics, budgets allocated, evaluation panels and so on. The goal of these concluding remarks, outlined below, is more modest. We wish to share some thoughts based on our particular experience.

Thoughts from own experience

The relative flexibility in allowing the bottom-up emergence of new themes for collaborative projects, initiatives which should be granted more possibilities given their success, has helped identify the new transdomain topics of landscape studies and heritage sciences. Understanding landscape as heritage thus means creating a new transdomain that spans two emerging transdisciplinary fields of their own. In our experience, though interdisciplinarity is a good thing we cannot turn our backs to specific disciplinary achievements, as long as these are useful in confronting common problems by adding to, not working apart from, common methodological frameworks. Landscape studies not only straddles many different disciplines and scales but also treads the ground between research and society by focusing on the social value of knowledge in on-the-ground activity related to planning, protection, management and dissemination of cultural heritage. Research is therefore not dependent on policy or social needs, but converges with them. Cultural heritage, a transdomain theme generated from the Humanities, must serve as a lever with which this domain asserts its importance. Initiatives such as HERA (Humanities in the European Research Area) are fully aware of this. A strong effort in coordinating cultural heritage studies throughout Europe, avoiding overlapping tasks, can only benefit the Humanities by giving them a competitive edge within the Framework Programme and the European Research Area. With landscape and heritage they can be reinterpreted into a new role which crosses existing academic frontiers, allowing the Humanities to scientifically lead transdomain projects, no doubt a challenge to traditional stances.

Ongoing projects should have fluid communication so that efforts are directed towards complementarity, not incongruity. If possible, efforts should be placed on adding to previous projects and building towards further objectives. Many scattered initiatives require a greater co-ordination effort so that work and objectives do not overlap and efforts can be maximized. In relation to this, and in order to avoid it, project results should be handily available. There is often an obscurity around them because of the lack of visibility mentioned before. Simplifying dissemination channels, internet, leaflets, brochures and pamphlets and texts in different languages would ensure higher visibility. Empowering formation programmes and mobility should be kept as a top priority. They normally mean so much more work for project members that they are rarely considered worthwhile.

The participation in European projects must serve as a stimulus to develop national networks by compelling partners to be national-level co-ordinators while at the same time being international representatives. Landscape studies have a territorial dimension which makes the integration of scales necessary.

Three axes for European collaboration
We have identified three main axes in which European collaboration is possible and beneficial: a. comparative perspectives based on selected case studies; b. design of integrative methodological approaches and; c. the establishment of efficient channels of knowledge transfer.

a. In landscape studies co-operation will fail when it seeks homogenization. On the other hand, it will succeed when it tends towards quality comparative approaches. Developing common frames such as region, not as the administrative unit but as a geo-historical one, diachronic perspectives and non-sectoral approaches will be helpful in establishing a common language with which dialogue can proceed. Finally, the examples of good practice, as well as the failures, can assist in clarifying the way forward. Above all, research on landscape must attempt to go before or beyond policy while always attempting to confront existing social needs.

b. Landscapes are a frame for understanding complexity, they deal with the effect of time, the interaction of humans and nature, the dialogue between culture and identity, etc. Complexity should not be simplified but embraced. Being at the forefront of research, landscape studies combine high-quality methodology with an unmitigated importance of transference to society. They confront the tendency of renewed regionalization within Europe with a multi-level perspective on the processes affecting local, regional and global realities. Cultural landscape studies have clearly marked the future steps to be taken. Among them we can highlight the role of geo-information technologies, for they are the tool necessary for recording the multivariate and complex data involved in landscape analysis. These, in turn, can serve as testing ground for developing more advanced protocols which add new dimensions such as time. Similarly, their role in research, management and dissemination of landscapes following standardized protocols, such as the Spatial Data Infrastructures (SDIs), can be perfectly integrated. With further collaboration and development in the field, research on historic landscapes can potentially follow a common methodology, thereby shedding light on the invisible relations which create them.

c. The social value of cultural heritage is clearly recognized as one of the main axes on which to build a sustainable landscape for Europe, a reality addressed by the Faro Convention (Faro Convention 2005). It is compatible with the society that inhabits the landscape, for the present and future become part of the historical process studied. Similarly, there is an ethical issue at stake when considering the dialogue between conservative practices and innovative solutions. By understanding and managing landscape we also shape it. The ultimate goal of studies on historic landscapes such as those dealt with in LANDMARKS is to reconsider the social and productive model we have so that cultural heritage can be protected and society benefits. Turning depressed landscapes into sustainable cultural landscapes is possible when specific challenges are met, such as the ordered planning of abandoned areas, recovery of traditional activities which contribute to heritage and environmental protection and economic revitalization.

NOTES

1   Research Group *Social Structure and Territory-Landscape Archaeology*. Centre for Human and Social Sciences (CCHS), CSIC. almudena.orejas@cchs.csic.es; guillermo.reher@cchs.csic.es. This paper is written as part of the research projects *Formation and transformation of the* civitas *in the Iberian Northwest/Formación y disolución de la* civitas *en el Noroeste peninsular (CIVITAS)* (AR2008-06018-C03-01/HIST) and *CONSOLIDER – Research Programme on Technologies for the conservation and valorization of Cultural Heritage/Programa de Investigación para la conservación y revalorización del Patrimonio Cultural (TCP)* (CSD2007-0058).

2   For general information and unpublished documents: COST website: http://www.cost.esf.org/; Action COST A27 LANDMARKS: http://www.soc.staffs.ac.uk/jdw1/costa27home.html; Action COST A27 Cultural Parks, Cultural Projects and Activities: http://www.unipg.it/COSTactionA27/parks-activities/.

REFERENCES

Bachtler, J., 2008: *Overcoming the barriers to transnational cooperation*, Aviemore (paper given at Launch of the Northern Periphery Programme 2007-2013, 21/02/2008).

Bartels, C./M. Ruiz del Árbol/H. van Londen/A. Orejas (eds.), 2008: *Landmarks. Profiling Europe's Landscapes*, Bochum.

Behrends, O./M. Clavel-Lévêque/D. Conso/A. Gonzales/J.-Y. Guillaumin/J. Peyras/S. Ratti/R. Compatangelo-Soussignan/L. Lévêque/O. Olesti/J.W.M. Peterson/F. Reduzzi/G. Tirologos (eds.), 2005: *Agennius Urbicus. Controverses sur les terres*, Napoli/Paris.

Bender, O./N. Evelpidou/A. Krek/A. Vassilopoulos (eds.), 2008: *Geoinformation Technologies for Geo-Cultural Landscapes: European perspectives*, London.

Compatangelo-Soussignan, R./J.-R. Bertrand/J. Chapman/P.-Y. Laffont (eds.), 2008 : *Marqueurs des Paysages et systèmes socio-économiques. Landmarks and socio-economics systems. Proceedings of the Le Mans Conference (7th-9th December 2006)*, Rennes.

Fairclough, G./P. Grau Møller (eds.), 2008: *Landscape as Heritage – The Management and Protection of Landscape in Europe, a summary by the Action COST A27 LANDMARKS*, Bern (Geographica Bernensia 79).

Faro, 2005: *Council of Europe Framework Convention on the Value of Cultural Heritage for Society*, Strasbourg (Council of Europe).

Final Report, 2008: *Action COST A27 "Understanding pre-industrial structures in rural and mining landscapes (LANDMARKS)". Final Scientific Report*, Madrid/Þingvellir.

Florence, 2000: *European Landscape Convention. Florence, 20 October 2000*, Strasbourg (Council of Europe).

Grande, E./A. Peschke, 1999: Transnational cooperation and policy networks in European science policy-making, *Research Policy* 28, 43-61.

Lévêque, L./M. Ruiz del Árbol (eds.), 2010: *Heritage, Images, Memory of European Landscapes*, Paris.

Lévêque, L./M. Ruiz del Árbol/L. Pop/C. Bartels (eds.), 2006: *Journeys through European Landscapes/ Voyages dans les paisajes européens*, Ponferrada.

MoU, 2004: *Memorandum of Understanding for the implementation of a European Concerted Research Action designated as COST A27 "Understanding pre-industrial structures in rural and mining landscapes (LANDMARKS)"*.

Muldur, U./F. Corvers/H. Delanghe/J. Dratwa/D. Heimberger/B. Sloan/S. Vanslembrouck, 2006: *A new deal for an effective European research policy: the design and impacts of the 7th framework programme*, Dordrecht.

Operational Guidelines, 2008: *Operational Guidelines for the Implementation of the World Heritage Convention WHC*, Paris (World Heritage Centre UNESCO), 173.

Orejas, A./D.J. Mattingly/M. Clavel-Lévêque, 2009a: Landscapes in European history. Some thoughts from the COST A27 experience, in A. Orejas/D.J. Mattingly/M. Clavel-Lévêque (eds.), *From present to past through landscape*, Madrid, 21-42.

Orejas, A./D.J. Mattingly/M. Clavel-Lévêque (eds.), 2009b: *From present to past through landscape*, Madrid.

Reduzzi, F. (ed.), 2007: *Sfruttamento, tutela e valorizzazione del territorio: dal diritto romano alla regolamentazione europea e internazionale*, Napoli.

Review 2004: *A Review of the EC Research on Environment Protection and Conservation of the European Cultural Heritage. 5th and 6th framework programmes projects*, EC Working Document.

Ruiz del Árbol, M./A. Orejas (eds.), 2005: *Landscapes as Cultural Heritage in the European Research. Proceedings of the Open Workshop (Madrid, 29th October 2004)*, Madrid.

Vermeulen, F./M. De Dapper (eds.), 2009: *Ol'man river: Geo-Archaeological Aspects of Rivers and River Plains. Proceedings of the International Conference Gent 2006*, Gent.

4. The Planarch experience

John H. Williams[1]

ABSTRACT

Planarch (PLANning and ARCHaeology) was a European Interreg project with partners from England, France, Belgium, the Netherlands and Germany which ran in two phases from 1999 to 2006. The aim was to improve the integration of archaeology in spatial planning through sharing experience and joint working. A project philosophy involving the cyclical process of identification, evaluation, management and promotion of the archaeological resource had understanding at its hub. Within the themes key work examined how to generate sound information bases (in particular the role of Historic Environment Records) for underpinning decision-making, the effectiveness of different approaches to archaeological field evaluation and the formulation of management strategies for embracing the historic environment within land-use planning, both at a strategic and a project level. A major study investigated current approaches to dealing with cultural heritage in Environmental Impact Assessment and drew up a series of Guiding Principles. The project underlined the importance of the iterative application of identification, evaluation, management and promotion in decision-making; understanding should be at the heart of decision-making, accepting that understanding can be personal and subjective, and effective communication, together with stakeholder involvement and ownership, is therefore essential from the early stages of any proposals.

KEY WORDS

Planarch; integration of archaeology in spatial planning; archaeological field evaluation; archaeological management strategies; Environmental Impact Assessment; communication

1. INTRODUCTION

The Planarch 1 project came into being in 1999, after a gestation period of about two years, and continued until 2002 with partners in southern England, northern France, the Netherlands and Belgium. For Planarch 2, which ran from 2003 to 2006, these same countries were involved, if with some changes in actual partners and with the addition of the Rhineland in Germany (Fig. 1-2). The projects were financed mainly by a combination of partner contributions and European Interreg funding for the North-West Europe region, the IIC stream for the first project and IIIB for the second. The following paper briefly introduces the philosophy behind the project and the subject areas covered; more detail is available in the various reports listed in the bibliography and referenced in the text. The contribution concludes with some personal observations that are hopefully of value in terms of the purpose of this volume and its focus on inter- and transdisciplinarity.

Planarch (PLANning and ARCHaeology) developed from the realization of a number of archaeologists involved in heritage management on either side of the southern North Sea that they were dealing with a common past within an evolving European political framework that on the one hand promotes

Fig. 1
Map showing showing the location of the Planarch partners.

social, political and economic harmony but yet fails to recognize adequately the transnationality of its prehistoric and historical roots. Indeed, while the European Union has a myriad of Directorates-General covering diverse areas of policy that include agriculture, education, the environment, justice, enterprise and economic and financial affairs, cultural heritage is relegated, under the subsidiarity principle, to being a matter normally dealt with nationally rather than transnationally. This is regrettable given that many of the frontiers of today are in fact recent constructs when related to the span of human history and that many cultural movements have paid little heed to national boundaries. Heritage does, however, figure prominently on the agenda of the separate Council of Europe as witnessed, for example in the

		Planarch 1	Planarch 2
Kent County Council (lead partner)	(E.)	●	■
Essex County Council	(E.)	●	■
Direction Régional des Affaires Culturelles	(Fr.)	●	
Rijksdienst voor het Oudheidkundig Bodemonderzoek	(Nl.)	●	■
Bureau Oudheidkundig Onderzoek Rotterdam	(Nl.)	●	
Province of East Flanders	(B.)	●	
Ministry of the Walloon Region	(B.)	●	
University of Ghent	(B.)	●	■
Institut National de Recherches Archéologiques Préventives	(Fr.)	●	■
Vlaams Instituut voor het Onroerend Erfgoed	(B.)		■
Landschaftsverband Rheinland	(D.)		■

Both projects were supported by English Heritage (E.)

Fig. 2
The partners for Planarch 1 and 2.

Fig. 3
Planarch 2 model: understanding at the centre of a cyclical process of identification, evaluation, management and promotion.

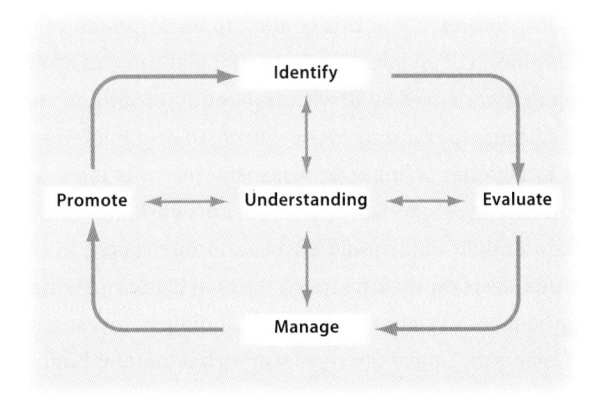

Valletta, Florence and Granada Conventions, which respectively deal with archaeology, landscape and architecture (Granada 1985; Valletta 1992; Florence 2000).

2. PROJECT DESIGN

Planarch 1 aimed to share experience and academic knowledge; develop methodologies for improving archaeological decision-making based on desk assessment, field evaluation and predictive modelling, both at a regional and a local level; integrate within the spatial planning process best practice for mitigation of impacts on the archaeological resource; and investigate approaches for conserving sites and presenting archaeology to the public.

For Planarch 2 there were similar aims, but now set within a model that recognized understanding as a hub around which there is a cyclical process of identification, evaluation, management and promotion (Fig. 3). Accordingly four activity areas focussed on identifying the resource, evaluating the resource, managing the resource and promoting the resource. The work undertaken and the lessons learned are examined below in section 4 (Results), utilizing the framework of the Planarch 2 model, but firstly it is profitable to make some observations about working in a multinational partnership.

3. INTEGRATION

A key objective of the initial phases of Planarch 1 was to increase awareness of the different organizational structures and legislative frameworks within which the partners operated (Cuming/Williams 2001; Evans/Williams 2001a) while at the same time examining commonalities and differences in terms of the archaeological resource itself. These actions were designed to enable the partnership to function more effectively through developing mutual trust and understanding, something that all disciplines and professions would find rewarding to embrace, even when working within a single region or country. Over the lifespan of the project, partnership became increasingly effective and while perhaps from time to time innate regional temperaments, academic philosophies, ways of working and governmental structures surfaced, increased awareness of alternative perspectives enriched discussion and led to increasingly consensual decision-making. Constructive diversity promotes fertile dialogue and leads to more effective shared outcomes.

It is interesting in this context to examine the role of language. Planarch was very much about the integration of archaeology in spatial planning and from day one 'policy' was an essential part of the dialogue, a word used by all with apparently a common view as to its meaning. Yet on one occasion, when the need came to translate 'policy' from an original English paper into French, there were alternative views as to whether *politique* or *réglementation* was more appropriate. This perhaps highlights a distinction between an Anglo-Saxon policy framework, utilizing precedent and providing a context within which action might and should ensue, and one rooted in the principles of the Napoleonic Code, setting out future decision-making much more in black and white. Again while *scientifique* might underpin French approaches to rigorous field and laboratory investigation, the (to some) seemingly academic overtones of 'scientific' make the word somewhat alien to English planning policy guidance. While the examples above involve translation from one language to another, can we always be certain that individual words and more extended messages have the same meaning for the speaker and the recipient? This can clearly be an issue when searching for significance in the world around us.

4. RESULTS

Throughout the Planarch project the importance of having sound information to underpin decision-making was very much recognized and attention was paid to the role of Sites and Monuments Records/Historic Environment Records as the basis for identifying the historical environment resource (Clarke 2001; Cuming/Evans/Williams 2001; Gilman *et al.* 2006). These Records may range from the presentation of point data to the mapping of sites utilizing polygons, to the more comprehensive and precise depiction of archaeological and historic features, perhaps on a 3-dimensional topographic background. In all cases the aim is to present information, but invariably there will be uncertainty as to how representative of the total historic environment resource is what is visible and known. In the case of the Netherlands, on account of the sometimes significant depths of alluvial deposits masking earlier archaeological horizons, recourse is had to predictive modelling, although it must be admitted that, particularly where the underlying historic topography is not uniform, the reliability of the methodology remains uncertain (Van Leusen/Kamermans 2005). In England, recent years have seen the development of historic landscape mapping and historic landscape characterization in an attempt to move away from individual sites to a broader landscape context. Again, while these are extremely valuable tools, the focus is on what from the past has survived into the landscape of the present day. What is still invisible and unrecognized? Giving true time-depth to a non-visual landscape presents many challenges not only of definition but also conceptually: how valid a determinant for future land-use planning is a perceived, or an imagined, landscape? The Planarch lesson, in no way unexpected, is that understanding will be increased the greater the quantity and accuracy of the information available and the clearer it is presented.

While historic environment databases provide an essential launch-pad for considering heritage issues in a spatial planning context, rarely is it possible to make informed decisions without recourse to further more in-depth evaluation and the Planarch project here had a particularly fruitful exchange of experience and best practice (Evans/Williams 2001b; Hey/Lacey 2001; Cuming/Evans/Williams 2001; Andrikopoulou-Strack *et al.* 2006; Blancquaert/Medlycott 2006; Dyson *et al.* 2006). Techniques considered included fieldwalking, augering, aerial photography, geophysical survey, test pitting and trial trenching. It was particularly useful for the English partners to see and experience the application of augering and boreholing applied to the investigation of deeply buried archaeological horizons in the wetland landscapes of Flanders and the Netherlands. Again the application of large-scale trial trenching in Kent, Essex and northern France stimulated constructive dialogue. The empirical modelling undertaken by Hey and Lacey (Hey/Lacey 2001) not unexpectedly demonstrated that it is easiest to find feature-rich, artefact-rich sites and also that the more extensive is the surface area exposed in evaluation, the greater is the certainty that the sample of the site exposed is representative of the totality of the archaeological resource within the evaluation area. It was particularly valuable to see a degree of certainty somewhat quantified, even if in terms of fairly crude trends. The work, however, further exposed a philosophical question about the role of field archaeology in investigating the past: should the focus just be on the key nodes of past human activity, either in spatial or chronological terms, or are relationships between nodes equally important? What is happening in the spatial or chronological spaces between the nodes? Is this important to understanding the past? Here techniques of large-scale stripping of sites, including that of strip, map and sample, provided much food for thought.

Armed with information from historic environment databases, with understanding enhanced by further evaluation, how can specialists and non-specialists appropriately manage the historic environment? Planarch devoted considerable energy to the issue of archaeological management strategies, looking at the issue from two perspectives: how to embrace heritage issues within a development area defined by modern economic and other factors and how, within a still recognizable heritage area such as an historic town, to define and then incorporate the sense of past place within a vision for the future (Waugh 2006). Studies considered examples such as the Thames Gateway in England, Erkelenz and Königswinter in the Rhineland, Mons and Charleroi in Wallonia and a variety of sites covered by the Belvedere project in the Netherlands. In all cases it was clear that the historic environment specialists involved had managed to gain enhanced understanding of the heritage assets involved and their place within their local historic context. This did not necessarily lead, however, to a sensitive incorporation of the assets within the development scheme. A major issue is obviously the tension between the economic and social motivations for development and the potentially inhibiting constraints, in financial and design terms, of incorporating surviving memorials of the past. This tension can be exacerbated by a lack of appreciation by non-specialists of the potential significance of the assets, to a greater or lesser degree influenced by the failure of the specialist to communicate that significance adequately. Even where there is a good dialogue there is a fundamental question as to how the past should be represented in the present for the future. At one end of the spectrum there is conservation of what has survived as it is, while further along the spectrum is the Belvedere philosophy of 'conservation through development'. More generally, to what extent can spirit of place be captured by retention of alignments of roads or selectively of other features in the landscape? How evocative can leitmotifs representing past glories be in creating real sense of identity and ownership? How can we blend the thread of time with the best of the present? To what extent is it physical reality as opposed to a feeling in the heart and mind that stirs us? Inevitably there will be subjectivity in all approaches, making it that much more difficult to measure success. In all the projects studied one could see a recognition that memory can contribute to placemaking but a range of approaches could be noted, from tokenism to something more substantial. Increasingly the information available to make informed decisions is more comprehensive and analytical but the level of engagement between heritage professionals and non-specialist planners and developers is variable.

In Planarch 2 a major study was undertaken of how cultural heritage is dealt with in respect of the European Union directives for Environmental Impact Assessment (85/337/EEC-European Commission (EC);

Fig. 4
The launch of Guiding Principles for Cultural Heritage in Environmental Impact Assessment at a reception at the European Parliament in Brussels in November 2005, with MEPs Richard Howitt (England) and Philippe Busquin (Belgium).

97/11/EC-EC 1997) and Strategic Environmental Assessment (2001/42/EC-EC, 2001) (Jones *et al.* 2006). As might be expected there was a lack of consistency in the way the directives were translated into national action, the standards applied, the degree to which heritage matters were considered and the quality of the work undertaken. Arising out of this analysis the partners produced a set of ten Guiding Principles 'intended to provide a rigorous, robust and reasonable framework for ensuring that cultural heritage is appropriately treated in the EIA process' (Planarch 2006). They were endorsed by the European Association of Archaeologists and the European Archaeological Council and launched at a reception in the European Parliament in November 2005 (Fig. 4). Although without legal status, the principles should provide a sound framework within which cultural heritage issues can be considered within the framework of EIA.

Promotion consisted of a series of seminars, a mobile exhibition, a publication looking at aspects of archaeology within the Planarch area (Williams/Evans 2001) and a website (www.planarch.org) in the four languages of the partnership, which hosts a very useful online library of reports and other materials relating to the Planarch project.

5. REFLECTIONS

Planarch, hopefully, made a serious contribution to the development of approaches to identifying, evaluating and managing the historic environment resource through exchange of experience and joint working; much, however, remains to be done in terms of developing methodologies and raising standards. It also enabled those taking part to recognize more clearly the shared nature of heritage and what its role should be within the environment we live in. There are a number of interrelated reflections, not new or earthshaking, that have wider application.

The iterative process at the heart of Planarch 2 of identification, evaluation, management and promotion, all constantly feeding and being fed by understanding, should underpin all ventures dealing with the historic environment. This process is indeed embedded in the frameworks evolving for research strategies in a number of countries.

It has to be admitted, however, that understanding does not have universal value and significance relates very much to the personal cultural values of a receptor. Heritage professionals, therefore, should not necessarily assume that all share their enthusiasm for their view of the past and its continuing role in the present and the future. Developing increased appreciation of the historic environment and of an individual's place in it may hopefully, however, stimulate the senses and the heart and lead to greater attachment to and ownership of the past and the present around us.

Communication is all important. It is desirable that messages mean the same thing to those giving and receiving them. It is also not enough to inform and tell. Rather communication is there for sharing stories and realizing common visions that everyone can appreciate and relate to.

In view of the above, for projects to work it is important that stakeholders are actively involved from an early stage and each one has ownership, both of the objectives and the implementation of the project. This applies not only to the specialists but to all. If Planarch had a failing it was in not engaging planners, developers and other non-historic environment specialists more in its deliberations.

Finally success is more likely where heritage assets can be creatively, yet appropriately, utilized within broader economic and social frameworks, but at the same time it is essential to safeguard the integrity and true meaning of the assets.

It is particularly rewarding to consider the changes in perspective during some ten years of Planarch journeying. At the start there were aspirations but uncertainties, a range of separate and individual objectives within a common framework, but perhaps a hesitancy with regard to systems and approaches beyond those to that date personally experienced by the participants. The voyage of discovery related both to an increased understanding of a common heritage around the southern North Sea but very importantly also to the need to work together to develop consistent standards and approaches. If then there is a general message it is that partnerships take time to develop but the effort can be very worthwhile.

NOTES

1 Chair of Planarch and Planarch 2 projects, as Head of Heritage Conservation, Kent County Council; now retired and Honorary Visiting Fellow at the Centre for Local History, the University of Leicester.

REFERENCES

Many of the reports cited below can be downloaded at no charge from the Planarch website www.planarch.org; two publications (Ghenne/Remy/Soumoy 2002; Ghenne 2007) have not been specifically referenced in the text but contain a variety of useful papers relating to the work of Planarch.

Andrikopoulou-Strack, N., with A.C. Ghigny/A. Letor/M. Meganck/J. Bourgeois/J. Plumier/H. Saunders/G. Blanqcquaert/G. Prilaux, 2006: *Archaeological Evaluation and Aerial Photography in the Planarch Area of North West Europe*, Maidstone.

Blancquaert, G./M. Medlycott, 2006: *Archaeological Evaluation of Rural Areas in the Planarch Area of North West Europe*, Maidstone.

Clarke, C. P. (ed.), 2001: *Protecting the past for the Future, The Development of SMRs in the Planarch Project Region and Beyond*, Chelmsford.

Cuming, P./K. Evans/J. Williams (eds.), 2001: *The Planarch Project in Belgium (Flanders and Wallonia), England, France and the Netherlands*, Maidstone.

Cuming, P./J. Williams (eds.), 2001: *Archaeological Legislation and Planning Frameworks in Belgium (Flanders and Wallonia), England, France and the Netherlands*, Maidstone.

Dyson, L./E. Heppell/C. Johnson/M. Pieters with C. Baeteman/J. Bastiaens/K. Cousserier/K. Deforce/I. Jansen/E. Meylemans/L. Schietecatte/ L.Theunissen/R. van Heeringen/J. van Laecke/I. Zeebroek, 2006: *Archaeological Evaluation of Wetlands in the Planarch Area of North West Europe*, Maidstone.

Evans, K./J. Williams (eds.), 2001a; *The Organisation of Archaeology in England, Belgium (Flanders and Wallonia), France and the Netherlands*, Maidstone.

Evans, K./J. Williams (eds.), 2001b: *Archaeological Evaluation Strategies in Belgium (Flanders and Wallonia), England, France and the Netherlands*, Maidstone.

Florence, 2000: *European Landscape Convention. Florence, 20 October 2000*, Strasbourg (Council of Europe).

Ghenne, M.-J. (ed.), 2007: *Le Projet Planarch 2, Archéologie et aménagement du territoire*, s.l. (Les Cahiers de L'Urbanisme, Hors-série Août 2007).

Ghenne, M.-J./H. Remy/M. Soumoy (eds.), 2002: *Le Projet Planarch, Archéologie et aménagement du territoire*, s.l. (Les Cahiers de L'Urbanisme, Hors-série Décembre 2002).

Gilman, P., with A. Bennett/O. Collette/P. Cuming/M.-J. Ghenne/F. Laurent/A. Letor/ Meganck/E. Meylemans/C. Thanos, 2006: *Development of Sites and Monuments (SMRs) in the Planarch Area of North West Europe*, Maidstone.

Granada, 1985: *Convention for the Protection of the Architectural Heritage of Europe. Granada, 3 October 1985*, Strasbourg (Council of Europe).

Hey, G./M. Lacey, 2001: *Evaluation of Archaeological Decision-making Processes and Sampling Strategies*, Oxford.

Jones, C./P. Slinn, with P. Burggraaff/K.-P. Kleefeld/G. Lambrick, 2006: *Cultural Heritage and Environmental Impact Assessment in the Planarch Area of North West Europe*, Maidstone.

Leusen, M. van/H. Kamermans, 2005: *Predictive Modelling for Archaeological Heritage Management: A research agenda*, Amersfoort (Nederlandse Archeologische Rapporten 29).

Planarch 2006: *Guiding Principles for Cultural heritage in Environmental Impact Assessment (EIA)*, s.l.

Valletta, 1992: *European Convention on the Protection of the Archaeological Heritage (Revised) Valetta, 16.I.1992*, Strasbourg (Council of Europe).

Waugh, K., 2006: *Archaeological management Strategies in the Planarch Area of North West Europe*, Maidstone.

Williams, J./K. Evans, 2001: *Aspects of Archaeology in the Planarch Region*, Maidstone.

WEBSITE

www.planarch.org

5. Management of knowledge within the international and intersectoral research project 'Cultural Landscapes'

Józef Hernik[1]

ABSTRACT

An international multi-disciplinary project entitled 'Protecting Historical Cultural Landscapes to Strengthen Regional Identities and Local Economies' (Cultural Landscapes), was developed between 2006 and 2009 within the European Union Interreg IIIB CADSES programme on cultural landscapes. This project involved 11 partners from 5 countries from central and eastern Europe, namely Poland, Austria, Germany, Romania and the Ukraine and aimed at the feasibility of extending its research and educational-training methodology of best practice on cultural landscapes across a much wider area. The primary function was that of developing best examples of the implementation of the European Landscape Convention in practice. In addition, the secondary function was to provide a source of advisory information for future interdisciplinary projects.

In the scope of the project management the original scientific concept 'before design and designing social approaches' was used to establish a research framework on the basis of the evaluation of several other projects. One of the main project results was the international catalogue of selected cultural landscape elements with a glossary of key terms. This approach involved a systematic mapping key (see section 3.4) on a register of iconic landscape elements based on a thorough survey of the cultural elements.

Communication inside and outside the project is very important for an efficient and effective running of the international project. The project website and the newsletters were the main form of information dissemination to those outside the project.

KEY WORDS

Cultural landscapes, central/eastern Europe, international catalogue

1. INTRODUCTION

Cultural landscapes have been shaped through evolving local and regional land use and, in turn, contribute towards shaping regional and local identity since they reflect the history and coexistence of people, the environment and nature. One of the most important factors of all landscapes is the way in which they have constantly evolved, a feature that must be both celebrated yet viewed with caution since, taking into consideration a conscious impact of humankind on the process of creating them, the rate of evolution in current and future times could lead to the elimination of their character, leading to a greater degree of unification and subsequent loss of diversity. In many areas it is evident how humankind has interfered with the environment to create a landscape that is both unique, regionally indicative and something that should be conserved wherever possible. Apart from negative examples of such influences there are also

Fig. 1 CADSES programme, showing project participants. *Source: INTERREG programme.*

instances that establish positive influences whereby people shape landscapes by means of traditional land use, taking into account natural conditions and making a conscious effort to preserve the landscape. Such landscapes have been especially preserved in rural areas. At present, in those communities where such valuable cultural landscapes are present there are added responsibilities in terms of spatial planning to permit their continued conservation and evolution as part of a process of appropriate and responsible management.

Thus, the diversity of these landscapes is currently under threat and to establish the degree of that threat, whilst emphasizing the regional importance of such landscapes, an international project entitled 'Protecting Historical Cultural Landscapes to Strengthen Regional Identities and Local Economies' (Cultural Landscapes), was developed between 2006 and 2009 within the European Union Interreg IIIB CADSES programme with the aim of protecting and developing such landscapes. This project involved 11 partners from 5 countries on a multi-disciplinary basis that reflected the holistic nature of cultural landscapes and the nature of the threats posed to them. Although the CADSES (Central, Adriatic, Danubian, South-Eastern European Space) programme covers a wide geographical area (website CADSES 2006;

Fig. 1), this particular project examined in greater detail a more restricted area as a means of providing a trial project to establish the feasibility of extending its methodology across a much wider area.

The most important stages of this project involved the fundamental research into the cultural landscapes of the participating countries leading to an identification of the iconic features that composed those landscapes while incorporating a number of pilot projects. This entire project emphasized the importance of interdisciplinary scientific exchange of both students and researchers in order to create networks that would be the forum for the exchange of experience from a local level through to international seminars and conferences.

2. INSTITUTIONAL STRUCTURE

The final institutional structure of the project partners was based around four universities (University of Agriculture in Kraków, Poland; University of Applied Sciences Erfurt, Germany; University Babes-Bolyai Cluj-Napoca, Romania; and National University Lviv Polytechnic, Ukraine), together with three associations (Heritage Association of Thuringia, Germany; Regional Planning Association East-Thuringia, Germany; and the Grazing Association Ramsar Site Valley Lafnitz, Austria), two municipalities (Municipality of Miechów, Poland; and the Municipality of Wiśniowa, Poland), one educational training unit (Environment Management, Austria) and one museum (Ethnographic Museum of Transylvania, Romania). The University of Agriculture in Kraków was the lead partner of this project. In terms of responsibilities, the universities were responsible for scientific research and creating an international research network with the participation of the remaining project partners whilst the results of the research project were implemented in four countries, Poland, Germany, Romania and the Ukraine. In turn, the educational training unit introduced the best practice on cultural landscapes for an effective implementation of these research results and the remaining project partners were responsible for the implementation of the project results under the supervision of the universities.

These partners were selected whilst preparing the application on the basis that their participation would support the achievement of the intended results and that the pilot projects could be implemented through the personal and economical potential to carry out the objectives determined in the project schedule.

3. INTEGRATION

3.1 Conflicting Epistemologies

One of the main project results was the international catalogue of selected cultural landscape elements. It was the result of an intensive co-operation during the whole project and the University of Applied Sciences, Erfurt, whose project group had already undertaken research on landscapes, first presented the unifying approach during the international seminar of experts in Kraków (Meyer *et al.* 2008a). This approach was a systematic mapping key (cf. section 3.4) based on a register of iconic landscape elements which was dependent on a thorough survey of the cultural elements. These were then mapped in the form of a hierarchical structure. During the expert seminar a similar approach was adopted with an emphasis upon applicability across all areas, given that different qualities of the elements need to be recorded at different scales and at different levels of selection. Throughout the project this evolved into a comprehensive catalogue of cultural landscape elements together with a glossary of terms (Meyer/Schmidt/Glink 2008b).

EU-Member States (Poland, Germany, Austria)	2006 (4–12)	2007 (1–12)	2008 (1–3)
Trans-national connections between CADSES cultural landscapes			
Trans-national feasibility study 'Strategies of CL valorization', preparing investments and pilot projects			
Catalogue of valuable, endangered cultural landscapes in the CADSES			
Guideline for European planning regulations and interactive regional planning instruments referring to the role of cultural landscapes in sustainable regional managements under structural changes			
Best practice compilation about CL valorization (results of research on pilot projects)			
Compendium of digital methods in CL survey			
Regional planning concept 'Middle Saale Valley'			
Curriculum: strategies of protection and use of cultural landscapes			
Common CADSES cultural landscape register (digital data base)			
Regional cultural landscape register (digital data base)			
Worldwide accessible open-source data base 'Landscape Wikipedia'			
Contributions to the open-source data base 'Landscape Wikipedia'			
Education-training centre for the use of renewable energy			
Demonstration plant 'product line for pellet production'			
Demonstration plant 'product line for briquettes production' (biomass)			
Landscape redevelopment project (exemplarily for sustainable agro-tourism)			
'Rural Regional Markets' involving 50 small scale enterprises (SME)			
Cultural Heritage Path (network of tourist foot path)			
Exemplary management concept for an eco-tourist recreational centre			
Local and regional meetings about details of cultural landscape valorization with representatives of local authorities, universities and 'local experts'			
International conferences, presenting outcomes and best practices of the project CULTURE LANDSCAPES to a wider CADSES audience			
International and regional workshops, discussing and presenting details of the project with regional and international experts			
Inter-regional development tours to present best practice examples for landscape valorization in the partner regions			
Trans-national network of organizations aiming at the protection and the development of cultural landscapes			
Regional networks of organizations aiming at the protection and development of cultural landscapes, involving local authorities, private economy and 'local experts'			

Fig. 2a.
Quantified main expected outputs of individual partners.

3.2 Development of common theory and methods

In the scope of the project management the original scientific method 'before design and during implementation by social approaches' was used to establish a research framework on the basis of the evaluation of several other projects. This scientific concept is understood as the whole of logically cohesive generalizations concluded on the base of the established scientific facts and connected with the current state of science. Its aim is to explain a cause or a system of causes, conditions, circumstances of creation and a given course of a project, in this case on landscape and heritage in their various forms. It is a summary of the results of detailed scientific works (Pieter 1967).

Among many kinds of research that are prepared before entering such a project dealing with landscape and heritage and during its implementation there is the importance of social research (Skalski 1990). The range, applied methods and tools of the research depend on a large number of factors and include the following stages (Pawłowska 2008): determination of work aims, analysis of present situation, definition of research problems, selection of research trial, selection and preparation of research tools, carrying out research, analysis and interpretation of research results and the presentation of research results.

In reflection of this, the most important stages of the project are the fundamental research on cultural landscapes, scientific exchange, exchange of students and researchers, the identification of historical and cultural landscapes, the development of pilot projects, protecting historical cultural landscapes by using them and strengthening their natural qualities and creating networks to take advantage of exchanges of experience, international seminars and conferences. These facets of the project, based upon a combination of theory and methodology (see Fig. 2a) which established a timeline of quantifiable expectations of the three EU member states (Poland, Germany and Austria) whilst similar and separate timelines are illustrated for the contributions of Romania and the Ukraine (Fig. 2b).

This in turn required the organization of frequent discussions, meetings, seminars and conferences that were a base for a development of common theory and methods. Through such a dialogue a formula was evolved that permitted the project partners to select and accept a common research method. This turned out to be of fundamental importance, since while carrying out the research we faced a variety of difficulties including the problems posed by different languages and meanings, the availability of data, means of acquiring data and the recording of those data across different landscape types. The accepted common method permitted us to solve these difficulties on time, which is of critical importance for international projects within a strict task schedule.

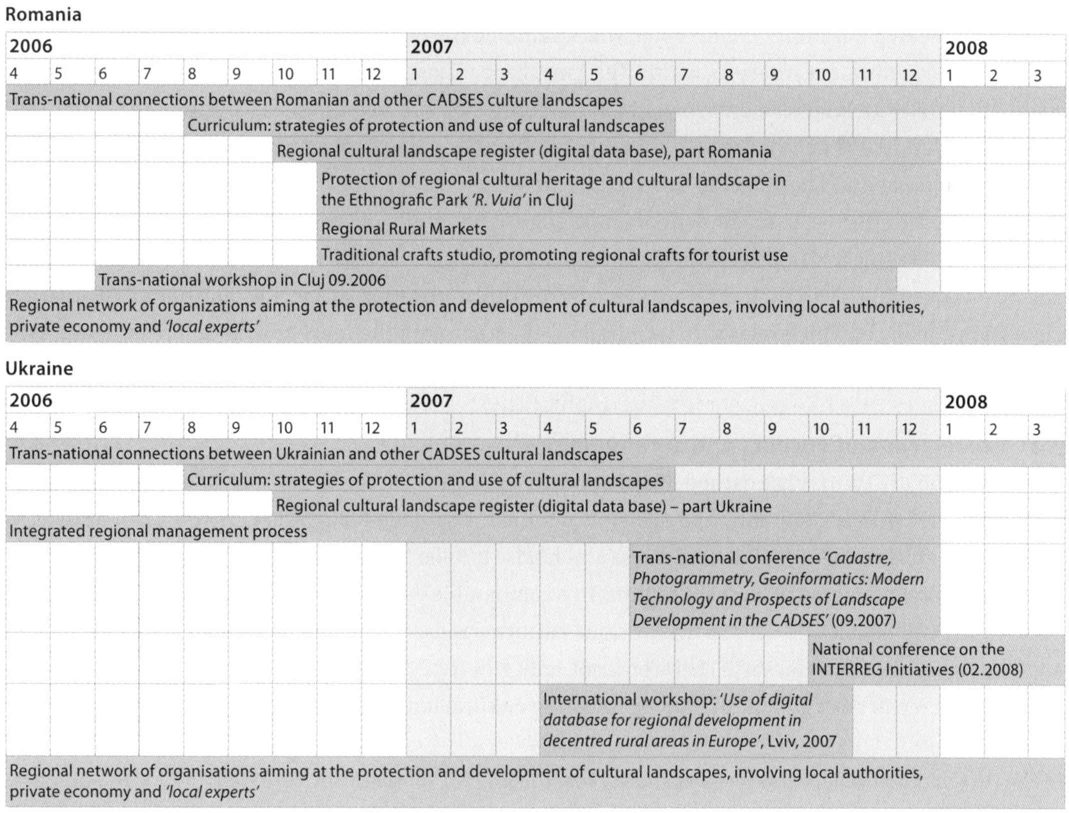

Fig. 2b.
Quantified main expected outputs of individual partners.

Fig. 3
A page from the International Catalogue of Selected Cultural Landscape Elements.
Source: www.cadses.ar.krakow.pl.

3.3 Finding a common research question

The recognition of the diversity of attitudes towards landscape and heritage was crucial because of the multidisciplinary nature of the landscape and cultural heritage. On the base of this diversity of attitudes a series of research questions was accepted that examined the relative perspective of different issues for those who have different interests within the landscape. These different actors in any particular area could potentially include residents, owners, local politicians from communes, counties and provinces, admirers of landscape and heritage from within and outside the area, tourists and various specialists related to landscape and heritage. In this way the answers were explored for the common research questions such as the effective management of knowledge to maintain and promote cultural landscapes.

We accepted a rule for the project that we would hold discussions about this common research question during our meetings, with each meeting preceded by the preparation of specific questions and areas for discussions, many of which related to terminology together with the mechanisms and techniques used to identify and record those landscape elements that would form part of the catalogue.

3.4 Agreement on Concepts and Terminology

The Catalogue of Cultural Landscape Elements with a Glossary of Terms consists of a catalogue of elements together with photographs and descriptions and the so-called mapping key which can be used as a methodological tool (Fig. 3). It includes cultural landscape elements which are typical of the participating regions or endangered in all these regions in a comparable way. Glossary entries are listed alphabetically, which will enable the user to find various cultural landscape elements and relevant descriptions and photographs in the glossary. Therefore, not only will it be of great use for practical field mapping activities but it will be of greater use for establishing cultural landscape cadastres.

In the project, the universities were primarily responsible for all scientific research and for the preparation and acceptance of a common research concept and terminology. Initially, the universities prepared a concept of research and terminology followed by a series of meetings organized by the universities with the participation of the remaining project partners and invited experts. Through the establishment of this iterative process, a common research concept was accepted in a way that had a positive effect on the quality of research.

4. COMMUNICATION

4.1 Communication and contact

Communication inside and outside the project is very important for an efficient and effective running of the international project. The University of Agriculture in Kraków, lead partner of the project, appointed the regular project office for internal communication. For the duration of the project, a secretary was employed to assist the project director in administrative and financial matters and provided a regular point of contact with the project partners and others. In addition, a scientific council was created to aid the project director on scientific matters. The project website, updated regularly, and the newsletters prepared and sent on regular basis, were the main form of information dissemination to those outside the project and is still maintained and functional after the conclusion of the project, displaying and making available the results of the project.

4.2 Additional Time Demands

International projects are often launched late due to the complicated contracting procedures. An agreement between an EU unit and a lead partner of a project is concluded and followed by a joint agreement between all partners of the project. This delay at the start of the project is an additional difficulty for running an international project and creates an additional time demand on the part of the project partners.

For the duration of the project, there was general acceptance of the rule of permanent monitoring of the tasks executed by the partners to ensure that an agreed timetable was adhered to. In addition, numerous meetings and visits had to be organized and the finances made available to pay the project partners. Despite numerous difficulties and troubles, especially in terms of the catalogue and pilot projects, we were able to find compromise solutions to allow additional time for the partners to complete their actions through a combination of discussions and agreements at both EU level and with the partners. The greatest difficulties comprised the determination of cultural landscape elements endangered within the CADSES area, whereas the greatest problems arose when receiving extra permissions, opinions and funds for pilot projects. What is important is that all the results of the project were achieved.

After the conclusion of the project it turned out to be effective and, more importantly, it was appreciated by the partners.

4.3 Leadership, Clear Role of Participants and Personal Chemistry

For the quality of the achieved project results it is very important for international and intersectoral projects to delineate clear and very precise roles and tasks for each project partner. The roles should be compiled in a written form as an additional project schedule. The clear delineation of the roles comes down to a very precise method of carrying out tasks and giving a person a clear deadline. Moreover, while conducting the project there are some temporal and relevant changes that require a constant delineation of revised roles and tasks for each project partner. This constant revision of the roles is very important and time consuming for any international and intersectoral project.

4.4 (Lack of) training and education

On the basis of an experience with international projects it can be stated that for interdisciplinary and intersectoral projects, their realization often means entrance into new fields of science and practice and by doing so all those directly involved in the project gain useful education and experience. The 11 representatives all had experience with national and international interdisciplinary and intersectoral projects on landscape and heritage. This experience allowed us to carry out and realize the project efficiently and effectively. Within the project many individuals had not been trained in interdisciplinary co-operation and it was the responsibility of the main representatives to give clear guidance and instructions so that their respective roles were clearly delineated. People leading and responsible for research must be highly educated and have experience, since leading an interdisciplinary and intersectoral group is very difficult and so is combining conflicting interests and views. This crucial problem was solved through intensive communication at all levels and an openness to accept that the opinions of other disciplines were equally relevant.

5. OUTPUT/ RESULTS

5.1 Application and Consultancy

For this interdisciplinary and intersectoral project the application of the achieved research results directly in practice was, on one hand, the greatest success of the project and, on the other hand, a serious difficulty to overcome. The difficulty was to complete all formalities in order to execute the tasks on time, particularly the preparation of the catalogue and the studies relating to the generation of farm tourism in the commune of Wiśniowa (Świtała/Hernik 2009). The success of the project lies in the current verification of research, paying special attention to the application in practice and having a solid basis for further research.

5.2 Achieving Integrated Products

For an interdisciplinary and intersectoral project it is very important to formulate a circle of people as authors and co-authors of the integrated products to respect the authors' rights. Often launching interdisciplinary and intersectoral research to achieve interesting integrated products is not valued, largely because of its crossdisciplinary nature. What needs to be recognized is that there is a significant need for a forum to bring together all forms of interdisciplinary and intersectoral research that address the general issues of land management in a holistic manner, and it is the belief of this author that this particular project has gone some small way in addressing that acceptance. At present, while the role of interdisciplinary research is expanding and sometimes produces surprisingly good results, this issue is very important. For example, the concept of multiple cultural landscapes (Van der Valk 2009), landscape evolution (Dixon-Gough 2009), the content of digital landscapes (Ionita/Lepadatu/Dumitrescu 2009) and the protection and preservation of hillsides of cultural landscapes (Hernik 2009b) are all exemplars of multidisciplinary research that takes a holistic approach to landscape and land management.

6. CONCLUSIONS

This paper discussed two essential functions based on the interdisciplinary and intersectoral approach of the project. The primary function was that of developing the best examples of the implementation of the European Landscape Convention in practice. The secondary function was to provide a source of advisory information for future interdisciplinary projects on the management of knowledge in order to achieve interesting integrated products.

A strong feature of the project was its interdisciplinarity and intersectorality, which made it possible to involve many specialists and experts from various scientific and practice fields. However, a weak side was the difficulty of generating precise results within interdisciplinary research. With respect to the results, the primary function of the project lay with the scientific element of the work, whilst the secondary function related largely to the pilot projects. The principal form of dissemination of the scientific results was through monographs and directly included the following works:
- *Cultural Landscape - Assessment, Protection, Shaping*, ed. J. Hernik and J. Pijanowski, AR Kraków, 2007;
- *Cultural Landscape - Protecting Historical Cultural Landscapes to Strengthen Regional Identities and Local Economy*, ed. J. Pijanowski and J. Hernik, PAN Kraków, 2008;
- *Cultural Landscape - Across Disciplines*, ed. J Hernik, Wydawnictwo Branta, 2009a;
- *Kulturlandschaftserfassung und Landschaftspflege in Mitteleuropa – Vergleichende Studie*, ed. H.-H. Meyer and B. Kolbmüller, 2007;
- *Kulturlandschaft Thuringen-Arbeitshilfe fur die Planungspraxis,* ed. H.-H. Meyer, C. Schmidt, R. Herrmann, M. Schottke and C. Glink, 2008;
- Journal of the Centre for Regional Geography 2007 vol. III;
- *Peisaje Culturale Istorice* 2008.

With respect to the secondary function, work has also been carried out within the following pilot projects:
- University of Agriculture in Kraków and Municipality of Miechów created a pilot project as an element of the Centre of Renewable Energies project;
- University of Agriculture in Kraków with the Municipality of Wiśniowa restored a small historical retention basin significant in terms of historical and cultural heritage as well as local landscape assets;
- 'Cultural Landscape' internet platform with a 'Cultural-Landscape Wiki' which allows integration of local experts and promotes public awareness for the quality of cultural landscapes;
- In co-operation with the association Grund Genug, a series of thematic markets for presenting regional products from the cultural landscape were organized and took place in May and December 2006 with the themes 'Everything about Bread' and 'Cultural Landscapes for the Senses'; the small regional Reinstädter Rural Market effectively communicated the connection between the products available and the conservation and valorization of the historical cultural landscape,
- Regional Development Concept 'Middle Saale Valley';
- Best-Practice-Beispiele der Kulturlandschaftserhaltung;
- Three curricula:
  - a curriculum for a five-day programme with the aim to motivate opinion leaders and decision-makers to realize projects to protect cultural landscape, giving information and showing best practice examples;
  - a curriculum for a 26 day training programme for managers and technical personnel in tourism which enables the participants to develop and realize measures in tourism which protect cultural landscape and have economic benefits;

- the University Babes-Bolyai Cluj-Napoca promoted the Faculty of Geography and Faculty of Environmental Science's curriculum at the conference on dynamics in spatial development in Kraków;
- The Ethnographic Museum of Transylvania organized two Folk Craftsmen Markets, developed a design for the structure and plan of the museum information centre and formulated initiatives for field trips for identifying and inventorying elements of cultural landscapes in Cluj and Alba;
- Tourist GIS by the National University Lviv Polytechnic.

The greatest potential problem of this project was related to the realization of pilot projects within the time specified in the project schedule. Above all, the difficulty was in fulfilling all the issues of the formal, administrative, and environmental criteria for the pilot projects. This caused a situation in which much time was dedicated to fixing these issues that had been difficult to predict beforehand. Moreover, in the countries where the euro was not a binding currency there were difficulties of often changing currency rates, which increased the beneficiaries' own share as a consequence.

NOTES

1   University of Agriculture in Kraków, Kraków, Poland.

REFERENCES

Dixon-Gough, R., 2009: Landscape Evolution of the Lake District National Park: conflicts between a working and cultural landscape, in J. Hernik (ed.), *Cultural Landscapes-Across Disciplines,* Bydgoszcz/Kraków, 141-172.

Hernik, J. (ed.), 2009a: *Cultural Landscapes-Across Disciplines,* Bydgoszcz/Kraków.

Hernik, J., 2009b: Protection and preservation of the mountainsides cultural landscapes threatened with water erosion, in J. Hernik (ed.), *Cultural Landscapes-Across Disciplines,* Bydgoszcz/Kraków, 311-321.

Hernik, J./J. Pijanowski (eds.), 2007: *Cultural Landscape - Assessment, Protection, Shaping,* Kraków.

Ionita A./C. Lepadatu/G. Dumitrescu, 2009: Digital cultural landscape content, in J. Hernik (ed.), *Cultural Landscapes-Across Disciplines,* Bydgoszcz/Kraków, 255-278.

Journal of the Centre for Regional Geography 2007 (Vol.III, 2), Presa Universitara Clujeana.

Meyer, H.-H./B. Kolbmüller, 2007: *Kulturlandschaftserfassung und Landschaftspflege in Mitteleuropa – Vergleichende Studie,* Erfurt.

Meyer H.-H./J.M. Pijanowski/R. Herrmann/M. Schottke/W. Schreiber/O. Dorozhynskyy/J. Hernik, 2008a: Catalogue of Cultural Landscape Elements with a Glossary of Terms, in J.M. Pijanowski/J. Hernik (eds), *CULTURAL LANDSCAPE. Protecting Historical Cultural Landscapes to Strengthen Regional Identities and Local Economies,* Kraków (Infrastruktura i Ekologia Terenów Wiejskich 2), 339-351.

Meyer H.-H./C. Schmidt/Ch. Glink, 2008b: A practical guide to using the international mapping key ("register") and glossary, in J.M. Pijanowski/J. Hernik (ed.), *CULTURAL LANDSCAPE. Protecting Historical Cultural Landscapes to Strengthen Regional Identities and Local Economies,* Kraków (Infrastruktura i Ekologia Terenów Wiejskich 12), 322-338.

Meyer, H.-H./C. Schmidt/R. Herrmann/M. Schottke/C. Glink, 2008: *Kulturlandschaft Thuringen - Arbeitshilfe fur die Planungspraxis, Band 3,* Erfurt.

Pawłowska, K., 2008: *Przeciwdziałanie konfliktom wokół ochrony i kształtowania krajobrazu,* Kraków.

Peisaje Culturale Istorice, 2008, Cluj-Napoca.

Pieter, J., 1967: *Ogólna metodologia pracy naukowej,* Wrocław.

Pijanowski J. M./J. Hernik (eds.), 2008: *CULTURAL LANDSCAPE. Protecting Historical Cultural Landscapes to Strengthen Regional Identities and Local Economies,* Kraków (Infrastruktura i Ekologia Terenów Wiejskich 12).

Skalski, K., 1990: *Humanistyka w projektowaniu,* Warszawa.

Świtała J./J. Hernik, 2009: Creating the model farm tourism homestead in Wiśniowa commune, in J. Hernik (ed.), *Cultural Landscapes-Across Disciplines,* Bydgoszcz/Kraków, 217-236.

Valk, A. van der, 2009: Multiple cultural landscape: research and planning for living heritage in the Netherlands, in J. Hernik (ed.), *Cultural Landscapes-Across Disciplines*, Bydgoszcz/Kraków, 31-60.

WEBSITES

CADSES Krakow 2007: *Protecting Historical Cultural Landscapes to strengthen Regional Identities and Local Economies.* Available at http://www.cadses.ar.krakow.pl (Accessed 26 November, 2009).

CADSES 2006. INTERREG III B CADSES Neighbourhood Programme. Available at http://www.cadses.net (Accessed 26 November, 2009).

6. 'Changing Landscapes': an interdisciplinary Danish research centre

Per Grau Møller[1]

ABSTRACT

This paper discusses issues of interdisciplinarity, multidisciplinarity and transdisciplinarity on the basis of the experience of the Danish Changing Landscapes Centre (1997-2002). The conclusion is that interdisciplinary research needs time for the involved researchers to evolve relevant research questions involving all disciplines. Multidisciplinarity is generally the most appropriate word to use to characterize the centre's research. Interdisciplinarity was unfolded within the six research projects, resulting in a book on five interdisciplinary research issues involving selected researchers. The research centre was strategic, involving governmental research institutions and museums, and in addition background groups were established with researchers, administrators, landowners and organizations, but on this basis no real transdisciplinary research was made. The centre was a success because all multidisciplinary goals were reached and interdisciplinarity was reached at a certain level. Good co-operation existed between the widespread researchers and this continued after the centre closed. Unfortunately, the political situation changed shortly after, so that the synergetic effects of this good co-operative basis could not be used because funding for environmental research was radically cut back. This is clearly the disadvantage of temporary research centres.

KEY WORDS

Multi-, inter- and transdisciplinarity; strategic environmental research; open research centre, research coordination

1. PROJECT DESIGN

'Changing Landscapes'[2] (in Danish: *Foranderlige Landskaber*) was a research centre established for the period 1997-2001 by a grant from the Danish Strategic Environmental Research Council (c. 40 million kroner in total, corresponding to c. 5 million euro). In Danish terms the word 'strategic' means applied or political and therefore the resulting research was primarily intended for a national audience in national governmental institutions and universities and an international research public. The purpose of grants in this programme was to fulfil strategic research purposes as basic research aims. The background for the Danish Strategic Environmental Research Programme was to pool research means from various ministries and traditional research councils in common programmes aiming at a wide range of environmental research themes. Furthermore it was aimed at achieving synergetic effects of research which would never be achieved on the basis of existing research institutions and research means.

The grant for Changing Landscapes belonged to a programme entitled 'Sustainable Land Use', which also financed three to four other corresponding research centres. This programme received an essential financial contribution from the Research Council for the Humanities, stressing a humanities approach to environmental research which hitherto had traditionally been a research field for scientific, technical and social science disciplines. The programme received several research proposals including a big application from a cultural historical group based in universities, governmental research institutions and museums ranging from archaeology to geobotany, history, cultural geography and ethnology. The result of the considerations of the leaders of the Strategic Environmental Research Council was to ask the cultural historical group to form a big new (temporary) research centre incorporating several of the other applications dealing with landscape issues. In practice this meant that we had about two months to form a new application for a certain amount of money involving several research applications from different research groups.

2. INTEGRATION

The process of preparing this application is essential in order to evaluate the degree of interdisciplinarity in the research centre (Tress/Tress/Fry 2006). What was possible to achieve within the group of leaders of the research programmes in the course of two months? It was decided that this process should be pragmatic and that the goals of the research centre should be realistic. It was the premise of the Strategic Environmental Research Programme that it should be a centre without walls, meaning that each research institution should still be the basis for its researchers but at the same time contribute to the centre. Against this background a centre concentrating on five research issues (later six as another research theme with a new research issue was integrated) was formed, based on the original applications of the research groups. No essentially new research questions based on common theoretical framework and common research traditions were formulated because this basis did not exist and first had to be developed. And two months were too short to discuss and agree upon these essential elements for interdisciplinary research.

A common approach concerning the selection of areas and different kinds of area-based landscape research was also established. This meant that four common inland areas were appointed and correspondingly three coastal areas, in which the research teams should try to elaborate their research questions. For some research groups certain areas were essential, for instance the archaeo-geobotanical group depended on the existence of lakes containing pollen and diatoms but other research groups could easily adjust to any areas. Another essential feature was the common use of the then relatively new GIS technology as essential for landscape research.

The six research themes/projects involved in the centre were the basis for organizing the research groups involving several subprojects (Fig. 1). The subprojects were mostly monodisciplinary, but different disciplines were involved in the research groups of the themes or projects so that on project level interdisciplinarity would be a right word to use, but typically they were within one faculty's disciplines, although there were some exceptions. From the outset it was decided to establish new research problems involving all research institutions at the new centre. It was clearly decided that the research should be based on the centre's themes or projects on the basis of the interdisciplinarity of the research groups. Within the established research groups various degrees of interdisciplinarity might be involved in solving the research questions, but not crossing the big traditional barriers between for instance humanistic and scientific disciplines. Taken as a whole, the centre involved the faculties of arts (humanistic), science and social science and on a broader level it is more appropriate to characterize it as multidisciplinary.

The reason for this initially limited kind of interdisciplinarity was that it takes time to establish interdisciplinary research themes and questions. It takes time for all the researchers involved to learn

Research projects	Subprojects	Institutions	Researchers
Strategic Studies in Cultural Environment and Landscape History	The Information Systems of the Cultural Landscape	2	3
	Historical Macro-Scale Relations between Human Impact and Landscape Variation*	1	3
	The Study of Regions in the Cultural Landscape and the Compilation of Cultural Landscape Regions in Prehistoric and Early Historical Periods	1	2
	Indicative models*	1	1
	The Colonized Landscapes, particularly Wetland Areas*	1	1
	Modern Agriculture and its Relationship to Elements and Structures of the Cultural Landscape	1	1
	The Manorial Landscape	1	1
	Coastal Management	1	1
	The Changing Danish Coastal Heritage*	1	1
Scenarios for Cultural Landscape Development	Methodologies for and Development of Landscape Scenarios	1	3
	Land Use Scenarios: Models and Methods for Scaling-up	1	3
	Computer-Based 3D-Visualization for Landscape Scenarios*	2	3
	Landscape and Ownership Structures	1	2
	Economic Analysis for Scenarios of the Development of Cultural Landscape	1	1
Nature Quality in Terrestrial Eco-Systems	A Terrestrial Biotopic Description	1	3
	The Influence on Mammal Fauna by the Landscape Structure	2	5
	An Integrated Landscape Model	2	2
Sustainable Nature Management in Coastal Areas		3	6
Landscape Resource Assessment		4	6

Fig. 1
Research projects and involved institutions and number of researchers.
* Ph.D. project

other colleagues' disciplines in terms of methodology and themes. Even if scholars are involved, they are traditionally educated in one discipline and learning the methodologies of others takes time before they become so familiar that it is possible to establish new essential research questions and define interdisciplinary methodologies on a realistic basis.

Correspondingly, the milestones of the new centre were established according to the milestones of each research group. The new centre was called 'Changing Landscapes' with the subtitle 'Centre for strategic studies in cultural environments, nature and landscape history', in this way trying to integrate some of the researchers' key words. The overall purpose of the centre was formulated in these sentences: "The aim of 'Changing Landscapes' is to create a scientific basis for understanding the historical background to the appearance of the present landscape. Equally important is to comprehend the processes of change occurring in the landscape. It is against this background that cultural historical and nature conservation interests will be evaluated in relation to human economic and recreational use of the landscape; particularly the culture-bound aspects of these dynamics will be analysed - including nature management." This is more a frame for research than specified basic research questions which were elaborated in the individual research groups.

3. CO-ORDINATION AND COMMUNICATION

In order to facilitate the centre as a functioning research unit, a relatively large sum, c. 12% of the research budget, was assigned to establishing common data like digitizing historical maps or buying external data for common use and for arranging internal meetings with all researchers and conferences open to external audiences. A group consisting of leaders from the various research groups was established as the board of the research centre under the guidance of the centre leader who was a historian from the University of Southern Denmark. A member of one of the governmental environmental institutions, The Danish Forest and Nature Agency, also had a seat on the board.

3.1 The start

When established, the Changing Landscapes research centre acted with the researchers situated in their traditional research institutions, either financing other researchers and teachers to take over their traditional tasks, especially universities, or partly financing their basic research. The big grant was formally given to the institution of the centre leader, who then made mutual agreements with all the institutions involved.

From the outset, the centre leader visited all institutions to make personal contact since most institutions were new to him and vice versa, and in the first months all involved researchers met to present their projects to each other and establish potential co-operation. E-mail communication facilitated co-operation within the research centre and especially from the centre leader to all groups and researchers. Annually there were internal meetings for all researchers, in addition to which meetings were arranged within the various subgroups, which were normally also inter-institutional.

Because of the strategic research theme an advisory group in connection to the centre was also established. It consisted mainly of landscape managers but some researchers from the universities were also invited. Annual meetings were held with this group in order to obtain good advice. The members were not involved in the research projects as such, but acted in such a way that the word transdisciplinarity can be used here. This was expressed by the wish of a few of them to be involved in the interdisciplinary book discussed below.

3.2 More interdisciplinarity

After eighteen months of research a conference was held with the common theme 'Agents in the landscape', the proceedings of which resulted in a book (Grau Møller/Holm/Rasmussen 2000). Another conference was held in May 2001 to present the results to a wide audience from the worlds of research, policy and landscape management.[3]

Fig. 2
The second and last book from the centre as a research entity: *Grau Møller et al.* 2002.

After the first conference in March 1999, the board of the research centre decided to promote more interdisciplinary research in the centre, even if it had not been promised in the application and the setup of the centre. It was noted that the centre's full potential was not being used and some researchers were thus asked to participate in five research issues across the established research groups. The themes were:
– nature in a cultural landscape: discourses on the concept of nature;
– integrated coastal zone management: a challenge in Danish management and research;
– cultural historical values in a future landscape;
– good quality soil: a natural and cultural phenomenon;
– sustainable land use: the cultural dimension in the landscape.

The challenge was well received by the researchers and the results were presented in the second and last book from the centre as a research entity (Fig. 2; Grau Møller *et al.* 2002). Interdisciplinarity was unfolded in different ways. In the first chapter two discourses were opposed to each other without reaching agreement or a common final conclusion. In the other chapters, the authors approached issues from a thematic perspective while raising their views on the common research questions. If the centre had not existed, these researchers would never have met and there would have been no opportunity for communication between different disciplines. A special grant for publication, granted by the leaders of the Strategic and Environmental Programme, was considered a success by both the authors and the funding body. Although the book had an attractive layout with many illustrations and multiple themes that might interest a wide audience, for instance the concept of sustainability, it was not well received by the public. Hardly any reviews appeared in newspapers and journals. Here the problem might be that it was definitely an interdisciplinary book, so that editors or reviewers within one discipline would not undertake to review a publication covering all disciplines.

4. RESULTS

From the perspective of the centre leader the centre was a success and fulfilled its original brief. Results were achieved from the research groups involved, communication within the centre was good and the interdisciplinary project, resulting in a book, was a success. Finally the centre inspired others inside and outside the centre to pursue interdisciplinary research in other projects.

The research groups have published individually and the total number of publications by the c. 40 researchers involved in the centre, both smaller and larger contributions, is more than 200. The publications are either in the field of basic research, generally in English, or in the field of strategic research. Furthermore two conferences were held, meant for a Danish audience, where we communicated with managers and researchers interested in the fields. Altogether many results, of a disciplinary as well as an interdisciplinary character, were produced and communicated.

Communication within the centre was good, especially because the relatively new e-mail technology facilitated easy communication and exchange of data. An internal GIS group involving all groups facilitated landscape studies and stimulated good discussions ranging from technical questions to disciplinary research questions facilitating the interdisciplinarity, since GIS data from one discipline can easily fit with data from other disciplines and common problems and issues can be visualized. The internal meetings usually lasted two days and involved professional discussions with the possibility of social discussions, which must not be disregarded as a precondition for achieving interdisciplinary results.

The centre's main focus was multidisciplinary research. This was a success, as noted above, further resulting into an interdisciplinary book. The process was rewarding for the researchers involved who had good discussions and learnt from their colleagues' methods. Although the book was almost ignored by the public, interdisciplinary research was developed in real terms.

Finally, some researchers from the centre, especially from the cultural-historical group, continued their work in another temporary research centre (1998-2003), called AGRAR2000, with the aim of describing and explaining the development of agricultural landscapes since the time of Christ (Odgaard/ Rømer 2009). The focus was also on interdisciplinary landscape research over a long chronological span, but within this whole group the disciplines involved were working more than just next to each other as there was one common issue to solve. The interdisciplinary co-operation within Changing Landscapes was one of the conditions of making this new co-operation a success. In the aftermath of AGRAR2000 and Changing Landscapes a network group was established focusing on historical maps and their use, specifically the access to digital versions. This group still exists and has a website where digital maps, especially in vector format, may be downloaded (www.hiskis.net).

5. REFLECTIONS

The strength of this research centre was that it was multidisciplinary in character, in the sense that so many researchers from different disciplines communicated with each other. This opened the eyes of the traditional monodisciplinary researchers to other issues and questions to be put to the landscape field, and specifically to the same research areas which they knew from their discipline's point of view. Even if there was no necessary obligation to take part in the common meetings, seen from the point of the individual research project, almost everyone took part in these meetings with open minds, presented his or her project and listened carefully to their colleagues' presentations. There was always a good and constructive mood at the meetings. This also meant that when the common book with the five interdisciplinary research themes had to be written, there was a good personal basis to build on for interdisciplinary work. While the centre's interdisciplinarity was deliberately of limited range, it was a great success. The strategic research theme also touched upon the transdisciplinary aspects of research involving the advisory group of landscape managers.

The weakness of this centre was that it was not organized to aim for interdisciplinary or transdisciplinary research. It might have been the first step towards this, if this goal had been set up. Interdisciplinary research needs time to prepare for good research questions, which are based on deep knowledge of the involved disciplines. The time needed for this was not available before starting the centre and the condition that everyone was in their own home institution did not promote insight into each other's way of researching. However, since this was not an original aim, it caused no immediate frustrations.

The opportunity offered by this centre was that in the long run a basis was created for interdisciplinary research within the landscape theme. People established personal relations which might be used in future co-operation, and actually that is what happened in the years after the centre closed. Furthermore, future strategic research co-operation may be tested without any further costs and this provides a basis for considerations to start new interdisciplinary research. Another opportunity is that Ph.D. researchers were also involved in the programme and could get an idea of interdisciplinarity, even if they were basically educated within their own discipline, in this way becoming interdisciplinary researchers.

The threat for the effectiveness of a centre like Changing Landscapes is that it was temporary. Even if large sums of money are spent on serious research questions, and even if it is a condition that some sort of integration in the involved institutions should take place, there is no guarantee that it will happen. Future prospects are uncertain in a changing political landscape, as was the case after the 2001 Danish elections, when one of the new government's political goals was to reduce environmental management and environmental research, including landscape issues. Therefore many of the institutions involved, especially governmental research institutions like NERI (National Environmental Research Institution) and the Research Centre for Forest & Landscape, faced dramatic budget cuts. Even if additional funding was given from the Strategic Environmental Research Programme meant for integration of researchers from Changing Landscapes programme in their home institutions, this would only provide a minimum of help in the situation. Furthermore, not all institutions were willing to accept the money if they had to promise a further financial involvement in the landscape field. The result is that many of the young researchers, in particular from Changing Landscapes, are no longer engaged in research but may be active in landscape management or in other fields.

NOTES

1   University of Southern Denmark, Odense, Denmark.
2   The centre has a website http://www1.sdu.dk/Hum/ForandLand/english/index.html, but the English version is meant more as a presentation of the centre, whereas the final results are integrated in the Danish version http://www1.sdu.dk/Hum/ForandLand/index.html.
3   *Sustainable Management of Changing Landscape*, held 29-30 May 2001 at Vingstedcentret.

REFERENCES

Grau Møller, P./P. Holm/L. Rasmussen (eds.), 2000: *Aktører i landskabet*, Odense.

Grau Møller, P./R. Ejrnæs/A. Höll/L. Krogh/J. Madsen (eds.), 2002: *Foranderlige Landskaber. Integration af natur og kultur i forvaltning og forskning*, Odense.

Odgaard, B./J. Rydén Rømer (eds.), 2009: *Danske Landbrugslandskaber gennem 2000 år. Fra digevoldinger til støtteordninger*, Aarhus.

Tress, B./G. Tress/G. Fry, 2006: Defining concepts and the process of knowledge production in integrative research, in B. Tress/G. Tress/G. Fry/P. Opdam (eds.), *From landscape research to landscape planning. Aspects of integration, education and application*, Dordrecht, 13-26.

WEBSITES

www1.sdu.dk/Hum/ForandLand/english/index.html (Short version in English)
www1.sdu.dk/Hum/ForandLand/index.html (Final results in Danish)
www.hiskis.net

7. The PDL/BBO research programme analysed from the perspective of knowledge management

Tom (J.H.F.) Bloemers[1]

ABSTRACT

The PDL/BBO research programme's knowledge management has been analysed from two perspectives. The first concerns the integrative approach of landscape research using the model of Tress et al. (Tress/Tress/Fry 2006) to handle challenges, the second is about the process of knowledge creation following Weggeman (Weggeman 2001[4], 28-41). He defines knowledge as "the partially unconscious capacity that is represented by the function of Information, Experience, Ability and Attitude of someone". Reflecting on the programme as an entity, the role of these four elements and the way they have influenced the creation of (new) knowledge is described.

The PDL/BBO programme (2000-2009) aimed at the development of social relevant scientific knowledge by establishing a meaningful link between scientific knowledge, archaeological-historical resource management and applied planning policy. The programme was divided into three types of research arranged in short (4-5 months) and long-term (4-5 years) studies: ten commissioned problem-oriented short-term, two conceptual studies and eleven strategic long-term projects selected in open competition. The concept of biography of landscape and the method of action research acted as anchor points for the assessment and selection of research proposals.

External assessments supported quality management and integration of knowledge. In 2003 NWO arranged for a mid-term evaluation by an international audit committee and in 2008/9 for an assessment of the societal impact. To strengthen the integration from 2006 onwards internal regional and thematic workshops were organized and the co-operation with the 'Onderwijsnetwerk Belvedere' started.

Newly created knowledge concerns the application of the biography concept in the four regionally oriented programmes, specific in the context of action in policy and practice to unify research and action. The new knowledge created by the thematic line of research can be labelled as interpretative heritage research, namely exploring data from an innovative research perspective and reflecting upon the process of giving them meaning and handling them.

The organization of the knowledge creation in the PDL/BBO research programme can be described as a 'fuzzy structure' in the sense of Weggeman. A fuzzy structure is more a non-structure than a structure, where learning and adapting are of great importance and various strategies are involved during the research process.

The result of the analysis of the PDL/BBO programme is that the value for money has been high, but that communication, especially external, has been a weak spot. Activities and the audience of the research programme and the Belvedere policy were complementary. Co-operation has created adequate conditions for the embedding of PDL/BBO insights in future going concerns. However, restructuration of heritage institutions during and after the lifetime of PDL/BBO creates the danger that the new insights and knowledge may be lost.

KEY WORDS

PDL/BBO programme: aims, structure; integration, assessment; fuzzy structure, SWOT

1. INTRODUCTION

One of the most unexpected personal experiences as one of the initiators of the PDL/BBO programme, as chairman of the Programme Committee and as participating researcher has been the absence of professional management expertise during the PDL/BBO research programme. The size, complexity and duration of a programme like this needs professional management to make the most of it. Management is not only the organization of the appropriate assessment of research proposals, of the allocation and control of the money flow and of reporting about progress and output. This is of course a basic condition for implementing research focused on specific new themes or lines and selected in a competitive environment, a task generally fulfilled by the funding research authority. But management must also care about that other basic research aim, creating new knowledge and insights within the proposed topic and its ambitions. This is what I have called in the context of the PDL/BBO programme 'the management of knowledge', a notion well known in business and organization studies and applied research as in industries and consultancy practice (Weggeman 2001[4]).

Management of knowledge as defined above is primarily the responsibility of the programme or project leader(s), generally participating researchers themselves. However, to my great surprise this seems to be no specific field of interest in the academic world, or at least in the humanities and social sciences. This might be logical, especially since in the humanities there is no strong tradition of organizing large-scale and complex research involving a greater number of researchers and even from 'paradigmatically' different disciplines. However, since the subject of the 'cultural landscape' by its very nature covers many different disciplines and involves research, practice and policy, the need for some form of specific knowledge management is evident. The answer to this need is, as a first step, to make explicit the experiences and tacit knowledge of researchers involved in relevant landscape research programmes. In this way a database would be created that can be exploited for further analysis and generalizations.

The PDL/BBO research programme is one of these sources that has been presented in this paper by applying two lines of analysis. The first concerns the inter- and transdisciplinary approach of landscape research as aimed for in this programme using the model of challenges for integrative research formulated by Tress *et al.* (Tress/Tress/Fry 2006). Here the focus is on creating the conditions for successful integrative research and the 'management history' of the PDL/BBO is analysed from this perspective. In addition, attention is given to the process of knowledge creation following the formula designed by Weggeman (Weggeman 2001[4], 28-41). He defines knowledge as "the partially unconscious capacity that is represented by the function of Information, Experience, Ability and Attitude of someone". Reflecting on the programme as an entity and its constituent subprogrammes and projects, the role of these four elements and the way they have influenced the creation of (new) knowledge is described.

2. THE PROJECT DESIGN

The project design covers the research design of the PDL/BBO programme, its institutional structure, research activities, the selection of proposals and researchers and the internal and external evaluation of the programme and its projects.

2.1 Research design

The research programme 'Protecting and Developing the Dutch Archaeological-Historical Landscape' (PDL/BBO) started in 2000 and was primarily aimed at the development of scientific knowledge in order to support the sustainable development of the Dutch archaeological-historical landscape. Consequently, the strategy focused on establishing a meaningful link between scientific knowledge, archaeological-historical resource management and applied planning policy in the Netherlands.

Formally the programme ran until the end of 2009, but most research appointments ended by 2008 and a considerable number of Ph.D. theses, final publications and spin-off products will be completed during 2010. A secondary aim has been the embedding of the inter- and transdisciplinary approach of cultural resource management and planning in the practice of heritage institutions, research and training.

The origins of the programme

The context of the origins of the programme during the late 1990s has been threefold: the national Belvedere policy (Belvedere 1999), the preparations for the implementation of the Valletta Convention (Valletta 1992) and the Nota Wetenschapsbudget 1997 (Wetenschapsbudget 1996).

By a joint effort of four ministries, Culture, Housing and Planning, Agriculture and Nature, and Transport and Public Works, in 1999 the Dutch government initiated the Belvedere programme and made available a sum of about 25 million euros for the following 4-5 years and another 25-40 million euros for the period 2005-2009 (Belvedere 1999). It has considered the three types of cultural historical resources, archaeological, historical-geographical and historical buildings, from an integrated perspective. Basic is the notion of archaeological-historical values as a resource for experiencing and expressing identity by preservation, innovation and design: a (re)source of inspiration, creativity and storytelling. Consequently, "cultural-historic identity is to be seen as a determining factor in the future spatial design of the Netherlands, for which the government shall aim to create appropriate conditions". The key concept of Belvedere has been 'conservation through development'. The PDL/BBO programme has adopted this concept, since the programme originated from the same motivation and engagement as the Belvedere policy and was seen by the initiators as complementary and supportive to Belvedere. Although one would expect that PDL/BBO would profit from the new policy, in this early phase it gradually also turned out to be a disadvantage since it was difficult to convince the same four ministries to invest once more in a research programme covering more or less the same field as Belvedere to which they had already committed themselves.

The Dutch preparations for the implementation of the Valletta Convention (Valletta 1992) focussing on the archaeological heritage, only completed in 2007, prepared the ground in another way. The Convention recommends 'the identification of the heritage and measures for protection' (art. 2) and 'the integrated conservation of the archaeological heritage' (art. 5). Although most time and energy was directed towards organizing protection by excavation, euphemistically called '*ex situ* conservation', attention increased for a preventive approach of '*in situ* conservation', which could match with the Belvedere concept of 'conservation through development'. Moreover, the invisibility of the archaeological heritage was considered as a disadvantage to integrate these resources with the more visible historical-geographical and historic built environment that Belvedere was promoting.

Finally, and crucial for the start of PDL/BBO, has been the Nota Wetenschapsbudget 1997 (Wetenschapsbudget 1996), presented by the Ministry of Education, Culture and Science and focussing on the funding of twelve strategic research themes combining excellent quality and social relevance. One of them was 'integrative use of space' and covered, among other things, 'conservation and prevention of the soil archive', a title not fully appropriate, but effective. Effective, because this budget granted 50% of the total costs of the programme on the condition that the other participating ministries would supply the remaining half. Again the argument was the threat to the archaeological resources and the problems with invisible heritage.

On 5th December 1997, Sint Nicolaas' birthday when in the Netherlands everyone gives and receives presents and poems, the first workshop was held as a start to prepare a full research programme to be presented to the Netherlands Organization for Scientific Research and the funding partners. Only two and a half years had passed since the rejection of a similar research programme including explicitly the historic built environment (Bloemers/Kerkstra/Van Voorden 1995)!

In 1998 and 1999 the design for the research programme was prepared and the negotiations between the funding ministries were started under the lead of NWO. The total amount as outcome of the funding process has been 3.000.000 euros.

The research design and the organizational structure

An interdisciplinary group representing archaeology, historical geography and planning prepared the design for the research programme that was presented to the funding partners and approved in 2000.

The aim was to develop a meaningful link between scientific knowledge, archaeological-historical resource management and applied planning policy in the Netherlands. The programme was divided into three types of research arranged in a mix of short (4-5 months) and long-term (4-5 years) studies (Fig. 1A). Two conceptual studies were commissioned and produced in 2001 to formulate the fundamental lines of research. Strategic inter- and transdisciplinary long-term research was selected in open competition from 2001 until 2003, a procedure lasting almost three years. Ten commissioned problem-oriented short-term projects on a variety of topics were carried out from 2002 until 2004.

Because of the focus on an integrative approach, four regionally oriented programmes, part of the strategic research, were selected to integrate and test the application of the conceptual and strategic lines in the context of differing archaeological-historical landscapes, spatial problems and developments and various political views. Moreover, the overall result of the programme should be more than the sum of its subprogrammes and projects.

The programme has been organized according to the structure normally used by the Netherlands Organization for Scientific Research. Heading the programme was a Steering Committee (SC) of eight members composed of the representatives of the six funding partners personifying the interdisciplinary ambitions and expectations (Ministry of Agriculture, Nature Management and Fisheries; Ministry of Education, Culture and Science; Ministry of Housing, Spatial Planning and the Environment; Ministry of Transport, Public Work and Water Management; the State Service for Archaeological Investigations; Netherlands Organization for Scientific Research). This group had the final responsibility for the programme and the authority to approve or reject the proposals presented by the Programme Committee (PC), a group with seven members. The PC originated from the group that prepared the research proposal and

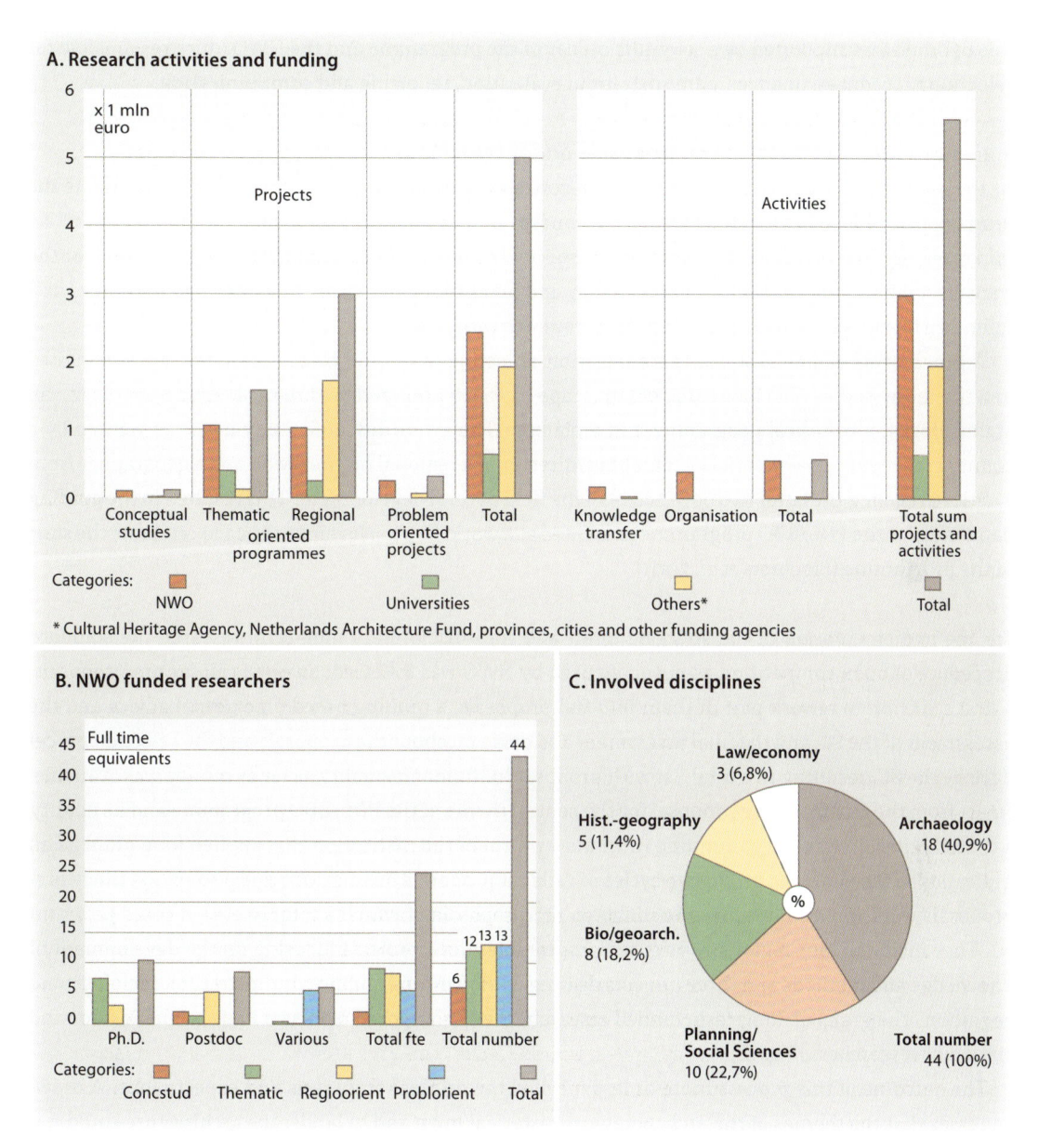

Fig. 1
Structure of the PDL/BBO programme.

included experts on architectural history, planning, and at a later stage human geography, all full professors from six disciplines and four universities. They have been responsible for developing the content of the research, the selection of proposals, their implementation and integration in the overall programme, the internal and external communication and international contacts. The formal leaders and researchers of the subprogrammes and projects, altogether over 50 persons, represented the intellectual resources of the PDL/BBO programme. All in all, over 70 people were united in the programme. The organization of this pyramid was supported by a scientific officer of the programme and the NWO office responsible for selection procedures, finances, administration, evaluation, reporting and communication.

2.2 Activities and selection of proposals and researchers

At the start of the programme, late 2000, two conceptual studies were commissioned to formulate the fundamental lines of research adopting the concept of biography of landscape and the method of action research. Together they should act as anchor points for the interdisciplinary integration and for the transdisciplinary link between research, policy and practice. At the same time, they had to be used as a reference for the assessment and selection of research proposals.

A group of six senior experts, its composition reflecting inter- and transdisciplinarity, were invited to write these studies. The biography of landscape has been prepared by three academic researchers: an archaeologist, a historical geographer and a planner. The action research study has been written by a county archaeologist, a historical geographer/director of a regional organization and a geographer from a national agency, the latter two both active in the field of rural development. This resulted in the guiding handbook for the PDL/BBO programme presented at a workshop in November 2001 to celebrate the start of the programme (Bloemers *et al.* 2001).

For the implementation of the strategic inter- and transdisciplinary long-term research the standard procedure of open competition as normally used by NWO was followed: an open call for pre-proposals, a first selection to rework part of them into full proposals, a ranking based on external advice and the assessment of the PC, and the final assessment and decision about the proposals and the selection procedure by the SC, resulting in a final list with proposals of fundable quality as far as money was available. Apart from the relevance of a proposal for the central theme of the PDL/BBO programme and its quality, a crucial criterion was the co-funding in whatever form of the institution that applied for a grant as an indication of its commitment. In two cycles of calls for proposals during 2001 and 2002-2003 thirty pre-proposals were received, resulting in nineteen full proposals of which a total of eleven could be granted. They included four regionally oriented programmes, four projects focusing on the development of knowledge and methods and three projects dealing with planning, public administration, sociology and cognition. The group of long-term funded researchers was composed of eleven Ph.D., eight Postdoc and six senior researchers (Fig. 1B).

The outcome of this process more or less fulfilled the original ambitions and expectations. A drawback was that the themes of the archaeological-historical town and of landscape architecture could not be covered because of the quality of the proposals, rather than lack of funding. Moreover, this can be considered as an indication that a balance was achieved between quality and money. A quite different issue was the conflict of interest between the role of senior researchers acting as applicants and members of the PC at the same time, which in an exceptional case raised suspicions about the integrity of the PC and the objectivity of the procedure. It reflects the limited size of the group of qualified experts available in the Netherlands to engage in an innovative field of research. However, in early 2002 and late 2003/early 2004 strategic research could really make a start in two phases.

Ten problem-oriented short-term projects on a variety of topics were commissioned by the Steering Committee as an expression of the policy orientation of PDL/BBO and its social relevance in the sense of the Wetenschapsbudget 1997. They ranged from an international survey of heritage policy and planning via specific planning issues such as urbanization, infrastructure, water management, non-destructive construction techniques and assessment methods for archaeological-historical urban areas into policy-oriented studies on decision-making processes, social-cost benefit analysis and experience of regional identities.

Communication activities were primarily oriented on the internal exchange between the researchers of the PDL/BBO programme by organizing annual one day thematic oriented and two day regionally oriented workshops with invited external guests. External presentations for the Dutch audience were organized at the beginning of the programme in 2000 and 2001 and at the end, in 2007. A range of activities was also developed on the international level. At the end of the programme in 2008 an international symposium was held with the participation, by special invitation only, of over thirty participants from all over Europe and about forty from the Netherlands. During the annual conferences of the European Association of Archaeologists from 2001 until 2006, round tables on sustainability, the European Landscape Convention and archaeological heritage management were initiated. From 2004 until 2008, six researchers actively participated in the European COST A27 programme LANDMARKS 'Understanding pre-industrial structure in rural and mining landscapes' (see Ch. VII.3). And finally the core aim of the PDL/BBO programme, the sustainable development of the archaeological-historical landscape, has become part of the Interdisciplinary Science Initiative 'New Perspectives on Landscape Studies' commissioned by the European Science Foundation and COST in 2007 and to be presented in 2010.

2.3 *External and internal assessments*

Late 2003, shortly after the completion of the second cycle of selecting and granting strategic research proposals, NWO arranged for a mid-term evaluation of the PDL/BBO programme by an external audit, a standard procedure for this type of programme. The committee was, for practical reasons, 'international' within the limits of Dutch-speaking members from the Netherlands and Belgium, since all proposals and reports were written in Dutch. The committee's interdisciplinary character was expressed by the mix of archaeological, cultural and economic geographical, architectural and rural planning expertise with an academic and national agency research background. The PC prepared a self-evaluation report following a NWO format, the external committee prepared a review based on the documentation about the PDL/BBO programme selected by the PDL/BBO Science Officer, the self-evaluation and an audit with representatives of the SC and the PC. After receipt of the review in January 2004, the SC and PC used the opportunity to formulate a reply on the review in March 2004.

Since at the time of the evaluation the main research work, with the exception of the conceptual studies, had just or had not yet started, the assessment focused on the intended implementation of the programme from the perspective of the granted research proposals. The main recommendations of the review and the follow-up given to them by SC and PC were the following.

The architectural and planning focus should be strengthened. Consequently an archaeological member of the PC was replaced by a human geographer with expertise on regional planning. In addition, the four regional programmes should aim for combinations with landscape architecture and planning by applying for special funding from the national Belvedere policy, especially the Netherlands Architecture

Fund (Stimuleringsfonds voor de Architectuur). During the following years, three of them were successful in achieving this in various forms.

It was recommended that the conceptual issues should be deepened to support the social embedding of the research results. In line with these recommendations the internal workshops were not only explicitly related to the concepts of biography and action research, but also more focused on both the regional and the thematic issues involved. The co-operation with local stakeholders and regional organizations should be intensified, particularly by the regionally oriented programmes.

To support the internal and external integration (see Van der Valk Ch. II.2) a communication strategy should be formulated. It was stressed by the SC that such a strategy could eventually be attached to the activities of the Belvedere project and the State Service for Archaeological Investigations, now part of the Cultural Heritage Agency. On the international level, the existing initiatives should be continued and extended when suitable opportunities were available. Both recommendations were implemented within the limits of time and money available.

A second form of evaluation was initiated by the PC and SC themselves to strengthen the inter- and transdisciplinary ambitions of the integrative research. They commissioned an analysis of three of the four regionally oriented programmes by studying the relevant documents and interviewing the researchers (Tress/Tress 2004). Points of analysis were the understanding of the conceptual approaches, experiences with integrative research, organization of the programmes, the integration of disciplines, expectations and personal experiences. The analysis resulted in thirteen recommendations about redefining ambitions, restructuring the organizational and managerial set up, increasing the expertise on integrative research, defining goals and output, supporting exchange and integration between the researchers, add senior researchers and developing an international publishing strategy.

The follow-up given to these recommendations was in line with those of the external evaluation. The communication strategy helped to focus the ambitions on the internal and external integration and activities like the congresses in 2007 and 2008 and related output. However, the intended creation of a programme website with links to the subprogrammes by NWO was delayed because of technical problems. To intensify exchange, strengthen integration and add senior expertise, half-yearly one and two day meetings were organized and a series of intensive workshops on the regional and thematic programmes was held in 2006 and 2007. The latter type of activity was crucial, since this is where the foundations were laid for the 2007 and 2008 external congresses.

A third form of assessing the programme was the visitation of the subprogrammes by selected members of the PC and reporting back to PC and SC. In fact this procedure has been limited to the first seven programmes granted. Afterwards this was replaced by the annual reports to the NWO office and the intensification of the plenary workshop meetings.

And finally quite an interesting assessment on the societal impact of the PDL/BBO research programme was carried out by the Humanities section of NWO during 2008 and early 2009 (Broek/Nijssen 2009). The aim of this type of impact assessment was to develop a methodology focused on the humanities and to test it by applying it to eight research programmes from different funding schemes of the Humanities section, one of which was the PDL/BBO programme, then in its final stage.

The focus of this assessment was on the societal impact of humanities research, a term the researchers prefer to use instead of the more general term 'valorization' (Broek/Nijssen 2009, 5-10). However, the two terms have a common background in a research policy that is interested in 'measuring' the use of scientific knowledge in practice and the way this knowledge can be made accessible and applicable. The impact assessment covered four 'value domains': economic value for the 'producing' society, social value for the 'coherent' society, cultural value for the 'learning' society, and democratic value for the 'arguing' society. The aspects to be measured and quantified were linked to dissemination activities in communication, teaching and co-operation expressed by their use value and factual utilization. This measured both the output by creating use value and effect by its utilization and the process of implementation of the dissemination activities. The societal effects of the utilization can take three forms: an instrumental one by direct and specific use, a conceptual one enhancing general understanding with an indirect and less specific influence, or a symbolic form legitimizing or criticizing existent positions. The BPI score used by the technological sciences was adapted and used for quantification.

The assessment report presents some interesting statements about the PDL/BBO programme. Its impact primarily covers the cultural and democratic value domains. The user value compared with the other programmes is average, probably because of the combination of the inter- and transdisciplinary ambition and the weaker score on the second activity. But its factual utilization has a high score because of the conceptual and symbolic effects by the fundamental concepts (Broek/Nijssen 2009, 54-64).

3. THE INTEGRATION AND DEVELOPMENT OF KNOWLEDGE

As already mentioned earlier, the research programme aimed at the development of scientific knowledge in order to support the sustainable development of the Dutch archaeological-historical landscape. Consequently, our strategy focused on establishing a meaningful link between scientific knowledge, archaeological-historical resource management and applied planning policy in the Netherlands using the central planning concepts of dynamics and quality expressed as sustainability, identity, diversity and coherence (Fig. 3). From the preparation of the research programme in the late 1990s, a structure gradually emerged of the underlying knowledge organization (Fig. 2). Essential in establishing the links

Fig. 2
The structure of the PDL/BBO programme.

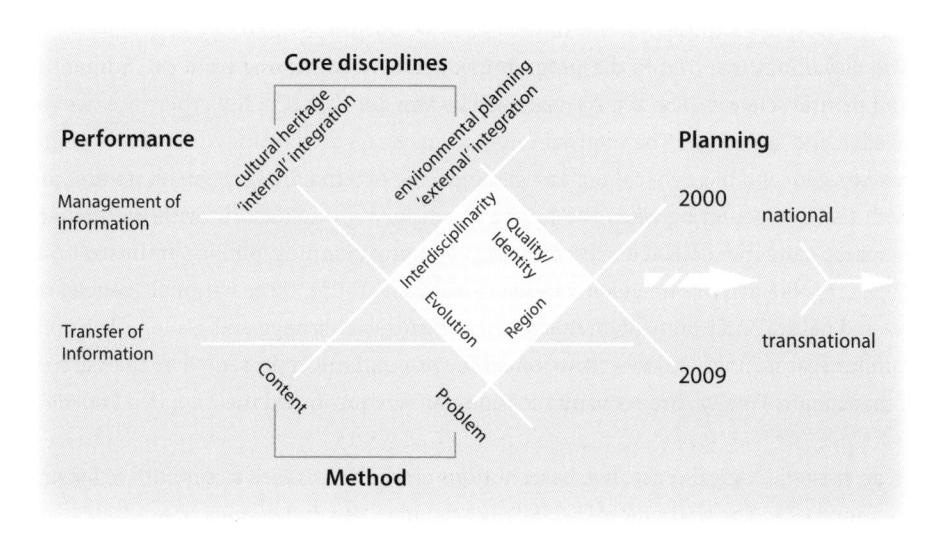

Fig. 3
Core concepts from Dutch environmental planning and their relevance for archaeological-historical heritage management (*Bloemers 2005, 75; idem 2006, 257*).

CORE CONCEPT	ENVIRONMENTAL PLANNING	ARCHAEOLOGY
Evolution		
Change	DYNAMIC evolution (dis)continuity	TRANSFORMATION
Quality		
Function	FUNCTIONALITY multi-use flexibility	FUNCTIONALITY
Meaning	PERCEPTION diversity quality of design coherency	PERCEPTION diversity identity
Future	FUTURE VALUE sustainability	FUTURE sustainability

between cultural or archaeological-historical heritage and planning and between research and policy has been the focus on inter- and transdisciplinary interaction between both domains. The methodology follows two lines, a problem oriented one and one on content or theme. The long-term perspective is expressed by evolution indicating the genesis and transformation of landscapes. The region is the entity where problems and content or themes interact and the integrative approach has to be practised. The management and transfer of knowledge is an aspect that permeates through all activities and interactions from the earliest beginning until the end of the programme. Although the focus is on the Netherlands, the world outside has to be taken into account as the wider context and source of inspiration.

3.1 Disciplines and epistemologies

The disciplines involved in the programme, about twelve, come from the humanities, social sciences and natural sciences (Fig. 1C). As described by Van der Valk (Ch. II.2), there are two forms of integration needed and aimed for. The internal integration covers archaeology, historical geography, architectural history, geo- and bioarchaeology and geology. The external integration on its first dimension has to do with the interaction between the before-mentioned group dealing with the archaeological-historical landscape and the social sciences: human geography, planning, public administration. This mix of disciplines represented five universities and six research groups, three national agencies dealing with the rural and natural environment, archaeological-historical heritage and geology. Four provinces, two semi-public organizations and two cities joined the programme, represented by their archaeological heritage departments. Finally, three consultancy companies contributed their applied knowledge.

In an epistemological sense, two basic notions can be considered as supportive for unifying the integrative approach. The first one is specifically related to the dimensions of landscape and environment as seen from a human perspective: time as reflecting genesis, social evolution, transformation, history; environment as a physical and natural phenomenon; and behaviour expressing human cognition and action. The second notion belongs to the world of social sciences and, according to Habermas, is about the functioning of society and action. It covers language, communication and related validity claims. It has to do with truth and justness or objectivity and subjectivity as has been described by During in the PDL/BBO conceptual studies (Korthals 1987, 160-163 and 169-173; During/Elerie/Groenendijk 2001, 114).

These two notions are characteristic of the difficulty of practising the interdisciplinary approach in PDL/BBO. The researchers from the humanities and natural sciences as cultural landscape specialists were trained in a very different paradigm from that of the social sciences researchers. Their languages were completely different, at the beginning they did not even understand the background of this issue and as a consequence did not appreciate what was communicated. It was especially difficult for those from the natural sciences, since they considered themselves as belonging to the hard sciences. However, it became clear that the cultural landscape and heritage theme was the unifying platform to gradually move towards each other. A surprising event was when a paper written by an archaeological science researcher about the role of perception in the research of ancient colours was discussed during one of the thematic workshops (Jones 2004). Suddenly it appeared that the social science paradigm also had relevance for science-based heritage approaches and that positivism and postmodernism could be understood and appreciated in their own right.

3.2 *Development of a common theory and method*

A meaningful link between scientific knowledge, archaeological-historical resource management and applied planning policy can be founded on the 'internal' integration of archaeology, historical geography and historic built environment and the 'external' integration with the design and analytical disciplines and with policy and technical sciences. To support this, two unifying concepts were used: the (cultural) biography of landscape and the action research approach (see Van der Valk Ch. II.2, 35-41).

The critical question now is whether these concepts worked out that way or not. For the four regionally oriented programmes the two concepts functioned quite well, although they were applied in very different ways. The result has been that the use of the biography concept in particular has been framed in a geographical setting, related to the specific context of achieving strategic alliances, communication, research or valorization (Van Beek *et al.* 2008, 179-184). These four programmes exemplify how the biography can be told to characterize the regions' specific long-term landscape history. However, in most thematic programmes the biography did not play a significant role. Action research has been applied in both regional and thematic programmes where both interdisciplinarity and transdisciplinarity were required. Examples of thematic studies are those by Kamermans and Verhagen, Van Assche, Duineveld and De Zwart. For the two multidisciplinary programmes on degradation and prospection the two concepts had a limited meaning, but they influenced aims and results by placing them in the wider context of heritage management.

The ultimate proof of the effectiveness of the two concepts lies in the synthesis of the overall programme expressed in particular by the content of this book and the synthesis it is presenting. The structure of the three themes presented in chapter III-V has been the outcome of the workshops aiming at establishing the meaningful link between scientific knowledge, archaeological-historical resource management and applied planning policy as represented in Fig. 4. In 2006 and 2007 two series of preparatory workshops

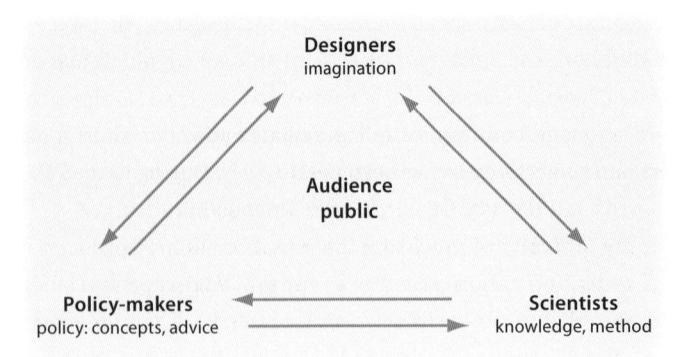

Fig. 4.
The core structure of this PDL/BBO volume: the interaction between knowledge, policy, imagination and practice.
(Courtesy of Heleen van Londen)

with three sessions each were held. One was for the researchers involved in the regionally oriented programmes chaired by Tom Bloemers and the other thematic series chaired by Arnold van der Valk. At the end a general meeting for the two types of research was organized to reconcile the two series of workshops. Researchers, including the leaders from each programme or project, had to present an overview of the actual state of the research and to focus on particular issues like problems encountered, factors influencing success or failure and directions of problem solving, illustrated by examples from the programme or project. In addition they had to suggest two publications which they considered as very relevant for the implementation of their research and the dilemmas they were facing. These papers had to be read before the sessions. A report was made of each session, sent and circulated before the next session and completed by a final overview of the series. This worked very well and laid a solid foundation for the final conferences in December 2007 and May 2008. However, the participants were not eager to spend their time on it for a number of reasons. They were focused on the progress of their own research and became aware that time was running fast and deadlines coming up towards the end of their appointment. Apart from this it was sometimes difficult for them to recognize the urgency of arriving at the synthesis of the overall programme as it was required by the Programme Committee and Steering Group.

4. CO-ORDINATION AND COMMUNICATION

Co-ordination and communication are of course crucial conditions that determine the success of complex and ambitious research programmes like PDL/BBO. Two characteristics of the group of researchers involved in various ways have to be recognized. First, the groups were distributed over six different locations in the country, most of them within a distance of about 100 kilometres, but their working areas were up to 200 kilometres apart. Thus, informal and spontaneous encounters between the members of the various groups did not happen frequently. Second, not all researchers had a full time research appointment for the PDL/BBO programme. Some of them worked part time, combining their research with other professional activities. Sometimes this had synergetic effects and sometimes this interfered in a negative way, but generally it meant that the time span involved to complete the research was longer than anticipated.

4.1 Co-ordination

The most important ambition has been that the overall result of the programme should be more than the sum of its subprogrammes and projects. As a consequence, co-ordination had go beyond current issues. From the perspective of knowledge management this has been the Programme Committee's major task. The full PC was always almost fully present at the Committee's meetings 2-4 times a year and at the plenary workshops. From 2006 onwards three members, the editors of this volume, invested extra time and energy in the organization of the two series of regional and thematic workshops. Together they personified the interdisciplinarity, being a bio- and geoarchaeologist, a planner and a cultural archaeologist. Prior to this, between late 2005 and mid-2007, an informal group had prepared the ground for the integration and the above-mentioned workshops. The eight members came from both regional and thematic research, had a natural and social sciences or humanities background and worked at a senior and postdoctoral level. The PC chairman played a central role together with the Science Officer. Fortunately, he could spend most of his time on the programme, since there was no special funding available for co-ordinating the programme.

The Steering Committee has been the high authority of the PDL/BBO programme. The eight members assembled twice a year and sometimes members attended the two-day regional workshops, enjoyed the discussions on landscape and contributed their expertise.

4.2 Communication

A communication plan that focused on the external world was developed in 2005 and 2006. The internal communication had to support this activity in the way previously described. For a number of reasons the external communication received special attention relatively late. First, the budget was too restricted to engage a special employee in the early phase, when all available time was invested in starting up the programme. Second, the overall feeling in the PC was that after communicating the start of the programme, initial preliminary scientific insights had to be developed before initiating a larger communication event. It was decided to limit external communication to the contacts directly related to the centrally organized regional workshops. Apart from that the individual programmes and projects were stimulated to organize their own external contacts, in some cases with additional funding from the central PDL/BBO budget. The programme on predictive modelling by Kamermans *et al.* is a fine example of organizing two workshops followed by two publications (Van Leusen/Kamermans 2005; Kamermans/Van Leusen/Verhagen 2009).

From 2006 onwards the co-operation with the Belvedere project gradually resulted in external effects. The new 'Onderwijsnetwerk Belvedere' had at that time started its activities under the leadership of the three Belvedere chairs at the universities of Wageningen (A. van der Zande), Amsterdam (VU University; J. Kolen) and Delft (E. Luijten) (Cerutti 2008). The co-operation with the chairs in Wageningen and Amsterdam has been particularly fruitful, transferring PDL/BBO knowledge to courses and handbooks. Furthermore, the additional funding of three projects linked to the regional programmes of the Drentsche Aa, the Oer-IJ and the Southern Netherlands by the Netherlands Architecture Fund (Stimuleringsfonds voor de Architectuur) had a strong effect on external communication and knowledge transfer by producing a regional historical website aimed at designers, a regional agenda for cultural landscape planning and a regional landscape vision also for cultural landscape development and management.

A very weak point was the lack of a website until about 2006. When finally available its function was very limited, following the basic NWO format with few illustrations and focused on the research community. However, some programmes and projects had developed their own websites in a much more appealing way.

4.3 Additional time demand and training

Within the PDL/BBO budget no specific funding was available for additional time for general co-ordination, communication and training participants, e.g. for doing inter- and transdisciplinary research. For general co-ordination a budget was envisaged but not effectuated to save this money for other purposes like communication. At the beginning of the programme it was not recognized that training for inter- and transdisciplinarity might be necessary. Halfway through the programme, as a result of the internal assessment of three regional programmes, this recommendation was implemented within the limits of time and money available by intensifying the workshop series.

4.4. Leadership

Leadership concerns two levels, that of the individual programmes, especially the larger ones like the regional research or the smaller thematic programmes, and that of the programme as a whole. Leadership of the individual programmes was in the hands of senior researchers, generally professors. Most of them had adequate experience of managing more complex research programmes with a focus on knowledge output. On the level of the whole programme and from the perspective of management of knowledge, the PC represented the most important echelon. All members were full-time professors with considerable experience in both assessing and managing research. The group showed excellent leadership both in terms of individual experts and as an interdisciplinary group.

5. KNOWLEDGE CREATION BY THE PDL/BBO RESEARCH PROGRAMME

Having discussed the PDL/BBO's research history, I will now focus on the research's crucial aspects, namely the new knowledge created by the programme. As referred to in the introductory paragraph, Weggeman defines knowledge as "the partially unconscious capacity that is represented by the function of Information, Experience, Ability (Dutch: *vaardigheden*) and Attitude of someone" (Weggeman 2001[4], 28-41 and expressed in the 'formula' $K=f(I.EVA)$. Weggeman defines information as meaning given to observed data, i.e. symbolic representations of quantities, facts and opinions; experience is the set of events a person has seen during his life; abilities have two forms, "exogenous" abilities of external communication and expression and "endogenous" or 'cerebral' abilities being analysis, intuition, imagination and reflection; attitude is the set of basic beliefs framing values and norms. Aside from reflecting on the programme as an entity and its constituent subprogrammes and projects, the role of these four elements and the way they have influenced the creation of (new) knowledge and its character are analysed in Ch. VI.

Using this knowledge perspective the two guiding concepts of the PDL/BBO research, biography of landscape and action research, are considered and their effects for the central planning concepts of dynamics and quality expressed as sustainability, identity, diversity and coherence. The data employed belong to the domains of the archaeological-historical heritage and of policy and practice. First we discuss this theme for the four regionally oriented programmes, then for the thematic projects.

5.1 The regionally oriented programmes

The biography concept in general was extensively described at the beginning of the programme (Hidding/Kolen/Spek 2001). The application of this concept in the individual regional programmes, however, resulted in the explication of its scientifically well-considered use in a particular context, i.e. the way to assess and select from the data the elements for the long-term narratives and of the various means to make them accessible and usable for planning and design. Moreover, the relationship between the biography and the action research concept could be explicated by considering them as the superstructure and infrastructure, a concept borrowed from the historical discipline. Superstructure is in our case the narration of the archaeological-historical landscape story by applying the metaphor of biography of landscape; infrastructure is the methodical way towards this narration exploring the sources and the biography's use in the context of heritage management, planning and design (see Ch. IV.1, 188 and IV.2, 211). The examples of the application of the biography concept in the four regionally oriented programmes illustrate its variety and the creativity involved as set out in the PDL/BBO programme's aims. In this way the biography concept has supported the aspects of sustainability, identity and diversity in a regionally specific context of landscape and policy.

The analysis of the application of the action research concept has yielded different insights, but clearly complementary to that of the biography concept. Here the biography concept has been applied in the context of action in policy and practice to unify research and action. It made itself felt for handling the issue of identity and for dealing with functionality in the sense of the Belvedere motto 'conservation through development' and with coherence, because of the integrative way of thinking about landscape and the planning and design process (e.g. Ch. IV.3 Fig. 7). The domain of experiences has yielded crucial new insights in the value of local knowledge (Elerie/Spek 2009) and of the existence of intermediary groups or institutions that link science and policy at the local or regional level in an effective way (Brede Overleggroep Kleine Dorpen in Drenthe: Ch. III.3, 90-91 and 109-110; Peelland: Ch. V.2, 402-403; Cultureel Erfgoed Noord-Holland: Ch. IV.2, 212). Another aspect concerns the phasing of science and policy cycles and the connections between them, especially on the regional or provincial level. Gradually it was realized that research and policy cycles had different starting points and durations resulting in asynchronic processes. Furthermore, one should be aware that although the two actors have common aims, they have partly different focuses and operate under specific conditions. As a consequence, only a limited set of activities are suited for co-operation (Bloemers et al. Oer-IJ: Ch. IV.2, 208-210). In the domain of endogenous abilities three programmes have shown activities each founded in long-term research involvement in the region concerned and together illustrating the diverse strands of knowledge creation. These activities are all externally directed and aim at the transfer of the biography concept, but also focus on different groups and aspects. In the Southern Netherlands programme the Zandstad project has developed a website that offers structured historical knowledge for planners and designers. The Agenda Oer-IJ presents the analysis of the process that a series of local and regional plans in a report and designs have gone through resulting in a recommendation for the follow up on the regional and local level towards an integrative approach. The field names project in the Drentsche Aa has field names considered as part of a living heritage and as a stimulus for cultural historical renewal. In this sense the field names have been collected in close co-operation with the local inhabitants of the region, interpreted from the perspective of various role models of the users and presented in a very appealing atlas.

Finally we come to the attitude and new insights gained in this domain, in the case of the PDL/BBO research programme characterized by the integrative, i.e. inter- and transdisciplinary, aims and approaches. Of course the awareness that this required a change in attitude has been confirmed and consequently it has been part of the management focus. However, the success of the resulting activities has not only depended on the PDL/BBO researcher, but also on the external partner in policy and planning on the regional or local level, both in research and action. Only when a partner is encountered who is able to cross the disciplinary and institutional boundaries is the potential for creating new knowledge success an option. This ability is related to the set policy conditions and the personal chemistry between the partners. Stakeholders at the local and regional level, e.g. in the form of a public-private institution, a non-governmental organization or one or more individuals combining knowledge and authority on this level, are essential for the embedding of the new attitude to secure the continuation of the new knowledge-creating process. It appeared that the action research activities lacked a framework of reference as a sort of 'rules of engagement' and as a consequence the need for an ethics of heritage management has been clearly felt.

5.2. *The thematic research perspective*

The new knowledge created by the use of the PDL/BBO guiding concepts of landscape biography and action research in the thematic projects is different from that in the regionally oriented programmes. This difference can be characterized as insights more focused on a specific issue or context resulting from a more in-depth analysis and interpretation of a relevant set of data. The insights relevant for the central planning concepts of dynamics and quality expressed as sustainability, identity, diversity and coherence stem not only from inter- and transdisciplinary research, but also from multidisciplinary science-based research on prospection and degradation.

None of the thematic studies focused on the biography concept in a specific way, but two of them, Van Assche (Signs in time; Van Assche 2004) and Smit (Valuable flints; Smit 2010), have touched upon it in combination with working in the domain of action research. Van Assche has concentrated on identity and identification as a social construction using history and a process with the outcome of the interaction between a person, a group and a place equating personality, culture or polity and space (Van Assche 2004, 168-169). Smit points to the potential of the biography to bridge the gap between present inhabitants and prehistoric land use, raising awareness of a forgotten or neglected past like that of early prehistoric hunter-gatherer landscapes and enriching the diversity of a region (Smit 2010). The biography concept can also be used to establish a link between an ecological and archaeological heritage policy for sustainable landscape management, as Smit indicates. This links up with Kars' research group working on the degradation of archaeological sites and landscapes, a primarily multidisciplinary approach explicitly directed at the sustainable development of this type of archaeological heritage. In this way a variety of data sets has been interpreted resulting in new information about their use and meaning from an unconventional heritage perspective.

Other programmes and projects have concentrated on the domain of action research alone. The interaction between data and information in the sense of Weggeman's knowledge formula is highlighted by Van Leusen *et al* critical study on the application of predictive modelling in current Dutch heritage policy (Kamermans/Van Leusen/Verhagen 2009). They explicitly criticize the quality of the data for the lack of time depth and spatial accuracy and for the limited possibilities to test predictions and predictive methods by fieldwork focused on developing the methodology related to its use in a policy context. These critiques also touch upon the abilities of the experts, since the spatial statistics generally used are not adequate for the type of predictions made. Kars' prospection programme also deals with abilities in the sense of Weggeman, especially the use of geophysical and geochemical survey methods in the typically Dutch wetland conditions and the potential and limitations for heritage management and conservation. The Ph.D. projects of Duineveld and De Zwart cover the combined aspects of abilities and attitude since they have studied the interaction between professional archaeology and the external world; in Duineveld's case the amateur archaeologists (Duineveld 2006), in De Zwart's case public authorities involved in the development of urban development (De Zwart Ch. V.7). Their analysis has revealed and criticizes the way in which archaeologists involved in heritage policy have carried out actions prior to the implementation of the Valletta Convention in the Netherlands, in the process losing public support for the process to establish a socially relevant archaeological policy that also protects heritage.

The new knowledge created by the thematic line of research can be summarized by using the label 'interpretative heritage research' introduced by one of the researchers involved, Duineveld. Exploring old and new data from an innovative research perspective and reflecting upon the process of giving them meaning and handling them in a specific social context is a form of reflective research, which is a must for heritage policy on all levels. This is illustrated by the presentation of the Archeologiebalans 2002 (Lauwerier/Lotte 2002) and the Erfgoedbalans 2009 (Beukers 2009), prepared by the national heritage authorities in the Netherlands. Van Assche's contribution in this volume (Ch. IV.5) on self- and heteroreference of a system, institution or sector is very appropriate in this context, since some of the 'critical' BBO researchers have been and still are confronted with sharp and sometimes vehement reactions from their colleagues. It is a surprising experience, showing the complexity of linking action and research.

5.3 The PDL/BBO research programme: a fuzzy structure

Looking back at the past ten years the organization of the PDL/BBO research programme can be described as a 'fuzzy' structure (*sensu* Weggeman) which characterizes knowledge-intensive organizations. A fuzzy structure is more a non-structure than a structure, since formal hierarchies and clear goals or results only exist on a limited scale and learning and adapting are of great importance. Related to a fuzzy structure are the various strategies involved during the research process. The research starts with the intended explicit and formal strategy, during the process an emergent strategy appears in an informal and opportunistic way, while at the end it gradually becomes clear which actions had a strategic value and have been realized (Weggeman 2001[4], 34). It is easy to recognize these three strategic phases when looking back at the PDL/BBO programme: the research design, the assessment phase, and the partly internal communication phase from 2006-2008. During the early formative phase of the programme the research preproposal and the intentions were explicitly described. The intended strategy was to focus on research for an integrated heritage policy including the historic built environment, which had been part of the proposal previously rejected in 1995 and was in agreement with the then new Belvedere policy. Since archaeology and to a lesser extent historical geography were considered to have a disadvantage compared to the historic built environment, the last was left out. This became what Weggeman calls the deliberate strategy as decided upon by the funding partners in 2000. During the later formative phase, when research proposals were selected and granted, the programme entered the phase of the emergent strategy which in a very recognizable way is characterized by Weggeman as being spontaneous, informal, opportunistic, implicit and using tacit knowledge. This is also the stage when research had to be adapted in terms of unrealized plans, for example the integration with the design disciplines. What we present in this volume represents the realized strategy, the pattern as we consider it by looking backwards, assessing and synthesizing the insights of the variety of subprogrammes and projects.

Considering the group of researchers from the perspective of age and discipline the mix has functioned well, but it has not been without risks. The senior researchers were pivotal in creating new knowledge related especially to the biography concept for the regional part of the research and action research. Their crucial assets were their relevant experiences and abilities like reflection, imagination and even intuition in combination with their action research attitude. The junior researchers were primarily involved in the collection and analysis of data in both regional and thematic research, using their specific abilities learned during their training phase. The postdoctoral researchers played an intermediary role in both research lines, combining assets of both senior and junior researchers in a mix of experiences and abilities with the action research attitude. It is to the credit of the junior and postdoctoral researchers that the involved risks, especially for the Ph.D. researchers with their focus on their thesis, only showed up in a very limited way. The internal assessment report made by Tress and Tress (Tress/Tress 2004, 33 recommendation 9) advised "...to avoid attracting further Ph.D. researchers ... and to strengthen the input of experienced researchers to realize the integration process and to guarantee for other programme outputs than Ph.D. theses.".

6. TO CONCLUDE: LESSONS LEARNED

As a conclusion, these reflections on the management of knowledge in the PDL/BBO programme will be examined from the perspective of the analysis of the strengths and weaknesses of the programme and the opportunities and threats as external conditions.

Clear strengths keeping the research in the intended direction and making good progress have been the engagement, focus and learning capacity of all participants on all levels, the presence of the two core concepts and the consistency of the research design that remained valid until the end of the programme. Considering that no specific attention has been given to training and education for practising inter- and transdisciplinary research, the junior researchers did a particularly fine job. The value for money has been high, as is stated in the Impact Assessment Humanities (Broek/Nijssen 2009, 60).

Communication, especially external, has been a weak spot, which has made the programme more invisible than intended or necessary. Taking into account the limited impact of the short-term studies, part of that funding would probably have been better allocated to communication activities. Another weak aspect noticed during the mid-term assessment, the engagement of landscape design, has been corrected by spin off activities of three regionally oriented programmes based on external funding, especially from the Netherlands Architecture Fund (Stimuleringsfonds voor de Architectuur). Surprising is the very limited interaction between the research programme and relevant research schools from archaeology and geography. The explanation might be the lack of interest in interdisciplinary research from the 'monodisciplinary' oriented institutions.

The Belvedere policy created an overall favourable climate for the core theme of the PDL/BBO programme. Although activities and audience were quite different, contact between both programmes was maintained during the whole duration. In the last phase co-operation between the Belvedere chairs and PDL/BBO was intensified. In combination with the merging of the national heritage organizations into one integrated Cultural Heritage Agency, this has created adequate conditions for the embedding of PDL/BBO insights in future concerns. However, similar restructurations of heritage institutions during the lifetime of PDL/BBO raised serious problems, since crucial stakeholders left these organizations or policy shifted in focus. This of course is a fact of life and researchers must learn to live with it, but it also creates the danger that the new insights and knowledge may be lost.

All in all, the PDL/BBO research has been a pioneering programme yielding major new insights in theory and application and showing the way forward for an exciting and intelligent combination of research, policy and practice.

NOTES

1 Amsterdam University, Amsterdam, the Netherlands.

REFERENCES

Assche, K. Van, 2004: *Signs in time. An interpretive account of urban planning and design, the people and their histories,* Wageningen (Ph.D. thesis Wageningen University).

Beek, R. van /J.H.F. Bloemers/L. Keunen/H. van Londen/J. Kolen, 2008: The Netherlands, in G. Fairclough/P. Grau Møller (eds.), *Landscape as Heritage. The Management and Protection of Landscape in Europe, a summary by the Cost A 27 project LANDMARKS,* Bern (Geographica Bernensia 79), 177-203.

Belvedere, 1999: *The Belvedere Memorandum. A policy document examining the relationship between cultural history and spatial planning,* The Hague.

Beukers, E. et al. (eds.), 2009: *Erfgoedbalans 2009. Archeologie, monumenten en cultuurlandschap in Nederland,* Amersfoort.

Bloemers, J.H.F., 2005: Archaeological-historical Landscapes in the Netherlands: management by sustainable development in planning, in M. Ruiz del Árbol/A. Orejas (eds.), *Landscapes as Cultural Heritage in the European Research. Proceedings of the Open Workshop Madrid, 29th October 2004,* Madrid, 69-85.

Bloemers, J.H.F., 2006: Kulturlandschaften in den Niederlanden - Erhaltung durch nachhaltige Entwicklung in der Raumordnung, in U. Matthiesen/R. Danielzyk/S. Heiland/S. Tzschaschel (eds.), *Kulturlandschaften als Herausforderung für die Raumplanung. Verständnisse - Erfahrungen -Perspektiven,* Hannover (Forschungs- und Sitzungsberichte der Akademie für Raumforschung und Landesplanung, 228), 253-273.

Bloemers, J.H.F./R. During/J.N.H. Elerie/H.A. Groenendijk/M. Hidding/J. Kolen/Th. Spek/M.-H. Wijnen, 2001: *Bodemarchief in Behoud en Ontwikkeling. De conceptuele grondslagen,* Den Haag.

Bloemers, J.H.F./K. Kerkstra/F.W. van Voorden 1995: Cultuurhistorisch landschap en ruimtelijke ontwikkeling. Een wetenschappelijke en toepassingsgerichte investering in de kwaliteit van de toekomstige omgeving. Een NWO-prioriteitprogramma?, Amsterdam/Wageningen/Delft.

Broek, S.D./A.J. Nijssen, 2009: *Impact Assessment Geesteswetenschappen,* Den Haag.

Cerutti, V., 2008: *Leerstoelen in de etalage. Review Onderwijsnetwerk Belvedere,* s.l.

Duineveld, M., 2006: *Van oude dingen, de mensen, die voorbij gaan. Over de voorwaarden meer recht te kunnen doen aan de door burgers gewaardeerde cultuurhistories,* Wageningen (Ph.D. thesis Wageningen University).

During, R./H. Elerie/ H.A. Groenendijk, 2001: Denken en doen: verpachten van wijsheid of delen van kennis? Pleidooi voor de verbinding van cultuurhistorische kenniseilanden en een relatie met de sociale wetenschappen, in J.H.F. Bloemers/R. During/J.N.H. Elerie/H.A. Groenendijk/M. Hidding/J. Kolen/Th. Spek/M.-H. Wijnen, *Bodemarchief in Behoud en Ontwikkeling. De conceptuele grondslagen*, Den Haag, 111-157.

Elerie, H./T. Spek, 2009: *Van Jeruzalem tot Ezelakker. Veldnamen als levend erfgoed in het Nationaal Landschap Drentsche Aa*, Utrecht.

Hidding, M./J. Kolen/Th. Spek, 2001: De biografie van het landschap. Ontwerp voor een inter- en multidisciplinaire benadering van de landschapsgeschiedenis en het cultuurhistorisch erfgoed, in J.H.F. Bloemers/R. During/J.N.H. Elerie/H.A. Groenendijk/M. Hidding/J. Kolen/Th. Spek/M.-H. Wijnen (eds.), *Bodemarchief in Behoud en Ontwikkeling. De conceptuele grondslagen*, Den Haag, 7-109.

Jones, A., 2004: Archaeometry and materiality: materials-based analysis in theory and practice, *Archaeometry* 46, 327-338.

Kamermans, H./M. van Leusen/P. Verhagen (eds.), 2009: *Archaeological Prediction and Risk Management*, Leiden.

Korthals, M., 1987: *Wetenschapsleer*, Heerlen.

Lauwerier, R.C.G.M./R.M. Lotte, 2002: *Archeologiebalans 2002*, Amersfoort.

Leusen, M. van/H. Kamermans (eds.), 2005: *Predictive Modelling for Archaeological Heritage Management: A research agenda*, Amersfoort (Nederlandse Archaeologische Rapporten, 29).

Smit, B.I., 2010: *Valuable Flints. Research strategies for the study of early prehistoric remains from the Pleistocene soils of the Northern Netherlands*, Groningen (Ph.D. thesis Groningen University).

Tress, G./B. Tress, 2004: *Analyzing and supporting the integration process in archaeological-historical landscape research in the BBO program (SINTAL)*, Wageningen.

Tress, B./G. Tress/G. Fry, 2006: Ten steps to success in integrative research, in B.G. Tress/G. Tress/G. Fry/P. Opdam (eds.), *From Landscape Research to landscape Planning. Aspects of Integration, Education and Application*, Dordrecht, 241-75.

Valletta, 1992: European Convention on the Protection of the Archaeological Heritage (Revised) Valetta, 16.I.1992, Strasbourg (Council of Europe).

Weggeman, M., 2001[4]: *Kennismanagement. Inrichting en besturing van kennisintensieve organisaties*, Schiedam.

Wetenschapsbudget 1996: *Topkwaliteit en relevantie. Samenvatting Wetenschapsbudget, 1997*, Den Haag.

8. Cultural landscapes in the mirror
What information systems reveal about information management and cultural landscape research

Sophie Visser[1]

ABSTRACT

Information systems on cultural landscapes and their broader contexts in European countries are not without problems. As this foremost relates to knowledge and information management issues, these issues are highlighted in this contribution. In doing so, the emphasis is on the information content, because this is decisive in what is possible and pertains to issues such as:
- What is modelled (or not) and from which cultural landscape research approach and aims, e.g. knowledge, values or characterizations. Which kinds of objects? What about typologies, etc.? Who are the makers and users?
- Levels of modelling, starting from a conceptual analysis or from logical or technical design and from higher or lower administrative levels.
- The adaptation to new or changing needs and landscape views and the integration of systems.
- What does the situation show about awareness and expertise as essential aspects in knowledge and information management?

Information systems and the overall information picture at the pan-European level and in the United Kingdom, the Netherlands, and Germany are discussed within this framework. This is mainly done from a historical-geographical perspective, although the archaeological information situation is also discussed with reference to the Netherlands.

In its current form, conceptual thinking is generally weak, although there seems to be more awareness of this in Germany and the United Kingdom than in the Netherlands. The differences in knowledge and information management seem bigger. This is much more an issue in the United Kingdom than in the Netherlands, with Germany in an in-between position. Germany takes the lead in discussions and reflection. At the European level, in both issues the situation is mainly dependent on the countries and their representatives.

KEY WORDS

Information system, usability; cultural landscape, modelling; conceptual, knowledge, values

1. INTRODUCTION

These days, information systems are a fact of life in practices concerning cultural and historical landscapes. While their purpose, to store and to provide knowledge, information and values, appears to be straightforward, their usability can be quite problematic. Usability means the ability to fulfill the information needs of (potential) users, which requires the makers to be well aware of what an information system really is about. But when circumstances change, be it in actors, purposes, concepts or otherwise, the information needs will change accordingly. Awareness of informational viewpoints such as these are core issues in disciplines like information systems science and information and knowledge management.

This contribution deals with information systems on cultural historical landscapes from an informational viewpoint. Therefore, at first, key concepts such as knowledge, information, values, etc. as well as other essential aspects from an informational viewpoint, are introduced. Based on this, a reference framework for positioning and discussing the systems is developed. This reference framework is used in a discussion of information systems and the overall information picture at the pan-European level and in the United Kingdom, the Netherlands, and Germany. This is primarily done from a historical-geographical perspective, but because of the PDL/BBO programme the Dutch archaeological information situation is also discussed.

2. KNOWLEDGE, INFORMATION, VALUES, AND INFORMATION SYSTEMS: CONCEPTS AND PRINCIPLES

2.1 *The concepts of knowledge and information*

Information systems, the general term for computer-based systems, encompass a very broad spectrum, including knowledge and data(base) systems, GIS systems, etc. The latter systems are about location-based information, handled by specialized Geographic Information technology. In many definitions the 'manual' or procedural information functions around the computer-based parts are also included.

Information is also the most common term, more than knowledge or data. Many definitions express information in terms of data and knowledge, for instance in information such as 'meaningful data' or as 'communicated knowledge' (Amin/Cohendet 2004; Pijpers 2006). Examples of definitions of knowledge are 'the body of meaningful concepts and associations' or 'a justified true belief'.

In this contribution the definition of information as 'communicated knowledge' is taken as a starting point. The reason is the implied relationship between the people on the sender side (the system developer and/or the landscape expert) and on the receiver side (the users) of the communication (Visser 2009). Both sides usually have their own perceptions and expectations of what is needed in information and communication. If those perceptions do not match, serious miscommunication and usability problems may result. In direct communication this can be solved by immediate feedback. Information systems, however, usually imply indirect communication, as they contain prefabricated messages for anonymous

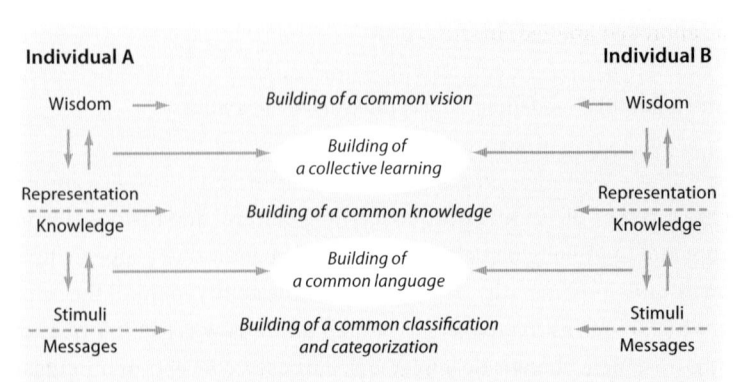

Fig. 1
Interactions between actors in the formation of knowledge
(Amin/Cohendet 2004, 26).

use later on. This makes the applied 'language', as in terms, categories or presentation, very crucial. Fig. 1 shows some general steps in acquiring knowledge by means of this kind of communicative interactions.

Information systems are, of course, only one way of transferring knowledge or information. They must therefore be positioned in this broader context of communication and information. A special aspect of cultural landscape systems is the emphasis on external communication, with other organizations (or their information systems) or with 'outside' people. This is different from internal systems in essential ways.

2.2 *Knowledge and values from an information perspective*

Knowledge is a complex concept because everything one gets to know, including values and characterization, becomes knowledge. However, from an informational perspective, there are essential differences between basic and derived knowledge or information. Basic knowledge is descriptive at a basic level, for example "that zone over there consists of water as a result of peat digging and was for some period part of a national defence line". Applying criteria like "national water defence lines are important" leads to judgements. The judgements lead to the designation of values like "this zone is valuable because it was part of a national defence line". Values can be seen as a combination of qualities, principally those of suitability, need and knowledge (Donaghey 2008, 10). They give some things significance over others, calling these 'heritage' (Clark 2006, 3), and have a selective function. Because values in this sense are a derived form of knowledge, they are essentially different from knowledge (see also Fig. 4):

- values can be derived from basic knowledge, but conversely, deriving basic knowledge from values is not possible;
- in landscape management basic knowledge is descriptive while values are meant to be prescriptive; (basic) knowledge is used upwards between scale levels, while values are used downwards;
- values often lead to making a selection of landscape objects, while for knowledge all the objects may be relevant;
- of course, values can be used as knowledge, but in that case, usually for different purposes, e.g. in value or heritage management.

From an information perspective, landscape characterizations are similar to values because they are the result of applying norms to landscape knowledge (Aldred/Fairclough 2002, 7). The indicators comprised in the judgements may also be values.

Which knowledge, values and characterizations become represented into data or information largely depends on the landscape analysis approach applied. In this sense, an approach may become more or less automatically represented in the information system. This includes differences as in bottom-up or top-down landscape analysis.

One and the same body of knowledge can be the basis for many different values, different over time, at different administrative levels, by different social groups, etc. Therefore, information systems are better (re)usable when they are knowledge-based, with values as a kind of addendum (Visser 2009; see also Bender 2009). It can even lead to separate (sub)systems for basic knowledge and for values, albeit within an overall information architecture.

The same or related knowledge may also be a part of other information systems such as digital heritage (old maps, archives, virtual museums, and archaeology and monuments, but usually not the cultural-historical landscape), digital libraries and historical GIS (HGIS, geography-related historical informa-

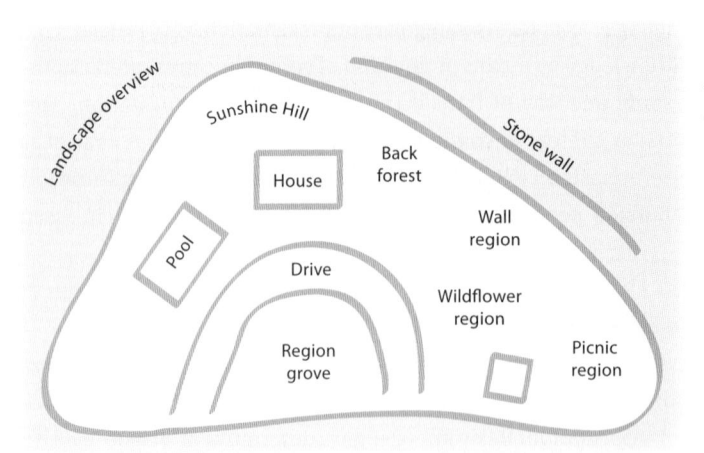

Fig. 2
Example of concepts and categories in a garden's design
(Stefik 1995, 17).

tion). Therefore, meta-knowledge, which describes the knowledge present within a system and where to find it, is an important aspect.

2.3 From knowledge to concepts to content in information systems

Knowledge *in* information systems is always explicit knowledge (that is, not tacit). All knowledge is built from perceived *concepts and associations* (like a mental map), with concepts seen as (natural) *categories* (Schuman 1994). To do so means codifying or describing the reality domain, in this case cultural-historical aspects of landscapes. This codification is usually done by means of classifications, typologies and characterizations.

Classifications, typologies, and characterizations are superimposed categories, purpose-made from specific viewpoints (Stefik 1995, 17). Fig. 2 shows some examples: 'house' is a natural category, 'pool' and 'drive' are application-specific categories for the natural categories 'water' and 'road', 'Sunshine Hill' is a named occurrence of a category and the 'regions' are superimposed characterizations. Apart from linguistics and semantics, there are all kinds of other methods for categorization and classification, as Read (Read 2007) shows with reference to archaeological artefact classification.

In designing a system, a first step is to unravel the relevant information needs and knowledge, pertaining to the relevant reality, domain into the underlying concepts and associations. The next step is the tuning and/or integration of all these components into a conceptual (information) model (see Fig. 3 for the example of the concept of 'building'). All (known) information needs to be taken into account, not just some specific ones. It is therefore essentially different from simple modelling, based on some specific view, output or user interaction (Morville/Rosenfeld 2006, 31). The more different views are present, as is the case with landscapes, the more important this is (e.g. Pedroli/Pinto Correia/Cornish 2004).

This integrative semantic model becomes the heart of the database and the system and forms the basis for the output and information needs. Every form of output reflects a specific view on this content. In communication with the users, both the content and (re)presentations, maps, text, images, lists, etc., are important. GIS is, of course, an essential tool for mapping and analysing, as well as for more advanced forms like landscape virtualizations in 3D and 4D including dynamics in time.

Despite this, integration with other information systems often comes into the picture at some point in time as well. In that case, there usually are technical, geo- or GIS standards to consider. However, the

Fig. 3
Schematized model of integrated views related to the concept 'building' in administrative systems (Laurini 2001, 73).

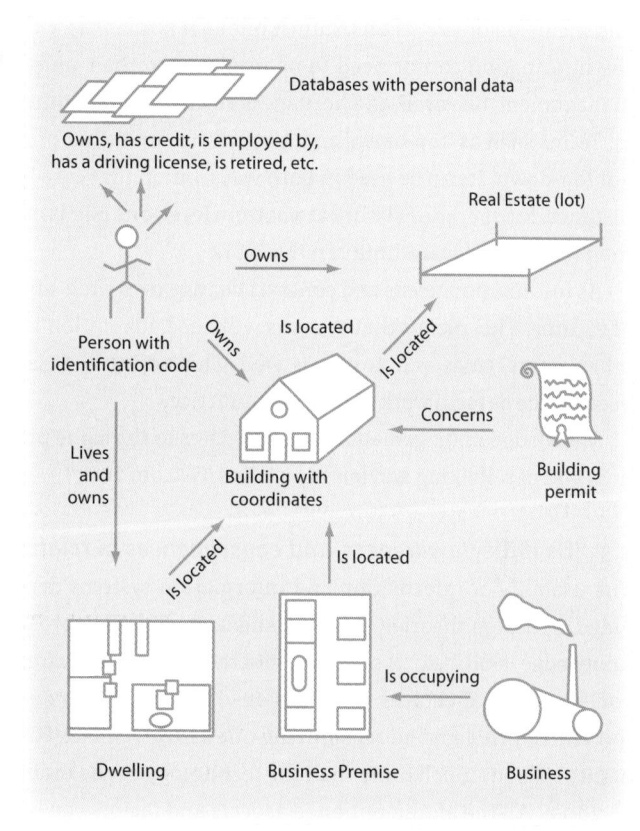

semantic heterogeneity in concepts, categories, language, etc., is usually at least as big a problem, albeit an often underestimated one (Bishr 2006). Solving this is a sensitive and complex process in which all parties are to be considered. As it appears, standardization is often only discussed from a logical or a technical level, not at a conceptual level. The logical level is the intermediate level between the conceptual and technical in which the system is technically designed and programmed. Many terms actually reflect logical or technical thinking, such as metadata, database, interoperability of data, or data quality. Data quality is about qualities like completeness, accuracy, reliability and consistency of data. Qualities can also be related to information (completeness, relevance, effectiveness, etc.; Pijpers 2006, 46) or knowledge, a main purpose in knowledge management.

Other terms seem, and originally were, conceptual, like semantics or ontologies. An ontology is a fundamental philosophical concept for considering 'what something is'. However, with the emergence of semantic information systems it has become a more or less logical technical term, used for categorizations and classifications.

2.4 Knowledge and information management

Information and knowledge management aim at providing the right information in the right amount at the right time in the right place to the right person. It aims, therefore, at giving answers to questions like which information is needed for a specific task (e.g. Chen/Chen 2006; Pijpers 2006). Who decides and can decide on this is a main issue. Therefore, information systems are also about power or dominance and inclusion or exclusion (Amin/Cohendet 2004, 154). Other questions pertain to scale levels at which the information can or need to be used and to their purposes, as in administrative levels. Landscape management, research, and heritage education and in communication between levels and purposes (Fig. 4). Terms such as 'top-down' and 'bottom-up' are rather problematic. Information is created bottom-up, not top-down. It can be used in both ways, but in that case it usually concerns different information. For instance, for operational work at a bottom level, one needs much more detailed and complete information than for higher-level administrative work.

As information needs and contexts change over time, an information system is more or less a product of its time. This means that systems will need adaptation to these new circumstances, that may include other actors, rules and norms as well. This adjustment is pivotal because information systems often become the *de facto* work standard in practice.

Knowledge management basically relates to the same principles but includes a higher level of awareness and of reflecting and learning (Hess/Ostrom 2007).

2.5 Usability, awareness, and consequences in relation to information systems

The usability of information and information systems depends on what is needed versus what is provided. In design theories, usability and user centred approaches are seen as crucial issues. Expertise like knowledge, skills, etc. is of course essential, but so is awareness of relevant aspects and factors. And the consequences of choices and decisions have to be considered as well. Awareness means recognizing a (potential) problem and recognizing one's involvement (Förster/Thierstein 2008, 25). It follows that usability is about much more than the technology or the evaluation of a user interface (as in Wachowicz *et al.* 2005). All the aforementioned aspects and factors can be at stake. The key word in this may be information system success, because "if users cannot use the system effectively and efficiently, it cannot be

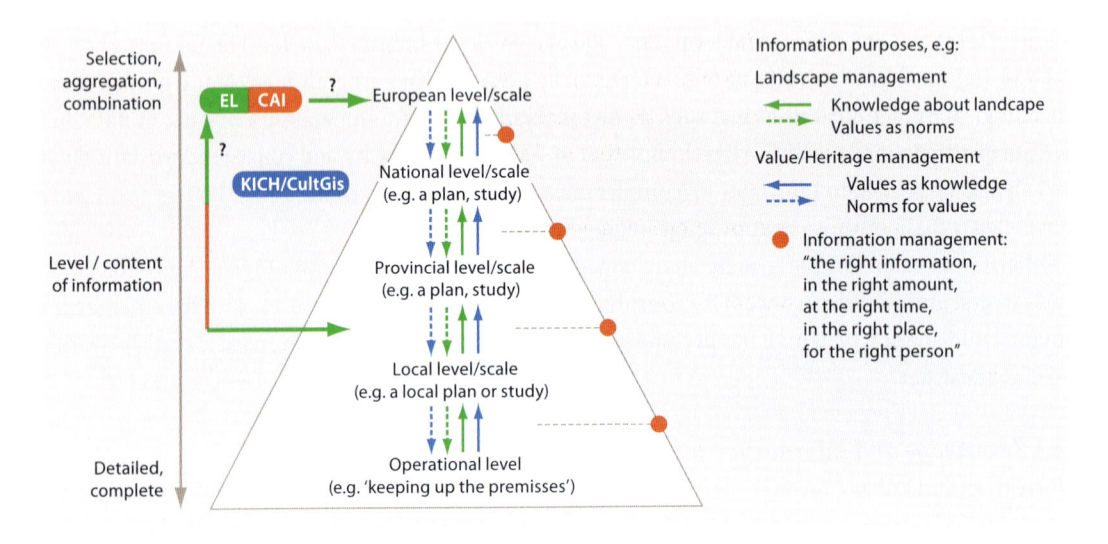

Fig. 4
Knowledge, values and information related to scale levels and purposes.

Fig. 5
Variables for information system usability from a stakeholder perspective *(after Elpez/Fink 2006)*.

User expectations of a task
• Task-technology fit
• Understanding the user's perspective (including cognitive style and mental model)
• Meeting user expectations or perceptions of the system

System usability
• Quality and effectiveness of the interface design
• Quality and effectiveness of user documentation and information
• Ease of use

User acceptance and ownership of a system
• Level of user involvement
• Participation in the development leading to greater commitment
• Extent of user involvement and participation
• Quality of user-developer communication
• Quality of the system and system reliability

deemed a success" (Elpez/Fink 2006, 221). From a stakeholders' perspective this translates into variables (Fig. 5).

Verification, as from 'in the box' thinking, is usually the main purpose of a usability evaluation. But falsification from 'out of the box' thinking should also be considered because often some user groups, purposes and uses are left out, deliberately or not. In that case people may come to ignore a system, work around the system or making one's own system. The last two will get reflected in the bigger information picture.

Therefore, both information systems, their documentation and the broader scenario can reveal much about the practices in which they came into existence and about information management issues.

3. A REFERENCE FRAMEWORK FOR POSITIONING AND DISCUSSION

A number of the above discussed aspects have been used as a kind of reference framework. This has been applied to discuss information systems as well as the bigger information situation in some European countries. The emphasis is on the content of the systems. What is not in the system cannot come out or, as the information systems discipline puts it, 'garbage in, is garbage out'. Content, therefore, is a main factor in the usability of a system. In this context, awareness about what the content really is and represents is crucial. One aspect that stands out is thinking and acting at a conceptual and semantic level (instead of at a logical or technical level). Another main aspect is selectivity and specificity in the content related to questions such as:

- does the information consist of knowledge, values, characterizations? If several, which one is/was leading?
- From which landscape analysis approach is the information the result? Was it a landscape inventory, a landscape characterization, a cultural landscape biography, etc.?
- Which (standards for) typologies, classifications, etc. are used and how selective are they?
- Is it basic or higher level information? Is it made in a top-down or bottom-up process? How is it made? For which uses is the information meant?

All these aspects will become represented in some way within an information system. For instance, people may feel the need to make their own system because of the selectivity and specificity in existing systems. The selectivity and specificity can be the result of a number of causes. The bigger picture, therefore, may serve as an indication for underlying problems in information (management) issues.

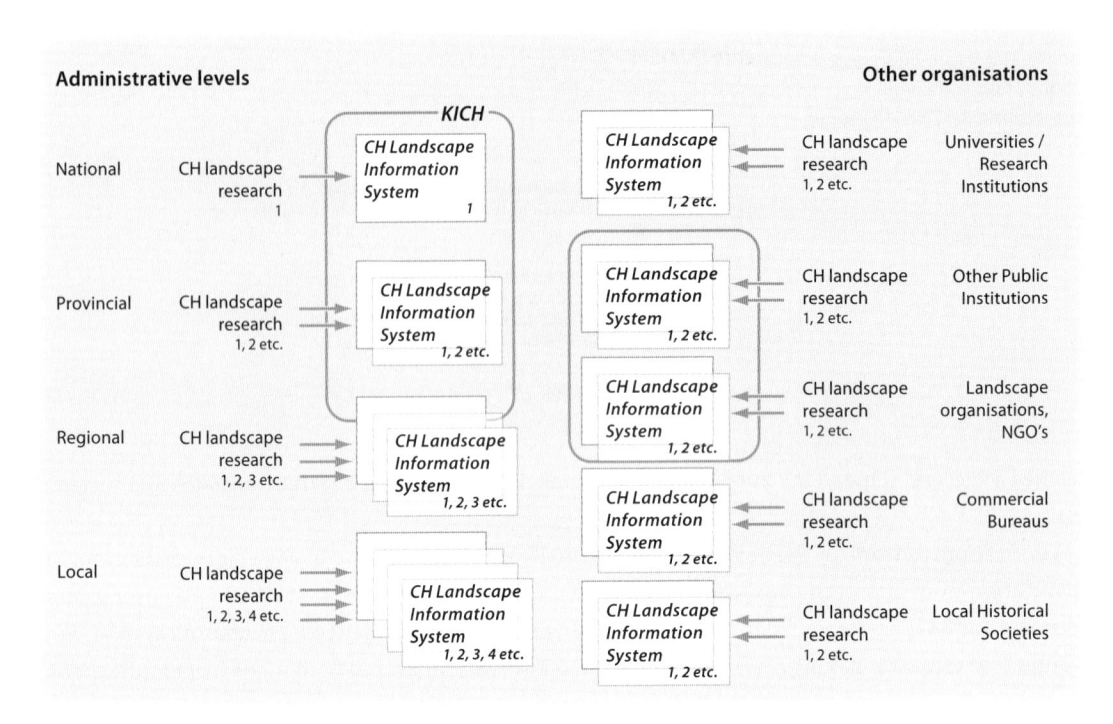

Fig. 6a
An information situation with many separate information systems and some infrastructures (CH=Cultural Historical).

The time dimension is important because all these aspects and factors may, and often will, change over time. To change systems accordingly, awareness is needed in the first place, next to the expertise to handle it properly. Of course, both awareness and expertise may change over time.

For the sake of the discussion, some specific systems are chosen from the selected countries. They were partly chosen because information was available. Therefore, they may or may not be typical. However, this discussion mainly is about the way some principles are worked out and the consequences of doing so. A comparison of the systems and their contexts is omitted, although some comparative remarks are made.

The broader context of information is primarily discussed from the perspective of information or knowledge management. This mainly pertains to the degree of coherence and interconnectedness of the involved information systems. What is done or not done for coherence between information systems can considerably weaken or strengthen a situation. As an example, two extremes are presented in Fig. 6. Both relate to the same situation comprising a multitude of contexts, organizations and systems. Fig. 6a shows the information situation as one with low degrees of coherence and interconnectedness. In such a case, the coherence is generally only at a logical or technical level. Fig. 6b shows the same situation as a coherent (example of an) information architecture, based on conceptual relations as well.

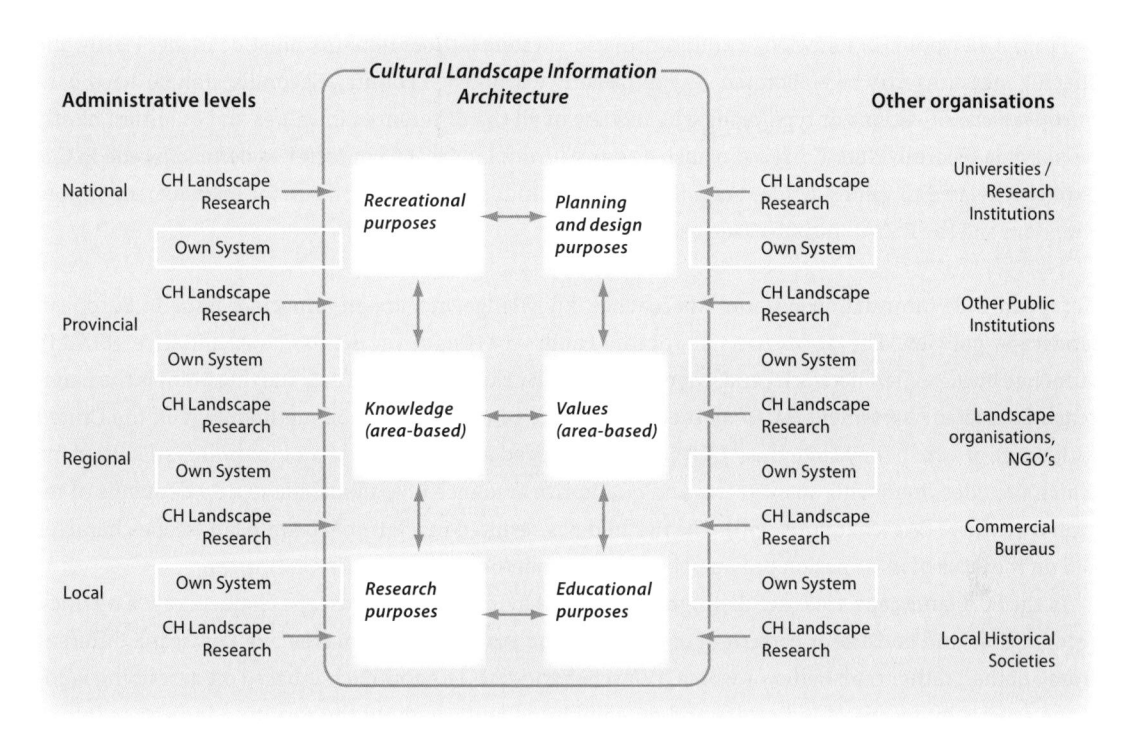

Fig. 6b
An example of an information situation as in an information architecture (CH=Cultural Historical).

4. THE SITUATION IN EUROPE AND IN THE UNITED KINGDOM, THE NETHERLANDS AND GERMANY

4.1 The European level

Since the 1990s, a number of initiatives concerning culture and landscapes has been implemented at the European level. The best known of these may be the European Landscape Convention (ELC; Florence 2000), which dates to 2000 and came into force in 2004. By mid-2009, most countries had signed and ratified the Convention, including the Netherlands (2005) and the United Kingdom (2006), although Germany has yet to sign.

In the ELC, landscape means "an area, as perceived by people, whose character is the result of the action and interaction of natural and/or human factors". Character is mainly a concept from the perspective of landscape protection, defined as "significant or characteristic features of a landscape, justified by its heritage value from its natural condition and/or human activities" (Florence 2000). Landscapes are seen as "an expression of the diversity of shared cultural and natural heritage, and a foundation of their identity", for which, next to involvement of regional and local authorities, etc., participation of the general public is essential. "Identification and assessment" is one of the specific measures to be taken by each Party, meaning that each Party has to identify its own landscapes, for which in the Explanatory Report GIS is mentioned, analyse the "characteristics" as well as "forces and pressures", and assess their quality. In order to guide these activities, "landscape quality objectives" are to be defined. Furthermore, Statement no. 22 in the Explanatory Report says "Official landscape activities can no longer be allowed to be an exclusive field of study or action monopolized by specialist scientific and technical bodies".

From a viewpoint of knowledge and information systems, three remarks must be made. Firstly, the specific measures may be elaborated very differently within each country. Secondly, standardized pan-European classifications or typologies will, in view of all the differences in values and qualities, hardly be possible (Pedroli/Pinto Correia/Cornish 2004). Thirdly, landscape character as defined by the ELC is explicitly related to values, while this aspect is mostly hidden in definitions in, for instance, the United Kingdom and the ELCAI initiative (see below).

European-wide information systems, approaches, knowledge, etc. are an important issue in European landscape policies. The 2000-2004 European Landscape Character Assessment Initiative (ELCAI), launched by the expert network Landscape Europe, is an example of this. Their starting point is the Landscape Character Assessment (LCA) methodology (since 1990 *the* landscape methodology in the United Kingdom), of which they state that "LCA [...] is recognized as an important tool for policy stakeholders, which provides them with quantitative and qualitative evidence [...], adjustable to new demands of regional identity" (Wascher 2005, viii). The method has resulted in a European-wide landscape character GIS on the basis of information provided by experts from the 14 participating countries.

In the LCA landscape areas are distinguished, each having its own landscape character as "a distinct, recognizable and consistent pattern of elements in the landscape that makes one landscape different from another, rather than better or worse" (Wascher 2005, 1). The approach is based on describing landscape aspects by means of indicators and on combining and weighing the resulting indicators into 'a character'. Existing landscape indicators and classifications, like the spatial framework of the European Landscape Classification (Landmap2), were taken as starting points, as was the Landmap2 mapping tool (see Wascher 2005, ix). ELCAI made use of over twenty landscape indicators, with geomorphology and land use as the most important ones. History/time depth and architecture/heritage were the only historical indicators. Questions concerning top-down or bottom-up aspects were avoided in the report because these terms have several usages in relation to LCA (Wascher 2005, 39).

As it emerges from the report, ELCAI is mainly meant to promote LCA and strengthen its position from and within an overall European viewpoint. The content, though, is at the much more detailed regional level. This raises the question at which level the system as such is aimed at and for which purpose (see Fig. 4). The result, though, is selective in some essential ways. One aspect is the underlying approach of viewing landscapes as a combined and possibly weighted ensemble of zones, one per indicator. For that, information needs to be more or less generalized as in e.g. land use. As may be clear, this approach may not provide the right information in contexts where all details count.

Another aspect is the use of this kind of indicators. Is it possible to handle all kinds of cultural and other non-natural aspects well enough through these? Much more is possible, as the United Kingdom shows in its complementing Historic Landscape Character (HLC) (see below). ELCAI aims at doing so as well, but they appear to see this quite unproblematically. Their statement is that, like the biophysical dimension, the socio-economic-technical, the human-aesthetic and the policy dimensions can be analysed in terms of a simple set of categories.

A related question is why just two historical indicators are taken into consideration. This may have a number of causes, e.g. cultural aspects not seen as particularly relevant by the information providing organizations or because of a lack of usable metrics information. In the last case it can be a matter of lagging behind the natural landscape information or as a consequence of problems in handling cultural landscapes in this way.

A similar culture-deprived approach in Norway leads to the remark that "[cultural aspects] are not a main factor in defining the regions, and the boundaries [...] do not reflect cultural-historical structures [...]. Consequently, the regions are rather useless for any landscape management or research that is focused on cultural historical aspects" (Jerpåsen/Ornland/Lindblom 2008, 210-212). It also leads to questions about the interpretation of a landscape's character in relation to its purpose, scale level, etc. It may be a main reason for 'diversity', rather than 'regional identity', as the central theme in ELCAI.

ELCAI, therefore, is selective in several respects. This means that if ELCAI were to be considered as a standard just because it exists, people involved in cultural landscapes would need to be aware of its selectivity. The development of further cultural indicators within ELCAI are another point of attention.

There are or have been other interesting initiatives. In the same period as ELCAI, the Pathways to Cultural Landscapes initiative (PCL; www.pcl-eu.de) was also ongoing, a result of the EU Culture 2000 programme. Examples include the Lancewad project, a co-operation between Germany, Denmark and the Netherlands, and the Spessart project in Germany. HLC was the common approach, resulting in the United Kingdom in more or less different results and GIS systems.

More recent projects, generally by experts, are the COST A27 project LANDMARKS and the Eucaland project. In the LANDMARKS report (Fairclough/Grau Møller 2008), information systems were only the main focus in the contributions from Germany and Austria (Bender/Schumacher 2008). In this project, this subject was an issue but mainly in the separate and rather technically oriented working group on virtual landscapes (Bender et al. 2009). The EucaLand project primarily aims at summarizing the state of knowledge about agricultural landscapes as a basis for further research and does not consider information systems so far (www.eucalandproject.eu).

Generally speaking, concluding from (the lack of) conferences, websites and other information sources, information systems on cultural landscapes are (much) less a subject in Europe than systems on archaeology or the built heritage. In so far as they are a subject, the emphasis is mostly logically or technically oriented, for instance on spatial data infrastructures. Conceptual relations with other systems are hardly considered.

4.2 United Kingdom

In the United Kingdom, since the early 1990s, one specific approach clearly took the lead in analysing cultural landscapes and developing information systems about them. This approach is the combined approach of LCA and HLC (Historic Landscape Characterisation), originating from co-operation between The Countryside Agency and English Heritage (see www.landscapecharacter.org.uk). The Scottish approach is similar (see Ch. III.5) but in Wales it is somewhat different.

LCA is more or less similar to ELCAI. HLC was, like LCA, originally developed for the county level but is also applicable at other levels. According to their website and documents, HLC concentrates on the present day landscape, on history not geography, and on areas not point data, and is mainly based on (landscape) archaeology. It involves first and foremost desktop research, although there is consultation with other, mostly official, stakeholders. In HLC all areas are seen as valuable, meaning that the whole administrative area is covered and split into characteristic areas according to specific criteria. The historic land-use types are important building blocks, each described by attributes such as form, function and period of origin. An area can, as a reflection of diachronic processes, have more than one type. Each county decides on its own landscape characters, types and criteria and creates its own GIS databases which are more or less similar in structure and content. Since the start at the county level, many have also been made at a local level. Therefore, nowadays these GISses start from the smallest areas, which are defined as polygons (GIS term for surface areas) with a number of attributes, including heritage data like archaeological sites, monuments, parks and gardens, etc. (e.g. Clark/Darlington/Fairclough 2004). As Fairclough (Fairclough 2007, 62) describes, HLC is an evolving approach, rather than a method, and is "being in the present, being outward- and forward looking (i.e. inclusive, democratic, purposive, interdisciplinary), being area-based and generalizing including turning away from 'sites', being more concerned with ideas (character, i.e. perception) than with stuff (fabric)."

Although HLC is seen as broadly usable, like ELCAI it can be problematic in activities where objects, point data and sites matter. One other remark pertains to the limitations of an HLC because of contemporary administrative units. This can mean a split in a real historic landscape, with two (somewhat) different characterizations on either side of the border. In order to solve this, Scotland has derived generalized higher level types and England is trying to come to some degree of standardization.

These questions, of course, are related to questions of top-down and bottom-up information analysis. LCA/HLC makes use of lower level data so the informational method is clearly bottom-up. The use of the characters, though, is for landscape planning and management issues, which is top-down. An interesting question is whether the basic information is kept or not, as this information also has other uses.

Apart from the landscape character information, there are information systems about heritage and the historic environment. At present, (almost) all are interconnected or brought together into web portals, for which a number of standards are developed. Providing overviews and meta-information about where to find which information are a strong point in the United Kingdom. Examples of information architectures and portals are MIDAS Heritage, MAGIC, HEIRnet, Historic Environment Records (HERs) and the Heritage gateway. They all have more or less their own purposes and user groups with a number of overlaps. The relations between the systems are mostly seen from a logical level and may be stronger when the conceptual/semantic relations are also taken into account.

However, these are not the only developments going on in the UK. New approaches are developing in, for instance, the Landscape & Environment Programme from the Arts & Humanities Research Council, oriented to themes like 'images, values and knowledge' and 'time, space and narrative', and in academic circles (www.landscape.ac.uk; www.landscaperesearch.org). Another recent development is the inclusion of local actors and public values in heritage policies (Clark 2006). Another main topic in the United Kingdom is Historical GISs (e.g. Gregory/Ell 2008). Although historical-geographers are involved in this programme, their relationship with the 'historic' in HLC is not very clear. Maybe this is a more structural issue, judging from the remark by Hooke (Hooke 2008), who stated that historical geographers should be concerned about their knowledge as archaeologists and historians seem to be winning in prominence.

An interesting question concerns the consequences of these developments for HLC and present practices in cultural heritage and related information systems. At present, evaluations are taking place (e.g.

Aldred/Fairclough 2002; Clark/Darlington/Fairclough 2004) within the HLC frame of reference. Furthermore, the official HLC institutions, especially English Heritage, are very dominant as can be concluded from numerous available information sources. Some critical remarks are heard, though, as in the Theoretical Archaeology Group (TAG) conferences in 2006 and 2007 (e.g. TAG07, http://sites.google.com/site/tag07york/home) and in Rippon's comparison of HLC and the wider concept of historic landscape analysis (Rippon 2007). Although information systems by local or regional history clubs seem absent, it is not clear whether this is a good or a bad sign.

All in all, the awareness of information management issues appears to be rather high and encompasses both the awareness of differences in local needs and situations and of integrative issues, although rather logically oriented. The awareness has been continuously developing as well (e.g. El Hassan/Elkadi 2002; Aldred/Fairclough 2002; Atkins Group 2006). However, it remains to be seen how the dominant HLC constructions can and will handle the new developments.

4.3 The Netherlands

The information situation in the historical-geographical field

In the Netherlands the present cultural landscape information situation in the historical-geographical field originated in 1990. Before 1990, nationwide inventories of historic landscape elements and structures on regional and local levels were planned and, at least partly, executed. Landscape elements were considered important for several reasons, one of these being the large-scale landscape restructuring processes of land reallocation and land-use development since the 1950s, in which elements were often the main historic 'leftovers'. The inventories were complemented by typologies, classifications and map legends resulting in some degree of standardization (e.g. Schuyf 1986; De Bont/Renes 1988). One of these was a national landscape typology which in reality was a generalized landscape characterization based on the physical landscape and on landscape structure and its genesis (Barends *et al.* 2000). As may be clear, the method was more or less bottom-up.

At the end of the 1980s, all of this was ready to be implemented into a GIS system. By then, the broader context was dramatically changing, as cultural landscapes and their values had become a main issue in national policy. The result was a switch to a top-down approach in which detailed inventories were seen as too time consuming.

The GIS system CultGis, developed in the 1990s, is a reflection of this development (Fig. 4). Cultgis was based on (inter)national values and was therefore very selective both in landscape areas and in landscape elements. Only the most 'typical' and 'authentic' elements, structures and regions were taken up. There was a selectivity in historical information as well, as for each object only one function from one period was taken into account (Visser 2007). This selectivity was translated in an information model, although the makers themselves wanted to include more. The decision-makers, however, decided otherwise.

In the implementation of the Belvedere Memorandum (Belvedere 1999), CultGis became the cultural-historical landscape system within the web-portal KICH just because it existed (Knowledge Infrastructure Cultural Heritage; Fig. 7; www.kich.nl; Visser 2007). KICH aimed at integrating knowledge on archaeological, architectural and landscape heritage at different administrative levels and for everyone involved. For this integration, the information model IMKICH was developed, the present version being IMKICH2008 (Wessels *et al.* 2008). IMKICH is foremost a model at a logical and technical level meant for information exchange. However, it also acted as a selective filter in the exchanged information content,

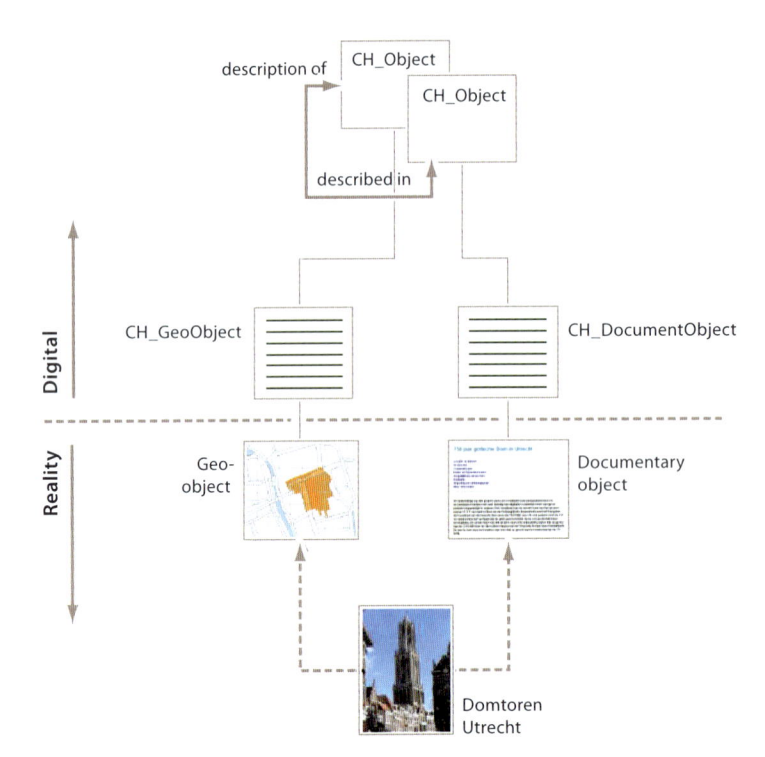

Fig. 7
Example of the association between a Geo-object and a Documentary object (below, as primary informational objects about a real object), in KICH ('digital') related through secondary KICH-information objects (*Wessels et al*. 2008, 15).
(CH=Cultural Historical)

although it has become more flexible in this regard over the years. KICH as such is still selective in some essential ways, though values are still the starting point and the users are mainly professionals (e.g. Wachowicz *et al*. 2005).

IMKICH is evolving but this is more in terms of catching-up rather than adaptation to changing contexts. An evaluation of KICH in 2007 stated that "the performance of KICH towards users urgently needs improvement" (Ministries of LNV etc. 2008, 108). Many informal accounts were/are not that positive. Very recently, the first steps have been taken to come to a thoroughly revised KICH by 2012, starting with a revised system for the built heritage (the KIMOMO project; Wiemer/Van Cappelleveen 2009). A semantic approach in the information modelling and taking all possible user needs into account are both main aspects in this project. As it may be clear, involvement of all kinds of actors ('users') will be pivotal in this.

CultGis is only one of many systems. Many other organizations and projects have created their own information systems. Wageningen University, for instance, did not agree with the top-down approach, at least not in relation to information systems, and instead developed its own system, Histland. All Dutch provinces have also created their own systems. Most of these started from what is seen as valuable landscape objects and structures, while showing much variation in their knowledge content. More recently, an increasing number of municipalities are developing their own systems and maps.

Apart from these official systems, a wide variety of institutions, planning and design bureaus, local history clubs and projects have developed their own cultural landscape systems. Some of these systems were created because of a lack of suitable official systems. The over 300 Belvedere projects on landscape research or planning and design may actually have contributed considerably to this situation since many created their own systems. Many systems contain information from approaches similar to the theory and praxis of the 1980s. A few other (and more recent) ones are the result of new approaches, like the cultural landscape biography (e.g. Fieldnames Atlas Drentsche Aa; Elerie/Spek 2000; www.veldnamendrentscheaa.nl; Zandstad (www.zandstad.nl).

The resulting information picture is one of both fragmentation and selectivity, with many gaps and overlaps and a more or less questionable usability beyond the mostly rather specific purpose they were made for (Visser 2007). New systems are constantly added, while the adaptation of existing systems to changing contexts does not seem to be very common. The many different categorizations and classifications are a major problem. It is mainly 'at the bottom' that these subjects get some public attention, as can be concluded for instance from the symposium on cultural landscape systems in 2008 by a local history and heritage platform (Landschap Erfgoed Utrecht 2008) and from the co-operation by land-owning NGOs concerning information systems (e.g. the 'Provincial Landscape' organizations).

The overall impression based on the previous period, therefore, is a general lack of both awareness and expertise in relation to conceptual aspects in information and communication issues. The future looks a bit more promising, though, if the KIMOMO project can realize its aims. The same may go for a knowledge infrastructure as meant by the 'Landscape 2.0' proposal by Van der Zande (Van der Zande 2009), although this will ask for careful consideration of its aims and realization.

The information situation in the archaeological field

In Dutch archaeology the situation is in many ways quite different from the one in the historical-geographical field. There is one central system, Archis, in which archaeological sites, finds and monuments are recorded. Archis dates from the period 1989-1992 and was the result of a co-operative development of the ROB (then the State Service for Archaeological Heritage) and three universities. Archis was meant for both scientific and heritage management purposes by professionals working at local, provincial or national levels (Zoetbrood et al. 1997). The main content comes from organizations which conduct archaeological investigations and are obliged to provide Archis with data (http://www.cultureelerfgoed.nl/werken/archis).

Archis was a new version of a partly computerized paper system dating from 1974, while registration as such had already started in the early 1800s (Zoetbrood et al. 1997). Archis primarily contains data about sites (locations), investigations (areas), observations, finds and complexes, as well as the main archaeological processes involved (excavation, depositing, etc.) and the geological and pedological contexts (Zoetbrood et al. 1997, 336). Over the years, the information-handling functions were expanded, resulting in the present web system Archis2 coupled with a Document Information System.

Archis can be seen as a system 'at the bottom' because it aims at completeness in sites, finds, etc., although it only contains a selection of the data known about these. Conceptual thinking has not been much of an issue in Archis. Discussions were very much restricted to the logical level, as may be concluded from terms like 'a normalized database' and 'data quality' aspects (Wiemer 2002). An evaluation in 2005 was mainly about the user interface (De Graaf/Klooster/Witjes 2005). The above-mentioned KIMOMO project will also relate to Archis, meaning that its conceptual aspects will get more attention.

Some specific expansions were related to archaeological monuments and to predictive modelling. Archaeological monuments have been part of Archis since 1994 and are a kind of shared heritage on both the national and provincial levels. An archaeological monument in Archis is a 'zone', which in itself consists of some added data about value, status, etc. The values are represented on the (standardized) Archeologische Monumentenkaart (AMK).

From 1997 on, Archis also served as the basis for nationwide predictive modelling as in the Indicatieve Kaart Archeologische Waarden (IKAW). Predictive modelling is about sites not yet discovered, which almost by definition are problematic to model, and makes using the proper archaeological knowledge in a proper way rather crucial (Lock/Harris 2006; Deeben 2008, 7). Apart from archaeological knowledge itself, this knowledge traditionally consists foremost of geological and other physical landscape knowledge and of (old) maps. Much of this knowledge is known to have biases and problems, although a number of these have been solved since the first generation IKAW in 1997, resulting in the second generation in 2001 and the third generation IKAW in 2006 (Deeben 2008, 7).

However, this traditional predictive modelling has always had its critics (e.g. Kvamme 2006), as noted in the 2002 PDL/BBO project "Strategic research into, and development of best practice for, predictive modelling on behalf of the Dutch Cultural Resource management" (Ch. V.5). In this project, the involved scientists criticized the common practice on issues like statistics, theory and data (Kamermans/Van Leusen/Verhagen 2009). One of the problems was the applied, primarily environmentally deterministic model and the need to expand this with human and cultural aspects, because people in the past may have chosen their locations for more reasons than just the physical landscape (Lock/Harris 2006, 44; Verhagen 2007, 20). So far, this has not been done (e.g. Kamermans/Van Leusen/Verhagen 2009, 11). The inherent conceptual modelling may also be interesting for modelling the reality domain of the cultural landscape in view of information systems in a broader sense.

In recent years, though, there have been some main developments outside Archis, resulting from the implementation of the Valletta Convention (Valletta 1992) and the revision of the Monuments Act of 1988. One consequence was the emergence of commercial archaeological companies and information systems developed by them in order to document their own excavations and results. Another consequence comprises the much bigger responsibilities of municipalities in archaeological heritage management (AHM). The resulting situation also led to the emergence of the quality issue, resulting in the Dutch Archaeological Quality Standard (KNA) (Willems/Brandt 2004). One result from this was a flexible structure for the documentation of excavations developed by archaeologists themselves (Sueur/Beestman/Wansleeben 2005). A more or less related development, the eDNA or Edna project, was the digital depositing of both documentary information and datasets at a central place in the DANS infrastructure (http://www.dans.knaw.nl/en/data/info_edna/; Van Oorsouw/Wansleeben 2005). Their ultimate aim is "one integrated digital research infrastructure for Dutch archaeology" based on unity in finds and documentation" (Wansleeben/Van den Dries 2008, 6). Although this remains a good example, there are some missing essential conceptual elements, such as the lack of discussion on links between the archaeological objects in both types of registration systems. Instead, in these studies the focus is information flows. It emerges as well in their view of Archis as 'less detailed', although supposedly the lack of completeness in data is meant.

As may be concluded, in the last decades in the Netherlands the information situations from historical-geography and archaeology have distinctly grown apart. One reason is the originally big difference in the legal position between historical geography and archaeology. Another appears to be the equally big difference in the decisions made in 1990 about information management in both fields, the continued bottom-up approach in archaeology and the switch to a top-down approach in historical geography, including a switch to cultural landscape thinking. More recently, though, the situation around Archis has become less clear. From this point of view, both fields may have some knowledge and information management weaknesses in common.

Unfortunately, the Belvedere and PDL/BBO programmes do not appear to have been very helpful in these matters. Knowledge, information, etc. have mainly been discussed in rather general and discursive ways, while leaving the acquisition of practical insights to (a few) specific projects. Apart from the conceptual and integrative issues, there are other unresolved issues in knowledge and information management such as:
- local (amateur) knowledge and users (e.g. Tress/Tress/Bloemmen 2003; Duineveld/Van Assche 2006; Van der Zande 2008);
- access to the necessary information for anybody involved; this pertains especially to archaeology where usually only archaeologists are mentioned as users and many restrictions apply to outsiders;
- information systems suitable for use in historical geography research because almost all their systems are meant for use by others for purposes like landscape design projects and spatial policy, rather than themselves.

Although not discussed here, integrative issues also affect the relationship of cultural landscape systems to landscape related systems used in landscape planning and design and in administrations like municipalities.

All in all, it is not that surprising that the recent PDL/BBO conference has acknowledged a serious knowledge and communication problem (see also Bosma 2008).

4.4 Germany

For decades, historical-geographical approaches and mapping were rather similar in Germany and in the Netherlands. First the Dutch adopted the German principles in landscape studies, while in the 1980s the Germans adopted the Dutch approach in identifying and mapping landscapes (e.g. Burggraaff 2007). Germany was also influenced by Austrian and Swiss methods like the Austrian landscape characterization based on dominant land use, natural factors, vegetation structures, etc.

This situation is reflected in the kinds of systems that are nowadays present in Germany. As may be seen in Fig. 8, showing some systems in German-speaking territories, they contain primarily discrete landscape elements, as in the Netherlands, (Bender/Schumacher 2008, 89). However, there are also systems based on historic landscape characterization, resulting from the Spessart (www.spessartprojekt.de) and Lancewad projects (www.lancewadplan.org/).

Most German systems are foremost inventories of landscape elements which may include landscape structures and heritage values. These can be combined with information on archaeology, the built heritage and the physical landscape, or contain meta-information about these (e.g. the aforementioned Spessart project). The KuLaDig and KLEKS systems are relatively important because both are used in more than one German state and regional projects. Inventories or cadastres like these can become rather complete and some may become complete enough to be used in 3D or 4D landscape virtualizations (e.g. Bender 2009). The information is mainly meant and used bottom-up in Germany, (much) more than in

Country/region	Cultural landscape history	Contents	Web address
Switzerland	IVS - Inventory of historical traffic routes in Switzerland	Discrete landscape elements of certain type: traffic routes	www.viastoria.ch
Rheinland, Germany	KuLaDig – digital cultural cadastre	Area-wide representation intended (several time slices) + discrete landscape elements	www.kuladignw.de
Neubrandenburg, Germany	KLEKS – cultural landscape elements cadastre	Discrete landscape elements	www.kleks-online.de
Tyrol, Austria	TIRIS - cultural landscape inventory Tyrol	Discrete landscape elements (of certain type: agricultural area) + analyses	tiris.tirol.gv.at

Fig. 8
Examples of cultural landscape inventories in German speaking regions *(after Bender/Schumacher 2008, 89)*.

the Netherlands. Many systems are developed by academics in co-operation with government bodies. There are a number of systems by other parties as well, like Thuringia (about fieldnames and their history, dating from 1999; see Rheinland/ARKUM 2005) and in the West-Bodensee area. This last project was initiated because they wanted information at a more detailed level than the official systems could provide (Rodat 2009).

In Germany, some information systems are connected to each other or brought together into portals, but concluding from conference proceedings, these are not common issues (see below).

All in all, as in the Netherlands, the resulting situation is rather fragmented and diversified but there are differences as well. Adapting information systems to changing needs seems more common than in the Netherlands. Furthermore, many German systems are generally less selective in landscape objects, as they often started from providing knowledge on the cultural historical landscape, not from providing values (e.g. Bender 2009, 137). The contexts in which systems get developed may also differ. In recent years in the Netherlands much cultural landscape analysis has been done as part of landscape planning projects in which selectivity and specificity are sometimes incorporated into the resulting system. In Germany, systems like KulaDig and KLEKS are the result of dedicated and research-based projects aimed at more generally applicable basic systems.

A complicating factor in Germany is the federal structure. Because each of the *Länder* is responsible for, amongst others, its own spatial policy as well as most of science, cultural landscape analysis and information systems may vary accordingly. Nation-wide standardization in these are therefore more difficult to obtain. This may be one, or maybe a main, reason why attempts at standardization, like that by Plöger (Plöger 2003), do not seem to have had much of an impact. However, in this case, there may be other important factors. Plöger thoroughly considered the GIS related aspects, his main topic, as well as solutions for dealing with categories for landscape elements. But he may have underestimated the standardization process, which usually involves much more than simple implementation. Furthermore, from a conceptual viewpoint, his proposed categorization is problematic. He designed one all-encompassing categorization, meaning that one view on the landscape gets priority over others, while his primary distinction was based on points, lines and polygons in GIS technology. This last distinction, though, is foremost related to information representation issues, meaning 'output' as on maps, not to modelling the reality domain of the cultural-historical landscape as such. Apart from this, it is also sensitive to changes in GIS technology.

Unlike the Netherlands, Germany holds regular conferences on cultural landscape systems (Matthiesen *et al.* 2006; BHU 2008; BHU/ARKUM 2009). Most conferences include contributions from the Netherlands. These conferences deal with systems and also engage in reflective and theoretical discussions.

As in the Netherlands, the amateur organizations have taken up an active role in coming to better information systems at a detailed level. Furthermore, the BHU (Bund Heimat und Umwelt in Deutschland), the overarching organization for local history and landscape organizations, is aiming at more connectedness as well. Their 2007 conference was meant as an initiative towards bringing together and standardizing insights as laid down in information systems (www.bhu.de, search on Tagung, Juni 2007). The bringing together worked out fine; however, the standardization issue remains unresolved.

All in all, there are a number of good and basic systems present in Germany. Furthermore, there is some awareness of their overall situation and the multitude of information systems, as well as willingness to discuss the situation. The administrative *Länder* situation, however, will not make conceptual issues and standardization any easier.

5. CONCLUSIONS

Concluding from the discussions of the situations in each country, conceptual thinking generally seems a more or less weak point. Especially questions of what, how and why to model a cultural historical landscape for representation into an information system are hardly considered. The same goes for the relation between this modelling and the used or to-be-used cultural landscape research method or approach. The United Kingdom, and other landscape character-based systems, as well as Dutch landscape biography systems presumably are most aware of what they are doing. In Dutch archaeology the landscape approach does not seem to be an issue, except in predictive modelling. In the other cases, what is done or not in relation to a system often seems a kind of common practice that is hardly reflected upon. However, recently conceptual thinking seems to be getting something of a (new) start because of the emergence of semantic systems, as in the Dutch KIMOMO project. As standardized yet flexible categories and classifications are put central, it will ask for a thorough conceptual analysis to come to broadly usable ontologies.

A second aspect is the adaptation of existing information systems to changing needs and situations. In the United Kingdom this appears to be a rather common practice. Despite this, in present systems the LCA approach is so dominant, that it remains to be seen how new developments may and can be handled in this sense. In Dutch historical-geographical information systems, new needs again and again lead to the creation of new systems (some exceptions include systems used in operational landscape management). In Dutch archaeology, archaeologists themselves have partly taken a lead in the development and adaptation of systems. The German situation comprises the adaptation of some main systems and the addition of new ones. Therefore, Germany seems to be in an intermediate position between the United Kingdom and the Netherlands.

Closely connected to this is awareness of what an information system can and cannot do, in view of purposes, activities, users and scale level(s). Systems, of course, are usually more or less selective in that sense and reflect what makers and decision-makers thought (un)necessary. These more or less individual decisions are reflected in the degree of fragmentation in the bigger information situation. This situation is more or less an issue in the United Kingdom, Germany and in Dutch archaeology, but much less so in the historical-geographical field in the Netherlands. A main factor in this is supposedly the combined choice of top-down thinking and the taking of values as the starting point in many, at least official, information systems. This almost by definition leads to unsuitable information for landscape activities at lower scale levels and other purposes than the systems aim at. It also may create the urge to create one's own system, thereby complicating the bigger information picture.

In all countries, the connections between systems are more or less an issue, but mostly at the logical or technical level. And it may be more from a viewpoint of information exchange than from conceptual coherence.

As all these (and more) countries are represented in working groups at the European level, the result at this higher level shows a mix of all these situations. The representatives in those working group and their views and approaches may be rather decisive in the specific situations in which methods, systems, and standards are developed.

As may be clear, both awareness and expertise are important. Decisions in the early 1990s were probably pivotal, as may be concluded from the information situation in Dutch historical geography when compared with other countries.

What is missing, therefore, is a serious and overarching discussion of what is done and what needs to be done. Both the Belvedere and PDL/BBO programmes have acknowledged some issues and aspects in communication, knowledge and information. However, statements were generally rather discursive, while practical insights were left to projects and information management issues and conceptual thinking were mainly missing. Thus, awareness of the actual situation and developments is needed, combined with the willingness to do something about it. Supporting and strengthening positive developments outside the official circles may also be a factor.

NOTES

1   Leiden, the Netherlands.

REFERENCES

Aldred, O./G. Fairclough, 2002: *Historic Landscape Characterization – taking stock of the method*, London/Swindon.
Amin, A./P. Cohendet, 2004: *Architectures of knowledge,* Oxford.
Atkins Group, 2006: *Historic Environment Local Delivery Report*, London/Swindon (Heritage Environment Enabling project no. 4634).
Barends, S./H.G. Baas/M.J. de Harde/J. Renes/T.Stol/J.C. van Triest/R.J. de Vries/F.J. van Woudenberg (eds.), 2000: *Het Nederlandse landschap*, Utrecht.
Belvedere, 1999: *The Belvedere Memorandum. A policy document examining the relationship between cultural history and spatial planning*, The Hague.
Bender, O., 2009: The concept of a historic landscape analysis using GIS with focus on central Europe, in O. Bender/N. Evelpidou/A. Krek/A. Vassilopoulos (eds.), *Geoinformation Technologies for Geocultural Landscapes: European Perspectives*, London, 129-144.

Bender, O./N. Evelpidou/A. Krek/A. Vassilopoulos (eds.), 2009: *Geoinformation Technologies for Geocultural Landscapes: European Perspectives*, London.

Bender, O./K.P. Schumacher, 2008: Germany and Austria, in G. Fairclough/P. Grau Møller (eds.), *Landscape as Heritage*, Bern (Geographica Bernensia 79), 77-127.

BHU, 2008: *Kulturlandschaftliche Informationssysteme in Deutschland. Erfassen – Erhalten – Vermitteln*, Bonn (Bund Heimat und Umwelt in Deutschland).

BHU/ARKUM, 2009: 'Kulturlandschaft' in der Anwendung, Bonn (Symposium 19-3-2009).

Bishr, Y., 2006: Geospatial Semantic Web, in S. Rana/J. Sharma (eds.), *Frontiers of Geographic Information Technology*, Heidelberg, 121-138.

Bont, C.H.M. de/J. Renes, 1988: *De historisch-landschappelijke kaart van Nederland, schaal 1:50.000: legenda en proefkarteringen*, Wageningen.

Bosma, K., 2008: *Het post-Belvederetijdperk: Cultuurhistorisch beleid verankerd in de ruimtelijke ordening en in de ontwerpopgave*, Den Haag.

Burggraaff, P., 2007: Kulturlandschaftserfassungen in Deutschland – ein kursorischer ausgewählter Überblick zur Forschungsgeschichte, in BHU, *Kulturlandschaftliche Informationssysteme in Deutschland. Erfassen – Erhalten – Vermitteln*, Bonn (Bund Heimat und Umwelt in Deutschland), 21-31.

Chen, M.-Y./A.-P. Chen, 2006: Knowledge management performance evaluation: a decade review from 1995 to 2004, *Journal of Information Science* 32, 17-38.

Clark, K., 2006: *Capturing the Public Value of Heritage*, London/Swindon.

Clark, J./J. Darlington/G. Fairclough, 2004: *Using Historic Landscape Characterisation*, London.

Council of Europe, 2000: *European Landscape Convention and Explanatory Report*, Strasbourg.

Deeben, J.H.C. (ed.), 2008: *De Indicatieve Kaart van Archeologische Waarden, derde generatie*, Amersfoort.

Donaghey, S., 2008: *A critical Exploration of Frameworks for Assessing the Significance of New Zealand's Historic Heritage*, Oxford.

Duineveld, M./K.A.M. Van Assche, 2006: Tweederangs burgers en de ogenschijnlijke democratisering van de Nederlandse ruimtelijke ordening, in M. Aarts/R. During/P. van der Jagt (eds.), *Te koop! en andere ideeën over de inrichting van Nederland*, 25-31.

El Hassan, R./H. Elkadi, 2002: *Information Systems Applications for Conservation Strategies*, Alexandria (UNESCO Virtual Congress), 125-130.

Elerie, H./Th. Spek (eds.), 2009: *Van Jeruzalem tot Ezelakker. Veldnamen als levend erfgoed in het Nationaal Landschap Drentsche Aa*, Utrecht.

Elpez, I./D. Fink, 2006: Information systems success in the public sector: Stakeholders' perspectives and emergent alignment model, *Issues in Informing Science and Information Technology* 3, 219-230.

Fairclough, G., 2007: *Being there* (session The Historic Landscape: more than just a character? Booklet Conference Theoretical Archaeology Group. Available on http://sites.google.com/site/tag07york/home.

Fairclough, G./P. Grau Møller (eds.), 2008: *Landscape as Heritage*, Bern (Geographica Bernensia 79). Florence, 2000: *European Landscape Convention. Florence, 20 October 2000*, Strasbourg (Council of Europe).

Förster, A./A.Thierstein, 2008: Calling for pictures, in A. Thierstein/A. Förster (eds.), *The Image and the Region – Making Mega-City Regions Visible!*, Baden (Switzerland), 9-34.

Graaf, V. de/B. Klooster/M. Witjes, 2005: *Klanttevredenheidsonderzoek ROB – Archis2*, Amersfoort.

Gregory, I.N./P.S. Ell, 2008: *Historical GIS – technologies, methodologies and scholarship*, Cambridge, UK.

Hess, C./E. Ostrom, 2007: *Understanding Knowledge as a Commons*, Cambridge, USA.

Hooke, D., 2008: *Understanding past landscapes for future conservation*, Lissabon, PECLRS Conference, available on www.tercud.ulusofona.pt/PECSRL/Presentations/PECSRL2008. (Accessed 20 May, 2009).

Jerpåsen, G./A. Ornland/I. Lindblom, 2008: Norway, in G. Fairclough/P. Grau Møller (eds.), *Landscape as Heritage*, Bern (Geographica Bernensia 79), 205-227.

Kamermans, H./M. van Leusen/Ph. Verhagen (eds.), 2009: *Archaeological Prediction and Risk Management. Alternatives to current approaches*, Leiden (ASLU 17).

Kvamme, K.L., 2006: There and Back Again: Revisiting Archaeological Locational Modeling, in M. Mehrer/K. Wescott (eds.), *GIS and Archaeological Site Location Modeling*, Boca Raton, 3-38.

Landschap Erfgoed Utrecht, 2008: *Cultuurlandschap op de digitale kaart gezet*, Utrecht.

Laurini, R., 2001: *Information Systems for Urban Planning*, London.

Lock, G./T. Harris, 2006: Enhancing Predictive Archaeological Modeling: Integrating Location, Landscape and Culture, in M. Mehrer/K. Wescott (eds.), *GIS and Archaeological Site Location Modeling*, Boca Raton, 41-62.

Matthiesen, U./R. Danielzyk/S. Heiland/S. Tzschaschel (eds.), 2006: *Kulturlandschaften als Herausforderung für die Raumplanung. Verständnisse – Erfahrungen – Perspektiven*, Hannover (Akademie für Raumforschung und Landesplanung 228).

Ministries of LNV, OC&W, VROM, V&W, 2008: *Evaluatie Belvedere*, Nijmegen.

Morville, P./L. Rosenfeld, 2006: *Information Architecture for the World Wide Web*, Sebastopol.

Oorsouw, M.F. van/M. Wansleeben, 2005: *Toekomstvisie Digitaal Archief voor de Nederlandse Archeologie – eDNA-project*. Available on http://www.edna.leidenuniv.nl/docs/edna_toekomstvisie.pdf.

Pedroli, B./T. Pinto Correia/P. Cornish, 2004: European landscape diversity, or how to turn scattered remains into a major asset, in *De la connaissance des paysages à l'action paysagère* (Conference Bordeaux, France, 1-4 december 2004), Bordeaux.

Plöger, R., 2003: *Inventarisation der Kulturlandschaft mit Hilfe von Geographischen Informationssystemen (GIS). Methodische Untersuchungen für historisch-geographische Forschungsaufgaben und für ein Kulturlandschaftskataster*, Bonn (Ph.D. thesis Bonn University).

Pijpers, G., 2006: *Information usage behaviour*, Den Haag.

Read, D.W., 2007: *Artifact classification. A conceptual and methodological approach*. Walnut Creek.

Rheinland/ARKUM, 2005: *Kulturlandschaft digital – Forschung und Anwendung*, Bonn/Aachen (Tagungsdokumentation).

Rippon, S., 2007: Historic Landscape Characterisation: Its Role in Contemporary British Archaeology and Landscape History, *Landscapes* 2, 1-14.

Rodat, C., 2009: Wasser, Wege, Wald und Weinberge – Kulturlandschaft am westlichen Bodensee, in BHU/ARKUM, *'Kulturlandschaft' in der Anwendung*, Bonn (Symposium 19-3-2009).

Schuman, B., 1994: *Synthetic dimensionality: concepts and concept structure*. Available on http://originresearch.com/sd/home.cfm. (Accessed 1 November, 2008).

Schuyf, J., 1986: *Plaats en waardering van fossiele elementen in het Nederlandse landschap*, Wageningen.

Stefik, M., 1995: *Introduction to Knowledge Systems*, San Francisco.

Sueur, C./J.W. Beestman/M. Wansleeben, 2005: *Digitale registratie en documentatie van opgravingen binnen de KNA*, Amersfoort.

Tress, G./B. Tress/M. Bloemmen (eds.), 2003: *From tacit to explicit knowledge in integrative and participatory research*, Wageningen (Delta Series no. 3).

Valletta, 1992: European Convention on the Protection of the Archaeological Heritage (Revised) Valetta, 16.I.1992, Strasbourg (Council of Europe).

Verhagen, Ph., 2007: *Case Studies in Archaeological Predictive Modelling*, Leiden.

Visser, J.S., 2007: Historische geografie en digitale vastlegging: een kritische analyse, *Historisch Geografisch Tijdschrift* 25, 15-26.

Visser, J.S., 2009: *Back to Basics. Cultural landscape analysis from an informational & perceptual perspective*, Kyoto (14th International Conference of Historical Geographers).

Wachowicz, M./W. Vullings/J.D. Bulens/H. de Groot/M. van den Broek, 2005: *Uncovering the Main Elements of Geo-Web Usability*, Lisbon (8th AGILE Conference on GIScience).

Wansleeben, M./M. van den Dries, 2008: *Wegwijzer Digitaal Deponeren Archeologie*, Amsterdam (DANS Data Guide 3).

Wascher, D.M. (ed.), 2005: *European Landscape Character Areas*, Wageningen (Alterra Report 1254).

Wessels, C./J.D. Bulens/R. Lokers/R. Wiemer, 2008: *Praktijkrichtlijn IMKICH2006 (meaning 2008!)*, Utrecht/Wageningen/Amersfoort.

Wiemer, R., 2002: Standardisation: the Key to Archaeological Data Quality, in G. Sanjuan/D.W. Wheatley (eds.), *Mapping the Future of the Past. Managing the Spatial Dimension of the European Archaeological resource*, Sevilla, 103-108.

Wiemer, R./E. van Cappelleveen, 2009: *Kennis Infrastructuur MOdernisering MOnumentenzorg*, Amersfoort.

Willems, W.J.H./R.W. Brandt, 2004: *Dutch Archaeology Quality Standard* (version 2.2), Den Haag. (Available on http//www.sikb.nl).

Zande, A. van der, 2008: Landschap vol betekenissen, in M. Stam (ed.), *Op historische gronden; erfgoed in een context van ruimtelijk ontwerp, planning en democratie*, Utrecht, 57-81.

Zande, A. van der, 2009: *Landschap 2.0*, Bathmen (Platformdag Stichting Netwerk Historisch Cultuurlandschap, 30 oktober 2009).

Zoetbrood, P.A.M./M.J.G. Montforts/I.M. Roorda/R. Wiemer, 1997: Documenting the Archaeological Heritage, in W.J.H. Willems/H. Kars/D.P. Hallewas (eds.), *Archaeological Heritage Management in the Netherlands*, Assen/Amsterdam, 330-345.

WEBSITES

www.bhu.de
www.cultureelerfgoed.nl/werken/archis
www.dans.knaw.nl/en/data/info_edna/
http://sites.google.com/site/tag07york/home
www.eucalandproject.eu
www.kich.nl
www.lancewadplan.org/
www.landscape.ac.uk;

www.landscapecharacter.org.uk
www.landscaperesearch.org
www.spessartprojekt.de
www.veldnamendrentscheaa.nl/
www.pcl-eu.de
www.zandstad.nl

VIII

AGENDA FOR THE FUTURE

Bergheider Lake (D): future recultivated post-mining landscape with industrial monument (conveyor bridge).
3D imaging: Philip Paar (Lenné3D GmbH, 2006).

1. Agenda for the future
What do we see and what do we take?

Tom (J.H.F.) Bloemers[1]

ABSTRACT

In the last section of this book I discuss the way forward in relation to the central theme. How and to what extent can we know past landscapes, how can we avoid considering only 'what we see' as known and how can we use this still hidden knowledge for the actual sustainable management of the landscape's cultural-historical values? This discussion has two basic dimensions that influence future developments in research and policy:
- managing the knowledge creation processes of the known, unknown and knowable past landscapes and
- integrating past, present and future perception of the historic visible and hidden environment in decision-making processes.

The answer is a change of thought and action towards integrative approaches and on European collaboration between research and policy, but closely linked with public participation and bottom-up actions. In the Netherlands the ideas and practices supporting the Belvedere motto 'conservation through development' are, after a decade, embedded in a network of researchers and practitioners in higher education, heritage institutions on national and regional levels and in private companies.

Regarding the focus on the (almost) invisible archaeological-historical landscapes, the PDL/BBO programme and related activities show a range of cases, methods and approaches as to how to explore and manage these landscapes. At the same time it is clear that in crucial parts of these landscapes, such as the historic urban areas, there remains much more to be achieved. A key issue is the development of partly existing methodologies and practices for the exploration and heritage management of urban areas. Another one is to intensify the collaboration with urban and landscape designers, in this way powerful alliances can be mobilized in order to make the hidden visible.

KEY WORDS

Future; integrative approaches; hidden (urban) landscapes; SWOT

1. AN AGENDA FOR THE FUTURE: WHAT DO WE SEE AND WHAT DO WE TAKE?

In many of the contributions in this volume on the archaeological-historical landscape and its heritage the authors have stated that the past has to be viewed from the present, with an eye on the future. Consequently, in the last section of this book we will consider the central theme of this volume and future directions. Koos Bosma will do so for the Dutch context, discussing the position of cultural heritage in spatial planning after a decade of Belvedere policy (Belvedere 1999) and its follow-up in the near future. Graham Fairclough and his co-author Heleen van Londen present their view on the European developments after the signing and ratification of the European Landscape Convention (ELC) in 2000 by most of the member states of the Council of Europe (Florence 2000). They also assess in this context the insights resulting from the Dutch Belvedere and PDL/BBO programmes for the ELC mission and relate them to future trends in research and policy on the European level. In this introductory contribution I will present my personal views starting from the context described in the subtitle of this volume: 'Protection and Development of the Dutch Archaeological-Historical Landscape and its European Dimension'. The Dutch combination of the national Belvedere policy with a strong focus on the mobilization of the design practice for cultural planning and the PDL/BBO programme with its emphasis on the knowledge-action nexus has been a fascinating and exceptional experiment.

Looking forward, we must first of all look backwards to the central problem formulated in Chapter 1 on the cultural landscape and heritage paradox. To protect or preserve our historic environment we have to collaborate with 'outsiders' and make our expert knowledge suitable for policy and society.

The central problem as formulated in Ch. I is how and to what extent can we know past landscapes, how to avoid only considering 'what we see' as known and how to use this still hidden knowledge for actual sustainable management of landscape's cultural-historical values. This is how in the late 1990s we perceived the problem of the modern Dutch context of the archaeological-historical landscape in a highly dynamic and wetland environment and how it was approached by the Belvedere policy and PDL/BBO research. This is a central problem that all countries in Europe are facing in similar but different ways and which has created the basis for a joint mission statement like the ELC. This central problem dealing with the archaeological-historical landscape in general has two basic dimensions that influence future developments in research and policy:
- managing the knowledge creation processes of the known, unknown and knowable past landscapes and
- integrating past, present and future perception of the historic visible and hidden environment in decision-making processes.

Both dimensions are relevant for all of us, researchers, policy-makers, practitioners and the public. Since we are all actors, albeit in different and often changing roles, and since we all have knowledge, interests, opinions and emotions, the preferred mode to approach this human resource for the PDL/BBO programme is action research. In the Dutch context special attention has also been given to the knowable value of the hidden or slightly visible archaeological-historical wetland landscapes. The reason was, and following Heleen van Londen's observation still is, that their invisibility is considered a disadvantage to integrate these resources with the more visible historical-geographical and historic built environment as promoted by the national Belvedere policy. The central problem as raised in Ch. 1 can thus be summarized as follows. In general, visible historic landscapes are just a small fraction of many more, diverse and older (almost) invisible, but knowable landscapes. Practising this awareness in combination with the momentum of the right opportunities to integrate cultural landscape heritage in spatial planning and design very much depends on the recognition that what we see is what we take as actors from research, policy, practice and public. Consequently the strategy must be to use the visible to attract interest from policy, practice and the public in order to introduce the potential and fascination of the invisible.

The cultural landscape and heritage paradox as described in Ch. 1 is in sharp contrast with the traditional and dominant paradigms of the heritage sector and of research as an objective and independent enterprise implemented and assessed by experts. It has also been said that this feeling might be typical of "the older, that is to say my, generation [that] has been 'educated by doing' in the world of research and legal heritage protection of the post-war decades from about 1960 onwards but [which] has also experienced the limitations and failures connected with it." This is the period "...in the 1970s and '80s when protection and rescue seemed crucial tasks ..." using as "... response ... 'Save!' or 'Rescue!'" as Fairclough rightly states (Ch. VIII.3 section 3, 663-664). And I have said in Ch. 1 that "Gradually they, or we, became aware of the need for a change of strategy from 'defensive' to 'proactive' and from a sectoral towards an integrated approach of the historic environment." Although I personally practised this change in research and practice by transforming my chair in about 2000 from pre- and protohistoric 'past-oriented' archaeology into 'future-oriented' archaeological heritage and landscape including the PDL/BBO programme, the feeling of surprise about the change from a defensive attitude towards collaboration in an anticipative one remains. This feeling embodies the paradox described in Ch. 1 and is what Fairclough and Van Londen described in their paper as 'steps on the way' in a wider context of adjustments that research, policy and practice have to make when they deliberately face the opportunities and challenges the ELC offers archaeology and related sectors.

The way to cope with the paradoxical elements in the shift from a defensive and exclusive towards a proactive and inclusive strategy and attitude is to recognize that it has to do with the management of change. This is not only in the sense of changes in landscapes and environments as meant in Fairclough's quote in Ch. 1 section 2.1, but also in attitudes of the actors towards research, policy and practice. Management of change in both senses can be 'learned through landscape' as Fairclough and Van Londen state in Ch.VIII.3, in other words learning by doing. This equals Van der Zande's comments in his inaugural lecture for the Wageningen Belvedere chair in 2006 about exploring the strategy for change. Not only is there a lack of knowledge about the meaning of cultural landscapes, but there is also a lack of democracy which has to be solved (Van der Zande 2008, 66-73). Civil society at large is considered by him as a major factor for change in the twenty-first century and calls for social-cognitive learning processes rather than a hierarchical top-down approach. In this context, Bazelmans' interpretation of heritage management as "the successful transfer of heritage between generations, despite the many risks that threaten it, allowing groups to define and maintain their identity" resonates with Van der Zande's observations on the lack of democracy and Fairclough's and Van Londen's recommendation to think bigger (Bazelmans 2006a, 16).

2. CHANGING EUROPEAN LANDSCAPES OF THOUGHT AND ACTION

Reading Fairclough's and Van Londen's fine contribution, or rather a well thought essay as I would prefer to call it, one gradually gets a view on changes we are part of as from an observatory, a Belvedere. As previously stated, these changes are not only related to the material landscapes themselves but also to the mental landscapes of our thoughts and actions. These changes are formally expressed in the acceptance by the Council of Europe of the Florence and Faro Conventions (Florence 2000; Faro 2005). In Fairclough's and Van Londen's view two crucial insights can be derived from the conventions. Landscape has an integrative force being 'a place for researchers and practitioners, a virtual *agora, thing or parlement*, within which landscape meanings and significances can be contested as well as agreed'. Here Van der Zande's views on a lack of democracy and civil society are particularly apposite. This links up with their second observation: '...landscape as customary territory, polity and community, ... land *to which* a community or collective group belongs, rather than land owned *by* someone.' Together with the ELC's focus on everyday, even degraded, landscapes this comprehensive view opens new ways of relating people to land in a democratic context. This offers great opportunities for the cultural history disciplines and sectors to integrate knowledge and action and in doing so create new knowledge and implement sustainable heritage management.

However, to grasp these opportunities the archaeological-historical disciplines and sector have to adjust their research, policy and practice in a fundamental way. Integrative, i.e. inter- and transdisciplinary research, as promoted by the ESF-COST Synergy Initiative is the main way forward (Synergy Initiative 2010). To implement this approach in practice, its value for society, aims and themes have to be specified. Fairclough and Van Londen are right in stating that cultural history has to convert the aims and core concepts of environmental agendas like quality, diversity, coherence, significance and sustainability into cultural specific and meaningful notions (Bloemers 2006, 268-271 on sustainability). Their argument that historical landscape studies have 'to think bigger' is even more convincing when we become aware of the fact that its core business is studying past landscape developments starting from the present. This qualifies landscape studies as an indispensable partner for future spatial developments and at the same time it legitimizes its participation and the risks possibly involved by doing so. Furthermore, this forces us to shoulder our responsibility and to play our role. Whether we do so or not depends on the capacity of the discipline(s) and sector(s) for self- and heteroreference as described by Van Assche (Ch. IV.5).

3. AFTER PDL/BBO AND BELVEDERE: THE KNOWN, UNKNOWN AND KNOWABLE

The PDL/BBO mission has two main aims, making the unknown, the (almost) invisible landscapes, manageable for heritage knowledge and action and 'thinking bigger' in terms of integrative approaches towards landscape and heritage as management of change. This is in agreement with the Belvedere mission and its motto 'conservation through development', but focuses in particular on the unknown and the invisible characterized by their potential for discovering the unimaginable and exploring its long time depth. What is the present state of the art about the known, unknown and unknowable after a decade of activities and what can we learn from it for the future, especially the next decade?

The attention to the management of invisible landscapes has resulted in innovative projects inside and outside the PDL/BBO sphere, extending the scope from the sedentary agricultural past landscape to the hunter-gatherer landscapes from earlier prehistory (Groenewoudt/Peeters 2006; Peeters 2007; Smit Ch. IV.9). Closely related is the research on the application of predictive modelling and its meaning for an anticipatory heritage strategy (Groenewoudt/Peeters 2006, 164-166; Verhagen/Kamermans/van Leusen/Ducke Ch. V.5).

The awareness of the need for management of change that we are facing is reflected by various lines of research inside and outside the PDL/BBO programme. The science-based development of methodologies for monitoring the physical conditions of archaeological-historical sites creates basic new knowledge about the processes of degradation and preservation necessary for a well directed heritage management practice, especially in a wetland environment (Kars *et al.* Ch. III.6; Kars/Kattenberg/Oonk Ch. III.4; Theunissen/Van Heeringen 2006; Huisman 2009).

The inventories of the stock of archaeological monuments (Zoetbrood/ Van Rooijen 2006) and the review of the archaeological (Lauwerier/Lotte 2002; Van Dockum/Lauwerier/Zoetbrood 2006) and the archaeological-historical heritage (Beukers 2009) are essential first steps facilitating the discussion about the management of change. Together they represent resources of information that support the development of interpretative heritage research as has been promoted by Duineveld (Ch. IV.6).

Finally, an important initiative has been the introduction of the methodology for the economic valuation of cultural values and its application in practice (Ruijgrok 2004; idem 2006; idem 2009).

For a fair view on the present state of the art of the two core issues, the unknown or invisible and the management of change, we must also consider some clear and basic weak points. After a decade there is still a divide between what I call 'traditional' or 'past-oriented' archaeology and archaeological heritage management, both as a field of research as well as action (Bazelmans 2006a, 16-17; Bloemers Ch. 1 section 2.2, 8-9 and Fig. 2). This divide exists, although the so-called management of archaeological resources cycle (AMZ cycle) formulated in the late 1990s has been widely accepted in Dutch archaeology (Willems 1997; idem 1998). A limitation of this AMZ cycle is its inward orientation which complicates its application in spatial planning (De Zwart Ch. V.7).

A very weak spot is the lack of research on the archaeological resource management of historic towns and villages. The PDL/BBO programme was unsuccessful in attracting research proposals with enough quality and dealing with this issue in some way or another. The first archaeological review (Lauwerier/ Lotte 2002; Van Dockum/Lauwerier/Zoetbrood 2006) did not consider this category of archaeological sites, although they were classified in the Belvedere Cultural-historical Values Map of the Netherlands (Belvedere 1999). And in the recent archaeological-historical heritage review (Beukers 2009) the historic towns fared badly in the view of expert critic Ed Taverne (Abrahamse 2009).

To a slightly lesser extent this also applies to the new urban development schemes, the rural landscapes transformed into urban ones. Although there are impressive examples of the conservation through development approach and the use of the archaeological-historical landscape as a source of inspiration for urban design as in Leidsche Rijn, Almere-Hout or De Dalemse Donken in Gorinchem (Bloemers/Van Schuppen 2009, 245-246; Linssen/Witsen 2010, 184; De Graaf s.a., 28-32) the integration of the archaeological-historical values in the urban area remains difficult (Van Loon/Nyst/Van Mispelaar 2006). This is also reflected by one of the dilemmas listed in the final Belvedere 'book of practice' which asks whether the conservation through development approach is applicable to the mostly invisible archaeological heritage (Linssen/Witsen 2009, 249). Of course the difficulty of exploring the subsurface hidden heritage, especially in historic towns and villages, is considerable but there are well-developed methods available to cope with this in an anticipative way. So it seems to be more a matter of focus than of possibilities.

Of a different but related kind is that initially the PDL/BBO programme was unsuccessful in attracting the design disciplines (Bloemers Ch. VII.7 section 2.2, 590). Although this was resolved in later stages, it might indicate a structural problem underlying the bridging of the world of research for designing the rural and urban landscape and the world of research in humanities and social sciences. Another structural weakness has been described in this volume as the synchronization of the cycles of research and policy (see e.g. Ch. IV.2 section 2.3-4 , 210-212; Van der Zande 2009, 49-50). They are not running parallel in real time, they mature in various tempi and there is a considerable difference in criteria for qualified output.

The opportunities and threats as we see them now are crucial for the future agenda. A good basis for the future is that the ideas and experiences of the PDL/BBO participants will be embedded and continued in different institutional contexts ranging from university groups like the new institute CLUE at VU University in Amsterdam and by the National Heritage Agency (Kennis 2010) to the Belvedere 'Onderwijsnetwerk' (Cerutti 2008) and regional follow-ups. The research theme itself has been integrated in the National Archaeological Research Agenda (NOaA) creating the conditions for full acceptance of heritage research by the scientific and heritage management community (Bazelmans 2006b, 61-62).

From the PDL/BBO experience it is clear that the conservation through development approach is suitable often for the (almost) invisible landscapes. It might be necessary to differentiate between the various types of spatial developments involved and their level of dynamics. An urban development scheme like Leidsche Rijn (Bloemers/Van Schuppen 2009, 245-246) or Almere-Hout (Linssen/Witsen 2010, 184) offer other opportunities and constraints than a linear structure like a railroad (Carmiggelt 2001) or a river reconstruction (Stoepker 2006). It will also be relevant to compare this approach with its counterpart development through conservation (Belvedere 1999, 33) and the maintenance of legal procedures (Vollmer-König Ch.V.9). The evaluation of the experiences from the last 10-15 years and the selection of a number of best practices could be a valuable result.

This evaluation of actual experiences combined with the results of the conservation through development approach should be considered as part of a long-term strategy aiming at the development of new knowledge and practice for heritage management by participating in spatial planning policy. This would fit very well in the chain of major steps forward made in the past by the archaeological discipline in the Netherlands, although more or less forced upon archaeology by the nation's socio-economic growth. The post-war urban building schemes in the 1950s and 1960s stimulated an upscaling of archaeological fieldwork into settlement archaeology, the large reclamation schemes of the 1970s and 1980s asked for a landscape level of research and heritage management (Bloemers 1999; Kolen 2005). The aims of the Valletta and Florence Conventions invite Dutch archaeology and adjacent disciplines, or rather urge them, to deliberately enter another phase of expansion and innovation.

Three serious threats are to be mentioned in relation to the two core issues, the unknown or invisible and the management of change.

First is the dominance of the visible over the invisible. This can happen when the historic built environment is considered as the only available or valuable relict of past landscapes. This can be stimulated by public perception, consideration of economic values or short-term visions of planners and designers.

The first threat particularly applies to the urban historic environment and its rich but invisible subsurface heritage. Its compact occupation, socio-economic value and the complexity of heritage management and planning can easily favour a neglect of an appropriate conservation strategy. This might also be fostered by the lack of awareness in policy and planning of the links between town and country resulting in sharp divides between the rural and the urban as we have seen in Dutch planning.

Second, the amount of archaeological sites is simply running out because of the unlimited destruction by excavation legitimized under the Valletta Convention of preservation *ex situ* and not being replaced by newly discovered sites.

The third threat could be a technocratic approach to the historic environment, neglecting or underestimating the importance of the human perspective on landscape and environment. An oppressive example of this is presented in a small booklet with papers by leading researchers and edited by persons from a prestigious institute (Bouma et al. 2008).

From what we have seen from these introductory observations on an agenda for the future, I conclude that it is crucial for the future of archaeological heritage to:
a. explicitly focus on the unknown and invisible and
b. to combine this strategy with the 'internal' integration of all cultural-historical disciplines and sectors and with the 'external' integration of relevant planning and design disciplines and sectors.

Managing the unknown and the invisible is more important than ever. The problem has not yet been solved, but PDL/BBO and similar research have broadened the horizons. The experiences gained from applying the knowledge-action nexus have differentiated the problem and presented case studies showing the way forward. A key issue is to develop already partly existing methodologies and practices for the exploration and heritage management of urban areas. Another one is to intensify the collaboration with urban and landscape designers aiming at a structured and well founded use of the imagination about the unknown past in the present. In this way powerful alliances can be mobilized in order to make the hidden visible.

The experiences with 'internal' and 'external' integration have prepared us for the 'thinking bigger' strategy. This requires a fruitful feedback between self- and heteroreference which is not self-evident. Extending this strategy to the European level will present surprising and unexpected views on a diversity of problems, approaches and solutions creating the conditions for a sustainable future of landscapes, their research and their management. And for 'learning through landscape'.

NOTES

1   Amsterdam University, Amsterdam, the Netherlands.

REFERENCES

Abrahamse, J.E., 2009: Ed Taverne: Geen behoud door stilstand. Een interview naar aanleiding van het verschijnen van de Erfgoedbalans 2009, *Vitruvius* 2, 8-11.

Bazelmans, J.G.A., 2006a: Value and Values in Archaeology and Archaeological Heritage Managament. Revolution in the Archaeological System, *Berichten van de Rijksdienst voor het Oudheidkundig Bodemonderzoek* 46, 13-25.

Bazelmans, J.G.A., 2006b: To what End? For what Purpose? The National Archaeological Research Agenda (NOaA) and Quality Management in Dutch Archaeology, *Berichten van de Rijksdienst voor het Oudheidkundig Bodemonderzoek* 46, 53-68.

Belvedere, 1999: *The Belvedere Memorandum. A policy document examining the relationship between cultural history and spatial planning*, The Hague.

Beukers, E., et al. (eds.), 2009: *Erfgoedbalans 2009. Archeologie, monumenten en cultuurlandschap in Nederland*, Amersfoort.

Bloemers, J.H.F., 1999: Regional Research Approach since the Early 70s in the Netherlands. A Fundamental Decision with Long-term Effects, in H. Sarfatij/W.J.H. Verwers/P.J. Woltering (eds.), *In Discussion with the Past. Archaeological studies presented to W.A. van Es*, Zwolle/Amersfoort, 317-27.

Bloemers, J.H.F., 2006: Kulturlandschaften in den Niederlanden - Erhaltung durch nachhaltige Entwicklung in der Raumordnung, in: U. Matthiesen/R. Danielzyk/S. Heiland/S. Tzschaschel (eds.), *Kulturlandschaften als Herausforderung für die Raumplanung. Verständnisse - Erfahrungen -Perspektiven*, Hannover (Forschungs- und Sitzungsberichte der Akademie für Raumforschung und Landesplanung, 228, 253-273.

Bloemers, J.H.F./S. van Schuppen 2009: Erfgoed en stedelijke transformaties, in: A. van der Zande/R. During (eds.), *Erfgoed en ruimtelijke planning*, Den Haag, 235-271.

Bouma, J./J.B. Opschoor/L.A. Groen (eds.), 2008: *De toekomst van het Nederlandse landschap. Wetenschappelijke bijdragen aan de toekomstige landschapskwaliteit*, Amsterdam.

Carmiggelt, A. (ed.), 2001: *Opgespoord verleden. Archeologie in de Betuweroute*, Abcoude.

Cerutti, V., 2008: *Leerstoelen in de etalage. Review Onderwijsnetwerk Belvedere*, s.l.

CLUE, 2010: *About CLUE (Research institute for the heritage and history of the cultural landscape and urban environment)*, Amsterdam.

Dockum, S. van/R.C.G.M. Lauwerier/P.A.M. Zoetbrood, 2006: Archeologiebalans (Archaeology Report). The National Review and Outlook, *Berichten van de Rijksdienst voor het Oudheidkundig Bodemonderzoek* 46, 41-52.

Faro 2005: *Council of Europe Framework Convention on the Value of Cultural Heritage for Society*, Strasbourg (Council of Europe).

Florence 2000: *European Landscape Convention. Florence, 20 October 2000*, Strasbourg (Council of Europe).

Graaf, K. de, s.a.: *Geschiedenis als onderlegger. Voorbeeldenboek projectontwikkeling and cultuurhistorie*, Utrecht.

Groenewoudt, BJ./J.H.M. Peeters, 2006: Assessment and Selection in Archaeological Heritage Management in the Netherlands. Past and Future, *Berichten van de Rijksdienst voor het Oudheidkundig Bodemonderzoek* 46, 159-170.

Huisman, D.J. (ed.), 2009: *Degradation of archaeological remains*, Den Haag.

Kennis, 2010: *Kennis voor de praktijk van de erfgoedzorg. Themaprogramma's 2004-2009. Kennisprogramma's 2009-2013*, Amersfoort.

Kolen, J., 2005: Hoofdlijnen in de Nederlandse landschapsarcheologie (1950-2005), in M.H. van den Dries/W.J.H. Willems (eds.), *Innovatie in de Nederlandse Archeologie. Liber amicorum voor Roel W. Brandt*, Gouda, 101-121.

Lauwerier, R.C.G.M./R.M. Lotte, 2002: *Archeologiebalans 2002*, Amersfoort.

Linssen, M./P. Witsen, 2009: *Belvedere.nu. Praktijkboek cultuurhistorie en ruimtelijke ontwikkeling*, Utrecht.

Loon, M. van/C.L. Nyst/A. van Mispelaar, 2006: The Role of the Cultural Heritage in Urban Development Projects, *Berichten van de Rijksdienst voor het Oudheidkundig Bodemonderzoek* 46, 225-242.

Peeters, J.H.M., 2007: *Hoge Vaart-A27 in context: Towards a model of Mesolithic-Neolithic land use dynamics as a framework for archaeological heritage management*, Amersfoort.

Ruijgrok, E., 2004: *Op weg naar een MKBA-methodiek voor de cultuurhistorie*, Rotterdam.

Ruijgrok, E., 2006: Cultural Heritage in Euro's; the three economic values of cultural heritage: a case study in the Netherlands, *Journal of Cultural Heritage* 7, 206-213.

Ruijgrok, E., 2009: Cultuurhistorie: omdat het wat waard is! in M. Linssen (ed.), *Het cultuurhistorisch argument. Essaybundel*, Utrecht, 41-45.

Stoepker, H., 2006: Risk Control, Knowledge Acquisition and Quality Management in an Archaeological Project. The Organisation and Results of the Maaswerken Field Evaluation, 1998-2005, *Berichten van de Rijksdienst voor het Oudheidkundig Bodemonderzoek* 46, 69-90.

Synergy Initiative 2010: *ESF-COST Synergy Initiative 'A European Network of Networks: New Perspectives on Landscapes'*, Strasbourg/Brussels.

Theunissen, E.M./R.M. van Heeringen, 2006: Hidden Heritage of the Dutch Delta. Thoughts about the Preservation Capacity of Wetlands and the Sustainability of the Archaeological Resource, *Berichten van de Rijksdienst voor het Oudheidkundig Bodemonderzoek* 46, 245-301.

Willems, W.J.H., 1997: Archaeological Heritage Management in the Netherlands: Past, Present and Future, in W.J.H. Willems/H. Kars/D.P. Hallewas (eds.), *Archaeological Heritage Management in The Netherlands. Fifty Years State Service for Archaeological Investigations*, Amersfoort, 3-34.

Willems, W.J.H., 1998: Archaeology and heritage management in Europe; trends and developments, *European Journal of Archaeology* 1, 293-311.

Zande, A. van der, 2008: Landschap vol betekenissen. Over het omgaan met historie in de ruimtelijke inrichting, in M. Stam (ed.), *Op Historische Gronden. Erfgoed in een context van ruimtelijk ontwerp, planning and democratie*, Utrecht, 57-81.

Zande, A. van der, 2009: Erfgoed en ruimtelijke ordening, in A. van der Zande/R. During (eds.), *Erfgoed en ruimtelijke planning*, Den Haag, 25-60.

Zoetbrood, P./C.A.M. van Rooijen 2006: Monuments in Balance. An Overview of the Stock of Archaeological Complexes at Archaeological Monument Sites, *Berichten van de Rijksdienst voor het Oudheidkundig Bodemonderzoek* 46, 171-179.

2. Heritage policy in spatial planning

Koos Bosma[1]

ABSTRACT

In response to the wave of nostalgia that accompanied the negative public response in the Netherlands to the huge number of infrastructural interventions, city extensions, agricultural concentrations and expanding business areas during the last quarter of the twentieth century, the Belvedere state policy (1999-2009) tried to implement a way to integrate the remembrance, rituals and material remnants of the past in spatial planning programmes.

The state wanted to transform the Netherlands, cope with the international competition and, at the same time, combine this transformation with a policy of reconciling preservation and renewal processes. Alliances between government, institutions, entrepreneurs and the public are indispensable for the realization of such aims, without such problems between owners and clients there would be no spatial planning and public space.

Such a policy also puts high demands on the designing disciplines. Their interventions and inventions could aim at autonomous enclaves within a new environment as a not recognizable or non-segregated element within a modern concept, or as a sublimated actualization of an old spatial or pattern-like arrangement, respectively transformation, recreation or recombination and perhaps even as loose traces and thus as historical references. The designer should also be able to uncover the invisible presence of the past, remixing the historical atmosphere. Thus surprising links may arise between physical and non-physical dimensions of a place in the sense of cross-overs. The unimaginable can produce a performance.

If the integration of historical remnants in spatial interventions is striven for, then cultural history is to obtain a firm position in the diverse configurations of spatial planning. A programme of knowledge development and knowledge education by means of a research agenda and an education programme is indispensable.

KEY WORDS

Body of knowledge; cultural renewal, education; heritage policy, identity, spatial planning

1. A CLOUD OF NOSTALGIA

1.1 Heritage as experience

The reconstruction of town and countryside in the Netherlands during the last decade was accompanied by ample attention to history and tradition. In full awareness of the risks and the transience in society, texts, images and matter evoked memories of the pretensions and magnificence of the Netherlands created by human hand. The search for the country of former times can be said to have worked as a balm for our pessimistic soul, while cultural pessimism revealed itself in mourning for the loss of the familiar chain of locally coloured identity and binding group cultures formerly discernible as a social reality in the structure and shape of settlement and landscape. Accelerating technical innovations, the impact of modernization, iconoclastic fury and natural disasters transformed our cities and landscapes in such a way that we perceive them as ruinous environments (Makarius 2004, 9). Under, between and next to the spatial manifestation of the Netherlands as a seemingly aimless enterprise, visually presenting itself as infrastructural slices, industrial premises with endless sheds, city extensions, intensive agrarian exploitation and cultural renewal, lies the ruin of the ancient Netherlands.

There is a large gap between the dynamism of groups attempting to antiquate or modernize the country. The interdepartmental document Belvedere Memorandum reacted to widely shared dissatisfaction with the 'silting up' of the Netherlands and the uniformity and loss of identity of cities and landscapes (Belvedere 1999). The Memorandum presented the plausibility and possibility of overcoming all these tokens of dissatisfaction and implied that the gap between the past and the future could be closed. The Memorandum spread the message that reshaping, recombining or transforming the ancient could become a hot spot in a modern environment. It remains to be seen whether or not the authors of the Memorandum have sufficiently realized that 'the dissatisfaction in society had deeper roots than the physical-spatial shaping of cities and landscapes' (Wallagh 2005, 18). The spatial order and the spatial planning of the Netherlands cannot undergo a positively appreciated modernization without involving sociocultural and mental factors. Without a different way of thinking and acting, the gap cannot be bridged.

Care for the ancient Netherlands has long led an autonomous and undisturbed existence with its own antiquity ideology, a specific framework, its own flow of money and its own institutional environment. Such autonomy along with a fixation on artefacts is under pressure because not only the institutional environment, but also the paradigm of the preservation of monuments and historic buildings is changing. Policies that advocate the development of old and new are hot issues (Modernisering Monumentenzorg 2008, 17). It is an uncertain step as well as a privileged perspective to expand and embed the fixation on artefacts in a more area-based approach. In the Belvedere approach our companionship with the ruin is revived. For spatial planning and public space the attempt is made to give the combination of preservation and renewal a structural place in the spatial order of the Netherlands. For the realization of such aims, alliances of government, institutions, entrepreneurs and the public are indispensable, without such problems between owners and clients there would be no spatial planning and public space. This policy has been the practice for some ten years and the question may be raised if and how it can be continued in the future. How do we deal with the past, individually and as a group? What fascinates us, how urgent is it? How can we integrate this fascination in the present? What ordering concepts are in operation when we value and appreciate the meaning of heritage? In what practices can perception and experience characterize our fascination with heritage?

1.2 Post-Belvedere

The Belvedere policy (1999-2009) was conceived as an instrument for linking the past and the present (Belvedere 1999). Cultural history is not launched in order to freeze historical processes, rather it detaches them from current interpretations, thus making them fit for adventurous experiments. In this sense the Belvedere policy strives for a culture break. Directed towards the future, professional groups are invited to look backward, and the historians that look backward in their official capacity are asked to take stock of the future. When both groups are willing to set aside their prejudices and adjust their sights, then a cultural break can become reality.

Next to systematic emphasis on new thought in the spatial sector, Belvedere started a sequence of projects that primarily existed in the collection of problems of space among owners, the facilitating of design workshops and the production of publications as in the *grands travaux* like the *limes*, the border of the Roman empire, (Colenbrander/MUST 2005), the New Dutch Waterline (Brons/Colenbrander 2009) and the sandy soils of the province of Noord-Brabant (Netherlands Architecture Fund 2007; www.zandstad.nl). Apart from the generating of knowledge, these projects were also aimed at methods of collaboration between designers and historians, the development of methods and techniques to link history and design and at visualizing historical meanings for major transformations. Moreover this body of knowledge was extended by a Belvedere committee of the Netherlands Architecture Fund which remunerated dozens of proposals that strived for impulses of design, culture and art in processes of spatial planning. In the Belvedere programme as a whole more than 300 projects have been executed in the past ten years. In itself, this imposing figure does not suffice for judgements about the efficiency and the continuity of the Belvedere policy. If the cultural history is to obtain a firm position in the diverse configurations of spatial planning, then a programme of knowledge development and knowledge education by means of a research agenda and an education programme is indispensable.

2. CULTURAL RENEWAL AND CULTURE PRESERVATION

2.1 *Culture injections*

The spatial diversity of the city as a social, physical and mental habitat is spreading far beyond the city due to urbanization processes. The historical fabric and the simultaneous existence of structures, ensembles and buildings from different eras are an expression of such processes. In a welfare state like the Netherlands these processes will continue to leave their traces in the near future. Linked to heritage claims, shrinking agricultural area, the spread of urbanization, claims on soils for water storage, the purchase of grounds to realize the national Ecological Main Structure, the image of a complex and endless transformation is indicated. As opportunities present themselves the cultural load requires sound and innovative planning and guidance. The official government policy is to grant heritage a strong position in plans for the future.

In the post-industrial era it is self evident that many culture forms participate. That is pure profit. Consciousness that cultural renewal can have a multiplier effect on regional or national image building, participation, planning and building processes can count on strong political interest. Cultural renewal gets its shape and meaning in an interaction between the existing, the possible and the unimaginable.

Along with traditional culture impulses several relatively new cultural peculiarities may be discerned. In contemporary marketing strategies such as 'creative city', 'cultural charisma', symbolism and the aesthetic qualities of buildings, places and areas, all being values of perception and experience, play a prominent role. In general the idea of a visual and spatial quality stands apart from the social strife for cultural diversity and continuity in processes of increase in scale and globalization and the Netherlands is seen as a cultural region in Europe. Politicians and planners also seek alliance with needs arising from the different cultural roles that individuals play: producer, consumer, civilian, tourist. Given free rein to the world of experience, the affinities and tastes of the public, including the nostalgic, aimed at local history, compose a substantial contribution to the legitimacy of bottom-up participation. Increasingly the public becomes co-producer of culture and co-owner of spatial problems and solutions (Mommaas 2001, 165-166). With successful culture injections, a broadening of the spatial agenda is inevitable.

2.2 Identities

Political and marketing discourses frequently champion the notion of 'identity' with a presupposed origin and discernable authentic features. This vision of local and historical identities being based on local or regional essences that can be inscribed is diametrically opposed to the view that the construction of identity is dealing with the appropriation of imported culture and that, historically seen, groups and individuals have revised traditions in a critical way (Herngreen 2002; *idem* 2005, 59).

It is feasible to discern (dynamic) identities at four levels:

1. Individual identity construction by (virtual) experience of town and country or as an ambiguous process. The individual interprets his/her surroundings and gives them historical depth. His/her views on the past and local identity are based on personal identity construction and tend to interpret one's region as immutable. The individual identity as lived authenticity is ultimately shaped by personal taste, individual experiences, attaching meaning and, of course, by the influence of group culture. We are unique and at the same we can be identified as members of a cultural group (partial identity);
2. Group identity as a distinguishing way of life has an interactive character that is attached to a region or mental landscapes and cityscapes through culture, subculture and multiculturality. Identity is composed of common features, shared behaviour and lifestyles, common meaning and a common conscience that is layered and multifocal. The collective rendering of meaning lapses in each era and for every person according to a certain common cultural logic with values as leading incentives. The Dutch for instance 'commemorate victimization, not heroism, at ceremonies we propagate the values charity and guilt, not the value courage.' (Enklaar 2007, 78).
3. The conviction that a spatial identity is anchored in buildings, spots, settlements and landscapes and which can be compared to a genetic code with an inalienable origin. Thanks to traditional behaviour, land use and building conventions, the identity stays loyal to itself within these limits. The existence of such a loyal identity in the sense of the *genius loci* as advocated by Norberg-Schulz, who considers natural features of an area determinative for a latently present identity (Norberg-Schulz 1979; *idem* 1996), has never been proven.
4. Regional and political identity with 'the' regional or national memory and 'the' historical canon as identifier. Politicians show themselves charmed by the 'aesthetic and intellectual, memorial (the historical memory), and political values (freedom, equality, participation and democracy) that shape the conscience of a shared national and if possible also 'European culture' (Frijhoff 2007b, 55). Both national and regional canons, seen as a national or regional identity, are in danger of being misused to legitimate the fixed uniform nation state or regional unity or to symbolize a simple expression of political unity. The stereotypical story of Dutch identity nowadays is usually 'a test of the deviation degree of immigrants' (Frijhoff 2007a, 26). Such a grim exclusive approach denies cultural developments and changes in a culture state that are influenced by immigrants and ethnic groups.

   It is striking that the four types of identity are mostly not recognized. In policy documents nobody seems to account for the fact that these strongly differing identity types and their ideological features must lead to differing policy priorities and a specific method of spatial practices (Mommaas 2001, 171-173).

2.3 Political consequences

Our heritage survives in the turbulence of flourishing culture insertions. In this climate, the antique and modern Netherlands need each other. Government organs, markets and the enterprising public have a responsibility for the guidance and promotion of visual, sustainable and sociocultural interests in the spatial planning of the country. It is self-evident that cultural renewal and culture preservation play a part that cannot be underestimated.

Sectoral thinking is a serious obstacle to collaboration between preserving and modernizing the Netherlands. Its results are the isolation of projects and collaboration is not sought. The separation of the spatial/visual, the social and the cultural dimensions and the negation of different spatial scale levels are detrimental for the contemporary landscape. Thus it is useful to scrutinize the transformation of the Netherlands and to outline a suitable spatial policy without the petrification and fragmentation of space.

Final responsibility for the sustainable 'system' in the Netherlands involves the obligation to define the general interest, to take the lead and to indicate the directions in which the state should be moving. In other words, its task is to phrase the frameworks and values for the integration of project areas in a larger order. When the responsibilities have been defined and divided, when the creativity and interdisciplinarity in decision-making and planning processes have been included, the interplay between the existing fabric, the potentials of the genius loci and the unimaginable can have great impact.

To understand ways in which the gap between the antique and the new can be bridged, it may be helpful to elucidate a number of once solid cornerstones of the traditional preservation of monuments and historical buildings that have in the meantime become much more flexible. When we accept that getting along with heritage ought to be dynamic and that identities are mutating (Mommaas 2001, 171-173; Kobylinski 2006), we can also accept the implication that the attitude in dealing with the past should not be that of a collector who caresses an immutable historical image that should be presented as a whole. A dynamic image of history and future needs the gardener who weeds and trims, demolishes, uproots, cleans up, knowing that in this manner the garden is incorporated in a living tradition. Dynamics may even mean the use of dynamite.

The aforementioned fixation on artefacts is based on the idea of maintainable authenticity and the intrinsic origins of objects that can be reconstructed by experts. This idea has lost much of its old evidence. The spectrum of opinions and lines of argumentation surrounding the terms authenticity or identity offers the officials who participate in the heritage industry more opportunities than ever to figure out concepts for an approach in which preserving and modernizing the Netherlands pursue variable relations.

To implement inspiring planning, participation and building processes, it is crucial that all participants in these processes are aware of the fact that the Netherlands has a long tradition of more or less radically pushing aside traditions.

3. BELVEDERE POLICY, SPATIAL PLANNING AND DESIGN
3.1 *Cultural history*

The original Belvedere policy was oriented towards the material meaning of cultural history. As a result of concentrating on the spatial order and planning of the Netherlands, it fell behind the developments in cultural-historical sciences. Since the 1970s historians have become more interested in history as such, their industrious research no longer serves religion, nationality, morality or sacrosanct institutions (Plumb 1969). Critical history goes further than collective memory, it seeks alternative threads in the task of (re)constructing the past. The result is special interest in deprived or neglected groups and individuals.

Since the 1980s, history and (collective) memory approach each other again, resulting in the re-evaluation of memory and oral tradition, precisely where the sources are silent and no evidence of individual experience is documented. Commemoration implies that people are remembering simultaneously and collectively, e.g. by ensuring their memories live on via the preservation of names and narratives. The memory revives a successful commemoration, while the worshippers of a commemoration think that the dead, not in shape but in essence, are brought to life."(Margalit 2006, 61). The primary impulse can be traced back to a desire for immortality, a fear for extinction and total oblivion. The commemoration can be seen as a life insurance that can trifle with time. Commemoration goes hand in hand with a solidarity of the memory of rare events. Commemorations also have a (sometimes heavily laden) message: "beside gratefulness, esteem and solidarity feelings, also rancour, hate and particularly a stereotypical impression of enemies is prolongated and kept alive." (Jonker 2001, 29-36; Von der Dunk 2007).

Seen from the perspective of memory, the writing of history can be extended in three ways (Assmann 2006, 24): the emotional dimension, the individual experience and the commemoration function. A moral function is also added to the critical and heroic. Therefore the preservation of authentic relics or places seems to have grown subordinate to the preservation, reinforcement or revival of non-material cultural values. Although the past cannot return it can be evoked on command.

3.2 *Heritage and spatial planning*

Material relics of a culture have a chance for a 'second life' outside the original context of use. Through the three dominant interpretations of the term 'heritage' (heritage as make over, heritage as a collection in a repository, immaterial heritage as cultural representation (Grijzenhout 2007), cultural renewal, culture conservation and traditional preservation of monuments and historic buildings can meet in spatial and infrastructural policy plans. Modernizing and preservation meet in the same design process. Joint action in the interdisciplinary arena of spatial planning did not work without friction, however, for two reasons. In the heritage sector the perception of its own vision of heritage is essentially different from the parties that strive for area development, preferring to allocate heritage a contemporary role. This does not make communication easy, as since 1990 spatial planning finds itself in a transitional phase from centralization to decentralization and from singular to multiple patronship. Currently this uncertainty does not favour cultural history which seeks a steady place in planning process in the sense of using cultural history as leverage in complicated planning processes. Developers and other big investors assess each case separately to see if cultural history deserves a place. Such a place is not self-evidently reserved but must be reasoned and rationally gained.

3.3 *Design and historicizing repertory*

The status of spatial design is strengthened partly as a result of the first three state memoranda on architecture, landscape, spatial quality and cultural history. Since the first memorandum on architecture (Ruimte voor architectuur 1991) a broadening of the architectural policy, building as a cultural commission, accompanied severe decentralization along with an increase in the importance of regional jobs and interlocal decision-making. Furthermore, the context in which architecture is produced has changed significantly. The sociocultural component is weakened and the building processes, seen financially, have stabilized. Questions remain: which combinations of modern and ancient are offered in design proposals? What does Belvedere mean for the professional ethics of designers, planners and clients in their contacts with the past in design and planning processes? In designer circles one was aware that old landscapes and ancient cities represent a collective symbolic capital as well as sources of collective identities. Between ignoring the past and canonizing it lingers a variety of freedoms for the designer. Assuming that initiators select some values that should not be erased and that deserve a place in the planning process means that concepts are conceivable that combine the ancient and the new. One thinks of a recognizable autonomous enclave within a new environment as a not recognizable or non-segregated element within a modern concept, or as a sublimated actualization of an old spatial or pattern-like arrangement, respectively transformation, recreation or recombination and perhaps even as loose traces and thus as historical references.

If the design makes it possible to visualize the relationship between the use of the visible and the invisible urban infrastructure of our habitat, it should also be possible that the designer uncovers the invisible presence of the past, samples the historical sphere and integrates it in his/her design. Thus surprising links may arise between physical and non-physical dimensions of a place in the sense of crossovers, overlap and cross-pollination with cross-bracings between arts, media, infotainment and heritage (Schwarz 2006, 24). The unimaginable can produce a performance.

Occasionally the interaction between political, commercial and cultural historical values of the region is difficult. Nevertheless building in a specific regional vernacular remains a growth market for architects. For many a designer the Belvedere discourse is a problem in that it sounds rather mechanical, suggesting that historically grown identities have been based on local or regional essences, something on which it seems evident to elaborate. As a counterproposal one may suggest that identity creation is concerned with appropriation of imported culture and that, historically seen, groups and individuals always treated the traditions in a critical way (Herngreen 2002; *idem* 2005, 59). Spatial identity does not exist in itself, it is determined by ideas and interpretations in an interactive process (Hague/Jenkins 2005, 6 ff.). To draw the mental significance of a place (*genius loci*) in a spatial transformation process, the aspired identity, with all its different layers of meaning, will have to be dissected, denoted, programmed, designed and maintained. Time and money need to be made available for this research.

3.4 *Policy and institutional design*

If the assumption that an understanding of historical processes can attribute to the plan for the future is correct, then this assumption challenges consideration of the role of the state, its memory and the future of institutional design, especially when the past and surviving remains are not treated like a collection of artefacts but in terms of processes (Rijksadviseur 2006, 5). The central government plays a leading and often persuading role in the execution of projects.

The design of public space is more than a real estate enterprise whose exclusive aim is profit. A vital city quarter, one that should prove its social face through a rich and attractive design, must frequently be the focus of endeavour. Heritage must play an important part. In the public domain the strategic design can be a powerful instrument in transmitting social engagement, especially when the user is not addressed as a passive consumer but is incited to involvement and reflection. Visualizing the public domain deals with collective interests. The design is meant to advance the communication between the public, authorities and organizations. The designer should anticipate the reactions of users. He/she is not just producing a visual product in a sensitive (historical) environment but also offers food for thought. Public space should provide the potential for exchange of (historical) knowledge, sensibility and emotions. The starting point of a meaningful social communication is a careful analysis of function, content and historical context of the commission. The potential of the existing fabric, the invention and the intervention of the designing disciplines make public space alive.

Alternative ways of thinking and alternative planning, participation and building processes result in different environments. Heritage of different sorts thus fulfils the role of support that could increase the return of investments. When involved parties, the administrators, planners, developers, designers, investors, users and managers test these alternatives, they have existing legislation at their disposal, like protecting nature monuments, landscapes, villagescapes and cityscapes. They can also utilize the freedoms of the market in order to create or reinforce combinations of old and new economic supports.

4. RESEARCH AND EDUCATION

4.1 *Research*

The degree of complexity in heritage projects such as the integration of heritage in spatial planning, the difficulties in sustaining a balance between conservation and contemporary styling or the use of historical knowledge for spatial design can increase enormously.

The original assumption of the authors of the Belvedere Memorandum, namely that in cases of practical spatial projects the needed historical knowledge would be available or could be gathered in a smart manner and then quickly be made fit for design commissions, has belied many Belvedere projects. Since the assignment and the problems to be solved differ at every turn and in every territory, new specific (historical) research is regularly needed which takes into account the advantage of elaborating on existing research results.

Analysis and the experience of finding significance in the ancient and the existing fabric in combination with a modern design requires a thorough preparation. Thus preliminary investigation deserves a strong position on the political agenda so that historians can contribute their knowledge of places and territories and designers can anchor their in(ter)ventions in the area in view on their drawing table and can anticipate transformations that are considered necessary. To observe designers who could, suiting their partly intuitive and tactile mode of operation, employ a personal concept, for instance in the contemporary transformation-assignments, is a thrilling prospect. Reflection on the extension of the set of instruments of the designer and the 'obligation' of preliminary survey could lead to an experimental association with history.

We can discern three types of research, fundamental knowledge development, surveys and best practices. Accompanying or generating from fundamental research stands the survey that borrows its urgency from clear-cut assignments or practical commissions. The survey focuses on the tracing of useful elements from the past, on all kinds of potential uses and functional potential and on the many-sided programming of contemporary activity. To that end, the survey cannot be restricted to morphology as the social and mental aspects need to be studied in both survey and planning. The responsibility of the heritage sector will then be added to constructive thinking about sectoral culture that promotes future-oriented thinking about making space, which is thus integrated in the conceptual framework (Bosma 1993; *idem* 2003).

Precisely because of careful attention to deregulating, the national government should reserve sufficient time and money for the creation of a framework within which combinations of old and new receive proper space. Politics and administrative and sociocultural institutions are indispensable to shaping an infrastructure of best practices that integrates the ancient and the modern.

4.2 Education

Designing surveys at both universities and at design offices with practical commissions would gain focus and depth when the context of the need for design (in relation to the major assignments), the programming (multiple land use, combination of the physical and non-physical) and reflection (the translation of ideas in concepts and the thinking about presentation modes) are more thoroughly embedded (Laurel 2003).

History and heritage normally have no place in the curriculum for the professional training that entertains planning for the future (real estate, planning, public administration, economy). Specialized and officially accredited Bachelor's or Master's courses, aiming at an adapted survival of heritage in processes of spatial planning, are few and far between. To achieve coherence in varied education programmes some fixed characteristics are necessary:
- a body of knowledge such as fundamental knowledge development, surveys and practices;
- consciousness that cultural history and heritage do not represent absolute values but regularly transform themselves and attain different meanings;
- a strong interaction between research and education;
- cultivation of town planning and landscaping traditions, conceived as the transfer of an average quality through a system of shaping, construing and material-technical conventions, skills, and knowledge of possibilities in the building sector;
- reflection on the building and design traditions (individual or collective artistic craftsmanship) implicates experiments with recombinations and radical breaks with the tradition;
- insight in policy, planning, participation and building processes.

In the education both of design and heritage, these generating fundamental knowledge (terms, context, history and design, traditions, valuation and selection), and the acquisition of competences to collect knowledge come under the title of transformation processes and products. These collect cultural baggage and contributions for the methods of the various disciplines. The core of the programmes is a design-oriented approach in which both preservation and renewal are taught.

The Belvedere project office has created a Belvedere education network in which three named professors (two at the design education universities at Delft and Wageningen and one at the Master's course for Heritage Studies at VU University in Amsterdam) are making efforts to integrate the Belvedere habitus in their education programmes.

Another recent development in this direction is the installation of the RMIT (2006) at Delft University. In collaboration with the chair of History of Architecture, a melting pot of history, restoration concepts and a design-typology of (re)combinations of ancient and new are employed.

Finally, in February 2008, the international and interfaculty research institute CLUE (Institute for the Heritage and History of Cultural Landscape and Urban Environment) started at VU University with the participation of more than fifty researchers (www.clue.nu). These most excellent institutions should be able to establish a national heritage education programme.

5. ANCHORING HERITAGE IN THE POST-BELVEDERE ERA

The rearrangement of the position of the state and the broadening of a territory-oriented approach asks for alliances with multiple clients and for programmes with clear structure and direction. Instead of hotchpotch spatial planning, the Belvedere habitus should be given a self-evident place in the existing chain of preparation of plans, decision-making and implementation practice. The Belvedere policy strives for the proclamation and awakening of a body of thoughts and the generating of a body of knowledge through education and research programmes through methods and techniques and an implementation practice in transformation arenas. The Netherlands has an established reputation for creativity through human interventions and *grands travaux*. The forthcoming major assignment is to anchor the cultural habitus in communal services, communal administrations and organs, individual companies and large firms. This means that in the post-Belvedere era the step must be taken towards a developing strategy that finds its self-evident combination of ancient and modern in the creation of projects with a layered, multiple land use programme in which culture preservation and cultural renewal are united.

NOTES

1 VU University, Amsterdam, the Netherlands.

REFERENCES

Assmann, A., 2006: *Der lange Schatten der Vergangenheit. Erinnerungskultur und Geschichtspolitik*, München.

Belvedere, 1999: *The Belvedere Memorandum. A policy document examining the relationship between cultural history and spatial planning*, Den Haag.

Bosma, K., 1993: *Ruimte voor een nieuwe tijd: Vormgeving van de Nederlandse regio 1900-1945*, Rotterdam.

Bosma, K., 2003: Het kennislichaam van de stedebouwkunde. Groei en krimp, *Stedebouw en Ruimtelijke Ordening* 5, 10-14.

Brons, R./B. Colenbrander (eds.), 2009: *Atlas of the New Dutch Water Defence Line*, Rotterdam.

Colenbrander, B./MUST (eds.), 2005: *Limes Atlas*, Rotterdam.

Dunk, H.W. von der, 2007: *In het huis van de herinnering. Een cultuurhistorische verkenning*, Amsterdam.

Enklaar, A., 2007: *Nederland tussen nut en naastenliefde. Op zoek naar onze cultuur*, Schiedam.

Frijhoff, W., 2007a: *Dynamisch erfgoed*, Amsterdam.

Frijhoff, W., 2007b: Hemels erfgoed: een reflectie, in F. Grijzenhout (ed.), *Erfgoed. De geschiedenis van een begrip*, Amsterdam, 45-56.

Grijzenhout, F., 2007: Inleiding, in F. Grijzenhout (ed.), *Erfgoed. De geschiedenis van een begrip*, Amsterdam, 1-20.

Hague, C./P. Jenkins (eds.), 2005: *Place identity, planning and participation*, London.

Herngreen, R., 2002: *De 8^e transformatie*, Wageningen.

Herngreen, R., 2005: Eenduidige cultuurhistorie ontkent dynamiek. Pleidooi voor de oningevulde ruimte, in R. Brons/J. Rodermond/G. Wallagh (eds.), *Ontwerpen aan geschiedenis. Een cultuur van ruimte maken*, Rotterdam, 58-60.

Jonker, E., 2001: Historische cultuur in Nederland, in I. Strouken/A. van der Zeijden (eds.): *Het verhaal achter het erfgoed. Regionale geschiedenis en volkscultuur als bindmiddel*, Utrecht, 29-36.

Kobylinski, Z., 2006: Challenges, conflicts and opportunities: cultural landscapes in Poland after the great socio-economic transformation, in W. van der Knaap/A. van der Valk (eds.), *Multiple Landscape. Merging Past and Present. Selected Papers from the fifth International Workshop on Sustainable Land Use Planning 7-9 June 2004*, Wageningen, 45-72.

Laurel, B. (ed.), 2003: *Design research: methods and perspectives*, Cambridge.

Makarius, M., 2004 : *Ruins*, Paris.

Margalit, A., 2006: *Herinnering. Een ethiek voor vandaag*, Amsterdam.

Mommaas, H., 2001: Over de culturele dimensie van de ruimte of hoe die te begrijpen en wat daarmee te doen…, in VROM, *Levende stad. Lagen en dimensies. Pijlers voor netwerkverstedelijking*, Den Haag.

Modernisering Monumentenzorg, 2008: *Modernisering Monumentenzorg*, Den Haag.

Netherlands Architecture Fund, the, 2007: *Podcasting cultuurgeschiedenis. Case: de toekomst van Zandstad*, Rotterdam.

Norberg-Schulz, C., 1979: *Vom Sinn des Bauens. Die Architektur des Abendlandes von der Antike bis zur Gegenwart*, Milan/Stuttgart.

Norberg-Schulz, C., 1996 (1993): *Highlands. Nordic building*, Cambridge/London.

Plumb, J.H., 1969: *The death of the past*, London.

Rijksadviseur voor het Landschap, atelier Rijksbouwmeester, 2006: *Institutioneel ontwerp: relict, revival of revisie*, Den Haag.

Ruimte voor architectuur, 1991: *Ruimte voor architectuur. Nota Architectuurbeleid*, Den Haag (Ministerie van VROM et al.).

Schwarz, M., 2006: Institutioneel ontwerpen herzien. Naar nieuwe design-benaderingen voor de netwerksamenleving, in Rijksadviseur voor het Landschap, atelier Rijksbouwmeester, *Institutioneel ontwerp: relict, revival of revisie*, Den Haag, 10-36.

Wallagh, G., 2005: Urgentie gezocht. Belvederebeleid te ver verwijderd van alledaagse realiteit, in R.J. Brons/J. Rodermond/G. Wallagh (eds.), *Ontwerpen aan geschiedenis. Een cultuur van ruimte maken*, Rotterdam, 19-22.

WEBSITES

www.clue.nu
www.zandstad.nl

3. Changing landscapes of archaeology and heritage

Graham Fairclough[1] & Heleen van Londen[2]

ABSTRACT

Florence and Faro (the European Landscape Convention and the Framework Convention on the Value of Cultural Heritage for Society) offer new lines of vision into archaeological heritage management. Unlike the Valletta Convention, neither of these two young conventions is specifically focused on archaeology and in fact the differences are much more fundamental. In conjunction with a more long-standing but recently maturing landscape dimension within heritage management and archaeologically/historically informed spatial planning, they offer a new context for archaeology and related disciplines. They open new channels into other landscape disciplines and into the integrated practice of landscape management. They suggest different approaches to understanding and responding to the past within the present. They expand the scale of theory and practice to the wider and more fluid concept of landscape itself, with a considerable impact therefore on conceptual frames. In three sections that look backwards, at current trends and at the future, and through the mirror of the PDL/BBO programme, this chapter explores the many faces that the ELC and the Faro Convention offer to archaeological practice, leading towards the introduction of a new European research agenda for ESF/COST focusing on landscape studies balanced between the humanities, the social sciences and the physical sciences.

KEY WORDS

Archaeology, heritage practice, landscape; ELC, social relevance, Faro; future

1. LANDSCAPES OF THOUGHT AND ACTION

1.1 *Metaphorical landscapes: disciplinary contexts and changing situations.*

Landscape can be object and subject, material as well as perceptual, metaphor as well as reality. Rather than dividing the field of research and practice, however, this diversity and multiplicity helps to provide a broad field of common ground. Landscape is above all a shared idea and creates an unparalleled nexus for debate, dialectic and difference within humanities and sciences. It is a place for researchers and practitioners from many varied fields to meet and discuss, using the idea of landscape as a virtual *agora*, *thing or parlement*, within which landscape meanings and significances can be contested as well as agreed. Landscape is an integrative force. It offers a way to dissolve some of the many divisions which have arisen in science, research, policy and practice over the past couple of centuries. This allows archaeological-historical knowledge and policy to be set within wider social contexts through which they will reach new levels of relevance. It might be said that landscape concerns everyday life whereas heritage is for holidays.

Metaphorical landscapes also change and this book clearly shows how the landscape of archaeological and historical research has changed in recent years, creating new ways for research and practice. This might be traced back to New Archaeology's discovery of 'landscape' or 'total archaeology' in the later

1960s or to older paradigms in historical geography and in 'field archaeology' from the 1920s at least. But since about 1990 a tidal wave of major literature, the vast majority, revealingly, being collaborative and often interdisciplinary, has greatly expanded the subject.[3] Not all these books use the word landscape, in Britain for example 'archaeology', 'environment' and 'countryside' were frequent proxies, e.g. Macinnes/Wickham-Jones 1992, but they nonetheless contributed to the emergent new paradigm that we see coming of age in the pages of this book. This reflects not only the PDL/BBO programme, but initiatives in other parts of Europe as well, in many cases facilitated by pan-European EC-funded projects and networks and even beyond.[4]

Archaeology's intellectual, social and organizational landscapes also change, as exemplified by the European Landscape Convention (ELC; Florence 2000). The ELC is 'a genuine innovation compared with other international documents on cultural and natural heritage' (Council of Europe 2008) that seeks to strengthen the democratic social role for landscapes and that is already stimulating new levels of interdisciplinary research and action (Landscape Research Group 2006). The ELC's definition of landscape, that it is "an area, as perceived by people, whose character is the result of the action and interaction of natural and/or human factor", is all-encompassing in its brevity, making room for the interests and concerns of all landscape disciplines and thus bringing archaeological and historical disciplines into synergetic debate and collaborations with other disciplines. The ELC also promotes a wider concept of landscape for archaeology than has been traditional and opens a way to re-visualize the practice of heritage in general.

The landscape of heritage is also changing. Like the ELC, it is responding to a sense of challenge and change at global scale and to broader ideas such as memory and belonging, and identity and community (e.g. Council of Europe 2009, Fairclough *et al.* 2008; Graham/Howard 2008; Sassitelli 2009). Another large recent bibliography, again often collaborative and interdisciplinary, testifies to the wide-ranging and widespread development of landscape ideas within heritage and beyond.[5]

1.2 *Interdisciplinary landscapes*

There is thus a wide and growing context for landscape-based historical and archaeological research and heritage action. The widespread adoption of landscape as a tool in practical spheres such as spatial planning (e.g. Sarlöv Herlin 2004; Selman 2006) has contributed to this, as has the adoption of landscape as a fundamental subject, in scalar or conceptual terms, in a large number of academic disciplines across all domains from humanities and arts to social and physical sciences, as evidenced by recent Position Papers of ESF standing committees and other networks. There is increasing recognition in the context of the European Research Area that in intrinsically interdisciplinary subjects like landscape the benefits of specialization can be outweighed by fragmentation, dissonance and needless tensions between disciplines. Merely multidisciplinary approaches are an insufficient answer, and explorations so far of inter- and transdisciplinary work have taken us little further. In terms of landscape we probably need to seek to be 'postdisciplinary'.

Disciplinary fragmentation has placed significant obstacles in the way of using landscape research to answer major social, economic and environmental challenges. A false distinction can arise between so-called curiosity driven and applied research. This, unfortunately, is especially the case in subjects such as landscape which have everyday practical relevance at all levels from the individual to the collective and in social, economic and environmental fields.

Effective interdisciplinary work is not easy to achieve. No discipline has a monopoly of landscape, but it is easy for a single discipline to see the ELC's definition of landscape as endorsing 'their' approach without noticing the full scope of its potential inclusivity. There will be conflicts between disciplines, of course, because the perspective of 'landscape' does not guarantee the same views and there are fundamental differences between scientific and humanities approaches (e.g. on the nature of data or the role of perception) and there can be conflicts or at least contradictions between cultural and natural heritage viewpoints. On the other hand, these differences could be used as a platform for *constructive* tensions, whilst interdisciplinary work offers reflexive advantages that help disciplines better understand themselves.

In the narrower, but interdisciplinary because of archaeology's theoretical and methodological reach, sphere of this book, landscape offers a new context for heritage management:

- The Belvedere Memorandum (Belvedere 1999) marked the rise of new policy and practice over the past ten years or more in the Netherlands. Alongside the more traditional heritage goals of preservation and awareness-raising, Belvedere stimulated the integration of historical landmarks into planning in order to create lasting improvement and a more socially sustainable and liveable environment.
- The research programme PDL/BBO (*Protecting and Developing the Dutch Archaeological-Historical Landscape*) had a time frame parallel to the Belvedere policy programme. As explained elsewhere in this volume, it aimed to study archaeological values in relation to historical-geographical and development values (see also Bloemers/Wijnen 2002, 4). Whereas Belvedere was about landmarks and planning in general, the BBO programme placed the archaeological-historical disciplines and practices in the planning context as its central focus.

After ten years of experience and self-evaluation, Belvedere openly questions the success of the policy for buried archaeological sites (Linssen/Witsen 2009, 249). On the other hand, Belvedere projects seem mostly to deal with sites or objects, not with landscape, so it is clear that more steps are needed down this road. Integrative strategies on a landscape level need to be further developed, as was done for instance by PDL/BBO. More strategic research is needed.

1.3 *Belonging and ownership: landscape and social archaeology*

'Landscape' in its ELC manifestation is a powerful concept which partly returns to an earlier manifestation of the concept of landscape before it was taken over by elite art and aesthetics since the Renaissance. This older 'everyman's' landscape is landscape as customary territory, polity and community, a view of landscape focused on shared use of land, community and fellowship - land *to which* a community or collective group belongs, rather than land owned *by* someone. Land can be owned, but landscape is always common; landscape can be kept with you in memory and thought, whereas land must be left behind, where it sits.

Although often referred to as a Nordic concept of landscape, because it is most recognized through the work of scholars in Scandinavia, notably of course Kenneth Olwig (e.g. Olwig 2002), it is tempting to assume that it also existed elsewhere in Europe. Britain, for example, has its 1000+-year old territories known as 'townships', farmed and exploited as a unit, and it is difficult not to start to search for its traces or survival further afield. It is a view of landscape with which the underlying mindset and objectives of archaeological research sit easily.

Recent approaches to archaeologically-informed understandings of landscape could be interpreted as reaching back to this sort of landscape. The idea of landscape as biography (Hidding/Kolen/Spek 2001; Van Londen 2006) showcased within the PDL/BBO programme connects with this older idea of landscape. It makes an explicit link between long time spans of environmental history and the individually short, but intergenerationally long, time spans of human lives and human biographies, lived between birth and death in many different ways. On the other hand, the more distanced 'vertical' perspectives of other types of landscape archaeology such as landscape characterisation give a second perspective. This is one that accepts our separation from the past but supports it with the basic notion of stratigraphy and historic processes through time afforded by the maps, aerial and satellite photographs used to understand landscape, either filtered interpretatively through characterisation or unmediated through *Google Earth* and *Bing Maps* (Fairclough 2003). A third approach is offered by more conventional empirical field survey approaches to landscape archaeology. This can go as far as treating landscape as a social place, embedding the researcher in the landscape itself, a form of lived, embodied landscape, bringing this approach closer than its practitioners often acknowledge to phenomenological approaches.

All these techniques illuminate ordinary lives lived and landscapes experienced in the past in a genuinely *longue durée* well beyond written history. They are also beyond written records in other ways because they capture things and events that historic documents never mention, the ahistoric as well as prehistoric aspects of landscape become of critical importance. They can also begin to guess at the cognitive, sensual and mental landscapes as well as the environments, a much simpler task, of our predecessors through the footprints they left on the land. They encourage archaeology and other historical disciplines to look beyond land as property, to go beyond landscape as image and to take up landscape's offer of a social context for understanding the past.

1.4 "The play's the thing...": landscape as context

This social context for archaeology fits well with the ELC's redefinition of landscape in terms of people. In the twenty-first century, most people living in Europe have lives and landscapes that are largely urban or urbanized, but conversely an individual's landscape is often more diverse than ever before, being multiple, polyvalent, mobile, virtual as well as real, multi-locational and global as well as local. Landscape research, even when its main focus is in the past, needs to relate to these altered relationships between people and land. The ELC relocates the idea of landscape in the realm of common current, present-day and everyday experience, or of embodiment and living; this is not very far removed from emerging new ideas of heritage either.

Whilst frequently equated with the 'local', indeed seen by many for policy purposes as the embodiment of local values, landscape can however also be seen as an instrument of global understanding and action and as a universal concept. A hundred and fifty years ago or so it was enlisted as a champion of nationalistic definitions, just as heritage was, but three hundred years ago it was adopted to symbolize the social and educational superiority of the landowning aristocracies. In this trajectory we perhaps see a gradual broadening out of the concept to a more democratic and universal level.

The ELC also reinforces landscape's characteristic dynamism and continuous change, summarized by the ELC as the 'action and interaction of humans and nature'; landscape is not a static depiction. Landscape changes all the time, whether we choose to define it as the world we see and sense around us or as what exists in memories and imaginations. Being dynamic, living, fluid and unfix(ed)(able) is actually central to landscape's very character. Its continuous transformations are not merely a change in the scenery, once a popular synonym for landscape in Britain (e.g. Stamp 1946), but are more far-reaching changes in screenplay, stage directions, cast, audience and performance; new stories are started as the old one ends. Some quality or character of landscape always endures through these transformations, however, and whilst it is always changing and changeable, malleable and vulnerable, with a dynamism that is embedded and immanent, landscape is also resilient. It will survive in one form or another as long as there are people to perceive it, whether or not they call it landscape, and of course in many parts of Europe they use other terms, such as *paysage*, *krajina*, *maisema* and various proxies such as countryside.

The ELC's is a view of landscape immediately recognizable to archaeological research, with people at its centre. But it asks archaeology to change. For example, it leaves little or no room for artificially constructed 'periods' or 'sites'. Working with landscape emphasizes like nothing else does both the temporal and the spatial seamlessness from past to future and across whole territories. In today's perceived landscape all periods of the past will co-exist whenever there is enough knowledge and understanding. Landscape archaeology needs to focus much less on trying to find 'Bronze Age', 'Roman' or 'Medieval' landscapes.

The ELC's definition of landscape encapsulates the interactions and relationships, not the 'balance', between humanity and the rest of the natural world, but understanding landscape historically reinforces its humanity. This is landscape as the opposite of environment – not merely a passive backdrop or stage on which human actors walk, but the play itself, the thing we imagine, write, design, choreograph and construct.

1.5 Frame, canvas, brush – landscape as tool

Landscape is not simply a larger type of archaeological site or historical monument, any more than it is simply a collection of habitats. Landscape is categorically different. It is a tool, a way of seeing, a lens, a filter, a scale, an explanatory model, a descriptive style, an agenda, that can be applied to many fields of research in humanities or sciences, as it often has been to archaeology. It simultaneously provides a frame, canvas and brush for research, for the communication of results to a wide range of audiences and users and for policy. It can help to solve significant current issues such as demographic change, new types of mobility, migration and social belonging, responses and results of climate change, recession and development. It is possible to manage change using landscape, through landscape, as well to manage changes to landscape.

The ELC reminds us that landscape is to be looked after, not simply for its own sake or for its own internalized values, but for wider public interests. Although the Convention refers to the threat of physical and environmental change in its preamble, its main concern can be seen to be more important social concerns, landscape as life, as part of identity and memory, sustainability as first and foremost a social aspiration within which the environmental fits. Some of these are spelt out in the Convention's Preamble, for example "(landscape, in) cultural, ecological, environmental and social fields …. constitutes a resource favourable to economic activity, contributes to the formation of local cultures and … is a basic component of… natural and cultural heritage, contributing to human well-being and … the European identity; (and) for the quality of life for people everywhere".

A second, even more recent, Convention approaches all the same issues, democracy, rights and responsibilities, social relations, the link between past and future, the balancing of change and preservation, social equity and environmental care, but from a different perspective, using 'cultural heritage' rather than landscape as its medium. The Faro Convention, a Framework Convention on the Value of Cultural Heritage for Society (Faro 2005), assesses heritage in terms of social, economic and environmental gains and in doing so it broadly redefines heritage not as something given to people by experts but something already existing, like landscape, in their world view and in their mentality. Experts can help in its understanding and construction but cannot define it. Faro, like Florence, should have a direct and significant bearing on the debates and ideas about archaeological and historical landscape research and practice contained within this book.

2. STEPS ON THE WAY

2.1 Adjusting research

The current conceptualization of landscape means that material aspects of landscape whilst not disregarded are filtered through perception in varying combinations dependent on the observer. Landscape is no longer only seen as an external object but as an idea and way of seeing. Landscape archaeology is adjusting to these newer ideas in many ways:

- Greater recognition that landscape and 'environment' are not the same, that landscape is not natural; tautological undertones of the term 'cultural landscape' are revealed, which 'landscapes' are not cultural?
- Landscape, viewed as culture, reflects its place within human intellect and emotion (perception) as well as in human actions of the past few thousand years.
- This 'culturalness' of landscape is linked to its embodied character. As well as being studied, represented and characterized, landscape is also lived. Distinctions between objectivity and subjectivity dissolve in landscape.
- It is now seen as axiomatic that landscape exists everywhere, not just in a few well-known places with good survival. The ordinary and the typical are seen as fundamental and the marginal can become central.
- In historical-archaeological terms, a landscape-centred research requires the abandonment of the traditional fragmentation of the past into constructs called 'site' and 'period'; the idea of bounded sites is irrelevant.
- Landscape is not always beautiful or green; 'ugly' landscapes-abandoned, post-industrial landscapes – and urban landscapes, the full extent of cities and towns, are seen as having their own values, notably evidential ones, an important open door for archaeology.
- There is no need to see landscape only as scenery. There are other important attributes such as context, biography, character, interest or familiarity that are more suited to historical research.
- A now commonplace recognition across many landscape disciplines that landscape components do not need to be visible. This broadens the link between archaeology and landscape to the seabed component of seascapes, for example, and the 'hidden-scapes' of buried archaeological and palaeo-environmental remains.

Other assumptions need reappraisal, such as that landscape is necessarily old. Landscape is also modern, expressed in concrete and tarmac as well as in trees and grass, by streets as well as by heathland. The recent or contemporary past is a fit subject and a necessary one for landscape and archaeological study. It is also a useful laboratory for addressing other heritage issues relating to the deeper past (Fairclough 2007; Penrose *et al.* 2007).

An ELC-type understanding of landscape makes it impossible to treat it as a field of study for any single discipline. Landscape has long been seen as a field which can bring together related sub-disciplines, for example in archaeology and history, but now it is becoming widely recognized as one of the key interdisciplinary fields that spans wider divisions, including the fundamental but obstructive divide between the humanities and the sciences, as well of course as the smaller divides between, for example, geography and history. The desirability of disciplines, indeed higher level domains, to reach out to each other is a current thread in the strategies of European Research Area bodies, and because of its interdisciplinary strength or at least its potential, landscape was chosen by two of them, the European Science Foundation and the COST Programme, to explore ways of bringing them together.

The ESF-COST Synergy Initiative: "A Network of Networks, New Perspectives on Landscapes" that was set up in 2008 to pursue this agenda took as a starting point the need to map out the interconnections between disciplines and domains, seek doorways through the walls between disciplines and identify social, environmental and economic policy challenges at European scale that the integrative landscape research could help to address. The 'network of networks' set up to achieve this new overview and to define ways forward produced a short "Science Policy Briefing" with *Landscape in a Changing World - Bridging Divides, Integrating Disciplines, Serving Society*' as its working title (Synergy Initiative 2010). It analyses the current strengths (e.g. a recent history of very robust theoretical and methodological development in many disciplines) and weaknesses, e.g. fragmentation, lack of inter-domain collaboration, of landscape research as an integrative discipline, and identifies key threats, notably a failure to capitalize on landscape research's great potential to help address major European policy challenges.

Landscape as concept offers much, its multiplicity and plurality, the way it absorbs and thrives on change, the humanity of landscape but also the environmental evolution and the lessons that we can draw from the past for the future. However, all these strengths are failing to be exploited in facing major social and environmental challenges such as demographic change, increased mobility and changes in how identities are being re-forged, urbanization and climate change responses. The Policy Briefing therefore identifies some of the ways that landscape engages with major policy issues, for instance its ability to contain multiple viewpoints, to link the past with the present through long term narratives and both materiality and mentality and to address change over the very long term. All these viewpoints, especially when integrated, give landscape research an unusual degree of purchase on twentyfirst-century socio-environmental and even demographic concerns. Major social and political issues, such as landscape as common good, the balance between private gain and public benefit, the effects of increased mobility and transience in the population and other demographic changes and the longterm transformations that are at the heart of the human-environment relationship, reside within and can be illuminated by landscape research.

As a result, *Landscape in a Changing World*, hopefully to be published at the same time as this book on the 10th anniversary of the ELC's publication, makes a strong statement of the need for more concerted efforts to be made at structural and institutional as well as academic levels to promote landscape research and its multiple social and environmental uses as a major interdisciplinary field. First steps would be to establish a forum for landscape studies in Europe, forge a vision of the way ahead and start to establish appropriately funded European wide programmes and networks of research.

A strengthened more integrative landscape research will become more fully and constructively interdisciplinary, enabling it to exploit the potential of landscape research to help address big human and political issues. In those spheres, too, a new revitalized idea of landscape is provoking adjustments, which the next section considers briefly.

2.2 *Adjusting policy and practice*

Like landscape research, landscape policy and practice is also evolving. The ELC includes many significant ideas which have the potential to change practice, but in our view the most significant are the democratic nature of landscape as common heritage, the plurality of perceptions and the overriding need for public *awareness* to be encouraged and used and for public *involvement* to be easily enabled. The Faro Convention with its notions of ownership and shared heritage is very relevant when read alongside the Landscape Convention. The issue of landscape is now less about land-use and more about concepts such as place (and placemaking), Quality of Life and *cadre de vie* and personal and collective identity; the ELC defines Landscape Quality Objectives as the aspirations of the public for the places where they live.

The idea, as mentioned above, that spatial planning or heritage management for example can work *through* landscape not simply *for* landscape (e.g. Selman 2006) is highly relevant. In other words, landscape can be used as a framework for shaping how we live in the world, one of the founding principles of Belvedere. This change of perspective can already be tracked in a number of ways:

- The growing influence of the ELC emphasis on landscape being everywhere, not just the special places, which places traditional heritage management (monumentalizing, authoritative and top-down, national, 'looking after the best') into a different context, calling for more widespread, localizing, contextualizing approaches.
- In terms of the ELC, Landscape Management, the management of change, and Planning, the enhancement and contextual creation of future landscapes, are more significant than Protection, which only works at the level of landscape component.
- The ELC has opened the question of agenda and aims. There exist few, if any, agendas specifically designed for landscape management or planning. Most are borrowed or recycled from other spheres, assuming for example that meeting biodiversity goals will necessarily also fulfil landscape objectives, or trying to adapt conservation approaches from building protection when many key issues (authenticity of fabric for example) do not translate into landscape.
- Faro insists that all individuals (alone but also collectively, in 'heritage communities') have both a right to their own cultural heritage and a responsibility to respect and look after other people's. This creates a multiplicity and diversity that challenges traditional heritage practice and indeed points policy further, beyond heritage (Council of Europe 2009).

The character and style of the Florence (Florence 2000) and Faro (Faro 2005) conventions reflects their content. The two conventions are different from the other Council of Europe conventions (Grenada, Valletta, Berne) because they neither prescribe nor prohibit. They recommend making no list of the special but instead to keep sight of the whole. They offer no particular protective measures but instead recommend more fluid ways of thinking whilst leaving detailed implementation to be tailored to national or local contexts. In some ways they even suggest a pulling back from control (although that is safer and easier at this moment in time in some European countries than in others), offering instead the idea that both landscape and heritage need to become issues for all strands of policy from environmental to economic, from social such as housing and placemaking to infrastructural.

They ask for changes in mentality, and offer new paradigms. In particular, unlike the Grenada, Valletta and Berne conventions, they begin with people not with things, fabric or wildlife. Their key is behaviour and human values. They see heritage as a resource and landscape as a way of relating to the world or adapting to changing environments and they are concerned first and foremost with people, being about mentality, discourse and values more than about things. They are socially embedded conventions, which makes them powerful and potentially radical.

2.3 *Reflecting on future objectives*

Future landscape and present-day and future changes are the key to the future of landscape studies, even for historically-focused disciplines. More work is needed on the strongest current drivers of change as they impact on landscape at the European scale, such as globalization, urbanization, transport policies, changing climates, the Common Agricultural Policy, and migration and mobility. Policy responses, e.g. to climate change, are major drivers for change in their own right.

Landscape can hold a mirror to assumptions about how archaeology or history is practised. Whereas traditionally archaeology and history aim to create ('recover') increasingly accurate knowledge about the past, Florence and Faro suggest that the past needs to be researched as part of the present, 'the present past'. The assumption that archaeology must protect its resource at all costs might therefore require further discussion. Where does the social relevance of archaeology sit?

We protect the authentic fabric of a historic building because its fabric is seen as central to its value. If we decide that change and dynamism and the subjectivity of people's perceptions are central to landscape's value, then we might need to reconsider what exactly we wish to protect and how. It might be argued that the way we have been looking after monuments and sites would be the wrong way to look after landscape and that conventional heritage principles and assumptions might not be transferable to landscape.

Archaeologically and historically informed goals for landscape as opposed to site management have rarely been defined, what agenda or ideologies might guide them? There is a habit of borrowing environmental (or 'natural') agendas, but if the crucial distinction between landscape and environment is not maintained then the value of landscape as a useful 'new' policy tool for heritage will be lost.

It is surely possible to devise distinctively archaeological or wider cultural agendas. These might be 'green' in the widest sense but they need not be identical to the aims of the biodiversity movement, which through rewilding or habitat recreation can cause as much damaging change to inherited landscapes as conventional 'development' such as forestry or housing. Where are the cultural, people-centred landscape policies to set alongside environmentally-based green objectives?

In article 1 the ELC identifies three complementary instruments, landscape protection, of course, and of greater relevance, landscape management (regular upkeep of a landscape) and landscape planning (forward-looking action to enhance, restore or create landscape). Whereas protection is focused on 'features' within the landscape, management and planning engage with the whole landscape. Whereas protection concerns the conservation of fabric, management and planning are concerned with managing change and perception and with shaping new landscapes in which the past also needs to be legible. The aims of Belvedere can be seen to be reflected in these formulations.

2.4 PDL/BBO themes revisited: learning through landscape

The insights from PDL/BBO programme have a strong resonance with the ELC. The three themes structuring the results and experiences of the BBO programme as presented in this volume focus on the actors and users that embody the knowledge supply-demand relationship and that represent this relationship within research and between research, policy, practice and public (Ch.VI).

The PDL/BBO programme and the related Belvedere policy are a fascinating illustration of the adjusting of research, policy and practice over a decade to the challenges and opportunities being presented to the historical landscape disciplines and sector by Dutch society. Although the PDL/BBO programme has adopted the central motto of Belvedere, 'conservation through development', it defined its own focus by linking research with action as expressed by the methodological concept of action research. In this way the participants in the programme, researchers and partners, have practised 'learning through landscape' by making use of the following three themes.

Linking knowledge and action

It is commonplace that knowledge of the past can, some would say should, underpin actions in the present (Rigney 2000, 7-9). For landscape, the knowledge we need is about the past *within* the present (the *'present past'*), rather than about the past *per se*. Landscape-led research in the archaeological and historical disciplines needs to be drawn towards a greater concern for the present and future. This will create more social and cultural relevance. Archaeologists (and historians) are not usually well-embedded in landscape policy and decision-making at a European level (or, often, at national levels), either in the academy or in the 'real' world, and neither in research nor practice. In most countries, for example, leadership in implementing the ELC is given to Nature or Environment ministries. Archaeologists and historians need to talk their way deeper into the landscape mainstream if the potential of landscape for archaeological heritage management is to be realized.

This should not be so difficult. There is a research role in all the stages outlined in the ELC implementation guidelines and there is potential for input from archaeological landscape research in all of them, from creating knowledge of the landscape, through defining and starting to achieve landscape quality objectives, to monitoring landscape change (Council of Europe 2008). But archaeological ideas and preoccupations need to be embedded more deeply into spatial planning at all scales and stages, and this means focusing on the present day as well as the past and on making archaeological data relevant to others. One of the implications of the ELC is that research disciplines should try to become more involved with public perception and awareness-raising and with the design and planning of new landscape.

Imagination: facts and constructions

Progress with this theme requires interdisciplinary work and additionally the combination of scientific knowledge of landscape with public understanding. This is problematic. The ELC definition of landscape contains a tension between materiality and perception and this does not necessarily privilege scientific ways of seeing. It is clear that the scientific and academic community cannot have a monopoly of knowledge about landscape and it is not possible to dictate which 'facts' people use in constructing their landscapes, but information can be offered that might modify or enrich how people know, see or understand the world around them. The Dutch policy to present and promote the 'canon' concept is an example of this and of the diverse reception it has received (Adams/Hendriks 2007; Van Oostrom 2007). It is clear from the spin-off of the canon policy and from the PDL/BBO experience, and in particular with activities related to historic narration and landscape biography, that imagination is a rich resource for mobilizing engagement and stimulating creativity from policy, practitioners and public. However, it has also become manifest that these activities have to be embedded in rules of engagement between the actors giving them scientific and democratic legitimation. Landscape can thus be shaped by changing perceptions as well as by changing the environment itself.

Sharing knowledge: stories, maps and designs

Archaeologists and historians or geographers might also ask themselves whether the ways they present their knowledge is best suited to help people construct their mental 'imagined' landscapes. We have learnt to 'read' landscape but are we yet adept at 'writing' it? Many new ways are being developed. Aside from the biography approach basic to the BBO, three books published in three separate countries in the space of less than two years have offered three other distinctive novel approaches (Le Du-Blayo 2007; Nord 2009; Blur/Santillo Frizell 2009). The process of sharing knowledge is two-way, it requires capturing other people's knowledge or perceptions, which as noted above might also mean allowing 'non-scientific' stories to reside next to scientific 'truths'. Landscape can contain both, just as it can contain competing and conflicting perceptions of the same area of land and as it challenges the dominance of expert, specialist or national criteria. Not every person sees or reads an area of land as landscape in the same way.

3. AGENDA FOR THE FUTURE AND THE ESF/COST NETWORK OF NETWORKS

3.1 *Needs and gaps, opportunities and challenges*

This book offers a series of challenges for landscape archaeology and related historical disciplines in terms of policy such as the Florence and Faro Conventions which challenge many heritage assumptions, and of new academic approaches, such as the various experiments being made using contemporary archaeology as a laboratory which fits well with the landscape paradigm. There are signs that a new more landscape-oriented heritage practice is emerging (Fairclough *et al.* 2008; Holtorf 2009), and the concept of social relevance is becoming a common debating point. What will replace the current essentially early twentieth century 'conservation' ethos?

In relation to archaeological practice, to start at the 'narrow' end, new challenges include:

- The increasing invalidity of constructs such as 'sites' and 'periods'; Grenada and Valletta are in particular focused on sites and monuments that are to a greater or lesser extent de-contextualized;
- The difficulty (undesirability) of maintaining emphasis on top-down measurements of significance, at least as traditionally defined (Grenada and Valletta both presuppose an established national canon), because both the ELC and Faro offer more democratic alternatives;
- The purely pragmatic impracticality of extending the traditional protectionist approaches, common to most European nation states and designed to deal with a limited number of special monuments, to a larger heritage defined, like landscape, as being widespread and everywhere and both universal and local.
- As the notion of heritage is broadened, the desirability of finding a more creative response than 'Save!' or 'Rescue!' becomes ever more critical. Heritage needs to be seen as something to be enjoyed, celebrated and used but not necessarily kept. This is the distinction between a heritage asset and a social resource and applies *par excellence* to landscape.

Archaeological research and heritage management also have their own challenges. The recent expansion of archaeological work in Europe since the 1980s, accelerated by the Valletta Convention in 1992 (Valletta 1992), shows us that there are archaeological remains everywhere. We are collecting more data than we can handle, with an ever greater need for research to be rigorously question-led. We have a different perspective now than in the 1970s and 1980s when protection and rescue seemed crucial tasks. Now understanding is most important, knowledge is seen as more than just data and as something that gains in value when transmitted beyond the discipline.

There is well-trodden ground here on the question of the identification (as the ELC calls it) of landscape, indeed there is a plethora of landscape survey and analysis techniques. More comparative work is needed on these methods of understanding, characterisation and assessment (see Fairclough/Rippon 2002; Fairclough/Grau Møller 2008), to be followed by more exchanges of expertise between countries and disciplines: "there is an acute awareness of the inadequacies of the most frequently used theoretical and methodological instruments for operational needs. Too often, they belong to *compartmentalized disciplinary universes*, while the landscape demands adequate responses within cross-disciplinary time and space constraints....." (Council of Europe 2008 with added emphasis).

The ELC also offers a framework to use understanding of landscape and perception for social and therefore economic and environmental goals, and Faro offers a similar framework for heritage. Old-fashioned archaeological data need to be converted into landscape synthesis in order to fit into these changing intellectual frameworks and paradigms. This is not landscape archaeology in its traditional sense, but archaeology using landscape as the PDL/BBO did to connect with current socio-political issues rather than merely heritage protection, and using landscape as Belvedere did for wider planning goals.

Even greater challenges were illuminated in 2008-2009 during the process of preparing the Landscape Science Policy Briefing for the European Science Foundation and the COST programmes mentioned above (Synergy Initiative 2010). Carried out through a multidisciplinary network of networks, with the contribution of 120 landscape researchers attending one or more of the network's five workshops, and through debates at other conferences and arenas, the Briefing was conceived as a collaborative exploration between a number of landscape disciplines within the Humanities to explore the scope for further interdisciplinary work.

There is already a strong drive within the European Research Area towards the lowering of boundaries between discipline and domains, and landscape was seen by the ESF Humanities committee, for example, as one of the primary spheres in which the humanities and the sciences might reach out to the physical, earth and social sciences where there are equally flourishing landscape disciplines. The network drawing up the Briefing located this drive for collaboration in the light of major social, economic, demographic and environmental challenges. It was felt that fully interdisciplinary approaches to landscape research, underpinned by the social and cultural aspirations of Florence and Faro, could begin to help address those big issues facing European and indeed global society.

3.2 Thinking bigger

The abiding message of Belvedere, the PDL/BBO programme and its results, the Landscape Convention and the papers within this book is that landscape archaeology and historical landscape studies need to "think bigger". The greatest general threat to landscape research was identified by the synthesis in the preceding chapter as being a potential failure to miss opportunities afforded by the current debate on major socio-environmental challenges. Rising to the opportunities those challenges offer to landscape research will need more ambitious agendas. The sites that landscape archaeology studies need to become regions. Fences need to be torn down to allow partnership with other landscape disciplines. Heritage should be seen as socially relevant, looking forward to tomorrow as well as back to yesterday. The contemporary relevance of studying the past needs to be stated ever more loudly and the history, achievements and mistakes of our predecessors over thousands of years need to be understood both for their own sake and for the lessons they have for life today and tomorrow.

Knowing the past prompts thought about the future, especially through the filter of landscape, which as archaeologists know is only one moment in a continuing transformation. What is the best way to make decisions about a landscape's future? Where do we put new motorways or runways, where do we build new houses as our populations grow, how do we fit new essentials such as wind turbines or nuclear reactors into inherited landscapes, how will we react to pressure from population growth, inward migration and loss of land to the sea?

Cherished ideals of 'saving' the special, the significant and the highly valued, especially in the most densely populated and pressurized of countries like the Netherlands, will be much less useful when the whole territory, as the ELC expresses it, must be looked after in some way. The Council of Europe's Faro Convention (Faro 2005) on the value of heritage for society with its notions of ownership and shared heritage becomes very relevant when read alongside the Landscape Convention (Florence 2000). Is it democratic to have less interest, less careful planning (at worst, unregulated development), in an 'undesignated' majority of each country that is usually where the bulk of the population lives?

New approaches would seem to be needed. One of these, as an example, might be to use the idea of sensitivity instead of significance, based on understanding the capacity of any landscape to absorb or benefit from change. Sensitivity, or its opposite, resilience, is perhaps a better tool for managing change in the landscape than significance or value. Unlike significance, sensitivity is usable in terms of all landscapes and is directly related to change and threats.

Florence and Faro whisper to us of the innate conservatism of heritage in its traditional and conventional paradigms. It is possible through the eye of landscape to question whether researching the past necessarily needs to be tied to preserving its remains. In the past few decades, 'rescue' and conservation were efficient platforms for the growth of archaeology as both discipline and practice, but being tied to preservationist goals might not necessarily be justified for landscape research or management.

Landscape often seems to be actually defined by being at risk, threatened or under pressure (Lozny 2006), rather than by its true intrinsic characteristics, one of which is change. Change is what archaeologists and historians study and find interesting, especially in landscape studies, and this is where archaeologists and historians can get most readily engaged with interdisciplinary landscape studies and policy. Evidence of change tells at least as much about the past as evidence of continuity does, and both can explain present landscape character and future landscape directions (Fairclough 2007).The ELC is also about change, encouraging us to look forward to new landscapes. One archaeological heritage agenda should be to explore how those new landscapes will in their turn be capable of future archaeological analysis, to determine how legible the past, our past and our future, will be within them in the future.

3.3 The biggest step – outside the academy?

More fundamentally, we might usefully ask how much is actually known about what landscape actually means to the wider population. There seem to be few well tested methods for securing community and civil society participation in creating landscape understanding or for capturing (or harvesting?) public views. There may be even fewer for *understanding* public views (what do people mean when they speak of beauty in the landscape?) or using them sensitively (how to align the non-scientific with the scientific, the myths and stories with the results of excavations or archival research, see e.g. Clark/Darlington/Fairclough 2004).

How precisely do people construct their mental landscape, in what way does the world around them, or heritage for that matter, help to create identities and belongings? What is most valued and why, and by whom? How does landscape differ in relation to family background, socio-economic status, degree of marginalization or alienation, position in relation to 'mainstream' society; what are the landscapes of migrant, displaced, mobile liminal communities? Where does landscape meet issues of equity, justice, property and governance? Seeing landscape simply as land or environment cannot address any of these socio-cultural questions, but landscape in its perceptual, people-centred guise can. Archaeological and historical researchers, if working in broad interdisciplinary and interdomain frames, can potentially offer insights to all these questions.

Such viewpoints suggest new roles for archaeologists and historians other than only using landscape as an archive to learn about the past and to be preserved as a scientific resource. They could for example learn to be a 'designing discipline', or to work in other ways to help shape the future. It might be said that such work belongs to other disciplines, but leaving it entirely to others risks marginalizing archaeological and historical perspectives. The ELC defines landscape quality objectives as "the formulation by the competent public authorities of the aspirations of the public with regard to the landscape features of their surroundings". Competent public authorities should include archaeological agencies, some members of the public are archaeologists or have archaeological interests and there are many two-way conversations that archaeologists need to have with the rest of society.

The new approaches and directions that landscape policy might take requires us to look at a bigger picture, to engage with the causes not the effects, for example, to focus on management and planning more than on protection, and to use landscape as a means to broader goals as well as being an end in itself. It requires research to start with people rather than with nature. Landscape primarily offers cultural services rather than ecological services, although these might follow as by-products, consequences or delivery mechanisms. There is perhaps an argument that it would more honestly reflect the state of the world to develop a cultural services approach with ecological benefits rather than an eco-systems approach. As mentioned above, it is necessary to be much more clear-sighted about the aims of historically/archaeologically informed landscape policy. Biodiversity for example is a product of human use of the land over many centuries, but that does not mean that its preservation or enhancement is automatically a *landscape* policy objective.

Landscape is first and foremost a cultural issue and it should be contributing to cultural ends, to mainstream socio-economic and socio-environmental aims. Landscape is an important concept. It raises and meets big challenges which we are only part way to meeting, we need to step further outside conventional ideas of what archaeology is, what it is for, and what it means to be an archaeologist. We need to 'think big'.

NOTES

1 English Heritage, London, England.
2 Amsterdam University, Amsterdam, the Netherlands.
3 Examples of recent major literature on landscape archaeology and heritage in the first author's country include, for example, Archaeologies of Landscape (Ashmore/Knapp 1999), Making English Landscapes (Barker/Darvill (eds.) 1997), Landscape: politics and perspectives (Bender 1993), Unravelling the Landscape (Bowden 1999), The Archaeology of Landscape (Everson/Williamson (eds.) 1998), Yesterday's World, Tomorrow's Landscape (Fairclough/Lambrick/McNab (eds.) 1999), Ideas of Landscape (Johnson 2007), All Natural Things: Archaeology and the Green Debate (Macinnes/Wickham-Jones (eds.) 1992), Approaches to Landscape (Muir 1999). In the the second author's country they include Landschap in meervoud: perspectieven op het Nederlandse landschap (Kolen/Lemaire (eds.) 1999), De Biografie van het Landschap (Hidding/Kolen/Spek 2001 in Bloemers et al. 2001), Bodemarchief in Behoud en Ontwikkeling, De conceptuele grondslagen (Bloemers et al. 2001), Sacrificial landscapes. Cultural Biographies of persons, objects and 'natural' places in the Bronze Age of the southern Netherlands (Fontijn 2002), Landscaping the Powers of Darkness and Light. 600 BC – 350 AD settlement concerns of Noord-Holland in wider persective (Therkorn 2004), De biografie van het landschap, drie essays over landschap, geschiedenis en erfgoed (Kolen 2005), Midden-Delfland. The Roman Native Landscape Past and Present (Van Londen 2006), The homecoming of religious practice: an analysis of offering sites in the wet low-lying parts of the landscape in the Oer-IJ area (2500 BC-AD 450) (Kok 2008), Living Landscape: Bronze Age settlement sites in the Dutch river area (c.2000-800 BC) (Arnoldussen 2008).
4 Examples of pan-European landscape-based research include Pathways to Europe's Landscape (Clark/Darlington/Fairclough (eds.) 2003), One Land, Many Landscapes (Darvill/Godja (eds.) 2001), Landscape as heritage COST A27 (Fairclough/Grau Møller 2008), Europe's Cultural Landscape: archaeologists and the management of change (Fairclough/Rippon (eds.) 2002), Envisioning Landscape Archaeology (Hicks/McAtackney/Fairclough 2007), Frühe Kulturlandschaften in Europa (Kelm (ed.) 2005), People and Nature in Historical Perspective (Laszlovszky/Szabo (eds.) 2003), The Archaeology and Anthropology of Landscape: Shaping your landscape (Ucko/Layton (eds.) 1999). Examples from other landscape disciplines such as geography, planning or ecology include Paysage: de la connaissance à l'action (Landscapes: from knowledge to action) (Berlan-Darque/Terrasson/Luginbuhl (eds.) 2007), Perception and Evaluation of Cultural Landscapes (Doukellis/Mendoni (eds.) 2004), Nordic Landscapes (Jones/Olwig (eds.) 2008), Multiple Landscape. Merging Past and Present (Van der Knaap/Van der Valk (eds.), Landscape Interfaces: Cultural Heritage in Changing Landscapes (Palang/Fry (eds.) 2003), Leggere il paesaggio. Confronti internazionali (Scazzosi (ed.) 2002) and Landscape (Wylie, 2008)
5 A few examples of landscape research in practice in spatial planning and heritage include: A Heritage Reader (Fairclough/Harrison/Jameson/Schofield (eds.) 2008, Cultural Landscape - across disciplines (Hernik (ed.) 2009): Stretching Beyond the Horizon: A Multiplanar Theory of Spatial Planning and Governance (Hillier 2007), Landscapes Under Pressure (Lozny (ed.) 2006), Landscape Ideologies (Meier (ed.) 2006), Planning at Landscape Scale (Selman 2006).

6 Far too many to cite, some examples include Landscape Archaeology – An Introduction to Fieldwork Techniques (Aston/Rowley 1974), Unravelling the Landscape, an Inquisitive Approach to Archaeology (Bowden 1999), The Future of Surface Artefact Survey in Europe (Bintliff/Kuna/Venclová (eds.) 2000).

REFERENCES

Adams, T./M. Hendriks, 2007: *Culturele canonvorming. Een eerste inventarisatie*, Amsterdam.

Belvedere, 1999: *The Belvedere Memorandum. A policy document examining the relationship between cultural history and spatial planning*, The Hague.

Bloemers, J.H.F/M.-H. Wijnen, 2002: *Protecting and Developing the Dutch Archaeological-Historical Landscape*, The Hague.

Blur, H./B. Santillo Frizell (eds.), 2009: *Via Tiburtina*: Space, Movement and Artefacts in the Urban Landscape, Rome.

Clark, J./J. Darlington/G. Fairclough, 2004. *Using Historic Landscape Characterisation*, London.

Council of Europe, 2008: *CM/Rec. (2008) 3: Guidelines for the Implementation of the European Landscape Convention.* (https://wcd.coe.int/ViewDoc.jsp?id=1246005).

Council of Europe, 2009: *Heritage and Beyond,* Strasbourg. (Accessed 19 December, 2009 at http://www.coe.int/t/dg4/cultureheritage/heritage/identities/beyond_en.asp).

Fairclough, G.J., 2003: The long chain: archaeology, historical landscape characterisation and time depth in the landscape, in H. Palang/G. Fry(eds.), *Landscape Interfaces: Cultural Heritage in Changing Landscapes*, Dordrecht, 295-317 (reprinted with revisions in Fairclough et al. (eds.) 2008, 408-424).

Fairclough, G.J., 2007: The contemporary and future landscape: change & creation in the later 20th century, in L. McAtackney/M. Palus/A. Piccini (eds.), *Contemporary and Historical Archaeology in Theory,* Oxford (Studies in Contemporary and Historical Archaeology 4, BAR International Series 1677), 83-88.

Fairclough, G./P. Grau Møller (eds.), 2008: *Landscape as Heritage. The Management and Protection of Landscape in Europe, a summary by the Cost A 27 project 'LANDMARKS,* Bern (Geographica Bernensia 79).

Fairclough, G.J./R.Harrison/J. Jameson Jr./J. Schofield (eds.), 2008: *A Heritage Reader,* London.

Fairclough, G./S. Rippon (eds.), 2002: *Europe's Cultural Landscape: archaeologists and the management of change,* Brussels.

Faro, 2005: *Council of Europe Framework Convention on the Value of Cultural Heritage for Society,* Strasbourg (Council of Europe).

Florence, 2000: *European Landscape Convention. Florence, 20 October 2000,* Strasbourg (Council of Europe).

Graham, B./P. Howard, 2008: *The Ashgate Research Companion to Heritage and Identity*, Aldershot.

Hidding, M./J. Kolen/T. Spek, 2001: De biografie van het landschap. Ontwerp voor een inter- en multidisciplinaire benadering van de landschapsgeschiedenis en het culturele erfgoed, in J.H.F. Bloemers,/R. During/J.N.H. Elerie/H.A. Groenendijk/M. Hidding/J. Kolen/Th. Spek/M.-H. Wijnen, 2001: *Bodemarchief in Behoud en Ontwikkeling. De conceptuele grondslagen*, Den Haag, 7-109.

Holtorf, C., 2009: World Heritage in Perspective [in Comments on Terje Brattli, 'Managing the Archaeological World Cultural Heritage: consensus or rhetoric' in NAJ 42(1)2009)], *Norwegian Archaeological Review,* 42, 196-200.

Landscape Research Group, 2006: Cultural Landscapes in the 21st Century, *Landscape Research*, 31(4) (themed issue on the ELC).

Le Du-Blayo, L. (with contributors), 2007: *Le Paysage en Bretagne: enjeux et défis.* Rennes.

Linssen, M./P.P. Witsen, 2009: <*Belvedere.nu*>. *Praktijkboek cultuurhistorie en ruimtelijke ontwikkeling,* Utrecht.

Londen, H. van, 2006: Cultural biography and the power of image, in W. van der Knaap/A. van der Valk (eds.), *Multiple Landscape. Merging Past and Present. Selected Papers from the fifth International Workshop on Sustainable Land Use Planning 7-9 June 2004,* Wageningen, 171-181.

Lozny, L. (ed.), 2006: *Landscapes Under Pressure: Theory and Practice of Cultural Heritage Research and Preservation,* New York.

Macinnes, L./C.R. Wickham-Jones, 1992: Time-depth in the countryside: archaeology and the environment. in L. Macinnes/C.R. Wickham-Jones (eds.), *All Natural Things: Archaeology and the Green Debate,* Oxford (Oxbow Monograph 21), 1-13.

Nord, J.M, 2009: Changing Landscapes and Persistent Places, *Acta Archaeological Lundensia,* Lund (Series in Prima Quarto, No 29).

Olwig, K.R., 2002: *Landscape, Nature, and the Body Politic. From Britain's Renaissance to America's New World,* Madison.

Oostrom, F. van, 2007: *A Key to Dutch History. Report by the Committee for the Development of the Dutch Canon,* Amsterdam.

Penrose, S. (with contributors), 2007: *Images of Change – an archaeology of England's contemporary landscape,* London.

Rigney, A., 2000: Introduction: Values, Responsibilities, History, in: J. Leerssen/A. Rigney (eds.), *Historians and Social Values,* Amsterdam, 7-15.

Sarlöv Herlin, I., 2004: New challenges in the field of spatial planning: landscapes. *Landscape Research* 29, 399 -411.

Sassitelli, M., 2009: *Becoming Europeans: Cultural Identity and Cultural Policies,* London.

Selman, P., 2006: *Planning at Landscape Scale,* London.

Stamp, L.D., 1946: *Britain's Structure and Scenery,* London.

Synergy Initiative 2010: *Landscape in a Changing World. Bridging Divides, Integrating Disciplines, Serving Society,* Strasbourg/Brussels (Science Policy Briefing by the ESF-COST Synergy Initiative 'A European Network of Networks: New Perspectives on Landscapes').

Valletta 1992: *European Convention on the Protection of the Archaeological Heritage (Revised) Valetta,* 16.I.1992, Strasbourg (Council of Europe).

WEBSITES: FINDING FLORENCE AND FARO

Council of Europe Framework Convention on the Value of Cultural Heritage for Society, European Treaty Series 1999: http://www.coe.int/t/dg4/cultureheritage/heritage/Identities/default_en.asp. (Accessed 19 December, 2009).

European Landscape Convention, European Treaty Series 176: http://www.coe.int/t/dg4/cultureheritage/heritage/Landscape/default_en.asp. (Accessed 21 December, 2009).

IX

SUMMARY

Las Médulas (ES): Canal from Roman period hydraulic network facilitating gold mining. *Photo: G.S. Reher.*

IX Summary

A. KEY WORDS

(Hidden) archaeological-historical landscapes, management of change, conservation through development paradox; European Landscape Convention, the Netherlands and Europe; inter- and transdisciplinarity, knowledge-action nexus, biography of landscape

B. SUMMARY

This book is about understanding and managing the archaeological-historical landscape and its heritage in the Netherlands and in Europe.

The basic problem is to what extent we can know past and mainly invisible landscapes and how we can use this still hidden knowledge for actual sustainable management of the landscape's cultural-historical values. The critical point is whether researchers, policy-makers, practitioners and society are aware of the fact that the visible historic landscapes are literally just a small proportion of many more, diverse and older (almost) invisible landscapes.

The widening scope of landscape and heritage research includes the 'ordinary' landscapes. It is also recognized that heritage management is increasingly 'the management of future change rather than simply protection'. This presents us with a paradox: to know and preserve our historic environment we have to collaborate with those who wish to transform it and in order to apply our expert knowledge we have to make it suitable for policy and society.

The answer presented by the Dutch PDL/BBO programme is an integrative landscape approach by applying inter- and transdisciplinarity and by establishing links between archaeological-historical heritage and planning and between research and policy. This is supported by two unifying concepts, biography of landscape and action research.

The synthesis of the results focuses upon the interaction between knowledge, policy and imagination centred around the public. Three types of action characterize this interaction, 'knowledge and action' covers the relationship between research, policy and public, 'imagination' focuses on the interaction between research and design and the role of facts and constructions of the past and the future; stories, maps and designs mediate the 'sharing of knowledge'.

Considering the integrative landscape approach in a European perspective makes us aware of the resourcefulness of the diversity of landscapes, social and institutional structures, various types of problems, approaches and ways forward. In addition, two related issues have been elaborated, the management of knowledge creation for landscape research and management and the prospects for the way forward in the near future. What they have in common is that we have to learn from the past through the landscape.

X
APPENDIX

Juminda (EE): 1941 sea mine aside a boatshed on the Baltic coast. *Photo: M. Kõivupuu.*

X.1 List of selected abbreviations

AHM	Archaeological Heritage Management
AMK	Dutch: Archeologische Monumenten Kaart
	English: Archaeological Monuments Map
AMZ	Dutch: Archeologische MonumentenZorg (= AHM)
BBO	see PDL/BBO
COST	European Cooperation in Science and Technology
CoE	Council of Europe
EC	European Commission
EIA	Environmental Impact Assessment
ELC	European Landscape Convention
ESF	European Science Foundation
GIS	Geographical Information System
HLC	Historic Landscape Characterisation
IKAW	Dutch: Indicatieve Kaart Archeologische Waarden
	English: Indicative Map Archaeological Values
KNA	Dutch: Kwaliteitsnorm Nederlandse Archeologie
	English: Dutch Archaeology Quality Standard
LANDMARKS	Understanding pre-industrial structures in rural and mining landscapes (Action COST A27)
MW	Dutch: Monumentenwet (1961 and 1988)
	English: Monuments and Historic Buildings Act (1961 and 1988)
NOaA	Dutch: Nationale Onderzoeksagenda Archeologie
	English: National Archaeological Research Agenda
NGO	Non-Governmental Organisation
NWO	Dutch: Nederlandse Organisatie voor Wetenschappelijk Onderzoek
	English: Netherlands Organisation for Scientific Research
PDL/BBO	Protecting and Developing the Dutch Archaeological-Historical Landscape
	Dutch: Bodemarchief in Behoud en Ontwikkeling
Planarch	Planning and archaeology (Interreg IIIB programme)
RACM	Dutch: Rijksdienst voor Archeologie, Cultuurlandschap en Monumenten
	English: National Service for Archaeology, Cultural Landscape and Built Heritage (integration of ROB and RDMZ)
RCE	Dutch: Rijksdienst voor het Cultureel Erfgoed
	English: Cultural Heritage Agency (successor of RACM)
RDMZ	Dutch: Rijksdienst voor de Monumentenzorg
	English: State Service for the Conservation of the Built Heritage
ROB	Dutch: Rijksdienst voor het Oudheidkundig Bodemonderzoek
	English: State Service for Archaeological Investigations
Wamz	Dutch: Wet op de Archeologische Monumentenzorg 2007
	English: Archaeological Heritage Management Act 2007

X.2 Glossary of specific subject-related concepts and terms used in this book

In this book a limited number of terms have been used that are specifically related to the subject and approach of the PDL/BBO programme. They are briefly explained here. A more extensive explanation, sometimes related to a specific research context, will be found in the various contributions in this volume.

ACTION RESEARCH

Action research is inquiry in which participants and researchers cogenerate knowledge through collaborative communicative processes in which the contributions of all participants are taken seriously. The meanings constructed in the inquiry process lead to social action, or these reflections on action lead to the construction of new meanings. Action research treats the diversity of experiences and capacities within the local group as an opportunity for the enrichment of the research/action process and produces valid research results. Action research is context centred; it aims to solve real-life problems in context.

Greenwood, D.J./M. Levin, 2003: Reconstructing the relationship between universities and society through action research, in N.K. Denzin/Y.S. Lincoln (eds.), *The Landscape of qualitative research: Theories and issues*, Thousand Oaks, 131-166.

Reason, P./H. Bradbury (eds.), 2001: *The SAGE Handbook of Action Research. Participative Inquiry and Practice*, London.

ARCHAEOLOGICAL-HISTORICAL LANDSCAPE

The cultural-historical landscape as an organic and cohesive combination of historic buildings and ensembles and historical-geographical and archaeological elements and structures without any particular limitation in time.

BELVEDERE

In a joint effort of four ministries (of Education, Culture and Science, of Housing, Spatial Planning and the Environment, of Agriculture, Nature and Food Quality, and of Transport, Public Works and Water Management) the Dutch government in 1999 initiated the so-called Belvedere programme, which was concluded in 2009 (Belvedere 1999). It considered the three types of cultural historical resources - archaeological, historical-geographical and historical - from an integrated perspective. Basic is the notion of archaeological-historical values as a resource for experiencing and expressing identity by preservation, innovation and design: a (re)source of inspiration, creativity and storytelling. Consequently, 'cultural-historic identity is to be seen as a determining factor in the future spatial design of the Netherlands, for which the government shall aim to create appropriate conditions'. The key concept of Belvedere has been 'conservation through development'.

Belvedere, 1999: *The Belvedere Memorandum. A policy document examining the relationship between cultural history and spatial planning*, The Hague.

BIOGRAPHY OF LANDSCAPE

The biographical approach as explored in the PDL/BBO programme follows a *geographical* (Van Beek et al. 2008, 179-184) line by integrating various insights from cultural geography (Samuels 1979; Meinig 1979; Thrift 1996), anthropology (e.g. Ingold 2000) and landscape archaeology (e.g. Bender 1993; Bradley 2002). A central topic is the interdisciplinary study of spatial formations and *trans*formations within landscapes and regions from the past up to the present. The geographical line of research can be explained in more detail by four observations on the various dimensions of landscape transformations, their contexts and the perceptions involved.

First, a starting point for biographical studies is that spatial transformations *always* involve complex interactions between physical structures on the one hand and changes in cultural values and mentalities on the other hand, that is between Samuels' landscapes of expression and landscapes of impression.

Second, all spatial transformations are 'multilayered' in the sense that they necessarily involve a reordering, reuse and re-presentation of the past, which lends an almost non-linear character to landscape processes.

Third, all societies develop distinctive, more or less culturally specific ways of dealing with their environment. Therefore landscape is never simply a *habitat* or a static built environment, but also a *habitus* reflecting, transmitting and renewing the spatial habits and values of culture.

Fourth, biography studies of landscape not only help us understand processes currently taking place in our environment, but also shed light on the development of heritage practices. Heritage is not a static spatial phenomenon, but it shapes itself around broader spatial developments and cultural changes (Lowenthal 1996; Rooijakkers 1999a).

Beek, R. van/J.H.F. Bloemers/L. Keunen/H. van Londen/J. Kolen, 2008: The Netherlands, in G. Fairclough/P. Grau Møller (eds.), *Landscape as Heritage. The Management and Protection of Landscape in Europe, a summary by the Cost A 27 project LANDMARKS*, Bern (Geographica Bernensia 79), 179-184.

Bender, B., 1993: Stonehenge - contested landscapes (medieval to present-day), in B. Bender (ed.), *Landscape - politics and perspectives*, Oxford/Providence, 245-280.

Bradley, R., 2002: *The past in prehistoric societies*, London/New York.

Ingold, T., 2000: The temporality of landscape, in T. Ingold, *The perception of the environment. Essays in livelihood, dwelling and skill*, London/New York, 189-208.

Lowenthal, D., 1996: *Possessed by the past. The heritage crusade and the spoils of history*, New York/London.

Meinig, D., 1979: The beholding eye. Ten versions of the same scene, in D.W. Meinig (ed.), *The interpretation of ordinary landscape*, New York/Oxford, 33-47.

Rooijakkers, G., 1999: Mythisch landschap: verhalen en rituelen als culturele biografie van een regio, in J. Kolen/T. Lemaire (eds.), *Landschap in meervoud. Perspectieven op het Nederlandse landschap in de 20ste/21ste eeuw*, Utrecht, 301-326.

Samuels, M.S., 1979: The biography of landscape. Cause and culpability, in D.W. Meinig (ed.), *The interpretation of ordinary landscapes*, New York/Oxford, 51-88.

Thrift, N., 1996: *Spatial transformations*, London.

CONSERVATION THROUGH DEVELOPMENT

'Conservation through development' is the key concept of Belvedere. "By seeking new uses, old landscapes and buildings can be saved. However, it is just as much a question of 'development through conservation'. By using our cultural heritage in a frugal and responsible manner, we are investing in the development and strengthening of our identity, knowledge, comfort, business climate and potential for tourism."

Belvedere, 1999: *The Belvedere Memorandum. A policy document examining the relationship between cultural history and spatial planning*, The Hague, 33.

CULTURAL HERITAGE

All those remains and remembrances which link us to our past, whether in the landscape around us or in the arts, languages or traditions. It includes especially the physical remains of the past: historic buildings and structures, archaeological sites, artefacts, palaeo-environmental deposits, historic landscapes and townscapes, and marine heritage.

Laarse, R. van der, 2005: Erfgoed en de constructie van vroeger, in R. van der Laarse (ed.), *Bezeten van vroeger. Erfgoed, identiteit en musealisering*, Amsterdam, 1-28.
Schofield, J., 2008: Heritage Management, Theory and Practice, in G. Fairclough/R. Harrison/J.H. Jameson Jr./J. Schofield (eds.), *The Heritage Reader*, London/New York, 16-20.

EIA: ENVIRONMENTAL IMPACT ASSESSMENT

The statutory assessment of the effects of certain public and private projects on the environment prior to deciding on their implementation.

See Jones Ch. V.6

EUROPEAN LANDSCAPE CONVENTION

The European Landscape Convention (ELC) was drawn up in 2000 by the Council of Europe. The ELC came into force in 2004. At present 36 states have signed or ratified the ELC, it was ratified by the Netherlands in 2005.

According to Article 1 "Landscape means an area, as perceived by people, whose character is the result of the action and interaction of natural and/or human factors."

The scope "covers natural, rural, urban and peri-urban areas. It includes land, inland water and marine areas. It concerns landscapes that might be considered outstanding as well as everyday or degraded landscapes." (Article 2). According to Article 5 of the Convention, signatories to the ELC are obligated to take the following steps:
- acknowledging landscape in legislation;
- involving the general public in the development of landscape policy;
- integrating landscape into land-use planning and other relevant policy fields;
- implementing spatial policy for landscape planning;
- maintaining and conserving landscapes, and;
- engaging in international co-operation.

The value of landscapes is spelt out in the Convention's Preamble, for example "(landscape, in) cultural, ecological, environmental and social fields .... constitutes a resource favourable to economic activity, contributes to the formation of local cultures and ... is a basic component of... natural and cultural heritage, contributing to human well-being and ... the European identity; (and) for the quality of life for people everywhere".

Florence, 2000: *European Landscape Convention. Florence, 20 October 2000*, Strasbourg (Council of Europe).
http://www.coe.int/t/dg4/cultureheritage/heritage/Landscape/default_en.asp. (Accessed on 26 March, 2010)

HISTORIC LANDSCAPE CHARACTERISATION (HLC)

Historic Landscape Characterisation is a methodology developed in England during the 1990s to assess the cultural-historical values for the management of change in historic landscapes. The principles behind the HLC are:
- it is the present-day landscape as history that is the main object;
- it is about landscape, not sites;
- all aspects of the landscape are taken into consideration;
- in a human landscape bio-diversity is considered as a cultural phenomenon;
- characterisation is a matter of interpretation and perception, not record and facts;
- collective and people's views are valued alongside more expert views;
- the aim is management of change, not preservation;
- the process of characterisation must be transparent and easy to understand;
- HLC results should be integrated into environmental and heritage management records.

Clark, J./J. Darlington/G. Fairclough, 2004: *Using Historic Landscape Characterisation, s.l.*, English Heritage and Lancashire County Council, 5-10.

INTERNAL AND EXTERNAL INTEGRATION

Integration as applied in the PDL/BBO programme has three dimensions. Within the world of research there is first the need for integration between the cultural historic disciplines, the 'internal' integration, and second for integration between the cultural historic disciplines (archaeology, historical geography, architectural history) and the other relevant disciplines from the social sciences, the design and construction disciplines and the natural and physical sciences, the 'external' integration. This is covered by interdisciplinarity. The third dimension has to do with integration of research with policy and public participation, a wider meaning of 'external' integration covering transdisciplinarity.

See Van der Valk Ch. II.2, 31-35.

MALTA (CONVENTION/TREATY)

See Valletta.

MULTI-, INTER-, TRANSDISCIPLINARY RESEARCH

Multidisciplinary research is characterized by parallel tracks, each situated within a particular academic field, between which there is only limited interaction; while knowledge is exchanged, it is not integrated. Instead, each field works within its own conceptual framework and according to its own methods.

Interdisciplinary research involves collaboration between various unrelated academic fields for the express purpose of crossing boundaries, such that researchers can create new knowledge (so-called unifying concepts) and achieve a common research goal. Here the adjective 'unrelated' indicates that the disciplines in question differ with regard to their research paradigms, for example differences regarding quantitative, qualitative, analytical or interpretative approaches.

In transdisciplinary research, academics from different unrelated disciplines collaborate closely with non-academics in order to achieve certain research objectives and to develop new knowledge. This approach is participative and usually leads to negotiated knowledge such as the common definition of problems, the identification of facts and the development of strategies (Tress et al. 2006, 15-17). Inter- and transdisciplinarity are labelled as integrative research approaches.

Tress, B./G. Tress/G. Fry 2006: Defining concepts and process of knowledge production in integrative research, in B. Tress/G. Tress/G. Fry/P. Opdam (eds.), *From Landscape Research to Landscape Planning. Aspects of Integration, Education and Application*, Dordrecht, 13-26.

PRESERVATION (OR CONSERVATION)

The preservation (or conservation) of archaeological-historical features and sites either *in situ* or *ex situ*. In the first case features and finds are kept at their original location (site = Latin: *situs*), which needs some form of maintenance and monitoring of the state of conservation. In the latter case features and materials are removed, ideally after extensive documentation by excavation, and the material and documents are kept in museums or depots. Consequently, preservation *ex situ* is also called 'preservation by record'.

SWOT STRATEGY MODEL

SWOT is an acronym for organizational (internal) strengths and weaknesses, and (external) opportunities and threats. Strategic planning in a corporate context uses the SWOT model as a means of establishing the organizational purpose, long-term objectives, action plans and resource allocation priorities.

Jain, R.K./H.C. Triandis, 1997: *Management of research and development organization. Managing the Unmanageable*, New York etc., 253-254.

VALLETTA CONVENTION (= MALTA CONVENTION/TREATY)

The Valletta Convention was adopted by the Council of Europe in January 1992 and came into force in May 1995. The aim is to protect the archaeological heritage as a source of collective European memory and as an instrument for historical and scientific study. The preservation and study will help to retrace the history of mankind and its relation with the natural environment. The archaeological heritage includes structures, constructions, groups of buildings, developed sites, moveable objects, monuments of other kinds as well as their context, whether situated on land or under water.

It is recommended that a legal system for the protection of the archaeological heritage be instituted to guarantee the scientific significance of archaeological research work by regulating archaeological excavations and other activities and to implement its physical protection. Integrated conservation of the archaeological heritage is aimed for by participation of archaeologists in planning policies designed to ensure well-balanced strategies for the protection, conservation and enhancement of sites of archaeological interest, preferably *in situ*. A provision should be made in major public or private schemes for covering the total costs of necessary related archaeological operations. The resulting archaeological information should be disseminated by and for the scientific community and for the public to develop its awareness of the value of the archaeological heritage for the understanding of the past and of the threats to this heritage.

Valletta, 1992: *European Convention on the Protection of the Archaeological Heritage (Revised) Valletta,* 16.I.1992, Strasbourg (Council of Europe).
http://conventions.coe.int/Treaty/en/Treaties/Html/143.htm. (Accessed 26 March, 2010).

X.3 Protecting and Developing the Dutch Archaeological-Historical Landscape/ Bodemarchief in Behoud en Ontwikkeling (PDL/BBO): projects and programmes

This is a list of research projects that have been funded by the PDL/BBO programme. Apart from these research projects, some other activities, especially workshops and conferences, related to one of the research themes of the PDL/BBO programme have been funded.

I. CONCEPTUAL STUDIES

PROTECTING AND DEVELOPING THE DUTCH ARCHAEOLOGICAL-HISTORICAL LANDSCAPE. THE CONCEPTUAL FOUNDATIONS.

Duration:	January-November 2001
Institutions:	Wageningen Universiteit; Brede Overleggroep Kleine Dorpen in Drenthe; Provincie Groningen; VU University, Amsterdam
Researcher(s):	R. During, J.N.H. Elerie, H.A. Groenendijk, M. Hidding, J. Kolen, Th. Spek.
Publication:	Bloemers, J.H.F./R. During/J.N.H. Elerie/H.A. Groenendijk/M. Hidding/J. Kolen/ Th. Spek/M.-H. Wijnen, 2001: *Bodemarchief in Behoud en Ontwikkeling. De conceptuele grondslagen*, Den Haag.

II. STRATEGIC RESEARCH

1-7 *Thematic studies*

II.1 SIGNS IN TIME: URBAN PLANNING AND DESIGN, THE PEOPLE AND THEIR HISTORIES

Duration:	January 2002-January 2006
Institution:	Wageningen University
Researcher:	K. Van Assche
Contact:	Assistant Professor, Land Use Planning, Planning & Culture, Community development program, St. Cloud State University, *Minnesota State Universities and Colleges*; 720, 4th Avenue South, 56301-4498 St Cloud, Mn; T. +1 320 308 3107; E: kvanassche@stcloudstate.edu.
Publication:	Assche, K. Van, 2004: *Signs in time. An interpretive account of urban planning and design, the people and their histories*, Wageningen (Ph.D. thesis Wageningen University).

II.2 ARCHEOLOGICAL HERITAGE AS EXPERIENCE

Duration:	March 2002-March 2006
Institution:	Wageningen University
Researcher:	M. Duineveld
Contact:	Postbus 47, 6700 AA Wageningen; T.: 0317-485770; E: martijn.duineveld@wur.nl.

Publication: Duineveld, M., 2006: *Van oude dingen, de mensen, die voorbij gaan*, Delft (Ph.D. thesis Wageningen University).

II. 3 STRATEGIC RESEARCH INTO AND DEVELOPMENT OF BEST PRACTICE FOR *PREDICTIVE MODELLING* ON BEHALF OF DUTCH CULTURAL RESOURCE MANAGEMENT.

Duration: February 2002-December 2006
Institutions/ Faculteit der Archeologie, Universiteit Leiden (H. Kamermans).
Researchers: Rijksuniversiteit Groningen (M. van Leusen); RAAP Archeologisch Adviesbureau/ Hendrik Brunsting Stichting, Vrije Universiteit (Ph. Verhagen); Rijksdienst voor Archeologie, Cultuurlandschap en Monumenten (now Rijksdienst voor het Cultureel Erfgoed; J. Deeben/D. Hallewas/P. Zoetbrood).
Contact: Hans Kamermans, Faculteit der Archeologie, Universiteit Leiden, Reuvensplaats 4, PO Box 9515, 2300 RA Leiden; T.: 071-527 2385; F.: 071-527 2429; E.: h.kamermans@arch.leidenuniv.nl
Publication(s): Leusen, M. van/H. Kamermans (eds.), 2005: *Predictive Modelling for Archaeological Heritage Management: A research agenda*, Amersfoort (Nederlandse Archeologische Rapporten 29).
Kamermans, H./M. van Leusen/P. Verhagen (eds.), 2009: *Archaeological Prediction and Risk Management. Alternatives to Current Practice*, Leiden (ASLU 17).
Verhagen, P., 2007: *Case Studies in Archaeological Predictive Modelling*, Leiden (Ph.D. thesis Leiden University; ASLU 14).

II.4 THE DEVELOPMENT OF A METHOD FOR THE PROSPECTION, CHARACTERIZATION AND INSPECTION OF ARCHAEOLOGICAL SITES AND LANDSCAPES IN THE NETHERLANDS, USING A MULTIDISCIPLINARY APPROACH.

Duration: September 2002-December 2006
Institutions: Instituut voor Geo- en Bioarcheologie, Faculteit Aard- en Levenswetenschappen, Vrije Universiteit; Amsterdams Archeologisch Centrum, Universiteit van Amsterdam; BIAX Archeobotanisch Adviesbureau, Zaandam; Rijksdienst voor Archeologie, Cultuurlandschap en Monumenten (now Rijksdienst voor het Cultureel Erfgoed); RAAP Archeologisch Adviesbureau.
Researchers: A.E. Kattenberg; S. Oonk; Ch. Sueur.
Contact: Henk Kars, Instituut voor Geo- en Bioarcheologie, Faculteit Aard- en Levenswetenschappen, Vrije Universiteit, De Boelelaan 1085, 1081 HV Amsterdam, T.: 020-598 7364; E.: henk.kars@falw.vu.nl
Publications: Kattenberg, A.E., 2008: *The application of magnetic methods for Dutch Archaeological Resource Management*, Amsterdam (Geoarchaeological and Bioarchaeological Studies 9) (Ph.D. thesis University of Amsterdam, Amsterdam).
Oonk, S., 2009: *The application of geochemical methods for Dutch Archaeological Resource Management*, Amsterdam (Geoarchaeological and Bioarchaeological Studies 11) (Ph.D. thesis VU University, Amsterdam).

II.5 SUSTAINABILITY AND ARCHAEOLOGICAL HERITAGE.

The deterioration of botanical (macro)remains with regard to the physical protection of archaeological sites and landscapes in the Netherlands.

Duration: October 2004-October 2008

Institutions: Instituut voor Geo- en Bioarcheologie, Faculteit Aard en Levenswetenschappen, Vrije Universiteit; Amsterdams Archeologisch Centrum, Universiteit van Amsterdam; BIAX Archeobotanisch Adviesbureau, Zaandam; Rijksdienst voor Archeologie, Cultuurlandschap en Monumenten (now Rijksdienst voor het Cultureel Erfgoed).

Researchers: J. Kool; M. van den Berg; H. van Haaster.

Contact: Henk Kars, Instituut voor Geo- en Bioarcheologie, Faculteit Aard- en Levenswetenschappen, Vrije Universiteit, De Boelelaan 1085, 1081 HV Amsterdam, T.: 020-598 7364; E.: henk.kars@falw.vu.nl

Publications: Berg, M.M. van den (in prep.): *The Dutch water-system and the implications for in-situ preservation of the archaeological record* (Ph.D. thesis VU University, Amsterdam).

Berg, M.M. van den/E.A. Hatzmann, 2005: *Water en archeologisch erfgoed,* Amersfoort (Nederlandse Archeologische Rapporten 30).

Berg, M.M. van den/G. Aalbersberg/R.M. van Heeringen, 2006: *Archeologische kwaliteit op peil. Bestaande grondwatermeetnetten en het erfgoedbeheer,* VU University, Amsterdam (Geoarchaeological and Bioarchaeological Studies 5).

II.6 VALUABLE FLINTS? THE ASSESSMENT AND SELECTION OF STONE AGE SITES IN THE NETHERLANDS

Duration: January 2004-December 2007

Institution: Groninger Instituut voor Archeologie, Rijksuniversiteit Groningen.

Researcher: Bjørn Smit

Contact: Cultural Heritage Agency; Smallepad 5, 3811 MG, Amersfoort P.O. Box 1600, 3800 BP, Amersfoort, The Netherlands; T.: 0031 33 421 76 03; E.: b.smit@cultureelerfgoed.nl; www.cultureelerfgoed.nl

Publication: B.Smit, 2010: *Valuable Flints. Research Strategies for the Study of Early Prehistoric Remains, from the Pleistocene Soils of the Northern Netherlands*, Groningen (Ph.D. thesis Rijksuniversiteit Groningen).

II.7 ARCHAEOLOGY AND SPATIAL PLANNING: A GOOD RELATION?

Duration: April 2002-July 2006

Institution: Amsterdams Archeologisch Centrum/Universiteit van Amsterdam.

Researcher: A. de Zwart

Publication: Zwart, A. de, in prep.: *Er op of er onder; de strijd om het bodemarchief. Over archaeologische monumentenzorg en de kwaliteit van de leefomgeving* (Ph.D. thesis University of Amsterdam, Amsterdam).

Contact: A. de Zwart, Hemonylaan 10/huis, 1074 BG Amsterdam; T.: 020-6647118; E.: anne.zwart@planet.nl

II. STRATEGIC RESEARCH

8-11 *Regional oriented studies*

8. THE BIOGRAPHY OF A SANDY LANDSCAPE: CULTURAL HISTORY, HERITAGE MANAGEMENT AND SPATIAL PLANING IN THE SOUTHERN NETHERLANDS

Duration: April 2002-April 2008
Institution: Archeologie en Kunstgeschiedenis/Vrije Universiteit Amsterdam.
Researchers: F.A. Gerritsen; C. van der Heijden; J.C.A. Kolen; N. Roymans; J.E. Bosma.
Contact: N. Roymans, Vrije Universiteit, Faculteit Letteren, De Boelelaan 1105, 1081 HV Amsterdam; T.: 020-5986369; E.: ngam.roymans@let.vu.nl.
Publications: Gerritsen, F.A./E. Rensink (eds.), 2004: *Beekdallandschappen in archeologisch perspectief. Een kwestie van onderzoek en monumentenzorg*, Amersfoort (Nederlandse Archeologische Rapporten 28).
Kolen, J., 2005: *De biografie van het landschap. Drie essays over landschap, geschiedenis en erfgoed*, Amsterdam (Ph.D. thesis VU University).
Kolen, J. (e.a.), 2004: *De Biografie van Peelland*, Amsterdam (Zuidnederlandse Archeologische Rapporten 13).

9. FROM OER-IJ ESTUARY TO METROPOLITAN COASTAL LANDSCAPE

Assessing and preserving archaeological-historical resources from 4000 years of living between land and water.

Duration: April 2002-April 2008
Institutions: Amsterdams Archeologisch Centrum/Universiteit van Amsterdam; Rijksdienst voor Archeologie, Cultuurlandschap en Monumenten (now Rijksdienst voor het Cultureel Erfgoed); Steunpunt Cultureel Erfgoed Noord-Holland; Deltares (until 1 January 2008 TNO Built Environment and Geosciences – Geological Survey of the Netherlands).
Researchers: G. Alders; J.H.F. Bloemers, R.M. van Heeringen, M. Kok; H. van Londen; L. Theunissen; P. Vos.
Contact: J.H.F. Bloemers, Amsterdam Archeologisch Centrum; Turfdraagsterpad 9-BG1, 1012 XT Amsterdam; T.: 020-525 5830; M.: j.h.f.bloemers@kpnmail.nl.
Publications: Bloemers, T./S. Husken/R. van Leeuwen 2009: *Een agenda voor het Oer-IJ. Het Oer-IJ op het snijvlak van cultuurhistorisch kennen en handelen*, Haarlem.
Heeringen, R.M. van/A. Smit/E.M. Theunissen 2004: *Archeologie in de toekomst: Nulmeting van de fysieke kwaliteit van het archeologisch monument in de Broekpolder, gemeenten Heemskerk en Beverwijk*, Amersfoort (Rapportage Archeologische Monumentenzorg, 107).
Kok, M.S.M., 2008: *The homecoming of religious practice. An analysis of offering sites in the wet low-lying parts of the landscape in the Oer-IJ area (2500 BC-AD 450)*, Amsterdam (Ph.D. thesis University of Amsterdam).
Londen, H. van, 2006: Cultural biography and the power of image, in W. van der Knaap/A. van der Valk (eds.), *Multiple Landscape. Merging Past and Present. Selected*

Papers from the fifth International Workshop on Sustainable Land Use Planning 7-9 June 2004, Wageningen, 171-181.

Alders, G.P., in prep.: *The archaeology of the Oer-IJ estuary in historical times. Modelling transformations and continuity in a metropolitan coastal landscape*, Amsterdam (Ph.D. thesis University of Amsterdam).

10. THE CULTURAL BIOGRAPHY OF NATURE.

Historical-ecological research and communicative planning in the Dutch National Landscape Drentsche Aa.

Duration;	October 2004-October 2007
Institutions:	Rijksdienst voor Archeologie, Cultuurlandschap en Monumenten (now Rijksdienst voor het Cultureel Erfgoed); Vereniging Brede Overleggroep Kleine Dorpen in Drenthe (VBOKD Drenthe); Wageningen Universiteit.
Researchers:	H. Elerie, Th. Spek.
Publications:	Elerie, H./Th. Spek (eds.), 2009: *Van Jeruzalem tot Ezelakker. Veldnamen als levend erfgoed in het Nationaal Landschap Drentsche Aa*, Utrecht.
	Elerie, H./T. Spek in druk: *Biografie van het Nationaal Landschap Drentse Aa. Een historich-ecologische benadering*, Utrecht.
Contact:	Th. Spek; Rijksdienst voor het Cultureel Erfgoed; Postbus 1600, 3800 BP Amersfoort; T.: 033-4217421; E.: t.spek@cultureelerfgoed.nl
	H. Elerie, Doornakkers 40, 9467 PR Anloo; T.: 0592-271334; E.: jnh.elerie@kpnmail.nl

11. THE CULTURAL BIOGRAPHY OF COVER-SAND LANDSCAPES OF SALLAND AND THE ACHTERHOEK

An integrated archaeological and historical-geographic research programme for rural planning, protection and management on ancient monuments and cultural landscapes.

Duration:	January 2004-January 2008
Institutions:	Wageningen Universiteit; Rijksdienst voor Archeologie, Cultuurlandschap en Monumenten (now Rijksdienst voor het Cultureel Erfgoed); Provincie Gelderland; Provincie Overijssel; Gemeente Zutphen; Gemeente Deventer.
Researchers:	R. van Beek; L. Keunen.
Contact:	J. Vervloet, Wageningen Universiteit, Postbus 47, 6700 AA Wageningen; T.: 0317-486114; M.: Jelle.Vervloet@wur.nl.
Publications:	Beek, R. van, 2009: *Reliëf in Tijd en Ruimte. Interdisciplinair onderzoek naar mens en landschap in Oost-Nederland tussen vroege prehistorie en middeleeuwen*, Wageningen (Ph.D. thesis, Wageningen University).
	Keunen, L.J., in press: *Eeuwig grensland. Een historisch-geografische studie van Salland en de Achterhoek*, Wageningen (Ph.D. thesis Wageningen University).

III. PROBLEM-ORIENTED SHORT-TERM PROJECTS

1. (INTER)NATIONAL SURVEY OF INTEGRATIVE CULTURAL-HISTORICAL POLICY AND RESEARCH

Duration:	July 2002-March 2003
Institution:	Rijksdienst voor Archeologie, Cultuurlandschap en Monumenten (now Rijksdienst voor het Cultureel Erfgoed).
Researcher:	T. de Groot
Contact:	T. de Groot; Postbus 1600, 3800 BP Amersfoort; T.: 033-4217421; E.: t.de.groot @ cultureeerfgoed.nl
Publication:	Groot, T. de, 2003: *(Inter)nationale verkenning naar beleidsnota's, stimulerings- en onderzoeksprogramma's op het gebied van archeologie, historische geografie en gebouwde monumenten*, (internal report Cultural Heritage Agency, Amersfoort/NWO, Den Haag).

2. (INTER)NATIONAL SURVEY OF POLICY, INCENTIVE AND RESEARCH PROGRAMMES CONCERNING ARCHAEOLOGY, HISTORIC GEOGRAPHY AND BUILT HERITAGE

Duration:	September 2002-April 2003
Institution:	Rijksdienst voor Archeologie, Cultuurlandschap en Monumenten (now Rijksdienst voor het Cultureel Erfgoed).
Researcher:	T. Fonds
Contact:	T. de Groot; Postbus 1600, 3800 BP Amersfoort; T.: 033-4217421; E.: t.de.groot @ cultureeerfgoed.nl
Publication:	Fonds, T., 2003: *Een internationale vergelijking van cultuurhistorisch beleid. Bezien vanuit een ruimtelijk perspectief*, (internal report Cultural Heritage Agency, Amersfoort/NWO, Den Haag).

3. PRESERVATION *IN SITU* OF ARCHAEOLOGICAL VALUES IN LARGE PROJECTS 1991-2001: INFRASTRUCTURE, HOUSING AND NATURE DEVELOPMENT

Duration:	July 2002-February 2003
Institution:	Rijksdienst voor Archeologie, Cultuurlandschap en Monumenten (now Rijksdienst voor het Cultureel Erfgoed).
Researcher:	R. Lotte
Contact:	P. Zoetbrood; Postbus 1600, 3800 BP Amersfoort; T. 033-4217421; E.: p.zoetbrood@ cultureelerfgoed.nl
Publication:	Lotte, R.M., 2003: *Evaluatie van grote projecten. Een studie naar het voorkomen van behoud in-situ bij grote infrastructurele projecten in het kader van het NWO-Stimuleringsprogramma Bodemarchief in Behouden Ontwikkeling (BBO)*, (internal report Cultural Heritage Agency, Amersfoort/NWO, Den Haag).

4. SUSTAINABLE MANAGEMENT AND PRESERVATION OF ARCHAEOLOGICAL VALUES IN HISTORIC-URBAN AREAS. BETWEEN PAPER AND PRACTICE.

Duration:	December 2002-September 2004
Institution:	Jacobs & Burnier Archeologisch Projectbureau
Researcher:	E. Jacobs

Publication:	Jacobs, E, 2005: *Duurzaam beheer en behoud van archeologische waarden in het stedelijk gebied. Tussen papier en praktijk*, Amsterdam (Standaard Archeologisch Rapport 44).
Contact:	E. Jacobs, Jacobs & Burnier Archeologisch Projectbureau, Veemarkt 186, 1019 DG Amsterdam; T.: 020-463 7300; E.: jenbbureau@zonnet.nl

5. CULTURAL-HISTORIC DECISION-MAKING AND IMPLEMENTATION OF INFRASTRUCTURAL PROJECTS: A LEGAL RESEARCH

Duration:	March 2003-May 2004
Institution:	Faculteit der Rechtsgeleerdheid, Universiteit van Amsterdam
Researcher:	E.S. Grimminck
Contact:	I.C. van der Vlies, Afdeling Bestuursrecht, Postbus 1030, 1000 BA Amsterdam; T.: 020-5254743; E.: vlies@uva.nl
Publication:	Grimminck, E.S., 2004: *Cultuurhistorie in besluitvorming en uitvoering van infrastructuurprojecten. Een juridisch onderzoek in het kader van het NWO Programma 'Bodemarchief in Behoud en Ontwikkeling'*, (internal report University of Amsterdam, Amsterdam/NWO, Den Haag).

6. STRENGTHENING THE POSITION OF CULTURAL HISTORY IN DECISION-MAKING: M.E.R. AND MKBA

Duration:	July 2003-March 2004
Institution:	Witteveen+Bos, Rotterdam
Researcher:	E.E.M. Nillesen
Contact:	E.C.M. Ruijgrok, Witteveen+Bos, Postbus 2397, 3000 CJ Rotterdam; T.: 010-2442800
Publication:	(Nillessen, L/E.C.M. Ruijgrok), 2004: *Verbetering van de positie van cultuurhistorie in de besluitvorming* (internal report Witteveen+Bos, Rotterdam/NWO, Den Haag).

7. PLANNING WITH CULTURAL HISTORY. INTEGRATION OF CULTURAL HISTORY AND URBAN DEVELOPMENT

Duration:	July-December 2003
Institution:	Rijksdienst voor Archeologie, Cultuurlandschap en Monumenten (now Rijksdienst voor het Cultureel Erfgoed).
Researchers:	T. Fonds and C. Nyst
Publication:	Fonds, T./C.L. Nyst 2006: *Plannen met cultuurhistorie. Integratie van cultuurhistorie en stedelijke ontwikkeling*, (internal report Cultural Heritage Agency, Amersfoort/University of Amsterdam, Amsterdam/NWO, Den Haag).
	Loon, M. van/C.L. Nyst/A. van Mispelaar, 2006: The Role of the Cultural Heritage in Urban Development Projects, *Berichten van de Rijksdienst voor het Oudheidkundig Bodemonderzoek* 46, 225-242.

8. THE NEOLITHIC OF PRESENT TIME. ABOUT EVERYDAY MEANING OF ARCHAEOLOGICAL HERITAGE IN THE POLDER 'DE GOUW' AND THE 'GROETPOLDER' (WEST-FRISIA)

Duration:	November 2003-June 2004
Institution:	Wageningen Universiteit
Researcher:	M. Koedoot
Publication:	Koedoot, M., 2004: *Het Neolithicum van nu. Over de alledaagse betekenis van archeologisch erfgoed in de polder de Gouw en de Groetpolder (West-Friesland)*, Wageningen.

9. WATER AND ARCHAEOLOGICAL HERITAGE

Duration:	September 2003-February 2004
Institution:	Instituut voor Geo- en Bioarcheologie, Vrije Universiteit, Amsterdam
Researchers:	M. van den Berg and E. Hatzmann
Contact:	H. Kars, Instituut voor Geo- en Bioarcheologie, De Boelelaan 1085-1087, 1081 HV Amsterdam; T.: 020-5987364; E.: karh@geo.vu.nl
Publication:	Berg, M.M. van den/E.A. Hatzmann, 2004: *Water en archeologisch erfgoed*, Amsterdam (IGBA Rapport 2004-06).

10. ARCHAEOLOGY AND CONSTRUCTION: KNOWLEDGE AND OPPORTUNITIES

Duration:	October 2005-December 2006
Institutions:	Instituut voor Geo- en Bioarcheologie, Vrije Universiteit, Amsterdam; Past2Present-Archeologic, Woerden
Researcher:	R. Isarin
Contact:	R. Isarin, Past2Present-Archeologic, Pelmolenlaan 12-14, 3447 GW Woerden; Tel.: 0348-437788; E.: r.isarin@archeologic.nl
Publication:	Isarin, R., 2007: *Archeologie en Bouwen, Kennis en Kansen*, Woerden.

11. ANALYZING AND SUPPORTING THE INTEGRATION PROCESS IN ARCHAEOLOGICAL-HISTORICAL LANDSCAPE RESEARCH IN THE BBO PROGRAMME (SINTAL)

Duration:	July-December 2004
Institution:	Wageningen Universiteit
Researchers:	G. Tress and B. Tress, Egenhofstrasse 27A, D-82152 München-Planegg, Duitsland; Tel.: 0049-8989 5563 95; E.: info@tress-tress.com; web: http:/www.tress-tress.com
Contact:	A.J. van der Valk, Postbus 47, 6700 AA Wageningen; T.: 0317-83696; E.: arnold.vandervalk@wur.nl.
Publication:	Tress, G./B. Tress 2004: *Analyzing and supporting the integration process in archaeological-historical landscape research in the BBO program (SINTAL)*, (internal report Wageningen University, Wageningen/NWO, Den Haag).

X.4 List of authors, fields of activity and addresses

Gerard Alders

Gerard Alders is an archaeologist who is specialized in Medieval and Post-Medieval Archaeology and in Archaeological Heritage. He has been professionally involved in the making of *Een agenda voor het Oer-IJ. Het Oer-IJ op het snijvlak van cultuurhistorisch kennen en handelen*, Haarlem 2009, an analysis of the effects of policy plans and landscape designs. At present he is completing his Ph.D. thesis as part of the PDL/BBO Oer-IJ programme.

Relevant publications:
Alders, G.P., in prep.: *The archaeology of the Oer-IJ estuary in historical times. Modelling transformations and continuity in a metropolitan coastal landscape*, Amsterdam (Ph.D. thesis Universiteit van Amsterdam).

Address:
G.P. Alders, Stichting Cultureel Erfgoed Noord-Holland, Stationsplein 112, NL-2011 LN Haarlem, The Netherlands.
Tel.:   +31 235 307 429
E-mail: gerardalders@cultureelerfgoednh.nl
Web: www.cultureelerfgoednh.nl

Kristoff Van Assche

Kristof Van Assche is currently associate professor at the community development and planning programme at Minnesota State Universities and Colleges – St. Cloud State. He is interested in the cultural, political and institutional embeddings of spatial planning and design, e.g. when studying heritage planning, environmental planning, transition and innovation in planning systems. He has worked extensively in the Low Countries, Eastern Europe and the Caucasus, and Minnesota.

Relevant publications:
Publications include an edited volume on city planning and city culture in Georgia (K.A.M. Van Assche/J. Salukvadze/N. Shavishvili (eds.), 2009: *City Culture and City Planning in Tbilisi: Where Europe and Asia Meet*, Lewiston/New York), papers in *Planning Theory, Memory studies, Ethnologia Balkanica, Anthropology of East Europe Review* and other journals, as well as book chapters. Forthcoming an edited volume (with Constantin Iordachi) on *Biopolitics in the Danube Delta*, Budapest, 2011).

Address:
Prof. Kristof Van Assche, Ph.D., Assistant Professor Land Use Planning, Planning & Culture, Community Development Program, St. Cloud State University, Minnesota State Universities and Colleges, 720, 4th Avenue South, 56301-4498 St Cloud, Mn., USA.
Tel.:   +1 320 308 3107
Cell: +1 320 237 4575

Fax: +1 320 308 5413
E-mail: kvanassche@stcloudstate.edu
Web: http://web.stcloudstate.edu/kvanassche

Jenny Atmanagara

Jenny Atmanagara focuses her current research on the topics landscape management, spatial planning, regional development, accessibility, tourism and transport. Since 2006 she has been a member of Forum Landschaft/Forum Paysage (CH; www.forumlandschaft.ch) and since 2009 a member of Landscape Research Group, Oxford (UK; www.landscaperesearch.org).

Relevant publications:

Bürgi, M./J. Atmanagara/M. Stuber/H.-R. Egli, 2008: Switzerland, in G. Fairclough/P. Grau Møller (eds.), *Landscape as Heritage - The Management and Protection of Landscape in Europe, a summary by the COST A27 project LANDMARKS*, Bern (Geographica Bernensia G79), 249-268.

Atmanagara, J., 2010, in print: Political Strategies and Best practices for Cultural Landscape Management in Switzerland, in K. Gawroński/J. Hernik (eds.), *Spatial Planning and Development as an Instrument for Shaping and Protecting Cultural Landscapes,* Kraków.

Address:

Dr Jenny Atmanagara, Institute of Geography, University of Bern, Hallerstr. 12, CH - 3012 Bern, Switzerland.

Tel.:   +41 316 318 838
E-mail: jenny.atmanagara@giub.unibe.ch
Web: www.geography.unibe.ch

Dr Jenny Atmanagara, Forststrasse 148, D-70193 Stuttgart, Germany.

Tel.:   +497 113 056 883
Cell: +491 609 465 768
E-mail: J.Atmanagara@t-online.de

Roy van Beek

Roy van Beek studied Prehistoric Archaeology of Northwestern Europe at the University of Leiden. Between 2004 and 2009 he did Ph.D. research on the long-term history of landscape and settlement of the Eastern Netherlands. Since 2009 he has been attached to the Cultural Heritage Agency as a postdoctoral researcher studying the settlement and landscape history of the river Vecht (Province of Overijssel, the Netherlands).

Relevant publications:

Beek, R. van/L. Keunen, 2006: A cultural biography of the coversand landscapes in the Salland and Achterhoek regions. The aims and methods of the Eastern Netherlands Project, *Berichten van de Rijksdienst voor het Oudheidkundig Bodemonderzoek* 46, 355-375.

Beek, R. van/J.H.F. Bloemers/L. Keunen/J. Kolen/H. van Londen/J. Renes, 2008: The Netherlands, in G. Fairclough/P. Grau Møller (eds.), *Landscape as heritage. The Management and Protection of Landscape in Europe, a summary by the Action COST A27 LANDMARKS* (Geographica Bernensia G79), Bern, 177-203.

Beek, R. van, 2009: *Reliëf in Tijd en Ruimte. Interdisciplinair onderzoek naar bewoning en landschap van Oost-Nederland tussen vroege prehistorie en middeleeuwen*, Wageningen (Ph.D. thesis Wageningen University).

Address:
Dr R. van Beek, Cultural Heritage Agency, Smallepad 5, P.O. Box 1600, NL-3800 BP Amersfoort,
The Netherlands.
Tel.:   +31 334 217 421
E-mail: R.van.Beek@cultureelerfgoed.nl
Web: www.cultureelerfgoed.nl

Martine van den Berg

Martine van den Berg (1973) studied physical geography at VU University Amsterdam and specialized in hydrology. After working in hydrology and GIS departments within engineering companies she joined the Institute for Geo- and Bioarchaeology in 2003. She participated in several interdisciplinary studies on nature management, water management and the preservation of archaeological remains. Today Martine works on monitoring studies of archaeological sites and she is preparing a Ph.D. thesis on the relation between water management and the preservation of archaeological sites and landscapes.

Relevant publications:

Berg, M.M. van de, in prep.: *The impact of changes in water management on the archaeological resources in the Netherlands: the development of a methodology for a risk assessment system approach*, (Ph.D. thesis VU University; Geoarchaeological and Bioarchaeological Studies).

Address:
M. van den Berg, Institute for Geo and Bioarchaeology, Faculty of Earth and Life Sciences,
VU University, De Boelelaan 1085, NL-1081 HV Amsterdam, The Netherlands.
E-mail: martine.vandenberg@falw.vu.nl

Raoul Beunen

Raoul Beunen is assistant professor at Wageningen University. His main research interests are the governance of nature (in particular the implementation of nature conservation policies in planning practices), grass roots planning (local and regional practices of spatial planning, citizen involvement and the integration of planning education and planning practices) and sustainable tourism (visitor surveys and management).

Relevant publications:

Beunen, R./W.G.M. van der Knaap/G.R. Biesbroek, 2009: Implementation and Integration of EU Environmental Directives. Experiences from the Netherlands, *Environmental Policy and Governance* 19, 57-69.

Beunen, R./J.E. Hagens, 2009: The Use of the Concept of Ecological Networks in Nature Conservation Policies and Planning Practices, *Landscape Research* 34, 563-580.

Beunen, R., 2010: *The Governance of Nature. How Nature Conservation Ambitions have been Dashed in Planning Practices*, Wageningen (Ph.D. thesis Wageningen University).

Address:
Dr R. Beunen, Wageningen University, Land Use Planning Group, P.O. Box 47 NL-6700 PB Wageningen, The Netherlands.
Tel.:   +31 317 482 697
E-mail: raoul.beunen@wur.nl
Web: www.raoulbeunen.nl; www.lup.wur.nl

Tom (J.H.F.) Bloemers
As a researcher Tom Bloemers has two main fields of research interests: the archaeology of the northwestern provinces of the Roman Empire and the relation between archaeological resource management, environmental planning and present day society focusing on issues like sustainability and environmental quality. Following from this second interest he has been one of the initiators of the national PDL/BBO research programme.

Relevant publications:

Bloemers, J.H.F., 2006: Kulturlandschaften in den Niederlanden - Erhaltung durch nachhaltige Entwicklung in der Raumordnung, in U. Matthiesen/R. Danielzyk/S. Heiland/S. Tzschaschel (eds.), *Kulturlandschaften als Herausforderung für die Raumplanung. Verständnisse – Erfahrungen – Perspektiven*, Hannover (Forschungs- und Sitzungsberichte der Akademie für Raumforschung und Landesplanung 228), 253-273.

Bloemers, T./A. van der Valk 2007: The Oer-IJ: a metropolitan wetland on Amsterdam's doorstep. The archaeological-historical landscape as inspiration for spatial planning, in B. Pedroli/A. van Doorn/G. de Blust/M.L. Paracchini/D. Wascher/F. Bunce (eds.), *Europe's living landscapes. Essays exploring our identity in the countryside*, Zeist, 160-176.

Address:
Prof. Dr J.H.F. Bloemers, Prins Frederiklaan 50, NL-3818 KD Amersfoort, The Netherlands.
Tel.:   +31 334 613 935
E-mail: j.h.f.bloemers@kpnmail.nl

Koos Bosma

Koos Bosma is professor of History of Architecture. His main research interest covers heritage studies, history of architecture and urban planning.

Relevant publications:

Bosma, J.E., 1996: European Airports, 1945-1995: Typology, Psychology and Infrastructure, in J. Zukowsky (ed.), *Building for Air Travel. Architecture and Design for Commercial Aviation*, Munich/New York, 51-65.

Bosma, J.E./H. Hellinga (eds.), 1997: *Mastering the City. North-European City Planning 1900-2000*, Rotterdam.

Bosma, J.E., 2000: *Housing for the Millions. John Habraken and the SAR (1960-2000)*, Rotterdam.

Address:

Prof. Dr J.E. Bosma, Faculty of Arts, History of Architecture/Research Institute CLUE, VU University Amsterdam, De Boelelaan 1105, NL-1081 HV Amsterdam, The Netherlands.

Tel.: +31 205 986 372

E-mail: je.bosma@let.vu.nl

Karoline Daugstad

Karoline Daugstad has a Ph.D. in human geography and is particularly interested in landscape studies. Her research explores landscape as symbol, representation, ideology, landscape policies and management balancing commercial use and protection, landscape and cultural heritage as an asset in tourism and debates on authenticity and value adding.

Relevant publications:

Daugstad, K./K. Rønningen/B. Skar, 2006: Agriculture as an upholder of cultural heritage? Conceptualizations and value judgements – A Norwegian perspective in international context, *Journal of Rural Studies* 22, 67-81.

Daugstad, K. 2008: Negotiating landscape in rural tourism in Norway, *Annals of Tourism Research* 35, 402-426.

Address:

Dr K. Daugstad, Centre for Rural Research, University Centre, NO-7491 Trondheim, Norway;

and Department of Geography, Norwegian University of Science and Technology, NO-7491 Trondheim, Norway.

Tel.: +47 773 591 658

E-mail: karoline.daugstad@svt.ntnu.no

Benjamin Ducke

Benjamin Ducke's field of research covers computational archaeology, statistics and quantitative archaeology, Geographic Information Systems, data capture, visualization and 3D data processing and formal models of past human behaviour (predictive modelling, territorial modelling, networks and visibility models).

Relevant publications:

Ducke, B./J. Müller, 2004: Die Geomagnetische Prospektion. Prospekcja geomagnetyczna, in J. Czebresczuk/J. Müller (eds.), *Bruszczewo. Ausgrabungen und Forschungen in einer prähistorischen Siedlungskammer Großpolens. Badania mikroregionu osadniczego z terenu Wielkopolski. I. Forschungsstand -- Erste Ergebnisse -- Das östliche Feuchtbodenareal. Stan -- Pierwsze wyniki -- Wschodnia, torfowa stanowiska*, Poznan/Kiel/Rahden (Westfalen), 61-68.

Ducke, B./U. Münch, 2005: Predictive Modelling and the Archaeological Heritage of Brandenburg (Germany), in M. van Leusen/H. Kamermans (eds.), *Predictive Modelling for Archaeological Heritage Management: A research agenda*, Amersfoort (Nederlandse Archeologische Rapporten 29), 93-108.

Ducke, B., 2007a: Ein Erosionsmodell für die brandenburgische Archäologie. Belege zur Akkumulation und Erosion am Beispiel des Fundplatzes Dyrotz 37, in J. Kunow/J. Müller (eds.), *Archäoprognose II*, Wünsdorf, 111-175.

Ducke, B., 2007b: Ein archäologisches Prädiktionsmodell für das Bundesland Brandenburg: Methoden, Datengrundlagen und Interpretationen, in J. Kunow/J. Müller (eds.), *Archäoprognose II*, Wünsdorf, 235-257.

Address:
B. Ducke, Oxford Archaeology, Janus House, Osney Mead GB-OX2 0ES, Oxford, U.K.
Tel.: +44 186 526 380 0
E-mail: benjamin.ducke@oadigital.net
Web: http://oadigital.net

Martijn Duineveld

Martijn Duineveld is assistant professor at the Socio-spatial Analysis Group at Wageningen University. After obtaining his Bachelor's degree at the International Agricultural School Larenstein he went to Wageningen University to study spatial planning. He obtained his Ph.D. degree in 2006 on a thesis on the politics of heritage. His current focus is on three interrelated lines of research: the multiple meanings of space and place, power strategies and the relationships between politics, policy and (scientific) knowledge. These three lines are used to study the mechanisms of meaning and power production in the fields of spatial planning and landscape architecture and tourism and heritage.

Relevant publications:

Duineveld, M., 2008: The Socio-political Use of Environmental Perception, Interpretation and Evaluation Research, in H.J. de Haan/V.R. van der Duim (eds.), *Landscape, Leisure and Tourism; Socio-spatial Studies in Experiences, Practices and Policies*, Delft, 245-257.

Duineveld, M./R. Beunen/K.A.M. Van Assche/R. During/R.G.H. van Ark, 2009: The relationship between description and prescription in transition research, in K.J. Poppe/C. Termeer/M. Slingerland (eds.), *Transitions towards sustainable agriculture and food chains in peri-urban areas*, Wageningen, 133-147.

Assche, K.A.M. Van/J. Salukvadze/M. Duineveld/G. Verschraegen, 2009: Would planners be as sweet by any other name? Roles in a transitional planning system: Tbilisi, Georgia, in K.A.M. Van Assche/J. Salukvadze/N. Shavishvili (eds.), *City Culture and City Planning in Tbilisi: Where Europe and Asia Meet*, Lewiston/New York, 243-317.

Address:

Dr M. Duineveld, Socio-spatial Analysis Group, Doevendaalsesteeg 3, Buildingnumber 101, NL-6708 PB Wageningen, The Netherlands.

Tel.: + 31 317 486 192
E-mail: martijn.duineveld@wur.nl
Web: martijn.duineveld@wur.nl

Hans Elerie

Hans Elerie is a historical geographer, columnist and former director of an umbrella organization of villages in Drenthe (BOKD). As such, he has a great deal of experience of local and regional environmental and planning policy. In his research he focuses on the connections between concepts and methods in historical ecology and historical anthropology. In 1998 he was awarded a doctorate for his historical ecological landscape research in southwest Drenthe. He has led the Drentsche Aa research and action programme over the past five years, alongside Theo Spek.

Relevant publications:

Elerie, J.N.H., 1998: *Weerbarstig land. Een historisch-ecologische landschapsstudie van Koekange en de Reest,* Groningen (Ph.D. thesis Wageningen University).

Elerie, H./Th. Spek, 2009: *Van Jeruzalem tot Ezelakker. Veldnamen als levend erfgoed in het Nationaal Landschap Drentsche Aa,* Utrecht.

Address:

Dr H.N. Elerie, Brede Overleggroep Kleine Dorpen in Drenthe, c/o Doornakkers 40, NL-9467 PR Anloo, The Netherlands.

Tel.: +31 592 271 334
E-mail: jnh.elerie@kpnmail.nl

Graham Fairclough

Graham Fairclough is an archaeologist engaged in heritage management and landscape issues, and is particularly involved in the development of Historic Landscape Characterisation (HLC). He has contributed to government heritage policy, such as the framework for archaeology in the planning process, the synergy of heritage and sustainability and a national sector-wide review that led to the publication *Power of Place: A future for the Historic Environment.*

He has contributed to the implementation at European level of the European Landscape Convention, and has worked within projects such as COST A27 Landmarks, Culture 2007 Eucaland, and the ESF-COST network of networks. He is currently a Board Member of the European Association of Archaeologists and a member of the External Advisory group of Le:Notre, a Europe-wide network of landscape architecture schools.

Relevant recent publications:

Edited volumes include *The Heritage Reader* (2008 with Harrison, Johnson and Schofield), *Landscape as Heritage* (2008 with P. Grau Møller), *Envisioning Landscape Archaeology* (2007 with Hicks/McAtackney),

Pathways to Europe's Landscape (2003 with Clark/Darlington), and *Europe's Cultural Landscape: archaeologists and the management of change* (2002 with Rippon). Publications include papers on landscape and heritage and chapters in books such as *Heritage and Beyond* (Council of Europe 2009), *Landscapes under Pressure* (Lozny 2007), *Landscape Ideologies* (Meier 2006), *Confronting Scale in Archaeology* (Lock/Molyneaux 2006), *Archaeological Resource Management in the UK* (Hunter/Ralston 2006[2]) and *Landscape Interfaces* (Palang/Fry 2003).

Address:
G. Fairclough, English Heritage, 1 Waterhouse Square, 138-142 Holborn, London, GB-EC1N 2ST, U.K.
Tel.: +44 707 331 24
E-mail: graham.fairclough@english-heritage.org.uk
Web: www.english-heritage.org.uk/characterisation

Fokke Gerritsen
Fokke Gerritsen's field of research is, among other things, landscape archaeology.

Relevant publications:
Roymans, N./F. Gerritsen 2002: Landscape, ecology and mentalités: a long-term perspective on developments in the Meuse-Demer-Scheldt region, *Proceedings of the Prehistoric Society* 68, 257-287.
Gerritsen, F., 2003: *Local identities. Landscape and community in the late prehistoric Meuse-Demer-Scheldt region*, Amsterdam (Amsterdam Archaeological Studies 9).
Rensink, E./F.A. Gerritsen/J. Roymans, 2006: Archaeological Heritage Management, Nature Development and Water Management in the Brook Valleys of the Southern Netherlands, *Berichten van de Rijksdienst voor het Oudheidkundig Bodemonderzoek* 46, 383-399.
Roymans, N./F. Gerritsen/C. van der Heijden/K. Bosma/J. Kolen, 2009: Landscape Biography as Research Strategy: The Case of the South Netherlands Project, *Landscape Research* 34, 337-359.

Address:
Dr F. Gerritsen, Faculty of Arts, Archaeology, Research Institute CLUE, VU University Amsterdam,
De Boelelaan 1105, NL-1081 HV Amsterdam, The Netherlands.
E-mail: fa.gerritsen@let.vu.nl
Web: http://www.let.vu.nl/en/about-the-faculty/academic-staff/staff-listed-alphabetically/staff-e-k/dr-f-a-gerritsen/index.asp

Per Grau Møller
Per Grau Møller's main areas of current research relate to landscape history, cultural heritage and planning, agricultural history, historical cartography.

Relevant publications
Grau Møller, P./R. Ejrnæs/J. Madsen/A. Höll/L. Krogh (ed.), 2002: *Foranderlige Landskaber – integration af natur og kultur i forvaltning og forskning*, Odense.

Grau Møller, P., 2004: Danish farmers and the cultural environment. Landscape management with a cultural dimension, in Palang H./H. Sooväli/M. Antrop/G. Setten (eds.), *European Landscapes: Persistence and Change in a Globalising Environment*, Dordrecht, 379-396.

Fairclough, G./P. Grau Møller (eds.), 2008: *Landscape as heritage: The Management and protection of Landscape in Europe, a summary by the COST A27 project LANDMARKS*, Bern (Geographica Bernensia G 79).

with Stein Tage Domaas, 2009: Technologies for integration and use of historical maps into GIS : Nordic examples, in O. Bender/N. Evelpidou/A. Krek/A. Vassilopoulos (eds.), *Geoinformation Technologies for Geocultural Landscapes: European perspectives*, Leiden, 145-168.

Address:
P. Grau Møller, Cartographical Documentation Centre, University of Southern Denmark, Campusvej 55, DK-5230 Odense M, Denmark.
Tel.: +45 655 021 04
E-mail: pgm@hist.sdu.dk
Web: http://www.sdu.dk/ansat/pgm.aspx

Henk van Haaster

Henk van Haaster (1952) graduated from VU University Amsterdam in 1985 with an M.Sc. in biology with a specialization in palaeo-ecology, physical geography and environmental archaeology. From 1994 onwards he has been a partner in BIAX Consult, a research company for biological archaeology and landscape reconstruction. In 2003 he completed his Ph.D. thesis on the food economy of the (post) medieval city of 's Hertogenbosch. His current fields of work and research interest are archaeobotany, palynology, palaeo-ecology and forensic botany.

Relevant publications:

Haaster, H. van/L.I. Kooistra/C. Vermeeren, 2001: Archeobotanie, in J.W. Oudhof/J. Dijkstra/A. Verhoeven (eds.), *Archeologie in de Betuweroute: Huis Malburg, Een middeleeuwse nederzetting in Kerk-Avezaath*, Amersfoort (Rapportage Archeologische Monumentenzorg 81), 279-328.

Haaster, H. van/L. Kubiak-Martens/P. van Rijn, 2001; Archeobotanie, in A.A.A. Verhoeven/O. Brinkkemper (eds.), *Archeologie in de Betuweroute: Twaalf eeuwen bewoning langs de Linge bij De Stenen Kamer in Kerk-Avezaath*, Amersfoort (Rapportage Archeologische Monumentenzorg 85), 519-608.

Haaster, H. van, 2008: *Archeobotanica uit 's-Hertogenbosch. Milieuomstandigheden, bewoningsgeschiedenis en agrarische ontwikkelingen in en rond een (post)middeleeuwse groeistad*, Groningen (Groningen Archaeological Studies 6).

Address:
Dr H. van Haaster, Research and Consultancy Service for Biological Archaeology and Environmental Reconstruction (BIAX), Hogendijk 134, NL-1506 AL Zaandam, The Netherlands.
E-mail: haaster@biax.nl

Robert van Heeringen
Robert van Heeringen (1953) graduated in Geology, Prehistoric and Urban Archaeology from the Universities of Leiden and Amsterdam in 1979. From 1975 onwards he held several positions at the former State Service for Archaeological Investigations (ROB). He received his Ph.D. from VU University Amsterdam in 1992 on The Iron Age in the Western Netherlands. From 1985-1997 he worked as the provincial archaeologist of the provinces of Zeeland and Zuid-Holland. From 1998 he was leader of several research programmes at the ROB on wetland research and monitoring of archaeological sites. In 2007 he moved to a position as senior advisor in commercial archaeology.

Relevant publications:
Heeringen, R.M. van/E.M. Theunissen (eds.), 2002: *Dessication of the Archaeological Landscape at Voorne-Putten*, Amersfoort (Nederlandse Archeologische Rapporten 25).
Heeringen, R.M. van/G.V. Mauro/A. Smit, 2004: *A pilot Study on the Monitoring of the Physical Quality of Three Archaeological Sites at the UNESCO World Heritage Site at Schokland, Province of Flevoland, the Netherlands*, Amersfoort (Nederlandse Archeologische Rapporten 26).
Smit, A./R.M. van Heeringen/E.M. Theunissen, 2006: *Archaeological Monitoring Standard. Guidelines for the non-destructive recoring and monitoring of the physical quality of archaeological sites and monuments*, Amersfoort (Nederlandse Archeologische Rapporten 33).

Address:
Dr R.M. van Heeringen, Vestigia BV Archeologie & Cultuurhistorie, Spoorstraat 5, NL-3811 MN Amersfoort, The Netherlands.
Tel.:   +31 332 779 200
E-mail: r.vanheeringen@vestigia.nl

Cor van der Heijden
Cor van der Heijden is a historian, publicist and secondary school teacher of history. His field of research is the social history of the southern Netherlands with emphasis on the 19th and 20th centuries.

Relevant publications:
Roymans, N./F. Gerritsen/C. van der Heijden/K. Bosma/J. Kolen, 2009: Landscape Biography as Research Strategy: The Case of the South Netherlands Project, *Landscape Research* 34, 337-359

Address:
Dr C. van der Heijden, Vooreind 7a, NL-5096 BC Hulsel, The Netherlands.
E-mail: c.van.der.heijden@chello.nl

Józef Hernik
Józef Hernik is a lecturer and researcher at the University of Agriculture in Kraków at the Faculty of Environmental Engineering and Land Surveying. He carries out research on cultural landscape and land management and he has coordinated international research projects such as the European Union pro-

gramme Protecting Historical Cultural Landscapes to Strengthen Regional Identities and Local Economies. He initiated and edited a series of monographs on cultural landscape.

Relevant publications:
Hernik, J./J.M. Pijanowski (ed.), 2007: *Cultural Landscape – Assessment, Protection, Shaping*, Kraków.
Pijanowski, J.M./J. Hernik (eds.), 2008: *Infrastructure and Ecology of Rural Areas: Cultural Landscape – Protecting Historical Cultural Landscapes to Strengthen Regional Identities and Local Economies*, Kraków.
Hernik, J. (ed.), 2009: *Cultural Landscape – Across Disciplines*, Bydgoszcz/Kraków.
Hernik, J./R. Dixon-Gough, in press: *Archiving the Complex Information Systems of Cultural Landscapes for Interdisciplinary Permanent Access – Development of Concepts*.
Hernik, J., in press: *Cultural Landscapes of River Valleys*, Branta.

Address:
Dr Józef Hernik, University of Agriculture in Kraków, Faculty of Environmental Engineering and Land Surveying, Department of Planning, Organization and Conservation of Agrarian Areas, ul. Balicka 253c, PL -30-149 Kraków, Poland.
Tel: +48 126 62 4 154
Fax: +48 12 633 11 70
E-mail: rmhernik@cyf-kr.edu.pl
Web: www.ur.krakow.pl
         www.rabalandscape.ur.krakow.pl
         www.cadses.ar.krakow.pl

Hans Huisman
Hans Huisman (1967) has a background in soil science and geochemistry. His Ph.D. thesis (Wageningen, 1998) was on the geochemical composition of subsurface sediments in the Netherlands. From 1998 to 2002 he worked as a geochemist at TNO-NITG/National Geological Service (Utrecht, the Netherlands). In 2003 he was appointed senior researcher at the Cultural Heritage Agency in Amersfoort (the Netherlands), working on monitoring and in situ protection of archaeological sites. He has edited a handbook on degradation processes in various archaeological materials. In addition to the use of a variety of geoarchaeological methods he studied anthropogenic soils using micromorphology. In 2009 he was appointed lecturer at the Faculty of Archaeology at Leiden University.

Relevant publications:
Huisman, D.J./E.M. Theunissen, 2008: Too good to be true? The unexpectedly good preservation of the Nieuw Dordrecht Neolithic peat trackway and its consequences, in H. Kars/R.M. van Heeringen (eds.), *Preserving archaeological remains in situ. Proceedings of the 3rd conference 7 - 9 December 2006*, Amsterdam (Geoarchaeological and Bioarchaeological Studies 10), 15-28.
Huisman, D.J. (ed.), 2009: *Degradation of archaeological remains*, Den Haag.
Huisman, D.J., 2009: Using soil micromorphology to evaluate the suitability of the burial environment for in situ protection, in K. Straetkvern/D.J. Huisman (eds.), *Proceedings of the 10th ICOM Group on*

Wet Organic Archaeological Materials Conference, Amsterdam 2007, Amersfoort (Nederlandse Archeologische Rapporten 37), 101-111.

Address:
Dr D.J. Huisman, Cultural Heritage Agency, P.O. Box 1600, NL-3800 BP Amersfoort, The Netherlands.
E-mail: H.Huisman@cultureelerfgoed.nl

Angelika Hunold
Angelika Hunold is an archaeologist and since 1997 she has worked on the project Vulkanpark Osteifel in Forschungsbereich VAT. Her research subject within the project is the archaeology of the Late Roman period. She was in charge of the excavation and presentation of the "Katzenberg" site, a Late Roman hill fort.

Relevant publications:
Hunold, A., 1997: *Der römische vicus von Alzey,* Mainz (Archäologische Schriften des Instituts für Vor- und Frühgeschichte der Johannes Gutenberg-Universität Mainz 5).
Hunold, A., 2010: *Die Befestigung auf dem Katzenberg bei Mayen und die spätrömischen Höhenbefestigungen in Nordgallien,* Mainz (Vulkanpark-Forschungen 8).

Address:
Dr A. Hunold, Forschungsbereich Vulkanologie, Archäologie und Technikgeschichte (VAT) des Römisch-Germanischen Zentralmuseums Mainz/Mayen, An den Mühlsteinen 7, D-56727 Mayen, Germany.
E-mail: hunold@rgzm.de

Ulf Ickerodt
Ulf Ickerodt conducted excavations, mainly in Germany, on prehistoric, medieval and modern sites and also in Burkina Faso. Recently he was the project coordinator of the trilateral LancewadPlan project at the Lower Saxon States Service. At present he is a lecturer in cultural heritage management, the history of prehistoric archaeology and theoretical archaeology at the Universities of Hamburg and Kiel. Currently he is deputy head of the heritage conservation organisation Archäologisches Landesamt Schleswig-Holstein.

Relevant publications:
Ickerodt, U., 2008: The spatial dimension of history: propagation of historical knowledge via open-air museums, leisure parks and motion pictures, *Public Journal of Semiotics* II, 73-102. (http://www.semiotics.ca/issues/pjos-2-2.pdf. Accessed on 24 April, 2009).
Ickerodt, U./M. Maluck, 2008: LancewadPlan - The Consideration of specific Processes in Landscape Development on the Wadden Sea Coast in an integrated Management of Cultural Heritage, in C. Bartels/C. Küppers-Eichas (eds.), *Cultural Heritage and Landscapes in Europe. Landschaften: Kulturelles Erbe in Europa. Proceedings of the International Conference, Bochum June 8-10, 2007,* Bochum, 401-423.

Ickerodt, U., 2010: *Einführung in das Grundproblem des archäologisch-kulturhistorischen Vergleichens und Deutens,* Frankfurt am Main etc.

Address:

Dr U. Ickerodt, Archäologisches Landesamt Schleswig-Holstein, Brockdorff-Rantzau-Strasse 70,

D-24837 Schleswig, Germany.

Tel.:   +49 462 138 723

Fax: +49 462 138 755

E-mail: Ulf.Ickerodt@alsh.landsh.de

Web: www.archaeologie.schleswig-holstein.de

Carys E. Jones

Carys Jones' research focuses on environmental assessment at both the project (EIA) and strategic (SEA) levels. Her main areas of interest relate to process, quality and linkages to landscape and cultural heritage. Carys is currently a Senior Lecturer in Environmental Planning in the School of Environment and Development (Planning and Landscape).

Relevant publications:

Jones, C.E./S. Jay/P. Slinn/C. Wood, 2007: Environmental Assessment: Dominant or Dormant? in J. Holder (ed.), *Taking Stock of Environmental Assessment: Law, Policy and Practice,* London, 17-44.

Jones, C./P. Slinn, 2008: Cultural heritage in EIA - reflections on practice in North West Europe, *Journal of Environmental Assessment Policy and Management* 10, 215-238.

Jones, C., 2009: L'avaluació dels impactes paisatgistics i visuals al Regne Unit, in Observatori del Paisatge (ed.), *Ordenació I gestió del paisatge a Europa,* Plecs de Paisatge, Eines 2, Catalunya.

Address:

Dr C.E. Jones, School of Environment & Development, University of Manchester, Oxford Road,

Manchester, GB-M13 9PL, U.K.

Tel.:   +44 161 275 625 5

E-mail: Carys.jones@manchester.ac.uk

Web: http://www.sed.manchester.ac.uk/planning/staff/jones_carys.htm

Hans Kamermans

Hans Kamermans is associate professor at Leiden University. He studied ecological prehistory and physical geography in Amsterdam and wrote his Ph.D. thesis on the use of land evaluation in archaeology. His research is in the field of computer applications in archaeology (predictive modelling, GIS, the use of computers in the field, sampling). In the 1980s he co-directed the Agro Pontino survey in Italy and he was involved in archaeological projects in Geleen, Boxgrove, the Vézère valley, Neumark and Ostia. From 2002 until 2008 he directed a research programme called "Predictive Modelling for Archaeological Heritage Management", a project within the Dutch PDL/BBO programme. In 2007 he received a grant for the project "EDNA II – Taking the electronic archive for Dutch Archaeology to the next level". Kamermans is a member of the steering committee of CAA (Computer Applications and quantitative methods in Archaeology) and a member of the International Advisory Editorial Committee of the journal Internet Archaeology.

Relevant publications:

Leusen, P.M. van/H. Kamermans (eds.), 2005: *Predictive Modelling for Archaeological Heritage Management: A research agenda,* Amersfoort (Nederlandse Archeologische Rapporten 29).

Kamermans, H., 2008: Smashing the crystal ball. A critical evaluation of the Dutch national archaeological predictive model IKAW, *International Journal of Humanities and Arts Computing* 1, 71-84.

Kamermans, H./M. van Leusen/Ph. Verhagen (eds.), 2009: *Archaeological Prediction and Risk Management. Alternatives to Current Practice,* Leiden (ASLU 17).

Address:
Dr H. Kamermans, Faculty of Archaeology, Leiden University, WSD, Reuvensplaats 3-4, NL-2311 BE Leiden, The Netherlands.
Tel.:   +31 715 272 385
E-mail: h.kamermans@arch.leidenuniv.nl
Web: http://archaeology.leiden.edu/organisation/staff/kamermans.html

Henk Kars

Henk Kars (1950) is an archaeological scientist with a background in petrology and geochemistry. After completing his Ph.D. thesis on provenancing stone artefacts found at early-medieval Dorestad (1984), he performed a variety of studies in provenancing (stone, ceramics), ancient technology (iron) and dating (archaeomagnetism) at the Cultural Heritage Agency (Amersfoort, the Netherlands).
In 1994 he was appointed to the first chair of Archaeometry in the Netherlands at VU University Amsterdam. Since 2002 he is director of the Institute for Geo- and Bioarchaeology within the Faculty of Earth and Life Sciences of VU University. Today he is an internationally acknowledged expert on the *in situ* preservation of archaeological remains.

Relevant publications:

Kars, H./E. Burke (eds.), 2005: *Proceedings of the 33rd symposium on Archaeometry, Amsterdam 2002,* Amsterdam (Geoarchaeological and Bioarchaeological studies 3).

Kars, H./R.M. van Heeringen (eds.), 2008: *Preserving archaeological remains in situ. Proceedings of the 3rd conference 7-9 December 2006, Amsterdam,* Amsterdam (Geoarchaeological and Bioarchaeological studies 10).

Address:
Prof. Dr H. Kars, Institute for Geo and Bioarchaeology, Faculty of Earth and Life Sciences, VU University, De Boelelaan 1085, NL-1081 HV Amsterdam, The Netherlands.
Tel.:   +31 205 987 364
Fax: +31 206 462 457
E-mail: henk.kars@falw.vu.nl
Web: http://www.falw.vu.nl/igba

Alette Kattenberg

Alette Kattenberg (1974) is an archaeological geophysicist with an interest in archaeological prospection in the wider sense of the word. After obtaining an MA in European Archaeology and an MSc in Archaeological Prospection she carried out her Ph.D. research on the application of magnetic methods for archaeological resource management in the Netherlands (University of Amsterdam 2008). She is currently employed as an environmental geophysicist in the Archaeology Department of the University of Highlands and Islands, based in Orkney (UK).

Relevant publications:
Kattenberg, A.E./G. Aalbersberg, 2004. Archaeological prospection of the Dutch perimarine landscape by means of magnetic methods, *Archaeological Prospection* 11, 227-235.
Kattenberg, A.E., 2008: *The application of magnetic methods for Dutch archaeological resource management*, Amsterdam (Ph.D. thesis University of Amsterdam; Geoarchaeological and Bioarchaeological studies 9, VU University).

Address:
Dr A. Kattenberg, University of Highlands and Islands, Geophysics Unit, Orkney College, KW15 1LX Kirkwall, Orkney, U.K.
E-mail: Alette.Kattenberg@orkney.uhi.ac.uk

Luuk J. Keunen

As a historical geographer, Keunen's research mainly focuses on the landscape history of the coversand and riverine landscapes of the southern and eastern Netherlands. He is performing contract research for several organizations. The majority of these projects results in interdisciplinary publications combining e.g. archaeology, palaeobotany, historical geography, medieval and post-medieval history, soil sciences and onomastics. Most of these publications also contain chapters about the use of historical data for spatial planning and about heritage management. Besides this, Keunen is finishing a Ph.D. thesis on the landscape and settlement history of Salland and the Achterhoek, two regions in the eastern part of the Netherlands.

Relevant publications:
Beek, R. van/L. Keunen, 2006: A cultural biography of the coversand landscapes in the Salland and Achterhoek regions. The aims and methods of the Eastern Netherlands Project, *Berichten van de Rijksdienst voor het Oudheidkundig Bodemonderzoek* 46, 355-375.
Beek, R. van/J.H.F. Bloemers/L. Keunen/J. Kolen/H. van Londen/J. Renes, 2008: The Netherlands, in G. Fairclough/P. Grau Møller (eds.), *Landscape as heritage. The Management and Protection of Landscape in Europe, a summary by the Action COST A27 'Landmarks'* (Geographica Bernensia G79), Bern, 177-203.
Keunen, L., in prep.: *Eeuwig grensland. Een historisch-geografische studie van Salland en de Achterhoek*, Wageningen (Ph.D. thesis Wageningen University).

Address:
L.J. Keunen, RAAP Archaeological Consultancy, P.O. Box 222, NL-7200 AE Zutphen, The Netherlands.
Tel.:   +31 575 567 876
E-mail: l.keunen@raap.nl
Web: http://www.raap.nl

L.J. Keunen, Van Uvenweg 144-II, NL-6707 BJ Wageningen, The Netherlands.
Tel.:   +31 317 842 486
E-mail: luuk.j.keunen@gmail.com
Web: http://www.luukkeunen.nl

Marju Kõivupuu
Marju Kõivupuu's main research interests lie in folkloristics and ethnology comprising mainly studies in local cultures, folkmedicine and ritual landscapes. She has been conducting ethnological fieldwork for over twenty years and several of her books have been awarded national prizes.

Relevant publications:
Kõivupuu, M., 2009: Natural sacred places in landscape: an Estonian mode, in S. Bergmann/P.M. Scott/M. Jansdotter Samuelsson/H. Bedford-Strohm (eds.), *Nature, Space and the Sacred. Transdisciplinary Perspectives,* Farnham, 223-234.
Kõivupuu, M., 2009: Roadside cemeteries, in M. Kõiva (ed.), *Media & Folklore,* Tartu, 313-344.

Address:
M. Kõivupuu, Centre for Landscape and Culture, Estonian Institute of Humanities, Tallinn University, Uus-Sadama 5, EE-10120 Tallinn, Estonia.
Tel.:   +37 261 995 37
E-mail: marju.koivupuu@tlu.ee
Web: www.tlu.ee

Marjolijn S. M. Kok
Marjolijn S. M. Kok is a senior researcher landscape and heritage at the AAC/projectenbureau of the University of Amsterdam, where she also completed her Ph.D. thesis. Since 2010 she is also a managing partner of the new foundation Institute of Landscape Archaeology and Heritage Studies. With Heleen van Londen she co-authored the content of four e-learning modules on European heritage management within the Leonardo da Vinci programme "E-learning European Heritage." Her research interests include archaeological theory and its practice, gender/identity, landscape and heritage. She is a member of the research group 'Heritage and Cultural Landscapes' of the Amsterdam Archaeological Centre.

Recent publications:

Kok, M.S.M., 2008: *The homecoming of religious practice. An analysis of offering sites in the wet low-lying parts of the landscape in the Oer-IJ area (2500 BC-AD 450)*, Amsterdam (Ph.D. thesis University of Amsterdam).

Londen, H. van/M.S.M. Kok/A. Marciniak (eds.), 2009: *E-learning Archaeology, Theory and Practice*, Amsterdam.

Therkorn, L./E. Besselsen/M. Diepeveen-Jansen/S.Gerritsen/J. Kaarsemaker/M. Kok/L. Kubiak-Martens/ J. Slopsma/P. Vos, 2009: *Landscapes in the Broekpolder. Excavations around a monument with aspects of the Bronze Age to the Modern*, Amsterdam.

Kok, M.S.M., 2009: Staging a soft landscape: how performative action created an understanding of the life-world, in L. Lévêque/M. Ruiz del Árbol/L. Pop (eds.), *Patrimoine, Images, Mémoire des paysages européens*, Paris, 203-214.

Kok, M.S.M./S. van Rossenberg (eds.), in prep.: *Fragmentation of perception/Perception of fragmentation: a queer perspective on art and archaeology*, Rotterdam.

Address:
Dr M. Kok, Institute of Landscape Archaeology and Heritage Studies, Maaskade 174-B, NL-3071 NT Rotterdam, The Netherlands.
E-mail: marjolijnkok@ilahs.org
Web: www.ilahs.org

Jan Kolen

Jan Kolen's field of research is Landscape Archaeology and Heritage Studies. He is director of the new Research Institute for the Heritage and History of the Cultural Landscape and Urban Environment CLUE at VU University in Amsterdam. In his Ph.D. thesis he presented a detailed analysis of the use of the 'biography of landscape' concept (Kolen, J.C.A., 2005: *De biografie van het landschap. Drie essays over landschap, geschiedenis en erfgoed*, Amsterdam).

Relevant publications:

Renes, J./J.Kolen, 2006: Entwicklung von Siedlung und Kulturlandschaft in den Sandgebieten der Südlichen Niederlanden unter Berücksichtigung von Siedlungsmodellen, *Siedlungsforschung. Archäologie – Geschichte – Geographie* 24, 251-273.

Kolen, J./M.Witte, 2007: A Biographical approach to Regions and its Value for Spatial Planning, in W. van der Knaap/A. van der Valk (eds), *Multiple Landscape. Merging Past and Present. Selected Papers from the fifth International Workshop on Sustainable Land Use Planning 7-9 June 2004*, Wageningen, 125-146.

Kolen, J., 2008: Regional Identity, *Architecture Bulletin* 2008, 45-63.

Roymans, N./F. Gerritsen/C. van der Heijden/K. Bosma/J. Kolen, 2009: Landscape Biography as Research Strategy: The Case of the South Netherlands Project, *Landscape Research* 34, 337-359.

Kolen, J., 2009: The "anthropologization" of archaeological heritage, *Archaeological Dialogues* 16, 209-25.

Address:
Prof. Dr J. Kolen, Faculty of Arts, Archaeology and Research Institute CLUE,
VU University, De Boelelaan 1105, NL-1081 HV Amsterdam,The Netherlands.

Tel.: +31 205 986 315
E-mail: jca.kolen@let.vu.nl
Web: http://www.clue.nu

Johan Kool
Johan Kool (1979) studied geology and geochemistry at Utrecht University, focusing on organic geochemistry and hydrology. He subsequently participated in organic and isotopic studies of fossilized wood and is the coauthor of several articles on this subject. He continued this line of work with a study on the preservation of archaeobotanical macroremains in situ at VU University in Amsterdam. He has expertise in pyrolysis-gas chromatography-mass spectrometry. In 2008 he changed career by developing software for Mac and iPhone through his company Koolistov.

Relevant publications:
Kool, J./I. Poole/P.F. van Bergen, 2009: How jet is formed: An organic geochemical approach using pyrolysis gas chromatography-mass spectrometry, *Organic Geochemistry* 40, 700-705.
Kool, J./H. van Haaster/G.D. Abbott/H. Kars/P. Buurman, 2009: How does organic geochemistry help to understand the degradation of botanical remains, in J.-F. Moreau/R. Auger/J. Chabot/A. Herzog (eds.), *Proceedings of the 36th International Symposium on Archaeometry, 2-6 May 2006*, Quebec City, 95-100.

Address:
J. Kool, Koolistov, Boskamp 105, NL-3343EC Hendrik-Ido-Ambacht, The Netherlands.
Web: johan@koolistov.net

Rob van der Laarse
Rob van der Laarse is associate professor of Heritage Studies at the Department of Art, Religion & Cultural Sciences at the University of Amsterdam. He lectures on cultural theory, heritage, memory, and landscape, and has published widely on the history of elites, country houses, memory landscapes, and tourist gazing. He is currently writing a study on the cultural history of Dutch court and landed society over the past 400 years, to be published under the title *Arcadiërs van de Republiek*. Other fields of research concern the intellectual roots and memory of the Holocaust. With Frank van Vree he recently initiated the NWO programmes *War Heritage and Memory - a dynamic perspective on the future of World War II* (2007-2013) and *Dynamic of Memory. The Netherlands in the Second World War* (2009-2014).

Relevant publications:
Laarse, R. van der (ed.), 2005: *Bezeten van vroeger. Erfgoed, musealisering en identiteit*, Amsterdam.
Laarse, R. van der/Y. Kuiper (eds.), 2005: *Beelden van de buitenplaats. Elitevorming en notabelencultuur in Nederland in de negentiende eeuw*, Hilversum.
Laarse, R. van/F. van Vree (eds.), 2009: *De dynamiek van de herinnering. Nederland en de Tweede Wereldoorlog in internationale context*, Amsterdam.
Laarse, R. van/J. Kolen (eds.), in press: *Landscape and Heritage. An introductory Reader*, Amsterdam.

Address:

Dr R. van der Laarse, Department of Cultural History of Europe, University of Amsterdam, Oude Turfmarkt 141, 1012 GC Amsterdam, The Netherlands.
Tel.: +31 205 257 278
E-mail: laarse@uva.nl

Rob van Leeuwen

Rob van Leeuwen (1949) is a landscape architect and writer. He worked at the research institute "De Dorschkamp", now Alterra, and the municipality of Amsterdam, before being employed by the urban planning office RBOI in Rotterdam, where he heads the design group Atelier R. He has taught at universities in the Netherlands and abroad, and presently teaches at the Amsterdam Academie van Bouwkunst. His publication topics range from historical analysis via methodological approaches to theoretical studies, together with reports and criticisms on recent design results.

Relevant publications:

Valk, A. van der/R. van Leeuwen, 2000: *Gespaard Landschap*, Amsterdam (Amsterdamse Raad voor de Monumentenzorg/De Balie).
Leeuwen, R. van, 2003: Het verbouwde landschap, in W. Dijkshoorn/E. de Jong/L. Odé (eds.), *Van Singel tot Singelgracht*, Zwolle, 31-69.
Leeuwen, R. van, 2009: Inleiding, in M. Steenhuis/F. Hooimeijer (eds.): *Maakbaar Landschap, Nederlandse landschapsarchitectuur 1945 – 1970*, Rotterdam, 24-65.
Bloemers, T./S. Husken/R. van Leeuwen, 2009: *Een agenda voor het Oer-IJ*, Haarlem.

Address:
R. van Leeuwen, RBOI Rotterdam bv, Postbus 150, NL-1030 AD Rotterdam, The Netherlands.
Tel.: +31 104 130 620
E-mail: r.vanleeuwen@rboi.nl

Martijn van Leusen

Martijn van Leusen is assistant professor of Landscape Archaeology at the University of Groningen. His research interests focus on the methodology of landscape archaeological research, including such topics as geoarchaeology, GIS modelling and fieldwork techniques. Martijn is currently compiling primary publications for the 5-year 'Hidden Landscapes' research project. He was a member of the editorial board of the European Journal of Archaeology from 2002 to 2008.

Relevant publications:

Leusen, P.M. van/H. Kamermans (eds.), 2005: *Predictive Modelling for Archaeological Heritage Management: a research agenda*, Amersfoort (Nederlandse Archeologische Rapporten 29).
Leusen, M. van/A.R. Millard/B. Ducke, 2009: Dealing with uncertainty in archaeological prediction, in H. Kamermans/M. van Leusen/Ph. Verhagen (eds.), *Archaeological Prediction and Risk Management. Alternatives to Current Practice*, Leiden (ASLU 17), 123-173.
Kamermans, H./M. van Leusen/Ph. Verhagen (eds.), 2009: *Archaeological Prediction and Risk Management. Alternatives to Current Practice*, Leiden (ASLU 17).

Address:
Dr M. van Leusen, Groningen Institute of Archaeology, Poststraat 6, NL-9712 ER Groningen, The Netherlands.
Tel.: +31 503 636 717
E-mail: P.M.van.Leusen@rug.nl

Heleen van Londen

Heleen van Londen's field of research covers landscape archaeology and heritage management. In her Ph.D. thesis she analysed the results from the large-scale regional field project in Midden-Delfland with a focus on the Roman period land use and field systems.

Relevant publications:
Londen, H. van, 2006: *Midden-Delfland: The Roman Native Landscape Past and Present*, Amsterdam (Ph.D. thesis University of Amsterdam).
Londen, H. van, 2006: Cultural biography and the power of image, in W. van der Knaap/A.van der Valk (eds.), *Multiple Landscape. Merging Past and Present. Selected Papers from the fifth International Workshop on Sustainable Land Use Planning 7-9 June 2004*, Wageningen, 171-181.
Bartels Chr./M. Ruiz del Árbol/H. van Londen/A. Orejas (eds.), 2008: *Landmarks. Profiling Europe's historic landscapes*, Bochum.
Londen, H. van/Orejas, A./Ruiz del Árbol, M., 2009: Historic landscapes in Europe: highlights and challenges, in A. Orejas/D. Mattingly/M. Clavel-Lévêque (eds.), *From present to past through landscape*, Madrid, 43-59.

Address:
Dr H. van Londen, Amsterdam Archaeological Centre, University of Amsterdam, Turfdraagsterpad 9, NL-1012 XT Amsterdam, The Netherlands.
Tel.: +31 205 255 830
E-mail: h.vanlonden@uva.nl
Web: www.uva.nl

Lesley Macinnes

Lesley Macinnes' field of research interests covers the understanding, conservation and management of the historic and cultural landscape, integration of natural and cultural aspects of landscape and conservation of historic battlefields.

Relevant publications:
Macinnes, L./C.R. Wickham-Jones (eds.), 1992 *All natural things: archaeology and the green debate*, Oxford.
Fairclough, G./L. Macinnes, 2003: *Understanding Historic Landscape Character*, (Topic Paper 5, published by the Countryside Agency and Scottish Natural Heritage, September 2003). This can be downloaded at http://www.landscapecharacter.org.uk/node/82.

Macinnes, L., 2004: Historic Landscape Characterization, in K. Bishop/A. Phillips (eds.), *Countryside Planning: New Approaches to Management and Conservation,* London, 155-69.

Macinnes, L., 2006²: Archaeology as land use, in J. Hunter/I. Ralston (eds.), *Archaeological Resource Management in the UK, an introduction,* Stroud, 229-257.

Macinnes, L., 2006: From past to present: understanding and managing the historic environment, in R. Davidson/C.A. Galbraith (eds.), *Scottish Farming, Forestry and the Natural Heritage: Towards a More Integrated Approach,* Edinburgh, 157-170.

Address:
Lesley Macinnes, Historic Scotland, Longmore House, Salisbury Place, Edinburgh GB-EH9 1SH, Scotland.

Tel.: +44 131 668 865 3
Fax: +44 131 668 889 9
Email: lesley.macinnes@scotland.gsi.gov.uk
Web: http://www.historic-scotland.gov.uk

Michael O'Connell

Michael O'Connell specializes in detailed pollen analytical investigations of lake sediment and peat cores, and mineral soils/overlying peats from archaeological contexts, with a view to reconstructing long-term human impact on landscapes and woodland dynamics during the Holocene in Ireland.

Relevant publications:

(with Karen Molloy and Ingo Feeser), in press: A new pollen record from east Galway: fresh insights into farming and woodland dynamics in mid-western Ireland from the Neolithic to recent times, in R.J. Schulting/N.J. Whitehouse/M. McClatchie (eds.), *Living landscapes: exploring Neolithic Ireland and its wider context,* Oxford (BAR).

(with Ingo Feeser), 2010: Late Holocene land-use and vegetation dynamics in an upland karst region based on pollen and coprophilous fungal spore analyses: an example from the Burren, western Ireland, *Vegetation History and Archaeobotany*. Published online DOI 10.1007/s00334-009-0235-5, Jan 2010.

(with Karen Molloy), 2007: Fresh insights into long-term environmental change on the Aran Islands based on palaeoecological investigations of lake sediments from Inis Oírr, *Journal of the Galway Archaeological and Historical Society* 59, 1-17.

(with Karen Molloy), 2001: Farming and woodland dynamics in Ireland during the Neolithic, *Biology and Environment (Proc Royal Irish Academy, Ser B)* 101, 99-128.

Address:
Prof. Michael O'Connell, Palaeoenvironmental Research Unit, School of Natural Sciences (Botany), National University of Ireland Galway, Galway, Ireland.

Tel.: +35 386 389 144 4
E-mail: michael.oconnell@nuigalway.ie
Web: www.nuigalway.ie/pru

Stijn Oonk

Stijn Oonk (1974) is an all-round chemist. His research has focused on analytical chemistry, geochemistry, mass spectrometry, proteomics, as well as archaeology, art, and defence and security issues. In 2009 he received a Ph.D. degree (VU University Amsterdam) through a research project on geochemical prospection in archaeology. Prior to and after this achievement he was trained and educated by a variety of top scientific institutions, including TNO, AMOLF-FOM, Merck, the University of York, VU University Amsterdam and the University of Amsterdam. At present Stijn is a scientist at TNO defence and security, conducting state-of-the-art research on bacterial and soil proteomics, geochemistry and mass spectrometry.

Relevant publications:

Oonk, S., 2009: *The application of geochemical prospection for Dutch archaeological resource management*, Amsterdam, (Ph.D. thesis VU University; Geoarchaeological and Bioarchaeological studies 11).

Oonk, S./C.P. Slomp/D.J. Huisman, 2010: Geochemistry as an aid in archaeological prospection and site interpretation: current issues and research directions, *Archaeological Prospection* 16, 35-51.

Oonk, S./C.P. Slomp/D.J. Huisman/S.P. Vriend, 2010: Effects of site lithology on geochemical signatures of human occupation in archaeological house plans in The Netherlands, *Journal of Archaeological Science* 36, 1215-1228.

Address:
Dr S. Oonk, TNO Defence, Security and Safety, Postbus 5050, NL-2600 GB Delft, The Netherlands.
E-mail: stijn.oonk@yahoo.com

Almudena Orejas

Almudena Orejas' research addresses the study of ancient rural landscapes (agrarian and mining) in the Iberian Peninsula in Roman Times. She is interested in the conceptual formulation and design of a specific methodology for the study of ancient landscapes and in the integration processes of peninsular territories and communities in Roman Times from a landscape archaeology perspective.

Relevant publications :

(with F.J. Sánchez-Palencia), 2002: Mines, Territorial Organisation and Social Structure in Roman Iberia : Carthago Nova and the Peninsular Northwest, *American Journal of Archaeology* 106, 581-599.

Orejas, A., 2001-2003: *Atlas historique des zones minières d'Europe, I & II*, Luxemburgo (OPCE, Comisión Europea).

A. Orejas/D. Mattingly/M. Clavel-Lévêque (eds.), 2009: *From present to past through landscape*, Madrid.

Address:
Dr A. Orejas, Instituto de Historia, Centro de Ciencias Humanas y Sociales, CSIC c/ Albasanz, 26-28, ES-28037 Madrid, Spain.
Tel.:   +34 916 022 486
E-mail: almudena.orejas@cchs.csic.es
Web: http://www.cchs.csic.es

Philip Paar

Philip Paar (1970) is a landscape planner and 3D modelling and visualization expert who studied at the Technical University Berlin (TUB). Research assistant at German Federal Agency for Nature Protection (BFN, 1996), and Leibniz Centre for Agricultural Landscape Research (ZALF, 1997 to 2002). Project manager of the joint research project on computer graphics assisted landscape planning (New Media for Landscape Planning – Lenné3D). Co-founder and managing director of the visualization & software company Lenné3D from 2005 to 2009. Occasionally, visiting researcher or lecturer, e.g. Chair of Landscape Architecture, University of Wageningen (WUR), University of Applied Sciences Eberswalde (FHE), and Anhalt University of Applied Sciences (HSA). From 2009 onwards, visiting fellow at National Singapore University (NUS) introducing GIS, landscape modelling, and visualization to MLA students. April 2010 onwards co-founder and managing director of the computer graphics start-up Laubwerk – Digital Botany.

Relevant publications:

Paar, P., 2006: Landscape visualizations: Applications and requirements of 3D visualization software for environmental planning, *Computers, Environment and Urban Systems* 30, 815-839.

Rekittke, J./P. Paar, 2006: Digital Botany, *Journal of Landscape Architecture* 2, 28-35.

Paar, P./W. Röhricht/J. Schuler, 2008: Towards a planning support system for environmental management and agri-environmental measures – the Colorfields study, *Journal of Environmental Management* 89 (special issue 'Our Shared Landscape), 234-244.

Address:
Philip Paar, Torstrasse 75, D-10119 Berlin, Germany.
E-mail: paar@laubwerk.com
Web: www.laubwerk.com

Hannes Palang

Hannes Palang's main research interests lie in geography and landscape studies. He has published on landscape change and its perception from various vantage points.

Relevant publications:

Palang, H./H. Alumäe/Ü. Mander, 2000: Holistic aspects in landscape development: a scenario approach, *Landscape and Urban Planning* 50, 85-94.

Palang, H./G. Fry (eds.), 2003: *Landscape Interfaces: Cultural Heritage in Changing Landscapes*, Dordrecht.

Palang H./H. Sooväli/M. Antrop/G. Setten (eds.), 2004: *European Rural Landscapes: Permanence, Persistence and Change in the Globalising Environment*, Dordrecht.

Address:
Dr H. Palang, Centre for Landscape and Culture, Estonian Institute of Humanities, Tallinn University, Uus-Sadama 5, EE-10120 Tallinn, Estonia.
Tel.:   +37 261 995 57
E-mail: hannes.palang@tlu.ee
Web: www.tlu.ee

Gísli Pálsson

Gísli Pálsson's main areas of current research relate to biomedicine (the new genetics, biobanks and genetic history), arctic exploration, property rights, environmental discourse, and the draining and reclaiming of wetlands.

Relevant publications:
(with Edward H. Huijbens), 2009: The Bog in Our Brain and Bowels: The Social Attitudes to the Carthography of Icelandic Wetlands, *Environment and Planning D: Society and Space* 27, 296-316.
(with Edward H. Huijbens), 2009: The Marsh of Modernity: Iceland and Beyond, in K. Hastrup (ed.), *The Question of Resilience: Social Responses to Climate Change*, Copenhagen, 48-69.
Gisli Pálsson, in press: Nature/Culture, in A. Gingrich (ed.), *Globalisation Face to Face: One Hundred Entries From Anthropology for Practitioners and Professionals*, Frankfurt am Main.
Pálsson's latest book is *Anthropology and the New Genetics*, Cambridge, 2007.

Address:
Prof. Gisli Pálsson, Department of Anthropology, University of Iceland, IS-101 Reykjavík, Iceland.
Tel.:   +35 452 542 53
E-mail: gpals@hi.is
Web: http://www2.felags.hi.is/page/gpals

Carsten Paludan-Müller

Carsten Paludan-Müller is General Director of NIKU, the Norwegian Institute for Cultural Heritage Research. His fields of research cover interdisciplinary research into the long-term development of the relationship between economic, political and symbolic organization of the physical environment, into empires and nation states as frameworks for economic, cultural and political diversity, and into the role of cultural heritage and the historical disciplines in the construction and deconstruction of identities and conflicts. Other activities concern working with the Council of Europe on the development and follow up of the European conventions on cultural heritage.

Relevant publications:
2008: The need for an archaeology of Europe. Reasons and perspectives, *Archaeological Dialogues* 15, 48-51.
2009: Europe – a constrained and fragmented space on the edge of the continental landmasses. Crossroad, battlefield and melting-pot, in *Heritage and Beyond*, Strasbourg, 75-83.
2010 in press: The Imperial Mirror, in C. Fenwick/K. Lafrenz Samuels/D. Totten (eds.), *Roman Spaces, Heritage Traces: Past and Present Roman Place-making*, Portsmouth/Rhode Island (JRA Supplementary Series).

Address:
Dr C. Paludan-Müller, NIKU, The Norwegian Institute for Cultural Heritage Research
P.O. Box 736 Sentrum, NO-0105 Oslo, Norway.
Tel. :   +47 233 550 00
Mobile: +47 932 668 41

E-mail: cpm@niku.no
Web: www.niku.no

Anu Printsmann

Anu Printsmann's main research interests lie in human geography and landscape studies combining geoinformatics with a biographical approach. She has been involved in projects regarding valuable, transboundary, suburban, protected, seasonal, bog and agricultural landscapes.

Relevant publications:

Palang, H./A. Printsmann/É. Konkoly Gyuró/M. Urbanc/E. Skowronek/W. Woloszyn, 2006: The forgotten rural landscapes of Central and Eastern Europe, *Landscape Ecology* 21, 347-357.

Palang, H./A. Printsmann, 2010: From totalitarian to democratic landscapes: the transition in Estonia, in J. Primdahl/J. and S. Swaffield (eds.), *Globalisation and Agricultural Landscapes: Change Patterns and Policy Trends in Developed Countries*, Cambridge, 169-184.

Address:
Anu Printsmann, Centre for Landscape and Culture, Estonian Institute of Humanities, Tallinn University, Uus-Sadama 5, EE-10120 Tallinn, Estonia.
Tel.: +37 261 995 39
E-mail: anu.printsmann@tlu.ee
Web: www.tlu.ee

Guillermo S. Reher

Guillermo S. Reher has a contract as project manager for the CSD-TCP network project on technological applications for heritage management. He was contracted by the coordination team to assist in organizing the international activity of the 16 groups integrated in the network. His Ph.D. research focuses on the study of ethnicity in the lower Tagus basin from pre-Roman to Roman times. His work is integrated in that of the Research Group *Social Structure and Territory: Landscape Archaeology*.

Relevant publications:

Alonso, F./A. Beltrán/B. Currás/J.L. Pecharromán/G.S. Reher/D. Romero, 2008: Leyendo paisajes culturales. Un modelo de trabajo desde el GI: EST-AP, in OrJIA (coord.), *I Jornadas de Jóvenes en Investigación Arqueológica: Dialogando con la cultura material*, OrJIA, Madrid, 549-554.

Reher, G.S., 2009: Estrategias de asentamiento ante la romanización en la cuenca baja del Tajo, in P. Sanabria (ed.), *Lusitanos y vettones. Los pueblos prerromanos en la actual demarcación Beira Baixa – Alto Alentejo – Cáceres*, Cáceres, 241-254.

Address:
Guillermo S. Reher, CSIC (Consejo Superior de Investigaciones Científicas = Spanish National Research Council), Instituto de Historia, Centro de Ciencias Humanas y Sociales, CSIC c/ Albasanz, 26-28, ES-28037 Madrid, Spain.
Tel.: +34 916 022 618

E-mail: guillermo.reher@cchs.csic.es
Web of the Institute: (http://www.cchs.csic.es/)
Web of the Research Group: (http://www.ih.csic.es/paginas/territorio/index.htm)

Jörg Rekittke
Jörg Rekittke (1966), landscape architect, studied at the Technical University Berlin and Ecole Nationale Supérieure du Paysage Versailles. He has been teaching assistant at RWTH Aachen University from 1997 until 2001 at the Department of Landscape Design, from 2001 to 2006 at the Department of Urban Design and Regional Planning. Doctorate from RWTH Aachen University in 2001. Co-founder and art director of Lenné3D GmbH (2005). Employed 2004-2006 as Associate Lecturer at Department of Town Planning, Urban- and Regional Planning, University of Siegen; 2006 as Associate Lecturer for the international Master's Programme in Landscape Architecture, Hochschule Anhalt. December 2006 to 2008 Assistant Professor at the Chair of Landscape Architecture, University of Wageningen, the Netherlands. Since 2009 Associate Professor and Director of the Master of Landscape Architecture Programme at the Department of Architecture, School of Design and Environment, National University of Singapore.

Relevant publications:
Rekittke, J./P. Paar, 2006: Digital Botany, *Journal of Landscape Architecture* 2, 28-35.
Rekittke, J., 2009: Grassroots Landscape Architecture for the Informal Asian City, in Lei Qu *et al.* (eds.), *The New Urban Question. Urbanism Beyond Neo-Liberalism*, Rotterdam (Conference Proceedings), 667-675.

Address:
Jörg Rekittke, Associate Prof. Dr.-Ing./Landscape Architect, Director NUS Master of Landscape Architecture Program, National University of Singapore, School of Design and Environment, Department of Architecture, 4 Architecture Drive, Singapore 117566.
E-mail: rekittke@nus.edu.sg
Web: www.arch.nus.edu.sg

Nico Roymans
Nico Roymans' fields of research cover landscape archaeology and archaeology of Western Europe. He is professor of Western European Archaeology at VU University in Amsterdam.

Relevant publications:
Roymans, N., 1995: The cultural biography of urnfields and the long-term history of a mythical landscape, *Archaeological Dialogues* 2, 2-38.
Theuws, F./N. Roymans (eds.), 1999: *Land and ancestors. Cultural dynamics in the Urnfield period and the Middle Ages in the Southern Netherlands*, Amsterdam (Amsterdam Archaeological Studies 4).
Roymans, N./F. Gerritsen, 2002: Landscape, ecology and mentalités: a long-term perspective on developments in the Meuse-Demer-Scheldt region, *Proceedings of the Prehistoric Society* 68, 257-287.
Roymans, N./F. Gerritsen/C. van der Heijden/K. Bosma/J. Kolen, 2009: Landscape Biography as Research Strategy: The Case of the South Netherlands Project, *Landscape Research* 34, 337-359.

Address:
Prof. Dr N. Roymans, VU University Amsterdam, Faculty of Arts, Archaeology
De Boelelaan 1105, NL-1081 HV Amsterdam, The Netherlands.
Tel.: +31 205 986 369
E-mail: ngam.roymans@let.vu.nl
Web: http://www.let.vu.nl/nl/organisatie-van-de-faculteit/wetenschappelijk-personeel/
medewerkers-alfabetisch/medewerkers-l-s/prof-dr-n-g-a-m-roymans/index.asp

Maria Ruiz del Árbol

Maria Ruiz del Árbol's research focuses on the study of the processes of change of the Iberian Peninsula's ancient social formations and the application of this research from a landscape archaeology approach to the management and planning of the studied regions.

Relevant publications:
(edited with L. Léveque/L. Pop/C. Bartels), 2007: *Journeys through European Landscapes*, Ponferrada.
(edited with C. Bartels/H. van Londen/A. Orejas), 2008: *Landmarks. Profiling Europe's Landscapes*, Bochum.
(directed with L. Lévêque/L. Pop), 2009: *Heritage, Images, Memory of European Landscapes*, Paris.

Address:
M. Ruiz del Árbol, Instituto de Historia, Centro de Ciencias Humanas y Sociales, CSIC c/ Albasanz, 26-28, EE-28037 Madrid, Spain.
Tel.: +34 916 022 703
E-mail: maria.ruizdelarbol@cchs.csic.es
Web: http://www.cchs.csic.es

Holger Schaaff

The archaeologist Holger Schaaff is head of Forschungsbereich VAT and has worked on the project "Vulkanpark Osteifel" since 1996. His research subject within the project is the history of the tuff stone industry from the Roman period. He was in charge of the excavation and presentation of the "Römerbergwerk Meurin" site.

Relevant publications:
Schaaff, H., 1993: *Die Altertümer der Merowingerzeit im Großherzogtum Luxemburg*, Luxembourg (Dossiers d'Archéologie du Musée National d'Histoire et d'Art 2).
Schaaff, H., 2000: Antike Tuffbergwerke in der Pellenz, in *Steinbruch und Bergwerk. Denkmäler römischer Technikgeschichte zwischen Eifel und Rhein*, Mainz (Vulkanpark-Forschungen 2), 17-30.

Address:
Dr H. Schaaff, Forschungsbereich Vulkanologie, Archäologie und Technikgeschichte (VAT) des Römisch-Germanischen Zentralmuseums Mainz/Mayen, An den Mühlsteinen 7, D-56727 Mayen, Germany.
E-mail: schaaff@rgzm.de

Bjørn Smit

From 2004 until 2008 Bjørn Smit researched at Groningen Institute of Archaeology (GIA), University of Groningen, early prehistoric surface scatters to assess the scientific value of these scatters both within a scientific environment and the context of archaeological heritage management. Attention was paid to how the research of surface scatters might be improved to gain scientific knowledge and also to creating a means of communicating the story of our early prehistory to a wider audience. From August 2008 he took on a new job at RAAP Archeologisch Adviesbureau BV, a commercial company which deals with several aspects of archaeological research in contract archaeology. The focus of his work is the research of archaeological remains dating to the Stone Age. As from mid-June 2010, he will take up a new position as senior researcher early prehistory at the National Cultural Heritage Agency of the Netherlands (RCE).

Relevant publications:

Smit, B.I., 2007. Oppervlaktevindplaatsen uit de steentijd rondom Wildervank (Gr.). *Paleoaktueel* 18, 43-51.

Raemaekers, D.C.M./B.I. Smit/M.J.L.Th. Niekus, 2008: Bewoning uit de vroege prehistorie: laat-paleolithicum tot en met vroege IJzertijd op Midlaren-de Bloemert, in J.A.W. Nicolay (ed.), *Opgravingen bij Midlaren, 5000 jaar wonen tussen Hondsrug en Hunzedal*, Groningen, 74-90.

Smit, B.I., 2010. *Valuable Flints. Research strategies for the study of early prehistoric remains from the Pleistocene soils of the Northern Netherlands*, Groningen (Ph.D. thesis University of Groningen).

Address:

Dr Bjørn Smit, Rijksdienst voor het Cultureel Erfgoed, Smallepad 5, NL-3811 MG Amersfoort, The Netherlands.
Tel.:   +31 334 217 421
E-mail: B.Smit@cultureelerfgoed.nl

Theo Spek

Theo Spek works as a senior researcher of landscape history and programme manager at the Cultural Heritage Agency of the Netherlands in Amersfoort, and is also professor of landscape history at the University of Groningen. His research focuses on the interdisciplinary connections between historical geography, archaeology, soil science and ecology. In 2004 he was awarded a doctorate for his study of the genesis of the Drenthe cultural landscape. In his daily work and outside interests, he advises on nature management, landscape management and heritage management. He has led the Drentsche Aa research and action programme over the past five years, alongside Hans Elerie.

Publications:

Spek, Th., 2007: Kulturlandschaftsentwicklung in den Eschdörferlandschaften der nordöstlichen Niederlanden (Provinz Drenthe), in W. Schenk/R. Bergmann (eds.), *Historische Kulturlandschaftsforschung im Spannungsfeld von älteren Ansätzen und aktuellen Fragestellungen und Methoden. Institutioneller Hintergrund, methodische Ausgangsüberlegungen und inhaltlichen Zielsetzungen,* Bonn (Siedlungsforschung 24), 219-250.

Spek, Th./W. Groenman-van Wateringe/ M.J. Kooistra/L.W. Bakker, 2003: Formation and landuse-history of Celtic fields in North-West Europe. An interdisciplinary case study at Zeijen, The Netherlands, *European Journal of Archaeology* 6, 141-169.

Address:
Prof. Dr T. Spek, Department of Landscape, Cultural Heritage Agency, PO Box 1600, NL-3800 BP Amersfoort, The Netherlands.
Tel.:   +31 620 136 689
E-mail: t.spek@cultureelerfgoed.nl

Institute of Architectural and Art History, University of Groningen, Oude Boteringestraat 34, NL-9712 GK Groningen, The Netherlands.
Tel.:   +31 503 638 951
E-mail: theo.spek@rug.nl

Liesbeth Theunissen
As a senior researcher Liesbeth Theunissen is responsible for the archaeological heritage from the Late Neolithic, Bronze and Iron Age. She participated in the creation of a national research agenda and contributed to the national heritage review on the subject of knowledge and knowledge growth. She carried out several assessments of sites *in situ* in the wetlands of the Netherlands. Currently, she is involved in a multidisciplinary project on the Single Grave Culture of North Holland. This project aims to unlock and integrate cultural and ecological information and research data in order to provide a sound basis for cultural modelling and development of heritage management strategies.

Relevant publications:
Heeringen, R.M. van/E.M. Theunissen, 2002: *Preserving the quality of the Archaeological Landscape at Voorne-Putten*, Amersfoort (Nederlandse Archeologische Rapporten 25).
Smit, A./R.M. van Heeringen/E.M. Theunissen, 2006: *Archaeological Monitoring Standard (SAM). Guidelines for the non-destructive recording and monitoring of the physical quality of archaeological sites and monuments*, Amersfoort (Nederlandse Archeologische Rapporten 33).
Theunissen, E.M./R.M. van Heeringen, 2006: Hidden heritage of the Dutch delta. Thoughts about the Preservation Capacity of Wetlands and the Sustainability of the Archaeological Resource, *Berichten van de Rijksdienst voor het Oudheidkundig Bodemonderzoek* 46, 246-273.
Huisman, D.J./E.M. Theunissen, 2008: Too good to be true? The unexpectedly good condition of the Nieuw-Dordrecht trackway and its implications, in H. Kars/R.M. van Heeringen (eds.), *Preserving archaeological remains in situ. Proceedings of the 3rd conference 7-9 December 2006*, Amsterdam (Geoarchaeological and Bioarchaeological Studies 10), 15-27.

Address:
Dr E.M. Theunissen, Ministry of Education, Culture and Science, Cultural Heritage Agency, Smallepad 5, 3811 MG, Amersfoort; P.O. Box 1600, NL-3800 BP, Amersfoort, The Netherlands.
Tel.:   +31 334 217 603

E-mail: l.theunissen@cultureelerfgoed.nl
Web: www.cultureelerfgoed.nl

Arnold van der Valk
Arnold van der Valk (1953) has been a full professor of land use planning at Wageningen University in the Netherlands since 2002. He has taken an MSc in human geography (specialization historical geography) and another MSc in urban and regional planning, both at the University of Amsterdam. His research revolves around planning theory, planning at the metropolitan scale, heritage and landscape. Since 1999 he has been leader of three major interdisciplinary research programmes sponsored by national research foundations.

Relevant publications:
Valk, A. van de, 2002: The Dutch planning experience, *Landscape and Urban Planning* 58, 201-210.
Knaap, W. van der/A. van der Valk (eds.), 2006: *Multiple Landscape. Merging Past and Present. Selected Papers from the fifth International Workshop on Sustainable Land Use Planning 7-9 June 2004*, Wageningen.
Valk, A. van der/T. van Dijk, 2009: *Regional Planning for Open Space*, London.

Address:
Prof. Dr Arnold van der Valk, Wageningen University, Landscape Centre, Land Use Planning, Building no. 101, Droevendaalsesteeg 3,NL-6708 PB Wageningen; P.O. Box 47, 6700 AA Wageningen,
The Netherlands.
Tel.:   +31 748 369 6; +31 206 840 947
E-mail: arnold.vandervalk@wur.nl ; a.vdvalk@chello.nl
Web: http://www.lup.wur.nl/uk/staff/valk

Philip Verhagen
Philip Verhagen (1966) graduated in Physical Geography in 1989, and has worked in commercial archaeology as a specialist in GIS from 1992 to 2005. From 1992 to 1998 he participated in the European Union-funded Archaeomedes and Rio Aguas projects in France and Spain. From the mid-1990s on he has actively participated in the development of predictive modelling for archaeological heritage management in the Netherlands leading to his thesis, completed in 2007. From around 2001, he has also worked on issues concerning the reliability of archaeological survey techniques for detecting archaeological sites, especially core sampling and (more recently) trial trenching. In 2008 Philip Verhagen obtained a VENI grant from NWO to extend his research in predictive modelling focusing on the social and cultural dimensions of past landscapes and of temporality.

Relevant publications:
Kamermans, H./M. van Leusen/P. Verhagen (eds.), 2009: *Archaeological Prediction and Risk Management. Alternatives to Current Practice*, Leiden (ASLU 17).
Verhagen, P., 2007: *Case Studies in Archaeological Predictive Modelling*, Leiden (Ph.D. thesis Leiden University, ASLU 14).

Verhagen, P., 2006: Quantifying the Qualified: the Use of Multicriteria Methods and Bayesian Statistics for the Development of Archaeological Predictive Models, in M. Mehrer/K. Wescott (eds.), *GIS and Archaeological Site Location Modeling,* Boca Raton, 191-216.

Address:
Dr P. Verhagen, CLUE, Faculty of Arts, VU University, De Boelelaan 1105, NL-1081 HV Amsterdam, The Netherlands.
Tel.:   +31 205 982 848
E-mail: jwhp.verhagen@let.vu.nl
Web: www.let.vu.nl/staf/jwhp.verhagen

Jelle Vervloet
Jelle Vervloet studied historical geography, prehistory and physical geography at the Vrije Universiteit at Amsterdam. Since 1974 he has worked as a historical geographer in Wageningen, specialized in heritage management and spatial planning of landscapes. He was attached as a researcher successively to the Soil Survey Institute, the Staring Centre and Alterra. In 1988, next to this job, he was appointed associate professor of historical geography (Socio-spatial Analysis Group) at Wageningen University. He is in charge of the Eastern Netherlands Project, one of the regional projects of the PDL/BBO programme.

Relevant publications :
Vervloet, J.A.J./J.H. Nijman/A.J. Somsen, 2005: Planning for the future; towards a sustainable design and land use of an ancient flooded military defence line, *Landscape and Urban Planning* 70, 153-163.
Vervloet, J.A.J., 2007: Some remarks about the changing position of landscape assessment, in Z. Roca/T. Spek/T. Terkenli/T. Plieninger/F. Höchtl (eds.), *Proceedings of the 21st Session of the PECSRL Conference "One Region, Many Stories: European Landscapes and Lifestyles: The Mediterranean Landscapes in a Changing Europe", Limnos/Lesvos 2004,* Lisboa, 433-439.
Vervloet, J.A.J., 2008: The position of cultural history and heritage management in a complex society, in H. de Haan/R. van der Duim (eds.), *Landscape, Leisure and Tourism. Socio-spatial Studies in Experiences, Practices and Policies,* Delft, 63-73.
Vervloet, J.A.J./A. van den Brink/J. Lengkeek, 2009: Agrarische cultuurlandschappen en erfgoed, in A. van der Zande/R.During (eds.), *Ons Erfgoed en Ruimtelijke Planning,* Den Haag, 273-294.

Address:
Prof. Dr J.A.J. Vervloet, Wageningen University and Research, Landscape Centre,
Socio-spatial Analysis, P.O. Box 47, NL-6700 AA Wageningen, The Netherlands.
Tel: +31 317 486 114
E-mail: Jelle.Vervloet@wur.nl
Web: www.sal.wur.nl

J. Sophie Visser
J. Sophie Visser graduated in Historical Geography at Utrecht University in 2006, after a career in information (systems) development, modelling, planning and strategy, and an MSc in Chemistry (specialization Chemometrics) in 1979. Currently she has her own consultancy firm LandZij, and is working on a Ph.D. thesis on information systems about cultural historical landscapes.

Relevant publications:

Visser, J.S., 2007: Historische geografie en digitale vastlegging: een kritische analyse, *Historisch Geografisch Tijdschrift* 25, 15-26.

Visser, J.S., in press: Back to Basics. Cultural landscape analysis from an informational & perceptual perspective, in *Proceedings 14th International Conference of Historical Geographers*, Kyoto.

Visser, J.S./H. Renes 2010: Angewandte Historische Geographie: alte Methoden und neue Fragen, in (s.e.), *Kulturlandschaft in der Anwendung*, Bonn (Bund Heimat und Umwelt in Deutschland), 51-59.

Address:
J. Sophie Visser, LandZij, Roomburgerweg 39, NL-2314 XN Leiden, The Netherlands.
Tel.:   +31 715 622 999
E-mail: landzij@planet.nl

Martin Vollmer-König
Martin Vollmer-König is an archaeologist with a pedological and historical background. His main theme of interest is the protection of archaeological heritage. As an instrument to reach better awareness in the long term his special aim is to make archaeological sites visible as parts of the recent landscape. For about sixteen years he has been responsible for archaeological heritage protection in the Rhineland, Germany.

Relevant publications:

Vollmer-König, M., 2005: Archäologie in Schloss Wickrath. Forschungsstand und bodendenkmalpflegerische Bedeutung, *Arbeitsheft der rheinischen Denkmalpflege* 65, 56-86.

Vollmer-König, M., 2008: Schützen, pflegen, sinnvoll nutzen - Bodendenkmalpflege und Planung, *Archäologie im Rheinland 2007*, 29-31.

Völlmer-König, M., 2008: Graefenthal in der Denkmallandschaft des Niederrheins, *Arbeitsheft der rheinischen Denkmalpflege* 72, 331-334.

Vollmer-König, M., 2009: Frühe Industrieobjekte und andere praemoderne Anlagen aus bodendenkmalpflegerischer Sicht, in H.-J. Przybilla/A. Grünkemeier (eds.), *Denkmäler3.de – Industriearchäologie, Tagungsband des interdisziplinären Kolloquiums vom 5.-7. November 2008 in Essen, Zollverein School*, Aachen, 97-106.

Address:
M. Vollmer-König, LVR Amt für Bodendenkmalpflege im Rheinland, Endenicher Straße 133, D-53115 Bonn, Germany.
Tel.:   +49 228 983 418 5

E-mail: m.vollmer-koenig@lvr.de
Web: www.bodendenkmalpflege.lvr.de

Peter Vos

Peter Vos is a Quaternary geologist employed with Deltares (until 1 January 2008: TNO Built Environment and Geosciences; formerly Geological Survey of the Netherlands) and a specialist in Holocene coastal geology, palaeogeography and geoarchaeology of northwest Europe.

Relevant publications:

Vos, P.C./R.M. van Heeringen, 1997: Holocene geology and occupation history of the Province of Zeeland (SW Netherlands), in M.M. Fischer (ed.), *Holocene evolution of Zeeland (SW Netherlands)*, Haarlem (Meded. NITG-TNO 59), 5-109.

Vos, P.C./D.A. Gerrets, 2004: Archaeology, a major tool in the reconstruction of the coastal evolution of Westergo (The Northern Netherlands), *Quaternary International* 133-134, 61-75.

Vos, P.C./C. Soonius, 2004: Het Oer-IJ estuarium, Archeologische Kennisinventarisatie (AKI), 4. Oude landschappen, in S. Lange et al. (ed.), *Het Oer-IJ estuarium, Archeologische Kennisinventarisatie (AKI)*, Amsterdam, 30-40.

Address:
P.C. Vos, Deltares, P.O. Box 85467, NL-3508 AL Utrecht, The Netherlands.
Tel.: +31 883 355 716 9
Mobile: +31 653 736 009
E-mail: peter.vos@deltares.nl

Mies Wijnen

Mies Wijnen has as former staff member of the Netherlands Organization for Scientific Research acted as secretary of the PDL/BBO research programme and its Steering and Programme Committees. She is an archaeologist by profession and completed her Ph.D. thesis on the prehistoric archaeology of Greece.

Relevent publications:

Bloemers, J.H.F./R. During/J.N.H. Elerie/H.A. Groenendijk/M. Hidding/J. Kolen/Th. Spek/M.-H. Wijnen, 2001: *Bodemarchief in Behoud en Ontwikkeling. De conceptuele grondslagen*, Den Haag.

Bloemers, J.H.F./M.-H. Wijnen (eds.) 2002: *Protecting and Developing the Dutch Archaeological-Historical Landscape*, The Hague.

Address:
Dr M.-H. Wijnen, Obrechtstraat 263, NL-2517 TX Den Haag, The Netherlands.
E-mail: Mies.Wijnen@kpnmail.nl

Willem J.H. Willems

Willem J.H. Willems is professor of Archaeological Resource management and of Roman Archaeology at Leiden University in the Netherlands, as well as dean of the Faculty of Archaeology. He studied at the University of Amsterdam and the University of Michigan, Ann Arbor. His work in Roman archaeology includes numerous articles and several monographs. He has worked mainly in archaeological heritage management, as provincial archaeologist, as project manager and State Archaeologist of the Netherlands (director of the ROB) and later as Chief Inspector at the State Inspectorate for Cultural Heritage. He has also published extensively on various aspects of archaeological heritage management. He served as President of the EAA, was the founding President of the Europæ Archæologiæ Consilium (EAC) and is currently co-President of the ICOMOS Committee for Archaeological Heritage Management (ICAHM).

Relevant publications:
(with H. Kars & D.P. Hallewas),1997: *Archaeological Heritage Management in the Netherlands*, Amersfoort/Assen.
(with H. Koschik), 1997: *Der Westwall. Vom Denkmalwert des Unerfreulichen*, Köln/Bonn (Führer zu archäologischen Denkmälern des Rheinlandes 2).
Willem, W.J.H., 1999: *The future of European Archaeology*, Oxford (Oxbow Lecture 3).
2000: *Challenges for European Archaeology*, Zoetermeer.
(with M. van den Dries), 2007: *Quality management in Archaeology*, Oxford (Oxbow).
(with H. van Enckevort and contributions of P. van den Broeke et al.), 2009: *VLPIA NOVIOMAGVS – Roman Nijmegen. The Batavian capital at the Imperial frontier*, Portsmouth/Rhode Island (JRA Supplementary Series 73).

Address:
Prof. Dr W.J.H. Willems, Faculty of Archaeology, Leiden University, P.O. Box 9515, NL-2300 RA Leiden, The Netherlands.
Tel.: +31 715 272 045
E-mail: w.j.h.willems@arch.leidenuniv.nl
Web: http://archeologie.leidenuniv.nl/

John H. Williams

During his professional life John Williams was much involved with cultural resource management, especially the integration of historic environment considerations within spatial planning. He held the chair of the Planarch and Planarch 2 projects while being Head of Heritage Conservation, Kent County Council. An ongoing area of research is that of the development of the medieval town, particularly the bringing together of documentary and archaeological sources. He is now retired and Honorary Visiting Fellow, University of Leicester, Centre for Local History.

Relevant publications:
In relation to spatial planning issues see the various contributions contained in the publications listed in the bibliography to his paper (Ch. VII.4). Also:

J.H. Williams, 2003: Managing the archaeological resource in England: the planning system in action, *Archäologiches Nachrichtenblatt* 8, 217-225.

Address:
Dr J.H. Williams, 25 Orchard Way, Horsmonden, Kent GB-TN12 8LA, England.
Tel: +44 189 272 301 3
E-mail: jhwms@btinternet.com

Anneke Marijke de Zwart
Anneke de Zwart is an art historian and archaeologist. Before she turned to archaeology she was a teacher of art history and managing director at an academy of arts in the Netherlands. She published, with others, some articles on the methodology of art history as an academic discipline. As an archaeologist she is interested in archaeological heritage management especially from a policy science perspective. She was involved in the Belvedere project right from the start and published some reports from the Belvedere workshops held in preparation for the Belvedere White Paper.

Her Ph.D. research is about Archaeological Heritage Management and spatial planning as a part of the Dutch PDL/BBO programme. She is a great lover of the cultural landscape, not from an archaeological point of view but as an experience. The best way to experience the Dutch landscape is on skates in the winter when all the waters are frozen. She performed the traditional and typically Dutch skating tour along the eleven cities of the province of Friesland.

Relevant publications:
Zwart, A. de, in prep.: *Er op of er onder; de strijd om het bodemarchief. Over archeologische monumentenzorg en de kwaliteit van de leefomgeving,* Amsterdam (Ph.D. thesis University of Amsterdam).
Zwart, A. de, 1996: *Laat maar zitten. Een onderzoek naar de mogelijkheden van een archeologisch beleidsplan,* Amersfoort/Amsterdam.

Address:
A.M. de Zwart, Hemonylaan 10/huis, NL-1074 BG Amsterdam, The Netherlands.
Tel.: +031 206 647 118
E-mail: anne.zwart@planet.nl

Subject index

Acculturation 410

Acidity 229-230

Action research 3, 8-9, 35-37, 69, 73-75, 80-81, 92, 191-193, 207-210 (Oer-IJ), 213, 283-284, 509-510, 517, 590, 595
(definition) 73, 679

Actors 53-55, 145-146, 207, 267-269, 273-274
(amateur archaeologists) 296-298
(public) 351

Aerial photography 417

Airborne laser scanning 418

Archaeobotany 161 ff.

Assessment 591

Augering 417

Authenticity 193-195, 255, 324, 645

Autopoiesis 274-279, 283

Belvedere (Memorandum/policy) 5, 7, 196, 587, 597 and 649 (Onderwijsnetwerk), 602, 632, 642, 642-643 and 650 (Post-Belvedere), 655, 679

BIC (Bien de Interés Cultural=Asset of Cultural Interest) 483-485

Biography of landscape 3, 11-13, 38-41, 71, 90, 107-108, 135-136, 190, 195-196, 209, 212-213 (definition and method), 333-335, 388-389, 508-510, 517, 590, 595, 680 (description)
(applications) 40-41, 83, 97-101 (Drentsche Aa), 212-222 (Oer-IJ), 232-233, 373-374 (Peelland, Zandstad), 399-404 (southern Netherlands), 401- 402 (Zandstad), 402-403 (Peelland), 409 (Zandstad and Peelland),
(supra-/infrastructure) 190, 213, 508-509

Bogs 341, 344 (blanket)

Boundary/ies (work) 30-31, 70, 282-283

Canon 196, 212, 644

Christianization (of landscape) 394-395, 408

Chromatography/mass spectrometry 164

Communication 366, 373, 379, 591, 597, 602

Community of practice 509, 550

Comparative approach 553

Complexity 553

Congruency 379, 469, 471, 473, 475

Conservation through/and development 3, 7, 196, 255-257, 284-285, 380, 488, 507, 561, 587, 634, 636, 681

Cultural Landscape programme 565 ff.

(Cultural) heritage/resource 70, 119-120 and 122 (rural built heritage), 120 (oral heritage), 263 ff., 400, 445, 447-448, 450-456, 482 (cultural and natural), 552, 558, 635 (urban), 641ff. (as experience), 646 (interpretations), 681 (definition)
(agricultural) 324-325, 376
(management) 69, 83, 332, 351-357, 358-359, 378, 379-380, 407, 409, 415-416, 426, 480 ff. (Spain), 561 (AHM) 432, 462-463, 635
(policy) 28

(Inter-/trans) Disciplinarity 83, 134 (inter), 141 (trans), 232 (trans), 529 ff. (interdisciplinary research), 548 and 550-551 (interdisciplinarity), 578, 580-583, 586, 683 (description)

(De-)differentation 276-281

Degradation: see preservation

Dehydration 230

Delta programme 536 ff., 543-544

(De-)democratization 291, 302-303

Desertification/deterioration 480-481

Design(ers) 241, 243, 248-252, 402, 410, 635, 646-648

Determinants 408, 410

Development
(blue/green) 332-333, 336, (sustainable) see sustainability

Diversity 247, 253

Emic 123-124, 126

Environment 6, 152-153 (historic), 636 (urban historic)

Environmental Impact Assessment 355, 375-376, 445 ff., 561

Epistemology 594-595

Ethics 199-200

Ethnicity 195, 211

Etic 124-126

European Landscape Convention 3, 368-369, 447, 504, 546, 565, 613, 654 ff., 654 and 656-657 (landscape definition), 681-682 (description)

Experience (of landscape) 25

Farmsteads 391, 408

Faro Convention 658, 663, 660

Fieldnames 105-107 (Drentsche Aa)

Florence Convention 20 (the Netherlands), 23

Framing 464

Function(ality) (of landscapes) 25

Fuzzy structure 601

GIS (modelling) 433, 436

Gradient zones 331, 333, 335

Grounded theory 376

Heath(land) 393, 395-397, 408

Heritage: see cultural heritage/resource

Heteroreference: see Self-(and hetero)reference

Historic land-use assessment 156-158

(Historic) Landscape Characterisation 155-156, 196-197, 508, 613-617, 682 (description)

Hunter-gatherer (societies/landscapes) 329-333, 336, 343

Identity 117, 125, 193-195, 222, 246, 324, 352, 389, 391, 399, 412, 587, 644

Imagination 189-190

Information (systems) 526, 605 ff., 612 (definition)

Infrastructure: see Super-(and infra)structure

Integration (in-/external) 11, 31-35, 410, 454-455, 461, 594-595, 682 (description)

Integrative approach/projects/studies 10, 512-513, 523-524, 534 ff., 644

Intermediary/ies 192

Interpretative (heritage research) 30, 197-198, 291-293, 302-303, 509, 585

Justness 191

Knowledge 365 ff., 369-370, 380, 521 and 586 (definition), 606 (definition), 607-610, 643 (body of knowledge)
(academic) 359
(to action) 69, 72-73, 503
(amateur/ layperson) 300, 537
(broker) 534
(creation process) 503-507, 522, 533, 598 ff., 632
(local) 83, 109-110, 142
(management) 585 ff., 586 (definition)
(production) 37
(explicit/tacit) 533

Lancewad 356

Land appropriation 389-391, 409, 412

LANDMARKS 373, 478, 524, 545 ff.

Land use 408-409, 412 (in-/extensification)

Landscape
(definition) 5, 53, 88, 90, 135-136 (authentic; real), 264-270 (emblematic), 344 and 346 (liminal), 368, 653-655 (metaphorical), 655-656 (ownership)
(archaeological-historical) 6, 679
(architecture) 83
Landscape Character Assessment (LCA) 614-617, 623
(cultural) 407, 410-411, 479, 565 ff. , 586, 605 ff.
(management) 83, 102-105 (Drentsche Aa), 153-155 (Scotland), 265-266 (Norway), 368, 412
(planning) 110, 368, 379-380, 412 (Switzerland)
(typology) 410-412 (of Switzerland)
(vision) 101-102 (Drentsche Aa)

Learning 366

Longue durée 389

Magnetometry/magnetic prosepction 415, 419, 421, 426

Materiality 505

Memory 63-64, 646

Mentality 352, 357

Micromorphology 168, 173

Migrants/-ation 408-410

Mining 177 ff.

Mitigation 453

Mobility 329-330

Monitoring 163, 168, 227 ff.

National Ecological Network (Ecologische Hoofdstructuur) 332-335

National/cultural Landscape/Park/Scenic Area 154, 156-157
Drentsche Aa 42, 76, 94-97
Lahemaa 76, 116 ff., 122 (Management Plan)
Las Médulas 484-486

Natives 409-410

Nature
(conservation) 84, 118
(management) 83, 109

Offering sites 223-226 (Oer-IJ)

Orders 55-62, 464

Paradigm 7, 9, 192, 369-370, 478 (mediterranean; northern), 586, 595, 654

Paradox 3, 7, 378, 437, 632-633

PDL/BBO (Protecting and Developing the Dutch Archaeological-Historical Landscape) 22-23 (central questions)

Participatory approach 123 (Lahemaa), 462

Philosophy 352, 357-359 (of science), 561

Planarch 446, 525

Planners 466

Planning 368, 642, 646
(Catholic) 398-399
(community/participatory) 83, 90, 97, 277, 286
(cultural/heritage) 13, 27, 192, 209, 211, 278, 280-282, 286, 507
(land-use planning) 26
(development planning) 27
(regional) 352, 354-357

Policy 241-242, 246-248, 292-294 (implementation), 366 (definition)

Positivist 29, 88

Practicioners 464-465, 529, 534

Prediction/predictive modelling 206, 224 (definition), 224-226 (Oer-IJ), 377-378, 431, 433-434, 438

Preservation/protection 78, 153-155 (Scotland), 163 ff., 168 ff., 227-231, 355-356, 368, 380, 416, 453, 463, 477 (Spain), 494-495, 588, 683 (description)
(degradation) 78, 162 ff., 173, 206, 227, 355, 360

Prospection 375-376, 416-417
(geochemical) 415, 422 (phosphate), 426

Public 357, 368, 454

Quality 206, 247, 416, 462
(of landscape) 25, 368
(spatial) 27-28, 594
(aesthetic quality plan/beeldkwaliteitplan) 243, 245
(biodiversity) 265
(quality norms) 440

Reactivity 198-199, 351

Reclamation 398 (Catholic)

Redox (probes/measurements) 169-170, 229, 231

Region(ally oriented projects) 36-37, 76, 352, 354-357 (planning), 507, 517, 599-600

Remote sensing 415, 418

Representation (before and after) 310-311, 322-323

Research
(applied) 533
(curiosity driven) 533
(strategic research) 533 (definition), 534, 577, 580

Resilience 665

Risk assessment 378, 431, 434

Scoping 450-451, 453

Self-(and hetero)reference 198, 275-280, 301-302

Semantic (model) 608-609

Sensitivity 665

Settlers 409

Social Cost Benefit Analysis 376-377

Super-(and infra)structure 190, 213, 509

(Social) Systems theory 274-277

Statistics/al methods 433, 434-437 (Bayesian), 435-436 (Dempster-Shafer)

Strategic Environmental Assessment 355, 445, 456

Strategy 611

Sustainability/sustainable landscape/sustainable development 24, 69, 70 (definition), 80, 207, 247, 487, 587

SWOT analysis 211-212, 513-516, 602-603, 635-637, 683 (description)

Synergy Initiative 659, 664

Transnationality 545 ff., 548, 550

Truth 191

Uncertainty 436, 541

Unifying concepts 71, 87, 192, 371

Urnfields 39-393, 408

Usability 605, 610-611

Valletta Convention 19 (the Netherlands), 294-296, 416, 446-447, 456, 462, 473-474, 504, 587, 620, 683-684 (description)

Valorization 593

Values 28, 613

VINEX 462

(3D) (landscape) visualization 309, 312, 314-318

Volcanism 178

Watching brief 453

Wetlands 205 ff. (in particular 215-231), 234

Index of places and regions

Achterhoek 34, 133-134

Aigues Mortes 59

Alaska 232

Amsterdam 204, 221, 243-244 (Stelling van Amsterdam), 251-253 (Stelling van Amsterdam)

Andernach 79, 177 ff.

Arnhem-Schuytgraf 472

Assendelft 254

Bangladesh 57

Barrees, Bear Peninsula 339, 342-346

Beemster 221

Beverwijk (-Heemskerk) 248

Blue Banana 61

Borgharen 425

Cairngorms National Park 157

Céide Fields 339, 341-342

Colmschate 35

Darfur 54

Dhaka 57

Drentsche Aa (National Landscape) 42, 76, 94-97

Eifel: see Vulkanpark Osteifel

Elst-Westeraam 467-472

Entlebuch 313

Estonia: see Lahemaa National Park

Franches Montagnes 411

Geiranger 267-268

Green Heart 25, 26-27

Heemskerk: see Beverwijk (-Heemskerk)

Iceland 233-235

Jericho 316-317

Kranenburg 496-497

La Balouta 481

Lahemaa National Park (Estonia) 76, 116 ff.

Las Médulas 484-486

Loch Lomond 156-157

Lough Boora Parklands 339, 342-343

London 61

Maghreb 54

Man(a)hattan 54, 60, 311

Mayen 79, 177 ff.

Mendig 181

Mönchengladbach 498-499

Napfgebiet 411

Netherlands
(East[ern]) 34-35, 77, 135 ff.
(South[ern]) 37-38

Nieuw-Dordrecht 169-171

Nijmegen-Waalsprong 473

Oer-IJ 38-39, 203 ff., 239 ff.

Orkney 157

Osteifel: see Vulkanpark Osteifel

Palestine 54

De Peel 402

Randstad 25, 61

Rees 497-498

Salland 34, 133-134

Scotland 77

Solway 157

Someren 390, 392

Spain: see Las Médulas

Swifterbant 169, 171-172

Tiel-Passewaay 424

Timisoara 58-59

Trossachs National Park 156-157

Velsen 220

Versailles 56-57

Vulkanpark Osteifel 79, 177 ff.

Warsaw 63

Washington DC 56-57

Western Ross 157

Wiśniowa 519, 572

Wrest Park Garden 314-315

LANDSCAPE & HERITAGE SERIES

Landscape & Heritage Series (LHS) is a new English-language series about the history, heritage and transformation of the natural and cultural landscapes, and built environment. The series aims at the promotion of new directions as well as the rediscovery and exploration of lost tracks in landscape and heritage research. These two theoretically oriented approaches play an important part in the realization of this objective.

Forthcoming Titles in 2010

Textbooks:
Jan Kolen & Rob van der Laarse
Reader in Landscape and Heritage
ISBN 9789089641854

Research:
Koos Bosma
Shelter City
ISBN 9789089642110